MARKETING

Strategic foundations

The Irwin Series in Marketing
Consulting Editor   Gilbert A. Churchill, Jr.
University of Wisconsin, Madison

MARKETING

Strategic foundations

Paul S. Busch
University of Wisconsin—Madison

Michael J. Houston
University of Illinois at Urbana–Champaign

1985

RICHARD D. IRWIN, INC.
Homewood, Illinois 60430

ISBN 0-256-02843-5

Library of Congress Catalog Card No. 84–82022

Printed in the United States of America

1 2 3 4 5 6 7 8 9 0 K 2 1 0 9 8 7 6 5

This book is dedicated to

Ann, Jennifer, and John
Max and Eleanor
Pat and Kerry
James and Claudia

Preface

Marketing: Strategic Foundations is a basic marketing textbook designed for the introductory marketing course. It comprehensively and thoroughly treats the basic conceptual and definitional elements of marketing. The text then challenges the student to adopt a strategic perspective by applying a strategic planning framework to each of the major marketing mix variables: product, price, promotion, and channels of distribution. Thus, this book covers the same principles of marketing found in other introductory texts but carries them to a higher level. Organizations in the United States today heavily emphasize strategic planning and management. It is appropriate, then, that students have a strategic perspective on the basic definitions and concepts of marketing in the introductory course. The phrase "build your introductory marketing course on a strategic foundation" effectively captures the message that we would like to communicate about the book.

A strategic perspective

The framework for strategic marketing planning used in the book comprises the following parts: (1) situation analysis; (2) establishment of objectives; (3) establishing product/markets and market segmentation; (4) budget determination; (5) management of the marketing program; (6) evaluation and control. This framework is introduced in Chapter 2 and applied in Chapter 13—Managing Products; Chapter 14—Channel: Basic Concepts and Strategies; Chapter 16—Pricing: Methods and Strategies; Chapter 19—Promotion: An Overview; Chapter 24—Multinational Marketing; and Chapter 25—Marketing of Services and Not-for-Profit Organizations.

The framework itself is derived from the literature on strategic planning and management. *Marketing: Strategic Foundations* differs from other introductory marketing books in that this strategic framework and perspective permeates the entire book rather than being limited to a discussion of strategic planning in an isolated chapter. The strategic planning framework serves as a key organizing device throughout the text.

A blend of theory and practice

Marketing: Strategic Foundations presents students with a solid blend of theory and practice. The authors believe that social science theory and research findings provide a sound basis for strategic management decision making. A major section of the book (Section Two, Chapters 4–8) contain up-to-date information on theory and research in consumer behavior decision processes and organizational buying behavior. In addition, social science research findings are presented throughout the text where appropriate. For example, Chapter 12 (on new products) contains a discussion on the adoption and diffusion of innovation, and Chapter 21 (on sales management) discusses expectancy value theory as it relates to sales management.

Key features of text

Several features of the book are designed to assist the student in learning the material.

1. Each section begins with an overview of the material within the sections. Each chapter contains a brief introduction and a detailed summary.
2. Key definitions and terms are highlighted by being set off in boxes and bold colored type.
3. Discussion questions and exercises at the end of the chapter are designed to apply the ideas and concepts presented in the chapter.
4. Key concepts and terms are listed at the end of each chapter.
5. Some 330 figures, charts, and tables illustrate important points and concepts in the text. In addition, more than 75 ads enhance the presentation and maintain student interest.
6. Two cases are included at the end of each section to highlight and illustrate topics discussed in that section. These 18 cases are based on actual experiences of for-profit and not-for-profit organizations that are well known to the students.
7. The legal aspects of marketing are discussed throughout the text. This is unlike many other introductory marketing texts, which confine the legal topics to a single chapter. The legal aspects of product,

price, promotion, and distribution are discussed in the chapters dealing with those topics.

Teaching aids

Instructor's Manual provides lecturettes for each chapter, answers to discussion questions, case solutions, true-false/multiple-choice testing materials, and transparency masters.
The Irwin Computerized Test Generator System.
Teletest.
Computest.

ACKNOWLEDG-MENTS

The development of a textbook is a collaborative effort involving many individuals who contribute in a variety of ways.

A very competent group of reviewers made many detailed and helpful suggestions. While we did not incorporate all their recommendations, we feel that their efforts did significantly improve the book. We owe a debt of gratitude to the following reviewers (all shortcomings are, of course, the responsibility of the authors): John Martin, Boston University; Donald Sciglimpalia, San Diego State University; Joe F. Hair, Jr., Louisiana State; Richard F. Yalch, University of Washington; Donald Shawver, University of Missouri—Columbia; and Peter C. Wilton, University of California—Berkeley.

We acknowledge the intellectual stimulation and ideas from our many fine colleagues at the University of Wisconsin—Madison. We especially recognize the ideas of Jack Nevin during the embryonic stages of this book.

Gil Churchill, University of Wisconsin, serves as consulting editor for the Irwin Series in Marketing. Gil's expertise and guidance are greatly appreciated, especially his encouragement during those difficult initial phases of the manuscript development.

Janet Christopher and Dorothy Peterson are acknowledged for their expert typing assistance. Betty Lane's secretarial assistance was a great help.

Surendra Singh's (University of Kansas) contribution to Chapter 24, Multinational Marketing, is gratefully acknowledged. Other individuals who helped with the sundry tasks of text development are: Scott Gerber, Diane Machut, John Murray, Laura Poduch, and Deborah Ruegger. A special thanks goes to Karen Burgess and Siew Meng Leong for their assistance with the cases.

Finally, we want to acknowledge the support and sacrifice from our families:

Special recognition is given to my mother, Eleanor, and to my father, Max, who died during the writing of this book. The love and support of my wife, Ann, and my children, Jennifer and John, is gratefully acknowledged and deeply appreciated. (P.B.)

My love and appreciation to Pat and Kerry, who recognized better than I that their presence was always desired but that their absence was sometimes needed. (M.J.H.)

Paul Busch
Michael J. Houston

Contents

SECTION ONE   **2**
The framework of marketing

    CHAPTER 1   **Marketing: An overview**   **4**
Why study marketing? *Marketing is a significant force in the economy and in society. Marketing is a major subsystem in an organization. Marketing is an employment opportunity. Marketing has personal relevance.* The nature and scope of marketing: *Positive versus normative. Macro versus micro. Profit versus nonprofit.* The role of marketing in the economy and in society: *Gap theory. Marketing as a matching activity. Marketing creates utility. Marketing and exchange. A macro definition of marketing.* Key elements of the macro system: *The functions of marketing. The concept of flow. Marketing institutions. Characteristics of functions performed by institutions. The role of specialization. Markets.* Marketing systems within the macro system: *Industries. Channels. Individual firms.* Marketing management: *Customer satisfaction and organizational objectives. Resources. Marketing philosophies. The marketing environment. A summary framework of marketing management.*

    CHAPTER 2   **The strategic role of marketing**   **40**
Strategic marketing planning: *Ongoing process. Process versus content of strategy. Organization levels. Objectives, strategy, and tactics.* The strategic marketing planning

process: *Situation analysis. Establishing objectives. Criteria for objectives. Product market. Budgeting. Market program positioning. Evaluation and control.* Strategic planning models: *Strategic business unit (SBUs) of analysis. Growth/ share matrix. Experience curve analysis. Industry attractiveness/business strength model. Profit impact of marketing strategy (PIMS).* Organizing the marketing department: *Functional organization. Product management organization. Market organization. Matrix approach.*

CHAPTER 3   The environment of marketing   70
Levels of the marketing environment: *Intraorganizational level. External support level. Macro level.* Nature of the macroenvironment. The impact of the macroenvironment. Strategic planning and the environment: *Environmental monitoring. Environmental adaptation. Sectors of the macroenvironment. The sociocultural sector. The economic sector. The competitive sector. The technological sector. The public policy sector.*

Cases for section one   105
Case 1:   Anheuser-Busch: A new soft drink encounters
             consumer protests   **106**
Case 2:   Eastman Kodak Company: An overview of corporate
             and marketing strategy   **107**

SECTION TWO   110
Describing and understanding buyers

**CHAPTER 4   Descriptive analysis of the U.S.
             consumer market   112**
Population size: *Household size.* Population age. Geographic distribution of the population: *Regional distribution. The "mobiles" as a market. Governmental definitions of concentrated market areas. Urban-suburban- rural distribution.* Socioeconomic characteristics: *Income. Engel's laws. The ratchet effect. Dual-income households. Education. Occupation.* Value of descriptive variables.

CHAPTER 5   Consumer behavior: The individual consumer   136
The nature and scope of consumer behavior. Why study consumer behavior? A behavioral science approach: *Assumptions of the behavioral science approach.* A framework for studying consumer behavior. Personal

factors: *Values.* Perception. *Perception in the marketplace. Beliefs and attitudes. Personality. Self-image.*

CHAPTER 6   **Consumer behavior: Social influences**   **170**
Sources of social influence: *Personal influence. Family influences. Reference group influence. Social class influence. Symbolic role. Lifestyle and psychographics. Culture and subculture.*

CHAPTER 7   **The consumer decision process**   **202**
The basic tasks of the consumer. The consumer decision process: *Stages of the consumer decision process. Variations in the overall process. Involvement. Problem recognition. Internal search. External search. Information receipt. Decision. Postdecision.* Consumer decision process and the classification of consumer goods: *Convenience goods. Shopping goods. Specialty goods.*

CHAPTER 8   **Organizational buying behavior**   **234**
Nature and structure of the organizational market: *Types of organizational buyers. Descriptive characteristics of the organizational market. Types of items bought by organizations. Demand characteristics of the organizational market.* Organizational buying practices: *Reseller buying practices. User buying practices. Participants in user buying.* Influences on organizational buying behavior: *Individual factors. Intraorganizational influences. Interorganizational influences. Environmental influences.* The organizational buying decision process: *Problem recognition. Internal search. External search. Information receipt. Decision. Postdecision.* Classification of organizational buying processes.

Cases for section two   **269**
Case 3: J.C. Penney and the working woman: Adapting to
            social and economic trends   **269**
Case 4: Xerox and Uniroyal and centralized purchasing: A
            case of organizational buying behavior   **271**

SECTION THREE   **274**
Segmenting and measuring markets

CHAPTER 9   **Market segmentation**   **276**
The nature of market segmentation: *Rationale of market segmentation. The market segmentation approach. Market*

*segmentation defined. Choosing a segmentation variable.
Homogeneity within and heterogeneity between segments.
Behavioral consequences. Marketing consequences.*
Necessary conditions for segmentation: *Measurability.
Substantiality. Stability.* Potential bases for segmenting
the market: *Descriptive characteristics of buyers—The
consumer market. Descriptive characteristics of buyers—The
organizational market. General behavioral characteristics—
The consumer market. General behavioral characteristics—
The organizational market. Product-specific behavioral
characteristics—The consumer market. Product-specific
behavioral characteristics—The organizational market.
Developing composite profiles of segments.* Pursuing the
market: *Aggregated strategy. Disaggregated strategy. Niche
strategy.* Steps in the segmentation process: *Step 1—
Identify market segments. Step 2—Collect research
information. Step 3—Develop composite profiles of segments.
Step 4—Ascertain behavioral and marketing consequences.
Step 5—Estimate market potential. Step 6—Analyze
marketing opportunity. Step 7—Decide if and how to pursue
the market. Benefits implied in the segmentation process.*

CHAPTER 10   Demand assessment   314
Key concepts in demand assessment. The role of demand
assessment: *Role of demand assessment in strategic
planning. Specific roles of demand assessment.* Methods for
current demand assessment: *Chain-ratio method. Market-
buildup method. Buying-power-index method.* Methods for
forecasting sales: *Judgment techniques. Time-series
techniques. Causal techniques.* Selection of forecasting
methods: *Factors to consider. The use of forecasting in
industry.*

Cases for section three   345
Case 5:   K mart: A market segmentation strategy   345
Case 6:   Midwest Hospital: Assessing current demand   348

SECTION FOUR   350
Product strategy

CHAPTER 11   Product: Basic concepts   352
What is a product? Classification of products. Consumer
goods: *Convenience goods. Shopping goods. Specialty goods.*

Product mix. Branding: *Reasons for branding. Characteristics of brand names.* Distributor and manufacturer brands: *Battle of the brands.* Branding strategy: *Individual brand name strategy. Family brand name strategy. Brand name becomes generic.* Unbranded goods. Packaging: *Protecting the product. Facilitating use of the product. Promoting the product. Labeling. Labeling and packaging legislation.*

CHAPTER 12 New-product development   374
What is a new product? Importance of new products. Why new products fail: *Lack of significant advantages. Failure to match company's strength. Changes in consumers' tastes. Insufficient market segment size. Competitive entry into market. Lack of channel support.* Organization for new-product development: *New-product committee. Product managers. New-product department. Venture team.* The new-product development process. Generation of new-product ideas: *Brainstorming. Benefit-structure analysis. Problem-inventory analysis. Attribute listing.* Screening of ideas. Business analysis: *Capital budgeting techniques.* Product-concept development and testing: *A comprehensive concept-evaluation procedure. Identification of market segment. Concept evaluation. Identification of key characteristics of various benefit segments. Assessing the concept's market positioning.* Product development: *Market testing. Minimarket test. Laboratory market tests. Statistical and mathematical models.* Commercialization. Consumer behavior and new products: *Product attributes that influence adoption. The consumer adoption process.*

CHAPTER 13 Managing products   410
Product life cycle: *Introduction stage. Growth stage. Maturity stage. Decline stage. Length of product life cycle. Theoretical foundation of product life cycle. Research on product life cycle.* Strategic marketing planning process applied to products: *Situation analysis. Product objectives. Product/markets. Budget determination.* Strategic product decisions: *Product life cycle and strategic planning. Product and brand positioning. Product cannibalization. Product deletion. Evaluation of product performance.* Legal aspects of products: *Product liability. Product warranty.*

Cases for section four   447
Case 7: Miller Lite: Product positioning   **448**
Case 8: Apple III: A new-product introduction   **449**

SECTION FIVE   450
Distribution strategy

CHAPTER 14   Channels: Basic concepts and strategies   452
              Characteristics of marketing channels: *The use of
              intermediaries. Types of channels. Marketing functions and
              flows.* Strategic marketing planning process applied to
              distribution channels: *Situation analysis. Establish channel
              objectives. Product/market strategy. Budget determination.
              Strategic channel decisions.* Management of
              interorganizational relations within channels: *Terms and
              concepts in channel relationships. Conflict. Conflict-
              management strategies.* Evaluation of channel
              performance: *Qualitative measures. Quantitative measures.*

CHAPTER 15   Retailing and wholesaling   490
              Nature and scope of retailing. Classification of retail
              structure: *Margin/turnover classification. Product mix
              classification. Method of operation. Nonstore retailing.
              Warehouse retailing, conglomerchant, hypermarkets.
              Geographic location. Form of ownership.* Retail institutional
              change: *Wheel of retailing. Retail accordion. Retail life cycle.*
              Strategic retail management decisions: *Store location. Store
              image. Merchandise, service, and atmosphere. Pricing.
              Promotion.* Wholesaling: *Wholesaling functions. Types of
              wholesalers.* Strategic wholesale management decisions:
              Location. Product/service mix. Pricing. Legal dimensions
              of channel, retail, and wholesale management: *Exclusive-
              dealing contracts. Tying contracts. Exclusive territories.*

CHAPTER 16   Physical distribution   526
              Nature of physical distribution: *Raw material to finished
              goods. Cross-functional area. Cost trade-offs. Reverse
              channel.* Customer service: *Order cycle. Percentage of
              demand to be satisfied. Quality control for order processing.
              Physical condition upon delivery.* Transportation: *Modes
              of transportation. Types of legal carriers.* Warehousing:
              *Location. Private and public warehouses. Developments in
              warehousing.* Inventory management and control:
              *Functions of inventory. Economic order quantity (EOQ).
              Inventory turnover and its impact on profits.* Current issues
              in physical distribution: *Computers. Inventory
              management. Material handling. Shared distribution.*

Deregulation. The role of physical distribution management in strategic planning.

Cases for section five 549

Case 9: Caterpillar Tractor: Dealer loyalty in an industrial channel of distribution 549

Case 10: GM and "just-in-time": Changing relationships in the channel of distribution 552

SECTION SIX 554
Pricing

CHAPTER 17 **Pricing: Basic considerations** 556
Importance of price in an individual firm's marketing strategy. Economic theory and pricing: *Monopoly. Oligopoly. Monopolistic competition. Pure competition.* Price elasticity of demand. Cost concepts: *Fixed costs. Variable costs. Average costs. Marginal costs.* Basic pricing decisions and administration: *New-product pricing. Discounts. Geographic pricing. Transfer pricing.* Legal aspects of pricing: *Horizontal price fixing. Vertical price fixing. Unit pricing.*

CHAPTER 18 **Pricing: Methods and strategies** 582
Cost-oriented pricing practices: *Markup pricing. Target-return pricing. Breakeven analysis pricing. Experience curve pricing.* Competition-oriented pricing: *Price leadership. Competitive bidding.* Demand-oriented pricing: *Perceived-value pricing. Price-quality relationships. Loss-leader pricing. Odd-numbered pricing. Price lining.* Strategic marketing planning applied to pricing: *Situation analysis. Establish pricing objectives. Product/market strategy. Budget determination. Strategic pricing issues. Distribution channels. Promotion. Evaluation of price performance.*

Cases for section six 615

Case 11: Braniff Airways: Deregulation and its impact on pricing in the airline industry 615

Case 12: Ford Motor Company: A reevaluation of pricing strategy 617

SECTION SEVEN 618
Promotional strategy

CHAPTER 19 **Promotion: An overview** 620
The role of promotion: *Promotion as a communications strategy. Inform, persuade, remind. Shifting the demand*

curve. Definition of promotional strategy. **The components of promotion:** *Advertising. Personal selling. Packaging. Public relations. Sales promotion.* **Promotional strategy.** **Factors influencing promotional strategy:** *Promotional resources. Nature of product. Push versus pull strategy. Life-cycle stage of product. Nature of the market. Product/market strategy.* **A communications model for promotional messages:** *Source. Encoding. Channel. Audience response. Noise. Feedback.* **Strategic planning in promotion:** *Situation analysis. Establishment of objectives. Product/ market. Determination of promotional budget. Management of program elements. Evaluation and control.*

CHAPTER 20   Advertising management   658
The nature and importance of advertising: *The role of advertising in an organization. Advertising expenditures. Types of advertisers. Types of advertisements. Advertising campaigns.* **Decision areas in advertising management:** *Advertising budgets. Selection and use of advertising agencies. Advertising objectives. Message formulation (the "creative" process). Message execution. Media selection. Media scheduling. Measuring advertising effectiveness.* **The regulatory environment of advertising:** *Self-regulation. Governmental regulation.*

CHAPTER 21   The personal selling process and
              sales management   704
Personal selling's role in marketing strategy. Boundary position of the salesperson. Classification of selling jobs. The selling process: *Prospecting. The preapproach. The approach. The presentation. Meeting objections. The close. The follow-up.* **Management of the sales force:** *Sales force objectives. Forms of organizing the sales force. Sales force size. Sales force compensation. Recruitment, selection, and retention. Sales training. Sales force supervision and motivation. Evaluation of sales force performance.* **Trends in personal selling:** *Team selling. Telephone selling. Women in personal selling careers. Research on personal selling. Dyadic studies.*

Cases for section seven   741
Case 13: Burger King, McDonald's, and Wendy's: Advertising
              in the fast-food industry   742
Case 14: Avis and Dow Corning: Using telemarketing to
              improve sales force efficiency and effectiveness   744

SECTION EIGHT   746
Evaluation of marketing performance

CHAPTER 22 **Control of marketing strategy**   748
Nature and definition of control: *Establishment of
standards. Interpretation and evaluation of actual
performance. Taking corrective action.* Characteristics of
effective control systems. Reasons for detailed analysis:
Iceberg principle. The 80/20 rule. Sales analysis. Variance
analysis. Marketing cost analysis: *Unit of analysis. Sales
per unit of analysis. Full-cost versus contribution margin.
Natural versus functional accounts. Construct unit profit
and loss statement.* PERT. Budgets. Strategic planning and
control: *Profit impact of marketing strategies (PIMS). Post-
action strategic control model. Contingency planning.
Steering Marketing Control Model (STEMCOM). The
marketing audit.*

CHAPTER 23 **Marketing research and information systems**   778
The role of information in marketing management.
Sources of marketing information. The nature and scope
of marketing research: *The role of marketing research in
society.* The marketing research process: *Formulate
problem. Propose research design. Assess value of research.
Implement research. Interpret findings. Prepare and present
report.* The marketing information system (MIS). *The
nature of a marketing information system. Components of
the MIS. Design factors in the MIS. The status of MIS in
industry.*

Cases for section eight   813
Case 15: Citizens & Southern National Bank: Using MBO
to establish a control and evaluation system   814
Case 16: AMP, Inc.: Effective use of a marketing information
system   815

SECTION NINE   818
Marketing in special fields

CHAPTER 24 **Multinational marketing**   820
Multinational marketing defined. Why firms go beyond
domestic markets: *Customers. Nature of the business. Lower
cost of operating abroad. Meeting the competition.
Environmental and ecological pressures. Incentives provided*

by the host country government. The stage in the product life cycle (PLC). Exchange rate fluctuations. Ways of entering foreign markets: *Exporting. Licensing. Joint ventures. Total ownership.* Developing multinational marketing strategies. Multinational environment: *Political environment. Other forms of political risk. Legal environment. Cultural environment. Economic environment. Technological environment.* Standardized versus nonstandardized marketing plans. Marketing mix variables in multinational setting: *Product considerations. Pricing considerations. Promotional considerations. Distribution considerations.* The role of multinational corporations.

CHAPTER 25   **Marketing of services and not-for-profit organizations**   848
Marketing of services: *The nature and importance of services. Characteristics of services. Classes of services. Strategic issues in service marketing. A comment on the marketing of professional services.* Marketing in nonprofit organizations: *The nature and scope of nonprofit organizations. The concept of exchange and nonprofit organizations. Strategic planning in nonprofit organizations.*

Cases for section nine   879
Case 17: Calvin Klein Jeans in Brazil: A case of
             multinational marketing   879
Case 18: Colleges and universities: An increasing
             use of marketing   881

Index of key terms and concepts   I–1

Index of names   I–7

Index of subjects   I–14

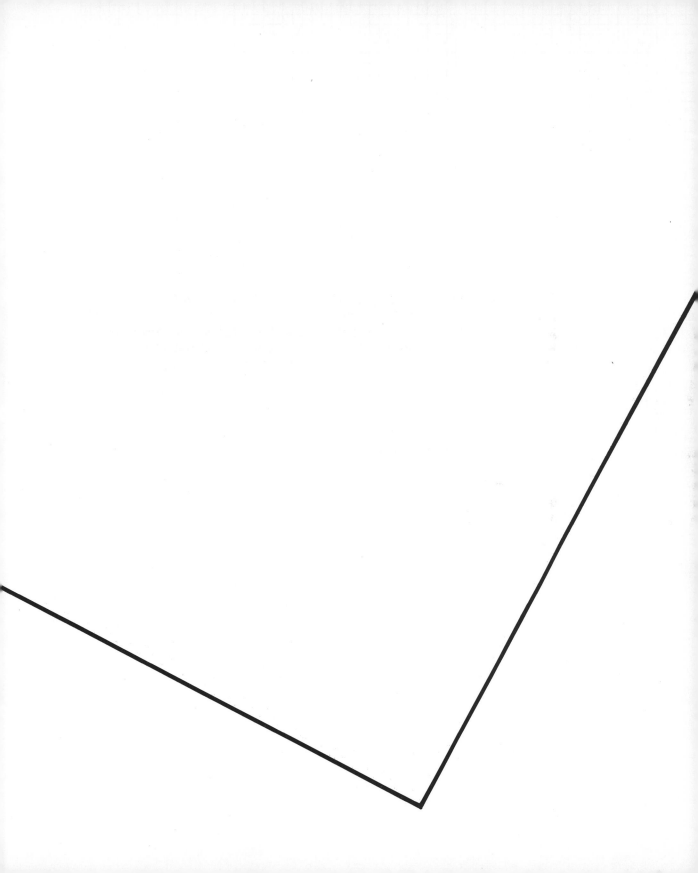

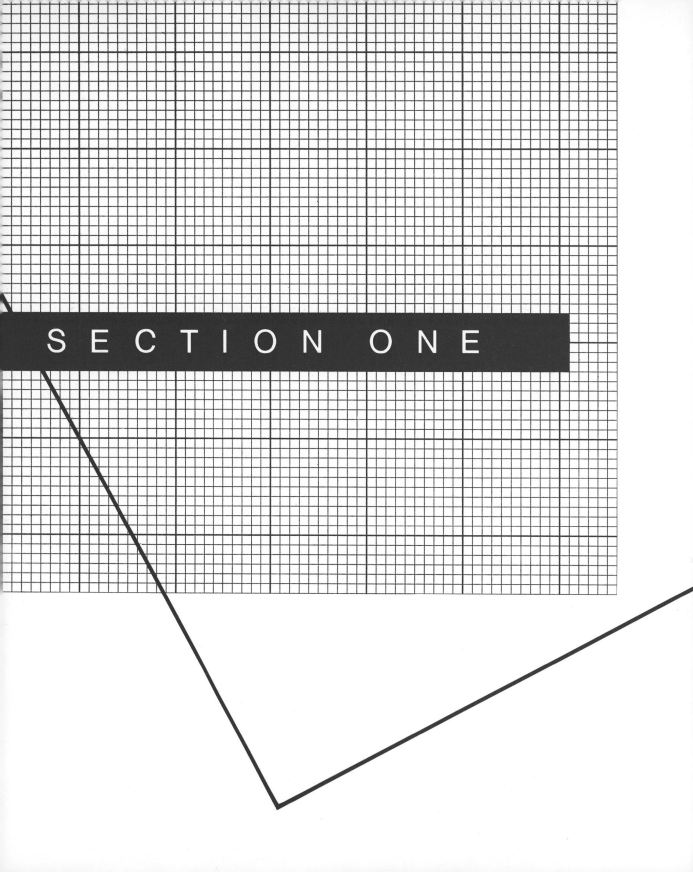

SECTION ONE

The framework of marketing

In this first section we present a framework for studying and understanding marketing that will serve as our foundation for the remainder of the book. Chapter 1 offers an overview recognizing two distinct views of marketing. One is that marketing is an influential force in both the economy and society as a whole—*a macro perspective on marketing.* The second view sees marketing as a major strategic activity within organizations—*a micro perspective.*

The strategic role of marketing is the dominant topic of this book. Chapter 2 suggests ideas to guide the planning, implementing, and control of marketing activities within an organization.

There is an important interplay between marketing within a firm and the broad environment within which it exists. Many economic and social forces influence the marketing activities of an organization. Chapter 3 discusses these environmental forces.

CHAPTER 1

Marketing: An overview

Why study marketing?
    Marketing is a significant force in the economy and in society
    Marketing is a major subsystem in an organization
    Marketing is an employment opportunity
    Marketing has personal relevance
The nature and scope of marketing
    Positive versus normative
    Macro versus micro
    Profit versus nonprofit
The role of marketing in the economy and in society
    Gap theory
    Marketing as a matching activity
    Marketing creates utility
    Marketing and exchange
    A macro definition of marketing

Key elements of the macro system
    The functions of marketing
    The concept of flow
    Marketing institutions
    Characteristics of functions performed by institutions
    The role of specialization
    Markets
Marketing systems within the macro system
    Industries
    Channels
    Individual firms
Marketing management
    Customer satisfaction and organizational objectives
    Resources
    Marketing philosophies
    The marketing environment
    A summary framework of marketing management

Summary

Key concepts

Discussion questions and exercises

After you have defeated a friendly opponent in a set of tennis, she buys you a brand of beer that you've never had before. You admire its rich flavor and smoothness and make a mental note to buy a six-pack of it the next time you buy beer. She remarks that the beer doesn't suit her tastes.

A major retail department store raises its prices on all goods 4 percent because of rising energy costs. A competitor incurring the same cost increase does not raise prices but does curtail the number of hours it stays open each week.

The Japanese automobile industry agrees to cut back the number of cars it exports to the United States each year. Mercedes Benz and BMW, two German auto producers, anticipate record sales in the U.S. market.

A major soft drink manufacturer slips in sales level compared to its main competitor. It hires a new ad agency to formulate an advertising campaign designed to regain its Number 1 position in the market. Its competitor increases its own promotional effort by selling eight-packs for the price of six-packs. Its purpose is to maintain its newly established Number 1 position.

Virtually everyone in the United States recognizes Smokey the Bear and what he stands for.

Deregulation of industries such as airlines, banking, professional services, and telecommunications is the recent sentiment of the federal government.

Societal changes are resulting in highly diverse, adult-oriented, individualistic lifestyles in which time is becoming a scarce resource.

All of these situations describe phenomena involved with or related to marketing. They are but a few of the countless events that occur within the domain of marketing. Marketing is diverse, perhaps more so than any other area of business. When you begin to study such a diverse field, you need a guide to help you tie together the array of concepts in it. And that is the major purpose of this book: *to introduce you to the diverse field of marketing in a structured, organized manner.*

WHY STUDY MARKETING?

When you begin to study a topic, one of the first questions may be, *Why* am I studying this? It's a fair question. Perhaps the only reason you know of so far is that this course is required as part of your major. Or you may be studying marketing as an elective. In any event there are several compelling reasons to study marketing—whether or not you anticipate a career in this field. (See Figure 1–1.)

Marketing is a significant force in the economy and in society

The set of activities known as *marketing* plays a significant role in determining the well-being of our economy and society. Our standard of living and the costs necessary to maintain it are partially determined by marketing activities. Roughly half of every consumer dollar spent

Figure 1–1: Reasons for the study of marketing

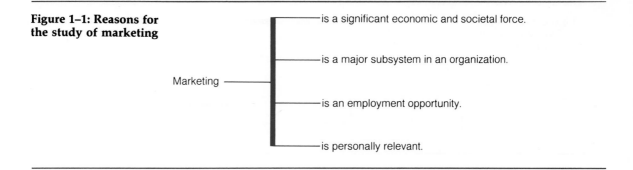

Marketing
— is a significant economic and societal force.
— is a major subsystem in an organization.
— is an employment opportunity.
— is personally relevant.

results from marketing activities in the economy. However, this doesn't mean that we would spend less if marketing didn't exist. Marketing plays a vital role in making life more efficient.

In general, marketing helps direct the allocation of resources. An understanding of marketing will lead to better decisions about these allocations.

Marketing is a major subsystem in an organization

An individual firm has three major **organizational subsystems.** (See Figure 1–2.) One is represented by the *accounting-finance* activities of the organization, which generate and manage its capital and operating funds. Another is the *production* activities of the organization, where the raw materials entering it are processed into goods or services the organization intends to deliver to the marketplace. Finally, there is *marketing,* which determines what is to be delivered and the manner of delivery.

Marketing's role among the three subsystems is revealed by Saab-Scania AB, the Swedish producer of Saab automobiles. For years its production processes have been innovative. Its financial situation has been stable and sound. But not until a major overhaul of its U.S. marketing effort did Saab begin to make a dent in the U.S. automobile market.[1]

In 1979 Saab introduced its 900 series—three models in the $10,000–17,000 price range. The following marketing plan was adopted:

1. Reposition Saab as a luxurious, high-performance automobile along the lines of BMW and Volvo rather than as an inexpensive compact.
2. Tell consumers about Saab's price range.
3. Use tough advertisements that make direct comparisons with the competition.

The results have been gratifying to Saab. Unit sales in the United States have risen dramatically since 1979 (a 42 percent increase from 1982 to 1983 alone).

---

[1] Bernie Whalen, "'Tiny' Saab Drives up Profits with Market-Niche Strategy, Repositioning," *Marketing News,* March 16, 1984, pp. 14–16.

**Figure 1–2: Major
subsystems in an
organization**

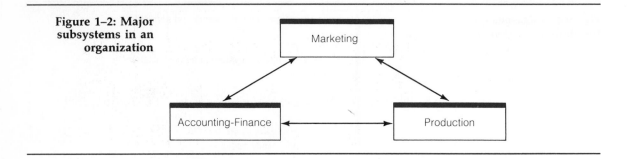

The point here is that Saab has for many years possessed the manufacturing and financial resources to do well in the United States. It was its
marketing subsystem that ultimately made the difference.

The three subsystems do not operate independently of each other.
Rather they interact, each subsystem influencing and responding to the
activities of the other two. Members of each subsystem must thoroughly
understand their own operation and have a working knowledge of the
operations of the other two subsystems. Saab's marketing effort occurred
within its manufacturing and financial capabilities. Thus, if you plan to
enter a career in marketing, your studies must lead to a thorough understanding of its role in an organization. If you anticipate entering other
areas of an organization, your study of marketing will help you understand
its interactions with these areas.

We must emphasize here that marketing's importance is not restricted
to commercial organizations; marketing activities are relevant to nonprofit
organizations as well. Charities, schools, museums, hospitals, and churches
are some examples of nonprofit organizations that can effectively use
marketing knowledge. If your career interest is in these kinds of organizations, you, too, have reason to study marketing. In fact, the nature of
these organizations is such that marketing may be the dominant subsystem
in many of them.

**Marketing is an
employment
opportunity**

Marketing's presence in organizations suggests the employment and
career opportunities associated with it. Marketing jobs are plentiful and
diverse. Roughly 25 to 33 percent of the work force is engaged in jobs
related to marketing. Marketing-related positions exist in sales, advertising, marketing research, product management, and distribution, to name
a few. And they exist at the manufacturing, wholesale, and retail levels
of trade. Marketing jobs appear to be the best route to the top. One
study of Fortune 500 firms reveals that more chief executive officers come
from the ranks of marketing than from any other field.[2] The study of

---

[2] Charles G. Burck, "A Group Profile of the Fortune 500 Chief Executive," *Fortune,*
May 1976, p. 172.

Your interest in a BMW, Volvo, Audi or Mercedes is completely understandable.

That's because you don't know about the Saab.

Saabs, in the words of *Car and Driver* magazine, "...are perpetual monuments to the more fundamental virtues of traveling by car."

So if you really have your mind set on one of those other cars, do yourself an enormous favor and don't test drive the Saab 900.

The Saab is so thoroughly, pragmatically, imaginatively and intelligently designed and built, it will only destroy your delusions about the car you want and create a lot of inner conflict.

We are not equipped to handle that.

SAAB
The most intelligent car ever built.

marketing can help direct you to a career in the field best suited to your interest and abilities.

Marketing has personal relevance

It is difficult to imagine a day going by without some aspect of marketing having a personal influence on you. The products and services we buy and consume, the prices we pay for them, the advertisements we see—in short, a significant portion of our whole being—result from marketing. The study of marketing can increase our understanding of the environment and how we exist in it. Perhaps some of your frustrations as a consumer will even be alleviated as you come to understand the complexities of the marketing system.

THE NATURE AND SCOPE OF MARKETING

The scope of topics, issues, and concepts relevant to marketing is exceedingly wide. Before embarking on the study of such a field we need to capture succinctly the important distinctions within the field.

One such view recognizes three dichotomies inherent in the study of marketing:

1. *Positive versus normative.* This dichotomy rests on the distinction between studying the *actual* conduct of marketing (positive) versus how it *should* be conducted (normative).
2. *Macro versus micro.* This refers to the distinction between the study of marketing as an aggregate economic activity within society (macro) and as a key managerial function within an organization (micro).
3. *Profit sector versus nonprofit sector.* This refers to the distinction between studying the role of marketing in an economic context (profit) and in a noneconomic context (nonprofit).[3]

When we combine the three dichotomies into an overall framework, there emerge eight distinct areas in the study of problems, issues, theories, and research related to marketing. (See Figure 1–3.) Let's take a closer look at each of the three dichotomies.

Positive versus normative

The ***positive-normative*** distinction recognizes that marketing can be examined from the standpoint of *what is* (positive) versus *what ought to be* (normative).

positive marketing

> **Positive marketing** attempts to describe, explain, predict, and understand the marketing activities, processes, and phenomena that actually exist.

---

[3] Shelby D. Hunt, "The Nature and Scope of Marketing," *Journal of Marketing,* July 1976, pp. 17–28.

Cells 1, 3, 5, and 7 of Figure 1–3 identify many of the types of issues found in positive marketing.

normative marketing

> **Normative marketing** attempts to *prescribe* what marketing organizations and individuals ought to do or what kinds of marketing systems a society ought to have.

Cells 2, 4, 6, and 8 identify many of the normative issues relevant to marketing.

The positive-normative distinction is interspersed throughout this book. Many topics entail a concern for what is and what ought to be. However, the positive perspective receives much greater weight. Through the collective use of industry examples, descriptive statistics, and theoretical material from the marketing literature, we hope to give you an understanding of the actual conduct of marketing. However, a normative framework—the strategic planning process—organizes our treatment of the conduct of marketing.

Macro versus micro

The role of marketing in the overall economy and as an important subsystem within an organization suggests the **macro-micro** distinction. It rests on the level of aggregation we take when examining marketing activities.

A macro perspective on marketing views the marketing system that results from the aggregate activities of all organizational units engaged in marketing. It examines how the nation's resources are allocated to serve its population. We can thus think of the macromarketing system as a social system and evaluate it accordingly—i.e., in terms of how well it serves society. This view means that each of the following would fit into the realm of macromarketing:

1. *The impact of marketing actions at a societal level of analysis.* Included here, for example, would be the correlation between total advertising expenditures and the consumer price index.

2. *The impact of society on marketing systems and actions.* This refers to the social and legal sanctions placed on marketing behavior. Examples include boycotts of products (social sanctions) and laws governing marketing actions of firms (legal sanctions).

3. *The study of marketing systems in their aggregate dimensions.* Examples include the role of wholesalers in the marketing system and comparative studies of different marketing systems (United States versus Japan).

Cells 3, 4, 7, and 8 of Figure 1–3 identify other macro issues.

The study of marketing from a micro perspective focuses on the management of marketing activities in the *individual organization*. At this

Figure 1–3: The scope of marketing

	Positive	Normative
Micro	(1) Problems, issues, theories, and research concerning: a. Individual consumer behavior b. How firms determine prices c. How firms determine products d. How firms determine promotion e. How firms determine channels of distribution f. Case studies of marketing practices	(2) Problems, issues, normative models, and research concerning how firms *should*: a. Determine the marketing mix b. Make pricing decisions c. Make product decisions d. Make promotion decisions e. Make packaging decisions f. Make purchasing decisions g. Make international marketing decisions h. Organize their marketing departments i. Control their marketing efforts j. Plan their marketing strategy k. Apply systems theory to marketing problems l. Manage retail establishments m. Manage wholesale establishments n. Implement the marketing concept
Profit sector **Macro**	(3) Problems, issues, theories, and research concerning: a. Aggregate consumption patterns b. Institutional approach to marketing c. Commodity approach to marketing d. Legal aspects of marketing e. Comparative marketing f. The efficiency of marketing systems g. Whether the poor pay more h. Whether marketing spurs or retards economic development i. Power and conflict relationships in channels of distribution j. Whether marketing functions are universal k. Whether the marketing concept is consistent with consumers' interests	(4) Problems, issues, normative models, and research concerning: a. How marketing can be made more efficient b. Whether distribution costs too much c. Whether advertising is socially desirable d. Whether consumer sovereignty is desirable e. Whether stimulating demand is desirable f. Whether the poor should pay more g. What kinds of laws regulating marketing are optimal h. Whether vertical marketing systems are socially desirable i. Whether marketing should have special social responsibilities

		(5) Problems, issues, theories, and research concerning: a. Consumers' purchasing of public goods b. How nonprofit organizations determine prices c. How nonprofit organizations determine products d. How nonprofit organizations determine promotion e. How nonprofit organizations determine channels of distribution f. Case studies of public goods marketing	(6) Problems, issues, normative models, and research concerning how nonprofit organizations *should:* a. Determine the marketing mix (social marketing) b. Make pricing decisions c. Make product decisions d. Make promotion decisions e. Make packaging decisions f. Make purchasing decisions g. Make international marketing decisions (e.g., CARE) h. Organize their marketing efforts i. Control their marketing efforts j. Plan their marketing strategy k. Apply systems theory to marketing problems
Nonprofit sector	**Micro**		
	Macro	(7) Problems, issues, theories, and research concerning: a. The institutional framework for public goods b. Whether television advertising influences elections c. Whether public service advertising influences behavior (e.g., Smokey the Bear) d. Whether existing distribution systems for public goods are efficient e. How public goods are recycled	(8) Problems, issues, normative models, and research concerning: a. Whether society should allow politicians to be "sold" like toothpaste b. Whether the demand for public goods should be stimulated c. Whether "low informational content" political advertising is socially desirable (e.g., 10-second "spot" commercials) d. Whether the U.S. Army should be allowed to advertise for recruits

Source: Shelby D. Hunt, "The Nature and Scope of Marketing," *Journal of Marketing,* July 1976, p. 21.

Marketing in the
nonprofit sector.

A new house and new dreams. Stay around to share those dreams.

You've saved and worked hard to buy your first house. Now you want to be around to enjoy it.

So if you have high blood pressure, don't take chances. Take your pills, control your weight, cut down on salt. Do whatever your doctor prescribes.

You can control your high blood pressure if you stay on your treatment every day, no matter how you feel.

High blood pressure. Treat it and live.

National High Blood Pressure Education Program. National Heart, Lung, and Blood Institute. U.S. Department of Health and Human Services

level the prime concern is that marketing helps an organization attain its overall goals (profit, growth, etc.). Marketing consists of a set of specialized activities that work together. Marketing management determines how each activity can best serve the interests of the organization. For instance, micromarketing issues include how much to spend on advertising, what price to charge for a product, or the selection of retailers to distribute a product to the consumer. Also of interest at the micro level is an understanding of the procedures for making such decisions. Cells 1, 2, 5, and 6 of Figure 1–3 identify additional micro issues.

The micro perspective dominates this book. Our major purpose is to examine the strategic foundations of marketing as they relate to the individual organization. A later section in this chapter considers macromarketing. Also, chapters 3 and 4 examine macroenvironmental issues relevant to strategic marketing.

Profit versus nonprofit

This ***profit-nonprofit*** dichotomy recognizes the relevance of marketing to both profit-seeking and nonprofit firms. Increasing numbers of nonprofit organizations (political parties and candidates, charities, museums, etc.) are using marketing to achieve their objectives.[4] Cells 5, 6, 7, and 8 of Figure 1–3 identify several issues relating to nonprofit marketing.

---

[4] For a specialized text on nonprofit marketing, see Philip Kotler, *Marketing for Nonprofit Organizations,* 2d ed. (Englewood Cliffs, N.J.: Prentice-Hall, 1982).

Marketing in its most sophisticated form occurs in the profit sector. Therefore, we concentrate mainly on marketing by profit-seeking firms. Examples of nonprofit marketing are provided in places. Chapter 25 contains a major section on nonprofit marketing.

THE ROLE OF MARKETING IN THE ECONOMY AND IN SOCIETY

We have recognized that marketing as an aggregate macro activity is a major force in the economy and society. In this section we will examine differing views of marketing and its role at the macro level. These views are compatible but state the role of marketing in different ways. Together they provide collective insight into the role of marketing.

Gap theory

An approach called **gap theory** has been offered to marketing. It is based on the premise that marketing need not exist until a social economy reaches the point where the producers of economic goods are not the consumers of these goods. In other words, marketing is unnecessary if everyone consumes what they themselves produce. But when goods are produced by someone other than consumers, there is a separation or gap. This gap must be closed for consumers to benefit from the consumption of these goods and for producers to realize revenue from their sale. The activity that unites producers and consumers—that bridges the gap—is marketing.

Figure 1–4: The separation of producers and consumers

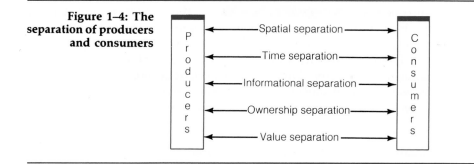

The tasks that marketing must perform to close the gap depend on the specific nature of the producer-consumer separation. McInnes uses five dimensions to characterize the nature of the separation (also see Figure 1–4):

1. **Spatial separation.** There is a geographic separation of producers and consumers. Automobiles produced in Detroit must reach consumers throughout the country.

2. **Time separation.** The geographic separation results in a time separation. The time lag between production and consumption of goods

is (at least) the time it takes to physically move goods from the point of production to the point of consumption. Consumers want the goods, however, when they need to use them. Thus, production must occur even when goods are not desired.

3. *Informational separation.* Consumers initially are unaware of the sources of goods; producers do not know where consumers are. Producers must be informed of the location and nature of consumers, and consumers must be informed of the nature and availability of goods.

4. *Ownership separation.* An exchange of goods cannot occur until the title of ownership (or right to use, in the case of leasing) is transferred from seller to buyer.

5. *Value separation.* Producers and consumers differ in what they seek from the exchange and in the sacrifices they make in entering the exchange. Consumers seek *utility* from products to satisfy needs. Producers seek *revenue* from products to recapture costs of production and contribute to profit. These differing values must be aligned to arrive at a price acceptable to each party in a mutually beneficial exchange.[5]

Marketing as a matching activity

Another classic view of the marketing role was provided by Alderson.[6] He, too, recognized the separate nature of the supply and demand sectors of the economy. Alderson suggested there are *heterogeneous supplies* in nature and *heterogeneous demands* on the part of society. On the supply side various human, technological, and material resources are available to serve society. On the demand side members of an advanced society possess diverse needs and wants. In fact, a trend of U.S. society is its increasing heterogeneity.[7] Different people want different things, and each person wants a multitude of things. Somehow our diverse resources must be shaped to fit society's diverse needs and wants.

marketing

Marketing is the process by which heterogeneous supplies in nature are matched with the heterogeneous demands of the marketplace.

This *matching process* is dynamic because neither supply nor demand is constant. At any one time the output of the marketing system is a massive array of goods from which an individual chooses an assortment

[5] William McInnes, "A Conceptual Approach to Marketing," in *Theory in Marketing,* 2d series, ed. Reavis Cox, et al. (Homewood, Ill.: Richard D. Irwin, 1964), pp. 51–67.

[6] Wroe Alderson, *Marketing Behavior and Executive Action* (Homewood, Ill.: Richard D. Irwin, 1957).

[7] John Naisbitt, *Megatrends: Ten New Directions Transforming Our Lives* (New York: Warner Books, 1984).

Figure 1–5: Marketing as a matching process

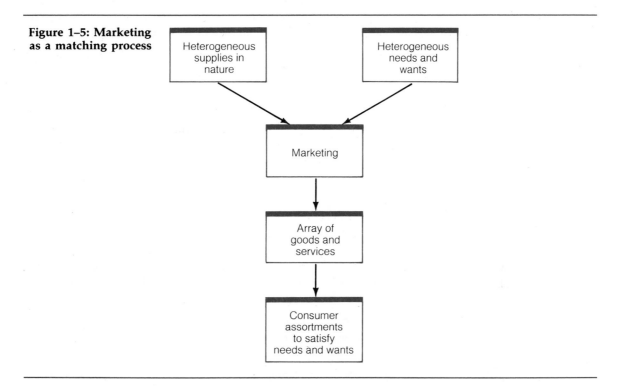

to satisfy his or her diverse set of needs and wants. (See Figure 1–5.) Ideally, this output will vary as available supplies and consumer needs and wants vary. As an example, consider the increased number of families in which both spouses work. This situation creates time pressures and demands for convenience. In response, more and more output of the marketing system is taking the form of convenience-oriented goods (microwave ovens) and services (house cleaning). During the last decade more than half of the new jobs created were in four industries: health, business services, finance, and eating and drinking places.[8]

Marketing creates utility

One of the older but still compelling views of marketing's role is that without marketing the utility of goods cannot be realized.

utility

> **Utility** refers to the capability of a good to satisfy consumer needs.

[8] Bruce Steinberg, "The Mass Market Is Splitting Apart," *Fortune,* November 28, 1983, pp. 76–82.

Figure 1–6: Types of utility

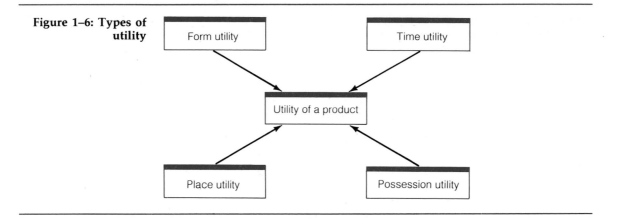

This need-satisfaction capability cannot be realized until specific types of utility are realized (also see Figure 1–6):

1. ***Form utility***—The functional nature of a product.
2. ***Time utility***—The availability of a product when it is desired by a consumer.
3. ***Place utility***—The availability of a product where it is desired by a consumer.
4. ***Possession utility***—The physical and legal possession of a product by the consumer.

This utility view of marketing is based on the premise that a product has no utility until it exists in the proper functional form, is available when and where the consumer wants it, and is in the hands of the consumer. Thus, certain processes must occur to provide form, time, place, and possession utility and to create the overall utility of a product.

Food products (wheat, corn, milk) do us little good until they are transformed to edible form and delivered to stores near our homes where they are available when we buy food. *Marketing* is primarily responsible for time, place, and possession utility. *Production* creates form utility by providing the physical product. However, to the extent that marketing activities collect information about what products to produce and their proper functional form, marketing contributes to form utility as well.

Marketing and exchange

Many people view marketing as "the science of exchange." The exchange process is central to the role of marketing; without it the gap between producers and consumers would not be closed, goods would not be matched with consumer needs, and the utility of a product would not be realized.

Figure 1–7: Some parties to exchange

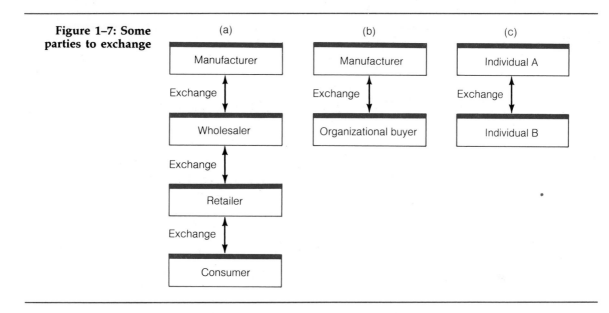

Kotler identifies five **conditions** that suggest the potential for **exchange:**

1. Two parties are involved.
2. Each party has something that could be of value to the other.
3. Each party is capable of communication and delivery.
4. Each party is free to accept or reject the opportunity.
5. Each party considers it appropriate or desirable to deal with the other party.[9]

Under these conditions an exchange occurs if the two parties can arrive at mutually agreeable terms. Terms will be mutually agreeable if each party expects the exchange to result in a situation better than the situation prior to the exchange. The marketing system's role is to perform the functions necessary to actualize the potential for exchange.

Exchange relationships are abundant in marketing. Exchanges occur between organizations involved in the distribution of goods to consumers and between retailers and consumers (Figure 1–7a); between organizations who sell and use (as opposed to resell) products/services (Figure 1–7b); and between individuals (Figure 1–7c) selling and buying used goods, for example. Furthermore, while exchange of products or services for money is the most frequent arrangement, many other types of exchange

---

[9] Philip Kotler, *Marketing Management: Analysis, Planning and Control,* 5th ed. © 1984, p. 8. Reprinted by permission of Prentice-Hall, Inc., Englewood Cliffs, New Jersey.

Figure 1–8: Examples of marketing exchanges

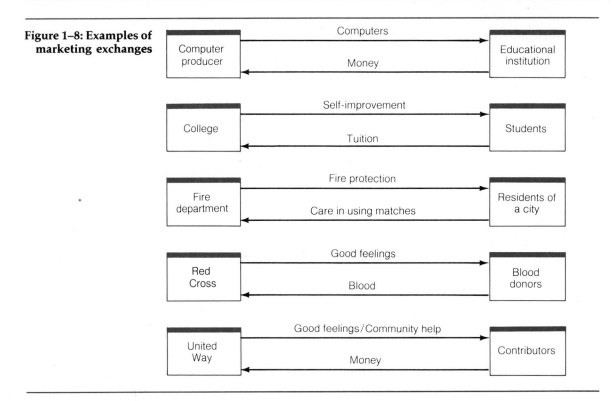

occur within marketing. Figure 1–8 identifies various types of exchanges and exchange parties.

Hunt views exchange fundamental to marketing:

marketing

> **Marketing** is the behavioral science that seeks to explain exchange relationships.

He then suggests that the study of marketing seeks to understand: the behaviors of buyers directed at consummating exchanges; the behaviors of sellers directed at consummating exchanges; the institutional framework directed at consummating and/or facilitating exchanges; and the consequences on society of the above behavior.[10] Figure 1–9 summarizes these four issues and the questions that must be answered to understand them.

---

[10] Shelby D. Hunt, "General Theories and the Fundamental Explanada of Marketing," *Journal of Marketing,* Fall 1983, pp. 9–17.

Figure 1–9: Marketing as the study of exchange

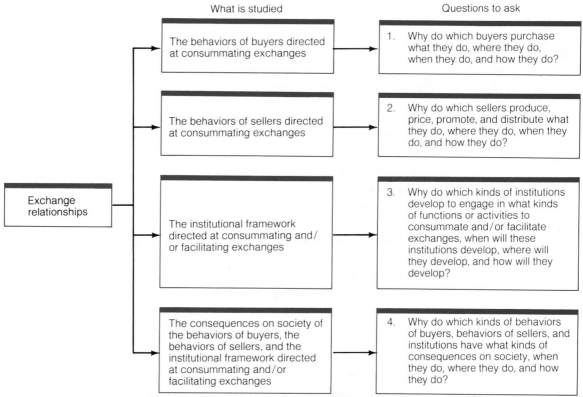

Source: Shelby D. Hunt, "General Theories and the Fundamental Explanada of Marketing," *Journal of Marketing*, Fall 1983, p. 13.

A macro definition of marketing

Now that we've examined several complementary views of the macro role of marketing, we can define marketing at a ***macro*** level.

marketing

> **Marketing** is the economic and social process by which society's needs are served through exchanges within the constraints of available and affordable resources.

The elements of this definition reflect much of the flavor of marketing. Marketing is an *economic process:* its participants seek gain, often of a monetary nature. It is a *social process:* its participants occupy well-defined roles that necessitate social interaction if the process is to work. The intent is to serve society: indeed, marketing can be evaluated in terms of how well it serves society. For society to be served, exchanges must occur. Finally, the process is *constrained* by the availability and cost of resources.

KEY ELEMENTS OF THE MACRO SYSTEM

Now that we have established the role of marketing at a macro level we must consider the way it performs that role. This section examines the key elements of the macromarketing system.

The functions of marketing

For producer-consumer gaps to be closed, goods to be matched with needs, utility to be created, or exchange to occur, eight *marketing functions* must be performed:

1. *Buying*—The search for and evaluation of goods and services.
2. *Selling*—The communication of information about goods and services to buyers. Advertising and personal selling are two prominent forms of the selling function.
3. *Transportation*—The physical movement of goods and services from the point of production to the point of consumption.
4. *Storage*—The holding of finished goods until an exchange occurs.
5. *Standardization and grading*—Standardization involves transforming goods to sizes or quantities appropriate for end-use requirements (quart containers of milk, six-packs of soda, 10-ounce cuts of beef). Grading involves categorizing goods by quality (Grade A beef).
6. *Financing*—The generation of cash to perform the other functions.
7. *Risk taking*—The fact that goods must be produced before they can be consumed requires suppliers to assume some degree of risk. There is no certainty that consumers will buy goods in the quantities produced.
8. *Market information*—The activities that provide information about the marketplace.

These functions vary in the role they play in the marketing system. Buying and selling play direct roles in that they are exchange functions. Transportation and storage also play direct roles of a distributive nature. The remaining functions are more indirect; they *facilitate* the performance of the exchange and distributive functions and indirectly contribute to certain types of utility. Table 1–1 summarizes the role of each function and the type of utility to which it is most relevant.

The concept of flow

The separation of producers and sellers and the marketing functions that overcome this separation suggest that the concept of *flow* is central to understanding the operation of the marketing system. Two types of

Table 1–1: Marketing functions

Function	Role	Utility created
Buying	Exchange	Possession
Selling	Exchange	Possession
Transportation	Distributive	Place
Storage	Distributive	Time
Standardization and grading	Facilitative	Form
Financing	Facilitative	Possession
Risk taking	Facilitative	Possession
Market information	Facilitative	Form

Figure 1–10: Flows in marketing

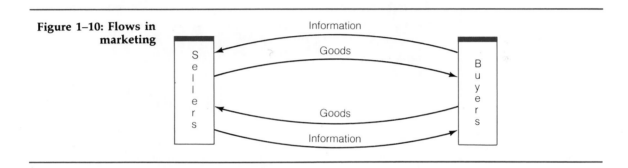

flow are inherent to marketing. (See Figure 1–10.) First, there is the physical *flow of goods* from the point of production to the point of consumption. This flow results from the transportation and storage functions and closes the spatial, time, and ownership gaps.[11] The flow of goods is mainly from producer to consumer, but the reverse also occurs, as in the case of defective goods.

Second, a *flow of information* results from the buying, selling, and market information functions. These functions help close the informational and valuation gaps. There is more of a two-way flow with information than with goods. Through the selling function, those with goods and services communicate with buyers. Through the buying function, buyers express their desire for goods. The market information function also allows sellers to obtain information from buyers.

---

[11] There are occasions when the ownership gap is closed by a flow of title that is separate from the flow of the good. Such an occasion occurs, for example, when an intermediary takes physical possession of a good (perhaps for storage purposes) but does not take ownership.

Offering the consumer
control of information
flow.

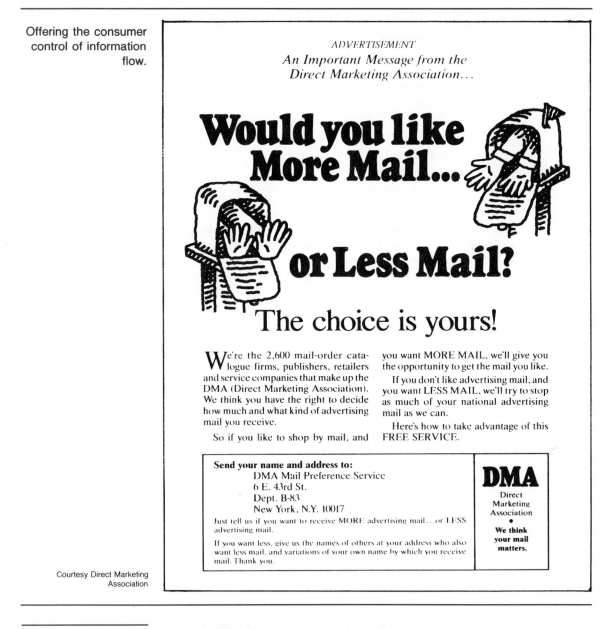

Courtesy Direct Marketing
Association

**Marketing
institutions**

Marketing functions are performed by various marketing institutions. While there are many marketing institutions, most can be placed in one of five categories:

1. ***Manufacturers***—Organizations that supply raw materials or trans-form them into finished goods suitable for consumption by end users.

2. **Wholesalers**—Intermediaries who buy goods and resell them to retailers.

3. **Retailers**—Intermediaries whose main role is to sell directly to the end user.

4. **Agents**—Institutions that specialize in one or more marketing functions (advertising agencies, marketing research agencies, warehouses).

5. **Buyers**—Individual consumers and organizational buyers who purchase and use products and services.

Characteristics of functions performed by institutions

Several important **characteristics of marketing functions** convey the manner in which they are performed in the marketing system. (See Figure 1–11.) First, all of the functions *must be performed.* Not one can be eliminated. Each function must be performed by at least one institution.

Second, the performance of a function *can be shifted* from one institution to another within the system. Thus, a function can be eliminated by one institution, but its performance must then be assumed by another.

Third, marketing functions are *divisible.* The performance of any one function can be shared by multiple institutions. For example, the transportation function for a particular product is generally shared by manufacturers, intermediaries, and even buyers. The burden of transporting many products from the point of exchange to the point of consumption is assumed by buyers. In this way buyers perform part of a marketing function. Other institutions transport goods from the point of production to the point of exchange.

Consider the performance of functions in the marketing of food items. A manufacturer such as Nabisco seeks out raw food supplies from farmers. An exchange (buying and selling) occurs probably at a central market

Figure 1-11: Characteristics of marketing functions

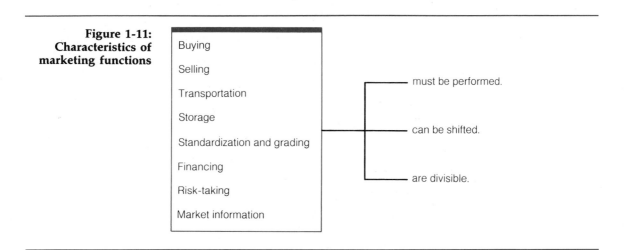

Buying

Selling

Transportation

Storage

Standardization and grading

Financing

Risk-taking

Market information

— must be performed.

— can be shifted.

— are divisible.

where the farmer delivered grain (transportation). Nabisco moves these supplies to its manufacturing plants (transportation). Based on research about consumer needs and wants (market information), it transforms these supplies into an array of finished goods in units suitable for transportation (standardization into cases). Some of the many Nabisco brands are listed in Table 1–2. For cost reasons it produces more quantities than are currently demanded (risk taking). Economies of scale in production and transportation are realized this way. Storage of the goods occurs until they are to be delivered.

Nabisco delivers its products to food stores carrying its brands (transportation). Items are left there. The retailer breaks the cases down (standardization) and places units on the shelves. Later Nabisco bills the retailer (financing of an exchange), who pays Nabisco (buying and selling). The retailer has bought more than required at that time (risk taking and storage). Throughout this time Nabisco advertises its products to consumers (selling). The retailer also advertises the availability of Nabisco brands in the store (selling).

Consumers come to the retailer and purchase some Nabisco products (buying). They take the products home (transportation) and put them in their pantries (storage) until they decide to consume them.

Notice the presence of all functions in the above scenario. All of them are divided to some extent among the institutions. Figure 1–12 identifies the functions performed by each institution. Now assume Nabisco decided

Table 1–2: Some Nabisco brands of food	Ritz crackers	Cream of Wheat hot cereals
	Premium saltine crackers	Nabisco shredded wheat
	Wheatsworth stone ground wheat crackers	Team flakes cereal
	Waverly wafers	Nabisco 100% bran cereal
	Chicken in a Biskit flavored crackers	Dromedary dates, pimientos, cake mixes
	Triscuit wafers	Royal desserts
	Wheat Thins snack crackers	Life Savers roll candy
	Snack Mate pasteurized process cheese spread	Bubble Yum bubble gum
	Chips Ahoy! chocolate chip cookies	Care* Free sugarless gum
	Oreo chocolate sandwich cookies	Blue Bonnet margarines
	Nilla wafers	Fleischmann's margarines
	Mallomars chocolate cakes	Egg Beaters cholesterol-free 99% real egg product
	Fig Newtons cookies	Chuckles candies
	Diggers popcorn snacks	Junior Mints candies
	Mister Salty pretzels	Charleston Chew candy bar
	Baby Ruth candy bar	Shreddies cereal
	Butterfinger candy bar	Planters nuts and snacks
	Fleischmann's active dry yeast	Moosehead imported Canadian beer
	Milk-bone brand dog biscuits	Foster's lager imported Australian beer
		Carlsberg lager imported Danish beer and other imported beers

Figure 1–12: The Allocation of marketing functions

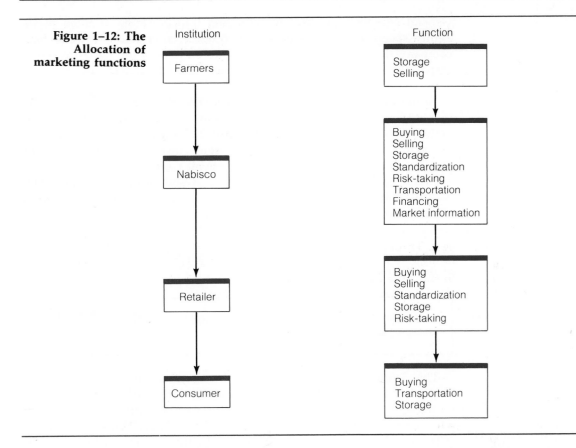

to stop transporting its products to retailers. That function would have to shift to another institution if the products were to reach the retailers. Perhaps some retailers would take it over. More likely, though, another institution—a wholesaler—would enter the situation and take over the function.

The role of specialization

The tasks and goals of the marketing system demand *specialization* in all but the simplest of economies. The heterogeneous needs and wants of society do not allow one firm to produce or market all the goods and services required to satisfy them. Instead, companies must specialize in the needs they satisfy. Producers do not specialize in products; they specialize in the *needs* products satisfy. Products are *means* by which needs are satisfied. Many times specialization is in the physical nature of the products that fill a specific need. Other times specialization is diverse products aimed at a general need. The production capabilities of General Motors are mainly devoted to automobiles. The production capabilities of Zenith are spread among televisions, radios, and stereos.

General Motors specializes in satisfying transportation-oriented needs; Zenith specializes in satisfying general home-entertainment needs. Each company develops a greater expertise in satisfying the needs in which it specializes. The results are more efficient and effective means of serving society.

In addition to product specialization, *functional specialization* occurs in marketing. Several diverse functions must be performed within a marketing system. Most firms would find it difficult to achieve expertise in every marketing function. Therefore, some institutions concentrate on the performance of one or a few of them. Certain intermediaries, for example, concentrate on the transportation and storage functions. This way they develop specialized functional expertise that results in a more efficient and effective performance.

Markets

The concept of a ***market*** is, of course, central to an understanding of marketing.

market

> A **market** is the set of all current and potential buyers of a particular product or service.

This definition has important implications about the nature of a market. Beginning with the latter part of the definition, markets are identified with a specific product or service. There are varying degrees of aggregation when considering the market for a product or service. Think of the liquid refreshment market. (See Figure 1–13.) Within it are markets for soft drinks, alcoholic beverages, fruit juices, etc. Within, say, the fruit juice market are markets for orange juice and grapefruit juice or markets for fresh versus frozen juices. We may ultimately identify the market for frozen Minute-Maid orange juice. Thus, we can move from very macro to very micro levels of identifying markets within this definition. Market boundaries will again be considered in Chapters 3 and 10.

The definition also implies an important aspect of markets: *opportunity.* By identifying both current *and* potential buyers, this definition recognizes that markets exist when a product satisfies certain needs and buyers will pay a price acceptable to producers. In other words, a market exists when there is *potential for exchange;* and the task of marketing is to actualize this potential. By identifying current and potential buyers, we define a market as the sum of realized and potential exchange involving a product or service.

The macromarketing system does not operate in random, unorganized fashion; there are important subsystems within it that perform marketing functions. The way these subsystems operate determines the specific nature of the total system.

Figure 1–13: The liquid refreshment market

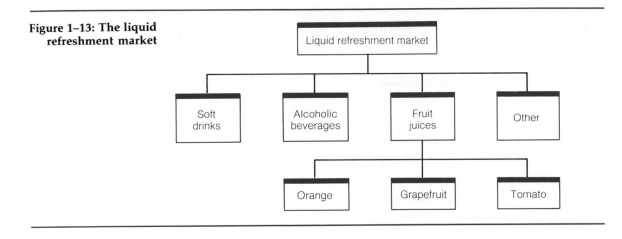

MARKETING SYSTEMS WITHIN THE MACRO SYSTEM

The entire macromarketing system contains certain identifiable marketing subsystems, including (1) industries, (2) channels, and (3) individual firms. The subsystems result from the specialization that is so critical to the performance of marketing tasks. They reflect how the operations of the entire marketing systems are allocated.

Industries

Consider the following definition of industry.

industry

> An **industry** is all firms involved in the production and marketing of similar goods and services.

We refer to the auto industry, the computer industry, the record industry, the insurance industry, and so on. But because of the myriad versions of many products and services, an industry is difficult to identify in practice. For example, should we think of the auto industry as a whole? Or is it more meaningful to think in terms of the small-car industry, the sports-car industry, the luxury-car industry?

If an industry comprises all firms involved in the production or marketing of similar products, then a disaggregated view of industries is probably most appropriate from a marketing perspective. While sports cars and luxury cars certainly have common attributes, they also are quite distinct. This distinctiveness requires them to be marketed differently; and it suggests they should be thought of as different industries—even though certain companies are common to both industries.

There certainly is no common structure to which all industries conform; nor are the operations of all industries standard. However, all marketing functions are performed in each industry. The pickup truck industry is composed of a small number of manufacturers who perform many of the marketing functions. They transport their goods directly to franchised

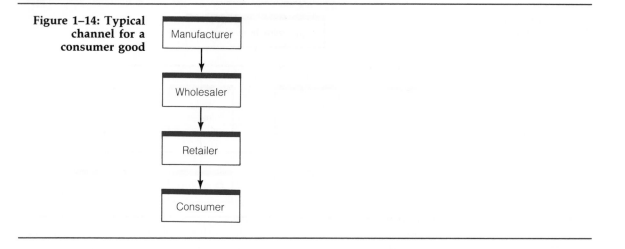

**Figure 1–14: Typical
channel for a
consumer good**

dealers, who sell to the end user. These dealers assume a significant part of the selling function. Usually, there is but one dealer for a particular brand of truck in a local market area.

Contrast the truck industry with the phonograph record industry and we see the substantial variations that can exist among industries. In the record industry producers distribute through a variety of intermediaries at the wholesale and retail levels. The selling and distribution functions are shared throughout the industry. A particular record will usually be available in several retail outlets in a local market.

An industry transforms raw materials into a set of similar products or services that serve as alternative choices to satisfy buyers' particular needs or sets of needs. Government regulations aside, an industry should not be thought of as managed. The essence of how industries operate is competition: competition between producers and between intermediaries that result in more efficiency and effectiveness in the creation of form, time, place, and possession utilities.

Channels

A marketing subsystem that takes on a managed nature is the ***marketing channel.*** Marketing channels exist within industries and involve only one specific product or service.

marketing channel

> A **marketing channel** is a set of interdependent organizations that by an exchange of outputs make a product or service available to buyers.[12]

The typical channel for many consumer goods is shown in Figure 1–14. A manufacturer sells its products to a wholesaler, who resells them

---

[12] Adapted from Louis W. Stern and Adel I. El-Ansary, *Marketing Channels,* 2d ed. (Englewood Cliffs, N.J.: Prentice-Hall, 1982), pp. 3–4.

to a retailer, who resells to the consumer. Channels are a major topic in Section Five. It is sufficient to say here that the major task of channel institutions is to allocate among themselves the marketing functions for a product.

Individual firms

The final marketing subsystem is the *individual firm.* Each marketing institution—whether a producer, retailer, or any other institution—is a marketing system. A firm reaches its markets through its marketing operations. These operations include product development, advertising, personal selling, pricing, and distribution. These activities are managed, and they represent means to achieve profit and growth objectives. At the level of a firm, marketing is a strategic force; and how well it is managed determines the firm's success. Strategic marketing management at the level of the firm is the main perspective of the remainder of this text.

As we move from discussion of the entire marketing system to discussion of industries, channels, and firms, we move to an increasingly micro level of analysis. (See Figure 1–15.) Each successive subsystem is a component of all the previous ones. You can understand each subsystem better by recognizing the larger system of which it is a part. With this in mind, we are now ready to examine the nature of marketing for individual organizations.

Figure 1–15: Macro-micro nature of marketing systems

Macro			Micro
Macro-marketing system	Industry	Channel	Individual organizations

MARKETING MANAGEMENT

marketing management

> **Marketing management** is the planning, decision making, organizing, directing, and controlling of an organization's resources to facilitate exchanges that satisfy customers and meet the organization's objectives.

Several aspects of this definition should be highlighted. First, *marketing management* involves five basic management functions: planning, decision making, organizing, directing, and controlling. *Planning* involves setting forth a sequence of actions to be carried out. *Decision making* involves identifying major problems, developing and analyzing courses of action, and decision implementation. *Organization* involves developing a formal structure, grouping activities into departments, and specifying relationships between departments and operating units.

The *organization function* is especially important in management of the sales force and in the firm's overall structure of function, products, or markets. The *direction function* involves the organization's philosophy about people and how to integrate the needs of individuals with those of the organization. The *control function* involves (1) developing standards of performance, (2) measuring actual performance, (3) comparing actual performance with norms or standards, and (4) taking corrective action to remedy substandard performance.

Customer satisfaction and organizational objectives

The purpose of marketing management activities is usually two-fold: (1) to satisfy customer wants and needs and (2) to achieve organizational objectives. For profit-making organizations, the overall objectives usually include attaining a special level of dollar sales volume or certain returns on investment. For nonprofit organizations, the major objective is often stated in public interest terms. For instance, a park commission wishes to increase the playgrounds in the community; a hospital wants to increase the number of health services it provides; a museum wants to offer new programs with broad public appeal.

Marketing management tries to develop products and services that specific groups of customers (often referred to as *target markets*) will find attractive. The intent is that these groups of consumers will be willing to exchange something of value (such as money or time) for the product or service. Profit-making organizations usually attempt to exchange a product or service for money. Nonprofit organizations may provide a sense of pride or some other psychological benefit in exchange for the customer's time or money.

Resources

The organization employs certain resources to achieve its objectives. In the broadest sense, the resources are labor and capital. But marketing management has developed much more specific resources to achieve its objectives. These resources are usually called the **marketing mix** or the firm's marketing decision variables. The marketing mix concept was developed by Professor Neil Borden of Harvard University.[13] The list of elements in the marketing mix can be very long. Therefore, the marketing mix is generally thought of in terms of four major decision variables: product, price, physical distribution, and promotion. Table 1–3 summarizes the detailed components of each.

To get an idea of a firm's marketing mix in operation, let's return to our earlier example of Saab automobiles. Table 1–4 identifies Saab's target market (as Saab defines it) and how it uses each area of marketing resources to appeal to this market.

[13] Neil Borden, "The Concept of the Marketing Mix," *Journal of Advertising Research,* June 1964, pp. 2–7.

Table 1–3: The marketing mix	Product	Promotion	Price	Place
	Quality	Advertising	List price	Channels of distribution
	Brand name	Ad copy	Discount	Physical distribution
	Packaging	Media placement	Allowances to:	Storage
	Services (before and after sale)	Personal selling	Retailers and wholesalers	Transportation
	Warranties	Managing sales	Rebates	Retailers
		Communication of sales message	Coupons	Wholesalers
		Publicity	Credit terms	Industrial distribution
		Press releases		
		Company newspaper		
		Plant tours		
		Sales promotion		
		Display		
		Trade shows		
		Product brochures		
		Package		

Table 1–4: Saab's marketing effort		
	Target market	Customers willing to pay more for distinctive automobiles, with performance, luxury, styling, and pure image.
	Product	900 Series. Three models, each in three-door hatchback and four-door sedan versions: Base 900 model, 900S model, 900 Turbo (turbocharger provides surge of power when needed). 900S and 900 Turbo offer many standard luxuries. Buyers get detailed explanation of operation of car, leatherette case with maintenance and warranty manuals, small flashlight, tire-pressure gauge, coffee mug, and thank-you card from president.
	Price	Base 900—$12,000; 900S—$16,000; 900 Turbo—$20,000.
	Physical distribution	326 dealerships and service centers in United States. Parts warehouses linked by computer to Sweden. Parts airlifted to United States.
	Promotion	$.5 million annually in national advertising, mostly in auto magazines and news weeklies. Dealer cooperatives spend about $2.5 million annually for ads in local TV, radio, and newspapers. Personal selling effort includes manufacturer's field representatives and dealer sales staff. Product brochures include four-page item with arty photographs of the car in unusual surroundings and a 50-page "Engineering Features" book.

Source: Bernie Whalen, " 'Tiny' Saab Drives up Profits with Market-Niche Strategy, Repositioning," *Marketing News*, March 16, 1984, pp. 14–16.

Marketing philosophies

Understanding management philosophy, or the way management views its task of managing the organization, is essential to understanding modern marketing management. Now, we might want to take for granted that management should try to satisfy the organization's customers. But some conditions have allowed management to follow other philosophies, or concepts.

Production concept. The ***production concept*** focuses on the factors necessary to manufacture or produce a product. The primary emphasis is on locating an adequate supply of raw materials and the necessary labor and/or power supplies and machinery and equipment. The idea that "supply creates its own demand" characterizes this concept. Management uses a production concept when there is more demand than supply and manufacturers are able to sell all they can produce. The production concept dominated U.S. business until the 1920s. During this time period the emphasis was on producing such basic items as clothing, food, and housing. Today firms may be able to operate under a production concept during periods of shortages. In some developing countries where demand exceeds supply, the economy may be dominated by a production-concept orientation.

Some companies mistakenly assume that producing a high-quality product insures success. Oftentimes an overemphasis on quality leads to products that are built to an unnecessarily high standard, which makes the product too expensive. Consider the following example. The manufacturer of office filing cabinets remarked that the company's filing cabinet should be selling better. The cabinets were built so well that they "could be dropped off a four-story building without injury." An observer stated, "customers don't intend to drop the cabinet off of a four-story building."

Sales concept. The ***sales, or selling, concept*** focuses on techniques to stimulate consumers to buy. Management emphasizes activities such as personal selling and advertising to persuade buyers to purchase what the firm has to sell.

The sales concept is often used when there is an excess of supply over demand. As competition increases and buyers become more affluent, management finds it necessary to become more aggressive in these efforts to persuade the market to purchase its products. Market intermediaries such as retailers, wholesalers, and industrial distributors are recognized as important in the selling effort. As a result, advertising and personal selling effort are directed at these intermediaries as well as at the final consumer or buyer of the products.

The sales concept relies on the "hard sell," which uses emotional appeals and pressure tactics. Used-car selling, some door-to-door, and telephone-selling programs are based on the sales concept. In the nonprofit area, political candidate campaigning and fund raising often use the sales concept.

Marketing concept. As the business environment has grown more competitive and consumer wants and needs more varied, organizations have had to adopt new philosophies. The philosophy consistent with the modern marketing-management approach is the ***marketing concept.***

marketing concept

> The **marketing concept** is a managerial philosophy that maintains an organization must integrate and coordinate its programs and resources to satisfy its customers in order to achieve its objectives.

Figure 1–16: Degrees of customer orientation

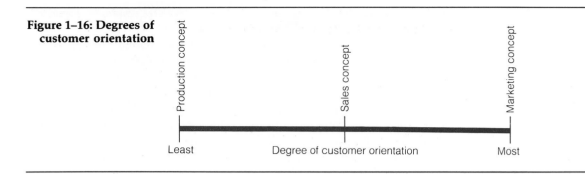

The marketing concept starts by determining the customer's needs and wants and then attempts to have the company develop products or services to satisfy the customer. In the production and sales concepts, the customer is considered after the product is made. The intent is to convince the customer to accept what the firm has already produced. See Figure 1–16 for an illustration of the degree of customer orientation for the production, sales, and marketing concepts.

The marketing concept has three distinct characteristics: a focus on customer wants and needs, a coordinated effort among the functional areas of the firm (i.e., production, marketing, finance, and personnel) as

Figure 1–17: Evolution of marketing concept at Pillsbury

Era	Description
Production concept 1869–1930	The formation of Pillsbury was based on the availability of the factors of production. The essence of the company production concept was captured in the following statement: "We are professional flour millers. Blessed with a supply of the finest North American wheat, plenty of water power, and excellent milling machinery, we produce flour of the highest quality."
Sales concept 1930–50	Pillsbury became highly conscious of the customer for the first time. A marketing research department was formed to provide information on the consumer. Management became more aware of the importance of retailers and wholesalers. The philosophy was "We are a flour-milling company, manufacturing a number of products for the consumer market. We must have a *first-rate sales organization which can dispose of all the products we can make at a favorable price.*"
Marketing concept 1950–60	Management realized that because of increased research and production capacities, literally hundreds of new and different products could be produced. It became necessary to have explicit criteria for deciding which products to produce. "And these criteria were, and are nothing more or less than, those of the consumer herself. . . ." The brand manager concept was introduced to implement the marketing concept.
Marketing control 1960–present	This era represents a more complete commitment to marketing and to the satisfaction of consumer wants. This philosophy is summarized as follows: "We are moving from a company which has the marketing concept to a marketing company."

Source: Robert J. Keith, "The Marketing Revolution," *Journal of Marketing,* January 1960, pp. 35–38.

the means of providing customer satisfaction, and attainment of organizational goals through customer satisfaction.

Some companies that have successfully implemented the marketing concept are Procter & Gamble, Pillsbury, General Electric, General Foods, General Mills, Caterpillar, John Deere Company, Avon Products, and IBM. Many others claim and/or attempt to employ the concept. But, relatively few have been truly successful in implementing it. The many reasons include a failure to understand the concept and a lack of resources to implement it correctly.

Figure 1–17 contains a summary of the evolution of the marketing concept at Pillsbury.

The marketing environment

Marketing management does not occur in a vacuum. Rather it occurs within a ***marketing environment*** consisting of three levels:

1. *Intraorganizational level*—Other departments in the organization and the overall culture of the organization.
2. *External support level*—Other institutions that facilitate the organization's marketing effort (wholesalers, retailers, agents).
3. *Macro level*—The diverse, dynamic, uncontrollable macro forces contained in five sectors (sociocultural, competitive, economic, technological, and public policy sectors).

The marketing environment influences the organization and its exchange process with customers in many ways. It imposes constraints and threats of detrimental consequences, but it also opens opportunities. The constraints limit the organization's use of the marketing mix elements. Regulation of advertising and pricing are good examples of these constraints. But other sectors (such as technology) may provide opportunities to make the organization more efficient or provide more effective ways to satisfy customers. Chapter 3 takes a closer look at the marketing environment.

A summary framework of marketing management

Figure 1–18 contains an overview of the exchange process between an organization and its market and the environment in which the exchange process takes place. The organization's management is guided by the marketing concept and the internal environment in developing the marketing mix offered to the market in exchange for money. In addition to the flow of goods, services, and money, there is an informational flow. The organization provides information on the product or service in many ways, including advertising and publicity. The consumer provides reactions to the product or service; and this information is usually gathered through the organization's marketing research efforts. Each flow may be facilitated by institutions in the external support environment.

As a strategic force in an organization, marketing requires careful plan-

Figure 1–18: Framework of marketing management

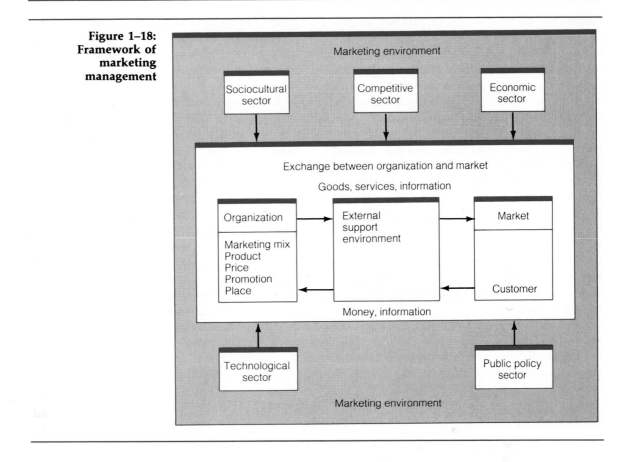

ning in line with organizational objectives. Chapter 2 will examine the strategic planning process in marketing management.

SUMMARY

Marketing is a highly diverse topic that deserves study because it is significant in the economy and individual organizations, is an employment opportunity, and is personally relevant. Three dichotomies capture the nature and scope of marketing. The positive-normative distinguishes between how marketing is actually conducted and how it should be conducted. Macro-micro distinguishes between marketing as an aggregate economic activity and a managerial function within an organiza-

tion. Profit-nonprofit recognizes its relevance to many types of organizations.

Several views reflect the role of marketing in the economy and in society. Gap theory suggests that marketing closes spatial, time, informational, ownership, and value separations between producers and consumers. A matching view suggests that marketing matches heterogeneous supplies with heterogeneous demands. Utility theory argues that marketing contributes to form, time, place, and possession utilities to create product utility. Exchange theory views marketing as the science of exchange. Together these views suggest that marketing at the macro level is the economic and social process by which society's needs are served through exchanges within the available and affordable resources.

Key elements within the macro system include marketing functions: buying, selling, transportation, storage, standardization and grading, financing, risk taking, and market information. These functions result in flows of goods and information. They are performed by marketing institutions: manufacturers, wholesalers, retailers, agents, and buyers. Each function must be performed but can be divided and shifted among institutions. Institutions specialize in the needs they satisfy or the functions they perform.

Markets are created by the potential for exchange. Industries include all firms involved in the production and marketing of similar goods and services to markets. A channel is a set of interdependent organizations that by an exchange of outputs make a product available to buyers in a market. Individual organizations are the most micro subsystem within the macro system.

At the organizational level marketing management is the planning, decision making, organizing, directing, and controlling of an organization's resources to facilitate exchanges that satisfy customers and meet the organization's objectives. Marketing resources include product, price, physical distribution, and promotion. The management of these resources is guided by the marketing concept—a philosophy of customer satisfaction as a means of goal achievement.

Marketing management occurs within an environment consisting of three levels: intraorganizational, external support, and macro. This environment is dynamic, diverse, and uncontrollable. It imposes constraints, suggests opportunities, and poses threats.

KEY CONCEPTS

Organizational subsystems	Time utility	Manufacturers
Positive-normative	Place utility	Wholesalers
Macro-micro	Possession utility	Retailers
Profit-nonprofit	Conditions for exchange	Agents
Positive marketing	Exchange relationships	Buyers
Normative marketing	Exchange definition of marketing	Characteristics of marketing
Gap theory	Macro definition of marketing	functions
Spatial separation	Marketing functions	Specialization
Time separation	Buying	Market
Informational separation	Selling	Industry
Ownership separation	Transportation	Marketing channel
Value separation	Storage	Marketing management
Heterogeneous supplies	Standardization and grading	Marketing mix
Heterogeneous demands	Financing	Production concept
Marketing as a matching process	Risk taking	Sales concept
Utility	Market information	Marketing concept
Form utility	Flows in marketing	Marketing environment

DISCUSSION QUESTIONS AND EXERCISES

1. Look back over the last 24 hours. Identify as many ways as you can recall that you came into contact with marketing.

2. Refer to Figure 1–3. Find a specific example for each of the eight cells in the figure.

3. Find a specific example of how society has shifted in the past decade or so. How have resources been shifted in response to this change? Be as specific as possible.

4. Pick one of the following statements and defend it.
   a. Marketing shapes society.
   b. Society shapes marketing.

5. The following two criticisms are frequently mentioned about marketing. Based on your reading of this chapter, can you counter these criticisms?
   a. Intermediaries (retailers and wholesalers) are unnecessary in the marketing system and only serve to increase the prices that consumers pay.
   b. Advertising results in higher costs to consumers.

6. Try to identify, based on your own experiences, knowledge, or impressions, an industry where the production concept seems to remain predominant. What about one where the sales concept is still common? Identify one where you think the marketing concept is prevalent. Why do you feel this way?

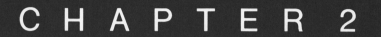

CHAPTER 2

The strategic role of marketing

Strategic marketing planning
    Ongoing process
    Process versus content of strategy
    Organization levels
    Objectives, strategy, and tactics
The strategic marketing planning process
    Situation analysis
    Establishing objectives
    Criteria for objectives
    Product/market
    Budgeting
    Market program positioning
Evaluation and control

Strategic planning models
    Strategic business units (SBUs) of
        analysis
    Growth/share matrix
    Experience curve analysis
    Industry attractiveness/business strength
        model
    Profit impact of marketing strategy (PIMS)
Organizing the marketing department
    Functional organization
    Product management organization
    Market organization
    Matrix approach

Summary
Key concepts
Discussion questions and exercises

STRATEGIC
MARKETING
PLANNING

This book emphasizes *strategic marketing planning.* Let's begin our discussion by defining that term.

**strategic marketing
planning**

> **Strategic marketing planning** is a process consisting of the following steps: (1) situation analysis, (2) establishment of objectives, (3) determination of product markets and market segmentation, (4) budget determination, (5) management of the marketing program, and (6) evaluation and control.[1]

Figure 2–1 shows this process. The intent of this chapter is to introduce the elements of the strategic marketing planning process and to indicate where the detailed discussions of these elements are found in the text.

We can highlight several aspects of our definition of strategic marketing planning.

Ongoing process

Strategic marketing planning is an ongoing process. The results of activities and actions in one part can and often do require changes in another part. For example, a firm may establish objectives only to find they need adjustment in response to competitive changes. This two-way relationship is illustrated by the arrows flowing to and from the components of Figure 2–1. The arrow must flow from performance evaluation and control (the last component) back to situation analysis (the first component).

**Process versus
content of strategy**

The strategic marketing planning framework presented here is a *process.* Applying this process should result in a statement of strategy *content.* Throughout this book we'll discuss the process of strategic marketing management, presenting the content of specific strategies for product, price, channel, and promotion management. For example, management's pricing strategy may be to set a high price relative to competition and make price a visible element in the advertising and personal selling. Called *high price/active strategy,* this strategy is followed by firms such as Curtis Mathes. (It's the most expensive television set and darn well worth it!)

Organization levels

The strategic planning process goes on at several levels throughout the corporation. Organizations can do strategic planning at the corporate, division, and product levels and at functional levels such as marketing. At the corporate level, planning emphasizes situation analysis and statements of corporate mission and objective. Division-level planning focuses on implementation of the strategic plan. Our focus in this book is on

---

[1] This definition is based on the strategic marketing literature and comes primarily from the following three sources: Derek F. Abell and John Hammond, *Strategic Market Planning* (Englewood Cliffs, N. J.: Prentice-Hall, 1979); David W. Cravens, *Strategic Marketing* (Homewood, Ill.: Richard D. Irwin, 1982); James Engel, Martin Warshaw, and Thomas Kinnear, *Promotional Strategy,* 5th ed. (Homewood, Ill.: Richard D. Irwin, 1983).

Figure 2–1: Strategic marketing planning process

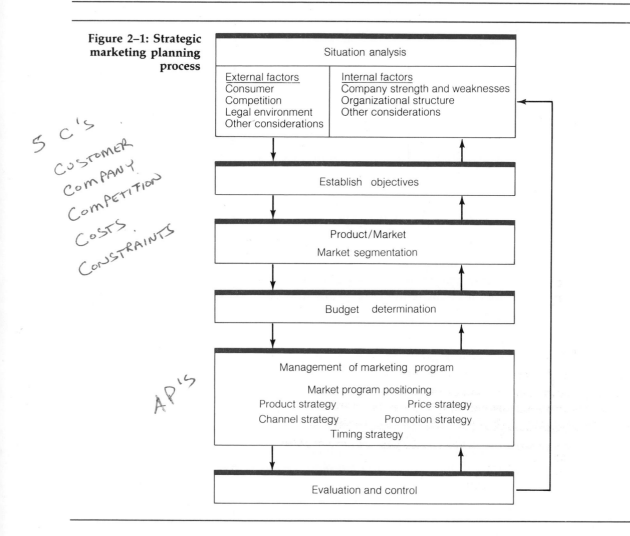

S C's
CUSTOMER
COMPANY
COMPETITION
COSTS
CONSTRAINTS

AP'S

the strategic management of the marketing function and on the development of strategies for the various elements of marketing.

Objectives, strategy, and tactics

These terms are important and are used frequently throughout this book, so let's define and discuss them.

objective

> **Objective** is the end result to be achieved.

Objectives may be stated in general qualitative terms; for example, "We want to be the industry leader in terms of quality and innovation."

Figure 2–2:
McDonald's—
Objective, strategy,
tactics

Objective	Increase the productivity of its restaurants
Strategy	Offer a breakfast menu to increase sales during off-peak hours
Tactic	Offer Egg McMuffin and a limited number of other breakfast-food items

However, to be more useful in guiding managerial action, objectives need to be stated in quantitative terms. (See the discussion later in this chapter.)

strategy

> **Strategy** is a general statement of the way in which an organization plans to achieve its objectives.

The strategy contains the basic approach but not the details of how a firm plans to attain its objectives. Strategies are usually established for the long term (5–10 years) and serve to guide short-term activity (less than 1 year).

tactics

> **Tactics** are specific actions taken to implement a strategy.

Usually a variety of tactics are employed. Tactics are very important to strategic marketing management because they help put plans into action.

To illustrate these concepts, let's consider the McDonald's hamburger chain. One of its corporate objectives is to increase the productivity of its individual fast-food restaurants. The restaurants represent substantial fixed costs, so to improve profitability management decided to increase the sales of individual restaurants during off-peak hours, especially during the morning. The company decided to offer the Egg McMuffin and a limited assortment of breakfast items.[2] Figure 2–2 specifies McDonald's objective, strategy, and tactics in this situation.

**THE STRATEGIC
MARKETING
PLANNING
PROCESS**

Now let's discuss each of the elements of the strategic marketing management process in more detail. The intent here is to introduce you to these elements and to indicate where in the book you'll find fuller discussion of them.

Situation analysis

Situation analysis deals with factors external and internal to the firm. External factors include consumer, competition, and legal environment.

---

[2] This example was adapted from Subhash C. Jain, *Marketing Planning and Strategy* (Cincinnati: Southwestern Publishing, 1981), p. 11.

Other external considerations are sociocultural, economic, technological, and public policy factors. These are discussed in Chapter 3. The factors internal to the firm are its basic strengths and weaknesses relative to competition and its organizational structure.

Consumer.   A well-conceived plan starts with an analysis of the consumer. The consumer or end user may be the ultimate household buyer or an industrial or organizational buyer. To develop effective marketing programs, we must understand two aspects of the consumer. First, we must identify influences on consumer decisions and their most likely time of occurrence. These influences include *personal factors* such as values, personality, and attitudes and *social factors* such as family and peer influence, social class, and culture.

Second, we should understand the processes by which individuals and organizations arrive at buying decisions. Consumers go through a goal-oriented, decision-making process. Marketing management's major challenge is to develop products and services that enable consumers to achieve their goals. Consumer needs play the central role in effective marketing, as we can see from the following example:

> *Divorced parents often face a space problem when their children visit. The solution is either to tolerate some crowding or to get an apartment with an extra bedroom. A St. Louis builder, the Mullenix Corporation, has included an economic answer to the divorced parents' problem. In 100 of 500 apartments it recently built, the builder installed a movable floor-to-ceiling partition that divides the living area to create a 10-by-20-foot bedroom. The partition disappears into the wall when not in use. Ivan Mullenix says divorced parents are a significant population whose special needs builders have ignored. So far, the units are selling and renting well.*[3]

A comprehensive analysis of the consumer is contained in Chapters 4 through 7.

Competition.   An important factor in formulating marketing strategy is competition. This can be structured in several important ways, including number of competitors, geographic scope of competition, and level of competition.

Competition may occur at a general or generic level where products strive to satisfy a similar need. For example, television, plays, and movie theaters compete to satisfy general entertainment needs. Manufacturers find that their brands compete against each other. Chapter 3 contains a detailed discussion of the types of competition and their relation to strategy.

---

[3] Reprinted by permission of *The Wall Street Journal.* © Dow Jones & Company, Inc., 1984. All rights reserved.

Legal environment. Here is another element to consider in strategic marketing planning. Legal concerns influence virtually every aspect of marketing management. For instance, management must consider the Robinson-Patman Act when making pricing decisions. This act prohibits granting different prices to different buyers of commodities of "like grade and quality" where it would reduce competition between seller and competitors, between a buyer and the buyer's competitors, or between a buyer's customers.[4] Robinson-Patman was enacted in the 1930s to protect smaller grocery stores from the strong price competition of large chains like A&P. Some critics feel that the Robinson-Patman Act decreases price competition and protects inefficient businesses. But it's the law and must be considered. The legal aspects of marketing are discussed in the following chapters: products in Chapter 13; channels, Chapter 14; pricing, Chapter 17; and promotion, Chapter 19.

Strengths and weaknesses. A key aspect of the situation analysis is the evaluation of the company's strengths and weaknesses. Some general categories or issues analyzed include the organization's financial status, production capacity and processes, plant location, share of market, product reputation and quality, size and quality of the labor force, and technological advantages.[5] In other words, how do the organization's strengths and weaknesses compare to those of competitors?

Organizational structure. The firm's existing organizational structure is another important internal factor that must be evaluated in situation analysis. Some internal factors the firm needs to consider are its financial and personnel resources and its current objectives. A detailed discussion of the various ways to organize the marketing function within the firm is presented at the end of this chapter.

Establishing objectives

After a complete analysis of the situation, management is ready to formulate objectives for the marketing program. These objectives are developed from the organization's statement of mission and corporate objectives, which are contained in the corporate strategic plan.

Mission statement. One of the most basic issues management must deal with is its statement of corporate mission and purpose. The corporate ***mission statement*** is a fundamental step in strategic planning at the corporate or overall organization level. The specification of this mission is one of the most challenging and difficult tasks facing management.

---

[4] David W. Cravens, Gerald Hills, and Robert Woodruff, *Marketing Decision Making: Concepts and Strategies* (Homewood, Ill.: Richard D. Irwin, 1980), p. 517.

[5] Merritt L. Kastens, *Long-Range Planning For Your Business,* 1978 AMACOM, a division of American Management Association, pp. 64–65.

Figure 2–3: Some major questions to be answered in formulation of mission statement	What business are we in? Who are our customers? What customers' needs should we satisfy? What are our resources and capabilities? How can we most effectively satisfy customers' needs? What environmental factors need to be considered?

Some of the major questions to be addressed are contained in Figure 2–3.

The mission should be stated in terms of meeting a need in the marketplace rather than in terms of producing a product. This is consistent with the marketing concept we discussed in Chapter 1, and many well-managed companies see their missions in these terms. Some examples of mission statements based on meeting marketplace needs are given in Figure 2–4.

Relationship between mission and marketing objectives. Once the corporate mission is established, it must be defined at more specific levels. First, an overall statement of corporate objectives is developed; then, specific marketing objectives are established; finally, marketing strategies follow. These relationships are illustrated by the hypothetical Shell Oil Company example in Figure 2–5.

Criteria for objectives Up to now we have discussed the role of objectives in strategic planning. The following *criteria* assist in the process of developing meaningful and workable objectives.

Priority. An organization usually has multiple objectives. It wants to increase sales, maintain financial stability, and hold or strengthen its competitive position. These objectives often conflict with each other. For example, the costs of increasing sales may undermine the objective of maintaining a strong financial position because additional money is spent on developing and advertising products. Prioritizing objectives reduces conflicts and helps management achieve its goals.

Figure 2–4: Possible mission statement for corporations	**Corporation**	**Mission**
	IBM	Meet the information-processing and problem-solving needs of business
	Shell Oil	Meet the energy needs of customers worldwide
	Marriott Hotels	Meet the food and housing needs for business and personal travelers
	Sony	Fulfill needs for home and personal entertainment

Figure 2–5: Relationship of corporate mission and objectives to marketing objectives and strategy for Shell Oil Company

Corporate mission	Meet the energy needs of mankind
Corporate objectives	Increase exploration for new energy sources
	Increase research and development for new energy products
	Develop new methods and practices for conserving energy
Marketing objectives	Increase sales from new products by 10% in next year
	Increase consumer awareness of major energy conservation practices
Marketing strategy	Introduce three new products to national market in next year
	Develop informational direct mailing and TV advertising on energy conservation practices

Measurable. Objectives should be measurable. An objective to "increase awareness of product" is too general. However, to "increase awareness of product from 20 percent to 40 percent" is specific and measurable. A statement of the means to measure the objective is also needed. Suppose brand X is a toothpaste best known for its decay-prevention ability. Then a statement of the means to measure the objective might be to "increase the percentage of respondents naming brand X from 20 percent to 40 percent when asked, 'Which toothpaste provides superior decay prevention?'"

Consistent. The objectives should be in harmony or consistent with each other. Firms shouldn't achieve results in one area at the expense of others. For example, a firm with the objective to maintain a high-quality image would probably not want to consider drastic price cutting to achieve short-term sales growth. Price cuts could suggest to potential buyers a reduction or loss of quality.

Reasonable. Objectives should be challenging but reasonable. They should be tailored to the individuals who must achieve them. Reasonable and challenging objectives offer a chance to gain a sense of achievement and encourage future performance.

Time period. Objective statements should specify a time period in which to accomplish given goals, and a specific time should be set to measure whether these objectives have been met. The toothtaste statement above could be expanded to read " . . . from 20 percent to 40 percent by November 1, 1986."

Product/market

The concept of ***product/market*** has been developed to facilitate strategic marketing.

product/market

> A **product/market** is a product (or group of products) that satisfies a particular need or want in a market.

A product/market may be defined quite broadly, such as "all products that provide transportation over short distances." By this broad definition automobiles, buses, trains, taxicabs, and bicycles would be competing products. The broad definition is useful when management finds it necessary to make a comprehensive analysis of competition. A narrower definition of a product/market includes products or brands that compete directly with each other—for example, the brands of subcompacts of the Big Three automakers that appeal to the same market.

Besides defining the competition for a product, the product/market concept facilitates the process of ***market segmentation.*** The organization can use the product/market concept to facilitate the process of matching the company's products and services with the needs of the market. Consider the case of a financial planning and securities corporation that provides investment, financial planning, and insurance services to three primary markets: individuals, small businesses, and large corporations. The company may decide to concentrate on three product/markets: investment services for small businesses, financial planning for individuals, and insurance for large corporations. (See Figure 2–6.) It may do so based on a

Figure 2–6: Product/ market grid

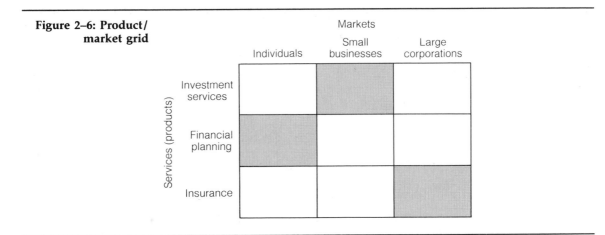

review of its own abilities, strengths, and sales growth potential and of the profitability of the markets.

   Market segmentation strategy.   After establishing the relevant product/markets, the firm must decide which particular product/market segments to serve. Market segmentation is useful in making this decision. Market segmentation divides a market into subgroups that are similar

A cologne advertisement is targeted toward the strong, silent male ("virile," "discreet") who has good taste at the same time ("masculine refinement").

Christian Dior
POUR HOMME

EAU
SAUVAGE

Virile. Discreet.

Refreshing. Uncompromising.

A fragrance of masculine refinement.

Exclusively Dior.

on some basis. It then develops marketing programs for one or more of these segments. The basis of forming marketing segments includes various traits of present and potential customers, their preference for certain product characteristics, and their use of the product. Chapter 9 is devoted to market segmentation.

The *target market* is the group of consumers to whom the organization's marketing program is directed. Once a market is segmented, an organization may direct its marketing effort at more than one target. For example, Charles of the Ritz, manufacturer of perfumes, designs its fragrances for certain target markets: Charlie perfume is aimed at the independent woman, Jontou at the "romantic" woman, Aviance at the housewife, and Senchal at the woman who wants advantage, luxury, and sex.[6]

Budgeting   Marketing management must consider the financial implications of its strategic plans. So *budgeting* is a key element in the process of strategic marketing management. Consider the following statement from some leading experts on strategic management:

> Finally, the [strategic] planning cycle ends with the determination of resource allocation and budgets for carrying out the plans.[7]

The allocation of financial resources to specific marketing programs represents some of the largest dollar expenditures made by corporations. For example, Procter & Gamble allocated over $726 million to advertising in 1982. Several of its individual brands had advertising budgets in excess of $20 million in 1982:[8]

Crest	$39 million
Folger	27
Crisco	22
Duncan Hines dessert mixes	20.5

Budgeting plays a role in the planning, implementation, and control aspects of strategic management. From a planning perspective, the organization's objectives must be considered in budget development. Financial analyses are made in the form of projected or planned income statements, balance sheets, and cash flow statements. Budgets provide the dollars for implementing the planned marketing programs. From a control perspective, comparisons are made between budgeted and actual expenditures. Significant differences can alert management to problem areas.

[6] Bill Abrams, "How Charles of the Ritz Knows What It Is that Women Want," *The Wall Street Journal,* August 20, 1981, p. 23.

[7] Abell and Hammond, *Strategic Market Planning,* p. 10.

[8] "100 Leading National Advertisers," *Advertising Age,* September 8, 1983, pp. 127–29.

The budget reflects management's belief in the ability of various marketing mix elements to achieve stated objectives. Consider the following example:

> In 1980, Avon had sales of $2.38 billion while Revlon's were $2.20 billion. Although the companies had a comparable level of sales, they had widely different budgets for advertising reflecting differences in management belief about the most effective way to market their products. Revlon spent over $105 million on advertising, while Avon spent $30 million. [9]

Financial resource allocation and budgeting are dealt with in Chapter 12 (on new-product strategy) and Chapter 20 (on advertising).

Market program positioning

A central concept in strategic marketing management is ***positioning.*** This means managing the marketing mix to shape the way consumers view the firm's product or brand relative to competing products. Usually position is regarded as a key element of the product strategy. (A detailed discussion of product positioning is presented in Chapter 13.) However, it is important to recognize that the other elements of the marketing mix—pricing, channels of distribution, advertising, personal selling—(promotion) are coordinated and integrated to establish and reinforce the product's position as perceived by the consumer.

Product strategy. The product is usually the basic element in the marketing mix. All subsequent decisions for other elements in the mix depend on the type of product being offered. With a high-quality product such as Michelob beer, an appropriate strategy would be a high price with heavy promotion to draw consumer attention to the beer's premium quality. Product and ***product strategy*** are discussed in Chapters 11, 12, and 13.

Marketing management of products involves both new products and existing products. A new product may be one that is new to the firm but not necessarily an innovation. A recent survey of 700 companies underscores the importance of new products to business. Between 1981 and 1986 it is estimated that new products will account for 31 percent of the firms' profits compared to 22 percent in the previous five-year period. In addition, new products will account for 37 percent of the firms' sales growth compared to 28 percent in the prior period. [10]

Existing products, of course, require management's continual attention regardless of how successful they may be. Consider the experience of

---

[9] Based on information from Gail Bronson, "Avon Lady Will Be Getting New Look in Drive for More Fashionable Image," *The Wall Street Journal,* January 19, 1981, p. 10; and "Advertising and Marketing Reports on 100 Top National Advertisers," *Advertising Age,* September 10, 1981, p. 129.

[10] Bill Abrams, "Despite Mixed Record Firms Still Pushing for New Products," *The Wall Street Journal,* November 12, 1981, p. 27.

General Foods with Jell-O dessert. When Jell-O's sales volume began falling 2 percent to 4 percent yearly, the company developed a new advertising campaign. The result was an increase in sales of 1 percent and an increase in market share from 70 percent to 71.4 percent—a major accomplishment given the competitiveness of the market and the dollar volume of sales involved.[11]

Channel strategy. A channel of distribution comprises a group of interdependent organizations that move a product or service from the producer to the ultimate consumer. The main purpose of the channel is to facilitate exchanges as the good or service moves from producer to ultimate consumer. To facilitate exchanges, intermediaries such as retailers and wholesalers are used. ***Channel strategy*** and retail and wholesale strategies are discussed in Chapters 14 and 15.

Major strategic decisions in channels involve the selection of the types and numbers of intermediaries to use. Other marketing decisions, particularly those related to product and price, are based on the channel. For example, Lenox Inc., using a channel of distribution comprised of leading department, jewelry, and specialty stores, has reinforced the Lenox image for high product quality and a premium price.[12]

Price strategy. Price is usually thought of as the amount of money an individual gives up to obtain a good or service from another individual. Price represents the value that buyer and seller assign to a good or service. Their agreement on this value is an inherent part of the exchange process and therefore an inherent part of marketing. Price and ***price strategy*** are discussed in Chapters 17 and 18.

Price is used in a variety of ways to help the firm reach specific objectives and implement strategies. Price can be used to defend against competitive threats. Xerox reduced its prices and intends to continue to do so to meet the fierce competition of the Japanese in the copier market.[13] A price increase can be used to reinforce a particular image for the product in the consumer's mind and to help increase profits as well. Hueblein raised the price of its Popov vodka by 8 percent. This resulted in 1 percent loss in market share. But Hueblein also saw 30 percent increase in profits.[14]

Promotional strategy. Marketing management communicates with its target market through ***promotional strategy.*** Promotional strategies

---

[11] Bill Abrams, "Jell-O's Revival Shows Sales Can Grow with Older Products," *The Wall Street Journal,* September 11, 1980, p. 23.

[12] David W. Cravens, *Strategic Marketing* (Homewood, Ill.: Richard D. Irwin, 1982) p. 263.

[13] Jeffrey H. Birnbaum, "Xerox Plans Further Price Cuts to Compete with Japanese Building Copier Market Share," *The Wall Street Journal,* May 22, 1981, p. 9.

[14] Jeffrey H. Birnbaum, "Pricing of Products Is Still an Art, Often Having Little Link to Costs," *The Wall Street Journal,* November 25, 1981, p. 25.

are based on a firm's integrating the elements of the promotional mix: advertising, personal selling, public relations, and sales promotion. Promotional strategies are designed to inform, persuade, and remind consumers of the benefits provided by the firm's products and services. Chapter 19 deals with the promotional mix, especially sales promotion and publicity. Chapter 20 is devoted to advertising, while Chapter 21 deals with personal selling and sales management.

The elements of the promotional mix should be used in an integrated way to achieve management's objectives. Consider the following example:

> The Twin City Bank of Little Rock, Arkansas, was attempting to increase its customers' use of Automatic Teller Machines (ATMs). The following promotional elements were used.
>
> Advertising. In newspapers, television (early morning and late evening), radio (especially during drive time and on weekends), statement stuffers, and point-of-sale displays in bank lobbies and offices.
>
> Sales promotion. Customers were rewarded with coupons on the back of the receipt generated by the ATMs. The coupons could be redeemed for a two-liter Coca-Cola, Godfather eight-inch pizza, or Baskin Robbins ice cream cone.
>
> Personal selling. Bank tellers and a special team of female senior citizens were hired to demonstrate the ATMs. Senior citizens were very successful demonstrators, not so intimidating as younger persons might have been.
>
> These promotional activities were effective. They increased ATM transactions 80 percent after the first month of promotional activity.[15]

Timing strategy.   A critical aspect of effective strategic planning is *timing.* Management decisions about the issues and questions in strategic planning are based on a dynamic analysis of factors. This dynamic analysis applies to the concept of *strategic windows.* There are limited periods of optimum fit between the key requirements of a market and the capabilities of a firm competing in that market. Investment in a product or market should be made when the strategic window is open. Conversely, a firm should consider discontinuing the manufacture of a product when the window has closed—that is, when market requirements are beyond the firm's capability to adapt.[16]

Four major categories of change affect the strategic window: the development of a new primary demand whose marketing requirements differ radically from existing marketing segments; market redefinition caused by changes in the definition of the product itself or change in the product/

---

[15] Kenneth J. Pennebaker, "How about Ice Cream, Coca-Cola, Pizza, and 'This Can't Be Yogurt,' " *Bank Marketing,* July 1983, p. 2.

[16] Derek F. Abell, "Strategic Windows," *Journal of Marketing,* July 1978, pp.21–25.

market strategies of competing firms; channel change; and new technologies that make existing ones obsolete.

> *An example of market redefinition is the case of Docutel, a manufacturer of ATMs. Docutel supplied virtually all ATMs in use until 1974. Then in 1975 a number of competitors—Burroughs, Honeywell, IBM—began to look at the banks' total electronic funds transfer system (EFTS) needs. These companies offered banks a complete package of equipment, of which ATMs were only one part. The competitors redefined the market in a way that made it increasingly difficult for Docutel to compete.[17]*

EVALUATION AND CONTROL

Evaluation of performance involves the establishment of criteria to assess performance and follow-up to determine what can be learned from the experience. To be most effective, the feedback criteria should be stated in quantitative terms and should assess the extent to which objectives have been met. Chapter 22 is dedicated to *evaluation and control.*

Consider the following example:

> *When Lever Brothers introduced AIM and Close-Up toothpastes and Beecham introduced Aqua-Fresh, the market share for Procter & Gamble's Crest toothpaste fell to 35 percent. To regain lost sales, Crest was reformulated, and advertising and promotion expenditures greatly increased. Since the objective was to recapture lost sales, market share was used as the measure of effectiveness. In one year's time, Crest's market share rose from 35 percent to an estimated 41 percent (near its original level), clearly showing the effectiveness of the reformulation and increased promotion.[18]*

Since sales volume results from the entire marketing plan, other measures can be used to evaluate selected parts of the marketing program. Consumer attitudes, advertising readership, and recall serve to measure communication results. Various expenses-to-sales ratios are criteria to evaluate personal selling and advertising. The point is that the measure used should adequately compare accomplishment and goal.

The marketing strategy's strengths and weaknesses should be evaluated. After the results of a plan are compared to the objective, a postmortem analysis should assess the experience. The findings of the postmortem should be used in future planning. It is particularly important that the management responsible for the successes be held accountable.

Procter & Gamble made effective use of its evaluation procedure with Pringle's potato chips. Pringle's losses exceeded $200 million[19]—quite near

---

[17] Ibid., p. 23.

[18] "Brands Gaining . . . Crest Sales Pick up . . . Industry Hoppers," *The Wall Street Journal,* January 14, 1982, p. 25.

[19] Dean Robart, "In Spite of Huge Losses, Procter & Gamble Tries Once More to Revive Pringle's Chips," *The Wall Street Journal,* October 7, 1981, p. 25.

the $250 million lost by Ford Motor Co. when it produced the Edsel. Like Ford, P&G was more concerned with product technology than with consumer needs. After some initial success, Pringle's failed because of consumer perceptions—fewer chips than in a normal bag, poor flavor, high cost, and too many preservatives and additives. Once P&G was aware of these perceptions it set out to change them by offering a better tasting, natural product and to communicate the changes through a new ad campaign. The results were encouraging, with a rise in market share of 1 percent and a $15 million increase in sales.[20] While this did not necessarily mean Pringle's would succeed, its chances for failure were much lower than if it had continued the previous marketing strategy. The evaluation and follow-up helped P&G avoid repeating their mistakes.

STRATEGIC PLANNING MODELS

Now, we turn to some strategic planning models, commonly referred to as *portfolio analysis models.*

portfolio analysis models

> **Portfolio analysis models** are strategic planning models used to classify products or product lines on such potential as sales growth and/or profitability. After classification, management allocates resources and develops strategies for products based on their potential.

Two widely used portfolio models are the **growth/share matrix** and the **industry attractiveness/business strength model. Experience curve** analysis is the foundation of portfolio analysis. The unit of analysis in these methods is commonly referred to as a **strategic business unit.**

Strategic business units (SBUs) of analysis

The concept of a strategic business unit (SBU) has been developed to facilitate strategic planning.[21]

SBU

> An **SBU** may be defined as a single product or brand or group of products or a mix of related products that serve a common market.

The management of the SBU should have control over the SBU's basic functions: engineering, manufacturing, marketing, and distribution.

Companies following the concept use widely different elements to compose SBUs. For example, General Electric's management took product lines from three separate divisions and formed an SBU to serve the house-

---

[20] Ibid.

[21] This discussion of SBU is adopted from Cravens, *Strategic Marketing,* p. 54; and William K. Hall, "SBUs: Hot New Topic in the Management of Diversification," *Business Horizons* 21, no. 1, February 1978, pp. 17–25.

**Figure 2–7: Growth/
share matrix**

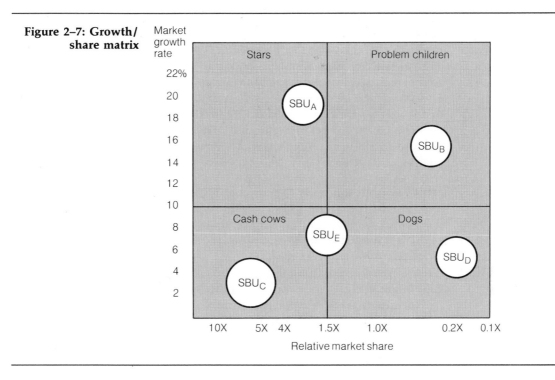

wares market. Another very small part of the Industrial Components Division was singled out as an SBU and now serves a distinct niche in the machine tool industry. At General Foods, SBUs were originally formed on a product-line basis. These product-oriented SBUs were redefined into menu segments like breakfast foods, beverages, main meals, desserts, and pet foods. The identification and definition of SBUs are managerial decisions that reflect the philosophical and programmatic answer to the question: "What are our businesses and what do we want them to be?"[22]

**Growth/share
matrix**

The Boston Consulting Group (BCG), a management consulting firm, developed the growth/share matrix. The growth/share matrix is based on two basic factors: market growth rate and relative market share. Market growth rate is the annual growth of the market in which the product competes. It is represented on the vertical axis of Figure 2–7. Relative market share is the company's share relative to its competition, shown as the horizontal axis of the figure. In Figure 2–7, the classification of SBUs into high- and low-growth categories is as follows: 10 percent or above is high growth; below 10 percent is considered low growth. We

[22] Hall, "SBUs: Hot New Topic," p. 19.

must point out, though, that the division between high and low market growth is arbitrary; the main consideration is that the criterion be made explicit to facilitate strategic planning.[23]

Market share in its simplest form is a given company's sales expressed as a percentage of industry sales. In the growth/share model a number of variations of market share measures may be used. One common variation is to compare the company's sales to those of its next largest competitor—the method used in Figure 2–7. This measure is simple to use and interpret. Relative market share is shown on a log scale. SBU_D, with a relative market share of 0.2X, has 20 percent of its closest competitor's share. SBU_C, with a relative market share of 5X, has five times the share of its closest competitor. The area of each of the circles in Figure 2–7 is proportionate to each SBU's contribution to total company dollar sales. An alternative measure of market share is to compare company share to the share of its three largest competitors. Both these measures provide information on the competition's structure. Regardless of the measure, often the dominant firm must have sales 1.5 times as large as its next largest competitor to ensure profitability.[24]

The growth/share matrix is divided into four quadrants, as shown in Figure 2–7. The label attached to each SBU within a quadrant, the nature of its cash flow, and the appropriate strategic action to be taken are discussed below.[25]

Stars.   Stars, represented by SBU_A, are high-growth, high-share SBUs. They usually require substantial cash to finance their rapid growth and to protect their share from competitors. Stars are the future cash cows, so scarce capital resources should be allocated to these SBUs.

Problem children.   Problem children are in a high-growth, low-share category, as shown by SBU_B. Generally they are a heavy cash drain on the company. The best strategic action here is to take quick steps to gain competitive strength and profitability—or else liquidate the SBU.

Cash cows.   Cash cows, as depicted by SBU_C, are in a low-growth, high-share category. Since they require little reinvestment to retain their market share and are highly profitable, SBUs in this category should generate a high cash flow. This cash should be allocated elsewhere.

Dogs.   Dogs are low-growth, low-share SBUs, as shown by SBU_D. They are not a large source of funds to the company, so the best strategy

[23] Yoram Wind and Henry J. Claycamp, "Planning Production Line Strategy: A Matrix Approach," *Journal of Marketing* 40 (1976), pp. 2–9.

[24] George Day, "A Strategic Perspective on Product Planning," *Journal of Contemporary Business,* Spring 1975, p. 10.

[25] Henry Claycamp, "Portfolio Approach Adds Missing Marketing Concept Element—Profit," *Marketing News,* November 17, 1978. p. 1.

here would be to liquidate the SBU or else to develop it slowly so more cash is available for the stars.

SBU$_E$ is an example of an SBU that does not fit clearly into one category, as it has intermediate levels of growth and market share. SBU$_E$ appears to be very close to making a profitable contribution to the company. The appropriate strategic action, then, would be to develop SBU$_E$ into a cash cow by gaining competitive strength.

Experience curve analysis

One foundation of portfolio analysis is the experience curve.

experience curve

> **Experience curve** analysis shows the relationship between per-unit costs and cumulative units of production. Specifically, each time the cumulative number of units produced doubles, per-unit costs decline by a specific percent. Experience is defined as the combined effects of learning, volume, investment, and specialization.

An 85 percent experience curve means that each time cumulative production doubles, costs decline 15 percent. If cumulative production doubles from 10 units to 20 units, per-unit costs decrease 15 percent (from $100 to $85). If production doubles again to 40 units, per-unit costs decrease 15 percent (from $85 to $72).

An important implication of the experience curve is that costs and market share appear to be related. As a result of the experience curve, if a firm produces more cumulative units faster than its competitors, its costs decrease faster. As its costs decrease, the organization is in a position to charge a lower price, which is likely to attract more customers and reduce costs even further. Consequently, as costs decrease, market share increases. The experience curve thus illustrates the importance of market share. The relationship of costs and market share shows the importance of market share in strategic planning models. Chapter 18 contains a discussion of the strategic implications of the experience curve to pricing.

Industry attractiveness/ business strength model

Strategic planning models other than the growth/share model have been developed. These models are sometimes referred to as ***multiple-factor screening methods.*** The most popular one was developed by General Electric working in conjunction with McKinsey and Company, a management consulting firm.[26] This model has all the advantages of the growth/share matrix plus some other benefits. The major differences between the two methods are the variables used to position an SBU and the strategic interpretation of that position. Specifically, factors in addition to market growth and market share are considered for both industry attractiveness and business strength. And, a grid position is assumed to

---

[26] Cravens, *Strategic Marketing,* p. 72.

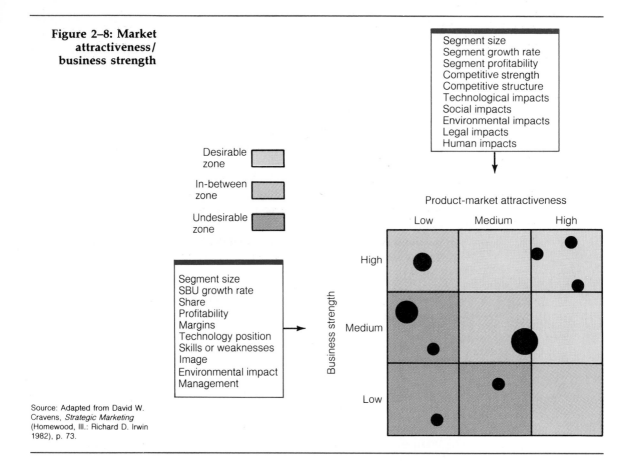

Figure 2–8: Market attractiveness/ business strength

Desirable zone

In-between zone

Undesirable zone

Segment size
Segment growth rate
Segment profitability
Competitive strength
Competitive structure
Technological impacts
Social impacts
Environmental impacts
Legal impacts
Human impacts

Segment size
SBU growth rate
Share
Profitability
Margins
Technology position
Skills or weaknesses
Image
Environmental impact
Management

Product-market attractiveness

Low   Medium   High

High

Medium

Low

Business strength

Source: Adapted from David W. Cravens, *Strategic Marketing* (Homewood, Ill.: Richard D. Irwin 1982), p. 73.

be linked to return on investment, not cash flow, which is the assumption of the growth/share matrix.[27]

Figure 2–8 is an example of a GE-type screening grid. GE uses 10 criteria to determine industry attractiveness: segment size, growth rate, and profitability; competitive strength and structure; and technological, social, environmental, legal, and human impacts. Ten factors are also used to assess business strength of competitive position. These are segment size and SBU growth rate, share, profitability, margins, technology position, skills or weaknesses, image, environmental impact, and management.[28] The variables are modified according to the requirements of each company. Management rates specific products or SBUs on each factor. Then the ratings are combined into an overall position for the product or SBU on the screening grid.

[27] Abell and Hammond, *Strategic Market Planning,* pp. 374–75.
[28] Hall, "SBUs: Hot New Topic," p. 20.

As with the growth/share matrix, there are strategic implications from the screening grid. According to Figure 2–8, SBUs in a high category are in a desirable zone, with presumably a high return on investment (ROI). The suggested strategy here would be to invest and to grow. Units in the diagonal categories fall in an in-between zone. The recommended strategy here would be to choose which products to develop and which to "milk" for cash. SBUs in the low categories are in the undesirable zone. Since they probably have a low ROI, the suggested strategy would be to liquidate or simply to get whatever return is possible in the short run.

There are a number of approaches in addition to the growth/share and industry attractiveness/business strength models. These include the product performance matrix used by International Harvester, which analyzes industry sales, product sales, market share, and profitability. The directional policy matrix used by Shell Oil incorporates the profitability of market segments and the firm's competitive position within the segment. For a more detailed discussion of these and other portfolio techniques, see the article by Wind and Mahajan.[29]

Profit impact of marketing strategy (PIMS)

An important input for strategic planning is the *Profit Impact of Marketing Strategy (PIMS)* project. PIMS is a research project that uses a computer model to analyze the strategic position and prospects of an individual business. PIMS is run by the Strategic Planning Institute (SPI). SPI has built an extensive data bank of strategy experiences for the variety of products and services of its members. From the computer analysis, members receive useful strategic planning information.

To obtain the strategic information, members must first submit a data form for each business component to be analyzed. For PIMS studies, a business component is any unit that sells a distinct set of products or services to an identifiable customer group with a well-defined set of competitors and for which revenues, costs, investments, and strategic plans can be separated out.[30] Data supplied on the business component includes characteristics of the market environment, the state of competition, the business strategy followed, and the operating results obtained. This information is confidential and is supplied in four different reports.

The PAR Report specifies the cash flow and return on investment normal for the business, given its market conditions and position, competition, technology, and budget allocations. The analysis is based on the past performance of other businesses with similar characteristics under comparable conditions. The PAR Report identifies the strengths and weaknesses of the firm that account for any deviation from "par." The Strategy

---

[29] Yoram Wind and Vijay Mahajan, "Designing Product and Business Portfolios," *Harvard Business Review* 59 (January–February 1981), pp. 155–65.

[30] *The PIMS Program* (Cambridge, Mass.: The Strategic Planning Institute, 1977), pp. 3–5.

Analysis Report shows the consequences of various strategic moves in the short and long term on various aspects of the firm. The Optimum Strategy Report predicts the combination of strategic moves that should produce optimal results for the business. The Report on Look-Alikes (ROLA) provides information on effective methods to attain objectives by analyzing the strategic moves of similar businesses.[31]

The PIMS program has found a number of significant influences on profitability and cash flow. One of the strongest relationships is between market share and return on investment. A 10 percent point difference in market share is, on the average, associated with a 5-point difference in pretax ROI.[32] Another influence on profitability is productivity or value added per employee. Value added is the amount the market value of the product or service is increased by the firm. Another influence is quality of the product or service as defined by consumers' evaluations comparing it to competitors. A fourth influence is cost push, which is the impact of the rates of increase in wages, salaries, and raw material prices. Other influences are investment intensity, growth of the served market, innovation, vertical integration, and the current strategic effort. These nine influences account for 80 percent of the determination of business success or failure.[33]

We said at the beginning of the chapter that we would discuss the issue of organization. Let's turn our attention to this topic now.

ORGANIZING THE MARKETING DEPARTMENT

Organization structure determines the flow of information and the flow of authority within the firm. *Information flow* is important in the development of the strategic plan. *Authority flow* determines who implements the plan. The marketing department can be organized according to functions, products, or markets. Each of these approaches is discussed in detail below.

Functional organization

The *functional organization* of a marketing department is the simplest and most common approach. As shown in Figure 2–9, the department is organized according to general marketing functions such as product development, marketing research, sales, advertising, and pricing. Most companies begin with this approach because of its simplicity. Functional organization works well on small businesses and on larger, centralized companies where both products and customers are few and similar in nature. The functional approach is not so suitable for large firms with decentralized marketing operations, as it can lead to coordination problems.

---

[31] Robert B. Buzzell, Bradley T. Gale, and Ralph G. M. Sultan, "Market Share—A Key to Profitability," *Harvard Business Review,* January–February 1975, p. 97.

[32] *PIMS Program,* pp. 11–12.

[33] *The PIMS Letter on Business Strategy* no. 1 (Cambridge, Mass.: The Strategic Planning Institute, 1977), p. 305.

**Figure 2–9: Functional
organization of
marketing department**

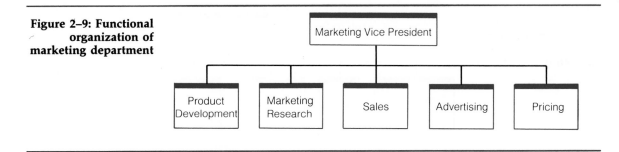

The **product management** form of organization enhances the functional system by adding a group of managers directly responsible for the individual products. (See Figure 2–10.) This system is used by companies with a large number of products because the functional form of organization does not allow managers to devote sufficient time and effort to individual products. Consequently, the product management system is established to ensure that products do receive individual attention.

Product management organization is widely used. It has been estimated that some 84 percent of consumer product firms use some form of this system. Consumer goods companies using product management organization include Procter & Gamble, Anheuser-Busch, Lever Brothers, Max Factor, Pillsbury, and General Mills.

The product management structure is used by manufacturers of industrial products also and by the service industry, as these organizations increase their emphasis on effective marketing management. In the industrial area, Union Carbide, Uniroyal, and Johns-Manville use product management. And commercial banks and the U.S. Postal Service are examples of service organizations that use product managers.[34]

Advantages of the product management system include: the ability to balance the functional inputs needed by a product; the ability to react quickly to problems in the marketplace; and more concentration on smaller brands that may be neglected in functional organizations.

The system is not without disadvantages, however. Conflict and frustration may result if the product manager is not given authority to match the responsibilities of the job. Second, the product manager becomes an expert in one product area but rarely has the chance to become an expert in functional areas such as advertising, marketing research, and sales.[35]

The product management system was originated by Procter & Gamble in 1927. One P&G brand, Camay soap, was doing poorly. Neil McElroy

**Product
management
organization**

---

[34] Richard T. Hise and J. Patrick Kelly, "Product Managers on Trial," *Journal of Marketing* 42 (October 1978), pp. 28–33.

[35] Philip Kotler, *Principles of Marketing* (Englewood Cliffs, N.J.: Prentice-Hall, 1980), pp. 409–11.

Figure 2–10: Product management organization of marketing department

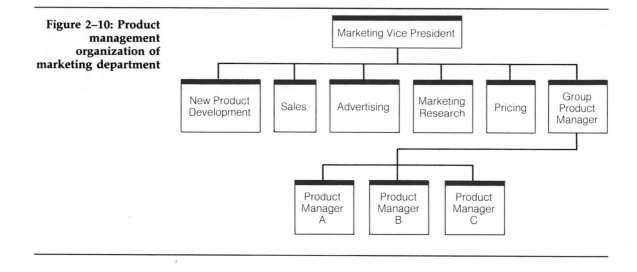

(later a P&G president) was assigned to devote exclusive attention to the brand. The approach worked so well that the company soon added other product managers.[36] Today Procter & Gamble has more than 50 brand groups, each with a product manager with one or two assistants.[37]

A survey of 97 large companies, including Dow Chemical, Johnson & Johnson, Quaker Oats, Reynolds Aluminum, Nabisco, Upjohn, and Weyerhaeuser, studied 198 product managers. The major findings: 62 percent of the product managers had profit responsibility, while 39 percent had staff positions with responsibility for providing information and coordinating marketing activities. Product managers had the most influence and involvement in decisions on product goals, sales forecasts for products, and means of achieving goals for products and the least influence on pricing, determining form of product, and distribution policies. Product managers had sufficient experience, with 78 percent having two or more years experience as a brand manager and 25 percent having six or more years in this capacity.[38]

A survey of sales, advertising and marketing research executives in leading consumer goods companies found that these executives rate their product managers as successful, effective managers even though they do not have full authority over the functional areas related to their products.[39]

---

[36] Kotler, *Principles of Marketing,* p. 408.

[37] Joel R. Evans and Barry Berman, *Marketing* (New York: MacMillan, 1982), p. 225.

[38] Hise and Kelly, "Product Managers."

[39] Jacob M. Duker and Michael V. Laric, "The Product Manager: No Longer on Trial," in *The Changing Marketing Environment,* ed. Kenneth Bernhardt et al. (Chicago: American Marketing Association, 1981), pp. 93–96.

The United States Postal Service offers a variety of services to its customers. Product managers are in charge of these services and help to ensure that they effectively meet the needs of customers.

How to get the Post Office to come to you

and a box full of ways to get the best of your Postal Service.

If you're on a rural delivery route, your letter-carrier does much more than deliver the mail. He or she can bring a wide range of postal services right to your door, and beyond that, your letter-carrier will prove to be a caring friend.

So all you have to do is open your mailbox, and a very special post office is right there for you.

How to find a stamp collection in your mailbox.

With our Philatelic Catalog, collecting stamps is as easy as reading your mail. Published six times a year, it includes a convenient order form and pre-addressed envelope. All you do is make your choices and send them in. The stamps will come to you. To get our catalog, write to the U.S.P.S. Philatelic Catalog, Philatelic Sales Division, Washington, DC 20265-9997

How to talk with your post office.

Postal people want to help you, and they know that an important part of helping is listening. So if you have any questions at all, ask a clerk. And feel free to fill out Consumer Service Cards, which you'll find at your post office, with your questions and comments. Or, if you want still more help, write to your

Consumer Advocate,
U.S. Postal Service,
Washington, DC
20260-6320

Talk to us, and we'll help you get our best.

We'll help you get our best.

This job advertisement highlights the challenges facing a product manager in a manufacturing firm in the health care field.

PRODUCT MANAGER
Medical Products

Medical products manufacturer has an immediate opening for an experienced Marketing Professional. Responsibilities will include developing marketing plans for current products and identifying viable new products, accessing potential new markets, establishing pricing and profit goals, providing sales and service personnel with training plus assisting with establishing annual sales forecasts and budgets. Technical degreed individuals with exposure to the healthcare construction and piping industry are preferred.

If you are interested in a challenging career in a fast-paced, growth-oriented organization, please forward resume in confidence to:

Market organization

Marketing departments may also be organized by types of market, as shown in Figure 2–11. *Market organization* works well for firms having several markets with different needs. Because the marketing activities and decisions for various markets differ considerably, this structure allows more efficiency in operations. In this organizational structure, marketing managers for each market report to the top-level marketing executive. Each marketing manager is responsible for most marketing activities for his or her specific market.

Geographical markets are commonly used in this organizational form, especially by large companies that market products nationwide. This form of organization is low in cost and clearly defines the responsibilities of each marketing manager.

Matrix approach

The *matrix approach* has developed in an attempt to manage firms with divergent products and markets. It involves a cross-classification scheme that enables two different factors, such as products and markets, to be emphasized. Product and market managers interact to enhance flexibility in response to different market influences. Where firms have multiple products in multiple markets, the matrix approach eliminates the need to find product managers with market or resource expertise, or market managers with specific product knowledge.

Source: Philip Kotler, *Principles of marketing*, © 1980, p. 181. Reprinted by permission of Prentice-Hall, Inc., Englewood Cliffs, N.J.

Figure 2–11: Market organization of marketing departments

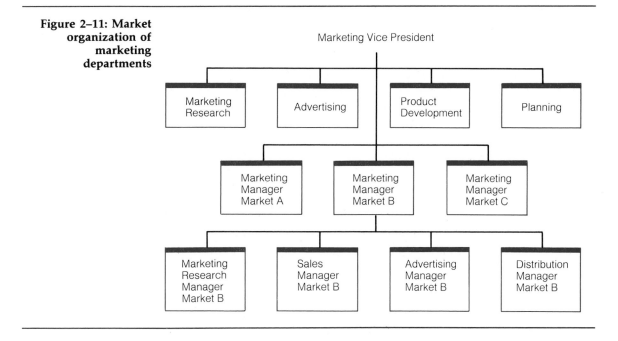

The most sophisticated version of the matrix approach is the product/market organization. Firms using this approach install product managers familiar with highly divergent products and market managers familiar with highly divergent markets.

Product managers are responsible for planning the sales and profits of their respective products. Their focus is primarily on short-run performance and usage of their products. They contact each market manager to determine sales estimates for their products in each market.

Market managers are responsible for developing profitable markets for existing and potential products. They are concerned with developing the

Figure 2–12: Du Pont's textile fibers division

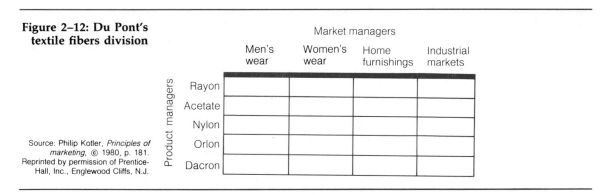

right product for their market rather than with pushing a specific product. Market managers contact each product manager to determine prices and availabilities of products in preparing their marketing plan.

The textile fibers division of Du Pont uses a product/market management system. (See Figure 2–12.) Product and market managers interact to manage the profits of their products and markets.[40] The 3M Company also uses this organizational structure.

SUMMARY

The strategic marketing planning process consists of the following steps: (1) analyzing the situation, (2) establishing objectives, (3) defining the product/market, (4) budgeting, (5) managing the marketing program, and (6) evaluating performance.

Various strategic planning tools can be used in this process. These tools include the growth/share matrix, the experience curve, the industry attractiveness/business strength model, and PIMS.

In strategic planning, it is important to understand the flow of information and authority within an organization. This flow is determined by the organizational structure. The marketing department can be organized according to (1) functions, (2) products, (3) markets, or (4) a matrix approach.

KEY CONCEPTS

Strategic marketing management	Product strategy	Stars
Process versus content of strategy	Channel strategy	Problem children
Objective	Price strategy	Cash cows
Strategy	Promotional strategy	Dogs
Tactics	Timing strategy	Experience curve
Situation analysis	Strategic windows	Multiple-factor screening methods
Mission statement	Performance evaluation and control	Profit Impact of Marketing Strategy (PIMS)
Criteria for objectives		
Product/market	Portfolio analysis model	Information and authority flows
Market segmentation	Growth/share matrix	Functional organization
Target market	Industry attractiveness/business strength model	Product management
Budgeting		Market organization
Market program positioning	Strategic business unit (SBU)	Matrix approach

<table>
<tr><td>DISCUSSION QUESTIONS AND EXERCISES</td><td>1.</td><td>Consider your experience as a consumer. Cite two examples of situations in which companies have carefully considered the needs and wants of the consumer in implementing their marketing strategies. Cite two examples in which the companies have neglected the consumer.</td></tr>
</table>

---

[40] Kotler, *Principles of Marketing,* p. 181.

2. Review a recent copy of *Business Week, The Wall Street Journal,* or some other business publication. Select an article on a particular company, and outline the firm's corporate and marketing strategy based on information in the article and your own knowledge of the company.

3. McDonald's was used in this chapter to illustrate the concept of objectives, strategy, and tactics. Consider some recent McDonald's marketing activities in your community. What strategies and tactics did McDonald's use in the areas of product, price, and promotion? How effective do you think these strategies and tactics were in your community? Why?

4. Discuss the relationship between evaluation and control and situation analysis in the strategic marketing management process.

5. What factors would cause a firm to change its mission statement and corporate objectives?

6. Construct a 3 × 3 product/market matrix for a bank.

7. Often, small market-share companies earn high ROIs. Does this undermine the validity of the experience curve and the PIMS finding? Discuss.

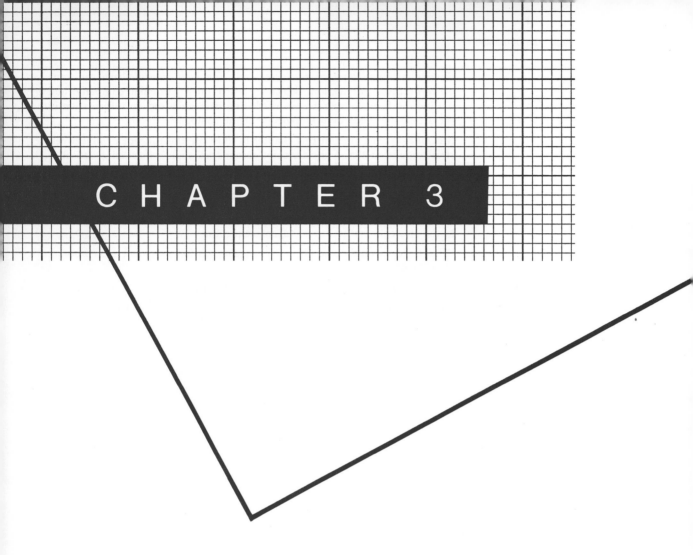

CHAPTER 3

The environment of marketing

Sectors of the macroenvironment
    The sociocultural sector
    The economic sector
    The competitive sector
    The technological sector
    The public policy sector

Summary

Key concepts

Discussion questions and exercises

Levels of the marketing environment
    Intraorganizational level
    External support level
    Macro level

Nature of the macroenvironment

The impact of the macroenvironment

Strategic planning and the environment
    Environmental monitoring
    Environmental adaptation

Chapter 2 described a planning process for developing an organization's marketing strategy. It began with a situation analysis. A key element here is an examination of the environment of marketing operations. What is the nature of the environment? How does marketing cope with it?

**LEVELS OF THE
MARKETING
ENVIRONMENT**

A firm's marketing operation should recognize three environmental levels: intraorganizational, external support, and macro. (See Figure 3–1). These are distinguished by their closeness and immediacy to marketing.

**marketing
environment**

> The **marketing environment** is a set of diverse, dynamic, and uncontrollable forces that impinge on an organization's marketing operations and opportunities.

**Intraorganizational
level**

The *intraorganizational level* includes all the forces *within* the company that affect marketing. We've seen that overall *corporate mission and objectives* must be considered in planning. *Departments* within the firm (finance, R&D) also exert influence. In fact, they're basic to marketing. We'll see their influences throughout this book.

One aspect of this level deserves special treatment.

corporate culture

> **Corporate culture** is the set of values shared by the managers and employees of a company.

**Figure 3–1: Overview
of the marketing
environment**

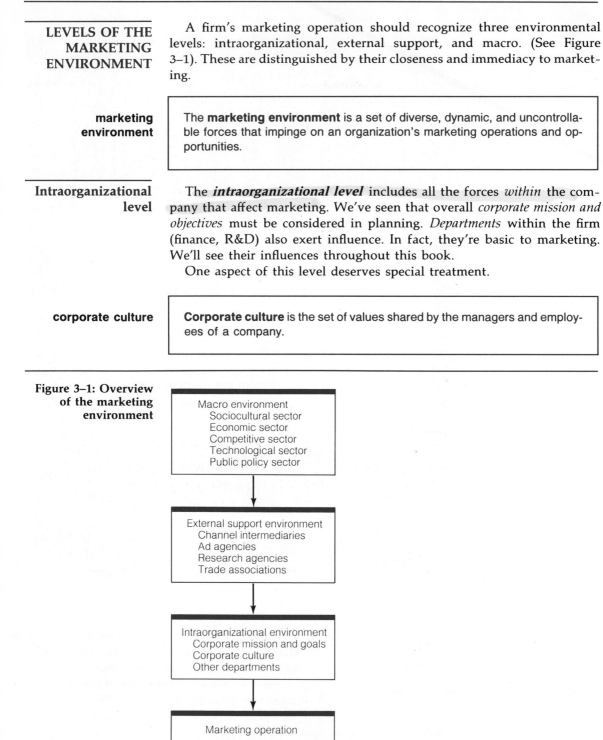

Macro environment
   Sociocultural sector
   Economic sector
   Competitive sector
   Technological sector
   Public policy sector

External support environment
   Channel intermediaries
   Ad agencies
   Research agencies
   Trade associations

Intraorganizational environment
   Corporate mission and goals
   Corporate culture
   Other departments

Marketing operation

Whirlpool
communicates its
corporate culture to
consumers through ads
like this one.

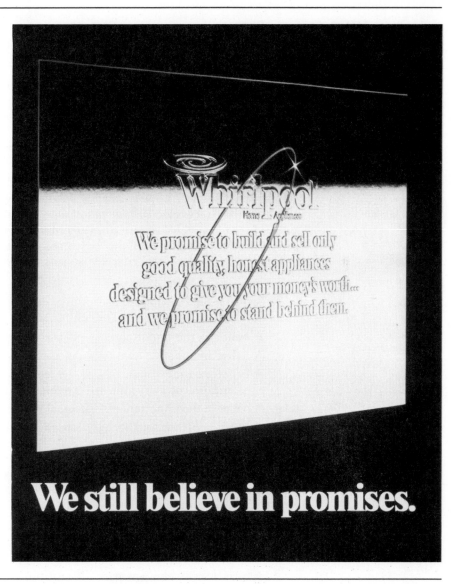

We still believe in promises.

Courtesy Whirlpool Corporation

A strong corporate culture doesn't always exist. However, Peters and Waterman observed it in their case studies of traits common to several excellent companies.[1] They emphasize that corporate culture must permeate the entire corporation. It should not be unique to top management.

---

[1] From *In Search of Excellence: Lessons from America's Best-Run Companies* by Thomas J. Peters and Robert H. Waterman, Jr. Copyright © 1982 by Thomas J. Peters and Robert H. Waterman, Jr. Reprinted by permission of Harper & Row Publishers, Inc.

	Company	**Core values**
Table 3–1:	Procter & Gamble	Business integrity; fair treatment of employees
Selected core values of companies	IBM	Customer service
	Delta	Family feeling within the company
Source: Extracted from Thomas J. Peters and Robert H. Waterman, Jr., *In Search of Excellence* (New York: Harper & Row, 1982).	Texas Instruments	Innovation
	Walt Disney Productions	Service through people
	Digital	Quality

Table 3–1 gives some of their observations about the core values of specific companies. Observe how marketing-related most of these core values are; how they recognize the *human element* within an organization. The values listed for each firm are not the only ones shared within the company. They are the most striking. In general, most of the companies share a similar set of values. Peters and Waterman summarize them as follows:

1. A belief in being the "best."
2. A belief in the importance of the details of execution, the nuts and bolts of doing the job well.
3. A belief in the importance of people as individuals.
4. A belief in superior quality and service.
5. A belief that most members of the organization should be innovators, and its corollary, the willingness to support failure.
6. A belief in the importance of informality to enhance communication.
7. Explicit belief in and recognition of the importance of economic growth and profits.[2]

External support level

The **external support level** of the environment contains the institutions with which the marketing operation interacts to achieve its strategic objectives. These institutions include:

1. *Channel intermediaries*—Manufacturers, wholesalers, and retailers who are sources of supply to the firm or aid the firm in distributing its products.
2. *Marketing service agencies*—Institutions that aid the firm in performing marketing activities. Two common types are ad and market research agencies.
3. *Trade associations*—Voluntary organizations of firms in a specific industry. These often provide their members important market and industry information (sales, prices, cost).

They may also lobby to federal and state governments for their members. Some associations may endorse codes of conduct. Prominent exam-

[2] Ibid., p. 285.

ples are the National Association of Manufacturers, the American Iron and Steel Institute, and the Association of Home Appliance Manufacturers.

Most of the institutions at this level influence specific aspects of marketing (channel management, promotion, research). So we'll consider the relevance of many of these when discussing their areas of impact.

Macro level

The *macro level* of the marketing environment represents the broad external forces that influence the marketing operations of a firm. The macroenvironment also influences each of the other levels. It is the most diverse, dynamic, and uncontrollable level of the environment. The remainder of this chapter explores the macroenvironment. We'll see how it impinges on the firm, how the firm behaves toward it, and the key changes that have occurred within it.

NATURE OF THE MACRO- ENVIRONMENT

The diversity of the macroenvironment is reflected in its multiple sectors. Macro-level forces come from a variety of sources. There are a number of classification theories, but for our purposes the macroenvironment will be viewed in five sectors:

1. *Sociocultural sector.* This sector contains the forces emanating from society as a whole. It includes both informal forces (the values of society) and more formally organized forces (those growing out of consumerism).

2. *Economic sector.* This includes forces associated with the macroeconomic environment. General factors like inflation, interest rates, and gross national product (GNP) are relevant here.

3. *Competitive sector.* This sector includes institutions the firm competes with in the marketplace.

4. *Technological sector.* Here are the forces associated with the knowledge and procedures of production and other business activities.

5. *Public policy sector.* This sector includes the forces imposed on the organization by legislation—the many laws governing a firm's marketing.

The macroenvironment is highly dynamic over time. As we will see, this creates both opportunities and problems. The environmental sectors vary in their pace of change. In some sectors change occurs slowly. Take, for example, the sociocultural sector. Societal values do not change overnight but over a span of years and even generations. On the other hand, some sectors change quite rapidly. The actions of competitors (for example, a price change in a competing brand) create change in the competitive sector in less than a day.

Figure 3–2: Interactive nature of changes in macro-level sectors of airline companies

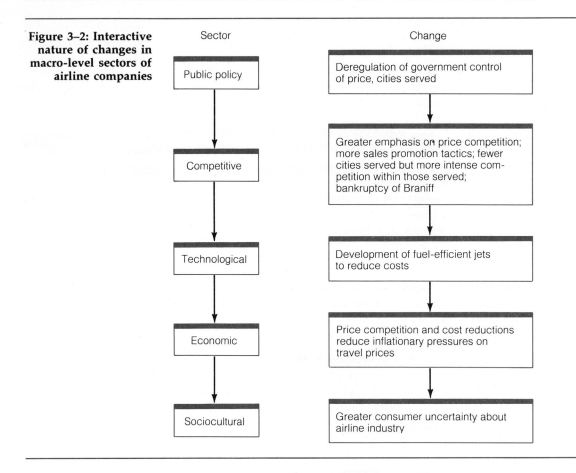

The dynamic nature of each sector causes their interrelatedness. Changes in one sector can create changes in others. Figure 3–2 reveals a chain of events across sectors that have recently occurred in the airline industry.

The uncontrollable nature of the environment means that the firm cannot manipulate it—the firm does not dictate the nature of the environment. But firms do influence the environment through their behavior. The competitive behavior of a firm *influences* how its competitors behave. It doesn't *control* their behavior. Organizations' lobbyists influence—but do not control—the behavior of legislators in the public policy sector.

THE IMPACT OF THE MACRO-ENVIRONMENT

The nature of the macroenvironment being what it is, its impact on the firm can be characterized in several ways. The scope of the impact takes in the entire set of marketing variables: neither product, price, physical distribution, nor promotion is immune. All may not be affected at

Figure 3–3: The marketing environment and its impact

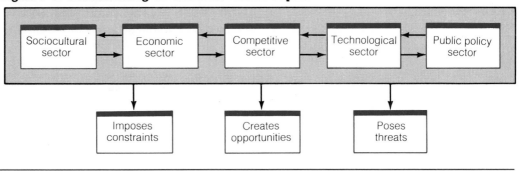

any one time. But in the long run all are subject to environmental influence. Figure 3–3 presents an overview of the discussion that follows.

The environment *constrains* a firm's marketing. It limits how the firm can act, especially how it can manipulate marketing decision variables. This is probably best seen in the public policy sector, where laws limit what a firm can do. Cigarette manufacturers, banned from TV ads, know this. Other sectors impose constraints more subtly. For example, the pricing behavior of competitors may limit the price a firm can charge for its own brand. Say the firm wants its brand to be priced no more than 5 percent above a competitor's price. Then its price is limited through the behavior of the competitor and its own policy.

A more positive impact is that *the environment creates marketing opportunities* for the firm. This happens through change. As the environment changes, new marketing action emerges. All the sectors create opportunity as they change—some more than others.

Perhaps the greatest opportunity emerging from environmental change is the creation of new markets (or the expansion of existing ones). Computer advances in the technological sector are probably the best example. Microcomputers have placed computer capabilities within the economic reach of households. The result has been the growth of the personal and home computer markets.[3]

Change can be bad, too. Disturbances in the environment often pose *threats* to the firm.

environmental threat

> An **environmental threat** is any environmental change that—in the absence of action by the firm—will have detrimental consequences on the firm's performance.

---

[3] For an extensive discussion of the marketing implications of home computers, see "Computer Stores: Tantalizing Opportunity Selling Computers to Consumers," *Business Week*, September 28, 1981, pp. 76–82.

Possible detrimental consequences include a decline in profitability or a loss of market share. Take the rapid increase in gasoline prices and interest rates in the 1970s, for example. Consumers cut back on their car buying. And those who did buy attached new importance to a model's fuel economy. Few American autos matched the fuel economy of foreign imports. So what happened? A period of huge operating losses and near-bankruptcy for some domestic manufacturers.

Often change creates opportunity for some firms and threatens others. One such change is the increased concern for physical fitness and health-consciousness in the sociocultural sector. This concern has altered the eating habits of many Americans. Figure 3–4 summarizes the impact on the consumption of certain types of foods. Clearly, opportunities are pres-

Figure 3–4: Percent change in per capita consumption of selected foods, 1976–82

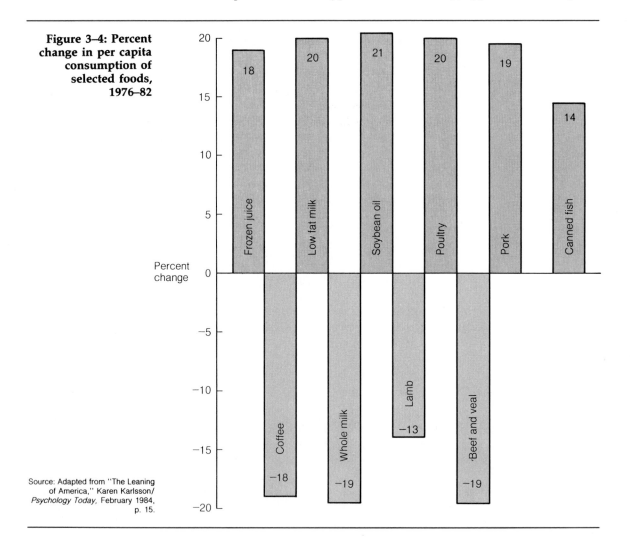

Source: Adapted from ''The Leaning of America,'' Karen Karlsson/ *Psychology Today*, February 1984, p. 15.

ent for manufacturers of fruit juices and leaner meats and fish. But threats are posed to the coffee, dairy, and red meat industries.

STRATEGIC PLANNING AND THE ENVIRONMENT

The dynamic, diverse nature of the environment makes it a fundamental concern in strategic planning. *The essential task in the formulation of strategy is to match a firm's strengths and weaknesses to the opportunities and threats in its environment.*

A firm can't sit idly. It must anticipate or recognize change and respond to it. Otherwise, opportunities will be missed, and threats will become setbacks. Long-run survival requires specific actions on the part of the firm.

Environmental monitoring

The firm must be able to identify or—better yet—anticipate environmental changes that have consequences for its marketing operation.

environmental monitoring

> **Environmental monitoring** occurs when a firm continuously monitors change and assesses whether it represents an opportunity, a threat, or an inconsequential event.

The firm should monitor the environment so as to receive a continuous inflow of environmental data. This data should enable the firm to identify immediate short-run changes or long-run trends. The firm should also assess these changes—and potential changes. That is, do they mean opportunities or threats? Are they inconsequential?

Monitoring short-run environmental changes is particularly important in the *competitive sector,* because the behavior of competitors can change so rapidly. It is also important in the broad *economic sector,* where changes are not usually as abrupt but can occur in short periods of time (e.g., the price of resources). The *public policy sector* seems to incur rapid change as new laws go into effect overnight. But there is usually such substantial forewarning of new laws that they really represent rather slow change.

Most sectors contain elements that change slowly over time, especially the sociocultural sector. Here the key monitoring task is to spot *trends* that in the long run may convert to opportunities or threats. Monitoring a slow rate of change in a sector is a two-fold task. First, the trend must be used to forecast the situation that will exist at a particular point in the future. Second, the forecasted situation must be translated into an opportunity, a threat, or an inconsequential event. The firm thus should monitor slow patterns of change so that it is in a position to *anticipate* a threat or opportunity. Because forecasting is subject to error, trends should be monitored continuously to determine whether movement is continuing as anticipated.

Societal changes in the sociocultural sector are prime examples of slow change whose ultimate state can be anticipated and interpreted as threatening, opportunistic, or inconsequential. For example, the birthrate in America has declined slowly in recent years. One result of this phenomenon has been a contraction of the market for baby goods, which obviously translates into a threat to baby-goods manufacturers. Another result of the slowing birthrate has been an aging of the population. The importance of the elderly segment of the market has increased. So have opportunities for companies who market to them. Again, we can see that the same significant long-run trend presents a threat to some firms and an opportunity to others.

Effective monitoring requires procedures that will provide the firm with a flow of environmentally relevant information. A variety of procedures are available, which differ for each of the sectors. We'll discuss some of these shortly.

Environmental adaptation

Once a firm has identified environmental change as an opportunity or a threat, it should respond accordingly.

environmental adaptation

> **Environmental adaptation** occurs when a firm responds to change by changing its own marketing operation.

The firm's marketing operation should adapt to the change to capitalize on opportunities or eliminate threats. Environmental adaptation is a fundamental behavior for a firm. Stagnant firms find it hard to survive. The firm that changes with the environment stands a much better chance of meeting its objectives and surviving in the long run.

Once a firm recognizes the need to adapt to an environmentally created opportunity or threat, it must ascertain how to do so. *Effective change* is crucial in responding to the environment; and it occurs through the manipulation of one or more of the marketing decision variables. The firm thus turns to the mix of the product, price, distribution, and promotion for effective response. Occasionally, the response will be simple, involving only one variable. A major competitor lowers price; the firm responds with its own price reduction. Another possible response to a competitive price reduction is a change in advertising to emphasize the superior quality of the firm's brand.

Many environmental changes necessitate a complex response involving most or all of the marketing decision variables. A recent case is the banking industry. Bankers have felt sweeping effects on marketing practices from abrupt changes in most sectors of the environment.[4] In the past, banks

---

[4] This discussion is taken from "Now Bankers Turn to a Hard Sales Pitch," *Business Week,* September 21, 1981, pp. 62–68.

performed well-defined, narrow roles requiring minimal marketing expertise. They served as depositories for consumer funds. Federal regulations
protected banks by limiting competition; only banks were allowed to
offer both checking and passbook savings accounts. Besides banks the
only other major sources of short-term loans were consumer finance companies. Finally, the interest rates paid and received by banks were defined
by law. Such a carefully defined and protected role meant narrow marketing practices as well. Bankers merely promoted. They advertised services,
gave gifts, and talked friendly. The services offered by banks were, in
fact, all about the same. There was little motivation for banks to be
innovative. Marketing, to the extent it existed, was simplistic. No more!

In recent years, changes have occurred in all environmental sectors:

1. *Public policy.* The cause of many of the changes has been deregulation. For example, banks are now allowed to offer interest-bearing
   checking (NOW) accounts. But this capability has also been extended to financial institutions formerly prevented from offering
   checking accounts at all. Ceilings on savings account interest rates
   are being phased out, too.[5]

2. *Economic.* High inflation in the late 1970s and early 80s made it
   difficult for savers to keep pace through traditional savings accounts.

3. *Competitive.* Deregulation has reduced the distinctive role of banks.
   Savings and loan institutions and credit unions can now offer services previously unique to banks. The development of money market funds has offered consumers new savings options. The competition is simply much tougher.

4. *Technological.* The new electronics have lowered costs of some transactions.

5. *Sociocultural.* The environmental changes offer consumers a greater
   array of services and institutions to meet their financial needs. People
   will probably use more criteria in choosing financial institutions.

These changes in the banking environment mean *opportunities* exist
to be more flexible in offering services and to lower the cost of transacting
business. But threats from more competition and changing consumer needs
are also evident. Bankers now have a much greater need for marketing.

Many banks are increasing the sophistication of their marketing operations by applying marketing tools common to major manufacturers. Specific examples of how banks are adapting through marketing:

1. Many banks are expanding services to keep existing customers and
   attract new ones. These services include insurance, free traveler's
   checks, automatic teller machines (ATMs), high-yield certificates

[5] For a fuller discussion of recent deregulation relevant to the banking industry, see
"The Depository Institutions Deregulation and Monetary Control Act of 1980," *Federal
Reserve Bulletin,* June 1980, pp. 444–51.

and repurchase agreements, and individual retirement accounts (IRAs).

2. Because of the increased competition in the retail market, some banks are shifting their emphasis to the corporate or small-business market. Others are focusing on the wealthy segment of the consumer market.

3. Promotional efforts are being expanded. Where once television advertising dominated, banks are moving into print media because of its ability to convey greater quantities of specific information. In the area of personal selling, one bank is using "relationship managers"—a customer deals with just one officer for all services.

**Figure 3–5:
Environmental
monitoring and
adaptation process**

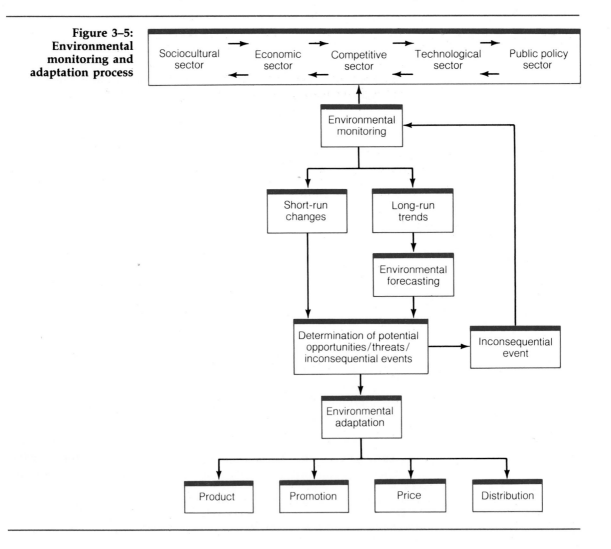

The changes in banks' marketing environment have been dramatic, and the way individual banks adapt will determine their long-run survival.

Figure 3–5 provides a summary framework of the environmental monitoring and adaptation process. First, it reflects the dynamic interplay between sectors. Then, environmental monitoring identifies short-run changes and long-run trends. The latter are projected to the future through forecasting and continuously monitored to determine if the trend is moving as forecasted. Changes and trends are translated into opportunities, threats, and inconsequential events. Environmental adaptation occurs through the manipulation of the controllable marketing strategy variables.

Success depends on an understanding of the sectors of the environment. In the following section we examine the nature of each sector. We'll identify changes that have occurred in it and discuss procedures for monitoring it.

SECTORS OF THE MACRO-ENVIRONMENT

The sociocultural sector

The sociocultural sector of the environment involves society as a whole and the forces emanating from it. It is perhaps the most important sector, for imbedded in it is the marketplace itself. The most crucial link a firm develops is with the marketplace. In the sociocultural sector we are concerned with the characteristics of society and their dynamic nature at the aggregate level. As we noted earlier, changes in the sociocultural sector are gradual. Abrupt changes seldom occur. Instead, we see minor shifts in short periods that ultimately lead to profound long-run changes. From a marketing standpoint, gradual shifts are desirable. They allow firms to monitor them better, to anticipate the future, and to develop long-run plans for adaptation.

The nature of the sociocultural sector and the changes in it can be examined in certain broad dimensions, often with marketing implications. These dimensions include the demography of society, its socioeconomic nature, its cultural values, and consumerism. (See Figure 3–6.)

Figure 3–6: The sociocultural sector

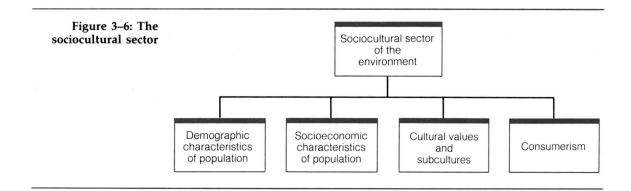

Demographics. The **demographics** of a society are the statistics that describe its aggregate nature in terms of population size, age distribution, sex distribution, family size, and geographic distribution. While these statistics are purely descriptive, they often have important marketing implications—especially as they change over time. Some demographic characteristics of American society and recent shifts within them include:

1. A large population marked by continuous growth.
2. Declining birthrates and corresponding reductions in average family size, including a growth in the number of single-member households.
3. An aging of the population, with relative size increase in older segments.
4. An uneven geographic distribution, with highly dense urban areas, suburban segments, and a rural population.
5. A flow of people from metropolitan to suburban and rural areas.
6. Significant shifts in the population to the Sun Belt states.

Changes in the demographic nature of society have had a tremendous influence on marketing opportunities and practice. The declining birthrate has threatened the success of manufacturers of baby goods. In response Johnson & Johnson, for example, now advertises its baby shampoo, baby oil, and baby powder for both adult and baby use. The aging of the population has created dramatic new opportunities for growth in certain firms. Remarkable success has come to Richardson-Vicks and its Oil of Olay brand of skin conditioner. From annual worldwide sales of $10 million in the early 1970s, the brand now realizes over $100 million in annual sales. This is due to the growth in the 30-to-45 age group. The company knows consumers start worrying about looking old when they enter that group.[6]

Socioeconomic characteristics. The **socioeconomic characteristics** of a society describe its members in terms of their economic and social status. Key socioeconomic characteristics include income, occupational distribution, and education. Understanding the sociocultural sector in terms of socioeconomic characteristics is important because of their strong relationship to overall consumption patterns. The major characteristics and their changes include:

1. An increasing percentage of white-collar over blue-collar workers.
2. An increased flow of women into the work force in general and into traditionally male-dominated occupations specifically.
3. A growing number of dual-income households as a result of more women in the work force.

---

[6] *Marketing News*, March 18, 1983, p. 23.

The increased number of working women has created growth opportunities for many firms. For example, business publications (*Business Week, Fortune*) are realizing growth from increased circulation to women. And the influx of women has buoyed undergraduate and graduate enrollments in college business programs.

The growth of dual-income households has created a heavy-spending market that emphasizes time and convenience in the products it buys and where it shops. Supermarkets are altering their operations in response. Safeway previously targeted its stores to "the family of four" in which "85 percent of the shopping was done by women on Saturday morning." The trend toward smaller families and dual-income households ate away at Safeway's target market. In Los Angeles from 1975 to 1980, Safeway's market share dropped 50 percent.

Safeway adapted. It now targets the 25–44 age segment. Stores stay open longer. New departments (bakeries, delis, and pharmacies) have been added to appeal to consumers with broad shopping needs and little shopping time. To reach its target market, Safeway has deemphasized newspaper advertising in favor of magazines, drive-time radio, and prime-time TV.[7]

Cultural values.   Values are enduring beliefs that guide behavior in specific situations. A value exists mainly at the individual level. But when a value is substantially shared throughout a society, it becomes a *cultural value.* Knowledge of the sociocultural sector in terms of cultural values is crucial to marketing, because cultural values influence the behavior of most individuals in consumption situations. As cultural values shift, so will motives for buying products. The firm that fails to recognize this will overlook opportunities for new products or changes necessary in existing ones.

Marketing-related shifts in cultural values of the last decade or so include:

1. *The changing role of women.* The role of women in society is expanding well beyond traditional boundaries, as women seek social and economic equality. Many women continue in the traditional housewife–mother role. But more and more women are pursuing careers—often those historically dominated by men. The women's movement has had far-reaching marketing consequences.[8] New markets have been created (women's business attire). Existing ones have expanded

---

[7] "Safeway Jilts 'The Family of Four' to Woo 'The Jogging Generation,'" *Business Week,* November 21, 1983, pp. 93–99. For a general discussion of trends affecting the retail industry, see J. N. Sheth, "Emerging Trends for the Retailing Industry," *Journal of Retailing,* Fall 1983, pp. 6–18.

[8] For an expanded discussion of the changes in the female population, see William Lazer and John Smallwood, "The Changing Demographics of Women," *Journal of Marketing* 41 (July 1977), pp. 14–22.

(microwave ovens). Many women have become highly critical of the way ads portray their sex.[9] The issue has become sensitive.

2. *An increased concern for the physical environment.* In the 1970s a strong movement emerged toward protecting the physical environment. The consequences to many firms go beyond marketing (e.g., disposition of industrial waste materials). Many consumers include ecologically relevant criteria when evaluating products.[10]

3. *Energy conservation.* The depletion of the world's energy resources and the rise in their prices have intensified societal concern for energy conservation. The marketing effects include new markets for energy-preserving products (solar heating systems) and the changes in old ones (automobiles).

4. *Physical fitness.* A large segment of society has shown an increased interest in health and fitness. The yen for exercise and special diets means markets for health clubs, exercise apparel, and "natural" foods.

America remains a melting pot. The sociocultural sector is vastly diverse, which implies another important trait of American society: its subcultures.

subculture

> A **subculture** is a segment of society whose members share many of society's cultural values while also sharing certain values distinctive to themselves, such as race, ethnicity, or religion.

Subcultures represent unique marketing opportunities to the extent that their distinctive values have marketing consequences. They must be monitored for change just as the entire sociocultural sector is. One such change is a rebirth of ethnic pride. A resurgence in ethnic foods, restaurants, and festivals has resulted.

Consumerism. This element of the sociocultural sector has direct relevance to the relationship between buyers and sellers.

consumerism

> **Consumerism** refers to the combined activities of government, business, independent organizations, and concerned citizens that protect and aid consumers in their exchange relationships in the marketplace.

---

[9] William J. Lundstrom and Donald Sciglimpaglia, "Sex-Role Portrayals in Advertising," *Journal of Marketing* 41 (July 1977), pp. 72–79.

[10] Karl E. Henion, Russell Gregory, and Mona A. Clee, "Trade-Offs in Attribute Levels Made by Ecologically Concerned and Unconcerned Consumers when Buying Detergents," in *Advances in Consumer Research,* vol. VIII, ed. Kent Monroe (Ann Arbor, Mich.: Association for Consumer Research, 1981), pp. 624–29.

Consumerism goes beyond the sociocultural sector of the environment. But it is first and foremost a social movement with roots in this sector.

Consumer movements have occurred at various times during the past 100 years or so.[11] In the 1960s, though, consumerism gained momentum as an organized social force with a variety of participants.

Consumerism aims to protect the **rights of consumers.** Perhaps the most famous set of consumer rights were outlined by President John F. Kennedy in 1962.[12] They remain the core of consumerism and help identify its dimensions. Figure 3–7 outlines these four plus a more recently identified consumer right. These rights and some activities designed to achieve them include:[13]

1. *The right to safety.* This right involves protection from products that are hazardous to health or life. It has been the impetus for numerous laws that protect consumers when they do not have sufficient knowledge to protect themselves. These laws are product-specific. They regulate such products as food, textiles, drugs, cosmetics, and tires, requiring that they not present a danger to the user. If danger exists through misuse, a clear warning must be provided. Laws of this type set auto tire performance standards, ban flammable material in clothing, mandate poison warning labels on cleaning liquids, and require safety belts in autos. Many of these laws resulted from the activities of consumer crusaders like Ralph Nader, who work to expose dangerous products.[14]

2. *The right to be informed.* This right has two dimensions. The first is protection against deception by sellers. Deceptive ads have long been a target of the Federal Trade Commission, and consumerism has greatly increased the activity in this area. The second dimension is directly attributable to consumerism and is one of the clearest results of the 1960s movement. It requires that the consumer receive enough information to make wise purchase decisions. Laws now require sellers to state the true rate of interest (truth-in-lending), the cost of food items on a per-unit basis (unit pricing), and the nutritional content of foods.

3. *The right to choose.* This right has been recognized for many years. It is based upon the principle that competition between sellers is in the best interest of consumers. Much antitrust legislation is designed to preserve this right.

4. *The right to be heard.* This right states that consumers should have a formal voice in the formulation of public policy. The Office of Consumer

---

[11] For a discussion of the history of consumer movements in the United States, see Robert O. Herrman, "The Consumer Movement in Historical Perspective," in *Consumerism: Search for the Consumer Interest,* 2d ed. David A. Aaker and George S. Day (New York: Free Press, 1974), pp. 10–18.

[12] As discussed in "Consumer Advisory Council: First Report," Executive Office of the President (Washington, D.C.: U.S. Government Printing Office, October 1963).

[13] Adapted from David A. Aaker and George S. Day, "Introduction: A Guide to Consumerism," in Aaker and Day, *Consumerism,* pp. xvii–xviii.

[14] For a classic example of an exposé of the automobile industry, see Ralph Nader, *Unsafe at Any Speed* (New York: Pocket Books, 1966).

**Figure 3–7: The rights
of consumers**

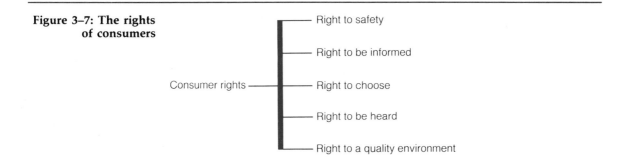

Affairs was established to this end. Many state and local governments and federal regulatory agencies have created similar departments. The right to be heard also demands channels through which other rights can be asserted. Such channels include consumer class-action suits, consumer hot lines, and special services to the poor (e.g., free legal advice).

A more recent, fifth right growing out of the increased concern for our physical environment can be added to Kennedy's original list:

5. *The right to a physical environment that protects the quality of life.* The pursuit of this right has led to the elimination of aerosol spray cans, the development and required use of unleaded gas, and tighter regulation of industrial waste disposal.

The many laws passed to protect and enhance consumer rights point out consumerism's impact. Government intervention is the most immediate means to rectify buyer–seller inequities in the marketplace. Later we'll examine public policy designed to aid consumers.

Still, the firm should not depend on government to guide its response to the consumer movement. It can respond on its own. And new opportunities may be created at the same time. For example:

1. *In 1970 Benner Tea Company, a midwest regional supermarket chain, instituted unit pricing as a competitive tool. (Right to be informed)*

2. *On the tentative evidence that its Rely brand of tampons was associated with an increased occurrence of toxic shock syndrome in women, Procter & Gamble recalled the brand. (Right to safety)*

3. *Many companies are creating ombudsman positions staffed by consumer-affairs specialists who represent consumers in the planning process. Also, specialized consumer-affairs agencies (similar to ad agencies) are being formed to help companies understand and respond properly to changing consumer concerns. (Right to be heard)*

Monitoring the sociocultural sector. Certain aspects of the sociocultural sector are easily monitored—the demographic and socioeconomic

Figure 3–8: Ten megatrends affecting our lives

1. The United States is shifting from an industrial society to an information society.
2. As technology increases its presence in our lives (high-tech), there will be a corresponding increase in the need for human touch (high-touch). The high-tech/high-touch principle symbolizes the need to balance our physical and spiritual reality.
3. The United States is shifting from an isolated, self-sufficient national economy to being part of an interdependent global economy.
4. Business planning is shifting from a short-term focus on the next quarter to a long-term planning horizon.
5. Our society and its organizations are shifting from a centralized structure to a decentralized structure.
6. A return to self-reliance and the entrepreneurial spirit rather than institutional reliance is occurring.
7. Citizens, workers, and consumers are demanding and getting a greater voice in governments, business, and the marketplace; i.e., a shift from representative to participatory democracy is occurring.
8. Because of the greater ease of communication, organizations are shifting from hierarchical to network structures.
9. Population flows from the North and Northeast to the South and Southwest are occurring.
10. Members of society are becoming more diverse in their demands; i.e., the marketplace is becoming more heterogeneous.

characteristics, for instance. Various publications like those from the Bureau of the Census often offer projections that make the firm's monitoring task easy.

Not so with the cultural values of society. These change slowly, are less quantifiable, and are more difficult to forecast. A judgmental, subjective task is required. Many firms depend on experts who make it a business to forecast changes in cultural values. A number of companies purchase the *Social Trends Monitor* of Daniel Yankelovich, Inc. Through an extensive survey research effort, the *Monitor* periodically measures 36 social-value trends, such as materialism, sexual freedom, hedonism, religion, and personalization. Many companies also purchase *The Trend Report,* a publication by futurist John Naisbitt. Recently, Naisbitt summarized his view of the future in terms of 10 "megatrends" in society. (See Figure 3–8.)

In addition to outside sources, some companies use internal departments to monitor social trends. General Motors has a Societal Analysis Department. Mead Corporation has a Human and Environmental Protection Department. PPG Industries created the position of manager of public policy research. These companies have established formal internal functions for monitoring social change. Scores of other companies perform this function informally.

The economic sector

The economic sector of the marketing environment contains the general macroeconomic forces that influence business operations. Most businesses recognize these influences. Many closely follow economic trends and the forecasts of econometric models of the macrostructure of our economy. Our treatment of the economic sector here is limited to a summary of some key factors contained within it that have characterized it in recent years:

1. *Rate of inflation.* The latter 1970s were marked by some of the highest inflation rates in the economy's history. Now, the effects of inflation are many and varied, but one sweeping effect is the increased cost-consciousness of consumers. In response, firms become more cost-sensitive in their marketing efforts. We saw the development of no-frills airline services in the 70s, and unbranded generic products emerged, too, as a significant marketing phenomenon. In the 80s, as inflation tapered off, less price-oriented marketing has occurred.[15]

2. *Interest rates.* Inflation and interest rates are related. When the 70s inflation was high, the prime-rate cost of borrowing money at times exceeded 20 percent. Home mortgage rates and installment loan rates reached 15 and 20 percent. This had a devastating effect in the housing industry, where demand for new homes plummeted in the late 70s and early 80s. Efforts to adapt to this situation included a greater use of land contracts, variable-rate mortgages, and innovative approaches like home raffling. As interest rates came down, traditional fixed-rate mortgages regained popularity.

3. *Resource shortages.* Critical shortages in key resources are developing. The primary example is, of course, oil and the products made from it. The increased cost of oil clearly contributes to inflation, but the oil shortage can be a problem aside from its cost consequences. Consider the plight of car rental agencies that provide gasoline in their rented cars. To increase rentals during gas shortages, Hertz had to adapt by shifting to smaller cars.

The economic sector is certainly dynamic. Fluctuations in interest rates, unemployment, inflation, and the like are ample evidence. Fortunately, though, the economic sector is characterized by quantifiable trends that lend themselves to short-run forecasting. **Leading indicators**—variables whose change signals looming change in other variables—come into use. For example, a decrease in wholesale prices signals a probable reduction in retail prices a few months hence.

The competitive sector

The competitive sector involves institutions a firm competes with in the demand and supply sides of the marketplace. On the demand side, firms compete for a share of buyer expenditures. Say, automakers compete for a share of consumer auto purchases. On the supply side, firms compete for favorable treatment from suppliers. That is, retailers compete for timely

---

[15] For an expanded discussion of inflationary effects on consumer behavior and marketing practice, see Zoher E. Shipchandler, "Inflation and Lifestyles: The Marketing Impact," *Business Horizons,* February 1976, pp. 90–96.

Figure 3–9: Forces driving industry competition

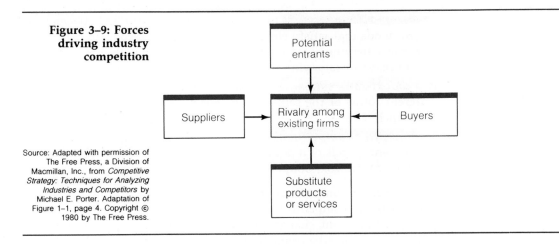

Source: Adapted with permission of The Free Press, a Division of Macmillan, Inc., from *Competitive Strategy: Techniques for Analyzing Industries and Competitors* by Michael E. Porter. Adaptation of Figure 1–1, page 4. Copyright © 1980 by The Free Press.

delivery of goods from manufacturers or wholesalers. One view of the array of forces affecting competition in an industry is presented in Figure 3–9. While a firm's marketing efforts are certainly relevant to supply-side competition, they are *crucial* to competition for buyers. Our focus here is restricted to competition on the demand side of the marketplace.[16]

The structure of the competitive sector. The competitive sector of the firm's marketing environment can be structured along several key dimensions. One is the type of demand for which the firm is competing. Another is the level at which competition occurs. The number of competitors and the geographic scope of competition are two more.

In structuring its competitive sector, a firm must recognize the different types of demand for which it is competing. Two types can be identified:

1. **Primary demand**—the demand for a particular generic product (the demand for televisions).
2. **Selective demand**—the demand for a specific version of a generic product. In this category we can distinguish between selective demand for a specific form of a generic product (a 25-inch console TV) and a specific brand of a generic product (Zenith).

Primary and selective demand imply a second dimension by which to structure the competitive sector: the different levels at which the firm competes. (See Figure 3–10.) A firm should identify its competitors at three levels: generic, product-form, and enterprise.

---

[16] A good joint discussion of competitive forces on the demand side and supply side of the marketplace can be found in Michael E. Porter, "How Competitive Forces Shape Strategy," *Harvard Business Review,* March–April 1979, pp. 137–45.

1. *Generic competition.* This level refers to competition between generic goods that satisfy similar needs. Televisions compete with stereos in satisfying home-entertainment needs and with movie theaters and plays in satisfying more general entertainment needs.
2. *Product-form competition.* This refers to competition between different forms of the same generic good: 19-inch TVs compete with 25-inch TVs.
3. *Enterprise competition.* This level refers to competition between different brands of a product. It is the competition between Zenith, RCA, Magnavox, Sony, etc.

These levels of competition offer the firm a framework for a complete assessment of its competitive environment. The firm is then less likely to overlook important changes in the competitive sector. Too often, a firm restricts its view of competition to the enterprise level. Watch out, though. This view fails to recognize threats or opportunities from changes at the generic or product-form level. Competition at these levels may actually lie within the firm itself! Many firms are multiproduct organizations whose products compete among themselves. The golf clubs marketed by a sporting goods company compete to some extent with the tennis rackets it markets. Furthermore, if the firm markets two or more versions of golf clubs, competition between these versions will occur. An important task in managing a multiproduct firm, then, is to anticipate how changing the marketing of one product may affect the marketplace status of its other products.

Two additional dimensions of the competitive sector are the number of competitors and their geographic scope. Some firms compete with a large number of competitors. Others face competition from a limited number. At the manufacturing level, aluminum producers have few competitors. Televisionmakers have relatively more. In general, though, most manufacturing industries have few competitors in an absolute sense.

The geographic scope of the competitive sector can vary considerably. It is largely determined by the geographic scope of the market being served. Some companies face competition at the global level (e.g., auto

Figure 3–10: Levels of demand and types of competition

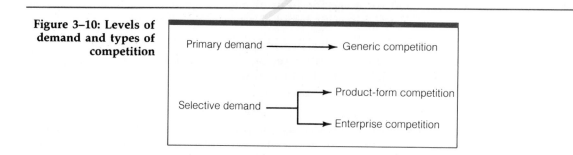

producers), while others find competitors concentrated at the regional or local level.

The nature of competition. It is important to consider the manner in which competition occurs within the structure of the competitive sector. Competition between U.S. firms is **nonprice** in nature. Nonprice competition means that the entire set of marketing strategy variables is the basis for competition. Price, of course, can be a formidable competitive weapon. But product, promotion, distribution, *and* price are the tools of competition. A firm can seek a competitive advantage through product differentiation, concentrated advertising and selling efforts, unique distribution, or service.

There are several reasons why nonprice competition is dominant in the U.S. economy:

1. *Dynamic, heterogeneous marketplace.* As we have noted, the marketplace is decidedly heterogeneous. Consumers are driven by motives extending well beyond the economic. Their affluence allows noneconomic motives to guide many of their purchases. Consumers are also dynamic in their strong desires for new and different products. Strict price competition, therefore, would not seem to be in the best interests of consumers or the firms that serve them.

2. *Selective weapon.* Related to the heterogeneity of the market is the need to be selective in approaching the marketplace. Firms may wish to pursue different segments of the market with unique marketing strategies. Nonprice efforts offer a better basis for developing these selective approaches.

3. *Difficulty of competitive reaction.* A firm that competes on a nonprice basis is less susceptible to retaliatory efforts from competitors. Duplication of a nonprice competitive move is quite difficult. A price reduction can be matched immediately by competition, but a change in product design or a new advertising theme cannot. Effective retaliatory action of a nonduplicative nature is often difficult and time-consuming to develop; and this allows the firm's nonprice strategy more opportunity to take hold.

4. *Stable industry conditions.* Nonprice competition is more likely to lead to stable industry conditions. Different price competition can lead to the chaos of price wars, but the stability of nonprice competition allows firms a better situation in which to plan and chart their operations.

While much competition is decidedly nonprice in nature, price does remain an important competitive weapon. In fact, some companies emphasize price over other variables in their competitive strategy. The Datril brand of nonaspirin pain reliever competes with Tylenol through a lower

This ad illustrates competing on a nonprice basis.

price. Note, however, that both Datril and Tylenol compete with aspirin-based pain relievers (Excedrin) on a nonprice basis at the product-form level.

Differential advantage. Whether price or nonprice factors dominate, the general objective of a firm is the same—to establish a ***differential advantage*** over its competition.

differential advantage	The **differential advantage** of a firm is the unique niche that it occupies in its competitive environment.

Table 3–2: Examples of approaches to the search for a differential advantage	Basis for differential advantage	Firm	Approach
	Market served	Richard D. Irwin	Publishes only college textbooks
	Product	Procter & Gamble	Emphasizes performance superiority of its products
	Service	IBM	Attempts to provide best customer service
	Distribution	Avon	Distributes only through personal home delivery
	Price	K mart	Across-the-board lower prices on major brands
	Selling	Electrolux vacuum cleaners	Door-to-door personal selling only

It is the search for differential advantage that guides the marketing effort. Through market segmentation, product/service design, distribution channels, selling approach, geographic location, and price, a firm seeks a differential advantage over its competition. Table 3–2 presents some examples of firms emphasizing different bases for a differential advantage.

A differential advantage serves to lessen the threats present in the competitive sector. It's hard for existing competitors to invade a niche. The same holds true for would-be competitors. In short, a strong differential advantage helps immunize a firm against competitive threats.[17]

Proliferation of opportunity. Too often, the competitive sector is seen only as a source of threats to the firm. But competitors' behavior can reveal opportunities to the firm as well. One concept—***proliferation of opportunity***—suggests firms that successfully enter new markets reveal opportunities in these markets for other firms.[18] Pursuit of these opportunities can occur in three ways: emulation, deviation, and complementation.

1. ***Emulation.*** Firms pursue the success of the original entrants by copying their behavior—usually by marketing functionally identical products. Several years ago the Miller Brewing Company very successfully opened the light-beer market with its Miller Lite brand. Other beer companies quickly followed with their own brands of low-calorie beer. The light segment is now one of the most competitive in the beer market.

2. ***Deviation.*** Firms pursue the opportunity by competing with a product and marketing strategy that deviate from that of the original firm. In the early 60s the success of foreign autos in the American small-car

---

[17] An extensive discussion of competitive forces and how to deal with them is found in Michael E. Porter, *Competitive Strategy: Techniques for Analyzing Industries and Competitors* (New York: Free Press, 1980).

[18] This concept was suggested by Wroe Alderson, *Dynamic Marketing Behavior* (Homewood, Ill.: Richard D. Irwin, 1965), pp. 198–200.

market revealed previously overlooked opportunities to American manufacturers. They responded with somewhat larger and roomier cars with bigger engines than their foreign counterparts yet distinctly smaller than their own full-size models. More recently, Japanese manufacturers have enjoyed success in the American market with small, economical, front-wheel-drive cars. The American response has been more an emulation strategy than previously.

Many successful companies have followed the deviation strategy. They allow other firms to take the first steps into a market and then respond with refined goods. Prominent examples include Hewlett-Packard, Digital, IBM, Caterpillar, and John Deere. The Hewlett-Packard approach, for example, has been described this way:

> The company is seldom first into the market with its new products. . . . The company's marketing strategy is normally that of a counterpuncher. A competitor's new product comes on the market and HP engineers, when making service calls on HP equipment, ask their customers what they like or dislike about the new product, what features the customer would like to have . . . and pretty soon HP salesmen are calling on customers again with a new product that answers their needs and wants.[19]

3. *Complementation.* Rather than pursue the opportunity by competing directly with the original entrant, firms may offer a good to be used in conjunction with the successful one (complementary good). Or they may serve as suppliers to the successful firm. For example, the burgeoning personal computer market has created a new software industry.

Monitoring the competitive sector.   The competitive sector is one of the most difficult to monitor. Naturally, competitors seldom voice their strategic plans openly. Adding to the difficulty is the broad scope of relevant competitor-related information.

New product plans, sales force organization, and advertising plans of competitors are just a few of the types of information needed to effectively monitor the competitive sector. Fortunately, the creative company can turn to a variety of key intelligence sources. Table 3–3 summarizes the nature of some of these.

The diversity of types and sources of information relevant to the competitive sector suggests the need for a *competitive intelligence system.*

competitive intelligence system	A **competitive intelligence system** is an integrated, systematic set of activities designed to find, store, and transmit to appropriate corporate decisionmakers information about the plans and actions of competitors.

---

[19] Kathleen K. Wiegner, "The One to Watch," *Forbes,* March 2, 1981, p. 60.

Table 3–3: Sources of competitive intelligence

Source	Example	Comment
Government	Government Contract Administration	Studying competitors' bids can reveal their technology, costs, bidding philosophy
Competitors	Annual reports, speeches of officers	Can reveal management philosophy, priorities
	Products	Reveal competitors' technology
	Employment ads	Can suggest technical and marketing directions based on type of person wanted
Customers	Customer engineers and officers	May be aware of competitors' plans
Professional meetings	Trade shows	Many competitors represented
Company personnel	Sales force, engineers	Can be trained to recognize and transmit relevant intelligence that they see
Other sources	Intelligence consultants	Perform monitoring task on fee basis

Source: Adapted from David B. Montgomery and Charles B. Weinberg, "Toward Strategic Intelligence Systems," *Journal of Marketing*, Fall 1979, p. 46.

Few companies presently maintain formal competitive intelligence systems. One company that does is GTE in its Sylvania Division.[20] Its management information of competitive strategies (MICS) system monitors the activities of 51 competitors. From Securities and Exchange Commission filings, articles from industry publications, and reports and analyses from GTE field staff, MICS compiles information in 17 strategic categories for each competitor. These categories include background of officers, management strategy, marketing strategy, pricing, legal matters, distribution strategy, R&D, and new technology. MICS receives its data from GTE's 30 SBUs. Field staff members feed the system with intelligence using 20-page forms. At GTE headquarters an analyst extracts useful information from the reports. This information goes into an on-line computer system accessible to authorized staff members only.

The GTE competitive intelligence system lacks the scope of information necessary for it to be a complete intelligence bank. But it's an excellent first step into the area of systematic competitive monitoring. As the system evolves, it will become even more useful.

The technological sector

In the simplest sense, technology is the knowledge and procedures that go into getting something done. At a more complex level, it is the knowledge and procedures used in the conversion of resources to a finished product.

A technological advance improves the knowledge or procedures of conversion. It can have two effects. First, improvements in knowledge or

---

[20] "GTE's Computer Records Secrets of 51 Competitors," *Marketing News,* September 16, 1983, p. 10.

procedures can lead to better finished products. Over time, functionally superior products are developed. Second, a technological advance can improve both the effectiveness and efficiency of the conversion process so that a superior product is produced at a cost lower than its predecessor. Color televisions are a classic example. Color TVs today are far superior to those 10 years ago (not to mention the original ones of 30 years ago). And they are produced with such improved efficiency that they cost less to consumers in *absolute* dollars than the original ones did.

Since World War II, technological advances have occurred faster and generated more improvements than in the entire history of humankind. Virtually no one has remained untouched by them. Electronics, telecommunications, medical equipment, computers, energy, artificial foods, and space exploration have all experienced rapid technological change. These areas are not unrelated. Technological advances in one area often result in advances in another. For example, some advances in medical equipment and telecommunications are direct results of the space program.

The impact of technology on society is virtually boundless. The modern home, with its microwave oven, personal computer, video recorder, freeze-dried coffee, cable TV hookup, and automatic garage-door opener, is a far cry from the home of 25 years ago.[21]

Technological change affects all aspects of marketing behavior. Of course, there are many new or improved products themselves. They create opportunities for new markets. The development of computer chips, for instance, has led to an array of new or improved products (hand-held calculators, minicomputers, video games).

But this is only the most visible effect. All aspects of the marketing operation are affected. Besides expanding the programming services available to consumers, cable TV improvements open new possibilities in non-store buying by consumers, more selective advertising messages, and improved marketing research surveys and experiments. We have already seen how electronic advances have increased the distribution capabilities of financial institutions. Finally, cost advantages in the marketplace can result from technology that improves the efficiency of production processes.

Technological change, however, is not without potential detrimental consequences. New products can render existing ones obsolete and threaten the survival of firms and industries. The railroad passenger industry is a mere shadow of its former self as a result of the automobile and passenger airplane. The development of computer disks for data storage will ultimately destroy the keypunch card.

The firm must decide how to deal with the many opportunities and threats posed by the technological sector. It has essentially two options.

---

[21] Interesting reading on the societal effects of technology is provided by Alvin Toffler, *The Third Wave* (New York: William Morrow, 1980).

It may attempt to operate at the forefront of technology by contributing to technological change. In this way it is in a better position to keep pace with or stay ahead of competition and more immediately realize the benefits of technological advances. Through internal development a firm may achieve patent rights on a process, thereby shielding itself from other companies matching its gain. The result can be more long-run pre-eminence in an industry.

The dominant means to this technological approach is through research and development (R&D) departments within a company. R&D departments are typically composed of scientists whose major task is to identify and pursue technological improvements. But often these scientists, without marketing expertise, fail to consider the marketing implications of their efforts.

R&D obviously incurs large expenses; therefore, these departments are usually found in large companies. In 1978 Texas Instruments, one of the world's most innovative companies, spent over $100 million on R&D, more than double what it had spent just three years earlier. Its sales virtually doubled during the same time period as well.[22] Then, in 1983, Texas Instruments pulled its version of the home computer off the market because of poor sales. Thus, within the same company we see both the benefits and the failure of innovation in the absence of effective marketing.

The second approach to technology is the opposite of R&D. A firm may leave efforts at technological change to others and attempt to capture the fallout from their efforts. This approach has the primary advantage of being without cost. It serves well for many small firms. The risk here is that the firm may not realize the benefits of technology or may realize them so late that it is too far behind the innovators to catch up.

It may seem at first that technology is not subject to environmental forecasting. There is, after all, a mighty rapid pace of change in this sector. However, while forecasting is not really as readily evident here as in other sectors, it does occur. One company, TRW, Inc., describes it this way:

technological forecasting

> **Technological forecasting** is "the prediction of likely inventions, specific scientific refinements, or discoveries in technology, including applications or products which may become possible."[23]

---

[22] For a discussion of the innovative nature of Texas Instruments, see "Texas Instruments Shows U.S. Business How to Survive in the 1980s," *Business Week,* September 18, 1978, pp. 66–92.

[23] B. Q. North and D. L. Pyke, " 'Probes' of the Technological Future," *Harvard Business Review,* May–June 1969, p. 69.

Technological forecasting cannot predict that a particular new product will appear at a specified time. Rather, it is designed to detect *trends* in technological levels and anticipate the general nature of potential new products.

The public policy sector

The public policy sector of the marketing environment encompasses the laws and regulations imposed by governments on the marketing operations of firms. This sector is extremely complex. The number of laws governing marketing is probably at an all-time high. All levels of government impose regulations on the behavior of firms. A broad array of federal laws govern businesses, but state and local governments have regulatory powers, too. States enact laws about minimum drinking ages, returnable bottles, and product pricing. Local laws govern when certain products can be sold. Some communities prohibit the sale of certain goods on Sunday; others prohibit the sale of packaged liquor after a certain hour. All of these laws and regulations have marketing consequences.

Historically, the general goal of the regulatory system has been to protect and promote competition. Competition was deemed to be in the best interests of society. Much early federal legislation involved **antitrust laws** designed to outlaw monopolies and regulate specific practices leading to them (collusion, price discrimination, tying contracts, predatory pricing). A summary of key antitrust laws and the amendments to strengthen them is given in Table 3–4. Of these, the amended Federal Trade Commission Act has probably the greatest impact on marketing practices.

In recent years the regulatory system, while maintaining its procompetitive stance, has also adopted a proconsumer stance by passing laws designed to **protect consumers.** Many of these laws are a direct result of the consumer movement of the 1960s and are designed to enhance the consumer's "right to know." They don't just prohibit deceptive practices. They also require certain practices that enhance the consumer-information environment. Table 3–5 provides a summary of these laws.

The impact of the public policy sector on the marketing activities of a firm is similar to that of the other sectors. It imposes constraints, creates opportunities, and poses threats. Its constraining influence is seen in antitrust and consumer-protection laws. This influence is felt throughout all of the marketing decision variables. The production, promotion, pricing, and distribution of products are all regulated by federal, state, and local governments. We'll consider specific public policy implications for each marketing decision variable as we discuss these variables.

The opportunities created by the public policy sector are often a result of regulations imposed on other industries. Many states, for example, have enacted laws requiring builders to install smoke alarms in new homes. The result has been a dramatic jump in the sales of smoke alarms. Antipollution legislation has created opportunities for makers of pollution-control equipment. Finally, tax incentive programs can increase the demand for certain products (e.g., energy-saving products).

Table 3–4: Significant antitrust legislation	Date	Law	Summary
	1887	Interstate Commerce Act	Outlawed railroads to divide markets, fix prices, and discriminate in price; established Interstate Commerce Commission as regulatory body
	1890	Sherman Antitrust Act	Outlawed monopolies as well as contracts, combinations, and conspiracies that restrain trade
	1914	Clayton Act	Regulated price discrimination, tying contracts, exclusive dealing, requirements contracts, reciprocal deals, and acquisition of stock of another company
	1914	Federal Trade Commission Act	Declared unfair methods of competition to be illegal; established Federal Trade Commission (FTC)
	1936	Robinson-Patman Act	Regulated price discrimination and discounts (i.e., advertising allowances, brokers' discounts)
	1938	Wheeler-Lea Act	Prohibited deceptive acts and practices as well as unfair methods of competition
Source: Adapted from Joe L. Welch, *Marketing Law* (Tulsa, Okla.: PPC Books, 1980), pp. 2–4.	1975	FTC Improvement Act	Expanded idea of trade regulation rules and remedial powers of FTC

The threats posed by the public policy sector are often severe. In 1981 the local government of Madison, Wisconsin, enacted legislation prohibiting the sale of carryout liquor after 9 P.M. This law effectively wiped out the major source of post-9 P.M. revenue for 24-hour convenience stores.

In the early 1980s the cries for less governmental regulation of business became louder. Federal spending cutbacks have also limited the activities of key regulatory agencies, such as the FTC. Will the movement toward deregulation gain momentum? What direction will it take? We don't know yet. It is enough to say here that deregulation in the public policy sector can have extensive marketing consequences. We have already seen the sweeping effects of deregulation in the banking and airline industries.

The dynamic nature of this sector requires that it, like the other sectors, be monitored. Most large companies maintain legal departments and lobbyists to keep abreast of, interpret, and even influence government regulations. Such activities are usually beyond the resources of small businesses, but the government and the press do a reasonably good job of keeping businesses informed of pending and new legislation. In fact, one study identified an eight-year pattern of development for public policy issues.[24]

[24] "Firms Hiring New Type of Manager to Study Issues, Emerging Troubles," *The Wall Street Journal,* June 10, 1982, p. 26.

Table 3–5: Selected consumer-protection legislation	Date	Law	Summary
	1906	Pure Food and Drug Act	Prohibited adulterations and misbranding of foods and drugs sold in interstate commerce
	1906	Federal Meat Inspection Act	Provided for government inspection and certification of meat in interstate commerce
	1914	Federal Trade Commission Act	Declared unfair methods of competition to be illegal; established Federal Trade Commission (FTC)
	1938	Federal Food, Drug, and Cosmetics Act	Established the Food and Drug Administration empowered to seize products found unfit for consumption and to prosecute persons or firms held in violation
	1953	Flammable Fabrics Act	Prohibited marketing of highly flammable materials for clothing
	1966	Fair Packaging and Labeling (Truth-in-Packaging) Act	Specified contents, name, and size or weight labeling requirements for many household products
	1966	Child Protection Act	Banned sale of hazardous toys and articles intended for children
	1966	National Traffic and Motor Vehicle Safety (Traffic Safety) Act	Provided for establishment of national safety standards for motor vehicles
	1970	Public Health Smoking Act	Banned cigarette advertising on radio and television and revised the caution label on cigarette packages
	1972	Consumer Product Safety Act	Established a Federal Consumer Product Safety Commission with authority to create federal standards for products that may pose an injury risk for consumers
	1975	Magnuson-Moss Warranty-FTC Improvement Act	Warranties on goods costing $5 or more must disclose the terms of the warranty in simple and readily understood language
	1977	The Equal Credit Opportunity Act	To ensure that credit is made available fairly and impartially; prohibited discrimination against any applicant for credit because of race, color, religion, sex, etc.
	1978	Petroleum Marketing Practices Act	Required that the octane rating of gasoline be disclosed to consumers
	1981	Cash Discount Act	Allowed merchants to offer discounts to customers paying with cash rather than credit cards
	1982	Motor Vehicle Safety and Cost Savings Authorization	Extended and revised motor vehicle safety requirements

Source: Adapted from Frederick D. Sturdivant, *Business and Society: A Managerial Approach,* rev. ed. (Homewood, Ill.: Richard D. Irwin, 1981), pp. 283–85.

For the first five years, the issues are low-key but occasionally evident in the press and some polls. In the fifth or sixth year, the national press latches onto the issue. By the eighth year, government action occurs. Such a pattern allows a firm to anticipate and adapt to public policy developments before they become "overnight" problems. For example, Sears, Roebuck foresaw the flammable-nightwear controversy and stocked nonflammable goods well before public policy was enacted. And S. C. Johnson stopped using fluorocarbons three years before their usage was prohibited.

Anticipating and responding to potential legal actions as Sears, Roebuck and S. C. Johnson did can lessen the disruptive effects of new laws and allow a smoother transition to new operations.

SUMMARY

The situation analysis stage of strategic planning requires an assessment of the marketing environment. The marketing environment is diverse, as reflected by its five sectors: sociocultural, economic, competitive, technological, and public policy. It is dynamic. Changes in one sector can cause changes in other sectors. Finally, it is uncontrollable. The firm cannot manipulate it, though the behavior of the firm can influence it.

The environment's impact on the firm occurs in several ways and encompasses a firm's entire marketing operation. The environment imposes constraints by limiting what the firm can do. But its dynamic nature also creates marketing opportunities for new markets. As the environment changes, it also poses threats that may have detrimental consequences to the firm. The environmental impact forces the firm to monitor change continuously. Firms must assess the opportunities or threats posed by change and, if necessary, respond through environmental adaptation (i.e., the manipulation of one or more marketing decision variables). This process is facilitated by a thorough understanding of each sector of the environment.

The sociocultural sector involves society as a whole. Its key dimensions are demography, socioeconomic characteristics, and the cultural values of society. Cultural values include the rights of consumers and the consumer movement designed to achieve them.

The economic sector includes the general macroeconomic forces that influence business operations. Such forces include inflationary rates, interest rates, and resource supply levels.

The competitive sector involves the institutions with which the firm competes in the marketplace. The structure of this sector is reflected by the types of demand for which the firm is competing (primary and selective), the levels at which competition occurs (generic, product-form, and enterprise), the number of competitors, and the geographic scope. The form of competition in the United States is decidedly nonprice in nature.

In the technological sector, advances in knowledge and procedures represent both opportunities and threats to firms. Opportunities for new or improved products and more efficient production evolve from technology. Threats of rendering the firm's product obsolete or less useful also emerge.

The public policy sector encompasses the laws imposed on firms by federal, state, and local governments. Laws with important marketing implications are designed to promote competition and to protect consumers.

KEY CONCEPTS

Marketing environment

Intraorganizational level of environment

Corporate culture

External support level of environment

Channel intermediaries

Marketing service agencies

Trade associations

Macro level of environment

Sociocultural sector

Economic sector

Competitive sector

Technological sector

Public policy sector

Environmental threat

Environmental monitoring

Environmental adaptation

Demographics

Socioeconomic characteristics

Cultural values

Subculture

Consumerism

Consumer rights

Leading indicators

Primary demand

Selective demand

Generic competition

Product-form competition

Enterprise competition

Nonprice competition

Differential advantage

Proliferation of opportunity

Emulation

Deviation

Complementation

Competitive intelligence system

Technological forecasting

Antitrust

Consumer protection

DISCUSSION QUESTIONS AND EXERCISES

1. Select a company of your choice. Interview three or four employees at various levels of the company, and try to get an idea of the presence and nature of a corporate culture.

2. The American automobile industry has been buffeted by a variety of environmental changes in the past decade or so. Identify as many of these changes as you can. What sectors do they come from? Is there a chain of events much like that described for the airline industry? How have domestic auto companies adapted to these events?

3. Find some additional examples of companies that have explicitly taken action directed at meeting the rights of consumers.

4. Look up a recent economic forecast for your state. What does it imply in the way of marketing threats and opportunities for the major industries in your state?

5. For a product of your choice, describe the structure of the competitive sector of the environment for a particular brand of the product.

6. Think of a recent major purchase you made. In your opinion, what was the differential advantage offered by the brand you chose?

7. In the early years of personal computers many companies existed in the industry. A large number have now gone out of business. What forces caused the failure of these companies?

8. Discuss the relationship between antitrust laws and consumer-protection laws.

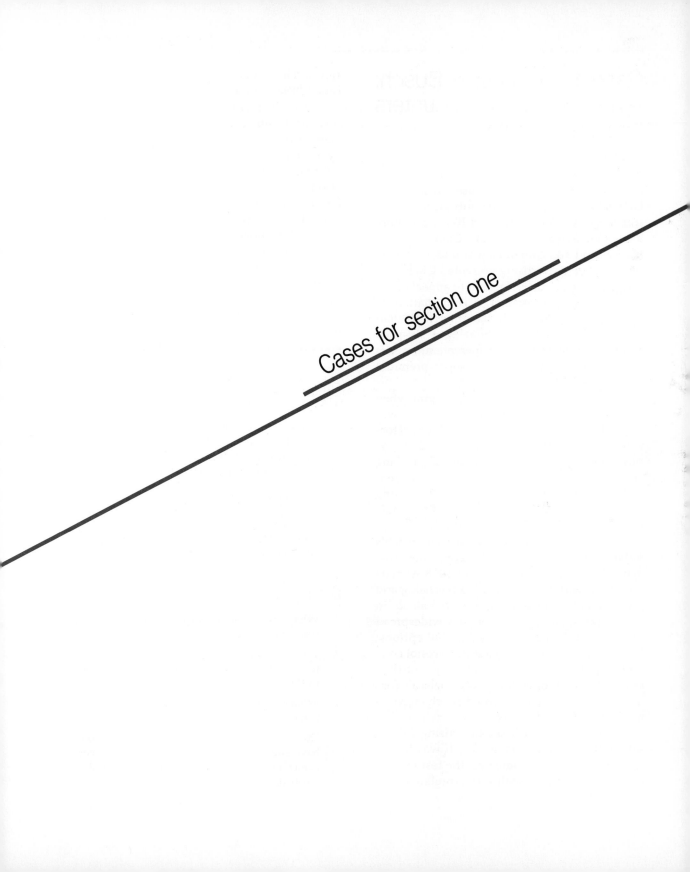

Cases for section one

Case 1: Anheuser-Busch: A new soft drink encounters consumer protests

In September 1978 Anheuser-Busch, the United States' largest brewer, introduced a new soft drink, Chelsea. Packaged like a premium beer with a foil bottle neck, Chelsea had a frothy head and contained just under 0.4 percent alcohol. Advertising presented Chelsea as the "not-so-soft-drink" meant to appeal to the urban adult. The product, a combination of ginger, lemon, and apple flavoring with malt flavoring base, sold for about $2 a six-pack and was intended to be a super-premium soft drink, much as Michelob is super-premium beer.

No sooner had test marketing begun when the protests started. In Virginia the drink was boycotted by clergy, nurses, and educators who claimed that the drink was aimed at getting young people into the habit of drinking alcoholic beverages. A school superintendent in Staunton, Virginia, was quoted as saying Chelsea was geared toward "socially conditioning" the young to take up drinking.

Despite rebuttals from Anheuser-Busch's public relations firm, some consumers remained critical, and in the fall of 1978 Anheuser-Busch withdrew Chelsea's advertising and promotional materials. Chelsea remained in test markets, and speculation was widespread regarding Anheuser-Busch's possible options. For example, it could increase the alcohol content to put it in the liquor category and thus out of the reach of children. Or Chelsea's formulation and packaging could be changed to make it look less like beer.

Withdrawal of Chelsea's advertising did not satisfy its critics. Anheuser-Busch was forced to pull the original product off the test market shelves, replacing it with a reformulated version in December 1978. The new Chelsea was called "the natural alternative" and described as a naturally flavored, less sweet, drier-tasting soft drink aimed at adults. The alcohol had been virtually eliminated in the new formula. Packaging was to be changed to eliminate any reference to alcoholic content. The bottles were also to be changed to make the product resemble a soft drink. Nonetheless, Chelsea's test markets could not produce consistent results, and in November 1979 test marketing was officially suspended.

Anheuser-Busch tried again to enter the soft drink market in 1981 with Root 66, a root-beer product. Despite heavy ad support and numerous promotional discount efforts, sales in test markets ranged from "good to awful," and production stopped in October 1981.

References

"Anheuser-Busch Halting Chelsea's Test Marketing," *The Wall Street Journal,* November 21, 1979, p. 4.

"Anheuser-Busch Removes Alcohol from 'Soft Drink.'" *The Capital Times,* December 13, 1978.

Marshall, Christy. "Anheuser-Busch Withdraws Chelsea Ads but Says Product to Stay in Test." *Advertising Age,* October 30, 1978, p. 2.

"Protest Brews over Malt Drink." *The Milwaukee Journal,* October 17, 1978, p. 1.

Reed, Robert. "Anheuser-Busch Signals End of Soft Drink Try." *Advertising Age,* October 5, 1981, p. 1.

Discussion questions

1. What environmental factors played a role in consumers' outcry against Chelsea?

2. What steps might have Anheuser-Busch taken to anticipate the reactions of consumer groups to the introduction of Chelsea?

3. What factors were likely to have motivated Anheuser-Busch to introduce a soft drink?

4. Do you think that any beer marketer would have encountered similar resistance from consumer groups if they attempted to introduce a soft drink?

Case 2: Eastman Kodak Company: An overview of corporate and marketing strategy

In 1983, Walter A. Fallon, chairman of Eastman Kodak, reflected on the appropriate strategy to adopt for his company. Some major challenges were facing the company: intense and disciplined Japanese competition, reduced growth rates in the demand for Kodak's basic products, and need for fundamental technological change. In 1982 Kodak spent about $143 million in advertising, a 41 percent increase over 1981. This resulted in worldwide sales of $10.82 billion—only a 5 percent increase over the previous year. Industry observers indicated that Kodak faced one of the greatest challenges in the company's history: to change its thinking, its corporate habits, and its reflexes to evolve into a company as successful in new markets as it had been in less competitive ones.

History

Unique circumstances allowed Kodak to develop a virtual lock on the market for photographic products. These included a creative, loyal, and nonunionized employee force; immense financial resources almost free of debt; and a strong research and development tradition. Indeed, in recent decades Kodak was able to monopolize the photography business. Attempts by such competitors as GAF Corporation, West Germany's Agfa-Gavaert, and Britain's Ilford Group Ltd., were easily thwarted. Polaroid Corporation stayed cautiously within its smaller, instant-photo market. In fact, Kodak successfully entered the instant-photo market when Polaroid's patents expired and has managed to maintain a 25 percent market

Exhibit 1: Annual percent increase in amateur pictures

Period	Growth
1980–81	4%
1979–80	4
1969–79	12
1959–69	13

Source: "BW Estimates," Business Week, February 1, 1982, p. 49.

share despite the depressed state of the market. To do so, Kodak introduced four new Kodamatic cameras and a high-velocity instant film, ASA 320. Kodak is hopeful of two other developments in the instant-camera field: (1) the Kodamatic Trimprint color film, and (2) the Instagraphic CRT imaging outfit. Instagraphic is a product for the professional or commercial market and takes pictures from still images projected on a video or computer screen.

The Instagraphic product marked Kodak's first departure from the amateur market in instant photography. Its introduction comes at a time when growth in the U.S. market in amateur pictures is declining (see Exhibit 1). This trend is a serious threat to Kodak, because amateur photography products provide the bulk of Kodak's profits (see Exhibit 2). Moreover, conventional photography is a maturing market. For decades, the force behind growth in picture taking has been the gradual changeover from black and white to color. This change is nearly completed. Thus, Kodak's traditional lines—conventional still cameras, silver halide film, photographic paper, Super 8 movie cameras, and slide and movie projection equipment—face a long-term threat from new electronic products, including electronic imaging cameras, magnetic tape or disk, video display,

Exhibit 2: Kodak's Sources of Profitability

	Film and paper	Other	Total
Sales	21%	79%	$10.65
Pretax profits	60	40	2.35

Source: Estimates of 1981 results by Merrill Lynch, Pierce, Fenner & Smith, Inc.

videotape cameras, and TV sets and video playback systems.

At the present time, Kodak faces a strong challenge from well-organized, financially strong Japanese companies led by Fuji and Konishiroku. Fuji holds 70 percent of the Japanese film market and is in the midst of a U.S. advertising blitz to build awareness in the United States. Konishiroku, a seller of private-label films to customers—including Fotomat Corporation—plans to introduce its own brand in the United States soon, with heavy advertising support. Both Japanese challengers feel that they have products as good as Kodak's but not its good name among consumers largely unaware of non-Kodak offerings. In addition, Kodak can marshal its immense resources in sales expertise—its detailed instruction booklet for salespersons has, for example, been considered an excellent sales tool.

Kodak plans an aggressive promotion of its new camera lines by increased advertising expenditures. Price cutting may be another effective tool that Kodak uses to compete against the Japanese. Currently, Kodak's U.S. wholesale price is about 10 percent higher than its competitors, and a more aggressive pricing strategy may be adopted. Kodak has historically had a somewhat rigid pricing structure. Powerful retailers who market Kodak products have been exerting more pressure on Kodak for lower prices and granting of volume discounts.

Already drug retailer Revco D. S., Inc., upset over Kodak's inflexible marketing bureaucracy, has approached Fuji with an offer to replace Kodak film with the Japanese substitute. Indeed, "lack of enthusiasm" and "arrogance" contributed to Kodak's losing the right to use the 1984 Los Angeles Olympic Games logo to Fuji, according to Daniel Greenwood, who was responsible for sponsorships for the 1984 Los Angeles Olympic Games.

Future directions

Chairman Fallon confronted the challenges facing his company. Several alternative strategies were under consideration or were under various phases of implementation. These included shifting into nonphotographic fields such as office copiers, blood analyzers, and high-speed electronic equipment; acquiring electronics companies; aggressively protecting Kodak's base in chemical-imaging know-how; and increasing film and paper market shares in foreign countries.

References

"Kodak Fights Back: Everybody Wants a Piece of Its Markets." *Business Week,* February 1, 1982, pp. 48–53.

Slinker, Barry H. "Eastman Kodak Company." *Advertising Age.* September 8, 1983, p. 48.

Discussion questions

1. Based on the information in the case and your own knowledge of Kodak, state in three or four sentences Kodak's corporate strategy.

2. What are the levels of competition—generic, product-form, or enterprise—Kodak is facing?

3. What environmental factors pose threats to Kodak's future?

4. What are Kodak's major strengths and weaknesses relative to the Japanese companies?

5. State the appropriate changes in pricing, promotion, product, and channel strategies for Kodak in view of the major challenges facing the company.

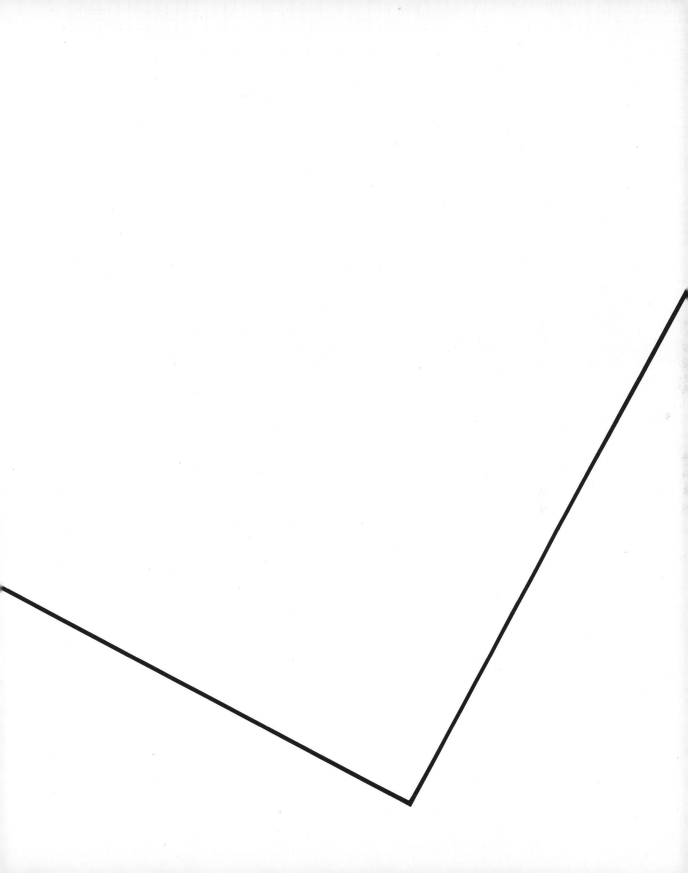

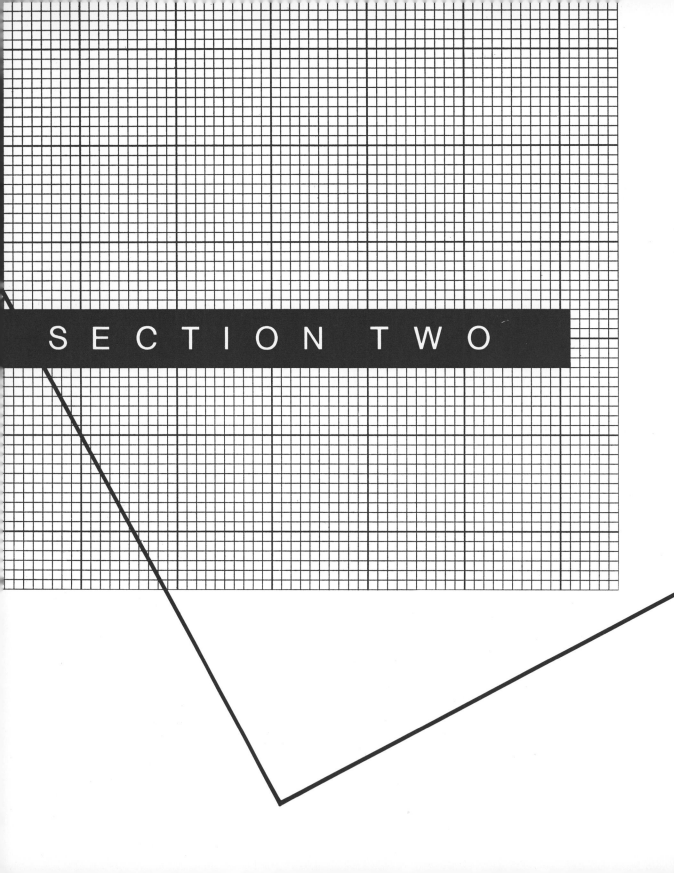

SECTION TWO

Describing and understanding buyers

Consistent with the philosophy of the market-ing concept, our starting point for examining the components of the marketing framework in greater detail is the marketplace—the sets of individuals and institutions to which prod-ucts and services are offered. Chapter 4 begins this section with a descriptive look at the over-all consumer market in the United States. It examines population size and distribution, as well as demographic and socioeconomic char-acteristics of the population. Chapters 5 to 8 serve as a framework for understanding buy-ers. Chapter 5 shifts to a behavioral science look at consumers, treating individual psycho-logical influences on individual consumers. Chapter 6 continues the behavioral perspective with a look at social influence on behavior. Our topic in Chapter 7 is the consumer buying process—the sequence of stages through which a consumer moves in the purchase and use of a product. In Chapter 8 we will consider organizational buyers—their nature, influences on their buying decisions, how they make buying decisions, and what they buy.

CHAPTER 4

Descriptive analysis of the U.S. consumer market

The ratchet effect
Dual-income households
Education
Occupation
Value of descriptive variables

Summary

Key concepts

Discussion questions and exercises

Population size
    Household size

Population age

Geographic distribution of the population
    Regional distribution
    The "mobiles" as a market
    Governmental definitions of concentrated
        market areas
    Urban–suburban–rural distribution

Socioeconomic characteristics
    Income
    Engel's laws

The answers to a number of questions about buyers yield considerable insight into proper marketing strategies for products or services. For instance:

1. *Who buys the product?* Is it used by a particular segment of society or by virtually all kinds of people?

2. *How much of the product is bought?* What quantity typifies an individual purchase?

3. *When is the product bought?* Is there a particular time of day, week, or year that it is typically bought?

4. *Where is the product bought?* Is it bought at a particular type of store?

5. *Why is the product bought?* What ends are sought in its purchase and use?

6. *How is the product bought?* What characterizes the decision process leading to and following purchase? Is it simple or complex?

These questions serve as guidelines for examining buyers and their relationships with products and services. The answers can encompass a wide scope of issues and topics. In Section Two we will address many of these topics, beginning here with a descriptive look at the overall consumer market. By considering its demographic and socioeconomic characteristics, we gain insights into "who buys the product."

POPULATION SIZE   In aggregate form the U.S. consumer market is of substantial size. In 1984 over 230 million people made up the population, and there has been steady growth. However, as Figure 4–1 shows, the rate of growth has been slowing. Recent and projected rates of growth are lower than have historically been the case. This means that the markets for products whose demand is tied to population size (staple items such as food) will

Figure 4–1: Total population of the United States, 1960–2000

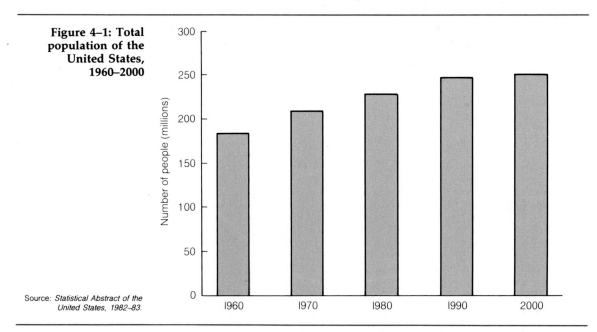

Source: *Statistical Abstract of the United States, 1982–83.*

Figure 4–2: Births per 1,000 population, 1950–1980

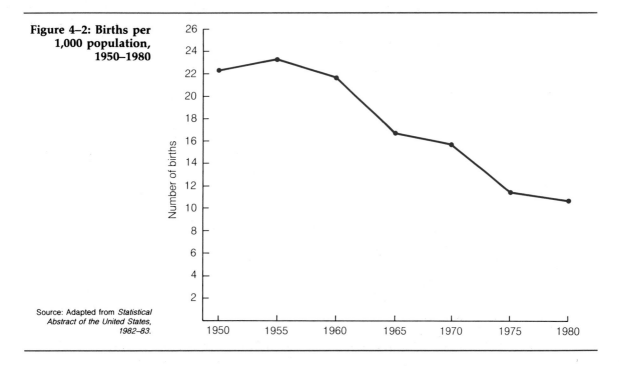

Source: Adapted from *Statistical Abstract of the United States, 1982–83.*

not grow much. Growth in the sales of individual brands of these products will have to come from improved competition and increased market share.

One factor contributing to the slowing of population growth is the declining birthrate. (See Figure 4–2.) Many couples are consciously limiting the size of their families. More and more are opting for no children at all. Some of this is due to the increase in dual-career families—which in itself has marketing relevance.

Declining birthrates are a prime example of a force directly affecting the marketing operations of certain firms whose target markets represent only a portion of the total population. The baby market is a target for many companies, notably Gerber Products, the largest baby food company. As the baby market becomes smaller, competition for a smaller total volume of sales becomes keener. Gerber recognized this in the mid-70s and adapted by developing nonfood baby items and marketing its baby products to adults.

Household size

One obvious effect of the declining birthrate is a reduction in the average household size. Substantial downward shifts in household size are evident. (See Table 4–1.) One impact is a reduction in the size of dwelling units. More consumers are interested in smaller, single-family homes and condominiums. The reductions in the size of families and their dwelling units require more compact products. Responding to this situation, General Electric downsized its microwave oven and modeled

	Year	Average household size	Single-person household as percentage of total
Table 4–1: Reduction of average household size and growth of single-person households, 1970–1980	1970	3.14	17.0
	1975	2.95	19.6
	1980	2.76	22.7

Source: *Statistical Abstract of the United States, 1982–83.*

it to hang beneath kitchen cabinets, thereby freeing valuable counterspace. As a result, GE went from a poor position in the microwave market to the second largest market share.

household

> **Household** refers to one or more persons occupying a "housing unit" (house, apartment), including related family members and any unrelated persons (lodgers, wards).

A phenomenon related to the shifts in household size is the growth of single-person households. Single persons, because of freedom from responsibility to others, typically have a broader perspective on the world around them. Spending less time at home, they often value convenience in meeting in-home requirements such as eating and home maintenance. Knowing this has offered marketers a better understanding of opportunities in this market and an improved ability to realize them.

Not only is this segment growing in size, however; its composition is also changing. It used to be that the single-adult market was quite identifiable, with distinct lifestyle and consumption patterns. Now there is increased heterogeneity of single adults, growing out of additional societal forces leading to single status. Once, adults remained single if they chose to postpone or not to enter marriage. Such persons still make up a substantial part of this segment of the population, but new types of one-person households are adding to the size of this segment—the divorced person and the widowed elderly female. These types of "singles" are quite different from the never-married and require different marketing attention. The lesson to marketers here is that an increase in the size of a demographic segment may result from new social forces rather than the ones that traditionally shaped it. Changes in marketing may thus be necessary.

POPULATION AGE

A fundamental demographic feature of a population is its age distribution—the number of people in various age categories. The age distribution of a population has far-reaching economic and social effects on a society.

Food companies develop products and direct advertising messages at certain types of consumers. Here we see Stouffer's offering conveniently prepared fine foods to the single-adult, urban male household.

Scene: Bachelor apartment, Chicago.
Time: 7:02 p.m.
Cast: One hungry guy. One T-bone done to a T.

And Stouffer's® **Fettucini Alfredo,**
in another outstanding performance.

Turn the side of your plate into a star attraction.
With Side Dishes. From Stouffers.

Courtesy Stouffer Foods Corporation

Labor force size, unemployment rates, government spending on societal needs, housing demand, and lifestyle patterns, to name a few, are all a function of age distribution.

From a marketing standpoint, a major effect of a population's age distribution is on the total assortment of goods it demands. Certain age groups follow certain consumption patterns; and the extent to which those patterns exist in the overall population is directly related to the size of the age group. One of the most fundamental forces in the economy, the demand for housing, is a prime example. Single-family homes are purchased most often by households in the early-30s age group. The expansion and contraction of this group over time explains some of the movement in the demand for housing.

Overall shifts in age distribution are crucial to forecasters and policymakers. There is no better time than now to realize the important effects of these shifts. The U.S. population is shifting drastically and with a variety of effects. Figure 4–3 and Table 4–2 reflect the nature of the shifts.

The most obvious change is that the population is growing older. The 1980s and 90s will see substantial growth in the older age categories—members of the population over 25. Correspondingly, the under-25 age groups will change little. As Table 4–2 shows, the median age of the

Figure 4–3: Age distribution of United States population, 1960–2025

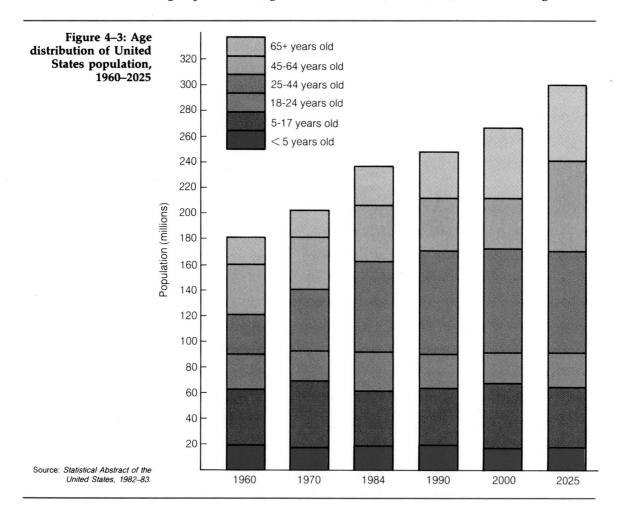

Source: *Statistical Abstract of the United States, 1982–83.*

Table 4–2:	Year	Median age
Median age of the population	1950	30.2
	1960	29.4
	1970	28.0
	1980	30.0
Source: *Statistical Abstract of the*	1990	32.8
United States, 1982–83.	2000	35.5

population will increase by over five years from 1980 to 2000. Many of these changes are due to the decline in birthrate, discussed above. Demographers foresee numerous effects on society resulting from the age shifts. Some of these are: a growing mood of conservatism as the youth culture wanes, a drop in the unemployment rate in the 1980s resulting from a decline in the number of new entrants in the labor force, and a decline in government spending on education.

It is important for marketers to recognize the gross shifts in the population age structure. But they must go further: they must ascertain the effect on living patterns and translate these effects into marketing implications. For example, the 25–44 age group will grow more than any other group. This group spends the most in general and on specific items, such as housing. Therefore, as this age group grows, the consumer-spending level should also increase. In turn, housing demand and thus the demand for household appliances, textiles, and do-it-yourself products should grow. Taking age trends as a whole, more dollars will go to small consumer durables, entertainment, travel, recreation, liquor, adult education, and convenience-oriented goods and services.

As the age structure shifts, the older segment of the population becomes a more attractive target market. The number of consumers in the 45–64 age range grows. More of this group have above-average incomes than in other age groups. Because households in this group have fewer financial obligations (many mortgages have been paid off), no children at home, and female heads that have returned to the work force, they have greater discretionary income. These households are becoming a prime target for companies marketing luxury goods, recreational products, and travel. Companies now recognize this group as an active, adventurous segment of society and are aiming many new products at it. New magazines such as *Prime Time* exist for the 45- to 65-year-old consumer. Existing magazines such as *Retirement Living* have gained many new readers. The popularity of the TV show "60 Minutes" is attributed to its appeal to older viewers.

The growing interest in older consumers will produce shifts in the nature of selling techniques. Older consumers are more experienced, less fad-oriented, and less likely to feel peer pressure. Consequently, these

The growing over-40 age segment is receiving more marketing attention. Here we see a product oriented to the special personal-care needs of women in this age group.

Introducing Affinity™ Shampoo for hair over 40

New Affinity Shampoo helps bring back fullness and shine the years take away. You'll notice the difference the first time you use it. Affinity brings back body and highlights. Reduces breaking and thinning, too.

Now there's no age limit to looking good!

NEW

Affinity Shampoo

BRINGS BACK BEAUTIFUL HAIR

Courtesy Johnson & Johnson

consumers will be influenced by demonstrations and facts contained in selling messages. Image-oriented, emotional appeals will be less effective and less frequent in marketing communications.

The aging of the population poses threats for firms marketing products and services to youthful market segments. One concerned industry is the soft drink industry. Soft drink sales are greatest in the younger age groups. As consumers grow older, they consume fewer soft drinks and more coffee, tea, and liquor. The strategic efforts of the major soft drink manufacturers include attempts to get consumers to continue the soft drink consumption patterns they developed in their youth. Pepsi-Cola hopes its consumers will think of themselves as members of "The Pepsi Generation" throughout much of their lives.

GEOGRAPHIC DISTRIBUTION OF THE POPULATION

"Where the people are" is a basic consideration in marketing strategy development, especially in distribution strategy. The geographic distribution of the United States has one overwhelming characteristic: It is uneven. The United States encompasses a large geographic area, but the population tends to be very concentrated. Certain geographic regions contain many more people than other regions. (See Table 4–3.) Furthermore, the population is concentrated within these geographic regions. For the United States as a whole, three out of every four people live within metropolitan areas that cover 16 percent of the total land area.[1]

The concentration of people has important implications for marketing at both macro and micro levels. For example, at the macro level the overall distribution structure of the economy is largely a result of population distribution. Also, a concentrated population allows firms of all sizes to exist. Local and regional firms can prosper and grow without extending the geographical boundaries of their operations because large numbers of consumers exist within a small geographic area. At the micro level many strategic decisions made by executives of national firms are shaped by the population distribution. Examples include the selection of test markets for new products, media placement of advertisements, and modes of transportation for physical distribution.

Regional distribution

Figure 4–4 shows the geographic divisions of the United States used by the Bureau of the Census. Table 4–3 shows the population distribution in these regions. Size differences alone suggest the relative potential of each as a distinct market.

Just as the age distribution of the population has been in a considerable state of flux in recent years, the geographic distribution has been changing as well. A significant portion of the population has shifted to the so-called Sun Belts of the southern and western regions. Reexamine Table 4–3 and notice where the greatest population growth has occurred: in the warmer regions. But influx of people into the Sun Belt is not shared equally by all states within this region. Figure 4–5 shows population growth figures on a state-by-state basis. Major growth states include Florida, Arizona, and Nevada. Thus, we see in the geographic shifts that are occurring a continued pattern of concentration.

---

[1] *Statistical Abstract of the United States, 1982–83.*

Table 4–3: Total population by geographical area, 1960–1980	Region	Population (000)			Percent change 1960–70	Percent change 1970–80
		1960	1970	1980		
	New England	10,509	11,848	12,348	12.7	4.2
	Middle Atlantic	34,168	37,213	36,787	8.9	−1.1
	East North Central	36,225	40,262	41,682	11.1	3.5
	West North Central	15,394	16,327	17,183	6.1	5.2
	South Atlantic	25,972	30,678	36,959	18.1	20.5
	East South Central	12,050	12,808	14,666	6.3	14.5
	West South Central	16,951	19,326	23,747	14.0	22.9
Source: *Statistical Abstract of the* *United States, 1982–83.*	Mountain	6,855	8,289	11,373	20.9	37.2
	Pacific	21,198	26,549	31,800	25.2	19.8

A number of factors account for these geographic population shifts. A central one is that the Sun Belt is where the employment opportunities are. Lower costs of doing business, especially energy costs, have induced many firms to establish operations in the warmer regions. This in turn creates employment opportunities, attracts workers, and increases the population. Circular effects result: the population growth then attracts

Figure 4–4: Geographic subdivisions of the United States

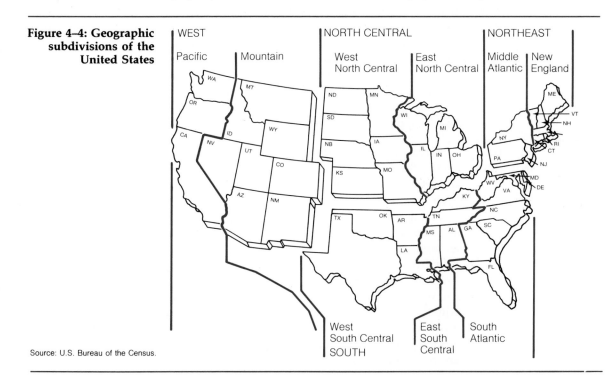

Source: U.S. Bureau of the Census.

Figure 4–5: State-by-state changes in population

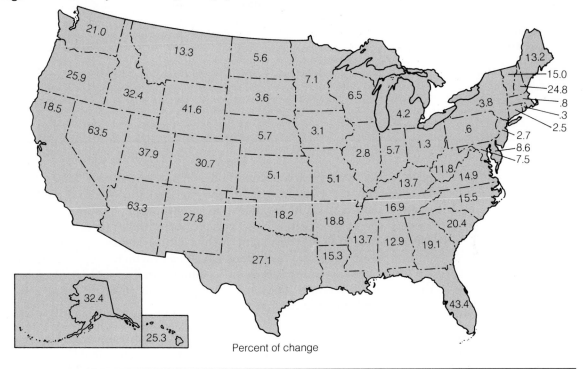

Percent of change

firms seeking expansion to new markets. For example, supermarket chains looking for new areas are focusing their attention on the Sun Belt. This phenomenon is not restricted to retail firms, though. The same principle applies to any regional manufacturer with an eye toward expansion into new geographical markets.

The "mobiles" as a market

The geographical shifts in population suggest a significant characteristic of the U.S. population—a high degree of mobility. Between March 1981 and March 1982, about 17 percent of the population (37 million people) moved to different residences. (See Table 4–4.) Fourteen million of these "mobiles" moved to a different county. While the share of the population that moves each year has declined somewhat over the last 20 years, the absolute number of movers is larger. Furthermore, a greater share of movers make long-distance moves.

This sizable group represents an attractive market. Much of it is created by the economic improvement of its members (job transfers, promotions). The dominant age group within it is a prime spending group. Movers

Table 4–4: Annual mobility rates, percentage of population moving to different house	Period	Within same county	Different county	Total
	1960–61	13.7	6.3	20.0
	1970–71	11.4	6.5	17.9
	1981–82	10.3	6.3	16.6

Source: Adapted from U.S. Bureau of the Census, "Geographical Mobility: March 1981 to March 1982," *Current Population Reports,* Series P–20, no. 384 (Washington, D.C.: U.S. Government Printing Office, 1983), p. 1.

have higher incomes and costlier homes than nonmovers.[2] These mobile households make an assortment of consumer decisions—who should move them, where to buy a house, where to shop for food, clothing, etc. Many moving companies keep a close eye on households preparing to move. They identify families who put their existing homes up for sale and inform them of their services. Banks in cities to which people are moving try to get advance information on incoming families and, again, inform them of their services. They may seek goodwill through, for example, gift subscriptions to a local newspaper.

Governmental definitions of concentrated market areas

Because the population continues to cluster within geographical areas, the federal government recently developed a new system to define concentrated population areas and replace the former Standard Metropolitan Statistical Area (SMSA). Future census reports will use this new system:

1. *Metropolitan Statistical Area (MSA).* An area is recognized as an MSA if it contains a city of at least 50,000 people, or if it includes an urbanized area of 50,000, with a total metropolitan population of at least 100,000 (75,000 in New England). An MSA includes the county containing the central city and any counties having close social and economic ties to the central county. At present 257 MSAs are recognized. Table 4–5 lists the 20 largest plus assorted others.

2. *Consolidated Metropolitan Statistical Area (CMSA).* Most of the largest metro areas having a million or more people and meeting certain other criteria are classified as CMSAs. These are sprawling metro areas with distinct subdivisions within them. At present the government recognizes 22 CMSAs. (See Table 4–6.)

3. *Primary Metropolitan Statistical Area (PMSA).* This is a distinct subdivision within the CMSA. PMSAs are major areas within the

---

[2] "Mobile Americans: A Moving Target with Sales Potential," *Sales and Marketing Management,* April 7, 1980, p. 40.

Areas currently identified as MSAs, CMSAs, and PMSAs.

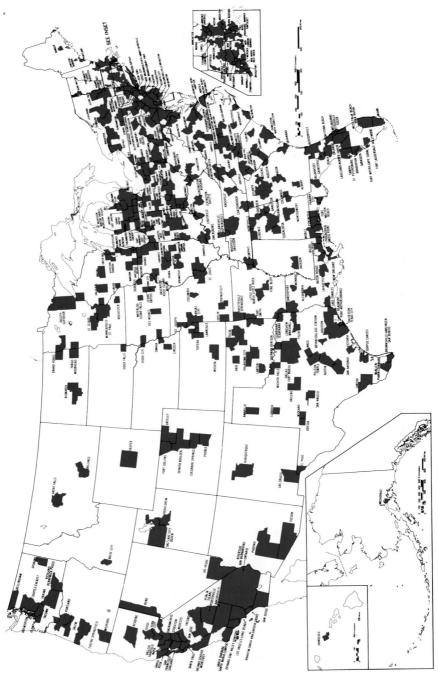

Source: U.S. Bureau of the Census.

Table 4–5:
Metropolitan statistical
areas

Twenty largest	Population
New York	8,274,961
Los Angeles	7,477,503
Chicago	6,060,387
Philadelphia	4,716,818
Detroit	4,488,172
Washington, D.C.	3,250,822
Boston	2,805,911
Houston	2,735,766
Nassau–Suffolk	2,605,813
Pittsburgh	2,218,870
Baltimore	2,199,531
Atlanta	2,138,231
Minneapolis	2,137,133
Dallas	1,957,378
Anaheim–Santa Ana	1,932,709
Cleveland	1,898,825
Newark	1,878,959
San Diego	1,861,846
St. Louis	1,808,621
Oakland	1,761,759

Selected Others

Indianapolis	1,166,575
Salt Lake City–Ogden	910,222
Tucson	531,443
Madison	323,545
Daytona Beach	258,762
Anchorage	174,431
Champaign–Urbana	168,392
Enid	62,820

Source: *County and City Data Book, 1983.*

sprawling CMSAs. Table 4–6 identifies the number of PMSAs within each CMSA. Table 4–7 identifies the specific PMSAs contained within two selected CMSAs.

As the Census Bureau begins to structure its statistical reports using these categories, marketing researchers will have useful information available on the variations between and within major market areas.

Urban–suburban–
rural distribution

Just because the population tends to concentrate does not mean no one lives outside the cities. Some population groups are identified by whether or not they are part of major metropolitan areas and by their location within the metropolitan areas. Three types of population groups are usually identified this way:

1. *Urban*—Those individuals living in the heart of a metropolitan area, the dwellers of the central city.

2. *Suburban*—Those individuals living in areas that are adjacent to the central city but that are considered a part of the overall metropolitan area. Most of these areas are separately governed and designated (e.g., Evanston, Illinois—a suburb of Chicago).

Table 4–6: Consolidated metropolitan statistical areas	CMSA	Number of PMSAs within CMSA	Population
	New York–Northern New Jersey–Long Island	12	17,539,324
	Los Angeles–Anaheim–Riverside	4	11,497,568
	Chicago–Gary–Lake City	6	7,937,329
	Philadelphia–Wilmington–Trenton	4	5,680,768
	Detroit–Ann Arbor	2	4,752,820
	Boston–Salem–Lawrence	6	3,971,736
	San Francisco–Oakland–San Jose	6	5,367,925
	Houston–Galveston–Brazoria	3	3,101,293
	Dallas–Ft. Worth	2	2,930,516
	Cleveland–Akron–Lorain	3	2,834,062
	Pittsburgh–Beaver Valley	2	2,423,311
	St. Louis–East St. Louis–Alton	3	2,376,998
	Seattle–Tacoma	2	2,093,112
	Miami–Ft. Lauderdale	2	2,019,200
	Cincinnati–Hamilton	2	1,660,278
	Denver–Boulder	2	1,618,461
	Milwaukee–Racine	2	1,570,275
	Kansas City, Mo.–Kansas City, Ks.	2	1,433,458
	Portland–Vancouver	2	1,297,926
	Buffalo–Niagara Falls	2	1,242,826
Source: *County and City Data Book, 1983.*	Providence–Pawtucket–Fall River	3	1,083,139
	Hartford–New Britain–Middletown	4	1,013,508

3. **Rural**—This designation connotes and includes the farm population, but for our purposes it includes everyone not living in or around a major metropolitan area. It thus includes people living in smaller cities and towns as well as those in the country.

Figure 4–6 indicates the population breakdown along urban, suburban, and rural dimensions. The large majority (75 percent) of the population is located in the urban and suburban categories.

Table 4–7: Two CMSAs and their PMSA breakdown	CMSA	PMSA	Population
	Chicago–Gary–Lake City (6 PMSAs)	1. Aurora–Elgin	315,607
		2. Chicago	6,060,387
		3. Gary–Hammond	642,781
		4. Joliet	355,042
		5. Kenosha	123,137
		6. Lake County	440,372
		Total CMSA	7,937,326
	Los Angeles–Anaheim–Riverside (4 PMSAs)	1. Anaheim–Santa Ana	1,932,709
		2. Los Angeles–Long Beach	7,477,503
		3. Oxnard–Ventura	529,174
Source: *County and City Data Book, 1983.*		4. Riverside–San Bernardino	1,558,182
		Total CMSA	11,497,568

Figure 4–6: Urban, suburban, rural distribution of the population, 1970–1980

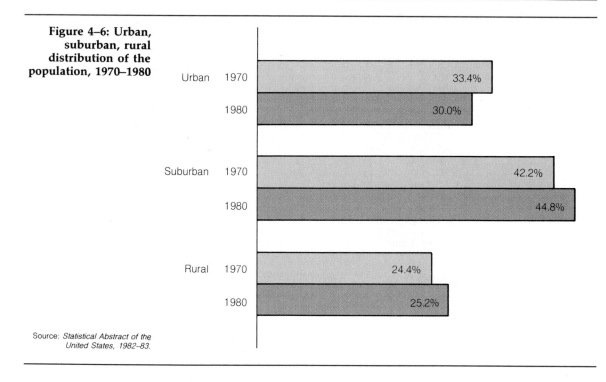

Source: *Statistical Abstract of the United States, 1982–83.*

The figures for 1970 and 1980 reveal the flight from the cities to the suburbs that is occurring.

People living in urban, suburban, and rural areas differ from each other in a number of ways, many of which relate to their consumption patterns. Table 4–8 indicates some consumption differences observed in a 1976 study. Some of these differences result from income differences. Other differences, however, result from the distinct lifestyles associated with living in these areas. For example, consider the heavier use of freezers by rural households. Their tendency to produce more of what they eat requires more long-term storage capabilities.

Table 4–8: Some consumption differences between urban, suburban, and rural households

Source: H. Axel, ed., *A Guide to Consumer Markets 1967–1977* (New York: The Conference Board, 1976), p. 182. Used with permission of The Conference Board.

Durable	Urban	Suburban	Rural
Washing machine	60.0%	77.0%	77.9%
Clothes dryer	39.6	61.6	55.0
Dishwasher	23.5	38.5	21.2
Refrigerator	98.4	99.1	99.2
Home food freezer	20.3	33.9	47.0
Kitchen range	97.8	98.8	98.8
Any TV	95.6	97.7	96.2
Color TV	56.1	69.4	57.0
Room air conditioner	33.1	32.2	30.1
Central air conditioner	17.3	23.4	14.5

SOCIOECONOMIC CHARACTERIS-TICS

Other descriptive characteristics of the U.S. consumer market point out variables related to the economic and social status of households. Distinct relationships exist between many of these variables and consumption patterns. What we mean here are income, education, and occupation.

Income

Income level plays perhaps the greatest role in determining the total consumption of goods and services in a market. The United States has been characterized by generally high income levels. Its total income level allows the highest aggregate level of consumption of any country.

More important, for our purposes, is the income level of households. To understand the impact of income on household consumptions we must first examine certain income-related concepts: ***absolute income, real income, disposable income,*** and ***discretionary income.***

absolute income

> **Absolute income** is the total dollars of income realized by a household.

Figure 4–7 shows the dramatic increase in the absolute-income level of households from 1970–81. This increase does not translate into corresponding increases in purchasing power. Real income provides a better index of changes in spending power.

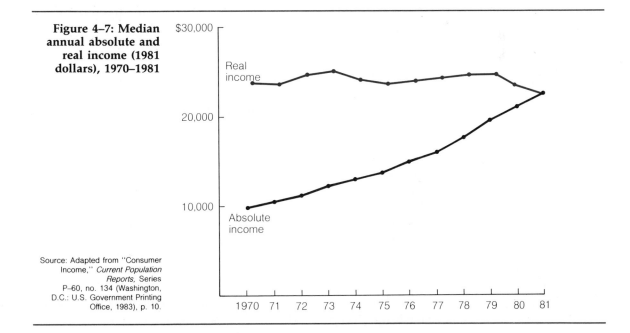

Figure 4–7: Median annual absolute and real income (1981 dollars), 1970–1981

Source: Adapted from "Consumer Income," *Current Population Reports,* Series P–60, no. 134 (Washington, D.C.: U.S. Government Printing Office, 1983), p. 10.

real income

> **Real income** adjusts absolute income by the overall price level of goods and services.

In other words, a 10 percent increase in income accompanied by 9 percent inflation gives very little increased spending power. Double-digit inflation would normally cause a *decrease* in spending power. The early 1980s were marked by *declines* in median household real income. (See Figure 4–7.)

The concepts of disposable income and discretionary income offer insights into the assortment of goods and services included in overall consumption.

disposable income

discretionary income

> **Disposable income** is that portion of income remaining after taxes are paid.
>
> **Discretionary income** is that portion of income remaining after providing for the necessities (taxes, food, clothing, and shelter).

Discretionary income provides for the "luxuries" of life. Households with the same total income vary in discretionary income depending on their situation. Single-adult households have greater discretionary income than a family of four because their necessities require less spending. The same is true of older couples whose children have left. Both are prime markets for products and services that contribute to the "comforts" of life.

Engel's laws

Further insights into consumer spending patterns are provided by *Engel's laws.* These are generalizations about a family's response to an increase in income. They imply that spending increases in all categories of goods as a result of an income increase but that percentage of spending in some categories increases more than in others. This results in a different overall allocation of income at the new level. Engel's laws state that as income increases, the percentage spent on food decreases; the percentage spent on housing remains constant; and the percentage spent on most other things increases.

Engel's laws make a very important point: while increases in income often improve prospects for sales in most product categories, some product categories realize a disproportionate share of increased consumption. Greater opportunities accrue to firms marketing these products.

The ratchet effect

The basic income–consumption relationship suggests that total spending changes in direct response to increases or decreases in income.

ratchet effect

> The **ratchet effect** suggests that the response to a decrease in income is not as great in an absolute sense as a response to an increase in income.

The absolute reduction in consumption from a decline in income is less than the absolute increase in consumption due to a corresponding increase in income. This phenomenon derives its name from the ratchet-like curve that results when it is depicted graphically. (See Figure 4–8.)

Notice that at point *A,* when income is $17,000, consumption equals $15,000. When income increases to $20,000, consumption increases to $16,000 (point *B*). When income drops back to $17,000 (point *C*), consumption declines to only $15,500. This is $1,000 more than the consumption level when income was $17,000 the first time. Thus, we see that a $3,000 increase in income elicits a $1,000 increase in consumption; but a $3,000 decrease in income elicits only a $500 reduction in consumption.

The rationale of the ratchet effect is that it is more difficult for a family to lower its standard of living than to raise it. Once a family becomes used to a certain standard of living, it becomes psychologically difficult for them to accept a lower standard and give up things associated with their lifestyle. On the other hand, the higher standard of living and perceived increase in status provided by an increase in income are much easier to accept.

The ratchet effect offers an important implication for marketing planning. Consumer response is faster and greater to increases than to decreases

Figure 4–8: The ratchet effect

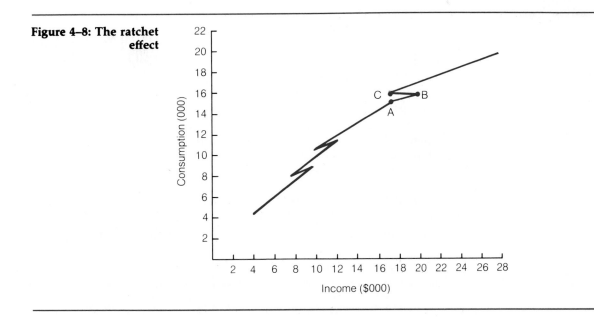

Table 4–9: Median income levels of types of couples, 1981	Type of couple	Median income	Percent
	All couples	$25,500	100%
	Only husband works	26,170	33
	Both work at least part time	28,560	62
Source: U.S. Bureau of the Census.	Both work full time	34,560	29

in income. Companies must be in a position to act quickly to realize the opportunities created by spending-power increases. Declines in spending power pose less immediate threats; companies have a longer time to plan the necessary adoptions in their marketing operation. Just as well. The strategies in response to decreased spending probably require more careful planning than those in response to increased spending.

Dual-income households

A very significant phenomenon related to the socioeconomic status of households is the growth in *dual-income households.* A 1984 Census Bureau study reports that both spouses work in 62 percent of all married couples—up from 50 percent in 1970 and 40 percent in 1960. Dual-income status dramatically influences the consumption patterns of a couple. There is, of course, the effect on total income (see Table 4–9)—raising it and allowing for greater affluency.

The effects of dual income go farther than just increasing total income. Consider two families, each realizing an income of $40,000 annually. In one, the income derives solely from one spouse's career. In the other, one spouse earns $25,000 as a sales representative; the other earns $15,000 as a high school teacher. While both families may spend similar amounts in total, the allocation of those expenditures will likely vary. The dual-income household is more likely to employ household help, entertain at home less, eat out more, and remain childless. The dual-income family is a different type of buying unit. One study found that dual-income spending patterns are geared toward living well now, not later. Only 2 percent of the dual-income families indicated they were saving for retirement.[3] The dual-income portion of the market represents a very attractive market, especially the nearly 30 percent of couples in which partners both work full time. They are prime consumers of luxury goods.[4]

Education

A second important socioeconomic variable to consider in examining the consumer marketplace is the educational level of its members. Certain geographic and ethnic segments of the population have significantly less

[3] "Changes Found in Attitudes, Shopping Behavior of United States Two-Income Couples," *Marketing News,* October 28, 1983, p. 12.

[4] For evidence on distinct consumption patterns of dual-income couples in Canada, see Charles M. Schaninger and Chris T. Allen, "Wife's Occupational Status as a Consumer Behavior Construct," *Journal of Consumer Research,* September 1981, pp. 189–96.

Table 4–10: Educational level of American population *(percentage of persons over age 25 at each educational level)*	**Educational attainment**	**1960**	**1970**	**1980**
	Less than 8 years	22.1	14.4	9.4
	8 years	17.5	13.4	8.2
	1–3 years high school	19.2	17.1	13.9
	4 years high school	24.6	34.0	36.8
	1–3 years college	8.8	10.2	14.9
	4 years college or more	7.7	11.0	17.0
Source: *Statistical Abstract of the United States, 1982–83.*	Median school years completed	10.6	12.2	12.5

education than the rest of the population; but the U.S. population, on the whole, is well educated. Perhaps more important, the educational level of the population is rising. (See Table 4–10.) During the period 1960 to 1980 the percentage of household heads with at least some college steadily increased; and the greatest increase occurred with the college-degree group. The percentage of household heads with less than a high school education continuously decreased during the same period.

The effects of increasing education levels on aggregate consumer behavior are widespread:

1. Educational improvements typically result in income improvement. Effects similar to those resulting from increases in income should accompany improvements in education.'

2. Educational improvements alter the lifestyles in the population. The population, as a whole, becomes more sophisticated. Increased sophistication causes a shift in the demand for certain leisure-time activities, residential preferences, home furnishings, the arts, etc.

3. Better-educated people are more sophisticated in *how* they buy. More careful buyers who use more product information sources will result.

Occupation

A final socioeconomic characteristic of the market is occupation. The diversity and complexity of the U.S. economy creates a similar diversity of occupations. This is often reduced to the distinction between the so-called blue-collar and white-collar workers. Shifts of workers across these two categories parallel the shift in educational levels. There is an increasing percentage of white-collar employees. A greater share of aggregate market expenditures should be directed toward products used in white-collar settings. Clothing companies will pay greater marketing attention to their fashion-oriented lines than their worker-oriented lines. For example, the classic blue-denim jean is now a relatively minor component of the Levi Strauss marketing effort.

VALUE OF
DESCRIPTIVE
VARIABLES

In this chapter we have examined several demographic and socioeconomic variables that can be used to describe the consumer market. Such a perspective is useful to marketing managers. But its usefulness is limited to the aggregate level of analysis. Aggregate shifts in these variables are valuable in predicting *long-run* changes in the consumption of *general* product categories. Their usefulness in reflecting short-run changes in consumption is minimal. Finally, these descriptive variables are only descriptive. They provide little *understanding* of the *individual consumer*. In the next three chapters we'll focus on variables that do provide insights into the "why" and "how" of consumer behavior at the micro level.

SUMMARY

A descriptive perspective on the consumer market reveals many of its important demographic and socioeconomic characteristics and significant shifts occurring within it. While the overall size of the market has continued to increase, in recent years the rate of this increase has slowed. The birthrate has dropped dramatically, resulting in a greater percentage of smaller households. The population is also getting older; the projected median age of the population in year 2000 is four years older than it was in 1950. The geographic distribution has shifted to the Sun Belt but has maintained its concentrated nature. The government has de-

veloped three categories of major population areas—MSAs, CMSAs, and PMSAs.

Socioeconomic variables such as income and education are also useful descriptors of the market. Income levels reflect effects on total spending and saving behavior. While absolute income has risen dramatically, real income (income adjusted by price levels) has not realized equivalent gains due to inflation. The educational level of the population has continued to improve, suggesting that shifts in what is bought and how it is bought are occurring. Occupational shifts to white-collar jobs have occurred.

KEY CONCEPTS

Household	Urban population	Disposable income
Metropolitan statistical area	Suburban population	Discretionary income
Consolidated metropolitan statistical area	Rural population	Engel's laws
	Absolute income	Ratchet effect
Primary metropolitan statistical area	Real income	Dual-income households

DISCUSSION
QUESTIONS AND
EXERCISES

1. Several demographic and socioeconomic trends of the U.S. population were described in Chapter 4. Using Census Bureau sources, trace the demographic and socioeconomic trends that have occurred in your hometown (or another

city of your choice). Do the trends match those of the population of the United States? If not, why do you think the area has not changed in the same way as the overall population?

2. Pick a product category that includes both users and nonusers. Describe what you think are the demographic and socioeconomic characteristics of users.

3. Based on the trends described in Chapter 4, identify markets for products that are growing and markets for products that are declining.

CHAPTER 5

Consumer behavior:
The individual consumer

Personality
Self-image

Summary
Key concepts
Discussion questions and exercises

The nature and scope of consumer behavior
Why study consumer behavior?
A behavioral science approach
    Assumptions of the behavioral science
        approach
A framework for studying consumer behavior
Personal factors
    Values
    Perception
    Perception in the marketplace
    Beliefs and attitudes

In Chapter 4 we identified the demographic and socioeconomic characteristics of the *over-all* market. We gave minimal attention to the individual consumer or household. In Chapters 5 to 7 the focus shifts to the micro, or individual, level. We examine behavioral concepts that can characterize individuals and distinguish them from other consumers. Our major goal in these chapters will be to acquire an *understanding* of consumer behavior. In short, we are addressing the "why" of consumer behavior.

THE NATURE AND SCOPE OF CONSUMER BEHAVIOR

The study of consumer behavior encompasses a wide range of concerns. Its nature and scope can be characterized as follows:

1. Consumer behavior deals primarily with the behavior of individuals in the marketplace—the manner in which they purchase and use products and services.

2. Consumer behavior is multidisciplinary. Its understanding is enhanced by contributions from such areas as psychology, social psychology, sociology, cultural anthropology, and economics.

3. Consumer behavior is concerned with factors that influence product purchase decisions and product usage.

4. Consumer behavior is concerned with the process by which consumers arrive at buying decisions and how that process differs across individuals and products.

5. Finally, consumer behavior includes postpurchase phenomena: satisfaction with the outcome of a purchase and usage behavior surrounding a product, for example.

WHY STUDY CONSUMER BEHAVIOR?

In general, studying consumer behavior contributes to the entire strategic planning process in marketing. As suggested by the marketing concept, the development of marketing strategy begins with an assessment of consumer needs and wants. It's imperative that we thoroughly grasp the nature of those needs and wants, why they exist, and how they can best be satisfied. The study of consumer behavior provides such an understanding; so it is an important part of situation analysis.

We can establish objectives by studying consumer behavior. We can, in fact, state many objectives in terms of consumer behavior. How the firm wants the consumer to view its products may be one way to do this. For example, a major objective of Campbell's Soup is to get consumers to perceive its soups as nutritional food items.

As we will see in Chapter 9, the study of consumer behavior is crucial to defining, analyzing, and understanding market segments.

Awareness of consumer behavior helps reduce the uncertainty inherent in any marketing program. It enables the firm to anticipate the effects of its marketing decision variables on consumers. Outcomes of a specific marketing strategy can be realistically predicted. The organization can then budget, implement, and manage the marketing strategy most likely to succeed.

Understanding consumer behavior allows a firm to *measure* the effects of a strategy. Thus, it is a basis for performance evaluation. It allows the assessment of more than just sales volume or profit. For example, a financial institution may know that local consumers place a high value on friendly service. The goal of its ad campaign would be to suggest to consumers the friendly nature of the institution. One measure of its effectiveness would be consumer perceptions of the institution on the friendliness dimension. This, in turn, contributes to the assessment of strengths and weaknesses in a subsequent situation analysis.

The value of understanding consumer behavior is not restricted to organizations that market goods and services. We use it also in formulating public policy designed to protect consumers. Government agencies such as the Federal Trade Commission (FTC) are interested in developing policy that helps consumers make wise purchasing decisions. They wish, for instance, to ensure that firms provide adequate information to consumers. To this end they consider various policies that would require manufacturers to provide certain product information in certain places. Understanding how consumers use information about a product enables policymakers to determine effective public policy.

As an example, consumer research helped determine the need for warnings in antacid TV ads.[1] Such brands as Alka-Seltzer and Maalox should not be used by people on salt-restricted diets. That information is given on the product labels or packages. And general warnings ("Read the label." "Use only as directed.") are visually presented for about three seconds in the middle of TV commercials. Researchers discovered, however, that most consumers don't read antacid labels or notice the warnings in commercials. The net effect was that consumers were not adequately informed. The researchers devised stronger warnings to be placed at the ends of commercials. Research showed these warnings to be more effective in alerting consumers to the restrictions on antacid usage. To date, the FTC has not required the inclusion of these warnings.

A BEHAVIORAL SCIENCE APPROACH

Microeconomists developed the first analytical approach to studying consumer behavior; but marketers have increasingly assumed a behavioral science perspective toward it.[2] This multidisciplinary perspective recognizes a number of influence factors. We'll discuss these, but let's first consider the assumptions underlying the behavioral science perspective. (See Figure 5–1.)

Assumptions of the behavioral science approach

Consumer behavior is human behavior. The most fundamental feature of the behavioral approach is that it recognizes consumer behavior as one form of ***human behavior.*** Therefore, many forces that shape human behavior also shape consumer behavior.

---

[1] Michael J. Houston and Michael L. Rothschild, "Policy-Related Experiments on Information Provision: A Normative Model and Explication," *Journal of Marketing Research,* November 1980, pp. 432–49.

[2] An excellent treatment of the microeconomic theory of consumer behavior can be found in S. Charles Maurice, Owen R. Phillips, and C. E. Ferguson, *Economic Analysis: Theory and Application,* 4th ed. (Homewood, Ill.: Richard D. Irwin, 1982).

Figure 5–1:
Assumptions
underlying the study of
consumer behavior

Consumer behavior is → human behavior.
Consumer behavior is ——→ goal-oriented.
Consumer behavior is ↘ rational.

human behavior

> **Human behavior** is the set of endeavors in which individuals engage to further their physical, social, and economic status in life in line with their individual values.

Consumer behavior is recognized as one such endeavor. The goals people seek as consumers are not unlike the goals they seek through other forms of behavior. And the same concepts and theories can explain both behaviors.

Consumer behavior is goal-oriented behavior. It is evident that consumer behavior is a goal-oriented or problem-solving process. Individuals—through their behavior in the marketplace—seek solutions to problems. They buy and use products and services as means to an end. They select one brand over another, for example, based on its perceived superiority as a means to reaching some desired state. Thus, consumers are problem solvers. And products, services, and stores are potential solutions.

Consumer behavior is rational. The behavioral approach assumes rationality on the part of consumers. But not the usual kind of rationality. The layperson sees rational consumer behavior as a careful, calculated process by which to reach a buying decision. Only nonemotional, objective criteria are used to evaluate products. The behavioral approach is much more flexible. It doesn't impose a particular decision process or set of criteria. Behavior is rational when its expected outcome exceeds its estimated costs. Whatever process the consumer uses to arrive at this cost-benefit analysis—whether it involves a careful consideration of all available information or a so-called impulse purchase—is irrelevant to the behavioral notion of rationality. As long as a favorable cost-benefit estimate results, it doesn't matter what process is involved. And the behavioral approach does not restrict what goes into estimates of value and cost. It recognizes differences between individuals in these choices. Emotions can enter into evaluating outcomes. The status of owning a particular brand adds to its value to some consumers. Price is not necessarily the sole consideration in determining cost. Time and effort count, too.

Essentially, we are saying that any form of behavior (given that it occurs) is rational—at least, in the mind of the performer. Others may

This ad is promoting a product's problem-solving benefits.

view someone's behavior as irrational, but they are imposing their own values and beliefs. To the person performing it, the behavior would be entirely reasonable in terms of his/her own values and beliefs. Later the person may look back and conclude that it was not worth it, but this does not make it irrational, either. It just means that the behavior was based on inaccurate estimates of the outcome or the costs.

The behavioral view is not useful in the sense of distinguishing rational from irrational behavior. It deems all behavior rational. Rather, it is useful in recognizing that individuals have different ideas of appropriate behavior. With this is mind, we can consider factors that help determine individual behavior.

A FRAMEWORK FOR STUDYING CONSUMER BEHAVIOR

In this section we offer a simple model of consumer behavior. We can use it as a framework to identify factors potentially relevant to understanding behavior toward a product or service. Not all of the factors are necessarily relevant to a specific product. We hope the model helps determine which factors are. Our goal is more efficient marketing strategy for a product—based on knowledge of consumer behavior.

In its simplest form the model can be expressed as:

$$\text{Behavior} = f(\text{Personal factors, social factors})$$

The terms in the model are defined as follows:

behavior

Behavior refers to any action a consumer takes toward a product or brand (buying or not buying it, expressing favorable or unfavorable "word-of-mouth" information about it).

personal factors

Personal factors are *internal* to the individual. They represent the unique psychological makeup of the individual (values, motives, needs).

social factors

Social factors refer to the influences that others have on an individual's behavior.

Thus, the model shows that behavior results from an interaction of the unique nature of an individual with his/her social environment. (See Figure 5–2.) As such, it is a framework for *studying* consumer behavior, which yields an *understanding* of it that serves as input to the planning, implementation, and control of marketing strategy and public policy. Let's turn now to a closer examination of the set of personal factors. (Social factors will be examined in Chapter 6.)

PERSONAL FACTORS

An individual's psychological makeup consists of values, motivation, perception, beliefs-attitudes, personality, and self-image.

Values

A fundamental factor that guides the behavior of an individual is a set of personal *values.*

Figure 5–2: A framework for understanding consumer behavior

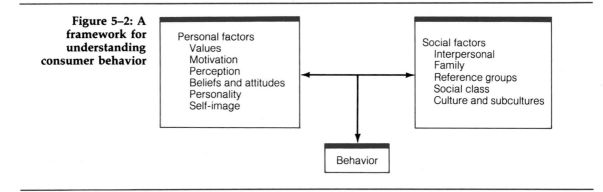

Personal factors
  Values
  Motivation
  Perception
  Beliefs and attitudes
  Personality
  Self-image

Social factors
  Interpersonal
  Family
  Reference groups
  Social class
  Culture and subcultures

Behavior

---

value

> A **value** is a centrally held, enduring belief that guides actions and judgments across specific situations and beyond immediate goals to more ultimate end states of existence.[3]

Each person holds a set of values arranged in hierarchical fashion according to their importance. This set of values develops as the individual goes through the socialization process. Differences in value systems help account for some of the differences between men and women, democrats and republicans, liberals and conservatives, buyers of large cars and buyers of small cars. Different values apply to different forms of behavior.

Vinson and colleagues offer a useful framework for applying the concept of values to consumer behavior.[4] They suggest that a value exists at one of three levels, depending on how centrally held it is and how specific it is to a particular behavior. ***Global values*** are the most centrally held and most general values.

global values

> **Global values** are abstract values that are generalizable to a wide variety of behavioral contexts.

Examples of global values include the desire for an exciting life, a clean environment, individual rights, etc. Global values are fewest in number; they typically number in the dozens.

At the next level we hold values that are ***domain-specific.***

---

[3] Milton Rokeach, *Beliefs, Attitudes, and Values* (San Francisco: Jossey-Bass, 1968), p. 161.

[4] D. E. Vinson, J. E. Scott, and L. M. Lamont, "The Role of Personal Values in Marketing and Consumer Behavior," *Journal of Marketing,* April 1977, pp. 44–50.

domain-specific values

> **Domain-specific values** guide us in certain domains or broad areas of behavior.

Such domains would include job behavior, religion, familial interaction, and consumption behavior. For each domain, the person develops a set of values relevant only to that domain. They result from the general values of the global level and from experience in the specific domain of concern. Domain-specific values related to consumer behavior would include:

Manufacturers should not pollute the environment.

Products should be nonpolluting.

Products should be fairly priced.

Companies should be progressive.

Products should be stylish.

Based on global and domain values and on experience in the product class, people develop ***product-specific values.*** This is the least centrally held and most specific type of value.

product-specific value

> A ***product-specific value*** is a belief about what is desirable or undesirable in a specific product class.

Product-specific values result in a set of ***evaluative criteria*** each of us uses to assess various brands in a product class. We determine what levels of each criterion are acceptable and unacceptable. We might value cars because they operate on unleaded gas, provide at least 30 miles per gallon of gas, or possess front-wheel drive. These product-specific values derive from domain-specific values which, in turn, grow out of global values. Thus, the individual with a global value of "a clean environment" is likely to hold a value in the consumption domain of "nonpolluting products." This, in turn, would lead to an automobile-specific value of "operates on unleaded gas." Figure 5–3 shows the functional linkage between the three levels.

The application of values in marketing is seen in pay-TV companies such as Home Box Office (HBO). Technological advances allow these companies to beam signals to local cable companies, who offer the service to subscribers for an additional fee. The existence of these services is based on a combination of two global values held by large numbers of people. The desire for entertainment as a significant component of life is one. A home orientation (in which families prefer relaxation at home) is another. As the first successful pay-TV service of its type, HBO appealed

Figure 5–3: Levels of values

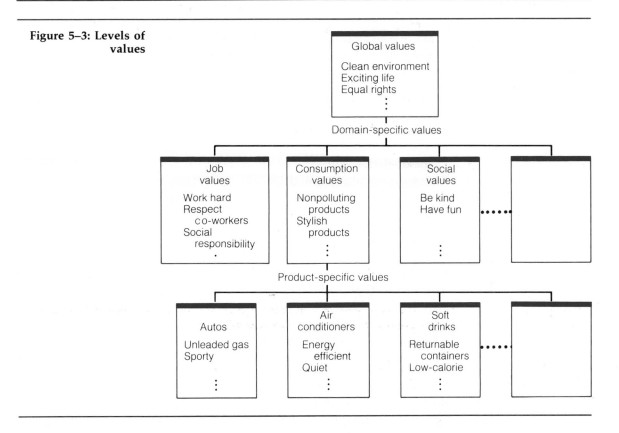

to a domain-specific value by offering recent movies as the form of entertainment. It appealed to a variety of product-specific values by providing a mix of G-, PG-, and R-rated movies.

The success of HBO has attracted other pay-TV companies. Some of them (e.g., Showtime) have emulated HBO by offering virtually identical forms of entertainment. Others appeal to different domain-specific values by offering sports, children's, "cultural," and sex-oriented programming. In fact, one company discovered how different domain-specific values can conflict. Cablevision initially packaged a cultural program channel with a sex-oriented channel. But they discovered that people who wanted one channel did not want the other. Consequently, neither channel sold well until Cablevision offered each as a separate service.[5]

Motivation. If consumer behavior is problem-solving or goal-oriented behavior, then we must consider what activates these processes. Perhaps the most insightful perspective is offered by the concept of ***motivation.***

[5] Laura Landro, " 'Ferocious' Rivalry Develops in Pay Services for Cable TV," *The Wall Street Journal,* August 12, 1982, p. 17.

motivation

> **Motivation** refers to a state of the individual in which energy is mobilized and directed toward the attainment of specific goals.

To better understand the role of motivation in consumer behavior we must examine a conceptual model of motivation, the nature of needs, and the role of products in the motivational process.

Need-reduction theory of motivation. A useful perspective on motivation is provided by *need-reduction theory.* (See Figure 5–4.) The premise of this theory is that a person has an array of needs that guides behavior. When these needs are satisfied, the individual is in a state of comfort or equilibrium and is not compelled to behave. When one or more needs are not met, the person is in a state of *tension* or disequilibrium. The discomfort of this state of tension creates a *drive* within the person to behave so that the need is satisfied and a state of comfort returns. The person then chooses a specific behavior to satisfy the need. Prior experience and knowledge help the individual identify behavior that potentially will satisfy the need and those not likely to do so. Implementing a form of behavior may or may not achieve satisfaction. If it does, the person's state of tension is eliminated or reduced to tolerable limits. If it does not, the state of tension remains or perhaps is increased.

Consumer behavior is a general domain of behavior for satisfying needs. Within it, a variety of specific forms of behavior are available. The hunger need can be met through the purchase and consumption of many alternative food items. Status needs can be fulfilled through alternative product categories (automobiles, houses, clothes) and alternative brands within a category (Cadillac, Mercedes Benz).

Figure 5–4: Need-reduction model of motivation

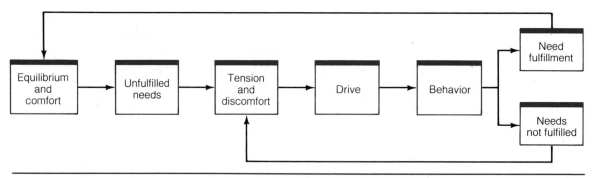

Table 5–1: Types of needs	Maslow	Bayton	Murray (partial listing)
	Physiological needs—hunger, thirst, sex, etc.	Affectional needs—relating to the formation and maintenance of emotionally satisfying relationships with others	Needs associated with inanimate objects—acquisition, conservance, retention, order, construction
	Security needs—protection from the physical environment	Ego-bolstering needs—relating to the enhancement and promotion of the self	Needs concerned with human power—dominance, deference, autonomy
	Love needs—affection (give and receive), friendship	Ego-defensive needs—relating to self-protection, i.e., avoiding physical, psychological, and social harm	Needs concerned with affection—affiliation, rejection, nurturance, play
	Self-esteem needs—success, prestige		Needs concerning power, ambitions
	Self-actualization—self-fulfillment		Sado-masochistic needs
			Needs concerned with inhibition
			Social-intercourse needs

The nature of needs. As you can see from our discussion, ***need*** is a central concept here.

> **need** | A **need** is a state of deprivation.

Needs exist in all individuals; their fulfillment is a goal common to all. To merely recognize that needs exist in a general sense is insufficient for marketing purposes. We must recognize the nature of needs, the specific types that exist, and their role in behavior. In this way we can better understand consumer behavior and determine marketing efforts that will satisfy consumers.

The foremost characteristic of human needs is their ***multiplicity.*** Each individual possesses an array of needs; and any one form of behavior may satisfy multiple needs within this array. A number of specific inventories of human needs exist in the literature. (See Table 5–1.) A classic is Maslow's hierarchy of needs.[6] He postulates five categories of needs: physiological, security, love, self-esteem, and self-actualization. Note that the first two categories represent primary or biological needs. The remainder represent secondary or psychological needs. Bayton concentrates on psychogenic needs in his three categories of affectional, ego-bolstering,

---

[6] Abraham H. Maslow, "A Theory of Human Motivation," *Psychological Review* 50 (1943), pp. 370–96.

and ego-defensive needs.[7] Finally, Murray's partial inventory reflects a more specific listing of individual needs.[8]

The role of products and services. In consumer behavior the purchase and consumption of products and services are the major means of need satisfaction. Thus, a critical perspective of this book is that *products and services are means to an end, not the end itself.* This perspective is critical to marketing management. One of the worst things a firm can do is assume it seeks profits through the *sale of products* and has achieved its goal once the sale is concluded. The firm is in business to make profits through the *satisfaction of consumers.* It offers, through its products, the means by which needs are satisfied. To obtain a sale is only partial marketing success. The true measure of success is whether the product, when consumed, satisfied the needs that motivated the purchase.

The use of products to satisfy needs should be viewed at multiple levels. Consumers determine that a particular *generic product* is an appropriate means to satisfy a need. They may decide that an auto, for example, is their best means to satisfy rapid-transit needs. Televisions satisfy entertainment needs. Steaks satisfy the hunger need. For other consumers, each of these needs may be satisfied with other generic products—motorcycles, movies, and hamburgers. The ability of alternative generic products to satisfy the same need creates competition between goods at the generic level.

Specific versions of a generic product are the means to satisfy certain needs. Often, these needs are not the same as those for using the generic product. The selection of a stylish auto involves different needs than the selection of an economic compact car. But both provide a means of transportation and compete with each other at the *product-form* level.

Finally, there is the selection of a particular *brand* of a product form within a generic product category. The selection of a Zenith TV over a similarly priced foreign model may involve a motive dealing with patriotism and the need for affiliation.

It is evident that the purchase of a particular product is often based on motives involving several needs. Autos are purchased on the basis of transportation, status, excitement, and other needs. Some of these needs play a role at one level of decision making but not at other levels. Transportation needs may be relevant at the generic level; status needs dominate at the product-form and brand levels. Figure 5–5 portrays how different needs can operate at each decision level and how consumers can behave differently in satisfying these needs.

---

[7] J. A. Bayton, "Motivation, Cognition, Learning—Basic Factors in Consumer Behavior," *Journal of Marketing* 23 (January 1958), pp. 282–89.

[8] H. A. Murray, "Types of Human Needs," in *Studies in Motivation,* ed. D. C. McClelland (New York: Appleton-Century-Crofts, 1955), pp. 63–66.

Figure 5–5: Needs operating at levels of purchase decisions

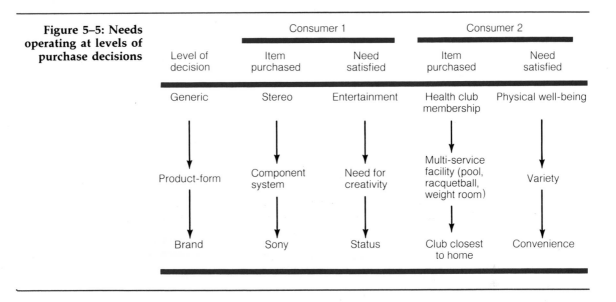

Level of decision	Consumer 1		Consumer 2	
	Item purchased	Need satisfied	Item purchased	Need satisfied
Generic	Stereo	Entertainment	Health club membership	Physical well-being
Product-form	Component system	Need for creativity	Multi-service facility (pool, racquetball, weight room)	Variety
Brand	Sony	Status	Club closest to home	Convenience

Needs versus wants. It should be evident that marketing does not create needs but rather the means to satisfy them. The firm does, however, wish to create ***wants.***

want

> A **want** exists when a consumer has an unfulfilled need state, has determined that a particular object offers the best means to satisfy it, but does not yet possess the object.

A want is, therefore, object-specific. It can exist at one or more of the generic, product-form, or brand levels. A major marketing task is clearly to create consumer wants.

We can understand the distinction between needs and wants by looking at one of the most compelling new products to hit the market in recent years—the personal computer. No one *needs* a personal computer. But many people do need to prepare, organize, and store their professional or personal records in efficient fashion. At an abstract level we are talking about the need for organization in our lives. Computers offer a means of satisfying that need. Suppose we decide that the personal computer offers our best means. Now we *want* it. (Another person might decide a typewriter and file cabinet are more suitable.) A major marketing task of Apple, IBM, Radio Shack, and other manufacturers is to show the ability of personal computers to satisfy the need for organization and the unique strengths of their brands as a means of doing so. In this way, they create *wants* for personal computers and for individual brands. The *needs* they are satisfying have always been there.

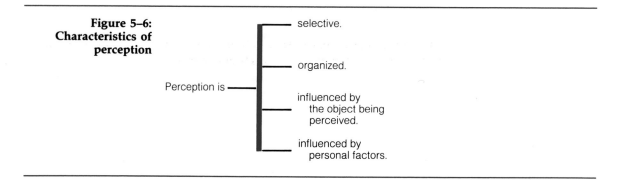

Figure 5–6:
Characteristics of
perception

Perception is

— selective.

— organized.

— influenced by
  the object being
  perceived.

— influenced by
  personal factors.

Perception

A critical determinant of the marketplace success of a brand or store is how it is perceived by consumers. In the study of consumer behavior it is important, then, to understand how consumers arrive at their *perceptions* of a product, brand, store, and so on.

perception

> **Perception** is the way in which we gather, process, and interpret information from the environment.

Understanding this process can provide considerable insight into developing marketing strategies for a brand or store.

Characteristics of perception.   Four major characteristics describe the nature of perception. (See Figure 5–6.) First, perception is *selective.* Humans are limited in their capacity to process all of the information in the environment. A person deals with a limited subset of the myriad objects and events in the environment. People attend to the aspects of the environment that relate to their personal concerns. They screen out the rest. The selective nature of perception reflects the difficulties encountered in advertising: consumers notice only a small subset of ads to which they are exposed. The ones they notice will likely involve products or brands that relate to their ongoing concerns. One study has estimated that a person is exposed to over 300 advertising messages daily, perceives only 76 of them, and responds in some fashion to maybe a dozen.[9]

A second characteristic of the perceptual process is that it is *organized.* A stimulus is not perceived in isolation from other stimuli. Stimuli are grouped into a pattern or configuration, forming a whole. Thus, when we attend to a stimulus, we attempt to organize and attach meaning to it. The sound of a distant siren, for example, is associated with a crime,

---

[9] Raymond Bauer and Stephen Greyser, *Advertising in America: The Consumer View* (Cambridge, Mass.: Graduate School of Business Administration, Harvard Univ. Press, 1968).

an accident, or a fire. In consumer behavior, low-priced brands are often perceived to be of lesser quality than their high-priced counterparts.

A third aspect of perception is that *what we perceive and the meaning attached to it are functions of the **stimulus** itself.* Factors associated with objects of perception that influence their perception include:

1. *Color.* Advertisements in color tend to capture greater attention than those in black and white. Also, color influences the meaning we attach to an object. That is, certain colors are symbolic. For example, red symbolizes fire; it is also used to refer to a financially unhealthy company. The success of Perdue Chickens reveals the impact of color. By feeding chickens marigold petals, they developed a distinct yellow color, which conveys succulence to consumers.

2. *Contrast.* The distinctiveness of an object within its surroundings increases its noticeability. The color ad is more likely to be noticed in a newspaper than in a magazine with many other color ads.

3. *Similarity.* While contrast allows stimuli to be distinguished from each other, stimuli similar to each other tend to be grouped together by the perceiver.

4. *Size.* Larger objects attract more attention than smaller objects of a similar nature. But doubling the size of an object does not double its attention-getting powers.

5. *Intensity.* More intense stimuli—louder sounds and brighter colors—attract more attention. As with size, doubling an object's intensity does not double its attention-getting powers.

6. *Movement.* Motion attracts attention. Thus, we see neon arrows flashing in the illusion of motion.

7. *Context.* The surroundings of an object influence its perception. For example, the placement of an ad in a prestigious magazine may elicit different perceptions of the advertised item than an ad in a low-prestige magazine.

Other stimulus factors that influence perception include the position of an object and its proximity to or isolation from other objects.

The fourth characteristic of perception is that *perception is a function of **personal factors**—those that derive from the nature of the perceiver.* A person's needs, values, motives, past experiences, attitudes, and personality combine to influence what is perceived and how it is perceived. Differences in physiological states, existing preferences, and values result in different meanings attached to the same object or event. In other words, what already exists within the individual plays a role in perception. Such a phenomenon is quite clear in consumer behavior, where individuals often differ widely in their perceptions of the same brand. The influence of personal factors on perception reflects the *subjective* nature of reality that exists in one's mind. We cannot expect consumers to view objects in the marketplace in a straightforward, objective way. The meaning attached to a product and the dimensions on which perception occurs differ across consumers because of differences in their psychological makeup.

The perceptual process in action is revealed in the blind taste tests often conducted in developing new food brands. In these tests a sample of consumers tastes the new item and other existing brands without knowing brand names. Often their perceptions change when given the brand names. Consumers trying Superman peanut butter blindly rated it high compared to other brands. Some people described it as very nutty. Those seeing the label described the product as watery. The dramatic effect that existing beliefs can have on perception was revealed when the same peanut butter, but labeled Jif, was rated even higher than in the blind tests.[10]

Just noticeable difference (JND).   A concept of perception that is highly relevant to marketing and consumer behavior—particularly when product changes are contemplated—is the *just noticeable difference (JND).* A JND is the minimal change in an object of perception needed to elicit perceptual change by the perceiver. Implicit to the JND concept is the principle that slight changes in an object can go unnoticed. The amount of change in an object it takes to elicit perceptual change varies. It depends on the intensity level of the original form of the stimulus. According to Weber's law, the greater the intensity of the original stimulus, the greater the amount of change necessary to produce a JND. Thus, high-priced products require a much greater absolute increase or decrease in price to create a JND than low-priced products.

Applications of the JND concept in marketing vary. A common one involves packaging. Marketers can effect considerable change in package design without causing consumers to think a different product exists. Yet a series of changes—each within a JND—can substantially modify the design! See Figure 5–7 for an example.

Perception in the marketplace

In this section we will consider some important features of consumer perceptions in the marketplace. Our discussion will include the perception of products and the concepts of brand image and perceived risk.

Fundamental objects of perception in the marketplace include those for which buying decisions are made—products, services, and stores. Understanding how perception of these objects occurs is critical if sellers wish to convey to consumers a certain meaning associated with their items. A key feature of the perceptual process for these objects is that it is *multidimensional* in nature. Seldom do consumers attach a single meaning to an object. Rather they attach meaning along several dimensions or attributes of the object. Thus, cars are perceived in terms of

---

[10] From a speech by Professor Bobby Calder at the 2d Annual Seminar on the Marketing Dynamics of Packaging on Consumer Purchasing Decisions, Chicago, 1983.

Figure 5–7: Sequential changes in packaging that fall below the JND

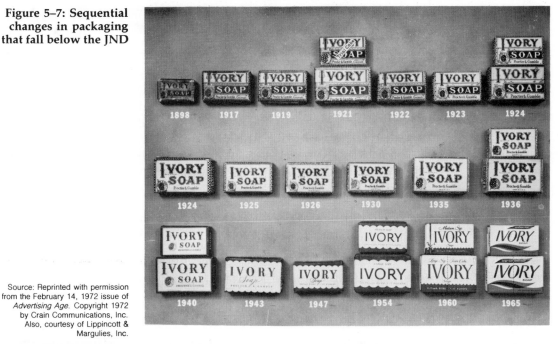

price, style, handling ease, and durability. Toothpastes are perceived in terms of decay-fighting, taste, and breath-freshening qualities. A store is perceived in terms of its array of goods, overall price level, who shops there, and convenience. It is critical for marketers to know which attributes or dimensions of the object consumers use in perceiving and evaluating it. These attributes become the consumer's *evaluative criteria* for the generic object and are used in making a purchase decision. And it is important to know the meaning attached to an object and its competitors along each of these dimensions. In this way perception of the object vis-à-vis its competition can be used to develop or evaluate marketing strategy.

The Mop & Glo brand of floor care effectively conveys the multiple criteria consumers use in choosing a floor-care product. In the development of the brand, the manufacturer recognized that consumers evaluated floor-cleaning products in terms of their abilities to clean and shine floors.

The multidimensional perception of objects includes a phenomenon that marketers need to recognize. *Halo effects* may occur in product perceptions.[11]

---

[11] For recent research on this phenomenon, see Joel Huber and John McCann, "The Impact of Inferential Beliefs on Product Evaluations," *Journal of Marketing Research* 19 (August 1982), pp. 324–33.

halo effect

> **Halo effect** is the tendency to attach meaning to an object on one dimension based on the meaning attached to another of its dimensions.

Although halo effects are evident in other types of product attributes,[12] it is probably most dominant in the ***price–quality relationship.*** Studies have shown that consumers use price to evaluate the quality of a product— at least in the absence of other distinguishing information.[13] Thus, firms seeking a quality image for a brand may charge a price higher than that of competitors. For several years Curtis Mathes has emphasized the high price of its televisions in an attempt to convey a high-quality image.

Another type of halo effect occurs when consumers base their evaluations of a brand's attributes on their general attitude toward the brand. This type of halo effect presents difficulties to marketers who try to improve their product. Consumers who disliked the product will tend to downgrade the improvement.

Brand image.   In the area of consumer perceptions of products, an important concept in marketing is ***brand image.***

brand image

> **Brand image** (translate to **store image** for retailers) refers to the array of subjective impressions a consumer holds of a product brand (or store).

It represents the meanings attached to a brand that could be elicited from the consumer by merely mentioning the brand name. Impressions of Mercedes Benz autos as expensive, durable, success symbol, or finely engineered represent their brand image. Impressions of a supermarket as moderately priced, clean, well stocked, friendly, or helpful represent its store image. Consumer images can be extended to broader areas as well to include company image (e.g., General Motors).

Consumer images of brands/stores are important to marketing strategy in a number of ways. First, they may be established as goals for marketing strategy. For example, in introducing a new product, a company may desire to associate a particular image with it. The introductory strategy for the product will be designed to convey this image. Second, image may serve as a basis for competing with other brands in the product class. In fact, for relatively standardized consumer goods, image may be the primary way brands get distinguished. Beer is an excellent example

---

[12] See, for example, Joel B. Cohen and Michael J. Houston, "Cognitive Consequences of Brand Loyalty," *Journal of Marketing Research* 9 (February 1972), pp. 97–9.

[13] For an extensive review of these studies, see Jerry C. Olson, "Price as an Informational Cue: Effects on Product Evaluations," in *Consumer and Industrial Buying Behavior,* ed. A. Woodside, J. Sheth, and P. Bennett (New York: North Holland, 1977), pp. 267–86.

of such a product class. It provides examples of both effective and ineffective uses of image. Budweiser, with its image-oriented slogan, "When you say Budweiser, you've said it all," maintained its position as the dominant brand of beer. Schlitz, on the other hand, slipped in sales a few years ago partially as a result of its macho-oriented approach of daring some unseen person to "take my gusto away." The image was conveyed but offended consumers.

Brand image can also help rejuvenate a brand's sales. Many companies try this. For example, Timex is trying to change its image by discontinuing the use of spokesman John Cameron Swayze and its familiar timepiece torture tests. A new image emphasizes fashion and technology.

As with many concepts in consumer behavior, brand image can be used to *evaluate* marketing strategy effectiveness. Two questions are relevant here. First, does the brand possess the intended image in the eyes of consumers? Consumer research can determine if the intended image is the actual image. And images of competing brands or stores can be examined vis-à-vis a firm's brand. The semantic differential technique of measurement is a useful way to measure and portray a brand's image and its similarity (or dissimilarity) to competing brands.[14] See Figure 5–8 for a hypothetical example of images of competing banks as expressed on a set of semantic differential scales. Second, is the intended image appropriate? Conveying the intended image does not assure its effectiveness, as shown by the Schlitz example. Evaluation of image effectiveness must be carried a step further to determine its effect on sales.

Finally, we should point out that brand image may result from factors other than marketing strategy efforts. For years the image of Harley-Davidson was based on its popularity with motorcycle gangs—something not intended by the company. This image left it open to competition from brands like Honda, which emphasized a more clean-cut user. Harley-Davidson is now attempting to alter its image by appealing to families.

Product positioning. A firm may attempt to establish brand image through a ***product-positioning*** strategy. This attempts to establish a unique meaning for a brand in the eyes of consumers—often a specific segment of the market. In some cases only a portion of the marketing strategy variables will be used to position a brand. For example, "The Uncola" was a simple but effective advertising theme that distinguished the 7up soft drink brand from its cola-based competition.

In other cases the entire set of marketing strategy variables will be used in a positioning strategy. Mead Johnson tried to reposition its Metrecal brand from a medically accepted product sold in drugstores to overweight people to a flavorful diet food sold in supermarkets to people

---

[14] Gilbert A. Churchill, Jr., *Marketing Research: Methodological Foundations,* 3d ed. (Hinsdale, Ill.: Dryden Press, 1983), pp. 258–61.

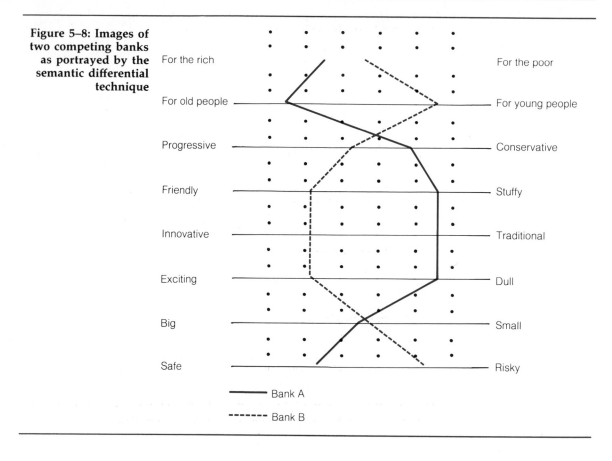

Figure 5–8: Images of two competing banks as portrayed by the semantic differential technique

trying to remain slim.[15] New versions of the product—such as flavored milk shakes—were introduced to supplement the basic diet drink. Advertising messages emphasized the taste and variety now available in a low-calorie food-store item.

Perceived risk. The element of risk in consumer decisions has led to a concept in the area of consumer perception known as ***perceived risk.*** This concept recognizes that consumer behavior involves risk in that any action of a consumer will produce consequences that he/she cannot anticipate with any certainty.[16] Implicit in this statement are the two components that determine the level of risk perceived by a consumer. (See Figure 5–9.) First, the *perceived severity of the consequences of a poor*

---

[15] Roger D. Blackwell, James F. Engel, and David T. Kollat, *Cases in Consumer Behavior* (New York: Holt, Rinehart & Winston, 1969), Mead Johnson and Co. (A), pp. 3–8, and Mead Johnson and Co. (B), pp. 113–20.

[16] The classic discussion of perceived risk is found in Raymond Bauer, "Consumer Behavior as Risk Taking," *Proceedings of the American Marketing Association,* ed. R. S. Hancock (Chicago: American Marketing Association, 1960), pp. 389–98.

choice contributes to perceived risk. The choice of an auto has potentially more severe consequences than the choice of a package of gum. It is, therefore, a riskier decision situation. In considering the perceived risk of a choice situation, a number of different types of consequences must be considered. The extent to which these consequences are relevant to a product class increases perceived risk. These types of consequences include:

1. *Functional consequences*—Those associated with the performance of the product. ("Will the floor wax provide the desired shine to my floor?")
2. *Physical consequences*—Those associated with physical harm to self or others that the product may pose. ("If this toy malfunctions, will it harm my child?")
3. *Financial consequences*—Those associated with the loss of money or time if the utility of the product falls short of what is expected. ("Is this new expensive restaurant really worth its prices and an evening out?")
4. *Social consequences*—Those associated with the embarrassment before others resulting from a poor choice. ("Will this new outfit look good to others?")
5. *Psychological consequences*—Those associated with the threat to the consumer's ego. ("Is this car really what I'm all about?")

The second component contributing to perceived risk is the *level of uncertainty* about the consequences of a particular choice. The greater the uncertainty, the greater the risk. Thus, purchasing a brand of automobile has potentially severe consequences; but if there is relative certainty that negative consequences will not occur, perceived risk is reduced considerably. Of course, when uncertainty about the consequences of purchasing a new candy bar is high, perceived risk remains quite low. The functional or financial consequences resulting from a poor decision in this case are not at all severe.

The effects of the level of perceived risk on consumer behavior are realized primarily in terms of the consumer decision process (to be dis-

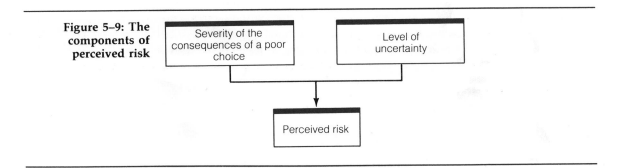

Figure 5–9: The components of perceived risk

| Severity of the consequences of a poor choice | Level of uncertainty |

Perceived risk

Clothes aren't just a
matter of style.

A running suit that's more comfortable than your birthday suit.

This nylon tricot chest band prevents chafing. A shirt that doesn't have it will rub you the wrong way.

Inside the shorts you'll find our famous built-in brief.

The back is all mesh. Spell that b-r-e-a-t-h-a-b-i-l-i-t-y.

Our overlapping sides open up to give your legs room to move.

You'd think running with no clothes would be more comfortable than running with clothes. It isn't. Because Bill Rodgers suits are designed to circulate air and keep you cool. So don't wear nothing. You won't be as comfortable. Besides, what would the neighbors say.

Bill Rodgers & Company, 86 Finnell Drive, Weymouth, MA 02188 (617) 335-2740

Courtesy Bill Rodgers & Company

cussed in Chapter 7). In decision making, consumers essentially attempt to reduce the risk associated with the purchase. A number of risk-reduction methods are available to consumers, but two seem to be most dominant.[17] When perceived risk is high, considerable *information-seeking* behavior occurs prior to purchase to reduce uncertainty. For many products, though, no information seeking will occur; consumers will use *brand loyalty* to reduce risk. That is, they will purchase a brand that has worked for them in the past.

---

[17] Ted Roselius, "Consumer Rankings of Risk-Reduction Methods," *Journal of Marketing* 35 (January 1971), pp. 56–61.

Beliefs and attitudes

Of all the factors influencing consumer behavior, beliefs, and attitudes have, without question, received the greatest attention in marketing.

belief

> A **belief** is the probability that a characteristic is associated with an object, event, idea, or person.

Two types of beliefs exist. A *descriptive* belief describes the nature of a product's objective characteristics (i.e., "The notebook is small"). An *evaluative belief*—the type most relevant to consumer behavior—attaches value (positive or negative) to an object (i.e., "This ice cream tastes good"). Since products are perceived in multidimensional fashion, consumers develop a *set* of beliefs about a product. Some of them are descriptive. Many of them are evaluative or judgmental and contribute to consumer images of the product. Thus, beliefs about the *attributes* of a product are developed. A consumer will form beliefs about attributes of a brand of toothpaste, such as price, decay prevention, or taste.

The set of beliefs individuals hold about an object form the basis for their attitude toward it.

attitude

> An **attitude** is an enduring positive or negative feeling toward an object that predisposes the individual to behave favorably or unfavorably toward it.

The attitude toward an object derives from the beliefs held about the object; it results in a feeling of affect (like or dislike) toward the object. This affective feeling guides the individual's behavior toward the object. An individual who "likes" an object is predisposed to behave positively with respect to it. Thus, a consumer who develops beliefs that a brand of toothpaste effectively fights decay, has a pleasing taste, and freshens breath develops a favorable attitude toward the brand and is more inclined to buy and use it. The enduring nature of an attitude suggests its resistance to change.

The relationship between beliefs and attitudes and, in particular, between attitudes and behavior indicate their importance to marketing. If our ultimate goal is to understand behavior, we must recognize and understand the factors that influence it. If attitudes are an important determinant, we must determine attitudes toward our brand and ascertain why they exist. Since attitudes derive from beliefs, we must identify the belief structure that underlies an attitude to understand why the positive or negative feeling results.

The existence of an attitude suggests, then, a three-level framework

This ad illustrates a
multi-attribute appeal.

Courtesy Beecham Inc.

within which to examine the feelings of a consumer about a brand. (See Figure 5–10.) First, the **cognitive level** represents the set of beliefs that the consumer holds about the brand. Second is the **affective level.** It represents the emotional side of the consumer's feelings—a liking or disliking of the brand. Third is the **conative,** or behavioral, level. This reflects consumers' likely behavior toward the brand—will they buy it? While

Figure 5–10: Three-level framework of development of consumer relationship with brands

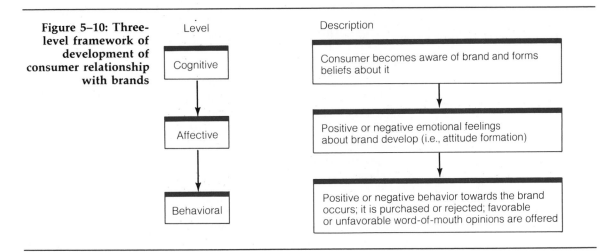

each level individually offers insight into the relationship between a consumer and a brand, the entire framework taken as a whole is more useful. Since each level is a result of the previous one, understanding any one level requires knowledge of the previous one.[18]

The cognitive–affective–conative framework represents the "hierarchy of effects" perspective often used when developing marketing strategy. The hierarchy indicates that the effects of marketing occur at different levels, beginning with the cognitive level. For effects at the behavioral level to be realized, consumers must first be influenced at the cognitive and affective levels. To develop a long-term inclination toward buying a brand, consumers must first develop a liking for it. This requires a set of favorable beliefs about the brand. As we will see, the establishment of realistic advertising objectives for a new product recognizes that the initial goals should center on creating favorable beliefs about a product rather than trying to get people to buy it immediately.

The multi-attribute model of consumer attitudes. A model that has received considerable attention in studying consumer attitudes is the ***multi-attribute model.*** Based on the work of Fishbein, the typical consumer behavior version of the model expressed in its algebraic form, as follows:[19]

---

[18] For more on the role of cognitive and affective factors in consumer behavior, see Robert B. Zajonc and Hazel Markus, "Affective and Cognitive Factors in Preferences," *Journal of Consumer Research* 9 (September 1982), pp. 123–31.

[19] M. Fishbein, "A Behavior Theory Approach to the Relations between Beliefs about an Object and the Attitude toward the Object" in *Attitude Theory and Measurement,* ed. M. Fishbein. Copyright © 1967 John Wiley & Sons, Inc.

$$A_{\text{Brand}} = \sum_{i=1}^{k} B_i I_i$$

where

A_{Brand} = The consumer's overall attitude toward a brand

B_i = The consumer's belief regarding the extent to which attribute i is associated with the brand

I_i = The importance to the consumer of attribute i in choosing a brand

k = Number of attributes used in evaluating brands in the product class

i = 1, 2, 3, . . . , k

This model, which has received considerable attention in consumer behavior research, has much intuitive appeal for several reasons:[20]

1. It recognizes the multidimensional nature of products in that it implies a *set* of beliefs about a brand.

2. It suggests that the evaluative criteria used by a consumer are not equal in determining attitudes. Some attributes are more important than others.

3. It suggests that a brand's poor performance on one attribute can be offset by superior performance on others.

4. It pinpoints key aspects of a consumer's cognitive structure regarding a brand that can serve as focal points for marketing strategy.[21]

The utility of the model to marketing management does not lie in its algebraic form. Rather, it is useful in suggesting a *framework* for studying consumer beliefs and attitudes. It suggests that we need to know what product attributes consumers use in making brand-choice decisions, their relative importance, and consumer beliefs about each attribute for both the company's and competing brands. Such information is useful for formulating and evaluating marketing strategy and selecting target markets.

Consider the hypothetical example in Table 5–2. The most favorable overall attitude exists for bank A. But in considering the values of the individual components of this score, we learn much about "why" this

---

[20] Excellent reviews of this body of literature are provided by W. Wilkie and E. Pessemier, "Issues in Marketing's Use of Multi-Attribute Attitude Models," *Journal of Marketing Research* 10 (1973), pp. 428–41; and R. Lutz and J. Bettman, "Multi-Attribute Models in Marketing: A Bicentennial Review," in Woodside, Sheth, and Bennett, *Consumer and Industrial Buying Behavior*, pp. 137–50.

[21] A series of marketing strategies based on the model can be found in H. Boyd, M. Ray, and E. Strong, "An Attitudinal Framework for Advertising Strategy," *Journal of Marketing* 36 (April 1972), pp. 27–33; and R. Lutz, "Changing Brand Attitudes through Modification of Cognitive Structure," *Journal of Consumer Research* 1 (March 1975), pp. 49–59.

| Table 5–2: | | Beliefs* | | | |
Multi-attribute framework for examining consumer beliefs/attitudes	Attribute	Importance*	Bank A	Bank B	Bank C
	Convenience	6	6	8	5
	Interest charged	8	5	6	6
	Interest paid	9	7	7	6
	Range of services	7	8	4	5
	Friendliness	3	9	5	5
	Overall attitude		222	202	182

* Hypothetical scores from a 1-to-9 rating scale with 1 being unfavorable and 9 being favorable.

attitude exists. The superiority of bank A in the consumer's mind derives primarily from its perceived advantage on the range of services offered. Bank A may then determine that customers who attach importance to service represent a segment of the market they effectively serve. They may define such a market segment as their target market. Banks B and C, on the other hand, may conclude that to compete more effectively they should expand their services or perhaps better inform consumers of the services they offer.

Determinant attributes. Our hypothetical example illustrates an important concept in the area of beliefs. A *determinant attribute* is that attribute of a product class that plays the greatest role in determining a consumer's brand choice.[22] The determinant attribute may be the most important one. But not always. The determinance results from consumers' perceived variations between brands on the attribute. If there are perceived variations between brands on the most important attribute, then it will be determinant. But if all brands are perceived equal on the most important attribute, then a less important attribute—but one in which variations are perceived—will be determinant. Such is the case with our hypothetical consumer. The most important attribute, interest paid, varies little between banks. Such is also the case with the second most important attribute, interest charged. Not until we get to the third most important attribute, services, are perceived variations between banks revealed. Range of services, though third in importance, is likely to be most determinant of the choice of banks by this consumer.

Personality

Personality, like attitude, is an enduring aspect of the individual. However, unlike attitude, it is not specific in its scope of concern. Rather, it is relevant to many situations.

[22] J. Myers and M. Alpert, "Determinant Buying Attitudes: Meaning and Measurement," *Journal of Marketing* 32 (October 1968), pp. 13–20.

personality

> **Personality** refers to the modal patterns of behavior exhibited by the individual.

It reflects the behavioral tendencies that are consistently elicited as the person is exposed to and copes with a variety of situations. There are a number of theoretical explanations of how personality develops, but many agree on our definition as a description of an individual's personality as it exists at any one time.[23]

The most common approach to the study of personality as it relates to consumer behavior is the so-called *trait approach.* This approach characterizes a person's personality by the extent to which he/she possesses traits such as self-control, sociability, conservatism, dogmatism, etc. Consumers are measured using a specific personality instrument (such as the California Personality Instrument) on a number of specific traits (sociability, self-control) and various aspects of their behavior as consumers (brand or store preference, new-product usage). Significant relationships between the personality traits and consumer behavior are then examined. Such a study might trigger the following statements:

Dogmatic individuals are less likely to be willing to try new products.

Beer drinkers preferring Michelob are outgoing and status conscious.

A broader approach to personality and consumer behavior is that of the *type approach.* This characterizes personality as more of a composite of traits and, thus, captures more of the totality of an individual. One classic type approach used in consumer behavior is that of Horney.[24] Her approach is concerned with the social orientation of individuals. Horney characterizes individuals by one of three orientations:

1. *Compliant*—Those who "move toward people" and want to be loved, appreciated, and needed by others.
2. *Aggressive*—Those who "move against people" and want to excel and achieve success through competing with others.
3. *Detached*—Those who "move away from people" and avoid relationships with others.

Cohen has applied Horney's typology of personalities to consumer behavior and observed some distinct purchasing patterns associated with each.[25] Compliant individuals, for example, use more mouthwash and soap. Wine is consumed by compliant types to a greater extent, also. Aggressive males are more inclined to use cologne and manual razors.

---

[23] For a review of these theories, see H. Kassarjian, "Personality and Consumer Behavior: A Review," *Journal of Marketing Research* 8 (November 1971), pp. 409–18.

[24] Karen Horney, *Neurotic Personality of Our Time* (New York: W. W. Norton, 1937).

[25] Joel B. Cohen, "An Interpersonal Orientation to the Study of Consumer Behavior," *Journal of Marketing Research* 4 (August 1967), pp. 270–78.

Detached individuals tend toward products that are against the main-stream (tea instead of coffee).

Conceptually, personality has much potential for explaining consumer behavior. Its enduring and comprehensive nature suggests that personality relates to a broad spectrum of behavior in a consistent manner over time. But its potential has not been realized in applying the concept of personality to consumer behavior. Studies have shown the personality–behavior relationship to be weak. One reason is that the personality inventories designed for clinical psychologists are far removed from consumer behavior. Few studies have used personality measures designed specifically to study consumer behavior.[26] Another reason for the limited practical usefulness of personality is the difficulty of developing and implementing marketing strategies aimed at specific personality types. Personality types are spread throughout society. Identifying individuals of a particular type and their unique needs, desires, and media behavior isn't easy. In short, perhaps the greatest difficulty is in defining market segments on a personality basis so that they are accessible to marketers.

Self-image

A concept rich in relevance to consumer behavior is ***self-image.***

self-image

> **Self-image** is the totality of the individual's thoughts and feelings that define for the individual what he or she is, has been, and hopes to be.

Two types of self-image are apparent in this definition. First, the *perceived self* refers to an individual's perception of how he/she actually is. Second, the *ideal self* is the individual's conception of what he/she would like to be and how he/she would like others to view him or her. The goal of the individual is to establish a congruency between perceived self and ideal self. A discrepancy between the two motivates the person to behave in a manner that achieves congruency between perceived and ideal self.

Two aspects of behavior are designed to achieve this congruency. First is the *external aspect.* Behavior conveys to others what the individual is all about. People want others to see them in a manner consistent with their ideal selves. They engage in behavior that portrays them in that light. Second is an *internal aspect.* Not only do people wish to convey to others a desired image, they want to feel good internally about themselves as well. They want to reinforce to themselves what they are all about. Figure 5–11 summarizes the role of self-image in consumer behavior.

---

[26] Exceptions include Cohen, *Journal of Marketing Research,* and G. Brooker, "The Self-Actualizing Socially Conscious Consumer," *Journal of Consumer Research* 30 (September 1976), pp. 107–12.

Appealing to self-image.

Good looks aren't everything.

Sure you've got a good job. A good income. A good-looking head on your shoulders. But do you have the American Express® Card? If not, you should. Because with the Card, you're welcomed at the finest hotels, resorts, restaurants and shops in the world. As well as at major airline and car rental counters.

In fact, the American Express Card does so much, it can eliminate the need to carry other charge, credit or travel cards.

So send in the attached application. Or call 800-528-8000. And get what even good looks can't buy. An American Express Card.

Behavior in the marketplace represents one domain of behavior that can be used to enhance self-image. The person seeks to build an assortment of products, services, and brands that convey the desired image. Some of these products are designed to symbolize to others the nature of the individual. Products used in the presence of others (clothes) often serve

Figure 5–11: The role of self-image in consumer behavior

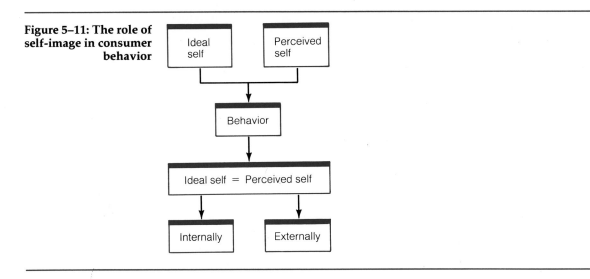

this function. Many products are purchased simply to confirm individuals' image to themselves. Products are used that enhance their internal feelings about themselves. Such products are not necessarily evident to others, but most would be. Most products relevant to image enhancement serve both the internal and external functions of image-oriented behavior.[27]

People determine the relevance of a product or brand to their self-image based on product or brand image. We seek an assortment of goods and services whose overall image matches our desired self-image. We don't buy incompatible brands and products.

The concept of self-image points out three important aspects of behavior:

1. Much human behavior seeks to protect and enhance self-image.
2. The purchase, display, and use of goods communicates symbolic meaning to the individual and others.
3. Consumer behavior seeks to protect and enhance self-image through the consumption of goods as symbols.

The concept of self-image offers a proper ending point for this chapter on individual influences on consumer behavior. Conceptually, self-image cuts across many of the areas previously discussed. Image enhancement is a goal or motive of behavior deriving from values. It is an object of perception that interacts with product and brand images to guide behavior. Attitudes are formed with ideal self in mind. Its enduring and comprehensive nature suggests self-image as a personality theory. However, it also

[27] An in-depth discussion of the role of self-image in consumer behavior is presented in M. Joseph Sirgy, "Self-Concept in Consumer Behavior: A Critical Review," *Journal of Consumer Research* 9 (December 1982), pp. 287–300.

recognizes the interaction between the individual and others as an influence on behavior. These social influences are a major topic in the next chapter.

SUMMARY

The multidisciplinary nature of consumer behavior recognizes a large number of factors that influence consumers. Understanding these factors aids the development and evaluation of marketing strategy and public policy. Two sets of factors, personal and social, interact to determine behavior in this approach. The emphasis in this chapter has been on the personal factors of values, motivation, perception, beliefs, attitude, personality, and self-image.

Values are enduring beliefs that guide behavior in a variety of situations. Values exist at the global, domain, and product levels. Motivation directs the consumer to the purchase of goods and services to satisfy needs. Individuals possess a multiplicity of needs at the physiological and psychological levels. Perception is the process by which meaning is attached to objects in the environment. It is selective, organized, and influenced by personal and stimulus factors. Consumers perceive products on a number of attributes and form brand images.

Perception results in beliefs about a product, which combine as the basis for an attitude, which directs *behavior*. The cognitive-affective-behavioral sequence represents the developmental process of consumer-brand relationships.

Personality refers to the modal patterns of behavior on the part of an individual. Personality traits and types have been related to consumer behavior. Self-image is a person's idea of what he or she is and would like to be. Many products are purchased to protect and enhance self-image.

KEY CONCEPTS

Human behavior	Want	Perceived risk
Behavior	Perception	Belief
Personal factors	Selective perception	Attitude
Social factors	Organized nature of perception	Cognitive level
Value	Stimulus factors of perception	Affective level
Global value	Personal factors of perception	Conative level
Domain-specific value	JND	Multi-attribute attitude model
Product-specific value	Multidimensionality of perception	Determinant attribute
Evaluative criteria	Halo effect	Personality
Motivation	Price-quality relationship	Personality trait
Need-reduction theory	Brand image	Personality type
Need	Store image	Self-image
Multiplicity of needs	Product positioning	

DISCUSSION QUESTIONS AND EXERCISES

1. Perform a self-analysis of the values that would guide your purchase of a stereo. Start at the product-specific level, and identify the evaluative criteria you would use. Then identify your domain-specific values from which the criteria emerged. Finally, identify the global values that determined your domain-specific values. How does all of this affect the way a company should market a stereo to you?

2. Using the evaluative criteria from Question 1 and a nine-point scale, attach importance weights to each attribute and belief score for each of three major brands. Compute your overall attitude for each brand.

3. What types of needs are you satisfying at the generic, product-form, and brand levels in your purchase of a stereo?

4. Devise and perform a taste test for Coca-Cola, Pepsi-Cola, and Royal Crown cola.

5. Find ads for three brands in the same product class that convey different brand images aimed at different self-images. Describe the nature of the self-images and how effective you think each ad is in appealing to the self-image involved.

C H A P T E R   6

Consumer behavior:
Social influences

The nature of social influence

Sources of social influence
    Personal influence
    Family influences
    Reference group influence
    Social class influence
    Lifestyle and psychographics
    Culture and subculture

Summary

Key concepts

Discussion questions and exercises

The proposition "No one is an island" certainly holds true for consumer behavior. Consumers, in reaching decisions, are beset by a number of external influences, many of which come from their social environment—family members, peers, etc. This chapter presents a framework for examining the nature and sources of social influences on consumer behavior.

THE NATURE OF SOCIAL INFLUENCE

Before examining the specific sources of social influence, it is important to recognize two major types of social influences.[1] (See Figure 6–1.) First, **normative social influence** refers to influence from others to conform to their expectations. People accept influence in order to maintain or enhance their status with others. They conform to others to gain approval from others.

---

[1] Paul W. Miniard and Joel B. Cohen, "Modeling Personal and Normative Influences on Behavior," *Journal of Consumer Research* 10 (September 1983), pp. 169–80.

Figure 6–1: Types of social influence

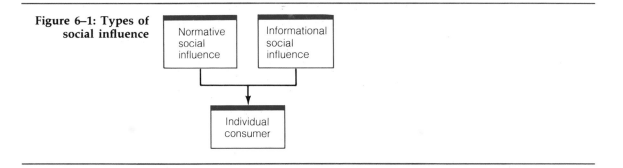

In consumer behavior "keeping up with the Joneses" applies to normative social influence. When we buy products that we feel make us look good in the eyes of others, normative social influence is at work. As you might expect, decisions about products that are highly visible are particularly susceptible to this type of social influence.

The second type of social influence is ***informational social influence—*** the acceptance of information from others as evidence of reality. It occurs when others are used as sources of information about what would be a good purchase. The individual is not seeking approval from others but evidence from them of behavior that will satisfy nonsocial needs. Informational social influence can occur in the purchase of a variety of product categories.

The following situation distinguishes between normative and informational social influence. Two families purchase homes in a neighborhood. Each family needs to buy a lawn mower. The person in each family who is responsible for buying the mower sees that many of the neighbors use the same brand and model of lawn mower. One buyer buys this same lawn mower in order to fit in with the neighbors and gain their approval. The other buys it because so many of the neighbors use this same type of mower and it must therefore cut grass well and be durable. The first buyer was subject to *normative influence*; the latter to *informational influence*.

These distinct types of social influence suggest different marketing strategies. For products whose purchase occurs to those seeking approval, the "social status" of a brand would be communicated to consumers. Communications using informational social influence would emphasize the number of people using the brand and perhaps include testimonials from its users.

SOURCES OF SOCIAL INFLUENCE

Social influence on individual consumers comes from a variety of sources. (See Figure 6–2.) These sources can be distinguished in terms of their level of aggregation. At the least aggregated level is the personal influence of a single person on another. The influence of culture is at

Incorporating
informational social
influence into the
marketing effort.

EVERYONE IS PICKING UP ON PILOT PENS
WATCH OUT FOR
THE ELEVATOR PLUCKERS

They know that the 89¢ extra fine Pilot Razor
Point Marker pen writes as smooth as silk. And
the custom-fit metal collar helps keep that point
extra fine page after page. That's why when it
comes to a Razor Point, it's love at first write.

PILOT

So thin...it's love at first write
National Sponsor of MDA/Jerry Lewis Telethon

RAZOR POINT
Extra-fine marker pen

Courtesy Pilot Corp. of America and
AMS Advertising Inc.

the most aggregated level. Moving from disaggregated to aggregated, we
discuss in this section the social influences of single persons, family, reference groups, social class, and culture and subculture.

Personal influence

Friends, neighbors, relatives, and co-workers are sources of personal
influence. The recipient of such influence may seek it out or may receive
it in the form of unsolicited advice.

personal influence

> **Personal influence** is a type of social influence in which a consumer's
> beliefs, attitudes, and behavior are swayed by another individual through
> informal interactions. It occurs through *word-of-mouth communications.*

Incorporating normative
social influence into the
marketing effort.

Personal influence is just that—influence. Advice offered by a friend or neighbor is not personal influence unless it has an effect. However, personal influence is usually a powerful factor in consumer behavior. Consumers generally regard friends and relatives as more credible and trustworthy than commercial sources of information. Thus, personal influence is primarily informational in nature.

Of course, the information can be positive or negative. Usually, it takes the form of an influencer's positive or negative experience with a brand—and it increases or decreases the probability of purchase.

Figure 6–2: Sources of social influence

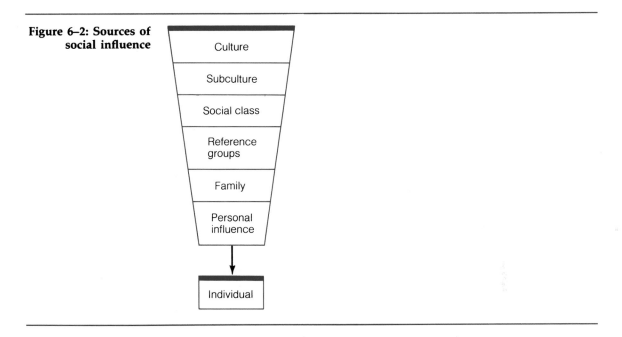

Advertisers may try to use personal influence in their ads by simulating word-of-mouth communications. Their strategy is to replace the consumer's need for direct contact with friends and relatives. By portraying typical consumers, they hope to enhance the credibility of their ad.[2]

Occasionally, word-of-mouth communications among consumers fuel the flames of crazy rumors about companies or their products. For example:

Poprocks, a General Foods candy, was rumored to cause children to explode.[3]

McDonald's was rumored to have cut costs by using red worms in their hamburgers; sales decreased by 30 percent in areas where the rumor circulated.[4]

Entenmann's, the world's largest baker of fresh cake products, was rumored to be owned by the Unification Church.[5]

Such rumors are detrimental (to say the least!), and it often requires a strategic effort to dispel them. Entenmann's (actually owned by Warner-Lambert) fought the rumors through advertising, press conferences, and letters of denial.[6]

[2] Henry Assael, *Consumer Behavior and Marketing Action,* 2d ed. (Boston: Kent Publishing, 1984), p. 427.

[3] Alice M. Tybout, Bobby J. Calder, and Brian Sternthal, "Using Information Processing Theory to Design Marketing Strategies," *Journal of Marketing Research* 18 (February 1981), p. 74.

[4] Ibid.

[5] "Entenmann's Fights Moonie Link," *Advertising Age,* November 23, 1981, p. 33.

[6] Ibid.

Figure 6–3: Two-step flow of communication

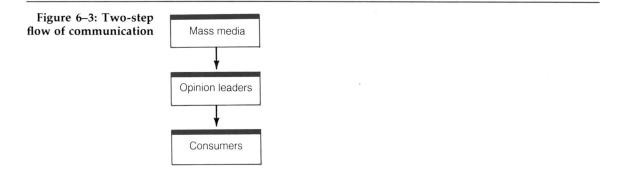

Opinion leadership.   A specific type of personal influence common in consumer behavior is opinion leadership.

opinion leaders

> **Opinion leaders** are individuals considered knowledgeable and objective in a particular area and to whom others look for behavioral guidance in that area.

When purchasing a product about which they have limited knowledge, consumers often turn to someone they believe knows more about the product category. Usually, they seek verbal advice. Opinion leaders can influence other consumers simply by their behavior. Sometimes they may not even be aware of their own influence.

Opinion leadership is category-specific. It tends to be restricted to a few product categories of a similar nature (e.g., sporting goods). Opinion leaders tend to have greater involvement with those products and know more about them than nonopinion leaders.[7] They also tend to be exposed to the mass media to a greater extent. This feature of opinion leaders suggests a *two-step flow of communication.* Figure 6–3 points out that much new-product information reaches consumers through opinion leaders who have learned of the product from mass media such as advertising.

The two-step flow of communication indicates an important marketing task. To the extent they can identify and reach them, firms should nurture opinion leaders with positive feelings toward their products. For instance, in 1983 Ford Motor Co. restyled its Thunderbird model, targeting it at prosperous professionals—car buffs with a taste for high-priced foreign cars. Then the company wrote some 400,000 executives and professionals, inviting them to drive a T-Bird for a day. Ford called this the VIP Program. Its strategy was to expose the car to these individuals and have them

[7] J. Jacoby and W. D. Hoyer, "What if Opinion Leaders Didn't Know More? A Question of Nomological Validity," in *Advances in Consumer Research VIII,* ed. Kent B. Monroe (Ann Arbor, Mich.: Association for Consumer Research, 1981), pp. 299–303.

Advertisements for a product can incorporate principles of identification by describing a specific individual who uses the product. Here Dewar's offers female scotch drinkers someone to identify with.

DEWAR'S PROFILE:

LISA BIRNBACH

HOME: New York City.

AGE: 27

PROFESSION: Writer, humorist, lecturer.

HOBBY: Attending weddings. "But only of people I know."

LAST BOOK READ: Robert Rimmer's *The Harrad Experiment.*

LATEST ACCOMPLISHMENT: Writing *Lisa Birnbach's College Book.* "After visiting students at 250 colleges and universities, I'm going through a second adolescence. Still, it beats growing up."

WHY I DO WHAT I DO: "A need to communicate and a penchant for voyeurism."

QUOTE: "Startling as it was to discover, there is life after writing *The Preppy Handbook.* Really."

PROFILE: Has a satiric wit but shows a remarkable sympathy for her victims.

HER SCOTCH: "Dewar's White Label, on the rocks. My father drinks Dewar's; so do I. Like Daddy, like daughter."

DEWAR'S "WHITE LABEL" • BLENDED SCOTCH WHISKY • 86.8 PROOF • ©1984 SCHENLEY IMPORTS

seen driving it at social functions. And the strategy paid off. During the last six months of 1983, almost 15,000 of these opinion leaders accepted Ford's invitation. Ten percent of these people indicated they intended to buy a T-Bird. Perhaps more important, over 80 percent said they would recommend the T-Bird to a friend.[8]

[8] "Ford Pushing Thunderbird With VIP Plan," *The Wall Street Journal,* November 19, 1983, p. 37.

Identification.   A more normative type of personal influence is one Kelman termed *identification.*[9]

identification

> **Identification** occurs when one person sees another as the type of person he or she would like to be and behaves accordingly.

While it may exist, a personal relationship between two people isn't necessary for identification to occur. Close friends and distant public figures can do equally well as role models. And the adopted behavior needn't be visible to the influencing person, for the influenced individual seeks internal gratification. Here we see the relationship between social influence and self-image. Promotional strategies based on identification can effectively market products by associating the products with types of individuals that consumers use as referents for self-image enhancement.

Family influences

Perhaps the greatest social influence on an individual comes from his or her family. Family influence on the individual can be viewed from both a long-run and a short-run perspective. A long-run perspective sees the family as a *socialization agent.*

socialization process

> The process by which an individual acquires the values, norms, and expected behavior patterns of a society is the **socialization process.**

The short-run perspective recognizes the interpersonal influences that family members exert on each other's behavior and on decisions made by the family unit.

The family as a socialization agent.   Socialization occurs so that the individual can effectively participate in and cope with the social environment. It is a long-run process. A person's social tendencies result from an accumulation of effects from a variety of socialization agents—i.e., those groups with which the individual has interacted in the past. One such group is, of course, the family. Many of the values and behavioral tendencies we carry through life result from family experiences over a number of years.

consumer socialization process

> A **consumer socialization process** occurs as, over time, one acquires skills, knowledge, and attitudes relevant to functioning as a consumer in the marketplace.[10]

---

[9] H. C. Kelman, "Processes of Opinion Change," *Public Opinion Quarterly* 25 (Spring 1961), pp. 57–78.

[10] Scott Ward, "Consumer Socialization," *Journal of Consumer Research* 1 (September 1974), p. 2.

Identification for the
black male consumer.

Courtesy TCB Division Alberto-
Culver Company

The family is significant in this process. Understanding how the family influences the development of an individual as a consumer can enhance understanding of an adult's consumer behavior. The shaping of public policy and consumer education programs can be enhanced, too. We see this in the increased governmental concerns over TV ads directed at children. One concern has been how the influence of these ads compares to parental influence.

Another long-run family influence occurs in the allocation of household tasks. Shaninger and Buss asked how newly married couples share grocery shopping, financial matters, household repair, and cleaning tasks.[11] They found task allocations were positively influenced by the behavior of the couple's parents. They also found that men were more influenced than women by their parents. Obviously, roles within the family will be an important aspect of its members' consumer behavior.

Family decision-making roles.   A short-run consideration: How does any one family member influence a purchase decision by the family as a unit? Much of the research in this area has focused on the relative influence of husbands and wives on certain purchase decisions. Three basic categories of husband–wife influence can be identified:

Husband-dominated. He carries the greatest weight in the purchase decision.

Wife-dominated. She carries the greatest weight.

Joint. Both share more or less equally in making the decision.

Products and services vary in the extent to which decisions about their purchase are husband- or wife-dominated or are made jointly. For example, purchasing decisions about autos and TV sets are typically husband-dominated. Wife-dominated decisions affect food and carpet buying. Joint decisions are usually made about housing and vacation spots. But not always. Like other consumer behavior, husband-wife influences are dynamic over time. A 1974 study by Cunningham and Green points this out.[12] It shows that over approximately two decades certain products have changed in terms of husband-wife influence patterns. (See Figure 6–4.) Automobile purchases are still husband-dominated. But they're now influenced to a much greater extent by wives. Thus, even by 1974, significant changes in family decision making had occurred. Since that time, trends toward later marriage, smaller families, two-job households, and so on suggest a trend toward more joint decision making as well. Many tradition-bound families still exist, of course. And they tend to have well-defined spousal roles in decision making.[13]

Knowledge of relative husband-wife influence is important to marketing strategy for a particular product. Product information should be directed at the influential spouse. But the task is more complicated than that. Husbands and wives may experience different media exposure pat-

---

[11] C. M. Schaninger and W. C. Buss, "Intergenerational Transfer of Task Allocation within the Family" (Paper presented at AMA Winter Educators' Conference, Fort Lauderdale, 1984).

[12] I. C. M. Cunningham and R. T. Green, "Purchasing Roles in the U.S. Family, 1955 and 1973," *Journal of Marketing* 30 (October 1974), pp. 61–64.

[13] Dennis L. Rosen and Donald H. Granbois, "Determinants of Role Structure in Family Financial Management," *Journal of Consumer Research* 10 (September 1983), p. 253.

Figure 6–4: Percentage of husband-dominated, joint, and wife-dominated purchase decisions in various product categories, 1955–1973.

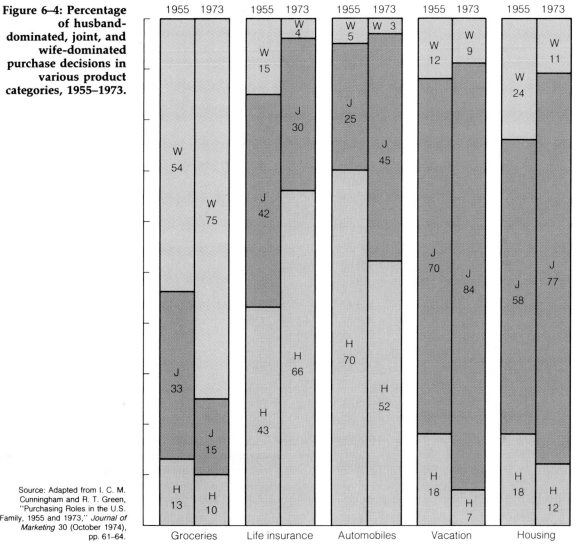

Source: Adapted from I. C. M. Cunningham and R. T. Green, "Purchasing Roles in the U.S. Family, 1955 and 1973," *Journal of Marketing* 30 (October 1974), pp. 61–64.

terns—so different media treatment may be needed. Evidence suggests that spouses also differ in their influence on different product attributes (style, price) at different stages in the decision process (problem recognition, information search) and at different stages of the family life cycle.[14] Marketers must sift these differences before designing and implementing a marketing strategy.

[14] Del I. Hawkins, Roger J. Best, and Kenneth A. Coney, *Consumer Behavior: Implications for Marketing Strategy,* rev. ed. (Plano, Tex.: Business Publications, 1983), pp. 252–66.

Figure 6–5: Flow of parent-child interaction in breakfast cereal selection

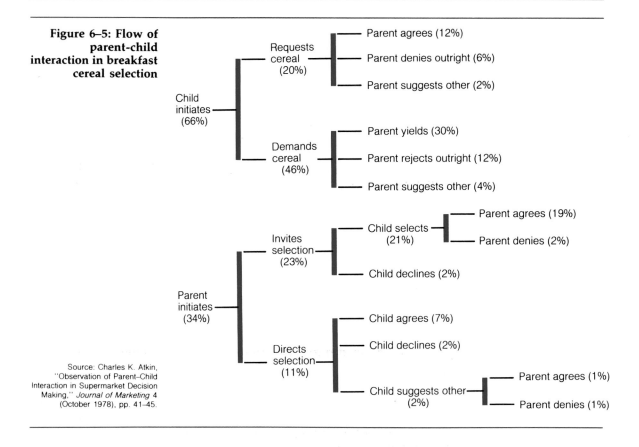

Source: Charles K. Atkin, "Observation of Parent–Child Interaction in Supermarket Decision Making," *Journal of Marketing* 4 (October 1978), pp. 41–45.

The influence of children.   Of course, spouses are not the only family members with influence. On a number of product decisions, children represent a major source of influence within the family. Their influence and parental yielding have been examined across a number of product categories.[15] Children's greatest influence is on the buying of food—especially breakfast cereals. Yet children frequently influence nonfood purchases. And parental yielding to requests only increases as children grow older.

In an interesting study of children's influence on breakfast cereal selection, Atkin observed parent-child interactions in a supermarket.[16] His flowchart (see Figure 6–5) reveals the types of parent-child interactions that occur. Most commonly, the child initiates the selection process through a demand, to which the parent yields. Clearly, advertising for

---

[15] Scott Ward and Daniel B. Wackman, "Children's Purchase Influence Attempts and Parental Yielding," *Journal of Marketing Research* 9 (August 1972), pp. 316–19.

[16] Charles K. Atkin, "Observation of Parent-Child Interaction in Supermarket Decision Making," *Journal of Marketing* 4 (October 1978), pp. 41–45.

breakfast cereals could be directed at children—it could stimulate them to initiate a request.[17] But this is a controversial notion; it's argued that advertising directed at children creates undesirable and unnecessary conflict between parent and child.

The other side of this issue is that learning to deal with advertising messages is an important part of the consumer socialization process for children. A legal ban on ads directed at children is unlikely. Still, such ads will probably be scrutinized by public policy officials for some time.[18]

Reference group influence

Influence on an individual by a group or body of individuals is known as ***reference group influence.***

reference group

> A **reference group** is used by the individual to evaluate self. It is a group whose standards are used as a comparison point for the individual's behavior.[19]

The importance of a reference group in a particular situation determines the extent to which its norm will influence the individual's actions.

Let's review some of the different types of reference groups. First, there are ***membership groups***—those to which the individual belongs. Face-to-face groups of a formal nature (social clubs, professional organizations) and an informal nature (co-workers, neighbors, social groups) are included here. So are groups of an ascribed nature. An individual automatically belongs to these by virtue of his or her inherent characteristics (age, sex). ***Aspiration groups***—those to which the individual does not belong but wishes to belong—are a second general type of reference group. Their influence operates in much the same way as membership groups.

Reference groups can exert a considerable amount of normative social influence on one's behavior. The desire to acquire or maintain a certain status within a group often requires the person to become aware of and conform to a group's behavior expectations. Bearden and Etzel present a useful framework to examine the normative influence of reference groups on consumer behavior.[20] In this framework the potential of refer-

---

[17] For evidence on the effects of advertising on children, see Gerald J. Gorn and Marvin E. Goldberg, "Behavioral Evidence of the Effects of TV Food Messages on Children," *Journal of Consumer Research* 9 (September 1982), pp. 200–205.

[18] For a discussion of some alternative regulatory approaches to children's advertising, see Deborah L. Roedder, "Age Differences in Children's Responses to Television Advertising: An Information-Processing Approach," *Journal of Consumer Research* 8 (September 1981), pp. 144–53.

[19] William O. Bearden and Michael J. Etzel, "Reference Group Influence on Product and Brand Purchase Decisions," *Journal of Consumer Research* 9 (September 1982), pp. 183–94.

[20] Ibid.

ence group influence is recognized at two levels of buying decision. First, reference groups can influence the decision to buy or not to buy a generic product (air conditioner, automobile). Second, reference groups may influence the choice of a particular brand of the product. The major feature of a generic product or brand determining its susceptibility to normative reference group influence is its **conspicuousness**. Not just its visibility but its ability to stand out, to be noticed.[21] Various combinations of the two levels of influence lead to four categories of reference group influence in buying decisions:

1. The decision to buy the generic product is strongly influenced, but brand choice is weakly influenced.
2. The decision to buy the generic product is weakly influenced, but brand choice is strongly influenced.
3. Both the decision to buy the generic product and the brand choice are strongly influenced.
4. Neither the decision to buy the generic product nor the brand choice is influenced.

Table 6–1 summarizes the nature of products falling into each of the four categories and their appropriate promotional strategies. Note that each category includes a variety of products—both durable and nondurable and with a wide range of prices. Thus, the physical nature and cost of a product are not critical in determining its susceptibility to reference group influence.

Reference group influence emphasizes an important point about consumer behavior: *much consumer behavior is symbolic.* The purchase and use of certain products and brands conveys information to others about the individual consumer. The product may symbolize self-image or adherence to group norms. In either case the communicative value of the product has played a major role in the decision to buy it.[22]

Reference groups may also exert informational influence. Here the group provides a benchmark to which we can compare ourselves to ascertain our status outside the group. For example, a household may compare how much it saves each month to savings in other households at a similar level of income. Members of the household do not feel compelled to save the same amount for status reasons. Rather, they make the comparison to determine if their savings behavior is sufficient for their income level. If it saves less, the household may become concerned about its

---

[21] F. Bourne, "Group Influence in Marketing and Public Relations," in *Perspective in Consumer Behavior,* ed. H. Kassarjian and T. Robertson (Glenview, Ill.: Scott, Foresman, 1968), pp. 289–96.

[22] For more on symbolic consumer behavior, see Michael R. Solomon, "The Role of Products as Social Stimuli: A Symbolic Interactionism Perspective," *Journal of Consumer Research* 10 (December 1983), pp. 319–29. Also see John Brooks, *Showing off in America* (Boston: Little, Brown, 1981).

Table 6–1: Categories of reference group influence on buying decisions	Category of influence		Nature of products	Appropriate strategies
	Generic product	**Brand**		
	Strong	Weak	Private luxuries: conspicuous products not owned by everyone and for which few brands exist (home video recorder, TV game, ice maker)	Stress social aspects of product to stimulate primary demand; stress unique features of brand (quality, price) to stimulate selective demand
	Weak	Strong	Public necessities: visible products owned by most but for which many brands exist (clothing, cars)	Less concern for primary demand needed; stress social aspects of brand ownership
	Strong	Strong	Public luxuries: conspicuous products not owned/used by everyone and for which many brands are available (cigarettes, beer, golf clubs)	Stress social aspects in stimulating both primary and selective demand
	Weak	Weak	Private necessities: inconspicuous products (canned goods, soap, mattress)	Stress utility of product and brand

Source: Adapted with permission from William O. Bearden and Michael J. Etzel, "Reference Group Influences on Product and Brand Purchase Decisions," *Journal of Consumer Research* 9 (September 1982), pp. 183–94.

financial situation and attempt to increase its savings. A financial institution that seeks to increase deposits may draw attention to this comparison. That is, it may show customers with small accounts or those with below-average deposits how they stack up against reference groups of equivalent income or age.

Social class influence

At a more aggregated level of social influence we have the concept of *social class.* In American society, social class identifies the social ranking of an individual or family.

social classes

> **Social classes** are subgroupings of a society whose members are approximately equal to each other in social prestige and status and share similar values, interests, and behaviors.

The placement of an individual or family into a social class is heavily determined by educational background and occupation. Social class differences are also revealed by social skills, status aspirations, community

Symbolic role of a
product.

NOTHING DEFINES A WOMAN LIKE ELEGANCE.

CROSS®
SINCE 1846

And what better definition for elegance than new Classic Black® writing instruments for women. With 22K gold electroplate appointments and convenient pen purse, in beautiful gift packaging. The satin black finish is the newest Cross for Women. Others come in 10K and 14K gold filled and sterling silver. All mechanically guaranteed for a lifetime. Suggested retail prices from $16.50.

Courtesy A. T. Cross Co.

Table 6–2:
Two recent views of
social class in America

Gilbert–Kahl	Coleman–Rainwater
Upper Americans	**Upper Americans**
The Capitalist Class (1%)—Their investment decisions shape the national economy; income mostly from assets, earned/inherited; prestige university connections	*Upper-Upper* (0.3%)—The "capital S society" world of inherited wealth, aristocratic names
Upper Middle Class (14%)—Upper managers, professionals, medium businessmen; college educated; family income ideally runs nearly twice the national average	*Lower-Upper* (1.2%)—The newer social elite, drawn from current professional, corporate leadership
	Upper-Middle (12.5%)—The rest of college graduate managers and professionals; lifestyle centers on private clubs, causes, and the arts
Middle Americans	**Middle Americans**
Middle Class (33%)—Middle-level white-collar; top-level blue-collar; education past high school typical; income somewhat above the national average	*Middle Class* (32%)—Average-pay white-collar workers and their blue-collar friends; live on "the better side of town," try to "do the proper things"
Working Class (32%)—Middle-level blue-collar; lower-level white-collar; income runs slightly below the national average; education is also slightly below	*Working Class* (38%)—Average-pay blue-collar workers; lead "working class lifestyle" whatever the income, school background, and job
Marginal and Lower Americans	**Lower Americans**
The Working Poor (11–12%)—Below mainstream America in living standard, but above the poverty line; low-paid service workers, operatives; some high school education	*"A lower group of people but not the lowest"* (9%)—Working, not on welfare; living standard is just above poverty; behavior judged "crude," "trashy"
The Underclass (8–9%)—Depend primarily on welfare system for sustenance; living standard below poverty line; not regularly employed; lack schooling	*"Real Lower-Lower"* (7%)—On welfare, visibly poverty-stricken, usually out of work (or have "the dirtiest jobs"); "bums," "common criminals"

Source: Reprinted with permission from Richard P. Coleman, "The Continuing Significance of Social Class to Marketing," *Journal of Consumer Research* 10 (December 1983), p. 267.

participation, family history, cultural level, recreational habits, and physical appearance.[23] Using these factors, the Coleman–Rainwater social class system was developed to reflect the contemporary social class structure of the United States. Table 6–2 provides a description of this view of American class structure. The Gilbert–Kahl view is also shown. Notice the strong similarity between the two. Both acknowledge three dominant groupings of Americans and offer similar socioeconomic profiles.[24] Either approach would be useful for marketing purposes. Presenting both here merely highlights the strong agreement on the meaning of social class.

Social class encompasses many aspects of a household— socioeconomic

[23] Richard P. Coleman, "The Continuing Significance of Social Class to Marketing," *Journal of Consumer Research* 10 (December 1983), pp. 265–80.

[24] For more on each view of social class, see Dennis Gilbert and Joseph A. Kahl, *The American Class Structure: A New Synthesis* (Homewood, Ill.: Dorsey Press, 1982); and Richard P. Coleman and Lee P. Rainwater, *Social Standing in America: New Dimensions of Class* (New York: Basic Books, 1978).

Table 6–3:
Social class differences in information usage patterns

Behavior pattern	Social class				
	Upper	Upper-middle	Lower-middle	Upper-lower	Lower-lower
Look for grocery specials in newspapers*	2.58	3.31	3.55	3.79	3.56
Grocery sale ads read carefully*	2.71	3.21	3.55	4.02	3.72
Mail coupon usage*	2.79	3.18	3.45	3.68	3.81
Newspaper coupon* usage	2.00	2.67	2.85	2.93	2.81
Hours watching evening TV	3.56	3.89	4.65	5.34	5.07

* 5-point rating scale measures.

Source: Charles M. Schanginger, "Social Class versus Income Revisited: An Empirical Investigation," *Journal of Marketing Research* 18 (May 1981), pp. 192–208.

Table 6–4:
Social class differences in consumption of generic products

Product category	Social class				
	Upper	Upper-middle	Lower-middle	Upper-lower	Lower-lower
Food/beverages (frequency of use)					
Bread	4.04	4.67	4.56	4.57	5.06
Margarine	2.41	3.48	3.12	3.18	3.45
Luncheon meat	2.67	3.65	3.58	3.70	4.00
Potato chips	1.96	2.58	3.15	3.08	3.30
Rice	4.63	4.12	4.00	3.43	3.09
TV dinners	1.11	1.32	1.35	1.53	1.76
Soda water	2.93	2.03	1.54	1.59	1.48
Scotch	2.85	2.18	2.08	1.61	1.55
Liquor	2.44	2.18	2.19	1.90	1.42
Cosmetic goods (frequency of use)					
Facial makeup base	1.22	1.51	2.04	1.37	1.09
Eyeshadow	1.67	1.44	1.79	1.12	0.82
Eyebrow pencil	0.18	0.59	1.47	0.63	0.88
Lipstick	2.52	2.74	3.19	2.47	2.33
Appliances (percent owning)					
Dishwasher	55.6	57.5	49.1	28.3	21.2
Freezer	40.7	70.0	66.0	66.7	36.4

Source: Charles M. Schaninger, "Social Class versus Income Revisited: An Empirical Investigation," *Journal of Marketing Research* 18 (May 1981), pp. 192–208.

characteristics, values, reference groups. It is therefore related to a variety of consumer behavior patterns:

1. *Media usage.* Individuals in the higher classes spend more time reading and listening to the radio and less time watching TV than those in lower classes. Content preferences also differ. People in the higher classes read more news magazines, nonfiction material, and editorial content.[25]

2. *Information search.* When evaluating purchase alternatives, consumers in lower social classes engage in less information search than other

[25] Hawkins et al., *Consumer Behavior,* pp. 195–97.

Table 6–5: Social class differences related to brand choice	Social class				
Product category	**Upper**	**Upper-middle**	**Lower-middle**	**Upper-lower**	**Lower-lower**
Frozen vegetables (usage frequency)					
Economy packs	3.15	2.23	2.40	1.87	1.52
National brands	2.81	3.50	2.92	2.67	2.03
Store brands	3.71	3.80	3.56	2.72	2.45
Beverages (usage frequency)					
Tang	1.63	1.74	1.77	1.64	2.82
Domestic wines					
Red	2.22	2.38	2.71	2.51	2.06
Rosé	1.44	1.90	2.31	2.10	1.82
White	1.85	2.15	2.25	2.08	1.52
Imported wines					
Red	4.22	3.00	2.77	2.20	1.52
Rosé	2.37	2.10	2.19	1.76	1.48
White	3.41	2.87	2.56	2.08	1.42
Clothing					
Number of dresses over $60 . .	0.78	0.60	0.33	0.16	0.21
Price of last men's suit bought . .	$170	$141	$148	$127	$106
Furniture					
Value of living room furniture . .	$2,316	$1,837	$1,227	$1,122	$1,014
Value of dining room furniture . .	1,589	1,032	789	574	494
Value of bedroom furniture . . .	1,098	843	687	599	550

Source: Charles M. Schaninger, "Social Class versus Income Revisited: An Empirical Investigation," *Journal of Marketing Research* 18 (May 1981), pp. 192–208.

consumers. They have limited access to information sources and less training in processing purchase-related information. Table 6–3 highlights some key differences in information usage across five social classes observed in a recent study.

3. *Store choice.* Social class influences the types of stores shopped. Schaninger found, for example, that lower-social-class families tend to buy matched living room furniture from discount department or regular furniture stores. Upper-middle-class families buy their furniture individually at separate times from specialized furniture stores.[26] Social class also relates to whether store shopping occurs at all. Higher social classes tend more to buy through mail or telephone orders.[27]

4. *Product consumption.* Social classes differ in the generic products they consume. The entire set of factors distinguishing social classes is at play: income, occupation, reference groups, values, etc. Table 6–4 summarizes some key differences.

5. *Brand choice.* Social class membership influences the specific types and brands of products chosen. Examples appear in Table 6–5.

---

[26] Charles M. Schaninger, "Social Class versus Income Revisited: An Empirical Investigation," *Journal of Marketing Research* 18 (May 1981), pp. 192–208.

[27] Hawkins et al., *Consumer Behavior,* p. 198.

The relevance of social class to marketing. The distinct composition of different social classes makes social class a useful basis for segmenting the market and developing unique marketing programs for the segments. This usage of social class is particularly evident at the retail level. Many department store chains orient their operations to a particular social class. K mart serves the lower classes; Sears, Roebuck and J.C. Penney serve the middle classes; Bloomingdale's and Neiman–Marcus serve the upper class. Social class also offers a basis for understanding behavior. This is evident in a study of social class and commercial bank credit card usage.[28] This study observed that lower-social-class members used bank cards (MasterCard, VISA) as convenient credit for rather significant purchases. Higher-class members used them as alternatives to cash for smaller, more frequent purchases. Here we see social class effects on the motives underlying behavior.

While social class offers a way to distinctly group consumers, it can still fall short of providing "clean" homogeneous groupings. This is especially true in the large middle class. As Coleman puts it:

> A "prototype" household of middle-class Middle American status has as its head a man employed in some lower-management office job, earning between $24,000 and $29,999 a year (1983 urban-average dollars), whose wife isn't working, so that is all the family income. Almost as likely to be middle class is a divorcee, with two years of college as educational credentials, who is trying to support two children on a legal secretary's salary of as little as $13,500—and who may be best friend and frequent bridge-playing chum to the wife in the first case. Another middle-class home will contain a working couple, both in office jobs earning a combined total of $42,000 or even $45,000 a year. A fourth might have as its head the owner of a bowling alley and restaurant whose wife may or may not be helping to run it—or the owner could be a widow, divorcee, or never-married woman; in any case, the living standard projected by house, car(s), and clothes suggest an income of $60,000 or $70,000 a year, yet the social status is still middle class because, through lack of mobility aspirations and/or social skills, no Upper American connections and acceptance have been established.[29]

Lifestyle and psychographics

Lifestyle offers a way to group consumers on a variety of factors that often overcomes the deficiencies of social class.

lifestyle

> **Lifestyle** refers to the overall pattern of living associated with an individual or family. It reflects patterns and interrelationships among the entire set of individual and social factors—i.e., the **psychographics** of an individual or family.

---

[28] H. Lee Mathews and J. W. Slocum, Jr., "Social Class and Commercial Bank Credit Card Usage," *Journal of Marketing* 33 (January 1969), pp. 71–78.

[29] Reprinted with permission from Richard P. Coleman, "The Continuing Significance of Social Class to Marketing," *Journal of Consumer Research* 10 (December 1983), p. 268.

Fitting a product to a
lifestyle.

"I'm too busy to take lazy vitamins."

The study of lifestyle attempts to identify groupings, or "clusters," of consumers who exhibit similar patterns among the many lifestyle dimensions. Researchers develop a battery of items encompassing an array of aspects of an individual's life. One popular approach examines activities, interests, and opinions (AIO). (See Table 6–6.) Consumers indicate their agreement or disagreement with a series of AIO statements. Then statistical analysis of these responses determines if distinct groupings of consumers exist. If they do, the result is a lifestyle profile of each of a set of market segments. This profile captures the nature of consumers

Table 6–6: Lifestyle dimensions	Activities	Interests	Opinions
	Work	Family	Themselves
	Hobbies	Home	Social issues
	Social events	Job	Politics
	Vacation	Community	Business
	Entertainment	Recreation	Economics
	Club membership	Fashion	Education
	Community	Food	Products
	Shopping	Media	Future
	Sports	Achievements	Culture

Source: Joseph T. Plummer, "The Concept and Application of Lifestyle Segmentation," *Journal of Marketing* 38 (January 1974), pp. 33–37.

in a segment and reveals their different product requirements. It's an excellent tool for matching products and consumer needs.

Lifestyle research can yield different typologies of consumers. Some capture the entire thrust of living. One such typology is emerging from the Standard Research Institute's (SRI) *Values and Lifestyle (VALS)* program. VALS offers a systematic classification of American adults. Its typology comprises four comprehensive groups, subdivided into nine lifestyles, each defined by a distinct array of values, drives, beliefs, needs, dreams, and special points of view.[30] (See Table 6–7.) The four comprehensive groups are:

1. *Need-driven groups.* These people are farthest removed from the cultural mainstream. They exist in extreme poverty and have no vision of or hope for the future. They deny rather than express values. They find rewards in the emotional and spiritual aspects of life. Two distinct subgroups make up the need-driven group: Survivors and Sustainers.

2. *Outer-directed group.* These people represent the mainstream. They respond to others and behave to please others. Their ways of life are geared to the visible, tangible, and materialistic. Their perspective includes a concern for others, affiliation with institutions, and a sense of the nation. The diverse array of values represented in the outer-directed group is reflected by its three subgroups: Belongers, Emulators, and Achievers.

3. *Inner-directed groups.* Internal forces drive the lives of these people. They are highly self-reliant and indifferent to social status and money. Many are active in social movements and support modern trends. Inner-directed people tend to be self-expressive, individualistic, concerned with people, and impassioned. Their diversity results in three distinct inner-directed lifestyles: I-Am-Me's, Experientials, and the Societally Conscious.

---

[30] Arnold Mitchell, *The Nine American Lifestyles* (New York: MacMillan, 1983).

Table 6–7: The nine American lifestyles

Need-driven groups

Survivor

Old, intensely poor; fearful; despairing; far removed from the cultural mainstream; misfits

Number: 6 million
Age: Most over 65
Sex: 77% female
Income: 100% under $7,500
Education: Median, 8th–9th grade

Sustainer

Living on the edge of poverty; angry and resentful; street-wise; involved in the underground economy

Number: 11 million
Age: 58% under 35
Sex: 55% female
Income: Median, $11,000
Education: Median, 11th grade

Outer-directed groups

Belonger

Aging; traditional and conventional; contented; intensely patriotic; sentimental; deeply stable

Number: 57 million
Age: Median, 52
Sex: 68% female
Income: Median, $17,300
Education: Median, high school graduate

Emulator

Youthful and ambitious; macho; show-off; trying to break into the system, to make it big

Number: 16 million
Age: Median, 27
Sex: 53% male
Income: Median, $18,000
Education: high school graduate plus

Achiever

Middle-aged and prosperous; able leaders; self-assured; materialistic; builders of the "American dream"

Number: 37 million
Age: Median, 43
Sex: 60% male
Income: Median, $31,400
Education: 32% college graduates or more

Inner-directed groups

I-Am-Me

Transition state; exhibitionist and narcissistic; young; impulsive; dramatic; experimental; active; inventive

Number: 8 million
Age: 91% under 25
Sex: 64% male
Income: Median, $8,800
Education: Some college

Experiential

Youthful; seek direct experience; person-centered; artistic; intensely oriented toward inner growth

Number: 11 million
Age: Median, 27
Sex: 55% female
Income: Median, $23,800
Education: 38% college graduates or more

Societally conscious

Mission-oriented; leaders of single-issue groups; mature; successful; some live lives of voluntary simplicity

Number: 14 million
Age: Median, 39
Sex: 52% male
Income: Median, $27,200
Education: 58% college graduates; 39% some graduate school

Combined outer- and inner-directed group

Integrated

Psychologically mature; large field of vision; tolerant and understanding; sense of fittingness

Number: 3.2 million

Source: Abridged with permission of Macmillan Publishing Company from *The Nine American Lifestyles* by Arnold Mitchell. Copyright © 1983 by Arnold Mitchell.

4. *Combined outer- and inner-directed groups.* These people combine the best qualities of the inner- and outer-directed. They blend the power of outer-directedness with the sensitivity of inner-directedness. They are psychologically mature, tolerant, self-confident, and self-actualizing, and they possess a world perspective. They are the Integrateds of the VALS typology.

The VALS typology represents a general view of lifestyle patterns. Much like social class, it offers a basis for segmenting the entire consumer market. Yet, it's often more useful to identify lifestyle segments in terms of a specific product class. In this approach users of a particular product are segmented into distinct lifestyle groups. A firm can then develop marketing programs for each segment of users. Wolverine World Wide doubled the sales of its Hush Puppies boots by recognizing that boots are no longer worn primarily by agricultural and industrial workers, but also by hikers, campers, and "urban cowboys."[31]

Culture and subculture

The most pervasive and enduring influence on an individual is **culture.** It is the most pervasive in that it cuts across virtually all aspects of one's life. It is the most enduring in that it exerts influence throughout an individual's life.

culture

> **Culture** refers to a set of learned beliefs, values, attitudes, habits, and forms of behavior shared by members of a society and transmitted from generation to generation.

Culture functions primarily as a normative influence on behavior. It establishes guidelines, or norms, for behavior and enforces them. Conformity is rewarded. Nonconformity or deviant behavior is punished. Norms that are important to a society become laws, and their violation results in criminal prosecution. Lapses in less important norms (proper eating behavior) are punished more informally (social embarrassment, ostracizing).

From a marketing management perspective, the relevance of culture is two-fold. First, though culture changes gradually, it does change. And often with implications for consumer behavior. In Chapter 4 we saw how cultural norms with respect to family size influenced the birthrate and the market for baby products—not to mention the overall age structure of American society. Marketers must anticipate such effects. And they must ascertain the relevance of change to their firms and industry. Second, culture is obviously tied to multinational marketing. A firm that markets to different cultures must recognize their differences and adapt marketing policies to their unique aspects. What will sell in Japan may

---

[31] "Squeeze More Profits out of Mature Markets," *Marketing News,* March 18, 1983, p. 23.

not sell in France. And what will sell in both may not necessarily be marketed in the same way. In Chapter 23 we will look more closely at the nature of international marketing.

The phenomenon of culture is most meaningful to marketing in the United States when *subcultures* are considered. Subculture members share many of the society's cultural norms but also share certain distinctive values and customs among themselves. These unique norms are learned within the subculture the same way overall cultural norms are learned by an entire society. Subcultures represent different segments of the market to the extent that their distinctive customs affect their behavior as consumers.

Subcultures in the United States can be defined along a number of dimensions. Perhaps the most common is ethnicity. The black and Hispanic subcultures, say, represent two prominent segments of American society. Other dimensions used to identify subcultures include national origin, religion, and age. Figure 6–6 identifies the major subcultures in the United States today. Each represents a unique segment of the overall consumer market that may serve as a target market. Two deserve special attention.

The black subculture.   The largest of American subcultures, blacks number over 28 million, representing approximately 12 percent of the population. The demographic and socioeconomic profile of this group (see Table 6–8) reveals the disadvantaged nature of the subculture. However, the black subculture still represents a viable market segment, with $150 billion in buying power. Also, more and more blacks are entering professions and realizing higher incomes.

Many companies now recognize the marketing opportunities in the black subculture. They are targeting products to fit the unique needs of this segment. The classic example is Ultra Sheen—a line of cosmetics aimed directly at black adults. Similarly, Fashion Fair, a quality cosmetic line for black women, recognizes the unique cosmetic shadings required by black women.

Figure 6–6: Subcultures of the United States

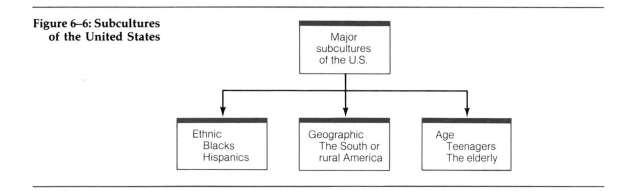

Marketing to the black consumer with a different ad but the same message.

	Characteristic	Black subculture	Hispanic subculture	Whites
Table 6–8: Demographic and socioeconomic characteristics of blacks, Hispanics, and whites	*Demographic*			
	Median age.	25.2	23.0	31.2
	Mean family size	3.7	3.4	3.2
	Percent urban	81.1	87.6	73.3
	Percent households with female head.	47.2	28.2	11.9
	Socioeconomic			
	Median income	$12,618	$14,711	$20,840
Source: *Statistical Abstract of the United States, 1983.*	Percent with 4+ years in college	8.4	7.7	17.2
	Percent white-collar job	37.8	21.6	54.3

In assessing the black subculture, a company should realize the unique marketing-related nature of this segment of consumers.

Blacks tend to distinguish themselves as consumers in a variety of ways:

1. *Spending behavior.* In black and white families of comparable incomes, blacks spend less and save more than whites.

2. *Product usage.* Blacks spend proportionately more than whites for clothing, personal care, and home furnishings. They spend less on medical care, food, and transportation. With respect to specific products, black households buy more record albums, orange juice, rice, and soft drinks than white households.

3. *Brand choice.* A 1981 study of 2,400 black consumers found a higher degree of loyalty to national brands among blacks than whites. Also, blacks are more loyal to certain specific brands— Listerine, Tide, SOS, Maxwell House, Minute Maid, Crisco, and Skippy.

4. *Shopping behavior.* Blacks make fewer shopping trips than whites. They attach more importance to a friendly atmosphere, convenience, and service. They are more likely to shop at discount stores and less likely to shop by mail or phone.

5. *Media exposure.* Blacks listen to radio and read magazines more than whites. There are magazines directed specifically at blacks (*Ebony, Essence*) as well as many black-oriented radio stations.[32]

An important cautionary note is appropriate here. The black subculture has a distinct racial identity related to some aspects of consumer behavior. But it possesses internal diversity approaching that of the overall market. In fact, one study has identified five distinct lifestyle groups within the black female population. (See Table 6–9.) Thus, it would be an oversimplification to treat the black subculture as a homogeneous segment in all cases. Segmentation within the black subculture may be necessary. For

[32] Assael, *Consumer Behavior,* pp. 311–13.

The Hispanic subculture can be reached through Spanish-language issues of magazines. Here we see Spanish-language and English-language versions of the same advertisement.

Table 6–9: Lifestyle differences among black females age 18–49	Segment	Size	Age	Income	Basic lifestyle attitude
	Conservative traditionalist	32%	Older	Higher	Views sex, drugs, and liquor as steps along the path to degeneration
	Fashion conscious	31%	Younger	Lower	Liberated in ideas about sex, liquor, and drugs; likes to try new hairstyles and would rather dress for fashion than comfort
	Independent	16%	Middle	Significantly higher	Outgoing and on the way up; financially secure and independent; prefer living in suburbs to city
	Girl next door	12%	Younger	Significantly lower	Described as the girl next door; she has strong moral values and likes trying new hairstyles as much as she likes to bake, which she often does
	Conservative thinker	9%	Older	Significantly lower	They shop for sales, disapprove of installment purchases, and believe that men should rule the household while women take care of it

Source: "New Survey Reveals Five Lifestyle Segments of Age 18–49 Black Women," *Marketing News*, August 21, 1981, p. 6.

example, Johnson Products (makers of Ultra-Sheen) segments the black market into two groups: those who strive for the middle-class lifestyle (strivers) and those who seek a separate identity (nonstrivers). They target products to both groups. Ads to the striver group emphasize middle-class lifestyle values. Ads to the nonstrivers emphasize ethnic identification.

The Hispanic subculture. Hispanics represent the second largest and fastest growing minority group in the United States. At close to 10 percent of the population, Hispanics already possess over $50 billion in purchasing power. The rapid growth of this subculture increases its attractiveness as a target market. But its demographic–socioeconomic profile is quite distinct from that of the general population. (See Table 6–7.)

A great degree of homogeneity characterizes the Hispanic subculture. Hispanics continue to use the Spanish language. They cling strongly to their original culture values, including paternal leadership and strong family ties. Stability should characterize this group even as it grows to become the largest minority group by 1990.[33]

[33] Danny N. Bellenger and Humberto Valencia, "Understanding the Hispanic Market," *Business Horizons*, May–June 1982, pp. 47–50.

Certain distinct buying patterns are evident in the Hispanic subculture:

1. An emphasis on quality.
2. A high level of brand loyalty.
3. Greater-than-average usage of packaged goods (beverages, canned goods, beauty aids).
4. Less price-consciousness than their income suggests and a disdain for coupons and premiums.
5. Heavy TV exposure and less-than-average magazine reading.[34]

As the Hispanic market grows, more and more products will be specifically targeted to it. One example is Del Monte's line of Mexican foods. To date, Hispanics' effect on marketing shows up mainly in specialized national advertising campaigns. There are also a national Spanish TV network (SIN), many local Spanish TV and radio stations, national Spanish magazines (*Vanidades*), and Spanish versions of such national magazines as *Cosmopolitan* and *Reader's Digest*. These vehicles enhance the ability to advertise specifically to Hispanic consumers.

---

[34] Assael, *Consumer Behavior*, p. 320.

SUMMARY

Consumer behavior is influenced by the social environment. The nature of social influence is two-fold. Normative social influence produces conformity to the expectations of others. Informational social influence effects the acceptance of information from others as evidence of reality. These influences come from a number of sources in the social environment.

Personal influence is exerted on the attitudes and behavior of one individual by another. Opinion leaders—individuals knowledgeable and objective in a particular area—are sources of personal influence. Another type of personal influence—identification—occurs when one adopts a behavior or opinion of another because it is consistent with a desired self-image.

The family represents a major source of influence in the long and short run. Over time the family serves as a socialization agent. It passes on consumer skills and knowledge. In the short run each family member possesses a relative degree of influence on certain purchase decisions. Wives or husbands may have more influence, or influence is equally shared. Children also exert influence.

Reference groups—membership or aspiration groups whose standards serve as a comparison point for the individual's behavior—can exert either normative or informational influence on an individual. Normative influence occurs through rewarding (or punishing) the individual for conformity (or nonconformity) to the group's norms. The purchase of highly conspicuous products/brands is particularly susceptible to reference group influence. Informational influence from reference groups occurs when an individual uses group norms to determine appropriate behavior not subject to group pressures.

Social class—groupings based on occupation, source of income, housing, and residential location—represent a broader source of influence. Distinct consumer behavior patterns exist between social classes, allowing marketers to treat an individual social class as a unique segment of the market.

Psychographics, the study of lifestyle, identifies clusters of consumers who exhibit similar patterns in their activities, interests, and opinions. Profiles that capture the totality of consumer behavior allow a closer match of products and consumers.

Culture is the set of values, beliefs, and behaviors shared by members of a society. It helps explain cross-national difference in consumer behavior. Subcultures contain people who share distinctive values and customs. Two major subcultures in the United States are the black and the Hispanic.

KEY CONCEPTS

Normative social influence	Socialization process	Conspicuousness of a product
Informational social influence	Consumer socialization process	Social class
Personal influence	Family decision-making roles	Lifestyle
Word-of-mouth communication	Reference group influence	Psychographics
Opinion leaders	Reference groups	VALS
Two-step flow of communication	Membership groups	Culture
Identification	Aspiration groups	Subculture
Socialization agent		

DISCUSSION QUESTIONS AND EXERCISES

1. For each of the following products analyze how you would be influenced by your social environment if you were going to buy the product: stereo, hair dryer, suitcase. Identify each likely source of influence and the nature of the influence it would exert on you.

2. Reference groups can be either aspirational groups or membership groups. Discuss the relevance of these two types of reference groups to the VALS lifestyle typology.

3. Looking back at Table 6–1, how might products shift over time from one category to another? Trace the movement for several product categories.

4. Develop a sales presentation for a particular product that incorporates informational social influence.

5. If you are married, describe recent family purchase decisions that were husband-dominated, wife-dominated, and jointly made. If you are single, try to do the same for your parents. Assume the patterns of influence for each purchase exist for many families. Then discuss the marketing implications for each product.

6. In this chapter retailing was identified as an area particularly concerned with social class distinctions in the marketplace. Discuss as many marketing differences as you can between department stores aimed at the lower, middle, and upper classes.

7. As the Hispanic subculture grows, more and more products will be developed specifically for this segment of the market. Identify what you think are some products that might be appropriate to aim at Hispanic consumers.

CHAPTER 7

The consumer decision process

The basic tasks of the consumer

The consumer decision process
    Stages of the consumer decision process
    Variations in the overall process
    Involvement
    Problem recognition
    Internal search
    External search
    Information receipt
    Decision
    Postdecision

Consumer decision process and the
    classification of consumer goods
    Convenience goods
    Shopping goods
    Specialty goods

A summary of consumer behavior

Key concepts

Discussion questions and exercises

The entire set of personal and social factors influences the process by which the consumer reaches a purchase decision. But these factors do not reveal the nature of the process itself.

Understanding the decision process can help marketers determine the role of marketing strategy variables: where and how they operate and the nature of their influence. Thus, an understanding of how consumers reach purchase decisions contributes mainly to the phase of strategic planning that involves marketing program management. It aids the formulation of strategies and tactics employing the marketing decision variables. Therefore, this chapter presents a framework for studying how consumers reach purchase decisions.[1]

THE BASIC TASKS OF THE CONSUMER

Suppose you are contemplating the purchase of a personal computer for home use. Ultimately, you must decide whether or not to buy a personal computer and, if so, which brand to buy. In order to reach these decisions, you must accomplish several consumer behavior tasks:

1. Determine the set of evaluative criteria to use in judging alternative brands.
2. Determine the set of brands to evaluate.
3. Obtain sufficient information on each brand to allow an evaluation.
4. Using this information, perform an evaluation of each brand in order to decide whether or not to buy a personal computer and, if so, which brand.

These tasks are not necessarily separate and distinct. Some of them may occur simultaneously. For example, while identifying and obtaining information on brands, you may discover important product attributes to use as evaluative criteria.

Some of these criteria may emerge as you perform other tasks as well. But the initial set results mainly from the needs the computer is intended to satisfy and your ability to pay. You will identify more evaluative criteria if you plan to use the computer for a variety of purposes than if your use of it will be limited. Also, the uses to which you will put the product will help determine the relative importance of each criterion. Table 7–1 summarizes your possible evaluative criteria for buying a computer for a wide variety of purposes and for only a few purposes.

Your intended uses for the computer will guide your choice of the alternative brands to consider. So will a variety of information sources (opinion leaders, ads, store visits, news articles).

The evaluative criteria (product attributes) and alternative brands together define the structure of the personal computer evaluation task. Figure 7–1 brings them together in matrixlike fashion. Figuratively speaking, you will have to complete enough cells of the matrix to allow yourself

---

[1] Space does not permit an exhaustive treatment of the process in this book. For a fuller treatment, see J. Bettman, *An Information Processing Theory of Consumer Choice* (Reading, Mass.: Addison-Wesley Publishing, 1979).

Table 7–1: Evaluative criteria for two types of personal computer buyers

	Extensive user (word processing, statistics, accounting, storage)	**Limited user (storage games, some word processing)**
	Memory capacity	Type of software included in purchase
	Number of disk drives	Portability
	Type of monitor	Price
	Modem connection	
	Type of software included in purchase	
	Compatibility with other software	
	Price	

to make a decision. You can then use this information to determine if one or more brands are worthy of purchase. If no brands are worthy, you may decide not to buy at all. If only one brand is worthy, both your determination to buy and your choice of brands may be made. If one or more brands are worthy, the decision to buy may be made but the brand choice still remains.

Figure 7–2 provides an abstract view of the structure of the consumer-choice task. It shows that multiple objects are available to the consumer as alternative problem-solving means. Depending on the level of decision to be made, the objects may be alternative generic products, product forms, or brands. The consumer uses a set of attributes to evaluate each object and different sets of attributes at each level of decision.

Again, we view the consumer's choice task in terms of a matrix. The consumer must fill the cells with evaluations or perceptions of the objects on enough attributes to be able to choose one (or none) of the objects. All of the cells need not be filled. But the consumer must fill enough to feel comfortable making a decision. For example, you may decide you won't spend over $4,000 for a personal computer. Once you fill in the

Figure 7–1: Structure of the personal computer evaluation task for extensive user

		Brands			
	Evaluative criteria	**IBM PC**	**Radio Shack**	**Apple**	**Hewlett-Packard**
	Memory capacity				
	Number of disk drives				
	Type of monitor				
	Modem connections				
	Software included				
	Compatibility with other software				
	Price				

Figure 7–2: Structure of the consumer-choice task	Objects			
Evaluative criteria	Object A	Object B	· · ·	Object Z
Attribute 1	A_1	B_1	· · ·	Z_1
Attribute 2	A_2	B_2	· · ·	Z_2
Attribute 3	A_3	B_3	· · ·	Z_3
'	'	'		'
'	'	'		'
'	'	'		'
Attribute n	A_n	B_n	· · ·	Z_n

Source: Steven H. Chaffee and Jack M. McLeod, "Consumer Decisions and Information Use," in *Consumer Behavior: Theoretical Sources,* edited by Scott Ward, Thomas S. Robertson, © 1973, p. 391. Reprinted by permission of Prentice-Hall, Inc., Englewood Cliff, New Jersey.

price cell for a brand costing over $4,000, you will probably not be concerned with other information about the brand and will ignore its other attributes.

The size of the matrix will vary across products, especially in terms of the number of evaluative criteria. Complex durable goods might have many evaluative criteria. For a simple food item (frozen orange juice) perhaps only price and taste would serve. Also, two consumers contemplating a purchase in the same product category will probably differ in the number and/or nature of evaluative criteria and the brands they consider. Many of the personal and social factors discussed in Chapters 5 and 6 contribute to variations in the matrix across consumers.

THE CONSUMER DECISION PROCESS

When performing the tasks we just discussed, consumers engage in a variety of activities. We need an organized framework to identify these activities.

consumer decision process

> The **consumer decision process** is a framework that organizes consumer problem-solving activities into a sequence of stages.

We use the consumer decision process to *study* consumer efforts in solving a problem. It should not be construed as a strict sequence. Every consumer won't adhere to it in purchasing every product. Some stages may be skipped entirely. The framework's usefulness lies in pointing out potential consumer activities.

Stages of the consumer decision process

Six stages make up the consumer decision process. (See Figure 7–3.) They are:

1. ***Problem recognition.*** A state of discomfort exists in the consumer sufficient in intensity to activate a search for a means to alleviate it.

2. ***Internal search.*** The consumer examines existing knowledge held in long-term memory to identify and evaluate alternative solutions.

3. ***External search.*** The consumer engages in an active search for information from external sources of information.

4. ***Information receipt.*** Various cognitive processes occur when the consumer deals with incoming information from external sources.

5. ***Decision.*** The consumer integrates in some way the preexisting and acquired information to form an estimate of the utility of alternative objects and to make a choice.

6. ***Postdecision.*** The consumer undergoes cognitive and behavioral phenomena after the decision has been implemented that influence the subsequent versions of the process for similar problems.

Figure 7–3: The consumer decision process

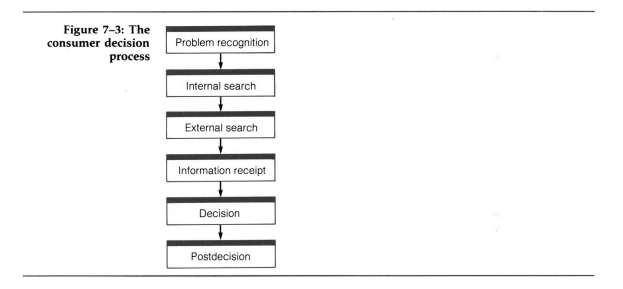

The extensiveness and complexity of each stage can vary, depending on the individual and the nature of the decision. For example, expensive or complex products, and those with social consequences associated with their use, involve an extensive, active information search. When consumers have considerable and existing knowledge in a product class, internal search will occur. This minimizes the need for external search.

Variations in the overall process

The consumer decision process can be characterized in terms of its overall complexity or extensiveness. Howard described these variations in the overall process:

1. ***Extensive problem solving*** occurs when a product class is new to a consumer. Existing knowledge is limited; the consumer is re-

quired to develop evaluative criteria and identify and evaluate alternative objects. An extensive external search process results.

2. ***Limited problem solving*** occurs when the consumer has previous experience in and considerable knowledge about a product class. When a change occurs in the product class (e.g., a new brand is introduced), limited effort is required to evaluate its relevance to the consumer.

3. ***Routinized response behavior*** occurs when the consumer, based on considerable prior experience in the product class, has developed a routine and virtually automatic response to a problem. The process is absent of any search and evaluation efforts.[2]

Howard suggests that these types of problem solving form an evolutionary process through which a consumer goes over time when dealing with a product class. (See Figure 7–4.) The first exposure to a product class requires extensive problem solving. Experience makes limited problem solving sufficient to deal with changes in the product class. Ultimately, once all changes have been dealt with, a routine solution is developed. Of course, the dynamic nature of many product classes often precludes a consumer from arriving at a routine response.

Personal computers serve to illustrate the evolutionary process. At first, consumers knew very little about their uses, capabilities, operating features, and so on. People contemplating a purchase engaged in extensive problem solving to fill these gaps in their knowledge. Many became computer buffs and developed extensive knowledge of personal computers. When IBM entered the market, these people possessed the knowledge structure to become easily acquainted with the IBM brand. They required only limited problem solving. However, the rapid changes in personal computer technology—not to mention their high prices—prevent consumers from developing a routinized response in this product category.

Routinized response behavior more likely develops with regard to frequently used, low-priced items—such as packaged foods, for instance. Consumers develop experience and knowledge of these items quite readily and find extensive or limited problem solving isn't worth the effort. A routinized response—always buying the same brand—is easiest.

The evolutionary nature of the decision process suggests some important tasks for marketing strategy. For example, when introducing a new brand in a product class for which routinized response behavior is common, the marketer must jolt the consumer into a limited problem-solving effort. This gets the consumer to consider the new brand and perhaps buy it. In part, the success of Miller Lite beer resulted from marketing's effectiveness in getting consumers to realize that a less filling, low-calorie

---

[2] John A. Howard, *Consumer Behavior: Theory and Action* (New York: McGraw-Hill, 1977), pp. 9–10.

**Figure 7–4:
Evolutionary
development of the
consumer decision
process**

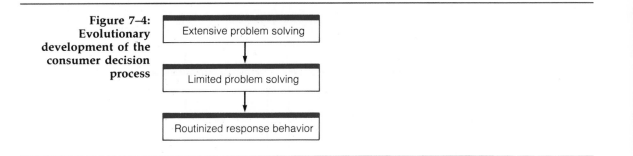

beer could provide a full flavor. Miller's success (and that of its followers) has created a segment of consumers who routinely drink low-calorie beers! Its task now is to preserve the routine response in these consumers.

Involvement

Involvement theory provides another view of variations in the overall decision process.

involvement

> **Involvement** refers to the economic and social importance of a purchase as viewed by the consumer.

High-involvement purchases include big-priced products relating to a consumer's self-identity. *Low-involvement purchases* include unimportant, low-priced products with no social meaning attached to them. High-involvement decisions entail an extensive decision process. The consumer has many attributes and alternative brands to consider as part of a substantial external search effort. For low-involvement purchases, it is not worth the consumer's time and effort to evaluate a large number of products on very many attributes. A limited decision process with little or no external search and a simple evaluation results. (See Figure 7–5.)

The involvement level of a purchase situation has important marketing implications. Take product presentation. For high-involvement purchases, the consumer wants a lot of information about a brand. Print media allow more information to be presented than broadcast media. Therefore, advertising in magazines occurs to a greater extent for products representing high-involvement purchases than for those representing low-involvement purchases. Broadcast media (TV, radio) dominate in the advertising of low-involvement products. They allow frequent repetition of simple messages.[3] A closer examination of the nature of each individual stage

---

[3] For more on involvement, see James F. Engel and Roger Blackwell, *Consumer Behavior*, 4th ed. (Hinsdale, Ill.: Dryden Press, 1982), Chapter 2.

Figure 7–5: High-involvement and low-involvement decision processes

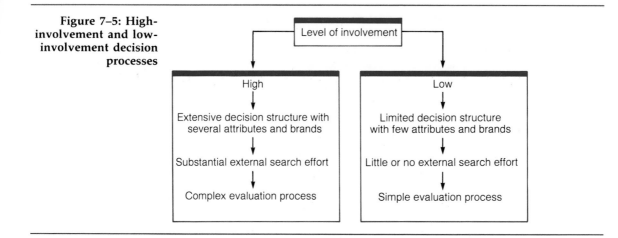

in the consumer decision process will be more insightful here. We need it to better determine the role of marketing-related activities within the process.

Problem recognition

The problem recognition stage activates the consumer decision process. Our previous discussion of motives and needs helps us understand this stage. A consumer is motivated to behave when a problem becomes intense enough to create a state of discomfort the consumer would like to alleviate. Problem recognition occurs when the consumer's existing state is perceived to be discrepant from a desired state. (See Figure 7–6.) The desired state derives from the motives of the individual, as we discussed in Chapter 5. This discrepancy between actual and ideal states activates the consumer to consider forms of behavior to bring them in line and alleviate the discomfort. Some levels of discomfort are tolerable, however, so not all problems result in a search for solutions.

Variations in the problem recognition stage result from the *magnitude* and *complexity* of the discrepancy between existing and desired states. Both factors influence the nature of the subsequent decision process. Substantial or complex discrepancies lead to extensive search and evaluation processes.

Running out of a frequently used product such as coffee creates a small, simple discrepancy that is easily resolved. On the other hand, a perceived discrepancy between actual and ideal self-image creates a substantial, complex problem. It is substantial because the discrepancy cannot be eliminated quickly. It is complex because of the scope of dimensions embodied in one's self-concept.

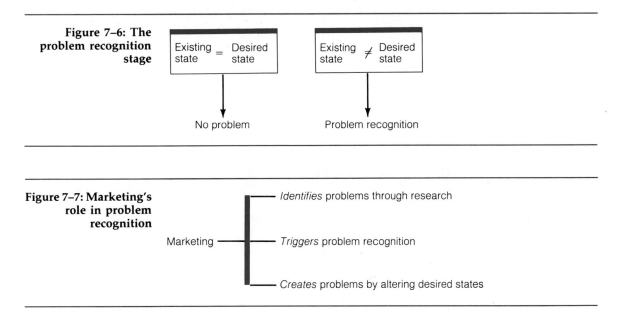

Figure 7–6: The problem recognition stage

Figure 7–7: Marketing's role in problem recognition

The relevance of problem recognition to marketing management emerges in three ways (also see Figure 7–7):

1. Firms need to conduct consumer research to *identify* problems that consumers face. Such research may reveal that consumers feel existing brands do not adequately provide the utility they want. An opportunity then exists for a company to provide this utility. Such an opportunity arose for the S. C. Johnson Company in the 1970s. Consumer research showed that many young women were unhappy with the way existing brands of shampoo solved hair oiliness problems. Accordingly, S. C. Johnson developed Agree shampoo and Agree creme rinse and coined the phrase "Fight the greasies" to communicate the products' benefits. Both products realized immediate consumer acceptance.[4]

2. Marketing efforts, mainly through advertising, can *trigger* problem recognition in consumers and direct them to brands that are potential solutions. The long-standing cry of "Ring around the collar" in ads for Wisk liquid detergent alerts consumers to a common problem.

3. Marketing efforts, mainly through the improvement of products, can *create* a discrepancy between actual and desired states. Here the approach is to alter the desired state by embellishing it so that a discrepancy exists. Kodak effectively used this strategy in the success of its disc cameras.

---

[4] "Key Role of Research in Agree's Success Is Told," *Marketing News,* January 17, 1979, p. 14.

Their research showed that amateur photographers were essentially satisfied with existing cartridge-loading cameras. Cartridge loaders were convenient, which seemed to make up for the occasional bad picture, as far as consumers were concerned. The disc camera altered the desired state by allowing consumers to take pictures where they previously could

First-time buyers of a product lack knowledge about what information to obtain in the external search stage. Smith-Corona offers buyers a structure for their external search and establishes its brand as a benchmark for comparison.

How to buy a typewriter.

-Clip and save-

Choosing a portable typewriter isn't hard if you know what to look for. This brief guide will help you make the best choice.

Test the feel. Check the slope and height of the keyboard. Check the size and shape of the keys. Make sure the controls are uncrowded and easy to reach.

Test the feel of a Smith-Corona® electric typewriter against several other brands. We welcome the comparison.

Try the touch. A responsive touch makes for better, easier typing. Look for a touch that is prompt, easy and dependable.

When you test a Smith-Corona, for instance, note how smartly the carriage returns. Press a button—zip—the carriage is back where it started.

Listen to the sound—the typewriter is trying to tell you something. If it sounds tinny, beware. This may indicate that the construction is too light.

Note the look of the type. Lines and individual letters should be straight. The impression should be crisp, clean and even. The print quality should not vary over the page.

Check the overall design. Good design is part of good value, so choose an attractive modern instrument. The Smith-Corona shown is an example of classic, good design.

Look at the carrying case. Does it have double walls for air-cushioned protection? Does it have sturdy latches and hinges? The Smith-Corona case does.

Check the price. A typewriter that sells for substantially less than others might be substantially less typewriter. If the price difference is minimal, you're probably better off paying a few dollars extra for the typewriter that tests best.

Ask who makes it. Smith-Corona makes every single typewriter that bears its name, which is not true of most other brands. So consider the maker's reputation. A company that has a solid reputation will still be around tomorrow and in the future to give your typewriter necessary service and maintenance.

A note about ribbon systems. Smith-Corona offers a unique cartridge ribbon and cartridge correction system. It lets you change ribbons in seconds without touching the ribbon. It also lets you correct typing errors neatly, quickly and easily. Not all correction systems produce equally good results. Test and compare.

Be sure to try the Smith-Corona carbon film ribbon. We offer a re-usable nylon fabric ribbon, excellent for ordinary typing jobs. This is the only kind of ribbon most portable typewriters offer. But Smith-Corona also offers carbon film ribbon in five colors. It's the kind of ribbon the most expensive office typewriters use, and it's perfect for jobs requiring a crisp, professional look such as term papers or a resume.

More people prefer Smith-Corona electric portables than all other brands combined. After these tests, we think you'll know why.

Patented Correction Cartridge

SCM SMITH-CORONA
SCM CORPORATION

Courtesy SCM® Smith-Corona

Figure 7–8: Relationship of internal search to external search

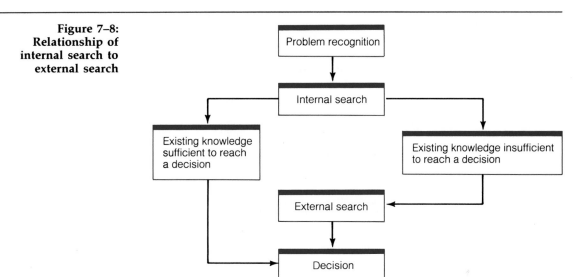

not. Many consumers apparently decided their existing state was no longer adequate, and disc cameras have enjoyed overwhelming success.[5]

Internal search

In the internal search stage, consumers examine the existing knowledge they possess to evaluate potential solutions and perhaps select one. In this stage the consumer essentially fills in as much of the decision matrix (Figure 7–2) as possible, based on what is already known about possible solutions to the problem. The consumer with sufficient existing knowledge skips the external search. If existing information is limited, external search occurs to obtain the necessary information not contained in memory. (See Figure 7–8.)

The nature of the internal search stage is revealed by the ***cognitive structure*** the consumer possesses for the problem at hand.

cognitive structure

> **Cognitive structure** is the framework, and knowledge contained within that framework, held by a consumer when evaluating objects in a product class.

The extensiveness of cognitive structure determines the role of internal search in the decision process. A more extensive cognitive structure allows greater reliance on internal search in finding a solution. An extensive

---

[5] "Credit Success of Kodak Disk Camera to Research," *Marketing News,*" January 21, 1983, pp. 8–9.

Figure 7–9: Limited and extensive cognitive structures for personal computers

a. Limited cognitive structure

	Brands		
Evaluative criteria	A	B	C
Price	$2,995	?	?
Memory capacity	64K	64K	?
Number of disk drives	2	?	?
Software included	?	?	?

b. Extensive cognitive structure

	Brands			
Evaluative criteria	A	B	C	D
Price	$2,995	$3,295	$3,495	$4,195
Memory capacity	64K	64K	64K	128K
Number of disk drives	2	2	?	1
Monitor	No color	No color	Color	Color
Modem connection	No	No	Yes	?
Software included	Much	Much	Some	?
Software compatibility	Very	Limited	Very	?

cognitive structure exists when the consumer: is aware of a large proportion of available brands in a product class, possesses a well-developed set of product attributes to use as evaluative criteria, has determined what is desirable and undesirable in each attribute, and holds beliefs about most or all of the brands on most or all of the criteria. A limited cognitive structure exists when the consumer: is aware of few brands, has not determined appropriate attributes to use as evaluative criteria or what is desirable in those attributes, and knows very little about the identified brands except that they exist. Figure 7–9 represents hypothetical limited and extensive cognitive structures for personal computers.

Two major factors influence the extensiveness of a consumer's cognitive structure for a product class:

1. *Prior experience.* Consumers who have frequently purchased and used a product in the past will possess well-developed cognitive structures.

2. *Nature of the product.* Consumers develop more extensive cognitive structures for complex, high-involvement products than for simple, low-involvement products.

External search   When internal search yields insufficient information, consumers engage in an active, purposeful search for information from external sources to

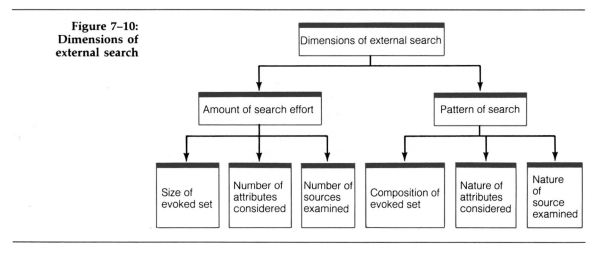

**Figure 7–10:
Dimensions of
external search**

aid in their choice. In this section we will examine two aspects of the external search state: (1) the dimensions that can be used to describe search behavior and (2) the correlates and determinants of search effort.

Dimensions of information search. Several variables can be used to describe the information search stage. These variables reflect two key dimensions of search—*amount* of effort and *patterns* of search behavior. (See Figure 7–10.)

One major feature of the search stage is the consumer's **evoked set.**

evoked set

> The **evoked set** consists of the brands the consumer focuses on in the search and comparison processes.

Usually, the brands for which information is sought include most, if not all, of the evoked set. Keep in mind, though, that a brand need not be searched to be in the evoked set, if the consumer's existing knowledge is sufficient to evaluate it. In any event, two important features of search behavior are the *size* and *composition* of the set of brands for which information is sought.

Vital to the success of any brand is inclusion in consumers' evoked sets. This means that marketing must not only make consumers aware of the brand but generate enough consumer interest in the brand for consumers to include it among those about which they seek information. Chrysler recognized this task in trying to reestablish its brands in the domestic auto market. As Lee Iacocca, head of Chrysler, put it:

Our biggest long-term job is to get people in [the showroom] to see how great these cars are—to get some traffic—and let them compare so we're going head-to-head on price and value.[6]

To accomplish this task, Chrysler improved its products, advertised heavily, and offered cash payments to consumers who would test drive a Chrysler product.

Another major dimension of search relates to the *type of information* sought on the brands being considered—that is, the number and nature of the attributes on which information is gathered. Obviously, the nature of the information sought varies across types of generic products; price information, though, is sought across most product categories. Generally, we would expect that product attributes of most importance to the consumer receive the most attention in search behavior. Also, determinant attributes—those the consumer expects to vary between brands—will receive attention during external search.

A final major dimension of search behavior involves the size and composition of the set of *external sources of information* from which information is sought. The consumer information environment comprises a variety of information sources. One major distinction is between **marketer-dominated** and **nonmarketer-dominated** sources.

marketer-dominated information sources

nonmarketer-dominated information sources

> **Marketer-dominated information sources** are those controlled by the organizations marketing products and services.
>
> **Nonmarketer-dominated information sources** are those organizations and individuals not involved with the marketing of products and services.

These two categories can be further broken down into personal (face-to-face) or nonpersonal sources. Figure 7–11 gives a breakdown of the potential sources of information a consumer might use in search efforts.

Consumer usage of information sources can be described in terms of scope and intensity. *Scope of usage* refers to the number of different sources utilized. *Intensity* refers to the effort required in using a source. Reading an article in *Consumer Reports* requires a more intense effort than perusing a quarter-page ad in a magazine.

A recent study of external search behavior by consumers in the purchase of certain home products reveals the kinds of information useful in marketing strategy development.[7] Some of its major findings include:

---

[6] R. Gray, "Chrysler Hinges Price on Popularity," *Advertising Age,* October 5, 1981, p. 7.

[7] "Study Tracks Housewares Buying, Information Sources," *Marketing News,* October 14, 1983.

1. In-store displays were a main information source for many products. They ranked highest as an information source for bathroom accessories and for serving and buffet products.

2. Print and TV ads were the primary sources for small electrical appliances and outdoor products.

3. Editorial articles in newspapers and magazines declined in usage as compared to findings from earlier studies.

4. Consumers were less likely to consult with a spouse or friend than previous studies showed.

One of the most compelling implications of this study is how marketer-dominated sources must complement each other. Advertising plays an important role in getting a brand into the evoked set. But, as the study indicates, point-of-purchase displays should be there to help close the sale.

Correlates/determinants of search effort. In general, an extensive information-seeking effort by a consumer involves a large number of brands for which information on several attributes is gathered from a variety of sources. As the number of brands, attributes, and sources diminishes in the search effort, a less extensive search stage occurs. One major determinant of extensiveness is, of course, the product itself. High-priced, complex, durable goods elicit more extensive searches than other products.

Figure 7–11: Potential sources of information for consumers

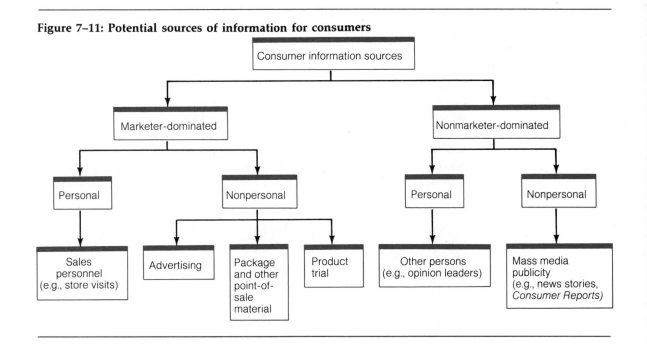

The perceived risk in the purchase of such goods is high; search is necessary to reduce uncertainty. Products for which style and appearance are important attributes also tend to involve greater search.[8]

Several variables related to the consumer appear to influence or correlate with search behavior. As we have said, the consumer's existing knowledge in a product class relates inversely to the need for information search. Better-educated and high-income consumers engage in greater levels of search behavior.[9] Finally, the personality variables of self-confidence and anxiety seem to influence information search patterns[10] as well as ultimate choice behavior.[11]

Knowing how consumers shop for information aids marketing strategists by allowing useful matchups between consumers, questions, and marketer-controlled information. If shoppers often ask salespeople about appliance features, appliancemakers will want to be sure salespeople are trained to answer fully.

Information receipt

In the information receipt stage, we recognize two important features of how consumers receive information. First, not all the information used by a consumer is acquired through an active search process. Second, consumers respond in various ways when receiving information.

Incidental learning. Consumers acquire a significant amount of information through *incidental learning.*

incidental learning

> **Incidental learning** occurs when product-related information is acquired by the consumer in a manner incidental to other forms of behavior.

Most incidental learning of products occurs when we watch TV or listen to the radio. Usually we are not purposely seeking product-related information when we do so. But we are exposed to the commercials on these media. We pay attention to those for products that interest us and ignore most of the others. When we do pay attention, information we obtain contributes to the total amount of information we have about a product. Thus, the total amount of information we obtain from external

---

[8] Joseph W. Newman, "Consumer External Search: Amount and Determinants," in *Consumer and Industrial Buying Behavior,* ed. A. Woodside, J. Sheth, and P. Bennett (New York: North Holland, 1977), p. 86.

[9] Ibid., p. 87

[10] W. B. Locander and P. W. Hermann, "The Effect of Self-Confidence and Anxiety on Information Seeking in Consumer Risk Reduction," *Journal of Marketing Research* 16 (May 1979), pp. 268–74.

[11] R. L. Horton, "Some Relationships between Personality and Consumer Decision Making," *Journal of Marketing Research* 16 (May 1979), pp. 233–46.

Figure 7–12: Processes contributing to knowledge about a product

Active external search $+$ Incidental learning $=$ Total knowledge from external sources

sources comes from incidental learning and an active search process. (See Figure 7–12.)

For some products much of what we learn comes from incidental learning. How much is primarily a function of the product class. Low-priced, frequently purchased items do not warrant an extensive search process. Differences between brands of such products are minimal, and the consequences of a bad choice for any one purchase are correspondingly small. Thus, marketers of such products depend heavily on media from which consumers acquire information passively. Usually, many repetitions of a message in the medium are needed to ensure receipt.

Responses to information. Another key concern in the information receipt stage is how consumers respond to the information conveyed to them. We know from our discussion of selective perception that consumers screen out many messages: they never receive them. Other messages do reach the consumer—and how the consumer responds to them is our concern here. These responses apply to both actively acquired and passively received information.

A sequence of responses occurs when a consumer deals with a source of information. (See Figure 7–13.) The first thing that must happen is ***reception.***

Figure 7–13: Sequence of responses to information

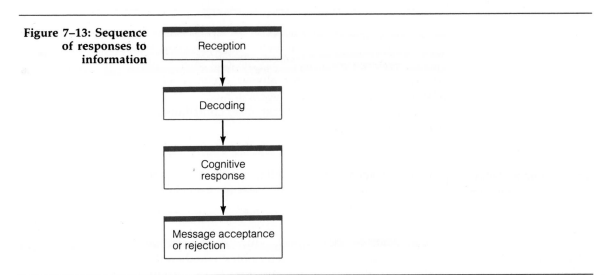

reception

> **Reception** occurs when the consumer notices and pays attention to the message.

When the consumer actively seeks information from a source, reception of the source's message definitely occurs. In the case of incidental learning, reception of a message is by no means automatic. Selective perception limits the stimuli to which an individual pays attention.

Once reception occurs, the consumer *decodes* the message.

decoding

> **Decoding** is the process by which the consumer attaches meaning to the message.

In decoding, the consumer interprets and translates the content of the message. The key concern here is whether the meaning attached to the message is the same as that intended by the source. Many psychological factors (values, attitudes) operate when consumers decode a message. They may serve to distort the content of the message when its intended content goes against the existing beliefs of the consumer.

Once interpreted, a message may elicit *cognitive responses* from the consumer.

cognitive responses

> **Cognitive responses** are spontaneous thought processes that occur in response to the perceived content of a message.

When the consumer agrees with the message, *support arguing* is a common cognitive response. When the consumer disagrees with the message, *counterarguing* or *source derogation* may be the cognitive response. Cognitive responses do not always occur. Their elicitation requires an existing belief structure in the consumer.

The previous sequence of responses contributes to *message acceptance or rejection.*

message acceptance/ rejection

> **Message acceptance/rejection** refers to the probability the consumer attaches to the content of the message being true.

A high probability means acceptance; a low probability means rejection. The degree of acceptance determines whether the message contributes to the consumer's cognitive structure in the product class.

The process that occurs in response to a message is highly relevant to marketing communication strategies. We will examine these issues more closely in our discussion of promotional strategy in Chapter 19.

Decision

Once the consumer has completed the search for and acquisition of information, he or she reaches the decision point. Based on knowledge contained in long-term memory plus actively and passively acquired information, the consumer must assess the expected utility of the brands remaining under consideration. Several features of the decision stage must be recognized:

1.   A decision *not to buy* might be reached.
2.   *Brand loyalty* might be the entire basis for the decision.
3.   Various ways of integrating information about brands can be used to arrive at a choice.
4.   A two-stage process of using decision rules might occur.

The decision not to buy.   Although it may be psychologically difficult after the sunk costs of search and evaluation, a decision not to buy (to maintain the status quo) might be reached. At least two explanations for a no-buy decision can be offered. First, the consumer determines that none of the options under consideration are worth buying. In the case of a personal computer, the consumer might decide that no brand of computer offers enough utility for its price. Affordability is not the issue. The consumer decides that he or she will simply not make sufficient use of the computer, given what the various brands have to offer.

A second explanation for a no-buy decision is that the consumer perceives that a purchase will result in a problem more severe than the one being solved. Typically, this occurs when expensive products are considered: the financial burden of a purchase could outweigh the original problem. Or, in the personal computer instance, the consumer may decide it takes too much time to learn to use the product—time better spent on more important matters. In either case the status quo is preferred, and a decision not to buy is reached.

Brand loyalty.   A phenomenon of consumer decision making of particular interest to marketers is ***brand loyalty.***

brand loyalty

> **Brand loyalty** refers to the tendency of a consumer to buy the same preferred brand each time a product is purchased.

Through an accumulation of prior experience in a product class, the consumer establishes a preference for a particular brand. When the desire for the product emerges, the consumer purchases the preferred brand with no comparison to or consideration of other brands. The consumer moves directly from internal search to the decision stage and employs a simple decision rule: buy the preferred brand. The internal search has been simplified to a preference for one brand, which, in turn, simplifies the remainder of the process.

The absence of an information search stage does not always mean brand loyalty exists. The consumer may hold enough knowledge about a product class in long-term memory that additional search is not needed. Brands are compared mentally, and a choice is made. If the choice proves unsatisfactory, this adds to the base of knowledge; on the next purchase occasion that brand may be rejected—again without search. Of course, if the chosen brand proves satisfactory, brand loyalty may begin to develop.

Brand loyalty is double-edged for those engaged in marketing. On the one hand, when a consumer develops loyalty to a company's product, the company has achieved the ultimate in marketing accomplishment with that consumer. The company's marketing tasks are not, however, completed. It must maintain that loyalty through continued reinforcement and provision of the utility from which the loyalty developed. Reminder advertising and in-package coupons redeemable on the next purchase are strategies designed to strengthen brand loyalty.

A more formidable marketing task results from loyalty's negative edge. When a consumer develops loyalty to a competitor's brand, the company faces a considerable barrier to inroads against the competitor. Consumers loyal to competitive brands are generally not receptive to information on other brands and do not search for such information. The company must jolt the consumer out of this loyalty by getting him or her at least to consider its brand. Heavy sales-promotion tactics are often used to accomplish this task. They include mail coupons and free samples. Thus, the phenomenon of brand loyalty requires separate marketing tasks: nurturing and strengthening loyalty to one's own brand and overcoming loyalty to competing brands. (See Figure 7–14.)

Consumer decision rules.   Of course, many consumer purchase decisions are not made on the basis of loyalty. Rather, consumers must somehow bring together their information on a set of brands and choose from this set or decide not to buy. A multi-attribute evaluation process must occur. That is, each alternative must be ranked vis-à-vis the others in terms of expected benefits. Consider the example in Table 7–2. The consumer must determine which of the four brands of toothpaste to buy based on the set of beliefs about each brand's attributes. A variety of procedures are available that range in complexity.

Multi-attribute evaluation processes fit into two general categories.

compensatory

> **Compensatory** procedures incorporate all of the attributes into the evaluation process. In so doing, good performance on one attribute can offset or compensate for poor performance on another.

noncompensatory

> **Noncompensatory** procedures may employ all or only some of the attributes, but their distinguishing feature is that good performance on one attribute does not offset poor performance on another.

Using the example of Table 7–2, let's consider various forms of compensatory and noncompensatory evaluation processes. (See Figure 7–15.)

Compensatory models. **Compensatory decision rules** are generally more complex to apply than noncompensatory rules. The simplest version of a compensatory rule involves a summation of beliefs across attributes for a brand:

$$A_j = \sum_{i=1}^{n} B_i$$

where

A_j = Consumer evaluation of or "attitude" toward brand *j*.
B_i = Consumer belief about attribute *i*.
n = The number of attributes employed in evaluating brands in the product class.

Employing this model, the consumer would evaluate brands A to D with scores of 34, 32, 33, and 35, respectively, and choose D.

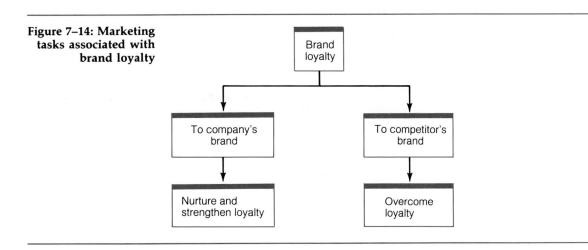

Figure 7–14: Marketing tasks associated with brand loyalty

Brand loyalty

To company's brand

To competitor's brand

Nurture and strengthen loyalty

Overcome loyalty

Table 7–2: A consumer's belief structure for brands of toothpaste*

| **Attributes** | **Importance weight** | **Brands** | | | |
		A	**B**	**C**	**D**
Cavity prevention	10	4	8	10	5
Teeth whitening	6	8	7	7	9
Breath freshness	6	9	5	6	9
Taste	7	8	6	5	8
Price	3	5	6	5	4

Table 7–2: A consumer's belief structure for brands of toothpaste*

* Scores represent subjective evaluations of each brand attribute on a 10-point scale where 1 = Poor and 10 = Excellent.

A more complex version would occur if the consumer incorporated importance weights for each attribute into the evaluation. It is unlikely that consumers attach equal importance to the five attributes of toothpaste. Based on a 10-point scale (ranging from 1 = Not at all important to 10 = Extremely important), a typical distribution of importance scores for the attributes is also presented in Table 7–2. The following decision rule could then be employed:

$$A_j = \sum_{i=1}^{n} W_i B_i$$

where

A_j, B_i, and n are defined as before.
W_i = The importance weight attached to attribute i.

Using this model, the consumer would score the four brands 213, 212, 228, and 226, respectively, and in this case, choose C. Note how, when

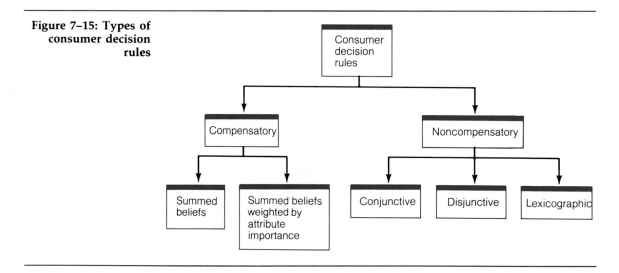

Figure 7–15: Types of consumer decision rules

the extreme importance of cavity prevention is considered, C's superior performance on that attribute compensates even more for its lack of superiority on other less important attributes.

Noncompensatory models. **Noncompensatory decision rules** generally are less difficult to employ than compensatory rules. The most extensive noncompensatory rule is the **conjunctive model,** whereby all of a product's attributes are considered. Here the consumer establishes minimum acceptable values that a brand must surpass on each attribute. A brand not meeting the minimum on any one attribute is eliminated from further consideration. Thus, poor performance on one attribute is not offset by superior performance on another. If a conjunctive rule is employed and no brand meets the minimum standard on all attributes, the result may be a decision not to buy. However, the consumer may relax the standards on an attribute so that a purchase results. If, in our example, a consumer established minimum cutoffs of 5 on all toothpaste attributes, brands A and D would be eliminated from further consideration.

A related but less extensive approach is a **disjunctive model,** whereby only a subset of all of the attributes is used. The consumer rejects brands not meeting certain standards of performance on this subset of attributes. For example, a consumer may determine that brands of toothpaste rated at less than 8 on cavity prevention will be rejected. Brand B and C remain as choices. The superior performance of brands A and D on three other attributes does not compensate for their inferior performance on cavity prevention.

A final noncompensatory approach is the **lexicographic model.** Here the consumer orders product attributes in terms of their importance. Considering the most important attribute first, the consumer chooses the brand most effective in providing that benefit. In our example such a rule would lead to a choice of brand C. If two or more brands were perceived equally effective on the most important attribute, the consumer might choose from these based on their ratings of the next most important attribute. Such a process would continue until all ties were broken and one brand remained.

A two-stage process. The consumer, of course, is not restricted to the use of just one decision rule. Nor is use of the rules restricted to the decision stage of the process. The likely situation is a **two-stage employment of decision rules:** a simple disjunctive rule is used at an earlier stage (external search) to discard brands from further consideration; a more extensive rule is used at the decision stage to choose from the remaining brands. (See Figure 7–16.) Consider the purchase of a home. A buyer will usually be exposed to several alternatives. Initially, many homes will be screened out on the basis of price alone. Then, others will be discounted because of style, size, or some other attribute. Finally,

Figure 7–16: Two-stage application of decision rules

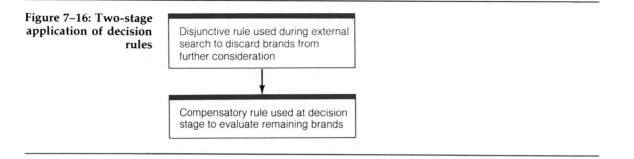

a set of two to three homes from which to choose will remain. These homes will be compared across several attributes, and the one offering the greatest expected utility will be chosen.[12]

Marketing implications. While consumers do not assign numerical values to attribute importance and brand beliefs, evidence exists to suggest they do engage in the *general type of thinking* indicated by these models.[13] In some situations consumers integrate brand information into an overall brand assessment—the process suggested by a compensatory rule. In other cases they concentrate on selected features and drop brands not performing at an acceptable level on these features—a noncompensatory rule.

A company needs to recognize these various ways in which consumers make brand-choice decisions. It can then determine if consumers frequently employ one particular rule when deciding about a product for which it has a brand. The type of rule used suggests the communications task the company faces. In compensatory evaluations consumers use a variety of information about a brand and seek an overall assessment. Here marketing communications should stress the *package* of benefits available in a brand and its overall quality performance. The use of a conjunctive rule suggests the need for a detailed account of a brand's features. The disjunctive and lexicographic rules suggest messages that focus on selected features of a brand—important attributes or attributes used early in decision making.

Postdecision

In the postdecision stage, the consumer realizes the consequences of his/her choice. The phenomena that occur at this stage are crucial in

---

[12] Evidence in support of a two-stage usage of decision rules is reported in J. W. Payne, "Task Complexity and Contingent Processing in Decision Making: An Information Search and Protocol Analysis," *Organizational Behavior and Human Performance* 16 (August 1976), pp. 366–87.

[13] See, for example, J. R. Bettman and C. W. Park, "Effects of Prior Knowledge and Experience and Phase of Choice Process on Consumer Decision Processes: A Protocol Analysis," *Journal of Consumer Research,* December 1980, pp. 234–48.

Cognitive dissonance can follow the purchase of a major item like a car. Postpurchase marketing efforts like the above can help alleviate these feelings and improve the prospects of future purchases from this seller.

Van Drunen Ford Co.
"SOUTHERN COOK COUNTY'S OLDEST FORD DEALER"

3233 WEST 183RD STREET   Phone 798-1668
HOMEWOOD, ILLINOIS 60430
Parts Phone 798-4100

Dear Customer:

I want to personally say "Thank You" for your business. It is my wish that the vehicle you purchased from Van Drunen Ford will give you pleasure and good service. Below are the people of Van Drunen Ford able to help you if any problems should arise.

SERVICE MANAGER - FRANK GULICK
ASSISTANT MANAGER - DAVE DYKSTRA

Talk to Frank or Dave for mechanical repairs. We believe our service department is the best anywhere. Frank, Dave, and their staff will be happy to answer your service questions.

BODYSHOP MANAGER - JACK SWAN
ASSISTANT MANAGER - BOB JOHNSON

We hope you will never need our bodyshop, but accidents do happen. Jack and Bob will give you an accurate estimate of required repairs and follow through with the highest quality workmanship available.

JUST IN CASE YOU DIDN'T KNOW...
We have expanded our facility, and we are now equipped to service most car makes. So, if you own a GM, Chrysler, or another brand car in addition to your Ford product, we can, in most cases, offer the same fine service and body repair which we have for over 50 years on Fords.

RENT-A-CAR - FRANKLIN VAN SOMEREN

Franklin will arrange for a new Ford Rent-A-Car at the most inexpensive rates available in the area. Rental by the day, week, and month can be arranged.

We value your business and want your experience with us to be a pleasant one. The people named above are experts in their fields.

Sincerely,

Marvin G. Van Drunen

MARVIN G. VAN DRUNEN
PRESIDENT

Business Goes Where it's Invited and Stays Where it is Well Treated.

determining the long-run relationship between the consumer and the chosen brand. The consumer's experiences with the chosen brand add to his/her knowledge and beliefs within the product class. Usage experience is probably the strongest influence on a consumer's set of beliefs about a brand. A satisfying experience with a brand will lead to stronger positive beliefs toward it. These beliefs become part of cognitive structure in a subsequent decision process. A favorable attitude toward the brand is strengthened, increasing the probability of purchase at the next decision. A series of satisfying experiences may lead to brand loyalty.

Of course, a dissatisfying experience has the opposite effect. Brand beliefs are revised in a negative direction. These beliefs, as part of cognitive structure, lower the probability of purchase—perhaps to zero—at the next decision sequence.

Cognitive dissonance.   An interesting aspect of postdecision phenomena is the anxiety a consumer may feel about a purchase that has occurred. Postpurchase anxiety is explained by the theory of ***cognitive dissonance.***[14] According to this theory, people often "second-guess" decisions they have made. In consumer behavior this can happen when someone has bought a brand that on the whole is satisfactory but is lacking in some specific respect (wrong color) or has rejected a brand with some positive feature (lower price). In either case a state of anxiety can result. A number of tension-reducing behaviors are available for these consumers. One is to seek information that is consistent with and confirms the chosen behavior—e.g., the consumer may notice some ads for the chosen brand that might have been ignored before.

Cognitive dissonance is more likely to occur when the purchase is important and the unchosen alternatives are relatively attractive. In consumer behavior, purchases of durable goods are thus most likely to result in dissonance. Marketers of such products should provide for easy confirmation of the consumer's decision. Brochures that accompany purchased brands often perform this role. An auto salesperson will often write or call a recent buyer to emphasize the wisdom of the choice. Such follow-up helps alleviate buyer anxiety.

CONSUMER DECISION PROCESS AND THE CLASSIFICATION OF CONSUMER GOODS

The amount of effort going into the consumer decision process varies. And the nature of the product being purchased is probably the biggest determinant of the amount of effort spent. One of the earliest approaches to categorizing consumer goods was based on the extensiveness of the decision process. This approach is the well-known scheme of Copeland, who identified three categories: ***convenience, shopping,*** and ***specialty*** goods.[15] Copeland's scheme has endured because of its intuitive appeal

[14] This theory was first proposed by Leon Festinger, *A Theory of Cognitive Dissonance* (Stanford, Calif.: Stanford University Press, 1957).

[15] Melvin T. Copeland, "Relation of Consumers' Buying Habits to Marketing Methods," *Harvard Business Review* 1 (April 1923), pp. 282–89.

	Type of goods	Strategy implications
Table 7–3: Types of consumer goods and marketing strategy implications	Convenience	Extensive distribution; heavy mass media advertising; point-of-purchase displays.
	Shopping	Selective distribution in large retail outlets; retailer assumes part of promotional effort.
	Specialty	Selective distribution; promotional strategy to maintain brand preference.

and the implications for marketing strategy that the placement of a good in a category suggests. (See Table 7–3.)

Convenience goods

Such goods are relatively standardized across brands, which explains the minimal effort consumers put into the purchase. Consumers gain little from extensive shopping so they buy readily accessible brands. They may prefer particular brands but will accept other brands in the absence of the preferred one. Frequently purchased, low-priced products (grocery items, soap) fall in the convenience category. As with the remaining categories, the *consumer's behavior* toward the product class (not the product class itself) describes a convenience good.

convenience goods

> **Convenience goods** include products the customer purchases frequently, immediately, and with minimum effort in comparing and buying.

As it turns out, goods similar in the above characteristics tend to elicit similar consumer behavior patterns. These behavioral patterns suggest distinct marketing strategies for a product in this category. First, since the consumer will accept any one of several substitutes, extensive distribution is necessary. Products must be distributed through all the types of retail outlets in which they are bought. The absence of a brand in a particular store will not cause a buyer to seek it elsewhere. The buyer will simply purchase a substitute.

The need for such extensive distribution in turn requires heavy use of marketing intermediaries and a long channel of distribution. Yet the responsibility for promoting a brand of convenience good lies primarily with the manufacturer. Retailers carry competing brands and do not promote any one of them. Heavy mass media advertising and point-of-purchase displays in retail outlets are necessary to inform buyers about the nature of a brand because buyers do not seek out such information on their own. Establishing brand preference through heavy promotion and satisfactory performance and making the brand readily accessible through extensive distribution are the keys to success in convenience good marketing.

shopping goods

> **Shopping goods** include products for which the consumer compares brands on one or more bases, such as suitability, quality, price, and style.

Shopping goods

Thus, an active search process characterizes a shopping good. The consumer perceives sufficient differences between brands to make a search worthwhile. Preference for a particular brand does not exist prior to the search effort. Shopping goods differ distinctly between brands in price, quality, and style. Also, they are usually high in price and infrequently bought. Examples include most durable goods (cars, furniture, appliances) and clothing items.

The behavioral patterns associated with shopping goods require less of a distribution coverage than convenience goods. Fewer but larger retail outlets are necessary for a brand. The burden of promoting a brand of shopping good, while assumed heavily by the manufacturer, does shift to some extent to a retailer. This effort is reflected in large part by the use of retail salespeople and by local advertising by the retailer.

specialty goods

> **Specialty goods** include any product with such unique characteristics and/ or brand identification that the customer will make a special effort to obtain it.

Specialty goods

Here the consumer holds a clear-cut preference for a particular version or brand of a product and will settle for no other. In such a case the consumer engages in whatever effort it takes to obtain the preferred brand. Generally, the consumer has had much experience in the product class, where significant variations exist across brands.

Many marketing strategies that are relevant to shopping goods are relevant to specialty goods. Basically, this is because, over time, a shopping good develops into a specialty good for some consumers. At any one time a specialty good to one consumer will be a shopping good to another, and marketing must be adjusted accordingly. Manufacturers should identify customers for whom their brand has achieved specialty status and develop a marketing program to maintain that status. A program designed to move the brand into specialty status should be developed for other consumers who treat the good as a shopping good. Thus, a major implication of the specialty good is that it reflects the ultimate marketing achievement and a long-run goal of a brand: to establish such a uniqueness and advantage for the brand that consumers will accept that brand alone.

A SUMMARY OF CONSUMER BEHAVIOR

To this point in our examination of consumer behavior we have discussed a variety of influences: internal and external to the individual, on behavior, and the process by which consumers reach and evaluate decisions. Our approach has been somewhat eclectic, drawing insights from each of several areas with no attempt to form a comprehensive theory of consumer behavior and establish interrelationships among all the variables. A comprehensive theory useful to both students and practitioners of marketing is the ultimate goal of the study of consumer behavior. It would establish the boundaries of the field of consumer behavior and allow researchers and managers to focus on the variables most relevant to its understanding. At this time, the field of consumer behavior is too complex—and knowledge of it too incomplete—for a useful comprehensive theory to develop. New variables relevant to its study and understanding are just emerging, and the value of many older ones remain in question.[16]

---

[16] This is not to say that attempts at a comprehensive theory of consumer behavior have not occurred. Two of the more notable ones include: John A. Howard and Jagdish N. Sheth, *The Theory of Buyer Behavior* (New York: John Wiley & Sons, 1969); and James F. Engel and Roger D. Blackwell, *Consumer Behavior,* 4th ed. (Hinsdale, Ill.: Dryden Press, 1982). The interested reader may wish to consult these sources in order to realize the structural nature and format that a comprehensive theory would assume.

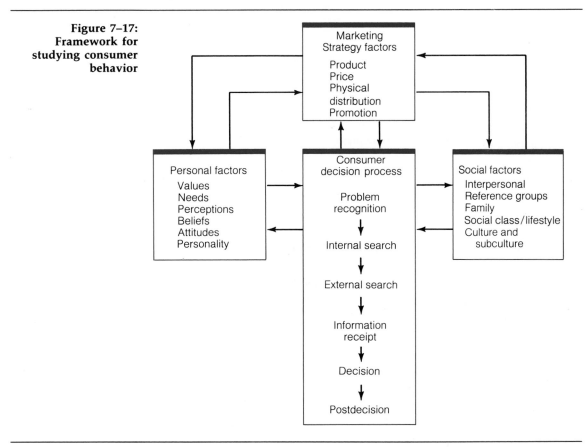

Figure 7–17: Framework for studying consumer behavior

In the absence of a comprehensive theory to use as an integrating device, Figure 7–17 presents an overview of the framework we have used to discuss consumer behavior. This diagram indicates the sets of factors that influence consumer behavior and the nature of the process they influence. It serves as our summary of Chapters 5–7 together.

The six stages of the consumer decision process are shown to be influenced by personal, social, and marketing strategy factors. As a consumer engages in this process, it in turn influences the personal, social, and marketing strategy factors. Decision-making experiences, for example, can result in the formation or modification of consumer beliefs and attitudes. They also can increase or decrease the attention consumers pay to the social consequences of their behavior. Finally, marketing strategy variables influence the personal and social factors and the decision process. Since marketing strategy is based in part on the nature of these factors and the decision process, we must recognize the influence they have on marketing strategy. This interplay between consumer behavior and marketing strategy is, of course, the essence of the marketing concept.

KEY CONCEPTS

Consumer decision process	Low-involvement purchases	Brand loyalty
Problem recognition	Cognitive structure	Compensatory decision rule
Internal search	Evoked set	Noncompensatory decision rule
External search	Marketer-dominated information sources	Conjunctive decision model
Information receipt		Disjunctive decision model
Decision	Nonmarketer-dominated information sources	Lexicographic decision rule
Postdecision		Two-stage usage of decision models
Extensive problem solving	Incidental learning	
Limited problem solving	Reception	Cognitive dissonance
Routinized response behavior	Decoding	Convenience goods
Involvement	Cognitive responses	Shopping goods
High-involvement purchases	Message acceptance/rejection	Specialty goods

---

DISCUSSION QUESTIONS AND EXERCISES

1. Construct hypothetical examples of consumer-choice tasks for decisions at each of the three decision levels: generic, product-form, and brand. What is happening to cognitive structure as you move from one level to the next?

2. Discuss the factors that contribute to variations in involvement level.

3. What is the role of marketing in problem recognition?

4. Develop a list of products for which you feel internal search would provide sufficient information for you to make a decision.

5. If you were considering the purchase of a personal computer, describe the likely amount and pattern of external search that you would use.

6. What consumer decision rule would you use when making the following decisions?

    a.   Brand of bicycle.

    b.   Restaurant at which to eat.

    c.   Physician to see.

    d.   A gift to buy for a young child.

    e.   An elective course to take.

    f.   Selection between two jobs.

7. Discuss the implications of the postdecision stage for marketing strategy.

8. Identify some products that for you would be convenience, shopping, and specialty goods.

CHAPTER 8

Organizational buying behavior

Nature and structure of the organizational
    market
    Types of organizational buyers
    Descriptive characteristics of the
        organizational market
    Types of items bought by organizations
    Demand characteristics of the
        organizational market

Organizational buying practices
    Reseller buying practices
    User buying practices
    Participants in user buying

Influences on organizational buying behavior
    Individual factors
    Intraorganizational influences
    Interorganizational influences
    Environmental influences

The organizational buying decision process
    Problem recognition
    Internal search
    External search
    Information receipt
    Decision
    Postdecision

Classification of organizational buying
    processes

A summary model of organizational buying

Summary

Key concepts

Discussion questions and exercises

Our look at buyer behavior has focused so far on individual consumers and households. But buying behavior is not restricted to these. Organizations buy goods and services, too. The organizational market represents a major marketing opportunity. Many differences exist between organizations and consumers in buying behavior. As a distinct component of the marketplace, organizational buyers deserve special attention.

NATURE AND STRUCTURE OF THE ORGANIZATIONAL MARKET

Our first goal in the study of these buyers is to describe the nature and structure of the organizational market. In this section we'll examine types of buyers, some descriptive characteristics of this market, and the types of goods and services purchased in it.

Types of organizational buyers

Various types of organizations represent potential buyers of goods and services. They can be categorized as follows:

1. *Manufacturers*—Those organizations that change resources into finished goods.
2. *Resellers*—Those that purchase goods for resale to other organizations or consumers. Retailers and wholesalers make up this group.
3. *Service organizations*—The commercial and nonprofit organizations that perform services for other groups or individuals. The diverse types include hospitals, trade organizations, schools, consulting firms, and charities, to name a few.
4. *Government*—Government agencies at the local, state, and federal levels.
5. *Farmers*—Agricultural organizations involved in producing and distributing raw food items.

The presence of **resellers** in this list suggests an important distinction within the market. The organizational buying practices of resellers include buying consumer goods for *resale*. Marketing consumer goods to resellers falls in the realm of consumer marketing. All the other categories purchase goods exclusively as **users.**

organizational users

> **Organizational users** purchase goods and services for their ongoing operations—to enhance the performance of their business activities.

Marketing goods and services to organizational users is part of industrial marketing. Since the distinction lies in what is bought for what purpose, wholesalers and retailers are organizational buyers of both types. However, marketing consumer goods to them as resellers is vastly different than marketing industrial goods to them as users.

Table 8–1: Size of the organizational market, 1979	Category	Number of organizations
	Producers	
	Agriculture, forestry, fisheries	3,970,000
	Mining	149,000
	Construction	1,422,000
	Manufacturing	503,000
	Transportation, communication, public utilities	539,000
	Finance, insurance, real estate	2,106,000
	Services	4,496,000
	Total	13,185,000
	Resellers	
	Wholesalers	613,000
	Retailers	2,664,000
	Total	3,277,000
	Government	
	Federal	1
	State and local	82,687
	Total	82,688
Source: *Statistical Abstract of the United States, 1982–83.*	Grand total	16,544,688

Descriptive characteristics of the organizational market

The size and distribution of the organizational market help characterize this important part of the marketplace.

Size. The importance of this market is probably best reflected by its size. The total number of organizational buying units in the U.S. economy is small compared to the consumer market. (See Table 8–1.) But the *aggregate dollar volume of purchases* by organizational buyers exceeds that of consumers. The dollar amount of a single purchase by an organization is usually much larger than a single consumer purchase. One source estimates that even small organizational buyers (excluding government and resellers) can spend at least $150,000 on goods and services each year.[1] Also, consider the following examples of recent federal government purchases:

> *Lockheed received a $65.2 million Air Force contract for supplies and services used in making wing parts for C-130 transport planes.*

> *NCR Corporation won a $61.8 million contract for data processing systems for Air Force commissaries.*

[1] Thomas V. Bonoma, Gerald Zaltman, and Wesley J. Johnston, *Industrial Buying Behavior* (Cambridge, Mass.: Marketing Science Institute, 1977).

Gentex was given an $11.6 million contract by the Defense Logistics Agency for helmets.

IBM received $10.2 million in contracts for installing and maintaining terminals.

Size distribution. The size of individual organizations is bunched at the small end. Using the number of employees as a measure of size, Figure 8–1 shows the percentage share of all firms in the manufacturing, wholesale, and retail sectors held by various sizes of firms. Clearly, most firms are not as extensive as General Motors, IBM, and the like. For the three types shown, the majority of firms employ less than 10 people.

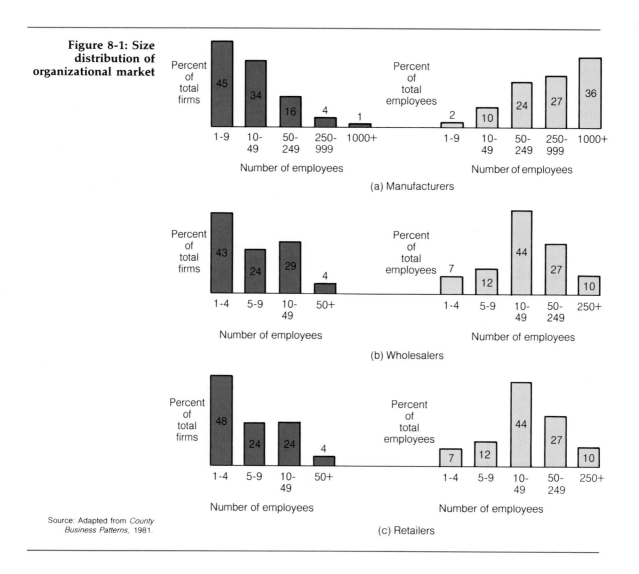

Figure 8-1: Size distribution of organizational market

(a) Manufacturers

(b) Wholesalers

(c) Retailers

Source: Adapted from *County Business Patterns*, 1981.

Figure 8–2: Percentage share of total dollar value added in size groups, manufacturers

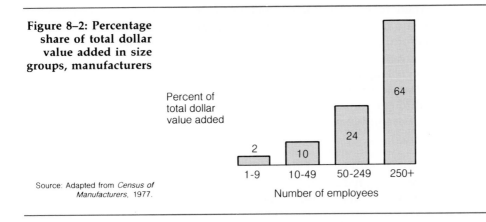

Percent of total dollar value added

| 2 | 10 | 24 | 64 |

| 1-9 | 10-49 | 50-249 | 250+ |

Number of employees

Source: Adapted from *Census of Manufacturers*, 1977.

Note, though, that larger firms account for a greater share of total employ-ees, especially in the manufacturing sector. Larger firms also account for much of the total business activity. Figure 8–2 shows the percentage of total dollar value added by each size group of manufacturers.

Geographic distribution. The geographic concentration of organiza-tions, especially manufacturers, is also quite pronounced. Most are located in or near major population centers. Buyers may operate out of the home office and purchase for several geographically dispersed plants, further concentrating the purchasing function.

Regional shifts in manufacturing activity correspond to those evident in the consumer market. Table 8–2 reveals relative business activity by geographic region and the changes that have occurred. Clearly, manufac-turer buying power is shifting to the Sun Belt.

Table 8–2: Regional shifts in manufacturing activity

Region	1982 percentage of total United States			Change in percentage points, 1973–82		
	Shipments	Total plants	Large plants	Shipments	Total plants	Large plants
New England	6.1	8.9	8.6	−0.3	1.3	0.1
Mideast	17.8	20.1	19.4	−4.2	−7.0	−3.9
Great Lakes	25.7	23.5	22.8	−3.2	0.5	−1.6
Plains	7.6	7.2	6.7	0.4	0.8	0.3
Southeast	20.6	20.4	24.0	2.1	3.2	2.3
Southwest	9.8	7.0	6.6	4.0	1.5	1.7
Mountain	2.0	2.0	1.6	0.4	0.5	0.4
Far West	10.5	10.8	10.3	0.8	−0.7	0.8

Source: *Sales & Marketing Management.* Survey of Industrial and Commercial Buying Power. Copyright July 25, 1983.

Certain types of industry tend to be concentrated in specific areas. Often the nearness of raw materials dictates. Steel in Pittsburgh, wine in California's Napa Valley, and "high tech" in California's "Silicon" valley are prime examples.

The geographic concentration of manufacturers allows efficiencies in marketing to them. A seller of industrial goods may realize nationwide sales through contact with one purchasing agent who buys for several plants. But this is equally easy for competition, and the market is intensely competitive.

Types of items bought by organizations

Three general kinds of items are purchased by organizational buyers: *consumer goods, industrial goods,* and *services.* Resellers purchase all three. Other buyers purchase industrial goods and services.

Consumer goods. ***Consumer goods*** are those that are ultimately bought and used by individual consumers. One reason for the large amount of aggregate dollar transactions in the organizational market is that a large portion of the goods bought by consumers have been first bought and resold by resellers (wholesalers and retailers). Consider a $60 dress purchased by a consumer at a women's clothing store. (See Figure 8–3.) The clothing store paid $32 to a wholesaler, who had paid $24 to a manufacturer. Thus, from a total of $116 in transactions for a single unit of a product, organizational buyers spent $56 to the consumer's $60. Resellers differ from other organizational buyers in why they buy. Their central motive is profit. They seek products that can be bought and sold to make money. Resellers seek goods that are demanded by consumers, though other considerations can enter into their buying decisions as well. These will be discussed later.

Industrial goods. Industrial goods differ from consumer goods in the purpose for which they are to be used.

industrial good

> An **industrial good** is any product that contributes to the operation of an organization (profit or nonprofit) that provides a product or service.

Figure 8–3: Organizational buyers' contributions to total dollar transactions in the sale of a consumer good

Transaction	Price
Manufacturer sells dress to wholesaler	$24 +
Wholesaler sells dress to retailer	$32 = $56 of organizational transactions +
Retailer sells dress to consumer	$60 = $60 of consumer transactions
Total transactions	$116

This ad illustrates an intermediary's promotion of accessory equipment to users.

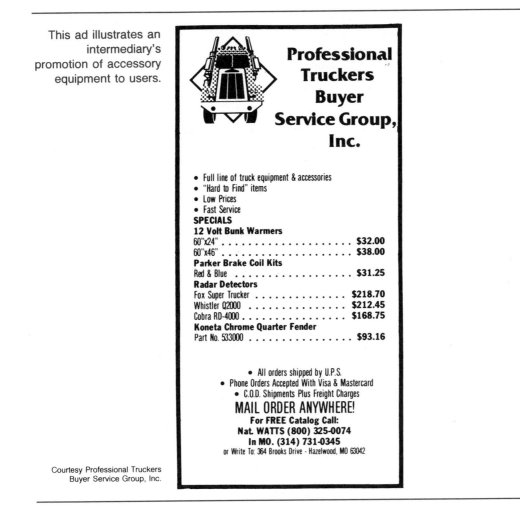

Courtesy Professional Truckers Buyer Service Group, Inc.

A typewriter bought for personal use by an individual is a consumer good. The same model bought for use by a manuscript typing service becomes an industrial good.

Generally, there are five categories of industrial goods:

1. *Raw materials*—Relatively unprocessed goods that in part or in whole become a portion of a final product.

2. *Component parts and materials*—Processed goods that enter into a final product.

3. *Major capital equipment*—Finished goods used in the production of a product but that do not enter the final product.

4. ***Accessory equipment***—Finished goods that indirectly contribute to production by performing a facilitative role.
5. ***Operating supplies***—Finished goods that facilitate maintenance, repair, and ongoing operations.

Table 8–3 provides a more detailed summary of these categories and their special characteristics. Note that for accessory equipment and operating supplies marketing intermediaries may aid the distribution of these goods to their users. Thus, intermediaries are not exclusive to consumer marketing.

Table 8–3: Categories of industrial goods

Category	Description	Examples	Special characteristics
Raw materials	Relatively unprocessed goods that in part or in whole become a portion of a final product	Farm products (wheat, tobacco) Natural products (animals, fish, land, minerals, forests, water)	Limited, nonreproducible supply; small number of producers; transportation is key marketing function
Component parts and materials	Processed goods that enter into a final product	Working parts of a final product (engines, springs, ball bearings, microchips)	High-volume purchases on long-term contractual basis; heavy competition between suppliers; require careful nurturing of a relationship with buyer
Major capital equipment	Finished goods used in the production of a product that do not enter the final product	Plant installations, machinery (printing press, oil rig)	Long-lasting and involved in the production of many units of final product over several years; involve large dollar outlays; capital budgeting committee often involved in purchase decision; sold direct from manufacturer to buyer
Accessory equipment	Finished goods that indirectly contribute to production by performing a facilitative role	Trucks, typewriters, safety glasses, welding equipment, conveyor belts	Enduring but less so than capital equipment; more standardized; more frequently purchased, less costly than capital equipment; less complex buying; intermediaries may be involved
Operating supplies	Finished goods that facilitate maintenance, repair, and ongoing operations	Office supplies, fuel, janitorial supplies	Analogous to consumer convenience goods; frequently purchased and consumed in a short time; standardized; very broad market; heavy involvement of channel intermediaries

Organizational services. A significant component of organizational spending goes to *organizational services.*

organizational services

> An **organizational service** is an act performed by an individual or organization for another organization.

Many different services are marketed to organizations. They include technical or marketing consulting, janitorial services, refuse removal, plant security, printing, and training of employees. The special nature of services for both consumers and organizations will be discussed in Chapter 25.

This ad is promoting capital supplier services.

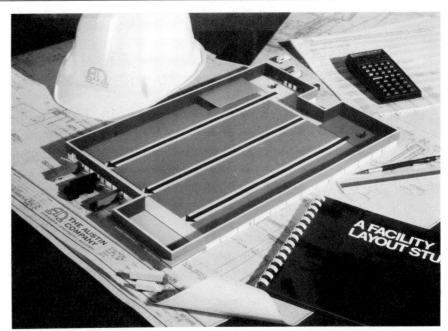

How Austin designs and builds facilities on time and within budget.

When it's time to expand your business, you want facilities that meet your needs, as soon as possible, and delivered under strict budget control. And that's what you get with The Austin Method.

Meeting your needs. How does Austin assure you of getting the building you need? First, by providing single-source responsibility for consulting, design and construction, we maximize your control over the project. We can work with you from feasibility studies clear through start-up or interior furnishing. You make your wishes known to us—and we're entirely responsible for carrying them out.

Secondly, we can add good ideas to the ones you already have. With more than

25,000 projects to our name, we've gained a lot of insight into design and construction for all kinds of industries.

Speeding your construction. Austin's single-source responsibility pays off in speed, as well. We can order hard-to-get materials as soon as our initial contract is drawn up, or begin construction while detailed engineering drawings are still being finalized. The Austin Method can often shave months off a project's construction schedule—and that can translate into important cost savings.

Working within your budget. Austin's management experience assures you of rigorous cost control. In over a hundred years of design and construction service,

Austin has amassed an impressive on-time, in-budget record.

If we didn't come through with what we promise, our clients wouldn't keep on coming back. And traditionally, returning customers account for 75 percent of Austin's business. For more information about our world-wide capabilities, contact The Austin Company, Cleveland, Ohio 44121.

THE AUSTIN COMPANY
DESIGNERS · ENGINEERS · BUILDERS

Courtesy The Austin Company

Demand characteristics of the organizational market

The basic characteristic of organizational buyers' demand is that it is a ***derived demand.***

Resellers' demand for a good to resell derives from consumers' demand for that good. Industrial goods demand derives from the demand for the products and services they help to produce. Changes in the demand for steel correspond to changes in the demand for the consumer goods into which it enters (e.g., automobiles).

derived demand

> **Derived demand** exists when the level of demand for a good or service is directly linked to the level of demand for another good or service.

Generally, the demand for industrial goods fluctuates more than the demand for the consumer goods from which it derives. Increases and decreases in consumer demand will cause correspondingly greater increases and decreases in industrial demand. The reason is that when consumer demand declines companies exhaust more of their industrial goods inventory. Further, the distribution of finished goods already in inventory will decline, allowing that stock to last longer. The overall effect is a reduced need for new materials and component parts and for other goods that facilitate production. When consumer demand increases, the organization must gear up rapidly to increase production. Inventories of goods entering production and finished goods will be exhausted more rapidly. The producer will have to purchase goods to replace those used up as well as to meet stepped-up production rates.

Because the demand for industrial goods is derived, marketers face at least three major implications:

1. Aggregate demand for an industrial good tends to be inelastic. It is not greatly affected by price. In turn, intense price-oriented competition between suppliers is not likely. Competition between industrial marketers is based more on the *quality* of goods and supporting services. An ex-chairman of Caterpillar stated,

> We adopted a firm policy that a Caterpillar product or component—no matter where it was built—would be the equal in quality or performance of the same product or component built at any other location . . . . [Furthermore] users can count on the availability of replacement parts regardless of where they operate . . . .[2]
> Caterpillar seeks a differential advantage through reliability, quality, and uniformity. One tactic it uses is to guarantee customers 48-hour delivery of parts anywhere in the world. If it fails, the part is free.[3]

---

[2] Thomas J. Peters and Robert H. Waterman, Jr., *In Search of Excellence* (New York: Harper & Row, 1982), p. 172.

[3] Ibid., p. 171.

While in general price is less of a competitive base than other factors, this is not the case with government. Government purchasing decisions are heavily influenced by price considerations.

2. Industrial marketers may want to direct some of their marketing effort at the consumer market. Industrial goods suppliers can increase demand for their offerings by stimulating consumer demand for goods that their goods enter or aid in production. For example, through a trade association manufacturers of glass containers advertise the benefits of bottles over other types of containers.

3. Since industrial product demand derives from consumer spending, industrial marketing needs to study shifts and trends in the consumer market. In this way, the industrial marketer can identify industries with a favorable derived demand for the long term and those facing a decline. The glass container manufacturers, for example, may want to shift their attention from baby-food producers to the beer and liquor industry.

ORGANIZATIONAL BUYING PRACTICES

The buying practices of organizations vary widely. One factor is the basic motive of the purchase—whether the product being purchased will be resold or used. Therefore, we'll organize our discussion of these buying practices around two categories: reseller practices and user practices.

Reseller buying practices

Several important features of reseller buying will help us understand it. (See Figure 8–4.)

Buying for someone else. A unique feature of resellers is that they buy for someone else—the individuals or organizations to whom they resell the goods they buy. As resellers, retailers are purchasing agents for the final consumer; wholesalers are purchasing agents for retailers. *Resellers buy what they think they can sell!* A careful examination of the needs and wants of their target buyers is critical to resellers' buying decisions. This is just as important to a reseller in deciding what to *buy* as it is to a manufacturer in deciding what to *produce*.

Figure 8–4: Important features of reseller buying practices

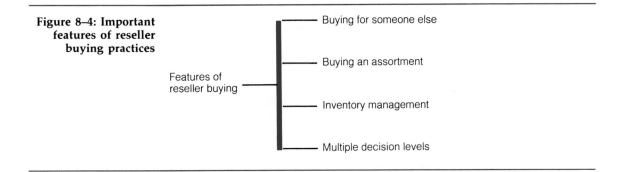

Features of reseller buying
- Buying for someone else
- Buying an assortment
- Inventory management
- Multiple decision levels

Thus, the marketing objectives and policies of resellers guide their buying practices. For example, major department stores (Sears, Roebuck; K mart; Neiman-Marcus) define target markets as do manufacturers. They buy products available from wholesalers and manufacturers that fit the needs and wants of their target markets. The marketing concept should guide the buying practices of resellers.

Buying an assortment. The buying decisions of resellers entail a wide variety of products. The reason is that both wholesalers and retailers offer buyers an *assortment of goods*. Consumers, as we have seen, seek to satisfy an entire array of needs and wants. They must search their environment for the mix of goods that will represent the best means for doing so. Through effective buying of an assortment of goods, retailers lessen the effort necessary for the consumer to perform this task. Wholesalers must perform a similar role for retailers.

Inventory management. The number and spread of products resellers buy make inventory management a key factor in buying decisions. Resellers seek the optimal level of stock on hand. Too much inventory results in unnecessary operating costs. Too little leads to opportunity costs from loss of present and future sales. Excess inventory effectively removes a reseller temporarily from the market as a buyer. Then even the most intense marketing effort by a supplier will not elicit a purchase.

The inventory management task of resellers offers their suppliers a servicing opportunity. Suppliers may offer guidance on inventory management, help take inventory, or arrange displays and shelves.

Levels of buying decisions. Resellers must decide what to buy, how much to buy, from what suppliers or vendors to buy, and what specific items to buy.

These interrelated decisions contribute to the reseller's total merchandise offering. In a merchandising plan resellers essentially seek to match the assortment of goods carried to those sought by their buyers. Decisions must be made about what generic products to stock, from what vendors to buy them, and what brand and product versions (size, style, color) to carry.

Implementing the buying function. Reseller size plays an important role in how the buying function is carried out. Small resellers usually have one person, the owner, responsible for the buying function. Large resellers, especially retail department stores, allocate the buying function by departments. The result is the glamorous, demanding, and sometimes tedious position of **retail buyer.**

retail buyer

> A **retail buyer** is an individual usually responsible for the entire marketing function of a department. Buyers perform the critical functions of determining the goods assortment to carry, promotion, pricing, and personnel management.

The scope of responsibility and its complexity make buying one of the more appealing career opportunities for marketing students.

The buying function in a large reseller organization may be performed by a **buying committee.**

buying committee

> A **buying committee** is a group of individuals who together authorize buying decisions and policies.

Buying committees are quite common in the food industry. One study reports that 71 percent of corporate chains and wholesale food operations use them.[4] A buyer may still exist, but the authority to make decisions about buying policies lies with the committee of divisional managers, their assistants, and other relevant people. The buyer presents the case for and against a vendor (in the absence of the vendor). The committee makes the decision. The greatest influence on the committee is usually the buyer's recommendations, if offered.

The presence of a buying committee poses a formidable marketing task, for supplier committee members are inaccessible as a group, except through a buyer. Furthermore, given the large number of buying decisions made, committees may not give a supplier's item deep consideration. For example, in one instance 49 items were considered in 50 minutes.[5] Well-targeted ads placed in reseller trade publications help overcome these problems.

The buying function may be performed by someone outside the organization. Many resellers work with *resident buyers.*

resident buyers

> **Resident buyers** are independent buying agents usually located in the city of the sellers (e.g., Paris, New York) who seek out vendors for the reseller. In particular, they reach the small suppliers who do not engage in a major selling effort.

---

[4] E. Mooney, *From the Buyer's Side* (Orleans, Mass.: Ed Mooney Company, 1979), pp. 160–61.

[5] Ibid., p. 163.

Resident buyers peruse the supply market, keeping a watchful eye out for new items that serve the reseller's needs. Resident buyers are paid a fee based on the amount of their purchases.

User buying practices

Almost any organization that performs a purchasing function is a user. Manufacturers, resellers, nonprofit organizations (hospitals, universities), and the government are included in this market. The basic role of the purchasing function is quite similar in all of these. They buy goods and services to enhance their ongoing operations. In essence, goods and services purchased serve as inputs to the process by which the organization generates its outputs. These outputs may be products, health care, education, or other services. Thus, the purchasing function is critical. It must be compatible with the mission of the organization. It is, therefore, a strategic management function designed to help the organization achieve its objectives.

The specific buying practices of all types of organizations are beyond the scope of this book. As organizational buyers, manufacturers face perhaps the most extensive and complex buying task. They buy virtually all of the types of industrial goods described above. Therefore, in discussing the buying behavior of organizational users we will concentrate on manufacturers. First, we'll identify several important features of industrial buying practices. (See Figure 8–5.)

Objectives of the buying function. As a strategic function, industrial buying occurs with objectives in mind. The general objective is to enhance the ongoing operations of the organization. More specifically, the objectives of purchasing can be thought of as "buying the right items in the

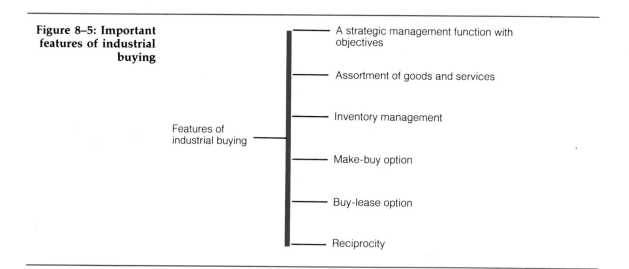

Figure 8–5: Important features of industrial buying

Features of industrial buying

— A strategic management function with objectives

— Assortment of goods and services

— Inventory management

— Make-buy option

— Buy-lease option

— Reciprocity

right quantity at the right price for delivery at the right time and place."[6] Thus, we see the same set of utilities present in organizational buying as in consumer buying.

Assortment of goods and services. Industrial users of products and services seek an assortment of goods and services to achieve their buying objectives. We have seen the various categories of industrial goods and the many services that organizations buy. Buying is complicated by the fact that items are purchased for all aspects of an organization's operation—engineering, production, marketing, finance, etc. The extent of the buying function is indicated by the B. F. Goodrich Company. In 1980 the company bought approximately 250,000 items, spending 62 percent of its sales dollars. As one executive put it, "No one area touches as much of the corporation's money as purchasing."[7]

Inventory management. Quantity buying makes inventory management an important feature of industrial buying practices. Effective inventory management lies at the heart of buying the right quantity of items for delivery at the right time. Inventory management is most crucial to the buying function when frequently purchased items—component parts, operating supplies—are involved.

Marketing to industrial buyers is made easier when a ***materials requirement planning*** function is incorporated into inventory management of purchased items.[8]

materials requirement planning	Materials requirement planning (MRP) is a technique of working backward from scheduled production runs to determine the necessary timing and quantities of purchases.

MRP incorporates information on new production plans, materials on order, and inventory on hand into a periodic computer run. The output of the program specifies the necessary quantity of items to be bought and when they are needed. MRP allows buyers to inform suppliers of their needs well in advance. Consequently, buyers can carry less inventory and keep costs down.

MRP allows a closer link, sometimes through computers, between buyer and seller. A computer linkage enhances the relationship between Dana, a supplier of drive shafts, and Ford. Dana delivers to Ford daily, knowing

---

[6] F. E. Webster, *Industrial Marketing Strategy* (New York: Ronald Press, 1980), p. 23.

[7] "New Status for Purchasing," *The New York Times,* June 2, 1981, p. 25.

[8] James B. Dilworth, *Production and Operations Management,* 2d ed. (New York: Random House, 1983), p. 239.

	Characteristic	Benefits to buyer
Figure 8–6: **Characteristics and benefits of a "just-in-time" system**	Frequent deliveries	Low inventory costs
	Small quantities purchased at one time	Quick detection of defects
	Long-term contracts	Less need for inspection
	Few suppliers	Quick response to engineering changes
	Close relationship with suppliers	

four days in advance how much each Ford factory will need.[9] This strong linkage makes it difficult for Dana's competitors to make inroads against the Dana-Ford relationship.

More and more firms are adopting the Japanese *"just-in-time" (JIT)* system to guide the MRP function for frequently purchased items. Characteristics of the JIT system include: frequent deliveries of small quantities, long-term contracts with suppliers, a small number of suppliers, and a very close buyer-seller relationship.[10]

Figure 8–6 summarizes the benefits of the JIT approach.

Make or buy.   A unique feature of the industrial market is that many industrial users have the internal capability to manufacture rather than buy some of the items they need. This is the **make-buy option.** Basically, the decision to make or buy rests with economic considerations. If it is economically advantageous to do so, the user will decide to start to make some of what it uses. Cost advantages *and* the opportunity to market the internally produced item contribute to the economic analysis of a make-buy decision.

A switch from buying to making occurs often. A few years ago NCR increased its production of semiconductor parts—components of its computer products. It increased its internal capacity from 40 percent to 60 percent of its requirements for the parts, cutting back its purchases by one third. NCR's motivation was to increase its control over this important component of its products.[11] The make-buy option stresses the importance of nurturing a long-term relationship with an organizational buyer. The essential task is to maintain a level of user satisfaction that keeps the make option out of the user's mind.

Buying versus leasing.   Another choice available to the user of industrial equipment is to rent or lease certain equipment—the *buy–lease op-*

---

[9] B. Charles Ames and James D. Hlavacek, *Managerial Marketing for Industrial Firms* (New York: Random House, 1984), p. 41.

[10] Richard J. Schonberger, *Japanese Manufacturing Techniques* (New York: Free Press, 1982), p. 163.

[11] *The Wall Street Journal,* July 18, 1980, p. 5.

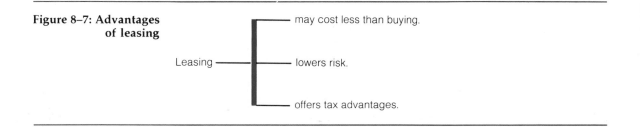

Figure 8–7: Advantages of leasing

Leasing
- may cost less than buying.
- lowers risk.
- offers tax advantages.

tion. Equipment leasing has been practiced for years by such firms as IBM. Leasing occurs in a variety of product categories in addition to major capital equipment: machine tools, cars, and trucks, to name a few. A variety of firms, including certain financial institutions, offer leasing arrangements. Some firms specialize in leasing (Leasco Computer, Inc.; National Equipment Leasing Corporation).

Users find various reasons for leasing instead of buying (also see Figure 8–7):

1. Some equipment costs too much to purchase. Leasing represents a lower-cost option. This factor is especially important when:
    a. The equipment offered is a new development.
    b. The equipment depreciates or becomes obsolete quickly.
    c. Specialized maintenance is often required.
    d. The need for the equipment is uncertain or sporadic.
    e. The company wishes to use its working capital elsewhere.
2. Leasing involves less risk. Unsatisfactory equipment can be returned.
3. Tax advantages are associated with leasing because it represents an operating expense usually in excess of the depreciation rate allowed by the IRS in the case of purchased equipment.

Reciprocity. One somewhat unfortunate relationship that can develop between industrial marketing firms is ***reciprocity.*** Firms may find that a potential supplier is also a potential buyer. A "You-buy-from-me, I'll-buy-from-you" situation may develop. Purchasing departments may be pressured by the sales department to develop a reciprocal relationship with a supplier. Reciprocity has negative effects on competition and free market operations. The government frowns on it.

Participants in user buying

The strategic importance of the buying function in organizations results in the need for specialized positions—***purchasing agents.*** However, the relevance of buying to many aspects of an organization means that multiple individuals get involved in the buying function. The concept of a ***buying center*** is important in organizational buying.

Purchasing agent. Large organizations often have purchasing agents.

purchasing agent

> **Purchasing agents** are specialists in buying, and part of the responsibility for buying is delegated to them.

In large firms they may head the purchasing department and be responsible for the entire scope of the firm's "materials management." In smaller firms the agent's duties may involve purchasing and other operational functions of the firm (e.g., marketing). The agent then becomes less of a buying specialist.

The scope of responsibility and authority delegated to purchasing agents varies considerably across firms. At a minimum, they coordinate the relationship with sellers. They become "detail people." That is, they make sure that the contractual relationship is carried out as agreed upon by the company in terms of trade, date of delivery, and so on. Seldom is the purchasing agent a major decisionmaker (unless he or she is the owner, which is often the case in a smaller firm). The purchasing agent will not decide what should be bought, how much, and from what vendors. Usually he or she may influence these decisions but will be responsible chiefly for implementing them.

The fact that purchasing agents usually are not decisionmakers in the purchase of major industrial goods does not lessen their importance as a contact for suppliers. Their influencer role is significant. Purchasing agents have experience with suppliers and are a quick source of information about them. They especially know the intangible features of suppliers—reliability, delivery speed, etc. Furthermore, purchasing agents influence virtually all organization buying decisions, although how central they are to the decision varies considerably.[12] Where decision making has become routinized, as with the purchase of operating supplies, the purchasing agent or a subordinate may play the dominant role in the buying process.

The buying center. The major reason that purchasing agents do not act alone in the buying function is that they are but one of a group of individuals to whom a purchasing decision is relevant. Take the case of capital equipment. Production, marketing, and finance departments all have concerns in the buying decision. Their concerns differ in nature, and they use different criteria to evaluate suppliers and their products. For example, production might be concerned with ease of use, dependability, and service. Purchasing might focus on cost, finance on return on investment, and marketing on any modifications necessary in the produced good. This, of course, increases the likelihood of conflict among the interacting parties.

---

[12] Wesley J. Johnston and Thomas V. Bonoma, "The Buying Center: Structure and Interaction Patterns," *Journal of Marketing,* Summer 1981, pp. 143–56.

The presence of multiple individuals in organizational buying decisions has given rise to the concept of a ***buying center.***

buying center

> The **buying center** refers to all organizational members involved in the purchase process for a product or service.

Webster and Wind have identified five ***key roles*** that exist among the members of a buying center:

1. *Users*—Those individuals and departments who will use the purchased goods. Their influence will likely occur at the beginning and end of the buying process. They may initiate the buying process by suggesting the need for the product. Also, they will provide postpurchase feedback regarding their satisfaction with the purchased item.

2. *Influencers*—Those members of the organization who exert influence by defining criteria that constrain the choices that can be considered or by providing information on alternative items. At the manufacturing level technical personnel (e.g., engineers) are often strong influencers, especially in the purchase of production equipment. They specify the technical requirements of production equipment.

3. *Buyers*—Those organizational members with formal authority for choosing the supplier and arranging the terms of the purchase. Such authority can often be limited by the influence of others who specify requirements that limit the choice of suppliers. The influence of buyers occurs throughout the buying process, once it has been initiated.

4. *Deciders*—Those members with formal or informal power to choose the ultimate supplier. Often buyers are deciders, but buyers may only implement the decisions of others.

5. *Gatekeepers*—Those members who control the flow of information into the buying group. Purchasing agents, because of their frequent interaction with various suppliers, are a prime example of gatekeepers. Others would include technical personnel who keep abreast of technological developments. The influence of gatekeepers occurs when they find alternative suppliers to evaluate.[13]

These roles are present in the network of interactions that characterizes organizational buying processes. Two or more roles can be performed by one individual. And the individuals performing each role and the

---

[13] F. E. Webster, Jr. and Y. Wind, *Organizational Buying Behavior* (Englewood Cliffs, N.J.: Prentice-Hall, 1972), pp. 78–80.

Table 8–4: Most central individual in buying center	Type of uses	Capital equipment		Industrial services	
		Product	**Individual**	**Service**	**Individual**
	Chemical manufacturer	Heat exchanger	Purchasing agent	Construction contract labor	Purchasing agent
	Steel manufacturer	Coke oven	Purchasing agent	Maintenance, repair	Buyer
	Machine tooling co.	Vertical boring mill	Vice president of operations	Fabricating work	Purchasing agent
	Power plant builder	Nuclear load cell	Job-shop order department manager	External building maintenance	Manager of facilities
	Steel manufacturer	River tow barge	Vice president of production	Employee food service	Plant labor relations manager
	Mining equipment manufacturer	Executive office desk	Purchasing agent	Training for first-line supervisors	General manager
	Chemical and scientific instruments distributor	Medical instruments	District vice president of sales	Management consultant	Senior vice president of sales
	Cement manufacturer	Forklift truck	General manager	Plant security protection	Assistant plant superintendent
	Home products manufacturer	Mixing machines	Buyer engineer	Drapery cleaning	Service manager
	Building materials manufacturer	Pump	Engineer	Engineering services	Executive vice president

Source: Adapted from Wesley J. Johnston and Thomas V. Bonoma, "The Buying Center: Structure and Interaction Patterns," *Journal of Marketing,* Summer 1981, pp. 150–51.

strength of their influence can vary across firms and buying situations. Table 8–4 reveals the most central individual in purchasing decisions for a variety of capital equipment and industrial services across different types of companies, as observed in a recent study of organizational buying centers. Table 8–5 shows the relative degree of influence of the various participants on different aspects of the buying process.

Research on buying centers reveals some useful findings. For example, Lillian and Wong, in a study of metalworking firms, found that individuals with some administrative responsibilities were more likely to be involved in buying.[14] Johnston and Bonoma found that firms with more formalized structures possessed larger, more strongly connected buying centers. Buying centers tended to be smaller for services and larger for more complex and important purchases.[15]

Such research aids industrial marketers by helping identify participants

---

[14] Gary L. Lillian and M. Anthony Wong, "An Exploratory Investigation of the Structure of the Buying Center in the Metalworking Industry," *Journal of Marketing Research,* February 1984, pp. 1–11.

[15] Johnston and Bonoma, "The Buying Center," pp. 151–53.

Table 8–5: Buying stages and role influence	Stage of buying process	User	Influencer	Buyer	Decider	Gatekeeper
	Problem recognition	XX	X			
	Criteria for evaluation	X	XX	XX	X	
	Identifying alternatives	X	XX	XX		XX
	Evaluating alternatives	X	XX	XX		
X = Moderate influence at this stage.	Decision	X	X	XX	XX	
XX = Strong influence at this stage.	Postpurchase feedback	XX	X			

in buying, their roles, and how the center changes according to the purchase situation. Such knowledge guides the development of suitable marketing efforts and helps identify who salespeople should contact.

INFLUENCES ON ORGANIZATIONAL BUYING BEHAVIOR

Our discussion of consumer purchase behavior shed light on a variety of influencing factors. Organizational buying behavior is a function of several factors as well (also see Figure 8–8):

1. **Individual factors**—Those relating to the psychological characteristics of each participant in the buying process.
2. **Intraorganizational factors**—Those relating to the structure, activities, objectives, technology, and other members of the firm engaged in buying.
3. **Interorganizational factors**—Those relating to the relationships between the buying organization and potential suppliers.
4. **Environmental factors**—Those relating to the external environment within which the buying firm exists.

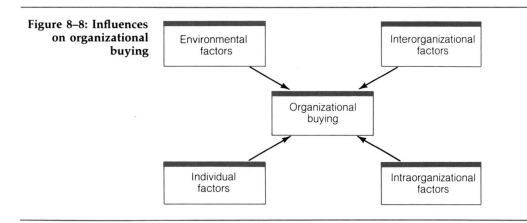

Figure 8–8: Influences on organizational buying

Appealing to an
industrial buying motive.

Over 60% of the top Fortune 200 companies have already purchased DOK-LOK* to prevent this costly accident.

we keep coming up best!

RITE·HITE

Courtesy Rite-Hite

Individual factors   Any organizational buying decision is a result of the interactions among several persons internal and external to the firm. Internal individuals act and interact on behalf of others in the firm or the overall firm itself. Organizational buying behavior is thus determined by the behavior of individuals; and their psychological characteristics operate as influences on buying.

The same general psychological influences that operate on consumer behavior (values, motives, perceptions, learning, attitudes, etc.) act on organizational buying behavior. The nature of their influence must be translated into an organizational context.

Values and motives. The specific values and motives that operate in organizational buying derive in part from the needs of both the firm and the individual. Values may relate to monetary matters. Motives relate to such goals as cost-minimization (in the purchase of operating supplies) and return on investment (in the purchase of capital equipment).

Motives relating to the welfare of the individual do operate in organizational buying. Such motives can be quite emotional. Fear is one motive. As an employee, the person involved in the buying process is concerned with job performance. He or she fears displeasing the boss, making wrong decisions, losing status, and even losing work. These fears often intensify the achievement motives in buying behavior. Motives relating to the welfare of the individual and the organization thus influence both the process by which a decision is reached and its outcomes.

Learning. Learning processes are for the most part similar in both organizational and consumer buying. Organizational buyers purchase items that have been successful for them in the past. Prior experience plays a major role in buying decisions, for dependability is of prime importance to organizations.

For some items organizational buying becomes habitual. A buyer who has had positive experience with a supplier over several purchases will return to this supplier. The supplier is dependable, and the habitual approach ensures a positive outcome with few demands on a busy employee's time. Habitual buying occurs for frequently purchased items that do not involve large dollar expenditures (e.g., operating supplies).

One distinction from consumer buying in the area of learning is that organizational buying involves very little trial-and-error learning. Consumers can learn about low-risk products through trial without losing much if products don't perform. But the magnitude of industrial purchases prevents such a learning process in organizational buying.

Perception. The perceptual processes relevant to consumer behavior also occur in organizational buying. Perception is selective, organized, and a function of stimulus and personal factors. Its context is different, though. Many processes governing the perception of advertisements are less relevant because advertising is less prevalent in industrial marketing.

The multidimensional nature of product perception is equally relevant. The nature of the dimensions on which products are perceived is different, however. Objective, easily defined dimensions (rather than the subjective ones of consumer perception) dominate in organizational buying. Buyers perceive products on dimensions such as operating convenience, price, dependability, operating costs, productivity, and service.

The concept of perceived risk is also relevant. Perceived risk in industrial purchasing decisions is probably greater in general than in consumer behavior. The risks pertain to both the firm and the individual. Purchasing decisions are an aspect of job performance. Good decisions contribute to the welfare of both the organization and the individual. The result is a strong need for certainty in buying decisions and a careful analysis of suppliers and their products.

Finally, the relevance of perception to corporate positioning strategies is just as strong for industrial marketing as for consumer marketing. Industrial marketers such as IBM, Du Pont, 3M, and Xerox seek a unique identity in the eyes of organizational buyers.

Beliefs and attitudes.   The hierarchy of effects used to examine the relationships among beliefs, attitudes, and behavior can be used in organizational buying behavior. Beliefs on various dimensions of suppliers and their products form the basis for an attitude toward them. More objective dimensions are used to evaluate industrial products. Also, attributes external to the product but relating to the supplier (e.g., speed of delivery) are more prevalent in organizational buying.

Organizational buyers on the whole use more objective criteria than consumers. But this does not mean they use no subjective or emotional factors. One study of homebuilders revealed such factors as the prestige of dealing with a supplier, friendships with salespeople, and personalities of salespeople in determining supplier selection.[16]

Personality.   Personality operates primarily as a factor in face-to-face, buyer–salesperson interactions. Salespeople need to consider the personalities of the buyers they call on. Also, personality influences how members of a buying center interact with each other.

Intraorganizational influences

The buying function occurs within a particular organization. Its general purpose is to help achieve the organization's goals. Therefore, certain features of the organization influence the performance of the buying function (also see Figure 8–9):

1. ***Interpersonal influences within the organization.*** The buying center concept recognizes that participants in buying do not act in isolation. Each takes part in a network of interactions between individuals and departments to whom a buying decision is relevant.

2. ***Organizational structure.*** This set of factors includes the communications network, authority, status, reward system, and work flow within the firm.

---

[16] G. R. Banville and R. J. Dornoff, "Industrial Source Selection Behavior—An Industry Study," *Industrial Marketing Management* 2 (June 1973).

Figure 8–9: Intraorganizational influences on buying

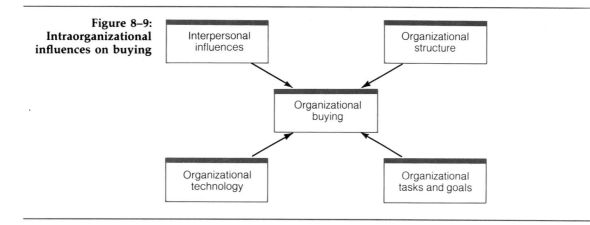

3. ***Organizational technology.*** The impact of technology on the buying function can be quite strong. For example, the computer plays a significant role in inventory management for both resellers and users.

4. ***Organizational goals and tasks.*** This set of factors encompasses the mission of the organization and the tasks necessary to accomplish the mission. Factors relating to whether buying occurs for resale or internal use, demand seasonality, the derived nature of demand, routinization of tasks, and the degree of centralization operate here.[17]

Organizations are complex units. Each of the four sets of intraorganizational influences would require individual chapters to convey more complete understanding. It's enough to say here that marketers need to understand the organization within which buying occurs. The nature of the organization says a lot about what guides the buying function.

Interorganizational influences

The major type of interorganizational influence on a firm's buying behavior comes from interactions with suppliers. These interactions are primarily interpersonal, as personal selling is the dominant form of promotion in industrial marketing. The personal contacts a supplier makes with a buyer are important in determining their relationship over time.

Supplier loyalty. Brand loyalty represents the ultimate goal in marketing to consumers. Supplier loyalty is the ultimate goal of industrial sellers with organizational buyers. Loyalty to a supplier exists when a buyer automatically turns to a particular supplier. As with brand loyalty,

---

[17] Based on F. E. Webster, Jr. and Y. Wind, "A General Model for Understanding Organizational Buying Behavior," *Journal of Marketing* 36 (April 1972), pp. 12–19.

Responding to change
in the environment.

THE IMPORTANT THINGS TO KNOW BEFORE BUYING A NEW BUSINESS PHONE SYSTEM:

1 There are at least 100 different manufacturers making over 2,000 different phone systems for you to choose from.

2 Some are not very good. Some are okay. A few are exceptional.

3 To sort out the good from the bad, the top engineers, technicians and customer consultants at Ameritech Communications studied and inspected hundreds of those systems to find the best-of-the-best.

4 They found the very few that were unquestionably the best-of-the-best in a variety of system sizes and types from smallest to largest and from the simplest to the most complex. From a variety of different manufacturers.

5 Then we put the Ameritech name on these few best-of-the-best systems.

6 You can only buy or lease one of these systems backed by the Ameritech name from the Bell Communications Companies in Illinois, Indiana, Michigan, Ohio and Wisconsin.

7 You can choose PBX, PABX, CPE or CPS— systems that have their operational hardware on your premises under your maintenance.

8 Or you can choose to go into THE CENTREX UNIVERSE—with systems, large and small, that make it easier, better and more economic than ever before.

9 Your phone company wants one thing for you: the world's best phone call. Every time, time after time. As for the Bell Communications Companies, that means doing all they can to sell you the best-of-the-best in business phone systems.

10 *Here's an offer:* As much as our Ameritech experts already knew about phones before they started their "best-of-the-best" search, they learned a lot more. We'd like to share what they learned with you. Find out "What The Phone Company Knows About Business Phones." Ask for our free book. It will make your own search easier and better, even if you don't buy from us.

AMERITECH
COMMUNICATIONS

serves you through:
**Illinois Bell Communications
Indiana Bell Communications
Michigan Bell Communications
Ohio Bell Communications
Wisconsin Bell Communications**

**We want to help you.
Give us a chance.
Give us a ring.**

1-800-562-2444

Or write: Ameritech Communications,
Box 2674 I, Highland Park, IL 60035

Courtesy Ameritech
Communications, Inc.

**Now that you don't have to buy your phones from the phone company,
isn't it nice to know you can?**

**Figure 8–10:
Environmental
influences on
organizational buying**

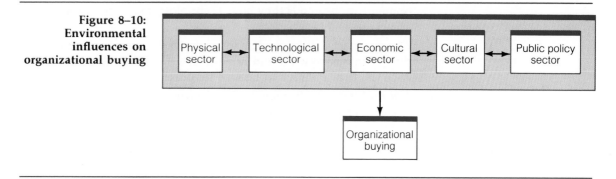

supplier loyalty results from a series of positive past experiences with a supplier—not the least of which is the personal contact with salespeople. Supplier loyalty is a risk-reduction mechanism in organizational buying just as in consumer behavior.

An important point is that supplier loyalty may develop for reasons other than those for which a supplier was initially chosen. Reasons for initially choosing a supplier may relate to price or product quality. Reasons for loyalty may have more to do with service and availability.

Opinion leadership. Interorganizational influences on buying by firms are not restricted to buyer–seller relationships. There is some evidence that an informal communications network can exist among alternative buyers of an industrial good. One study showed this to be true in a group of steel producers considering the adoption of a new production process.[18]

**Environmental
influences**

In Chapter 3 we discussed several environmental variables that influence the marketing operations of a firm. These same factors influence the firm's buying behavior. The general nature of these factors remains the same, also. They are dynamic, and as they change they may require the firm to adapt its buying procedures.

Environmental sectors relevant to organizational buying include (also see Figure 8–10):

1. *Physical sector.* Natural resources dictate the availability of certain goods. This sector influences where the firm can locate if it must purchase certain raw materials. Ecological concerns also mean the firm must consider the physical sector in what it buys.

2. *Technological sector.* Organizations must keep up with new devel-

[18] J. A. Czepiel, "Word-of-Mouth Processes in the Diffusion of a Major Technological Innovation," *Journal of Marketing Research* 11 (May 1974), pp. 172–80.

opments in the goods they buy. Technology may alter the selection criteria.

3. *Economic sector.* Because demand is derived, general economic conditions influence what and how much is bought. They also influence the firm's ability to finance its purchases.

4. *Cultural sector.* Cultural values and norms influence the individuals engaged in the buying process.

5. *Public policy sector.* Legal constraints can influence what is bought. For example, pollution standards dictate the use of certain goods in the production process.

Marketers need to monitor the environment's effects on potential buyers. This may reveal potential threats and opportunities associated with buyers' adaptive responses.

THE ORGANIZATIONAL BUYING DECISION PROCESS

The influences on organizational buying behavior affect not only what is bought but how it is bought. As with consumer behavior, we can identify a process by which organizational buying decisions are reached and implemented. The same stages that describe consumer decision processes can describe organizational buying decisions. Furthermore, the same task faces the organizational buyer—filling in the cells of an attributes-by-objects matrix to the point at which a decision can be made.

Problem recognition

Conceptually, organizational buyers recognize problems in the same way as consumers. A discrepancy between an actual and desired state triggers the recognition of a problem and a desire to alleviate it. A range of simple to complex phenomena can trigger the recognition of a problem. Simple phenomena include maintaining a certain level of inventory. In many firms a predetermined rule specifies when it is time to buy. For example, when operating supplies reach a prespecified level of existing inventory, it is time to replenish the supplies. Here, problem recognition is routinized.

A variety of factors can operate to trigger more complex problem recognition. Increased market demand may suggest a need for increased production. The firm might feel a need to buy new equipment or a new plant. Technological advances may suggest new cost-saving production processes. Generally, problem recognition processes become more complex when capital equipment purchases are suggested.

Marketing efforts can trigger problems by raising the level of the desired state. For example, Advance Lifts, a manufacturer of hydraulic lift equipment, developed portable dock lifts to make it easy for customers who lease facilities to move the lifts with them.[19] It hopes that mobility becomes a desired state for dock lifts in this segment.

---

[19] "Marketing Program Leads to Dominance," *Marketing News,* October 28, 1983, p. 6.

Internal search

Based on existing knowledge, the organizational buyer structures the problem to be solved. Potential suppliers and evaluative criteria are identified. The buyer searches existing knowledge for evaluations of suppliers on attributes. The experience of purchasing agents plays an important role here. Several factors determine the nature and number of evaluative criteria and their relative importance. First, the nature of the product being purchased influences the evaluative criteria used. For example, for operating supplies the dominant criterion might be speed of delivery. For capital equipment, evaluative criteria include product quality, technical services, price, and geographic proximity of the supplier. More complex industrial products generally yield more evaluative criteria than less complex ones.

A second set of factors relate to the characteristics of the buying organization. For example, size variations among buyers may result in different criteria. One study showed that the worst supplier problem for small industrial buyers was late delivery.[20] This finding suggests that delivery time is more important to small buyers than to large buyers.

External search

If existing knowledge is inadequate for decision making, members of the buying center will actively search for information to increase their knowledge base for a decision. As with consumers, behavior at this stage can be described in the extent and patterns of search.

In general, the extent of external search is a function of how well-developed the internal search stage is. The more well-developed it is, the less is the search effort. This relationship derives from the level of prior experience the buyer has. When considerable prior experience exists, less search will be needed.

Because more complex industrial goods entail more evaluative criteria, they will elicit consideration of more types of information in the search stage.

The sources of information available to the organizational buyer are of the same general types available to consumers. There are marketer- and nonmarketer-dominated, personal and nonpersonal sources. There are differences in the specific nature of some of these types. (See Figure 8–11.) Marketer-dominated personal sources include, of course, supplier salespeople. Trade shows are a personal source of information unique to organizational buying. Nonpersonal, marketer-dominated sources include advertising that is restricted largely to the print media (e.g., trade journals, brochures, and magazines). Nonmarketer-dominated personal sources include knowledgeable members of the buying center and buyers in other firms. There is evidence that word-of-mouth influences between companies—while they do occur—are not that frequent.[21] Nonpersonal

---

[20] M. M. Bird, "Small Industrial Buyers Call Late Delivery Worst Problem," *Marketing News,* April 4, 1980, p. 24.

[21] F. E. Webster, Jr., "Informal Communications in Industrial Markets," *Journal of Marketing Research* 7 (May 1970), pp. 186–89.

Figure 8-11: Sources of information for organizational buyers

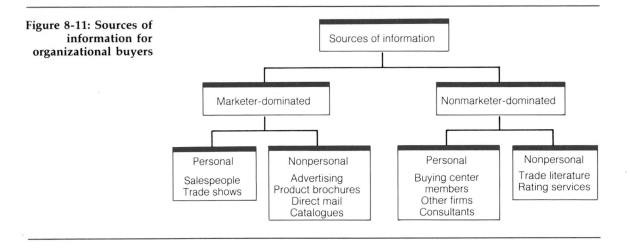

sources in this category fall into the publicity category—articles in trade media.

Research evidence suggests that most of these sources are used to some extent by industrial buyers.[22] It also suggests that the most frequently and intensely used source is the supplier's sales force.[23] Multiple contacts with the same salesperson are quite common in a purchase decision. Salespeople must have abundant knowledge of their products and their customer's organizations to be effective in these situations.

Information receipt

The dominant role of the salesperson as an information source for organizational buyers suggests that information is transmitted to and received by buyers within a *dyadic* situation (where two individuals interact with each other). In such a situation, especially where two individuals have interacted frequently in the past, a number of factors determine the buyer's receipt of information. A buyer will more readily accept information from salespeople perceived as credible and knowledgeable. Also, to some extent the personality of the salesperson can influence the manner in which the information is received.

A second feature of the information receipt stage for organizational buyers is the specificity and precision they require. The attributes used in decision making—technical features, service offerings, price, delivery time—warrant such precise information. The seller cannot be elusive or ambiguous.

Further, because of the strong interpersonal flavor to information re-

---

[22] Rowland T. Moriarity, Jr. and Robert E. Spekman, "An Empirical Investigation of the Sources Used during the Industrial Buying Process," *Journal of Marketing Research* 21 (May 1984), pp. 137–47.

[23] See, for example, U. B. Ozanne and G. A. Churchill, Jr., "Adoption Research: Information Sources in the Industrial Purchasing Decision," in *Marketing and the New Science of Planning,* ed. R. L. King (Chicago: American Marketing Association, 1968), pp. 352–59.

ceipt by organizational buyers and the demands they place on its form, incidental learning is much less common than in consumer behavior. Organizational buyers are purposeful as they consider information. They seldom receive it incidental to other forms of behavior. Little TV advertising is directed at these buyers. Some industrial advertising on drive-time radio occurs, though.

Decision

The task of the organizational buyer at the decision stage is that of the consumer—to integrate the various bits of knowledge on each alternative supplier so that utility estimates can be made and a decision reached. The various models described for consumer behavior are available to the organizational buyer as well. It is likely that organizational buyers would use more complex versions of these models (e.g., compensatory or lexicographic versions). To the extent that source loyalty occurs, a simple decision process would also occur. In the end, reciprocity might prevent use of any at all.

Postdecision

As with consumers, an organization's experiences with a chosen supplier go a long way in determining future behavior toward the supplier. If a chosen supplier performs well, the buyer will likely consider the supplier in subsequent purchases of the same or a different product.

The goal of the industrial marketer at postdecision should be to ensure a favorable reaction from the buyer and to maintain or enhance this feeling. This is, of course, the same goal in consumer marketing. However, in industrial marketing the approach is quite different. Consumer marketing depends heavily on advertising to accomplish this long-run goal. Personal selling is used in industrial marketing. Salespeople must ensure adequate postpurchase service in delivery, technical advice, maintenance, etc. It fact, in some situations the role of personal selling may be greater after the purchase than before it.

CLASSIFICATION OF ORGANIZATIONAL BUYING PROCESSES

Organizational buying processes can be classified in terms of the extent of effort put into the decision process. Three distinct classes can be identified (also see Table 8–6):

1. ***Straight rebuy.*** A routine purchase occurs that usually will have been made several times before. There would likely be no search for new information or consideration of new suppliers. Source loyalty might be strong because of its ease. The majority of purchases would be of this type, but buyers would spend little time on these purchases.

2. ***Modified rebuy.*** In this case the buyer has considerable information but does not make a routine decision. Additional information is acquired, evaluative criteria may be modified, and new suppliers may be considered.

Table 8–6:
Organizational buying
situations

		Buying situation		
		Straight rebuy	Modified rebuy	New-task
	Description	Routine purchase; no external search; source loyalty likely	Well-informed buyer; some new information acquired; new evaluative criterion; new supplier considered	Satisfying new need; little or no experience; much information needed
	Product example	Office supplies	Many services; office furniture	New capital equipment
	Marketing implications	Maintain loyalty or jolt buyer into modified rebuy	Emphasize uniqueness in price, service relative to other suppliers	Major marketing task

3. ***New-task buying.*** Here the organization is trying to satisfy a new need. Little or no experience exists, and the buyer must develop evaluative criteria, identify alternative suppliers, and acquire information on each criterion for each supplier.[24]

These three classes are analogous to routinized response behavior, limited problem solving, and extensive problem solving in consumer behavior. Similar marketing implications also exist. In straight rebuy situations the marketing task of the preferred supplier is to maintain loyalty. Other suppliers must jolt the organization into a modified rebuy situation by offering the buyer a reason to consider new suppliers. In new-task buying a major marketing task occurs, with much information presented to buyers, considerable negotiation, and a strong postpurchase follow-up effort.

A SUMMARY
MODEL OF
ORGANIZATIONAL
BUYING

Figure 8–12 identifies the major components of organizational buying behavior. Environmental factors can influence buying through all other factors. Interorganizational factors (which include supplier marketing efforts) influence buying through individual and intraorganizational factors. Individual and intraorganizational factors merge within the buying center, which carries out the decision process. Other more complex, comprehensive models of organizational buying behavior—notably the Webster–Wind and Sheth models—have been developed. Moriarity presents a useful summary of these models.[25]

[24] P. J. Robinson and C. W. Faris, *Industrial Buying and Creative Marketing* (Boston: Allyn & Bacon, 1967), Chapter 2.

[25] Rowland T. Moriarity, *Industrial Buying Behavior* (Lexington, Mass.: Lexington Books, 1983)

Figure 8–12: A summary model of organization buying

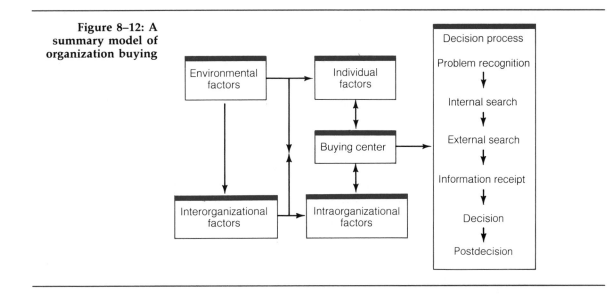

SUMMARY

Organizational buyers—users and resellers—represent a major marketing opportunity, with a dollar volume in excess of that of the consumer market. Two general types of goods are bought by organizational buyers. Resellers buy consumer goods. Industrial goods are bought by both resellers and users. A major characteristic of the demand of organizational buyers is that it is derived from the demand for the goods sold by their firms.

Although many organizations have individuals who specialize in buying, several people are usually involved in a buying decision. A set of factors influences their buying decisions. These factors include the nature of each individual and intraorganizational, interorganizational, and environmental factors.

The organizational buying process follows the same stages used in consumer behavior—problem recognition, internal search, external search, information receipt, decision, and postdecision. But the nature of each stage differs. Organizational buyers use more objective evaluative criteria, use personal sources of information more often, engage in less passive receipt of information, and may use reciprocity as a basis for supplier choice. They also have the option to buy, lease, or make goods that they use.

Organizational buying procedures can be placed in one of three categories, depending on the extensiveness of the process—straight rebuy, modified rebuy, and new-task buying.

KEY CONCEPTS

Resellers	Industrial good	Capital equipment
Users	Raw materials	Accessory equipment
Consumer good	Component parts and materials	Operating supplies

Organizational service	Buy-lease option	Environmental factors
Derived demand	Reciprocity	Interpersonal influence
Retail buyer	Purchasing agent	Organizational structure
Buying committee	Buying center	Organizational technology
Resident buyer	Buying center roles	Organizational goals and tasks
Materials requirement planning	Individual factors	Straight rebuy
Just-in-time (JIT) system	Intraorganizational factors	Modified rebuy
Make-buy option	Interorganizational factors	New-task buying

DISCUSSION QUESTIONS AND EXERCISES

1. Choose a particular industrial marketing industry and develop a descriptive profile of it.

2. To what extent should the firms in the above industry follow trends in the consumer market? Why?

3. For each of the following industries, identify some key sources of derived demand:
   a. Steel.
   b. Lumber.
   c. Rubber.
   d. Architectural services.
   e. Builders of communication satellites.
   f. Mobile phone manufacturers.

4. Interview buyers in a major department store about their buying practices.

5. Interview a purchasing agent about his or her responsibilities and roles in various situations. Pick one of these situations and see if, with the purchasing agent, you can construct the buying center.

6. Describe the "just-in-time" system.

7. Is the make-or-buy decision relevant to organizational services? Discuss.

8. Discuss the information sources available to organizational buyers.

Case 3: J. C. Penney and the working woman: Adapting to social and economic trends

J. C. Penney; Sears, Roebuck; and Montgomery Ward & Co. have been direct competitors for years. All of these stores have offered a wide range of products (from evening gowns to garbage disposals) at low to moderate prices. Sidney Stein, market research manager at Penney, says, "Our customers told us that they saw our stores as functional, institutional, unattractive, unexciting [and] dull." Penney is trying to forge a new image to compete with department stores rather than with Sears and Wards.

Part of Penney's about-face has come from the realization that they were missing out on an important social and economic trend. Working women exist today in greater force than ever before. Later marriages and higher divorce rates lead to more single working women, and over 40 percent of married women are employed outside the home. A primary target market for Penney is the young, affluent working woman. Through market research, Penney found that this customer was buying at Penney for linens and household goods, but was turning to other department stores for fashion. To capture more of the working woman's fashion expenditure, Penney signed a reported $1 million, six-year deal with designer Halston for an exclusive line of Halston designs, Halston III.

Halston III is geared toward the fashion-conscious working woman with money to spend. Its five groups include denim, casual wear, active wear for sports participation, sports wear for work and weekends, career wear for office dressing, and PM wear for evenings and special occasions. Prices are on a par with department store offerings. A Halston III blouse sells for $34, a dress for $90. To showcase Halston III, special attention has been paid to the design of a boutiquelike area in each Penney store. This is part of a $1 billion remodeling effort to upgrade Penney's layout and fixtures. In addition, the square footage of all women's clothing departments has increased by over 50 percent per Penney store.

Overall, sales of Halston III are brisk. Atlanta's district manager, R. H. Seaman, indicates that sales of brand name clothing are up 88 percent. Penney's long-term goal is to lift sales per square foot from its present $120 to the $200 range, on a par with Macy's. To accomplish this, Penney plans to continue its use of Halston designs, expanding into men's wear, jewelry, and children's clothing.

References

Blyskal, Jeff. "Better Slow than Never." *Forces,* October 10, 1983, pp. 153–54.

"The Halston–Penney Liaison: A Couple to Watch." *Stores,* August 1983, pp. 26–27.

Kotler, Philip. *Marketing Management,* 1980, p. 106.

"J. C. Penney Goes after Affluent Shoppers." *The Wall Street Journal,* February 15, 1983, p. 33.

"J. C. Penney Shops for a Trendier Image." *Business Week,* February 6, 1984, p. 58.

"Penney Pitches to a Different Base." *Chain Store Age Executive,* March 1983, pp. 23–25.

"Penney Shifts Strategy." *Dun's Business Month,* March 1983, p. 21.

Discussion questions

1. As part of its new focus, Penney is phasing out automotive, hardware, and appliance departments. Is there a problem involved with a change of this magnitude? How risky is it? How would you suggest Penney minimize the risk?

2. At $200 for a woman's suit, $34 for a blouse, $90 for a dress, do you think Halston prices are too high? Is Penney likely to gain or lose customers overall? Will sales revenue increase or decrease?

3. Penney is also emphasizing store brand "designer" names in an effort to provide fashion and quality at a less expensive price. Is this a good idea? Does it reduce the risk involved with the other changes?

4. How do you think Sears and Wards will react? What about department stores?

5. What effect will this liaison have on Halston's image?

Case 4: Xerox and Uniroyal and centralized purchasing: A case of organizational buying behavior

A buying center is the decision-making unit for an organization's purchasing function. Whether buying centers should be "centralized" or "decentralized" has been a controversial subject for many years. In a centralized system, the purchasing department operates at a corporate level, making all the buying decisions and then allocating resources to divisions and plants. Recently, with the advent of profit centers—where strategic business units and their managers are evaluated as if they were free-standing entities—purchasing has been largely decentralized. However, two major companies, Uniroyal and Xerox, have recently made the switch to centralized purchasing in an effort to cut costs and have the purchasing function help to meet overall corporate goals.

Uniroyal previously had a problem with lack of coordination in purchasing. Don Tieken, the purchasing director, said,

> As of January 1982, there was some corporate buying, some divisional buying, and, of course, some plant buying. These three different layers of buying existed quite independently of one another. Corporate people tended to buy things that went across divisional lines; the divisional people bought things that were just for the division; and plants bought for just the plant. There wasn't a unified approach to purchasing.

As a result, Uniroyal failed to take advantage of the buying leverage of a company with $2.5 billion in annual sales. There was no formal cost-savings program, and they made little use of the efficiencies possible from their large-scale operations.

To help overcome these problems at Uniroyal, the purchasing function was centralized in an innovative fashion. The system involves a central council of division purchasing managers. Each division is responsible for the procurement of companywide requirements for which that division is the biggest user. National contracts for major raw materials are negotiated through headquarters, and the council functions as the clearinghouse for worldwide requirements, supplying small divisions with materials procured by larger divisions.

The new system clearly delineates purchasing responsibility. Each product has a single manager who is responsible for it. As a result, buying leverage is maximized, and cost-reduction goals can be realistically identified and met.

Purchasing manager Tieken comments, "We've had a lot of consolidation at Uniroyal—efficiencies and cutbacks—so people became more efficient." With the new system, Uniroyal went from a $119 million loss to a net profit of $51 million in 1981, of which $30 million was savings attributable to the new purchasing system.

Xerox Corporation also made the switch to centralized buying in a campaign to "drive expenses down." Their strategy includes worldwide centralization of purchases, with a reduction in the number of suppliers. In the past, Xerox buyers, called "commodity managers," bought for the plants in their own country. Under the new plan, each commodity manager buys a particular product for all plants, with most purchases being on a "sole-source" basis. For example, transformers that used to be supplied by U.S. and European companies will be purchased in Hong Kong, and rubber products from the United Kingdom and Dutch sources will be bought in the United States. The central commodity managers will be located in the countries where their vendors are. As part of this consolidation, Xerox halved their 5,000 suppliers. In the long run, they plan to reduce to about 600.

A Xerox contract is a valuable asset for a supplier; they typically are long-term—two to three years. Xerox, however, anticipates that good suppliers can expect to keep their contracts indefinitely.

Under the new system, economies of scale have allowed Xerox suppliers to reduce their prices. Xerox reports that their goal was a 15 percent price reduction, and many commodities have exceeded that goal.

References

Dowst, Somerby. "Xerox Centralizes Buys for Cost Fight." *Purchasing,* October 7, 1982, pp. 56–59.

Temin, Thomas R. "Purchasing at Uniroyal Takes New Approach." *Purchasing,* October 7, 1982, pp. 61–64.

Discussion questions

1. What is the difference between "centralized" and "decentralized" purchasing?

2. What are the reasons for Uniroyal's and Xerox's switch to centralized purchasing?

3. What are potential problems with decentralized purchasing?

4. Are there problems with the centralized system? If so, can you think of ways in which these problems can be surmounted?

5. What environmental factors recently have made centralized buying attractive to large corporations?

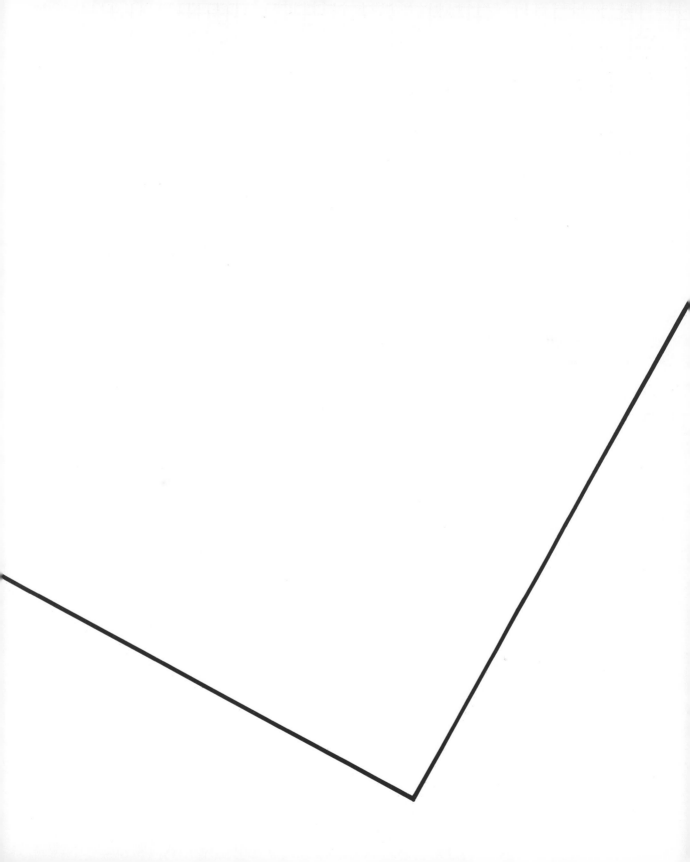

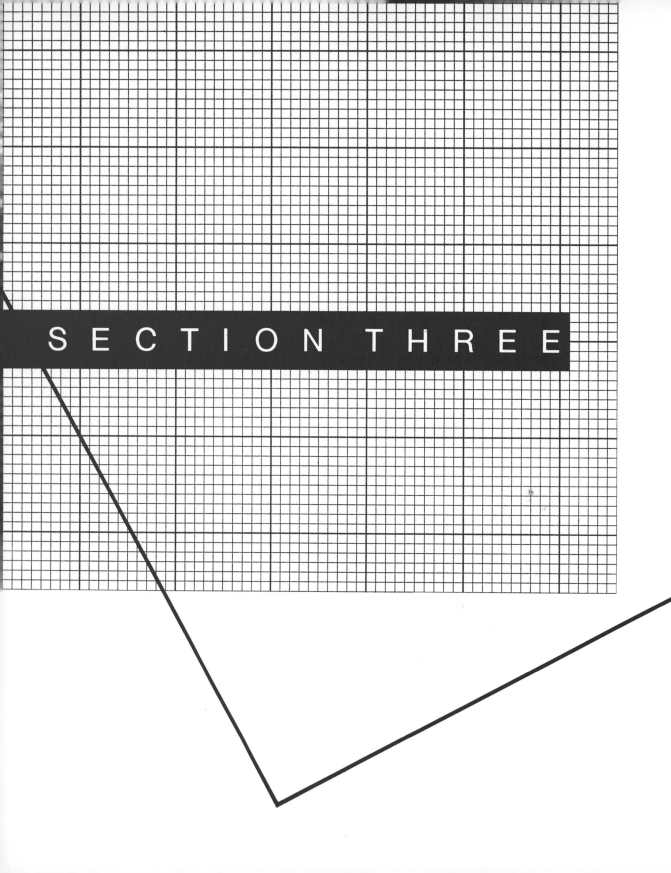

SECTION THREE

Segmenting and measuring markets

The heterogeneity of the marketplace makes it infeasible to implement the marketing concept using a single marketing strategy aimed at all buyers. Instead, market segmentation occurs. That is, distinctive marketing strategies aimed at one or more targets are developed. Chapter 9 takes a close look at the market segmentation process.

The attractiveness of a market to an organization rests partially on its level of demand. Chapter 10 examines the role of demand assessment and the procedures available for assessing demand.

CHAPTER 9

Market segmentation

The nature of market segmentation
    Rationale of market segmentation
    The market segmentation approach
    Market segmentation defined

Choosing a segmentation variable
    Homogeneity within and heterogeneity between segments
    Behavioral consequences
    Marketing consequences

Necessary conditions for segmentation
    Measurability
    Substantiality
    Stability

Potential bases for segmenting the market
    Descriptive characteristics of buyers—The consumer market
    Descriptive characteristics of buyers—The organizational market
    General behavioral characteristics—The consumer market
    General behavioral characteristics—The organizational market

Product-specific behavioral characteristics—The consumer market
Product-specific behavioral characteristics—The organizational market

Developing composite profiles of segments

Pursuing the market
    Aggregated strategy
    Disaggregated strategy
    Niche strategy

Steps in the segmentation process
    Step 1—Identify market segments
    Step 2—Collect research information
    Step 3—Develop composite profiles of segments
    Step 4—Ascertain behavioral and marketing consequences
    Step 5—Estimate market potential
    Step 6—Analyze marketing opportunity
    Step 7—Decide if and how to pursue the market
    Benefits implied in the segmentation process

Summary

Key concepts

Discussion questions and exercises

In Chapter 2 we saw that an important stage in the strategic planning process was the development of the firm's product/market concept. This concept designates the particular need or want of a group of buyers that a product (or group of products) attempts to satisfy. We saw that a financial planning and securities company identified three groups of buyers—individuals, small business, and large corporations—and three types of services—investment, financial planning, and insurance. The company decided to concentrate on three product/markets: financial planning for individuals, investment services for small businesses, and insurance for large corporations. (See Figure 9–1.) The three product/markets define the company's marketplace approach—how it will achieve its corporate objectives. The company has identified three target markets and wants to tailor a marketing program to each. The company's approach represents the dominant way of thinking about marketing strategy today. As one ad agency executive put it:

> The mass market has splintered . . . . Every market [is] breaking into smaller and smaller units, with unique products aimed at defined segments.[1]

This approach to the market requires **market segmentation**—a very useful process to a firm that identifies one or more target markets and wants to tailor a marketing program to each. Market segmentation is quite evident in the consumer market. It is also relevant to firms marketing to organizational buyers. In this chapter we'll consider the nature of the process, its underlying rationale, the benefits it offers, ways to segment the market and the criteria for choosing them, and procedures for pursuing a segmented market.[2]

THE NATURE OF MARKET SEGMENTATION

Rationale of market segmentation

Two factors suggest the need for market segmentation. (See Figure 9–2.) First, market segmentation is an outgrowth of the marketing concept, which emphasizes the satisfaction of buyer needs as the focal point of marketing. Second, market segmentation is an outgrowth of **market heterogeneity.** Buyers vary in the needs that are important to them. And buyers with similar needs can vary in what they see as the best means to satisfy those needs. Market segmentation provides a way to adapt the firm's marketing programs accordingly. The result is a more effective implementation of the marketing concept.

As an example, consider the U.S. food market. The recent trend toward weight consciousness has created at least four different types of food buyers: (1) Those not concerned about their weight; (2) Those who go

---

[1] "Marketing: The New Priority," *Business Week,* November 21, 1983, p. 97.

[2] Particularly helpful in the development of this chapter was W. L. Wilkie and J. B. Cohen, "A Behavioral Science Look at Market Segmentation Research," Working Paper, Center for Consumer Research, University of Florida, 1976.

Figure 9–1: Product/ market strategy

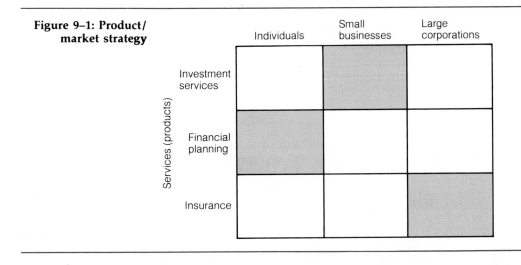

on and off diets; (3) Those who consistently try to contain their calorie intake; and (4) Health-food addicts.

Food companies are broadening their product lines to better serve some of these types. Health-food lines have been developed for the health-food addicts, for instance. But the greatest growth appears to be in prod-

Figure 9–2: The need for market segmentation

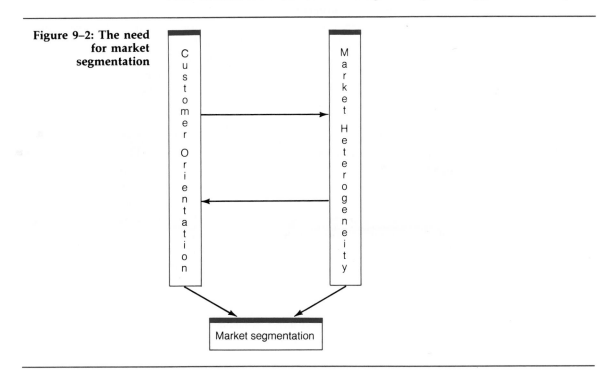

ucts designed to serve the third group. Many foods not considered diet-oriented (for example, cheese, catsup, cookies, pancakes, mayonnaise) are now available in "light" form, with one-third to one-half fewer calories than the regular form. Campbell's is now reminding consumers of the low-calorie benefits of several of its soups that have been on the market for years.

The market segmentation approach

In taking a segmented approach, a firm seeks to establish: distinct customer groupings within the marketplace and linkage between the nature of each group of customers and the appropriate marketing programs to direct at the group.

Customer groupings. The marketplace has a broad array of variables. *Consumers* differ in demographic, socioeconomic, psychological, and behavioral variables including how they respond to marketing efforts. *Organizational buyers* differ in type and size of business, geographic location, and their responses to marketing efforts. Each customer and organization probably has a unique combination of these variables and could thus be treated as a unique market segment. For most firms, though, treating each buyer uniquely would be overwhelming and inefficient.[3] A more reasonable approach would focus on one or a few variables. It would form groupings of buyers who are similar to each other on these variables but who differ from members of other groups. A firm might disaggregate the consumer market into segments based on, say, income. The result might be six distinct segments: households earning (1) less than $10,000 per year, (2) between $10,000 and $14,999, (3) between $15,000 and $19,999, (4) between $20,000 and $24,999, (5) between $25,000 and $29,999, and (6) $30,000 or over.

Linkage to marketing practice. Once market segments are identified, their unique nature and differing response to marketing strategies should be considered. We will see later that differences in response to marketing strategies may even serve as the basis for segmentation. The firm seeks to match the segment's nature with the most appropriate marketing program. The result is a more efficient and effective use of the firm's resources to influence market demand. Thus, to merely *describe* differences between buyers is not sufficient. A complete market segmentation strategy *analyzes* the differences and determines whether the differences can be translated to a product/market strategy.

---

[3] Exceptions in the consumer market would include the housing industry, while in the organizational market any industrial marketer selling to a few large buyers might take such an approach.

market segmentation

> **Market segmentation** is the process by which an organization attempts to match a total marketing program to the unique manner in which one or more customer groups behave in the marketplace.

Market segmentation defined

We should go further with this important definition. (See Figure 9–3.) The definition recognizes segmentation as a *process* involving a sequence of steps: identify the segments, analyze the nature of each segment to determine its uniqueness, translate these differences into the appropriate marketing strategy, and select target markets. We'll discuss specific features of this process later.

Second, market segmentation is an *attempt* to market products more effectively. The mere process does not ensure its success.

Third, the nature of a segment has implications for all the marketing decision variables. Firms should think in terms of an *entire marketing program* for a segment. Variations in marketing programs across segments may involve all of the decision variables or only a portion of the marketing mix. In the automobile industry we see extensive variations between marketing programs aimed at different segments. Physical variations (sizes, style) and functional variations (engine size, extra features) are evident in the product. Corresponding variations in purchase price, operating costs, and promotional tactics accompany these product differences. They result in distinct overall marketing strategies aimed at the various segments. Less extensive variations in marketing programs between segments are indicated in the bank credit card area mentioned in Chapter 6. Here a study revealed differences between social class segments in the motive underlying the use of bank credit cards. Lower social classes use the card as convenient credit. Higher social classes use the card as a cash substitute. Variations in marketing strategy would be restricted to the

Figure 9–3: Key features of market segmentation

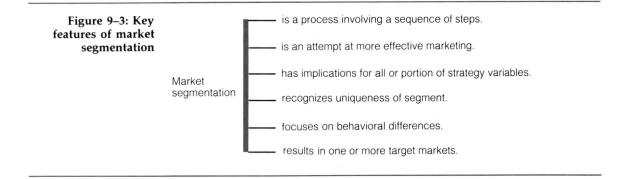

Market segmentation
- is a process involving a sequence of steps.
- is an attempt at more effective marketing.
- has implications for all or portion of strategy variables.
- recognizes uniqueness of segment.
- focuses on behavioral differences.
- results in one or more target markets.

promotional area. The basic product and its conditions and costs of use would remain constant over segments.

Fourth, market segmentation must recognize the *uniqueness* of segments. It deals with and is predicated on the differences among buyers. Without differences there is no need to segment.

Fifth, the firm may develop marketing programs for each of *one or more segments* of the market. It may develop marketing programs for each of the segments, only a portion of them, or just one of them. These alternatives are discussed more fully in a later section, as well.

Finally, the firm must focus on crucial *behavioral differences* between segments. Segments may be formed on the basis of some descriptive characteristic, such as age of consumers. However, to be meaningful, the age differences between segments must correspond to behavioral differences between the segments. Unless age differences relate to what buyers want in a product, how they buy it, their media exposure patterns, or some other type of behavior, age won't be a very useful segmentation variable. Mere differences in consumers' ages are insufficient for segmentation purposes.

There are different levels at which we might consider behavior among segments. Buyers make decisions between different generic products, between different forms of a generic product, and between different brands. At each of these levels there may be important differences between buyers that are related to preferences. Consider how a bank might segment the market at different levels. (See Figure 9–4.) At the generic level it could be interested in spending versus saving behavior. That is, it might identify two segments—spenders and savers. The bank would then examine the financial services needed by each group.

At the product-form level, segments could be based on the preference for banks versus savings-and-loan institutions. Both spenders and savers could be further segmented in terms of their usage of one type of institution over another. At the next decision level—the selection of a specific financial institution—segments could be based on consumers' preferences for large versus small financial institutions.

CHOOSING A SEGMENTATION VARIABLE

The diversity of the market provides a vast array of potential variables that can be used to identify market segments. Segments can be based on one or a combination of variables. Figure 9–5 shows the effects of increasing the number of variables used to segment the market. In (*a*) only one variable—income level—is used, and three segments emerge. In (*b*) income and age, when used together, generate nine segments. In (*c*), when we add the education variable, we get 18 segments. As you increase the number of variables used, you increase the number and precision of segments. Of course, there is a practical limit to the number of segments that should be formed. As you increase the number of segments

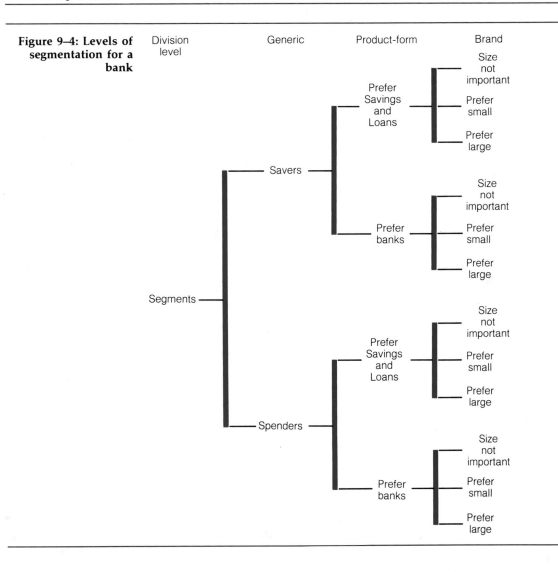

Figure 9–4: Levels of segmentation for a bank

you rapidly experience diminishing returns with respect to cost efficiencies and varying responses to marketing strategies. The ultimate number of segments could be attained by treating each buyer as a separate segment. But, as we said, this is usually impractical.

There are no hard, fast rules for selecting segment variables. But there are some guidelines for evaluating their potential usefulness. These guidelines are useful in the search for the "ideal" segmentation variable. They are relevant to both consumer and organizational markets. Table 9–1 summarizes these guidelines.

Figure 9–5: Single and multiple variable market segments

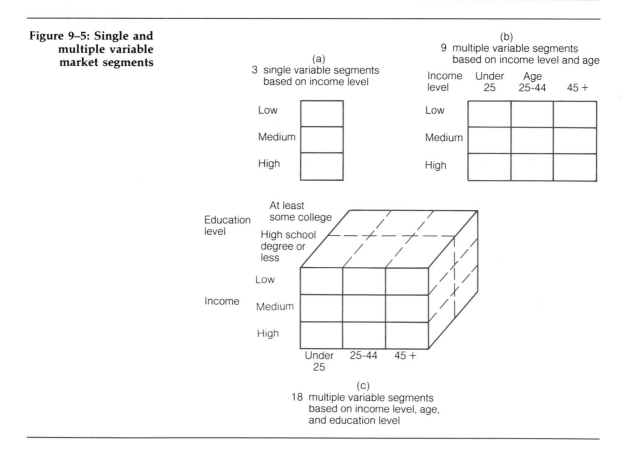

(a)
3 single variable segments based on income level

Low
Medium
High

(b)
9 multiple variable segments based on income level and age

Income level	Under 25	Age 25-44	45 +
Low			
Medium			
High			

Education level
At least some college
High school degree or less

Income
Low
Medium
High

Under 25   25-44   45 +

(c)
18 multiple variable segments based on income level, age, and education level

Homogeneity within and heterogeneity between segments

Two general, interrelated criteria should be kept in mind when considering a basis for segmenting the market and applying some of the subsequent criteria. First, a segmentation variable should provide for ***homogeneity within segments:*** the members of a segment should be as similar to each other as possible on as many relevant variables as possible. Rele-

Table 9–1: Guidelines for choosing a segmentation variable

Criterion	Ideal situation
Homogeneity within and heterogeneity between segments	Buyers within each segment very similar to each other and very different from buyers in other segments
Behavioral consequences	The segmentation variable is highly correlated with behavioral differences between buyers
Marketing consequences	Behavioral differences should be translatable into distinct marketing programs for each segment

vant variables include the one being used to identify segments and others that are used to analyze the nature of a segment.

Second, a segmentation variable should provide for ***heterogeneity between segments*** on the same variables for which homogeneity within segments is sought. In market segmentation we want buyers within each segment to be similar to each other but clearly different from buyers in other segments.

One increasingly popular basis for segmenting the market for direct-mail marketing reveals the potential for violating this guideline. ZIP code location is a relatively easy way to segment the market in geographic terms. Commonly, there are important differences among ZIP code areas in the composition of residents. Income, age, ethnicity, and home ownership represent a few of the characteristics on which ZIP code areas differ. Not always, though. Many ZIP code areas are quite heterogeneous, containing a range of incomes, ages, ethnic groups, homeowners, and renters. Consequently, many ZIP code segments would not meet the homogeneity-within criterion. Direct-mail marketers face difficulties with a single marketing strategy aimed at these heterogeneous segments.

Behavioral consequences

The mere identification of customer groupings based on some variable is insufficient. The segmentation variable also should reflect similarity within and differences between segments in some type of marketplace behavior. If age is used to segment the market, it should be correlated with some type of behavior—so that buyers in a segment are similar but differ from members of other segments in that behavior. It would be important that age groups differed in terms of media exposure patterns, product-usage rate, or other consumer-related behavior patterns.

A variety of types of marketplace behavior can be associated with a segmentation variable. They include purchase-related behavior (product or brand preferred, usage rate), decision-process behavior (information sources consulted, general media exposure patterns), and existing brand perceptions, to name a few. In considering a variable, the marketing manager should be alert to the entire range of ***behavioral consequences*** that might be associated with the variable.

Many companies segment markets using variables with built-in behavioral consequences. Behavioral differences between buyers are the basis for segmentation. For example, an airline company can identify segments based on frequency of flying—infrequent fliers (less than once a year), moderately frequent fliers (one to three times per year), and frequent fliers (four or more times per year).

Marketing consequences

The behavioral consequences of a segmentation variable should result in ***marketing consequences.*** The behavioral differences between segments should suggest distinct marketing programs for each segment. Variations in the combination of marketing mix components across segments should be indicated by the behavioral differences. Thus, differences should be suggested in product design, communications strategies (message content, media), price (if legally feasible), and/or product distribution across segments. The key point here is that buyers within a segment should be similar in how they respond to marketing mix variables but different from how other segments respond. In short, the behavioral consequences of a segmentation variable should translate into an overall product/market strategy. Without these marketing consequences, there is no need for a market segmentation strategy.

Frequency of flying as a segmentation variable for the airline industry has marketing consequences. Frequent fliers respond to marketing programs that offer free trips once a certain number of miles have been traveled on an airline. Airlines attempt to establish brand loyalty with these programs. Less frequent fliers do not respond to these programs. Instead, "super saver" discounts on individual trips are more likely to appeal to them.

NECESSARY CONDITIONS FOR SEGMENTATION

The above guidelines represent normative criteria to consider in the search for a way to segment the market. A variable that meets these criteria must meet certain other conditions that are necessary to implement a segmentation plan and strategy using this variable. These conditions include **measurability, substantiality,** and **stability.** (See Table 9–2 for an overview.)

Measurability

To be identified as a segment, a buying unit—whether an individual consumer, household, or organization—must be measurable on the chosen variable. It must be clearly identifiable in terms of the segment of the market to which it belongs. In this way buyers in each segment can be distinguished from other segments. Now, we might want to choose personality as our variable. It could suggest to us important differences. But we would find personality a difficult variable to measure in ways meaningful to marketing.

Table 9–2: Necessary conditions for the implementation of segmentation

Condition	Description
Measurability	Buying units must be identifiable in terms of the segmentation variable
Substantiality	Segmentation must yield at least one segment with sufficient profit potential
Stability	Segments must remain stable from when they are analyzed to when a strategy based on that analysis is implemented

Substantiality   The segmentation process must yield at least one segment that is sufficiently large in profit potential to make it worthwhile as a target market. A segment may meet all the above criteria but be too small to be a profitable target market. An extreme example of a less-than-substantial segment would be belts developed for individuals with 60-inch waists or more. Few individuals fall into this group. Thus, a very high price would be necessary. But the consumers are probably unwilling to pay the price that would have to be charged for it to be a profitable target market.

Stability   The sequence of steps in the segmentation process usually encompasses a considerable range of time. In particular, there will be a gap between when segment information is collected and analyzed and when a marketing strategy based on this information is implemented and performance objectives can be realized. It is necessary then for a market segment to be highly stable with respect to the appropriate marketing strategy. The segment must remain much the same from when information is analyzed to when the appropriate strategy for it is implemented. If the segment is unstable, the marketing strategy directed at it can become inappropriate, and the benefits of segmentation may be less than otherwise. They may even become negative. Indeed, one reason offered for the failure of the Edsel is that the target segment had changed by the time strategy for it was implemented.[4]

POTENTIAL BASES FOR SEGMENTING THE MARKET

Now that we have examined the guidelines and conditions for segmenting the market, we can consider the vast array of segmentation variables. In both the consumer and the organizational market, three general categories of segmentation variables are available:

1. *Descriptive characteristics of buyers.* These are variables that *describe* customers in terms of the characteristics they possess.
2. *General behavioral characteristics.* These are behavioral patterns exhibited by customers in the marketplace that are not unique to a product class but rather cut across their behavior in the marketplace in general.
3. *Product-specific behavioral characteristics.* These are behavioral patterns exhibited by customers that are specific to the product in question.

We can now consider specific variables within each of these categories for both the consumer and the organizational market. Table 9–3 provides an overview of the discussion.

[4] David W. Cravens, Gerald E. Hills, and Robert B. Woodruff, *Marketing Decision Making,* rev. ed. (Homewood, Ill.: Richard D. Irwin, 1980), p. 177.

Table 9–3: Overview of segmentation variables	**Category**	**Consumer market**	**Organizational Market**
	Descriptive characteristics	Demographics Family life cycle Socioeconomic status Social class Geography Subculture	Type of business Size Geography
	General behavior characteristics	Media exposure patterns Personality Lifestyle	Media exposure patterns Nature of buying center Buyer sophistication
	Product-specific characteristics	Loyalty patterns Deal-proneness Usage rate Benefits sought Information search patterns User lifestyles	Source loyalty Usage rate Benefits sought

Descriptive characteristics of buyers—The consumer market

Demographic and socioeconomic variables. The demographic and socioeconomic characteristics of consumers are frequently used as variables for segmenting the market. *Demographic variables* include age, sex, family size, marital status, etc.; *socioeconomic variables* include income, occupation, and education. The popularity of these variables as segmentation bases derives from their ease of measurement and often strong correlations with behavior in the marketplace.

Levi Strauss has used demographic bases for segmenting the market in its efforts to broaden its product line.[5] It defines its total market as individuals of both sexes from ages 4 to 60. It segments this total market using a combination of sex and age; and for the adult market it adds occupation as a basis for further breaking down the market. The result is a series of jean products and other apparel items directed at each segment. Denim and corduroy jeans are directed at men, women, and children for casual wear. Professional men are targeted for the company's brand of dress suits, blazers, and slacks. Similar variations in products (casual to dressy) are offered to women. Children's apparel is offered to both sexes; it includes items for back-to-school, play, and dress-up uses.

The marketing consequences of the Levi Strauss approach to segmentation is particularly evident in the media used in its advertising. Men's products are advertised through TV, radio, and print media. Women's products make heavy use of national TV and print. Children's products are advertised exclusively through radio.

---

[5] "The Cowboy Who Became a Lady," *Marketing and Media Decisions,* Spring 1982, pp. 33–49.

Going after the dual-
income household.

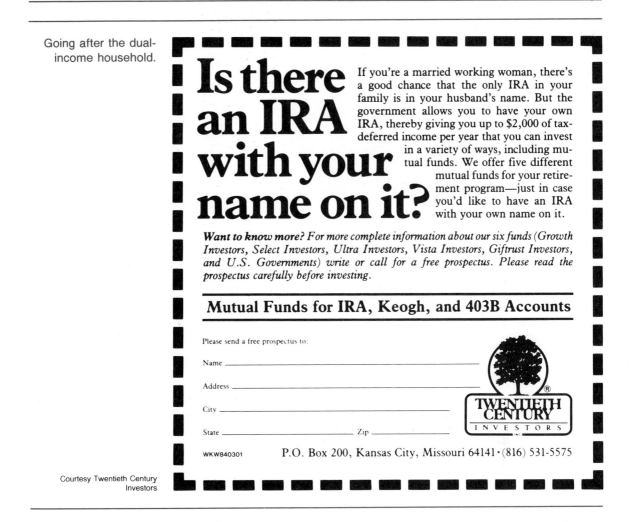

Is there an IRA with your name on it?

If you're a married working woman, there's a good chance that the only IRA in your family is in your husband's name. But the government allows you to have your own IRA, thereby giving you up to $2,000 of tax-deferred income per year that you can invest in a variety of ways, including mutual funds. We offer five different mutual funds for your retirement program—just in case you'd like to have an IRA with your own name on it.

Want to know more? For more complete information about our six funds (Growth Investors, Select Investors, Ultra Investors, Vista Investors, Giftrust Investors, and U.S. Governments) write or call for a free prospectus. Please read the prospectus carefully before investing.

Mutual Funds for IRA, Keogh, and 403B Accounts

Please send a free prospectus to:

Name _____

Address _____

City _____

State _____ Zip _____

TWENTIETH CENTURY INVESTORS ®

WKW840301   P.O. Box 200, Kansas City, Missouri 64141 · (816) 531-5575

Courtesy Twentieth Century
Investors

Another company using demographics to segment the American market is Mazda, a Japanese auto manufacturer.[6] Its total market is defined as the imported car buyer, men 18 to 48, college educated, with $20,000 or more annual income. It then defines the segment for the RX-7 model as 18 to 34 years old, college educated, with at least a $30,000 annual income.

Geographic location. In marketing some products it is often useful to recognize geographic location differences among consumers. Geographic bases for segmenting the market can be defined in a variety of ways— urban–suburban–rural, states, counties, cities, climate, etc. Important geo-

---

[6] "How Mazda Came Back," *Marketing and Media Decisions,* September 1979, p. 75.

Figure 9–6: Geographic difference in most popular motor vehicle

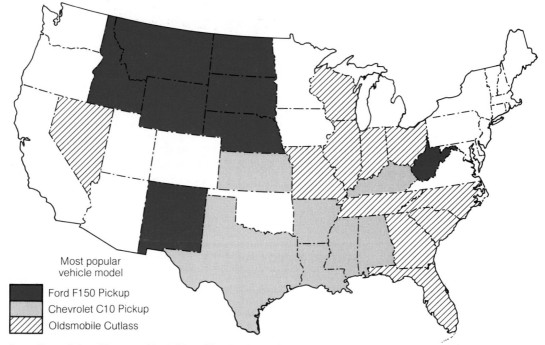

graphic differences in buying patterns can suggest different marketing programs for such segments.

Distinctive geographic patterns of consumer behavior are evident in the motor vehicle market. (See Figure 9–6.) In several states the most popular vehicle is a pickup truck. This "pickup belt" runs from the upper Midwest to the Gulf states. Interesting variations in brand preference exist within this area. In the northern portion Ford trucks sell the best. Chevrolet is the leader in the southern states.

Geographic variations in car sales are also apparent. Ford has traditionally been strong on the West Coast; Buick sells better in Chicago than anywhere else. But the one model with distinct geographic popularity is the Oldsmobile Cutlass. It is the best-selling vehicle in a cluster of Great Lakes states and in a cluster of south Atlantic states. (See Figure 9–6.)[7]

Of course, the mere geographic location of consumers does not *explain* these patterns of vehicle preference. To understand distinctive geographic

---

[7] Eugene Carlson, "Personality of Area's Drivers Offers Key to Auto's Success," *The Wall Street Journal*, December 13, 1983, p. 33.

Table 9–4: Capsule summaries of the nine nations	**Nation**	**Description**
	The Foundry Capital: Detroit	Industrialized, urban; losing population, jobs; heavy unionism; old technology; work-oriented. On the decline but will bounce back because of water resources; Emulators, Inner Directeds, I-Am-Me's.
	Mexamerica Capital: Los Angeles	Heavy Hispanic culture; mix of high- and low-educated; hard-working, entrepreneurial spirit; growth-oriented. Becoming most influential nation; Emulators, Achievers, Societally conscious.
	The Islands Capital: Miami	Caribbean and Latin American influence; heavy illegal drug trade; young and old live here; has little in common with rest of Florida and Dixie; diverse population.
	Quebec Capital: Quebec City	French-speaking Canada; steeped in history, tradition, ethnic pride; very homogeneous culture; plentiful resources; diversified economy; fiercely independent.
	Dixie Capital: Atlanta	Trying to catch up; smalltown way of life; undergoing rapid social and economic change; economy-minded. Need Drivers, Belongers.
	New England Capital: Boston	Poorest nation but "high-tech" influx bringing it back; politically diverse, cautious, brand loyal. Inner Directed, Societally conscious, Achievers.
	The Empty Quarter Capital: Denver	Wide-open spaces, energy-rich, mineral-rich; largest area, smallest population; frontier ethic; major economic growth foreseen; hard-working, conservative, blue-collar; Inner Directed.
	Ecotopia Capital: San Francisco	"High-tech," interest-rate-based economy; quality of life important; mottos: Leave me alone, Small is beautiful; young, educated, affluent; Inner Directed, Experientials.
Source: Adapted from "Capsule Summaries of the Nine Nations," *Marketing News,* January 21, 1983, p. 18.	Breadbasket Capital: Kansas City	Agricultural economy; mainstream America; stable, at-peace-with-itself population; conservative; Conformist Belongers.

patterns of buying, marketers must more deeply examine the underlying values and lifestyles common to a geographic region.

A major step in this direction has been provided by Joel Garreau.[8] He argues that an array of economic, social, cultural, political, topographical, and natural resource factors have worked to create the *"nine nations" of North America.* (See Table 9–4.)

The Ogilvy and Mather advertising agency studied the eight nations contained in the United States. (See Figure 9–7.) They applied the VALS framework to identify the distinct lifestyle nature of each segment.[9] Some

---

[8] Joel Garreau, *The Nine Nations of North America* (New York: Avon Books, 1981).

[9] *Listening Post,* no. 57, December 1983.

Figure 9–7: The eight nations of the United States

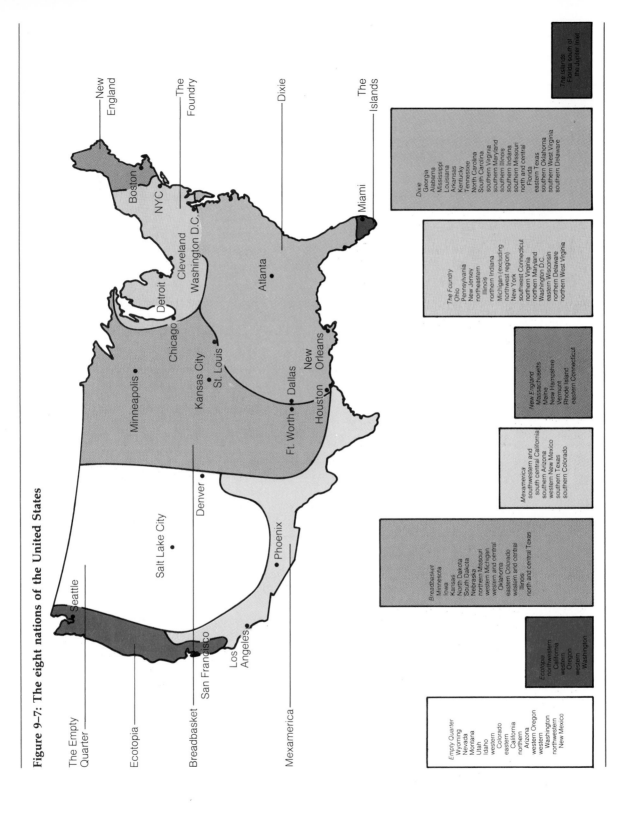

The Empty Quarter

Ecotopia

Breadbasket

Mexamerica

Seattle

Salt Lake City

Denver

Phoenix

San Francisco

Los Angeles

Minneapolis

Chicago

Kansas City
St. Louis

Ft. Worth · Dallas

Houston

New Orleans

Atlanta

Detroit

Cleveland
Washington D.C.

Boston

NYC

Miami

New England

The Foundry

Dixie

The Islands

Empty Quarter
Wyoming
Nevada
Montana
Utah
Idaho
western Colorado
eastern California
northern Arizona
western Washington Oregon
northwestern New Mexico

Ecotopia
northwestern California
western Oregon
western Washington

Mexamerica
southwestern and south central California
southern Arizona
western New Mexico
southern Texas
southern Colorado

Breadbasket
Minnesota
Iowa
Kansas
North Dakota
South Dakota
Nebraska
northern Missouri
western Michigan
western and central Oklahoma
eastern Colorado
western and central Illinois
north and central Texas

New England
Massachusetts
Maine
New Hampshire
Vermont
Rhode Island
eastern Connecticut

The Foundry
Ohio
Pennsylvania
New Jersey
northeastern Illinois
northern Indiana
Michigan (excluding northwest region)
New York
southwest Connecticut
northern Virginia
northern Maryland
Washington D.C.
eastern Wisconsin
northern Delaware
northern West Virginia

Dixie
Georgia
Alabama
Mississippi
Louisiana
Arkansas
Kentucky
Tennessee
North Carolina
South Carolina
southern Virginia
southern Maryland
southern Illinois
southern Indiana
southern Missouri
north and central Florida
eastern Texas
southern Oklahoma
southern West Virginia
southern Delaware

The Islands
Florida south of the Jupiter Inlet

of their findings are incorporated in the capsule summaries of each nation in Table 9–4.

Garreau offers some insights into the marketing implications of his view of North America: (1) The notion of "suburb" is strictly a Foundry phenomenon. In a lifestyle sense, however, everything is a suburb in the Southwest. (2) One reason the domestic auto industry reacted slowly to imported cars was that Detroit-based executives failed to see the trend toward Japanese cars in California. They looked out their windows and saw gas guzzlers.[10]

Subcultures. Different subcultures may represent distinct market segments. We saw in Chapter 6 the growing importance of black and Hispanic segments of the markets. They offer opportunities to develop products oriented specifically to a particular subculture (cosmetics developed especially for blacks) or special promotional campaigns directed at a subculture (an ad campaign for Coca-Cola aimed at Hispanics).

Social class. As discussed in Chapter 6, social class represents a composite of socioeconomic variables. Each social class represents a potential market segment.

Family life cycle. The concept of ***family life cycle*** traces the evolution of a family from its formation to its ultimate dissolution. It defines several distinct stages through which a family passes over time. (See Table 9–5.) Each stage reflects changes in age, family size, and marital status. Because these changes have an important impact on the purchasing patterns of the family (i.e., behavioral consequences), market segments can be formed for each stage in the life cycle.[11]

Financial institutions such as banks can make effective use of life-cycle stages to segment their markets. The financial needs of families change as they move through the life-cycle stages. Early in the cycle families are spenders more often than savers; they thus are prime candidates for loans. Later in the cycle, as their financial positions improve, families become more concerned with saving. They become targets for the various deposit services that a financial institution offers.

Descriptive characteristics of buyers—The organizational market

While less plentiful than in the consumer market, descriptive characteristics of buyers in the organizational market can be useful ways to form customer segments. Some of these variables are discussed below. Keep in mind that most of them are relevant to both the reseller and the user market.

---

[10] "The Nine Nations of North America," *Marketing News,* January 21, 1983, p. 17.

[11] P. E. Murphy and W. A. Staples, "A Modernized Family Life Cycle," *Journal of Consumer Research* 6 (June 1979), pp. 12–22.

Table 9–5: The family life cycle	Stage	Identifying characteristics	Behavioral consequences
	Bachelor	Young, single, not living at home	Few financial burdens; fashion opinion leaders; recreation-oriented; buy basic household goods, cars, travel.
	Newly marrieds	Young, no children	Better off financially than in the near future; high purchase rate of major items.
	Full nest I	Youngest child under six	Low liquid assets; dissatisfied with financial position and amount of money saved.
	Full nest II	Youngest child at least six	Financial position improved; wife may work; less influenced by advertising.
	Full nest III	Older couples with dependent children	Financial position further improved; more luxury items purchased.
	Empty nest I	Older couples, children moved out, head in labor force	Interested in travel, recreation, self-improvement; best financial position.
	Empty nest II	Older couples, head retired	Usually a drastic cut in income.
	Solitary survivor	Widow or widower	Convenience-oriented.

Type of business.   One common descriptive characteristic of organizations used to form segments is the type of business in which the business is engaged. In general, we may identify individual segments composed of manufacturers, service organizations, wholesalers, retailers, nonprofit groups, and governmental agencies or institutions. Advance Lifts, the hydraulic-loading marketer, uses this approach to segment its market. In developing new products it considers the special needs of retailers, hospitals, mass merchandisers, and other types of institutions.[12]

The federal government has developed the ***Standard Industrial Classification (SIC) system*** to classify business organizations. The SIC system categorizes organizations according to their economic activity. An example for manufacturers of fabricated structural metal buildings is shown in Table 9–6. It should be pointed out the SIC categories have limitations. Many firms, because of their multiple business activities, fit into the system rather loosely.

Size of organization.   Segments based on an organization's size can often reveal important differences between organizational buyers. The

---

[12] "Marketing Program Leads to Dominance," *Marketing News,* October 28, 1983, p. 6.

Table 9–6: Structure of the Standard Industrial Classification System	Classification	SIC number	Description
	Division	D	Manufacturing
	Major group	34	Manufacturers of fabricated metal products
	Industry subgroup	344	Manufacturers of fabricated structural metal products
	Detailed industry	3441	Manufacturers of fabricated structural steel
	Manufactured products	34411	Manufacturers of fabricated structural metal for buildings
	Manufactured products	3441121	Manufacturers of fabricated structural metal for buildings—Iron and steel (for sale to companies): industrial

Source: Adapted from Office of Management and Budget, *1972 Standard Industrial Classification Manual* (Washington, D.C.: U.S. Government Printing Office, 1972); U.S. Bureau of the Census, *1977 Census of Manufacturers: Fabricated Structural Metal Products* (Washington, D.C.: U.S. Government Printing Office, 1980).

size of an organization may be represented in several ways: number of employees, number of establishments, and volume of goods sold. The seller should use the measure of size most closely related to purchase behavior.

Many banks segment the organizational market on the basis of size. They charge lower interest rates on commercial loans to large businesses than to small ones. Competition between banks for the business of large firms is much keener than for the small segment.[13]

Geographic concentration. The geographic concentration of some industries suggests that geographic classifications can be used for segmenting. Government buyers tend to be clustered in the heavily populated states. And, as noted before, specific industries can be concentrated geographically—oil in Texas and Oklahoma, steel in Pittsburgh and Chicago, "high-tech" in California. This concentration allows a much sharper geographic focus in the marketing effort directed at such industries.

General behavioral characteristics—The consumer market

Many consumer behavior patterns are not associated with a single product class but occur consistently as part of an individual's overall behavioral pattern. Segmenting a market by one of these characteristics thus automatically builds in behavioral consequences. The extent to which these behavioral differences suggest marketing consequences to a particular seller becomes a crucial issue.

Media exposure patterns. One general behavioral characteristic that suggests variations in marketing communications strategy is the pattern of exposure to the various media. Media exposure patterns are reflected by a number of variables:

---

[13] T. D. Schellhardt, "Interest-Rate Gap on Business Loans Riles Small Concerns that Must Often Pay More," *The Wall Street Journal,* October 13, 1983, p. 35.

Marketing to different segments of the industrial market.

Courtesy International Business Machines Corp.

1. *Amount and nature of television-viewing behavior*—Time spent watching TV, network and local programs watched.
2. *Amount and nature of radio-listening behavior*—Time spent with radio on, time of day, station preferred, AM or FM preferred.
3. *Print media exposure*—Magazines read, newspapers read, section of paper read most thoroughly.

Media exposure patterns can be examined for national, regional, or local markets. For example, local retailers can examine newspaper readership, TV viewing, and radio listening within the local market to determine the appropriate advertising strategy for a segment. In developing radio advertising, segments of drive-time listeners versus listeners at other times might be examined.

Personality. Personality, as a broad behavioral characteristic, might be useful as a segmentation variable. Many products reflect a personality orientation in their advertising appeals and in product design. Liquor companies use this orientation to establish an image for their brand. And variations in the styles of automobiles partially have a personality base. Unfortunately, personality—while rich in potential—is difficult to measure in ways meaningful to marketers; thus it hinders the identification of personality-based segments.

Table 9–7:
Eight male lifestyle
segments

Group I. "The Quiet Family Man" (8 percent of total males)
He is a self-sufficient man who wants to be left alone and is basically shy. Tries to be as little involved with community life as possible. His life revolves around the family, simple work, and television viewing. Has a marked fantasy life. As a shopper he is practical, less drawn to consumer goods and pleasures than other men.
Low education and low economic status, he tends to be older than average.

Group II. "The Traditionalist" (16 percent of total males)
A man who feels secure, has self-esteem, follows conventional rules. He is proper and respectable, regards himself as altruistic and interested in the welfare of others. As a shopper he is conservative, likes popular brands and well-known manufacturers.
Low educational and low or middle socioeconomic status, the oldest age group.

Group III. "The Discontented Man" (13 percent of total males)
He is a man who is likely to be dissatisfied with his work. He feels bypassed by life and dreams of better jobs, more money, and more security. He tends to be distrustful and socially aloof. As a buyer, he is quite price-conscious.
Lowest education and lowest socioeconomic group, mostly older than average.

Group IV. "The Ethical Highbrow" (14 percent of total males)
This is a very concerned man, sensitive to people's needs. Basically a puritan, content with family life, friends, and work. Interested in culture, religion, and social reform. As a consumer he is interested in quality, which may at times justify greater expenditures.
Well-educated, middle or upper socioeconomic status, mainly middle-aged or older.

Group V. "The Pleasure-Oriented Man" (9 percent of total males)
He tends to emphasize his masculinity and rejects whatever appears to be soft or feminine. He views himself as a leader among men. Self-centered, dislikes his work or job. Seeks immediate gratification for his needs. He is an impulsive buyer, likely to buy products with a masculine image.
Low education, lower socioeconomic class, middle-aged or younger.

Group VI. "The Achiever" (11 percent of total males)
This is likely to be a hard-working man, dedicated to success and all that it implies, social prestige, power, and money. Is in favor of diversity, is adventurous about leisure-time pursuits. Is stylish, likes good food, music, etc. As a consumer he is status-conscious, a thoughtful and discriminating buyer.
Good education, high socioeconomic status, young.

Group VII. "The He-Man" (19 percent of total males)
He is gregarious, likes action, seeks an exciting and dramatic life. Thinks of himself as capable and dominant. Tends to be more of a bachelor than a family man, even after marriage. Products he buys and brands preferred are likely to have "self-expressive value," especially a "Man-of-Action" dimension.
Well-educated, mainly middle socioeconomic status, the youngest of the male groups.

Group VIII. "The Sophisticated Man" (10 percent of total males)
He is likely to be an intellectual, concerned about social issues, admires men with artistic and intellectual achievements. Socially cosmopolitan, broad interests. Wants to be dominant and a leader. As a consumer he is attracted to the unique and fashionable.
Best educated and highest economic status of all groups, younger than average.

Table 9–7 (concluded)   *Product and media use by psychographic group*

	Psychographic group percentages							
	I	**II**	**III**	**IV**	**V**	**VI**	**VII**	**VIII**
Drink beer	45	56	57	51	75	59	80	12
Smoke cigarettes	32	40	40	29	54	42	51	18
Air travel outside United States	4	4	6	7	5	8	12	19
Air travel, domestic	14	15	14	26	19	12	20	42
Use Brand X deodorant	7	7	6	8	14	10	9	12
Used headache remedy in past four weeks	53	60	66	61	61	64	65	61
Read current issue of:								
Playboy	8	11	8	13	25	27	16	30
National Geographic	21	13	11	30	13	28	16	21
Time	17	8	7	16	9	26	17	29
Newsweek	17	14	8	20	11	18	13	22
Field & Stream	10	12	14	8	12	9	13	3
Popular Mechanics	11	6	9	9	9	9	8	6

Source: William D. Wells, "Psychographics: A Critical Review," *Journal of Marketing Research,* May 1975, pp. 196–213.

Lifestyle.   Lifestyle is the broadest representation of a consumer's behavior patterns. Measures of activities, interests, and opinions (AIOs), and sophisticated statistical procedures are used to form consumer lifestyle segments. Consumption behavior with respect to product classes, brands of these products, benefits desired, etc., is then examined for each segment. The outcome is a rich description of each segment's "way of life" and consumption behavior. We have seen the VALS lifestyle framework for the entire adult population. Table 9–7 shows lifestyle segments of men and the information provided by lifestyle segmentation.

In 1981 R. J. Reynolds used a lifestyle-oriented strategy to rejuvenate its Camel brand of cigarettes. A theme, "Where a man belongs," conveyed masculinity, independence, self-assurance, and a sense of adventure and excitement. The theme was incorporated into an ad campaign that emphasized the outdoor life—backpacking, aviation, mountain climbing, winter camping, and hiking. This strategy, which seems directed at segment VII in Table 9–7, was quite effective: the Camel brand realized a 24 percent growth in sales during a time when the entire industry grew only 1 percent.[14]

General behavioral characteristics—The organizational market

Broad patterns of behavior as bases for market segmentation are less plentiful in the organizational market. However, from our discussion in Chapter 8, certain potential bases can be suggested.

Media exposure patterns.   As with consumers, organizational buyers can be characterized in terms of media exposure. In this market it is

---

[14] "Positioning Camel Where It Belongs," *Marketing and Media Decisions,* Spring 1982, pp. 173–86.

predominantly print media related to the organization's business—trade journals, for example.

Nature of the buying center. We have noted that a firm's buying decisions result from a network of interactions among members of its buying center. It could be very useful to segment the market by the nature of the buying center—its size, the nature of the participants. For example, segments might be based on the role of the purchasing agent in the buying unit—by the amount of influence the agent has on buying decisions. The result might be one segment where purchasing agents are simply detail persons and one where they are major "gatekeepers" for the organization. Segments defined this way would suggest alternative strategies for the sales force. In the former, salespeople would be concerned with purchasing agents after the sale. In the latter, purchasing agents would be a focus before the sale.

Buyer sophistication. Members of the buying center might be segmented in terms of their buying sophistication. One study identified three groups of buyers in the organizational market—sophisticated, moderately sophisticated, and unsophisticated.[15] Table 9–8 summarizes the key characteristics of each segment. These profiles suggest the marketing consequences of this segmentation approach. For example, ads in trade publica-

Table 9–8: Industrial buyer sophistication segments	Sophisticated	Moderately sophisticated	Unsophisticated
	Top management	Middle management	Lower management
	Heavy exposure to trade/ professional magazines	Some exposure to travel, professional magazines	No exposure to trade/ professional magazines
	Next heaviest readers of consumer magazines	Heaviest readers of consumer magazines	Infrequent readers of consumer magazines
	Large majority are members of professional association	Half are members of professional association	Few are members of professional association
	Large majority go to trade shows	Half go to trade shows	Few go to trade shows
	Middle level of education	Highest level of education	Lowest level of education
	Oldest and most experienced	Middle in age and experience	Youngest and least experienced
	Slightly less confident than moderately sophisticated about buying decisions	Most confident about buying decisions	Least confident about buying decisions

Source: Adapted from Nancy J. Church and Ronald McTavish, "Segment Buyers 'Sophistication' to Reach Industrial Markets Efficiently," *Marketing News*, September 16, 1983, p. 8.

[15] Nancy J. Church and Ronald McTavish, "Segment Buyers 'Sophistication' to Reach Industrial Markets Efficiently," *Marketing News*, September 16, 1983, p. 8.

tions and exhibits at trade shows would be appropriate to reach sophisticated buyers. The moderately sophisticated buyer would be better reached through a blend of trade and consumer magazine ads and personal selling. The unsophisticated buyer would be most receptive to a phone call or demonstration by a salesperson.

Advertising to the sophisticated buyer often requires an appeal based on several attributes.

MEET OTTO.

THE MOST OBLIGING AGV GOING. AND GOING. AND GOING

OTTO™ IS TOUGH. Here's a driverless vehicle that can take it. More payloads and punishment than any other. Rugged chassis comes in a variety of functional designs to suit customer needs — with a load range of 1000 to 6000 lbs. Otto runs on American industrial batteries for longer staying power. And his maintenance-free, easy-to-service construction makes him your hardest worker.

OTTO IS SMART. He's engineered with NDC Controls that provide extremely accurate, reliable performance. User programmable, Otto can easily be "taught" to do so much more. Quickly integrates with and expands your systems capability. In storage. Work-in-process. And everywhere in between. Otto can operate on uneven and ramp surfaces. Smooth speed controls permit precise on-line placement and assembly applications.

(Standard and custom models available)

OTTO IS SENSIBLE. His high performance and versatility mean he is a low risk investment. Most important, this AGV really reduces indirect labor and the need for costly lift truck fleets. So, if you're ready to automate…you need to Otto-mate.

BECAUSE YOUR BUSINESS CAN'T WAIT…send for full line literature and cost comparisons. Call or write INTECH SYSTEMS, Copeland Industrial Park, P.O. Box 9287, Hampton, VA 23670. (804) 838-6010.

INTECH SYSTEMS™

Intech Systems Group of Unimet Corporation

83-6

Automation you can live with.

Courtesy Intech Systems

Product-specific behavioral characteristics—The consumer market

In this section we consider several behavioral variables that can be examined on a product-specific basis. In this approach we segment according to how or why consumers buy the product of concern. With behavioral consequences built into these bases, the crucial issue again becomes the marketing consequences of the segments that result.

Customer loyalty. One meaningful difference between consumers in a product class is whether they are loyal to the particular brand or switch from brand to brand over several purchase occasions. The loyal segment can be further broken down into segments of customers loyal to each brand. In this way a firm can examine customers loyal to its brand, customers loyal to competing brands, and those not loyal to any brand. Strategies can be developed to keep the firm's loyal customers (cents off the next purchase) and to lure customers away from other brands (free samples). Similar loyalty segments can be identified for stores, also.

Loyalty at the product-form level could be incorporated into the identification of market segments. For example, some customers are loyal to frozen juice over canned orange juice. And then some customers are loyal to Tropicana frozen orange juice, others to Minute-Maid, and so on. Figure 9–8 portrays the loyalty segments for orange juice.

"Deal-prone" consumers. In many product classes there may be a segment of consumers whose purchase behavior is largely determined by the availability of a "deal" for a brand (sale price, coupon, premium). Such buyers typically switch brands from purchase to purchase, based

Figure 9–8: Consumer loyalty segments for orange juice

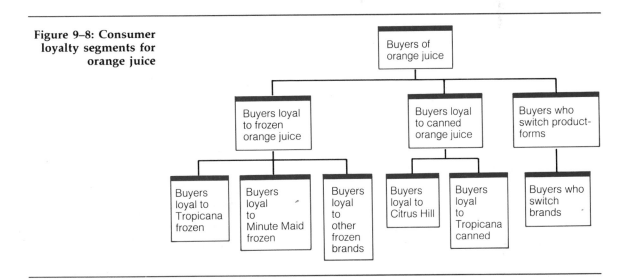

on the best deal available. Knowledge of this segment would help maximize sales of a brand during the time a deal was offered.[16] To the extent that there's a segment of consumers who are deal-prone in many product categories, it may be a useful general behavioral characteristic for segmenting the market.

Product-usage rate. One of the most meaningful product-specific variables to use in segmenting a market is the usage rate of the product. The heavy users of a product are distinguished from the light users. The classic "80-20 principle" of the beer industry suggests the value of segmentation by usage rate. Eighty percent of the beer is consumed by 20 percent of the beer drinkers. This pattern holds true for many products. Different marketing strategies for segments of heavy and light users are likely to be appropriate in markets such as airline travel, long-distance phone calls, soft drinks, and coffee, to name a few. The heavy-user segment requires a greater advertising effort, more extensive distribution, more competitive pricing, and greater sales-promotion effort.

Benefit segmentation. One increasingly popular approach is to segment by the primary benefit a consumer desires in a product.[17] In this approach **benefit segments** are defined by the most important product attribute sought by consumers. A prime example of this exists in the toothpaste industry. Segments of the primary benefit desired by toothpaste users have been formulated, and certain brands are directed at each of these segments. Crest toothpaste is directed at the cavity-prevention segment. Ultra-brite is directed at the segment concerned with teeth-whitening benefits. Close-Up seems designed for consumers concerned with both teeth whitening and breath freshness. Of course, each of these brands faces competition from others directed at the same segment.

Recognizing that segments based on desired product benefits can be formed in the food market, H. J. Heinz made a major acquisition in 1978. The increasing concern for weight control by a significant portion of the population has created a market segment that desires low-calorie food items. To realize immediate revenue from this segment, Heinz purchased Weight Watchers International and Foodways National (which produces Weight Watchers frozen food products) for $121 million. The acquisition gave Heinz immediate access to a growing benefit segment in the food market.[18] Stouffer's took the opposite approach; it spent six

---

[16] A study of the "deal-prone" segment is reported in R. Blattberg, T. Buesing, P. Peacock, and S. Sen, "Identifying the Deal-Prone Segment," *Journal of Marketing Research* 15 (August 1978), pp. 369–77

[17] A classic reference is Russell I. Haley, "Benefit Segmentation: A Decision-Oriented Research Tool," *Journal of Marketing* 32 (1968), pp. 30–35; also see Roger J. Calantone and Alan G. Sawyer, "The Stability of Benefit Segments," *Journal of Marketing Research,* November 1978, pp. 395–404.

[18] "Heinz Leaps into Low Calories," *Business Week,* March 5, 1979, pp. 57–58.

to eight years internally developing its Lean Cuisine line for this benefit segment.[19]

Information search patterns. If consumers differ in how they acquire information about the product, information search segments may be identifiable. A recent study of automobile dealers revealed six distinct segments of car buyers based largely on their information search patterns.[20] Figure 9–9 provides profiles of each of these segments.

Product-specific lifestyle segments. We have seen lifestyle segments of the entire population (VALS) and, earlier in this chapter, lifestyle segments of males. Both approaches formed lifestyle segments without a specific product in mind. Product-specific lifestyle segments can also be formed. Here, the users of a product or service are segmented into lifestyle groups. This approach offers a penetrating look at how the product or service fits into a consumer's pattern of living.

In the hotel industry a recent study of frequent business travelers commissioned by MasterCard reveals three lifestyle segments of business travelers and the role hotels play in their lifestyle while on the road:

1. *Extravert affluents.* This group (30 percent of frequent business travelers) buys first-class products and services, is not very concerned with saving money while traveling, likes to have a good time, stays at fashionable hotels, and wants good service from a friendly staff.

2. *Cost-plus.* This group (34 percent) is extremely cost-conscious, forms attachments to particular hotels, makes plans, and enjoys meeting others who share similar interests.

3. *No-frills.* This group (36 percent) is very careful with money, not interested in hotel activities, and not concerned with personal service. They want a clean room at a fair price.[21]

Product-specific behavioral characteristics—The organizational market

Product-specific behavioral characteristics can be applied to segmentation of the organizational market. Kodak, for example, segments the industrial market for office copying machines. The Kodak brand, Ektaprint, is less well known to the general market than Xerox and Canon. But this is because their marketing efforts focus on the heavy-user segment of the copy machine market. This high-volume end of the market includes such buyers as the government, law firms, and retail printing shops. Through a selective strategy that emphasizes personal selling, Ektaprint

[19] Kevin Higgins, "Meticulous Planning Pays Dividends at Stouffer's," *Marketing News,* October 28, 1983, p. 1.

[20] David H. Furse, Girish N. Punj, and David W. Stewart, "A Typology of Individual Search Strategies among Purchasers of New Automobiles," *Journal of Consumer Research,* March 1984, pp. 417–31.

[21] "Survey Reveals Three Types of Business Travelers," *Wisconsin State Journal,* March 18, 1984.

Figure 9–9: Information search segments of new-car buyers

Segment 1 (low search)
Spend least time of all segments in search-related activities

Greatest prior purchase experience

Have owned more cars than average

More satisfied with previous purchases

Most certain would get a good deal without information search

More likely to know in advance the manufacturer and dealer from whom they wish to purchase

Reason for purchase more likely to be feeling that it is good to trade cars every few years

Older

Highest income of all segments

Search for and purchase cars in a higher price range

Most likely of segments to consider full-sized, four-door models

More likely to consider products made by Ford and General Motors (e.g., Cadillac)

Less likely to consider Chrysler products or imports

Segment 2 (purchase pal assisted)
Least-experienced car shoppers

Have owned the fewest cars previously

Most likely to indicate a father was involved in decision

Tend to involve another who is perceived as knowing cars (purchase pal)

Express little confidence in their ability to judge cars

Likely to be less satisfied with most recent car purchase

May know manufacturer but not dealer from whom they will purchase

Largest percentage of single respondents in this segment

Tend to work in clerical and sales jobs

Most likely to be buying because had no car or because they feel it is good to trade cars every few years

More likely to purchase a two-door model

Car purchased more likely than for any other segment to be outside of original size and price set of models considered at the outset of formal search

Segment 3 (high search)
Spend the greatest amount of time (their own and others') in search activity

Have lowest confidence of any segment in their ability to judge cars

Believe extensive information search is necessary to get a good buy

Least satisfied of all segments with previous purchase

Postpurchase satisfaction with new car is below average

Tend to involve others in search activities, but these other individuals may have no particular expertise

Car actually purchased has the lowest average sticker price of all segments

Less likely to have a trade-in or get a high trade-in price

Best educated of segments but of moderate income

More likely than other groups to be female (although over half are male)

More likely to consider subcompacts, compacts, and hatchbacks

Likely to consider popular imports

Least likely of the segments to select General Motors as the preferred manufacturer, although a majority still prefer GM products

Segment 4 (self-reliant shopper)
Spend the greatest amount of own time in search process but do not involve others in search

Consider a large number of automobile makes and models

Less likely to know in advance the dealer from whom car is purchased

Less likely to have a trade-in

Well educated with moderate to high income

Male

Most likely to be purchasing new car for fuel efficiency or because they want a car for a different purpose from that of previous car

Most likely to consider subcompacts and compacts

Most likely to consider imports, Ford products, and Dodge

Less likely than average to consider General Motors products

Segment 5 (retail shopper)
Largest number of decisionmakers involved—especially the wife when she is not the principal decisionmaker (this group has the highest percentage of married individuals)

Unlikely to know dealer in advance

Less likely to have a trade-in

Consider a large number of makes

Large amount of "other" involvement in the search process

Well-educated but not necessarily high-income

Common occupations are managers, government officials, or proprietors

Principal reasons for new-car purchase are desire for greater fuel efficiency or the fact that the old car quit working and needed replacement

Pay highest average price of all segments for car

Prefer intermediate-sized sedans made by GM or Ford (Oldsmobile and Pontiac are particular favorites)

More likely to buy outside of initial manufacturer set but less likely to buy outside of original price set

Segment 6 (moderate search)
Devote below-average amount of time to search activities

High certainty that they could obtain a good deal without information search

Very likely to know manufacturer in advance but not necessarily the dealer

Least likely to involve others in search process

Tend to be older males with higher income than average

Most likely to receive a high trade-in price

Principal reasons for purchase are desire for greater fuel efficiency and feeling that it is best to trade cars every few years

Most likely to consider four-door models

Most likely to buy outside of initial price set

Preferences for manufacturers well distributed among members of this group

Source: Adapted with permission from David H. Furse, Girish N. Punj, and David W. Stewart, "A Typology of Individual Search Strategies Among Purchasers of New Automobiles," *Journal of Consumer Research,* 3 (March 1984), p. 422.

has achieved high awareness in the target market. In five short years it became the third-best-selling brand in the heavy-user segment.

DEVELOPING COMPOSITE PROFILES OF SEGMENTS

We have identified a variety of potential variables to use in identifying segments of the market. A firm may select one or a combination of these variables to form segments. Once the variables are selected, though, the remaining variables are not disregarded. They become the basis for an in-depth examination of each segment that provides the information needed to develop the marketing program.

The purpose of the examination is to provide a ***composite profile*** of a segment: who buys, what they buy, why, how, etc. Answers are provided by many of the remaining variables not used in forming the segments. (See Figure 9–10.) A composite profile of an income segment, for example, would include descriptions of its age, distribution, educational levels, lifestyle, media exposure patterns, and benefits desired in the relevant product class. Differences in these profiles between segments are the basis for different marketing strategies. If meaningful differences are found between the profiles, a segmented approach to the market may be necessary.

For marketing strategy development, the variables most useful for composites are the general and product-specific behavioral characteristics. These variables reflect behavioral and marketing consequences. The descriptions of the lifestyle segments in Table 9–7 are a prime example of segment profiles. Note that segments V and VII are prime markets for beer. *Playboy* magazine is read more by these segments than by most other segments. Both segments would appear to choose brands of beer on the basis of image, but they would buy brands with different images.

Figure 9–10: What the segmentation variables tell you

	Who buys	What they buy	How much they buy	How they buy	Why they buy
Demographics	X				
Socioeconomic	X				
Life cycle	X				
Lifestyle	X	X			
Personality	X				
Subcultures	X				
Media exposure patterns				X	
Opinion leaders	X			X	
Innovators	X				
Deal-proneness				X	X
Loyalty		X		X	
Benefits desired					X
Usage rate			X	X	
Beliefs/attitudes					X
Information search				X	

Both brands might be advertised in *Playboy,* but TV advertising would occur on different programs, because viewing behavior probably differs between the two segments.

PURSUING THE MARKET

Once the product market has been segmented and the segments analyzed for demand potential and appropriate marketing strategies, the firm must decide the overall strategy it will use to pursue the market. Of course, one potential decision is to not pursue the market at all. This decision would be appropriate if the overall market or each of its segments lacked sufficient demand potential or marketing opportunity for the firm. When the segmentation procedures do suggest that the overall market or one or more of its segments warrant marketing attention, alternative strategies are available for pursuing the market.

Aggregated strategy

In some situations it is appropriate to pursue a market for a product with one strategy directed at the entire market. This **aggregated strategy** is appropriate when *no meaningful difference—with marketing consequences—exists between buyers.* Segment profiles may not suggest distinct marketing approaches to one or more of the segments.

There are positive features to an aggregated strategy. When a single combination of marketing decision variables is used to pursue the market, marketing costs are minimized—and this carries over into cost advantages in production and inventory management.

But given the diversity of the marketplace, aggregated marketing strategies are the exception rather than the rule today. They are probably most appropriate for new products or services for which distinct segments have yet to emerge. The new express mail services (e.g., Federal Express) began with aggregated strategies.

Disaggregated strategy

A disaggregated pursuit of a market occurs when a firm develops individually tailored marketing strategies for two or more segments of the market. A **fully disaggregated** approach occurs when strategies are developed for each of the identified segments (i.e., the firm pursues the entire market). A **partially disaggregated** approach occurs when two or more but less than all of the segments are pursued with distinct strategies. It is appropriate when a firm lacks the resources to pursue all segments or when some segments lack sufficient market potential.

Examples of fully and partially disaggregated strategies abound in business today. Manufacturers of consumer durable goods are prime examples, with their variations in product styles, functional features, prices, etc. The auto industry is a particularly good example. General Motors, as a whole, takes a fully disaggregated approach to the market for automobile buyers. Each of its divisions (e.g., Chevrolet, Cadillac) takes a partially disaggregated approach. At the retail level the Limited, Inc., takes a highly

Figure 9–11: The Limited, Inc.

The Limited, Inc. is a growth company focused exclusively on women's apparel. The company's primary business is to provide fashion, quality, and value to the American woman through multiple retail formats:

Limited stores. There are 500 Limited stores in over 125 major markets throughout the United States. Limited stores sell medium-priced fashion apparel tailored to the tastes and lifestyles of fashion-conscious contemporary women 20 to 40 years of age. The majority of Limited stores are located in regional shopping centers with the remainder in key downtown locations.

Limited Express. Distinguished by a unique store design and merchandise selection, Limited Express stores offer an exciting assortment of popular-priced sportswear and accessories designed to appeal primarily to fashion-forward women 15 to 25 years of age. Currently there are 45 Limited Express stores located in regional shopping centers in California, Texas, and the Midwest.

Lane Bryant. Lane Bryant is the nation's leading retailer of women's special-size apparel. The 223 Lane Bryant stores specialize in the sale of medium-priced fashion, basic, and intimate apparel designed to appeal to the special-size woman, with particular emphasis on those over 25 years of age. The stores are located in regional shopping centers throughout the United States.

Brylane Mail Order. The nation's foremost catalogue retailer of women's special-size apparel and shoes, Brylane Mail Order publishes five catalogues, each directed to a specific special-size customer. The catalogues include *Lane Bryant, Roaman's, Tall Collection, Nancy's Choice,* and *LB For Short.*

Victoria's Secret. Through retail stores and a nationally distributed mail-order catalogue, Victoria's Secret offers European and American designer lingerie for the fashionable contemporary woman 25 to 45 years of age. The 12 stores are located in the San Francisco, Boston, Columbus, Dallas, Chicago, and New York metropolitan areas.

Sizes Unlimited. This newly established division is an off-price retailer of women's special-size apparel. Composed of Sizes Unlimited and Smart Size stores, the division offers nationally known brand and private-label merchandise designed to appeal primarily to women 25 to 50 years of age. The 77 stores are located in smaller shopping centers throughout the East and Midwest.

Mast Industries. Mast Industries is a large, international supplier of moderate-priced apparel for fashion-conscious women. The Commercial Division employs a worldwide network of 150 contract production facilities to produce merchandise against specific orders from retailers, wholesalers, and manufacturers. Through sales offices in New York and Los Angeles, as well as a field sales force, the Wholesale Division supplies a wide variety of apparel products to department and specialty stores throughout the United States.

Source: Reprinted from Roger D. Blackwell and W. Wayne Talarzyk, "Lifestyle Retailing: Competitive Strategies for the 1980s," *Journal of Retailing,* Winter 1983, pp. 7–26.

disaggregated approach to the women's apparel market. (See Figure 9–11.)

A disaggregated approach loses the cost advantages of an aggregated approach. Variations in the marketing decision variables mean higher marketing, production, and inventory management costs. But the precise adjustments of the marketing program to the nature of each segment increase the likelihood of purchases within each segment. Thus, a disaggregated approach increases the total revenue of the firm to the point where, it is hoped, it offsets the added costs.

Niche strategy

In a ***niche strategy,*** a firm identifies only one segment as its target market and focuses its entire marketing effort on that segment. The niche

Segment	Percentage of market	Number of competitors	Proportionate market share of new firm
A	50	9	$\dfrac{50 \text{ percent}}{10} = 5 \text{ percent}$
B	12	1	$\dfrac{12 \text{ percent}}{2} = 6 \text{ percent}$

Table 9–9: Why the largest segment may not be the most attractive

strategy is appropriate when a firm lacks the resources to pursue more than one segment or when just one segment deserves marketing attention (i.e., the other segments lack sufficient demand potential). For example, initial inroads by foreign auto manufacturers into the American market were achieved through a niche strategy aimed at the small-car segment. As their success grew and resources increased, these manufacturers moved into a more disaggregated approach. Our Kodak example is also one of a company entering a market with a niche strategy.

A niche strategy realizes advantages similar to those of the aggregated strategy—one standardized approach with its attendant cost advantages. Furthermore, the focus on one segment increases the chances of more precisely meeting the needs and wants of that segment. Unfortunately, the niche strategy is risky. Unlike the disaggregated approach, failure in one segment cannot be offset by success in others.

In taking a niche strategy, caution is necessary in selecting the target segment. A firm should avoid the so-called majority fallacy, which warns that the largest segment attracts the most competitors. In some cases a smaller segment with fewer competitors may represent the greatest marketing opportunity. Consider the following situation (also see Table 9–9):

> The largest segment of a market (segment A) contains 50 percent of the total market, with nine firms currently competing within it. A smaller segment (B) contains 12 percent of the total market, with only one existing firm serving it. Assuming that a new firm entering either segment can ultimately realize a proportionate share of the segment, segment B is the more attractive. It will result in a 6 percent share of the total share. Segment A will result in 5 percent.

One company that recognizes the opportunity in a niche strategy aimed at a small segment is Windham Hill Records. Windham Hill avoids the large rock segment of the music market. Instead it concentrates on a small but avid segment of jazz listeners (4 percent of the retail market for albums). With prices below the industry average and an unorthodox distribution system that includes health-food stores and florists, Windham Hill realized annual sales gains ranging from 180 to 600 percent during a three-year period when the record industry was in a severe slump.[22]

[22] Robert Guenther, "Windham Hill Records Prospers by Producing Soft Jazz for Music Lovers Who Can't Stand Rock," *The Wall Street Journal,* December 13, 1983, p. 56.

STEPS IN THE SEGMENTATION PROCESS

Based on our discussion to this point, we can now delineate the sequence of steps in the *market segmentation process.* Figure 9–12 presents an overall view of the process.

Step 1—Identify market segments

The initial task is to identify the segments of the market for further analysis. Companies typically use one of two approaches to do this:

1. *A priori segmentation design.* Management selects a basis for segmentation (age, income, usage rate) and designates the levels of the variable that will represent each segment. For example, age might be selected as the segmentation variable with four segments designated: 18–24, 25–44, 45–59, and 60 and over.
2. *Cluster segmentation design.* Buyers are measured on a *set* of relevant variables. Clusters of buyers similar on the set of variables are identified as segments. Lifestyle segmentation is a form of cluster segmentation.[23]

The key distinction between these approaches lies in the way the basis for segmentation is selected. In the a priori approach the basis for identifying segments and the number and type of segments are known in advance. In the cluster approach all that is determined in advance is the set of variables on which to measure buyers. The number and nature of segments emerge from the homogeneous customer groupings that exist with respect to the set of variables.

It may be useful to use the two approaches in combination. For example, customers could first be divided into heavy and light users. Then, customers in each segment could be clustered according to lifestyle.

The variables used in either approach are selected from the three categories of segmentation variables discussed previously. While all three categories offer candidates for use, managers increasingly use product-specific variables. They are most closely tied to marketing decision variables. Therefore, they more readily suggest marketing consequences. Within the product-specific category, the type of marketing decision to be made helps guide the selection of the specific variable. Table 9–10 identifies the variables most relevant to certain marketing decisions.

Step 2—Collect research information

In the a priori approach to segmentation, this step follows the identification of segments. In the cluster approach it must precede the identification of segments because research information is needed to cluster buyers. In either case the information to be collected includes the entire array of descriptive, general behavioral, and product-specific characteristics of buyers, as well as the size of each segment.

---

[23] Yoram Wind. "Issues and Advances in Segmentation Research." *Journal of Marketing Research,* August 1978, p. 317.

Figure 9–12: The market segmentation process

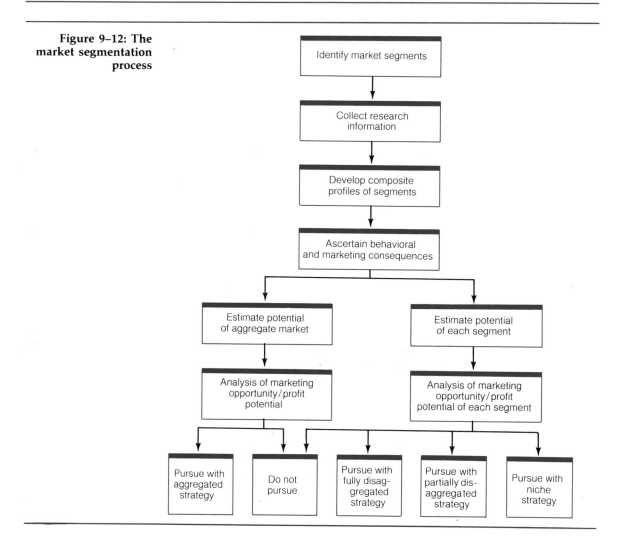

Step 3—Develop composite profiles of segments

The collected information should be analyzed to provide a composite profile of each segment. Each segment is profiled in terms of who buys, what they buy, where, why, how much, and how they buy.

Step 4—Ascertain behavioral and marketing consequences

From the segment profiles any differences between segments in terms of product-specific behavior and general marketplace behavior are identified. If such differences do exist, the extent to which they suggest unique marketing strategies for any of the segments is determined. Depending upon whether marketing consequences exist, the firm from this point on concerns itself with the market in aggregate form or with each of the individual segments.

	Situation	Useful variables
Table 9–10: Segmentation variables useful in certain marketing situations	General understanidng of a market	Benefits sought Product purchase patterns Usage rate Needs Brand/source loyalty and switching
	Product positioning	Usage rate Brand preference Benefits sought
	New-product decisions	Innovativeness Benefits sought
	Pricing decisions	Price sensitivity Deal-proneness
	Advertising decisions	Benefits sought Media usage Information search Lifestyle
Source: Adapted from Yoram Wind, "Issues and Advances in Segmentation Research," *Journal of Marketing Research*, August 1978, p. 320.	Distribution decisions	Store loyalty Store benefits sought

Step 5—Estimate market potential

Based on the research results, the expected level of demand for the market or each segment can be estimated. If no marketing consequences were ascertained, the estimate is for the market as a whole. If they were suggested, it is for each segment. Chapter 10 discusses procedures relevant to Step 5.

Step 6—Analyze marketing opportunity

The firm must now determine its opportunity in the market. This analysis requires (1) an examination of the competitive situation in the overall market or in each segment and (2) the determination of the appropriate marketing program for the market or each segment. Combined, this information provides a basis to estimate the revenue potential for the firm and the costs of generating it. The net result is an estimate of profit potential for the market as a whole or for each segment.

Step 7—Decide if and how to pursue the market

The estimate of profit potential now serves as the basis for the product/market strategy. If the firm is treating the market as a whole, it is an all-or-nothing decision. Adequate profit potential leads to the pursuit of the entire market with an aggregated strategy. Inadequate profit potential leads to the decision to discard the market as a marketing opportunity.

If the firm treats the market on a segmented basis, profit potential is estimated for each segment. If all segments reflect adequate profit potential and the firm's resources enable it to do so, the entire market is pursued with a fully disaggregated strategy. Or, if only a portion of the segments reflect sufficient opportunity, the firm selects two or more as target markets and pursues the market with a partially disaggregated strategy. Finally, if resources limit it to one segment—or if only one segment possesses adequate potential—the firm selects that segment as a target market and pursues it with a niche strategy.

Benefits implied in the segmentation process

The process described above reflects a well-planned approach to the market, and it implies certain key benefits to a firm's marketing operations. First, the segmentation process provides valuable input to the analysis of marketing opportunities. Multiple opportunities can be identified and compared. Second, such information about a market results from the process. This provides a deep understanding of the market. Third, the efficiency and effectiveness of the firm's total marketing program are enhanced. The firm can tailor its product and surrounding marketing effort more precisely to the nature of the market. The ultimate outcome becomes the implementation of the marketing concept in line with the heterogeneity of the marketplace—which, as you may recall, is the *raison d'être* of market segmentation.

SUMMARY

The heterogeneity of the marketplace suggests that market segmentation would enhance the effectiveness of the marketing concept. Marketing segmentation is the process by which a firm attempts to match its total marketing program to the unique way one or more customer groups behave in the marketplace. Three categories of variables are available as bases for forming customer groupings: descriptive characteristics of buyers, general behavioral characteristics, and product-specific behavioral characteristics.

Several criteria should guide the selection of one or a combination of these variables as a basis for segmenting the market. The variable should provide for homogeneity within and heterogeneity between segments. Behavioral consequences should be linked to the variable. The behavioral consequences should reflect marketing consequences (i.e., variations in appropriate marketing strategy between segments). The variables used to form segments must be measurable so that individual customers can be placed in the proper segment. It should yield one or more segments substantial enough in opportunity to warrant marketing attention. Finally, segments must be suffi-

ciently stable over time so that their potential may be realized.

In assessing the opportunities in each segment, it is important to construct composite profiles. These profiles are constructed using variables other than the ones used to form the segments. The profiles are the basis for determining the opportunity existing in a segment and the nature of the marketing effort that will most effectively serve it.

Once the existing opportunity has been assessed, several alternative strategies can be used to pursue this opportunity if it is deemed adequate. First, if the segmentation process suggests that no variations in marketing strategy between segments are appropriate, the firm can use an aggregated strategy, where the entire market is pursued with a standardized strategy. If variations in marketing strategy are warranted, the firm may employ a fully disaggregated strategy. Here all of the segments are pursued, each receiving a unique marketing strategy. A partially disaggregated strategy may be used where more than one segment is pursued with a unique strategy directed at each segment. Finally, a niche strategy directed at only one segment may be employed.

KEY CONCEPTS

Market segmentation
Market heterogeneity
Homogeneity within segments
Heterogeneity between segments
Behavioral consequences
Marketing consequences
Measurability
Substantiality
Stability
Descriptive characteristics
General behavioral characteristics
Product-specific behavioral
    characteristics

"Nine nations" of North America
Family life cycle
Standard Industrial Classification
    (SIC) system
Benefit segment
Composite profile
Aggregated strategy
Fully disaggregated strategy
Partially disaggregated strategy
Niche strategy
Market segmentation process
A priori segmentation design
Cluster segmentation design

DISCUSSION QUESTIONS AND EXERCISES

1. How would you say each of the following firms segments the market? What strategies might they use in pursuing the segmented market?

    a. K mart.
    b. Mercedes Benz.
    c. Toyota.
    d. Zenith.

2. Describe how you think the market should be segmented for each of the following products:

    a. Hair shampoo for women.
    b. Dentures.
    c. Hotels.
    d. Scientific instruments.
    e. Water softeners.

3. Summarize the advantages and disadvantages of aggregated, disaggregated, and niche strategies for pursuing a market.

4. Which of the "nine nations" contains your hometown? Discuss the extent to which you feel your hometown possesses the characteristics described for its region.

5. Find 10 heavy users and 10 light users of a product of your choice. Gather information from each that can be used to draw a composite profile of the two segments.

CHAPTER 10

Demand assessment

Methods for forecasting sales
    Judgment techniques
    Time-series techniques
    Causal techniques

Selection of forecasting methods
    Factors to consider
    The use of forecasting in industry

Summary

Key concepts

Discussion questions and exercises

Key concepts in demand assessment

The role of demand assessment
    Role of demand assessment in strategic
        planning
    Specific roles of demand assessment

Methods for current demand assessment
    Chain-ratio method
    Market-buildup method
    Buying-power index method

Throughout our discussion so far, marketplace demand for a product has been an important consideration in the strategic planning of a company's marketing program. Knowing the level of demand contributes to virtually every phase of the strategic planning process: from identifying opportunities and threats in situation analysis to arriving at control standards for performance evaluation. Thus, *demand assessment* is a crucial activity in marketing management.

demand assessment

> **Demand assessment** refers to the process by which a firm arrives at a quantified estimate of the level of demand for a generic product or brand that exists or will exist during a given time period.

Demand assessment provides a quantified measure of demand that is useful in the development of both short- and long-run plans. Short-run plans rely on measures of *current* demand. For long-run plans, a measure of the demand that will exist during a *future period* is appropriate. Thus, demand *forecasting* becomes an important activity for long-run planning. A variety of methods are used to estimate current or forecast future demand. In this chapter we'll examine these methods. However, we must first clarify some key concepts relating to demand assessment and—more specifically—examine its role.

KEY CONCEPTS IN DEMAND ASSESSMENT

To assess demand, we must understand certain key concepts relating to the demand for a product. (See Table 10–1.)

market potential

> **Market potential** is the maximum sales of a generic product, product-form, or service for an entire industry in a market during a given time period, presuming a given environment and a maximum marketing effort by all marketers.

Market potential refers to the total sales for a generic product (automobiles) or a version of it (subcompacts) available to those firms marketing the product. Market potential may be estimated for an entire market or a particular segment within it: for all U.S. buyers or only buyers in a certain customer group (as in a certain income group) or a specific geographic area. Finally, market potential is defined by a specific time period: a particular month, quarter, year, or even decade. The concept of market potential refers to the *maximum limit* that sales can reach for an industry. It does not necessarily indicate the actual sales that will be realized.

Table 10–1: Key concepts in demand assessment	Concept	Definition
	Market potential	Maximum industry sales under maximum marketing effort by all firms in the industry, given a particular environment
	Market forecast	Estimated actual industry sales under expected marketing effort and expected environment
	Sales potential	Maximum sales of a company under maximum company effort
	Sales forecast	Expected sales of a company under intended marketing effort

market forecast

> **Market forecast** is an estimate of the expected sales of a product or service that will be realized by the industry in the market (or portion thereof) during a specified time period.

This concept recognizes that usually only a portion of market potential will be realized by an industry. Market potential sets the upper limit for industry sales under a *maximum* marketing effort by the industry. The market forecast incorporates expected actual industry effort (typically less than the maximum) and expected environmental conditions to arrive at an estimate of the portion of market potential that will be realized.

sales potential

> **Sales potential** refers to the maximum sales available to a company under maximum marketing effort by the company for a given time period.

Sales potential is the share of market potential that a company would expect to achieve if it maximized its marketing effort. Theoretically, sales potential is limited by market potential. That is, the most a company could achieve is the entire sales of the industry. This theoretical limit realistically exists only for true monopolies.

sales forecast

> **Sales forecast** is an estimate of a company's actual sales that will be realized in a market during a given time period under a planned marketing program and expected environmental conditions.

At the company level the planned marketing program will typically be less than the maximum available. The sales forecast incorporates the *intended* marketing effort and *expected* environmental conditions into a forecast of sales that a company expects to achieve. The sales forecast can be made with respect to an individual product or service or an entire line.

market share

> **Market share** is the ratio of actual company sales to actual industry sales.

Market share is a fundamental concept in marketing. It is a measure of a company's marketing performance, and many firms track it continuously. Marketing objectives also may be defined in terms of market share.

Virtually all companies that actually measure market share compute several versions of it. These differ in terms of the boundaries of the market being analyzed. General Foods, for example, might compute each of the following:

1. The share of aggregate market expenditures on food that its combined sales of all food items realize.

2. The share of consumer expenditures on all canned goods that its sales of canned goods realize.

3. The share of consumer expenditures on coffee that its line of coffee brands realizes.

4. The share of consumer expenditures on ground coffee that its Maxwell House brand realizes.

Market shares at even more generic levels might be computed. For example, the airline industry might want to compute the share of total travel expenditures going to commercial airlines.

These concepts recognize that demand assessment can involve primary or selective demand. They recognize, too, that primary or selective assessment can occur for an entire market or a specific segment within it. Together they provide a framework for a company's approach to demand assessment. Based on its specific planning and/or control needs, a company should choose within this framework the specific demand-estimation task that is appropriate.

Figure 10–1 presents a logical flow of steps that the demand assessment

**Figure 10–1:
Steps in demand
assessment**

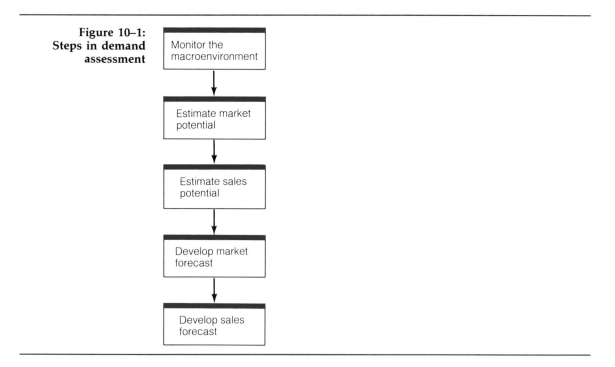

process might follow. First, input from monitoring sectors of the macroenvironment helps set the environmental conditions that can be expected during the time period for which demand is to be assessed. Second, given these conditions, estimates are developed of maximum sales available under maximum industry effort (market potential) and maximum company effort (sales potential). Expectations of competitors' marketing effort and knowledge of the company's marketing capabilities can then be blended to forecast actual market sales and actual company sales. This process yields estimates of potential and actual sales that serve a variety of strategic purposes.

THE ROLE OF DEMAND ASSESSMENT

Demand assessment serves purposes in several areas of strategic management. We'll consider them first in the broad context of strategic planning and then in terms of more specific business decisions.

Role of demand assessment in strategic planning

Several broad marketing management activities occur within the strategic planning process. Those activities to which demand assessment contributes are listed below, followed (parenthetically) by the stage of the strategic planning process to which the activity is relevant.

1. *Evaluation of markets.* A company may desire estimates of market or company potential or of expected sales in a market it is currently serving. Such estimates may help determine whether modifications in the marketing program are necessary and what these changes should be. Demand assessment may be used to evaluate and compare potential markets. (Situation analysis)

2. *Market segmentation.* The substantiality of a market segment is a critical factor in a market segmentation strategy. Demand assessment contributes to estimates of the viability of one or more segments. (Product/market)

3. *Setting of objectives.* Demand assessment can provide a realistic idea of how a firm might perform in the marketplace. From such information, sales and market share performance objectives can be set. (Establish objectives)

4. *Conditional analysis.* Depending on the specific technique being used, demand assessment can be used to estimate sales under different marketing programs. For example, a company might want to assess demand for a brand at different levels of advertising effort. The resulting schedule of demand would aid the determination of the optimal advertising program. (Management of marketing program)

5. *Budgeting.* Demand assessment can pinpoint the amount of effort a firm must expend to operate during a particular period and allows the firm to budget its production and marketing efforts. (Budget determination)

6. *Setting control standards.* With realistic expectations of sales perfor-

mance from demand assessment, appropriate standards can be developed against which to compare actual performance. (Performance evaluation)

These categories encompass a variety of specific strategic decisions. Within each, the demand assessment process might be used for several decisions.

Specific roles of demand assessment

The specific decisions to which demand assessment applies depends on whether estimates of current demand or forecasts of future demand are being used.

Role of current demand estimates. Estimates of current demand gauge the level of demand at the time of estimation or in the near short-run future. There is no standard time frame for defining the short-run future. For some products (many convenience goods) the near short run is only one or two months. For others (expensive industrial goods) the near short run may encompass the following year.

In general, "current" demand encompasses the length of time in which the level of sales cannot be altered by the actions of companies or changes in the environment. Thus, an estimate of current sales is a single number that assumes a given level of company or industry effort and the existing environment.

These estimates are useful in making decisions on current operations. Usually estimates of sales that the company and the industry will realize, they can be used to make decisions regarding: production levels, inventory levels, procurement of raw materials and component parts, sales goals, advertising budgets, sales force and personnel requirements, working-capital requirements, and price-setting and distribution needs in geographic markets.

Role of demand forecasts. Long-run forecasts of demand attempt to assess the level of demand that will exist well into the future—usually one to five years down the road. Such forecasts include estimates of actual sales and/or market and sales potential. They enable long-run decisions about new markets to pursue, existing markets with growth potential or decline potential, expansion or reduction of production plants, ripe areas for research and development, and organizational changes.

A few companies' forecasts cover periods up to 25 years into the future. These forecasts become the basis for defining a company's overall mission.

It is clear that demand assessment plays an important role in determining a company's present and future operations. One marketing executive characterized the sales forecast as "the most important piece of data which is presented to management." Another called it "the basic core of our planning effort."[1]

---

[1] Stanley J. Pokempner and Earl L. Bailey, "Sales Forecasting Practice: An Appraisal," in *Experiences in Marketing Management,* no. 25 (New York: The Conference Board, 1970), p. 1.

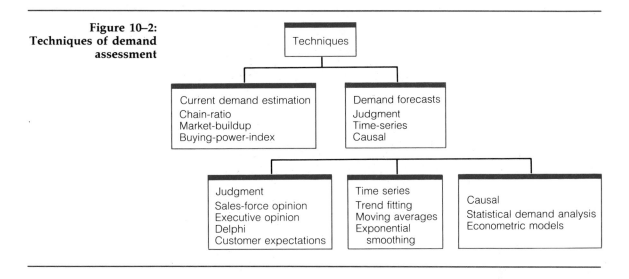

**Figure 10–2:
Techniques of demand
assessment**

Given the importance of demand assessment, marketing managers should be familiar with the techniques available. Let's turn our attention to these techniques. Figure 10–2 provides an overview of those we will discuss.

METHODS FOR CURRENT DEMAND ASSESSMENT

The first task in measuring demand for a product or brand is to establish the *boundaries of the market.* In other words, we must clearly specify what characterizes the product's users or potential users. Such characteristics are usually stated as relevant demographic, socioeconomic, or geographic variables. The market for a new sailboat, for example, might consist of households with heads between the ages of 25 to 55 years, with annual incomes in excess of $20,000, and who live within 35 miles of a body of water. If 2 percent of such households engage in or are interested in sailing, we then have a basis for estimating market potential.

Our second task is to determine the *consumption rate of a unit of the product.* Variations across products in the expected life of a unit of a product must be recognized if accurate demand estimates are to be attained. Those who purchase sailboats do not purchase them every year. Replacement purchases may occur every 15 years. Other products have quite rapid consumption rates. Soft drinks, for example, might be consumed at the rate of more than a six-pack per week. The demand estimate must consider these things. That is, we want an estimate that includes both new and replacement demand.

Chain-ratio method

A method of current demand assessment that incorporates user characteristics and consumption rates is the ***chain-ratio method.*** This method begins with an aggregate measure of demand and, through the application of a series of ratios or usage rates, arrives at an estimate of demand for a product or brand. In our sailboat example, the chain-ratio method might be applied as follows:

Total households with head aged 25–55, income over $20,000, and within 35 miles of water	2,000,000
Percent who sail or are interested in sailing	× 2%
Total sailing market	40,000
Percent who are first-time buyers	× 10%
Total first-time buyers	4,000
Replacement demand (6% of 40,000)	+ 2,400
Total market demand	6,400
Estimated company share	× 20%
Unit sales	1,280
Average unit price	× $15,000
Total revenue	$19,200,000

The expected revenue of $19.2 million can be compared to estimated costs to determine if the new sailboat represents a sufficiently profitable venture.

The accuracy of the chain-ratio method depends, of course, on the accuracy of the ratios and consumption rates that go into it. The sources of these figures vary. For existing products, historical data may be used to estimate the key ratios. Market surveys—in which users or potential users are asked about their rate of consumption or interest in the product—can be used for existing or new products.

Market-buildup method

The ***market-buildup method*** for assessing demand is used to estimate market potential. The basic procedure is to estimate market potential in each of several identifiable markets. The estimates are then added together to arrive at total market potential. A key requirement of the method is that sales in each market can be estimated using a common denominator across markets. The need to identify distinct markets and relate sales to some common factor across these markets makes the market-buildup method more amenable to estimating potential in industrial markets than in consumer markets.

Industrial marketers can identify distinct market segments using the Standard Industrial Classification (SIC) codes discussed in Chapter 9. The common denominator on which sales are estimated is usually some measure of size or activity across the markets: number of employees, number of production facilities, or dollar value of goods sold.

Figure 10–3 summarizes the steps in the market-buildup method. As an example of this method, consider a firm that markets safety glasses for industrial workers. Its new version of the product is meant specifically

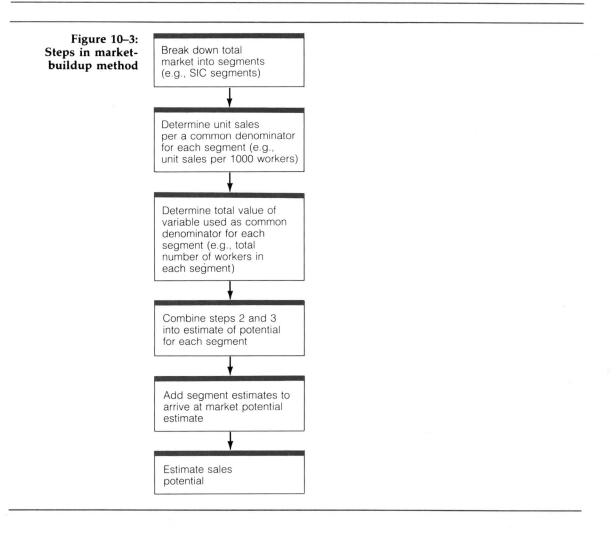

Figure 10–3: Steps in market-buildup method

Break down total market into segments (e.g., SIC segments)

Determine unit sales per a common denominator for each segment (e.g., unit sales per 1000 workers)

Determine total value of variable used as common denominator for each segment (e.g., total number of workers in each segment)

Combine steps 2 and 3 into estimate of potential for each segment

Add segment estimates to arrive at market potential estimate

Estimate sales potential

for the construction industry. Using SIC codes, the firm breaks the market into three segments:

SIC Code 15—Building construction

SIC Code 16—Construction other than building

SIC Code 17—Special trade contractors

In each segment, the firm uses number of employees as a common denominator. It determines the demand for safety glasses per 1,000 workers in each segment. Historical data on purchases of safety glasses by each segment would be the likely source of such information. Commercial information services like Economic Information Services, Inc., provide this type of information for a fee. For each segment the resulting data reveal annual purchases per 1,000 workers as follows:

SIC code	Sales per 1,000 workers
15	20
16	10
17	7

From external secondary sources (e.g., *Census of Manufacturers, County Business Patterns*), the firm can determine the number of workers in each segment for the entire country or for a specific geographic area. Assume that it determines the following number of workers in each segment:

SIC code	Workers (000)
15	4,500
16	3,200
17	1,450

Table 10–2 combines the two sets of information to arrive at an estimate of market potential. The company next determines sales potential. Actual sales are a function of company potential, marketing efforts devoted to safety glasses, and the environment.

The accuracy of the market potential estimate of 132,150 units is a function of several things. First, the number of employees in each market must be accurate and up to date. Second, the expected sales per 1,000 workers must be accurate, and, since it is based on historical figures, it must be expected to remain stable for the time period in which market potential is being assessed. A firm with experience in the market of interest will be in a better position to determine the sales per 1,000 workers and whether it can be expected to remain stable.

If the figures going into the market-buildup method are available, the method becomes a very useful technique beyond just estimating aggregate potential. By developing estimates on a segment-by-segment basis as

Table 10–2: Market-buildup method using hypothetical safety glasses firm	(1) SIC Code	(2) Number of employees (000)	(3) Sales potential per 1,000 workers	(2 × 3) Market potential
	15	4,500	20	90,000
	16	3,200	10	32,000
	17	1,450	7	10,150
				132,150

part of the method, managers can compare segments on their potential. This comparison would help identify particularly strong segments in the event a niche or partially disaggregated segmentation strategy would be followed.

Buying-power-index method

A useful procedure for estimating market potential in a specific geographic market is provided by *Sales & Marketing Management,* a marketing trade publication, in their "Annual Survey of Buying Power." They provide an "index of buying power" for well-defined geographic areas.

The ***buying-power index (BPI)*** is a type of demand-estimation procedure in which estimates of demand are derived from the values of factors believed to be related to the level of demand (i.e., a corollary-index method). Specifically, this method provides the relative buying power of regions, states, and metropolitan areas through the following calculation:

$$BPI = 0.5Y + 0.2P + 0.3R$$

where

BPI = Proportion of aggregate national buying power contained in the area

Y = Proportion of aggregate national disposable personal income contained in the area

P = Proportion of national population contained in the area

R = Proportion of aggregate national retail sales occurring in the area

For example, Texas contains 6.69 percent of the aggregate national disposable income, 6.56 percent of the national population, and 7.52 percent of national retail sales.[2] Its BPI is, therefore:

$$0.5(6.69) + 0.2(6.56) + 0.3(7.52) = 6.91$$

The BPI is a useful basis for estimating the geographic market potential for an entire industry because its three factors—income, population, and retail activity—are tied to the level of demand for many consumer products. It is particularly useful to large retailers offering a wide assortment of goods. Estimating the market potential for a specific type of product may require an adjustment in the weights applied to each factor. These weights can be estimated using statistical procedures such as multiple regression. As with any estimate of *market potential,* the BPI does *not* reflect the level of demand for a particular brand.

The editors of *S&MM* have extended their "Survey of Buying Power" concept to include a "Survey of Industrial Purchasing Power." It serves as an aid to industrial marketers in assessing the market potential available. The "Survey of Industrial Purchasing Power" analyzes markets by both geographic area and SIC code. Several factors relating to demand for

[2] "1983 Survey of Buying Power," *Sales & Marketing Management,* October 31, 1983.

Sales & Marketing Management's Survey of Buying Power presents useful information for estimating market potential in various geographic consumer markets.

Courtesy Sales & Marketing Management

industrial goods are presented for a specific geographic area or SIC category. They include:

1. Total number of manufacturing plants with 20 or more employees.
2. Total number of plants contained in factor 1 with 100 or more employees.
3. Dollar value of goods produced in the market.
4. The percentage of the dollar value of all goods produced in the United States that factor 3 represents.
5. The percentage of the market's manufacturing output produced by the plants contained in factor 2.
6. Average value of goods produced per plant.

Factors 1, 3, and 4 provide indexes of industrial activity in a market and reflect market potential. Factors 2, 5, and 6 indicate how concentrated this activity is. They have implications for marketing strategy. For example, a higher percentage of activity concentrated in large plants would suggest the need for a smaller sales force.[3]

METHODS FOR FORECASTING SALES

A variety of methods are used to estimate future sales. These methods vary in their time horizons, costs, technical ability required, and the use of judgment. But they are consistent in that each provides an estimate of actual sales that will be realized for an industry, company, or brand at a future time.

Sales-forecasting methods can be classified into the following categories:[4]

1. *Judgment techniques.* These techniques make use of qualitative data, relying primarily on judgments from those participating in the forecasting process. They attempt to bring objectivity to nonstructured situations and to treat relevant information in a systematic way. Information about the past may or may not be used.

2. *Time-series techniques.* These techniques rely entirely on historical data in the form of past sales. They incorporate the movement of sales over time by discerning and measuring the regular, repetitive patterns of sales. These techniques (unlike judgmental ones) are highly structured and objective. The fundamental assumption of time-series forecasting is, of course, that past sales are a basis for estimating future sales.

3. *Causal techniques.* These techniques also rely on historical quantitative data. But rather than focusing on the historical pattern of sales alone, an attempt is made to link movements in sales to movements in other factors. The result is a statistical model that specifies the relationship,

---

[3] For more on industrial purchasing power as a basis for demand assessment, see "1983 Survey of Industrial Purchasing Power," *Sales & Marketing Management,* April 25, 1983.

[4] George C. Michael, *Sales Forecasting* (Chicago: American Marketing Association, 1979).

if any, between sales and other variables. Causal techniques go a step beyond time-series procedures. Rather than merely *describing* the past sales patterns and extending them into the future, they seek to *understand* past sales and use this to forecast future sales.

Let us now consider some of the specific techniques in each of these categories.[5]

Judgment techniques

Survey of customer expectations. The *survey of customer expectations* method, as its name indicates, goes to the marketplace to obtain judgments of buying intentions. Typically, structured survey instruments are administered to a sample of buyers through interviews. Each buyer is measured in terms of the strength of intent to buy and, if appropriate, the number of units that will be bought. For estimates of aggregate sales, the measure would center on the purchase of a generic good without regard for the brand. For estimates of company sales, additional questions can focus on the most likely brand. If the proper sampling techniques have been used, the findings of the sample can be extrapolated to the market to arrive at a market estimate.

The survey of customer expectations method is best suited to estimating future sales of products whose buyers typically formulate purchase plans based on an assessment of their requirements for the product. Such products include industrial goods and consumer durables (although the latter are subject to a greater instability of purchase intent). The use of the method is further enhanced when the number of potential buyers is small and each buyer can be distinctly identified. In general, well-defined small markets for industrial goods are best suited for this method.[6]

Perhaps the greatest advantage of buyer expectation surveys is the penetrating examination of the market that they allow. Measures of variables beyond purchase intention can be included in the survey form. Forecasts specific to certain types of buyers and geographic areas can be made by including appropriate measures. Attitudinal variables can also be examined, thus allowing meaningful profiles of the market or its segments. Such information becomes particularly useful when the method is used to forecast new-product sales.

Major disadvantages of the method include buyers' inability or unwillingness to articulate their purchase intentions, the limited time horizon (buyers cannot be expected to anticipate their purchases much beyond

---

[5] More complicated treatments of these techniques are available in many of the specialized books on the subject. See, for example, Spyros Makridakis and Steven C. Wheelwright, *Forecasting: Methods and Applications* (New York: John Wiley & Sons, 1978).

[6] For further discussion of the use of this method for forecasting sales of industrial products, see Richard Rippe, Maurice Wilkinson, and Donald Morrison, "Industrial Market Forecasting with Anticipation Data," *Management Science* 22 (February 1976), pp. 639–51.

a year or so), and cost. Buyer expectation surveys, when conducted properly, represent major market research projects. These surveys require a considerable amount of time, money, and research expertise.

Several firms used customer expectation surveys to estimate sales for cellular mobile phones. These new phones can be used in cars. Because of technological advances, they will be available to many more users than previously. Several firms (MCI, Western Union, and others) assessed demand for these phones in several major metropolitan areas.

MCI's approach involved telephone surveys of households earning $20,000 or more annually. Other firms interviewed businesses only. MCI surveyed households because it felt that expected use for business and personal reasons could be measured. Each household head was asked his or her level of interest in this type of product. (See Figure 10–4.) The key question asked respondents their likelihood of purchase (Figure 10–4) at each of three price levels ($75, $125, $175 per month). Additional questions focused on locations of use (commuting to work or home, during business travel), desirable features (call waiting, call forwarding), and the amount of business versus personal use.

Market sales were estimated from answers to the intent-to-subscribe question. Asking intentions at each price level permitted a schedule reflecting the elasticity of demand. To take into account errors by respondents in estimating their probabilities, the percentage of the market subscribing at each price level was estimated as follows:

$$(\% \text{ Definitely subscribe} \times 0.60) + (\% \text{ Probably subscribe} \times 0.30) + (\% \text{ Probably not subscribe} \times 0.05) + (\% \text{ Definitely not subscribe} \times 0) = \% \text{ of Target market representing potential subscribers}$$

Figure 10–4: Customer expectation measure for mobile phones

Level of interest

If cost were not a factor, how much interest would you have in having this new mobile telephone service? Would that be:

_____ A great deal of interest
_____ Some interest
_____ Little interest
_____ No interest at all
_____ Don't know

Purchase expectations

If the new mobile telephone service and equipment were available at a total cost of about $175 per month, how likely is it that you or your firm would subscribe to the service for *your* use? Would you or your firm:

_____ Definitely subscribe
_____ Probably subscribe
_____ Probably not subscribe
_____ Definitely not subscribe

Table 10–3: Customer expectations forecast of mobile phone sales

Price level	Strength of interest	Percent responding	×	Adjustment factor	=	Estimated Percent	Percent of market subscribing
$75	Definitely will	10.2%		.60		6.1%	
	Probably will	22.3		.30		6.7	
	Probably will not	22.1		.05		1.1	
							13.9%
$125	Definitely will	3.0		.60		1.8	
	Probably will	14.8		.30		4.4	
	Probably will not	29.8		.05		1.5	
							7.7
$175	Definitely will	1.4		.60		0.8	
	Probably will	11.7		.30		3.5	
	Probably will not	31.0		.05		1.5	
							5.8

These adjustments assume that many people who say they will subscribe actually will not and that a few who say they will not actually will.[7] Table 10–3 summarizes the findings at each price level for one major market area. Figure 10–5 shows the demand curve associated with price variations. Total unit sales at each price level can be estimated by applying the market percentage to the total number of target-market households in the geographic area. The optimal price would be determined by estimating net revenue at each price level based on sales and costs.

Composite of sales force opinion. As its name implies, initial input to this technique comes from members of the sales force (i.e., those individuals closest to the marketplace on a day-to-day basis). Each salesperson estimates how much he or she will sell during the time period for which sales are being forecasted. The estimates are then reviewed and adjusted at various levels of marketing management. (See Figure 10–6.) Ex-Cell-O Corporation makes use of the sales force composite in its forecasting efforts. Ex-Cell-O manufactures an assortment of industrial goods—machinery, precision parts and assemblies, aerospace parts, and expendable tools and accessories. One line of goods, machine tools, ranges in price from a few thousand dollars to $400,000 or more. They are sold by Ex-Cell-O's own sales force of approximately 50 salespeople and 100 independent distributors. Each salesperson and distributor forecasts expected orders in each of the next five quarters, repeating the process every three months. The regional manager reviews the forecast with each salesperson

---

[7] Evidence in support of this type of adjustment is reviewed in Manohar U. Kalwani and Alvin J. Silk, "On the Reliability and Predictive Validity of Purchase-Intention Measures," *Marketing Science,* Summer 1982, pp. 243–86.

Figure 10–5: Demand schedule for mobile phones

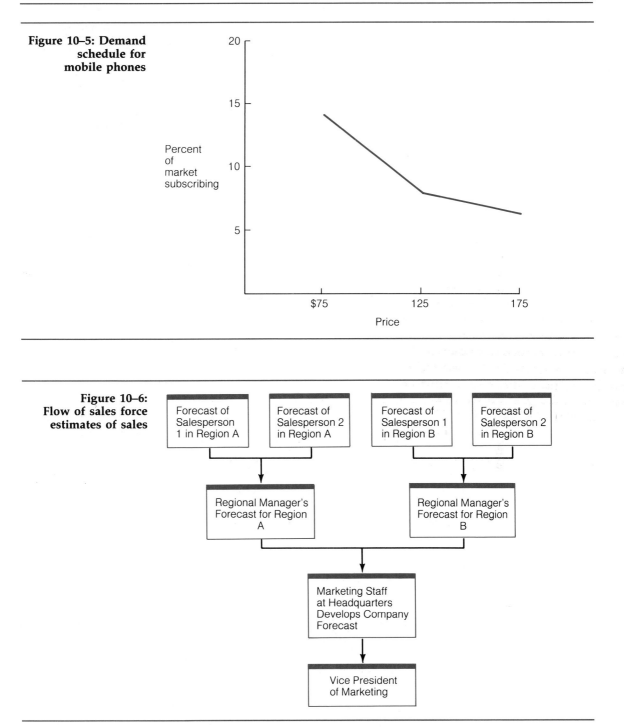

Figure 10–6: Flow of sales force estimates of sales

and distributor. Disagreements among them are resolved, and the agreed-upon forecast is then forwarded to the marketing staff at headquarters.[8]

The sales force composite method has a limited time horizon. That is, salespeople cannot be expected to forecast their sales much beyond the next year. For short-term forecasts, though, it does have some distinct advantages. Not the least of these is that salespeople are one type of expert on the marketplace. Also, this procedure entails a form of participatory management. Salespeople take part in a process that has consequences for them, often in the form of sales quotas. The method also lends itself to the development of customer, product, territory, or sales force breakdowns.

The technique is not without major disadvantages, and a key one is the accuracy of sales force judgment. Salespeople are often unaware of general economic conditions that influence demand. They may be overly optimistic when sales have been good and overly pessimistic when sales have been bad. Furthermore, there are occasions when it is to their advantage to underestimate sales. When quotas for salespeople are established from forecasts, lower forecasts will result in lower sales quotas, which are easier to meet. One study suggests that overly optimistic forecasts from the sales force are more common than errors on the low side.[9] It also found that a key factor in determining the accuracy of sales force estimates is the existence of a structured, formalized forecasting participation process.

Jury of executive opinion.   This method employs the experience and knowledge of the firm's key executives in arriving at a sales forecast. Each executive provides an estimate of sales for a future time period. These estimates are combined in some fashion to arrive at a final estimate. The procedure may entail the simple computation of an average or an extensive discussion in a group meeting until consensus is reached. Sometimes the jury of executive opinion is the only basis for arriving at a forecast. In other cases, forecasts prepared by other means serve as input to the executives, who adjust them (if necessary) based on their expert opinion and knowledge.

Like the sales force composite method, the jury of executive opinion is best suited for relatively short-run forecasts. But it can be used for a time horizon beyond that appropriate for the sales force composite method—especially when used in conjunction with another method—because the jury will usually have knowledge of important company plans. The ease and short amount of time required in this approach are its key advantages. In addition, the collective wisdom of important executives

[8] David L. Hurwood, Elliot S. Gorman, and Earl L. Bailey, *Sales Forecasting* (New York: The Conference Board, 1978), pp. 40–44.

[9] Thomas R. Wotruba and Michael L. Thurlow, "Sales Force Participation in Quota Setting and Sales Forecasting," *Journal of Marketing* 40 (April 1976), pp. 11–16.

encompasses a diverse base of knowledge about company plans and environmental factors.

The major disadvantage of this method, other than its limited time horizon, is the aggregate form of the estimate. It is not very amenable to territorial, product, or salesperson breakdowns of expected sales. Thus, the uses to which forecasts based on executive opinion can be put are limited. Furthermore, the process itself is prone to rather unique error factors. Politics, for example. Too much weight can be attached to a powerful executive's estimate, though it be no better (or worse) than a lesser executive's estimate based on greater expertise.

Delphi technique. A variation of the method that overcomes the problems of group dynamics but maintains the role of important executives or experts is the so-called ***Delphi technique.*** In this approach a panel of experts is questioned in successive stages through the use of anonymous questionnaires. The results of each stage are fed back to each expert, who can revise his or her estimate in light of the collective wisdom of the remainder of the group. (See Figure 10–7.) In this way the unique knowledge of each expert is available to the group as a whole. The anonymity of each estimate allows equal weight for each participant's response. Over a series of stages the participants should move toward greater agreement, although the average of the final-stage estimates will probably need to be computed to arrive at a single estimate.

The Delphi technique preserves and enhances many of the advantages of the jury of executive opinion and eliminates some of its disadvantages. Expert opinion is used more objectively, and there is a greater time horizon for forecasting. The time and costs involved in Delphi procedures are potentially substantial. One major corporation used Delphi to develop a 10-year forecast for component parts it planned to make. The nearly

Figure 10–7: Operation of Delphi process

Forecaster

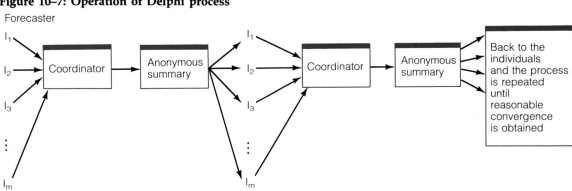

Source: Gilbert A. Churchill, Jr., Neil M. Ford, and Orville C. Walker, *Sales Force Management*, rev. ed. (Homewood, Ill.: Richard D. Irwin, 1985).

year-long study involved three stages and 40 experts. The company was very pleased with the parts and impressed with the process by which they were generated.[10]

The Delphi technique is highly flexible. It has been used, for instance, to forecast postnuclear war conditions and general social conditions in the 21st century. In 1981 ESIS Inc., a risk-management information firm, established a Delphi panel consisting of over 300 risk-management and insurance professionals from around the world. The purpose of the panel is to provide a forum for debate and discussion of key risk-management issues and to forecast long-term risk-management trends. In its first year the panel accurately predicted movements in the prime interest rate.[11]

Time-series techniques

The time-series techniques all rely on known, quantitative measures of past sales over a series of points in time. Each technique projects sales to a future point based on past sales. The techniques vary in their statistical treatment of historical patterns of sales. Depending on the availability of total industry and company sales figures, time-series procedures can forecast at market or company levels.

Trend fitting. The simplest form of time-series analysis is ***trend fitting.*** This method fits a trend line to a series of sales data. Forecasting occurs by simply extending the fitted line to the time period for which sales are being estimated. If sales have shown relatively stable rates of growth over the time series, the trend line can be a straight, linear one. Sales rarely follow so straightforward a pattern, however. Thus, curvilinear trend lines must often be explored and used. (Figure 10–8 provides an example of a linearly fitted trend line.) Accurate trend fitting requires a large number of past sales figures to which the trend line will be fitted. This procedure also attaches equal weight to each entry in the series. If future sales are influenced more by most recent sales, serious errors can occur.

Moving averages. The method of ***moving averages*** also attaches equal weight to the entries in the time series included in the forecast. However, as more entries become available from actual sales results, early entries in the time series are dropped. Thus, in a sense, more recent entries are weighted more heavily because historically distant sales results are given no weight at all.

The procedures in the moving average method are quite simple. As the name suggests, a forecast is determined by averaging the actual sales figures for the most recent set of time periods on which the forecast is

---

[10] Michael, *Sales Forecasting,* p. 12.

[11] Kip D. Cassino, "Delphi Panel: A Practical 'Crystal Ball' for Researchers," *Marketing News,* January 6, 1984, p. 10.

Figure 10–8:
Forecasting by trend
fitting

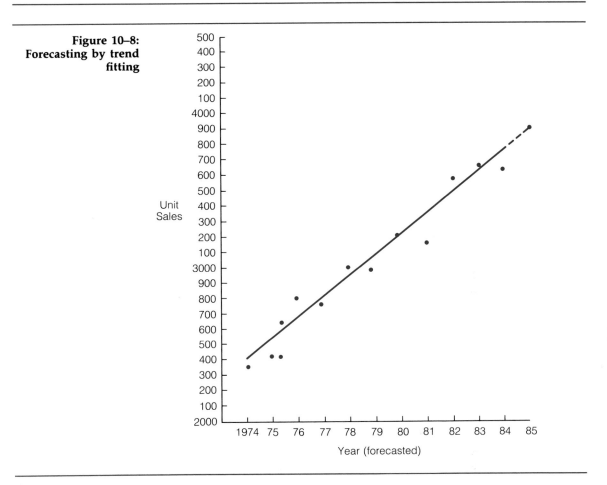

based. If a four-year moving average is used, then forecasted sales for 1985 would be the average of actual annual sales realized for 1981–84. "Moving" reflects the fact that—as time progresses and actual sales for 1985 become available—the 1981 entry is dropped and the basis for forecasting 1986 sales "moves" to the period 1982–85. Table 10–4 shows forecasts that would occur from a hypothetical set of sales figures using two-year and four-year moving averages. Figure 10–9 portrays them graphically.

A critical issue in the moving average method is the number of most recent time periods to use to compute an average. Clearly, four-year moving averages require more data than two-year moving averages. With relatively new products the forecaster is forced to use a smaller number of years. For well-established products with several years of sales data available, the number of time periods selected should be based on the

Table 10–4: Annual sales and forecasted sales using two-year and four-year moving averages

		Forecasted sales	
Year	Actual sales	Two-year moving average	Four-year moving average
1965	4,200	—	—
1966	4,410	—	—
1967	4,322	4,305	—
1968	4,106	4,366	—
1969	4,311	4,214	4,260
1970	4,742	4,209	4,287
1971	4,837	4,527	4,370
1972	5,030	4,790	4,499
1973	4,779	4,934	4,730
1974	4,970	4,905	4,847
1975	5,716	4,875	4,904
1976	6,116	5,343	5,128
1977	5,932	5,916	5,395
1978	5,576	6,024	5,684
1979	5,465	5,754	5,835
1980		5,520	5,772

volatility of historical sales. When actual sales have shown a rather stable pattern, a larger number of time periods can be used. But a volatile sales history with large, rapid fluctuations in sales suggests the use of fewer time periods. This way the forecast is more sensitive to the changes that are occurring.

Exponential smoothing.   A special type of moving average technique, *exponential smoothing* attaches the greatest weight to the most recent sales figures. It is logically sound in that the most recent sales figures should contain the most information about the future. The algebraic form of the exponential smoothing procedure is:

$$\hat{S}_{t+1} = \alpha S_t + (1 - \alpha)\hat{S}_t$$

where

S_{t+1} = Forecasted sales for period $t + 1$.
S_t = Actual sales for the previous period.
$\hat{S}_t$ = Forecasted sales for the previous period.
α = Smoothing constant between 0 and 1.

At first glance it may seem that only the previous time period's sales value is being used in arriving at a forecast. However, the use of the last time period's *forecasted* value implicitly incorporates more distant sales figures.[12]

---

[12] The algebraic proof for this assertion is provided in Steven C. Wheelwright and Spyros Makridakis, *Forecasting Methods for Management,* 2d ed. (New York: John Wiley & Sons, 1977), p. 36.

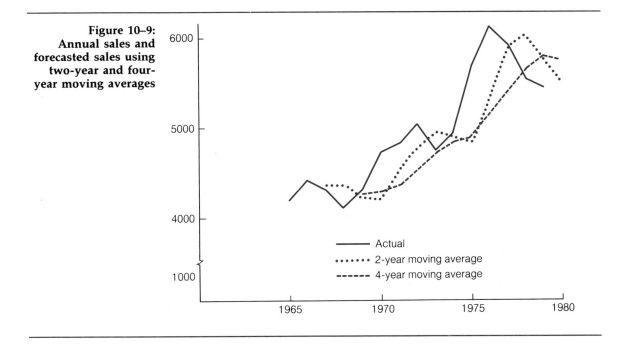

**Figure 10–9:
Annual sales and
forecasted sales using
two-year and four-
year moving averages**

The crucial issue in the use of exponential smoothing is the value given to ∝ *(smoothing constant).* Larger values (i.e., closer to 1) mean more weight is being given to the last time period's sales patterns. Smaller values give more weight to earlier time periods; they are appropriate when sales are more stable over time. For example, Hewlett-Packard discovered that a smoothing constant of 0.5 was superior to 0.3 when forecasting monthly demand for component parts of electronic equipment whose demand was rapidly growing (because of their newness) or whose demand had abruptly dropped (because of an association with recently obsolete equipment).[13] Table 10–5 provides forecasted values from a hypothetical time series using smoothing constants of 0.2 and 0.5. (Also see Figure 10–10.)

Advantages and disadvantages of time series. The appeal of time-series procedures lies in their simple elegance and precise output. They seem sophisticated, but they are based on simple logic and (with the use of computers) are easily applied. Their output is a precise quantitative representation of the future not subject to the whims of an individual. However, they are only as good as the quality of the assumption that

[13] Robert Stanton and Edward A. Drury, "Forecasting at Hewlett-Packard: Finding a Better Way," *Management Accounting,* June 1981, pp. 45–49.

Table 10–5: Annual sales and forecasted sales using exponential smoothing and various values for the smoothing constant α

Year	Actual sales	Forecasted sales α = 0.2	Forecasted sales α = 0.5
1965	4,200		
1966	4,410	4,200	4,200
1967	4,322	4,242	4,305
1968	4,106	4,258	4,314
1969	4,311	4,228	4,210
1970	4,742	4,244	4,260
1971	4,837	4,343	4,501
1972	5,030	4,441	4,669
1973	4,779	4,559	4,849
1974	4,970	4,603	4,814
1975	5,716	4,676	4,892
1976	6,116	4,883	5,304
1977	5,932	5,129	5,710
1978	5,576	5,289	5,821
1979	5,465	5,346	5,699
1980	—	5,370	5,583

underlies them: the future is strongly linked to the past. If the marketplace is volatile in the influences on demand, the assumption is tenuous. The mere passage of time does not explicitly recognize new competitors, the loss of old ones, or relevant internal changes in the firm. Causal forecasting techniques are an attempt to overcome this potential deficiency.

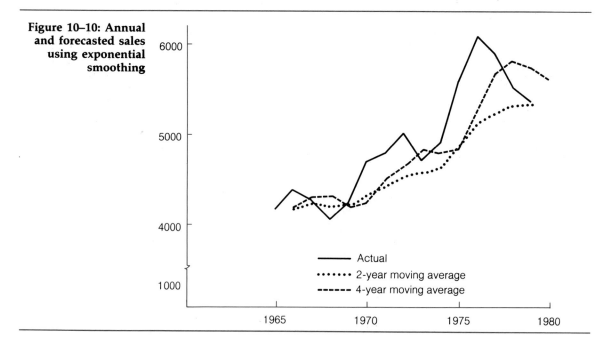

Figure 10–10: Annual and forecasted sales using exponential smoothing

Legend:
——— Actual
·········· 2-year moving average
------ 4-year moving average

Causal techniques   Causal techniques attempt to incorporate factors that influence demand into forecasting models. In doing so, they can provide a basis for understanding movements in demand as well as for forecasting demand. The procedures are readily adaptable to the industry or company level.

Statistical demand analysis.   Perhaps the most widely used causal technique for forecasting sales is *statistical demand analysis.*[14] In this technique, regression analysis is used to estimate an equation that relates sales to a set of independent predictor variables. The procedure used to derive the model determines the number of units of sales that will change for every unit change in each predictor variable. Through the appropriate statistical procedures, the relative importance of each predictor variable in forecasting sales can also be determined.

A somewhat dated but still excellent example of statistical demand analysis as a forecasting method is provided by Palda, who developed the following model to forecast sales of Lydia Pinkham's vegetable compound from 1908–60:[15]

$$S = -3649 + 0.665 PS + 1180 \log A + 774 D + 32 T - 2.83 Y$$

where

S = Yearly sales in thousands of dollars.
PS = Previous year's sales in thousands of dollars.
A = Yearly advertising expenditures in thousands of dollars.
D = A dummy variable that receives a value of 1 for the years 1908–25 and a value of 0 for all subsequent years.
T = A time-series variable with 1908 = 0, 1909 = 1, 1910 = 2, and so on.
Y = Disposable personal income in billions of dollars.

The equation highlights many advantages and disadvantages of statistical demand analysis as a forecasting method. As a major advantage, statistical demand analysis accommodates a variety of variables to include as predictors. Such variables include:

1.   *Marketing strategy variables.* In the Palda model advertising effort (A) is such a variable. Other possibilities include price and product modifications.

2.   *Previous year's sales.* Note that in the equation the previous year's sales can easily be included to capture the information they contain.

---

[14] Causal is somewhat of a misnomer. No statistical procedure can actually prove causation. However, good logic in combination with statistical demand analysis can provide insights into causal influence on sales.

[15] Kristin S. Palda, *The Measurement of Cumulative Advertising Effects* (Englewood Cliffs, N.J.: Prentice-Hall, 1964), pp. 67–68.

3. *Dummy variables.* These variables receive a value of 0 or 1 for a given year. They are used to reflect abrupt and otherwise nonquantifiable changes. For example, war years might be given a 1 and other years a 0.

4. *Passage of time.* Time-series influences from the mere passage of time can be included, as in the case of T in the Palda model.

5. *General economic conditions.* Variables that reflect economic conditions are readily included, as disposable income is included above. Other possibilities include interest rate levels.

6. *Competitive factors.* While not included in the Palda model, factors such as competitors' prices and advertising effort can be incorporated, if the information is available.

These types of variables together can provide a deep understanding of the marketplace factors that influence sales. Many variables can be tested for their significance as influences. Key factors that are uncovered then provide a strong foundation for strategic planning.

Statistical demand analysis has weaknesses that can render it dangerous or unusable. It can be dangerous if the relationships uncovered in building the model do not hold into the period for which the forecast is being made. Serious forecast errors can then result. It can be unusable if information on the value of one or more of the predictor variables is unavailable for the forecast time period. For example, in the Palda model knowledge of future advertising effort and disposable-income levels would be necessary to forecast from the model. In many instances these variables themselves will have to be forecasted before the forecast of sales can occur!

Econometric models in forecasting are an extension of statistical demand analysis. Instead of a single equation model, a system of interdependent equations is used to examine the causal phenomena affecting sales or demand level. The equations indicate an overall set of relationships that are relevant to the understanding of movements in sales. The statistical nature of this approach is quite sophisticated and well beyond the intended scope of this text.[16] But we should still recognize the distinct advantages and disadvantages of this approach. The basic advantage of the econometric approach is its ability to incorporate a large number of variables relevant to the understanding of demand. A major disadvantage also results from the large number of variables involved. The technique can require a considerable amount of historical data, which may not be available. It also requires a high level of statistical expertise.

---

[16] There are many textbooks that explain the statistical requirements of econometric modeling. For one of the better ones, see J. Johnston, *Econometric Methods,* 2d ed. (New York: McGraw-Hill, 1972).

SELECTION OF FORECASTING METHODS

Factors to consider

With three general categories of forecasting techniques (judgmental, time-series, and causal) and several specific approaches contained within them, a key managerial issue remains: Which method of forecasting should be used? The general rule is to use the technique that best fits the forecasting situation. The specific factors to consider when making this decision are:

1. *Accuracy.* Some situations for which forecasting is used require more forecast accuracy than others. The need for accuracy is indicated by the use to which the forecast will be put. For example, the accuracy of a forecast of first-year sales of a new product is more critical than that of a one-week forecast of the inventory necessary for a low-cost consumer good.

2. *Cost.* This is related to accuracy. More accurate forecasts simply cost more to perform. Generally, the more important the decisions to which the forecast is relevant, the more the firm should spend on it.

3. *Desired precision.* This factor refers to the manner in which the forecast will be expressed. Some forecasts are expressed as a range of values, others as a single quantitative value. The form of the forecast should be based on who will be using it. A forecast prepared for the sales force should probably be communicated differently than one prepared for a corporate president.

4. *Time horizon.* The period of future time that the forecast will cover is an important consideration. Some techniques are suitable for the short term; others become appropriate for the long term.

5. *Requirements of the technique.* The nature of the technique should be considered in terms of its data requirements. Some techniques require substantial amounts of historical data. Others require virtually none. Another aspect to consider is the extent to which it allows users of the forecast to participate in its development. One study showed that managers were willing to trade off accuracy for participation of personnel who would be affected by the forecast.[17]

The specific techniques we've discussed vary in how well they perform on these factors. Table 10–6 ranks the techniques on each factor.

The use of forecasting in industry

The results of two studies on the extent to which various forecasting techniques are actually used by companies are summarized in Table 10–7.[18] Certain key observations emerge from these results. First, it is evident

[17] Pokempner and Bailey, "Sales Forecasting," p. 32.

[18] See Douglas J. Dalrymple, "Sales Forecasting Methods and Accuracy," *Business Horizons,* December 1975, pp. 69–73; and Steven C. Wheelwright and Darral G. Clarke, "Corporate Forecasting: Promise and Reality," *Harvard Business Review,* November–December 1976, pp. 40ff.

Table 10–6: Forecasting techniques ranked from best to worst on selection factors

Categories of forecasting techniques	Accuracy	Cost	Desired precision	Time horizon	Data requirements	Involvement of users
Judgmental	Delphi Customer expectations Executive opinion Sales force composite	Delphi Customer expectations Executive opinion Sales force composite	Customer expectations Remainder are equivalent	Executive opinion Delphi Sales force composite Customer expectations	All are equivalent requiring little historical data	Sales force composite Executive opinion Delphi Customer expectations
Time series	Exponential smoothing Moving average Trend fitting	Exponential smoothing Moving average Trend fitting	All are equivalent, providing precise values	Trend fitting Moving average Exponential smoothing	All are equivalent, requiring at least two years of data	All are equivalent, providing very little involvement
Causal	Econometric Statistical demand analysis	Econometric Statistical demand analysis	All are equivalent, providing precise values	Econometric Statistical demand analysis	Econometric requires most	All are equivalent, providing very little involvement

Source: Adapted from George C. Michael, *Sales Forecasting* (Chicago: American Marketing Association, 1979), pp. 34–35.

Table 10–7: The use of forecasting in industry

Technique	Percentage of firms indicating they use	
	Dalrymple study	Wheelwright and Clarke study
Judgmental		
Sales force composite	48%	67%
Executive opinion	52	77
Delphi	Not measured	Not measured
Customer expectations	15	48
Time series		65*
Trend fitting	28	Not measured
Moving average	24	Not measured
Exponential smoothing	13	Not measured
Causal		
Statistical demand analysis	17	70
Econometric	Not measured	57

* Only a summary measure of the use of some time-series procedures was provided

that some type of forecasting procedure is used by the substantial majority of firms. Thus, forecasting is a common activity in U.S. corporations. Second, while both studies show markedly different results in some respects, a consistent finding is that participatory procedures (i.e., composite of sales force opinion and jury of executive opinion) are most often used. Finally, it is clear that many firms use more than one technique. Generally, these firms are also more accurate in their forecasts.

SUMMARY

Demand assessment is a crucial activity in the situation analysis stage of the strategic planning process. It is how a firm arrives at a quantified estimate of the level of demand for a generic product or brand that exists (or will exist) during a given time period. Key concepts relevant to demand assessment include market potential, market forecast, sales potential, sales forecast, and market share. Estimates of the values of these concepts serve as useful input to the short-run and long-run planning efforts of the company. Specifically, demand assessment plays a role in the evaluation of markets, planning and budgeting, setting of objectives and control standards, and conditional analyses.

There are techniques of demand assessment to estimate current demand and forecast future demand. Techniques for estimating current demand include the chain-ratio method, the market-buildup method, and the buying-power index method. Methods for forecasting future demand fall into three categories: judgmental techniques, time-series techniques, and causal techniques. Judgmental techniques include a composite of sales force opinion, jury of executive opinion, Delphi, and surveys of customer expectations. Time-series procedures include trend fitting, moving averages, and exponential smoothing. Causal techniques include statistical demand analysis and econometric modeling.

Important factors to consider in the selection of a forecasting technique include accuracy, cost, desired precision, time horizon, and requirements of the technique.

KEY CONCEPTS

Demand assessment	Buying-power index (BPI)	Delphi technique
Market potential	Judgment techniques	Trend fitting
Market forecast	Time-series techniques	Moving averages
Sales potential	Causal techniques	Exponential smoothing
Sales forecast	Sales force composite method	Smoothing constant
Market share	Jury of executive opinion method	Statistical demand analysis
Chain-ratio method	Survey of customer expectations	Econometric models
Market-buildup method		

1. For each of the following situations, discuss how useful the concepts of market potential, sales potential, market forecast, and sales forecast would be to a marketing manager in a particular firm facing the situation. Then, for each concept that you consider useful, discuss the technique best suited for estimating the value of the concept.
    a. A new generic product to be introduced by the firm.
    b. A new brand of an existing generic product.
    c. A mature brand.
    d. A new service to be offered to organizational buyers.

2. Given the following observations of unit sales, develop sales forecasts using:
    a. A two-year moving average.
    b. A four-year moving average.
    c. A smoothing constant of 0.2.
    d. A smoothing constant of 0.4.

Year	Sales	Year	Sales
1970	2,150	1978	2,635
1971	2,085	1979	2,795
1972	2,120	1980	2,910
1973	2,310	1981	3,145
1974	2,285	1982	3,080
1975	2,375	1983	3,195
1976	2,545	1984	3,215
1977	2,515		

3. Identify the variables that you would consider for inclusion in a statistical demand analysis model to be used to forecast market sales of pickup trucks. Explain the rationale for each variable. What variables would you include in such a model to forecast sales of Ford pickup trucks?

Case 5: K mart: A market segmentation strategy

When K mart made its debut in 1962, the company focused on selling brand name items. Gradually, K mart began selling house brands in the belief that consumers would be attracted to the lower-priced items which, the company believed, were as good as the well-known brands. The strategy worked for years. Sales grew at a 20 percent annual rate between 1962 and 1980, from about $500 million to $13 billion. Net income also increased 23 percent compounded annually over the same period.

345

The K mart success is due primarily to its emphasis on low cost. In fact, of 12 highly successful service companies, K mart has been considered the only one with cost as its prime distinguishing feature. Comparative price studies made over the years by Goldman Sachs, an investment analyst company, and *Chain Store Age* showed K mart prices usually several percentage points below its competitors.

K mart has significantly increased the number of its retail outlets. Two hundred new stores per year were opened during the 1970s to total 1,968 stores by late 1981. K marts are in 48 states and in 261 of 275 SMSAs. The stores range in size from 40,000 to 96,000 square feet, with an 84,000 standard.

Recently, regional discount chains with more attractive stores and more fashionable products have begun to erode K mart's market share (see Exhibit 1). New kinds of discounters have picked off other pieces of the K mart domain. For example, specialty stores began selling sports equipment, drugs and beauty products, books, apparel, and shoes, while catalog showroom houses engaged in selling small appliances and jewelry. By the late 1970s it became evident that K mart's style and quality did not keep pace with consumer tastes. Its aging stores, cluttered with vending machines offering ice cream, gum balls, and popcorn, made it look outdated and tacky.

The "saving place" became less flatteringly known as the "polyester palace." In 1980, K

mart's profits fell 27 percent to $261 million despite sales reaching a record $14.2 billion. A primary reason for this was that K mart's overhead expenses outpaced its sales for 7 out of the 10 preceding years.

New strategy

In 1980, K mart management implemented a new strategy. It slowed the rate of expansion to 170 new stores in 1981 and to about 120 in 1982. Instead, it began to concentrate on increasing the profitability of existing outlets by remodeling, stocking a broader range of more fashionable merchandise, and raising productivity, as measured by sales per employee hour.

K mart unveiled its new look in nine stores in Indianapolis in November 1980. A new theme color, "poppy red" was chosen. Unattractive interiors cluttered with signs were refurbished with wide aisles, new racks, and larger counters. Remodeling costs ran from $75,000 to $500,000 per store, depending on store size, age, and extent of refurbishment required.

K mart's decision to place greater emphasis on fashion resulted in a need to stock and restock its shelves more quickly. To accomplish this, K mart has built 10 large, mainly automated distribution centers which reduce merchandise delivery time by two or three weeks. A new information system, KIN (K mart Information Network), handles inventories, orders,

Exhibit 1: Comparative analysis of financial performance of major discount chains (1980)

	K mart	Wal-Mart	Target	Goldor
Sales ($000)	$14,204,381	$1,643,199	$1,531,700	$666,530
Number of stores	1,968	368	148	75
Sales per square foot	$104	$120	$154	$129
Sales growth	11.6%	31.6%	36.7%	18.4%
Gross margin	26.7%	21.6% (est)	26.7% (est)	22.2%
Overhead (percent of sales)	23.4%	15.3% (est)	20.5% (est)	15.6%

Source: *Fortune,* September 21, 1981, p. 80.

shipments, payrolls, accounting, and other operations.

Market segment

K mart management has also decided to target as its market middle-income, home-owning, younger- to middle-age consumers—specifically, families between the ages of 25 and 44, with incomes in the $15,000 to $35,000 bracket. This group is expected to grow rapidly in the 1980s. Indeed, between 1977 and 1990, the number of households occupied by this segment of the middle class is projected to increase 55 percent to 18.3 million.

New products for the market segment

To attract these customers, K mart has returned to brand name products while maintaining its customary lower-cost brands. Thus, K mart stocks designer clothing and French perfumes, among other top-line items, and still sells them at discounts ranging from 10 percent to 15 percent for French perfumes to 50 percent for designer jeans. Some have even argued that K mart has begun to take Sears' traditional place by also offering "value at a decent price," Sears' long-time philosophy.

In addition, K mart is offering increasingly diversified merchandise. For example, 180 pharmacy departments were opened in new and existing K marts in 1979, along with 21 optical departments, plus expanded automotive service centers and a prototype "do-it-yourself" department bringing together home-improvement items. Another important aspect of the diversification program has been the establishment of shoe departments in 1,584 K marts.

Assessment of market segmentation strategy

Experts disagree about what will happen to K mart and its new strategy. One management consultant sees a fundamental weakness in K mart's plan that has more to do with demographics and economy than with the strategy. The consultant expects good times for retailers if inflation remains at a low level and real income grows. But he argues that the K mart customer will not benefit as much as others because "he is a mid- to down-scale customer from a family with one wage earner and several children."

However, K mart CEO Bernard M. Fauber disagrees and states that the majority of K mart customers are "roughly representative of their communities and include many people with incomes in the $30,000 to $50,000 range," instead of the common misconception that they come mostly from the lower-income group.

Another consultant agrees with Fauber and paints an optimistic future for K mart. He assumes that the "discount department store industry has become and will remain the principal delivery vehicle for popular-priced general merchandise in the United States in the 1980s." K mart is by far the biggest of these discount chains and is "brilliantly positioned" based on such "fundamentals" as efficiency, low-cost stores, and good locations in almost every major market in the United States. K mart's reputation for value, price, and merchandise quality is another strong point.

References

Cravens, David W. *Strategic Marketing.* Homewood, Ill.: Richard D. Irwin, 1982, pp. 165–66.

Main, Jeremy. "K mart Plans to Be Born again." *Fortune,* September 21, 1981, pp. 74–85.

Peters, Thomas J., and Robert H. Waterman, Jr. *In Search of Excellence.* New York: Harper & Row, 1982, p. 192.

Discussion questions

1. What factors contributed to K mart's recent market share erosion?

2. How does K mart segment the market? Who is their target? How is K mart trying to attract them?

3. What is K mart's future?

Case 6: Midwest Hospital: Assessing current demand

Midwest Hospital owns and operates a hospital serving a midwestern city and primarily four other counties in the surrounding region. In addition, it operates three satellite clinics serving two rural areas. Early in May 1980, Dr. Jim Farr, Midwest's chief administrator, was examining the results of a market research study he had commissioned to determine Midwest's market share. The research was to be used for strategic planning purposes. Therefore, Farr knew that his interpretation was critical to Midwest's future position as a provider of health-care services.

The market research study

BLC Inc., a local market research firm, was hired by Farr to estimate Midwest's market share. As a first step, the marketing consultants attempted to define the geographical boundaries of Midwest's service area. The county was the most common geographic unit used in market share calculation for hospitals. However, BLC used ZIP codes in their research.

BLC felt that the subdivision of counties into ZIP codes was more meaningful, particularly since much of Midwest's operations were conducted in primarily rural counties with generally small populations. BLC identified a total of 10 ZIP codes that Midwest served in the geographic area of interest. Of these, six were serviced by its central hospital facility and the remaining four by its satellite clinics.

Market share calculation

In estimating Midwest's market share, BLC reviewed its patient records for a one-year period to obtain the number of patients who were admitted to its hospital and the number who visited a physician at its clinics. With this information, BLC had the absolute number of patients served from surrounding communities but did not know what proportion of the total hospitalizations or total physician visits those number of patients represented. A search of the state's Bureau of Health Statistics revealed that 781,000 people were discharged from the state's hospitals in 1979, which converts to 167 hospitalizations per 1,000 residents.

BLC then obtained Midwest's market share using the following formula:

$$M_z = \frac{H_z}{P_z \times D/1{,}000} \tag{1}$$

Exhibit 1: Midwest's market shares (1979)

Hospital		Clinic		
			Market share	
ZIP code*	Market share	ZIP code	Formula 2	Formula 3
1	25%	7	14%	18%
2	18	8	12	14
3	10	9	17	20
4	6	10	6	8
5	4			
6	3			

* Each of the ZIP codes has been recoded to preserve anonymity. ZIP codes 2 through 6 get progressively further away in distance from Midwest's hospital facility in ZIP code 1.

where

M_z = Midwest's market share for a particular ZIP code z.

H_z = Hospital's number of annual discharges for ZIP code z.

P_z = Population of community with ZIP code z.

D = Discharges per 1,000 people for a particular geographic area, such as a state.

To estimate the market shares of each of Midwest's satellite clinics, two different formulas were used that eliminated the D variable. They were:

$$M_z = \frac{Q_z}{P_z} \qquad (2)$$

where

M_z = Clinic's market share for ZIP code z.

Q_z = Number of patients who visited the clinic during the year for ZIP code z.

P_z = Population of community with ZIP code z.

and

$$M_z = \frac{F_z}{L_z} \qquad (3)$$

where

M_z = Clinic's market share for ZIP code z.

F_z = Number of families who had at least one member visit the clinic during the year in ZIP code z.

L_z = Number of households within the community for ZIP code z.

Exhibit 1 presents Midwest's market share in each of the ten ZIP codes of interest.

Conclusion

Jim Farr pondered over the results contained in BLC's report to Midwest. He was particularly concerned about the implicit assumptions underlying the market share calculations and the accuracy of the estimates. Thus, he intended calling the BLC consultants for clarification of these issues before presenting his findings to the board of directors of Midwest in three days' time.

Reference

Busch, Paul, and James Farrell. "Market Share's Role in Health-Care Management." In *The Changing Market Environment: New Theories and Applications,* ed. Kenneth Bernhardt. Chicago: American Marketing Association, 1981, pp. 74–76.

Discussion questions

1. What is demand assessment and what is the role of market share information in the demand assessment process?

2. Three methods were presented for assessing market share. Which method do you think is best and why?

3. Which other methods presented in Chapter 10 could be appropriate for assessing demand for Midwest Hospital?

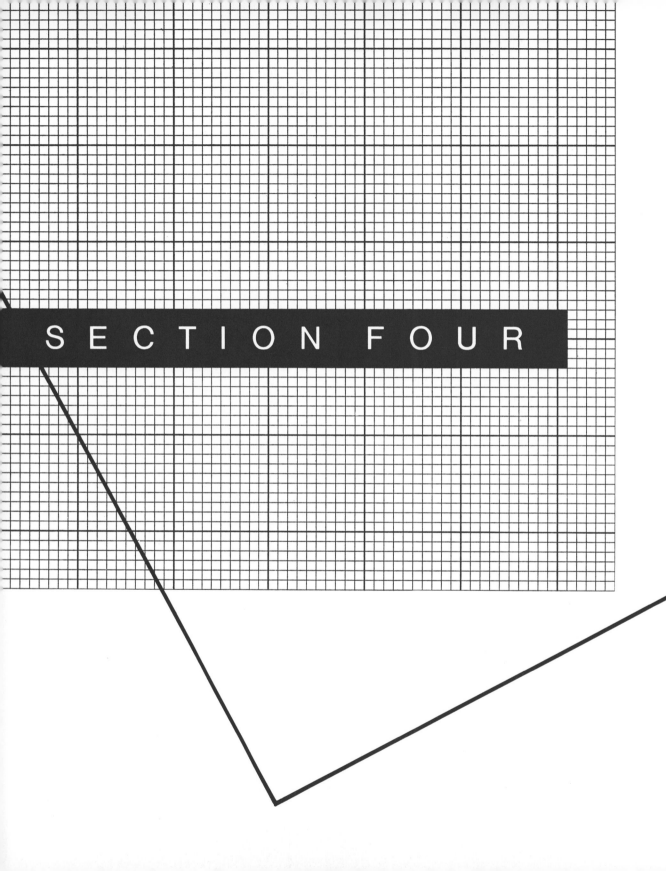

SECTION FOUR

Product strategy

In this section we turn to the product. Chapter 11 begins with a discussion of basic product terms, followed by a look at branding decisions, packaging, and labeling.

Chapter 12 deals with the introduction of new products. We will cover various organizational structures firms may adopt for product development and the seven stages of the development process, as well as factors affecting consumers' decisions to adopt new products.

In Chapter 13 we'll look at various areas of managerial concern related to products. These include the product life cycle, product and brand positioning, cannibalization, and product deletion. The responsibility of the firm to its customers is clearly shown as we discuss product safety, liability, and warranties.

CHAPTER 11

Product:
Basic concepts

What is a product?

Classification of products

Consumer goods
    Convenience goods
    Shopping goods
    Specialty goods

Product mix

Branding
    Reasons for branding
    Characteristics of brand names

Distributor and manufacturer brands
    Battle of the brands

Branding strategy
    Individual brand name strategy
    Family brand name strategy
    Brand name becomes generic

Unbranded goods

Packaging
    Protecting the product
    Facilitating use of the product
    Promoting the product
    Labeling
    Labeling and packaging legislation

Summary

Key concepts

Discussion questions and exercises

This chapter introduces the product portion of the marketing mix, with a focus on basic concepts and terms. First we'll discuss contemporary marketing management views of what constitutes a product. We'll discuss brands next and examine the major managerial decisions related to them. Our focus will be on packaging and labeling.

WHAT IS A PRODUCT?

The most important element of the marketing mix is the ***product.***

product

> A **product** is anything capable of satisfying a consumer want or need. A product can take a variety of forms, including a physical object, a service, a place, an organization, an idea, or a personality.

Decisions on pricing, channels of distribution, and promotion—all depend on the product. For example, if marketing management decides to produce a quality product, one of its logical strategies would be premium pricing. It might choose a heavy promotional effort to inform and convince consumers that the product is worth the extra money. It would select a channel of distribution such that channel members understood the product's benefits and could communicate them to potential buyers.

We must understand the term *product* in all its dimensions. Typically, when we use the term in ordinary conversation, we mean some physical object—a car, an appliance, or a piece of clothing. But from the marketing management perspective, product means much more than that. It also means the prestige and reputation of the object's manufacturer, the credit available to facilitate its purchase, and the information and instruction given for its proper use.

What we need, then, is a more accurate and comprehensive definition.

total product concept

> The **total product concept** is the entire set of benefits the product provides to the consumer.

The total product concept is illustrated in Figure 11–1. At its center is the physical object. Other dimensions, such as quality and reputation of the manufacturer, enhance the benefits and satisfaction users derive from the object.

To further grasp the total product concept, consider the following example. Suppose you are going to purchase an Apple computer. You could buy the computer from a full-service retailer like Computerland or from a mail-order house. Each could provide the same physical object. But Computerland can give you considerable product information, training on how to use the computer, and after-sale service. The mail-order house might provide none of these additional benefits. As a buyer, would you

Figure 11–1. Total product concept

Quality	Reputation of manufacturer	Packaging
Credit	Physical object	Information
Warranty	Service after the sale	Delivery

prefer the complete set of benefits you'd get from the purchase of an Apple computer at Computerland? Or would you rather save several hundred dollars and get fewer benefits by purchasing from the mail-order house?

Understanding the total product concept is important, for it is consistent with the marketing concept and sound marketing management practice. Adopting the total product concept allows consumer needs to be met more effectively. Management can differentiate their products from the competition and thus capture a position within the market.

CLASSIFICATION OF PRODUCTS[1]

The most basic classification scheme for products divides them into *consumer goods* and *industrial goods.*[2]

consumer goods

Consumer goods are products used by the ultimate consumer or households and in such forms that they can be used without further processing.

industrial goods

Industrial goods are products that are to be sold primarily for use in producing other goods or rendering services, as contrasted with goods destined to be sold primarily to the ultimate consumer.

The product's ultimate (end) use determines its classification, and a product may be classed as either of the two types of goods. For example, a typewriter bought by a consumer to type personal letters is a consumer product. If a retailer buys it to type business-related correspondence, it is an industrial product.

Marketing management usually develops different marketing programs for consumer and industrial products. Understanding how its customers use the product is crucial to effective marketing management.

---

[1] The classification of consumer goods is discussed in Chapter 6 and related to consumer decision processes. We discuss consumer goods in this chapter for two reasons: (1) to refine the classification by discussing impulse goods, emergency goods, etc., and (2) to relate the classification to managerial decisions on promotion, price, and distribution. A detailed presentation of industrial goods is found in Chapter 7 and is not dealt with here.

[2] Committee on Definitions of American Marketing Association, *Marketing Definitions: A Glossary of Marketing Terms* (Chicago: American Marketing Association, 1960).

Suppose a company produced a cleaning product for both consumers and businesses. For the consumer market, the company would package the product in small quantities, advertise on TV and in consumer magazines, and sell the product through supermarkets. For the business (industrial) market, the company would package large quantities, use a sales force to promote the product, and sell directly to businesses.

Another common approach classifies products as either **durable goods** or **nondurable goods** based on the number of times the product is used. Durable goods are used repeatedly over a long time. They include major appliances, autos, and home furnishings. Nondurable goods are consumed in one or a few uses—bread, newspapers, and soft drinks, for instance. Our examples so far are all consumer goods, but industrial products may be classed as durables and nondurables as well.

CONSUMER GOODS

Traditionally, consumer goods have been further subdivided based on the amount of shopping effort consumers expend in buying these products. Shopping effort involves activities such as visiting retail stores to compare price and product features, evaluation of product information contained in ads and publications such as *Consumer Reports,* and trial use of the product such as test driving a car or in-home demonstration of the product.

In general, **convenience goods** are purchased with a minimum of effort. Considerable effort is expended in the purchase of **shopping goods. Specialty goods** are products for which consumers are unwilling to accept substitutes. Consumers typically do not expend much shopping effort for specialty goods; they know what they want and go directly to the seller. Figure 11–2 compares convenience and shopping goods based on the amount of shopping effort involved.

Convenience goods

As we said, convenience goods are purchased with a minimum of shopping effort. They include cigarettes, magazines, chewing gum, and many food items. They usually are purchased frequently and in small quantities, are low in price, and are available in many retail outlets.

Marketers of convenience goods usually make them available in as many retail outlets as possible. Convenience goods manufacturers often use TV and magazine ads to stimulate consumer demand. In-store advertising also reminds consumers of such products and their benefits. Because their prices are usually low, convenience goods require a large sales volume

Figure 11–2: Shopping effort for convenience and shopping goods

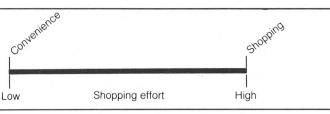

to ensure adequate profit for the manufacturer and retailer. Convenience goods can be classified as staple, impulse, and emergency items.

Staple goods. These products are purchased routinely, with some preplanning to minimize the time and effort to make the purchase. Many food items (bread, milk, cereal, and soft drinks) are in this category.

Impulse goods. These products are purchased without planning prior to entering the store. Common examples are chewing gum, candy, and magazines. Store ads or those seen on TV or in a magazine may have created a vague desire for the product but not an explicit plan to purchase on a particular shopping trip. Once the consumer is inside the store, the product itself or some in-store advertising may trigger a purchase response.

Emergency goods. These products are required to meet an unexpected need. Items such as bandages, tire repair kits, plumbing services, and electrical fuses are examples of emergency goods.

Shopping goods

Shopping goods are products for which the consumer expends considerable effort comparing suitability, price, quality, and style. Examples of shopping goods are furniture, bicycles, and women's suits.

Marketers of shopping goods usually place more emphasis on personal selling than on advertising. Salespersons can emphasize a product's features that make it better than competing products. Ads for shopping goods often emphasize the attributes consumers look for when making the purchase decision. Maytag, for example, advertises the dependability of its washers and dryers. Compared to convenience goods, shopping goods are available in fewer retail outlets. Because of their higher price, financing the purchase is often a significant aspect of marketing shopping goods. General Motors established its General Motors Acceptance Corporation (GMAC) to finance auto purchases, and today GMAC is a significant aspect of that automaker's business.

Specialty goods

Specialty goods are products for which consumers are unwilling or unable to accept substitutes. Consumers may become very loyal to a particular brand of product. Typical examples of specialty products include expensive stereo and photographic equipment and antiques. Other types of specialty products might include medicine or medicinal supplies for which no reasonable substitute exists.

Marketers of specialty goods usually restrict the distribution of the product to a limited number of outlets. This restriction enhances the product's unique image and usually doesn't decrease sales because customers are willing to exert time and effort to obtain the product. Promotional expenditures are used to inform consumers of where to buy the product.

Table 11–1: Product classification schemes	**Product classification system**	**Basis of classification system**
	Convenience, shopping, specialty	Consumer shopping effort
	Durable, nondurable	Number of repeated uses of product
	Consumer, industrial	The use (household or business) to which the product is put

Prices of specialty goods are usually high because buyers are willing to pay a premium to obtain them. Table 11–1 contains a summary of the product classification schemes and their basis for classification.

PRODUCT MIX

Certain terms are basic to the discussion of product.

product mix

> **Product mix** refers to the set of all product lines and items that a particular seller offers for sale to buyers.

product line

> A **product line** is a group of products within a product mix that are closely related either because they function in a similar manner, are sold to the same customer groups, are marketed through the same types of outlets, or fall within given price ranges.

product item

> A **product item** is a distinct unit within a product line that is distinguishable by size, price, appearance, or some other characteristic. The item is sometimes called a stockkeeping unit, product variant, or subvariant.[3]

The product mix can be further described in terms of width, depth, and consistency. *Width* is the number of product lines within the product mix. *Depth* is the number of product items per line. *Consistency* is the degree to which the products are related.

These terms are illustrated in Figure 11–3, which contains a partial product mix for General Foods. The mix shown contains six product lines. The average depth of the lines is calculated by dividing the total number of products by the number of lines (in this case 24/6 = 4). All products in the mix are highly related in price, packaging, and distribution, so the product mix is highly consistent.

BRANDING

A major product-related decision is branding. Before we begin the discussion of branding, we must define the relevant terms.

---
[3] Ibid.

Figure 11–3: General Foods product mix

Coffee	Beverages	Breakfast foods	Dessert and topping	Main meal	Pet foods
Maxwell House	Kool-Aid	Alpha Bits	Jell-O	Minute Rice	Gaines Burger
Sanka	Country Time Lemonade	Honey Comb	Cool Whip	Stove Top Stuffing	Gravy Train
Brim	Tang	Grape Nuts		Shake 'n Bake	Top Choice
Maxim		Raisin Bran			Puppy Choice
Yuban		Bran Flakes			Cycle 1
Max Pax					

Product mix width

Product line depth

brand	A **brand** is a name, term, sign, symbol, design, or combination of them that identifies the goods or services of one seller or group of sellers and differentiates them from those of competitors.
brand name	**Brand name** refers to that part of a brand that can be vocalized (Crest, Mustang, Tide).
brand mark	**Brand mark** refers to the part of a brand that cannot be vocalized, such as its symbol, design, or distinctive packaging (the GM symbol, the Green Giant).
trademark	A **trademark** is a brand or part of a brand that is given legal protection because it is assigned exclusively (Buick and Michelob).

Reasons for branding

A manufacturer engages in branding for several reasons. The company's objective is to achieve repeat purchases, and branding provides an opportunity to develop a favorable relationship with consumers. The manufacturer hopes the relationship will result in a higher market share and increased profitability. If consumers demand the product, the manufacturer can exercise more control over its price and distribution. Branding also enables a manufacturer to develop a specific market position for a product. For example, Hart Shaffner & Marx men's suits are positioned as high-quality products. Their pricing, distribution, and promotion reinforce this high-quality position.

Branding is also helpful to the consumer. A familiar brand name represents a number of important product attributes, and it enables the consumer to make a decision with a minimum of effort. Manufacturers who brand their products are concerned that their brand names represent a certain standard of quality and consistency. A brand may give the consumer pride and satisfaction in owning a well-known and high-quality product.

Characteristics of brand names

To be effective, a brand name should possess certain characteristics. The brand name should be readily recognizable and easily remembered. So short names, easy to pronounce and to spell, are desirable (Tide, Aim, Gleem, Cheer). An effective brand name tells the consumer something about the product's benefits (Allerest, NoDoz, Ultra-brite, Hamburger Helper). The name should be markedly different from other similar products (Impala, Winston, Zenith). Finally, management should develop a brand name that can be legally protected. The Lanham Act of 1946 applies to goods shipped in interstate or foreign commerce; it specifies the types of marks and brand names that can be protected by law.[4]

---

[4] Joe L. Welch, *Marketing Law* (Tulsa: Petroleum Publishing Company, 1980), p. 136.

The Luvs brand name is short, easy to pronounce and spell. Moreover, the brand name projects a favorable connotation about the product's benefits.

Luvs® added a second row of flexible gathers to add to your baby's comfort.

Now Luvs is more comfortable for babies than ever before.

As you can see, New Luvs has two rows of flexible gathers.

They snuggle up around your baby's legs more gently than our one row ever did.

There's something else new about

Old Luvs   New Luvs

Luvs. You can't see it, but you can feel it. It's Luvs new, softer lining. And it's more comfortable next to your baby's tender skin.

New Luvs, with two rows of flexible gathers plus a softer lining. It all adds up to a new, more comfortable Luvs for your baby.

New
Luvs

Luvs

Your baby's comfort begins with Luvs.

© 1984 Procter & Gamble

No one brand name meets all the criteria for effectiveness. Trade-offs are usually necessary. For example, Miller Brewing Company first introduced a low-calorie beer called Lite. The name is easy to pronounce and tells the consumer about the product's major benefits. However, Miller was not able to retain exclusive use of the term *light beer.*

DISTRIBUTOR AND MANUFACTURER BRANDS

Brands are classed as **manufacturer** or **distributor** brands depending on who is responsible for the major naming, promotion, pricing, and product-quality decisions. For manufacturer brands, the producer assumes these responsibilities. Distributor brands are developed by the wholesaler or retailer, who assumes the major responsibilities for them. Manufacturer brands are also known as *national brands;* distributor brands are sometimes called *private brands.*

Manufacturer brands are usually the best-known items in the product category. Familiar examples include Budweiser beer, Marlboro cigarettes, Edge shaving gel, and L'Eggs panty hose. Manufacturers of branded products are sophisticated and effective marketers. Their excellent reputations for marketing expertise are widely known and well deserved (companies like Procter & Gamble, General Mills, and S. C. Johnson, for example). The marketers of manufacturer brands stress quality, rely heavily on advertising and sales promotion, and usually price products 10 to 20 percent higher than distributor brands.

Distributor brands are usually less well known. They are not heavily advertised, and their distribution is limited to areas in which the retailer or wholesaler sells. Examples of distributor brands are K mart and A&P. Distributors brand products because they are highly profitable compared to manufacturer brands. Typically distributor brands cost less for distributors to purchase. Therefore, the gross margin is higher. The lower cost is possible because the distributor's brand is not advertised or promoted heavily, and raw materials may be of lesser quality than the manufacturer brand. The distributor has great control over the pricing of the product. All these factors make distributor brands attractive to the intermediary.

Battle of the brands

The competition between manufacturer and distributor brands is referred to as the **battle of the brands.** The battle is likely to continue as intermediaries, especially retailers, grow more aggressive in developing their own brands. In the automobile tire market, retailer brands such as K mart and Sears account for 40 percent of the sales volume. In the grocery products market, 30 percent of sales is in retailer brands.[5] Sears sells over 90 percent of its sales volume under its various distributor brand names like Kenmore (appliances) and DieHard (automobile batteries). Manufacturers will no doubt continue to stress product quality and innovation in product design and packaging to compete with distributor brands. Price reductions through cents-off, couponing, and 2-for-1 deals are likely to be used by distributors as short-term tactics to compete with manufacturer brands.

---

[5] E. B. Weiss, "Big Stores, Non-Foods, and Private Brands Wane in Supermarket Field," *Advertising Age,* January 5, 1976, p. 32.

BRANDING STRATEGY

Branding strategy involves two major issues: marketing options and selection of brand names. The first requires the manufacturer to select one of three major options: (1) Market products exclusively under manufacturer's brand name; (2) Market products exclusively under distributor's brand name; or (3) Market products under a mixture of manufacturer and distributor brand names.

After making this choice, the firm must select its brand names. The two major approaches here are the ***individual brand name strategy*** and the ***family brand name strategy.***

Individual brand name strategy

A company may select an individual brand name strategy whereby each brand has a distinctive name not associated with the company or with its other products. Procter & Gamble chose this strategy for its laundry detergents (Tide, Cheer, Oxydol, Gain, Bold). So did most cigarettemakers. Phillip Morris, for one, markets Marlboro, Parliament, Merit, Virginia Slims, and Benson & Hedges.

The major advantage of individual branding is that a brand failure is not easily associated with the company's name or the names of its other products. If a consumer is dissatisfied with a brand, the dissatisfaction is not likely to spread to the firm's other brands. Individual branding also enables the company to market several products that compete with each other. There are several reasons for this practice. It enables a firm to compete more effectively in markets where consumers frequently switch from one brand to another. It also enables a firm's products to meet different consumer tastes and preferences. Coca-Cola markets a variety of soft drinks, including Tab, Sprite, Mr. Pibb, and Mello Yello, to satisfy buyers looking for different tastes (cola, lemon and lime) and types (regular and diet). Marketing several brands also creates opportunities for advancement and growth within the company. The company's managers compete with each other and can learn more about specific products and markets when their company has several brands in the same markets. Finally, a manufacturer can exert more control over the distribution and retailing of products when marketing several brands. Specifically, the manufacturer would occupy more shelf space (always in limited supply) and thus make it more difficult for competition to market their products. The major drawback to individual brand name strategy is the cost of advertising and promoting a new product that cannot capitalize on the established reputation of an existing brand name or company name.

Family brand name strategy

The second naming approach—the *family brand name strategy*—puts a family name on all products manufactured by the firm. This strategy involves making a name (usually the manufacturer's company name) prominent on each product itself or on its packaging, advertising, and promotional materials. Companies like Campbell Soup, General Electric, and H. J. Heinz use the family name strategy.

P&G laundry list of
major products in 1980.

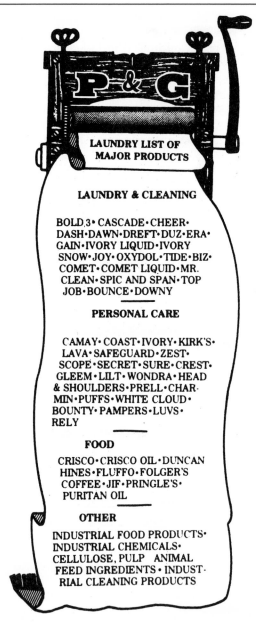

LAUNDRY LIST OF MAJOR PRODUCTS

LAUNDRY & CLEANING

BOLD.3• CASCADE•CHEER•
DASH•DAWN•DREFT•DUZ•ERA•
GAIN•IVORY LIQUID•IVORY
SNOW•JOY•OXYDOL•TIDE•BIZ•
COMET•COMET LIQUID•MR.
CLEAN•SPIC AND SPAN•TOP
JOB•BOUNCE•DOWNY

PERSONAL CARE

CAMAY•COAST•IVORY•KIRK'S•
LAVA•SAFEGUARD•ZEST•
SCOPE•SECRET•SURE•CREST•
GLEEM•LILT•WONDRA•HEAD
& SHOULDERS•PRELL•CHAR-
MIN•PUFFS•WHITE CLOUD•
BOUNTY•PAMPERS•LUVS•
RELY

FOOD

CRISCO•CRISCO OIL•DUNCAN
HINES•FLUFFO•FOLGER'S
COFFEE•JIF•PRINGLE'S•
PURITAN OIL

OTHER

INDUSTRIAL FOOD PRODUCTS•
INDUSTRIAL CHEMICALS•
CELLULOSE, PULP   ANIMAL
FEED INGREDIENTS • INDUST-
RIAL CLEANING PRODUCTS

The strategy has seen several refinements. Some firms use *separate family names* for *product lines.* For example, Sears uses its Craftsman brand on hand and mechanic's tools and Kenmore on major appliances. A firm may use separate family brand names for product lines of different price levels as well, or it may use a *family name combined with individual product names.* Ralston Purina Co. uses this approach for its Purina Dog Chow, Purina Puppy Chow, and Purina Special Dinners (cat food).

The family branding approach has several advantages that account for its being the most frequently used naming strategy. For one thing, new brands are easier and less expensive to introduce. The firm need not incur the expense of research for a brand name. More significantly, the advertising and promotion costs for new brands are lower. The firm can capitalize on its reputation and on the investment it made in advertising its existing products. The Campbell Soup Company frequently introduces new soups with relative ease because of consumer awareness of the family brand and its quality image, created in part by Campbell's long-term advertising expenditures.

Ralston Purina has effectively used the family brand name approach for the company's pet and animal foods. Individual brand names such as Cat Chow and Kitten Chow are associated with the family brand name. Effective use of the family brand name approach eases the process of introducing new products.

Courtesy Ralston Purina

Family branding does have some drawbacks. If one product using the brand name proves unsatisfactory to buyers, it may damage the reputation and sales of other products using the same name. Firms that use the family brand approach assume a greater burden of maintaining consistent quality across all products than do users of individual brand names.

Brand name becomes generic

Sometimes a brand name becomes synonymous with a product category. A firm's promotional efforts with a brand are sometimes so effective that consumers learn to use the brand name generically. You may have found yourself saying, "Please give me a Kleenex" or "I need a Band-Aid." In either case you may have meant a *product* (facial tissue, adhesive bandage) of no particular brand name. The marketers of these brands have done such an effective job that their brand is often used as a general or **generic** name for the entire product class. When a brand name becomes a generic name, the government may prohibit the firm's exclusive use of the name.

A company's brand name can become a generic name when a patent expires and there is no other practicable product name for the public to use.[6] This happened with shredded wheat, nylon, and cellophane. Legally protected brand names that have been heavily promoted and are used generically by consumers include Vaseline, Xerox, Frigidaire, Levi's, Styrofoam, Fiberglass, and Jeep.

A company can take several actions to prevent losing its exclusive use of a brand name through generic usage. First, its ads may stress that the brand name belongs exclusively to the company. (See Figure 11–4.) Second, a firm may couple the brand name with the company name. For example, Eastman Kodak has run a series of ads stating: "If it doesn't say Eastman, it isn't a Kodak." These ads remind consumers that the Kodak name belongs exclusively to Eastman. Third, the use of the symbol ® near the brand informs consumers that the name is a registered trademark. Finally, the U.S. Trademark Association recommends that a firm always spell the brand name with a capital letter and use the name as an adjective for the product class, such as Jell-O gelatin dessert or Kleenex facial tissue. A firm may use all these methods to protect its brand name. For a recent example of a company losing its trademark see the discussion of the *Monopoly board game* case.

UNBRANDED GOODS

A recent phenomenon in the packaged goods industry has been the introduction of **unbranded** goods. Unbranded goods are also known as *no-name, generics, no-frills,* or *plain-wraps.* They were introduced in France in 1976 by the Carrefour chain. Within two and a half years, generics

---

[6] W. J. Stanton, *Fundamentals of Marketing,* 6th ed. (New York: McGraw-Hill, 1981), p. 197.

achieved widespread consumer acceptance and captured a considerable share of the French market. One reason for this success is that France had no private-label products. Consequently, generics met an important need for a low-cost alternative to nationally branded products.

Jewel Food Stores was the first to offer generics in the United States when they introduced them to the Chicago market in October 1977. Esti-

MONOPOLY: MORE THAN A GAME

Manufacturers spend millions to build name recognition for their products, and sometimes succeed only too well. Over the years, the courts have invalidated such trademarks as shredded wheat, aspirin, zipper, yo-yo, cola, and cellophane on the ground that the public had come to accept them as generic, "common descriptive" terms for actual products rather than as brand names. Last week the popular board game Monopoly joined the list of overachievers when the U.S. Supreme Court refused to hear an appeal of a lower-court ruling stripping Parker Brothers and its parent, General Mills, of the trademark issued in 1935.

The decision seemed to uphold a controversial twist given to trademark law by the U.S. Court of Appeals for the Ninth Circuit. In a ruling last August on a case brought by the makers of Anti-Monopoly, a once-popular parody of the Parker Brothers' game, the court invalidated Parker Brothers' claim because, it said, actual and potential Monopoly buyers were motivated more by desire to play the game than by loyalty to the maker. Critics said the decision might, for example, allow any soap manufacturer to bring out a detergent called Tide, if surveys showed that consumers did not connect the original product with Procter & Gamble Co. But Monopoly's makers need not worry about exact replicas flooding the stores: the game itself is still copyrighted. Even so, Parker Brothers still faces hearings on antitrust charges filed by the Anti-Monopoly forces saying that the company tried to interfere with the marketing of the similarly named board game.

mates are that approximately one third of the nation's 33,000 supermarkets now carry some generic products and achieve average unit market share of nearly 11 percent in these product categories.[7] Initially, generics were offered in about 30 food and nonfood product categories, and they typically sold in one (usually large) size. But some retailers who have enjoyed success with no-brands plan to increase the generic product categories to 150. Generics' penetration has been greatest in canned fruits and vegetables, paper and plastic products, and soaps and detergents. The least penetration has occurred in soft drinks, pet products, and other specialty categories.[8]

The major virtue of generics for the consumer is lower price. Compared to national brands, typical savings range from 10 percent to 35 percent,[9] with some product categories offering savings up to 50 percent.[10] Compared to private labels, the savings are usually smaller. There are a number of reasons for the lower prices of generics:

[7] M. Yao, "Generics Are Winning Noticeable Share of Market from National Brands," *The Wall Street Journal,* August 10, 1979, p. 6.

[8] J. W. Cagley, L. A. Niedell, and L. E. Boone, "The Wheel of Retailing Squeals but Turns: Generic Labeling in Supermarkets," in *1980's Marketing Changes and Challenges,* ed. Richard P. Bagozzi et al. (Chicago: American Marketing Association, 1980), pp. 184–87.

[9] J. S. Coyle, "Why Jewel Did It, How Consumers Respond, What Risks Are, Where It All Goes from Here," *Progressive Grocer,* February 1978, pp. 75–8.

[10] J. S. Coyle, "To Jewel, Its Controversial Generics Line Is More than Merely Defensive," *Progressive Grocer,* February 1978, p. 34.

1. The product may not be consistent in color or size.

2. Color and fragrance have been eliminated from paper products.

3. Container size is limited, usually to the larger size.

4. Items never go on sale, so the cost of markdowns is eliminated.

5. The products are sold with limited advertising.[11]

Consumers must consider the drawbacks of generics. The most significant has been the lack of consistent product quality. Other disadvantages are restriction of packages and containers to larger sizes, lack of availability, and low prestige of product compared to national brands.

Retailers can use generics to appeal to the price-conscious consumer. Generics may also help build store traffic and increase the purchase of branded product items. A number of leading retail chains (A&P, Pathmark, Jewel) have concluded that—at least for the short run—generics are profitable. While the evidence is mixed, it does appear that generics are purchased by consumers who would typically buy national rather than store or private brands.[12] Retailers could thus preserve the market shares of their store brands and still enjoy the benefits of marketing generics. Some retailers are so committed to generics that they use distinctive symbols or colors to identify their store's generics (Jewel). Other retailers have established "generic brand names." No Brand (Food Town), Valu Time (a Topco registered trademark), and No Frills (Pathmark) have been copyrighted by supermarket chains.[13]

Some retailers have found success with generics. But we stress that this success depends on a commitment to adequate levels of advertising, inventory, and stocking and display of the products.

Generics do pose a significant challenge to manufacturers of national branded products, especially in product categories where generics have made the greatest penetration. The national brands have fought back in several ways.

Sales promotion tactics, such as 2-for-1 sales, have been used to "load up" consumers so they need not buy generics.

Clorox has stressed the quality of its national brand over generics: "Our product (Clorox) is more pure, more stable, more consistent in quality."

J. M. Smucker offered larger discounts to supermarkets on case sales of two-pound jars of grape jelly and strawberry jam because generics posed the greatest threat on those items.
Libby, McNeill & Libby placed more emphasis on specialty products that have not appeared in generics.

---

[11] C. Moore, "No-Brands Foods Slow to Catch on Here," *Wisconsin State Journal,* August 31, 1978, sec. 4, p. 5.

[12] Yao, "Generics Are Winning Noticeable Share," p. 6.

[13] R. Parcels, "An Unadvertised Brand? The 'Generic' That Never Was," *Advertising Age,* December 17, 1979, p. S–2.

While the future of generics is uncertain, they seem to have found a definite niche in the market. Given the current pressures on consumers' budgets, generics are likely to continue to be significant for consumers, retailers, and manufacturers.

PACKAGING

Packaging is the container or wrapping for a product item. Because a brand's package is a highly visible part of the product, packaging assumes a major role in marketing the product. Some consumer goods companies place so much importance on the product's container or wrapping that they have vice presidents in charge of packaging. A study of packaging's influence on consumer decision making in drugstore purchases sheds additional light on the significance of packaging. Approximately 38 percent of respondents making an initial purchase said that the package had "great influence" on purchases of cosmetic or toiletry products.[14]

The three basic functions of a product's package are protecting the product, facilitating use of the product, and promoting the product.

Protecting the product

The most basic and original purpose of packaging is to protect the product in transport and in storage at the manufacturer, wholesaler, retailer, and consumer levels. The product may be exposed to extremes of cold, heat, or moisture during transportation and storage. It must be protected against being crushed, dropped, or punctured during its physical handling.

Facilitating use of the product

Increasing the ease of opening and usefulness of the package is a major chance for marketers to differentiate their product from competitors. No-drip spouts, squeeze bottles, resealable soft drink bottles, and tear tapes are package improvements designed to facilitate use. Marketing research can play a central role by analyzing how consumers use products and the problems they encounter with packaging. This research can help identify specific ways to improve packaging.

Promoting the product

The extent to which the package protects and facilitates product use increases the package's sales and promotional value. Improved packaging can be an effective way to attract new customers. For instance, research has shown that 30 percent of the purchasers of cosmetic and toiletry products switched brands for a better package.[15]

Occasionally a company uses packaging as a strategic variable to promote its product to a specific market segment. Pittsburg Brewing and Huber Brewing of Monroe, Wisconsin, have made frequent design changes on their beer labels to appeal to beer can collectors. For small breweries,

---

[14] "Drugstore Packages," *Sales Management,* September 15, 1970, pp. 41–52.
[15] Ibid.

sales to collectors have become an important means of increasing sales.[16]

The package is one element of the firm's comprehensive strategy for marketing products. The Hanes Corporation developed a consistently high-quality panty hose, priced it at 30 percent above competing products, and used aggressive sales promotion to achieve success. The unique egg-shaped package for its L'eggs product helped distinguish the product from its competition.[17] The L'eggs package is an example of using the package as in-store or point-of-purchase promotion for the product. Procter & Gamble's bright orange Tide box is another example.

| Labeling | *Labeling* is often an important part of the package. It allows management to communicate with those who purchase—or might purchase—the product. |

Labeling

Labeling is often an important part of the package. It allows management to communicate with those who purchase—or might purchase—the product.

There are three types of labels:

1. *Grade labels* indicate the product's quality. For example, meat may be graded as choice or prime. Canned fruits are grade-labeled A, B, or C.

2. *Descriptive labels* tell how the product is to be used or maintained; e.g., clothing labels might give laundering instructions. Labels on power lawn mowers tell how to safely operate the product.

3. *Brand labels* identify the brand itself. Brand labels include the brand name, symbol, sign, or some combination of these elements.[18]

Labeling can be a means of gaining a competitive edge. Del Monte Corporation introduced nutritional labeling before it was required by federal law; and the company enjoyed an advantage over competitors who did not provide this information.[19] Informative and distinctive labeling can be used to set a product apart. **Open dating** indicates the product's useful life and helps consumers avoid spoiled products. Dairy products, for example, are stamped with the last date the product should be sold to ensure freshness.

Labeling and packaging legislation

As marketers responded to competitive pressures, consumer needs, and opportunities in the market, the numbers and types of packages and labels proliferated. This resulted in a number of problems. Consumer groups and governmental agencies complained about the safety of medication packaging. Confusion developed over the meaning of phrases like "king size" and "giant economy size"; and the wide range of package sizes made price comparisons extremely difficult. These problems and others led to federal regulation of packaging.

---

[16] Lawrence Ingrassia, "Some Breweries Find New Market to Tap When Sales Are Flat," *The Wall Street Journal,* November 14, 1978, p. 1.

[17] "Our L'eggs Fit Your L'eggs," *Business Week,* March 25, 1972.

[18] Stanton, *Fundamentals of Marketing,* p. 205.

[19] William Pride and O. C. Ferrell, *Marketing Basic Concepts and Decisions,* 2d ed. (Boston: Houghton Mifflin, 1980), p. 208.

In 1966 Congress passed the Fair Packaging and Labeling Act, which resulted in changes that affected marketing management. Federal agencies like the Food and Drug Administration were given the power to set packaging regulations where it was deemed necessary. Industry was encouraged to voluntarily set packaging and labeling standards to reduce the number of sizes and thus simplify comparisons between packages and brands. Mandatory labeling requirements were established.[20]

The legislation and voluntary actions have brought definite improvements. The Poison Prevention Packaging Act of 1970 required many household products to be packaged in child-resistant containers. According to the Consumer Product Safety Commission, which administers the law, the accidental consumption of aspirin preparations by children has since dropped by 41 percent.[21]

The number of detergent package sizes was reduced from 24 to 6; the number of toothpaste sizes was reduced from 57 to 5.[22] To make packaging more ecologically compatible, some states (Oregon and Michigan) enacted laws requiring returnable beverage containers. Marketing management can expect demands for improved packaging to continue. Responsible management will view this challenge as an opportunity to better serve consumer needs and improve product profitability.

---

[20] Warren A. French and Leila O. Shroeder, "Package Information Legislation: Trends and Viewpoints," *MSU Business Topics,* Summer 1972, pp. 39–44.

[21] Lawrence Woods, "Child-Resistant Packaging Is Praised," *The Wall Street Journal,* May 11, 1978, p. 42.

[22] "Nutrition by Numbers," *Time,* October 30, 1972, p. 49.

SUMMARY

The term *product* involves several dimensions, and understanding each is vital because of the impact products have on all decisions concerning the marketing mix. The total products concept is the physical product along with its many related dimensions, such as quality, information at time of sale, and prestige of ownership. Such concepts as product mix, product line, and product item help us understand the various levels at which firms group and manage their products.

Although a product's end use determines its classification, the most basic product categories are consumer and industrial goods. Consumer goods can be further categorized as convenience, shopping, and specialty items.

Branding is a critical product-related decision. It takes in such concepts as brand, brand name, brand mark, and trademark. Brands are either distributor or manufacturer brands. The "battle of the brands" is the struggle between these two types. The growth of unbranded goods, or generics, represents a major competitive threat to traditional branded goods companies.

Packaging plays a major role in product marketing. Besides offering protection, a package promotes the product and facilitates its use. An important part of the package is its label. A label can indicate product quality, product composition, and use, and it can serve as a competitive tool. Labeling and packaging legislation helps protect consumers, the economy, and the environment.

KEY CONCEPTS

Product	Product line	Battle of the brands
Total product concept	Product item	Individual brand name strategy
Consumer goods	Width, depth, consistency of	Family brand name strategy
Industrial goods	product mix	Generic name
Durable goods	Brand	Unbranded goods
Nondurable goods	Brand name	Packaging
Convenience goods	Brand mark	Labeling
Shopping goods	Trademark	Open dating
Specialty goods	Distributor brands	
Product mix	Manufacturer brands	

DISCUSSION QUESTIONS AND EXERCISES

1. Construct a product mix for one of the Big Three automobile companies. What conclusions about the company's marketing strategy can you draw based on such things as the width and depth of the product mix?

2. Review the total product concept. Develop a list of benefits you would derive from purchasing a used car from an individual seller versus a large reputable automobile dealership.

3. Make a list of five products that are physically identical but could be classified as either consumer or industrial goods based on their use.

4. Select a well-known branded durable product (e.g., Maytag washing machines) and a well-known branded nondurable product (e.g., Coca-Cola). Compare and contrast the marketing mix elements of product price, promotion, and distribution for these two brands.

5. "Specialty goods may have been shopping goods for an individual consumer at a particular point in time. However, over time the shopping good may evolve into a specialty good." Discuss how this process may occur.

6. Consider a branded product that you frequently purchase. What are the major benefits you derive from the branded product? Does the branded product you buy meet the criteria for effective brand names as presented in the text?

7. Define "battle of the brands." How does the introduction of generic (no-name or brandless) products fit into the "battle of the brands"? Discuss.

8. Have you ever purchased generic or no-brand products? If so, compare these products to their branded equivalents.

9. The next time you are in a supermarket, note products with new packages. Which of the three basic functions of packaging do the new packages illustrate?

CHAPTER 12

New-product development

What is a new product?

Importance of new products

Why new products fail
  Lack of significant advantages
  Failure to match company's strength
  Changes in consumers' tastes
  Insufficient market segment size
  Competitive entry into market
  Lack of channel support

Organization for new-product development
  New-product committee
  Product managers
  New-product department
  Venture team

The new-product development process

Generation of new-product ideas
  Brainstorming
  Benefit-structure analysis
  Problem-inventory analysis
  Attribute listing

Screening of ideas

Business analysis
  Capital budgeting techniques

Product-concept development and testing
  A comprehensive concept-evaluation
    procedure
  Identification of market segment
  Concept evaluation
  Identification of key characteristics of
    various benefit segments
  Assessing the concept's market
    positioning

Product development
  Market testing
  Minimarket test
  Laboratory market tests
  Statistical and mathematical models

Commercialization

Consumer behavior and new products
  Product attributes that influence adoption
  The consumer adoption process

Summary

Key concepts

Discussion questions and exercises

Our purpose in this chapter is to present a comprehensive overview of the new-product development process. Starting with the definition of a new product, we'll follow with a discussion of new products' importance and the reasons why new products fail. Next we'll summarize how to organize for new products. Then we'll make detailed analysis of each of the seven steps in the new-product development process. Finally, we'll look at the relationship between consumer behavior and the adoption of new products.

WHAT IS A NEW PRODUCT?

The term *new product* can mean many things. Sometimes it means a major innovation such as the automobile or television. Other times, it refers to a small modification in the feature or packaging of an existing product. To discuss new products systematically, we will use a classification system based on how new products influence the behavior of the consumer using them.[1]

continuous innovations	**Continuous innovations** are minor product changes that have little influence on established consumer behaviors.
dynamically continuous innovations	**Dynamically continuous innovations** are more disruptive changes and include major product changes and creation of some new products.
discontinuous innovations	**Discontinuous innovations** establish new products and new patterns of consumer behaviors.

Examples of continuous innovation are brand-line extensions like Taster's Choice decaffeinated coffee and Michelob Light beer. Examples of dynamically continuous innovations are the electric toothbrush, the Mustang automobile, and the Touch-Tone telephone. Discontinuous innovations include the introduction of television and computers. (See Figure 12–1.)

We define a new product as something that the company is producing for the first time. Most new products are continuous or dynamically continuous innovations. Discontinuous innovations are rare.

---

[1] Thomas S. Robertson, "The Process of Innovation and the Diffusion of Innovation," *Journal of Marketing,* January 1967, p. 15.

Figure 12–1: Types of new products

Discontinuous innovation   Dynamically continuous innovations   Continuous innovation

Most   Disruptive influence on consumer behavior   Least

IMPORTANCE OF NEW PRODUCTS

The development of new products is clearly one of the firm's most critical activities. A major reason for developing new products is to achieve growth in the firm's sales and profits. It is not uncommon for 30 to 40 percent of a firm's current sales dollars and profits to come from products that were not in its product portfolio five years ago.[2] Such growth is a key element of effective strategic planning and management of the firm's product portfolio.

Robots represent a current example of a discontinuous innovation. This ad informs potential industrial buyers of the wide range of Prab robotic applications.

Courtesy Prab Robots, Inc.

---

[2] Richard T. Hise, Charles Futrell, and Donald Snyder, "University Research Centers as a New-Product Development Resource," *Research Management* 23 (October 1980), pp. 25–28.

Positive consumer reaction to a competitor's new product may be another reason for a firm to introduce its own. After Miller Brewing successfully introduced Lite beer, all major brewing companies reacted by introducing their own brands. New products may also be introduced to replace obsolete or unsuccessful ones. This is common in industries where technology is rapidly improving, such as the camera and computer industries. Smoothing out seasonal sales fluctuations, exploring new opportunities, and using excess plant capacity are additional reasons for developing new products.[3]

WHY NEW PRODUCTS FAIL

It is often stated that there is a high rate of failure for new products. Estimates of failure range from 20 to 80 percent of new-product introduction.[4] But comprehensive review of 31 studies conducted since World War II found the failure rate considerably lower than is commonly thought. About 25 percent of all new industrial products and 30 to 35 percent of all consumer products fail to meet the expectations of managers who develop them.[5]

Estimates of failure rates vary depending on the method used to define a new product, the sample of firms used in the studies, and how a failure was determined.[6] For our purposes, failures occur when a new product does not meet projected financial goals, especially a specified return on investment. Research indicates that new-product failure rates are higher among consumer products than among industrial products. Some of the best-known new-product failures and their financial losses are listed in Table 12–1.

Lack of significant advantages

Many reasons have been given as causes of failure for new products.[7] Research has shown, for instance, that a product is likely to fail if it lacks a significant price or performance advantage over existing competi-

---

[3] Richard T. Hise, *Product/Service Strategy* (New York: Mason/Charter Publishers, 1977), pp. 136–39.

[4] For research on new-product failures, see Betty Cochran and G. Thompson, "Why New Products Fail," *The National Industrial Conference Board Record,* October 1964, pp. 11–18; Robert D. Buzzell and Robert E. M. Nouse, "Product Innovation in Food Processing, 1954–1964" (Boston: Harvard Business School, 1967); David S. Hopkins and Earl L. Bailey, "New-Product Pressures," *The Conference Board Record,* June 1971, pp. 16–24; C. Merle Crawford, *New-Product Management* (Homewood, Ill.: Richard D. Irwin, 1983), pp. 25–28.

[5] C. Merle Crawford, "New-Product Failure Rates—Facts and Fallacies," *Research Management,* September 1979, pp. 9–13.

[6] Robert D. Hisrich and Michael P. Peters, *Marketing Decisions for New and Mature Products: Planning, Development, and Control* (Columbus, Ohio: Charles E. Merrill Publishing, 1984), p. 15.

[7] J. Hugh Davidson, "Why Most New Consumer Brands Fail," *Harvard Business Review,* March–April 1976, pp. 117–22.

Table 12–1: New-product failures

Product	Estimated dollar loss ($000)
Ford's Edsel	$350,000
Du Pont's Corfam (synthetic leather)	100,000
Scott Paper's Baby Scott (disposable diapers)	12,800
Hunt's pizza- and hickory-flavored catsup	11,200
General Foods' freeze-dried fruit cereals	5,000
American Home's Easy-Off household cleaner	850

tive brands. One study of 100 new grocery brands in 38 different product categories found that 74 percent of the successes offered the consumer *better performance* at the same or higher price. Only 20 percent of the failures fit this category![8] At the same or a higher price, the vast majority of failures (80 percent) gave the *same performance* as other brands already on the market. The major implication here is that marketing management should avoid introducing *parity products*—that is, those no better than the competition.

Failure to match company's strengths

A new product may fail because it doesn't match the company's unique skills, talent, or background. The term *imbricative* (or overlapping) *marketing* has been coined to describe the need to overlap customer needs, a firm's creative talents, and profitable opportunities to ensure product success.[9] Many industrial companies fail with consumer product ideas because of a lack of reasonable overlap with their present distribution system.

Changes in consumers' tastes

Frequently, a change in consumer preference accounts for new-product failure. One reason the Edsel failed was that consumers turned from big to small cars. Research to support the introduction of the Edsel was adequate, but it took Ford over three years to bring the car to market. Meantime, consumer preferences shifted. Continued monitoring of consumer attitudes is one way to avoid a similar costly mistake.

Insufficient market segment size

Sometimes marketing management overestimates the size of the target market for the product. This is especially a problem when a firm tries

---

[8] The discussion of reasons for new-product failure is adopted with modification from Glen L. Urban and John R. Hauser, *Design and Marketing of New Products* (Englewood Cliffs, N.J.: Prentice-Hall, 1980), pp. 42–46.

[9] Andrew G. Kaldor, "Imbricative Marketing," *Journal of Marketing,* April 1971, pp. 19–25.

to oversegment a market. The resulting segments can violate the criterion of substantiality; that is, they are not profitable enough to warrant a separate marketing effort. (See Chapter 9 for a discussion of substantiality of a market segment.)

Competitive entry into market

A successful new product almost always prompts the competition to introduce its own version of the product. Sunbeam's electric skillet was copied so widely that the market became saturated within a few years. Lestoil, a liquid household cleaner, had an outstanding sales record of $25 million annually. After competitive entries by Procter & Gamble with Mr. Clean, Lever Brothers with Handy Andy, and Colgate-Palmolive with Liquid Ajax, Lestoil sales quickly dropped to $16 million.[10] To deter competitors, management should design products so well that other firms can only introduce parity products.

Lack of channel support

A product may fail because channel members are unwilling or unable to support the product. Retailers and wholesalers are independent businesses; they make decisions according to their customers' needs and their own financial criteria. A firm should research reaction of these intermediaries to a new product. Such research is usually done in the market-testing phase of the new-product introduction process. Manufacturers who try to introduce the third or fourth brand of a new product are most likely to encounter a lack of channel support.

ORGANIZATION FOR NEW-PRODUCT DEVELOPMENT

A firm can adopt a variety of organizational structures for new-product development. The four main types are covered below.[11] The structure that the firm uses depends on the importance of new products to the firm, its existing organizational structure, and its objectives. No single structure is inherently better than another. Each company adopts a structure (or some combination of structures) to best meet its needs.

New-product committee

The *new-product committee* is probably the most common form of organizational structure for managing new products.[12] The committee is formed from top-management ranks. Usually its members represent the firm's major functional areas, including manufacturing, finance, accounting, engineering, and marketing. The committee tends to be structured on an informal basis and meets as the need arises.

The new-product committee's functions vary considerably among companies, but four general types of functions can be identified:

[10] Hisrich and Peters, *Marketing Decisions for New and Mature Products,* p. 126.
[11] Ibid., p. 29.
[12] Ibid.

1. *Search teams*—Responsible for idea generation.
2. *Screening teams*—Charged with evaluation of product proposals.
3. *Project teams*—Entrusted with controlling and coordinating the development of ideas into full-fledged products.
4. *Product teams*—In charge of test marketing and introducing new products.[13]

The new-project team can be used to function along with the new-product department. This approach helps to provide a sufficient number of permanent employees to handle the full evolution of all new-product proposals. Otherwise, it would be impractical to staff the new-product department with enough permanent employees to process such proposals.[14]

There are advantages and disadvantages to the new-product committee. On the plus side, top management is involved, and so its ideas and expertise are pooled. Conflicts between line and staff are reduced. The firm is likely to accept the committee's decision because they have been made by the firm's own management. The committee is also flexible in terms of when it meets and the function it performs.

There are a number of drawbacks to the new-product committee approach, though, and it should be used carefully. The committee activity takes valuable executive time from other responsibilities. A lack of clear lines of authority and responsibility may result in buck-passing. Committee members tend to be more concerned with their own departmental objectives than with the firm's overall goals, which could result in a narrow view of the committee's purpose. In many cases, new-product planning and development should be a full-time job because of its importance to the firm.[15]

Product managers

New-product managers may assume the responsibility for planning and development. For many categories of consumer goods, new products are simply minor modifications of existing products. For example, the Ralston Purina Co. introduced Sugar Chex and followed with New Sugar-Frosted Chex and Super Sugar Chex. The product manager for the original brand could effectively manage these new products since they required only minor product, package, and advertising changes.

There are distinct advantages—and disadvantages—in having the product manager of an existing product line assume responsibility for new products. The product manager is sensitive to product opportunities, so

---

[13] Eberhard S. Schewing, *New-Product Management* (Hinsdale, Ill: Dryden Press, 1974), p. 47.

[14] Ibid., p. 49

[15] The discussion of the new-product committee's advantages and disadvantages is based on Hisrich and Peters, *Marketing Decisions for New and Mature Products,* p. 32.

new products are likely to meet customer needs. The product manager can manage the new product from the idea stage to the marketplace. Finally, some companies recognize the vital role that product managers can play in strategically managing a product/market segment. One vice president of an office equipment firm says that his company's product managers are not only responsible for specific product models but said they "automatically have implicit responsibility for a market segment and a market share. They know this market and will be the first to detect an erosion of segment or share. Therefore, they can initiate new products earlier, before the erosion becomes critical."[16]

The major disadvantages arise from the product manager's dual responsibility for new and existing products. Often the existing products receive the major attention; new-product planning and development may be neglected or receive secondary emphasis. The result may be an emphasis on me-too products that require only modest change and are sold to familiar markets. What's more, new-product efforts may be short-range and hurried. Product managers also may lack the broad perspective, especially in technical and other nonmarketing considerations.[17]

These disadvantages have led some firms to limit the scope of their new-product managers to a single division or product line. The new-product manager may report directly to the general manager of a division. Once a new product has been successfully introduced, responsibility for it is turned over to the manager of other established products in the line.[18]

Another option is to assign a manager for special projects that represent major new-product opportunities for the firm and require an extraordinary financial commitment. This approach is common in the auto and food industries. The person in charge of the new product is called the project manager and may be assigned to the first product in a line (like Ford's Mustang) from its inception throughout its life cycle. The manager's career often rises or falls with the product's success.

New-product department	The ***new-product department*** is common in firms that assign priority to new-product development as a corporate goal. These departments are assigned a variety of names (growth and development, new-product development, or market development) to emphasize their role in developing new products as a source of growth for the firm.

The new-product department may be structured as either a line or a staff unit. As a staff function, the department is placed high in the organization and may report to the president or executive vice president. The

---

[16] David S. Hopkins, "Options in New-Product Organization," Report no. 613 (New York: The Conference Board, 1974), p. 20.

[17] Ibid., p. 19.

[18] Schewing, *New-Product Management,* p. 49.

emphasis is on duties such as coordination and control of the new-product development process. As a line function, conflict can develop between the new-product department and other departments, such as marketing, engineering, finance, or production. Whether the department is line or staff, it is essential that channels of communication and authority be clearly established so that new-product planning and development may proceed with a minimum of internal conflict. The continual support of top management can be a major factor in successfully dealing with potential conflict.[19]

The functions of the new-product department include: recommending new-product objectives, planning exploration of new-product ideas, screening new-product ideas, assisting in development of new-product specifications, recommending and implementing market testing, and coordinating interdepartmental effort during the evolution of the product.[20]

Venture team

The freshest organizational structure for management of the new-product process is the *venture team.* This approach is used by firms to develop products or services that are entirely new to the firm and are to be sold to markets the firm has never served.

A recent study of about 100 venture teams in consumer and industrial goods companies revealed something of their nature. (See Figure 12–2.) Venture team members are organizationally separated from the existing structure of the firm. This fosters a spirit of creativity and innovation. The team members are drawn from the various functional areas in the firm and remain together until the team's assigned objectives are achieved.[21]

One problem of the venture team—the placement of authority to make final decisions—can be solved by granting the venture team manager authority to make major decisions about the product and by giving the manager direct access to top management.

Another conflict may occur if a department head feels that department members are spending too much time on the venture team project rather than devoting time and effort to departmental responsibilities.[22]

THE NEW-PRODUCT DEVELOPMENT PROCESS

The general process for developing new products includes seven stages: Product-idea generation, Screening of ideas, Business analysis, Product-concept development and testing, Product development, Market testing, and Commercialization.

---

[19] Hisrich and Peters, *Marketing Decisions for New and Mature Products,* p. 30.

[20] *Management of New Products* (New York: Booz, Allen & Hamilton, 1968), p. 20.

[21] Richard M. Hill and James D. Hlovacek, "The Venture Team: A New Concept in Marketing Organization," *Journal of Marketing,* July 1972, p. 46.

[22] Hisrich and Peters, *Marketing Decisions for New and Mature Products,* p. 41.

Figure 12-2: An example of a venture team in a hypothetical organization

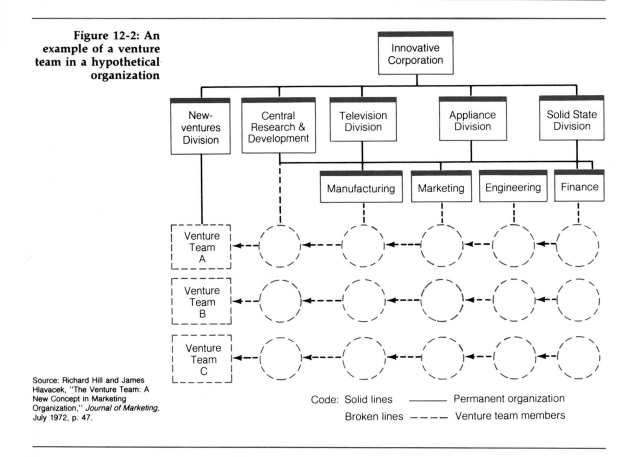

Source: Richard Hill and James Hlavacek, "The Venture Team: A New Concept in Marketing Organization," *Journal of Marketing*, July 1972, p. 47.

Code: Solid lines ———— Permanent organization

Broken lines – – – – Venture team members

We'll discuss each of these stages in detail below, presenting specific methods and techniques that enhance the effectiveness of the new-product development process. Table 12–2 contains an overview of stages and their purposes in the process.

GENERATION OF NEW-PRODUCT IDEAS

The starting point for the new-product development process is the ***product idea.*** In 1968 the consulting firm of Booz, Allen & Hamilton found that it took 58 product ideas to generate one new successful product. In 1981 the company conducted a study of 700 companies to update its previous study. It found that only seven ideas were required for every successful new product. Booz, Allen & Hamilton states that the significant improvement is due to more rigorous and sophisticated procedures for generating new-product ideas. Management now concentrates its efforts on those product ideas that appear to be most promising. (See Figure 12–3.)

Table 12–2: An overview of the new-product development process	Stage	Purpose	Comments
	Idea generation	Develop a large number of product ideas	Techniques used: Brainstorming Reverse brainstorming Forced relationship Benefit-structure analysis Problem-inventory analysis Attribute listing
	Screening	Evaluate and reduce the number of product ideas	Rating of new product ideas according to specific criteria
	Business analysis	Evaluate the financial aspects of new products	Capital budgeting Payback Average rate of return Present value
	Product concept	Develop the subjective meaning the company hopes to communicate about the product	Process: Identify market segments Concept evaluation Identify characteristics of market segments Concept positioning
	Product development	Development of the physical product	Detailed information is developed in manufacturing and costs
	Market testing	Fine-tuning the marketing mix for a new product by marketing it in a limited geographic area	A major commitment to the product is made by top management
	Commercialization	Introduction of the product to the national market	Requires maximum coordination among marketing, manufacturing, and physical distribution, as well as major expenditures

New-product ideas come from sources internal and external to the organization. Primary internal sources are the organization's departments of engineering, marketing, production, and research and development. The most important external sources are customers and competition. Note that often the identification of a product idea results from the joint efforts of internal sources (the marketing research department) and external sources (customers). Given the high mortality rate of new products, management has sought ways to improve the number and quality of product ideas.

Brainstorming

Brainstorming is a method in which a group of individuals, usually managers, meet for the sole purpose of generating lots of ideas. The groups usually have 6 to 10 members, and meetings last about an hour. Experts are not involved because they tend to view problems in a preconceived

Figure 12–3: Product-idea decay curve in product development process

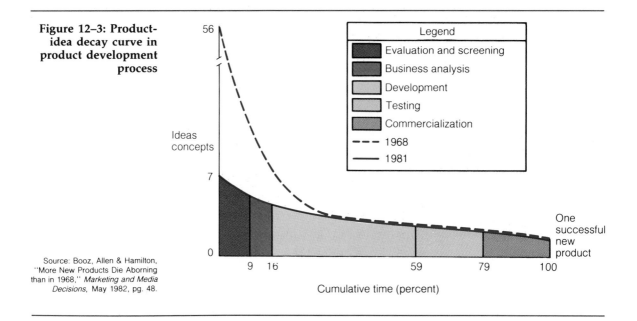

Source: Booz, Allen & Hamilton, "More New Products Die Aborning than in 1968," *Marketing and Media Decisions*, May 1982, pg. 48.

way. Negative evaluation from an expert may also inhibit group members from offering their own ideas. There are four rules for the most effective use of brainstorming:

1. *No criticism.* Ideas are critically evaluated at a later time.
2. *Free-wheeling is encouraged.* The wilder the idea the better, since it is easier to tame down ideas than to think them up.
3. *Quantity is wanted.* The greater the number of ideas the higher the probability of finding a useful and marketable idea.
4. *Combinations and improvements are sought.* Participants are encouraged to suggest how the ideas of others can trigger more ideas.[23]

A modification of brainstorming called **reverse brainstorming** takes a particular product (such as a refrigerator or a dishwasher) and generates a list of things wrong with it.[24] The list of negatives provides direction for product improvement.

Benefit-structure analysis

A procedure developed to identify new-product opportunities and ideas in very broad or service categories is **benefit-structure analysis.** Consum-

---

[23] Alex F. Osborn, *Applied Imagination,* 3d ed. (New York: Charles Scribner's Sons, 1963), p. 156.

[24] John W. Hoefele, *Creativity and Innovation* (New York: Reinhold Publishing, 1962), p. 145.

This new product from Fleischmann's offers consumers a healthful benefit (no cholesterol) and a convenience benefit (squeeze bottle).

Courtesy Nabisco Brands, Inc.

ers are surveyed for their reaction to the specific benefits desired from a type of product or service and to its physical characteristics. Their reactions are recorded in terms of *desire for* and *perceived deficiencies in* each benefit and characteristic. Product opportunities are identified by comparing the percentage of respondents who desire a specific benefit but did not receive it from existing products. Benefit-structure analysis has been successfully applied in a variety of product categories, including foods, beverages, and recreational vehicles.[25]

Problem-inventory analysis[26]

Problem-inventory analysis rests on two basic assumptions. First, it is much easier for consumers to relate known products to suggested problems than to generate problems for a given product. Second, the general ways that products and services can solve problems are rather limited.

In problem-inventory analysis, a list of statements is prepared, each of which mentions a problem but not a product. For example, "Preparing _____ leaves so many pots to clean." Sentence completion is a projective technique in which consumers are asked to indicate the product that immediately comes to mind, given a specified problem. The data can be obtained through mail surveys in which respondents are asked to complete self-administered questionnaires.

Table 12–3 shows some results obtained from a problem-inventory analysis conducted in the food industry. But be careful interpreting these. In some cases, the findings may only provide clues about new-product opportunities. Further research may be warranted.

The table data show that 49 percent of those surveyed said cereal packages don't fit well on the shelf. Based on these findings, General Foods introduced a compact cereal box, but it failed to win consumer acceptance. The interpretation here is that this "problem" is of little importance to consumers. Another 16 percent of the respondents indicated that it was difficult to get catsup to pour easily. It's not likely, though, that many consumers would prefer a runny catsup.

Attribute listing

In *attribute listing* all the existing product attributes (characteristics) are listed and then modified until a new combination of attributes emerges that will improve the product.

Suppose your company makes pallets. (These are low, portable platforms on which materials can be stacked during storage or transportation.) You want to improve your product and so must analyze it. You would first list the attributes that defined the existing pallets: wood composition, rectangular runners, and accessibility on two sides by a forklift. Then you might change the wood to plastic, lowering the price. The rectangular runners might be replaced by cups for easier storage and to allow the new pallet to be accessible on all sides by a forklift truck.[27]

[25] James H. Myers, "Benefit-Structure Analysis: A New Tool for Product Planning," *Journal of Marketing,* October 1976, pp. 23–32.

[26] This discussion of problem-inventory analysis is based on Edward M. Tauber, "Discovering New-Product Opportunities with Problem-Inventory Analysis," *Journal of Marketing,* January 1975, pp. 67–70.

[27] Hisrich and Peters, *Marketing Decisions for New and Mature Products,* p. 58.

Table 12–3: Results of a problem-inventory study about food

Questions asked and percent of respondents answering

1. The package of _____ doesn't fit well on the shelf.

Cereal	49%
Flour	6

2. My husband/children refuse to eat _____

Liver	18%
Vegetables	5
Spinach	4

3. _____ doesn't quench my thirst.

Soft drinks	58%
Milk	9
Coffee	6

4. Packaged _____ doesn't dissolve fast enough.

Jello/gelatin	32%
Bouillon cubes	8
Pudding	5

5. Everyone always wants different _____

Vegetables	23%
Cereal	11
Meat	10
Desserts	9

6. _____ makes a mess in the oven.

Broiling steaks	19%
Pie	17
Roast/pork/rib	8

7. Packaged _____ tastes artificial.

Instant potatoes	12%
Macaroni and cheese	4

8. It's difficult to get _____ to pour easily.

Catsup	16%
Syrup	13
Gallon of milk	11

9. Packaged _____ looks unappetizing.

Hamburger helper	6%
Lunchmeat	3
Liver	3

10. I wish my husband/children could take _____ in a carried lunch.

Hot meal	11%
Soup	9
Ice cream	4

Source: Edward M. Tauber, "Discovering New-Product Opportunities with Problem-Inventory Analysis," *Journal of Marketing*, January 1975, pp. 67–70.

Questions often used in attribute listing to generate new-product ideas are shown in Figure 12–4.

The main drawback to the attribute-listing method is its focus on existing products. This method, then, is not likely to generate totally new product ideas but modifications of existing ones.

Figure 12–4: Questions used in attribute-listing approval	Put to other uses	New ways to use as is? Other uses if modified?
	Adapt	What else is this like? What other idea does this suggest? Does past offer parallel? What should I copy? Whom could I emulate?
	Modify	Change meaning, color, motion, sound, odor, form, shape? Other changes?
	Magnify	What to add? More time? Greater frequency? Stronger? Higher? Longer? Thicker? Extra value? Plus ingredient? Duplicate? Multiply? Exaggerate?
	Minify	What to subtract? Smaller? Condensed? Miniature? Lower? Shorter? Lighter? Omit? Streamline? Split up? Understate?
	Substitute	Who else instead? What else instead? Other ingredient? Other material? Other process? Other power? Other place? Other approach? Other tone of voice?
	Rearrange	Interchange components? Other pattern? Other layout? Other sequence? Transpose cause and effect? Change pace? Change schedule?
	Reverse	Transpose positive and negative? How about opposites? Turn it backward? Turn it upside down? Reverse roles? Change shoes? Turn tables? Turn other cheek?
Source: Alex F. Osborn, *Applied Imagination*, 3d ed. (New York: Charles Scribner's Sons, 1963), pp. 286–87.	Combine	How about a blend, an alloy, an assortment, an ensemble? Combine units? Combine purposes? Combine appeals? Combine ideas?

SCREENING OF IDEAS

In the *screening* stage of the new-product development process, the major objective is to evaluate the number of product ideas previously developed. This reduces the number of product ideas to those that can undergo further detailed analysis.

In general, three basic criteria are used to evaluate new-product ideas. First, product ideas must be consistent with the firm's objectives. If the firm has decided to restrict itself to nondurables, it will not consider durable products. Second, the technical, financial, and managerial capabilities of the firm must be considered. Third, a sufficient market potential must exist for the product.[28] The emphasis in analyzing market potential is on the financial prospects and not exclusively on the number of consumers in the market. These general criteria provide a beginning for analyzing product ideas. But to systematically evaluate a number of ideas, management usually needs a more detailed and structured framework.

A common approach that provides this structure is a checklist and rating form for evaluating new-product ideas, as shown in Table 12–4. Column 1 of the table contains product-idea criteria considered relevant to a decision to add a new product. This list is not exhaustive but serves

---

[28] David B. Montgomery and Glen L. Urban, "Screening New-Product Possibilities," in Corporate Strategy and Product Innovation, 2d ed., ed. Robert Rothberg (New York, Free Press, 1981), pp. 313–31.

Table 12–4: Checklist and rating for screening new-product ideas

1 Product-idea criteria	2 Importance weights	3 Product-idea rating scale										4 Overall rating (col. 2 × col. 3)
		0.1	0.2	0.3	0.4	0.5	0.6	0.7	0.8	0.9	1.0	
Marketability												
Relation to present channel of distribution	0.50				X							0.20
Relation to present product line	0.20								X			0.16
Price–quality relationship	0.80			X								0.24
Durability												
Breadth of market	0.60		X									0.12
Stability of market	0.90						X					0.54
Resistance to seasonal and cyclical fluctuations	0.40							X				0.28
Productive ability												
Equipment necessary	0.90	X										0.09
Raw materials availability	0.90		X									0.18
Growth potential												
Product category stage of life cycle	0.90					X						0.45
Competitive situation	0.30										X	0.30
Total												2.56

Source: This checklist is adapted with modification from the following sources: J. T. O'Meara, "Selecting Profitable Products," *Harvard Business Review*, January–February 1961, pp. 83–89; and Barry M. Richman, "A Rating Scale for Product Innovation," *Business Horizons*, (Summer 1962), pp. 37–44.

as an example of the major considerations. A firm would, of course, develop a list to meet its own specific needs.

Column 2 of the table contains the importance weight for each product-idea criterion. The ratings are based on a 10-point scale ranging from 0.1 to 1.0. The importance could represent an average of the weight assigned by the members of the new-product committee. Managers use the product-idea rating scale to evaluate the idea on a specific criterion. For example, the score of 0.8 for "Relation to present product line" means that the product idea under consideration complements the existing product line well.

The next step is to multiply the importance weight and the rating scale score (Column 2 × Column 3) to compute the overall rating (Column 4). Finally, the values in Column 4 are summed to arrive at the idea's total score. The group in charge of new products may establish minimum score criteria for evaluating new-product ideas. For example, a product may have to score 2.0 to receive further consideration. Products scoring above 6.0 may be given increased attention since they could represent outstanding opportunities. As the new-product group gains experience, they should begin to see a relationship between scores on their screening device and the sales and profitability success of the product ideas they have approved. The major challenge of the screening phase is to avoid approving product ideas that ultimately fail and to avoid rejecting ideas that may have proved successful or are successfully developed by competition.

If a company has no specific rating device to evaluate a product, then usually some set of general questions must be asked before the company can proceed to develop the product. For example, the L'eggs division of Hanes Corporation has five criteria against which it evaluates new-product items. The company will add a new product if (1) it can be sold through food and drug outlets, (2) it will be purchased primarily by women, (3) it will sell for less than $3, (4) it can be packaged easily and distinctively, and (5) it is part of a retail market segment not already dominated by other producers.[29]

BUSINESS ANALYSIS

The basic purpose of the *business analysis* stage is to determine the financial aspects of the new-product introduction. Typically, a firm has established specific financial criteria for this analysis. For example, a firm might set a minimum acceptable return on investment or a minimum time period for repayment of investment in the new product.

The following sections review the major tools marketing managers use in the business analysis of new products.

Capital budgeting techniques

A survey conducted of the nation's 500 largest manufacturing firms has shown that marketing management uses *capital budgeting* techniques for decision making.[30] In new-product development, 81 percent of the responding firms have used *payback, average rate of return,* and *present value.* Each of these techniques is discussed below, using a cash flow analysis of a new toy. The cash investment in the product is $1.3 million and comprises the following elements: product equipment, $1 million; training salespeople, $100,000; promotional materials, $10,000; and inventory and accounts receivable, $190,000. Table 12–5 details the new toy's projected sales, costs, and profits.

---

[29] Charles D. Schewe and Reuben M. Smith, *Marketing Concepts and Applications* (New York: McGraw-Hill, 1980), p. 74.

[30] V. H. Kirpalani and Stanley J. Shapiro, "Financial Dimensions of Marketing Management," *Journal of Marketing* 37 (July 1973), pp. 48–53.

Table 12–5: Cash flow analysis of new toy introduction ($000)

	Year 0	Year 1	Year 2	Year 3	Year 4	Year 5
1. Cash investment	($1,300)					
2. Sales volume		$600	$1,000	$1,200	$1,000	$800
3. Cost of goods		(180)	(300)	(360)	(300)	(240)
4. Expenses		(100)	(100)	(100)	(100)	(100)
5. Depreciation		(200)	(200)	(200)	(200)	(200)
6. Before-tax profit (sum of lines 2, 3, 4, and 5)		120	400	540	400	260
7. After-tax profit (line 6 times 52%)		62	208	281	208	135
8. Depreciation added back		200	200	200	200	200
9. Recovery of investment in inventory and accounts receivable						190
10. Cash flow (sum of lines 7, 8, and 9)		262	408	481	408	525
11. Discount factors (10% per year)	1.00	0.91	0.83	0.75	0.68	0.62
12. Discounted cash flow (lines 1 and 10 times line 11)	(1,300)	238	339	361	277	325

Source: Adapted from Leon Winer, "A Profit-Oriented Decision System," *Journal of Marketing* 30 (1966), pp. 38–44.

Payback period.

payback period

> The **payback period** is defined as the number of years required to recover the initial cash investment in a project. It is calculated as follows:
>
> $$\text{Payback period} = \frac{\text{Initial fixed investment}}{\text{Annual cash inflow for recovery period}}$$

Thus, a project requiring an initial fixed investment of $40,000 and generating annual cash inflows of $12,000 would have a payback period of 3.3 years (40,000/12,000). The annual cash inflows generated by many projects are not equal, however. In such cases, the payback period calculations are somewhat more complex. Referring to the new toy example in Table 12–5, we find the following cash inflows for years 1 to 3:

Year 1:	$262,000	Initial investment: $1.3 million
Year 2:	408,000	
Year 3:	481,000	
	$1,151,000	

The inflow in year 4 is $408,000, only $149,000 ($1,300,000 − $1,151,000) of which is needed for the recovery of the initial investment.

The payback period for this example is thus:

$$3 \text{ years} + (149{,}000/408{,}000) = 3 + 0.37 = 3.37 \text{ years}$$

This is a realistic figure, as consumer goods companies frequently establish three to four years as a targeted payback period.

Average rate of return.

average rate of return

> The **average rate of return** for a new product is calculated as follows:
>
> $$\text{Average rate of return} = \frac{\text{Average annual profits after taxes}}{\text{Total investment}}$$

Using the figures from Table 12–5, the average rate of return divided by total investment in the project would be $178.8/1{,}300 = 0.1375$, or 13.75 percent. It is common for firms to seek a 20 to 25 percent rate of return on new products.

Present-value method.   Another criterion to evaluate new-product decisions is the *present-value* method. In this method, the new cash flows for each year of the recovery period are discounted using a factor representing the time value of money. To discount cash flows, we need simply to know the cost of capital to the firm and then refer to tables that give the appropriate factor for a given cost of capital and the year of the recovery period with which we are concerned.[31] This method allows us to determine whether the proposed investment will return more than the capital that is put into it.

---

[31] A present-value table is simply a bond-yield table that takes account of compound interest. For example, the present value of $1 received at the end of year n is

$$PV = \frac{1}{(1+i)n}$$

where PV is present value and i is discount rate. One year from today, at 10 percent interest, $1 would be worth:

$$PV = \frac{1}{1+0.10} = 0.909$$

After two years:

$$PV = \frac{1}{(1+0.10)^2} = \frac{1}{1.21} = 0.826$$

For further discussion on present values and discount factors, see O. Maurice Joy, *Introduction to Financial Management* (Homewood, Ill.: Richard D. Irwin, 1983), chap. 3.

In Table 12–5, we find net cash flows for the proposed investment of $262,000, $408,000, $481,000, $408,000, and $525,000 (line 10). Assuming a cost of capital of 10 percent, we would use the discount factors found in line 11, multiplying them by the net cash flows to arrive at the discounted cash flows in line 12.

Once the discounted cash flows have been calculated, they may be summed and then compared to the initial investment to determine whether the proposal is acceptable. If the sum of the discounted cash flows exceeds (or equals) the amount of the investment, the product will generate enough income to incur a profit, or at least to cover the cost of capital. If the discounted cash flows total less than the amount of the investment, the project would be unsatisfactory. In our example, the discounted cash flows total $1,540,000. Our new toy would be an acceptable investment.

PRODUCT-CONCEPT DEVELOPMENT AND TESTING

It is important to distinguish between a ***product idea*** and a ***product concept.***

product idea

> A **product idea** is a potential product described in objective, functional terms.

product concept

> A **product concept** is the subjective meaning about a product that the company tries to communicate to the consumer.[32]

For example, a product idea might be a powdered product that adds considerable nutrition when mixed with milk. This product idea could be expressed as several product concepts: an instant breakfast, a snack treat for children, a diet meal, or a health food.[33] In general terms, the relationship between a product idea and product concept can be expressed as follows:

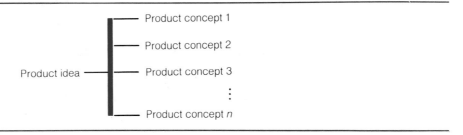

---

[32] Phillip Kotler, *Marketing Management: Analysis, Planning, and Control,* 3d ed. (Englewood Cliffs, N.J.: Prentice-Hall, 1976), p. 207.

[33] Edward M. Tauber, "What Is Measured by Concept Testing?" *Journal of Advertising Research,* December 1972, pp. 35–37.

A product concept can be presented to consumers as a prototype of the product, a written or broadcast ad, a package, or a simple written description. The written description is probably the most common form of presentation, but the form actually used depends on management's objective for the concept test. If the objective is to rank a number of product concepts, it's best to provide a written, factual description of the product. Research has shown that the written description yields the same information (that is, rankings) as the most elaborate and costly advertisement. If the objective is to measure the initial product-trial level attainable through promotion, the form of presentation should closely simulate that which would be used in the product introduction. If a product will be introduced through TV ads, then that method of communication should be used. When in-store exposure is the most frequent source of inventory information, the package presented in real or simulated stores may be used. And personal-selling presentations may be the most effective concept test for industrial products sold by industrial salespersons.[34]

A comprehensive concept-evaluation procedure

Usually concept tests involve collecting three types of basic information: (1) a measure of respondent's affect, or feelings of liking or disliking, for the concept; (2) a measure of respondent's behavioral intent to purchase the product concept; and (3) open-ended questions to obtain information and insight about the reasons for feelings of liking or disliking and behavioral intention.[35]

A comprehensive procedure for concept evaluation has been developed that includes, in addition to the information listed above: (1) an analysis of how many market segments exist, their characteristics, and their reactions to various concepts, and (2) the relevant competitive setting of the given concepts over the most desirable positioning for the concepts.[36] (See Table 12–6.)

Identification of market segment

Table 12–6 gives an overview of the major objectives and data used in the comprehensive product-concept test. Of the many possible bases for segmentation, two are especially useful to marketing management: (1) consumers' positive or negative reactions to the concept and (2) the benefits sought by consumers from products in a given product class.

Concept evaluation

A number of specific steps are taken to thoroughly evaluate the product concept:

1. For each product concept, the percentage of consumers with positive intention to buy is calculated.

[34] Ibid., p. 37.

[35] Bill Iuso, "Concept Testing: An Appropriate Approach," *Journal of Marketing Research,* May 1975, pp. 228–31.

[36] Yoram Wind, "A New Procedure for Concept Evaluation," *Journal of Marketing,* October 1973, pp. 2–11.

		Objective of analysis		**Data**

Table 12–6: Objectives and data used in comprehensive product-concept test

Objective of analysis		Data	
1.	Identify relative market segments	a.	Rank of product benefits
		b.	Consumer reactions to product concepts
2.	Concept evaluation	a.	Intention to buy the concept
		b.	Selection of concept in forced-choice situation
		c.	Frequency of occurrence of various occasions
		d.	Overall preference rankings of concepts or brands
		e.	Overall liking of concepts
		f.	Rating of concept attributes on evaluative scales
		g.	Concept "likes" or "dislikes"
3.	Identify the characteristics of the market segments	a.	Demographic and socioeconomic
		b.	Lifestyle and attitudes toward concept
		c.	Product- and brand-usage data
4.	Concept positioning	a.	Concepts and control brands rated according to (1) overall preference, (2) their appropriateness for various occasions, and (3) the various product benefits

Source: Yoram Wind, "A New Procedure for Concept Evaluation," *Journal of Marketing,* October 1973, pp. 2–14.

2. To identify the *hard-core potential buyers,* intention to buy is measured.

The product concept is also placed in a forced-choice situation in which consumers are asked to make a selection from among several product concepts. The results of the intention-to-buy and the forced-choice situation tests are analyzed carefully. Consider the following example:

Assume that 200 respondents are sampled. For the intention-to-buy scale, the results are as follows:

$n = 50$	$n = 60$	$n = 30$	$n = 40$	$n = 20$
Definitely will buy	Probably will buy	Undecided	Probably won't buy	Definitely won't buy

The interpretation is that 55 percent $\left(\frac{50 + 60}{200} = \frac{110}{200}\right)$ have positive intention to buy. However, the data analysis yields the following result:

		Intention to buy				
		Definitely will	**Probably will**	**Undecided**	**Probably won't**	**Definitely won't**
Selected in forced-choice situation	**Yes**	30	20	10	20	10
	No	20	40	20	20	10
		50	60	30	40	20

The interpretation is that only 25 percent $\left(\dfrac{30+20}{200}=\dfrac{50}{200}\right)$ would be identified as hard-core loyalists to the product concept. The data analysis produces a lower estimate of the size of the market segment than does the measure of behavioral intentions alone.

3. The anticipated occasion usage of the concepts is calculated. Occasion usage measures the number of times a product is used for a specific purpose within a given time period. Intention to buy for each occasion is weighted by the frequency of occurrence of the given occasion.

4. Measurements establish the relative preferences for the concepts or for **control brands** for specific and overall occasion usage. Control brands are existing brands that serve as a frame of reference for the product concepts being tested. Unless the concept receives higher ratings than control brands, there is no basis to proceed with the development of the concept. Management does not want to develop a product that is inferior to existing brands or that does not provide an opportunity to gain an advantage over the competition.

5. Product attributes important in explaining consumer reactions are assessed by multiple regression analysis for the overall sample and for each market segment.

6. A content analysis of open-ended questions on likes and dislikes about the concept, when supplemented by the multiple regression results, gives some clue to the aspects of the concept that led to its being liked or disliked.

Identification of key characteristics of various benefit segments

This analysis identifies the key characteristics and provides better insight into the nature of the segments. Separate analyses are conducted for (1) socioeconomic and demographic data, (2) product-usage data, and (3) general and product-specific lifestyle and attitude data. The major findings of these analyses are combined to determine the most important characteristics for the market segments.

Assessing the concept's market positioning

Three major data inputs are necessary for this analysis: consumer ratings of concepts and control brands by (1) overall preference, (2) appropriateness for various occasions, and (3) degree of achievement of desired product benefits. The results of this analysis give a clear profile of the market structure. The relative position of each concept compared to existing brands and the position of both concepts and brands on a set of product benefits are specified.

PRODUCT DEVELOPMENT

During **product development,** the physical product takes shape. Heretofore, it existed only in the form of drawings, word descriptions, or crude models. Information developed in the product development stage includes technical details of manufacturing the product and the costs of producing it. While general cost estimates have already been made, the product development stage provides detailed information on component parts, manufacturing, and overhead costs.

Organizationally, the product development stage presents a major challenge to management. The separate organizational units must be closely coordinated in this stage. At a minimum, the departments of marketing, research and development (R&D), engineering, and manufacturing or production must coordinate and integrate their efforts. The number of organizational units or departments deeply involved in this stage may greatly expand, depending on the nature of the product innovation and company policy.

A number of factors should be considered to complete a successful product development effort, starting with a clear statement of the objectives to be met by the product. This statement will help R&D, engineering, and production personnel take the steps necessary to ensure the product objectives are met. Marketing personnel must also ensure that the product is consistent with the organization's overall objectives.

Effective communication must be maintained among the groups involved, and clearly stated objectives facilitate this. Also, management should consider the physical proximity of the groups, especially those involved in R&D. Researchers have studied how the physical distance between R&D people affects the probability of weekly communication. It has been found that beyond a separation of 30 feet, the probability is less than 10 percent. If people are on different floors or in different locations, the chances for communication are even less.[37]

Finally, technical groups such as R&D, engineering, and production must be given sufficient time and money to complete their tasks. Quality research usually takes considerable time and effort, especially in new-product development. The following indicate how long it can take from the time a product idea is born until it is converted to a physical product to be market tested or marketed: Crest toothpaste, 1945–55—10 years; DeCaf instant coffee, 1947–53—6 years; Lustre Creme liquid shampoo, 1950–58—8 years; Polaroid color camera, 1948–63—15 years.[38]

Market testing

Several major objectives are accomplished by a market test. For one, it serves as a control function for management. The company can gain

---

market testing

> **Market testing** is the introduction of a product in limited geographic areas to determine if the product should be introduced to the national market.

---

[37] J. Allen, *Managing the Flow of Technology* (Cambridge, Mass.: MIT Press, 1977).

[38] L. Adler, "Time Lag in New-Product Development," *Journal of Marketing Research,* January 1966, pp. 17–21.

information and experience with the product before marketing it on a large scale. For another, market testing predicts sales for the product.[39] The product's dollar and unit volume of sales are closely monitored during the market test; reaction to and evaluation of the product is sought from consumers, wholesalers, and retailers.

The decision to market test a product depends on many factors, including the financial and managerial resources of the firm, time pressures imposed by competitors, and the innovativeness of the product itself.

When recycling an existing brand, there is usually little reason to market test it. But marketing management may feel that a major repackaging or a repositioning of some other significant factor in an existing brand are bases to market test.

The most common situation for market testing is when the firm enters an existing product category with a new brand. The need to market test is great when the new brand is priced higher than the competition or involves a new method of packaging, shelving, or distribution.

Market testing is especially important for new-product categories in which there are no direct substitute products. (This is rare in the consumer goods area.) The market test serves as a pilot operation and helps predict national sales of the product.

The decision to market test represents a major managerial commitment to the product, and it is based on a high probability of the product's success. When estimating the probability of success, the director of marketing at Clairol states, "The batting average ought to be somewhere between 65 and 75 percent."[40] Why, then would management incur the cost and time of a market test when it believes the product has a high probability of success in a national market? The answer is that the market test can improve the effectiveness of the marketing plan. Management can see ways to enhance the effectiveness of promotional, pricing, and advertising strategies. This is consistent with the control objective for market testing.

The cost of market testing a packaged good in one city typically is $1 million; and some firms spend $1.5 or more.[41] There are direct (or out-of-pocket) expenses and indirect costs. Direct costs involve manufacturing the product on a limited scale, broadcast and print media, point-of-sale materials, couponing, sampling, and higher trade allowances to obtain distribution.[42]

---

[39] Alvin A. Achenbaum, "Marketing Testing: Using the Marketplace as a Laboratory," in *Handbook of Marketing Research,* ed. Robert Ferber (New York: McGraw-Hill), pp. 4–31.

[40] Jay E. Klompmaker, G. David Hughes, and Russell I. Haley, "Test Marketing in New-Product Development," *Harvard Business Review,* May–June 1976, pp. 128–38.

[41] Glen L. Urban and John R. Hauser, *Designing and Marketing of New Products* (Englewood Cliffs, N.J.: Prentice-Hall, 1980), p. 419.

[42] Klompmaker, et al., "Test Marketing," p. 129.

The indirect costs are usually not quantified when calculating the market test expenditures. But they are substantial. Revealing a new product to a competitor can be costly. If better organized for new-product introductions, the competitor can beat the original firm to the national market. Another indirect cost is the loss of corporate reputation if the product fails. This is especially true when promoting a family brand. The company name and brand name both may be subject to a negative evaluation. Finally, the diversion of management attention and employee effort from existing products is another major indirect cost.[43]

The problems and costs of market testing have promoted the development of alternative methods, including *minimarket tests, laboratory market tests,* and *statistical and mathematical models.*

Minimarket test

The major differences between minimarket and traditional market tests are the geographic area of distribution and the method of distribution. Minimarket testing uses smaller geographic areas to test the product. For example, instead of distributing the product through several hundred retailers in a metropolitan area, only 40 or 50 retailers might be used. Unlike the traditional market test, in which the cooperation of intermediaries must be gained through personal-selling efforts, the minimarket test guarantees retail distribution. The company using the minimarket approach usually hires an outside research agency that has a contract with a group of retailers to "rent" shelf space for research purposes.

The minimarket's advantages are speedier assessment of consumer sales, reduced cost per market, and greater secrecy.[44] A conventional market test takes from 8 to 12 weeks for products to go through regular channels of distribution (from manufacturer to wholesaler to retailer). In minimarkets, the time is reduced to two weeks. Minimarkets are not usually audited by marketing research companies such as A. C. Nielsen. This makes it more difficult for a competitor to obtain information on the sales of a product in a minimarket test.[45]

When a marketer introduces a truly innovative product, and especially if the company is small and unknown, retailers may resist the product because of the risks involved. Supporters of minimarket testing feel that it offers these companies an effective means to test the product.[46] But minimarkets have been criticized for lacking predictive capability because the minimarket is not representative and is limited to one geographic area.[47]

---

[43] Ibid.

[44] Achenbaum, "Marketing Testing," p. 449.

[45] Sally Scanlon, "Zeroing in on Profits," *Sales and Marketing Management,* March 1978, pp. 61–76.

[46] Ibid., p. 69.

[47] Achenbaum, "Marketing Testing," p. 452.

Laboratory market tests

Another alternative to traditional testing is the laboratory market test. A number of marketing research companies have developed procedures to laboratory market test, including Yankelovich, Skelly, and White's "Laboratory Test Market," Management Decision Systems' "Assessor," and Elrick and Lavidge's "Comp." In these procedures consumer trial is measured by exposing consumers to commercials and then allowing them the opportunity to purchase the product in a simulated retail store. The product is used in the normal setting of the home, and a follow-up interview is conducted. The purpose of the interview is to determine the degree of satisfaction and repurchase intention. Most of the procedures allow an optimal repurchase opportunity after the product is used in the home.

While there are variations in methods used by different companies, some common elements exist. Once target consumers have been identified, they are brought into a lab situation, which may be a permanent facility or a temporary setting in a shopping mall. The consumers are shown commercials for the existing brands and the new product. Then they are taken to a simulated store and given money to purchase products. They are free to buy either the test product or competitive brands. If the test product is not purchased, it may be given as a free sample. The product is taken home; and follow-up interviews are conducted to measure attribute ratings, satisfaction, and intention to repurchase. Usually, optional repurchase opportunities are provided after the home replacement.[48]

Laboratory market tests offer the following advantages over conventional market tests:

1. They can predict on a par with standard or full-scale market tests.

2. Results are obtained quickly. In most instances a laboratory market test can conduct a full market evaluation in 12 to 14 weeks. Standard market tests usually run from 6 to 12 months.

3. They are confidential. Competitors do not have the opportunity to preempt test brands or to disrupt market tests.

4. Various marketing mixes can be inexpensively tested.[49]

The major weakness of the laboratory market test is that it relies on post-trial intentions or attribute shifts to predict repeat-purchase behavior. Research has shown that these intentions are not very reliable and at best predict only the first repeat purchase. To overcome these problems, some tests offer multiple opportunities over extended periods of time to purchase the product.[50]

The following examples provide additional insight into the ways com-

[48] Edward M. Tauber, "Forecasting Sales Prior to Test Markets," *Journal of Marketing* 1 (1977), pp. 80–84.

[49] G. E. Meredith, "Test Markets Succumb to the Defense," *Advertising Age,* February 4, 1980, pp. 24–27.

[50] Tauber, "Forecasting Sales," p. 82.

panies use laboratory market testing as a final screening before going to a standard market test.[51]

John Newman, marketing research director of the Betty Crocker division of General Mills, says, "We use it routinely and have been for several years. The primary function is to screen project candidates for test, as test marketing is extremely expensive."

Joel Levine, corporate director of research for Pillsbury, uses the company's own Supertest system. Pillsbury kills one out of three products on the average after the Supertest. "We use the Supertest to get some feel, some perspective on how good the market is. The objective is to be more selective with what you take into the test."

Statistical and mathematical models

A number of attempts have been made to develop quantitative relationships between predictor (or independent) variables such as promotional spending and consumer awareness and dependent variables such as trial, repeat purchase, and market share. Multiple regression analysis has been used to analyze the relationships between predictor variables and dependent variables. The best-known models of this type are the N. Y. Ayer model and the National Purchase Diary model. The regression models are most applicable to continuous innovations such as brand-line extensions.[52]

Mathematical simulation models have been used to estimate market share, payback period, and return on investment. A model may be used in sequence. First, the model may be used to estimate the payback period. In this stage, the inputs may be executive judgment. Second, product test data replace executive judgment in the next estimate of payback period. Third, data from extended product use and communication tests are used to supplement market testing in several ways. Prior to testing management may critically and systematically consider all the relevant marketing variables that influence a criterion variable, such as market share. Simulation models can project market test results so that tests may be stopped sooner. The models also can identify aspects of a product's market plan that may need improvement.[53]

COMMERCIALI-ZATION

Commercialization requires maximum coordination and integration among the firm's functional areas. In particular, the areas of marketing, manufacturing, and physical distribution must work together very closely during this period. Frequently, sizable expenditures are made on production facilities for the new production. For example, Miller Brewing Company spent over $240 million on production plants and equipment for Miller Lite beer.

---

[51] These examples are from Jennifer Alter, "Lab Simulations: No Shot in the Dark," *Advertising Age*, February 4, 1980, pp. S-1 to S-26. Reprinted with permission. Copyright 1980 by Crain Communications, Inc.

[52] Tauber, "Forecasting Sales," p. 81.

[53] Klompmaker et al., "Test Marketing."

commercialization

> **Commercialization** is the last phase of the new-product introduction process. It is also known as the *launch* for the product.

Besides the cost of production facilities, large sums are spent to promote the new product. The promotional expenditures include heavy introductory advertising, allowances and incentives for retailers, free samples, and coupons. Phillip Morris spent $40 million to introduce Merit cigarettes; Procter & Gamble spent $15 million on Pringles.

When introducing a new product, companies often use a ***roll-out*** procedure, meaning that the product is introduced in selected geographic regions rather than nationally. The selected areas usually are company sales territories. When the product achieves a specific level of sales in a given territory, it is then "rolled out" to another geographic area.

Effective planning is essential to achieve the necessary coordination and integration.[54] The plan should include the timing of production, introduction, and the use of the marketing mix elements.

A useful technique to manage launch timing and coordination is ***critical-path method (CPM).*** CPM structures the sequence of activities and identifies those most critical to the success of the timing. See Figure 12–5 for an example of a critical-path method for a new-product introduction.

Figure 12–5: Critical-path method for a new product

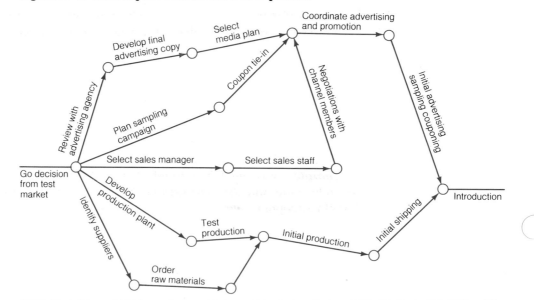

Source: Glen L. Urban and John Hauser, *Design and Marketing of New Products* (Englewood Cliffs, N.J.: Prentice-Hall, 1980), p. 469.

---

[54] Urban and Hauser, *Designing and Marketing,* pp. 465–66.

CONSUMER BEHAVIOR AND NEW PRODUCTS

Now that we've analyzed the new-product development process from the marketing manager's perspective, we can turn to the factors that influence the consumers' decision to buy a product. Specifically, we will analyze (1) product attributes that influence the adoption and (2) the consumer adoption process.

Product attributes that influence adoption

The rate of consumer acceptance of new products varies considerably. Fad or novelty items (hula hoop, skateboard) achieve widespread acceptance in their target markets very rapidly. Other products (especially dynamically continuous or discontinuous innovations) take considerably longer to be accepted. These varying acceptance rates are found in both consumer and industrial markets.

In designing marketing strategies and plans for products, information on the factors that influence the acceptance rate would be useful to marketing management. Research has found five product characteristics that influence the rate of adoption: (1) relative advantage, (2) compatibility, (3) complexity, (4) trialability, and (5) observability.[55]

Relative advantage is the degree to which consumers perceive the new product as superior to existing ones. The relative advantage is usually expressed in economic terms; but it may be seen in other attributes, such as greater convenience or superior performance. For example, passive solar systems may provide savings of up to 75 percent on monthly energy bills, and steel-belted radial tires provide consumers with superior durability.

Compatibility is the degree to which potential consumers perceive the product as consistent with existing values, past experiences, and needs. Compatibility provides greater security and less perceived risk for the consumer. For instance, a concept test for a lipstick designed to last one month showed that women found the idea incompatible with their current habits and experiences with lipstick. The concept test revealed that long-lasting lipstick seemed more like a hair dye in terms of permanence. As a result, the product concept received no further evaluation. If a product fits in little with consumer needs and past experiences, it has a slim chance, indeed, of being adopted readily.[56]

Complexity is the degree to which a product is perceived as difficult to understand and use. The greater the complexity, the less likely that it will be adopted. Therefore, one way to increase the product's acceptability is to make it easier to understand and use. Polaroid's One-Step camera,

---

[55] The discussion of product attributes that influence adoption is based on Everett M. Rogers and F. Floyd Shoemaker, *Communication of Innovations,* 2d ed. (New York: Free Press, 1971), chap. 7; and Leon G. Schiffman and Leslie L. Kanuk, *Consumer Behavior* (Englewood Cliffs, N.J.: Prentice-Hall, 1978), pp. 405–7.

[56] Bill Iuso, "Concept Testing: An Appropriate Approach," *Journal of Marketing Research,* May 1977, pp. 228–31.

which offers simplicity, ease of use, and instant development of pictures, is an excellent example.

Trialability is the degree to which a product may be experimented with on a limited basis. A product trial enables the consumer to evaluate a product and learn about its use and effectiveness. Marketing management has devised many ways for consumers to try products. Free samples,

Industrial marketers like Videojet use ads like this to stimulate product trial among its target market buyers. Industrial buyers can reduce their risks by evaluating new products and services on a free-trial basis.

Courtesy Videojet Systems International, a Division of A. B. Dick Company

money-back guarantees, and test drives all allow the consumer to try a product on a limited basis.

Marketers can also encourage consumers to try new products by offering small quantities. One study found that 63 percent of new-brand triers purchased a smaller quantity than they did on the average for established brands. This finding was consistent for five different new brands.[57]

Observability is the degree to which the results of a product are visible to others. The higher the observability, the greater the rate of adoption. An interesting example of observability is in the agricultural industry. Preemergent weed killers were designed to be sprayed on a field before weeds emerged. Midwestern farmers were slow to adopt this idea, despite its relative advantage. There were no dead weeds the farmers could show their neighbors.[58]

The consumer adoption process

Researchers have found that an individual's decision about an innovation is not a single act. Rather, it is a process that occurs over time and consists of a series of actions. The stages of the **consumer adoption process** are:

1. *Awareness*—The individual learns of the existence of the new idea but lacks information about it.

2. *Interest*—The individual develops an interest in the innovation and seeks additional information about it.

3. *Evaluation*—The individual makes a "mental trial" of the product to present and future situations and then decides whether or not to try it.

4. *Trial*—The individual actually applies the new idea on a small scale to determine its utility to his/her own situation.

5. *Adoption*—The individual uses the new idea continuously on a full scale.[59]

The adoption process is easy to understand, and it has helped marketers determine the types of information sources consumers find most important at specific decision stages. Mass media sources are most important for creating initial product awareness. But as a consumer moves through the adoption process, the importance of interpersonal sources (friends, salespeople, and others) increases.

Shortcomings of the adoption process.   The adoption process model has a number of shortcomings:

---

[57] Robert W. Shoemaker and F. Robert Shoaf, "Behavioral Changes in the Trial of New Products," *Journal of Consumer Research,* September 1975, p. 104.

[58] Rogers and Shoemaker, *Communication of Innovations,* p. 156.

[59] Schiffman and Kanuk, *Consumer Behavior,* p. 415.

1. The model's name is misleading because it implies that the process always ends in a decision to adopt. In reality, a decision to reject is more likely. Also, further information seeking may reinforce the reject decision, or the individual may later shift from adoption to rejection.

2. The five stages don't always occur in the order specified. Some stages, especially trial, may be skipped.

3. Evaluation occurs throughout the process rather than just at one of the five steps.[60]

---

[60] Rogers and Shoemaker, *Communication of Innovations*, p. 101.

SUMMARY

The term *new product* has varied meanings, the most common of which is a *continuous innovation*. This type least disrupts established patterns of consumer behavior and is exemplified by brand-line extensions.

New-product development is crucial for an organization. Firms may introduce new products to achieve sales and profit growth, as a reaction to a competitor's action, or to replace obsolete or unsuccessful products. New products are not always winners, however. Reasons for failure include lack of significant advantages to consumers, failure to match the firm's strength, changes in consumer tastes, insufficient market size, a competitor's entry into the market, and lack of channel support.

A company can adopt a variety of organizational structures for new-product development: new-product committee, product manager, new-product department, or venture team. It is the responsibility of the chosen structure to guide the firm through the new-product development process, which consists of the following stages: (1) product-idea generation, (2) idea screening, (3) business analysis, (4) product-concept development and testing, (5) product development, (6) market testing, and (7) commercialization.

New products affect not only the firm but also the consumer. Several factors influence a consumer's decision to buy a product, including product attributes that influence adoption and the adoption process.

KEY CONCEPTS

Continuous innovation	Brainstorming	Payback period
Dynamically continuous innovation	Reverse brainstorming	Average rate of return
Discontinuous innovation	Benefit-structure analysis	Present value
New-product committee	Problem-inventory analysis	Product concept
New-product manager	Attribute listing	Hard-core potential buyer
New-product department	Screening	Control brands
Venture team	Business analysis	Product development
Product idea	Capital budgeting	Market testing

Minimarket test	Roll-out	Trialability
Laboratory market test	Critical-path method (CPM)	Observability
Statistical and mathematical model	Relative advantage	Consumer adoption process
Commercialization	Compatibility	Forced relationship
Launch	Complexity	

DISCUSSION QUESTIONS AND EXERCISES

1. Review the concepts of continuous, dynamically continuous, and discontinuous innovation. Name two examples of each in addition to those given in the text.

2. Suppose that you've just accepted a position with a company as an assistant product manager. The company has committed itself to introducing three to five new products per year. Discuss the likely nature of these new-product introductions. Are they likely to be continuous, dynamically continuous, or discontinuous innovations? Discuss the significance of these new-product introductions to you as a new employee.

3. In a recent copy of *Business Week, The Wall Street Journal,* or a similar publication, locate an article about a new-product failure. How many of the reasons given in text for new-product failure were operative in the failure that you located? Do you see other reasons beside those listed for the new-product failure?

4. The next time you have an assignment, such as a term paper, that requires group interaction and the generation of creative ideas, consider applying the techniques discussed in the idea-generation phase of the new-product introduction process. Brainstorming, reverse brainstorming, and attribute listing may be especially useful.

5. Review the checklist in Table 12–4 for evaluating new-product ideas. Suggest additional criteria that could be used in this phase.

6. Compare and contrast the payback, average rate of return, and present-value methods of evaluating new products. Which procedure is best? Why?

7. Budweiser introduced a beer, LA, which has one half the alcohol of regular beer. What are the various ways that LA could be concepted?

8. What does the term *hard-core loyalist* mean as presented in the comprehensive product-concept test? Why is this concept important in estimating market share?

9. Evaluate the personal computer according to five product characteristics: relative advantage, compatibility, complexity, trialability, and observability.

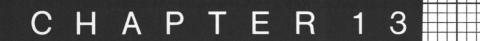

CHAPTER 13

Managing products

Product life cycle
    Introduction stage
    Growth stage
    Maturity stage
    Decline stage
    Length of product life cycle
    Theoretical foundation of product life cycle
    Research on product life cycle
Strategic marketing planning process applied
    to products
    Situation analysis

Product objectives
Product/markets
Budget determination
Strategic product decisions
    Product life cycle and strategic planning
    Product and brand positioning
    Product cannibalization
    Product deletion
    Evaluation of product performance
Legal aspects of products
    Product liability
    Product warranty

Summary

Key concepts

Discussion questions and exercises

The ***product life cycle*** is our first topic in this chapter. We'll be dealing with the stages of the life cycle, variations in it, and the theoretical foundation of and research on the life cycle. The second part of the chapter deals with the strategic marketing planning process applied to the product decision. Finally, the legal aspects of products are presented, with a focus on product liability and product warranties.

PRODUCT LIFE CYCLE

Figure 13–1 graphs the ***classical life-cycle curves*** of sales and profits throughout the four stages.

product life cycle

> The **product life cycle** is the sales history of a product. It is usually presented graphically in four distinct stages: introduction, growth, maturity, and decline.

The concept of product life cycle applies to varying definitions of a product or units of analysis. It can be applied to *product classes* (cigarettes), *product forms* (plain filter cigarettes), and *brands* (Philip Morris regular, nonfilter). Figure 13–2 illustrates the product life cycle applied to these definitions of a product.

Introduction stage

In the introduction stage, both the sales growth rate and the level of sales are low. The slow sales growth results from one or more of the following situations: delays in the expansion of production capacity, technical problems in the product or in production, delays in achieving ade-

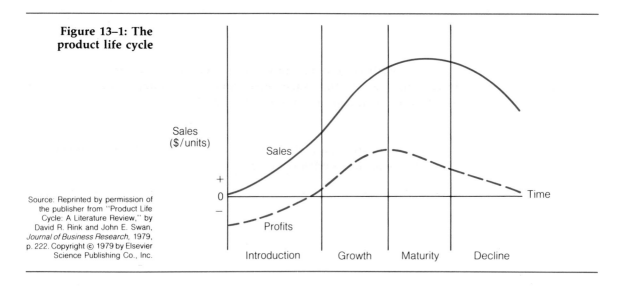

Figure 13–1: The product life cycle

Source: Reprinted by permission of the publisher from "Product Life Cycle: A Literature Review," by David R. Rink and John E. Swan, *Journal of Business Research*, 1979, p. 222. Copyright © 1979 by Elsevier Science Publishing Co., Inc.

Figure 13–2: Product life cycle applied to varying definitions of product

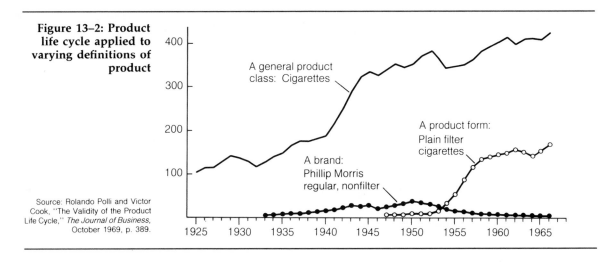

A general product class: Cigarettes

A product form: Plain filter cigarettes

A brand: Phillip Morris regular, nonfilter

Source: Rolando Polli and Victor Cook, "The Validity of the Product Life Cycle," *The Journal of Business*, October 1969, p. 389.

quate distribution through retail outlets, and customer inertia due to reluctance to change established patterns of behavior.[1]

Typically, the firm has considerable investments in research and development, marketing research, and initial promotional expenses for the product. These large initial investments combine with the low level of sales, usually placing the firm in a negative cash flow position during a product's introduction. In fact, for consumer products the ratio of promotional expenditures to sales is highest in the introduction stage of the cycle. When a new brand is introduced, the company usually engages in a promotional blitz, spending heavily on mass media advertising, free samples, and coupons. This effort is needed to inform consumers about the product, to induce initial product trial, and to stimulate repeat purchases. Promotional efforts directed toward the retailers and wholesalers include increased personal selling and dealer incentives.

Growth stage

The growth stage of the product life cycle is characterized by rapidly increasing sales. In this stage, price should be maintained at a high level to allow the company to improve its cash flow position. Advertising and other promotional expenditures remain high compared to expenditures for established products.[2]

On an industry level, the major characteristic of the growth stage is the increase in the number of competitors. As competition increases, individual firms must attend to a number of other factors as well. These include changes in product features, new advertising campaigns, and addi-

---

[1] Robert D. Buzzell, "Competitive Behavior and Product Life Cycles," in *Educators Conference Proceedings*, ed. John Wright and Jack Goldstucker (Chicago: American Marketing Association, 1966), pp. 46–47.

[2] Ibid., p. 53

tional channels of distribution. A downward pressure on prices also begins when competitors try to attract new customers to their brands.

As more consumers accept the product, new channels of distribution open up. For example, in their introduction phase, wristwatches were sold primarily in jewelry and department stores. In the growth phase, such mass-merchandising retailers as discount stores began to market them. The purpose of advertising at this stage is to inform consumers of the merits of one brand over another; and developing a reputation for high product quality, supported by adequate production capacity, can help the firm secure a large market share. This is just what Zenith did in the black-and-white television market.[3]

Some firms adopt a **used-apple policy.** They deliberately let other firms develop markets for new products and then come in during the growth phase.[4] Of course, the innovating firm assumes the major burden of risk for the product's development and initial advertising. Once it's clear that the product has a market, the used-apple companies introduce their own brands.

Maturity stage

In the maturity stage, sales growth rates decline dramatically and the sales curve levels off. The first firms into the market have recovered the investment in their respective brands. But the increase in competitors places even greater downward pressure on prices and margins for both manufacturers and intermediaries.

The key elements of successful marketing in the maturity phase are more difficult to define than in the introduction and growth stages. Programs to reach more consumers and to find and promote new uses for mature products become important means of competing.[5] For example, when the sales of Johnson's baby shampoo leveled off due to declining birthrates, the company successfully marketed the shampoo to adults. And General Foods upheld the sale of Jell-O gelatin dessert by introducing new flavors and promoting new recipes.

Reducing price to make the product affordable to more buyers is another important marketing element during this phase. Companies with a large market share are usually in the best position to do this profitably. Typically, they also have a lower unit cost resulting from economies of scale and from experience in the production and marketing of their brands.

Market **saturation** is the first sign of the maturity phase of the product's life cycle. Saturation means that most companies or households who were

---

[3] Donald K. Clifford, "Managing the Product Life Cycle," in *Marketing Management and Administrative Action,* 4th ed., ed. Stewart H. Britt and Harper Boyd (New York: McGraw-Hill, 1978), pp. 237–43.

[4] Theodore Levitt, "Exploit the Product Life Cycle," *Harvard Business Review,* November–December 1965, pp. 81–94.

[5] Clifford, "Managing the Product Life Cycle," p. 20.

Jell-O brand gelatin dessert and pie filling are in the mature stages of their life cycle. The company introduced Jell-O Pudding Pops frozen pudding on a stick as a new product to increase sales and capitalize on its well-established brand name. Jell-O and Pudding Pops are registered trademarks of General Foods Corporation.

Courtesy General Foods Corporation

prospects now own or use the product.[6] Market saturation is an especially difficult problem for durable goods marketers since additional sales come primarily from replacement of existing products.

Since few, if any, new purchasers are forthcoming in the maturity

---

[6] Levitt, "Exploit Product Life Cycle."

phase, firms must try to sway competitors' customers to their brands. The result is intensified competition based on reduced prices or small differences in product attributes. For example, Olympia entered the light beer market stressing the calorie content of its brand compared to Miller Lite, the market share leader. Olympia's light beer had 72 calories; Miller's had 96.

Decline stage

Unit and dollar sales in the product category begin to decline in this phase. Cost control becomes very important, for the company with the lowest unit costs and the most extensive distribution often enjoys an extended period of profitability.[7]

The decline stage has been described as the shakeout period because the firms with lower market share and those with marginal product quality are likely to be forced out of the market. The difficult competitive struggle during the decline phase has been effectively described as follows:

> Few companies are able to weather the competitive storm. As demand declines, the overcapacity that was already apparent during the period of maturity now becomes epidemic. Some products see the handwriting implacably on the wall but feel that with proper management and cunning they will be one of the survivors after the industrywide deluge they so clearly foresee. To hasten their competitors' eclipse directly, or to frighten them into early voluntary withdrawal from the industry, they initiate a variety of aggressively depressive tactics, propose mergers or buyouts, and generally engage in activities that make life thanklessly burdensome for all firms, and make death the inevitable consequence for most of them. A few companies do indeed weather the storm, sustaining life through the constant descent that now clearly characterizes the industry. Production gets concentrated into fewer hands. Prices and margins get depressed. Consumers get bored. The only cases where there is any relief from the boredom and gradual euthanasia are where styling and fashion play some constantly revivifying role.[8]

A firm in an industry with declining sales may diversify to boost its own sales. For instance, after the steady sales growth rates of the 1950s and 60s, the food industry reached a plateau. In 1975 industry sales actually declined. General Mills foresaw this trend in the 1960s and decided to pursue growth by diversifying into other industries. It became the largest company in the game and toy business after acquiring the Lionel and Parker Brothers companies.[9]

Length of product life cycle

The length of stages within the product life cycle may vary considerably. A fad item may enjoy a very short period of growth (less than

---

[7] Clifford, "Managing Product Life Cycle," p. 240.

[8] Levitt, "Exploit Product Life Cycle," p. 83.

[9] Glen L. Urban and John R. Hauser, *Designs and Marketing of New Products* (Englewood Cliffs, N.J.: Prentice-Hall, 1980), p. 5.

Table 13–1: Product life cycle: Shortening over time	Time Period	Introductory (years)	Growth (years)
	1922–42		
	1. Clothes washers	12	37
	2. Total coffeemakers	18	40
	3. Hotplates	6	23
	4. Gas ranges	7	14
	5. Electric ranges	15	40
	6. Refrigerators	7	44
	7. Irons	13	28
	8. Toasters	15	43
	9. Vacuum cleaners	18	40
	10. Waffle irons	9	18
	11. Heating pads	15	37
	12. Portable electric heaters	15	42
	Mean	12.5	33.8
	1945–69		
	13. Air conditioners	16	19
	14. Bed coverings	8	9
	15. Broilers	6	20
	16. Can openers	0	12
	17. Gas clothes dryer	5	21
	18. Electric clothes dryer	5	22
	19. Corn poppers	4	22
	20. Dishwashers	11	16
	21. Disposers	8	24
	22. Home freezers	3	26
	23. Fry pan skillets	0	21
	24. Food mixers	13	28
	25. Gas water heaters	9	18
	26. Electric water heaters	11	24
	27. Blenders	10	13
	28. B/W TV	3	17
	Mean	7.0	19.5
	1965–79		
	29. Calculators	2	6
	30. ADC coffeemakers	1	6
	31. Curling irons	0	7
	32. Digital watches	0	7
	33. Hand-held hair dryers	3	6
	34. Hair setters	0	4
	35. Electric knives	1	3
	36. Slow cookers	0	7
	37. Color TV	11	15
	Mean	2.0	6.8

Source: William Qualls, Richard W. Olshavsky, and Ronald E. Michaels, "Shortening of the PLC—An Empirical Test," *Journal of Marketing*, Fall 1981, p. 77.

six months), followed by a rapid decline and withdrawal from the market. Hula hoops spun swiftly at first, then spiraled from sight. Other products reach maturity and then stay in that stage for an extraordinarily long time. Procter & Gamble introduced Ivory soap in 1881, and Ivory has been on the market continuously ever since.

A study of ethical drugs revealed the stages in the product life cycle for a typical brand: introduction, 1 month; growth, 6 months; maturity,

15 months. There wasn't sufficient data to thoroughly analyze the length of the decline stage. However, "It seems likely that average length of this stage [decline] is longer than the other three stages combined."[10] Length of the product life cycle depends on rate of technical change, rate of market acceptance, and ease of competitive entry.[11]

A study of consumer durable goods found that the introduction and growth stages of the product life cycle are shortening. For consumer durables introduced between 1922 and 1942, the mean introduction period was 12.5 years. The figure shrank to 2.0 years in the 1965–79 time period. (See Table 13–1.)

A study of 140 brands of health, personal-care, food, and tobacco products found that 26 percent of brands studied could be classified in the growth stage, while over 50 percent were in the maturity stage.[12]

Product life-cycle stages don't necessarily follow each other predictably or in sequence. Some brands may never grow beyond the introduction stage. For example, Pillsbury's Apple Easy was withdrawn during the introduction stage when it became apparent that the product was not going to succeed.

After a period of decline, some brands experience a sales increase. A study of 258 ethical drug brands found it a common practice to increase promotional expenditures sharply when a brand reaches the end of its maturity stage. In fact, the most common type of product life-cycle curve was the one found for some 39 percent of the brands studied.[13] This form of the product life cycle is called the *cycle–recycle curve.* (See Figure 13–3.) A similar pattern was found for food and household products[14] and for industrial fluid-measuring devices.[15]

Theoretical foundation of product life cycle	The theory of adoption and diffusion of innovations provides the theoretical foundation for the product life cycle. Studies have shown that upon introduction, a new idea or product is usually accepted by a small number of innovators (adoption). Then others may begin to adopt it.

adoption process

> The **adoption process** comprises the decision-making phases the consumer goes through when accepting a new product: awareness, interest, evaluation, trial, and adoption. It applies to the *individual* consumer and therefore is *micro* in perspective.

[10] William E. Cox, Jr., "Product Life Cycles as Marketing Models," *The Journal of Business,* October 1967, pp. 375–84.

[11] Joel Dean, "Pricing Policies for New Products," *Harvard Business Review,* November–December 1950, pp. 45–53.

[12] Rolando Polli and Victor Cook, "The Validity of the Product Life Cycle," *Journal of Business,* 1969, pp. 385–400.

[13] Cox, "Product Life Cycles."

[14] M. T. Cunningham, "The Application of Product Life Cycles to Corporate Strategy: Some Research Findings," *British Journal of Marketing,* Spring 1969, pp. 32–44.

[15] Joel Hinkle, *Life Cycles* (New York: Nielsen, 1966).

**Figure 13–3: Cycle–
recycle pattern**

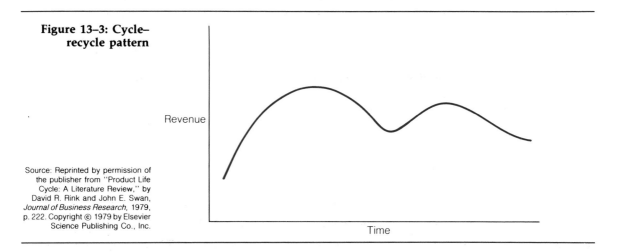

Source: Reprinted by permission of
the publisher from "Product Life
Cycle: A Literature Review," by
David R. Rink and John E. Swan,
Journal of Business Research, 1979,
p. 222. Copyright © 1979 by Elsevier
Science Publishing Co., Inc.

diffusion process

> The **diffusion** process, on the other hand, applies to the way a product is accepted by a *group* of consumers, usually the target market, and is *macro* in perspective.

While marketing management must evaluate and respond to both adoption and diffusion, the major focus is usually on diffusion since this process relates most directly to unit sales for a brand or product class. Figure 13–4 shows a distribution of consumers classified according to the diffusion of a new idea or product.

**Research on product
life cycle**

To summarize a comprehensive review of the literature on the product life cycle:

1. The emphasis in product life-cycle research has been on consumer nondurables and durables. More specifically, the research has concentrated on products that are frequently purchased, low in price,

**Figure 13–4: Time of
adoption of
innovations**

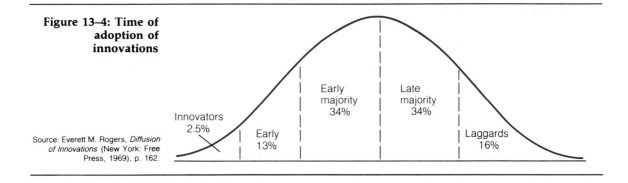

Source: Everett M. Rogers, *Diffusion
of Innovations* (New York: Free
Press, 1969), p. 162.

widely distributed, and not subject to wide variations on the supply side.

2. Some 15 studies of consumer products and 4 studies of industrial goods provide substantial evidence to validate the classical product life cycle. (See Figure 13–1.) However, a total of 11 different cyclical shapes were found.

3. Research has concentrated on product classes and forms. Brands have largely been ignored.

4. Little is known about the length and sequence of product life-cycle stages. Some success has been claimed for methods designed to forecast the transition from one product life-cycle stage to another.

5. The research on product life cycles was conducted during periods of economic stability and growth. Therefore, how recession and prolonged periods of inflation influence the product life cycle is unknown.

6. Very little is known about the impact of the firm's characteristics on the product life cycle. Only one study empirically investigated how the product life cycle is used in business planning.[16]

STRATEGIC MARKETING PLANNING PROCESS APPLIED TO PRODUCTS

The discussion that follows involves the application of the strategic planning process to the product decision. We plan to focus on those aspects of strategic planning that relate directly to the product management. See Figure 13–5 for an overview of the strategic marketing planning process as applied to the product decision.

Situation analysis

Consumer. The consumers or buyers in the firm's target markets should be the starting point for developing effective product strategy. Product strategy is directly linked to market segmentation strategy. Its goal is to provide the benefits sought by a group of consumers within a market segment. Some examples of successful new products that effectively provide consumer benefits are:

> The Polaroid Land camera provides the benefit of immediate availability of a picture.
>
> The Sony Walkman provides the benefits of high-fidelity sound with portability.
>
> Stouffer's Lean Cuisine provides the benefits of low calories, good taste, and convenience.[17]

---

[16] David R. Rink and John E. Swan, "Product Life-Cycle Research: A Literature Review," *Journal of Business Research* 7 (September 1979), pp. 212–19.

[17] Peter Engel, "Implementation, Quality Spell Success for New Products," *Marketing News,* January 20, 1984, p. 5.

Figure 13–5: Strategic marketing planning process applied to product decision

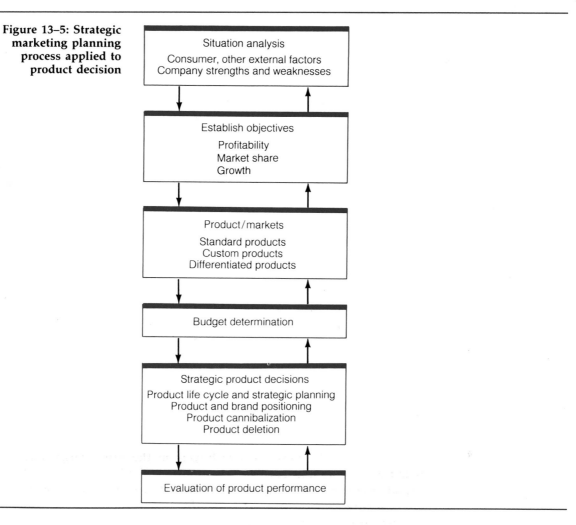

Situation analysis

Consumer, other external factors
Company strengths and weaknesses

Establish objectives

Profitability
Market share
Growth

Product/markets

Standard products
Custom products
Differentiated products

Budget determination

Strategic product decisions

Product life cycle and strategic planning
Product and brand positioning
Product cannibalization
Product deletion

Evaluation of product performance

Other external factors.   Economic, technological, social, and legal issues play a role in the strategic product decision. The impact of double-digit inflation on consumer purchasing power was a major factor in the development of generic, or brandless, products. Generics provide satisfactory quality at prices 10 to 35 percent below the price for nationally branded products.

Technological advances often are a primary factor in the development of new products. Technology played a major role in developing the automobile, which has spawned a host of new products and services. A more recent example is the ongoing development of robots. At Ford Motor

Co. robots test engines. General Motors uses robotic welders. Some government agencies use robots to pick up and deliver mail.[18]

New products have developed to meet changing social conditions, too. For example, women's business attire products have been significantly expanded to meet the needs of the growing number of women in the work force. The market for certain time-saving products has also increased.[19]

The legal aspects of product management are dealt with at length at the end of this chapter.

Company strengths and weaknesses.   Management must critically analyze the company's strengths and weaknesses when making product decisions. Strategic decisions in the product area are related very closely to the overall corporate mission and definition of the business. Consider the following example:

> *It is particularly interesting to note that Bic's decision to define their business as inexpensive consumer disposables led them to razors and lighters. Their initial success with disposable pens could have led them into stationery supplies or office equipment—natural additions, given their channel of distribution. Leveraging their production capability of plastic disposables rather than their distribution channel was a critical strategic decision.[20]*

Management must carefully evaluate its resources when making strategic product decisions. Critical evaluation of the market may identify many consumer needs and profitable opportunities. But management should pursue only those the firm has the internal resources to pursue. Bic is a good example of a company effectively matching market opportunities with internal resources.

Product objectives   Most often, ***product objectives*** are defined in terms of profitability, market share, and growth.[21] Depending on circumstances internal and/or external to the organization, a company may pursue such other objectives as technological leadership, social contribution, or international economic development.

Usually companies use a combination of objectives. However, smaller firms, because of limited resources, may have to constrain their efforts to the pursuit of one major objective. Let's discuss the three common objectives that firms establish for their products.

---

[18] John Naisbitt, *Megatrends* (New York: Warner Books, 1982), p. 22.

[19] William Lazer and John Smallwood, "The Changing Demographics of Women," *Journal of Marketing* 41 (July 1977), pp. 14–22.

[20] Edward M. Tauber, "Brand Franchise Extension: New Product Benefits from Existing Brand Names," *Business Horizons* 24 (March–April 1981), p. 38. Copyright, 1981, by the Foundation for the School of Business at Indiana University. Reprinted by permission.

[21] This discussion of product objectives is based on Sabhash C. Jain, *Marketing Planning and Strategy* (Cincinnati: South-Western Publishing, 1981), pp. 184–89.

Profitability.   Profitability may be expressed in terms of some specific absolute or dollar amount or in terms of a percentage of capital employed. Profits provide a measurable criterion against which management can evaluate product performance.

In implementing the profit objective, firms usually follow three basic steps:

1. Determine the desired rate of return on the amount invested in the product.
2. Forecast the number of units to be sold over a specified time period, such as one year.
3. Calculate the dollar amount to be added to costs to provide the desired profit level.

Market share.   Research has shown that market share is positively related to profitability.[22] Therefore, market share is seen as a viable objective for products. Market share has been traditionally defined in absolute terms. But this doesn't always work. When the industry is concentrated in the hands of only several major competitors, a relative measure is often used—say, a company's share relative to the largest or three largest competitors.

The reason for pursuing market share as an objective is the experience curve. The underlying logic is that higher share allows the company to accumulate more experience. The greater accumulated experience often translates into lower costs and provides management with a competitive cost advantage. Of course, higher market share doesn't automatically mean lower costs. It would be more accurate to say that higher market share creates conditions allowing management to capitalize on the experience curve effects. Companies known for their concentration on market share are Texas Instruments Incorporated in consumer products and Harnischfeger, a manufacturer of rough-terrain cranes.[23]

Growth.   When growth is a stated objective for products, it is usually in terms of units or dollar amount of sales. The reasons for pursuing growth as an objective come from a variety of sources, including:

1. *Customers*—Developing related products to serve a specific market; or production capacity is not enough to fill needs of important customers, who may themselves be growing.
2. *Competition*—To maintain or better position in specific product or market areas where competition is making strong moves; or to permit more competitive pricing ability by greater volume.

---

[22] "Profit Impact of Marketing Strategy," (Strategic Planning Institute, 1977).
[23] Michael E. Porter, *Competitive Strategy* (New York: Free Press, 1980), pp. 36–37.

3. Channels of distribution—To make additions necessary to obtain needed attention and selling effort from existing distributors, dealers, and agents.

Perhaps the strongest reason for pursuing growth comes from within the company itself. Often management attempts to fulfill its own growth expectations. Management may be attempting to capitalize on its unique growth opportunities because of specific corporate strengths and competencies. For example, in the late 1970s Time, Inc., was in a very strong cash position. The company acquired Book-of-the-Month-Club, Inc., American Television and Communications Corporation, and the *Washington Star* newspaper.[24]

Product/Markets

How do different types of products—standard, custom, and differentiated—relate to the various product/market strategies? Let's highlight the different types and the overall strategic perspective and try to illustrate the role that the product plays in the strategy.

Standard products. When a company uses an aggregated product/market strategy, it offers essentially the same marketing mix to the entire market. That is, the company offers a ***standard product*** to all market members. Management makes two assumptions when using the aggregated strategy: (1) All or most of the customers have similar needs for the product, and (2) The organization can offer a single marketing mix that satisfies these needs.

From a strategic perspective, firms that offer a standard product are attempting to compete on a cost-leadership basis. Management tries to achieve a large sales volume, which offers an opportunity to lower costs and attain higher profits. The experience curve plays an important role in the effective marketing of standard products.

The classic example of the standard product was Henry Ford's Model T. Ford assumed that customers preferred a low-cost, standard automobile to one that had features more closely matched to individual buyer's needs and wants. He was right for a time. Ford sold millions of Model Ts in the 1910s and 20s. But then General Motors saw the opportunity to offer different styles and colors in varying price ranges. GM's strategy ultimately proved effective.

The standard product approach is based, as we said, on cost leadership. Some recent examples of companies that have used cost leadership are Black & Decker Mfg. Co. and Du Pont.

Custom products. A company that uses a niche strategy offers a marketing mix appealing to a small group or segment of the entire market.

[24] Time, Inc., "A Bold Bid for Growth in All Four Lines of Business," *Business Week,* March 20, 1978, p. 130.

Rolls-Royce is an excellent example of a company using a niche strategy. Their expensive automobiles are targeted to the very rich.

There are only 10 people in the world who know how to make the Rolls-Royce grille.

You don't know Dennis Jones. Pity. Because Dennis is one of the few men still walking on this earth who can, with good conscience, call themselves master craftsmen of the old school.

Dennis Jones is a man who uses his extraordinary skill to magically sculpt by hand a fair amount of cold steel into the sparkling silver grille of the finest motor car in the world.

The Rolls-Royce. Dennis will slowly and carefully work on a Rolls-Royce grille for days. And in the end, in an unobtrusive corner inside the grille, where it may never be seen by another human being, he will put his initials. A sign of pride in his work.

A celebration of a job well-done.

Dennis Jones typifies the small band of rare craftsmen who practically hand build the Rolls-Royce.

This is why we can say without hesitation: While ordinary cars may come in and out of vogue, the Rolls-Royce lives forever.

It lives forever because there are craftsmen with the skills

and dedication of a Dennis Jones working on every inch of every Rolls-Royce. Craftsmen who lovingly assemble the Rolls-Royce engine by hand.

The Rolls-Royce you acquire today combines the skill of these master craftsmen along with the most recent technological advances of this day.

In the end, the work of all these craftsmen will produce a motor car that Charles Stewart Rolls or Frederick Henry Royce would be proud to have bear their names.

A motor car to be driven into the next century by someone of great accomplishment who believes, "I give the world my best, I desire its best in return. I drive the Rolls-Royce."

Rolls-Royce. Simply the best motor car in the world.

For information, contact your local authorized Rolls-Royce dealer or the Rolls-Royce Midwestern Zone Office (312) 991 7455). © Rolls-Royce Motors Inc. 1984. The names "Rolls-Royce" and "Silver Spur" and the mascot, badge, and radiator grille are registered trademarks, as are the Bentley name, mascot, and badge.

Courtesy Rolls-Royce Motors, Inc.

The basis of the niche strategy is to define the target market very narrowly and then efficiently and effectively meet its needs. Often, highly specialized *custom products* are a key ingredient in the niche strategy. However, a firm can implement a niche strategy by concentrating on another element of the marketing mix, such as distribution.

Concentration on the needs and wants of a small segment of the market

Table 13–2: Key characteristics of standard, custom, and differentiated products		**Standard products**	**Custom products**	**Differentiated products**
	Cost relative to competitors	Low	High	Intermediate
	Usual product market strategy	Aggregated	Niche	Disaggregated
	Number of market segments appealed to	All*	One or two	All†
	Extent to which product is made to customer specifications	Low	High	Intermediate

* When using a standard product in the aggregated strategy, the firm does not develop market segments, but rather offers the same product to all customers.
† In disaggregated marketing the firm uses differentiated products to appeal to all major market segments.

is the key ingredient for success in the niche strategy. Measurex Corporation is a manufacturer of computer-based process control equipment. The company concentrated on developing their product to meet the needs of a single industry—paper. Measurex's systems range in price from $150,000 to over $1 million.[25]

In the automobile industry, Rolls-Royce practices the niche strategy with its unique product offering. Its opulent cars are prestigious, costly to produce, and expensive to purchase. Clearly, Rolls-Royce targets the ultra rich.

Differentiated products.   A company that uses a disaggregated product/market strategy offers different marketing mixes to serve various market segments. The company offers products that have been designed to provide benefits to members of various target markets. ***Differentiated products*** with widely varying features are developed to satisfy the needs of the various segments. Differentiated products are obviously a compromise between standard products and custom products. In some cases a firm starts with a standard product and then offers the customer a variety of options.

GM, Ford, and Chrysler use the notion of differentiated products in their marketing strategies. They offer many different types of cars, each available with a wide variety of options. Their objective is to build brand loyalty to their company and its products.

Table 13–2 contains a comparison of standard, custom, and differentiated products based on four key characteristics.

Budget determination   The budget and financial implication of products usually represent the largest dollar expenditure made by corporations. For example:

---

[25] David W. Cravens, *Strategic Marketing* (Homewood, Ill: Richard D. Irwin, 1980), p. 170.

RCA Corporation spent $150 million to develop and market SelectaVision, a videodisc player. RCA hopes to claim a strong market position in the $8 billion videodisc market that is expected to develop in the 1980s.[26]

R. J. Reynolds spent over $40 million on its Real brand of cigarettes. Covered in these costs were newspaper and magazine ads, 25 million sample packs, and 130 boxcars of in-store displays. Another $1 million was spent on extensive research involving more than 10,000 smokers. Despite these efforts, Real failed to reach its projected market share of 1 percent of $100 million dollars in sales, and it was taken off the market.[27]

Digital Equipment Corporation made a $150 million investment in the company's data processing products and technology in order to adapt their product and marketing mix to more effectively satisfy the needs of the office market.[28]

Product decisions usually involve commitment to large capital expenditures over extended time periods. When making product decisions, management often spends funds on plant and equipment, inventory, and advertising and promotional materials. Capital budgeting techniques are often used when making the critical strategic decisions. We discussed these techniques in detail in Chapter 12.

STRATEGIC PRODUCT DECISIONS

Product life cycle and strategic planning

The product life cycle is a major dimension of various strategic planning models. The product portfolio or growth/share matrix uses market growth rate as one of its major dimensions.[29] The market attractiveness/business strength matrix by General Electric uses market growth rate and seven other factors to assess the market attractiveness dimension.[30]

In the strategic planning models, the market growth rate or stage of the product life cycle is regarded as a situational variable to which management must adjust its marketing mix variables. In these models, we deal with a product class or product-form level of aggregation. Thus, the product life cycle at these levels of aggregation is appropriately regarded as an *independent* variable. That is, marketing management cannot control it. On the *brand* level, though, the most strategically useful perspective is that the brand's life cycle is a *dependent variable* that can be controlled through effective management of the brand's marketing mix.

Treating the brand's life cycle as a dependent variable has been recom-

---

[26] Ellen Klugman, "Dealers Gripe about Sluggish Sales of RCA's New SelectaVision Player," *The Wall Street Journal,* July 6, 1981, p. 14.

[27] John Koten, " 'Real' Cigarettes Prove True Disappointment despite Their Merit," *The Wall Street Journal,* February 26, 1980, p. 1.

[28] "Two Giants Bid for Office Sales," *Business Week,* November 9, 1981, p. 86.

[29] George S. Day, "Diagnosing the Product Portfolio," *Journal of Marketing,* April 1977, pp. 29–38; George S. Day, "The Product Life Cycle: Analysis and Application Issues," *Journal of Marketing,* Fall 1981, pp. 60–68.

[30] Yoram Wind and Vijay Mahajan, "Designing Product and Business Portfolios," *Harvard Business Review,* January–February 1981, pp. 155–66.

Figure 13–6: Life-cycle stages of various product classes

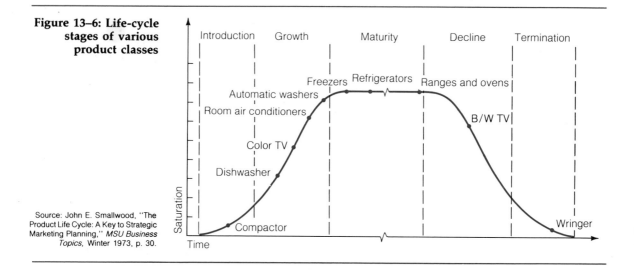

Source: John E. Smallwood, "The Product Life Cycle: A Key to Strategic Marketing Planning," *MSU Business Topics*, Winter 1973, p. 30.

mended by several marketing scholars.[31] A model for planning product-line strategy that systematically evaluates a brand's market share, profitability, and company and industry sales trends was developed. The model is useful in planning for an industrial product line and is, in fact, employed by International Harvester.[32]

An interesting application of the product's life cycle at the product-category level is presented by the Whirlpool Corporation. Products are grouped into various stages of life cycle based on the estimated saturation level of the market for a particular product. Note in Figure 13–6 that freezers and refrigerators are in the mature stage. Whirlpool management estimates that freezers have a potential of only one third of occupied households and have achieved 90 percent of that market. Refrigerators have a much higher potential but have achieved 99 percent of their market. Automatic clothes washers have a potential of about four fifths of occupied households and so are only at about 70 percent of their potential; consequently, they still have potential for additional sales and are classified in the growth stage.

Whirlpool has its own brands in many of these product categories. The placement of the product categories into various stages of the product life cycle enables Whirlpool management to determine which of its brands are competing in high- and low-growth markets. Accordingly, Whirlpool's management may allocate most of its marketing dollars to the brands

---

[31] Peter Doyle, "The Realities of the Product Life Cycle," *Quarterly Review of Marketing,* Summer 1976, pp. 62–73; and Ben Enis, Raymond La Grace, and Arthur Prell, "Extending the Product Life Cycle," *Business Horizons,* June 1977, pp. 46–56.

[32] Yoram Wind and Henry Claycamp, "Planning Product-Line Strategy: A Matrix Approach," *Journal of Marketing,* January 1976, pp. 2–9.

competing in product categories in the introduction and growth stages. These categories include trash compactors, dishwashers, and room air conditioners. (See Figure 13–6.) The dollars generated by sales of brands in the decline stage (black-and-white TV) may be used to support brands with the greatest potential for growth.

Product and brand positioning

One critical strategic decision made about a product is its positioning.

product positioning

> **Product positioning** is a process in which a firm tries to create a perception in a consumer's mind as to where a given product or brand fits in relation to competing products or brands.

Product positioning is a major strategic decision. But it's important to stress that positioning ultimately takes place in the minds of consumers. Marketing management may develop products and promote them to achieve a specific position, but the ultimate determination of the product's position is the consumer's perception of it.

Conceptually, positioning occurs on two levels: the product-category level and the brand level. The *product category* contains the products that will satisfy the same general need. The *brand* level refers to the offerings of different companies within a product category. An example will illustrate the differences between the two.

Assume that a company is considering introducing an instant breakfast drink.[33] On the product-category level, the product would compete against other breakfast foods, such as bacon and eggs and breakfast cereals. In order to understand the position of the instant breakfast drink in relationship to other breakfast foods, a **product-positioning map** could be constructed. Figure 13–7 contains such a map, using two dimensions—cost and preparation time. The instant breakfast drink stands alone in a distinctive part of the market because the consumer perceives it as a low-cost and quick-preparation breakfast food.

If the company entered the market after it was formed, a brand-positioning map could be formed as well. Suppose that companies A, B, and C had brands on the market. Consider the brand-positioning map for these three companies in terms of price per ounce and caloric content. (See Figure 13–7B.) The new company entering the market might consider positioning itself low in calories and in price per ounce. None of the competing brands occupies that position currently. We must stress that the data used to construct these maps should be based on *consumer perceptions* of the products and brands. Therefore, marketing research must be done to collect the appropriate information. A serious positioning deci-

---

[33] This example and figure is adapted from Philip Kotler, *Marketing Management: Analysis, Planning, and Control,* 4th ed. (Englewood Cliffs, N.J.: Prentice-Hall, 1980), p. 322.

Figure 13–7: Product and brand positioning

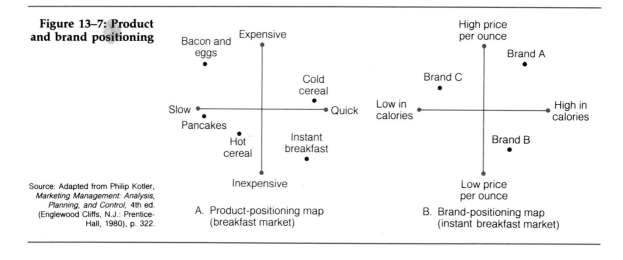

A. Product-positioning map (breakfast market)

B. Brand-positioning map (instant breakfast market)

Source: Adapted from Philip Kotler, *Marketing Management: Analysis, Planning, and Control,* 4th ed. (Englewood Cliffs, N.J.: Prentice-Hall, 1980), p. 322.

sion error could occur if based on *managerial perceptions* of the product and brands and not on consumer perceptions.

Marketing management usually concentrates on brand positioning, since most products are in the mature stage of the life cycle and multiple brands exist. Effective positioning is especially important when the physical characteristics of the brands are very similar. Other situations when positioning or repositioning (i.e., trying to change existing perceptions of brands) is important are (1) when a competitor enters a brand that takes market share from an existing brand and (2) when a shift in customer preferences occurs.

Effective positioning involves the identification of physical attributes of the brand or product that can be communicated, usually through advertising, to create a specific perception (or location) in the consumer's mind. One of the most brilliant and financially successful positioning strategies was developed for the Seven-Up Company. You can appreciate the brilliance of their "Un-Cola" campaign if you realize that, when the campaign started, two out of three soft drinks consumed in the United States were colas. Seven-Up linked its product to what was already in the consumer's mind, and the Un-Cola position established 7-Up as an alternative to a cola drink![34]

Often the industry leader in terms of market share enjoys a unique position in the consumer's mind. This position makes it difficult if not impossible for competitors to make strong inroads. For example, the computer "position" in the minds of consumers is filled by a company called International Business Machines Corp. (IBM). Consumers reject the mes-

[34] Jack Trout and Al Reis, "The Positioning Era," (Reis Cappiello Colwell, Inc., undated), p. 18.

**Figure 13–8:
Positioning map for
automobiles**

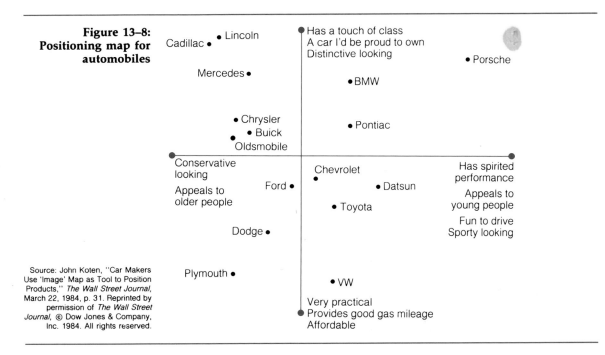

sage of a commercial that says "NCR means computers." IBM means computers; NCR means National Cash Register.[35]

A strong market share position does not guarantee an effective position. Consider the following:

> *Take the position of Scott in paper products. Scott has about 40 percent of the $1.2 billion market for towels, napkins, toilet tissues, and other consumer paper products. But Scott, like Mennen with Protein 21, fell into the line-extension trap.*
>
> *ScotTowels, ScotTissues, Scotties, and Scottkins, even Baby Scott: All of the names undermined the Scott foundation. The more products hung on the Scott name, the less meaning the name had to the average consumer. When Procter & Gamble attacked with Mr. Whipple and his tissue squeezers, it was no contest. Charmin is now the No. 1 brand in the toilet tissue market.*
>
> *In Scott's case, a large "share of market" didn't mean they owned the position. More important is a large "share of mind." The householders could write "Charmin, Kleenex, Bounty, and Pampers" on their shopping lists and know exactly what products they were going to get. "Scott" on a shopping list has no meaning. The actual brand names aren't much help, either: Which brand, for example, is engineered for the nose—Scotties or ScotTissue?*

[35] Ibid., p. 11.

Volkswagen has the reputation of producing practical cars but not very exciting ones. In this ad, VW positions its Scirocco as having high performance while retaining the image of quality at an affordable price. See Figure 13–8 for VW's position compared to other car makers.

It's the fastest you can go at 55 mph.

55 mph in a 1984 Volkswagen Scirocco is faster than 55 mph in a mere car.

Faster in terms of its speed of reaction.

Underneath its aerodynamic body (made by Karmann Coachworks in Osnabrück, West Germany) is an engine and suspension system designed to directly communicate with you.

So it responds to your commands immediately. Whether you're maneuvering at a city crawl. Or on a German Autobahn, where there are no speed limits. Of course, in the U.S., there is a speed limit. But in a Scirocco, there's no limit on the fun you can have while you're observing it. **It's not a car. The 1984 Scirocco $10,870. It's a Volkswagen.**

Seatbelts save lives. *Mfr's sugg. retail price includes a 12-month unlimited mileage, limited warranty. Transp., tax, license, dealer prep add'l. © 1983 Volkswagen of America

Courtesy Volkswagen of America

In positioning terms, the name *Scott* exists in limbo. It isn't firmly ensconced on any product ladder.[36]

Brand-position map for automobiles. Fuel-efficiency requirements have narrowed the design and performance characteristics for cars. As a result, the auto companies have had to turn to more subtle ways of drawing distinctions between different models. The brand-positioning map

[36] Jack Trout and Al Reis, "How to Position your Product," in *Advertising Management Practical Perspective,* ed. David A. Aaker (Englewood Cliffs, N.J.: Prentice-Hall, 1975), p. 114.

Figure 13–9: Sources of new-product revenue

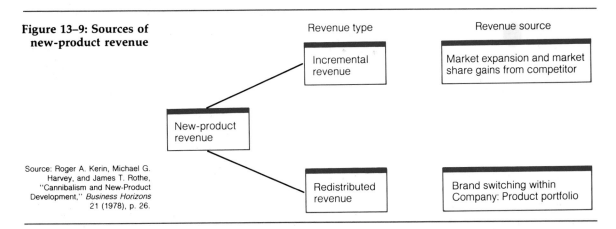

Revenue type

Revenue source

Incremental revenue

Market expansion and market share gains from competitor

New-product revenue

Redistributed revenue

Brand switching within Company: Product portfolio

Source: Roger A. Kerin, Michael G. Harvey, and James T. Rothe, ''Cannibalism and New-Product Development,'' *Business Horizons* 21 (1978), p. 26.

contained in Figure 13–8 is one tool being used to help separate one auto manufacturer's product from others.

The real advantage of the map is that it looks at cars from the consumer perspective while retaining a tangible product orientation. By plotting on the map strong areas of consumer demand, an auto manufacturer can tell if its cars are on target. By analyzing the concentration of dots representing competition, management can assess how much opposition it is likely to get in a specific territory on the map.

Product cannibalization[37]

An important dimension in the strategic management of a firm's product portfolio is ***product cannibalization.***

product cannibalization

> **Product cannibalization** is the process in which a company introduces a new product whose sales are partially derived from the sales of the company's existing products.

Product cannibalization is frequently overlooked when planning and managing the new-product development process. But unless consideration is given to the sources of sales for the new product, management might greatly overestimate its profits. In order to better understand the cannibalization issue, consider Figure 13–9. A new product has three sources of revenue: (1) new consumers who were not previously buyers of the product, (2) consumers of competitive products, and (3) consumers who switch

---

[37] This section is adopted from Roger A. Kerin, Michael G. Harvey, and James T. Rothe, "Cannibalism and New-Product Development," *Business Horizons* 21 (October 1978), pp. 25–31; and Michael G. Harvey and Roger A. Kerin, "Diagnosis and Management of the Product Cannibalism Syndrome," *University of Michigan Business Review,* November 1979, pp. 18–24.

from a company's existing product to its new one. The first two sources of revenue represent increment volume for the product portfolio because they come from market expansion and capturing market share. But redistributed revenue (cannibalization) is the third revenue source; it results when the company's existing customers merely substitute one item for another in the company's product portfolio.

This is *inadvertent cannibalization,* and it occurs in the early stages of the product's life cycle. However, there are two other types of cannibalization: planned and preemptive. *Planned cannibalization* may be used to delete an existing product from the portfolio. Products in the late stages of the product life cycle may be replaced by new or improved products in order to maintain market share. The replacement of the wringer-type washing machine by automatic washing machines is an example of planned cannibalism.

Preemptive cannibalization is similar to planned cannibalism. The difference is that preemptive cannibalism usually occurs during the maturity stage of the product life cycle. There are three sources of preemptive cannibalism: (1) increased consumer dissatisfaction with the product, (2) technological developments within the firm that enable it to produce a new product, and (3) lack of adequate raw materials for the present product. An example of preemptive cannibalism is the case of Bristol-Meyers' introduction of Datril to compete with McNeil Laboratories' Tylenol. Bristol-Meyers held a large market share in the aspirin segment of the analgesic market with its Bufferin and Excedrin brands. However, while growth in the aspirin market plateaued, the anti-inflammatory-compound segment was growing substantially—and taking away former and potential aspirin consumers. Bristol-Meyers introduced Datril in hopes of attracting consumers switching from Bufferin and Excedrin. In other words, let's help consumers keep buying a Bristol-Meyers product, not switch to McNeil Laboratories' Tylenol.

The theoretical foundation of product cannibalism is the cross-elasticity of demand, which analyzes the substitutability of one product for another. Cross-elasticity of demand is commonly applied when analyzing the impact of price changes. That is, if a competitor changes the price of its product, how will your product be affected? In fact, if you reprice one of your own products, how will that affect others in your product portfolio?

The financial consequences of cannibalization should be carefully considered when assessing the introduction of a new product. The amount and the source of potential new-product volume must be calculated and their effect on the overall profitability of the product portfolio considered. One way to consider the effect of cannibalization is to subtract the gross margin dollars produced by the new product. The following formula can be used to calculate the number of units of the new product necessary to offset the effects of cannibalization:

Total number of
new-product units
necessary to offset $=$ $\dfrac{\text{Cannibalized}}{\text{volume}}$ $\times$ $\dfrac{\text{Gross margin of existing product}}{\text{Gross margin of new product}}$
the effects of
cannibalization

To illustrate, suppose that

Cannibalized volume $\quad = 400{,}000$ units
Gross margin existing product $= \quad \$2.00$
Gross margin new product $\quad = \quad \$1.00$

Therefore,

$$800{,}000 \text{ units} = 400{,}000 \times \frac{\$2.00}{\$1.00}$$

The existing product would have to sell 800,000 units to offset the effects of cannibalization and keep the company in the same gross margin dollar position as it would have been had it not introduced the new product. Market management could use this information to estimate the market share necessary to achieve the 800,000-unit sales volume. It may be that this unit volume translates into a difficult-to-achieve market share position. If so, management may reconsider introducing the new product.

Product deletion

As products reach the decline stage of their life cycles, management must evaluate their roles in the company's product portfolio and consider eliminating them. **Product deletion** requires careful planning, for it can have serious consequences for a company's production, finance, and sales departments. And dropping a product may have undesirable effects on the buyers of the product.

A variety of benefits accrue to the company for dropping products that are small contributions to profit, overhead, and total sales volume. The direct financial benefits can be substantial. Consider the following examples:

> *Hunt-Wesson Foods, the canner of vegetables and fruits, began to cut its 30-odd product lines in 1947. By 1958 it had only three products: fruit cocktail, tomato products, and peaches. The company's sales went from $15 million to $120 million. Along with cutting the number of products, Hunt-Wesson began a diversification program which helped to increase sales as well.*

> *A company with annual sales of $40 million dropped products accounting for 8 percent of sales. Within three years, its profit increased by 20 times.*[38]

---

[38] The examples are from Philip Kotler, "Phasing out Weak Products," *Harvard Business Review*, March–April 1965, pp. 109–10.

Additional benefits of dropping weak products include freeing executive time for more profitable products, forcing management to give thorough consideration to why products failed, and making scarce resources (such as raw materials) available for more promising products.[39]

A survey of the marketing vice presidents of *Fortune* 500 companies revealed that the main reasons for dropping a product usually revolved around the product's sales or financial performance.[40] The most important reasons are shown below (figures in the parentheses are the percent of respondents giving a response):

1. Future sales volume appears poor (68 percent).
2. Return on investment is below a minimum acceptable level (56 percent).
3. Past sales and volume are declining (48 percent).
4. Past sales volume is not up to expectations (48 percent).
5. Future market potential for products of this type is not favorable (34 percent).
6. Costs exceed revenues (29 percent).
7. Market share is declining (25 percent).

When a firm produces and markets a large number of individual product items, the screening of items is complex and time-consuming. Computer models have been developed to assist marketing management in the task of identifying products for deletion. The **Product Review and Evaluation Subsystem (PRESS)** model is such an approach. (See Table 13–3.) The model uses standard cost-accounting data that would be readily available in most companies. The key factor is the product's contribution margin (Sales minus Directly assignable costs). The model is used to generate product rankings in terms of a selection index (SIN), which is computed as follows:

$$SIN_i = \frac{CM_i/\Sigma CM_i}{FC_i/\Sigma FC_i} \times (CM_i/\Sigma CM_i)$$

where

SIN_i = Selection index number for product i.
CM_i = Contribution margin for product i.
FC_i = Facilities cost for product i.
ΣCM_i = Summation of contribution margin of all products.
ΣFC_i = Summation of facilities costs of all products.

---

[39] Richard T. Hise and Michael A. McGinnis, "Product Elimination: Practices, Policies, and Ethics," *Business Horizons* 18 (June 1975), p. 25.

[40] Ibid., p. 28.

Suppose a product item's contribution margin is 5 percent of the total contribution for all products but it uses 10 percent of the company's resources or facilities. The product's effective contribution in terms of return on investment, then, is small. For this product:

$$\text{SIN} = \frac{.05}{.10} \times .05 = .025$$

This product uses double the percentage of facilities it produces in revenues. The SIN number awards it one half the value of its percentage of contribution margin. If a product's use of facilities is less than its percentage of contribution margin, it will show a higher SIN number than its unadjusted percentage of contribution margin.

The PRESS model is used to develop a ranking of products according to their SIN indexes. Table 13–3 contains an example of these rankings. Management would select products with low SIN scores (1 or less) for possible deletion. The PRESS model has subsystems that can be used to examine price–volume relationships, sales trends, and product complementarity and substitutability.

Once management has identified a weak product, additional analysis

	Product	Total contribution margin	Percent of contribution margin	Cost of facilities utilized	Percent of facilities utilized	SIN
Table 13–3: PRESS model rankings of products	810	37065.60	15.45	60.15	4.78	49.94
	927	20021.80	8.35	22.16	1.76	39.56
	812	24948.10	10.40	95.64	7.60	14.22
	801	16909.80	7.05	52.19	4.15	11.98
	813	9229.59	3.89	24.33	1.93	7.82
	802	14919.10	6.22	62.77	4.99	7.75
	815	11767.60	4.91	48.26	3.84	6.27
	811	12740.90	5.31	65.27	5.19	5.44
	807	12026.60	5.01	58.69	4.66	5.39
	808	11315.10	4.72	55.25	4.39	5.07
	914	9049.04	3.77	41.90	3.33	4.27
	959	9581.52	3.99	55.62	4.42	3.61
	951	5275.66	2.20	17.54	1.39	3.47
	806	6273.96	2.62	25.59	2.03	3.36
	805	5843.32	2.44	25.83	2.05	2.89
	960	4635.12	1.93	20.00	1.59	2.35
	923	5048.00	2.10	27.41	2.18	2.03
	809	5311.16	2.21	34.53	2.74	1.79
	814	5392.80	2.25	36.40	2.89	1.75
	803	3757.65	1.57	71.73	5.70	.43
	926	1325.35	.55	9.05	.72	.42
	952	3242.56	1.35	107.88	8.57	.21
Source: Paul W. Hamelman and Edward M. Mazze, "Improving Product Abandonment Decisions," *Journal of Marketing*, April 1972, pp. 20–26.	917	2802.95	1.09	76.53	6.08	.19
	922	837.25	.35	76.63	6.09	.02
	804	655.98	.27	86.82	6.90	.01
			100.00%		100.00%	

is usually needed before the final decision to drop. In fact, a number of factors can cause management to resist making the final drop decision. For instance, management may be considering modifications that could improve the product and its sales and profitability. Or alternatives in the product's marketing program (advertising, channels of distribution, or price) may be under consideration as a way to improve its performance. The product's poor performance may be attributed to an unfavorable economic condition, and the firm hopes that, as the economic situation strengthens, the product's performance will, too. The sales department may exert pressure to keep the product because personal selling is easier with a full line of products. And the production department may need the product to use excess plant capacity and allocate overhead expenses to it. The list of reasons for maintaining the product can grow considerably, with the result that management doesn't drop as many products as it should.

This conclusion is based on a survey of product deletion and on the *80/20 principle,* which states that 80 percent of the items in a firm's product mix generate 20 percent of the firm's sales and profits. It is reasonable to assume that most companies experience the 80/20 phenomenon. Research has shown that 47 percent of survey respondents eliminated five or fewer products in a recent year,[41] which suggests that with the prevalence of the 80/20 principle, a large number of weak products are retailed by firms.

To deal with the problem of carrying too many weak products, the product mix should be systematically and regularly evaluated. A two-step approach to deleting products has been suggested.[42]

First, develop basic criteria to evaluate all products, to identify candidates for deletion. The criteria would include declining gross margins, declining sales in relation to total company sales, or low contribution margin. As we discussed earlier, PRESS is one example of a computer model designed to identify weak products on the basis of contribution margin.

The second step involves establishing more extensive and less quantifiable criteria that management can use to evaluate the products singled out in the first step. These criteria could include (1) future market potential, (2) potential improvement through production modifications, (3) improvement from marketing strategy modification, (4) the amount of useful executive time released by abandoning the product, and (5) the quality of the firm's alternative opportunities. An annual systematic analysis of a company's product mix is an effective means to identify weak products. Eliminating these products can provide substantial rewards for marketing management.

---

[41] Ibid. p. 28.
[42] Kotler, "Phasing out Weak Products," pp. 107–18.

Evaluation of product performance

Evaluation of performance involves comparing plans and actual results. After this evaluation is made, management is in a position to determine if action is necessary to bring actual results in line with the plans. In evaluation of product strategy, a standard procedure is to conduct a *sales variance analysis,* which identifies the sources of variation from planned price and volume standards. When evaluating the product, the major emphasis is on projected sales or volume changes.

A strategic framework for analyzing volume changes attempts to determine if the changes were due to poor planning or inadequate execution of the plans. Poor planning usually means that there was an error in forecasting product sales. The source of the error more specifically is usually associated with failure to accurately estimate market potential or to identify a major environment factor. Poor execution may mean that the product's pricing, channel, or promotional strategies are inadequate. Alternatively, the problem may be inherent in the product. Its quality may be poor. At any rate, effective strategic control attempts to pinpoint the nature of the error and assign responsibility to either the planning or the execution.[43]

LEGAL ASPECTS OF PRODUCTS

The two major legal aspects of products are product liability and product warranty. We'll discuss product liability first.

Product liability

The fact that product liability has become and is likely to remain a major managerial problem is indicated by the following figures:

The number of product liability suits has been rising. There were 50,000 suits per year in the mid-60s; by the mid-70s the number had risen to 200,000 a year. The administrative office of the U.S. District Court reports a 26.4 percent increase in product liability filings in fiscal 1980 over fiscal 1979.[44]

The average settlement has jumped from $12,000 to $79,000. A study of large losses (those amounting to $100,000 or more) indicated that average cost per claimant had risen 68 percent, to $364,587, from 1975 to 1979.[45]

In 1962, only one million-dollar award in a product liability case was recorded. By the late 1970s million-dollar awards were rendered at an average of one per week.[46]

---

[43] James M. Hulbert and Norman E. Toy, "A Strategic Framework for Marketing Control," *Journal of Marketing* 41 (April 1977), pp. 12–20.

[44] J. Geisel, "Product Liability Suits Jump in 80, Court Report Says," *Business Insurance,* October 6, 1980, p. 1.

[45] "Large Product Claims Get More Expensive," *Business Insurance,* September 29, 1980, p. 3.

[46] Paul Busch and Roger A. Formisano, *Managing Product Liability in the 1980s,* unpublished manuscript.

product liability

> **Product liability** is management's legal responsibility for defective products that cause injury to consumers.

An individual injured by a product has four theories of liability by which to sue the manufacturer or seller of the product:[47] negligence, breach of warranty, strict liability, and misrepresentation or fraud.[48] Under **negligence theory,** the injured must prove that the manufacturer was careless and that this carelessness caused the injury. Originally, "priority of contract" between the manufacturer and buyer was necessary. (*Priority* means direct relationship between persons who are party to the same contract.) Most manufacturers were immune from suit because few sold their products directly to consumers. However, in 1966 all states adopted the 1916 ruling of the *MacPherson* v. *Buick Motors Company* case. This ruling stated that a manufacturer is liable for negligently-built products that are reasonably certain to place life and limb in peril, even though consumers do not buy directly from the manufacturer.[49] The negligent manufacturer is thus potentially liable to any user of the product.

Breach of warranty may be based on either express or implied warranty. An *express* warranty is an explicit statement in writing or conversation or in advertising, labeling, or any other form of promotion. Most courts hold that even though some warranties are not express, they are *implied* by law. (We will discuss warranties and legislation affecting them in more detail in a following section.)

Strict liability theory was greatly expanded in the *Greeman* v. *Yuba Power Products* case.[50] In this case the Supreme Court ruled that "a manufacturer is strictly liable when an article he places on the market knowing that it will be used without inspection proves to have a defect that causes injury to a human being." Under strict liability theory, an injured party need only prove that the product is defective and that the defect caused the injury. In strict liability it is not necessary to prove the manufacturer was careless or negligent; the focus is on the product, not the manufacturer's conduct.

Misrepresentation or fraud occurs when a manufacturer engages in deception to secure an unfair or unlawful gain. In a product liability situation this might involve presenting the product as able to perform specific functions it is not designed to perform.

A major role of the marketing department is to control the words

---

[47] Lawrence A. Benningson and Arnold I. Benningson, "Product Liability: Manufacturers Beware!" *Harvard Business Review,* May–June 1974, pp. 122–32.

[48] William L. Trombetta and Timothy L. Wilson, "Foreseeability of Misuse and Abnormal Use of Products by the Consumer," *Journal of Marketing,* July 1975, pp. 48–55.

[49] *MacPherson* v. *Buick Motor Company* 217 N.Y. 382 (New York Court of Appeals, 1916).

[50] *Greeman* v. *Yuba Power Products, Inc.,* 59 Col. 2d 57 (California Supreme Court, 1963).

written and spoken about the product—both to improve safety and to reduce liability.[51] In an era of strict liability, the concept of **product defect** has been expanded to include inadequate instructions on product use and/or failure to provide adequate warnings on product-related dangers. Extravagant advertising claims or an overzealous salesperson may create an express or implied warranty that is not intended by the manufacturer; and breach of this unintended warranty may become the basis for a product liability claim. Typically, the plaintiff has a lighter burden of proof with a breach of warranty than with negligence as the basis of a product liability claim.[52]

The use of superlatives and promises of absolute safety should be avoided: statements like "fail-safe," "absolutely safe," and "harmless" should not be used in advertising copy or other promotional material. For example, a Wyoming court ruled that a sanitation worker was entitled to $114,300 for hand injuries when his hand was drawn into a garbage truck hopper and he was unable to turn off the machine. In promoting the product, the manufacturer had claimed the equipment was safely designed and that even a careless worker could not get hurt.[53]

Promotional material should picture the product with safety equipment in place and should promote safe usage of the product. Consider the following incident from a product liability case.

> *A boy and his father were operating a feeder auger. The boy walked on the auger and tripped, and his foot was mangled. They recovered $480,000.*
>
> *The manufacturer's promotional literature was prominent in the case. This type of auger should have been covered when being operated, but the manufacturer wanted a potential buyer to see a photograph of the auger in its actual state— uncovered. The brochure contained such a picture.*[54]

Expert testimony can become very technical and confusing to a jury. But juries can readily relate to the wording of an ad or to poorly written assembly instructions, for they may have experienced these things themselves. For this reason, advertising and other promotional materials often play a pivotal role in product liability court cases.

The sales force can take a number of positive steps to reduce liability and promote safety. The salesperson, in constant contact with the customers and their day-to-day use of products, can watch for product-usage situations that require additional safety features or design changes. Their

---

[51] This section is adopted from Busch and Formisano, "Managing Product Liability," pp. 16–20.

[52] Tom V. Hallett, "Word Control and Products Liability," *Risk Management,* January 1977, pp. 15–18.

[53] *Insurance Facts,* Insurance Information Institute, 110 Williams St., New York, N.Y. 10038 (March 1977).

[54] "An ounce of prevention is worth a pound of reliability," *Iron Age* 220, no. 5 (August 1, 1977) pp. 140–43.

recommendations should be made to the product safety unit, who in turn should encourage and facilitate this type of communication. The salesperson should check the warnings placed on products to be sure they are intact. Warnings that have been removed should be replaced, and the sales representative should record such findings and the actions taken in the sales call report. Sales representatives should always recommend safety options to prospective customers and include them in proposals and quotations. If a safety option is not purchased, the salesperson should document in the sales call report that it was the buyer's choice not to purchase the option. As new safety devices become available, they should be offered to all known customers.

Sales representatives should be cautious about creating oral warranties. A case has been reported in which a company tape-recorded a salesperson making an oral guarantee that went beyond the product's written warranty. The oral guarantee was found to be legal, and it did expose the supplier to additional liability when the product failed.[55]

Warnings should be used when the manufacturer recognizes an inherent hazard associated with the reasonable and foreseeable use of the product. Of course, the warning should be used only after exhaustive efforts to remove the inherent hazard have proved unsuccessful. The warnings should generally be placed in product manuals and on the product itself. In the case of chemicals and pharmaceuticals, the warning may be included in advertising.[56]

The criteria for effective warnings are (1) to catch the attention of a reasonably prudent person in circumstances of use, (2) to be comprehensible to the average user, and (3) to convey the exact nature and extent of the danger.

In some cases, the use of warnings may not be sufficient. In the *Incollingo* v. *Ewing* case, Parke-Davis included label warnings indicating that blood disorders could develop from using a particular drug.[57] However, the company was found negligent on three counts: (1) the salesperson nullified the label warning by minimizing the drug's danger when presenting it to the physician; (2) the company failed to promote the warning through the salesperson; and (3) Parke-Davis did not take steps to limit the drug's distribution.[58] The major implication of this case is that sales representatives may have to supplement the label warning in order to fully communicate the hazards associated with a product.

Courts look at the substance of a warning and the method of delivery. Salespersons should emphasize a warning in their sales presentations.

---

[55] "Buyers Can Help Block Product Liability Suits," *Purchasing,* February 22, 1977, p. 15.

[56] Hallett, "Word Control," p. 18.

[57] *Intercollingo* v. *Ewing,* 282 A 2d 206 (1971).

[58] W. L. Trombetta and T. L. Wilson, "Foreseeability of Misuse and Abnormal Use of Products by the Consumer," *Journal of Marketing,* July 1975, p. 51.

When the number of purchasers is relatively small (as in many industrial-buying situations), the company may consider sending a letter via certified mail to reinforce the label warning on a product.[59]

The marketing department should consult with the firm's legal counsel on labels, warnings, advertising, and personal-selling messages. The intent of this exchange is to eliminate product liability problems created by the written and spoken word.

Marketing research can play a major role in identifying the product's potential users and their physical and intellectual abilities. Such data can be extremely helpful in identifying possible unintended misuses of the product. It can be conveyed to design and engineering personnel—and may improve the product's design by eliminating the chance of misuse. If the hazard cannot be eliminated in the design phase, then management might consider warnings to inform consumers.

Product warranty

A product warranty is an assurance by the seller of the quality or performance of a product. As we mentioned above, warranties may be either express or implied. Express warranties make explicit assurances either in written or spoken words. Most often they are written. Under the Uniform Commercial Code (which is in effect in all states but Louisiana), most sales of tangible goods are covered by implied warranties of merchantability and fitness—even in the absence of an express warranty. An *implied warranty of merchantability* warrants that a product is fit for the ordinary purpose for which it is sold, is properly packaged and labeled, and conforms to any promises or affirmations made on the label. An *implied warranty of fitness* applies where a buyer relies on the warrantor's judgment that the product will be fit to use for a particular purpose.[60]

Product warranties provide specific advantages to companies that use them properly. A warranty can be a very effective way to differentiate a product, especially in a highly competitive market. For example, when American Motors introduced their Buyer Protection Plan, they clearly distinguished their product from the competition. The American Motors warranty became a model for the industry and enabled American Motors to exert a leadership position on the warranty aspect of its product.

In the services area, several companies have used warranties to compete more effectively. Holiday Inns Inc. offered a money-back guarantee on accommodations that helped the company gain a second chance with unhappy customers and helped to improve its service. A Holiday Inns spokesperson states: "Before we started offering the guarantee there was a good chance someone might leave one of our hotels mad without ever

[59] W. L. Trombetta, "Product Liability: What the New Court Rulings Mean for Management," *Business Horizons,* August 1979, p. 72.

[60] Lawrence P. Feldman, "New Legislation and the Prospects for Real Warranty Reform," *Journal of Marketing,* July 1970, p. 41.

telling us what was wrong. That probably meant we would lose them forever as customers."

In 1984, Republic Airlines offered its customers who flew to Florida and southern California a free round-trip ticket if they traveled on this airline only to have it rain during most of their vacation. The warranty or guarantee is providing Republic with a welcome alternative to a price reduction.[61]

Closely related to the differentiation is the promotional value that a warranty can offer. For example, Curtis Mathes television sets have a four-year warranty, the "longest in the business," which is stressed in its advertising. A written warranty may stimulate legitimate consumer complaints that become a valuable source of information about product defects. This information can be used to improve products and increase the company's chances for success with new-product introduction. And for the consumer, a warranty is a means of reducing the risk associated with purchasing a specific product.

A number of practices have led to consumer problems with warranties: (1) misleading representations, (2) lack of access (i.e., the ability to read and study a warranty before purchase), (3) difficult-to-understand terms, (4) unreasonable burden on consumers to exercise the warranty, and (5) lack of performance by the warrantor in fulfilling the obligation set forth in the warranty.[62]

The 1975 *Magnuson Moss Warranty Act* was passed to accomplish two major goals: (1) to spell out the obligation of warrantors in the event of a malfunctioning product and (2) to indicate the type of recourse available to consumers and to the FTC (which administers the act) when consumer complaints are not satisfied.[63]

---

[61] John Koten. "Aggressive Use of Warranties in Benefiting Many Careers." *The Wall Street Journal.* April 5, 1984, p. 33.

[62] Ibid., pp. 42–43.

[63] Ibid., p. 44.

SUMMARY

The management of a firm's products involves a variety of dimensions, one of which includes the product life-cycle approach. This approach classifies a product as in an introductory, growth, maturity, or decline stage and suggests appropriate action for each.

Product life cycles may vary greatly in length and shape. For instance, fad items often exhibit a short growth stage, followed by rapid decline and withdrawal from the market. The product life-cycle theory is based on the theories of adoption and diffusion of innovations and is a popular research area due to its implications for strategic planning.

Product and brand positioning is a critical strategic aspect of product management. Positioning is a marketing strategy that involves locating a product or brand in the consumer's mind in relation to competing products. The most brilliant product idea is doomed if consumers fail to perceive it as appropriate.

Cannibalization is another concern in the strategic management of a firm's product portfolio. It results when sales of a newly introduced product are gained at the expense of sales of the company's existing products. Cannibalization must be an important consideration when a firm introduces new products, for it may distort their true profit implications.

Firms must also know when to delete products that are in the decline stage of the life cycle. Because of the effects deletion may have on a firm's production, finance, and sales departments and on its customers, the process requires careful planning. Many firms follow elaborate screening and evaluation procedures; the PRESS model is an example. Regular evaluation of the entire portfolio is necessary to identify products for potential deletion because weak products may usurp valuable company capital and time.

Firms have legal responsibility for defective products that cause injury. Product liability is a major managerial problem; but firms can take steps to protect themselves by using label cautions, warnings, advertising, and personal-selling messages.

Warranties are a seller's assurance about the quality or performance of a product. Used properly, they are advantageous to a firm. Warranties can be an effective means of product differentiation and a useful promotional tool. They are also stimuli for legitimate consumer complaints, which may become a valuable source of information about product defects. Consumers see warranties as a way to reduce the risk associated with purchasing a specific product.

KEY CONCEPTS

Product life cycle	Product cannibalization	Strict liability
Classical life-cycle curve	Inadvertent cannibalization	Misrepresentation or fraud
Used-apple policy	Planned cannibalization	Product defect
Saturation	Preemptive cannibalization	Implied warranty of merchantability
Cycle–recycle curve	Product deletion	Implied warranty of fitness
Diffusion process	PRESS model	Magnuson Moss Warranty Act of 1975
Product objectives	80/20 principle	
Standard product	Product liability	Product class
Custom product	Negligence theory	Product form
Differentiated product	Breach of warranty	Brand
Product positioning	Express warranty	Adoption process
Product-positioning map	Implied warranty	

DISCUSSION QUESTIONS AND EXERCISES

1. The product life cycle is applicable to product classes, product forms, and brands. Assume that you are a product manager at Procter & Gamble for Crisco cooking oils. What benefits would you derive from having information on the life cycle of your brand compared to the product class of shortenings versus product form (solid or liquid shortenings)?

2. The hula hoop had a life of less than one year. Ivory soap has been on the market for over 100 years. Make a list of at least five factors affecting the length of the product life cycle. When making your list, be sure to be explicit as to whether you are discussing the product class, product form, or brand.

3. Most of the studies that have analyzed the product life cycle have been conducted during periods of economic stability and growth. In what ways do you think recession and prolonged periods of inflation would influence the product life cycle?

4. Name at least two companies that are effectively marketing a standard product or service.

5. Draw a two-dimensional brand-positioning map for light beers. Decide on the two dimensions, and then place the top five light beers in your local market on the map. What conclusions can you draw from the positioning map regarding the marketing of light beers in your local market?

6. What is product cannibalization? What are the consequences of failing to recognize product cannibalization when evaluating a new-product introduction?

7. What is the 80/20 principle? What is the major implication of this principle for deletion decisions?

8. Compare and contrast the four theories of liability. Which theory places the most burden on the manufacturer or marketer of a product? Why?

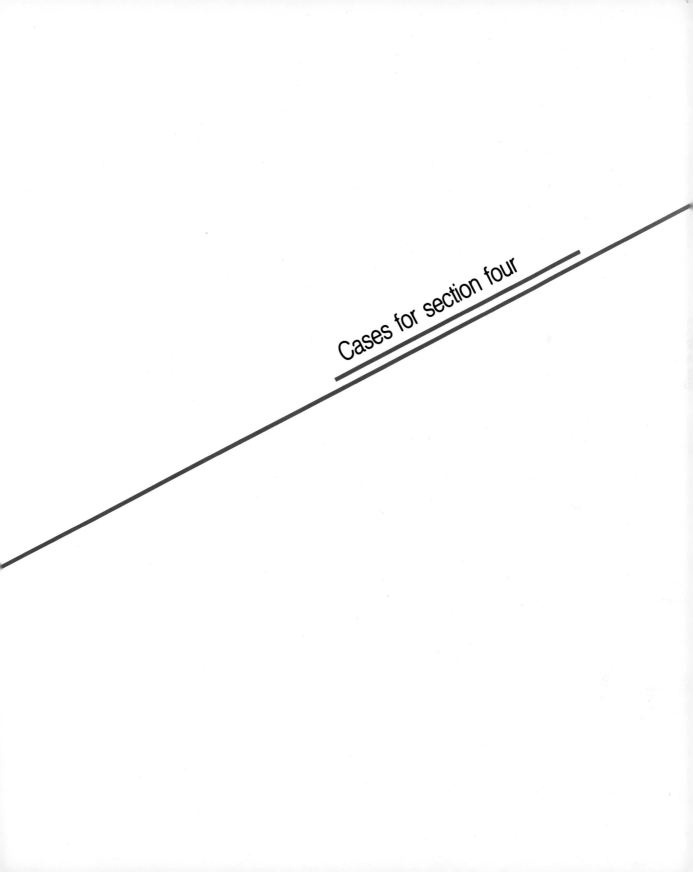

Cases for section four

Case 7: Miller Lite: Product positioning

From the moment Philip Morris Incorporated acquired the Miller Brewing Company in 1970 there has been a shake-up in the beer industry—in particular, light beers. In 10 years Miller has succeeded in developing a 15-million-bbl. market for a product which was traditionally thought to be a marginal item appealing to women and infrequent beer drinkers.

Miller's success stemmed from a well-researched market-positioning plan. Research on one of Miller's unsuccessful "diet" beers, Meister Brau Lite, uncovered one geographic market where the traditional views of light beer did not hold. Many heavy beer drinkers in the steel town of Anderson, Indiana, drank Meister Brau Lite because it didn't "fill them up as much as regular beers." This was found to be a welcome attribute for heavy beer drinkers nationwide—as long as the taste was comparable to regular beers. Thus was formulated the basic strategy for the introduction of Miller Lite beer. Miller's strategy has focused on positioning the brand to the heavy beer drinker, using well-known personalities whose appearance and fame would establish Lite beer as acceptable to men.

The success of their product positioning was shown after only 18 months. Miller Lite was 40 percent ahead of its volume and share objectives. The other major beer producers continued to be unaware of the market potential for light beers for some time—contributing to the success of Miller Lite by allowing it to capture a large share with little or no competition.

Since the successful introduction of Miller Lite, more than 40 low-calorie beers have been introduced. Anheuser-Busch has introduced three: Michelob Light, Natural Light, and the latest, Budweiser Light. In spite of Miller's current 60 percent market share, Miller's marketing staff has no delusion of security. Competition, especially from the nation's number 1 beer producer and number 2 *light* beer producer, Anheuser-Busch, has been intense and is likely to continue.

References

"A-B's Natural Exits Macho Fray." *Advertising Age,* October 19, 1981.

"Research Unlocked the Key to Proper Positioning of Lite Beers." AMA *Marketing News,* July 8, 1983.

Discussion questions

1. What caused Miller to be successful in mass marketing a light beer when other firms had failed?

2. Why has Anheuser-Busch's positioning been relatively unsuccessful against Miller?

3. What do you suppose were the two major product attributes Miller used to position Miller Lite? Construct a product-positioning map using those two major attributes as the axes and attempt to place the top five competitive brands on your map. What information does this map provide to you?

4. What can Miller Lite's marketing team do to maintain their superior position?

5. What can the small, regional beer producers do in the face of such strong competition?

Case 8: Apple III: A new-product introduction

The success of the Apple Computer Company has been a page out of the American dream. From its beginnings in a California garage early in 1976, Steven Jobs and Stephan Wozniak have taken their company to $335 million plus in 1982. In early 1980 Apple went public, and the stock issue was bid up 30 percent in the first day. In spite of the entry of such companies as IBM, Xerox, and others, Apple has remained the market leader with over 20 percent share of the small-computer market.

This phenomenal success story has not been without its problems. Apple's first problem was the ill-fated initial introduction of the Apple III—an up-graded version of their highly successful Apple II computer. Before going public in 1980, the Apple III had been announced and samples had been shipped. Pressure from new investors had encouraged the premature introduction of the Apple III. The problem with the Apple III was that there were still bugs in the system and virtually no software available to run on the computers. Product availability was low, and early purchasers had their machines repaired in the field. Because of the Apple III's introduction, 40 mid-and lower-level managers lost their jobs as well as then-president, Michael M. Scott. Apple stock slipped from a high of 36 to a low of 13.5 over the year of the Apple III introduction.

Finally, in November 1981 the Apple III was relaunched at a base price of about $4,000 for a typical system. Management has been reshuffled, production problems have been worked on, and finally top management has been able to focus attention on the 1983 introduction of Lisa—their newest computer, priced in the $10,000 range.

References

"As Competition Grows, Apple Computer, Inc. Faces Critical Period." *The Wall Street Journal,* November 11, 1981, p. 1.

"How Apple Will Keep Growth Going." *Business Week,* February 8, 1982, pp. 66–71.

"Shiny Apple Got Some Bruises." *The Milwaukee Journal,* December 13, 1981, p. 4.

Discussion questions

1. Why did the Apple III initial introduction fail?

2. What is top management's role in new-product introduction? How can they avoid being pressured into early introduction of a product?

3. How can a firm's growth rate affect its ability to introduce new products? And, conversely, how can new products affect a firm's growth?

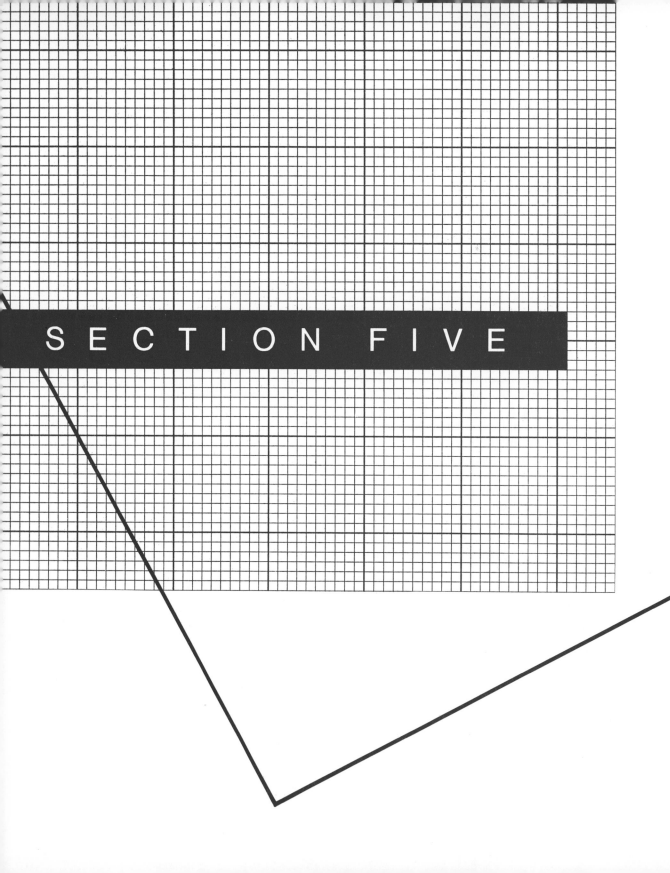

SECTION FIVE

Distribution strategy

In this section, we turn to essential elements of the distribution strategy. Chapter 14 begins with an analysis of channel characteristics, followed by a discussion of channel member functions, types of channels, and major managerial considerations.

Chapter 15 deals with retail and wholesale management. First, we'll look at the nature of retailing and various types of retail institu-

tions, theories of institutional change, and strategic management decisions. A section on wholesaling concentrates on wholesaling functions, types of wholesalers, and strategic management decisions. Finally, the legal aspects of channel, retail, and wholesale management are discussed.

Chapter 16 focuses on elements of physical distribution. We first discuss the total cost approach to physical distribution and then the major elements of customer service. The chapter ends with an evaluation of transportation, warehousing, and inventory management and control as major dimensions of the physical distribution functions.

C H A P T E R 1 4

Channels: Basic concepts and strategies

Product/market strategy
Budget determination
Strategic channel decisions
Management of interorganizational relations within channels
Terms and concepts in channel relationships
Conflict
Conflict-management strategies
Evaluation of channel performance
Qualitative measures
Quantitative measures

Characteristics of marketing channels
The use of intermediaries
Types of channels
Marketing functions and flows
Strategic marketing planning process applied to distribution channels
Situation analysis
Establish channel objectives

Summary

Key concepts

Discussion questions and exercises

453

We begin this chapter with a description of channel characteristics and explain why intermediaries (retailers and wholesalers) are used. Then we'll discuss the functions performed by channel members and the various types of channel structures. Finally, we'll apply the strategic marketing planning process to the channel decision.

CHARACTERISTICS OF MARKETING CHANNELS

We should emphasize two aspects of this definition. First, the term *interdependent organizations* includes manufacturers, wholesalers, and retailers, as well as consumers and industrial users. Second, the definition indicates that both *products* and *services* have channels. Traditionally, channels are most often discussed in terms of physical products. But services (like medical care and banking) have channels of distribution as well.

channel of distribution

> A **channel of distribution** is a set of interdependent organizations involved in the process of making a product or service available for use or consumption.[1]

In this chapter, we use the terms ***reseller*** and ***intermediary*** interchangeably. Table 14–1 lists definitions and common characteristics of intermediaries in marketing channels for consumer and industrial goods.

The use of intermediaries

Intermediaries are used in the channel of distribution for a number of reasons. One of the most basic is that they perform functions that would otherwise have to be assumed by manufacturers or consumers. For example, a wholesale food distributor usually transports food products from a processing plant to the retailer's store or warehouse. The transportation of the food is obviously necessary to make the food physically available to consumers. If this function was not performed by the wholesaler, it would most likely be shifted to either the food processor or the retailer.

The use of intermediaries creates efficiencies that would be difficult (or impossible) for individual manufacturers and retailers to achieve. These include expertise and specialization, economies of scale, and the contact function. The example in Figure 14–1 explains the ***contact efficiency.*** Without an intermediary, there are 15 contacts between three manufacturers and five retailers (3 manufacturers × 5 retailers). Introducing one intermediary (in this case a wholesaler) reduces the number of contacts to eight (three manufacturers and five retailers). We must caution, how-

---

[1] This definition is adapted from Louis W. Stern and Adel I. El-Ansary, *Marketing Channels* (Englewood Cliffs, N.J.: Prentice-Hall, 1982), p. 3.

Table 14–1: Definitions and characteristics of common intermediaries	Intermediary	Definition	Distinguishing characteristics
	Retailer	Merchant, or occasionally an agent, whose main business is selling directly to ultimate consumer.	Size of units in which retailer sells is incidental rather than a primary element in character; sells typically to ultimate consumer.
	Wholesaler	Business unit that buys and resells merchandise to retailers and other merchants and/or to industrial, institutional, and commercial users.	Many operate on a very small scale and in small lots; habitually sell for resale; do not sell in significant amounts to ultimate consumers; significant portion of sales to industrial users.
	Industrial distributor	Merchant engaged primarily in selling industrial goods.	Specialized types include *metal warehouses*, which handle about 20 percent of total steel tonnage; operates on the differential between mill prices for standard lots and smaller quantities and mill supply houses, which handle as many as 20,000 items in 600 product lines.
	Manufacturer's agent	An agent who generally operates on an extended contractual basis; often sells within an exclusive territory; handles noncompeting but related lines.	May be authorized to sell a definite portion of the output of principals represented; also known as "manufacturer's representative."
	Sales agent	Intermediary in title-passing process, characterized by responsibility for disposing of principal's entire output on an extended contractual basis.	The only functional intermediary frequently involved in financing the principal.
	Rack jobber	A limited-function wholesaler who supplies merchandise and sets up displays.	Receives payment only for items sold; usually puts merchandise in retail stores on a consignment basis; provides special services of selective brand and item merchandising; most prevalent in food business.
	Facilitating agent	Performs or assists in performance of one or several of marketing functions.	Takes neither title to goods nor negotiates purchase of sales; includes bankers, graders, inspectors, advertisers, marketing researchers, packers, shippers.

Sources: Irving J. Shapiro, *Marketing Terms*, 3d ed. (West Long Branch, N.J.: S-M-C Publishing, 1969); and *Marketing Definitions: A Glossary of Marketing Terms*, compiled by the Committee on Definitions of the American Marketing Association, 1960.

**Figure 14–1:
Distributor's effect on
contactual efficiency**

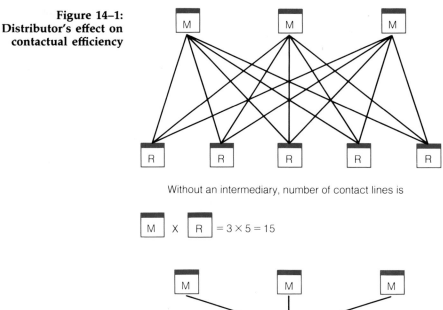

Without an intermediary, number of contact lines is

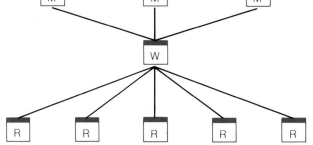

With an intermediary, number of contacts becomes

M = Manufacturer
R = Retailer

ever, that using more and more intermediaries is subject to diminishing returns.[2]

Intermediaries facilitate the exchange process between consumers and manufacturers of products or providers of services. Specifically, intermediaries do this by performing a *sorting* function for providers of goods

_____
[2] Ibid., p. 222.

and services and by assisting in the searching process.[3] The sorting function comprises the following activities:

1. *Sorting out* is breaking down a heterogeneous supply into separate stocks that are more homogeneous, as in the grading of agricultural products.

2. *Accumulation* is the bringing of similar stocks together into a larger homogeneous supply.

3. *Allocation* is breaking a homogeneous supply into smaller lots. At the wholesaler level, this allocation process is known as "breaking bulk": wholesalers take carload lots and then break them down into smaller units to be sold to retailers.

4. *Assorting* is building up an array of products for use in association with each other. Wholesalers build assortments of goods for retailers. Retailers build assortments for their customers.

The searching process involves producers' search for consumers' wants and needs and consumers' attempts to locate goods and services to meet their needs.[4] Marketing intermediaries ease the search process by offering producers a way to present goods and services to consumers. The producers receive valuable feedback that allows them to make appropriate adjustments in goods and services. Retailers try to select the goods and services that best meet their customers' needs. And—thanks to the retailer's assortment of goods—consumers are able to compare four or five brands of frozen dinners in a supermarket or three or four brands of suits in a clothing store.

Types of channels

There are a great number and variety of distribution channels. To increase our understanding of the nature of a channel, we can examine certain basic types. In this discussion, we'll examine the institutional levels involved in the channel for consumer and industrial goods.

Consumer channels. Figure 14–2 shows several basic *consumer goods channels.* Channel A (producer–consumer) is a direct marketing channel: producers market their goods or services directly to the consumer. Products that are highly perishable (eggs, fruit, vegetables) or that require considerable personal selling effort (encyclopedias, cooking ware, life insurance) are often marketed this way. Companies that market their products through the mail also engage in direct-channel marketing. Some of the best-known direct-channel marketers are Avon Products, Fuller Brush, and Electro-Lux.

---

[3] For a detailed discussion of sorting and searching functions, see Wroe Alderson, "Factors Governing the Development of Marketing Channels," in *Marketing Channels for Manufactured Products,* ed. R. M. Clewett (Homewood, Ill: Richard D. Irwin, 1954), pp. 5–22.

[4] Stern and El-Ansary, *Marketing Channels,* p. 220.

Figure 14–2: Basic channels of distribution for consumer products

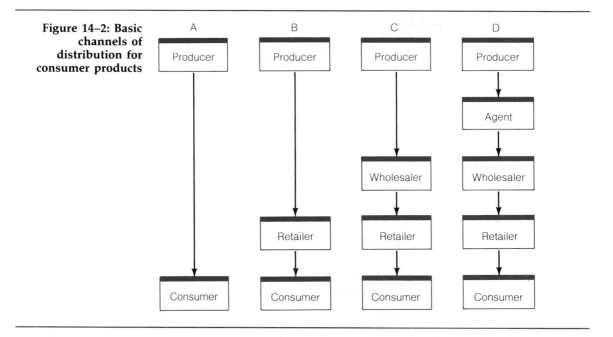

Channel B (producer–retailer–consumer) is common in consumer markets. Products such as clothing, gasoline, and automobiles are sold through this channel. General Motors, Ford, and Chrysler sell their automobiles through independent retailers. Clothing manufacturers such as Levi Strauss and Arrow employ sales reps to call on department stores and clothing retailers who sell these products to consumers.

Products that require widespread distribution—groceries, hardware, tobacco, and drugs—use channel C (producer–wholesaler–retailer-consumer). Producers often require the services of a wholesaler because the cost of contacting all the potential retailers would be prohibitive. Retailers also rely on wholesalers to provide such services as transportation, credit, storage, and the purchase of small quantities.

Channel D (producer–agent–wholesaler–retailer–consumer) is used when the producer has a narrow or single product line and the market is widely dispersed geographically. This situation is common among food canners who process only foods native to their locations but whose market is widespread and is reached only through wholesale and retail accounts. An agent (usually called a food broker) makes contacts for the canner and brings buyer and seller together. These are services that the canner could not perform efficiently alone.

Industrial channels. *Industrial goods channels* appear similar to those for consumer products but there are important differences because of

Figure 14–3: Basic channels for industrial products

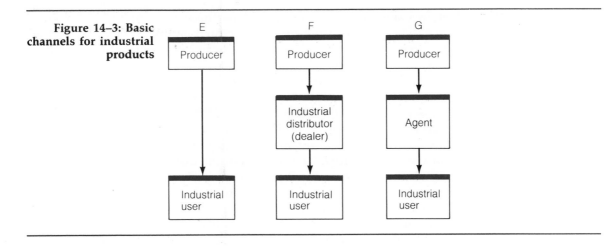

(1) the nature of industrial products and markets and (2) the types of intermediaries involved. Figure 14–3 shows some of the most common channels of distribution for industrial products. As illustrated by channel E (producer–industrial user), producers of industrial products frequently market their products directly to their customers. A common arrangement is for the industrial manufacturer to have its own sales force in direct contact with the company's customers. Products that are technically complex or need technical support are frequently marketed using a channel E arrangement. The industrial user needs the direct contact to make effective use of the product, and the manufacturer prefers the direct contact as a way of ensuring its effective use. By employing its own sales force, the manufacturer can maintain an aggressive personal selling effort, often important when marketing industrial products. A geographically concentrated market is another consideration favoring a direct marketing channel for industrial products.

In channel F (producer–industrial distributor–industrial user), the industrial distributor is similar to the wholesaler in the marketing channel for consumer goods. To understand the industrial distributor's role, it helps to analyze the reasons industrial users buy from them.[5]

Industrial distributors provide speedier delivery than manufacturers can. Distributors usually have warehouses located nearer the industrial buyer and typically operate more warehouses than a manufacturer could afford. Speedy delivery reduces the industrial buyer's investment in inventory and storage space.

A distributor may also enable a buyer to reduce paperwork costs. A

---

[5] The discussion of these reasons is adapted from Ralph S. Alexander, James C. Cross, and Richard M. Hill, *Industrial Marketing* (Homewood, Ill: Richard D. Irwin, 1967), pp. 223–37.

metalworking firm, for example, was purchasing 144 supply and maintenance items directly from 66 manufacturers. A survey showed that all these items could be bought from four or five distributors at competitive prices. The distributor would deliver many items in a single shipment and bill on one invoice. Buying directly from manufacturers required 30 times as much paperwork as did buying from the distributors!

In some cases the distributor can actually offer lower prices than those available directly from the producer. For example, a power and light company was buying bolts for machine replacement parts at $1 per dozen from the manufacturer. The price from the distributor was 52 cents per dozen. If the industrial distributor can offer a lower price than the manufacturer, it's usually because of transportation charges. The distributor usually delivers with his or her own equipment without a specific charge; the manufacturer ships FOB factory, which means that the buyer must pay freight.

An industrial distributor also provides better service to buyers. A distributor of metal products, for example, can cut products to the specification of the small buyer—a service that the manufacturer can't afford to provide except to its largest buyers.

The industrial distributor provides further benefits to customers: (1) a readily available source of product information, (2) a convenient and liberal source of credit, and (3) easy-to-make adjustments on complaints about products, billing, or service.

Channel G (producer–agent–industrial user) agents are frequently used by manufacturers of industrial products. Agents usually work on commission for a limited number of manufacturers. They do not take title to the products they handle, although some agents may carry an inventory of the products they sell.

Agents offer specific advantages to manufacturers. One of the most important is that their costs are low compared to those of industrial distributors or manufacturer branch offices. Agents are helpful in introducing new products, especially in markets in which the manufacturer has not previously sold. A small manufacturer who lacks experience in marketing may be able to sell the company's entire output through one agent. An agent usually provides better sales service than an industrial distributor. The distributor may have a catalog of 30,000 items made by hundreds of manufacturers. Its sales force can devote little time or effort to selling any one product. In contrast, the agent handles a much more limited number of items, usually not more than two dozen.

Agents do have drawbacks, though. Industrial sales managers feel they cannot control agents' promotional activities as completely as they can those of their own sales force. It is especially difficult to induce agents to engage in selling that doesn't immediately result in commissions. Agents are also criticized for lack of flexibility in situations that require competitive bidding. When a manufacturer's product requires technical service in selling, installation, or maintenance, the agent may be unwilling or unable to provide it. Overall, the use of agents may be viable only when the sales volume with the agent is small. The sales commission on large-volume business may cause the manufacturer to switch to another channel structure, such as direct selling (channel G) through the company's own sales force.

You can see that industrial manufacturers have many trade-offs to consider when selecting a channel for their products. And different channels may have to be used as circumstances change (say, due to fluctuations in sales volume or introduction of new products). Now, let's turn our attention to the channel member functions.

Marketing functions and flows

marketing function

> A **marketing function** is a task performed by an intermediary in the channel of distribution to create form, time, place, and possession utilities.

Form utility is the satisfaction consumers derive from a product that has been converted into a usable state. For example, raw cotton can be processed and formed into a shirt. The creation of form utility usually takes place in the manufacturing and processing stage of the channel, although wholesalers and retailers may create form utility when involved in the process of assembling products. *Time utility* is the satisfaction consumers derive from having a product available when they want it. It is created through the storage of products. *Place utility* is created by satisfying a want based on geographical considerations. Transportation creates place utility by moving an item from where it has been produced, grown, or mined to where it is desired. *Possession utility* is the satisfaction derived from using the product as required or needed. The title transfer function in the channel creates possession utility.[6]

marketing flow

> The **marketing flow** is similar to a function: *flow* describes the movement created by the performance of function in the channel of distribution.

Figure 14–4 shows eight important flows in a marketing channel. The flows are illustrated in the context of a channel for consumer goods, but the concept is applicable to channels for industrial goods as well.

---

[6] The definition of the types of utilities is based on Irving J. Shapiro, *Marketing Terms: Definitions, Explanations, and/or Aspects* (West Long Branch, N.J.: S-M-C Publishing, 1973).

Figure 14–4: Major flows in the channel of distribution

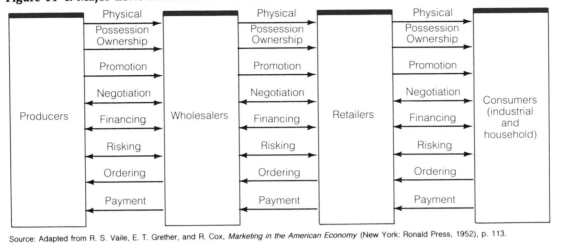

Source: Adapted from R. S. Vaile, E. T. Grether, and R. Cox, *Marketing in the American Economy* (New York: Ronald Press, 1952), p. 113.

Physical possession, ownership, and promotion are forward flows from producer to consumer. For example, promotional effort moves from producer to wholesaler, who promotes the product to a retailer, who directs advertising and personal selling efforts at the consumer. Negotiation, financing, and risk taking are reciprocal flows. They move in both directions. Ordering and payment are backward flows, originating at the channel's end and moving in reverse order in the channel. Lets take a closer look at each of these flows.[7]

Physical possession is the actual movement of the physical product from the producer to the final consumer. *Ownership flow* is the movement of the product's title (or ownership) from one marketing institution to another. The movement of the flow of the physical product may be different from the flow of title. A product may physically move from producer to transportation company and warehouse to consumer, but the title may move from producer directly to consumer.

Promotional flow may take various forms, including advertising, personal selling, public relations, and publicity. A company may decide to use a push or a pull promotional strategy. (See Figure 14–5.) The *push strategy* directs promotional efforts at the intermediaries involved in the channel. The usual types are personal selling and sales promotion efforts (price reductions in the form of cash discounts) and incentives (prizes or all-expense-paid trips). The purpose of the push strategy is to move the product through the channel to make it physically available. Retailers

_____

[7] The discussion of marketing flows is adapted from Stern and El-Ansary, *Marketing Channels*, p. 15.

Figure 14–5: Pull versus push promotion strategies

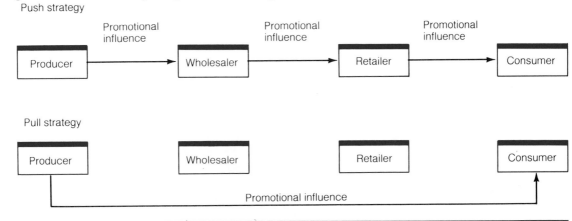

try to attract customers to their stores and use personal selling to complete sales.

The **_pull strategy_** focuses promotional efforts directly at the consumer or user of the product. The goal is to create demand for the product at the end of the channel, causing the product to be pulled through the channel as wholesalers and retailers try to profit by accommodating the needs of consumers. Advertising is usually the most commonly used promotional tool in a pull strategy.

Negotiation occurs at all levels in the channel, and all aspects of exchange may be negotiated. For industrial products, the manufacturer's purchasing agent does the negotiating with prospective suppliers and vendors. The process is usually started with a bid modified to reflect factors pertinent to the company's needs, such as price, technical specifications for the product, delivery, and financing.

Financing occurs whenever inventories are held by one member of the channel. When the wholesaler takes title and assumes physical possession of a portion of the manufacturer's output, the wholesaler is financing the manufacturer. The financing function may be shifted among channel members. For example, in the furniture industry, traditional furniture retailers operate on a sold-order basis only and do not participate in the backward financing flow. Alternatively, "warehouse" furniture retailers do participate in this flow directly and receive benefits from manufacturers in the form of lower prices and preferential treatment.[8]

Risking or **_risk taking_** is similar to negotiation in that it occurs at all levels within the channel and may involve all aspects of the exchange. A retailer who makes prepayment for goods assumes the risk of having

---

[8] Ibid., p. 16.

This ad is directed at retailers and is encouraging them to handle Aloe Essence Scent Arrid Extra Dry deodorant. This is an example of a push strategy.

America's #1 deodorant brand launches a major new product.

Introducing

New Arrid Aloe Essence Scent

The MAGIC OF ALOE has added dramatic growth to many H&BA categories.

Now Arrid is the first anti-perspirant/deodorant with New Aloe Essence Scent.

• Heavy TV schedule—special Aloe Essence Scent commercials.
• FSI with scratch n' sniff trial device.
• 44,500,000 25¢ coupons.
• In-store display with scented tear pads.
• Introductory trade allowances.

STOCK NEW ARRID ALOE ESSENCE SCENT IN SPRAY, SOLID AND ROLL-ON.
Tough on wetness and odor, with a clean, fresh scent.   © 1984 Carter-Wallace, Inc.

Courtesy Carter-Wallace, Inc.

the goods delivered on time and without damage. A manufacturer who provides money to a retailer for advertising in that retailer's market assumes the risk of having the retailer perform according to the terms of agreement. The greatest risks usually derive from taking physical possession and/or title to products.

Through advertising directly to consumers and the use of coupons, management uses a pull strategy to market Sunlight dishwashing liquid.

Courtesy of Lever Brothers Company

Orders are usually written requests from a customer to the retailer or other channel member to purchase a product. Ordering is simply the flow of orders through the channel. The promotional flow's objective is to stimulate orders. Salespeople usually consider the customer's signing of the order a major objective of the personal selling effort.

Payment is the actual transfer of money from the consumer to the retailer, who in turn pays the wholesaler, etc., backward-financed through the channel. Payment may be directly to a retailer; or, if the customer financed the purchase, the payment may flow from bank to retailer, with the customer repaying the bank. Banks and other credit institutions play major roles in facilitating the payment flow in channels of distribution.

Multiple channels. Companies may begin with simple marketing channels, such as selling directly to consumers or industrial users. As the company grows and develops, however, need also grows to add marketing channels. A major reason for using *multiple channels* is to reach new markets with products of varying prices. A Kentucky distiller, for example, bottles bourbon under 4,000 labels per year. The differences in the products are age (new to 20 years old) and alcoholic content (80 to 100 proof). A private club in Tallahassee, a supermarket in Cleveland, and a liquor distributor in St. Louis—each may have its own label of bourbon, and all from the same distiller's barrel.[9]

Multiple channels may be needed to meet the varying sales volumes and profitability generated by different geographic market segments. In Chicago, for example, an industrial parts manufacturer sells through its own sales force directly to users in the immediate area. The Chicago market is geographically concentrated, purchases are large, and sales reps can make as many as a dozen calls per day. But in rural areas, the manufacturer uses agents because the sales volume and profits are too small to support full-time sales representatives.[10]

The type of market and the degree of control the manufacturer wants may be another reason to use multiple channels. Warner & Swasey of Cleveland, Ohio, manufactures construction equipment, machine tools, and textile machinery. The construction equipment is sold through industrial distributors, who sell a complete line of products to a wide variety of markets (such as contractors of all sizes and federal, state, and municipal governments). However, a direct marketing channel is used to sell machine tools and textile machines. Direct selling here is more efficient and less costly and affords Warner & Swasey a greater degree of control.[11]

Figure 14–6 shows the multiple channels used by a phonograph record manufacturer. These channels were developed as the demand for records expanded and new product segments developed. Specific channels had to be developed to reach the jukebox, teenage, and classical markets, etc. To improve promotional efficiency, record clubs were developed and operated by manufacturers and retailers. Jukebox locations were serviced by specialized firms such as jukebox operators. The rack jobber was used to service specific retail accounts. (See Table 14–1 for a definition of *rack jobber.*) While the complexity of the distribution structure greatly in-

---

[9] Robert E. Weigand, "Fit Products and Channels to Your Markets," *Harvard Business Review* 55, no.1 (January/February 1977), p. 103.

[10] Ibid., p.100.

[11] Joseph T. Bailey, "From Product Creation to Servicing—Successful Marketing Is a Team Effort," *Industrial Marketing,* April 1975, p. 54.

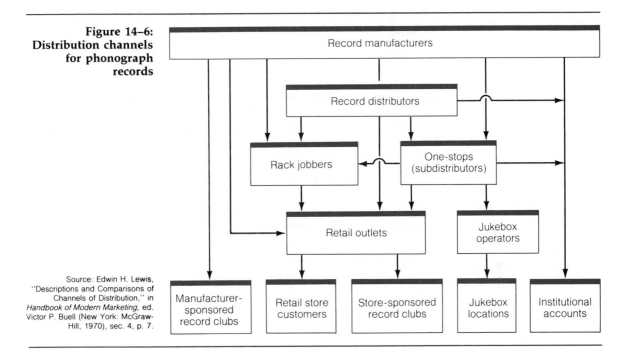

Figure 14–6: Distribution channels for phonograph records

Source: Edwin H. Lewis, "Descriptions and Comparisons of Channels of Distribution," in *Handbook of Modern Marketing*, ed. Victor P. Buell (New York: McGraw-Hill, 1970), sec. 4, p. 7.

creased, so did the efficiency of the marketing channel for phonograph records.

STRATEGIC MARKETING PLANNING PROCESS APPLIED TO DISTRIBUTION CHANNELS

The following discussion applies the strategic planning process to the channel decision. Our goal is to focus on those aspects of the strategic planning process that relate directly to channel management. Figure 14–7 provides an overview of the process as applied to the channel decision.

Situation analysis

The consumer. A thorough understanding of the consumer's shopping and buying habits is important when developing channel strategy. Basic questions regarding consumer or industrial buying behavior must be answered:

1. How many buyers are there in the target market and where are they located?
2. What changes are occurring in purchasing patterns for the product?
3. When and where is the product purchased?
4. Where and how is the product consumed or used?

5. How much effort will the consumer expend in the search for the product?

6. What are the informational and technical product-support needs of the buyer at time of purchase?

7. What are the buyer's needs after the sale for technical and product information?

Let's discuss several of these questions.

A basic consideration is the number of buyers. A&W Root Beer was initially marketed at the company's drive-in restaurants. But the company

Figure 14–7: Strategic marketing planning process applied to channel decision

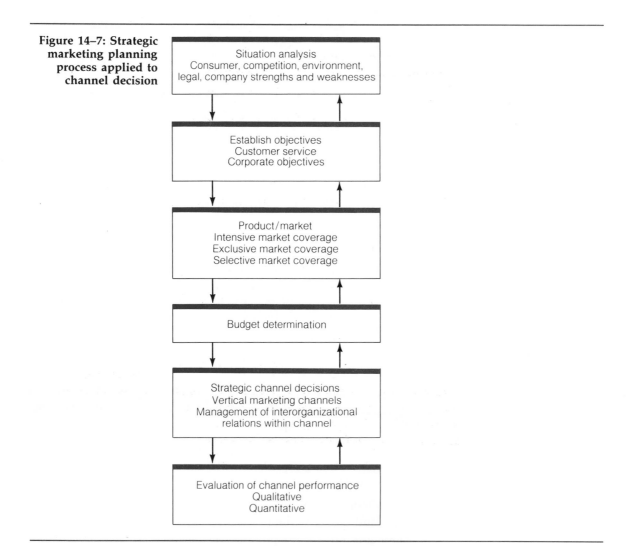

felt it could increase the number of buyers and the frequency of purchases by marketing its root beer through supermarkets and other food stores.[12]

Geographic location and dispersion of buyers is another factor affecting channels. Selling to buyers in many locations is more expensive than selling to the same number of buyers concentrated in a few geographical centers. Virginia National Bank opened 30 neighborhood self-service branches to improve its service to the singles and young-married market, which was dispersed throughout the metropolitan area.[13]

Customer purchasing patterns influence the type of channel as well. For example, as more women have become wine buyers, wine manufacturers have placed more emphasis on distributing their products in supermarkets in addition to the traditional retail outlet, the liquor store.[14]

The competition. A producer's channel design is also influenced by channel competition of four different types: (1) between channel members, (2) among channel members, (3) between channels, and (4) between channel members for the use of channel members. Although Revlon sells through various types of outlets, such as drug stores, Esteé Lauder restricts its distribution to department store cosmetic counters in order to reach a more sophisticated market.[15] Competition may require new channel designs that provide more services or efficiency.

The environment. Environmental conditions also have a strong impact on channel design. Business and economic conditions, technology, the extent of international marketing, and social and ethical elements—all affect channel design. Philip Morris and R. J. Reynolds have found distribution channel operations the major obstacle in their attempts to ensure their respective cigarette shares in the Brazilian market. Expensive direct distribution is necessary because no acceptable indirect-channel structure exists in Brazil to handle the product.[16]

Legal issues. The legal issues in channels are discussed in Chapter 15.

Company strengths and weaknesses. The general categories or issues involved in analyzing a company's strengths and weaknesses are: the organization's financial status, production capacity and processes, plant location, share of market, product reputation and quality, size and quality of the labor force, and technological advantage.

---

[12] "The Rising Tide of A&W Root Beer," *Sales Management,* February 18, 1974, p. 36.
[13] "Marketing Observer," *Business Week,* August 9, 1976, p. 31.
[14] "Wine: Selling the Mass Market," *Business Week,* February 23, 1974, pp. 64–70.
[15] "Esteé Lauder's Golden Give-Aways," *Forbes,* July 15, 1975, p. 41.
[16] "Marketing Observer," *Business Week,* October 4, 1976, p. 104.

Several of these issues are very prominent within the beer industry. By acquiring the Jos. Schlitz Brewing Co., Stroh's significantly increased its own strength. The major advantages to Stroh's were the increase in production capacity and the strong channel of distribution. Stroh's was able to increase its 11-million-barrel annual capacity by some 18.8 million barrels, for a total capacity of 29.8 million barrels. However, more significant was the acquisition of Schlitz's very strong distribution channels in the South and Southwest.[17] Stroh's also acquired F&M Shaefer Corporation for $32 million in 1981. This move expanded Stroh's distribution to the Northeast and helped the company build on its strong position in the Midwest. These acquisitions were a major final step for Stroh's in becoming a national brewer, and that's what it takes to survive for the long term in the highly competitive beer industry.[18]

Establish channel objectives

Channel objectives are based on two primary sources: (1) a specified level of customer service and (2) the overall corporate objectives.

Customer service. The channel of distribution is established to provide for a specific type and level of customer service. The level of service can be specified for all members of the channel including other manufacturers, intermediaries such as retailers and wholesalers, and the final buyer or consumer. The dimensions of customer service are many and varied but include such things as (1) the time needed to process and fill orders, (2) the percentage of orders to be filled from inventory, and (3) the quality and physical condition of goods upon delivery. (Customer service levels are discussed in detail in Chapter 16.)

Failure to meet customer service level is a major problem facing U.S. steel manufacturers. Major steel buyers, such as Ford Motor Co., Senco Products, and G. F. Business Equipment, are concerned that the quality of products and services will decline further as U.S. manufacturers diversify into other industries. These concerns have prompted some buyers to protect themselves by entering into long-term relationships with Canadian steelmakers.[19]

Corporate objectives. A continued level of sales growth is a common objective for many corporations. Development of the channel and selected intermediaries can play a key role in achieving this type of objective. In the early 1980s, sales of personal computers were increasing at rates of 50 percent to 100 percent each year. In order to achieve its 1982 goal of selling 200,000 personal computers, IBM used several independent re-

[17] "Schlitz Board to Meet Soon on Stroh Offer . . . ," *The Wall Street Journal,* March 30, 1982. p. 4.

[18] "Stroh's Gamble in Swallowing Schlitz," *Business Week,* April 26, 1982, p. 31.

[19] "Buyers' Market? Now Steel's Customers Are Taking Their Turn at Jolting the Industry," *The Wall Street Journal,* May 21, 1982, p.1.

Figure 14–8: Relationship between market segmentation strategies and market coverage	Strategy		
	Aggregated	Disaggregated	Niche
Market coverage	Intensive	Selective	Exclusive
Number of intermediaries used in a given geographic area	As many as possible	A limited number	One

tailers, including Computerland. IBM also planned to add more independent retailers in North America and Europe.[20]

Product/market strategy

The product/market is a product or group of products that satisfies a want or need in the market. The product/market concept facilitates the process of market segmentation.

The three strategic approaches to the market are aggregated, disaggregated, and niche. The primary channel consideration in implementing these strategies is the extent of market coverage, which is the number of intermediaries used to service the market. The relationship between these strategies and market coverage is illustrated in Figure 14–8.

Intensive distribution. An *intensive distribution* policy means that the maximum possible number of retailers is used to distribute the product. Generally, this policy suits manufacturers of convenience goods that consumers purchase frequently and with a minimum of effort. Examples of these convenience products are newspapers, candy, cigarettes, and soft drinks. In the industrial market, products such as standardized parts are marketed intensively in that a manufacturer tries to have the product available in as many outlets as will carry it. The manufacturer using an intensive distribution policy enjoys certain advantages. Greater product recognition and more impulse buying are likely due to broad exposure of the product to buyers. This, of course, can mean increased sales volume. However, some disadvantages of intensive distribution may prevent sales from reaching their highest potential volume. Retailers may not cooperate fully with a manufacturer's marketing program because the retailer doesn't have an exclusive right to handle the product. Retailers would compete with each other, and this could cause conflict between retailers as well as between the manufacturer and selected retailers. Another problem with intensive distribution is that it may encourage orders too small to be profitable.

[20] "IBM Home Computer Starts Strong, but Competitors Are Still Thriving," *The Wall Street Journal*, February, 1982, p. 19.

Exclusive distribution. ***Exclusive distribution*** means that only one retailer or wholesaler in a geographic area carries a product. Usually there is a contractual agreement between the manufacturer and the intermediary covering the details of this type of arrangement. Products marketed by exclusive distribution tend to be very high-quality and among the highest-priced in their product categories. Companies using the exclusive approach are Ethan Allen, Inc. (furniture) and Curtis Mathes (television). Caterpillar

Because only one retailer in a geographic area carries the brand, Lois sportswear is an example of a company using exclusive distribution.

ILLUSTRATION BY BILL RIESER   © LOIS 1984

L'AGENCE

Courtesy LOIS

MACY'S NEW YORK • BULLOCK'S • B. ALTMAN • JORDAN MARSH

tractors are an example in the industrial market. The main advantage of exclusive distribution is the close cooperation that can be developed between the manufacturer and intermediary. The manufacturer relies exclusively upon the wholesaler or retailer to implement the distribution and promotional program for the product. The main disadvantage to the manufacturer is that success of the product's distribution and promotion program depends on how well that one retailer or wholesaler performs. The manufacturer has put all the eggs into one basket. Careful selection and explicit contract terms can do much to eliminate the dangers of poor performance from a retailer or wholesaler, though.

Selective distribution.   **Selective distribution** is a compromise between the extremes of intensive and exclusive types. In practice, it can vary from nearly intensive to nearly exclusive. Usually, shopping goods that consumers purchase infrequently and compare considerably on price and product features are distributed selectively. When selecting resellers, the manufacturer usually has a set of criteria (capital requirements, order size, annual sales volume, inventory turnover rates) the resellers must meet. Selective distribution is used for certain types of automobiles. You've probably noticed there are usually several Ford and Chevrolet dealers within a metropolitan area. Arrow shirts and Zenith and RCA also use selective distribution. The advantages and disadvantages of the selective approach are similar to those for exclusive distribution.

Budget determination

The budget and financial aspects of channels are significant because of (1) the long-term nature of channel investments and (2) the large dollar expenditure involved in channels.

Compared to other marketing mix variables, establishing or changing a distribution channel requires a longer time. For example, a franchiser-franchisee agreement typically runs 15 to 20 years. In contrast, prices can be established or changed within a comparatively shorter time, while promotional and product decisions require a moderate length of time to be effected. Research emphasizes the differences of the marketing mix variables on the time dimension. One study found that capital budgeting techniques were employed in 90 percent of the decisions concerning distribution channels as against 81, 64, 50, and 50 percents for product development, sales management, advertising, and marketing research decisions, respectively. The average payback period for investment in channels was 7.6 years, or over twice the 3.8 years for new-product development.[21]

The large dollar expenditure involved in channels is illustrated by the Caterpillar dealer organization.

[21] Richard T. Hise and Robert H. Strawser, "Application of Capital Budgeting Techniques to Marketing Operations," *MSU Business Topics,* Summer 1970, pp. 69–76.

Some observers say the dealers have made the company. Competitors privately concede that their own dealer networks can't approach Caterpillar's in size or service. The company has 122 dealers in the United States and 148 abroad, operating out of 900 places of business. The average dealership's net worth is around $8 million, and some dealers have sales of more than $100 million per year. One such dealership is the John Fabick Tractor Company of Fenton, Missouri, near St. Louis. Fabick has more than 400 employees operating out of Fenton and four branches in Missouri and Illinois. Besides large facilities for repairing machines, the dealer also maintains a fleet of 100 trucks on 24-hour call to minister to ailing equipment. Each truck, specially equipped, costs about $50,000.[22]

Strategic channel decisions

Now let's turn our attention to the two major strategic channel decisions: (1) the development and management of vertical marketing channels, or systems, and (2) the management of interorganizational relations within the channel.

Conventional versus vertical marketing channels. Up to this point we've discussed *conventional marketing channels* to develop your understanding of their basic framework. We must stress, though, that conventional channels oversimplify the realities of more complex channels. Moreover, conventional channels have been plagued with problems caused by a lack of coordination and cooperation among channel members. As one noted authority stated, conventional marketing channels are:

Highly fragmented networks in which loosely aligned manufacturers, wholesalers, and retailers have bargained with each other at arm's length, negotiated aggressively over terms of sale, and otherwise behaved autonomously. For the most part, the firms participating in these provisional coalitions have traditionally operated on a relatively small scale and performed a conventionally defined set of marketing activities.[23]

In contrast, *vertical marketing systems* have been developed to deal with problems of traditional marketing channels. Vertical marketing systems are defined as:

Professionally managed and centrally programmed networks [that are] preengineered to achieve operating economies and maximum market input. . . . Stated alternatively, these vertical marketing systems are rationalized and capital-intensive networks designed to achieve technological, managerial, and promotional economies through the integration, coordination, and synchronization of marketing flows from points of production to points of ultimate use.[24]

[22] Harlan S. Byrne, "What Recession? A Leaping Caterpillar Is a Wondrous Thing, Even Its Rivals Agree," *The Wall Street Journal,* April 19, 1976, p. 12. Reprinted by permission of *The Wall Street Journal,* © Dow Jones & Company, Inc., 1976. All rights reserved.

[23] Bert C. McCammon, Jr., "Perspectives for Distribution Programming," in *Vertical Marketing Systems,* ed. Louis P. Bucklin (Glenview, Ill: Scott, Foresman, 1970), p. 43.

[24] Ibid.

Table 14–2: Organizational dimension of conventional and vertical marketing systems

Dimension	Conventional	Administered	Contractual	Corporate
Relation of units to an inclusive goal	No inclusive goals	Units with disparate goals, but informal collaboration for inclusive goals	Units with disparate goals but some organization for inclusive goals	Units organized for achievement of inclusive goals
Locus of inclusive decision making	Within units	In interaction of units without a formal inclusive structure	At top of inclusive structure, subject to unit ratification	At top of inclusive structure
Locus of authority	Exclusively at unit level	Exclusively at unit level	Primarily at unit level	At top of hierarchy of inclusive structure
Structural provision for division of labor	No formally structured division of labor within an inclusive context	Units structured autonomously, may agree to *ad hoc* division of labor, without restructuring	Units structured autonomously, may agree to a division of labor, which may affect their structure	Units structured for division of labor within inclusive organization
Commitment to a leadership subsystem	Commitment only to unit leaders	Commitment only to unit leaders	Norms of moderate commitment	Norms of high commitment
Prescribed collectivity-orientation of units	Little or none	Low to moderate	Moderate to high	High

Source: Adapted from Roland L. Warren, "The Interorganizational Field as a Focus for Investigation," *Administrative Science Quarterly* 12 (1967), pp. 396–419; and Louis W. Stern and Adel I. El-Ansary, *Marketing Channels*, 2d ed. (Englewood Cliffs, N.J.: Prentice-Hall, 1982), p. 357.

There are three types of vertical marketing systems—administered, contractual, and corporate. Each represents a varying degree of integration in a formal ownership sense.[25] Table 14–2 shows the conventional marketing channel compared to the three major vertical marketing systems.

Administered vertical marketing system. In an ***administered vertical marketing system,*** the manufacturer of the largest market share or most prestigious brand assumes a leadership position to achieve coordination and cooperation with the channel. A common way to obtain this coordination is through a merchandising program where a manufacturer develops displays, shelf-space arrangements, promotions, and pricing policies to be used by wholesalers and retailers. These programs have been used successfully by General Electric in major appliances, Sealy with its Posturepedic mattresses, and Vilager in the dress and sportswear line.[26]

Contractual vertical marketing system. In ***contractual vertical marketing systems,*** integration occurs where the various stages of production and distribution are independently owned but the relationships between

[25] Stern and El-Ansary, *Marketing Channels,* p. 394.
[26] Ibid., p. 398.

vertically adjacent firms are covered in a contractual arrangement.[27] While there are many specific forms of contractual systems, they can be divided into three major types: (1) wholesaler-sponsored voluntary groups, (2) retail-sponsored cooperatives, and (3) franchise systems.[28]

A *wholesaler-sponsored voluntary group* is an arrangement in which a wholesaler bands together a number of independently owned retailers in a contractual agreement that specifies the products and services to be provided by the wholesaler. The result is that the goods and services can be provided much more economically than the same retailers could provide by acting individually. A well-known wholesaler-sponsored voluntary is the Independent Grocers Alliance (IGA). Others include Western Auto (automobile accessories) and Ben Franklin (general merchandise) markets.

A *retail-sponsored cooperative* is also a voluntary association, but the initiative to organize comes from the retailers rather than the wholesalers. The retailers operate their own wholesaler company, which performs services for member retailers. Retail cooperatives are common in the grocery field. Associated Grocers and Certified Grocers are examples.

Franchising is an arrangement in which an organization that has developed a successful product or service extends to others—for a fee—the right to engage in the business, provided they accept the terms of a written agreement.[29] (Chapter 15 contains a more detailed discussion of franchising.) There are four major types of franchise arrangements:

1. The manufacturer–retailer franchise, common in automobile and gasoline industries. Ford and General Motors have franchise contracts with independent businesses who agree to market autos in compliance with the contract.

2. The manufacturer–wholesaler franchise, exemplified by Coca-Cola, Pepsi-Cola, and Seven-Up. The manufacturers sell soft drink syrups to franchised wholesalers, who, in turn, bottle and distribute soft drinks to retailers.

3. The wholesaler–retailer franchise, exemplified by Rexall Drug Stores.

4. The service sponsor–retailer franchise, common in a variety of industries and probably the best-known type of franchise. Examples include McDonald's and Kentucky Fried Chicken in fast foods; Avis and Hertz in car rentals; Howard Johnson's and Holiday Inns in lodging and food; Midas and Aamco in auto repair; and Manpower in temporary employment.[30]

---

[27] Donald N. Thompson, "Contractual Marketing Systems: An Overview," in *Contractual Marketing Systems*, ed. D. N. Thompson (Lexington, Mass.: Heath: Lexington Books, 1971), p. 5.

[28] Stern and El-Ansary, *Marketing Channels*, p. 400.

[29] Shapiro, *Marketing Terms*, p. 69.

[30] William P. Hall, "Franchising: New Scope for an Old Technique," *Harvard Business Review*, January–February 1964, pp. 66–72.

Servicemaster is an example of a service retailer franchise. It operates throughout the United States.

ISN'T THIS THE DAY
To Call
SERVICEMASTER
**FOR HOME AND OFFICE
PROFESSIONAL CLEANING**

—Maid Service
—Fire & Smoke Clean-up
—Carpet
—Furniture (including velvets)
—Walls and Ceilings
—Tile & Wood Floors
—Smoke & Odor Removal
—House Wide Cleaning
—Complete Janitorial Service
—Drapery Cleaning
—FREE ESTIMATES

SERVICEMASTER
OF PARK FOREST, INC.
747-1962
73148

Courtesy Servicemaster of Park Forest, Inc.

Corporate vertical marketing system. In *corporate vertical marketing systems,* coordination and control are achieved through single corporate ownership of successive stages of production and distribution. A corporate system can be established through forward integration in which a manufacturer assumes wholesale and retail functions.

The Sherwin-Williams Company operates over 2,000 retail outlets, and Hart Shaffner & Marx operates about 200 stores. International Harvester and Goodyear have also used forward integration. Backward integration occurs when a retailer or wholesaler assumes ownership of institutions that normally precede them in the channel.[31] At the retail level, Sears is an example of backward integration. In 1974, Sears held a financial interest in 31 of its 12,000 suppliers, which included such companies as Armstrong Rubber, Whirlpool, and DeSoto. The 31 suppliers had combined sales of $4.2 billion and supplied about 29 percent of Sears' purchases.[32]

The corporate vertical marketing system offers significant advantages. It provides operating economies and absolute control over the activities of other channel members. The corporate system centralizes decision making and authority while assuring long contact and development of relationships with customers and suppliers.[33]

---

[31] Stern and El-Ansary, *Marketing Channels,* p. 420.

[32] Ibid.

[33] Ibid., p. 423.

Comparative analysis of conventional and vertical marketing systems. The conventional channel can be compared with the administered, contractual, and corporate forms of the vertical marketing system (VMS) along six dimensions. (See Table 14–2.)

The first dimension concerns how individual units in a marketing channel relate to systemwide channel objectives. At one extreme, represented by the conventional marketing channel, the units involved are isolated and autonomous, having no system-related goals. At the other extreme, the corporate VMS has units specifically organized to achieve overall channel objectives. The intermediate firms of a VMS reflect an increasing degree of collaboration and coordination aimed at achieving systemwide goals.

The second dimension deals with where decisions are made concerning channel activities. Generally, individual units in a conventional channel focus on cost, volume, and investment relationships at their own stage of the distribution process. However, as one proceeds along the VMS continuum, decisions concerning overall channel activity become more formal, centralized at the top of the interorganizational channel structure.

The marketing systems also vary along the third dimension, where authority over channel decisions resides. It is located exclusively within individual units in a conventional channel but becomes gradually concentrated at the top of the interorganizational channel structure in a corporate VMS.

The fourth dimension is structural provision for division of channel activity. This concerns the degree to which channel operations are formally integrated and synchronized within a marketing system. The conventional channel has no formally structured division of labor, as each member performs a traditionally defined set of marketing functions. At the other extreme, a corporate VMS usually handles marketing transactions by administrative processes and achieves coordination by centralized control procedures.[34]

The fifth dimension, the degree of commitment to a leadership subsystem, refers to a power focus in the system that provides for channel leadership, role specification, coordination, control, and conflict management. In conventional and administered channels, commitment is directed only to one's own organization. The contractual and corporate forms of a VMS are marked by moderate and high degrees of commitment, respectively.

The final dimension focuses on the systemwide orientation of channel members. Conventional channel units are totally self-oriented, as they pursue their own goals. However, systemwide orientation increases along the continuum of VMS forms.

---

[34] John Arndt, "Toward a Concept of Domesticated Markets," *Journal of Marketing* 43 (Fall 1979), pp. 69–75.

The emergence of vertical marketing systems is one of the most important developments in contemporary marketing.[35] In contrast to the conventional marketing channel, the vertical systems provide improved coordination through detailed planning and programs. For the corporate and contractual systems, membership loyalty is assured through the use of specific arrangements or ownership. Consequently, the channel tends to be more stable. There is more reliance on scientific decisions, with an emphasis on using sophisticated marketing concepts and tools.[36] The trend toward vertical marketing systems is likely to continue as marketing managers pursue ways to control costs and improve efficiency in the channel.

To complete our discussion of integration, we should briefly consider horizontal integration.

Horizontal integration. *Horizontal integration* occurs when two or more organizations at the same level in the channel of distribution combine resources to accomplish an objective. Two manufacturers may engage in a joint effort to advertise their products and create a synergistic effect by creating a "new product." For example, Hueblein, a vodka producer, teamed with Seven-Up to produce and promote the Smirnoff Mule. The idea was to do for vodka what the martini did for gin and the daiquiri did for rum. Horizontal integration may also occur at the retail level. For example, the independently owned and operated Ford dealers of Wisconsin and the Upper Peninsula of Michigan have combined their promotional campaign efforts to create higher advertising impact in the markets they serve. Horizontal integration is likely to continue as firms seek ways to reduce costs and improve efficiency.

MANAGEMENT OF INTERORGANIZATIONAL RELATIONS WITHIN CHANNELS

The major objectives of channel management are to satisfy customers and to achieve a desired level of profitability. Achieving these objectives requires an understanding of the goals and behavior characterizing the interactions between organizations within a distribution channel. Two of the major dimensions of channel member goals and behaviors are cooperation and conflict.[37] Cooperation is the joint striving toward an objective—the process of working with others for a goal or value or mutual benefit.[38] Conflict, in contrast, is opponent-centered behavior in which the major concern is to overcome the opponent or counterpart to serve a goal.[39]

[35] William R. Davidson, "Changes in Distributive Institutions," *Journal of Marketing* 34 (October 1970), pp. 7–10.

[36] McCammon, "Perspectives," p. 44.

[37] L. W. Stern and T. Reve, "Distribution Channels as Political Economics: A Framework for Comparative Analysis," *Journal of Marketing* 44 (Summer 1980), pp. 52–64.

[38] L. W. Stern, "Antitrust Implications of a Sociological Interpretation of Competition, Conflict, and Cooperation in the Marketplace," *The Antitrust Bulletin* 16 (Fall 1971), pp. 509–30.

[39] Ibid.

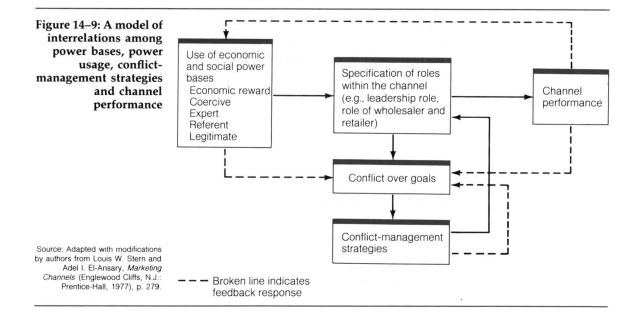

Figure 14–9: A model of interrelations among power bases, power usage, conflict-management strategies and channel performance

Source: Adapted with modifications by authors from Louis W. Stern and Adel I. El-Ansary, *Marketing Channels* (Englewood Cliffs, N.J.: Prentice-Hall, 1977), p. 279.

– – – Broken line indicates feedback response

Cooperation and conflict are separate processes, although they are highly interrelated. For example, customer–supplier relationships ordered by long-term contracts reflect basically cooperative behavior, but conflicts regularly arise regarding the interpretation of contractual details and problem-solving approaches.[40] Thus, conflict and cooperation exist simultaneously in all channels. The task then becomes to manage the relationships between organizations within a channel to achieve maximal cooperation and minimal conflict. To do this, we present a model of key relationships among channel members in Figure 14–9.

Before we begin our discussion of channel relationships, some terms and concepts used in the model must be discussed.

Terms and concepts in channel relationships

Power. **Power** should be thought of as a relationship between or among persons or organizations. While many definitions of power exist, the following is generally accepted.

power

> A has **power** over B to the extent that A can get B to do something that B would not otherwise do.[41]

---

[40] Stern and Reve, "Distribution Channels."

[41] Robert A. Dahl, "The Concept of Power," *Behavioral Science,* July 1957, pp. 201–18.

Bases of power. A *base of power* is a source of influence in a relationship.[42] The following power bases have been identified in the relationships among channel members:[43]

1. *Economic power* is a form of reward power and is based on the perception that one channel member can administer economic rewards to another. Economic rewards typically used in the channel include lower prices and money for advertising and other promotion.

2. *Coercive power* is based on the perception that one channel member will punish another for failure to cooperate. The forms of punishment include reductions in margins, withdrawals of promotional allowances, and denials of exclusive territorial rights.

3. *Expert power* is based on the perception that one channel member has special knowledge that could help the channel. For example, retailers usually expect manufacturers to have special knowledge and expertise about new products and promotion and to use this expertise to assist the retailers.

4. *Referent power* is based on the perception that it is desirable to join or to be a member of a given organization. For example, suppose an individual is simultaneously considering a Mercedes Benz dealership and a Volkswagon dealership. Assume that both dealerships would provide the same rate of return on investment and that the management of both companies would give comparable support in promotion, training service representatives, etc. It is likely that the individual will choose the Mercedes Benz dealership and that, in turn, the Mercedes Benz organization would be able to exercise referent power relative to its new dealership.[44]

5. *Legitimate power* is based on the perception that one channel member has the right to make specific decisions and to expect compliance from another channel member with regard to these decisions. For example, in a relationship covered by written contracts, a manufacturer may provide money to a retailer to advertise the manufacturer's product in the local retail market. The manufacturer expects the retailer to comply with the terms of the agreement and is said to exert influence based on legitimate power.

Role. Within a channel, a member's position is determined by the channel member's goals, expectations, or values. For example, if a member's goal is to earn 20 percent return on investment and if such a return

---

[42] John French and Bertram Raven, "The Bases of Social Power," in *Studies in Social Power,* ed. D. Cartwright (Ann Arbor: University of Michigan Press, 1959).

[43] The discussion of power bases is adapted from French and Raven, "Bases of Social Power"; Frederick J. Beier and Louis W. Stern, "Power in the Channel of Distribution," in *Distribution Channels: Behavioral Dimensions,* ed. Louis W. Stern (Boston: Houghton Mifflin, 1969); and Michael Etgar, "Selection of an Effective Channel Central Mix," *Journal of Marketing* 42 (July 1978), pp. 53–56.

[44] This is from Stern and El-Ansary, *Marketing Channels,* p. 290.

is not possible in retailing or wholesaling, then manufacturing may be a more attractive position for the member to assume.

| role | A **role** is the pattern of actions expected of an individual (or organization) in activities involving others resulting from the position an individual (organization) occupies in the social structure.[45] |

The roles associated with a position define the behavior of the individual or organization occupying it. Through knowledge of the roles assumed by channel members, occupants of counterpart positions can anticipate their behavior.[46] The importance of roles and position in the channel of distribution is illustrated as follows:

> A wholesaler and a retailer in a distribution channel are aware of each other's role and are able to anticipate behavior. The retailer knows that salespeople will call at specific times, that goods will be delivered when needed and in good condition, and that special deliveries can be counted on to meet unexpected shortages. The wholesaler expects payment for the merchandise after a certain time period and knows the retailer will carry out promotional plans and that a helper will be provided to unload delivered merchandise. Marketing channels cannot function without such sustained cooperation, in which each party knows what to expect from their opposite number.[47]

Channel leadership is another important role in channels of distribution. The channel leader—sometimes called the "channel captain"—can organize and influence the actions of other channel members. The role of channel captain may be assumed by manufacturer, wholesaler, or retailer. In the auto industry, the channel leaders are generally considered to be General Motors and Ford. Because of their size and the large number of consumers who buy from them, large retailers such as J. C. Penney, K mart, and Sears often assume a leadership role. If a manufacturer who supplies one of these large retailers fails to perform in product quality or reliability of delivery, the retailer may switch to another manufacturer. An example of a wholesaler assuming the channel leadership role is the Independent Grocers Alliance (IGA), a wholesaler-sponsored voluntary chain. The wholesaler performs many functions for the retailer, including purchasing, transporting, promoting, and pricing. Through the performance of these functions, the wholesaler exerts expert and economic reward bases of influence upon the retailers.

---

[45] Keith Davis, *Human Behavior at Work* (New York: McGraw-Hill, 1972), p. 26.

[46] Stern and El-Ansary, *Marketing Channels,* p. 280.

[47] Lynn E. Gill and Louis W. Stern, "Roles and Role Theory in Distribution Channel Systems," in *Distribution Channels: Behavior Dimensions,* ed. Louis W. Stern (Boston: Houghton Mifflin, 1969).

Conflict

Conflict within a channel occurs when channel member A perceives member B as engaging in behavior that interferes with A's goals and performance.[48] One such source of conflict occurs when an intermediary such as a wholesaler engages in behavior that interferes with the manufacturer's goals. This type of conflict occurred between Coca-Cola and its wholesale distributors, or bottlers. From 1965 until 1975, Dr Pepper, the manufacturer of the leading cherry-flavored soft drink, persuaded about 24 percent of Coca-Cola's bottlers to distribute Dr Pepper. Coca-Cola wanted its bottlers to handle its Mr. Pibb, which competed directly with Dr Pepper. The conflict was resolved when Coca-Cola was able to persuade their bottlers to handle Mr. Pibb rather than Dr Pepper.[49]

A comprehensive review of the literature on channel conflict found several causes of conflict in the channel of distribution:

1. *Failure to achieve financial goals.* Channel members pursue a variety of goals, including price or market share leadership, growth, or a prestigious reputation. In the final analysis, these goals are pursued to achieve the basic financial objectives of profitability and return on investment. If channel members are not meeting their financial objectives, they will negotiate aggressively on individual transactions and increase the level of conflict.

2. *Varying assessments of risk.* Conflict may arise as channel members have differing opinions on the amount or type of risk they perceive in a situation. Usually smaller, more aggressive members are more willing to take risks than are the larger, more established channel members.

3. *Joint decision areas.* These are topics in which two or more channel members have input into a decision. If it isn't clear who makes the final decision, though, conflict is likely to arise.

4. *Sources of power.* The use of expert and referent power sources may reduce conflict; the use of coercion or the threats of coercion tend to increase it.

5. *External factors.* Factors such as changing technology, intense competition, and shortages of supply that are external to the channel itself may cause conflict.

6. *Poor communication.* Differences in the amount of information received or in information-processing capabilities and procedures used in the channels may result in communication problems among channel members. The content, frequency, source, and receiver of communication should be taken into consideration when designing communication programs to reduce conflict among channel members.[50]

---

[48] Raymond W. Mack and Richard C. Snyder, "The Analysis of Social Conflict—Toward an Overview and Synthesis," *Journal of Conflict Resolution,* June 1957, pp. 214–48.

[49] "Dr Pepper: Pitted against the Soft-Drink Giants," *Business Week,* October 6, 1975, p. 70.

[50] The discussion of sources of conflict is based on Robert F. Lusch and James F. Horrell, *Sources of Conflict in Distribution Channels,* paper presented at the 1977 meeting of the American Institute of Decision Sciences, Chicago; and Joseph B. Mason and Morris L. Mayer, *Modern Retailing Theory and Practice* (Plano, Tex.: Business Publications, 1981), pp. 454–55.

Figure 14–10: Means for solving channel conflict

	Degree of perceived vertical interdependence		
	High ◄───► Low		
			Bargaining and boundary negotiation
	Supraorganizational	**Interpenetration**	
	Superordinate goals	Membership	Diplomacy
	Conciliation and mediation	Exchange-of-persons	bargaining
	Arbitration	or programs	strategy
	Special-purpose	Ideological	
	mechanisms	Education	
	Commissions of inquiry	Propaganda	
	Observers	Membership	
		cooperation	

Source: Louis W. Stern, "Potential Conflict Channels: An Interorganizational Analysis, in *Contractual Marketing Systems,* ed. Donald N. Thompson (Lexington, Mass.: Heath-Lexington Books, 1971), p. 114.

Conflict-management strategies

A variety of conflict-management strategies and tactics can be used, depending on the cause of the conflict, the amount of power one channel member has over another, and the degree of interdependence among channel members. The model in Figure 14–10 contains various types of conflict-management strategies based on the degree of interdependence among channel members. On the high end of the interdependence continuum are the most integrated vertical marketing systems (such as the corporate ownership type used by Sherwin-Williams). The low end of the continuum is represented by the conventional marketing channel.

Supraorganizational means of managing conflict refer to those actions that influence the entire channel as opposed to a single level in it. The most important specific actions include: the establishment of goals for the entire channel, the use of conciliation and mediation, arbitration, and special-purpose actions, such as the creation of commissions to inquire into problems within the channel. Let's discuss and illustrate some of these.

Superordinate goals are those that the actors caught in the conflict desire to achieve but which cannot be met by the resources and energies of parties separately; they require the concerted efforts of all parties involved.[51] Consider the following example. In the U.S. liquor industry, distillers and small retailers have established the superordinate goal of preventing large discounting retailers from gaining a significant market share. To carry out this objective, small retailers have endorsed price controls in an attempt to prevent price competition, while distillers have provided continued small-retailer support to ensure leadership and thus resist the power of large retailers.[52]

---

[51] Muzafer Sherif, *Social Interaction* (Hawthorne, N.Y.: Aldine Publishing), p. 457.

[52] Stern and El-Ansary, *Marketing Channels,* p. 306.

Conciliation is a passive role. It attempts to bring cooperation to a negotiation over conflicting issues; it primarily involves adjustment of the dispute by the parties themselves. In the U.S. pesticide industry, manufacturers and distributors belong to the national Agricultural Chemicals Association, which frequently acts as a conciliator for issues within the industry. *Mediation* suggests a more active intervention by a third party who makes procedural or substantive recommendations in order to secure a settlement. Industries with a history of conflict among channel members should consider the establishment of mediation boards staffed by respected individuals (such as retired judges, professors, or consultants).[53]

Arbitration is a process wherein parties submit their disputes to a third party whose decision is final and binding. Arbitration can be compulsory or voluntary. The courts have acted as arbitrators in channel conflicts—such as in cases where the government has settled disputes between auto dealers and manufacturers and between resellers and drug manufacturers where fair-trade pricing was a conflict issue.[54]

Interpenetration strategies increase the number of meaningful interactions among channel members. These interactions provide an important source for conflict reduction. The U.S. television receiver industry provides an example of interpenetration strategy:

> The lack of communications in the channel of distribution was one of the major dealer complaints. Another was the lack of product knowledge and the lack of understanding of the dealers' problems on the part of the distributor salespeople. The approach used to correct the lack of communications was to invite the manufacturers to become members of the National Appliance and Radio TV Dealers Association (NARDA). Twelve of the major manufacturers are not members, and representatives of these and other companies now attend NARDA conventions. Manufacturers' relations meetings are a regular convention feature. Executives of manufacturing organizations are regular speakers at NARDA training seminars and at the regular convention.[55]

Ideological penetration uses information, propaganda, and educational activities to manage conflict. A manufacturer may act as a channel propagandist or educator to seek some sort of ideological change in another channel member. For example, a manufacturer may try to change retailers' thinking from gross profit margins to return on investment. This type of change would result in changes in retail operating methods.

Bargaining is the usual mechanism used to handle conflict within a channel. It involves making commitments, offering rewards, or threatening punishment between and among channel members. There are two key issues in bargaining: (1) the amount of control necessary to concede to

---

[53] Ibid., p. 305.

[54] Ibid.

[55] Ibid.

another channel member and (2) how one party can be induced to accept less favorable terms than it wants to achieve.

Effective conflict management should produce increased performance and satisfaction for channel members. In the long run it should be a major determinant in the survival and growth of a channel system.

EVALUATION OF CHANNEL PERFORMANCE

Performance of any channel system can be evaluated along several dimensions. The framework in Figure 14–11 shows that channel system performance can be evaluated qualitatively and quantitatively. A qualitative assessment of channel system performance is generally subjective in nature and involves the perceptions of individual channel members regarding the flow of operations and quality of relations within a channel system. A quantitative appraisal is based on objective data collected over the course of channel operations.

Qualitative measures

Major components of the qualitative approach include the quality of interorganizational relationships, the availability of information about various operational characteristics within the distribution channel, and other measures of the degree of flexibility and innovation in the channel concerned.

Several measures exist that assure the quality of interorganizational relationships. These may include the degree of channel coordination, co-

Figure 14–11: Qualitative and quantitative measures of channel system performance

Channel system performance

Qualitative measures

I Quality of interorganizational relationships

 1. Degree of channel coordination.
 2. Degree of cooperation.
 3. Degree of conflict.
 4. Degree of development of channel leadership.
 5. Degree of commitment to channel.

II Availability of information about

 1. Physical inventory.
 2. Product characteristics.
 3. Pricing structure.
 4. Promotional data.
 5. Market conditions.

III Other

 1. Assimilation of new technology.
 2. Flexibility in shifting functions.

Quantitative measures

I Customer service

 1. Customer service level (by products, by market segment).
 2. Percent of damaged merchandise.
 3. Percent of lost and/or delayed shipment.

II Cost per unit (CPU)

 1. Total distribution CPU.
 2. Transportation CPU.
 3. Warehousing CPU.
 4. Production CPU.

III Other

 1. Distribution turnover.
 2. Number and percent of new distributors.
 3. New markets entered—number, percent sales volume.

Source: Adapted from Adel I. El-Ansary, "A Model for Evaluating Channel Performance," unpublished paper, Louisiana State University, 1975, pp. 10–11; reported in Douglas M. Lambert, *The Distribution Channel Decision* (New York: National Association of Accountants, 1978), p. 41.

operation, conflict, commitment, and leadership. Another useful qualitative performance measure is the extent to which information concerning physical inventory, product characteristics, pricing structure, promotional data (such as personal selling assistance, advertising, point-of-purchase displays, and special promotions), and market conditions are available among the channel members.

Other qualitative performance criteria may include the degree of flexibility of the channel structure or, more specifically, the extent to which channel functions can be shifted among channel members without loss in efficiency. The greater this flexibility, the better able the channel system is to respond to environmental changes. Another factor that may be considered in this connection is the degree of innovativeness in distribution generated within the channel.

Quantitative measures

Several classes of quantitative measures of channel system performance are available. The most important one is customer service. Objective measures of this factor include the level of customer service by product and by market segment; the percent of damaged, lost, or delayed shipments of merchandise; the number of customer complaints; percent of stockouts; accuracy of sales forecast; and number of errors in order filling.

Costs are incurred in providing these services to customers. These include the total distribution cost per unit and the cost per unit of transportation, warehousing, and production. Since these costs escalate as the level of customer service increases, a channel leader or manufacturer may have to determine the optimal cost-benefit trade-off for each product.

Other quantitative measures of channel system performance may include the distribution turnover (or the number and percent of discontinued channel intermediaries over a specific time), the number and percent of new distributors, and the number of new markets entered.[56]

[56] Adapted from Adel I. El-Ansary, "A Model for Evaluating Channel Performance," unpublished manuscript, Louisiana State University, 1975, pp. 10–11; reported in Douglas M. Lambert, *The Distribution Channel Decision* (New York: National Association of Accountants, 1978), p. 41.

SUMMARY

Marketing channels consist of sets of interdependent organizations involved in the process of making products or services available to consumers. Intermediaries facilitate the exchange process and create a variety of efficiencies that would be difficult for individual retailers or manufacturers to achieve.

Intermediaries perform several tasks in a channel in order to create form, time, place, and possession utilities. These tasks create forward and backward channel flows, such as promotion and ordering.

Channel systems may be conventional or vertical. Vertical channels, in turn, may be administered, contractual, or corporate.

The strategic marketing planning process is applicable to the channel decision as well. A situation analysis is first performed to determine consumer shopping and buying habits, channel competition, environmental conditions, and company strengths and weaknesses. Following the situation analysis, channel objectives can be established based on (1) a specified level of customer service and (2) overall corporate objectives. The company can then be in a position to decide whether to have intensive, exclusive, or selective market coverage for its products. This establishes the num-

ber of intermediaries used in a given geographic region.

Strategic channel decisions can then be facilitated in regard to (1) development and management of vertical marketing channels or systems and (2) the management of interorganizational relations within the channel. Finally, channel performance can be evaluated on qualitative and quantitative considerations.

KEY CONCEPTS

Channel of distribution
Reseller
Intermediary
Contact efficiency
Sorting
Retailer
Wholesaler
Industrial distributor
Manufacturer's agent
Sales agent
Rack jobber
Facilitating agent
Marketing function
Marketing flow
Physical possession
Ownership flow
Promotional flow
Push strategy
Pull strategy
Negotiation

Financing
Risk taking
Orders
Payment
Multiple channels
Intensive distribution
Exclusive distribution
Selective distribution
Conventional marketing channels
Vertical marketing systems
Administered vertical marketing system
Contractual vertical marketing system
Wholesaler-sponsored voluntary group
Retail-sponsored cooperative
Consumer goods channels
Industrial goods channels
Franchising

Corporate vertical marketing system
Horizontal integration
Power
Base of power
Economic power
Coercive power
Expert power
Referent power
Legitimate power
Role
Conflict
Conciliation
Mediation
Arbitration
Bargaining
Form utility
Time utility
Place utility
Possession utility

DISCUSSION QUESTIONS AND EXERCISES

1. List and briefly discuss the major reasons why intermediaries are used.

2. Assume that there are four producers and five consumers. Each producer wants to sell or at least make contact with each consumer. How many contacts are necessary if there is no intermediary involved? If an intermediary is added, what is the decline in the number of contacts made?

3. Compare and contrast the wholesaler with the industrial distributor.

4. Distinguish between a marketing flow and a marketing function.

5. Consider the allocation of funds to the various elements of the promotional budgets for firms A and B:

	Firm A	Firm B
Advertising	85%	5%
Personal selling	5	90
Sales promotion	10	5

Which firm is using a pull strategy? Which is using a push strategy? Explain.

6. Discuss the risk-taking function performed by retailers in the channel of distribution. State two specific risks that are assumed by
   a. Supermarkets.
   b. Clothing retailers.
   c. A heavy equipment distributor.

7. What are multiple channels and why are they used?

8. Compare and contrast the conventional channels and vertical marketing systems.

9. Why does conflict occur within the channel of distribution? Discuss the major strategies for managing conflict within the channel of distribution.

CHAPTER 15

Retailing and wholesaling

Nature and scope of retailing

Classification of retail structure
    Margin/turnover classification
    Product mix classification
    Method of operation
    Nonstore retailing
    Warehouse retailing, conglomerchant, hypermarkets
    Geographic location
    Form of ownership

Retail institutional change
    Wheel of retailing
    Retail accordion
    Retail life cycle

Strategic retail management decisions
    Store location
    Store image
    Merchandise, service, and atmosphere
    Pricing
    Promotion

Wholesaling
    Wholesaling functions
    Types of wholesalers

Strategic wholesale management decisions
    Location
    Product/service mix
    Pricing

Legal dimensions of channel, retail, and wholesale management
    Exclusive-dealing contracts
    Tying contracts
    Exclusive territories

Summary

Key concepts

Discussion questions and exercises

This chapter begins with a discussion of the nature and scope of retailing. We then explore retail structures in the context of various classifications, which include margin/turnover, product mix, method of operation, and geographic location. We'll be examining institutional change in terms of the wheel of retailing, accordion, and life-cycle theories. Then we'll cover several strategic decision areas of retailing, including location, image, pricing, and promotion.

Wholesaling is discussed next, beginning with its several functions. We'll be describing various types of wholesalers for both consumer and industrial products. Finally, we'll explore strategic decision areas involving location, product/service mix, and pricing, and some legal dimensions of channel, retail, and wholesale management.

NATURE AND SCOPE OF RETAILING

According to the last Census of Retailing in 1977, there were 1,855,068 retail stores in outlets operated by 1,567,071 retail firms. Over 97 percent of these firms operate only one establishment (single unit), but they had only 52 percent of the sales of all retail firms in business at the end of 1977. Multi-establishment firms operated only 17.9 percent of retail establishments but accounted for 48 percent of sales.[1] See Table 15–1 for a listing of sales of high-volume (multi-establishment) retailers versus low-volume (single-establishment) retailers.

Table 15–1: Average dollar sales of high-volume versus low-volume retailers	Average sales in 1977 ($000)
High-volume retailers (multi-establishment)	
Department store	$9,000
New-car dealer	4,100
Grocery store	900
Low-volume retailers (single-establishment)	
Florist	$89
Drinking place (bar)	87
Gift shop	84

Source: Bureau of Census, *1977 Census of Retail Trade Vol. 1* (Washington, D.C.: U.S. Department of Commerce, June 1981), "Summary of Findings," p. 1.

Retailing is a major source of employment in the United States. Approximately 15 million individuals work in retailing, making it the third-largest employer (manufacturing employs 20 million, and service industries, 18 million). For many individuals, working in a retail establishment provides their first valuable work experience.[2] Retailing employs individuals in a

---

[1] Bureau of Census, *1977 Census of Retail Trade Vol. 1* (Washington, D.C.: U.S. Department of Commerce, June 1981), "Summary of Findings," p. 1.

[2] *County Business Patterns—United States* (Washington, D.C.: U.S. Government Printing Office, July 1983), p. 1.

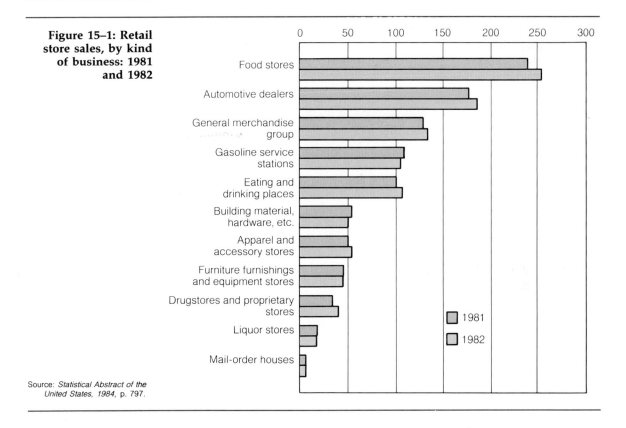

Figure 15–1: Retail store sales, by kind of business: 1981 and 1982

Source: *Statistical Abstract of the United States, 1984*, p. 797.

wide variety of selling situations. Figure 15–1 shows retail store sales by kinds of business for 1981 and 1982.

Retailing keeps the entrepreneurial spirit alive by providing an opportunity for people to establish their own businesses. But with the opportunities for high earnings and independence come the risks in owning one's own business. Eating and drinking places, which are generally individually owned and operated, have the highest failure rates among retail businesses.[3]

Most retailers operate on a small scale in terms of number of employees, number of retail outlets, and dollar sales volume. About 64 percent of all U.S. retail establishments in 1977 had five or fewer paid employees.[4] In stark contrast are the large retailers, which represent some of the most significant businesses within our U.S. economy in terms of sales.

Now let's turn our attention to the various schemes for classifying retailers.

---

[3] Dun & Bradstreet, Business Economic Division, *Monthly Business Failure,* February 29, 1980, p. 2.

[4] Bureau of Census, *1977 Census of Retail Trade Vol. 1,* pp. 1–3.

Figure 15–2:
Margin/turnover
classification

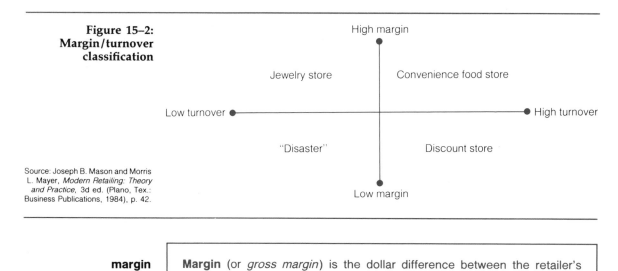

Source: Joseph B. Mason and Morris
L. Mayer, *Modern Retailing: Theory
and Practice*, 3d ed. (Plano, Tex.:
Business Publications, 1984), p. 42.

---

margin	**Margin** (or *gross margin*) is the dollar difference between the retailer's cost of purchasing a product and the retail selling price.
turnover	**Turnover** relates to sales volume and is the number of times that the average inventory is sold in a given time period, usually one year.

CLASSIFICATION OF RETAIL STRUCTURE

Margin/turnover classification

A margin/turnover classification is useful in retail formulation.

Figure 15–2 shows four categories of margin and turnover for classifying retail establishments. The "Disaster" store has the double problems of low margins and low turnover. The store lacks a specific strategic advantage and therefore is likely to be a financial failure.

Management can determine which category a particular retail outlet most logically fits in and develop appropriate strategies based on that category. The most important elements in retail management strategy based on margin/turnover are: whether merchandise is presold before the customer enters the store or sold in the store through retail personal selling, the types and varieties of services, location, type of promotion, price level, and the organizational structure.[5]

Beyond the margin/turnover classifications, retailing institutions can be classified in a variety of other ways. For our purposes, we classify retailers according to (1) the product mix they offer to their customers, (2) the method of operation, (3) the form of ownership or control, and (4) location. See Figure 15–3 for a listing of these classifications.

Product mix classification

Department stores. ***Department stores*** (Gimbel's, Macy's, Marshall Field's) carry many product lines, including furniture, clothing, sporting

---

[5] Ronald R. Gist, *Retailing: Concepts and Decisions* (New York: John Wiley & Sons, 1968), pp. 37–40.

Figure 15–3: **Classification of major types of retailers**	**Product mix**	**Method of operation**	**Location**	**Form of ownership**
	Department store	Full service	Central business	Independent
	Specialty	Supermarket	District	Chains
	Variety	Discount store	Shopping center	Franchise
		Convenience store	Regional	Voluntary cooperative
		Nonstore retailing	Community	Retail sponsored
		Direct marketing	Neighborhood	Wholesale sponsored
		Door-to-door		
		Vending		
		Other		
		Warehouse retailing		
		Conglomerchant		
		Hypermarkets		

goods, jewelry, and toys. Their product mix is usually the widest of any retailer. Depth within each line is considerable, but the product lines are not as deep as those offered by specialty stores.

An analysis of the organizational structure of department stores provides insight into the managerial functions of retail stores and is the model for other types of retailing institutions, like discount stores.

Many department stores use a four-function plan that divides the store's activities into the following groups: (1) merchandising, (2) publicity, (3) store management or operations, and (4) accounting and control. This organizational structure is called the *Mazur plan* in honor of its proponent, Paul Mazur, an investment banker and chairman of a National Retail Dry Goods Association special committee on store organizations.[6]

The *merchandising division* is usually considered the heart of a department store's business. It is responsible for all buying and selling activities and receives the most attention from top management. The *publicity division* is responsible for all promotional efforts (advertising, display, and public relations) except for personal selling, which is the responsibility of merchandising. The *operations division,* headed by the store manager or superintendent, handles all activities not assumed by one of the other groups, such as store maintenance and security, warehousing, shipping, and delivery. The *accounting and control division,* headed by the controller or by the treasurer, protects the company's assets and obtains adequate working capital. The controller's responsibilities have increased in recent years because of increased credit transactions, the use of electronic data processing, and the growing complexity of tax and other regulations.

The full-service department store was once the most prestigious retailing institution in the United States. But the population shift to the sub-

[6] Delbert J. Duncan and Stanley C. Hollander, *Modern Retailing Management: Basic Concepts and Practices* (Homewood, Ill.: Richard D. Irwin, 1977), pp. 184–89.

The Foot Locker is an example of a specialty store. It offers great depth in a limited product mix.

The world's greatest athletic shoes compete in our arena everyday.

It's Nike vs Adidas vs Puma vs Converse vs Pony vs Saucony vs a dozen others. The greatest selection of top name sports shoes ever assembled. Anywhere.

With that kind of a lineup, and with Foot Locker's trained sales pros, we can guarantee you the right shoe for your game. Whether it's serious or social.

That's the name of our game in America's athletic shoe arena.

America's Most Complete Athletic Footwear Store™

Courtesy of Foot Locker, a division of Kinney Shoe Corporation

urbs, the decline of the central cities, and inept management have greatly reduced the prestige and profitability of many department stores. To compete more effectively, most department stores have opened branches in suburban shopping centers: by 1974, department stores with sales of over $1 million obtained about 75 percent of their sales from branch locations.[7] Department stores have also eliminated slow-moving and low-margin products (especially such durable goods as washers and refrigerators) and have adopted more profitable items (like fashion clothing). And many have tried to expand business by leasing departments to outside individuals or firms when store management could not handle new lines successfully. Leased departments are common for (1) products with complicated inventory problems (shoes), (2) products and services that require technical knowledge (watch repair, camera and photo supplies), and (3) services with operating problems (restaurants and snack bars).[8]

Specialty stores. **Specialty stores** offer great depth within a limited number of product lines. Examples of specialty stores are The Athlete's Foot (sports apparel), Merle Norman (cosmetics studios), and Tiffany's (jewelry). Figure 15–4 shows an example of the sporting goods product

[7] Jay Scher, "Financial and Operating Results of Department Stores in 1974" (New York: National Retail Merchants Association, 1975).

[8] Robert Drew Bar, *Mass Merchandising: Revolution and Evolution* (New York: Fairchild Publications, 1970), pp. 272–75.

Figure 15–4: Width and depth of sporting goods product mix in department and specialty stores

Department store

	Width				
	Jogging shoes	**Warmup suits**	**Tennis rackets**	**Baseball gloves**	**Tennis balls**
Depth	Nike Elites Brooks Vantage Adidas Country	Speed-O Winning Ways	Spaulding Natural Wilson T-3000 Head Vilas	Wilson Rawlings MacGregor	Wilson Spaulding Penn

Specialty store

	Width	
	Jogging shoes	**Tennis rackets**
Depth	Adidas Dragon Adidas TRX Converse Pro-Keds Nike Tailwind Nike Roadrunner Brooks Vantage Brooks Vantage Supreme	Wilson T-5000 Spaulding Accomplice Spaulding Big Boss Dunlop Yamaha Head Master Head Edge Head Professional

Source: Adapted by authors from Lawrence Golden and Donald Zimmerman, *Effective Retailing* (Chicago: Rand McNally, 1980), p. 138. Copyright © 1980 Houghton Mifflin Company. Adapted with permission.

mix found in a specialty store. We can see the effectiveness of the strategic planning of specialty stores by looking at the key factors in the success of specialists in sporting goods:

1. Complete selection of equipment and apparel for every sport from tennis and lacrosse to camping and backpacking, in broad price ranges.

2. Expert sales assistance by a sales staff who use the equipment and apparel they sell.

3. Private-label merchandise designed to ensure high quality and exclusiveness for the distinct market segmentation pursued by the superspecialists.[9]

Specialty stores are likely to become more important as consumer markets are more effectively segmented. Specialty store management is usually better informed about customer needs and is more flexible in responding to them than are other types of retailers (such as department stores).

Variety stores. *Variety stores* handle a wide range of low-price products. Usually operated on a self-serve or self-selection basis, these stores were once known as "5- and 10-cent stores." F. W. Woolworth and Ben Franklin are examples. The variety store is generally regarded as a dying institution. Severe competition is at fault.

---

[9] Doreen Morgan, "How the Specialists Demonstrate Sporting Goods," *Stores*, July 1979, pp. 32–36.

Method of operation

Full-service retailers.   Retailers can provide a full range of services that include a wide mix of products, personal selling assistance, credit, product information, delivery, alterations (clothing), and installation (washers, dryers). Department stores and specialty stores usually provide many of these services and are, therefore, *full-service retailers.* But as they eliminate services, retailers can lower overhead and other costs and thus reduce prices.

Supermarkets.   Supermarkets as we know them today emerged in the late 1920s. Most commonly they retail grocery and food items, although marketers of toys and liquor also use the supermarket concept. In food retailing, supermarkets usually feature large buildings, self-service, and large amounts of space for such categories as delicatessens, liquor, and cosmetics, plus sacking and drive-up delivery services. Examples of such supermarkets are Jewel and Kroger. As a whole, supermarkets are experiencing competition from fast-food organizations as Americans increase their tendency to eat away from home. Some supermarkets have made efforts (such as adding delicatessens) to stabilize or increase market share, but the success of these strategies has not been demonstrated conclusively. Supermarkets face competitive challenges and cost pressures as well as problems of scarce equity capital, high energy costs, and labor productivity.

A&P is an example of a supermarket victimized by competitive pressure. In failing to keep abreast of trends, management allowed its stores to become antiquated; and many A&P stores were small, cluttered, and in poor locations. Lacking space to allow larger sales volume, A&P's stores could not stock high-margin general merchandise items. As a result, A&P lost about $42 million on $6 billion in sales within a six-month period in the early 1970s.[10]

Discount stores.   Discount stores were originally small, unadvertised retail outlets selling branded electrical appliances, watches, luggage, jewelry, cameras, and similar items at reduced prices. Those featuring wearing apparel rather than "hard" goods appeared in the early 1950s, quickly attracting many price-conscious buyers. Today, discount stores are likely to have the following characteristics: broad merchandise assortments, including hard and soft goods and food; assortments limited to popular items, colors, and sizes in each product classification; emphasis on price as main sales appeal, aimed at low- and middle-income families; self-service operations; limited customer services; long hours; large stores, ranging from 50,000 to 200,000 square feet or more; large, free-parking area; and relatively simple buildings.[11]

The most successful firm in discount retailing is S. S. Kresge with its

[10] Eleanor Johnson Tracy, "How A&P Got Creamed," *Fortune,* January, 1973, pp. 103–4.

[11] Duncan and Hollander, *Modern Retailing Management,* pp. 22–23.

K mart stores. Discount stores, though, do face competition from specialty discount outlets, combination supermarkets and drugstores, and catalog showrooms.

Discount retailing has become so popular that conventional retailers (like department stores) have tried to capture some of this market segment by opening discount operations or operating budget departments, usually in their store basements. Discount retailing is competitive, though, and not all such efforts are successful. In 1981, J. C. Penney decided to dispose of its 34-store Treasury discount chain after seven years of unprofitability and fiscal 1981 loss of $14 million.[12]

Convenience stores. ***Convenience stores*** are a variation of the conventional limited-line food stores. Stock is limited to such convenience items as bread, milk, ice cream, and snack foods. Convenience, rather than a wide assortment, is the major attraction of these stores. As for price: they often charge 10 to 20 percent above nearby supermarkets. The number of these stores has risen rapidly in recent years, from 2,500 in 1960 to 27,500 in 1977.[13]

Nonstore retailing

There are three major types of ***nonstore retailing:*** direct marketing, vending machines, and door-to-door selling.

Direct marketing

direct marketing

> **Direct marketing** or direct response marketing describes a variety of approaches a marketer uses (such as direct-mail, telephone, or TV or radio ads) to directly promote the product and elicit an immediate response to buy from the consumer.

A good example of direct marketing is Ronco's program for products such as the Vegomatic vegetable slicer, the smokeless ashtray, and the Popeil pocket fisherman. Ronco's approach is to use TV ads to demonstrate the product and tell viewers where it can be purchased. The products are available in 23,000 retail outlets, including drug and discount stores, supermarkets, hardware, and chain stores like Sears.[14] Other direct-marketing programs include: (1) the mail-order approach, which is used by Sears and Wards to distribute catalogs on a variety of merchandise; (2) the producer/direct marketer approach, which is used by manufacturers to supplement their other channels of distribution, such as the record

---

[12] "Penney's Will Shed Treasury Stores, Its Discount Unit," *The Wall Street Journal,* February 14, 1981, p. 14.

[13] "Convenience Stores: A $7.4-Billion Mushroom," *Business Week,* March 21, 1977, pp. 61–64.

[14] Helen Pauly, "Readers! Act Now! Share Ronco's Story," *The Milwaukee Journal.* September 27, 1981, p. 4.

club established by manufacturers in the recording industry; and (3) the department store or specialty shop, which solicits direct-response business through special newspaper advertising and seasonal catalogs.[15]

Vending machines. **Vending machines** are popular for products such as candy, cigarettes, and soft drinks. This type of retailing has grown steadily in volume and in the variety of products offered. Gas stations, bus terminals, airports, and motels use vending machines to serve the needs of travelers by selling such items as toothbrushes, headache remedies, and combs.

Door-to-door selling. **Door-to-door selling** is another popular method of nonstore retailing. Avon Products and Shaklee are examples of successful personal, in-home selling operations.

Warehouse retailing, conglomerchant, hypermarkets

Warehouse retailing has become increasingly popular in a variety of retail trades, including furniture, lumber, general merchandise, and supermarkets. Warehouse markets, or "box stores," are discount, no-frills, reduced-service operations in huge attached warehouses used for merchandise display and/or storage. Well-known examples include Red Owl stores (food), Levitz (furniture), 84 Lumber, and Osco (drug).

Warehouse markets offer the consumer prices from 4 to 6 percent lower on food items and as much as 25 percent lower on nonfoods such as furniture. Efficient store layouts make goods easy to locate, and goods like furniture are usually sold on a cash-and-carry basis. Disadvantages of this retail concept include lack of customer service, smaller selection, and little, if any, post-sale service.

For manufacturers and suppliers, warehouse markets offer relatively assured markets, large-volume sales, and operating efficiencies. The major disadvantage is that many warehouse retailers purchase a limited number of brands within a product category and often will buy only one or two brands from a given manufacturer. A manufacturer thus does not achieve full-line representation for all brands.

The ***conglomerchant*** approach to retailing is one in which multimart retailers develop different stores to appeal to different market segments. They do not, however, allow the various stores in the total store portfolio to compete with each other. This precise and permanent positioning is used especially by retail holding companies and national chains. An example of the conglomerchant approach is Federated department stores, a conglomerate with 18 divisions, including Bloomingdale's (New York), the Boston Store (Milwaukee), and Ralph's supermarkets (West Coast).[16]

---

[15] Maurice I. Mandell and Larry J. Rosenberg, *Marketing,* 2d ed. (Englewood Cliffs, N.J.: Prentice-Hall, 1981), p. 405.

[16] Duncan and Hollander, *Modern Retailing Management,* p. 194.

Hypermarkets, or superstores, are large, self-service stores of at least 250,000 square feet that sell a mixture of foods and general merchandise in a warehouse-type setting. Many of the goods are displayed in wire baskets and metal racks stacked to a height of 12 to 15 feet.

The closest approximation to a hypermarket in the United States has 245,000 square feet and 68 checkout registers. Other companies have shown an interest in the concept, but there is some concern as to whether such stores can develop the sales volume necessary to compete with conventional supermarkets and discount department stores.

Geographic location

Shopping districts or locations known as *shopping centers* have emerged due to the growth of subdivision communities, the shift of families from urban to suburban areas, and the rising revenue costs of downtown locations. Shopping centers feature accessibility, free parking, and bright, clean stores.

Neighborhood shopping centers consist of several convenience stores. They usually include a supermarket, drugstore, hardware store, laundry, and gas station, among others. They normally serve 7,500 to 40,000 people living within 6 to 10 minutes' driving distance.

Community shopping centers are larger and offer some shopping stores as well as convenience stores. They normally serve 40,000 to 150,000 people within a three- to four-mile radius and usually include a small department store.

Regional shopping centers emphasize shopping stores and goods. They include one or two large department stores and as many as 200 smaller stores. Usually found near suburban areas, they serve at least 150,000 people with a five- to six-mile radius.

The *central shopping district* contains many of the urban area's leading shopping and specialty goods stores, as well as numerous convenience goods retailers. Serviced by public transportation, the central shopping district draws customers from the entire metropolitan area. Some specialty stores catering to a traditional clientele may obtain greater success in these downtown areas than in suburban malls. Secondary shopping districts are similar to the central districts and have the same types of stores, but they are usually smaller and fewer in number.

Free-standing stores are located apart from other retail establishments. They may draw customers from a considerable distance by offering unique merchandise, such as imported goods or exotic foods. Most survive, however, by selling convenience goods to customers who cannot or do not want to travel greater distances for better value.

Form of ownership

Retailing institutions can be classified on the basis of ownership or control. The major retailer classifications are independents, chains, franchises, and voluntary cooperatives, both retail- and wholesale-sponsored. (We discussed cooperatives in Chapter 14.)

Independents. About 85 percent of retail establishments are classed as ***independents:*** they are owned by individuals or firms with only one store in the same general kind of business. Independents account for 55 percent of all retail sales, making them the predominant retail form, both in numbers and in total sales volume.[17]

Independents usually are able to compete with larger retailers for several reasons. First, the independent frequently has a lower cost of doing business because of low rents, location in isolated neighborhoods, and ownership by the proprietor. Second, the store is usually located closer to customers than is possible for a larger chain store. Finally, the personal relationship between customer and owner allows the store to develop a unique personality and customer loyalty. But the failure rate among independents is high. The culprits here are inexperience, incompetence, and other management inadequacies.[18]

Chain stores. Technically, a ***chain store*** system is an organization consisting of two or more stores that are centrally owned or managed. However, many merchants who consider themselves small-scale independents operate two or three stores. It may be more meaningful, therefore, to consider a larger minimum number of units when categorizing a store as a chain—for example, 11 or more units (one of the categories used by the Census of Business).[19]

The sales volume of chains with 11 units or more is 35 percent of all retail sales, but the amount of retail sales by chains within various retail categories varies considerably. For chains with 11 or more units, the sales figures vary as follows: department stores—88 percent of sales; variety stores—81 percent; grocery stores—57 percent; drugstores—38 percent; and furniture stores—14 percent.[20]

Chain stores are characterized by the sale of similar merchandise and by similar architectural formats, centralized buying, and common ownership. Centralized buying is a key feature. It allows economies of scale and lower prices.

Chains typically feature staple merchandise for which there is little variation in customer preference. The chain store manager is basically involved with selling and has little control over the merchandise carried. Higher overhead expenses, less operational flexibility, and greater legislative regulation are disadvantages of chain stores.[21]

---

[17] Ibid., p. 17.

[18] Joseph B. Mason and Morris L. Mayer, *Modern Retailing: Theory and Practice,* 3d ed. (Plano, Tex.: Business Publications, 1984), p. 47.

[19] William J. Stanton, *Fundamentals of Marketing,* 4th ed. (New York: McGraw-Hill, 1975), p. 351.

[20] Duncan and Hollander, *Modern Retailing Management,* p. 19.

[21] Mason and Mayer, *Modern Retailing,* p. 47.

Franchises

franchise

> A **franchise** is a contractual agreement in which a parent company (franchisor) grants an individual or a relatively small company (franchisee) the right to do business in a prescribed manner over a certain period of time in a specified place.

Rights granted in the franchise agreement include sale of the product, use of company name, and adoption of methods, trademarks, and architecture. (See Chapter 14 for a discussion of different types of franchise arrangements.)

Franchising holds advantages for both the franchisor and the franchisee. It allows the franchisor to create rapid, extensive distribution and to benefit from the franchisee's knowledge of the locale. Profits are relatively secure in a shorter time with smaller risk and less investment than would be incurred in a solo venture. The franchisor avoids routine managerial tasks and enjoys revenue from several sources.

The franchisee is able to share a proven business idea and benefits from the franchisor's management and guidance in such areas as purchasing and location techniques. The franchisee also enjoys the opportunity to act as an independent business owner with only modest investment outlays and royalty payments and with less risk of failure.

In 1983 there were an estimated 465,000 franchised establishments totaling $465 billion in retail sales.[22] About 20 percent of franchises are owned by the parent company, while 80 percent are franchisee-owned. General Motors' ownership of a Buick dealership is an example of a company-owned franchise.

RETAIL INSTITUTIONAL CHANGE

Retailing is a dynamic industry, and retail management must be willing and able to adapt to the many changes confronting it. Retailers are affected by changes in consumer markets as well as by management practices. As evidence of the rapid changes in retailing, consider the example of the growth in factory retail outlet stores: In 1972 there were about 350 such outlets in the United States. By 1981 the number had grown to 7,000, which represents a 2,100 percent increase in less than 10 years! This dramatic increase has been caused by consumer demands for lower prices and by the efforts of manufacturers to dispose of their overruns and defective merchandise in more profitable ways.[23]

Several theories have been advanced to explain changes in retail institu-

---

[22] U.S. Department of Commerce, *Franchising in the Economy, 1981–83* (Washington, D.C.: U.S. Government Printing Office, 1979), pp. 12, 34.

[23] Jeffrey H. Birnbaum, "Discounting Outlets Increasing in Malls," *The Wall Street Journal,* October 14, 1981, p. 25.

tions. Three of the most popular theories are the wheel of retailing, the accordion theory, and retail life cycles.

wheel of retailing

> The **wheel of retailing** hypothesis states that new retailers usually enter the market as low-status, low-margin, and low-price operators.

Wheel of retailing

Gradually, they acquire more elaborate establishments and facilities, which require both increased investments and higher operating costs. Finally, they mature as high-cost, high-price merchants, vulnerable to newer retailers (who, in turn, go through a similar wheel pattern).[24] Examples of retail institutions that follow the wheel of retailing pattern are discount houses and supermarkets. Not all types of retailing institutions follow the wheel pattern. Nonconforming examples include vending machines, department store branch operations, and shopping centers. These retailing institutions started as high-cost, high-margin, and high-convenience types of operations.

There are several explanations offered by the wheel pattern:

1. *Retail personalities.* This explanation states that retail institutions are originally started by highly aggressive and cost-conscious entrepreneurs. However, as they gain wealth and grow older, they relax their vigilance and control over cost. The result is that their successors may be less cost-conscious and competent, and thus there is a deterioration in management, which causes a movement along the wheel.

2. *Misguidance.* This explanation suggests that in retail trade, advertising causes retail management to engage in superfluous modernization and to install overly elaborate facilities, both of which increase cost.

3. *The secular trend.* This explanation indicates that rising living standards promote more affluent tastes and motives. Price thus becomes less important, and more emphasis is placed on improved services and facilities. But some groups are still susceptible to low-price innovations. Thus, the wheel continues to move as innovative retailers respond to this low-price segment.

4. *Imperfect competition.* This explanation states that as the retail institution matures, competitive measures are focused on nonprice factors such as credit, service, location, and appearance. Less emphasis is placed on price, and this enables new price-conscious competitors to open the market.

Retail accordion

The ***accordion theory*** of retail development focuses on changes in the *width* of the product mix offered by the types of retail institutions.[25]

---

[24] Stanley C. Hollander, "The Wheel of Retailing," *Journal of Marketing,* July 1960, pp. 37–42.

[25] Mason and Mayer, *Modern Retailing Theory,* pp. 68–69.

accordion theory

> The **accordion theory** states that retail institutions offer a product mix that is first very wide, then much narrower, and then returns to a wider product mix.

The proponents of this theory think that modern retailing began with the general store with a very wide product mix. The department store replaced the general store with a somewhat more narrow and specialized product mix. The mail-order store, which tended to be still more specialized, developed after the department store. With the population concentration in urban areas, the opportunity to develop specialty stores increased. Consequently, single-line and specialty stores developed for books, phonographs, drugs, and garden supplies. But since the late 1950s, retailers have added product lines to their mixes, making the product mixes more generalized (wider). Grocery stores have added product lines unrelated to their basic grocery business, such as magazines, panty hose, school supplies, and selected hardware items. These retailers have tried to attract more customers and improve profit margins by offering a more generalized product mix.

Retail life cycle

The *retail life-cycle theory* states that retail institutions have life cycles similar to the cycles of products.[26]

retail life cycle

> The **retail life cycle** consists of four stages: early growth, accelerated development, maturity, and decline.

In the *early growth stage,* a new type of retail institution emerges. It usually represents a drastic change from existing retailing approaches and offers consumers a significant advantage. Often the advantage is lower price, but it may also include a distinctive product assortment, ease of shopping location, or different advertising and promotion methods. The supermarket that emerged in the 1930s is an excellent example of a retail innovation based on cost and price advantage. Supermarkets were able to operate on a gross margin of only 12 percent, compared with 20 percent for conventional food outlets. Moreover, supermarkets produced a net margin that was 50 percent higher than conventional outlets, and they generated as much sales volume in two weeks as many conventional stores did in an entire year.

---

[26] William R. Davidson, Albert D. Bates, and Steven J. Bass, "The Retail Life Cycle," *Harvard Business Review* 54, no. 6 (November/December 1976), pp. 89–96.

In the *accelerated-growth stage,* both sales volume and profits grow rapidly. This growth usually attracts many competitors. For example, once the discount department store was established as a permanent retailing institution, mature competitors such as Kresge, Woolworth, and Federated started their own discount operations. The influx of these new competitors frequently necessitated higher levels of investment to sustain growth.

In the *maturity stage,* sales growth and market share level off. Several major problems confront retailers in this stage of the life cycle. First, the entrepreneurs who started the retail institution find it difficult to control the larger and more complex organization. Second, excess capacity becomes a problem if retailers expand beyond levels justified by the size of the total market and thereby increase the amount of square footage to unprofitable levels. Finally, new forms of competition usually confront the retailers at this stage.

In the *decline stage,* sales drop dramatically and profits are low or negative. Retailers may struggle to avoid decline by repositioning their stores or by modifying their marketing approach. Such changes may only delay their inevitable end.

Now, let's summarize the major implications of these various theories of change in retail institutions. The wheel of retailing contends that changes in retailing are brought about by changes in the external environment, but a competent and forward-looking retail management can effectively adapt to these changes. The accordion theory stresses the pivotal role of changes in the width of the retailer's product mix as a way to adapt to change. Several implications of the retail life-cycle theory are important to retail management. First, because of shortening life cycles, management must remain flexible by adopting new management ideas and practices. For example, when Federated department stores established their Gold Circle discount division, they established an autonomous management task force that was completely free to explore new ideas and procedures. This enabled the Gold Circle group to try new concepts and operating procedures that ultimately proved successful. Other implications of the retail life-cycle theory are that management should place greater emphasis on research and on trying to analyze risk and profits in their decision making. Another sound practice is to try to extend the maturity stage of the life cycle. For example, department store managers have effectively extended the maturity stage by focusing on the sale of fashion apparel as well as on home furnishings. This adaptation has enabled them to achieve acceptable rates of profitability and growth.

Research indicates that the life cycles of retail institutions are becoming shorter. (See Table 15–2.) For example, variety stores took 60 years to reach their maturity stage in the early 1960s, but recent retail concerns (such as catalog showrooms) reach such maturity in just 10 years. Newer forms of retail selling will soon be confronted with intense competition, price pressures, and diminishing profit margins—all characteristics of the decline stage of the life cycle.

Table 15–2: Life cycles of retail institutions	Retail institutions	Intro-duction	Maturity	Approximate time required to reach maturity
	Department stores	Mid-1860s	Mid-1960s	100 years
	Variety stores	Early 1900s	Early 1960s	60 years
	Supermarkets	Mid-1930s	Mid-1960s	30 years
	Discount department stores	Mid-1950s	Mid-1970s	20 years
Source: Adapted from Bert C. McCammon, Jr., "The Future of Catalog Showrooms: Growth and Its Challenges to Management" (working paper, Marketing Science Institute, 1973), p. 3.	Fast-food service outlets	Early 1960s	Mid-1970s	15 years
	Home-improvement centers	Mid-1960s	Late 1970s	15 years
	Furniture warehouse showrooms	Late 1960s	Late 1970s	10 years
	Catalog showrooms	Late 1960s	Late 1970s	10 years

STRATEGIC RETAIL MANAGEMENT DECISIONS

Retail management makes strategic decisions in the areas of (1) store location; (2) store image; (3) merchandise, service, and atmosphere; (4) pricing; and (5) promotion.

Store location

The selection of a *store location* is one of the most crucial long-term decisions that retail management makes. Good locations can partially off-set poor retail management, but poor locations seriously impede even the most skillful retail managers. The location decision involves the selection of (1) a city or trading area and (2) the particular site within it. Specific quantitative criteria usually guide the location decision, too. For example, Denny's, a California-based chain of restaurants, demands that new restaurants be located in the suburbs of metropolitan areas with 100,000 people or more. Specific sites must be on commercial lots 150 feet wide, fronting on streets traveled by at least 20,000 cars each day. The median family income within a three-mile radius of a Denny's location must be $12,000.[27]

Although retail management agrees that location is a critical decision, the money spent on location analysis and research is woefully inadequate.[28] As the costs of location increase, though, so will the need for sound location research and analysis.

Store image

The customer forms this image from the store's attributes, such as merchandise, service, and physical facilities. Table 15–3 contains a listing of nine dimensions and their 20 components that represent the major attributes of a retail store's image.

store image	**Store image** is the *customer's perception* of the store's personality or character.

[27] "Denny Takes Its Menus East," *Business Week,* September 19, 1977, p. 114.
[28] Duncan and Hollander, *Modern Retailing Management,* p. 93.

	Dimension	Component
Table 15–3: The dimensions and components of store-image attributes	Merchandise	Quality Selection Style Price
	Service	Lay-away plan Sales personnel Easy return Credit Delivery
	Clientele	Customers
	Physical facilities	Cleanliness Store layout Shopping ease Attractiveness
	Convenience	Location Parking
Source: R. Hansen and T. Deutscher, "An Empirical Investigation of Attribute Importance in Retail Store Selection." Journal of Retailing, Winter 1977–78, pp. 59–73. Used with permission.	Promotion	Advertising
	Store atmosphere	Congeniality
	Institutional	Store reputation
	Post-transaction	Satisfaction

One research project expanded the 20 store-image components into 41 specific attributes frequently used in store-image studies.[29] Consumers were asked to rate the importance of each attribute for grocery stores. Table 15–4 shows their importance rankings.

Retail management could use this type of research to tailor its marketing efforts to meet the expectations of its target market. For example, based on the results found in Table 15–4, management could adopt procedures to ensure dependable products, clean stores, and easy-to-find items and could promote and advertise these attributes to customers. As customers become familiar with the store, these attributes would help to shape the customers' image of it.

Failure to achieve a distinctive image among consumers may mean disaster for a retailer. In 1975, W. T. Grant was a 1,200-store chain with sales over $2 billion. The company went bankrupt for a variety of reasons, including heavy indebtedness and ill-conceived plans for expansion. Another major factor, though, was the lack of a definable and distinctive store image.[30]

---

[29] Robert Hansen and Terry Deutscher, "An Empirical Investigation of Attribute Importance in Retail Store Selection," *Journal of Retailing,* Winter 1977–78, pp. 59–73.

[30] Robert F. Hartlye, *Marketing Mistakes* (Columbus, Ohio: Charles E. Merrill Publishing, 1976), p. 51.

Table 15–4: Top 10 and bottom 5 store attributes for grocery stores

Store attribute	Rank	Mean importance rating*
Dependable products.	1	9.50
Store is clean	2	9.33
Easy to find items you want	3	9.27
Fast checkout	4	9.23
High-quality products.	5	9.10
High value for the money	6	9.05
Fully stocked.	7	8.94
Helpful store personnel.	8	8.88
Easy to move through store	9	8.88
Adequate number of store personnel	10	8.87
.	.	.
.	.	.
.	.	.
Many friends shop there.	37	4.18
Store is liked by friends.	38	4.07
Easy to get credit	39	2.58
Lay-away available.	40	2.09
Easy to get home delivery	41	1.93

Source: R. Hansen and T. Deutscher, "An Empirical Investigation of Attribute Importance in Retail Store Selection." *Journal of Retailing,* Winter 1977–78, pp. 59–73. Used with permission.

* The importance of each attribute was rated from 0 (no importance) to 10 (very important) by 215 consumers.

Merchandise, service, and atmosphere

The total product offering of the retailer comprises three major elements: the merchandise, the service, and the atmosphere. The most basic element is the merchandise or product mix, which can be thought of as wide or narrow, depending on the number of product lines. The offering within specific lines can be either deep or shallow. As we discussed earlier, department stores usually have a wider product mix than specialty stores, while specialty stores usually have much deeper product lines, giving customers a greater choice of brand names, quality, and price within product lines.

The merchandise the retailer offers to target consumers plays a major role in developing consumers' image of the store. In the early 1980s J. C. Penney added a line of women's apparel exclusively designed for the company. To promote this new line and create an overall trendier image, Penney's increased national advertising from $35 million in 1983 to $50 million in 1984. The goal is to boost sales per square foot from $120 to about $200, which is comparable to the higher-margin retailers such as Macy's.[31]

Retail management has adopted the practice of ***scrambled merchandising,*** which means selling product lines unrelated to the basic lines the retailer carries. For example, grocery supermarkets now carry such non-food items as greeting cards, magazines, assorted household and hardware

---

[31] "J.C. Penney Shops for a Trendier Image," *Business Week,* February 6, 1984, p. 58.

items, school supplies, and motor oil. Retailers have resorted to scrambled merchandising to improve their gross margin (the difference between selling price and cost of goods sold) and profits. The after-tax profit margin in supermarkets is about 1 percent of each dollar's worth of products sold. The typical gross margin on most food items is about 20 percent, while the gross margin on many nonfood items adopted in a scrambled merchandising approach is 40 to 50 percent. Supermarkets and drugstores have been especially active in scrambling their merchandise.

The services a retailer offers are a major form of nonprice competition and another important element in developing a positive store image. A retailer can offer varied services: delivery, gift wrapping, credit, money-back or complete-satisfaction guarantees, personal selling, and adequate parking. The decision to offer services is determined by a number of factors. Competition often forces a retailer to provide comparable or compensating advantages. The type of merchandise being marketed often influences the types of services offered: for example, bulky and heavy products like furniture and major appliances usually require the retailer to provide delivery service. The store's pricing policy also often affects services. Discount store customers don't expect many services, while customers of higher-priced department stores do.[32] Retailing services will probably increase as retailers provide more of them to customers in an attempt to improve store profitability. Indeed, one estimate is that by 1990 services will provide 50 percent of sales revenue in general merchandise stores.[33]

Store atmosphere is the general quality of design, which expresses the store's character and results in a store image that is readily recognizable by consumers.[34] There are two major elements to atmosphere: (1) the interior decor (walls, ceilings, floor, lighting, fixtures), customer services, and merchandise; and (2) exterior design, which often draws customers to the store by identifying the type of quality of the firm.[35] The interior and exterior elements should be in harmony with and reinforce each other.

The atmosphere should be designed to satisfy the target market.[36] For example, college bars are usually loud, hectic, and active; bars designed for middle-aged customers are more quiet and subdued. Retail management must decide which atmospheric variables will create the utilities sought by consumers in the target market. The overall store atmosphere is a major factor in developing the store's image.

---

[32] Duncan and Hollander, *Modern Retailing Management,* pp. 514–15.

[33] "Future Shock/Customer Services," *Chain Store Age,* September 1975, p. 124.

[34] Adolph Novak and James Toman, *Store Planning and Design* (New York: Lebhan Griedman Books, 1977), p. 222.

[35] Mason and Mayer, *Modern Retailing,* pp. 611–12.

[36] Philip Kotler, "Atmospherics as a Marketing Tool," *Journal of Retailing,* Winter 1973–74, p. 50.

| Pricing | Retail management makes pricing decisions on the strategic and tactical levels, and success demands that the pricing decisions be integrated with the retailer's overall strategy. The price of merchandise should be consistent with the retailer's strategy and should reinforce the image the retailer is trying to project. The role of price in the overall strategy of K mart is stated by its chairman of the board: "Sell the basic necessity items. Buy it narrow. Stock it deep. Price it low."[37] |

On a tactical level, retailers must make decisions on such issues as the frequency of sales, the amount of markdowns or reduction from original selling price, and the use of loss leaders. *Loss-leader pricing* refers to the pricing of selected products at prices lower than consumers expect. The main objective is to build traffic in the store. The logic of loss-leader pricing is that the promotional appeal of the loss leaders will bring in more customers, who will then purchase merchandise besides the loss-leader item. Products frequently used as loss leaders in grocery stores are milk, soft drinks, and eggs.

| Promotion | Retail management uses the basic promotional tools: advertising, personal selling, publicity, and sales promotion. These should be coordinated and integrated in order to achieve clearly defined objectives. The objectives for promotion in general and advertising in particular fall into two categories: (1) the accomplishment of some communication objective such as increased awareness or comprehension of advertising messages and (2) the attainment of sales. |

Much retailing advertising is designed to prompt consumers to buy in the immediate future. The large, multipage ads run by supermarkets that feature weekly specials are designed to elicit an immediate sale. Newspapers carry about 75 percent of all U.S. retail ads, and most of them are meant to attract sales. But some department stores advertise to communicate a specific image, and recently the trend has been to use television as the medium to convey this image.[38]

Advertising can frequently motivate retail employees to achieve specific objectives. Retailing is a service-oriented business—and the service is only as good as the people who provide it. Consider the example of Pathmark, a food chain in the eastern United States. The company learned through marketing research that consumers were skeptical about the freshness of its meats, produce, and other perishables. Management responded with a program of renewed commitment to freshness in every department. Realizing that employees must be fully informed and committed to the new program, management completely integrated employees

---

[37] "The New Growth for Discounters," *Chain Store Age Executive* 5 (September 1975), p. 67.

[38] Jefferey H. Birnbaum, "Retailers Buy More Ads on TV," *The Wall Street Journal*, August 14, 1980, p. 17.

Table 15–5:
Types of wholesalers

Full-function
  Merchant wholesalers
    General-line
    Specialty-line
  Sales office and branches
  Agents
    Manufacturer's
    Selling
  Brokers and commission houses

Limited-function
  Drop shipper
  Truck distributor
  Mail-order wholesaler
  Cash-and-carry
  Cooperatives
  Rack jobbers

Industrial
  Sales branches
  Industrial distributors
    General-line
    Specialty-line
    Combination-house
  Manufacturer's agents
  Brokers

into the program from its start. Before advertising was shown to the public, it was shown to the store's 25,000 employees. The result was a "fanatic attention to the details of freshness." Follow-up research showed that consumers no longer questioned the freshness of Pathmark's perishables.[39]

wholesalers

> **Wholesalers** are intermediaries who sell to other intermediaries, who buy for resale or for industrial use.[40]

WHOLESALING

According to this definition, a manufacturer may not be part of the wholesale *trade* but may perform a wholesaling *function* if it sells products to other manufacturers. A retailer could not be a wholesaler, although the retailer may perform a wholesale *function* by marketing to other retailers.[41]

[39] Zal Venet, " . . . Retail Ads Should Emphasize Employee Pride," *Marketing News,* October 30, 1981, p. 5.

[40] Irving J. Shapiro, *Marketing Terms: Definitions, Explanations, and/or Aspects* (West Long Branch, N.J.: S-M-C Publishing, 1969), p. 183.

[41] Ronald W. Hasty and R. Ted Will, *Marketing* (New York: Canfield Press, 1975), p. 206.

Wholesalers are an important factor in the U.S. economy. In 1977 wholesale sales topped $1.2 trillion, while retail sales were about $1 trillion. Wholesale prices are substantially lower than retail prices; but total wholesale sales exceed total retail sales because products are sold several times at wholesale levels before they reach the retailer.[42] There are some 382,000 wholesalers in the United States, and they maintain about $82 billion of inventory. About 4 million people are employed in wholesaling.[43]

Wholesaling functions

Wholesalers perform a variety of functions essential to the marketing process; and frequently they are able to perform these functions more effectively and at a lower cost than are other members of the distribution channel. A great variety of wholesalers perform some or all these functions, depending on their role and the needs of the other members in the channel.

Buying and breaking bulk. The primary function of the wholesaler is to purchase in large quantities and then sell smaller quantities to other intermediaries—a process called *breaking bulk.* The wholesaler interacts with many suppliers and tries to select an assortment of goods that best meets the needs of the wholesaler's customers. In the industrial area, for instance, an electrical supply firm or wholesaler may handle some 60,000 product items made by as many as 300 different manufacturers.[44] As you can easily see, the individual electrician is well served by the electrical supply firm, which provides at one convenient location the product offerings of several hundred manufacturers.

Transportation. Wholesalers frequently assume the function of delivering products to retailers. Since the wholesaler is physically located closer to the retailer than the manufacturer is, the wholesaler can perform the delivery function more quickly. Besides delivering the product, the wholesaler may also stock the retailer's shelves. For example, the rack jobber, one of the newest types of wholesalers, stocks the shelves for retailers and frees the retailer's personnel from this task. Rack jobbers usually serve supermarkets and drug stores and handle such lines as housewares, cosmetics, toys, and novelty items.

Storage and inventory maintenance. Wholesalers provide a warehousing or storage function that benefits both manufacturers and retailers. Manufacturers benefit because the warehousing done by the wholesaler

[42] William H. Cunningham and Isabella C. M. Cunningham, *Marketing: A Managerial Approach,* (South-Western Publishing Co.: Cincinnati, 1981) p. 471.

[43] U.S. Bureau of the Census, *Census of Wholesale Trade, 1977* (Washington, D.C.: U.S. Government Printing Office, 1980).

[44] Ralph S. Alexander, James Cross, and Richard Hill, *Industrial Marketing* (Homewood, Ill.: Richard D. Irwin, 1967), p. 229.

Material Flow is a wholesaler selling industrial products to warehouses, industry, and government. Here the company employs a postage-paid form to generate interest in its catalog.

Courtesy Material Flow, Inc.

reduces the manufacturer's cost of physical distribution and the capital needed to store larger inventories. The retailer benefits because the smaller inventory that can be carried results in higher turnover and less inventory investment.

Market information.   The manufacturer of a product often has no regular direct contact with its customers. The wholesaler can serve as a communication link, supplying information to manufacturers about customers' reactions to new products, competitors' new products, and price changes. And the wholesaler provides its customers valuable product information from the manufacturers.

Finance.   Wholesalers perform two important financial functions. They often provide credit to their customers—usually for a period of 30 days, with a discount for early payment. And wholesalers provide financial assistance to manufacturers by placing orders early and by paying their bills promptly.

Promotion.   Wholesalers engage in several promotional activities, including personal selling, advertising, and sales promotion. Of these, the personal selling function is often the most valuable to manufacturers. Advertising usually involves developing sales catalogs for convenient inspection of product items and placing ads in trade journals. A common sales promotion activity is to set up point-of-purchase displays and shelf tags informing retailers' customers of price-reduced specials.

Risk taking. The wholesaler assumes the risk associated with taking title and physical possession of goods and thus relieves the manufacturer of some risks. Wholesalers' risks lie in the possible obsolescence of the product, theft, and destruction by fire or other natural disasters. When granting credit, the wholesaler assumes the risk of the retailer or industrial buyer not paying for the goods.

Management advice and services. Wholesalers frequently have contact with hundreds or even thousands of industrial accounts. Wholesalers thus learn a great deal about successful and unsuccessful business practice, and this experience and knowledge is often passed on to the wholesaler's

The Wholesale House is a top-of-the-line wholesaler. This ad demonstrates the depth of the product line in bathroom accessories.

Courtesy Top of the Line/The Wholesale House.

𝒢LAMOROUS BATHROOM ACCESSORIES *BY STYLEBUILT*
ARE AS WONDERFULLY PRACTICAL AS THEY ARE BEAUTIFUL!

You'll delight in the whimsical *Golden Butterflies* that have alighted on the brushed florentine finish of dazzling gold. These opulent accessories are designed to give your bath or powder room the true touch of regal elegance!

A. Waste Basket of glittering gold with three butterflies caught in mid-flight. Meas. 10½" high × 8½" wide. #ST01XDF, Suggested Retail $40.00, **Your Price $34.50.**

B. Toothbrush and Tumbler Holder to keep your sink beautifully neat. #ST01XDC, Suggested Retail $25.00, **Your Price $21.50.**

C. Boutique Tissue Box, exquisite on your bedside table too! #ST01XDE, Suggested Retail $24.00, **Your Price $19.50.**

D. Tissue Holder for standard tissue box, with two butterflies on top. #ST01XDV, Suggested Retail $28.00, **Your Price $21.50.**

E. Soap Dish rests gracefully on four gold legs decorated with two delightful butterflies. #ST01XDA, Sug Retail $22.00, **Your Price $16.50.**

F. Finger Towel Holder is a magnificent way to keep your guest towels wonderfully at hand. #ST01XDY, Sugg. Retail $23.00, **Your Price $17.50.**

BASKETS have never been more gorgeous. The sumptuous gold finish is intricately and wonderfully woven into these lustrous *Basketweave* accessories that will add the decorator's touch to your home.

G. Wastebasket looks wonderful in any room! Meas. 11½" high × 10½" wide. #ST02XDF, Sug Retail $40.00, **Your Price $31.50.**

H. Boutique Tissue Box, a marvelous holder you'll display with pride. #ST02XDE, Suggested Retail $22.00, **Your Price $16.50.**

I. Toothbrush & Tumbler Holder is both efficient and a lovely bath decoration. #ST02XDC, Sug Retail $25.00, **Your Price $18.50.**

J. Tissue Holder, a man-size tissue holder that will add a note of grace to your breakfast room or den. #ST02XDV, Suggested Retail $26.00, **Your Price $19.50.**

K. Fingertip Towel Holder presents your guest towels in a most beautiful way. #ST02XDY, Suggested Retail $23.00, **Your Price $17.50.**

L. Soap Dish, a delicately footed container for soaps, china interior for easy cleaning. #ST02XDA, Sug Retail $20.00, **Your Price $15.50.**

M. Perfume Tray, a special feminine touch that's perfect for your bureau, too! #ST02XDL, Sugg. Retail $40.00, **Your Price $31.50.**

customers. Some wholesalers conduct seminars to discuss trends and to present new products and techniques to improve business operations. In addition, wholesalers provide many other services, such as assisting in store layout, training sale clerks, setting up in-store displays, and inventory control.

Types of wholesalers

Different types of wholesalers have developed to meet the specific needs of customers. Some wholesalers provide the full range of services we discussed earlier; others provide almost no services other than order taking and processing. In the following section we discuss the various wholesalers listed in Table 15–5, beginning with the three basic types of full-function wholesalers: merchant wholesalers, sales offices and branches, and agents, brokers, and commission houses.

Merchant wholesalers. There are 307,000 **merchant wholesalers** in the United States, and their total sales in 1977 were $676.1 billion.[45] This makes merchant wholesalers the largest group of wholesalers as measured by number of establishments and dollar sales.

Wholesale merchants represent what is commonly meant when the term *wholesaler* is used. They usually sell to retailers and provide the full range of wholesaler services. The major types of wholesalers are general-line and specialty-line. **General-line wholesalers** carry only one or two lines of products but have great depth within the lines. Hardware wholesalers are an example. **Specialty-line wholesalers** are even more narrow than general-line wholesalers. They carry only part of a product line but provide greater depth for that part of the line. Specialty-line wholesalers frequently handle products such as cheese, beer, and frozen foods.

Sales offices and sales branches. A manufacturer-owned **sales office** may operate with only one or two employees. No inventory is held, and all deliveries of merchandise sold go directly from manufacturer to buyer. Firms may choose this method for economic reasons or because an effective wholesaler is not available. A sales office gives the manufacturer complete control of the marketing of its products.

Manufacturer's **sales branches** are similar to sales offices except that the branches do carry inventory, which allows quicker delivery to the customer. Because sales branches are often much larger than sales offices, they can provide more services. For example, General Electric Supply, a subsidiary of GE, maintains several sales branches throughout the United States. They differ from other electrical supply wholesalers in that they carry primarily General Electric products.[46]

---

[45] U.S. Bureau of the Census, *Census of Wholesale Trade, 1977.*

[46] Richard H. Buskirk, *Principles of Marketing,* 4th ed. (Hinsdale, Ill.: Dryden Press, 1975), p. 364.

Table 15–6: Wholesale trade statistics by type of operation, 1977	Number of establishments	Sales ($ billions)	Number of employees (000)	Payroll ($ billions)
Wholesale trade	382,800	$1,258.4	4,397	$58.2
Merchant wholesalers	307,300	676.0	3,368	42.0
Manufacturer's sales branches and offices	40,500	451.8	806	13.2
Merchandise agents and brokers	35,100	130.4	222	2.9

Source: *Statistical Abstract of the United States, 1984,* p. 907.

Agents, brokers, and commission houses.   Merchandise agents and brokers do not take title to merchandise they sell. Their payment is usually a fee or commission. There are four main categories in this group.

Manufacturer's agents sell part of a manufacturer's output on a contractual basis. They have little or no influence on price and usually have exclusive selling rights in a region. Since payment is not on a salaried basis, these agents offer advantages to small manufacturers and to firms whose markets are too geographically dispersed to make a company sales force economical. Manufacturer's agents are familiar with buyers, and they can be influential in opening new markets.

Selling agents handle a firm's entire output. They usually have more authority over price and may have some financing responsibilities. Because they are reimbursed on a commission or fee basis, selling agents are especially advantageous to the small manufacturer. But selling agents are responsible for the entire selling and distributing task: firms using them give up most of their control over marketing activities.

Brokers specialize within some particular line and provide intermittent buying and selling services for a principal. They have little, if any, authority over price or terms of sale but serve as a liaison between buyers and sellers until an agreement is reached. Brokers can offer professional advice to firms as well as economic advantages to manufacturers.

Commission houses take physical possession of merchandise, arrange delivery to buyers, negotiate prices, and collect and remit proceeds of sales. They are common in the marketing of perishable goods (primarily fruits and vegetables) and in the marketing of livestock such as hogs and cattle. See Table 15–6 for a listing of the number of establishments, sales, number of employees, and payroll for the various types of full-function wholesalers.

Limited-function wholesalers.   There are six basic types of limited-function wholesalers: (1) drop shippers, (2) truck distributors, (3) mail-order wholesalers, (4) cash-and-carry wholesalers, (5) cooperatives, and (6) rack jobbers.[47]

---

[47] Adapted from E. Jerome McCarthy and William A. Perreault, Jr., *Essentials of Marketing,* 8th ed. (Homewood, Ill.: Richard D. Irwin, 1984), pp. 425–27.

The **drop shipper** takes title to goods and extends credit to customers but does not handle, stock, or deliver the goods. This wholesaler is merely an assembler of transactions, ordering goods directly from the manufacturer to be shipped directly to buyers. A drop shipper commonly sells products that are so bulky that additional handling would be expensive and possibly damaging. Because drop shippers do not handle the goods, they can operate at lower markup than full-service wholesalers.

Truck wholesalers provide most of the same functions as the full-service wholesaler. They deliver goods stocked in their own trucks—usually perishable goods such as candy, tobacco, and salad dressings. Truck wholesalers often carry goods that regular wholesalers prefer not to carry; and they call on small service stations and "back-alley" garages who often forget to order small items from a full-service wholesaler. Because of the amount of service they provide, truck wholesalers' operating costs are relatively high.

Mail-order wholesalers do everything full-service wholesalers do except send a sales force into the field. Instead, they distribute catalogs to their customers, who are often small industrial buyers or retailers who might not be called on by other wholesalers. Mail-order wholesalers are common in hardware, jewelry, sporting goods, and general merchandise lines.

Cash-and-carry wholesalers do not send out sales representatives but require customers to come to the warehouse, pick up orders, pay cash, and transport their own purchases. The shifting of these costs to retailers reduces the wholesaler's costs and prices and is an economical way to serve low-volume retailers who are too small to be served profitably by a full-service wholesaler.

Producers' cooperatives operate much like service wholesalers, but profits here go to the co-op's customer members. Successful cooperatives emphasize the sorting-out process to improve the quality of products offered to the market. Examples of producers' cooperatives include Land-O-Lakes Creameries, and the Sunmaid Raisin Growers Association.[48]

Rack jobbers specialize in nonfood items sold through grocery stores and supermarkets. They concentrate on narrow lines such as housewares, cosmetics, toys, and novelties, often displaying them on racks that they own in the retailing stores. Rack jobbing is a fairly expensive service, with operating costs about 18 percent of sales; but this service frees retail management from merchandising the items involved. An example of a successful rack-jobber operation is the L'eggs boutique (hosiery).

Industrial wholesalers.   Many wholesalers used in consumer product marketing are also used in industrial product channels. Examples are man-

---

[48] Ibid., p. 263.

ufacturers' sales offices and agents. Sales branches maintain an inventory to meet a substantial portion of demand from a given geographic area. Many branches also include a service installation when pre-sale or post-sale service is part of the marketing program. Sales branches are usually used by large manufacturing concerns; they offer the possibility of lower marketing costs than other types of industrial wholesalers. These savings could be passed on to customers to gain a competitive advantage.

A manufacturer may choose between industrial distributors, agents, and brokers. **Industrial distributors** are full-service merchant wholesalers selling primarily to industrial markets. They perform all or most of the marketing functions and stock the products they sell. Their products include maintenance, repair, and operating supplies; original equipment supplies; operating equipment; and machinery. For the manufacturer, they provide intensive market coverage and advice on local markets, convenient warehousing, and customer credit and billing. For the customer, industrial distributors act as purchasing agents, store and deliver goods, extend credit, provide service, and supply information. There are three types of industrial distributors: (1) **general-line distributors,** which carry a complete assortment of goods in one line; (2) **specialty distributors,** which concentrate on a limited range of products in a given line (such as bearings, abrasives, or cutting tools); and (3) the **combination house,** which is involved in other forms of wholesaling in addition to industrial distribution.[49] An example of the latter is an electrical distributor who sells to the construction industry, manufacturers, and retailers.

Manufacturers' agents are the most numerous of all intermediaries and are second in total sales. The typical agent handles several brands of related but competitive goods and provides technical sales development as a principal service. Price, sales territory, and terms of sale are set by the manufacturer. Manufacturer's agents are often used where sales potentials are not sufficient to warrant direct-sales efforts, in cases of new-product introduction, and when seasonal demand fluctuations occur.

Brokers are the most important functional intermediaries in terms of sales volume. They buy or sell on behalf of their principals. A broker operates on a single-transaction basis or on a series of related transactions. The principal service provided is price negotiation, so brokers tend to be concentrated in highly standardized lines that can be bought or sold by description, such as agricultural raw materials.

Circumstances favoring the use of a broker are wide seasonal variations in output and the desire for buyer or seller anonymity.

---

[49] Frederick E. Webster, "The Role of the Industrial Distributor in Marketing Strategy," *Journal of Marketing,* July 1976, pp. 10–16.

STRATEGIC WHOLESALE MANAGEMENT DECISIONS

Location

The two major decisions confronting the management of wholesaling operations involve the general area or location and the particular sets within the general area. Wholesalers are concentrated in highly populated areas. Almost half of all wholesale sales are made in the 15 largest Standard Metropolitan Statistical Areas (SMSAs). Wholesalers are concentrated because the industries they serve are concentrated: for example, furniture manufacturers are concentrated in North Carolina and Michigan; clothing and textiles are concentrated in New York and North Carolina. Wholesalers locate near their target markets to meet their customers' needs quickly and reliably. Wholesalers need the warehousing, financing, and transportation facilities available in metropolitan markets to provide these services.

Wholesalers usually locate in low-rent areas of the community. Every effort is made to hold down the costs of building and land—those aspects of wholesale operations usually not visible to customers, who are most interested in the lowest possible price. Inexpensive facilities help wholesalers maintain their net profit margins (usually from 1 to 2 percent of sales). In summary, the wholesale strategic location decision is to locate near customers; on a tactical level, the decision is to minimize the land and building costs of the particular site.

Product/service mix

The types of products wholesalers usually handle (1) are nonperishable, (2) are simple (not technically complicated), and (3) can be purchased from stock rather than custom-made. Products without these characteristics usually cannot be handled effectively and efficiently by wholesalers. For example, technical equipment like a computer is usually sold directly by the manufacturer to the industrial user.

A major strategic decision facing the wholesaler involves the completeness of the product mix and services to provide to customers. A key factor in this decision is the profitability of specific products and services. So is the relative importance of a given customer who requests a specific product or service. Consider the following example:

> McDonald's, the fast-food franchisor, wanted one of its wholesalers, Golden State Foods, to provide McDonald's entire food and nonfood supplies. Golden State derived 80 percent of its $66 million in annual sales by supplying burgers, buns, potatoes, and other secondary items to 432 of McDonald's 2,200 outlets. As you can surmise, Golden State did add a complete line of paper products and other nonfood items to provide the product mix requested by its largest customer.[50]

The services that a wholesaler provides are determined by the needs of its customers. For example, as retailers trim costs in order to compete

---

[50] "A Fight for All of McDonald's Business," *Business Week,* February 17, 1973, pp. 42–46.

in the discount segment of retailing, poor shelf displays and out-of-stock problems increase. Manufacturers then have an increased need for in-store services such as replenishment of shelf stocks, checking inventory in retail outlets, and tidying displays. Often these wholesaler services produce a doubling or tripling of retail sales for manufacturer clients:

> In general, the promotional services provided by wholesalers have not been very effective. The use of advertising in particular has been done without strategic planning guidance. Personal selling at the wholesale level usually lacks the effectiveness provided by the team approach employed by manufacturers like IBM and Xerox.[51]

Pricing

Pricing at the wholesale level is a cost-oriented approach in which wholesalers mark up the products they purchase from manufacturers and suppliers. The markup varies according to the type of product and services performed; it commonly ranges from 20 percent to 40 percent of the wholesaler's cost of goods sold for a full-service wholesaler such as the merchant wholesaler. Food brokers earn a commission of about 2 percent on items like sugar to 7 percent on new-product specialty items.

From a manufacturer's perspective, establishing the price at which to sell products to wholesalers involves setting functional trade discounts. These discounts are based on the wholesaler's place in the channel; they represent payment for performing certain marketing functions. A wholesaler may also receive larger discounts based on the competitive situation: if competition has reduced the wholesaler's margin on a product, the wholesaler might be able to negotiate a greater discount in return for helping implement the product manufacturer's program.

Wholesalers are often squeezed between manufacturers or suppliers (who offer small trade discounts) and their customers (who demand lower prices). In fact, research indicates that industrial distributors believe too much emphasis on price is the problem most often encountered with their customers.[52] As wholesalers improve operations through the use of computers, they should grow more sophisticated in pricing their products.

LEGAL DIMENSIONS OF CHANNEL, RETAIL, AND WHOLESALE MANAGEMENT

When manufacturers or suppliers establish relationships with channel members such as wholesalers or retailers, legal questions may arise. In the following sections we discuss the major legal issues confronting channel retail and wholesale management.

---

[51] James L. Hesket, *Marketing* (New York: MacMillan, 1976), p. 317.

[52] John Convar, "They Buy, They Sell—Here's What They Tell," *Purchasing*, May 8, 1973, pp. 32–37.

Exclusive-dealing contracts

Exclusive dealing is the practice of a seller agreeing to sell through one intermediary and the intermediary agreeing to sell the products of one manufacturer. ***Exclusive-dealing contracts*** are not illegal per se. But they are considered illegal if (1) the manufacturer's sales volume represents a substantial percent of the total sales volume for a particular product class in the affected market or (2) competition is substantially lessened because the dealer in the exclusive deal has a dominant position in the market.[53]

In the *Standard Oil of California* case, the court applied the quantitative substantiality test.[54] This test states that if an exclusive contract prevents a substantial share of the market from competing, the contract is an unreasonable restraint of trade and, therefore, illegal. In the *Standard Oil* case, the company sold 23 percent of the gasoline marketed in the western United States and had exclusive contracts with 16 percent of the retail outlets, accounting for approximately 7 percent of that area's gasoline sales. Consequently, the amount of trade affected was considered substantial.[55]

Tying contracts

A ***tying contract*** is one in which the seller agrees to sell one product (the tying product) only if the buyer agrees to buy the seller's other product (the tied product). Tying contracts are subject to prosecution under Section 3 of the Clayton Act if they substantially lessen competition. Full-line "forcing" is a type of tying contract in which a manufacturer requires an intermediary to purchase an entire product line when only one or several product items are desired by the intermediary.

American Can leased its patented can-closing equipment to canners only if they were willing to buy their cans from American Can. This tying contract was found to violate the Sherman Antitrust and the Clayton acts because it restricted competition between American Can and any other canner for the business of the companies who leased American's equipment.[56]

Exclusive territories

Exclusive territories exist when a manufacturer gives an intermediary the exclusive right to sell in a specified territory. Exclusive-territory arrangements are also referred to as ***vertical divisions of the market.*** Too little is known about the economic effects of vertical divisions of the market to make a summary judgment; so the courts have applied the rule of reason or a case-by-case analysis when judging the vertical agreements. In contrast, a ***horizontal agreement*** is one in which intermediaries

[53] Joe L. Welch, *Marketing Law* (Tulsa: Petroleum Publishing Company, 1980), p. 29.

[54] *Standard Oil of California* v. *The United States,* 337 US 293 (1949).

[55] Welch, *Marketing Law,* p. 30.

[56] *U.S.* v. *American Can Company et al.,* 87 F. SUPP. 18 (1949).

get together and divide the market among themselves. The court has ruled that horizontal agreements are illegal.

The *Schwinn Bicycle Company* case is helpful in understanding the legal dimensions of exclusive-territory arrangements.[57] Schwinn used a multiple-channel approach in distributing its bicycles, parts, and accessories (1) through distributors, (2) directly to retailers on consignment (retailer takes possession but not title to the product), and (3) directly to retailers. Schwinn assigns specific territories to its distributors and instructs them to sell only to franchised accounts in the distributor's territory. The Supreme Court ruled that requiring distributors to sell only to franchised dealers was illegal and a violation of Section 1 of the Sherman Antitrust Act.[58] In order to control distributors' territories, Schwinn had to either sell only on consignment or vertically integrate. In *Schwinn*, the Court ruled that if title passed to an intermediary, it is a per se violation to restrict territories. The exception to this rule would be if reasonable restriction were imposed by a failing company or by a newcomer to the market.[59] If title does not pass to an intermediary (such as a manufacturer's agents), then the manufacturer could restrict territories as well.

In 1977, the *GTE Sylvania* case overruled the per se ruling established in *Schwinn*. In this landmark decision, the Supreme Court established that the rule of reason must be applied when evaluating the impact of exclusive-territory arrangements on competition. Sylvania had a network of independent franchisees that sold Sylvania products in restricted territories. One of the franchisees became dissatisfied with the Sylvania policy of restricting the location at which franchisees could sell Sylvania products. After several confrontations, Sylvania terminated the franchise agreement with the disgruntled franchisee. The Court upheld the GTE Sylvania position because, even though the franchise description reduced the amount of *intrabrand competition* for Sylvania TV sets, it increased Sylvania's ability to engage in *interbrand competition.* The Court felt that the net effect was a more competitive marketplace, with Sylvania's market share increasing from 1 percent to about 5 percent because of the advantages provided by the territorial restrictions.

The key to understanding the *GTE Sylvania* case is understanding the difference between interbrand and intrabrand competition. **Interbrand competition** is competition among producers of television sets. **Intrabrand competition** is competition among intermediaries selling a particular brand—for example, competition among retailers selling Zenith television sets.

---

[57] *U.S.* v. *Arnold, Schwinn & Co.,* 388 U.S. 365 (1967).

[58] Welch, *Marketing Law,* p. 48.

[59] James R. Burley, "Territorial Restriction in Distribution Systems: Current Legal Developments," *Journal of Marketing,* October 1975, p. 52.

SUMMARY

Retailing is a major source of employment in the United States. Structural classifications include margin/turnover, product mix, nonstore retailing, geographic location, and form of ownership.

Retailing is a dynamic industry, characterized by constant institutional change. The wheel of retailing, accordion, and life-cycle theories help explain these changes and their implications for retail management.

Several strategic decision areas for retail management include store location, image, merchandise, service, atmosphere, pricing, and promotion.

Wholesaling is an important function in the channel of distribution. Wholesale intermediaries perform various tasks, including buying and breaking bulk, transportation, storage, inventory maintenance, market information, financing, promotion, risk taking, and management advice.

There are various types of wholesalers. Full-function wholesalers include merchant wholesalers, sales offices and branches, agents, and brokers. Drop shippers and rack jobbers are examples of limited-function wholesalers. Wholesalers used for industrial products include sales branches and manufacturer's agents. Wholesale management requires decision making in such strategic areas as location, product/service mix, and pricing.

There are several legal dimensions of channel, retail, and wholesale management. Issues that may confront management include exclusive-dealing and tying contracts and exclusive territories.

KEY CONCEPTS

Margin	Conglomerchant	Wholesalers
Turnover	Hypermarket	Breaking bulk
Department store	Shopping center	Merchant wholesaler
Mazur plan	Neighborhood shopping center	General-line wholesaler
Merchandising division	Community shopping center	Specialty-line wholesaler
Publicity division	Regional shopping center	Sales office
Operations division	Central shopping district	Sales branch
Accounting and control division	Free-standing store	Manufacturer's agents
Specialty store	Independent	Selling agents
Variety store	Chain stores	Brokers
Full-service retailer	Franchise	Commission houses
Supermarket	Wheel of retailing	Drop shipper
Discount store	Accordian theory	Truck wholesaler
Convenience store	Retail life cycle	Mail-order wholesaler
Nonstore retailing	Store location	Cash-and-carry wholesaler
Direct marketing	Store image	Producers' cooperative
Vending machine	Scrambled merchandising	Rack jobbers
Door-to-door selling	Store atmosphere	Industrial distributor
Warehouse retailing		

General-line distributor

Specialty distributor

Combination house

Exclusive-dealing contracts

Tying contracts

Exclusive territory

Vertical divisions of the market

Horizontal agreement

Interbrand competition

Intrabrand competition

Schwinn bicycle case

GTE Sylvania case

DISCUSSION QUESTIONS AND EXERCISES

1. What factors make retailing a significant institution in our economy?

2. What is the margin/turnover classification of retail stores? What are two or three strategic implications of the margin/turnover classification?

3. Compare and contrast the product mixes for each of the following stores:
    a. R. H. Macy's.
    b. The Athlete's Foot.

4. Name at least one major benefit that each of the following types of retailers provides to the consumer:
    a. Full-service retailer.
    b. Supermarket.
    c. Discount.
    d. Convenience.
    e. Vending machine.
    f. Hypermarket.

5. What is the wheel of retailing theory? Has the development of Sears, Roebuck followed the wheel of retailing pattern? Explain.

6. What is retail store image and what role does it play in the strategic management of a retail institution?

7. Compare and contrast wholesalers to retailers in terms of the following:
    a. Markets served.
    b. Functions performed.
    c. Nature of their operations.

8. Assume you are the marketing vice president for a manufacturer of a wide variety of automobile and truck parts and accessories, such as wheels and filters, spark plugs, etc. What are the specific benefits that each of the following wholesalers would offer to you?
    a. General-line merchant wholesalers.
    b. Specialty-line merchant wholesalers.
    c. Rack jobbers.
    d. Manufacturer's agents.

CHAPTER 16

Physical distribution

Nature of physical distribution
    Raw material to finished goods
    Cross-functional area
    Cost trade-offs
    Reverse channel

Customer service
    Order cycle
    Percentage of demand to be satisfied
    Quality control for order processing
    Physical condition upon delivery

Transportation
    Modes of transportation
    Types of legal carriers

Warehousing
    Location
    Private and public warehouses
    Developments in warehousing

Inventory management and control
    Functions of inventory
    Economic order quantity (EOQ)
    Inventory turnover and its impact on profits

Current issues in physical distribution
    Computers
    Inventory management
    Material handling
    Shared distribution
    Deregulation
    The role of physical distribution
        management in strategic planning

Summary

Key concepts

Discussion questions and exercises

In this chapter we begin our coverage of *physical distribution* with a discussion of its nature. We'll also be talking about customer service, transportation, warehousing, inventory control, and current issues in physical distribution.

NATURE OF PHYSICAL DISTRIBUTION

"Physical distribution" and "logistics" both refer to functions aimed at the physical transfer of products. The National Council of Physical Distribution has defined physical distribution as follows:

> *Physical distribution management* is the term describing the integration of two or more activities for the purpose of planning, implementing, and controlling the efficient flow of raw materials, in-process inventory, and finished goods from point of origin to point of consumption. The activities may include, but are not limited to, customer service, demand forecasting, distribution communications, inventory control, materials handling, order processing, parts and service support, plant warehouse site selection, procurement, packaging, return goods handling, salvage and scrap disposal, traffic and transportation, and warehousing and storage.[1]

Figure 16–1 is an overview of the institutions and the physical flow of the product in the physical distribution system. Let's discuss some of the important distribution aspects.

Raw material to finished goods

As defined here, physical distribution involves the movement of raw materials from suppliers to manufacturers and finished goods from manufacturer to warehouse and storage facilities. This perspective allows management to identify opportunities to improve customer service or reduce costs across a very broad range of activities, from the raw material stage to the finished product stage.

Cross-functional area

Physical distribution involves activities cutting across various functions or departments within the firm. For example, suppose that customer order processing is the responsibility of the firm's accounting function, while traffic or transport management is handled by manufacturing and warehousing is the responsibility of the marketing department. The result is that total physical distribution costs are in a managerial purgatory. No single executive is responsible for them.

Cost trade-offs

The costs of physical distribution are highly interrelated. Changing costs in one area usually means cost changes in one or more other areas. For instance, a firm may consider reducing transportation costs by switching from high-cost air freight to lower-cost trucking. Yet the firm may

---

[1] This is the definition of physical distribution accepted by the National Council of Physical Distribution. It is found in John H. Campbell and Masao Nishi, *Logistics: Issues for the 80s* (Shaker Heights, Ohio: Corinthian Press, 1982), p. 9.

Figure 16–1: An overview of the institutions and flow of product in physical distribution system

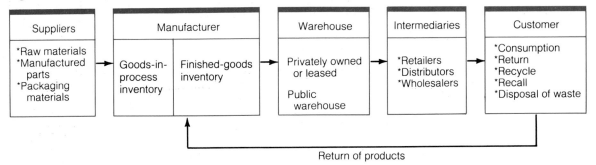

Source: Adapted with modification from Bernard J. La Lande, John R. Grabner, and James F. Robeson, "Integrated Distribution Systems: A Management Perspective," in *Business Logistics*, ed. P. M. Van Buytenen, M. G. Christopher, and G. S. Wills (The Hague, The Netherlands: Martinus Nijhoff, 1976).

incur higher inventory costs because finished products spend more time in transportation and storage. Figure 16–2 demonstrates the *cost trade-off* idea by presenting total distribution costs as various sized integrated elements within a physical distribution system.

Management often underestimates the real impact distribution costs

Figure 16–2: Trade-offs among types of physical distribution costs

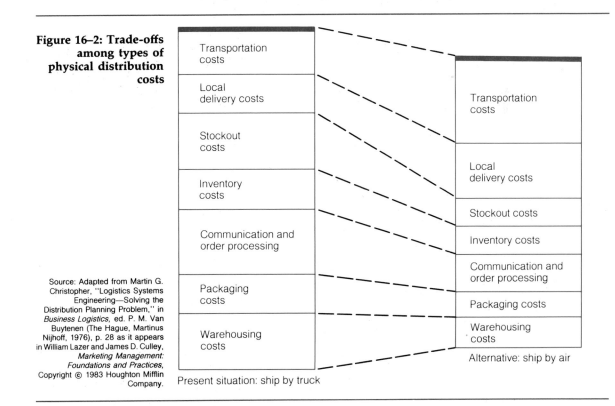

Source: Adapted from Martin G. Christopher, "Logistics Systems Engineering—Solving the Distribution Planning Problem," in *Business Logistics*, ed. P. M. Van Buytenen (The Hague, Martinus Nijhoff, 1976), p. 28 as it appears in William Lazer and James D. Culley, *Marketing Management: Foundations and Practices,* Copyright © 1983 Houghton Mifflin Company.

have on profits. Companies that have studied distribution-related costs have found them significantly greater than management estimated. Distribution costs in the petroleum industry constitute 29 percent of sales revenue.[2] In the supermarket industry, profits are only 1 percent of sales. If a company cuts distribution costs by $100,000, the impact on profits would be the same as a $10 million sales increase!

Reverse channel

Most distribution systems are designed for forwardbound, one-way movement of products. However, the reverse flow of products from consumer back to producer has recently grown in importance. There are a variety of reasons, including (1) greater attention to the environment and to the need for recycling, (2) improved customer service that allows buyers to return damaged goods, and (3) trends toward consumer protection and the return of unsafe products through product recalls.

Reverse channel is the movement of goods from consumer back to producer. This movement is depicted in Figure 16–1.

A number of reverse channels have developed. For example, central processing warehouses developed by existing intermediaries in traditional channels handle, store, and process trash.[3] Reclamation, or recycling, centers are modernized "junk yards" conveniently located for customers, who are paid an equitable amount for their waste goods. Initial processing of these wastes is also performed at these centers.[4] Aluminum producers, canmakers, and beverage distributors alone have set up more than 2,000 recycling centers in the United States.[5] Indeed, the growing number of federal, state, and local laws directed toward environmental protection may firmly establish reverse marketing channels as a permanent feature of the distribution structure in this country.[6]

CUSTOMER SERVICE

Effective physical distribution requires the establishment of standards for the types and levels of service that are important to channel members. Manufacturers frequently state physical distribution objectives in terms of some level of *customer service* they guarantee to provide. For instance, a manufacturer of earth-moving equipment promises to fill 87 percent of customer orders for parts from existing earlier inventories. A manufacturer of office equipment promises 24-hour delivery of parts and services

[2] James I. Puccini, "Managing Distribution for Profits," *Business Quarterly* 47 (August 1982), pp. 58–64.

[3] "Tomorrow's Markets: Refuse Disposal, Trash Removal, Traffic Jam," *Sales Management,* November 10, 1969, pp. 24–26.

[4] L. W. Stern and A. I. El-Ansary, *Marketing Channels,* 2d ed. (Englewood Cliffs, N.J.: Prentice-Hall, 1982), p. 572.

[5] "Recycling Ease Gives Aluminum an Edge over Steel in Beverage-Can Market Battle," *The Wall Street Journal,* January 2, 1980, p. 28.

[6] Peter M. Ginter and Jack M. Starling, "Reverse Distribution Channels for Recycling," *California Management Review,* Spring 1978, pp. 77–78.

anywhere in the country. Many types of services can be provided by physical distribution. Nine common service concerns that are often important to channel members at the wholesale and retail levels are: time from order receipt to order shipment, order size and assortment constraints, percentage of items out of stock, percentage of orders filled accurately, percentage of orders filled within a given number of days from receipt of the order, percentage of orders filled, percentage of filled orders that arrive in good condition, order cycle (time from order placement to order delivery), and ease and flexibility of order placement.[7]

Determining an appropriate customer service level means setting objectives for various dimensions of service. These dimensions are many and varied, but four are generally considered especially important: (1) order cycle, (2) percentage of demand to be satisfied, (3) quality control for order processing, and (4) physical condition of goods upon delivery.[8]

Order cycle

From the channel member's viewpoint, the lower the average time of the order cycle and the lower the dispersion or variation around that average time, the better the service level.

order cycle

> **Order cycle** refers to the total time elapsed from placing an order to receiving the goods.

The importance of accurately forecasting demand and the risk of lost sales both increase as the order cycle lengthens. Assume, for example, that a supplying firm's order cycle is 45 days. If a customer runs out of stock 5 days after placing an order, he or she will stay out of stock and lose sales for 40 days, until the order arrives. If the supplier's order cycle were only one day, no customer would be out of stock more than 24 hours. Physical distribution management must use faster order-processing and improved physical-handling procedures to reduce the average order cycle. Quality control procedures similar to those used in manufacturing can also lower the dispersion around the average delivery time.

Percentage of demand to be satisfied

Another major dimension of customer service is the percentage of demand for which a supplier decides to maintain inventory. If a firm maintains inventory sufficient to fill 100 percent of its orders, then inventory costs increase. If a firm lowers inventory costs by keeping a stock level to fill only 80 percent of demand at peak periods, the firm either increases

---

[7] James L. Heskett, Nicholas A. Glaskowski, and Robert M. Ivie, *Business Logistics,* 2d ed. (New York: Ronald Press, 1973), pp. 250–51.

[8] The discussion of customer service level is adapted from Richard J. Lewis, "Physical Distribution: Managing the Firm's Service Level," in *Readings in Basic Marketing,* ed. E. Jerome McCarthy, John F. Grashof, and Andrew A. Brogowicz (Homewood, Ill.: Richard D. Irwin, 1975), pp. 220–23.

the time necessary to fill some orders or it loses sales. In industries where firms sell highly similar products (say, commodity items like steel or lumber), there is greater chance for lost sales due to out-of-stock situations.

Figure 16–3 shows the general relationship between the percentage of orders filled from existing stock and the increase in inventory cost. In general, as the service level (percentage of orders filled from existing inventory) approaches 100 percent, inventory costs increase sharply. For example, a $500,000 inventory would be necessary to fill 85 percent of orders. A 5 percent increase (to 90 percent) in orders to be filled from existing inventory would require a $100,000, or 20 percent, increase in inventory investment. If orders fillable from inventory increased another 5 percent (to 95 percent), the required investment in inventory would increase another $200,000, to $800,000. This graph tells management only the relationship between inventory cost and customer service level. It doesn't indicate whether or not an increase in customer service level is warranted. Management would have to analyze the impact on customer satisfaction—and, ultimately, upon sales and profits—to determine if an increase in inventory level can be justified.

Figure 16–3: The relationship between percent of company's orders filled through existing inventory and investment in inventory

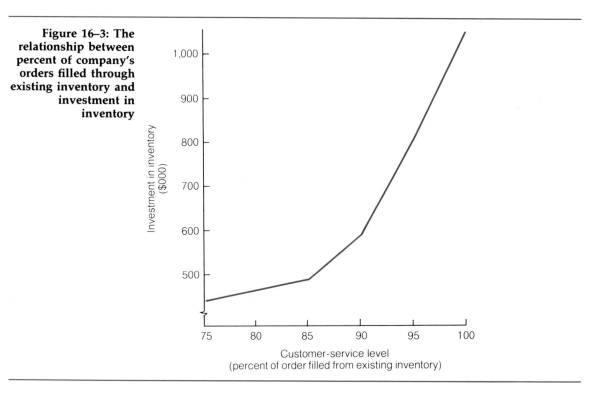

Quality control for order processing

The customer hasn't been effectively serviced unless the right item, color, size, etc., have been shipped to the right place. Several checks and cross-checks are necessary to insure that the order and shipment are matched exactly. Quality control procedures similar to those found in manufacturing are necessary to insure accurate order processing. Most firms today seem to have done an effective job in designing systems for the outflow of their goods. But few seem to have spent adequate time and effort in designing a system to return goods when an incorrect order is processed. Perhaps they simply devote too much attention to designing and controlling their outbound flows. In any case, firms must realize that when a customer receives an incorrect shipment, they can ill afford to compound the mistake by having poorly defined and slow procedures for correcting the situation.

Physical condition upon delivery

All efforts to ensure prompt delivery of the ordered items can be nullified if the products arrive in a damaged or unsalable condition. And as the length of the channel increases, so does the risk of physical damage. By selecting adequate packaging, storage, and transportation, suppliers can see to the physical protection of goods. One large consumer goods manufacturer instituted a "get-well policy" to deal with damaged products. The company immediately makes financial adjustments to retailers and assumes the responsibility for determining where the damage occurred and who, if anyone, will ultimately be held responsible for financial loss.

TRANSPORTATION[9]

Transportation is the element of the physical distribution system that links geographically separated markets and facilities. Most firms spend more dollars on transportation than on any other element of physical distribution.

Modes of transportation

There are five basic modes of transportation: rail, highway, water, pipeline, and air. Railroads account for about 37 percent of the nation's total intercity ton-miles. Their outstanding characteristic is their ability to move very large tonnages efficiently over long distances. Railroads can also offer such important services as stop-off privileges and pickup and delivery. The high fixed cost of operations, along with the nature of rail power, results in a relatively low variable cost.

Highway transportation has grown rapidly due to greater flexibility of door-to-door operations and greater speed of operation compared to railroads. Motor carriers require a relatively small investment in technical facilities and owned right-of-way. But their variable costs (individual

[9] The discussion of transportation and warehousing is adapted from Stern and El-Ansary, *Marketing Channels*, pp. 138–201; and Donald J. Bowersox, *Logistical Management* (New York: MacMillan, 1974), pp. 137–57.

The CF Company uses multiple modes of transportation, including trucking, air, and rail to service the diverse freight transportation needs of its customers.

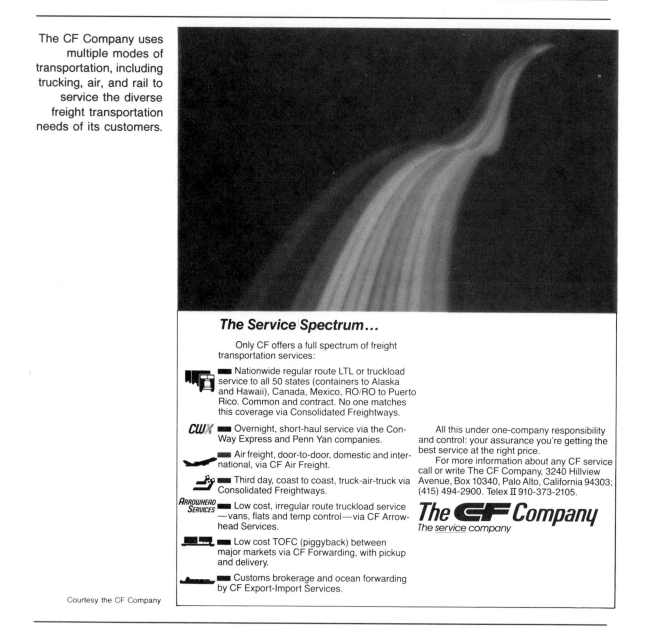

The Service Spectrum...

Only CF offers a full spectrum of freight transportation services:

■ Nationwide regular route LTL or truckload service to all 50 states (containers to Alaska and Hawaii), Canada, Mexico, RO/RO to Puerto Rico. Common and contract. No one matches this coverage via Consolidated Freightways.

CWX ■ Overnight, short-haul service via the Con-Way Express and Penn Yan companies.

■ Air freight, door-to-door, domestic and international, via CF Air Freight.

■ Third day, coast to coast, truck-air-truck via Consolidated Freightways.

ARROWHEAD SERVICES ■ Low cost, irregular route truckload service —vans, flats and temp control—via CF Arrowhead Services.

■ Low cost TOFC (piggyback) between major markets via CF Forwarding, with pickup and delivery.

■ Customs brokerage and ocean forwarding by CF Export-Import Services.

All this under one-company responsibility and control: your assurance you're getting the best service at the right price.

For more information about any CF service call or write The CF Company, 3240 Hillview Avenue, Box 10340, Palo Alto, California 94303; (415) 494-2900. Telex II 910-373-2105.

The *CF* Company
The *service* company

Courtesy the CF Company

trucks, labor) are high. As a result, motor carriers are more economically suited to handle smaller shipments moving shorter distances.

The main feature of water transport is the ability to move extremely large shipments. But water transportation offers limited flexibility and comparatively slower speeds. Then, too, unless the source and destination

	Operating characteristic	Transportation mode				
		Rail	Highway	Water	Pipeline	Air
Table 16–1: Relative operating characteristics of five basic transportation modes	Speed	3	2	4	5	1
	Availability	2	1	4	5	3
	Dependability	3	2	4	1	5
	Capability	2	3	1	5	4
	Frequency	4	2	5	1	3

Source: Reprinted with permission of Macmillan Publishing Company from *Logistical Management*, 2d ed. by Donald J. Bowersox. Copyright © 1978 by Donald J. Bowersox.

Rating scale: 1 = Performs well
.
.
.
5 = Performs poorly

of movement are adjacent to the waterway, additional transportation by truck or rail is needed. Still, the capability to haul large tonnage at low variable costs puts this mode in demand when low rates are desired and speed is of secondary importance.

Pipelines have the highest fixed cost and the lowest variable costs of all transportation modes. Because pipelines operate around the clock, they are the most dependable mode. Pipeline transport offers very low loss and damage rates as well. But pipelines provide a limited range of services and capabilities: their main use has been in moving petroleum products.

Air is the newest and least utilized mode of transportation for shipping products. Although it offers unmatched delivery speeds, it is limited by the lift capacity and availability of aircraft. The relatively high cost of aircraft and the erratic nature of freight has limited the assignment of planes to all-freight operations. Air transport is second only to highway in low fixed cost; but variable costs are extremely high because of fuel, maintenance, and labor requirements. A summary of the operating characteristics of the five transportation modes is given in Table 16–1.

Coordinated, or **intermodal,** transportation arrangements offer point-to-point services on a regularly scheduled basis using a combination of two common carriers of different modes. The most widely used intermodal system is the *piggyback* (truck trailer on railroad flatcar). Other combinations include *fishyback* (trailer on ships or barges), rail–water, truck–air, and truck, rail, or water with pipeline.

Types of legal carriers

Transportation alternatives may be classified by the legality of carrier operating rights. The four basic types of legal carriers are common, contract, private, and exempt. Each may exist within any of the five basic modes.

The most frequently encountered category of legal transportation is common carrier. A **common carrier** is a firm that makes its transportation services available to all shippers and accepts responsibility for carrying goods any time or any place. Rates charged must be made public and be identical for similar types of freight.

Contract carriers make their services available on a selective basis. Contracts between shippers and carriers call for a specified transportation service at a specified cost. The contract becomes the basis for receipt of a permit by the carrier, allowing that carrier to transport specified goods over specified routes. Contract carriers may service more than one shipper and may charge different rates to different customers.

Private carriers are firms that provide their own transportation service. Firms generally must own (or control through lease) the transport equipment and the goods being shipped. The shipping itself must be incidental to the primary objective of the business.

Exempt carriers are not subject to direct regulation of operating rights and pricing policies; but they must comply with licensing and safety laws in the states in which they operate. Exemptions may be granted for certain commodities and geographic areas and to select associations.

WAREHOUSING

Warehousing decisions determine the number, size, and location of storage facilities needed to service customer demand. Warehouses are a critical element of a firm's total strategy for creating time and place utility.

Location

The location of production facilities and of the market to be served largely determine a warehouse's physical location. Three types of distribution formats may be considered when adopting warehouses.

The *market-positioned warehouse* replenishes retail store inventory and merchandise delivered to customers. The market-oriented warehouse offers maximum transport economies from shipping points with fairly short product movements in local delivery. These warehouses may be owned by a retailer or a manufacturer or may be independently owned— and the basic purpose varies accordingly.

Production-positioned warehouses serve as collection points for many products manufactured at different plants. These warehouses are located near production plants, and shipments to them are usually the result of product allocation. The basic reason for product-positioned warehouses is the desire of a manufacturer for maximum customer service. Products flow from each plant to a collection center (the warehouse), which in turn fills customer orders, thus providing superior service for a total product assortment. Production-positioned warehousing is used in the food-processing industry by such firms as Pillsbury and Nabisco.

Intermediately positioned warehouses are located *between* customers and manufacturing plants. They are similar to production-oriented warehouses and are justified economically on the basis of increased customer service. The warehouse operation is basically one of breaking bulk and regrouping. The objective is to move large quantities in and customized assortments out as efficiently as possible. Important to this objective are the *movement* functions (receiving, transfer, assembly, and shipping) and the *storage* function (which may involve temporary or permanent storage).

Private and public warehouses

Warehouses are normally classified as private or public. **Private warehouses** are owned or leased by the firm; they allow the firm complete control over the activities of the facility. Private warehouses are desirable when a firm (1) must be able to adapt to rapidly changing market or product conditions; (2) has special storage and handling requirements; and (3) has a relatively constant, high volume of goods moving into large metropolitan areas.

Public warehouses are operated by professional warehousers and provide a range of services to a number of firms on a fee basis. Public warehouses may be the choice for a firm that desires freedom from operational and management problems, location flexibility, and lower freight rates (through consolidation of small shipments).

Table 16–2 summarizes the basic trade-offs involved in choosing between public and private warehousing.

Developments in warehousing

Although relatively limited in scope, public warehouses have experienced a steady growth rate. This is due to their ability to provide services to firms with varied needs and to developments in engineering, management, and data processing. As a consequence, both large and small compa-

Table 16–2: Decision variables in choosing among types of warehouses

Decision variables	Types of warehousing arrangements		
	Private		
	Owned	**Leased**	**Public**
1. Fixed investment	Very high	Moderate, depends on the lease's terms	No fixed investment is involved
2. Unit cost	High, if volume is low	High, if volume is low	Low, since facilities are on "for hire as needed" and fixed costs are widely distributed among users
3. Control	High	High	Low managerial control
4. Adequacy to product line	Highly adequate	Moderately adequate	May not be convenient
5. Flexibility	Low	Low	High; termination of usage can be easily arranged

Source: Louis W. Stern and Adel I. El-Ansary, *Marketing Channels*, 2d ed., Copyright © 1982, p. 167. Adapted by permission of Prentice-Hall, Inc., Englewood Cliffs, New Jersey.

Table 16–3: Companies and their reasons for using public warehousing facilities	Companies using public warehouses	Reason(s) for using public warehousing facilities
	Balanced Foods, Inc.	Obtaining greater amount of warehouse space allocated to its products
		Use of sophisticated equipment it could not otherwise afford
		Reduction in order cycle
	Mead Johnson & Company	Space flexibility
	Tonka Corporation	Space flexibility required due to fluctuating demand for toys
	Alcoa	Increased speed of delivery to customer

Source: Adapted from Walter F. Friedman, "Physical Distribution: The Concept of Shared Services," *Harvard Business Review* 53 (March–April 1975), p. 26. Copyright © 1975 by the President and Fellows of Harvard College; all rights reserved.

nies, particularly in the household goods industry, are making increased use of public warehousing. Examples of such companies and their reasons for using public warehousing are shown in Table 16–3.

The emergence of distribution centers is a major development in the private warehousing area. These are major, centralized operations that serve regional markets, process and regroup products into customized orders, maintain full product lines for customer distribution, and are highly automatic. Distribution centers are concerned more with the movement of goods than with their storage. Their objective is to maintain a company's product in a constant, efficient flow.

Many of the world's largest corporations now operate distribution centers as an integral part of their physical distribution systems. For example, Caterpillar Tractor's Morton Center is an automated distribution center carrying a 60-day inventory of more than 200,000 parts and is the basis of an elaborate computer network linking dealers and depots worldwide. With such support, Caterpillar dealers are able to order any part they need for delivery the next day.[10] Similarly, Levi Strauss has a large distribution center in Little Rock, Arkansas, which handles its 48,000 product items from its 10 U.S. manufacturing plants and ships to distributors in 70 countries and more than 17,000 domestic stores.[11] IBM has its World Trade Distribution Center (WTDC), which is one of the biggest and most sophisticated of its kind anywhere. Located in New York, the WTDC uses a complex communications network to control the annual movement of more than 23 million pounds of equipment, parts, and supplies.[12]

Clearly, the trend in private warehousing is toward increasing sophisti-

---

[10] "Caterpillar: Sticking to Basics to Stay Competitive," *Business Week,* May 4, 1981, pp. 77–78.

[11] Jim Dixon, "Streamlining Storage and Distribution," *Distribution Worldwide,* May 1975, p. 32.

[12] Janet Bosworth Dower, "How IBM Distributes-Worldwide," *Distribution Worldwide,* October 1973, pp. 51–54, 58–60.

cation. With the availability of high-speed computers capable of providing rapid customer service and the raising of income tax depreciation allowances for such capital expenditures, companies are encouraged to seek more productive equipment in their reevaluation and redesign of private warehousing facilities.[13]

INVENTORY MANAGEMENT AND CONTROL

Because marketing's chief concern is to provide a high level of customer service, inventory planning is crucial. Unless they maintain inventories, firms can experience marketing problems in customer relations and revenue generation. As we saw, though, inventory costs rise at an increasing rate as the customer service level nears 100 percent. So carrying enough stock to guarantee no stockouts would be unrealistic from a cost standpoint. Thus, inventory management requires careful decisions about when and how much to order. Before these decisions can be made, though, one must understand the functions of inventory.

Functions of inventory

Although the basic function of inventory is to increase profitability through marketing and manufacturing support, four underlying functions may be specified.[14]

1. Inventory allows **geographic specialization** of individual operational units of the firm. The most economic location for manufacturing may be quite far from the prime target market due to such factors as raw materials and sources of power. The manufacture of specific components of a finished product may also be geographically separated, as can physical distribution. Collecting an assortment of goods from various manufacturing sites to offer a mixed variety of all products to a customer in a single shipment is an example. Inventory is crucial to the degree that geographic separation provides economic specialization between manufacturing and distribution.

2. **Decoupling** provides maximum efficiency of operations in a single locale. It allows each product to be manufactured and distributed in economically sized lots and all products to be offered to consumers as an assortment.

3. Inventory serves to *balance supply availability with demand requirements.* Examples include balancing seasonal production with year-round consumption—and year-round production with seasonal consumption. The balancing function requires investment in seasonal stock, but it allows mass consumption (or manufacturing) of all products with seasonal patterns.

4. *Safety stock* concerns short-range variation in demand or the capacity of the operation to replenish inventories. The need for safety stocks arises

---

[13] Stern and El-Ansary, *Marketing Channels,* pp. 170–71.

[14] The following discussion is adapted from Bowersox, *Logistical Management,* pp. 182–85.

from uncertainty about future sales and inventory replenishment; and it necessitates planning an inventory position.

Planning an inventory position consists of estimating sales and determining the desired degree of protection against forecast variation. The amount of inventory committed as protection is known as *safety* or *buffer stock.* Safety stock must protect against two types of variation: (1) sales that occur at random in excess of those estimated for the planning period and (2) random time delays that occur in excess of the normal time for replenishing inventory stocks. Statistical and mathematical techniques are available for planning safety stocks. One of the most common models for inventory planning is *economic order quantity (EOQ).*

Economic order quantity (EOQ)

The solution for inventory models consists of three steps:

1. To identify and reduce to a formula one set of costs that decreases as inventory increases (ordering costs).
2. To identify and reduce to a formula one set of costs that increases as inventory increases (carrying costs).
3. To find the minimum cost point for the sum of these two sets of costs (defined as the point at which the rate of decrease equals the rate of increase).

The simplest inventory model involves determining the EOQ by solving the equation

$$Q = \sqrt{\frac{2DC}{V_p}}$$

where

Q = Quantity to be found
D = Known demand or usage rate
C = Fixed cost of placing a purchase order
V = Unit value of item
p = Inventory carrying cost (as a percentage of value of inventory carried)

The EOQ model assumes (1) known supply and demand and (2) constant supply and demand during the planning period.

Ordering costs are those that decrease as inventory increases. If D = Known year demand and Q = Quantity ordered, then D/Q = Number of orders per year. If C = Cost per order, then $C \times D/Q$ = Total annual ordering costs.

Carrying costs increase along with inventory. Because demand is known and constant, there is no safety stock. Average inventory is, therefore, $Q/2$. Thus, $V \times Q/2$ = The value of average inventory, and $V_p \times Q/2$ = Total annual carrying costs.

The sum of the ordering costs, DC/Q, and carrying costs, $QV_p/2$, is the total combined cost to be minimized:

$$\frac{DC}{Q} + \frac{QV_p}{2} = DCQ^{-1} + \left(\frac{V_p}{2} \times Q\right)$$

To solve this problem, the derivative (a formula for rate of change) of this expression must be found and then solved for the value of Q for which the rate of change equals zero. The resultant expression for Q is

$$Q = \sqrt{\frac{2DC}{V_p}}$$

The following example illustrates the use of the EOQ formula:

$D = 100{,}000$ units
$C = \$5$
$V = \$10$
$p = 10$ percent

$$Q = \sqrt{\frac{2(100{,}000)(\$5)}{(\$10)(.10)}}$$

$$= \sqrt{\frac{1{,}000{,}000}{1}}$$

$$= 1{,}000 \text{ units}$$

The relationships among total cost, ordering cost, and carrying cost are represented in Figure 16–4. Here, the total cost curve C is comprised of the two components—curves A (order cost curve) and B (carrying cost curve). The minimum value of C occurs at $Q = 1{,}000$ units, which lies above the intersection of the component curves.

Inventory turnover and its impact on profits

The frequency of **stock turnover** has important implications for a firm's profitability. For example, if one manufacturer's product has a gross margin on an item of 10 percent and the inventory turns over three times annually, the yearly gross margin is 30 percent. However, if the number of inventory turns for a similar competitive product item also with a 10 percent gross margin is six times per year, the annual gross margin obtained is 60 percent. Thus, there is greater pricing flexibility on high-turnover items.

CURRENT ISSUES IN PHYSICAL DISTRIBUTION

An effective physical distribution system can add significantly to customer service and satisfaction and is an excellent way for a firm to differentiate its product. Physical distribution is a major issue with marketing

Figure 16–4: Total cost, ordering cost, and carrying cost curves

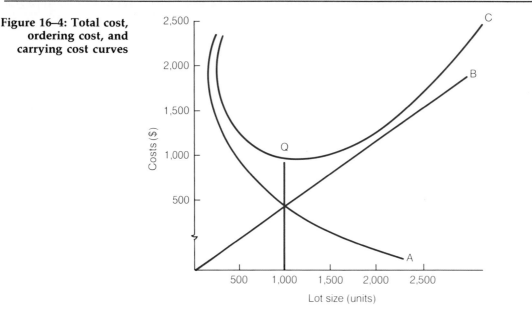

A = Ordering costs; B = Carrying costs; and C = Total costs.

management: a survey of 216 industrial buying agents showed physical distribution ranking second (behind product quality) as a factor in their buying decision.[15]

Computers

Computers are becoming an integral part of the physical distribution system of many companies. Kellogg, for example, has used them successfully in its order-processing system. The computerized system kept Kellogg's orders virtually error-free in 1977. The company was able to fill 98 percent of its orders in their entirety during the first 10 months of 1978, providing a distinct competitive advantage for its field sales force.[16]

Computer simulation, or modeling, is also used extensively. Hunt-Wesson Foods designed a model to increase distribution capacity for its many products. The model enabled 3 of its 12 distribution centers (serving 14 production facilities) to be modified immediately, reassigning many of its customers to new centers. As a result, Hunt-Wesson saved over $1 million a year with no decline in customer service quality.[17]

[15] William D. Perreault, Jr., and Frederick A. Russ, "Physical Distribution Service in Industrial Purchase Decisions," *Journal of Marketing,* April 1976, pp. 3–10.

[16] "*S&MM* Excellence Awards," *Sales and Marketing Management,* January 1979, p. 44.

[17] Arthur M. Geoffrion, "Better Distribution Planning with Computer Models," *Harvard Business Review,* July–August 1976, pp. 92–99.

Inventory management

Improving inventory management is also of concern. Many companies have half their stock tied up in items representing only 20 percent of unit sales—with the highest-volume items selling four time faster than low-volume items. Reducing inventories of slow sellers to the point where their turnover rates approach those of the fast sellers can have a major impact. Inventories of slow-moving items can be reduced by 75 percent, for an overall reduction in inventory of 37.5 percent.[18]

Honeywell once distributed its 18,000 catalog parts and pieces through 100 warehouses to 5,000 distributors. Few of these distributors carried adequate replacement stocks. To avoid losing sales due to inadequate stocks, Honeywell adopted a program to improve inventory levels and maintenance by its distributors. The program helped Honeywell achieve increased sales and better control of customer service levels.[19]

These cases make it obvious that manufacturers are moving toward central warehousing, substituting distribution centers for warehouses, and introducing a variety of buy plans to decrease inventories and shift them to resellers. These trends were particularly evident in the early 1970s, when inventory management was severely affected by the recession, rising cost of funds, increasing need for customer service, and desire to lower cost.[20]

Material handling

Improved *material handling* and shipping is another dimension of efficient physical distribution. One new method is *containerization.* Here, goods are shipped in metal boxes that can be moved by and transferred between two or more transportation modes. Rail and water carrier service is often used; it eliminates costly reloading, rechecking, and security requirements.

Shared distribution[21]

Shared distribution is a promising cost-saving concept whereby two or more firms cooperatively establish and use joint warehousing, transportation, and/or other logistics facilities or whereby one firm performs a full range of physical distribution services for others. Shippers' associations are one important form of this concept.

Shared distribution may become more important due to several factors. First, the high cost and security of capital are encouraging firms to seek ways of acquiring assets and otherwise perform functions with lower capital investment. Shared distribution is one method of either gaining

[18] James L. Heskett, "Logistics—Essentials to Strategy," *Harvard Business Review,* November–December 1977, p. 89.

[19] Ibid., p. 93.

[20] Charles J. Teplitz, "Manufacturers Shift the Inventory Carrying Function," *Industrial Marketing Management* 11 (July 1982), pp. 225–30.

[21] The discussion in this section is based on the articles by Joseph L. Cavinato, "Shared Distribution," in *Logistics: Issues for the 80s,* ed. John H. Campbell and Masao Nishi (Shaker Heights, Ohio: Corinthian Press, 1982), pp. 105–12.

Toyota features the broad array of industries that its forklifts may serve.

LIFT TRUCKS FOR A TO Z

Toyota supports its position as the number one lift truck manufacturer in the world with the capabilities required to serve a full range of industries which handle materials and products like these. Join them. Call (800) 421-2101* now!

use of needed assets or assuring a more intensive use of existing assets. Second, the concept is attractive when top management is marketing- or finance-oriented and an avoidance of internal physical operations is desired. Such is the case with some fast-food chains and high-growth firms. Third, hiring full logistics services from a single source is feasible in high-product-markup situations and when items involved can be set into explicit specifications.

Deregulation[22]

Deregulation has caused some major changes in the transportation sector. Air travel has been deregulated for several years, while the deregulation bill for the motor carrier industry was passed in 1980. But deregulation has had mixed results, short of the expectations of its proponents.

The effects of deregulation on airline pricing and scheduling are twofold. First, because fares have risen substantially for those who must travel at set times and on short notice, those traveling on business are subsidizing those who travel for pleasure. Second, a very limited number of large-city pairs—like New York to Los Angeles—enjoy favorable rates; less popular destinations cost more to get to. Thus, it appears that the place discrimination prevalent on railroads in the last century has been reestablished.

Reduction in the number of scheduled flights by the trunklines has had a negative effect on air freight service and the activities of air forwarders. Indeed, some forwarders have had to shift directly into air freight to maintain a level of service that would sell.

The savings expected by deregulation of motor carriers have not been entirely satisfactory. The increase in haulers has disrupted the balances established by general commodity haulers. The percentage of "empty miles" rose sharply for many carriers. This, in turn, meant that service had to be reduced and rates raised on movements of the less-than-truckload traffic to offset the increased empty mileage.

The role of physical distribution management in strategic planning[23]

Several recent events have increased the role of physical distribution management in strategic planning. First, managers at all levels have become exposed to the concept, which has caused many firms to at least experiment with the process, if not wholly integrate it into their overall strategy. The relaxation of transport regulation has helped develop (1) a more complex and dynamic environment for carriers and shippers, (2) more flexible rates and routes, (3) more and varied levels of service, and (4) more types of carriers.

[22] The discussion in this section has been drawn from an article by L. L. Waters, "Deregulation—For Better, or For Worse," *Business Horizons* 24, no. 1 (January–February 1981), pp. 88–91.

[23] The following discussion is based on an article by Gary N. Dicer, "The Role of Logistics Management in Strategic Planning," in *Logistics: Issues for the 80s*, ed. John H. Campbell and Masao Nishi (Shaker Heights, Ohio: Corinthian Press, 1982), pp. 121–29.

Furthermore, capital has become costly, not to mention hard to find. Inventory control has become a crucial financial consideration. Capital expenditure decisions on such items as material handling equipment, field warehouses, and new plants are closely analyzed for possible system trade-offs to save scarce and costly capital.

Energy costs and availability are new concerns that reinforce the need for a physical distribution role in strategic planning. Of particular importance are the various location-related issues that arise in a strategic planning process. Can new market areas be served profitably? Where should the firm look for its raw material? These questions require input from physical distribution managers.

Finally, the new operating environment has produced a trend toward changed distribution service standards. Now, firms appear to offer a variety of service/cost combinations to their customers. Many carriers offer such options in their pricing structures. New customer service strategies have to be developed, especially by firms in industries susceptible to distribution competition.

For firms oriented toward strategic management, the implications of physical distribution are clear. First, PD connects the firm to the outside world in both the inputs provided and the outputs delivered. The more important these external relationships are to the firm, the more important PD becomes in the planning process.

Physical distribution is becoming an important cost center for many firms, mainly because of the effects of high interest rates and energy costs. Thus, PD is having a greater impact on corporate profitability.

Physical distribution decisions have become strategically important because of their long-term nature. For example, the construction of plants, warehouses, and other fixed facilities involves long-run depreciation.

Several other factors have also increased the importance of physical distribution in planning strategy. Distribution service may be a competitive tool for a firm. Intercorporate and subsidiary relationships can be made more efficient with appropriate physical distribution coordination, such as pooling or intercorporate hauling. Finally, the multinational nature of much of today's business activities forces closer integration of strategic planning with physical distribution alternatives.

SUMMARY

In this chapter, we defined physical distribution as involving the movement of raw materials from suppliers to manufacturers and finished goods from manufacturer to warehouse and storage facilities. Physical distribution activities cut across various functional areas, such as accounting, manufacturing, and marketing. Moreover, the uses of physical distribution are highly interrelated. Other characteristics of physical distribution are its significant impact on profitability—which management often underestimates—and its frequent design as a forwardbound, one-way channel. Reverse channels may become more prevalent as legislation directed toward environmental protection increases.

Establishing standards for types and levels of customer service is essential. The dimensions of customer service levels include order cycle, percentage of demand to be satisfied, quality control for order processing, and physical condition of goods upon delivery.

Transportation is another important consideration in physical distribution management. The five basic modes of transportation—rail, highway, water, pipeline, and air—vary considerably in their ability to meet distribution needs.

Warehousing decisions determine the number, size, and location of storage facilities needed to service customer demand and involve the choice between private and public warehouses. New developments in warehousing (such as distribution centers) are also affecting management's distribution decisions.

The four underlying functions of inventory are geographic specialization, decoupling, balancing supply availability with demand requirements, and provision of safety stock. Inventory planning can be aided by such techniques as the economic order quantity (EOQ) model. The impact of stock turnover on profits can also be a major management consideration.

Finally, current issues in physical distribution include the increased role of computers in physical distribution, the need to improve inventory planning and material handling, the concept of shared distribution, the impact of deregulation on the transportation sector, and the increased influence of physical distribution management in strategic planning.

KEY CONCEPTS

Physical distribution
Cost trade-off
Reverse channel
Customer service
Order cycle
Intermodal transportation
Common carrier
Contract carrier
Private carrier
Exempt carrier
Market-positioned warehouse

Production-positioned warehouse
Intermediately positioned
  warehouse
Private warehouse
Public warehouse
Geographic specialization
Decoupling
Safety (buffer) stock
Economic order quantity (EOQ)
  model

Stock turnover
Material handling
Containerization
Shared distribution
Deregulation
Percentage of demand satisfied
Highway transportation
Water transportation
Pipeline transportation
Air transportation

DISCUSSION QUESTIONS AND EXERCISES

1. One of the central aspects of physical distribution is the interrelationship among costs. Consider the following functional areas: marketing, transportation, and accounting. Identify costs in each area and discuss how the costs in one area might affect costs in another.

2. What is the reverse channel? Why has it grown in importance? What is the likely future of the reverse channel?

3. How is the customer service level defined? How would you go about setting a specific level of customer service?

4. When would a company like Caterpillar use air transportation as its physical distribution system?

5. Review the pros and cons of public versus private warehousing.

6. What are the basic costs involved in inventory management? How do these costs relate to transportation?

7. Discuss the role that physical distribution might play in a company's overall strategy.

Case 9: Caterpillar Tractor: Dealer loyalty in an industrial channel of distribution

"Forty-eight-hour parts service anywhere in the world—or Cat pays." This motto clearly states Caterpillar's confidence in the reliability and quality of the machines and in its mammoth dealer network. The Cat dealers constitute probably the biggest obstacle to competitors trying to breach Caterpillar's markets around the world. Cat's dealer organization is so substantial that their combined net worth—$3.6 billion—slightly exceeds that of the Caterpillar Tractor Corporation itself.

In 1982, Cat's dealers did suffer losses. However, in 1981, the average U.S. dealer had sales of $65 million (within a range spanning

$8 million and $308 million) and aftertax profits of 2.7 percent on sales, or about $1.75 million. Foreign dealers are even bigger. Worldwide, the dealers deliver Cat an estimated 50 percent market share in the machines it manufactures. Indeed, the emergence of the exclusive, full-line dealer offering financing and service has brought about consolidation among earth moving equipment manufacturers, with Caterpillar the major beneficiary.

Cat's dealers are consistently mentioned by customers as a prime reason for purchasing its products. There is a pattern of long-standing loyalty among dealers to Cat, with many in their second and third generations of affiliation. In the words of former Caterpillar president and chairman William Black, "We have a tremendous regard for our dealers. We will not bypass or undercut them. Some of our competitors do and their dealers quit. Caterpillar dealers don't quit; they die rich." Cat dealers are also treated like "members of the family."

All of Cat's dealerships are independently owned; but a competitor's chance of wooing any dealer away seems negligible. "Our average dealer can count on a steady income from service, maintenance, and used-machine business generated by at least several thousand machines operating in his territory, and competitors who don't have that base can't afford the investment it takes to provide first-class services," maintains E. C. Chapman, executive vice president for marketing. Attesting to the success of the Cat dealership is the fact that they have blossomed into rich and diversified companies in their own right. With the strong encouragement of Caterpillar, many of the 93 domestic and 137 overseas dealerships have established related businesses that add to their service capability and profits.

Present chairman Lee L. Morris considers Cat's dealers as "partners," not "agents or middlemen." Further, he says that Cat worries "as much about their performance as they do themselves." Dealers, on the other hand, praise Caterpillar for its consistent supply of "superior products and a high-quality program of parts and product information," says Frank O. Moyle, executive vice president of Pattern Industries, Inc., a dealer in Chicago's Elmhurst suburb.

Strong customer relations

However, the strength of the dealer system lies less in the relations with Caterpillar than in the dealers' relations with customers. To ensure that these relations remain cemented, Caterpillar stands ready to provide backup support for its products from their inception, giving the dealers confidence to devote ample promotional dollars to new products. Moreover, the Morton Center, with its automated warehouse carrying a 60-day inventory of more than 200,000 parts, forms the basis of an elaborate computer network linking dealers and depots worldwide. With such support, dealers are able to order any part they need for delivery the next day. Cat also repurchases parts the dealers do not sell and then paces its introduction of new products according to dealers' capabilities. For example, because many dealers are still preparing to handle the expansion of machine sales, Cat intends to limit its new-product introductions over the next few years, although it has been developing a four-wheel-drive farm tractor.

Cat also conducts many training programs for dealers and product demonstrations for their customers. Indeed, it even conducts a course to encourage dealers' children to remain in the business!

Market contenders

Yet, Cat is not without competition. Many industry observers expect Komatsu to make further headway in the near future. Currently,

Cat's products sell at a price premium while Komatsu is already strong in certain geographic areas like Japan, the Middle East, and Southeast Asia.

In the United States, however, Cat still reigns supreme. An example of this can be found in the bulldozer segment, where the Komatsu product introduced 14 years ago has a market share of only 6.7 percent against Cat's probable 50 percent. However, Komatsu has boosted its U.S. network to 60 dealers—a move that may pay off in the limited categories of crawler tractors and loaders, where it holds an estimated 5 to 8 percent market share. Further, Komatsu intends to broaden its product line by exhibiting a huge off-highway hauler and a hydraulic shovel at a recent trade show. "We believe we can increase our market share in the United States to about 20 percent within five years," said T. Anada, president of Komatsu's U.S. subsidiary in 1981.

In 1983, the new Komatsu president N. Murai implicitly acknowledged the difficulties of building a dealer network sufficiently strong to handle its products exclusively. Nonetheless, Komatsu dealers are known to deal aggressively. In addition, Cat faces similarly intensive activities from Fiatallis (controlled by Lagnellis of Italy) and International (a product line that Dresser Industries bought in 1982 from International Harvester).

Cat's response

To meet the competition, Cat and its dealers have become more aggressive in pricing. It is thought that a large part of the battle between Cat and Komatsu is going to focus on price. In 1983, a Komatsu D155A bulldozer with standard equipment sold for $243,000—which is 12 percent below the $276,000 price tag on the comparable Cat machine, the D8L. Caterpillar has cut prices to dealers to help the deal-ers hold their business. The dealers, in turn, have become very aggressive in price bids that they submit. One dealer recently told a buyer soliciting bids on a multimillion-dollar order that he simply wouldn't be undersold. He wasn't either, as his bids were very competitive.

Some dealers complain about the rigid bureaucratic structure at Cat's Peoria headquarters. This sentiment was expressed by one dealer. "I only wish they had things set up in Peoria so you get the help a little more easily, without every deal having to go to the seventh floor for an executive decision."

References

"Caterpillar: Sticking to Business to Remain Competitive." *Business Week,* May 4, 1981, pp. 74–78.

Loomis, Carol J. "High Stakes in the Cat Fight." *Fortune,* May 2, 1983, pp. 66–68.

Peters, Thomas J., and Robert H. Waterman, Jr. *In Search of Excellence.* New York: Harper & Row, 1982.

Porter, Michael E. *Competitive Strategy.* New York: Free Press, 1980, p. 202.

Discussion questions

1. Why does a financially strong company like Caterpillar, with a net worth of over $3.5 billion, rely on dealers to market their products? In other words, what are the advantages to Caterpillar of using a dealer network as opposed to marketing the Caterpillar machines themselves?

2. Caterpillar is known for superior product quality and outstanding service or parts, maintenance, and repair. Which of these two elements (product or service) of their marketing program is more important and why?

3. Evaluate Caterpillar's price cutting in order to compete more effectively with the Japanese and Italian competitors.

4. Will Cat suffer the same loss of sales and prestige that U.S. automakers did due to Japanese competition?

Case 10: GM and "just-in-time": Changing relationships in the channel of distribution

At the heart of the Japanese production management and productivity improvement system is the concept of "just-in-time." In a nutshell, with JIT, you "produce and deliver finished goods just in time to be sold, subassemblies just in time to be assembled into finished goods, fabricated parts just in time to go into subassemblies, and materials just in time to be transformed into fabricated parts."

Proponents of JIT claim myriad benefits, starting with reduced manufacturing costs. They also say workers begin to feel personally responsible for the quality of their output when it goes directly into the next stage without becoming absorbed by buffer inventory, since defective parts are obvious to both user and supplier. With this kind of responsibility on the part of the workers, they have an interest in improving the quality of their work, and suggestions for streamlining production processes and cutting setup times should be forthcoming. Fewer defective parts lead to minimal wasted materials and less direct labor wasted on rework.

General Motors has applied the just-in-time concept to its materials management system. Robert Stone, vice president of materials management, outlined the eight requirements of a successful JIT program:

1. The supplier should be within one day of the user.

2. There should be no unusable parts.

3. There should be long-term contracts and few suppliers.

4. The user needs careful control of the transpor-

tation system, allowing flexible scheduling of delivery.

5. The supplier should have manufacturing flexibility.

6. The lot sizes should be small.

7. The user should have an efficient receiving and materials handling system.

8. User management must be willing to commit necessary resources.

One implication of JIT is the switch from competitive bidding by suppliers to preselection of sources. This cuts down the lead time and allows GM and the supplier to work closely on setting up the manufacturing system and quality control, but the element of competition is lost. This effect is heightened by long-term contracts.

In addition, JIT puts a burden on suppliers. Since the user does not carry inventory, the supplier must smooth out fluctuations in demand. In essence, this is merely switching the cost from one part of the chain to another. Despite GM's intent to use long-term contracts, one vice president of a supplier to Detroit says, "Car makers haven't learned how to forecast their needs well enough to give the commitments that the Japanese give to their suppliers." Moreover, GM's emphasis on zero defective parts and perfect quality control is a new facet of manufacturing for suppliers; the system GM requires is expensive and time-consuming.

Small suppliers are likely to suffer if JIT becomes widespread. It is difficult for them to compete on the large scale required by JIT; and if they are slow to react, they may get frozen out of the market entirely.

From the user's point of view, JIT can shut out new technology and the new suppliers that normally come with aggressive competition. In addition, the reduction in supplier base tends to magnify any errors made in supplier selection. Implementation of JIT can be difficult from a physical distribution viewpoint as well; transportation is difficult when suppliers are geographically dispersed, and few plants in the United States have the kind of receiving and materials handling setup required.

From the consumer's point of view, the jury is still out on GM's experiment with just-in-time. The theory behind JIT and its associated quality control is appealing; but it is too early to say if the adjustments required in the American system to make JIT run smoothly can be made. If JIT is a success at GM, car prices will fall and quality improve—a definite benefit to the consumer.

References

Dollar, William E. "The Zero Inventory Concept." *Purchasing,* September 29, 1983, p. 43.

"GM Turns to Just-In-Time." *Automotive Industries,* June 1982, p. 21.

Hoeffer, El. "GM Tries Just-in-Time American Style." *Purchasing,* August 19, 1982, p. 67.

Mather, Hal F. "The Case for Skimpy Inventories." *Harvard Business Review,* January–February, 1984, p. 40–46.

Schonberger, Richard J. "Why the Japanese Produce Just in Time." *Industry Week,* November 29, 1982, pp. 57–60.

Discussion questions

1. What is "just-in-time"?

2. What are GM's requirements for a successful JIT system?

3. What burdens does JIT place on the suppliers?

4. Does JIT fit in with the American open market, free competition system of business?

5. Do you think that the quality control and innovation by workers in the JIT system offset its lack of open market competition?

6. Do you think just-in-time is a fad, or will it have a long-lasting effect on American business?

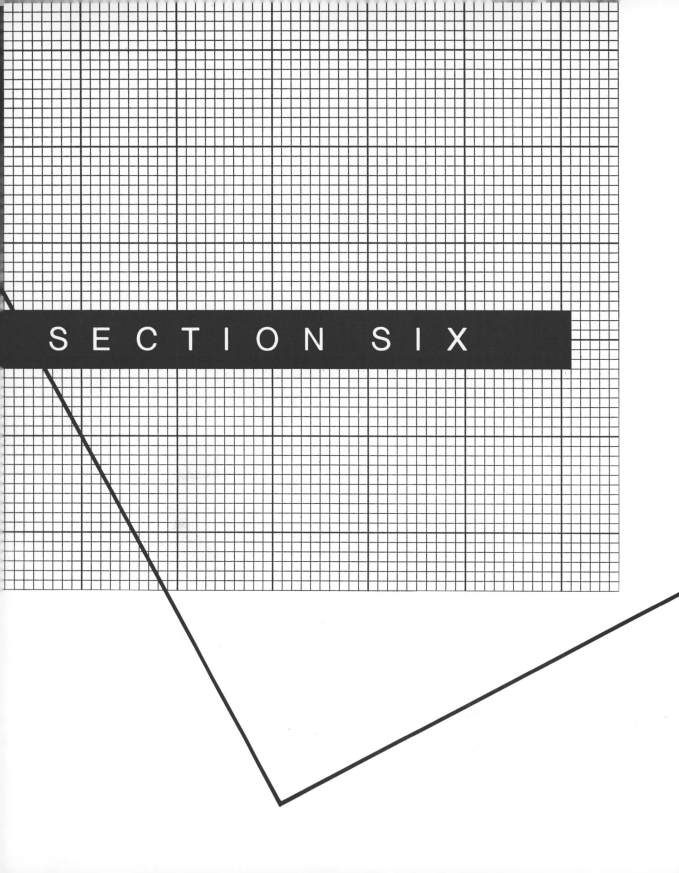

SECTION SIX

Pricing

In this section we'll address the critical issues in pricing strategy. Chapter 17 begins with market structure and pricing, then treats price elasticity, the different types of costs, and

the pricing decision. Finally, we'll present the legal aspects of pricing.

Chapter 18 deals more specifically with the methods and strategies used in pricing. First, we'll focus on the three orientations of pricing—cost, competition, and demand. We conclude with a discussion of the strategic marketing planning process applied to the pricing decision.

CHAPTER 17

Pricing: Basic considerations

Cost concepts
    Fixed costs
    Variable costs
    Average costs
    Marginal costs

Basic pricing decisions and administration
    New-product pricing
    Discounts
    Geographic pricing
    Transfer pricing

Legal aspects of pricing
    Horizontal price fixing
    Vertical price fixing
    Unit pricing

Summary

Key concepts

Discussion questions and exercises

Importance of price in an individual firm's
    marketing strategy

Economic theory and pricing
    Monopoly
    Oligopoly
    Monopolistic competition
    Pure competition

Price elasticity of demand

Price has many names. The price for the services of a bank is the interest charged on loans and service fees on checking accounts. The price for using a turnpike is a toll. Tuition, salary, rent, tips, donations, and taxes are a few other names for price in the exchange process.

price

> **Price** is the value assigned to the utility one receives from products or services. Usually price is the amount of money that is given up to acquire a given quantity of goods or service.[1]

An individual may give up other valued things—such as time or effort—to obtain something of value. Price is inherent in the exchange process and, therefore, is an inherent part of marketing. The parties to an exchange must establish a price in order for the exchange to take place, and the price for a good or service must be satisfactory to both buyer and seller. The buyer must feel that the good or service is worth the price. The seller, in turn, must feel that a fair value is being received for the good or service exchanged.

Price can be an effective means of allocating goods and services among potential purchasers. Only customers who feel the product is worth the price will purchase it. Price thus determines who purchases what. Moreover, price determines what sellers produce and in what quantities.

Often, however, the price of a particular product is not established scientifically. The pricing of products is more an art than a science; pricing decisions are often quite arbitrary, in fact. While manufacturers do consider costs, potential demand, and prices of similar products, the final decision on the price of the product is often no more than a "good guess."[2]

IMPORTANCE OF PRICE IN AN INDIVIDUAL FIRM'S MARKETING STRATEGY

Price is one of the most crucial elements in marketing strategy. Pricing decisions directly affect every element of the marketing mix. For instance, a high-priced product requires a distribution channel and a promotional strategy quite different from those required by a low-priced product. Price is influenced by cost, demand, and competitive factors. Consequently, pricing is a complex and crucial decision area for marketing management.

Research has examined the relative importance of various marketing activities to a firm's success. A 1964 study found that price was *not* one of the top five variables most mentioned by business executives as crucial

---

[1] Kent B. Monroe, *Pricing: Making Profitable Decisions* (New York: McGraw-Hill, 1979), p. 5.

[2] For a discussion of unsystematic pricing procedures, see Jeffrey H. Birnbaum, "Pricing of Products Is Still an Art often Having Little Link to Costs," *The Wall Street Journal,* November 25, 1981, pp. 25, 33.

Table 17–1: Ranking of marketing activities in importance for marketing strategy	Marketing activity	Order of importance 1975	Order of importance 1964
	Pricing	1	6
	Customer services	2	5
	Sales personnel management	3	3
	Product research and development	4	1
	Marketing cost budgeting and control	5	9
	Physical distribution	6	11
	Market research	7	2
	Marketing organization structure	8	7
Source: Robert A. Robicheaux, "How Important Is Pricing in Competitive Strategy?" in *Proceedings of the Southern Marketing Association, 1975.* ed. Henry W. Nash and Donald P. Robin	Advertising and sales promotion planning	9	4
	Distribution channel control	10	8
	Extending customer credit	11	10
	Public relations	12	12

to the firm's marketing success.[3] The reason was that firms found nonprice variables such as product research and development, market research, and promotion were most successful in meeting the needs of the consumers.

However, a study in 1975 produced drastically different results.[4] Pricing became the most important marketing variable. Table 17–1 compares the rankings obtained by the two studies. The conflicting results are attributed to the different economic conditions in 1964 and 1975. Due to inflation, 1975 consumers had become much more price-conscious. That trend is likely to continue.

ECONOMIC THEORY AND PRICING

Economists have developed models that specify how market structure affects pricing strategy. **Market structure** describes factors such as the number of buyers and sellers, the buyers' knowledge, and the amount of product differentiation. The models of market structure are monopoly, oligopoly, monopolistic competition, and pure competition. Let's examine each of these models and their implications for pricing strategy.

Monopoly

A **monopoly** exists when there is a single producer of a product for which there are no close substitutes. The following conditions characterize a monopoly: (1) there must be only one seller, (2) there must be no acceptable substitutes for the product in the market, and (3) barriers to

---

[3] Jon G. Udell, "How Important Is Pricing in Competitive Strategy?" *Journal of Marketing,* January 1964, p. 48.

[4] Robert A. Robicheaux, "How Important Is Pricing in Competitive Strategy?: Circa 1975," in *Proceedings of the Southern Marketing Association,* ed. Henry W. Nash and Donald P. Robin, 1975, pp. 55–57.

**Figure 17–1: Demand
curves for four basic
market structures**

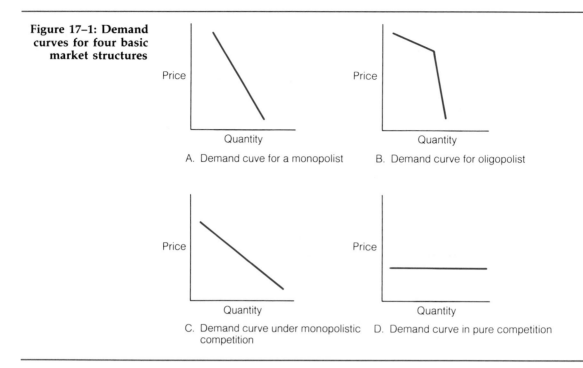

A. Demand cuve for a monopolist   B. Demand curve for oligopolist

C. Demand curve under monopolistic   D. Demand curve in pure competition
    competition

entry in the market must be extremely difficult, if not impossible, to overcome.

The demand curve for a monopolist is shown in Figure 17–1A. Since the firm that holds a monopoly is the only producer in the market, its demand curve is the industry's demand curve. The monopolist has a great deal of control over prices.

Although a pure monopoly is highly unusual in today's market, it can occur in several situations.[5] First, a monopoly can occur when a firm has control over the sources of raw materials. For example, at one time the Aluminum Co. of America (Alcoa) had a monopoly in aluminum production: it owned almost every source of bauxite, which is needed to produce aluminum. Second, patents can result in a monopoly by giving a firm the exclusive right to produce a product. E. I. du Pont de Nemours and Co., for example, had a monopoly in cellophane production due to a patent. Third, efficient, large-scale production can result in monopolies like those we see in some public utilities. Finally, monopolies can occur because of a contract between the government and a firm. Some public utilities fit this type of monopoly, too.

_____

[5] This discussion is based on J. P. Gould and C. E. Ferguson, *Microeconomic Theory* (Homewood, Ill.: Richard D. Irwin, 1980), pp. 247–48.

Oligopoly   A more common market structure is an ***oligopoly.*** An oligopoly occurs when only a few firms produce a product, which can be differentiated or undifferentiated. Examples of oligopolies are the automobile industry (General Motors, Ford, and Chrysler), and the cigarette industry (the three major producers being American Tobacco, Liggett and Myers, and R. J. Reynolds).

Since there are only a few firms in the market, the actions of one firm directly influence the other firms. For example, if one firm lowers its price, the other companies must follow in order to remain price competitive. But if one firm raises its prices, the others may not. This produces a kink in the oligopolist's demand curve, as shown in Figure 17–1B. In formulating a pricing strategy, then, a firm in an oligopolistic industry must consider competitors' reactions.

Monopolistic competition   ***Monopolistic competition*** is a market comprising many small sellers producing a differentiated product. A firm does have some control over the price of its product, depending on the product's degree of differentiation. Consequently, its demand curve (Figure 17–1C) is similar to the monopolist's.

Since substitute products are available, firms in monopolistic competition must rely heavily on the marketing mix to help differentiate the product. Examples of this type of market structure are retailers such as grocery stores, tailor shops, and clothing stores.[6]

Pure competition   The polar extreme of monopoly is ***pure competition.*** Pure competition is characterized by:

1. A large number of buyers and sellers, none of whom is large enough to affect price in any way.
2. No product differentiation.
3. No barriers to entry.
4. Perfect knowledge of market information and perfect substitutes.
5. Instantaneous adjustment to supply and demand changes.
6. No collusion.
7. Mobility of resources.
8. Buyers who act to maximize utility and sellers who act to maximize expected profits.[7]

In pure competition, the market determines the price a firm charges for its product. The firm has no discretion in setting the price. Since so many competitors are producing the same product, a firm must accept the going market rate. Consequently, the demand curve for a company

---

[6] Mark I. Alpert, *Pricing Decisions* (Glenview, Ill.: Scott, Foresman, 1971), p. 9.
[7] Ibid., p. 6.

Figure 17–2: Models of market structure based on the number of sellers

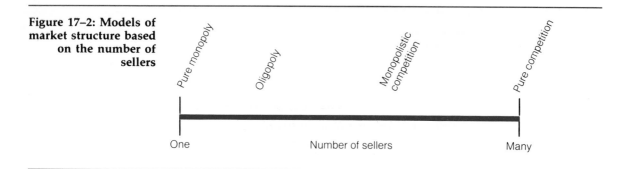

in a pure competition market structure is a horizontal line, as shown in Figure 17–1D.

Because products are usually differentiated in some way, pure competition is rare. Agriculture is probably the closest thing to a purely competitive market structure. The prices of such products as tomatoes and apples are determined by market factors that approach pure competition. There are many small farmers who have little influence on market price. Standardized grading of farm products tends to eliminate product differentiation because all products within a standard grade are identical to one another.[8] Figure 17–2 shows the models of market structure arranged according to the number of sellers.

PRICE ELASTICITY OF DEMAND

Price elasticity of demand measures how demand changes in response to a price change.[9] In its simplest terms, price elasticity can be expressed as follows:

$$\frac{\text{Price elasticity}}{\text{of demand}} = \frac{\text{Percent change in quantity demanded}}{\text{Percent change in price}}$$

In more precise mathematical terms, the following formula is used to calculate the ***coefficient of price elasticity of demand:***

$$Ed = \frac{\left(\dfrac{\left(\dfrac{Q_0 - Q_1}{Q_0 + Q_1}\right)}{2}\right)}{\left(\dfrac{\left(\dfrac{P_0 - P_1}{P_0 + P_1}\right)}{2}\right)} = \frac{\left(\dfrac{\left(\dfrac{\Delta Q}{Q_0 + Q_1}\right)}{2}\right)}{\left(\dfrac{\left(\dfrac{\Delta P}{P_0 + P_1}\right)}{2}\right)}$$

---

[8] Alpert, *Pricing Decisions.*

[9] Kent B. Monroe, *Pricing: Making Profitable Decisions* (New York: McGraw-Hill, 1979), p. 26.

where

Ed = Coefficient of price elasticity of demand.
Q_o, Q_1 = Original and new quantity demand, respectively.
P_o, P_1 = Original and new price, respectively.

It'll help, here, if we calculate a sample coefficient. Assume that a manufacturer of electric razors sold 400,000 units at \$20 per unit. The next year the manufacturer lowers the price to \$18 and sells 426,087 units. The coefficient of price elasticity would be calculated as follows:

$$Ed = \frac{\left(\dfrac{\left(\dfrac{400{,}000 - 426{,}087}{400{,}000 + 426{,}087}\right)}{2}\right)}{\left(\dfrac{\left(\dfrac{20 - 18}{20 + 18}\right)}{2}\right)} = -0.6$$

In the following year the price of the razor was reduced to \$16, resulting in sales of 663,162 units. Again, the price elasticity is calculated as follows:

$$Ed = \frac{\left(\dfrac{\left(\dfrac{426{,}087 - 663{,}162}{426{,}087 + 663{,}162}\right)}{2}\right)}{\left(\dfrac{\left(\dfrac{18 - 16}{18 + 16}\right)}{2}\right)} = -3.7$$

The minus sign reflects the fact that for most products the quantity demanded and the product's price are inversely related. That is, as price decreases, the quantity demanded increases. However, for some products the sign of the coefficient of price elasticity of demand may be positive. The positive sign indicates an unusual situation—quantity demanded increasing with an increase in price. For luxury products, higher prices may indicate greater prestige, which may generate increased quantity demanded.

We can interpret the coefficient of price elasticity of demand more easily if we look at the absolute value of the coefficient. The absolute value is symbolized by $\|$ and disregards the sign of the coefficient.

If $Ed < |1|$, demand is inelastic

If $Ed > |1|$, demand is elastic

In our first case, the price elasticity, $Ed = |0.6|$, is less than one; thus, the product's demand is defined as **_price inelastic._** In the second case, the price elasticity, $Ed = |3.7|$, is greater than one and is defined as **_price elastic._**

To further evaluate these definitions, we can use the total revenue test. If a product's demand is inelastic, a drop in price results in a decrease in total revenue. Demand for the product changes little, but people are paying less for it. However, a price decrease for a product with elastic demand results in an increase in total revenue. More consumers are buying it. This becomes obvious when looking at total revenue generated from our earlier example.

Example 1: Inelastic demand

Old price: $20/unit $\times$ 400,000 units = $8,000,000 (total revenue)

New price: $18/unit $\times$ 426,087 units = $7,669,566 (total revenue)

Example 2: Elastic demand

Old price: $18/unit $\times$ 426,087 units = $7,669,566 (total revenue)

New price: $16/unit $\times$ 663,162 units = $10,610,592 (total revenue)

Management must also look at the relationship between total cost structure and the product's price elasticity of demand. Without considering the total cost structure, management may lower the price on a product that has elastic demand and thereby increase revenue. But cost may increase by a larger percent and thereby reduce profits. This can occur when additional production capacity requiring a large increase in fixed costs is needed to meet higher demand for the product.

Elasticities vary by product types as well as by the price range. For example, in the mid-1970s it was estimated that a 50 percent increase in the price of gasoline from 38 cents to 57 cents reduced demand by 7.5 percent.[10] This resulted in a coefficient of elasticity of -0.15, which indicated inelasticity. However, when gas prices rose to $1, consumers looked for ways to reduce gasoline costs, such as purchasing smaller cars or diesel engines.[11] This indicated an increase in gasoline's price elasticity. Research has shown that price elasticity is greater for individual brands than it is for an entire product category. The average coefficient of price elasticity for individual brands of soft drinks and food products was -1.74, while for the entire product category the coefficient was -0.7.[12]

Three factors determine the degree to which a product is price elastic or inelastic. The first factor is whether substitute products are available.

---

[10] Sharon Sabin, "Don't Fill 'Er up: With Gasoline Higher, Motorists Buy Less, Surprising Experts," *The Wall Street Journal,* August 1, 1974, p. 1.

[11] Amanda Bennett, "Small Cars and Diesels Get Rush from Buyers amid Gas Price Fears," *The Wall Street Journal,* March 12, 1979, p. 1.

[12] Scott A. Neslin and Robert W. Shoemaker, "Using a Natural Experiment to Estimate Price Elasticity: The 1974 Sugar Shortage and the Ready-to-Eat Cereal Market." *Journal of Marketing* 47 (Winter 1983), pp. 44–57.

If consumers can select from a large variety of alternative products, any given product tends to be more elastic. However, products with few close substitutes tend to enjoy relatively inelastic demand. The second factor is whether the product is a necessity. If the product is one consumers must have, such as medical service, the product tends to be more inelastic. Nonnecessity or luxury goods, such as fine food or expensive vacations, are more elastic. And finally, the third factor is the size of the purchase relative to the consumer's budget. Purchases that require a significantly large proportion of a consumer's budget, such as a new car or a home, tend to be elastic. Small, routine purchases, then, tend to be relatively inelastic.

As you can see, price elasticities can provide managers with useful information. In most situations it is difficult to measure price elasticity precisely. But the actual shape of the demand curve usually is unknown, and estimates are used to calculate the elasticity. Still, price elasticity is useful in indicating how consumer demand responds to price changes. And that information, even if not precise, can be very useful to marketing management.

COST CONCEPTS

Costs are often an important element in price decision making. Therefore, we need to understand their nature. One of the most fundamental aspects of costs is their relationship to changing level of production. Costs that remain the same over different levels of production are **fixed costs.** Costs that change over the level of production are called **variable costs.** Other cost concepts that are relevant for effective price decision making are *average costs* and *marginal costs.* Let's look at each of these concepts.

Fixed costs

Fixed costs remain constant over a range of production or sales regardless of the volume of production or sales. Example of fixed costs are executive salaries, property taxes, and depreciation of building and equipment. The sum of a firm's fixed cost is the total fixed cost. Over the long term no costs are considered fixed. But in the short term—usually regarded as less than one year—some costs, such as executive salaries, are fixed for practical purposes. In Table 17–2 the cost concepts are illustrated using an example based on electric razor manufacturing. The total fixed costs are $400,000 (see column 2) and remain constant over the production range of 0 to 100,000 units.

Variable costs

Variable costs vary directly with production output or sales volume. Examples include raw materials used in manufacturing a product, wages paid to production employees, and sales commissions paid to the sales force. The total variable cost is the sum of all variable costs. In Table 17–2, total variable costs for the electric razor (column 5) range from $0 to $600,000 over the quantity produced.

Table 17–2: Cost structure for electric razors

(1) Quantity produced (000)	(2) Total fixed costs (TFC) ($000)	(3) (col. 2 ÷ col. 1) Average fixed costs (AFC)	(4) Average variable costs (AVC)	(5) (col. 4 × col. 1) Total variable costs (TVC) ($000)	(6) (col. 2 + col. 5) Total cost (TC) ($000)	(7) (col. 6 ÷ col. 1) Average cost (AC)
0	$400	$ 0	$ 0	$ 0	$ 400	$ 0
10	400	40.00	6.00	60	460	46.00
20	400	20.00	6.00	120	520	26.00
30	400	13.33	6.00	180	580	19.33
40	400	10.00	6.00	240	640	16.00
50	400	8.00	6.00	300	700	14.00
60	400	6.67	6.00	360	760	12.67
70	400	5.71	6.00	420	820	11.71
80	400	5.00	6.00	480	880	11.00
90	400	4.44	6.00	540	940	10.44
100	400	4.00	6.00	600	1,000	10.00

Average costs

Management is frequently interested in cost per unit rather than total cost. Costs per unit are called *average costs.* Average cost per unit is computed by dividing total cost by the quantity sold or produced. Average fixed cost is obtained by dividing total fixed cost by quantity. The average variable cost is derived by dividing the total variable cost by the quantity produced.

In Table 17–2, the average cost per electric razor ranges from $46 at a production level of 10,000 units to $10 at a production level of 100,000 units. The reason for the reduction in average cost is that the fixed cost of $400,000 is allocated over more units. The average fixed cost per electric razor decreases from $40 to $4 as production increases from 10,000 to 100,000 units. The average variable cost is $6 per unit and is constant over the entire range of production.

Marginal costs

Marginal cost is the cost of producing and marketing one more unit of a product. For example, if it costs $460,000 to produce 10,000 units and $460,050 to produce 10,001 units, the marginal cost for the additional unit is $50.

An understanding of these different types of costs can be very useful to marketing management when making price decisions. For example, marketing management may set a price that covers only marginal costs and not total costs. If a firm had an average total cost of $100 and variable costs of $60 per unit, the firm may price at a level slightly in excess of $60—say, $65. This would be done because the $65 price would cover the variable costs or out-of-pocket expenses, and the difference between selling price and variable cost would make a contribution to overhead. Setting a price based on marginal cost would be done when the firm

Figure 17–3: Range of possible prices

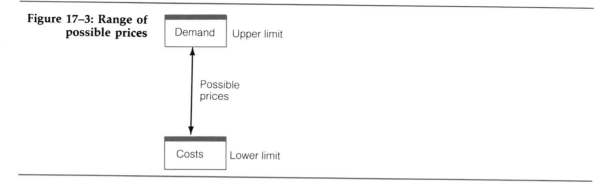

has excess capacity and high fixed cost. For example, an airline might price tickets in this manner on lightly traveled routes in order to generate revenues that would contribute to fixed costs.

When using marginal cost pricing, management must be careful not to merely switch customers who paid for the higher-priced (and, hopefully, higher-profit products) to the lower-priced products. This is an important limitation to the use of marginal cost pricing as a way of setting prices and stimulating demand.

The price a firm sets for its products or services is influenced by many factors. Three of the most important are costs, demand, and competition. The major approaches to setting prices have been organized around these factors. To illustrate these general approaches, we'll discuss specific procedures.

It's useful to think of costs as setting a lower limit for prices while demand sets an upper limit. Within these limits lies the range of possible prices that marketing management might consider when making a pricing decision. (See Figure 17–3.)

BASIC PRICING DECISIONS AND ADMINISTRATION

Now we turn to basic pricing decisions and the administration of pricing programs. In this section we analyze new product pricing. Price structure involves developing an appropriate set of discounts and determining whether buyer or seller pays the cost of transporting a product. We'll cover these issues as well. Finally, this section will consider the price to be charged for products transferred between separate divisions of the same company.

New-product pricing

There are two major policies for pricing products that are major innovations: skimming price and penetration price.[13] A ***skimming price policy***

---

[13] The discussion of skimming versus penetration policy is based on the classic article by Joel Dean, "Pricing Policies for New Products." *Harvard Business Review,* November–December 1976, pp. 141–53. This is a reprint of the original *Harvard Business Review* article in the November–December 1950 issue.

uses a high price in the early stages of the product's life cycle when the market is developing. There are several reasons why skimming is a successful pricing policy.

First, a large enough segment of consumers is willing to pay a premium price for a novel product. Second, skimming is an effective means of dividing the market into segments that differ in price elasticity of demand. Initially, the high price generates more per unit sales dollars from consumers who respond to the product's newness and distinct characteristics. In later stages of the life cycle, management can lower the price and appeal to more price-sensitive segments. Third, skimming is considered a safe policy. If the initial price is too high and sales forecasts are not met, management can easily lower the price. Buyers, however, are usually much more resistant when a price initially set too low is raised. And finally, a high price may help management keep the demand within the limits of the company's production capabilities.

A *penetration price policy,* in contrast to skimming, uses a low price to capture a large market share. There are several reasons why penetration is also a successful policy.

Probably the most compelling reason for using penetration pricing is the threat of competition. A low price helps the innovating firm capture a large market share. In addition, the low price usually means low per unit profit. These factors discourage competitors from entering the market. Second, a low price is effective when the market is highly sensitive to price and responsive to a low per unit price. Third, penetration pricing is effective when there is substantial savings in production costs resulting from increased volume.

Some companies use a skimming policy when introducing a product and then switch to a penetration policy in later stages of the product life cycle. For example, Du Pont used a high price and targeted fashion designers like Dior, Cardin, and Givenchy when introducing Dacron. As competitors entered the market and Du Pont increased sales volume, the initial price of Dacron at $2.20 per pound fell to 40 cents per pound over a 20-year time span.[14]

Discounts

Discounts are reductions from selling price. Consumers and channel members may receive discounts for a variety of reasons. Channel members may receive a discount for performing certain functions such as transporting, storing, and promoting products. Discounts may be received for paying bills promptly or for purchasing in large quantities. The major types of discounts are trade or functional, cash, promotional, and quantity.

Trade or functional discounts. A *trade* or *functional discount* is a list-price reduction granted to channel members for various tasks they perform. The *list price,* or suggested retail price, is the price that final consumers or industrial buyers are charged for products. In marketing

---

[14] "Pricing Strategy in an Inflation Economy," *Business Week,* April 6, 1974, pp. 43–49.

A display allowance is another name for a price reduction. Here a publisher encourages retailers to provide a favorable display for one of its publications, *American Health*.

RETAIL DISPLAY PLAN

A Retail Display Plan is available to all retailers who purchase AMERICAN HEALTH Magazine from suppliers other than American Health Partners. Under the plan, participating retailers receive a display allowance of 25¢ per copy resold, for performing required display services. Interested retailers can obtain details and a copy of the formal plan by writing to: Warner Publishers Services, Retail Display Allowance, 666 Fifth Avenue, New York, NY 10103.

industrial products, the manufacturer usually publishes a list price and then discounts from it. The discounts are granted to retailers and wholesalers based on the type of function they perform.

When a manufacturer quotes a price to channel members, the quotation is usually in the form of a chain discount. A *chain discount* is a series of discounts from the list price. For example, consider the terms "30, 10" quoted to a wholesaler by a manufacturer. If the list price is $100, then the wholesaler's selling price (to the retailer) would be $100 — 0.30($100) = $70. The manufacturer's selling price would be $70 — 0.10($70) = $63. The size of the discounts is based on the type and quantity of functions performed and expenses incurred by various channel members.

Trade discounts can be advantageous to distributors. If the discount is large enough, distributors can sell below the list price; and this can be an effective means of stimulating sales, if consumers perceive the price decrease.

Distribution channels are becoming more complicated, though. And it is becoming more difficult to develop an appropriate trade discount. As new types of wholesalers and retailers emerge, the role of each becomes less distinct. Unique distribution functions cannot be identified with specific channel members (wholesaler, retailer). Then it becomes difficult to justify a trade discount structure based on unique cost differentials.

Cash discounts. A *cash discount* is a reduction of the purchase price if a bill is paid within a specified time. The cash discount is usually applied after any trade or quantity discounts have been deducted.

For example, a manufacturer may quote "1/10, net 30" terms to a wholesaler. This means the wholesaler can deduct 1 percent of the price from the invoice if it is paid within 10 days of the invoice date. Otherwise, the full amount is due within 30 days. Now assume the invoice, dated June 2, indicates the wholesaler owes the manufacturer $1,000 after all applicable trade discounts. If the wholesaler pays by June 12, the amount due is only $990. But if the wholesaler waits until July 2, the full $1,000 must be paid.

At first a 1 percent discount may not appear too significant. However, by disregarding the discount and paying on July 2, the buyer in effect, borrows $1,000 for 20 days at an 18 percent annual interest rate (360 days in a year/20 days = 18 20-day periods in a year; 18 periods × 1 percent = 18 percent annual interest rate). Management should thus take advantage of this discount whenever possible. Further, offering cash discounts benefits sellers, too, by encouraging early payment of accounts receivable and improving their cash flow.

Promotional discounts. A ***promotional discount*** is an allowance to channel members for promoting the manufacturer's products. The promotional allowance may take a number of forms: price reductions, display materials, cooperative advertising payments, or complimentary samples of the product. As an example, a department store advertising a manufacturer's clothing line in a local newspaper may pay only half the advertising costs. The manufacturer may also offer a price reduction and in-store promotional material.

Both wholesalers and retailers find these discounts helpful in marketing products. Manufacturers use promotional incentives to encourage channel members to promote their products in specific ways.

Quantity discounts. The most common form of discount is the quantity discount—a price reduction based on the size of purchases, measured either in dollars or units. Quantity discounts may be noncumulative or cumulative.

A ***noncumulative quantity discount*** applies only to individual purchases, with the amount of the discount based on the dollar or unit size of the purchase. For example, a manufacturer offers a 1 percent discount on the purchase of 1,000 units and a 2 percent discount on the purchase of 2,000 units. Here, a noncumulative quantity discount encourages larger orders. Generally, this means fewer but larger orders are processed, which decreases the manufacturer's administration, production, and distribution costs.

A ***cumulative quantity discount*** applies to the total volume of goods purchased over a period of time, usually one year. Table 17–3 gives an example of such a cumulative quantity discount schedule. In this example, a distributor receives a 1 percent discount when total purchases for the year are between $50,000 and $100,000. If the distributor purchases goods worth $275,000 during the year, a discount of 1.5 percent, or $4,125, is received. Since cumulative quantity discounts do not encourage larger,

Table 17–3: Cumulative quantity discount schedule	Purchase volume ($000)	Percent discount
	Above 50–100	1.0
	Above 100–300	1.5
Source: Ashok Rao, "Quantity Discounts in Today's Markets," *Journal of Marketing* 44 (Fall 1980), pp. 44–51.	Above 300–500	2.0
	Above 500–700	2.5
	Above 700–1,000	3.0

less frequent orders, they may result in cost inefficiencies. They may, however, increase customer loyalty.

In today's changing environment, it becomes very important to periodically update the company's discount schedules. With changing environmental factors like inflation, corporate mergers, and an increasingly sophisticated buyer, a discount schedule can become a liability.[15] Assuming inflation was 10 percent annually, last year's cumulative purchases of $275,000 would increase to $302,500 this year. According to the discount schedule in Table 17–3, the total discount would increase. Furthermore, when companies merge, they can combine their individual purchases and receive an even greater quantity discount. Computer programs have been developed that enable purchasing agents to determine the quantity to purchase from each supplier in order to maximize the total quantity discount they can receive. Therefore, when developing or updating a discount schedule, the rate of inflation, the incidence of mergers between buyers, and the level of buyer sophistication are important considerations.

Geographic pricing

Geographic pricing deals with the issue of who pays the costs of transporting a product from the seller to the buyer. Deciding who bears the freight costs can have a significant impact on the seller's marketing strategy. The geographic size of the market, profit margins, location of production plants, source of raw materials, and the competitive strength in certain markets are affected by this decision. Generally, the type of geographic pricing used depends on industry practice. There are two major types: *FOB factory pricing* and *delivered pricing*.

FOB factory pricing. With *FOB (free-on-board)* factory or FOB mill pricing, the buyer incurs all costs and responsibility of shipping. The buyer selects the transportation mode and the specific carrier, handles any damage claims, and pays for all transportation charges. The seller pays only the costs of loading the merchandise on the carrier. This is what is meant by "free on board." Once the merchandise is on board,

---

[15] Ashok Rao, "Quantity Discounts in Today's Markets," *Journal of Marketing* 44 (Fall 1980), pp. 44–51.

the buyer has title to the goods. With this approach, the seller receives the same return from every sale.

The FOB factory approach can restrict a firm's growth in distant markets. To avoid this, firms may use a modified approach known as **freight absorption** or **freight equalization** pricing. With freight absorption pricing, the seller pays part of the freight costs. The seller's objective is to make the delivered price equivalent to the price charged by the competitor closest to the buyer. Of course, the seller's net return varies from customer to customer. This practice is legal only when used to meet a competitive price and when done without collusion.

Delivered pricing. In **delivered pricing,** the seller is responsible for all transportation charges. There are several forms of delivered pricing: uniform delivered, zone delivered, FOB freight allowed, and basing-point.

Uniform delivered pricing. Under **uniform delivered pricing,** all buyers are charged the same price regardless of their location. Consequently, the seller's net return on a sale depends on the location of the buyer and the corresponding transportation costs. In effect, the price includes the cost of production and the average transportation charge. So, buyers located near the seller are overcharged, and buyers located far from the seller are undercharged. This practice is legal only if the same price is quoted for the seller's entire geographic market. In practice, a uniform delivered price is usually used when a product is advertised nationally. In this case, transportation costs are typically a minor part of the product's total price.

Zone delivered pricing. A variation of uniform delivered pricing is **zone delivered pricing.** The seller's market is divided into smaller geographic zones. Each zone has a uniform delivered price. The transportation component of the uniform delivered price is, then, an average freight charge for each zone. This system is similar to the zone rate system used for pricing long-distance telephone calls. However, management must be cautious to avoid price discrimination charges since zone boundaries must be drawn so that all competing buyers are in one zone.

FOB with freight allowed. Another variation of delivered pricing is **FOB with freight allowed.** With this approach, the buyer arranges and pays for all transportation. Those charges are then deducted from the buyer's invoice, and the buyer pays only the net amount. The net price paid to the seller varies.

Basing-point pricing. A final variation of uniform delivered pricing is **basing-point pricing.** The delivered price is the factory price plus the freight costs from the basing point nearest the buyer. A *basing point* is a location where the product is produced and from which all sellers' delivery prices are computed. Generally, the basing point is the area of greatest production. The actual shipping point is not considered in determining the delivered price.

Figure 17–4: Basing-point pricing

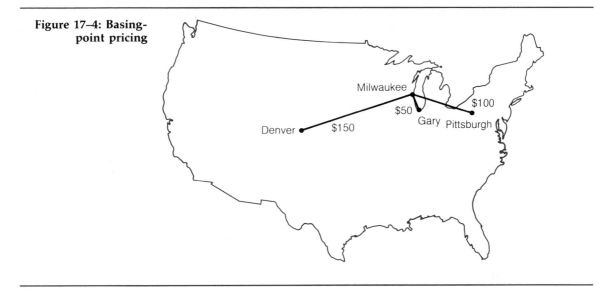

A single or a multiple basing point may be used. For many years, the steel industry used a single basing-point system known as the Pittsburgh-plus system. The delivered price for any steel product from any steel manufacturer was equal to the factory price plus freight from Pittsburgh, regardless of the seller's actual location. For example, assume a steel manufacturer has plants in Pittsburgh, Denver, and Gary, Indiana, as shown in Figure 17–4. For a buyer located in Milwaukee, freight charges for a product selling for $300 are $50 from Gary, $100 from Pittsburgh, and $150 from Denver. However, since Pittsburgh is the basing point, the delivered price would be $400 even if Gary was the actual shipping point. The Gary manufacturer would then receive an additional $50 for freight charges not incurred. This $50 is referred to as *phantom freight.* If the actual shipping point was Denver, the delivered price would still be $400, but the Denver manufacturer would have to absorb $50 in freight costs.

A multiple basing-point system uses several basing points. The basing point used to calculate the delivered price is the one that results in the lowest cost to the buyer.

Generally, basing-point systems are used by oligopolistic industries that produce basic, undifferentiated products where price is most important and brand name is least important to the buyer. Sugar, cement, plate glass, and lumber products are examples of industries that have used this system.

There are several advantages to a basing-point pricing system.[16] First,

---

[16] Monroe, *Pricing,* p. 186.

price competition is not based on different transportation costs. In addition, a firm is not prevented from expanding its geographic market because of transportation costs.

But there are also a number of disadvantages associated with a basing-point price system. It provides no incentive for the buyer to use the least expensive mode of transportation, and sellers often may have to absorb freight costs. Because of the variance in actual freight costs and charges, the seller's net return varies from sale to sale. Phantom freight charges and the elimination of price competition are major problems with basing-point pricing.

Furthermore, the legality of the system is questionable. Currently, single basing-point pricing is illegal. The legality of multiple basing-point pricing is still uncertain. A firm can probably avoid legal problems if the system does not result in phantom freights, varying net returns, or price fixing. The main considerations are whether the system is a means for sellers to fix prices and whether competition among buyers is reduced because of price discrimination. Because of the administrative and legal problems of basing-point pricing, most firms have switched to FOB factory pricing.

Transfer pricing

Transfer pricing involves the establishment of a price when one division of a company sells products to another division within the same company. Management establishes transfer pricing when one division manufactures components used or sold by another division. Both divisions must contribute to overall corporate profits. Therefore, price for the components is established that is profitable for the selling division and fair for the buying division. Transfer prices are most commonly established by using the going market price or a cost-based price.[17]

Using the market price is the simplest method. With this approach, the price need not be negotiated between divisions. It has the added benefit of making the selling division more cost-conscious to remain competitive with other manufacturers and to increase contribution margins. The market price is also a way to demonstrate the real contribution the division is making to corporate profits.

Using a cost-based method, the transfer price is established by adding a specified profit margin to the standard unit cost of the product. *Standard costs* are the estimated costs of producing a product under normal conditions. The use of standard costs forces the division producing the product to control costs since it must sustain any losses if actual costs are greater than standard costs. The buying division cannot be penalized, then, for the inefficiencies of the selling division. This approach is generally used if a market price has not been established for the product.

Regardless of the method used, the transfer price should be realistic

---

[17] Robert N. Anthony and John Dearden, *Management Control Systems* (Homewood, Ill.: Richard D. Irwin, 1976), pp. 280–83.

and fair to all divisions concerned. Then, transfer prices provide an effective means of evaluating the performance of each division.

LEGAL ASPECTS OF PRICING

The legal aspects of pricing are complicated and have received much attention from government agencies. We have already discussed some of the legal issues involved in geographic pricing and minimum markup laws. In this section we focus on two price-fixing practices. First, we analyze collusion among channel of distribution members who are at the same level within the channel, such as retailers. This is called ***horizontal price fixing.*** Second, we analyze price-fixing practices among members at different levels of the channel—such as collusion between a manufacturer and a wholesaler. This is ***vertical price fixing.*** Finally, we explore the issue of providing price information to consumers under the topic of *unit pricing.*

Horizontal price fixing

Horizontal price fixing occurs when two or more competitors act jointly to fix prices. For example, two gasoline retailers might collude and fix prices on gasoline.

Horizontal price fixing is illegal per se under Section 1 of the ***Sherman Antitrust Act,*** which states: "Every contract, combination . . . or conspiracy, in restraint of trade or commerce among the several States, or with foreign nations, is hereby declared to be illegal." Horizontal price fixing is also illegal under the ***Federal Trade Commission Act,*** which made "unfair methods of competition" illegal. It was made illegal because it allowed conspirators to charge unreasonable prices if they desired.

Horizontal price fixing can take a variety of forms. The most common form is conspiring to stabilize or increase prices. Other forms include agreeing to:

Rotate bids in order to divide a market.[18]

Maintain a certain markup or discount.[19]

Lower or maintain prices by providing competitors with price information.[20]

Raise prices indirectly by removing slow-selling merchandise from distribution.[21]

All of these acts are illegal per se. Furthermore, this applies to all levels within the channel of distribution—manufacturer, wholesaler, or retailer.

---

[18] *Las Vegas Merchant Plumbers Association* v. *U.S.,* 210 F.2d 732 (9th Cir.), cert. denied, 348 U.S. 817 (1954).

[19] *California Retailer Growers and Merchants Association* v. *U.S.* 139 F.2d 978 (9th Cir., 1943), cert. denied, 322 U.S. 729 (1944).

[20] *United States* v. *Utah Pharmaceutical Assoc.,* 371 U.S. 24 (1964).

[21] *U.S.* v. *Sacony-Vacuum Oil Co.,* 310 U.S. 150 (1940).

Penalties for violating price-fixing laws can be quite severe. Lawyers' fees, company fines, executives' personal fines, civil suits, and prison sentences can be quite substantial. The costs to company morale and company image are incalculable.

An example of the severe consequences of price fixing is provided by the folding-carton industry.[22] In one of the largest antitrust suits ever brought before the Justice Department, 70 percent of the companies in the folding-carton industry were found guilty of conspiring to fix the prices of corrugated cardboard boxes and folding cartons. Jail terms, probation, and fines were imposed on 47 of the 48 executives who were charged with conspiracy. The companies were fined the maximum—$50,000 each—for a misdemeanor violation. In addition, many customers of these companies filed civil suits to obtain compensation for overcharges. One company reported that the legal fees involved were greater than the earnings of its folding-carton division in the five years prior to the lawsuit!

A more recent example of horizontal price fixing is the case of two crayon firms.[23] Binney & Smith, maker of Crayola crayons, and Milton Bradley were accused by the FTC of fixing prices of wax crayons and other school supplies. An initial settlement of $200,000 was made by Binney & Smith.

Numerous conditions facilitate the occurrence of horizontal price fixing.[24] One condition that favors it occurs when competing products are undifferentiated. Price becomes the major means of competition, and to avoid a price war and low profit margins, there is great temptation to collude. This is also true when overcapacity exists in an industry and competitors engage in price wars to obtain more business. In addition, collusion is much easier when only a few firms compete in an industry— in other words, when oligopoly exists.

Price fixing may also occur as a result of factors internal to a firm. Price agreements are a common practice in many companies. Individual performance evaluations based solely on profits and volume almost encourage it. This type of evaluation forces marketing management to achieve the bottom-line results regardless of what is involved. The decentralization of pricing decisions also makes horizontal price fixing more likely: top management may not be fully aware of lower-level decisions. Finally, close-knit trade associations can facilitate price agreements.

Vertical price fixing

Vertical price fixing occurs when two or more firms in a channel of distribution act jointly or collusively to fix prices. Unlike horizontal price

[22] Jeffrey Sonnefeld and Paul R. Lawrence, "Why Do Companies Succumb to Price Fixing?" *Harvard Business Review,* July–August 1978, pp. 145–56.

[23] Jeffrey H. Birnbaum, "Prospect Is Waxing of Two Crayon Firms Settling Price Case," *The Wall Street Journal,* February 29, 1980, p. 6.

[24] The following discussion is based on Sonnefeld and Lawrence, "Why Do Companies," pp. 146–50.

fixing, the vertical type involves firms at different levels in a channel of distribution.

At one time, vertical price fixing was legal under the **Miller-Tydings Act** of 1937 in states that exempted vertical price fixing from the antitrust laws. As a result, many states passed resale price maintenance, or fair-trade, laws. The fair-trade laws allowed manufacturers and wholesalers to fix the price retailers could charge for their products. These laws were designed to aid the small, independent retailer in its battle with chain stores and discount stores, which were able to charge lower prices.

Very few manufacturers took advantage of these laws. In fact, 90 to 95 percent of all retail goods during this time were never fair traded.[25] Manufacturers felt that fair trading would create a price umbrella and that short-term profits would increase competition. Furthermore, it was up to the manufacturers to enforce the retail price of their products. Since it was not to the manufacturers' advantage to sue their distributors, the fair-trade laws were not enforced.

The fair-trade laws did not protect the small retailer as they were designed to do. In fact, they aided the chain stores by allowing them to avoid price cutting during the Depression. Moreover, the fair-trade laws may have been a key factor in the growth of discount stores and private brands.[26]

As a result, in 1975 Congress passed the **Consumer Goods Pricing Act,** which repealed the Miller-Tydings Act. This made vertical price fixing illegal per se under the Sherman Antitrust and Federal Trade Commission acts.

Another aspect of vertical price fixing is *price discrimination.* Price discrimination is prohibited under the **Robinson-Patman Act.** Robinson-Patman prohibits a seller from selling two or more different commodities of like grade and quality at different prices where the result may be to substantially lessen competition or create an injury to competition. The act had four primary goals:

1. To make it illegal for anyone involved in interstate commerce to discriminate in price between purchasers (business purchasers as opposed to consumers of goods of like grade and quality).

2. To protect independent retailers, manufacturers, and the public from unfair competition.

3. To prohibit the granting of brokerage firms to large buyers who purchase directly from producers or through "dummy" brokerage houses run by the purchasers' employees.

---

[25] E. Jerome McCarthy, *Basic Marketing,* 4th ed. (Homewood, Ill.: Richard D. Irwin, 1971), p. 690.

[26] L. Louise Luchsinger and Patrick M. Dunne, "Fair-Trade Laws—How Fair?" *Journal of Marketing* 42 (January 1978), pp. 50–53.

4. To prohibit payment to a customer unless that payment is made on proportionately equal terms to all competing customers.[27]

According to the Robinson-Patman Act, any price differences must be based on actual cost differences or on the need to meet competition. Furthermore, any promotional or advertising allowances must be provided the same proportionately to all customers.

An example of application of Robinson-Patman is provided by the *Borden* case.[28] In this case, the Borden Company sold evaporated milk under its own label and under a private label at different prices. Borden was charged with price discrimination because it sold evaporated milk of like grade and quality to different purchasers at higher prices than private labels. Borden argued that the products were not of like grade and quality because the different brand names were perceived differently by consumers. But the Court ruled that the economic factors in brand names and advertising should not be considered in a test of like grade and quality.

The *Perkins* case added another dimension to the Robinson-Patman Act.[29] In this case, Perkins—a wholesaler and a retailer—charged that Standard Oil of California had sold it gasoline at a discriminatorily higher price than to another firm, Signal Oil Company. Signal sold the gasoline to Western Hyway, which sold it to Regal, a competitor of Perkins' retail outlets. Perkins charged that Regal was able to charge lower prices because of the lower price passed on to it from Signal. Standard argued that Regal was "so far removed from Standard in the chain of distribution" that Robinson-Patman did not apply. The Court ruled that Perkins suffered damages because it could not compete with Regal due to the lower price charged to Signal. The distance of Standard and Regal in the distribution chain was not a proper defense for price discrimination.[30]

Unit pricing

The increase in the number of package sizes and shapes has made it increasingly difficult for the consumer to make price and value comparisons. ***Unit pricing*** presents price information enabling the consumer to make price comparisons quickly and easily. With unit pricing, the product's price and the price per unit (such as an ounce, pound, or hundred count) are presented. For example, unit-pricing information for liquid dishwashing detergents might be presented as follows:

Ivory	22 oz.	56 cents	81.5 cents per quart
Lux	22 oz.	45 cents	65.5 cents per quart
Ivory	32 oz.	80 cents	80.0 cents per quart
Lux	32 oz.	63 cents	63.0 cents per quart

[27] William G. Nickels, *Marketing Principles,* 2d ed. (Englewood Cliffs, N.J.: Prentice-Hall, 1982), p. 597.

[28] *FTC* v. *The Borden Co., U.S. Supreme Court Reports,* vol. 383 (1966), p. 367.

[29] *Clyde A. Perkins* v. *Standard Oil of California,* 395 U.S. 642 (1969).

[30] Ray O. Werner, "Marketing and the U.S. Supreme Court, 1968–1974," *Journal of Marketing* 41 (January 1977), p. 36.

The consumer could readily determine that the 32-ounce Lux is the best buy on a cost-per-quart basis. However, other factors such as brand name, cleaning power of the liquid, etc., would enter into the buying decision. About 100 chain stores have voluntarily adopted unit pricing; some states require it by law.[31]

Unit pricing has implications for retailers and consumers. The major disadvantage to retailers is the cost of making unit-price computations, displaying the information, and maintaining computer records. These costs equal less than 0.1 percent of sales for the average supermarket; but this amounts to approximately 10 percent of retailers' profits.[32] These costs must be weighed against the advantages. Giant Foods, a Washington, D.C., supermarket chain, found that their unit-pricing system resulted in considerable savings from a reduction in marking errors, better inventory control, and improved space management.[33]

The major consumer advantage of unit pricing is that it makes price comparisons easier. The comparisons help consumers identify the lowest-cost brands and may thus lower their expenditures. One study found that listing unit prices resulted in a 3 percent consumer savings and a 5 percent increase in the market share of the lower-cost-per-unit store brands.[34] Another study found that unit-pricing information provided the following benefits: (1) consumers were able to determine the most economical item, and (2) it helped consumers purchase the most economical product items when they sought to achieve this goal.[35] While a final answer has not been reached, the evidence does suggest that price lists are the most effective means of providing unit-price information to consumers.

---

[31] Joseph B. Mason and Morris L. Mayer, *Modern Retailing and Practice* (Plano, Tex.: Business Publications, 1981), p. 743.

[32] J. Edward Russo, "The Value of Unit-Price Information," *Journal of Marketing Research* 19 (May 1977), pp. 193–201.

[33] Esther Peterson, "Consumerism as a Retailer's Asset," *Harvard Business Review* 52 (May–June 1979), p. 97.

[34] Russo, "Value of Unit-Price Information," p. 193.

[35] Michael J. Houston, "The Effect of Unit Pricing on Choices of Brand and Size in Economic Shopping," *Journal of Marketing* 36 (July 1972), pp. 51–69.

SUMMARY

The market structure facing a firm will have a significant impact on a firm's pricing strategy. A monopolist's demand curve is the industry demand curve; thus, monopolists have a great deal of control over prices. In an oligopoly, the few firms in the industry must consider competitive reaction in formulating pricing strategy. The tendency to lower prices but not to raise prices to meet competitors has led to what economists call a "kinked" demand curve. Monopolistic competitors rely on product differentiation to attempt to develop some degree of monopoly power. In pure competition, the price a firm charges is totally determined by the market, since there are always perfect substitutes and perfect knowledge of the market. Both pure competition and monopoly are rare forms of market structure.

Price elasticity will also have an impact on the pricing decision. Elasticity is a measure of demand sensitivity to changes in prices. Three major factors determine degree of price elasticity: (1) availability of substitutes, (2) extent to which a product is a necessity, and (3) relative ease of purchase.

How much a product costs will often limit how low a product can be priced. It is important to understand how fixed, variable, average, and marginal costs vary over different levels of production.

New products can be priced under either skimming price or penetration price methods. Skimming generates more per unit sales dollars initially. Penetration pricing attempts to capture a large market share quickly.

Discounts from the selling price can provide a monetary incentive for channel members or consumers to behave in ways beneficial to a firm. Trade or functional discounts are given to channel members for the type of functions they perform for a manufacturer. Cash discounts are an incentive for paying a purchase invoice in a timely manner. Promotional discounts help a channel member promote a manufacturer's product. Quantity discounts are given based on the size of purchases and may be cumulative or noncumulative.

Costs of transporting a product from seller to buyer often are significant, so the price charged should reflect those additional costs or lack of them. FOB factory and delivered pricing are two different geographic pricing methods for treating those transportation costs.

Transfer pricing refers to the price charged when transferring a product from one division to another within a company. Transfer prices commonly used are the market price and cost-based price (when a market price is not available).

Legal problems with pricing are often related to price fixing. Horizontal price fixing occurs when two or more competitors collude to fix prices, and it is illegal per se. Vertical price fixing occurs when members of a channel of distribution join to fix prices, thus harming other members of the channel. It is also illegal per se. Vertical price *discrimination* is legal, but only when based on actual cost differences or on the need to meet competition. Unit pricing helps consumers to be better informed about the pricing of products; it is required by law in some states. While unit pricing does help consumers make comparisons, its cost is a significant portion of retailers' profits.

KEY CONCEPTS

Price	Fixed costs	Promotional discount
Market structure	Variable costs	Noncumulative quantity discount
Monopoly	Average costs	Cumulative quantity discount
Oligopoly	Marginal costs	Geographic pricing
Monopolistic competition	Skimming price policy	FOB factory pricing
Pure competition	Penetration price policy	Freight absorption pricing
Price elasticity of demand	Discounts	Delivered pricing
Coefficient of price elasticity of demand	Trade or functional discount	Uniform delivered pricing
	List price	Zone delivered pricing
Price inelastic demand	Chain discount	FOB with freight allowed
Price elastic demand	Cash discount	Basing-point pricing

Transfer pricing

Horizontal price fixing

Vertical price fixing

Sherman Antitrust Act

Federal Trade Commission Act

Miller-Tydings Act

Consumer Goods Pricing Act

Price discrimination

Robinson-Patman Act

Unit pricing

DISCUSSION QUESTIONS AND EXERCISES

1. Price is an expression of the value that buyer and seller attach to whatever is being exchanged in a marketing transaction. Consider the following situations:

   a. Your *starting salary* when you graduate.

   b. The *tuition* you pay to your college or university.

   c. The *interest* you pay on a bank loan.

   Price is represented by each of the italicized terms. In each of the above situations, what is being exchanged for the price paid?

2. What is the role of price in our economy?

3. In this chapter we presented research showing that executives placed much more importance on price in 1975 than they did in 1964. What do you think is the relative status of price today in the marketing strategy of leading companies in the United States?

4. The Ajax Company sold 100 units of their product at $10 per unit. The company then dropped the price to $5 per unit and sold 150 units. Compute the coefficient of price elasticity of demand using the formula presented in the text. Is the demand elastic or inelastic? Was the price reduction a sound idea? Why or why not?

5. Define and provide an example of each of the following types of costs:
   a. Fixed. b Variable. c. Average. d. Marginal.

6. What is a skimming price policy versus a penetration price policy? What conditions favor each of these?

7. What is a functional discount? Who usually grants the functional discount and why?

8. A manufacturer quotes the following terms to a wholesaler: "2/20, net 60." On an invoice of $2,000, what would the wholesaler pay if the discount was taken? If the wholesaler does not take advantage of the discount, what is the annual interest rate for failing to take the discount?

9. What's the difference between FOB factory pricing and delivered pricing?

10. Compare and contrast horizontal price fixing to vertical price fixing.

11. What is unit pricing? Describe the advantages and disadvantages of unit pricing to:
    a. Consumers.
    b. Retailers who provide the unit price information.

CHAPTER 18

Pricing: Methods and strategies

Cost-oriented pricing practices
  Markup pricing
  Target-return pricing
  Breakeven analysis pricing
  Experience curve pricing
Competition-oriented pricing
  Price leadership
  Competitive bidding
Demand-oriented pricing
  Perceived-value pricing
  Price-quality relationships

Loss-leader pricing
Odd-numbered pricing
Price lining
Strategic marketing planning applied to pricing
  Situation analysis
  Establish pricing objectives
  Product/market strategy
  Budget determination
  Strategic pricing issues
  Distribution channels
  Promotion
  Evaluation of price performance

Summary

Key concepts

Discussion questions and exercises

In this chapter we'll discuss the three major methods for establishing a specific price: cost-oriented, competition-oriented, and demand-oriented. The second major part of this chapter deals with the strategic marketing management framework applied to the pricing decision. The focus is on those aspects of the process that are unique to the pricing decision.

COST-ORIENTED PRICING PRACTICES

Cost-oriented approaches to setting prices are the most common. There are four techniques: markup, target-return, breakeven analysis, and experience curve pricing.

Markup pricing

Markup pricing is the most common technique used by retailers and wholesalers. A price is determined by adding a predetermined percentage to the cost of a product. This dollar amount is the *markup* on the product. Markup is the difference between a product's cost and its selling price. In other words, the amount added to the cost of the product to cover expenses and provide a profit.

Department stores typically determine markup as a percentage of selling price. To determine the markup percentage, the dollar markup is divided by the original selling price. A markup of 40 percent of retail value is common for many soft goods and apparel sold in department stores.[1] Smaller stores determine markup as a percentage of cost. They divide the dollar markup by the product's cost. As an example, the markup for hardware retailers is usually 50 percent of cost.[2]

The following example illustrates markup pricing. Assume a product costs $1. If a company has determined that it needs a 25 percent markup on cost (or a 20 percent markup on retail value) to cover expenses and provide a profit, the selling price of the product is set at $1.25.

Markup pricing focuses on costs rather than on demand in arriving at a specific price. It is a highly popular practice for several reasons. It's easy to use. It helps reduce price competition because retailers have similar costs, apply similar markups, and arrive at very similar prices. Finally, markup pricing is regarded as equitable to both buyer and seller. Generally, retailers keep markups at the same level even during periods of high demand. This allows the retailer to cover costs and earn a reasonable profit.

Target-return pricing

Target-return pricing involves establishing price so that a predetermined return is attained on the capital used in producing and distributing a product.[3] The target return is based on a *standard volume*—the volume expected to be sold during a specific time period, usually a year.

---

[1] William R. Davidson, Alton F. Doody, and Daniel J. Sweeney, *Retailing Management*, 4th ed. (New York: John Wiley & Sons, 1978), p. 241.

[2] Ibid.

[3] Kent B. Monroe, *Pricing: Marking Profitable Decisions* (New York: McGraw-Hill, 1979), p. 214.

In determining a selling price by this approach, per unit labor and material costs associated with the standard volume are estimated. Next, the per unit fixed costs are determined. To obtain the selling price, these costs are then added to the per unit return desired on the capital used to produce the product. Mathematically:[4]

$$P_r = DVC + \frac{F}{X} + \frac{rK}{X}$$

where

P_r = Selling price determined when the target-return formula is used.
DVC = Direct unit variable costs.
F = Fixed costs.
X = Standard unit volume.
r = Profit rate desired.
K = Capital (total operating assets) employed.

For example, if per unit labor costs are estimated to be $2.15, and per unit material costs are $2.05 based on a standard volume of 500,000 units, then direct unit variable costs are $4.20. If fixed costs are estimated to be $500,000, and a 15 percent rate of return on $1 million in capital employed is desired, the selling price is $5.50. In equation form:

$$P_r = \$4.20 + \frac{\$500,000}{500,000} + \frac{15 \text{ percent } (\$1,000,000)}{500,000}$$

$$= \$4.20 + \$1.00 + \$0.30$$

$$= \$5.50$$

The classic 1958 study on pricing practices found that achieving a specific rate of return on investment was the dominant goal of such large corporations as General Motors, U.S. Steel, Alcoa, Exxon, and Du Pont.[5] Target-return pricing is often associated with the automobile industry, especially the market share leader, General Motors.

There is a major problem with target-return pricing. If demand is less than estimated, a firm may raise prices in order to achieve the target rate of return. Of course, raising prices in the face of declining demand is the opposite of what economic theory prescribes. During 1974–75, the automobile industry was caught in the difficult situation of declining demand on one hand and target-return pricing on the other. Auto prices rose an average $1,000 per auto, while sales fell 25 percent.[6]

The auto industry has used target-return pricing and has been criticized

[4] Ibid.

[5] Robert F. Lanzillotti, "Pricing Objectives in Large Companies," *American Economic Review* 78 (May 1958), pp. 921–40.

[6] "Detroit's Dilemma on Prices," *Business Week,* January 20, 1975, p. 82–87.

because of its inflexible pricing approach. Specifically, the industry has strongly resisted price reductions. In fairness to automakers, we should say that rebates have increased pricing flexibility. But in 1981 the use of rebates failed to increase sales enough to deliver operating profits for any U.S. automaker.[7]

Breakeven analysis pricing

Another cost-oriented approach is ***breakeven analysis pricing.*** Breakeven analysis determines the number of units required to generate the sales dollars to equal the total fixed and variable costs at a specific unit price. At the breakeven point there are neither profits nor losses. The breakeven point can be calculated in units or dollars. The equation for determining the breakeven point in units is:

$$BEP = \frac{FC}{SP - VC} = \frac{FC}{UCM}$$

where

BEP = Breakeven point in units.
FC = Fixed cost.
SP = Unit selling price.
VC = Unit variable cost.
UCM = Unit contribution margin = $SP - VC$.

With this approach, management can determine how many units must be sold at a given price in order to break even. This information can be very useful when establishing the price for a product. The breakeven points for a number of selling prices can be compared. So, while breakeven analysis is based on cost, it can be adapted to consider market factors. This is helpful in selecting the price that is likely to exceed its breakeven point and maximize its contribution margin.

For example, suppose a firm wants to reprice its electric razor. The costs associated with this razor are shown in Table 18–1. In breakeven analysis, we assume that total fixed costs and average variable costs remain constant. If the firm were to price the product at $18, the breakeven point would be:

$$BEP = \frac{\$400,000}{\$18 - \$6} = \frac{\$400,000}{\$12} = 33,333 \text{ units}$$

For every electric razor sold at the $18 price, $12 is contributed to fixed costs. To completely cover the $400,000 in fixed costs, 33,333 units must be sold or $599,994 in sales revenue must be generated. If any more units are sold, the $12 per unit contribution margin is considered profit.

---

[7] "Why Detroit Can't Cut Prices," *Business Week,* March 1, 1982, pp. 110–12.

A breakeven chart is usually drawn to illustrate the relationship between revenues and costs. The breakeven chart for this example is shown in Figure 18–1. The breakeven point is where the total revenue curve for a given price level intersects the total cost curve. Figure 18–1 shows that the total revenue curve for an $18 price intersects the total cost curve when 33,333 units are sold or $599,994 in revenue is produced. Above the breakeven point, profits are made. Below the breakeven point, losses are incurred.

To determine the best price for this electric razor, the breakeven point at each of several prices was calculated. Since the price must at least cover the average variables costs, a price of $6 or less was not considered. The prices considered and their breakeven points appear in Table 18–2. Based on this and other available information, management decided that a sales level of 33,333 units was attainable and, therefore, set the price for the electric razor at $18.

Breakeven analysis is a useful tool in pricing decisions. As the previous example indicates, price is evaluated by the volume it must generate to cover costs. This allows various pricing alternatives to be compared. Breakeven analysis forces management to consider the relationship between revenues and costs and to consider the interaction between costs and demand. It also shows how fast profits can be attained once the breakeven point is passed and the losses that can be sustained if it is not reached.

Breakeven analysis has also been criticized as a pricing tool. The main criticism is that it assumes costs are static. But average variable costs usually fluctuate, depending on the volume level produced. And total fixed costs are constant for only a limited volume range. Furthermore, breakeven analysis assumes all costs can be separated into fixed and variable costs.

Table 18–1: Cost structure for electric razors

Quantity sold (000)	Total fixed costs (TFC) ($000)	Average fixed costs (AFC)	Average variable costs (AVC)	Total variable costs (TVC) ($000)	Total cost (TC) ($000)	Average cost (AC)
–0–	$400	$ 0	$ 0	$ 0	$ 400	$ 0
10	400	40.00	6.00	60	460	46.00
20	400	20.00	6.00	120	520	26.00
30	400	13.33	6.00	180	580	19.33
40	400	10.00	6.00	240	640	16.00
50	400	8.00	6.00	300	700	14.00
60	400	6.67	6.00	360	760	12.67
70	400	5.71	6.00	420	820	11.71
80	400	5.00	6.00	480	880	11.00
90	400	4.44	6.00	540	940	10.44
100	400	4.00	6.00	600	1,000	10.00

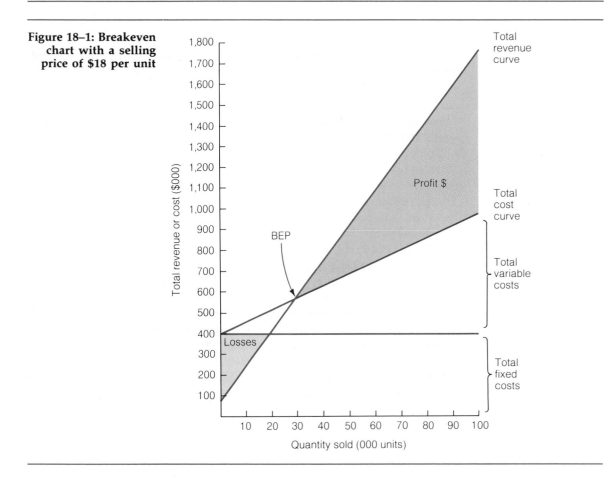

Figure 18–1: Breakeven chart with a selling price of $18 per unit

In addition, breakeven analysis doesn't consider demand properly. The breakeven chart assumes that any quantity of electric razors can be sold at $18 each. It assumes a constant relationship between revenue and output.[8] It fails to recognize that profits are dependent on such factors as demand and marketing efforts. This approach also fails to take account of risk. To overcome some of these objections, a range of breakeven points at a given point can be estimated.[9]

Despite these shortcomings, breakeven analysis is a useful tool for firms in oligopolistic industries where prices are "sticky," plants are large and have excess capacity, and variable costs are constant and represent

[8] V. H. Kirpalani and Stanley T. Shapiro, "Financial Dimensions of Marketing Management," *Journal of Marketing* 37 (July 1973), pp. 40–47.

[9] Bill P. Darden, "An Operational Approach to Product Pricing," *Journal of Marketing* 32 (April 1968), pp. 29–33.

Table 18–2: Breakeven point under several selling prices	Selling price (SP)	Average variable costs (AVC)	Contribution margin (UCM = SP − AVC)	Total fixed costs (TFC) ($000)	Breakeven point (TFC ÷ CM) (units)
	$10	$6.00	$ 4.00	$400	100,000
	15	6.00	9.00	400	44,444
	18	6.00	12.00	400	33,333
	23	6.00	17.00	400	23,529
	30	6.00	24.00	400	16,667

a low proportion of the final selling price. Examples of such industries are petroleum refining, steel manufacturing, and production of industrial chemicals.[10]

Experience curve pricing

Experience curve pricing uses the experience curve as a strategic tool in establishing price. The experience curve illustrates the relationship between cumulative production and per unit costs. As more units are produced, per unit costs drop in a predictable fashion. Specifically, each time the cumulative volume of units produced doubles, per unit costs decline by a fixed percentage. *Experience* is defined as the combined effects of learning, volume, investment, and specialization.

The experience effect is shown graphically by plotting the total accumulated units produced on the horizontal axis and the cost or price per unit on the vertical axis. Figure 18–2 shows an 85 percent experience curve. An "85 percent" curve means that every time cumulative output doubles, costs per unit drop to 85 percent of their preceding level. In other words, per unit costs decline 15 percent with each doubling of cumulative production. This is a typical relationship for many products and services.

Consider the example in Table 18–3. Suppose that a firm initially produced 10 units at a $100 cost per unit. If cumulative production doubles to 20 units, per unit costs would decrease 15 percent to $85 per unit. If cumulative production doubles again, per unit costs decrease by 15 percent of the previous $85 per unit cost—that is, to $72.

Normally, the experience curve is plotted on a log-log scale. The experience effect then becomes a straight line, as shown in Figure 18–3. The slope of this line represents the experience rate.

As per unit costs decline with increased production, management has the flexibility to reduce prices and remain profitable. Ideally, price decreases should parallel cost decreases and, therefore, should follow the same experience curve slope. Consequently, the experience curve can be illustrated by plotting the unit price and cumulative units produced. To

[10] Kirpalani and Shapiro, "Financial Dimensions," p.42.

**Figure 18–2: An
85 percent
experience curve**

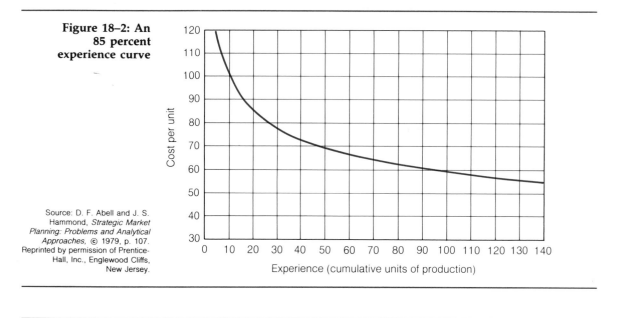

Source: D. F. Abell and J. S.
Hammond, *Strategic Market
Planning: Problems and Analytical
Approaches*, © 1979, p. 107.
Reprinted by permission of Prentice-
Hall, Inc., Englewood Cliffs,
New Jersey.

**Table 18–3: Cost
reductions due to
increased experience**

Cumulative units of production	Cost per unit	Cumulative cost reduction per unit
10	$100	—
20	85	$15
40	72	28
80	61	39
160	52	48

illustrate, the 85 percent price experience curve for the Ford Model T from 1909 to 1923 is shown in Figure 18–4.

Texas Instruments' digital watch provides another example of the parallel movement of prices and costs down the experience curve. In just five years, the price of the digital watch had declined from $2,000 to $10! This decrease was due to a 60 percent decrease in initial production costs as volume increased.[11]

The experience curve provides a way to estimate the relationship among costs, prices, and accumulated experience. This can have significant implications when evaluating various pricing strategies. It is particularly crucial to understand this relationship when the critical factor to success in an industry is production costs. In such a situation, a firm must gain a cost advantage over competitors in order to gain market leadership—which means moving down the experience curve faster than competitors. Gener-

---

[11] "The Great Digital Watch Shake-Out," *Business Week,* May 2, 1977, pp. 78–80.

Figure 18–3: An 85 percent experience curve on a log-log scale

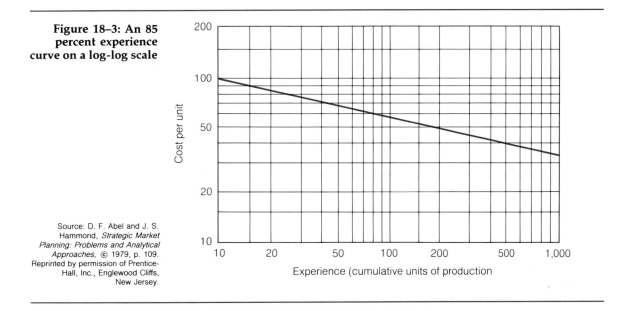

ally, market share is proportional to experience. As a result, competitors' costs must decrease at the same rate as the leader's if they are to survive.

For example, consider Figure 18–5. Here, three competitors are moving down the same experience curve. Firm A is further down the experience curve and thus has lower costs than Firm B. Firm B, in turn, has lower costs than Firm C. As the current industry price declines with experience,

Figure 18–4: The 85 percent price experience curve for the Ford Model T

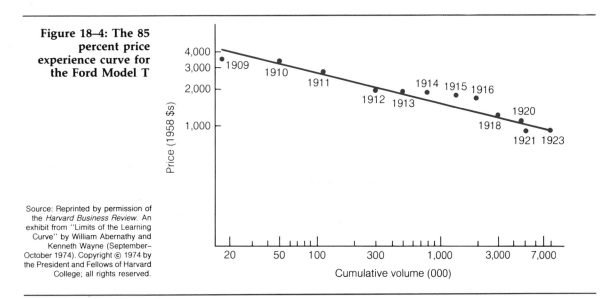

Figure 18–5: Profitability advantages of greater experience (market share)

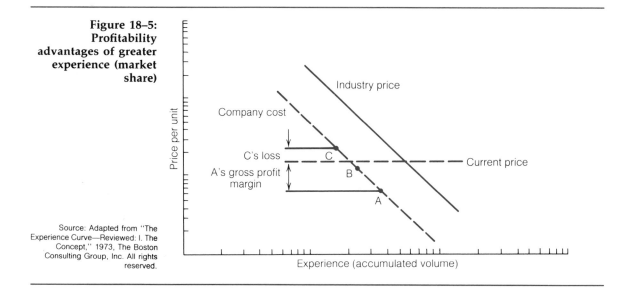

Firm C will have a loss. It has not accumulated enough experience to reduce its cost below the industry price. Firm B will have a slight profit; Firm A will have a substantial one. Both firms' costs have moved down the experience curve with price. If Firm A were to reduce its prices even further, it could easily force Firm C out of the market and cut Firm B's profit margin.

When using the experience curve in pricing strategy, a company must consider two factors: (1) competitors' positions on the experience curve and (2) how fast the company can move down the curve itself. This second factor is determined mainly by the market growth rate, stage of the product life cycle, and the number of competitors already in the market.

COMPETITION-ORIENTED PRICING

In competition-oriented pricing, the major considerations are the prices charged by the firm's main competitors. The exact price established may be above, below, or the same as the price charged by major competitors.

Competition-oriented pricing is used for several reasons. The established market price represents the total managerial experience within the industry. This experience is based on costs as well as demand factors. Therefore, the going price is usually regarded as fair to buyers and sellers. Competition-oriented pricing may be necessary for maintaining customers and sales level. If a competitor lowers its price, a firm may have to meet that lower price or lose sales. The need to meet a competitor's price reduction is especially strong for products and services that consumers perceive

The emphasis on price-oriented competition in the airline industry is highlighted by this Mexicana ad.

Courtesy Mexicana Airlines

as equivalent. For example, United Airlines was forced to reduce its $296 regular round-trip coach fare from Cleveland to New York to meet the $90 fare offered by New York Air.[12]

Within competition-oriented pricing, two major approaches are price leadership and competitive bidding.

Price leadership

Price leadership is a situation in which a dominant firm has a strong influence on industry price levels and initiates industry price changes.[13] The price leader is usually a firm with a large market share and whose actions are respected by competitors.

In general, other firms in the industry follow the price established by the industry leader. This leader-follower relationship reduces the chance of a price war. Price followers generally are conservative companies with smaller market shares.

Price leaders' actions can have drastic effects on an entire industry.

---

[12] John Curley, "Decontrol of Airlines Shifts Pricing from a Cost to a Competition Basis," *The Wall Street Journal,* December 4, 1981, p. 27.

[13] Ibid.

For example, the computer industry has operated under the price leadership of IBM. When IBM introduced its 4300 series of mainframe computers at a low price, one competitor was forced out of business and others were seriously hurt.[14] Competitors were unable to match IBM's price and performance standards. If IBM had continued to sell at a low price, competition in the computer industry would have been much more aggressive and profits would have been lower. To avoid this, IBM increased prices 5 to 7 percent—which improved IBM's earnings and those of its troubled competitors.

Competitive bidding

Competitive bidding is a practice in which several companies submit prices (or bids) at which they could provide a product or service to a business or the government. Such businesses as original equipment manufacturing and defense contract work set prices this way. Competitive bidding is almost always used when dealing with the government.

In a competitive-bidding situation, a company's pricing strategy is based on its perceptions of how competitors will price. Costs and demands do not directly influence the bidding price. In most cases, price is the only means by which a firm can differentiate itself from competitors. Thus, if a particular contract is desired, the bidding price is set lower than competitors' expected bids to increase the probability of winning the contract. However, a firm can't set prices too far below costs if it wishes to remain profitable. On the other hand, if it bids too far above costs, chances are the bid will be higher than competitors' bids and the contract will be lost. To come up with a bid that has a reasonable chance of being selected and still be profitable, the firm must find a balance between these two extremes.

Mathematical models based on the **expected profit concept** are used to determine the optimal price in a competitive-bidding situation. The expected profit concept derives from the notion that as the bid increases, profit increases but the probability of winning the contract decreases. Expected profit at a specific bid is the profit at that bid times the probability of getting the contract with that bid. Assuming a firm wishes to maximize expected profits, it actually bids a price that provides the highest expected profit.

To determine the maximum expected profit, a firm must examine a range of bids. It is relatively easy to measure profits under various bids, as costs for all bids are the same. But it may be difficult to estimate the probability of winning the contract. To do so requires information on competitors' bids. Often this can be estimated by examining past bidding situations involving the same competitors.

Table 18–4 shows the expected profit for a number of bids for a contract

---

[14] "Why IBM Reversed Itself on Computer Pricing," *Business Week,* January 28, 1980, p. 84.

Table 18–4: Expected profit concept

Bid ($000)	Cost ($000)	Profit ($000)	Probability of getting the contract	Expected profit
$40	$50	<$10,000>	0.99	<$9,900>
50	50	0	0.95	0
55	50	5	0.85	4,250
60	50	10	0.70	7,000
65	50	15	0.50	7,500
70	50	20	0.35	7,000
75	50	25	0.25	5,000

that would cost $50,000 to fulfill. In this example, if a firm were to bid $50,000 for a contract that cost $50,000, it would probably get the contract but no profit. If a company wishes to maximize its expected profits, it should submit a bid of $65,000. This would yield an expected profit of $7,500. the highest expected profit in this example. The chances of gaining this contract would be 50-50.

Since this approach assumes a firm wants to maximize expected profits, it is most useful to larger firms that submit many bids in a year. Smaller firms may be willing to accept a less-than-maximum expected profit for a number of reasons.[15] First, a company may have excess plant capacity it wants to use. By bidding $55,000 it increases to 0.85 the probability of gaining the contract and using this available capacity. Second, a company may need a contract to survive. If it bid $50,000, it would at least cover its variable costs until more business can be obtained. Third, a company may bid lower than $65,000 in the hopes of gaining more profitable future contracts.

DEMAND-ORIENTED PRICING

Demand-oriented pricing deals with pricing methods and tactics that marketing management uses to affect consumer perceptions or behavior. The major demand-oriented pricing methods and tactics are perceived-value pricing, price-quality relationship, loss-leader pricing, odd-numbered pricing, and price lining.

Perceived-value pricing[16]

In 1974, when the government's price controls were removed, most U.S. companies increased prices to protect or improve profit margins. The job of the sales force was to convince customers that these increases

[15] Stephen Pranka, "Competitive Bidding Strategy," *Business Horizons,* June 1971, pp. 39–43.

[16] This section on perceived-value pricing is based on Philip Kotler's *Marketing Management: Analysis, Planning, and Control,* 4th ed. (Englewood Cliffs, N.J.: Prentice-Hall, 1980), pp. 391–94; and Daniel A. Nimer, "Pricing the Profitable Sale Has a Lot to Do with Perception," *Sales Management,* May 19, 1975, pp. 13–16.

were justified. Unfortunately, customers were not convinced, and sales declined. These companies disregarded the marketing concept by failing to recognize the importance of consumers' perceptions of price setting.

Production costs are important and must be considered when establishing a product's price. But the most important consideration is the consumer's perception of the value of the product or service. This value is expressed in terms of the price —or the amount of money—that consumers are willing to exchange for that good or service. In order to recognize the importance of the consumer in pricing decisions, some companies have adopted a *perceived-value pricing approach.* Perceived-value pricing establishes the price for a product based on the buyer's perception of the value of the product or service. It is the soundest approach to pricing from a strategic marketing perspective because it is consistent with consumer perceptions and product positioning.

At this point let's say a few words about the relationship between product positioning and perceived-value pricing. Positioning a new product involves analyzing the attributes that consumers within a market segment use when evaluating a product. A company's product is then compared to competitors' products. The positioning analysis enables a firm to establish a price relative to the competition. A product's value is determined by such variables as quality, service level, and price. After the positioning analysis is completed, management can forecast product sales. These forecasts are major inputs in the calculation of the required investment in working capital and production facilities. All this information is used in projecting profit and loss statements for the product, which form the basis for making the go and no-go decision to market the product.

Du Pont and Caterpillar are examples of companies that use perceived-value pricing. Du Pont used it when introducing a new synthetic carpet fiber. By comparing the existing carpet material with the new fiber, Du Pont was able to show its retail customers that they could earn the same profit even when the new fiber was priced at the relatively high level of $1.40 per pound. Du Pont then sold the product at a price lower than $1.40 per pound, which enabled its customers to increase their profit margins. In a contrasting approach, Caterpillar prices its tractors at a premium level compared to its competitors. Caterpillar's marketing efforts attempt to convince potential customers that Cat's products provide superior durability, reliability, service, and warranties on parts. When customers evaluate this bundle of attributes, Caterpillar's management hopes they perceive the tractors as well worth the premium price.

A numerical example of perceived-value pricing should help here. Assume that companies A, B, C, and D each produce an electric razor. Consumers evaluate these products on four attributes: durability, ease of use, closeness of shave, and the company's reputation for quality. Research indicates that consumers weight the importance of these attributes as 20 percent, 25 percent, 45 percent, and 10 percent, respectively. Assume

Table 18–5: Perceived-	Weighted		Products				
value pricing:	importance	Attribute	A	B	C	D	Total
Importance and							
attribute ratings	0.20	Durability	25	25	25	25	100
	0.25	Ease of use	20	20	30	30	100
	0.45	Closeness of shave	30	15	35	20	100
	0.10	Company reputation	30	15	40	15	100

that researchers have asked consumers to rate the attributes by dividing 100 points among the four products for each attribute. The summary of the importance weights and the ratings are shown in Table 18–5.

The first step in this pricing procedure is to calculate the perceived value for each product. For example, for product A, we would multiply the importance weights by the attribute ratings and then sum the products:

$$\frac{(25)(0.20) + (20)(0.25) + (30)(0.45) + (30)(0.10)}{5 \quad + \quad 5 \quad + \quad 13.5 \quad + \quad 3} = 26.50$$

You can check the calculations to see that the perceived value of products B, C, and D are 18.25, 32.25, and 23, respectively.

In step two, the perceived value for a specific product is divided by the average perceived value and then multiplied by the average price of a razor. In this example, with four products, the average perceived value would be 25 (100/4). Say that the average selling price of electric razors is $20. The calculations would be:

$$\frac{\text{The perceived value of a specific product}}{\text{The average perceived value}} \times \begin{array}{c}\text{Average selling} \\ \text{price}\end{array}$$
$$= \text{Price proportional to the product's perceived value}$$

For product A,

$$\frac{26.50}{25} \times \frac{\$20}{} = \$21.20$$

For products B, C, and D the price proportional to the perceived value would be $14.60, 25.80, and 18.40, respectively. These calculations are useful when a company evaluates alternative prices. If the actual price is higher than the perceived-value price, then the product is overpriced and the company is likely to lose market share. On the other hand, if the actual price is lower than the perceived-value price, the company is likely to gain market share from competitors. If all companies price proportionately to perceived value, then the market should be in a state of balance and market shares should remain stable.

Price-quality relationships

The concept of a *price-quality relationship* states that consumers associate high price with high quality and low quality with low price. From a managerial perspective, the price-quality relationship has been summarized by a marketing executive from Sony Corporation of America, the New York-based subsidiary of the Japanese television manufacturer: "A premium price adds an air of prestige to a product . . . ."[17]

A number of research studies have investigated the price-quality relationship. In the first group of studies, subjects had only price information to use in evaluating a product's quality. These studies found that when the identical product was priced differently, different quality levels were associated with it. In one study subjects were asked to rank the quality of three samples of unlabeled beer with different prices on them.[18] Subjects ranked the highest-priced beer as the highest quality and the lowest-priced beer as the lowest quality. All samples were the same brand! This finding supported the notion of a positive price-quality relationship.

Another group of studies gave the consumer additional information, such as the brand name and the product itself.[19] These studies found little evidence of a price-quality relationship. Consumers did rely on brand name when judging a product's quality, however.

Findings like these have major implications for both consumers and market management.[20] For the consumer, these studies indicate that consumers who rely solely on price as an indicator of quality may pay a high price for low quality. But for management to assume that higher price is always perceived as implying higher quality is too simplistic. Consumers use brand name, advertising, store reputation, and other variables when forming an opinion about the quality of a product. Management should not assume price is the only one used by consumers to infer quality and neglect the other indicators of quality.

Loss-leader pricing

Loss-leader pricing is the practice of setting prices on selected products at low levels that generate less than the usual profit margins in order to increase the sale of other products within a retail store or product line. For retailers, the objective is to increase store traffic so they can sell other products at traditional profit margins. For manufacturers, the

---

[17] Paul Ingrassia, "In a Color-TV Market Roiled by Price Wars, Sony Takes a Pounding," *The Wall Street Journal,* March 16, 1978, pp. 1, 6.

[18] J. Douglas McConnell, "Effect of Pricing on Perception of Product Quality," *Journal of Applied Psychology* 52 (September 1968), pp. 331–34.

[19] Ben M. Enis and James Stafford, "The Price-Quality Relationship: An Extension," *Journal of Marketing Research* 6 (November 1969), pp. 256–58; Jacob Jacoby, Jerry Olson, and Rafael Haddock, "Price, Brand Name, and Product Composition Characteristics as Determinants of Perceived Quality," *Journal of Applied Psychology* 55 (December 1971), pp. 470–79; David M. Gardner, "Is There a Generalized Price-Quality Relationship in an Experimental Setting?" *Journal of Advertising Research* 21 (August 1981), pp. 49–52.

[20] John E. Swan, "Price-Product Performance Competition between Retailer and Manufacturer Brands," *Journal of Marketing* 38 (July 1974), pp. 52–59.

goal is to attain greater consumer interest in the overall product line.[21] Products that are used as loss leaders are usually well-known, branded, and frequently purchased. For grocery retailers, common loss-leader items are milk, soft drinks, and beer. Within manufacturing, camera makers have sold cameras at low prices and then charged higher prices for film or camera accessories.

Loss-leader pricing may be illegal if it results in violation of minimum markup laws enacted in many states. These laws were designed to protect the small retailer from predatory pricing practices of large retailers. However, research has shown that the minimum markup laws have no effect on the viability of small retail firms.[22] This conclusion holds for retail markets in general and in the specific retail segments of grocery, apparel, variety, automobile dealers, furniture, and liquor. It appears that small retailers compete on the basis of nonprice factors such as convenience, location, delivery service, and friendliness rather than price.

Odd-numbered pricing

Odd or ***odd-numbered pricing*** is the practice of setting price below even-dollar amounts. For example, a clothing manufacturer sold its jeans for $9.86. Products over $50 often sell for $1 or $2 less than even-dollar amounts.

The use of odd pricing has become common for two main reasons. The practice originally developed as a means of controlling theft by retail employees. The odd price usually forced the employee to open the cash register, record the transaction, and return change to the customer. It was felt that these actions made it more difficult for the employee to pocket the money. Second, some retailers believe consumers perceptually round the $2.00 price down to $2. A $2.99 price, then, makes the item appear less expensive than if it were priced at $3. The evidence supporting this assumption is inconclusive.[23] At best, we can say that odd prices are distorted downward for only some products in some but not all circumstances.

Price lining

Price lining is the practice of selling merchandise at a limited number of predetermined price levels. The practice is common among retailers, so we'll discuss it here in a retailing context rather than in a manufacturing or wholesaling context. Each price level is intended to represent a certain level of quality: for example, a retailer may sell sweaters at $12.95, $18.95, and $26.95. This practice aids consumer decision making by grouping

---

[21] Joel R. Evans and Barry Berman, *Marketing* (New York: Macmillan, 1982), p. 539.

[22] Michael J. Houston, "Minimum Markup Laws: An Empirical Assessment," *Journal of Retailing* 57 (Winter 1981), pp. 98–113.

[23] Zarrell V. Lambert, "Perceived Price as Related to Odd and Even Price Endings," *Journal of Retailing* 51 (Fall 1975), pp. 13–22.

This ad for Spaulding shoes demonstrates effective use of price lining (the $19.99 and $24.99 lines) as well as odd-numbered pricing.

Courtesy Lane Bryant

the merchandise assortment.[24] The consumer first decides how much to spend and then looks at the products within that price range.

Price lining simplifies the pricing structure and allows the retailer to carry less inventory. The retailer needs to stock merchandise only in the predetermined price lines, which eases stock planning. The store's overall

[24] Kent B. Monroe, "Buyers' Subjective Perceptions of Price," *Journal of Marketing Research* 10 (February 1973), pp. 70–80.

sales may increase because a wider variety of goods can be carried at fewer price levels.

Price lining may be difficult to maintain when costs are rising rapidly. Unless prices are increased across the entire product line, profit margins may be cut and the differences in the price points may be changed. The differences in the price line may also be disrupted by markdowns or sales.

STRATEGIC MARKETING PLANNING APPLIED TO PRICING

The following discussion applies the strategic planning process to the pricing decision. Our purpose is to focus on those aspects of the strategic planning process that relate directly to the management of pricing. See Figure 18–6 for an overview of the strategic marketing planning process as applied to the pricing decision. (Legal considerations—part of situation analysis—are discussed in Chapter 17.)

Situation analysis

Consumer. The consumers in the firm's target market are a basic consideration in establishing a product's price. In many situations, management tries to emphasize nonprice factors such as product quality, service, and the product's image. By emphasizing nonprice variables, management achieves more flexibility in establishing price and increases the chances of marketing the product at a profit. Brand image is heavily emphasized in the marketing of cosmetics. A bottle of perfume retailing for $100 may have only $4 to $16 worth of ingredients and production costs.

The emphasis on nonprice factors isn't limited to consumer goods. In the industrial area, Caterpillar's products are usually priced about 10 percent above competitors'. Caterpillar emphasizes the product quality and service aspects of its product and dealer distribution network. One of the key factors in Caterpillar's strategy is that the company spends 3 to 4 percent of its sales dollars for research and development compared to 1 to 2 percent for its competitors.[25]

Company strengths and weaknesses. When making a pricing decision, the major variables in assessing a company's strengths and weaknesses are its financial status and its product reputation and quality. If consumers see a particular firm's products as high in quality, the firm may charge a price above the industry's average. Cadillac commands a premium price because of its prestige image, high trade-in value, and excellent reputation for quality.

Establish pricing objectives

The establishment of price is a critical decision in the formulation of a marketing strategy for a product or service. Price influences a number of variables critical to a firm's success. Price influences sales volume, prof-

[25] Harlan S. Byrne, "What Recession? A Leaping Caterpillar Is a Wondrous Thing, Even Its Rivals Agree," *The Wall Street Journal,* April 19, 1976, pp. 1, 12.

Figure 18–6: Strategic marketing planning process applied to the pricing decision

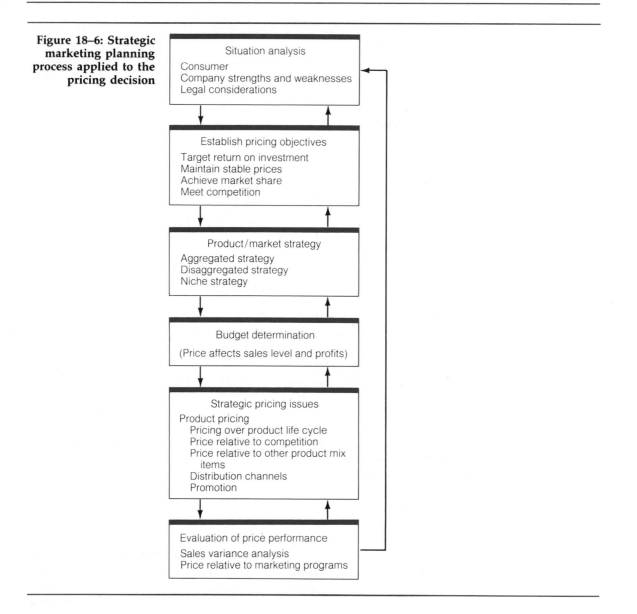

Situation analysis

Consumer
Company strengths and weaknesses
Legal considerations

Establish pricing objectives

Target return on investment
Maintain stable prices
Achieve market share
Meet competition

Product/market strategy

Aggregated strategy
Disaggregated strategy
Niche strategy

Budget determination

(Price affects sales level and profits)

Strategic pricing issues

Product pricing
   Pricing over product life cycle
   Price relative to competition
   Price relative to other product mix
     items
   Distribution channels
   Promotion

Evaluation of price performance

Sales variance analysis
Price relative to marketing programs

its, cash flow, inventories, brand image, the possibility of government regulation, and market competitiveness.[26]

Consequently, before any pricing decisions are made, ***pricing objectives*** must be established. Pricing objectives help clarify the role of price in a company's long-term plans and strategy. Pricing objectives flow from

[26] Alfred R. Oxenfeldt, *Pricing Strategies* (New York: AMACOM, 1975), pp. 42–43.

the company's objectives. When establishing objectives, management must consider a variety of factors; the most important ones are costs, target-market, and competition.

A major study examined the pricing objectives of large companies and found that most companies have one major and several secondary pricing objectives.[27] Four major pricing objectives are to: (1) achieve target return on investment, (2) maintain stable prices, (3) achieve target-market share, and (4) meet competition.

Target return on investment. One pricing expert estimated that about 80 percent of corporations worldwide price to achieve a specific return on investment (ROI) or sales.[28] The classic Lanzillotti study on pricing objectives found that about 50 percent of the leading corporations surveyed use ROI as their principle pricing objective.[29] In a study of manufacturing firms, "a satisfactory return on investment" was the overwhelmingly most popular pricing objective.[30] The Lanzillotti study found that average after-tax return was 14 percent, with a range of 8 to 20 percent.

Under target-ROI pricing, a price is determined that provides a specified rate of return on capital used in making a product. Specifically, profits associated with a specific price and marketing strategy are estimated. If the return meets or exceeds the target return, the pricing structure is accepted. If not, the price and other marketing mix variables are adjusted to attain the required return. Some firms that use target ROI as their pricing objective are General Electric, Du Pont, General Motors, and International Harvester.

Target ROI is commonly used for pricing new products. New products usually do not have close competitors, so often there is no other basis for a pricing decision. Furthermore, to justify their introduction, new products are expected to generate a predetermined level of ROI. This level is generally higher than that for established products. Alcoa, Du Pont, and General Foods use target ROI for pricing new products.

Maintain stable prices. Maintaining stable prices is a major objective in industries that experience large or frequent fluctuations in demand. Prices are not reduced significantly during poor economic conditions, nor are they increased significantly during prosperous ones. A primary reason to maintain stable prices is to avoid price wars in which firms attempt

---

[27] Lanzillotti, "Pricing Objectives," pp. 921–40.

[28] Daniel A. Nimer, "Developing Pricing Strategies in an Uncertain Environment," *Proceedings of 58th International Marketing Conference* (Chicago: American Marketing Association, April 1975), pp. 9–14.

[29] Lanzillotti, "Pricing Objectives," pp. 921–40.

[30] Saeed Samiee, "Pricing Objectives of U.S. Manufacturing Firms," in *Proceedings of Southern Marketing Association,* ed. R. S. Franz, R. M. Hopkins, and Al Toma (University of Southwestern Louisiana, Ponchatoula, LA., 1978) pp. 445–48.

to win customers by undercutting competitors' prices. Usually, companies that lead their industries in sales and reputation for quality have price stability as a goal. U.S. Steel and Kennecott have stated price stability as an objective in setting prices.

Achieve market share. Another common objective in pricing is to achieve a specific market share. With this approach, companies can relate their activities to the size of the market. Larger companies may limit the size of their market share in order to avoid antitrust action. For example, it has been suggested that Procter & Gamble deliberately allowed its share of the shampoo market to drop from 50 to 20 percent to avoid antitrust problems.[31] It is much more common to attempt to increase market share, though A&P executives state that they attempted to increase market share through low pricing.

Meet competition. Firms may establish a price with the objective of meeting the competition. Often, the role of competition is a key factor when marketing a standardized product or commodity-type item. For example, in an aggressive effort to increase sales in the United States, Alcan Aluminum, Ltd. of Canada cut prices 6 percent on aluminum sheets used in the manufacture of beverage cans. Consequently, the industry leaders—Alcoa, Reynolds Metals Co., and Kaiser Aluminum and Chemical Corporation—promptly lowered their prices to meet this competitive threat.[32]

Occasionally, firms may price to prevent or discourage competition from entering a market. A&P is a classic example of this type of action. In the 1930s, A&P reduced prices in some local markets to make it difficult for competitors who were opening stores in those areas.

Product/market strategy

The product/market is a product or group of products that satisfies a want or need in the market. The product/market concept defines the competition for a product and facilitates the process of market segmentation. Pricing relative to competition is discussed in the section on strategic pricing issues. The focus here is on market segmentation strategy and the establishment of price.

Strategically, a firm may approach a market with three different market segmentation strategies: aggregated, disaggregated, or niche.

Aggregated strategy. In this strategy, one marketing program is offered to all consumers. In this case, the product or service would be

---

[31] See Paul N. Bloom and Philip Kotler, "Strategies for High Market Share Companies," *Harvard Business Review* 53 (November–December 1975), p. 69; and Nancy Giges, "Shampoo Rivals Wonder When P&G Will Seek Old Dominance," *Advertising Age,* September 23, 1974, p. 3.

[32] Thomas F. O'Boyle, "Aluminum Can Sheet Contest Intensifies," *The Wall Street Journal,* May 17, 1982, p. 40.

offered at only one price to all who wish to purchase it. The best-known example is Henry Ford's marketing of the Model T Ford: one color, one price. A more recent example is Federal Express, which offers an overnight pickup and delivery service for small, high-value packages. The market for this service is small, and the service is offered to all customers under a uniform marketing and pricing program.[33]

Disaggregated strategy.   A second strategic option is to offer different marketing programs to various market segments. This option is called *disaggregated strategy.* For some products, traditional price lines have developed so that all marketing activities are based on price levels. The market for products such as clothing, cosmetics, automobiles, and appliances has developed to the extent that markets have become segmented into price lines. Strategic consideration of these markets demands that all product and marketing decisions are contingent on the price line offered.[34]

Niche strategy.   Finally, an organization may decide to use a *niche strategy* in which it concentrates on only one segment of the market. Usually, one marketing program, well tailored to meet the needs of a specific target-market group, is developed. In the highly competitive pocket calculator market, Hewlett-Packard equips its products with special features and offers them at above-industry-average price to the market segment comprising technical and professional individuals.[35]

Budget determination

Price has a direct effect on the sales level and profitability of a firm. The gross income for a firm is simply the number of units sold times per unit price. A change in price has a direct—often major—impact on sales revenue and profitability. For example, Hueblein, the maker of Popov brand vodka, raised its price by 8 percent to an average of $4.10 per fifth. While the company lost 1 percent market share, profits increased by 30 percent because of the higher prices.[36] Sometimes a lower price can increase the sales volume and thereby improve profitability. In the airline industry, during the first nine months of 1981, 65 percent of the air travel was on discount fares, which were 45 percent lower than full fare. The airline industry followed American Airlines, which introduced the "supersaver" fare. To the surprise of the industry, the initial reduction in fares did generate new business, so the discounted fares were profitable.

---

[33] David W. Cravens, *Strategic Marketing* (Homewood, Ill.: Richard D. Irwin, 1982), p. 168.

[34] Shirley Young, Leland Ott, and Barbara Feigin, "Some Practical Considerations in Market Segmentation," *Journal of Marketing Research* 15 (August 1978), pp. 405–12.

[35] "Flexible Pricing," *Business Week*, December 12, 1977, p. 84.

[36] Jeffrey Birnbaum, "Pricing Products Is still an Art," *The Wall Street Journal*, November 25, 1981, p. 25.

However, it remains to be seen whether the industry can continue its deep discounting and remain profitable.[37]

Strategic pricing issues

There are many strategic issues regarding the relationship between product and price. Three of the most important are (1) the pricing decisions during the product's life cycle; (2) the position of price relative to competition and whether price has an active or passive role in the marketing program; and (3) the price of a product relative to other items in the product mix.

Pricing over the product life cycle. Since the internal and external environment changes as a product matures, management must strategically consider a product's price during all stages of its life cycle. In doing so, many firms use a skimming strategy, which introduces a product at a high initial price and then lowers price as the product progresses through the growth and maturity stages of its life cycle. In this way, the firm attempts to achieve a high level of short-run profitability by maintaining high profit margins. Then, as competitors enter the market, prices drop to protect market share. Du Pont used this strategy when it introduced Dacron. The product, introduced in 1953, was priced at $2.25 per pound. But by 1974 that price had dropped to about 40 cents.[38]

Another commonly adopted strategy is the penetration strategy. When using this strategy, a firm sacrifices short-run profit by offering a product at a low price. Consequently, the firm initially builds a large market share and offsets the lower profit margin with higher volume. Dow Chemical uses this strategy. During initial product introduction Dow stresses low price (and, therefore, low profit margins) to build a dominant market share. Once established, the company turns its emphasis to maintaining sales volume over time.[39]

As a product matures, competitive products usually enter the market. Price may serve as a substitute for elements of the marketing mix. For instance, to meet the threat from generic (no-brand) products, Colgate-Palmolive stopped advertising some of their weaker brands while cutting price at the same time. In this case, the price reductions were used as a substitute for advertising.[40]

Price positioning relative to competition. The choice of pricing strategy reflects how management is positioning the product relative to competition and how actively or passively price is promoted. *Active* simply

[37] John Curley, "Decontrol of Airlines Shifts Pricing from a Cost to a Competition Basis," *The Wall Street Journal,* December 4, 1981, p. 27.

[38] "Pricing Strategy in an Inflation Economy," *Business Week,* April 6, 1974, pp. 42–49.

[39] Ibid., p. 44.

[40] "No-Frills Food: New Power for the Supermarkets," *Business Week,* March 23, 1981, pp. 70–80.

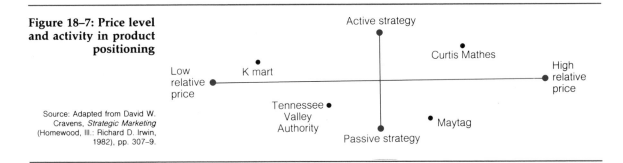

Figure 18–7: Price level and activity in product positioning

Source: Adapted from David W. Cravens, *Strategic Marketing* (Homewood, Ill.: Richard D. Irwin, 1982), pp. 307–9.

means price is emphasized strongly in advertising, personal selling, and other promotional activities. To develop or evaluate alternative strategic options, we can use the matrix found in Figure 18–7. The matrix poses the questions, "Is price used actively in the marketing program, or is it left in the background?" and, "What is the price level relative to competition?"

High active strategy. The **high active strategy** is used most often with high-prestige products. When a buyer has little information to evaluate the product, a high price is used to signal superior quality. Thus, Curtis Mathes, the television manufacturer, uses its slogan ("It's the most expensive television, and darn well worth it") to reinforce product quality and dependability.

High passive strategy. The **high passive strategy** is used when product performance and quality are most important. By emphasizing these non-price factors, management tries to relate the product characteristics to consumers' perceived needs. The Maytag Company, known as the "dependability people," use this strategy to position their products as high-quality while charging a premium price over competitive products.

Low active strategy. The **low active strategy** is very common and assumes that price is an important factor to consumers. So, the company offers the price-conscious consumer a low price and acceptable quality. The low active strategy may lead to a price war. However, retailers like K mart actively promote their low prices and have been very successful.

Low passive strategy. The **low passive strategy** is the least common and is frequently used by companies with product quality lower than their main competitors'. By minimizing the awareness of low price, management also minimizes the potential danger that consumers will associate low price with low product quality. Nonprofit organizations like the Tennessee Valley Authority also use this strategy.

Price relative to other items in the product mix. Since most firms are multiproduct firms, managers must understand the interrelationship

Sales of Johnson's 50/1 lubricant would be related to increased sales or usage of Johnson Outboard Motors. The lubricant is an example of a complementary product.

TEAM MATES

When we build an outboard we build a lube to match.

Johnson

50/1 lubricant

OMC
PARTS AND ACCESSORIES
A DIVISION OF OUTBOARD MARINE CORPORATION

Johnson

Courtesy Outboard Marine Corporation

among the prices of products in the product mix. The products within the mix may be complements to or substitutes for each other.

Complementary products. A **complementary product** is one whose sales increase simultaneously with a sales increase of a related product. Thus, as sales for Gillette razors increase, so do the sales of Gillette replacement razor blades. Complementary sales result from four basic situations:

1. *Related use.* This occurs when the purchase of one product is dependent on that of another product. For example, buying a camera leads directly to the purchase of film.

2. *Enhance value.* This occurs when a product upgrades the value or use of another product. The purchase of a flash unit would allow greater utilization and easier operation of the camera.

3. *Quality supplements.* This occurs when products are designed to repair, maintain, or assist in operating a product. Lens cleaners, dust brushes, and the like are in this way tied to a camera purchase.

4. *Broader assortments.* Products totally unrelated may be complementary if bought from the same distributor just to minimize customer effort. In this case, a customer may purchase video cassettes from a camera store simply to avoid another shopping trip.[41]

Substitute products. **Substitute products** satisfy the same needs of similar consumers. A common example is found in different brands of coffee and tea, all of which satisfy a similar need for a hot drink. When a company offers a number of substitute products in its product mix, each with a differing level of quality, price differentials must be used to reinforce product quality and consumer segmentation. Managers must be careful to differentiate prices widely enough to be noticeable and closely enough to encourage trading up.

When a company's product mix has a number of substitute products distinguished by quality and price, management must be careful to avoid *product cannibalism.* If current customers simply switch from one product to another within the same company's product mix, both market share and profits may decrease. For example, in 1959 the standard-sized Ford and Chevrolet automobiles each enjoyed a 22 percent market share. Then, both companies introduced a new compact car. Ford introduced its Falcon, and Chevrolet, the Corvair. By year end, the Falcon claimed 30 percent of the compact-car market; the Corvair, 13.5 percent. Unfortunately, the Ford Falcon achieved higher penetration at the cost of the standard-sized Ford. On the other hand, Chevrolet's Corvair represented totally new business. While the standard-sized Chevrolet maintained its 22 percent market share, the standard-sized Ford share dropped to 13.5 percent in 1960. The Falcon was positioned too close to the standard Ford. Cannibalism—and lower total sales—resulted.[42]

Distribution channels

The relationship between a product's price and its distribution channel is a major strategic consideration. The manufacturer of a product must recognize that a pricing decision involves pricing to the channel members as well as through the channel. In other words, a price (or series of prices) must be established at which the product is sold to channel members, as well as the retail price, which is the final price to consumers at the channel's end.

A major strategic factor in establishing a channel is the degree of control that the manufacturer wishes to exert over the marketing and pricing of the product. Products or services are technical, require considerable

[41] Joseph P. Gultinan and Gordon W. Paul, *Marketing Management Strategies and Programs* (New York: McGraw-Hill, 1982), pp. 205–6.

[42] William Copulsky, "Cannibalism in the Marketplace," *Journal of Marketing,* October 1976, pp. 103–5.

personal selling effort, and are high-priced and frequently marketed through a direct channel. IBM has been very successful in marketing computers through a direct channel employing its well-trained and highly compensated sales force. This direct channel allows IBM to exert considerable control over the selling and pricing of its products.

In many instances, manufacturers have neither the resources nor the opportunity to market directly. Management then is faced with the task of establishing a series of trade or functional discounts for channel members, as well as a final retail price. The manufacturer's problem of effectively controlling price in these circumstances can be substantial. For example, consider the problems of Sony, the TV manufacturer. Sony successfully stressed the quality of its TVs and sold them through such prestigious retailers as Bloomingdale's of New York, Famous Barr of St. Louis, J. L. Hudson of Michigan and Ohio, and the May Company in California. However, when fair-trade laws were repealed in 1976, Sony was unable to control retail prices. In addition, smaller retailers engaged in a practice called **transshipping.** Transshipping works like this: A small-volume retailer purchases twice as many sets from Sony as it thinks it can sell in order to obtain the volume discount that would normally go to only big stores. The little store then sells half the shipment to another small-volume retailer at a small profit. Both little stores obtain the sets more cheaply than if they bought directly from Sony without the volume discount. Each store then has more flexibility to reduce prices and remain profitable.[43]

Besides the control issue, several other major strategic issues arise in considering channels. These are whether to use conventional channels or vertically integrated systems, the distribution intensity, and the number of levels and intermediaries to use in the channel.[44]

Promotion

Marketing management must consider the relationship of price to the elements of the promotional mix, which include advertising, personal selling, publicity, and sales promotion.

From a strategic standpoint, research has shown that it's important to coordinate pricing and advertising in order to achieve satisfactory profit levels. More specifically, a premium price and high levels of advertising expenditures usually work in combination to achieve optimal market share and profit margin results. This strategy has been summarized by Richard B. Patton, president of H. J. Heinz, makers of Heinz ketchup:

> Our feeling is that consistency in advertising and pricing strategies is important to the success of any consumer product. Heinz ketchup is premium-priced because it is made from more expensive ingredients and also because it is perceived by consumers as being a superior value compared with competitive products.[45]

---

[43] Ingrassia, "Color T.V. Market Roiled," pp. 1, 6.

[44] Cravens, *Strategic Marketing,* pp. 270–75.

[45] Paul Farris and David J. Reibstein, "How Prices, Ad Expenditures, and profits Are Linked," *Harvard Business Review,* November–December 1979, p. 174.

A competitor of Heinz attempted to use an inconsistent price and promotion strategy. The competitor increased advertising and other promotion expenditures and simultaneously lowered price. The company did increase market share. But the combination of lowered prices and increased promotion caused profits to suffer, and the company eventually abandoned the strategy.[46] Research shows that the consistency of the price-advertising relationship affects return on investment. Return on investment varied from 5.86 percent for companies with low consistency to 15.76 percent for those companies with a high degree of price-advertising consistency.[47]

Evaluation of price performance

The evaluation of performance means comparing plans and actual results. In the evaluation of a price strategy, a standard procedure is to conduct a *sales variance analysis,* which identifies the sources of variation in planned results from price and volume changes. Another major aspect of price evaluation is to analyze the price in relationship to other major elements in the marketing program.

First, let's review a specific example of sales variance analysis. Consider our earlier example involving electric razors. Suppose that the firm decided to price the razor at $18 and the projected sales volume was 33,333 units. However, due to competitive market circumstances, the company sold only 25,000 razors at a $15 price. A sales variance analysis enables the company to determine how much of the decline was due to a price cut and how much was due to a failure to sell the projected number of units. Consider the following sales variance analysis calculations:

Variance due to price decline ($18 − $15)(25,000) = $ 75,000   33.7%

Variance due to volume decline ($18)(33,333 − 25,000) = $149,994   67.3%

$224,994   100.0%

The failure to achieve projected volume accounted for two thirds of the sales variance. The company should investigate the reasons for the shortfall in sales volume. Management should explore such key strategic variables as price, market share, and market size in making this evaluation.[48]

Management must also evaluate price in relationship to the product, promotion, and channels employed in the marketing program. Recently, a number of industry-leading companies lowered price and reduced expenditures on advertising and sales promotion to give consumers better value. Lever Brothers reduced the price of Lux bar soap and quadrupled sales of the brand over several years. Campbell Soup didn't raise prices for approximately one year in the early 1980s and reduced the number

[46] Ibid., p. 173.

[47] Ibid., p. 180.

[48] James M. Hulbert and Norman E. Toy, "A Strategic Framework for Marketing Control," *Journal of Marketing,* April 1977, pp. 19–20.

of its trade deals and the average price of its cents-off coupons.[49] Lower prices and reduced promotion spending are major ingredients in developing consistency in a company's marketing strategy.

---

[49] Bill Abrams, "Consumer Goods Firms Turn to Price Cuts to Increase Sales," *The Wall Street Journal,* May 13, 1982, p. 29.

SUMMARY

There are three major approaches to setting prices for products: cost-oriented, competition-oriented, and demand-oriented. Under the cost-oriented approach, the specific methods are markup, target-return, breakeven analysis, and experience curve pricing. Markup is most often used by retailers. Target-return pricing involves establishing a price so that a predetermined return is obtained on capital used in producing and distributing the product. Breakeven analysis determines how many units must be sold to generate sales dollars to equal the total fixed and variable costs at a specific unit price. Experience curve pricing involves establishing a relationship between cumulative production and per unit costs. Often, the firm with the most experience enjoys a cost advantage that increases gross margin dollars when products are priced at the prevailing market level.

Price leadership and competitive bidding are competition-oriented pricing approaches. Price leadership occurs in industries where a dominant firm exerts a strong influence on industry price levels and initiates price changes. Competitive bidding is the practice in which several companies submit prices, or bids, at which they would provide a product or service to a business or the government. Competitive bidding is commonly used for defense contract work and original equipment manufacturing.

Of the demand-oriented approaches to pricing, perceived-value pricing is the soundest approach from a strategic marketing perspective because it is consistent with consumer perceptions and product positioning. Perceived-value pricing establishes the price for a product based on the buyer's perception of the value of the product or service.

The concept of a price-quality relationship states that consumers associate high price with high quality and low price with low quality. Research has shown that, besides price, consumers use brand name, advertising, and retail store reputation when forming an opinion about a product's quality.

Loss-leader pricing sets low prices on selected products for less-than-usual profit margins in order to increase the sale of other products within a retail store or product line. Common loss-leader product items for grocery retailers are milk, beer, and soft drinks.

Odd-numbered pricing is the practice of setting price below even-dollar amounts. It was used originally as a means of controlling retail employee theft. Retailers also assume that consumers round odd prices downward: for example, a $2.99 price would be rounded down to $2. Research evidence supporting this assumption is inconclusive, though.

Price lining is the practice of selling merchandise at a limited number of predetermined price levels. The practice benefits consumers by grouping the merchandise assortment. Price lining simplifies the pricing structure and allows the retailer to carry less inventory.

The strategic marketing planning process as applied to pricing starts with a situation analysis of the consumer and the firm's strengths and weaknesses. Major objectives for pricing are achieving a target return on investment, maintaining stable prices, achieving a market share, and meeting competition. The product/market analysis facilitates market segmentation and helps management decide on an aggregated, disaggregated, or niche marketing segmentation strategy. Price is a major factor in budget determination because a change in price has a direct—and often major—impact on sales revenue and profitability.

Management of the marketing program involves coordinating price with product, distribution, and promotion. The major considerations in the product-price relationship are pricing over the product's life cycle, price positioning relative to competition, and pricing relative to other products in the product mix.

Key pricing considerations for the channel of distribution are establishing a price or prices at which the product is sold to channel members and the retail price (the final price to consumers at the channel's end). A major strategic variable is the degree of control that a manufacturer wishes to exert over the marketing and pricing of the product.

For the promotion mix, an important strategic issue is to achieve consistency between the price level and promotion expenditures. Specifically, a premium price and high level of advertising are usually used together to achieve optimal market share and profit margin results. A low level of advertising and low price are also considered consistent. A price reduction may be regarded as a substitute for advertising and as a means of stimulating demand.

The evaluation of price performance includes a sales variance analysis and evaluation of price in relationship to other major elements in the marketing program. Sales variance analysis identifies the sources of variation in planned results from price and volume changes. Management must make sure that price is coordinated and integrated with the other elements of the marketing mix. For example, high levels of advertising expenditures and premium prices have been used together to achieve optimal market share and profit results.

KEY CONCEPTS

Markup pricing	Expected profit concept	High active strategy
Target-return pricing	Perceived-value pricing	High passive strategy
Standard volume	Price-quality relationship	Low active strategy
Breakeven analysis pricing	Loss-leader pricing	Low passive strategy
Experience curve pricing	Odd-numbered pricing	Complementary product
Price leadership	Price lining	Substitute product
Competitive bidding	Pricing objectives	Transshipping

DISCUSSION QUESTIONS AND EXERCISES

1. What is markup pricing and why is it so widely used among retailers and wholesalers?

2. A clothing retailer purchased a suit of clothes for $80. The store maintains a markup of 35 percent on cost. Compute the dollar amount of markup and the selling price.

3. If a product is marked up 50 percent on cost, what is the percent of markup based on retail?

4. Assume the following information on a new product:
   a. Per unit labor costs = $1.50.

    b. Per unit material costs = $1.60.

    c. The firm plans on a standard volume of 400,000 units and has fixed costs of $2 million.

    d. The firm has $5 million in capital invested in the new product and wants to earn a 20 percent return on capital invested.

Calculate the price using the target-return pricing formula.

5. In the above problem, how many units would the company have to sell to break even? What is the breakeven point in terms of dollars?

6. Review the advantages and disadvantages of target-return pricing. What do you regard as the most significant advantage and disadvantage of target-return pricing?

7. Assume a firm produced 100 units of a product and per unit costs were $200. If the firm was operating under an 80 percent experience curve, what would its costs be for the 400th unit produced?

8. What are the components of the experience curve effect? What are the major implications of the experience curve for pricing? Which companies appear to do an effective job of using the experience curve in their pricing strategies?

9. What is price leadership? To what extent do you feel that price leadership is operative today in American industry?

10. Assume that there are three competing automobiles produced by three different automobile manufacturers, A, B, and C. A research project was conducted that asked consumers to allocate 100 points among each of the cars for each of four attributes. The results were as follows:

Importance weight	Attribute	Cars		
		A	**B**	**C**
0.30	Style	60	20	20
0.40	Miles per gallon	45	30	25
0.15	Safety	45	15	40
0.15	Handling	20	25	55

The average price of a car is $8,000. Using the perceived-value pricing model, calculate the following:

    a. Perceived value for each product.

    b. Price for each product relative to its perceived value.

Which cars should be losing or gaining market share?

11. Think about a purchase you have made. Did the notion of a price-quality relationship play a role in the purchase? Explain.

12. Cite two examples of loss-leader pricing in your local market.

13. Review the matrix in Figure 18–7 regarding the strategic arena for pricing. Name two examples of other companies or products that follow each of the strategic options. You should have difficulty coming up with examples of companies following a low passive strategy. Why? Which is probably the most common strategy followed?

Case 11: Braniff Airways: Deregulation and its impact on pricing in the airline industry

On October 24, 1978, the Airline Deregulation Act of 1978 was signed into law. The Carter administration's goals in deregulation were to liberalize charter rules, expand service, encourage U.S. airlines' entry into international markets, expand nonstop service, and encourage price competition and new price and service options.

Braniff Airways made the most of deregulation, "invading new markets with almost reckless abandon." At the time of deregulation, Braniff was well-equipped to expand, having recently purchased 17 new 727s. All the competition were short on planes, thus limiting the steps they could take when deregulation went into effect. Airline analyst Julius Maldutis believed at that time that Braniff's chairman Harding Lawrence was on the verge of an historic coup, and commented, "In his aggressive response to deregulation, he has made another brilliant, strategic move that should put Braniff in splendid shape for the 80s."

Maldutis was wrong; Lawrence's risky move did not pay off. All airlines were burdened with rising fuel costs and decreased demand, but Braniff had to contend with the costs of expansion, as well. The airline was forced to cut prices deeply in an attempt to build volume and sway customers away from their major competitors—especially American Airlines. American responded by cutting prices, and the fare war was launched. Braniff and American were typical of airline marketing at that time. Prior to the 1978 deregulation, airlines differentiated themselves on the basis of service. After 1978, the move was toward competition on the basis of price.

By 1982, Braniff and American were dueling to the death. An example of this came on May 10, 1982, when Braniff announced a one-week ticket sale during which passengers could buy two round-trip tickets at full fare, and receive one bonus round-trip ticket for use at a later time for only $1. American's response: the same offer—but the bonus ticket was free. One securities analyst commented, "It became a bleeding contest. And Braniff bled to death faster."

On May 13, 1982, Braniff filed for bankruptcy under Chapter 11, with over $336 million in losses over the preceding three years and over $700 million in debts. Industry consensus was that, despite claims to the contrary, Braniff was dead.

However, on March 1, 1984, Braniff was reborn, with a new attitude toward competition and pricing. Braniff is starting small, with 82 flights to 18 cities from Dallas/Fort Worth. There is room for competition in this market, and Braniff does not plan to be a cut-rate carrier or even offer special introductory fares. American and Delta, the competition, have not lowered prices either; instead, they have fine-tuned their schedules in the area and concentrated on motivating travel agents. Braniff does have the advantage of much lower rates than American or Delta and, therefore, lower operating costs. However, Braniff president Slattery says the airline needs to fill 48 percent of their seats to turn a profit; and airline analysts feel that without discount prices to build traffic, Braniff is going to have a tough time.

Despite Braniff's apparent commitment to avoiding price wars, one analyst predicts "Soon we'll see what [lower costs] can do. The answer may be much, much lower fares."

References

"Braniff, American Air Heat up Fare War . . . ." *The Wall Street Journal,* May 11, 1982, p. 27.

"Braniff Is Coming back to Some Tough Competition." *Business Week,* February 27, 1984, pp. 37–41.

"Braniff Is Making the Most of Deregulation." *Business Week,* March 19, 1979, pp. 131–33.

Carley, William M. and Brenton R. Schlender. "Conditions that Did in Braniff . . . ." *The Wall Street Journal,* May 14, 1982, p. 1.

"Grounding the Bright-Colored Birds." *Fortune,* June 14, 1982, pp. 7–8.

"How Deregulation Will Change Air Service." *Business Week,* October 30, 1978, p. 57.

"The Last Roundup." *Forbes,* June 7, 1982, p. 62.

"U.S. Airlines Brace for Open Skies." *Business Week,* September 11, 1978, p. 55.

Williams, John D. "Airlines Give up Image Ads to Promote Cut-Rate Prices." *The Wall Street Journal,* April 15, 1982, p. 29.

Discussion questions

1. What were the federal government's goals in deregulation of the airlines? Did they meet their goal as far as price competition?

2. What was Braniff's downfall? What environmental factors contributed? Could things have worked out differently for Braniff if environmental factors had changed?

3. Are fare wars necessarily the result of price competition? What other things could happen? Do you think there was incentive for price collusion in the airline industry?

4. On the basis of the information given in the case, do you think Braniff, American, and Delta will continue to compete on a nonprice basis?

5. Can you think of any other examples of price wars? What conditions are necessary for a price war?

6. Has deregulation of the airlines benefited the consumer?

Case 12: Ford Motor Company: A reevaluation of pricing strategy

Ford Motor Co. top management has broken away from automobile manufacturer's time-honored ROI pricing strategy. One manager says, "In the old days, our business plans called for getting a certain return on investment. Now they call for improving quality first, on the theory that returns will follow."

Quality has not been considered Ford's strong point. It has a reputation for producing boring, boxy cars, and for being slow to introduce popular innovations. Worse, in the 1970s, there were lawsuits charging that the Ford Pinto gas tank exploded easily in a collision. Publicity surrounding this left consumers with the impression that Ford cars are poorly designed.

The long-term game plan now calls for totally new designs and a new emphasis on quality. In 1984 Ford introduced five new cars with a radically different aerodynamic style. Ford engineers believe that automobiles would have become more aerodynamic over time. Ford is hoping to start the trend, not follow it.

The emphasis on quality is not just pep talk. For example, in the 1970s, some assembly lines would run 154 hours per week. Now, the same lines will run only 106 hours per week at a maximum, and less if management feels that quality is suffering. In addition, the Dearborn engine plant closed for two weeks in the summer of 1984 rather than hiring temporary workers to replace vacationing skilled workers. The plant manager says, "Staying open lowers costs and increases mistakes."

Ford hopes that its trend setting styling and improved quality will attract consumers, thereby increasing its market share. Only time will tell if their new perspective will pay off.

Reference

Nulty, Peter. "Ford's Fragile Recovery." *Fortune,* April 2, 1984.

Discussion questions

1. Why is ROI pricing no longer appropriate for Ford? Is it still appropriate for other automobile manufacturers?

2. How is Ford trying to increase its market share? Is this a long-run or short-run strategy?

3. What other tactics might have been used?

4. How difficult will it be for Ford to convince consumers that their cars are of good quality? How long do you think it will take?

5. What recent developments in the automobile industry forced Ford into reevaluating their long-term strategy? Shifting consumer tastes and foreign competition are two things to consider. Can you think of others?

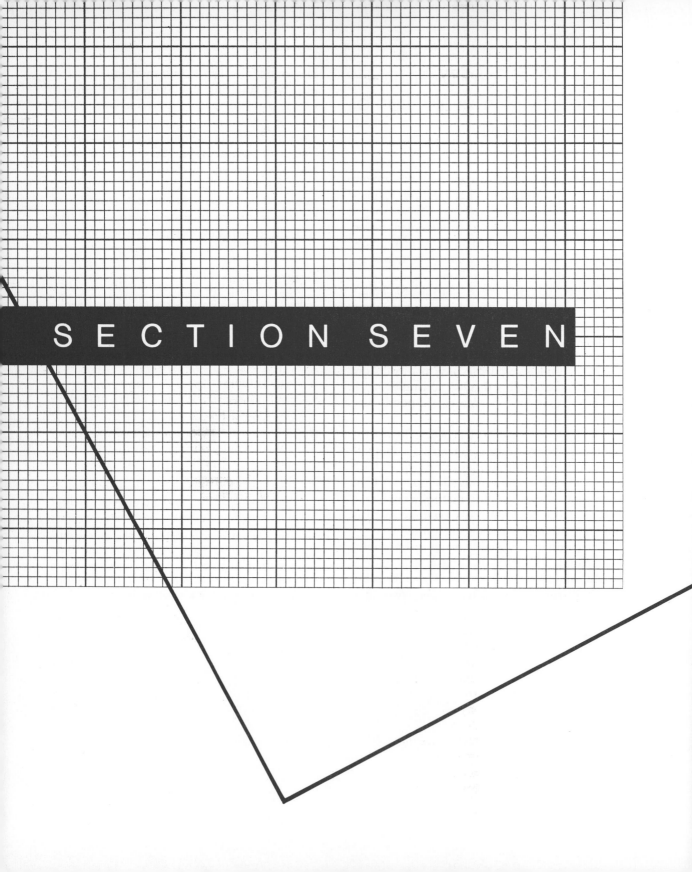

SECTION SEVEN

Promotional strategy

To this point we've examined three crucial elements in a marketing strategy—product, price, and physical distribution. Considering these elements, we see that it is important to (1) develop a product consistent with consumer needs and desires, (2) price it in accordance with costs and the buyer's willingness to pay, and (3) deliver it to the place of exchange through an effective, efficient distribution system. While these aspects of marketing strategy must be present, they are not suffi-cient. An element of marketing strategy that informs buyers of the nature and availability of the product and convinces them of its appropriateness must also exist. Marketing activities that stimulate interest in and demand for a product must be coordinated with the elements of product, price, and distribution. Such activities fall under the general rubric of *promotion*—the topic of this section.

Chapter 19 provides an overview of promotion. Key topics include the strategic role of promotion, the various promotional methods, and the conceptual foundations of communication strategy. Chapter 20 discusses the management of perhaps the most visible form of promotion—advertising. Chapter 21 closes the section with an examination of key managerial issues relating to personal selling.

CHAPTER 19

Promotion: An overview

The role of promotion
    Promotion as a communications strategy
    Inform, persuade, remind
    Shifting the demand curve
    Definition of promotional strategy
The components of promotion
    Advertising
    Personal selling
    Packaging
    Public relations
    Sales promotion
Promotional strategy
Factors influencing promotional strategy
    Promotional resources
    Nature of product

Push versus pull strategy
Life-cycle stage of product
Nature of the market
Product/market strategy
A communications model for promotional
    messages
    Source
    Encoding
    Channel
    Audience response
    Noise
    Feedback
Strategic planning in promotion
    Situation analysis
    Establishment of objectives
    Product/market
    Determination of promotional budget
    Management of program elements
    Evaluation and control

Summary
Key concepts
Discussion questions and exercises

The set of activities that a firm employs to communicate to buyers in an attempt to stimulate their demand composes its ***promotional strategy.*** Just as the overall marketing strategy of a firm contains a mix of elements, the firm's promotional strategy, as one of those elements, also contains a mix of elements. In this chapter, we'll examine:

The role of a firm's promotional strategy.

The various types of promotion that combine to represent a promotional strategy.

The major factors that determine the optimal combination of the promotional types.

The underlying communications theory on which promotional strategy is based.

A framework for decision making in promotional strategy.

THE ROLE OF PROMOTION

There are several views of the role of promotion; here we'll examine the major views. By examining each view of promotion's role in a firm's marketing strategy, we hope to gain a better appreciation of why promotion exists than if we adopted a single perspective of the collective roll of advertising, personal selling, public relations, packaging, and sales promotion.

Promotion as a communications strategy

Perhaps the most salient characteristic of any type of promotional activity is that it is a form of communication. In marketing, it is communication from seller to potential buyer. As such, any single communication has the general objective of *eliciting from a target buyer a reaction favorable to the source of the communication.* The desired reaction can be one of a large number of possibilities (creating awareness, stimulating interest, reinforcing behavior). As a form of communication, promotion seeks to influence the recipient through the use of informative and/or persuasive forces (as opposed to physical ones).

Inform, persuade, remind

The role of promotion can be viewed in terms of the desired impact on buyers. From our earlier discussion of buyer behavior, we know that there are different stages in the development of the relationship between a buyer and a product. The buyer must first become aware of and knowledgeable about the product (cognitive structure), develop a favorable attitude toward the product (affective structure), and ultimately buy it (behavioral structure). This sequence suggests a three-tiered view of the desired impact of promotion. (See Figure 19–1.)

At the first level, promotion seeks to *inform* buyers of the availability and nature of a product. When a new product is introduced to the market, an initial major marketing task is to make buyers aware of its nature

Figure 19–1: Levels of
desired impact of
promotion

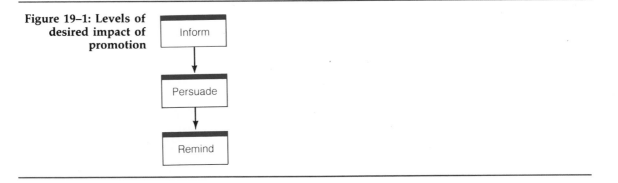

and existence. The informational role of promotion is not restricted to new products. Because buyers differ in the stage of their relationship with a product, products that have been on the market for several years also require informational support. Three situations show the need for the informational role of promotion for an existing product.

1. Many products that have been around for some time realize first-time buyers. Most durable goods are of this nature, as well as some services (e.g., insurance). Households do not buy a particular good until they reach a certain age, stage of the family life cycle, or level of income. A firm's promotional effort must keep these first-time buyers in mind if it is to effectively compete for their purchases.

2. We know that firms may seek growth through market development; that is, they direct an existing product at a new segment of the market. Buyers in the new segment must then be informed of the product and its benefit.

3. When an existing product is modified, buyers must be informed of this change and its positive consequences.

Once buyers are informed of a product, they must then recognize the value of buying it relative to other forms of behavior. Promotion must *persuade* them that positive consequences will be realized from consumption of the firm's product—consequences more positive than those of competitors' brands. Promotion attempts to develop a positive set of beliefs about the product's important attributes.

The task of promotion is not completed when consumers are aware of and have positive feelings toward a product. Competitors constantly seek to make inroads on a brand's position. A firm cannot disregard these efforts and maintain its preeminence in the consumer's mind. It must *remind* buyers of the positive consequences associated with its brand. The consumers' favorable cognitive feelings toward a product must be reinforced continually.

The informational, persuasive, and reminder roles of promotion grow directly out of its communications role. They represent the reactions to communications efforts that are favorable to the sender (i.e., the firm). Usually the promotional program will be seeking all three effects. Some

Smokey Bear—In his
debut and now.

Courtesy U.S. Department of
Agriculture

of the promotional effort will have an informational role; some will be directed at persuading or reminding. And any *one message* may contain elements that seek all three effects.

One of the best promotional campaigns to inform, persuade, and remind a target audience is the forest fire prevention campaign using Smokey Bear as its symbol. Started in 1944, the Smokey Bear campaign now includes reminder signs and posters in forested areas, television spots, personal appearances by Smokey, costumed forest rangers, parade floats, and a giant Smokey Bear balloon. Research shows that 98 percent of the people know who Smokey is; a large majority know what he stands for. Most important, in persuading and reminding people to be careful, the campaign is credited with reducing forest fires by 50 percent since 1944.[1]

Shifting the demand curve

An *economic* view of the role of promotion—entirely consistent with the behavioral view discussed above—can also be taken. The economic goal of promotion is to influence the shape and/or position of the firm's demand curve. (See Figure 19–2.) Promotion seeks to influence the position of the demand curve by shifting it further to the right (Figure 19–2A). In this way greater sales are realized at a given price. Promotion seeks to influence the shape of the curve by making it more inelastic at higher

[1] "Only He Can Prevent Forest Fires," *Psychology Today,* May 1984, p. 14.

**Figure 19–2: The goals
of promotion**

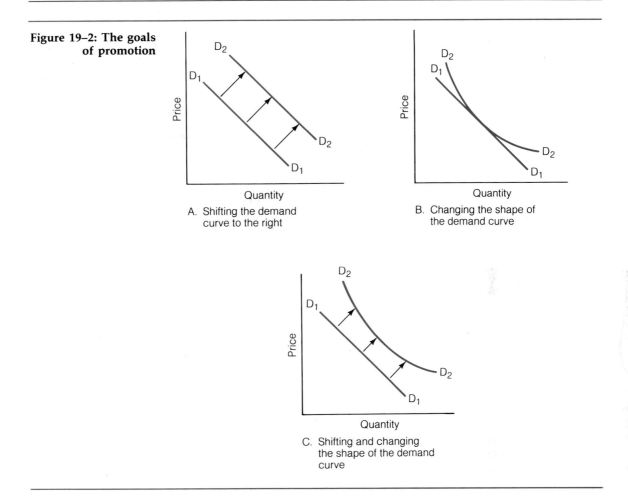

A. Shifting the demand
curve to the right

B. Changing the shape of
the demand curve

C. Shifting and changing
the shape of the demand
curve

prices and more elastic at lower prices (Figure 19–2B). In this way nonprice factors operate at higher prices, but when price is decreased it has an effect. And promotion can effect both the shape and position of the demand curve (Figure 19–2C) simultaneously.

promotional strategy

> **Promotional strategy** is that portion of an organization's overall marketing strategy designed to communicate to the marketplace, usually through a set of activities, the nature of the organization and its market offering.

**Definition of
promotional strategy**

Within this definition we can see several aspects of promotional strategy. First, a promotional strategy exists within a total marketing strategy. Thus, its nature and objectives must be compatible with the overall marketing program. Second, promotional strategy is the communications arm of the marketing program. Third, promotion is directed at the marketplace, which includes users as well as resellers as target audiences. Fourth, promotional strategy consists of a set of activities, each assigned a specific role within the overall promotional scheme. Ideally, these activities represent a coordinated whole (as opposed to independent, isolated communication efforts). Finally, the ultimate objective of this coordinated whole is to communicate the nature of the organization in general and its specific offerings to target audience members.

THE COMPONENTS OF PROMOTION

The components of promotion include *advertising, personal selling, packaging, public relations,* and *sales promotion.* (See Figure 19–3.)

advertising

> **Advertising** is any *paid* form of nonpersonal communication of ideas, goods, or services by an identified source.

Advertising

Its goals run the gamut from informing to reminding an audience. It involves a variety of media that (for the most part) are designed to reach larger masses of buyers. These include television, radio, magazines, and newspapers. Advertising probably allows the greatest latitude of creativity in message design, and its varied nature requires substantial management.

personal selling

> **Personal selling** involves the face-to-face communication of information from a seller to a prospective buyer.

Personal selling

Its key feature is its *personal* element. Personal selling occurs throughout the channel for a consumer good—from manufacturers to resellers, resellers to resellers, and resellers at the retail level to the final consumer. It is the dominant form of promotion in industrial marketing.

Figure 19–3: Components of promotion

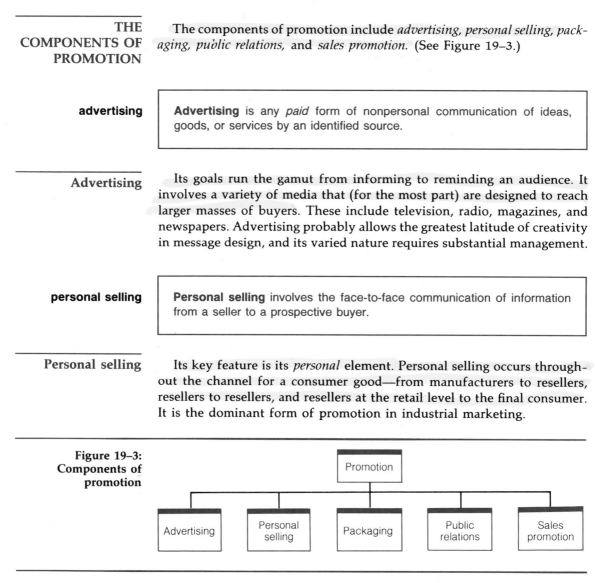

For some firms, personal selling involves the management of human resources (the sales force) to a greater extent than in any other function of marketing. Other firms have a smaller sales force. Either way, the sales job is a unique position within a firm, and managing its occupants is a difficult task. (We will examine sales force management at greater length in Chapter 21.)

Packaging

Often, the package is viewed as simply an extension of the physical product. Because of its protective and sometimes functional roles (e.g., pouring spouts), the package is properly viewed as a dimension of the product variable. But for many products the package has promotional properties, too.

The **promotional properties** of a package derive mainly from the use of color, lettering, and illustrations. An effective package design can convey persuasive, informational messages that create awareness, increase recognition, generate interest, and even convince a consumer to buy. Illustrations and wording generate interest by describing the package contents. Informational wording on the package can provide directions for use or consumer warnings. As a component of promotion, packaging plays several strategic roles. (See Figure 19–4.)

Consumer goods, shelved next to competitors in a retail store, depend—more than any other type of product—on packaging for promotional support. They depend on packaging for shelf impact. This role of packaging led to the "sea of green" effect created with the packaging design of the Green Giant frozen vegetable line. Green packaging was used to unify more than 40 products and achieve visual impact in the freezer cases of supermarkets.[2]

As a promotional device, packaging can take on symbolic properties. A symbolic package played a key role in the success of L'eggs panty hose. The egg-shaped package was unique and stood out; but, perhaps more important, the egg association symbolized a fragile yet protected fashion item.

Packaging is a key consideration in repositioning a mature or failing

Figure 19–4: Strategic roles of packaging

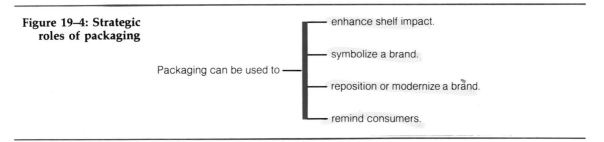

Packaging can be used to
- enhance shelf impact.
- symbolize a brand.
- reposition or modernize a brand.
- remind consumers.

[2] "Sea of Green Look Adopted in Green Giant Repackaging," *Marketing News,* March 4, 1983, p. 4.

brand. In fact, the rejuvenation of the Right Guard brand of deodorant was based almost entirely on a new package.

Finally, frequent exposure to a package allows it to play a reminder role. The Campbell Soup Company estimates the average consumer sees its label 76 times a year—twice the exposure delivered by TV and worth an estimated $30 million.[3]

Public relations

Public relations (PR) is an activity of a firm that can be part of—but is not restricted to—its promotional program.

public relations

> **Public relations** is the management function of an organization designed to elicit from one or more publics a general positive feeling toward the organization and its products.

Usually, PR takes the form of service to the general public or a specific group. It seeks to establish goodwill. Examples of public relations activities include the donation of scholarship money to a college or university, Macy's Thanksgiving Day parade, grand-opening parties thrown by retailers, free city-bus rides on New Year's Eve, and sponsorship of a youth athletic team.

In small firms PR activities are often handled informally by one or two employees who have other, more formal duties. In large firms public relations departments are common. They are composed of individuals whose sole responsibility lies in public relations. These "PR types" assess public attitudes, develop and execute PR programs, and evaluate their effects.[4]

Publicity. As the communications arm of public relations, *publicity* is considered part of the promotional program.

publicity

> **Publicity** is any message concerning an organization appearing in the mass media as a news item for which the organization does not pay and is not generally considered to be the source.

Publicity is crucial to public relations. It is the means by which the public service activities of the organization are communicated. It does little good (from a public opinion standpoint) to donate a scholarship if only the recipient and the scholarship office of a university are aware

[3] Kevin Higgens, "Economic Recovery Presages Packaging Explosion," *Marketing News,* February 3, 1984, p. 20.

[4] For a discussion of public relations and its relationship to marketing, see J. N. Goodrich, R. L. Gildea, and K. Cavanaugh, "A Place for Public Relations in the Marketing Mix," *MSU Business Topics,* Autumn 1979, pp. 53–57.

of it. To achieve publicity, the PR department will issue a press release to the news media in the hope that it will be printed and/or broadcast.

Publicity is also used to enhance the marketing of a specific product of a firm. Any favorable news story about a product will likely increase consumer awareness and interest. Again, firms can increase the publicity surrounding a product by preparing news releases. Such an effort can be particularly useful when a firm is introducing an innovative product. A good example of a carefully planned publicity campaign for a new product is provided by the IBM PC jr, IBM's entry into the home computer market. Prior to introducing the "Peanut," IBM leaked tantalizing bits of information about the product to the press. IBM so whetted the appetites of the press that, when the full information was made available, feature stories about the Peanut appeared in several major magazines.

Publicity, as a form of promotion, has certain distinctive features. (See Figure 19–5.) First, as noted before, it is free. Publicity messages appearing in the media are not paid for by the subject firm. Second, publicity messages are typically more believable. This is due to their news-story format and the fact that the subject firm is not viewed as the source. Thus, their impact is usually greater than a corresponding message presented in a paid advertisement. Third, the news-story format improves the ability of the message to get through to the audience. Selective defenses against advertising are down, and receptivity to news stories is present. Finally, the organization has less control over publicity than over other forms of promotion. Certainly a firm *influences* publicity by providing impetus in the form of a press release. Whether the story is printed is determined by the media, however. Also, publicity can occur without the efforts of the subject firm: brand ratings in *Consumer Reports* represent publicity. And a news exposé about a firm's apparent disregard for the environment is publicity. Thus, publicity can be positive or negative in the way it portrays an organization.

Sales promotion

Once referred to as the "stepchild" of marketing because it was often an afterthought in developing promotional strategy, sales promotion is now taking on greater importance. In fact, aggregate annual expenditures on sales promotion exceed those for advertising and are increasing at a greater rate, as well.[5] Sales promotion is defined by the American Marketing Association as:

> Those activities other than personal selling, advertising, and publicity that stimulate consumer purchasing and dealer effectiveness, such as displays, shows and exhibitions, demonstrations, and various nonrecurrent selling efforts not in the ordinary routine.[6]

[5] Roger A. Strang, "Sales Promotion—Fast Growth, Faulty Management," *Harvard Business Review,* July–August 1976, pp. 115–24.

[6] *Marketing Definitions: A Glossary of Marketing Terms* (Chicago: American Marketing Association, 1960), p. 20.

Figure 19–5:
Distinctive features of
publicity

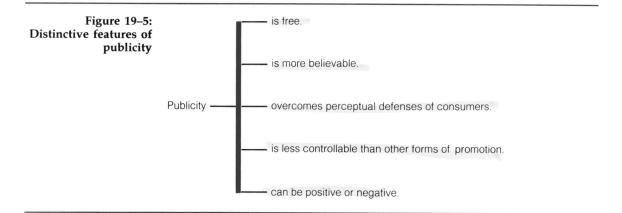

Publicity
- is free.
- is more believable.
- overcomes perceptual defenses of consumers.
- is less controllable than other forms of promotion.
- can be positive or negative.

Most sales promotion attempts to support and complement other forms of promotion. But, in some cases, a sales-promotion device may be the major marketing impetus for a new product or the major tactic to save a failing one. Either way, sales promotion must be planned, implemented, and evaluated with the same care devoted to other promotional forms. The diversity of available sales-promotion devices alone suggests a careful approach to their selection and use.

Types of sales promotion devices. We can categorize sales-promotion devices by their sources and targets. (See Table 19–1 for an overview.)

In the first category we have ***manufacturer-to-consumer*** sales promotion. Generally, these efforts have one of two possible purposes.[7] First, there are sales-promotion efforts designed to increase the tendency of consumers to try a *new product.* These efforts aim to get the product into the hands of the consumer with the hopes that the consumer, in using the product, will develop a favorable attitude toward it and continue to purchase and use it. New-product sales promotion includes free samples, cents-off coupons, introductory sale prices, and cash rebates. Manufacturers also direct sales promotion at consumers to reinforce or increase the purchase of *established products.* These efforts may be necessary to shore up a failing brand or to respond to competitive pressures. The essence of these approaches is that they offer consumers a more favorable value–cost ratio. Examples are cents-off coupons included in the package, premiums (i.e., gifts or low-cost products offered in conjunction with the purchase of a product), contests, sweepstakes, and cash rebates. Also included here would be a frequent-flyer program in which, after a certain number of miles flown on an airline, the flyer qualifies for a free trip.

A second general category of sales promotion includes ***manufacturer-to-industrial user*** devices. For technically oriented firms such efforts may involve user brochures, design guides, and product premiums (e.g., small

---

[7] John F. Luick and William L. Ziegler, *Sales Promotion and Modern Merchandising* (New York: McGraw-Hill, 1968).

Table 19–1: Type of sales promotion categorized by source and target

Source	Consumers	Organizational users	Wholesalers	Retailers
Manufacturers	Free samples Coupons Introducing low price Cash rebates Premiums Contests and sweepstakes	User brochures Design guides Product premiums Gifts Trade shows	Buying allowances Contests Trade shows	Buying allowances Contests Advertising and display allowances Trade shows
Wholesalers		Buying allowances		Buying allowances
Retailers	Coupons Contests Gifts Trading stamps			

(Target)

pieces of equipment, such as tape measures). In industrial markets perhaps the most common type of sales promotion is a gift. Gifts are compatible with the more permanent, closer buyer-seller relationships that often develop in industrial markets.[8]

A third category of sales promotion is the ***manufacturer-to-wholesaler*** type. This attempts to increase wholesaler handling of a product or the marketing attention resellers devote to a product. One common device used to increase reseller purchases of a product is a ***buying allowance***— an offer to a wholesaler of a certain sum of money for a certain quantity of a product purchased (thus contributing to the profit margin of the wholesaler). Sales contests are another sales promotion aimed at increasing wholesaler attention to a product.

Manufacturer-to-retailer sales promotion also includes buying allowances and sales contests. Another popular device is an ***advertising and display allowance.*** Here a retailer is compensated for advertising a manufacturer's product or providing a ***point-of-purchase (POP) display.*** Manufacturers increasingly seek POP support from retailers. Much like packaging, POP displays act as silent salespersons, giving consumers information on the product that the retail salesclerk doesn't have the time or knowledge to provide. L'eggs effectively combined its unique package with its panty hose "boutique" (a POP display). The success of the L'eggs brand allows its POP display a permanent spot in most retail outlets.

Ralston Purina provides an interesting variation on the manufacturer-to-retailer sales promotion. Through veterinarians, the company distrib-

---

[8] Benson P. Shapiro, "Improve Distribution with Your Promotional Mix," *Harvard Business Review*, March–April 1977, p. 123.

uted Puppycare Kits, which included samples of Ralston Purina products and a booklet on the care of puppies. The kits became so popular that Ralston Purina now sells them to vets for $1 each.[9]

Trade show exhibitions represent a sales-promotion device used by manufacturers to reach industrial users, wholesalers, and retailers. Trade shows allow manufacturers to reveal their latest products. Often they represent the first exposure of a new product to the market.

Two less common categories of sales promotion are the ***wholesaler-to-organizational user*** and ***wholesaler-to-retailer*** varieties. Buying allowances may occur here.

A final category of sales promotion—***retailer-to-consumers***—is used by retailers to increase traffic in their stores. A once-popular retail sales-promotion device was the use of trading stamps. Retailer coupons, contests, sweepstakes, and gifts represent more current forms of retail sales promotion.

The uniqueness of sales promotion. The inclusion of sales promotion in the promotional elements of a firm results primarily from the use of the term *promotion* in its name. Most sales-promotion devices differ from those of other forms of promotion. They include more than a communication dimension. For example, a free sample delivered by mail to consumers is a combination of pricing and physical distribution strategies. Contests are an extension of the product strategy. Cash rebates represent a pricing strategy.

PROMOTIONAL STRATEGY

The development of a promotional strategy must consider all forms of promotion as an integrated whole. A major task of marketing management is to determine the optimal way to integrate the forms of promotion into an overall promotional strategy. The resulting blend of ingredients complement each other and work together toward the achievement of promotional goals. Thus, the management of promotion requires a coordinated approach to decisions involving the various forms of promotion.

FACTORS INFLUENCING PROMOTIONAL STRATEGY

An infinite number of possibilities are available to a firm developing a promotional blend. Several factors should be examined in determining the extent to which a particular form of promotion should play a role. These factors represent a joint consideration of certain aspects of the firm and of the market. A promotional blend that fits these constraints is best suited for the firm and the market it serves. Table 19–2 summarizes these factors and their efforts.

---

[9] Donna Sammons and Bruce Smith, "To Market, To Market," *INC,* June 1983, p. 59.

	Factor	Effect
Table 19–2: **Factors influencing** **promotional strategy**	Resources	More resources allow more diverse forms of promotion.
	Product	Industrial goods, technical goods, and costly consumer goods require more personal selling. Advertising, supplemented by packaging and sales promotion, dominates low-priced, frequently purchased goods.
	Push versus pull strategy	Push requires heavy personal selling. Pull requires heavy advertising and sales promotion to consumer.
	Life-cycle stage of product	See Figure 19–6.
	Nature of market	Personal selling is important for organizational buyers; advertising for consumers. Smaller and geographically concentrated markets allow more personal selling.
	Product/market strategy	Diversification requires more forms of promotion.

Promotional resources

One aspect of the firm that places an immediate limitation on its promotional blend is the amount of money it can spend on promotion. A small promotional budget limits the use of certain costly forms of promotion (e.g., network-TV advertising). Large budgets allow promotional blends with diverse forms of promotion; small ones allow fewer promotional forms. With its resources, Procter & Gamble makes heavy use of advertising and sales promotion to consumers and personal selling to resellers and pays close attention to packaging.

Nature of product

Another aspect of the firm that influences its promotional strategy is the nature of its products. *Technical* products generally require more personal selling than nontechnical ones. Much more information must be communicated about such products—and a personal selling situation can accommodate this requirement better. This is not to say that other forms of promotion (e.g., advertising) are not used to promote technical products. But personal selling does play a greater role here than it does for less complex products.

The *price* of a product also influences its promotional blend. High-priced products are greeted by a greater degree of perceived risk on the part of their buyers. The buyers want more information before buying. Personal selling again must play a greater role in promotion; and greater profit margins on these products allow for its use. Low-priced, low-risk products can rely on advertising.

Technical nature and price reflect important differences in the appropriate promotional blends for industrial and consumer products and for different types of products in each category. Generally, industrial goods are more technical and priced higher than consumer goods. Personal selling thus plays a more substantial role in the promotion of industrial goods; its importance increases with more technical, costly products (capital goods, heavy machinery). Advertising supplements personal selling, primarily in specialized print media (trade magazines).

Consumer goods rely more heavily on advertising than do industrial goods. And more diverse media are used to advertise them. Again, though, the more technical, higher-priced durable goods require personal selling to a greater extent than lower-priced convenience goods. The self-service nature of convenience goods restricts their consumer promotional blends to advertising, packaging, and point-of-sale materials. But personal selling is important when promoting convenience goods to resellers. Salespersons can play an important role in maintaining inventory levels and increasing retail shelf space devoted to their brands. For example, in an attempt to increase supermarket exposure of its food products, Quaker Oats increased its sales force by 25 percent in the late 1970s.[10]

Push versus pull strategy

The relative presence of each form of promotion is influenced by whether a *push* or *pull* strategy is necessary. The push–pull distinction refers to different ways a manufacturer tries to get resellers to carry its product.

---

push strategy

A **push strategy** occurs when each member of the channel attempts to persuade the member below it to carry and promote the product.

pull strategy

A **pull strategy** occurs when the manufacturer attempts to stimulate consumer demand for the product, thereby making it profitable for resellers to handle the product.

A push strategy makes heavy use of personal selling at each stage of the channel. Little national advertising occurs by the manufacturer, but local advertising by retailers is important. Each channel member aids the subsequent member in developing the promotional effort. Shopping goods such as household furniture are commonly promoted in push fashion. A pull strategy requires heavy advertising and manufacturer-to-consumer sales-promotion efforts to influence consumer demand. Packaged goods are commonly promoted in pull fashion.

Life-cycle stage of product

As a brand progresses through the stages of the product life cycle, its appropriate promotional blend changes. (See Figure 19–6.) This is because the role of promotion—what it is trying to achieve—changes from

---

[10] "Quaker Oats Retreats to Its Food Lines," *Business Week,* February 25, 1980.

Manufacturer-to-consumer sales promotions play an important role in a pull strategy.

Courtesy The Procter & Gamble Company

stage to stage. In the introductory stage, the role of promotion is to create awareness and stimulate trial of the new brand. Advertising, publicity, and sales promotion are major components of the promotional blend. In the growth stage, publicity and sales promotion slack off; advertising assumes a greater burden of the promotional task. Incentives for trial

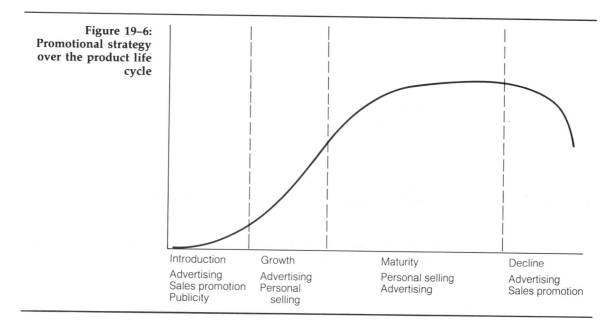

Figure 19–6: Promotional strategy over the product life cycle

Introduction	Growth	Maturity	Decline
Advertising	Advertising	Personal selling	Advertising
Sales promotion	Personal	Advertising	Sales promotion
Publicity	selling		

are less necessary; advertising reinforces trial and word-of-mouth processes among buyers. Personal selling aimed at resellers intensifies. In the maturity stage, personal selling becomes important; advertising serves a reminder function (unless product modifications have occurred). Finally, at the decline stage, advertising continues at reminder levels. Personal selling attention becomes minimal. Sales promotion may increase.

Nature of the market

Various characteristics of the market being served by a company influence its promotional blend. As we have seen, organizational buyers receive more personal selling attention; consumers receive more advertising attention. (Avon is a line of consumer goods, however, that is promoted heavily through personal selling directed at the consumer.)

Other aspects of the market influencing the promotional blend include its size and concentration. A market with few buyers can receive personal selling attention more efficiently; large numbers of buyers require advertising attention. A firm serving a local market can use personal selling readily. But as its geographic scope widens, advertising and sales promotion become more prevalent. However, in a wide geographic market where buyers tend to be concentrated in a few clusters, personal selling again becomes more feasible.

Product/market strategy

The firm's product/market strategy influences its promotional blend. A product/market strategy involving several diverse segments requires more forms of promotion. For example, with products aimed at consumers and industrial segments, IBM makes heavy use of both advertising and personal selling. A company focusing exclusively on industrial segments would use much less advertising.

A COMMU-NICATIONS MODEL FOR PROMOTIONAL MESSAGES

A fundamental aspect of promotion is that it involves communications: messages are developed and communicated to an audience. Therefore, promotional strategy can be enhanced by a sound understanding of communications theory. A useful model for understanding the communications process is shown in Figure 19–7. It shows the process by which a

Figure 19–7: A model of the communications process

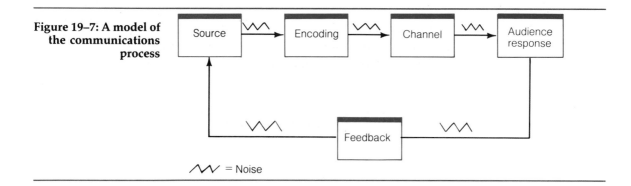

∧∨∨ = Noise

single message is developed and communicated. This is a general model; any specific form of promotion can be applied to it.

source | The **source** is the sender of the message.

Source

In promotion, the source can be any institution engaged in marketing activities. The source enters the communications process seeking a response from a target audience that will help achieve the general objective of promotion. Three important points must be made about this first stage of the process. (See Figure 19–8.) Each point is important because it affects what happens in the remainder of the process.

Figure 19-8: Key issues concerning message source

Source ─── Message objective
Target audience
Source credibility

1. Message objective. The source must establish a specific objective of its communication effort in terms of the desired response to its message. The inform–persuade–remind framework of the role of promotion (discussed above) is the basis for determining this response. The purpose of the message influences its content and the manner in which it is delivered. Message content designed to create awareness will be less extensive than that designed to inform an audience of the features of a brand. It will probably be delivered in different fashion, too.

2. Target audience. The source must clearly define the target audience from which it is seeking a desired response. The nature of the target audience (e.g., market segment) influences the appropriate content and mode of delivery of a message.

3. Source effects. The source of a message—and *source credibility*—can influence response to a message. Generally, highly credible sources are more effective in eliciting attitude change in the desired direction. But a highly credible source becomes ineffective when the audience is highly involved with a message topic. Highly involved audiences are more resistant to persuasion.[11] Therefore, the use of source credibility in promotion may be most effective in the case of new products.

[11] H. H. Johnson and J. A. Scileppi, "Effects of Ego-Involvement Conditions on Attitude Change to High- and Low-Credibility Communicators," *Journal of Personality and Social Psychology* 13 (1972), pp. 31–36.

Figure 19–9: Factors contributing to source credibility

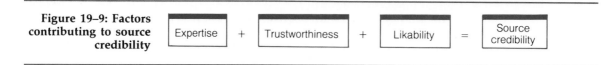

Three factors (see Figure 19–9) generally contribute to source credibility: expertise, trustworthiness, and likability. Firms strive to use spokespersons high on these factors to communicate their messages. For example, Arnold Palmer, a professional golfer and successful businessman who rates high on all three factors, is a popular spokesman for golf equipment, business products, and other goods.

encoding

> **Encoding** is the process by which the source translates the information to be transmitted into words and symbols.

Encoding

In short, message formulation occurs. In formulating a message, three important elements must be considered: content, structure, and format. (See Figure 19–10.) These three elements blend to determine the effectiveness of the message.

Message content

content

> The **content** of a message refers to the appeal, idea, or theme that provides the basis for the audience to respond in the manner desired by the source.

A variety of approaches to formulating the message content is available:
1. *Rational appeals.* These messages are directed at the reasoning capabilities of the audience. They offer a basis for behavior that is in the

Figure 19–10: Elements of a promotional message

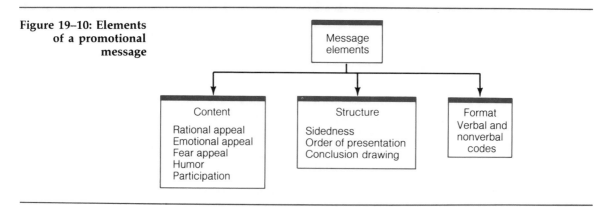

How to control a world you can't always predict.

Cullinet's integrated manufacturing software.

Cullinet has a software system that provides manufacturers with the one thing they could use more of: control.

A Cullinet Manufacturing Software System consists of eight applications from Master Production Scheduling to Shop Floor Control. They can be purchased separately or as a completely integrated system.

As a net-change, closed-loop MRP II system, Cullinet's Manufacturing Software provides manufacturing personnel with an accurate reflection of – and easy access to – constantly changing information about the manufacturing cycle. At any point in the cycle.

With this kind of timely information, variables that might influence inventory, resources, personnel, production, distribution, indeed, the very profitability of a manufacturing concern can be accounted for. And, once accounted for, controlled.

A very flexible system, Cullinet's Manufacturing Software can bring high-level control to any manufacturing environment however unique or personal your individual style and approach. It can provide single or multi-plant controls. Control for process manufacturing, make-to-order, make-to-stock, or repetitive manufacturing. In other words, it is equally capable in any manufacturing environment.

So even if your world changes in unpredictable ways, we can give you control over it. Cullinet's Manufacturing Software.

Cullinet

audience's best interests. Objective information in support of the suggested behavior is emphasized. Rational appeals in promotion stress the functional superiority of the product. Quality, value, and performance are emphasized. Rational appeals are well suited when the audience is organizational buyers or consumers of technical, high-priced goods.

2. *Emotional appeals.* Messages attempt to elicit feelings of guilt, shame, anger, pride, etc., so that the desired behavior occurs. Such appeals have been used in safety-related areas (e.g., getting people to use safety belts in cars). Texas uses the theme "Drive Friendly" for its highway system.

3. *Fear appeals.* These messages suggest to the audience that behaving (or not behaving) in a certain way will have undesirable consequences (e.g., cancer from smoking, cavities from not brushing your teeth). One marketing source concludes that fear appeals based on moderately negative consequences are most effective.[12] But another source suggests strong fear appeals are superior when an audience's loved ones are threatened.[13] Thus, life insurance promotion often stresses the consequences on one's family from not having it.

4. *Humorous appeals.* Well-executed humorous messages can be memorable and persuasive. Poorly executed humor may detract from comprehension. A classic example of effective humor is the Miller Lite ad campaign on TV. The use of humor in advertising appears to be on the increase.[14]

5. *Participation appeals.* Participation of the audience in the message enhances its persuasive effect. Participation is felt to increase attention and learning. Merely describing the features of a car would probably be less effective than doing so while the prospective buyer is test-driving it.

Message structure

---

message structure | **Message structure** refers to the manner in which the content of a message is organized.

Sidedness, order of presentation, and conclusion-drawing are important dimensions of message structure to be considered in developing a persuasive message.

1. *Message sidedness.* The issue of whether a one-sided or two-sided message is more persuasive has received considerable research attention. In a one-sided message, only one view is presented—the source's position on an issue. A two-sided message presents both the source's position and an opposing view. It points out the relative strengths and weaknesses

---

[12] M. L. Ray and W. L. Wilkie, "Fear: The Potential of an Appeal Neglected by Marketing," *Journal of Marketing,* January, 1970, p. 57.

[13] M. Karlins and H. I. Abelson, *Persuasion,* 2d ed. (New York: Springer Publishing, 1970), pp. 9–10.

[14] John Koten, "After Serious 70s Advertisers Are Going for Laughs Again," *The Wall Street Journal,* February 23, 1984, p. 29.

The use of humor in a message.

Courtesy Selchow & Righter Co.

SCRABBLE® is the registered trademark of Selchow & Righter Co., Bay Shore, NY, for its line of word games and entertainment services.

of each position. An example of a two-sided promotional message would be a comparative ad in which superiority is claimed on certain attributes of the source's brand but is disclaimed on other attributes. The attributes on which superiority is disclaimed should be relatively unimportant. Generally, the effectiveness of a two-sided message results from a greater level of *believability* granted the source by the audience.

Certain conditions determine whether a one-sided or two-sided message will be more persuasive. A two-sided message is more effective with better-educated audiences. A second moderating condition is the *initial position* of the audience. When the audience already advocates the position of the message, a one-sided message is more effective. The message reinforces the position. If the audience is initially opposed to the position of the message, a two-sided message results in greater movement toward the source's position. Thus, promotion messages directed at existing users of a brand should be one-sided; a two-sided message is more appropriate when the target audience includes users of a competing brand.

2. *Order of presentation.* This refers to whether the major points of the message should be presented early or late in the message or, in a two-sided message, whether the pro position precedes or follows the con position. Research suggests that when audience interest in the issue is low, the major points should come early; when audience interest is high, they should be placed near the end of the message. Thus, in promotion messages about low-interest products, or messages placed in low-interest media, the major points should be placed at the beginning of the message.[15]

3. *Conclusion drawing.* Another issue in message structure is whether a message should explicitly draw a conclusion for the audience or allow the audience to do so on its own. In general, it is more effective to explicitly draw a conclusion. However, allowing the audience to draw its own conclusions is more persuasive under certain conditions. This is best with a highly intelligent audience or one that is personally involved with the issue of the message.[16]

Message format.   A final consideration in the development of a message is the format within which its ideas are to be expressed.

message format
> **Message format** refers to the codes or symbols used to express the content of a message.

Two general types of codes are available for message expression: verbal and nonverbal. *Verbal codes* involve the spoken and/or written word. Verbal codes are virtually necessary to convey information and express ideas. Effectively arranging verbal codes into slogans or themes ("The Quality Goes in before the Name Goes on") can convey the essence of a message as well as enhance recall and recognition.

Nonverbal codes are symbolic in nature and can be either visual or auditory. To convey meaning, a nonverbal code must have a common meaning among people. Examples of nonverbal codes include facial expressions, body language, music, color, and pictures. Nonverbal codes can be effective in eliciting emotional reactions to a message but appear to contribute most to the memorability of a message. Childers and Houston show that pictorial messages are remembered better than verbal messages, especially when the audience focuses on the appearance rather

[15] M. Wayne DeLozier, *The Marketing Communications Process* (New York: McGraw-Hill, 1976), p. 91.

[16] Ibid., pp. 98–99.

This message uses a visual referent to convey an important product attribute.

Announcing a bloom of perfect color for your lips. It's our rare lipstick formula drenched with natural moisturizers, for color that stays very fresh. Very silky.
Imagine the pleasure of perfect, in twenty-four glorious shades.

Cutex Perfect Color

Reprinted with the permission of Chesebrough-Pond's Inc., the owner of the registered trademark CUTEX.

than the content of the message. Thus, messages for low-involvement products should depend more heavily on visual codes.[17]

The outcome of the encoding process is a message that, it is hoped, combines message content, structure, and format effectively to achieve its intent. Once formulated, it must be delivered through a channel.

---

[17] Terry L. Childers and Michael J. Houston, "Conditions for a Picture-Superiority Effect on Consumer Memory," *Journal of Consumer Research,* September 1984, pp. 643–54.

Channel

In promotion, channels of communication are represented by the various forms of promotion: advertising, personal selling, packaging, etc. Earlier we discussed the strengths and weaknesses of the forms of promotion in terms of achieving desired effects (awareness, reinforcement, etc). Thus, the selection of a channel as a delivery medium must consider the purpose of the message. We also saw that the nature of the target audience is an important factor in the form of promotion chosen: organizational buyers require more personal selling than advertising attention. Therefore, message intent and the target audience jointly influence the choice of a channel.

channel

> The **channel** in the communications process represents the medium through which the message is delivered to the audience.

An additional point about the channel is that the various forms of promotion place constraints on message formulation. The promotional forms vary in what they allow in the way of message content, structure, and format. Advertising and packaging are more limited than personal selling in the quantity of content that can be delivered. Also, there are differences in the nature and number of nonverbal codes that can be utilized. Radio advertising is probably most limited in the use of nonverbal codes. Personal selling is probably the most flexible form for transmitting a message.

Thus, the development of a promotional message involves a dual consideration of the nature of the message and the channel. If an organization develops a particular message to send, the nature of this message (i.e., its content, structure, and format) may limit—or even dictate—the choice of a channel. On the other hand, if budgetary limitations preclude the use of more costly channels, the message may have to be adapted to the constraints of a less expensive channel.

Audience response

The end result of the communications process is *audience response* to the message—it may or may not be the response desired by the source. The desired response may be of a cognitive, affective, or behavioral level. The hierarchy of effects model becomes appropriate, then, as a framework for examining responses to a communication (and, as we have noted before, a basis for establishing message objectives). An expanded version of the hierarchy of effects model presented in the context of communication effects is presented in Figure 19–11. This version indicates the sequence of effects that must occur for a message to be received and have some level of effect.

Exposure.   For a message to influence a member of an audience, there must first be *exposure.*

Figure 19–11: Audience response to a communication

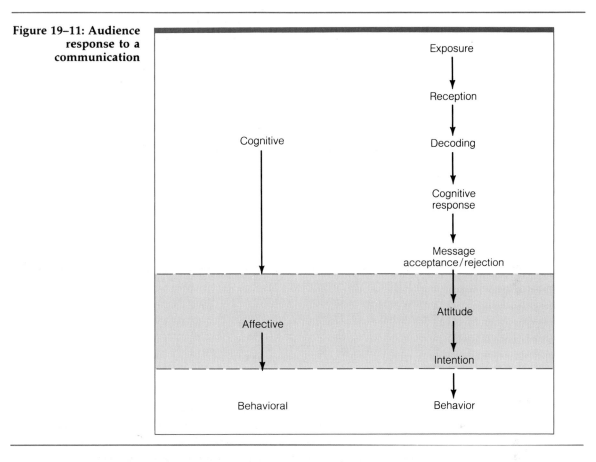

exposure

> **Exposure** occurs when the message is present in the individual's physical environment.

Whether message exposure occurs is primarily a function of the channel through which it is delivered. Messages must be delivered through a medium that will reach the target audience. Therefore, knowledge of media exposure patterns of a target audience is important input to the selection of a channel of communication.

Reception

reception

> **Reception** occurs when the individual notices and *pays attention* to the message.

The process of selective perception limits the stimuli to which an individual pays attention. The mere presence of a message in an individual's environment does not ensure its reception. The probability of reception is higher when the message deals with an issue of interest to the audience.

Decoding

decoding   **Decoding** is the process by which a receiver attaches meaning to a message.

The codes or symbols of the message are interpreted and translated into the receiver's own language based on the receiver's experience. The success of the message depends on whether the receiver interprets the message as intended by the source. If not, then a response other than the desired one is more likely.

The nature of the *decoding* process suggests several important points to keep in mind when *encoding* a message. First, it is important to make the decoding task as easy as possible. A message that requires a lot of mental effort to interpret is likely to be discarded rather than interpreted. Second, the decoding task becomes easy when the message is encoded into the language of the receiver. This, in turn, increases the likelihood that the message will be interpreted as intended. It is crucial, then, to understand the language of the audience and encode the message accordingly.

Cognitive response. The impact of a message is determined by the ***cognitive responses*** it elicits from the receiver who has confronted and decoded the message.

cognitive responses   **Cognitive responses** are the receiver's spontaneous thought processes in response to the perceived content of the message.

These processes are considered to be a primary mediator of whether a message is accepted or rejected.

Three types of cognitive responses to marketing communications have been extensively studied by Peter Wright:

1. ***Counterarguments.*** This occurs when the receiver compares message content to existing beliefs and notes a discrepancy. The receiver counters the message by recalling a negative aspect of the topic not presented in the message. For example, a consumer may counterargue an ad emphasizing the teeth-whitening ability of a

toothpaste brand by recalling his or her belief that the brand's ingredients destroy the protective enamel of teeth.

2. **Source derogation.** This occurs when the receiver focuses on a negative thought about the source. The message is rejected because the source is viewed as biased, untrustworthy, lacking in expertise, etc.

3. **Support argument.** Not all cognitive responses resist a message. Support arguing is positive. The receiver notes a congruency between message content and existing beliefs. Such a response serves to reinforce existing positive beliefs. For example, a consumer might recall a dentist's favorable comment about the toothpaste brand.[18]

Message acceptance/rejection. The nature of cognitive responses suggest that their occurrence depends on an existing belief system about the topic of the message. When a message relates to a topic the receiver knows about, cognitive responses are more likely to occur; they become the primary determinant of *message acceptance or rejection.* In the absence of existing beliefs (when a topic is new to the receiver), cognitive responses are less likely to occur. Factors relating to the source or the message itself (e.g., appeal, structure) are the primary determinants of message acceptance or rejection.

The acceptance or rejection of a message influences an individual's beliefs by reinforcing existing beliefs or creating new ones. Rejection of a message through counterarguing or source derogation reinforces existing negative beliefs; acceptance by way of support arguing reinforces existing positive beliefs. Newly created beliefs (positive or negative) result when cognitive responses are minimal or absent.

The factors that determine message acceptance or rejection help reveal the difficult task of persuasion that a promotional message faces. Messages that are incompatible with the existing beliefs of a receiver tend to be rejected. Effective marketing communications reinforce existing attitudes and behavior or stimulate people already predisposed to behave in the desired manner. Thus, marketing communications work with and through a variety of factors to realize an effect. In isolation, a promotional message has limited influence.

Attitude, intention, and behavior. The remainder of the sequence of effects derives from the relationships between beliefs, attitudes, behavioral predispositions, and behavior (discussed in Chapter 5). The effect

---

[18] See, for example, Peter Wright, "Message-Evoked Thoughts: Persuasion Research Using Thought Verbalization," *Journal of Consumer Research,* September 1980, pp. 151–75. Also see George E. Belch, "The Effects of Television Commercial Repetition on Cognitive Response and Message Acceptance," *Journal of Consumer Research,* June 1982, pp. 56–65.

on beliefs from message acceptance/rejection serves to strengthen an existing positive/negative attitude or create a new attitude. Attitude then affects behavioral intent, which, in turn, determines ultimate behavior.

noise

> **Noise** is anything within the communications process that interferes with it, making it less than 100 percent effective in achieving its desired effect.

Noise

Noise can occur throughout the process at any stage. It occurs when the source incorrectly defines the target audience, improperly encodes the message, or chooses a channel that does not reach the target audience. It occurs when the receiver misinterprets the message, counterargues it, or derogates the source. Noise is anything that distracts the receiver. A dominant form of noise is a competing message (e.g., a package of a competing brand on the shelf).

Feedback

The presence of noise, among other things, necessitates *feedback.*

feedback

> **Feedback** is any information provided to the source about the impact of the message.

It is the communications process in reverse. The receiver of the original message becomes the source of the feedback; the source of the original message becomes the receiver of the feedback. This process is also subject to the effects of noise.

Feedback measures the effectiveness of a message. It can be informal or gathered in a conscious, systematic fashion. Personal selling, as a form of promotion, can provide informal, instantaneous feedback if an astute salesperson is involved. Marketing research provides formal, systematic collection of information about the effectiveness of a firm's promotion.

The effects of promotion can be measured at any of the levels of the hierarchy of effects—awareness, recall, beliefs/attitudes, sales. The procedures used to measure the effectiveness of advertising and personal selling and key variables to measure will be considered in our separate discussions of advertising management, sales management, and marketing research.

STRATEGIC
PLANNING IN
PROMOTION

As with the other strategic areas of marketing, the strategic planning process can be applied to the promotional area. Figure 19–12 presents the strategic planning process adapted specifically to promotional strategy.

Situation analysis

Demand and competition are aspects of situation analysis particularly relevant to promotional strategy. In promotion it is crucial to understand

Figure 19–12: Strategic planning for promotion

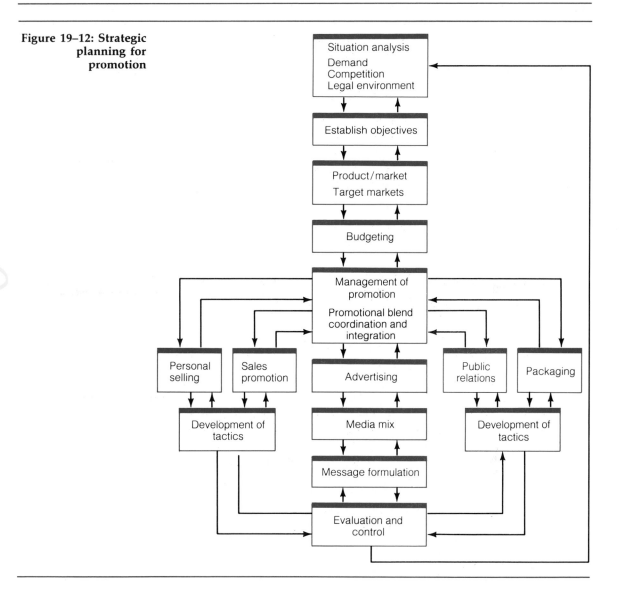

the nature of demand—cultural and social influences, attitudes, decision processes, etc. The nature of competition (e.g., markets served, product strategies) reflects how demand is being served by other organizations. The joint analysis of demand and competition suggests the opportunities and constraints faced by the organization. They help define the promotional task. The legal environment places constraints on how the task can be accomplished.

The analysis of demand and competition played a key role in defining the promotional task faced by Apple in the 1984 introduction of the Apple IIc computer. While designed for use in the home, the IIc is not labeled a home computer. This is because Apple discovered that consumers had developed a negative view of home computers. Brands previously offered as home computers (Texas Instruments, Timex, and Mattel) failed when consumers discovered they could not do much more than play video games on them. Apple's analysis of competition showed the brands remaining in the market faced difficulties because of these consumer feelings. Atari was struggling. Sales of IBM's PC jr fell short of that firm's hopes. Apple's general promotional task was to inform consumers of the wider scope of utility a home computer offered. We'll focus on Apple's approach as we discuss the strategic planning process.[19]

Establishment of objectives

Based on overall corporate and marketing objectives, along with other information obtained during situation analysis, promotional objectives are established. Since an important part of marketing management is the evaluation of whether objectives are being met, it is necessary to state promotional objectives in concrete, quantitative, measureable terms. From situation analysis it will be evident what the focus of promotion should be—increasing awareness, increasing trial, changing attitudes, etc. Then measureable objectives for promotion can be established. Examples of specific promotional objectives might include: increasing awareness from its present 40 percent of target customers to 70 percent within six months and to 90 percent within a year, establishing the belief within 50 percent of target customers that our brand is superior on a particular attribute, and achieving 20 percent new-trial purchases in the next six months.

For its IIc model, Apple set a marketing objective of 400,000 units sold in the first eight months. While its specific promotional objectives are unavailable, Apple's general promotional objective was to change consumers' attitudes about the utility of computers in the home by informing them of the IIc's use for personal finance (taxes, home budgeting), word processing (letter writing, creative writing), and educational uses. Apple wanted to distinguish the IIc from inexpensive game machines.

Product/market

The product/market strategy of the firm substantially influences the nature of its promotional strategy. A disaggregated segmentation strategy, in which multiple target markets exist, requires distinct promotional strategies for each market. As discussed earlier, the specific nature of a target market is a key factor influencing the appropriate promotional blend.

In Apple's case the target market for the IIc was defined as the serious home computer user—20 million college-educated professionals, many

---

[19] This example is based on Carrie Dolan, "Apple Faces Challenge Selling New Computer for Home Use," *The Wall Street Journal,* May 3, 1984, p. 27.

with school-aged children. Since Apple employs a partially disaggregated approach to the computer market, a major professional task was to distinguish the IIc from its other models—the IIe and the Macintosh. The IIe, with a lower price and less memory than the IIc, is targeted at schools and hobbyists. The Macintosh, at twice the IIc's price and with more speed and power, is aimed at offices and universities.

Determination of promotional budget

A tentative budget, based on promotional objectives and available resources, must be set that will provide the resources to implement an overall promotional strategy. This initial budget will likely be revised as subsequent stages of the strategy-formulation process occur.

Several budget-setting procedures are available. Usually, a procedure emphasizes either the promotion task or the available resources in arriving at a monetary figure. Unfortunately, no one procedure balances the two considerations in arriving at a budget—which, of course, is the more practical approach to budget determination. Some procedures for budget determination are discussed below.

Equimarginal approach. This approach employs a fundamental principle of microeconomics—the equimarginal principle. It recognizes that the ultimate purpose of promotion is to generate revenue. The ***equimarginal approach*** states that expenditures on promotion should occur to the point where the marginal revenue generated by promotion is equal to its marginal cost. To put it another way, promotion should occur right up to the point at which it stops contributing to profit.

In practice, the equimarginal approach has limitations. It requires a quantitative measure of the effect of promotion on sales. But such a measure is not readily available. Promotion does not act in isolation; it interacts with other variables to affect sales. Also, promotion that is designed to create awareness or change attitudes is difficult to translate into sales effects. Furthermore, the equimarginal approach treats promotional expenditures as operating cost; it fails to recognize the investment-like quality of certain forms of promotion. Advertising, for example, has long-run effects, where advertising in one period generates sales in subsequent periods.

Nonetheless, in principle the equimarginal approach is not without value. It imposes the thought that there is a finite limit to the effects of promotion. It forces managers to recognize that additional promotional expenditures become unnecessary beyond a certain point.

Return on investment approach. The ***return on investment (ROI) approach*** does recognize the long-run benefits of promotion. It argues that promotional managers should compete for their funds on the same basis as for funds categorized as capital expenditures: long-run returns. Unfortunately, because of the inexact science of estimating these returns, only guesses at the expected dollar return from promotion can be offered. However, other areas of budgeting are no more exact. Again, in spite of its practical limitations, the ROI approach, like the equimarginal approach, imposes an important perspective on promotion when determining its budget—in this case, the investmentlike nature of promotion.

Percentage of sales approach.   A practical and commonly used approach to promotional budget determination is the ***percentage of sales (POS) approach.*** In this approach the proportion of the sales dollar allocated to promotion in the past is calculated. A budget is arrived at by applying this percentage to the previous period's sales or forecasted sales for the upcoming period.

The POS approach is popular for its practical utility. It is easy to administer and express the budget as a quantitative portion of sales. Furthermore, it is a financially conservative approach: it limits the availability of funds when revenue is down and increases them when revenue is up.

But the POS approach has a fundamental flaw. *It reverses the intended relationship between promotion and sales!* The POS approach treats promotion as a function of sales when, in fact, the ultimate purpose of promotion is to influence sales. How can forecasted sales be the basis for establishing one of its major determinants? Promotional efforts will be limited when sales are expected to be down—the very situation calling for more intensive promotion!

The POS approach would be adequate when the firm exists in a stable, unchanging environment and wishes to maintain its position—an uncommon situation, to say the least. At best, then, the POS approach is useful as a starting point in budget determination. It can be fine-tuned based on objectives and expected changes in the environment.

Competitive-parity approach.   The essence of the ***competitive parity approach*** is that the promotional budget is based on what competitors are spending. The organization determines what competition is spending (perhaps an industry average) and matches it. The value of this approach is that it explicitly considers an important part of the environment that was examined in situation analysis. Its major flaw is that it does not base the budget on the specific tasks that promotion must perform for the firm. Different firms may require different promotional tasks which, in turn, require different budgets.

Market share approach.   The ***market share approach*** is based on the premise that the market share realized by a firm is equal to its share of the promotional dollars spent in the industry. Therefore, if a firm desires a 15 percent market share, its promotional budget should equate to 15 percent of total industry promotional expenditures. Here we have an approach that establishes a task to perform and determines the necessary expenditures to achieve it. Unfortunately, there is no real support for the underlying premise that market share equals share of promotion. In fact, recent evidence suggests this is seldom the case.[20]

All-you-can-afford approach. In the ***all-you-can-afford approach*** the promotional budget is based on available liquid resources. Essentially, management spends as much of these liquid resources as it can afford without impairing its financial liquidity. While a safe approach in a financial sense, it bears no relationship to what *should* be spent on promotion. The result is likely to be an inadequate—or excessive—budget.

Objective and task approach. To this point the budget-setting procedures discussed fall short in one or more respects. They are either impractical, bear no relationship to the tasks of promotion, or potentially misuse available funds. While less than perfect, the ***objective and task approach*** does strike somewhat of a balance between these considerations. The essence of this approach is that the promotional budget is based on the tasks that promotion is to perform. The budget grows directly out of the specification of promotional objectives.

A straightforward sequence of steps is involved in the objective and task approach. Objectives are stated in specific, realistic fashion. The promotional effort necessary to attain these objectives is then determined. The costs of this promotional effort are estimated; this figure represents the budget. The financial resources of the company may enter the process to establish an upper limit to the budget. In this way available funds are being used at their maximum feasible level of effectiveness.

The difficulty with this approach lies in determining what promotional effort is necessary to accomplish promotional objectives. Often, research is needed to estimate the necessary promotional effort. Experimentation, in which alternative programs are tested, would be best as a preliminary basis for determining the necessary effort. But this capability will not exist in many organizations, especially smaller ones; and so this scientific approach to budget determination, while appealing, is limited to large firms with technical know-how and financial resources. Using the thinking implied in the objective and task approach, Apple arrived at a $20 million promotional budget for the IIc model.

Budget practices in industry. A recent study of promotional budgeting reports that increased sophistication in budgeting practices is occurring among the largest advertisers. Table 19–3 reveals the percentage of firms

---

[20] "Advertising and Sales Relationships: A Current Appraisal," *The Nielsen Researcher* 1 (1980), pp. 2–9.

	Method	Percent of firms using each method
Table 19–3: Budgeting practices of large advertisers	Objective and task	63%
	Percent expected sales	53
	Percent past sales	20
Source: Charles H. Patti and Vincent Blasko, "Budgeting Practices of Big Advertisers," *Journal of Advertising Research*, December 1981, pp. 23–29. Reprinted from the *Journal of Advertising Research* © Copyright 1981, by the Advertising Research Foundation.	Affordable	20
	Match competitors	24
	Quantitative methods	51
	Arbitrary	4

reporting the use of certain methods for setting budgets. The results point out that many firms use a combination of methods.[21]

Management of program elements

Once the overall budget is established, the focus turns to the development of strategies and tactics for each form of promotion within the promotional mix. The factors influencing the promotional blend (discussed earlier) must be considered here. Specific decisions with respect to advertising, personal selling, and the other elements are made. A sequence of decisions that might occur for advertising is shown in Figure 19–12. Analogous sequences would exist for other elements. (Key decision areas in advertising and personal selling will be examined in greater depth in the following chapters.)

An outcome of the process by which objectives and strategies for each form of promotion are developed is an allocation of the total budget to each form. Budgets will be established based on the tasks to be performed by each form of promotion. Often, this will require a modification in the overall budget.

Coordination and integration. The implementation of each form of promotion requires a coordinated, integrated approach to the management of promotional strategy. Two important considerations are evident here. First, individual forms of promotion should complement each other: advertising should enhance the personal selling effort, and vice versa. Second, managerial talent should be skillfully used, especially when outside agents (e.g., advertising agencies) are used. The use of outside agents requires an appropriate division of responsibility between internal and agent personnel.

Difficulties encountered in coordinating the promotional effort may require modifications in one or more of the individual forms of promotion. Such modifications may range from changes in a message to simply per-

---

[21] Charles H. Patti and Vincent Blasko, "Budgeting Practices of Big Advertisers," *Journal of Advertising Research,* December 1981, pp. 23–29.

sonnel replacement. Significant modifications may necessitate a budgetary revision.

For the Apple IIc, advertising and sales promotion directed at dealers were major elements in the initial promotional program. For sales promotion, Apple spent $2 million on a one-day show to introduce the IIc to dealers. The show was a blend of pep rally, rock concert, and revival meeting for 4,000 attendees.

Apple directs advertising for the IIc at parents and children. Commercial messages promote the huge amount of software available for the IIc. Apple makes direct comparisons to IBM on this feature. Market research by Apple showed that children influence the purchase of a computer by a family. Therefore, Apple placed ads for the IIc in children's magazines.

Evaluation and control

A key element in any strategic management process is an evaluation of the implemented strategy. Information feedback that assesses the effectiveness of promotional strategy should therefore be incorporated into the management of promotion. The ultimate measure of effectiveness is sales. However, to separate the effects of promotion on sales is difficult because sales result from the impact of the entire marketing program. Therefore, much of the assessment of promotion focuses on measures relating to its communication effects—exposure, recall, readership, etc. (Specific measures of the effectiveness of advertising and personal selling will be discussed in the next two chapters.) However, early returns on the IIc suggested a major impact of promotion on sales. In the first seven hours of its debut, Apple took orders for 50,000 units of the IIc. By comparison, it took Apple 2.5 years to sell that many units of the original Apple.

The evaluation of the effects of promotion is part of the control process. When these effects fall short of desired levels, modifications in the promotional program are usually necessary. This possibility is indicated in Figure 19–12 by an upward flow of arrows through the framework.

Each implementation of this strategic process adds to the experience of the organization in formulating promotional strategy. The strengths and weaknesses of the promotional plan should be analyzed in a postmortem analysis. They should be used in further implementations of the process during the situation analysis stage. The accumulation of experience should enhance future promotional planning if procedures for systematically incorporating it into the process are established.

SUMMARY

Promotional strategy is the set of activities within a total marketing program that an organization employs in communicating to buyers in the attempt to stimulate demand for the organization's offering. Promotion is a communications strategy; it seeks to inform, persuade, and remind buyers so that a preference on the part of buyers is established. The ultimate effect is to influence the demand curve for the offering of the organization.

Promotional strategy consists of advertising, personal selling, packaging, public relations, publicity, and sales promotion. These activities blend together to represent the overall promotional program. The optimal promotional blend is a function of promotional resources, nature of the product, push–pull strategy, life-cycle stage of the product, and nature of the market.

Since promotion represents a form of communication, insights into its use are provided by communications theory. A useful model of the communications process includes source, encoding, channel, audience response, feedback, and noise. The model applies to the communications process for an individual message.

Systematic planning of the overall promotional program is important. Situation analysis followed by establishment of promotional objectives should occur. A tentative budget for the program should be estimated. Individual promotional activities should be developed and managed in coordinated, integrated fashion. Feedback regarding the effects of promotion should be provided. Finally, an evaluation of the strengths and weaknesses of a program should serve as input to subsequent planning efforts.

KEY CONCEPTS

Promotional strategy
Advertising
Personal selling
Packaging as promotion
Public relations
Publicity
Sales promotion
Manufacturer-to-consumer sales promotion
Manufacturer-to-industrial-user sales promotion
Manufacturer-to-wholesaler sales promotion
Buying allowance
Manufacturer-to-retailer sales promotion
Advertising and display allowance
Point-of-purchase (POP) display
Wholesaler-to-organizational-user sales promotion
Wholesaler-to-retailer sales promotion

Retailer-to-consumer sales promotion
Push strategy
Pull strategy
Source
Source credibility
Encoding
Message content
Rational appeal
Emotional appeal
Fear appeal
Humorous appeal
Participation appeal
Message structure
Message sidedness
Message order of presentation
Conclusion drawing
Message format
Verbal code
Nonverbal code
Channel

Audience response
Exposure
Reception
Decoding
Cognitive response
Counterargument
Source derogation
Support argument
Message acceptance/rejection
Noise
Feedback
Equimarginal approach
Return on investment (ROI) approach
Percentage of sales (POS) approach
Competitive parity approach
Market share approach
All-you-can-afford approach
Objective and task approach

DISCUSSION QUESTIONS AND EXERCISES

1. What is promotion trying to accomplish in its influence on the position and shape of the demand curve?

2. Examine the package of a product that you recently bought. Analyze the package in terms of its informational, persuasive, and reminder content. Which of these roles does its nonverbal content play?

3. Find examples of positive and negative publicity about a company or one of its products. For the positive examples try to ascertain from the content of the message how public relations played a role in the publicity.

4. What types of sales promotion, if any, would be appropriate in the following situations?
   a. Introduction of a new packaged good.
   b. Building brand loyalty to a convenience good.
   c. Building brand loyalty to a shopping good.
   d. Introduction of new capital equipment.

5. What promotional blend would be appropriate in the following situations?
   a. New brand of frozen orange juice.
   b. Mature industrial good.
   c. Pushing a new style of furniture.
   d. A new small retail business.
   e. A declining brand of a consumer shopping good.
   f. A firm marketing to organizations in the "Silicon Valley."

6. Using the communications model as a framework, develop the personal selling message for this course. Link each element of the model to the message. Who is the source? What is the target audience? What appeal, structure, and format are you using? What cognitive responses can you expect?

7. Interview a businessperson responsible for promotional decision making. Using the strategic planning process as a framework, determine how this person makes promotional decisions.

CHAPTER 20

Advertising management

Decision areas in advertising management
    Advertising budgets
    Selection and use of advertising agencies
    Advertising objectives
    Message formulation (the ''creative''
        process)
    Message execution
    Media selection
    Media scheduling
    Measuring advertising effectiveness

The regulatory environment of advertising
    Self-regulation
    Governmental regulation

Summary

Key concepts

Discussion questions and exercises

The nature and importance of advertising
    The role of advertising in an organization
    Advertising expenditures
    Types of advertisers
    Types of advertisements
    Advertising campaigns
    Types of advertising decisions

Of all the promotional activities conducted by businesses and other organizations, advertising is probably the most evident because it touches the greatest number of consumers. Of course, this ability to reach large numbers of buyers with a single exposure is the dominant reason for its use as a form of promotion. Advertising is *mass communication*. It conveys product-related information to millions of buyers, often at a cost of less than a penny for each buyer reached.

On the surface, advertising seems simple. It is nonpersonal, and it usually has a rather brief message. However, a deeper look reveals a great deal of complexity. Advertising comes in many forms, is used for a variety of purposes, and occurs in several media. Many decisions are inherent in the use of advertising as a form of promotion. This chapter takes a deeper look at advertising by considering its nature and importance, the major decision areas faced in using advertising, procedures for assessing its performance, and the legal constraints placed on its use.

THE NATURE AND IMPORTANCE OF ADVERTISING

Perhaps the best way to appreciate the nature and importance of advertising is to consider its role in an organization. (See Figure 20–1.)

The role of advertising in an organization

Advertising informs, persuades, reminds. Advertising, of course, performs the same general roles of promotion as a whole: it informs buyers of the existence and nature of a product, may attempt to persuade them to purchase the advertised brand, and reinforces the buying behavior of the brand's existing users. In general, advertising is more effective in building awareness of a brand and maintaining conviction toward it. The development of favorable attitudes and initial brand preference results from factors other than advertising (personal selling, direct experience).

Advertising can substitute for personal selling. Advertising is a form of promotion, just as personal selling is. It performs functions that personal selling performs—but in much different fashion. Advertising is mass communication. One ad can reach thousands, even millions, of consumers.

Advertising complements personal selling. Most organizations use a blend of promotional activities, including both advertising and personal selling. While advertising may substitute for personal selling, it usually exists in conjunction with it. Therefore, advertising's more dominant role

**Figure 20–1:
The role of advertising in an organization**

Advertising
— informs, persuades, reminds.
— can substitute for personal selling.
— complements personal selling.

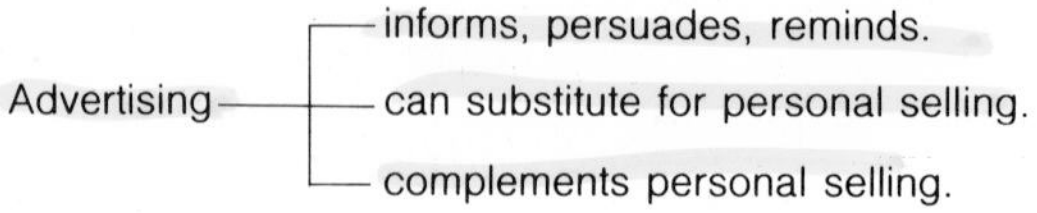

"I don't know who you are.

I don't know your company.

I don't know your company's product.

I don't know what your company stands for.

I don't know your company's customers.

I don't know your company's record.

I don't know your company's reputation.

Now—what was it you wanted to sell me?"

MORAL: Sales start **before** your salesman calls—with business publication advertising.

McGRAW-HILL MAGAZINES
BUSINESS • PROFESSIONAL • TECHNICAL

is to complement and enhance personal selling. Advertising informs buyers and creates interest; then the personal selling activity must take over to convince a buyer of the product's virtues and close the sale. Without advertising, the task of the salesperson is more difficult—a point excellently depicted in a classic McGraw-Hill ad. (See Figure 20–2.)

Advertising expenditures

Another way to appreciate the importance of advertising is to consider the dollars spent on it by major national advertisers. (See Table 20–1.) Substantial expenditures—reaching well into the hundreds of millions of dollars—reflect the importance these firms attach to advertising in their promotional efforts.

Several points are worth noting about these advertising budgets. First, the firms in Table 20–1 are the *biggest* advertisers at the national level. They are not representative of the large majority of American companies; most companies spend considerably less than these firms. Second, while these advertising budgets are large, notice how small a percentage of total sales revenue they represent. Most of the budgets are less than 10 percent of sales, and the majority of them are under 5 percent. Finally, consider the diversity of industries represented in the list. Major retailers, auto companies, companies offering wide lines of household and food items, tobacco companies, oil companies, communication companies, and entertainment companies are all represented. Also note the presence of the U.S. government. Clearly, advertising is a vital activity to a broad spectrum of organizations.

Table 20–1: Major advertisers in 1982

Rank	Company	Advertising expenditures in $ millions	Sales in $ millions	Advertising as a percent of sales
1.	Procter & Gamble	726.1	12,452.0	5.8
2.	Sears, Roebuck	631.2	30,020.0	2.1
3.	General Motors	549.0	60,025.6	0.9
4.	R. J. Reynolds	530.3	13,057.0	4.1
5.	Phillip Morris	501.7	11,716.1	4.3
6.	General Foods	429.1	8,256.4	5.2
7.	AT&T	373.6	65,757.0	0.6
8.	K mart	365.3	16,772.2	2.2
9.	Nabisco	335.2	5,871.1	5.7
10.	American Home Products	325.4	4,580.0	7.1
11.	Mobil	320.0	64,137.0	0.5
12.	Ford Motor Co.	313.5	37,062.2	0.9
13.	PepsiCo	305.0	7,449.0	4.1
14.	Unilever U.S.	304.6	2,954.9	10.3
15.	Warner-Lambert	294.7	3,246.0	9.1
25.	Warner Communications	232.2	3,990.0	5.8
29.	U.S. Government	205.5	n.a.	n.a.
41.	CBS	159.0	4,122.8	3.9
49.	Time, Inc.	130.1	3,564.0	3.7
63.	American Express	95.5	8,093.0	1.2
74.	IBM	75.0	34,364.0	0.2
86.	20th Century-Fox	65.0	560.7	11.6
97.	Wendy's	44.9	1,632.4	2.8
99.	Gallo Winery	42.9	620.0	6.9

Source: Reprinted with permission from the September 8, 1983, issue of *Advertising Age.* Copyright 1983 by Crain Communications, Inc.

Types of advertisers

advertiser

> An **advertiser** is any organization or individual who communicates, in non-personal fashion through various media, a message directed at a target audience.

There are virtually no limits to the types of organizations that advertise. All types of producers (consumer goods, industrial goods, services) advertise. Retailers, of course, advertise heavily to consumers. Nor is advertising restricted to commercial firms. Nonprofit organizations (military services; charities; political parties and candidates; health organizations; federal, state, and local governments) also need to communicate information to individuals and influence their behavior. This chapter will consider advertising primarily in the context of commercial organizations, however.

Types of advertisements

The nature of advertising is further reflected by the various types of advertisements that can be used. These types are distinguished by the content and purpose of the ad, the target audience, and the sponsors of the ad. Figure 20–3 summarizes the type of advertisements.

Product advertising. This type of ad is concerned with a product or service.

product advertising

> **Product advertising** presents information and/or persuasive appeals about products and services.

Figure 20–3: Types of advertisements

Type	Description
Product	Presents information and/or persuasive appeals about products and services
Pioneer	Presents messages about a product class to stimulate primary demand
Competitive	Presents brand-oriented messages designed to stimulate selective demand
Comparative	Makes direct comparisons between advertised and competing brands
Institutional	Seeks to enhance the overall image of and build goodwill for an organization
Trade	Seeks to stimulate reseller demand through messages in trade media
Cooperative	More than one party shares in cost of advertising
Horizontal cooperative	Group of retailers sponsors a common ad for a product
Vertical cooperative	Manufacturer shares in cost of retail ad

Stimulating primary demand in the industrial market.

Rail contracts are changing the way America moves freight.

Throughout the U.S., hundreds of companies of all sizes ship large quantities of a broad variety of goods by rail every year. They're taking advantage of the innovative changes in the way railroads do business. One change is the dramatic increase in contracts negotiated between railroads and their customers. These contracts give rail users predictable rates, schedules and services, and give railroads flexibility to meet the demands of a highly competitive marketplace. Contracts allow innovative rates and services tailored to the customer's needs, and railroads can make more efficient and cost-effective use of rail equipment. America's modern freight railroads are responding to the challenges of the private enterprise system in fresh and exciting ways. Contracts with rail customers are one of those ways and more than 9,000 have been negotiated in the last three years. For more information, write: New Incentives, Dept. 102, Association of American Railroads, 1920 L St., N.W., Washington, D.C. 20036.

ASSOCIATION
OF AMERICAN
RAILROADS

Some 50% of all passenger vehicles produced in the U.S. are moved safely, efficiently and cost effectively by railroad rack cars.

FREIGHT RAILROADS ARE ON THE MOVE.

Courtesy Association of American Railroads

Product advertising can be further distinguished by the level of demand it attempts to stimulate.

pioneer advertising

Pioneer advertising consists of messages about a product class and is designed to stimulate primary demand.

Luxury can be promoted at the generic level or the brand level. Here we see an effort to stimulate primary demand for a generic luxury item.

Real gold.
Once you get the feel of it nothing can touch it.

FOR A FREE BROCHURE ON BUILDING A KARAT GOLD JEWELRY WARDROBE WRITE: INTERNATIONAL GOLD CORPORATION, LTD., 900 THIRD AVENUE, NEW YORK, N.Y 10022

14K KARAT GOLD

Nothing else feels like real gold.

Courtesy International Gold Corporation, Ltd.

The need to stimulate primary demand exists when a new product class is introduced to the market. Thus, in recent years manufacturers of such products as personal computers and VCRs faced the task of stimulating primary demand. However, pioneer advertising is not restricted to new products. Often sponsored by trade associations, pioneer advertising occurs to increase the consumption of products that have been around for years. For example, faced with declining demand in their product classes, trade associations for milk and coffee have sponsored pioneer advertising for their products.

competitive advertising

> **Competitive advertising** consists of brand-oriented messages designed to stimulate selective demand.

Competitive ads are the ones we see the most. An increasingly popular form of competitive advertising is *comparative advertising.*

comparative advertising

> **Comparative advertising** makes direct comparisons between the advertised brand and one or more competing brands, usually across several attributes.

Lincoln and Samli reviewed the research on the effectiveness of comparative ads and concluded that these are most effective for convenience goods and for new brands.[1] Comparative ads offer brands a potentially effective way to make inroads on the leading brand in a market. For example, Pepsi-Cola's series of "Pepsi Challenge" ads helped the company take over the lead from Coca-Cola in food-store sales.

Institutional advertising. Rather than focusing on the products or services of an organization, some ads promote the organization as a whole.

institutional advertising

> **Institutional advertising** seeks to enhance the overall image of and build goodwill for the organization.

For example, an ad by Exxon pointing out its efforts to find new sources of energy is an institutional ad; an ad emphasizing the engine-cleansing abilities of Exxon's gasoline is a product ad. Institutional ads are often

---

[1] D. J. Lincoln and A. C. Samli, "Empirical Evidence of Comparative Advertising's Effects: A Review and Synthesis," in *1979 Educator's Conference Proceedings,* ed. N. Beckwith, M. Houston, R. Mittelstaedt, K. Monroe, and S. Ward (Chicago: American Marketing Association, 1979), pp. 367–72.

This is an information-type ad

IN 1980, HANDGUNS KILLED 77 PEOPLE IN JAPAN. 8 IN GREAT BRITAIN. 24 IN SWITZERLAND. 8 IN CANADA. 23 IN ISRAEL. 18 IN SWEDEN. 4 IN AUSTRALIA. 11,522 IN THE UNITED STATES.

GOD BLESS AMERICA.

The pen is mightier than the gun.
Write Handgun Control, Inc. Now.
810 18th Street N.W., Washington, D.C. 20006
Or call (202) 638-4723

STOP HANDGUN CRIME BEFORE IT STOPS YOU.

Courtesy Handgun Control, Inc.

Motivation with psychological appeals is often necessary with standardized products like perfume

ENJOLI
MIDNIGHT
THE MYSTERIOUSLY ROMANTIC FRAGRANCE...
FOR THE OTHER 8 HOURS IN YOUR LIFE.

© CHARLES OF THE RITZ GROUP LTD. 1984

CIMARRON '84
THIS ONE'S GOT THE TOUCH.

The Cadillac touch. It's Electronic Fuel Injection, matched by
a tenacious Touring Suspension that comes to grips with the road.
It's leather-faced front bucket seats with lumbar support behind
a leather-trimmed steering wheel that lets you know you're in control.
It's new grille and taillight styling. Laser-accurate quality fits.
It's Cimarron '84...with something no other car in its class has.
The Cadillac touch.

BEST OF ALL...IT'S A CADILLAC.
Let's Get It Together...Buckle Up.

Courtesy Cadillac Motor Car Division

A common approach showing the product in use

Go Bass or go barefoot.

Courtesy G. H. Bass & Co.

The brand
familiarization
approach often involves
only the brand name
and a visual
presentation of the
product

NUNN BUSH

Nunn Bush Shoe Company, Milwaukee, Wisconsin 53201

Courtesy Nunn Bush Shoe Company

The symbolic association approach can be used to convey a key attribute of the product

Courtesy Leading Edge Products, Inc.

A comparative ad.

NEC/3510	QUME/Sprint 11	DIABLO/630	DAISYWRITER 2000
$2290	$1990	$2340	$1495

Price doesn't count.

Productivity is everything. And when it comes to printing,
the letter-quality Daisywriter 2000 outperforms the competition by
producing a lot more pages a day. Every day!
Why does the Daisywriter 2000 cost less?
The real question is why pay more?
Simply send your business card for complete information,
or call toll free. 800-255-5550, ext. 500.
In Colorado: 303-799-4900, ext. 500.

daisywriter®
The printer you'll judge others by.

 **Computers International Incorporated**
3540 Wilshire Boulevard, Los Angeles, CA 90010 / Tel: (213) 386-3111 / TWX/Telex: 910-321-4209

Summary of Daisywriter 2000 comparative testing available upon written request.

Courtesy Computers International
Incorporated

directed at audiences other than buyers—investors and employees, for example. Institutional ads can also be used to retain an organization's identity as it diversifies into new markets.

Trade advertising. Consumer goods manufacturers face a dual marketing task: they stimulate demand for their products both from the consumer marketplace and from the resellers who distribute them. The stimulation of reseller demand—while in large part a task of personal selling—may also involve **trade advertising.**

An institutional ad.

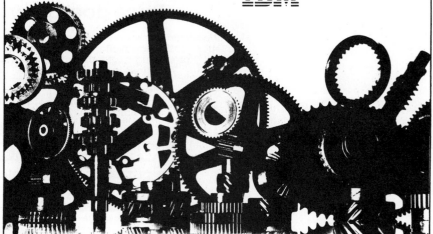

Helping engineers change gears.

The relentless ingenuity of America's engineers has made technological revolution commonplace.

But today, manufacturing engineers face a relentless challenge: to produce goods of ever-higher quality at ever-lower cost. The marketplace, domestic and foreign, demands it.

To meet that challenge, engineers need state-of-the-art training and state-of-the-art tools. This, of course, is a job best done by America's universities. But universities can't do it alone. All sectors of society must help.

That's why IBM is giving $50 million in money and equipment to 22 universities for the creation and expansion of engineering programs in manufacturing systems. The curricula, in part, will include computer-aided design and manufacturing, robotics and lasers, quality control, systems management, and automation.

We expect this investment in education to pay off by helping to keep America's manufacturing in high gear.

And that will pay off for all of us. **IBM**

Courtesy of International Business
Machines Corporation

---

trade advertising

> **Trade advertising** consists of messages directed at resellers that appear in specialized trade publications (e.g., *Progressive Grocer*) or are sent through the mail.

Cooperative advertising. A cost-saving approach to promotion is provided by ***cooperative advertising.***

A cooperative ad.

Courtesy Budget Rent a Car and
United Air Lines

---

cooperative advertising	**Cooperative advertising** occurs when the costs of an advertising message are shared by more than one party.

There are two major forms of cooperative advertising. *Horizontal cooperative advertising* occurs when a group of retailers sponsors a common ad for a brand of a product they carry. Horizontal cooperative advertising is not a common practice because most retailers compete with each other and carry multiple brands. *Vertical cooperative advertising,* on the other hand, is more common. It occurs when advertising that is initiated and implemented by retailers is paid wholly or in part by a manufacturer. It is usually part of an overall program of promotional support provided by a manufacturer. Thus, vertical cooperative advertising is actually sales promotion directed at retailers by manufacturers.

Advertising campaigns

Many advertisers use *advertising campaigns* in their promotional programs.

> An **advertising campaign** is an integrated advertising effort for a product that extends over time. It involves multiple messages (often placed in multiple media) with a common underlying theme.

advertising campaign

The repeated exposure to campaign messages increases consumer learning and reinforces a brand's position in the consumer's mind. A campaign is often a crucial component of a positioning strategy for a brand.

The soft drink industry provides an excellent history of memorable advertising campaigns. Major soft drink brands are advertised with different messages in each media (e.g., magazines, television, radio). The Coca-Cola brand has used a series of effective themes. (See Figure 20–4.) During the 1970s, the 7up brand used a campaign—with "The Uncola" theme—designed to distinctly position it among other product forms and brands.

Figure 20–4: A history of Coca-Cola's campaign themes

1886	Drink Coca-Cola
1905	Coca-Cola revives and sustains
1906	The Great National Temperance Beverage
1922	Thirst knows no season
1925	Six million a day
1927	Around the corner from everywhere
1929	The pause that refreshes
1938	The best friend thirst ever had
1948	Where there's Coke there's hospitality
1949	Along the highway to anywhere
1952	What you want is a Coke
1956	Makes good things taste better
1957	Sign of good taste
1958	The cold, crisp taste of Coke
1963	Things go better with Coke
1970	It's the real thing
1971	I'd like to buy the world a Coke
1975	Look up, America
1976	Coke adds life
1979	Have a Coke and a smile
1982	Coke is it

Source: *The Wall Street Journal,* February 5, 1982, p. 14. Reprinted by permission of *The Wall Street Journal,* © Dow Jones & Company, Inc. 1982. All rights reserved.

Brands in other generic product categories that have been supported by consistently effective campaigns include Volkswagen, Marlboro, Alka-Seltzer, L'eggs, Budweiser, and Avis, to name a few.

DECISION AREAS IN ADVERTISING MANAGEMENT

A variety of key decisions must be made in advertising management. These decisions include: determination of an advertising budget, the decision to use and selection of an advertising agency, determination of campaign and message objectives, the formulation of messages, selection of advertising media and the development of a media mix and schedule, and evaluation of advertising performance. These decisions are made and implemented within the constraints of a regulatory environment. For the remainder of this chapter, we'll focus on important issues within these decision areas and on the nature of the regulatory environment.

Advertising budgets

The advertising budget grows with advertising's importance as a component of promotional strategy. Therefore, our discussions in Chapter 19 of factors influencing promotional strategy and promotional budgeting practices highlight the key issues in setting advertising budgets.

Selection and use of advertising agencies

Most major advertisers use advertising agencies to help manage their advertising programs. An ad agency helps a firm develop and implement advertising strategy. The biggest, *full-service advertising agencies* (see Table 20–2) provide a variety of advertising-related services to clients: the creative dimension (positioning strategy, message appeal, copy preparation), media selection and scheduling, consumer research, consultation about branding and packaging, publicity planning, and preparation of point-of-sale material. *Limited-service advertising agencies* ("boutiques") offer more specialized services.

Traditionally, ad agencies realize their income through a combination of commissions and services fees. Commissions are earned by placing ads in the media: recognized agencies receive a 15 percent discount on the price of time or space bought but bill clients for the full amount. If, for example, an agency purchases $100,000 of TV network time for a client, the network will bill the agency $85,000. The agency bills its client the full $100,000, realizing a gain of $15,000. Other agency services (e.g., research, copy preparation) are offered on a cost-plus-fee basis, with the fee determined through agency–client negotiations.

The traditional 15 percent commission approach appears to be declining in use. A recent study reports that strict adherence to the commission approach is uncommon. The increasing diversity of services offered by agencies is moving more and more of them to a negotiated-fee basis for billing clients.[2]

---

[2] "The 15 percent Media Commission Is on the Way toward Becoming a Relic in Ad Agency Compensation Plans," *Marketing News,* June 10, 1983, p. 9.

Table 20–2: Ten largest advertising agencies in U.S. income, 1983

Rank	Agency	Gross income ($ millions)	Some client brands gained and lost in 1983	
			Gained	Lost
1	Young & Rubicam	274.4	U.S. Postal Service Pabst Extra Light	Spic & Span Atari computers
2	Ted Bates	244.4	Pizza Time	HBO Coors beer
3	Ogilvy & Mather	204.1	Polaroid Barclay cigarettes	Pabst Extra Light Schwinn bicycles
4	BBDO	199.0	Apple computers HBO	Camel cigarettes Thom McAn shoes
5	J. Walter Thompson	189.9	Ameritech Computerland	Sears, Roebuck Miles Labs
6	Foote Cone & Belding	158.9	Kimberly-Clark Colgate-Palmolive	Ramada Hotel Group Fotomat
7	Doyle Dane Bernbach	146.0	Michelin tires Parliament cigarettes	Bulova American Cyanamid
8	Leo Burnett	135.0	American Dental Association Seven-Up	Parliament cigarettes
9	Grey Advertising	125.1	Arby's Clairol	Sentry Insurance Computerland
10	McCann-Erickson	95.4	Diet Coke Alka-Seltzer	Western Airlines *New York Times*

Source: Adapted with permission from the March 28, 1984, issue of *Advertising Age.* Copyright 1984 by Crain Communications, Inc.

In theory, advertising agencies are similar to channel intermediaries: they offer services that firms would otherwise perform themselves. Agencies offer expertise in advertising-related matters. They offer a breadth of experience in a diversity of industries plus the objectivity of an outsider. Therefore, ad agencies can typically offer a higher-quality service than advertisers can achieve on their own at an equivalent cost. The decision to hire an ad agency to perform all or some of the advertising function should be based on such a principle—the extent of marginal benefits to be realized from using an agency versus not using one.

The decision to use an agency also involves choice of the specific agency. Ad agencies are an intensely competitive industry. Competition is based primarily on the quality and extent of services offered. When an advertiser seeks an agency, it typically solicits proposals for a campaign and ancillary services from several agencies. Each agency prepares and presents its proposal to the potential client, who then makes a selection on the basis of the presentations. Bozell & Jacobs reportedly spent $1 million on a presentation to win the American Airlines account.[3]

---

[3] Tom Boyer, "Bozell's American Pitch," *Advertising Age,* June 8, 1981, p. 3.

The key figure in the agency is the *account executive,* the individual who is in closest day-to-day contact with the client. An account executive (AE) is likely to be assigned full time to a client's brand. He or she represents the agency to the client and the client to the agency. As a result, the AE needs a thorough knowledge of both the client's business and the operations of the agency to organize and control the flow of work on the account from initial planning through execution. The AE's responsibilities include collecting, analyzing, and interpreting all relevant facts on the brand; developing strategy; presenting the agency's plans and creative work; coordinating the implementation of these plans; and monitoring the results.

Advertising objectives

The objectives of an advertising message or campaign relate to (1) the specification of a target audience and (2) the establishment of message or campaign purpose—what the advertiser is trying to accomplish in the message or campaign. Both of these considerations should grow out of the overall marketing objectives for a brand. (See Figure 20–5.)

Target audience. The nature of the target audience must be considered in determining message purpose, message content, and the media. Thus, a profile of the target audience, much like profiles of market segments (Chapter 9), should be drawn up. The target audience should be

Figure 20–5: Determining advertising objectives

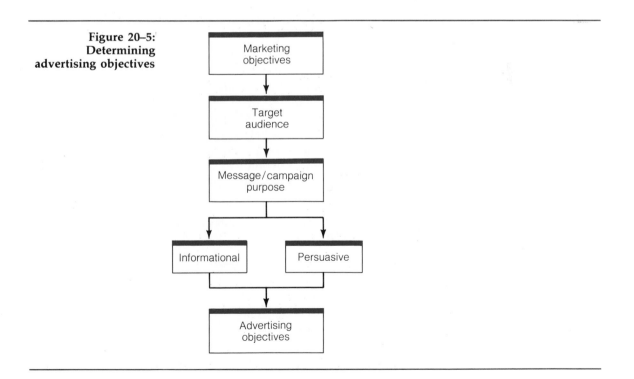

defined in terms of demographic (age, sex, etc.), socioeconomic (income, education, etc.), and marketplace behavior (e.g., media-usage behavior) characteristics to the fullest extent possible. Then, the other aspects of the advertising strategy can be determined more effectively—and the result will be a matching of message purpose, message content, and media with the target audience.

Message/campaign purpose.   The second important consideration is what you want to achieve through the message or campaign. Two broad distinctions are often made in the purpose of an advertising communication. First, the message may be ***informational.*** It does not seek immediate action on the part of the audience; rather it seeks to inform the audience of the availability and/or nature of the product. Second, the purpose may be ***persuasive.*** Here the message or campaign has the explicit purpose of increasing sales through persuasion.

These two objectives suggest that the "hierarchy of effects" (awareness, interest, evaluation, trial, adoption) is a useful framework for determining the purpose of a specific message or campaign as well as for understanding the overall role of advertising. Informational messages seek effects early in the hierarchy; persuasive messages seek effects at later levels. Therefore, in determining the purpose of a message or campaign it is important to know the current level of the target audience with respect to the brand to be advertised. The general purpose then becomes to move the audience to the next level. Thus, if the audience is unaware of the brand, the primary purpose of the campaign is to create awareness. If the audience is aware but lacks interest, the purpose is to create interest. If favorable attitudes exist, the purpose may be to convert them to preference. As the purpose of advertising moves from creating awareness to influencing behavior, it moves from an information to a persuasive orientation.

Advertising objectives should be stated in precise, quantitative terms that allow measurement of their achievement. Informational objectives generally fit these requirements better than persuasive objectives because it is difficult to separate advertising's contributions to sales from the contributions of other marketing decision variables. Nonetheless, the following examples of how advertising objectives might be stated include informational as well as persuasive objectives:

1. Increase brand awareness from 50 to 75 percent in the target audience (informational).
2. Shift consumer beliefs of the quality level of our brand from average to above-average quality (informational and persuasive).
3. Get 20 percent of nonusers in the target audience to make a trial purchase (persuasive).
4. Increase heavy users of our brand by 15 percent (persuasive).

Message formulation (the "creative" process)

In the "creative" process, an advertising message or campaign is formulated from knowledge of the target audience and the stated objectives of the message or campaign. ("Creatives" translate ad objectives into an actual message.) This creative process includes the selection of appeals, message conceptualization, nonverbal elements of the ad, graphics and design, and production.

Message content.   Simon presents eight *approaches to message content* as ways to activate buyer behavior toward a product.[4] These approaches provide general guidelines to message content and have implications for message appeal, structure, and format:

1. *Information.* In this approach the ad presents straightforward facts and nothing else. Arguments based on the facts or implications drawn from the facts are not presented. Information ads are frequently found in, but are not restricted to, the Yellow Pages of a telephone directory and the classified section of a newspaper. Ads that present nothing more than the price of a product are one form of information ads.

2. *Argument.* The argument approach provides a "reason-why" type of content. Facts are presented as reasons to buy. Generally, such ads must present relatively large amounts of information in order to shape an argument. And therefore, to be effective, they must be read thoroughly by the audience. Comparative ads are a form of argument ads.

3. *Motivation with psychological appeals.* This approach attempts to attach emotional value to a product. It is frequently used with relatively standardized consumer products (perfume, beer) whose primary basis for differentiation is the image that the brand connotes for its users.

4. *Repeated assertion.* This approach employs a hard-sell technique in which one simple message is repeated and repeated. Over-the-counter drugs make frequent use of the repeated-assertion ad because few people have an intrinsic interest in these products or in messages about them. Frequent repetition of a simple line (e.g., "Plop, plop, fizz, fizz, oh, what a relief it is") becomes necessary for learning.

5. *Command.* This type of ad simply directs the audience to behave in a certain way and—like the repeated-assertion—requires frequent repetition. It is often a hard-sell approach, but not necessarily so. An example of a command would be "Drink Dr Pepper." Command ads serve a reminder purpose for relatively well-known consumer brands.

6. *Brand familiarization.* In this approach the purpose is to keep a brand name in the eyes of the public (a reminder purpose again) and essentially present only the brand name (and perhaps an illustration of the product). Unlike information ads, no information about the brand

---

[4] Julian L. Simon, *The Management of Advertising* (Englewood Cliffs, N.J.: Prentice-Hall, 1971), pp. 174–83.

is presented. Brand familiarization ads are used frequently in billboard advertising.

7. *Symbolic association.* This approach is the soft-sell version of repeated assertion. Here, one single message is conveyed in symbolic rather than direct fashion. The principle is to link the brand to a place, person, event, or other symbol that will have a positive connotation for the target audience. With this linkage repeated over time, the symbol begins to stand for the product. A classic example of symbolic association is the "Marlboro Man." Symbolic association ads are appropriate for standardized consumer goods where physical differences between competitive brands are minimal.

8. *Imitation.* In social psychology it is recognized that a significant portion of human behavior is shaped through imitation of others. We behave as we feel others whom we seek to be like behave. Imitation ads apply this aspect of behavior by associating a brand with a celebrity or with an unknown person with whom the audience can identify.

These approaches to ad content are by no means mutually exclusive. The use of one approach in an ad does not preclude the use of another. An ad can incorporate two, or even more, of the approaches. Furthermore, the more emotional approaches can have one effect on one person and a different effect on another. For example, the Marlboro Man may have a symbolic-association effect on one person and an imitation effect on another.

Implications for message appeal, structure, format.   Simon's classification scheme for ads is particularly useful because each approach suggests implications for types of appeals, message structure, and message format. (See Table 20–3.) Rational appeals are suggested by information, argument, and, to some extent, motivation. Emotional appeals are associated with motivation, symbolic association, and imitation. Fear appeals will likely use an argument and/or motivation approach.

The different approaches accommodate the dimensions of message structure to varying extents. One-sided messages fit all of the approaches, but a two-sided message requires an argument or motivation approach. Conclusion drawing is implicit in argument, motivation, and even repeated assertion.

Finally, with respect to message format, the approaches will vary in the extent to which they use verbal versus visual codes. Verbal codes will be used to a greater extent in information, argument, motivation, repeated-assertion, and command ads. Visual codes will be more dominant in brand-familiarization, symbolic-association, and imitation ads.

Factors influencing appropriateness of each approach.   Several factors suggest the appropriateness of any one of the approaches to ad content. (Also see Table 20–4.) These are not hard-and-fast rules:

Table 20–3: Relationship of ad message dimensions to Simon's types of ads	Dimensions of ad message	Appropriate types of ads
	Appeal	
	Rational	Information, argument, motivation
	Emotional	Motivation, symbolic association, imitation
	Fear	Argument, motivation
	Structure	
	One-sided	All
	Two-sided	Argument, motivation
	Conclusion-drawing	Argument, motivation, repeated-assertion
	Format	
	Verbal	Information, argument, motivation, repeated-assertion, command
	Visual	Brand familiarization, symbolic association, imitation

Table 20–4: Factors influencing appropriate type of ad	Factor	Appropriate types of ads
	1. Industrial versus consumer good	Industrial: Information, argument Consumer: All; subsequent factors narrow choice
	2. Characterization of product	
	Style goods	Imitation, symbolic association
	Mechanical goods	Information, argument
	Sensory	Imitation, symbolic association
	Services	Information, argument
	Hidden benefits	Information, argument, motivation
	3. Necessity, convenience, or luxury goods	Necessity and convenience: Most types are appropriate but must stress brand differentiation and be competition-oriented Luxury: Motivation, argument
	4. Target audience	Intelligent audiences require information, argument
	5. Stage of generic product acceptance	New generic products require information, then move to argument, and finally motivation
	6. Stage of brand acceptance	New brands: Information, then argument, then brand familiarization Established brands: Symbolic association, command, repeated-assertion, imitation
	7. Price range	High price: Information, argument, motivation Low price: Reminder-oriented (e.g., repeated-assertion)
	8. Purchase frequency	Parallels price range
	9. Homogeneity of competing brands	Standardized: Symbolic association, imitation, motivation Heterogeneous: Argument, motivation

Source: Extracted from Julian L. Simon, *The Management of Advertising* (Englewood Cliffs, N.J.: Prentice-Hall, 1971), pp. 184–91.

1. *Industrial or consumer good.* The motives and values underlying industrial buyers are usually different from those of consumers. The quality and service orientations of industrial buyers suggest the information and argument approaches are most appropriate for ads directed at the industrial market. For consumer goods, a diversity of approaches might be used. The remaining factors should help narrow them down for a particular situation.

2. *Best way to characterize product.* Simon suggests that the general nature of a product should be considered in determining the appropriateness of an approach. He identifies the following ways to characterize the general nature of a product:

   a. *Style.* Style goods are those whose purchases are dominated by their visual nature (e.g., fashion goods, furniture). More emotional approaches to ad content become appropriate (e.g., imitation, symbolic association).

   b. *Mechanical.* Goods with a strong mechanical nature usually require ads with a dominant information or argument approach.

   c. *Sensory.* A sensory good is one whose benefits are realized by the user through any of the five senses. It is difficult to verbally describe sensation; therefore, symbolic-association and imitation ads are useful for sensory goods.

   d. *Services.* Because of their intangible nature, services often defy illustration and must be verbally described. Argument and information become useful approaches.

   e. *Hidden benefit.* These goods provide benefits that are not visible (e.g., medicine, nutritious food). Information, argument, and motivation become useful approaches to revealing these hidden benefits.

3. *Necessity, convenience, or luxury good.* Necessity and convenience goods often require brand-differentiation and competition-oriented approaches in their ads. A luxury good, by definition, is unnecessary; people must be motivated to buy it. Motivation ads become more appropriate for luxury goods.

4. *Intelligence and sophistication of target audience.* The intelligence of an audience influences the types of persuasive messages that would be effective. More intelligent people are less likely to be swayed by generalities, commands, and irrelevant material. Information and argument work better here.

5. *Stage of product class acceptance.* Generic products new to the market may not require attention-getting efforts. People are interested in the product because of its newness and the attendant publicity surrounding a new generic product. They want facts. New generic products, therefore, require information ads. Over time, the straight facts, as they become known, must be tied together to form an

argument. As the argument becomes old, the motivation method may create new reasons for those who have yet to use the product to try it.

6. *Stage of brand acceptance.* Even when the generic product is old, new and modified brands often enter the marketplace. They, too, must be advertised in an information manner initially and proceed through motivation and brand familiarization. Well-established brands will make greater use of symbolic association, command, repeated assertion, and imitation.

7. *Price range.* The higher the price of the product, the greater the prepurchase deliberation. High-priced products, therefore, must accommodate the buyer's need for a "rational" decision process through the use of information, argument, and motivation. Low-priced products bought in more spontaneous fashion can use more reminder-oriented approaches.

8. *Frequency of purchase.* Generally, the level of repeat purchases of a product correlates strongly with price level in an inverse manner. Thus, advertising approaches for frequently versus infrequently purchased products parallel those for low- versus high-priced products.

9. *Homogeneity of competing brands.* When real differences exist between brands, argument and motivation can effectively be used to point out these differences. However, standardized competing brands establish their distinctiveness through symbolic association, imitation, and motivation.

Message execution

Once the overall approach to an advertising message has been formulated, the next task is to execute the approach. Three important aspects of **message execution** must be considered: copy, nonverbal elements, and layout.

Copy

copy	Copy refers to the verbal codes of an advertising message.

Copy can be broken down into the following components, as shown in the accompanying Neutrogena ad:

1. **Headline.** Much like in a news story, the headline is the "grabber" and sometimes all that is read or heard. It must capture the essence of what is to follow. The headline can perform various roles: provide news, make product claims, give advice, identify the target audience, arouse curiosity, or identify the product or company

The components of message copy.

Headline → **SKIN-SMOOTHING.**

Subheadline → **WALK OUT OF THE SHOWER WITH UP TO 28% SMOOTHER SKIN.**

Body copy →

Smoother skin all over your body isn't a claim, not a hope, but a Neutrogena® fact.

Tests have proven that women with normal skin actually had 12-28% smoother skin after using Neutrogena Rainbath® Shower and Bath Gel.

Rainbath is truly a product with a purpose, hard to compare to all of the frilly bath and shower indulgences sold today.

Rainbath functions. Performs. If you have dry or rough skin, you can expect smoother, softer skin every time you use it. Rainbath also does two functions at once. When used in a shower or bath, Rainbath not only brings your skin to a much higher degree of smoothness, softness, silkiness, but cleans your skin with the famed Neutrogena effectiveness and mildness.

Unlike soaps you may have used, Rainbath isn't drying or skinstripping, leaving virtually no filmy, soapy residue to clog your pores or cause skin irritation.

Neutrogena Rainbath. It's not a bath or shower luxury. It's a skin necessity, if smoother, cleaner, more beautiful skin is what you want to see and feel.

And who doesn't.

NEUTROGENA ← Signature

Courtesy Neutrogena Corporation

name.[5] Any one headline may perform several of these roles simultaneously.

2. **Subheadline.** The subheadline reinforces or extends the headline and links it to the remainder of the ad.

3. **Body copy.** This is the heart of the verbal portion of the ad. Here main points of the ad are delivered, often in paragraph form.

4. **Signature.** The signature closes the ad by naming (or renaming) the sponsor, perhaps accompanied by a slogan.

Nonverbal elements. The **nonverbal elements** should complement the verbal content so that the impact of the ad is enhanced. Various forms of, or roles that can be played by, nonverbal elements include:[6]

---

[5] J. F. Engel, M. F. Warshaw, and T. C. Kinnear, *Promotional Strategy,* 5th ed. (Homewood, Ill.: Richard D. Irwin, 1983), p. 597.

[6] Adapted from ibid., pp. 604–12.

1. *The product alone.* Many products require no visualization beyond their mere presence. Distinctive, well-known brands fit this category.

2. *The product in a setting.* Showing the product in a setting can enhance its appeal—especially when symbolic association is sought—and the attention-getting power of the ad.

Showing the product in use.

Courtesy Bausch & Lomb

3. *The product in use.* Perhaps the most popular form of visualization, showing the product in use can readily portray the manner in which its benefits can be realized and explain how to use it most effectively.

4. *Benefits of the product.* Showing the outcome of using the product can be particularly effective. Before–after products with multiple uses especially can use this form of visualization.

5. *Featuring product details.* Here new or important features of a product are focused upon visually. Technical products might use this form of visual display.

6. *Dramatizing the headline.* Often it is useful to enhance the power of the headline by dramatizing it in a visual manner.

7. *Dramatizing evidence.* If evidence of claims is being presented, it can be effective to visualize this evidence by showing the test in progress or visualizing its results.

8. *Color.* Although it increases cost, color, with its eye-catching powers, esthetic appeal, and dramatization capabilities, usually makes a more effective ad.

9. *Sound.* In broadcast advertising (especially radio ads) sound is a crucial element. Music, pleasant voices, special effects all create a mood, symbolize the product, dramatize its presentation, and make the ad more memorable.

The use of nonverbal elements in advertising messages is taking on greater importance than ever before. As consumers are increasingly bombarded with advertising, advertisers will depend more heavily on nonverbal elements to distinguish their messages.

Figure 20–6: Integrating copy and nonverbal elements into message layout

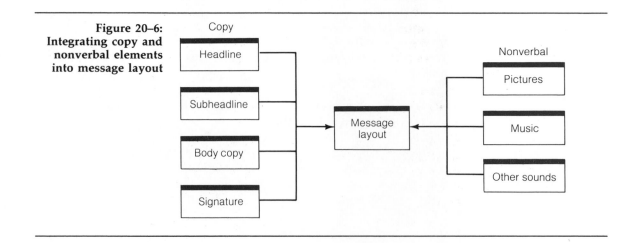

Layout

layout	The **layout** of an ad is the manner in which the elements of copy and the nonverbal portions of the message are arranged to form an integrated whole. (See Figure 20–6.)

There is considerable flexibility in this aspect of the creative process. But advertisers often try to carry the audience through a sequence of stages within the ad itself by using the *AIDA* approach: they must first capture Attention, develop Interest, create Desire, and induce Action. Using the AIDA structure, the roles of the various message components can be assigned (see Table 20–5) and the most effective layout developed. Keep in mind that AIDA suggests the *roles* to be performed within the ad, not the order or position in which the elements appear. For example, headlines are designed to capture attention and create interest. They may do so at either the beginning, middle, or bottom of the ad. The AIDA structure is, of course, similar to the hierarchy of effects in the overall role of advertising; it may guide the overall advertising program as well as develop individual messages.

Media selection

An advertising program is no better than the *media* used to deliver it. A message, no matter how well conceived, will have no impact if it fails to reach its intended audience. Therefore, media selection is a crucial decision within the area of advertising. In this section we will consider the major types of media available to advertisers, the concept of the *media mix,* criteria to guide the development of a media plan, and the scheduling of advertising through the media.

Types of media.   The major categories of media are identified in Table 20–6, with estimated dollar expenditures in each category from 1980 to the year 2000.

Table 20–5: Message elements and their likely roles	**Elements**	**Roles**
	Headline	Attention, interest
	Subheadline	Interest
	Body copy	Interest, desire, action
	Signature	Action, reinforcement
	Nonverbal	Nonverbal elements can be used to perform any of the roles

Table 20–6:
Media types and
estimated revenues—
1980–2000

	Dollar revenue ($ billions)			
Media type	**1980**	**1990**	**2000**	**Percent increase (1980–2000)**
Newspapers	15.9	35.5	74.2	366.7
Magazines	3.4	9.2	21.0	517.6
Television	12.4	38.7	98.9	697.6
Radio	3.8	8.9	17.8	368.4
Direct mail	7.6	15.8	27.5	261.8
Business and farm publications	1.9	3.9	5.4	184.2
Outdoor and transit	0.6	1.0	1.3	116.7

Source: *Advertising Age*, April 30, 1980, p. 259.

Newspapers. Historically, newspapers have realized the largest share of combined local and national advertising revenues. The newspaper is primarily a local medium whose audience is restricted to the community in which the paper is published and its outlying areas. Much of its advertising revenue, therefore, comes from local retailers. While newspapers will realize substantial growth in advertising revenue, they will ultimately by replaced by television as the No. 1 medium in revenue.

Magazines. Perhaps the most diverse media type is the consumer magazine. Its diversity is reflected in the four major subdivisions of magazines: (1) general-audience magazines (*Readers' Digest*), (2) special-audience magazines (*Modern Maturity, Redbook, Seventeen*), (3) shelter magazines (*Better Homes and Gardens*), and (4) special-interest magazines (*Motor Trend, Golf Digest*).

Note from Table 20–6 that magazines are second only to television in expected growth as an ad medium. A major factor contributing to this growth is the increasing need for advertisers to reach segmented markets. Magazines offer this capability perhaps more than any other medium.

Television. Television has become a powerful promotional tool. It offers advertising capabilities at the local (spot advertising) and national (network advertising) levels. It is the only major medium offering both video and audio capabilities.

Technological advances will contribute to the expected rapid growth of TV as an ad medium. Cable TV, satellite transmissions, and viewer-sender interaction represent technical developments that should enhance television as a marketing force.

Radio. Once a major national advertising and entertainment medium, radio has survived the birth of TV by becoming a predominantly local advertising medium and by using primarily a music-and-news format. The dynamics of radio (more specialized stations, the growth of FM stations) should preserve it as an ad medium.

Direct mail. After newspapers and TV, direct mail realizes the greatest dollar expenditures as a medium. Used by retailers, magazine publishers, and book clubs (to name a few), direct mail offers great selectivity in whom an ad reaches. But direct mail must overcome its "junkmail" image to be effective.

Business and farm publications. This category includes trade magazines directed at professional, occupational, and institutional audiences such as doctors, executives, retailers, and farmers. Much like consumer magazines, trade magazines can be categorized into general-audience types (*Business Week, Fortune*) and special-audience types (*Progressive Grocer, Iron Age*). Industrial marketers, of course, concentrate much of their advertising in these media.

Outdoor and transit. Outdoor advertising (billboards) and transit advertising (buses, taxis) have been around a long time. Outdoor advertising has been attacked by environmentalists for scarring the land but appears to have withstood these attacks.

Miscellaneous. A variety of other minor types of media exist. They include, among others, movie screens, skywriting, and the Yellow Pages.

Media mix. Much like the marketing decision variables form a mix and promotional tools blend into a promotional mix, a major decision within advertising is the development of a **media mix.**

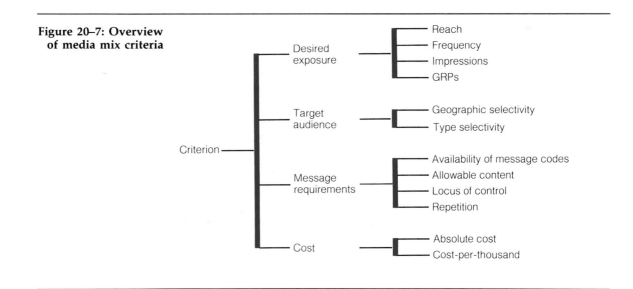

Figure 20–7: Overview of media mix criteria

media mix	The **media mix** of an organization is the blend of general types of media and specific vehicles within each type used to convey its advertising messages.

The determination of the media mix involves strategic decisions at two levels. First, the extent to which each general type of media will be used, if at all, must be determined. (To what extent will the organization use television, radio, magazines, direct mail?) Second, the specific vehicles within each media category must be determined. If consumer magazines are to be used, for example, then the selection must be made of the specific magazines in which to advertise. The use of TV requires decisions about the network, station, and programs on which to advertise.

As with virtually all marketing decisions, the determination of the media mix is made under certain constraints. The most obvious constraint is budgetary: media expenditures must be allocated within a dollar limitation imposed by the promotional budget. Other constraints relate to the physical limitations of any one medium or vehicle. Some media or vehicles restrict the number of messages that can be placed in them over a specified time period. Given these constraints, a major task in advertising management is the selection of a media mix that maximizes the probability of achieving advertising objectives. It is not an easy task. Certain key criteria can guide the media selection, though.

Criteria in media selection.   In this section we consider the important criteria in the media mix decision and the capacity of the major media to meet these criteria. Four key criteria guide the determination of the media mix: (1) desired exposure, (2) target audience, (3) message requirements, and (4) cost. See Figure 20–7 for an overview.

Desired exposure.   The function of advertising media is to deliver a message to a target audience. In formulating the media mix, we should think in terms of a desired level of exposure provided by the media mix. Media objectives can be stated in terms of a desired number of exposures within a target audience.

Several concepts help us understand the exposure level generated by a medium. (Also see Figure 20–8.)

reach	**Reach** is the number of different households (individuals) exposed to at least one message during a given time period (usually four weeks).

For example, if an ad in a local newspaper is seen by 50,000 readers, its reach is 50,000. The size of a medium's audience contributes to its

Figure 20–8: Key concepts relating to exposure level of a medium

Concept	Definition	Calculation example
Reach	Number of different households exposed to at least one message during a given time period	Newspaper ad is seen by 50,000 readers, Reach = 50,000.
Frequency	Average number of times the message reaches a household during a given time period	$\dfrac{(10{,}000 \times 1) + (20{,}000 \times 2) + (15{,}000 \times 3) + (5{,}000 \times 4)}{50{,}000} = 2.3$
Impressions	Total number of exposures delivered by a media plan	$50{,}000 \times 2.3 = 115{,}000$
Gross rating points	Adjusts impressions by percent of market reached	$67 \times 2.3 = 154.1$

reach. Network television provides more reach than other media. Newspapers provide high levels of reach within local markets.

---

frequency | **Frequency** is the average number of times the message reaches a household during the given time period.

For example, if the newspaper ad reaches 10,000 of the 50,000 readers once, 20,000 of them twice, 15,000 three times, and 5,000 four times, frequency would be:

$$\text{Frequency} = \frac{(10{,}000 \times 1) + (20{,}000 \times 2) + (15{,}000 \times 3) + (5{,}000 \times 4)}{50{,}000}$$

$$= \frac{115{,}000}{50{,}000}$$

$$= 2.3$$

Frequency captures the *intensity* of exposure provided by a medium. Through repetition within a time period, television provides intense exposure. And magazines provide frequency to the extent that a single issue is picked up more than once by an individual. Outdoor ads can provide high levels of frequency when placed on frequently traveled routes.

Reach and frequency combine to provide *impressions.*

---

impressions | **Impressions** are the total number of exposures delivered by a media plan.

Impressions are calculated by multiplying the number of individuals who see a message by the average number of times it is seen (Reach × Frequency). In the newspaper example the impressions would be:

$$50,000 \times 2.3 = 115,000 \text{ impressions}$$

Impressions are often translated into **gross rating points (GRPs)** to account for the percentage of a target audience reached. If the market our newspaper ad is trying to reach consists of 75,000 households, then the newspaper has a rating of 67 percent (50,000/75,000) of these households. GRPs are then determined by:

$$\text{Rating} \times \text{Frequency} = 67 \times 2.3 = 154.1$$

The concepts of reach, frequency, and GRPs can be used to state media objectives. For example, if an advertiser determines that it is necessary to reach 60 percent of the market with a frequency of 2.5 in order to achieve an advertising objective of, say, 40 percent awareness, media objectives can then be specified in terms of $60 \times 2.5 = 150$ GRPs. A media mix that delivers 150 GRPs must then be formulated.

Target audience. The target audience that the organization wants to reach through its advertising effort is a crucial factor in determining the media mix. Because of market segmentation, the target audience is often a segment of the overall consumer population. Messages must be placed in media vehicles to which members of the target market are exposed at the necessary level. Therefore, a general guideline in developing the media mix is to match the media to the unique media exposure patterns of the target market.

This guideline suggests that the *selectivity* of a medium is an important criterion to consider in evaluating whether inclusion in the media mix is warranted. The selectivity of a medium refers to its ability to reach a certain segment of the population and not others.

Two dimensions of selectivity should be considered. First, the **geographic selectivity** of a medium refers to its ability to reach only certain geographic areas. This capability is important when advertisers wish to reach only one geographic area or when they wish to send a distinct message to each of several geographic areas. Second, the **type selectivity** of a medium refers to its ability to reach a certain type of consumer and not others. The type of consumer may be defined in terms of any of the bases for market segmentation (demographics, socioeconomic variables, product-usage rates, lifestyle). Type selectivity is important when a firm develops a unique marketing strategy for one or more target markets.

The general types of media and the specific vehicles within them vary in their selectivity. Direct mail is probably the most selective. Few households beyond those receiving an ad in the mail will be exposed to it. Thus, for example, many retailers identify their best customers through sales invoices and design a direct-mail campaign aimed exclusively at them. Mailing-list companies develop and market lists of households fitting certain demographic or socioeconomic categories. Direct-mail advertisers buy these lists and aim mail campaigns exclusively to those on the lists.

This radio station offers programming directed at a very selective audience.

Magazines offer the most versatility for reaching selective audiences. Geographic selectivity is provided through the growing number of magazines developed for certain geographic regions (e.g., *Southern Living, Texas Monthly, California*). Also, many national magazines offer regional editions in which the advertising content differs for each region.

Many national magazines offer type selectivity through different editions based on the type of consumer. For example, *Time* varies its advertising content by the occupational status of the subscriber. It also has a unique ad content for its student subscribers.

It is the special-interest magazines (*Golf Digest, Runner's World, Yachting, Personal Computing*) that offer a way to reach distinct lifestyle segments or special markets. Specific magazines also vary in the demographic and socioeconomic nature of their readers. Readers of *The New Yorker* differ in occupation and income from readers of *Argosy*.

Television, while falling short of the selective capabilities of magazines, is not without selectivity. Heavy TV viewers are different than light TV viewers. Also, many individual programs differ in the demographic and socioeconomic makeup of their viewers. Radio also offers selectivity, especially for reaching younger markets. Anheuser-Busch used radio extensively to improve the position of Budweiser in the young-adult segment.[7]

Finally, of all the media, outdoor advertising is probably the least selective.

The need to match the media mix to the media exposure patterns of the target market requires substantial market research data on the nature of the audiences of specific media vehicles. Fortunately, a number of media research firms provide such data. One popular media research firm, Simons Market Research Bureau (SMRB), provides audience profiles for many magazines and newspapers, TV and radio exposure data, and even outdoor data. Audiences are profiled by demographic and psychographic characteristics, usage levels of products, and brand loyalty.

Message requirements. Often, the choices of media must be adapted to the requirements of the message. The major types of media vary in the restrictions they place on what can be done with a message. These restrictions include availability of message codes, message content and length, and recognition.

The media vary in the number of codes available for use in the message. Television, because of its joint audio and video capabilities, has the greatest number of codes available. It can present verbal and nonverbal codes through both video and audio means. The strictly audio nature of radio and the strictly visual nature of print limit the codes available to them (although microencapsulation allows some print media to appeal to the sense of smell in unique nonverbal fashion).

Media also differ in the nature of message content they allow, and some types of content are more suitable for certain media than others. A prime example of this restriction and its effect on the media mix is provided by the Jockey men's underwear line.[8] In the 1970s Jockey began to position its men's underwear as a fashion item, providing a variety of colors, patterns, and styles in the brand. This strategy required that

---

[7] Kevin Higgins, "Musical Commercials Revive Bud in Young-Adult Segment," *Marketing News*, December 10, 1982, p. 1.

[8] "Why Jockey Switched Its Ads from TV to Print," *Business Week*, July 26, 1976, pp. 140–41.

advertising portray the brand as other fashion items are portrayed in ads: being worn. The need for this type of message required Jockey to shift its media mix from almost exclusively television, where issues of good taste prevented the product from being shown in the desired manner, to almost exclusively magazines, where it was more acceptable to show men and women in their underwear. As societal values change, however, TV will likely become available as a medium for Jockey.

Another difference between print and broadcast media that affects both message content and length lies in the locus of control over the processing of the message. Print media are **receiver-controlled media:** they allow the receivers to dictate their processing of the message. That is, receivers can spend as much or as little time with the message as they desire. Broadcast media, on the other hand, are **media-controlled:** they have inherent limitations on the time spent with a message (e.g., most TV commercials are 30 seconds long). In this case, the medium dictates the extent to which the receiver can process the message. As a result, more information and lengthier messages can be presented in print than in broadcast.

A final message requirement that influences the media mix is the amount of repetition desired. Broadcast media allow the greatest amount of message repetition within a given time period. Outdoor advertising also allows for a large number of repeated exposures to the same message. The number of exposures provided by magazines and newspapers is limited by the number of times any one issue is picked up by the same individual and by the length of time between issues. Direct mail allows the least repetition.

Cost. The final consideration in media planning is cost. The media and specific vehicles within them vary in costs, making cost comparisons important in evaluating alternative media mixes.

Absolute costs must be considered when evaluating media because they may be prohibitive to some firms. Many firms simply can't afford, for example, approximately $500,000 for a minute of network TV during the Super Bowl.

Major advertisers typically make cost comparisons using a figure that captures the efficiency of a medium. Media cost comparisons are based on the **cost per thousand (CPM)** of target prospects reached. The CPM is determined by dividing the total cost of the medium for a message by the number of thousands of target prospects reached. For example, if a magazine ad cost $25,000 and the magazine was delivered to 1,200,000 target customers, the CPM would be 25,000/1,200 = $20.83.

Generally, the major broadcast media (prime-time network TV and network radio) offer the greatest efficiencies. The CPM of prime-time network TV averages between $5 and $6; for network radio it is $2 to $3. Consumer magazines are in the $7-to-$8 range. Within each medium variations exist between specific vehicles. For example, in 1981 the CPM

Table 20–7: Media mixes of selected companies in selected industries, 1980

Company (by industry)	Measured total ad expenditures ($ millions)	Media percent of total dollars							
		News-papers	Maga-zines	Farm publi-cations	Spot TV	Net-work TV	Spot radio	Net-work radio	Out-door
Airlines									
TWA	$ 54.4	36.5%	8.0%	—	14.8%	24.6%	0.3%	14.7%	1.1%
Delta	46.0	53.6	1.7	—	—	15.2	—	25.5	4.0
Appliances									
RCA	84.4	33.5	27.7	—	22.7	10.4	1.4	3.9	0.4
General Electric	49.5	12.2	20.8	—	58.5	6.6	0.4	0.8	0.7
Automobiles									
Ford	288.3	15.8	20.4	1.2	44.7	7.7	2.2	7.6	0.4
Toyota	98.5	15.8	11.1	—	21.6	45.5	0.2	3.7	2.1
Chemicals									
Du Pont	44.7	4.5	48.3	7.6	27.8	6.6	1.9	4.4	—
Food									
General Mills	230.2	1.8	7.6	—	40.7	46.6	0.8	2.4	0.1
Retail chains									
Sears, Roebuck	188.2	—	27.2	0.1	54.5	9.3	5.9	3.0	—
K mart	56.1	—	15.9	—	57.8	14.6	1.4	10.0	0.3
Soaps, cleaners									
Procter & Gamble . . .	609.4	1.4	4.9	—	64.1	29.4	—	0.2	—
Soft drinks									
PepsiCo	196.3	1.5	4.8	—	38.6	44.7	1.4	8.4	0.6
Coca-Cola	174.2	2.5	3.3	—	50.1	34.1	0.1	8.1	1.8
Liquor									
Anheuser-Busch	204.4	1.6	5.1	—	46.8	23.0	3.1	18.0	2.4
Seagram	110.2	8.9	56.3	—	12.5	7.7	—	—	14.6
U.S. government	101.4	6.6	31.3	—	26.7	17.9	9.1	7.2	0.9

Source: Reprinted with permission from the September 8, 1983 issue of *Advertising Age*. Copyright 1983 by Crain Communications, Inc.

for *Business Week* was approximately $7; for *Fortune* it was around $11.[9]

You can see that the media mix decision is a complex one. In arriving at a media mix, media must be evaluated in terms of the number and nature of customers they reach, their ability to accommodate certain types of messages, the amount of repetition they allow, and their efficiency. Table 20–7 presents the media mixes of selected companies in selected industries.

Media scheduling

The media mix decision basically determines *how* to reach the members of a target market. Another important decision is *when* to advertise to your market. **Media scheduling** is concerned with the timing of advertis-

---

[9] *Media Costs and Coverage* (Chicago: Leo Burnett USA, 1981).

ing messages and should be considered from both a long-range and a short-range view.

Long-range timing. The long-range media scheduling problem deals with the timing of advertising expenditures over a year's time. When a seasonal product is involved, advertising messages are often concentrated just before or during the peak demand period. For example, many snowblower brands are advertised only during or just prior to the winter season. Minimal advertising (or none at all) occurs during the remainder of the year. Some products, while not seasonal in a functional sense, realize a peak demand period at one point in the year, with lower, stable demand levels throughout the remainder of the year. The demand for toys, for instance, exists throughout the year but peaks during the Christmas buying season. The bulk of advertising by toy manufacturers occurs at that time.

In some situations, advertising for a seasonal product is timed opposite to the fluctuations in demand. Advertising is concentrated in the off-season, in other words. This happens when demand is so strong in the peak period that advertising is unnecessary at that time. Advertising then tries to stimulate demand in the off-season to even out over time the use of the firm's total capacity. Resort areas often engage in such a strategy by advertising more heavily and offering reduced rates during the off-season.

A special consideration in the long-range timing of advertising is the case of a new product. Advertising must be closely coordinated with distribution. The general rule is not to advertise a product until it is available, except for some durable goods. For some new brands and especially new-season models (e.g., autos), heavy advertising precedes distribution in an attempt to build an anticipatory mood in the consumer.

Short-range timing. The short-range timing decision involves the scheduling of messages over short time periods: a month, a week, or even a day. A key issue here is whether to distribute messages throughout the given time period or concentrate them at one time with little or no advertising during the remainder of the period. The former, a ***continuous advertising schedule,*** would be appropriate when there is a need to reach buyers on a continuous basis (e.g., for a high repeat-purchase type of product). Concentrating messages—often referred to as ***flighting***—is appropriate when a heavy short-run impact is desirable. A restaurant may find that major expenditures by individuals eating out occur on Fridays and Saturdays. Demand during the rest of the week is a function of nonpromotional factors, but demand on the weekends is affected by advertising. The owner would perhaps spend the entire weekly advertising budget on Thursdays and Fridays, when individuals are deciding if and where to eat out.

Flighting is also appropriate when the advertising budget is limited.

Figure 20–9: Three approaches to media scheduling

Continuous advertising

Flighting

Pulsing

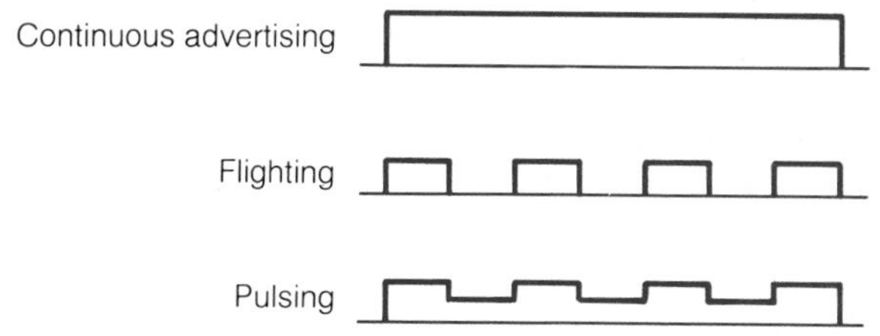

Distributing the budget throughout the time period might result in a level of advertising effort at any one point in time that would not be noticeable. But by concentrating the budget at one point, the level of effort at that time is substantial enough to have a significant impact that may carry over to the nonadvertising period. Thus, the total impact of advertising during the short-run period is greater through flighting than it otherwise would be. Combine this with the media discounts that can result from heavier expenditures at a point in time, and the advertising dollar is working harder.

When flighting is to be used, a key decision is how far apart to space the flights. Important information for this decision is the carryover rate of advertising's effects on buyers. If strong carryover effects exist, the spacing of the advertising effort can be wider. Weak carryover effects require shorter nonadvertising intervals of time.

A scheduling approach that combines continuous advertising and flighting is *pulsing*. Here, advertising occurs continuously but is marked by periodic bursts of greater advertising effort. Pulsing is appropriate when demand is continuous but rises and falls over time. For example, supermarkets realize sales throughout a month, but during certain periods within the month sales go up.

Figure 20–9 summarizes the nature of continuous, flighting, and pulsing approaches to media scheduling. Keep in mind that these approaches can be used for both long-range and short-range media scheduling decisions.

Measuring advertising effectiveness

Any marketing activity designed to affect the marketplace should be evaluated in terms of its potential and actual success. Advertising is no exception. With the large expenditures that are often placed in advertising and the important role it plays in marketing strategy, information on its effectiveness is critical to the sound management of a marketing program.

But this is easier said than done. There is no single, generally accepted method for measuring advertising effectiveness but rather an array of methods or procedures. There are differences in *what* to measure and *when* to measure it. Differences in *what* is measured result from examining

**Figure 20–10:
Procedures for
measuring advertising
effectiveness**

	Pretests	**Posttests**
Communications- oriented	Consumer jury Portfolio tests Physiological tests	Recall Recognition
Sales- oriented	Controlled market experiments	Statistical estimation

the communications effects of advertising versus its effects on sales. Dif-ferences in *when* advertising's effects are measured result from the impor-tance of having information as input to the development of an advertising campaign and feedback about the effects of an implemented campaign. Thus, we have a two-dimensional scheme for categorizing methods of measuring the effectiveness of advertising. (See Figure 20–10.) There are methods focusing on the communications effects of advertising before and after a campaign has been implemented and corresponding before-and-after methods focusing on sales effects. Before measures are called **pretests;** after measures are called **posttests.**

Communication effects

Pretests. In measuring the communication effect of advertising, the focus is on the impact of the content. Pretests of communication effects attempt to identify the strengths and weaknesses of an ad prior to its full-scale implementation. Three procedures for pretesting the communi-cation effects of an ad are the consumer jury, portfolio tests, and physio-logical tests.

The **consumer jury** involves a sample of consumers (50 to 100), each of whom evaluates a set of alternative ads in terms of likelihood of reading each ad, its interest-generating abilities, how convincing the ad is, and how effective it would be in causing a purchase. The outcome of the procedure is the relative effectiveness of alternative ads as seen by the intended audience.

In **portfolio tests** consumers are given a portfolio of ads consisting of a mix of the ads being tested and dummy ads. They are told to examine the ads for as long as they wish. The portfolio is then taken away, and the respondents are asked to recall the ads they saw and describe their content. The test ad eliciting the greatest recall is rated the most effective.

Physiological tests measure consumer reaction to ads as shown by galvanic skin response, blood pressure, pupil dilation, salivation, and even brain wave activity. These measures reflect attention-getting capabilities of ads rather than any impact on beliefs or attitudes—although salivation level in response to a food ad would seem to suggest more than just attention.

Posttests. The two major posttests of ad campaigns are recall and recognition tests. Both tests examine responses to ads that have appeared in the media.

Recall tests use a sample of consumers who regularly use a media source in which several ads appear. Respondents are asked, in unaided or aided fashion, to recall advertisers and products they saw in the media source under study (usually a print vehicle) and the nature of the message. The result is a measure of the relative ability of ads to attract attention and have the message retained.

Recognition tests ask consumers to indicate for a specific print medium whether certain ads in the issue were noticed and read. The **Starch readership measures** are the most commonly used. The syndicated Starch service annually examines approximately 30,000 ads appearing in nearly 1,000 publications. The Starch method results in three key readership scores for each ad:

1. *Noted*—The percentage of readers who remember seeing the ad.
2. *Seen-associated*—The percentage of readers who remember any part of the ad identifying the product or brand.
3. *Read most*—The percentage of readers indicating they read at least one half of the advertisement.

Despite their popularity, recall and recognition tests do have limitations. These are primarily methodological and relate to the survey nature of the procedures. Interviewer effects and social desirability factors can lead to underreporting or overreporting of exposure. There is also the obvious limitation of the memory capabilities of individuals. Nonetheless, these procedures can provide useful, if only approximate, measures of the relative attention-getting and communication abilities of a company's ads and those of its competitors.[10]

Sales effects

Pretests. Much like the potential sales of a new product can be assessed through test markets, the sales effects of a new campaign can be pretested, too. The general procedure is to identify *matched test markets* (markets that are as similar as possible in factors that might influence sales) and designate one or more of them as test areas in which the campaign will be implemented and one or more as control areas in which it will not. If the test and control markets are identical except for the presence and absence of the campaign, then any sales differences between them can be attributed to the campaign.

---

[10] For more on recall versus recognition, see Surendra N. Singh and Michael L. Rothschild, "Recognition as a Measure of Learning from Television Commercials," *Journal of Marketing Research,* August 1983, pp. 235–48.

These **controlled market experiments** can provide accurate estimates of the sales effects of advertising. However, it is a costly and time-consuming procedure. The tests must run long enough (at least six months to a year) for cumulative advertising effects to occur. As a result, controlled experimentation is available to only large firms. One of the first firms to use experiments was Du Pont.[11] In one experiment, industrial advertising was implemented in all but two states. Sales effects were measured by examining the differences in sales increases between the two control states and the test states.

Posttests. Measurement of the effects of advertising on sales in posttest fashion is difficult because of the need to separate out the effects of the multitude of other marketing factors that influence sales. Still, attempts to assess advertising's contributions to past sales are not uncommon.[12] The typical approach is to build a statistical demand analysis model expressing sales as a function of current and past advertising expenditures and other variables that influence demand. This procedure is limited, however. It is restricted to an "effort" orientation in that expenditures can only be examined. The effects of the creative, qualitative aspects of advertising cannot be tested.

As you can see, the measurement of advertising effectiveness is an inexact science. Each technique, while useful, has its limitations and cannot capture the whole picture. Advances and refinements in this area will continue. It is unlikely, however, that the ultimate measure of ad effectiveness will emerge in the near future.

THE REGULATORY ENVIRONMENT OF ADVERTISING

The prominence of advertising as a marketing tool and the strong creative element within it make advertising a candidate for misuse and abuse by those who implement it. As a result, advertising efforts come under close scrutiny by regulatory agencies and consumer activists in an extensive regulatory system. The purposes of this regulatory system are similar to those of business regulation as a whole: (1) to preserve competition by preventing unfair competition in the use of advertising and (2) to protect consumers from abusive practices of advertisers. The regulatory system comprises self-regulation from within the advertising industry and government regulation at the federal, state, and local levels. (See Figure 20–11.)

Self-regulation

The advertising industry has a long history of attempts at self-regulation. Over the years the intensity of self-regulation has increased. Early

---

[11] "Who Says Ad Impact Can't Be Measured?" *Sales Management,* April 19, 1963, pp. 37–43.

[12] For a recent one, see Robert P. Leone, "Modelling Sales-Advertising Relationships: An Integrated Time Series-Econometric Approach," *Journal of Marketing Research,* August 1983, pp. 291–95.

Figure 20–11: The regulatory environment of advertising

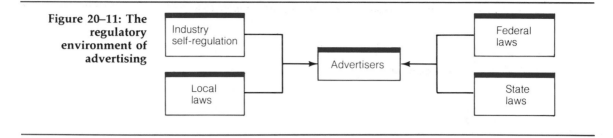

on, the major instrument of self-regulation was the *code of conduct*—a statement of ethical guidelines for the implementation of advertising. For example, the American Association of Advertising Agencies has offered a "creative code" for its members to follow for almost 60 years. This code urges, among other things, the avoidance of false or misleading claims and testimonials, unfair comparisons with a competitive product, insufficiently supported claims, and statements that offend public decency. But codes of conduct, while useful, have no enforcement capabilities and often are simply plaques on a wall; and as a result, formal bodies with more clout in the area of self-regulation emerged.

The first major body to achieve some degree of enforcement power in its code was the National Association of Broadcasters (NAB). In 1952 the NAB developed strict and comprehensive standards of good taste and acceptability in radio and TV advertising and programming. Stations that do not comply with the advice of the NAB review panel and carry commercials rated as unsatisfactory face expulsion and denial of the privilege to display the membership seal. Through the efforts of the NAB, liquor advertising (except for wine and beer) has been kept off the air. Also, it was the NAB that eliminated the "man-in-white" commercials in which simulated physicians extolled the virtues of a health product.

In spite of the success of the NAB in certain areas, advertising abuses continued, and public criticism of the industry increased. As a result, the National Advertising Review Board (NARB), a broad-based regulatory agency that encompasses many segments of the industry, was created in 1971. It has become the major body of self-regulation in the industry. The NARB screens ads for honesty and responds to—and encourages—consumer complaints. Its review panel, which includes public representation, offers a verdict on disputed ads. When the verdict is against an ad, the advertiser usually removes it, even though the NARB has no real power to enforce its removal. If a firm does not comply, the NARB publicizes the issue and reports it to the Federal Trade Commission, the major governmental agency with regulatory power over advertising. The success of the NARB has led to the development of similar bodies at the community level which regulate local advertising.

The value of self-regulation in the advertising industry is two-fold.

First, self-regulation can pinpoint questionable ads early in their exposure. Removal of these ads avoids the time-consuming and costly legal procedures that might follow if the ads come under the scrutiny of the government. Second, self-regulation can pursue the problems of taste, which are ticklish legal issues. The portrayal of women in ads is one area where self-regulation can be more effective than governmental regulation.

Governmental regulation

Unfortunately, self-regulation cannot completely eliminate abusive practices in advertising. Governmental regulation at the federal, state, and local levels further limits these practices.

Federal Trade Commission. The Federal Trade Commission (FTC), created by the FTC Act of 1914, is the governmental agency with the greatest regulatory power over advertising. Its initial sweeping mandate was to prohibit unfair acts in commerce, including false advertising. However, the FTC's real clout was provided by the Wheeler-Lea Amendment of 1938, which allowed the commission to act without proving intent on the part of the advertiser. Other changes in the amendment include:

1. "Unfair acts" was expanded to include "deceptive" acts or practices.
2. The FTC was empowered to issue cease-and-desist orders that become binding after 60 days.
3. Specific jurisdiction was granted over false advertising of foods, drugs, and cosmetics.
4. The FTC was granted power to issue injunctions to halt improper food, drug, or cosmetic advertising when harm to the public was possible.

For most of its history the FTC has assumed a reactive stance in its regulation of advertising. It would monitor advertisements in an attempt to identify questionable or false claims or receive complaints from injured parties. If an ad was deemed false or misleading, a cease-and-desist order would be issued. For example, in 1967 the FTC issued a cease-and-desist order against the maker of Geritol that prohibited advertising the product as an effective remedy for tiredness, loss of strength, run-down feeling, nervousness, or irritability.

The activities of the FTC have extended beyond the mere stoppage of false ads. They have included programs that place a greater burden of responsibility on potentially offending firms and firms whose ads have been deemed inappropriate. The **substantiation of claims program** requires that advertisers provide, on demand, studies that substantiate advertising claims about the price, safety, or performance of a product. For example, in 1979 the FTC ruled that Bristol-Meyers lacked a scientific basis for stating that the pain reliever Bufferin worked faster than its competition, caused less stomach upset, and offered tension relief.

The **corrective-advertising program** of the FTC is probably its strongest stance in reacting to inappropriate claims in ads. This program allows the FTC to require advertisers to run ads at their own expense to correct the effects of advertising that has been deemed deceptive. Perhaps the most prominent case to date in the corrective advertising program involves the Listerine brand of antiseptic. FTC action against Listerine began in 1971, when the FTC issued a complaint that Listerine ads claimed the product was an aid in preventing colds. Medical evidence did not substantiate such a claim. The manufacturer (Warner-Lambert) was required to run ads to correct any false beliefs formed by consumers as a result of the deceptive ads. Ideally, the corrective ads were designed to alter any false beliefs about Listerine's cold-preventing abilities *without affecting positively or negatively any other beliefs about Listerine as a product or Warner-Lambert as a company.* The results of several studies are mixed as to the ability of a corrective ad to isolate and alter beliefs about one attribute of a brand without affecting other beliefs.[13]

The most sweeping powers of the FTC come from its right to issue **Trade Regulation Rules (TRRs)** as granted by the Moss-Magnuson Act of 1975. TRRs establish rules and guidelines that are applicable to an entire product category or industry.

Recent changes at the FTC.   In 1984 the FTC adopted a controversial new interpretation of the FTC Act as it relates to protecting the public from false advertising. The FTC will now decide whether an ad is deceptive by requiring proof that a "reasonable consumer" suffered actual injury. Such proof must be furnished before an advertiser can be charged with false advertising. Previously, an ad was considered deceptive if it had the capacity or tendency to deceive a substantial number of consumers. Endorsed by the advertising industry but denounced by others, the new policy is designed to reduce the number of trivial lawsuits against advertisers.[14]

Other federal agencies.   While the FTC possesses the most sweeping powers over advertising, several other federal agencies regulate advertising and other promotional practices. They include:

1. *The Food and Drug Administration (FDA).* Under the Food, Drug, and Cosmetic Act of 1906 and subsequent amendments, the FDA is empowered to require truthful disclosure of ingredients and prohibit false labeling and packaging of foods, drugs, cosmetics, and devices. Procedures providing for premarketing approval of claims and labels for prescription drugs have been established.

---

[13] For a review of these studies and a description of perhaps the most extensive study addressing this issue, see R. W. Mizerski, N. K. Allison, and S. Calvert, "A Controlled Field Study of Corrective Advertising Using Multiple Exposures and a Commercial Medium," *Journal of Marketing Research,* August 1980, pp. 341–48.

[14] Pravat Choudbury, "FTC Interpretation of Deception Giving Advertisers New Latitude," *Marketing News,* April 27, 1984, p. 11.

2. *Federal Communications Commission (FCC).* The Communications Act of 1934 empowers the FCC to issue licenses to operators of radio and TV stations and impose character qualifications for licensees. It prohibits lotteries, fraud, and obscenity. Also, it can impose criminal penalties for concealing instances in which a station has been paid to mention a product or service.

3. *Treasury Department (Bureau of Alcohol, Tobacco, Firearms).* It is the governing body that regulates the advertising of liquor products.

State and local regulations. Most of the regulation at the federal level is sweeping in its scope of relevance. Federal laws, in other words, are not confined to specific industries or media. At the state and local levels, however, individual laws pertaining to advertising are restricted to certain products, industries, or media. For example, many states and municipalities have their own unique laws pertaining to the liquor industry. Some states place restrictions on the use of outdoor advertising. Certain states prohibit the advertising of some products. All of these laws, however, must exist within the constitutionality of the federal government. For example, a long-standing prohibition of advertising of prescription drug prices in several states was deemed unconstitutional by the Supreme Court in 1976.

The diversity of state and local regulations on advertising prevents the description of a general framework of regulation at this level. The state law that approaches a generalized view of state regulation is the one based on the 1911 Printer's Ink model statute that has been adopted in original or modified form by 44 states. This statute sets forth what constitutes deceptive advertising and the punishment for it. Since this statute is essentially redundant with respect to federal legislation—and state legal systems have more pressing legal issues than isolated cases of fraudulent advertising—litigation at the state level based on Printer's Ink has been infrequent.

SUMMARY

As a form of promotion, advertising informs, persuades, and reminds buyers and can substitute for or complement personal selling. In spending what can be a substantial amount on advertising, advertisers use product, pioneer, competitive, comparative, institutional, trade, horizontal cooperative, and vertical cooperative advertising. They develop ad campaigns in which the advertising effort for a product involves multiple messages with a common theme.

Promotional budgeting procedures discussed in Chapter 19 can be used to set the advertising budget. Advertisers use ad agencies to develop their advertising strategy.

The objectives of advertising strategy relate to the specification of a target audience and the establishment of message or campaign purposes. These purposes can be informational or persuasive.

Message formulation includes the determination of message content. Eight approaches to content are information, argument, motivation with psychological appeals, repeated assertion, command, brand familiarization, symbolic association, and imitation. These approaches have different implications for message appeal, structure, and format. Factors to consider in choosing an approach include industrial or consumer good; best way to characterize the product (style, mechanical, sensory, service, hidden benefit); necessity, convenience, or luxury good; intelligence of audience; stage of product class and brand acceptance; price range; frequency of purchase; and homogeneity of competing brands.

Message execution involves bringing together the copy (verbal components) and nonverbal elements (pictures, sounds, etc.) into the layout of the message. Within the layout, attention, interest, desire, and action can be influenced.

Media selection occurs within a variety of media types: newspapers, magazines, television, radio, direct mail, business and farm publications, outdoor and transit, and miscellaneous media. A media mix is determined based on desired exposure levels, target audience, message requirements, and cost.

Long-range and short-range media scheduling considers demand fluctuations and carryover effects of advertising. Continuous advertising, flighting, and pulsing approaches to scheduling are available.

The effectiveness of advertising can be measured from a communications or sales orientation. Effectiveness can be measured using pretests or posttests.

The regulatory environment of advertising includes industry self-regulation and governmental regulation at federal, state, and local levels. The Federal Trade Commission is the major regulatory body of the federal government.

KEY CONCEPTS

Advertiser

Product advertising

Pioneer advertising

Competitive advertising

Comparative advertising

Institutional advertising

Trade advertising

Cooperative advertising

Horizontal cooperative advertising

Vertical cooperative advertising

Advertising campaign

Full-service advertising agency

Limited-service advertising agency

Account executive

Informational message

Persuasive message

Approaches to message content

Information

Argument

Motivation with psychological appeals

Repeated assertion

Command

Brand familiarization

Symbolic association

Imitation

Message execution

Copy

Headline

Subheadline

Body copy

Signature

Nonverbal elements

Layout

AIDA

Media

Media mix

Reach

Frequency

Impressions

Gross rating points (GRPs)

Geographic selectivity

Type selectivity

Receiver-controlled media

Media-controlled media

Cost per thousand (CPM)

Media scheduling

Continuous advertising schedule

Flighting

Pulsing

Communications-oriented measures of effects

Sales-oriented measures of effects

Pretest

Posttest

Consumer jury

Portfolio test

Physiological test

Recall test

Recognition test

Starch readership measures

Controlled market experiment

Substantiation of claims program

Corrective-advertising program

Trade Regulation Rules (TRRs)

DISCUSSION QUESTIONS AND EXERCISES

1. Discuss the role of advertising in an organization.

2. Consider the various types of advertising: product, pioneer, competitive, comparative, institutional, trade, and cooperative. To what extent do you feel each would be appropriate in the following situations:
   a. Marketing household robots.
   b. Changing the name of a major corporation.
   c. The No. 2 brand trying to take over the top spot.
   d. Marketing a new brand of soap.
   e. A company trying to overcome negative publicity about its pollution of the environment.

3. Find examples of each of Simon's approaches to advertising content. Using Table 20–4 as a reference, try to explain why each of your example companies is using its particular approach.

4. For each of the eight examples you choose for question 3, identify the elements of copy in the advertisement.

5. If a media vehicle reaches one half of a target market of 150,000 consumers at a frequency of 3.5, calculate its reach, impressions, and GRPs.

6. Go back to Table 20–7. Pick five companies in five different industries. Using the criteria for media selection, try to explain the media mix for each company that you chose.

7. For each of the following businesses or products, discuss the extent to which continuous advertising, flighting, or pulsing would be appropriate:
   a. Soft drink.
   b. Travel agency.
   c. Writing pen.
   d. Packaged meat.
   e. Office furniture.
   f. Home furniture.
   g. Washer–dryer combination.
   h. Professional football team.

8. Discuss the advantages and disadvantages of the various procedures for measuring the effectiveness of advertisements.

9. What is your opinion of the FTC's recent softening on what constitutes deceptive advertising?

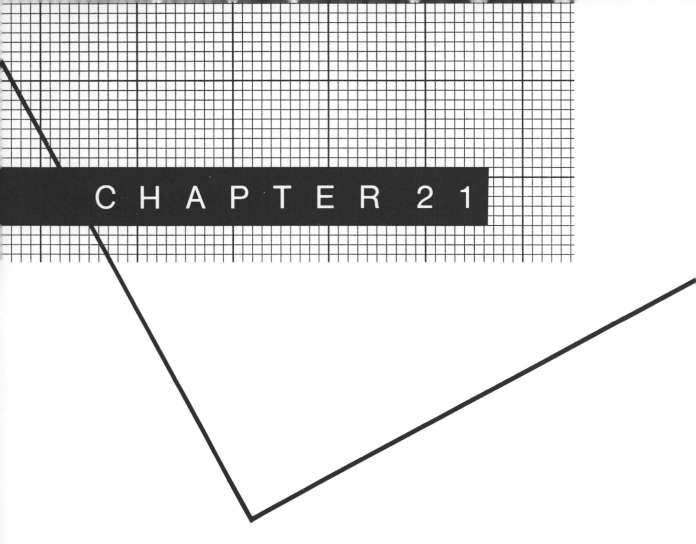

CHAPTER 21

The personal selling process

and sales management

Personal selling's role in marketing strategy

Boundary position of the salesperson

Classification of selling jobs

The selling process
    Prospecting
    The preapproach
    The approach
    The presentation
    Meeting objections
    The close
    The follow-up

Management of the sales force
    Sales force objectives
    Forms of organizing the sales force
    Sales force size
    Sales force compensation
    Recruitment, selection, and retention
    Sales training
    Sales force supervision and motivation
    Evaluation of sales force performance

Trends in personal selling
    Team selling
    Telephone selling
    Women in personal selling careers
    Research on personal selling
    Dyadic studies

Summary

Key concepts

Discussion questions and exercises

Our purpose in this chapter is to provide an overview of the role of personal selling in marketing strategy and analysis of the major issues in managing the sales force.

First, we'll discuss the role of personal selling in marketing strategy. We'll then describe the salesperson's position in the company, a system to classify sales jobs, and the selling process itself.

The topics discussed under sales force management include objectives, organization, size, compensation, recruitment and selection, training, supervision and motivation, and evaluation of the sales force. Finally, we'll address current trends in personal selling.

Substantially more resources are allocated to personal selling than to advertising. About 6.3 percent of the U.S. labor force—6.01 million people—are employed in personal selling; about 500,000 are employed in advertising.[1] In 1980, U.S. profit and nonprofit firms spent nearly $55 billion on advertising.[2] It is estimated that the amount spent on personal selling is 2.5 times greater than expenditures for advertising. This means that U.S. firms spent about $137.5 billion on personal selling in 1980.

PERSONAL SELLING'S ROLE IN MARKETING STRATEGY

Personal selling is only one factor in an organization's marketing strategy; and it may be a primary element or may play only a secondary role. Consider the examples of Avon and Revlon, both very successful cosmetics manufacturers. In 1980, Avon had sales of $2.38 billion; Revlon's sales were $2.20 billion. Avon's basic strategy uses a direct marketing program that relies heavily on personal selling. The firm employs 415,000 sales representatives in the United States and 1.2 million worldwide to implement it. By paying a 40 percent commission on sales, Avon's expenditure for personal selling is estimated at $925 million.[3] In contrast, Revlon uses a more conventional channel: 10,000 retail stores (including department and drug stores) market its brands. Revlon uses sales reps to call on retailers, but its $2 billion sales level relies heavily on consumer advertising. Revlon's 1980 advertising expenditures were about $105 million, almost 5 percent of sales. Avon spent $30 million, about 1 percent of sales, on advertising in 1980. Much of Avon's advertising features its personal representatives. But the company also directs considerable advertising effort toward recruiting sales reps. Avon's promotional strategy would be characterized as a push strategy; Revlon's is a pull strategy. The point is that personal selling can be used in various ways to implement marketing strategy.

[1] U.S. Bureau of Census, *Statistical Abstract of the U.S.: 1979*, 100th ed. (Washington, D.C.: U.S. Government Printing Office, 1979).

[2] See Courtland L. Bovee and William F. Arens, *Contemporary Advertising* (Homewood, Ill.: Richard D. Irwin, 1982), p. 21. The figure is based on estimates that the $13 billion spent by the 100 largest advertisers is 23.8 percent of total ad expenditures.

[3] The information for these examples is from Gail Bronson, "Avon Lady Will Be Getting New Look in Drive for More Fashionable Image," *The Wall Street Journal*, January 19, 1981, p. 10; and "Advertising and Marketing Reports on 100 Top National Advertisers," *Advertising Age*, September 10, 1981, p. 129.

A key element in Avon's success is the effective use of personal selling. This ad is used to recruit Avon representatives.

"If you're thinking of going back to work, don't settle for a 9 to 5 job. Avon's got a better idea."

Courtesy Avon Products, Inc.

When you're an Avon Representative, *you* set your goals, *you* pick your hours. What we've done is make your earning opportunities better than ever before. So you can earn more money as an Avon Representative than ever before.

We'll even start you off with the training to help make your new venture a success. And remember, it's your own business...one you can tailor to suit your life-style.

There has never been a better time to become an Avon Representative!

Ask your Representative to be your sponsor. Or send in the coupon below.

I'd like to know more about the new Avon Earning Opportunity. I understand there is no obligation.

Name_____

Address_____

Phone_____

My Representative's name is_____

Have you ever been an Avon Representative? Yes___ No___

Mail to: Avon Products, Inc., 2200 Cotillion Drive, Atlanta, Georgia 30338.
Applicant must be 18 years or older and a resident of the Continental U.S., Alaska, or Hawaii.

BOUNDARY POSITION OF THE SALESPERSON

Sales reps occupy a ***boundary position:*** that is, they serve as the interface between the company and its customers. The salesperson must try to satisfy the expectations and demands of both and, as a result, is often caught between their conflicting demands.

Role conflict and role ambiguity often occur. Role conflict results from incompatible job demands from management, customers, family, and other persons with whom the salesperson must interact.[4] When the sales rep is not sure about how he/she is expected to perform the job, role ambiguity steps in.[5]

Research has shown that high levels of role ambiguity lead to greater job dissatisfaction and high turnover.[6] In order to reduce these effects,

---

[4] Orville C. Walker, Jr., Gilbert A. Churchill, Jr., and Neil M. Ford, "Organizational Determinants of the Industrial Salesman's Role Conflict and Ambiguity," *Journal of Marketing* 39 (January 1975), p. 32.

[5] Ibid.

[6] James H. Donnelly, Jr., and John M. Ivancevich, "Role Clarity and the Salesman," *Journal of Marketing* 39 (January 1975), pp. 71–74.

management must provide a clear understanding of job requirements and company expectations.

Other research has assessed the impact of various factors on role ambiguity and role conflict.[7] It found that role conflict and role ambiguity decreased as salesperson experience increased. And role ambiguity decreased when the sales rep was more closely supervised. Supervision was measured by the extent to which the sales supervisor watched how much salespersons traveled, which customers they called on, the content and form of the sales presentation, and so on.

CLASSIFICATION OF SELLING JOBS

Personal selling jobs differ greatly in the technical knowledge and creativity they require. One classification system identifies four types of selling jobs:

1. *Trade sellers.* Their main responsibility is to increase business from present and potential customers by providing *promotional and merchandising assistance.* Trade sellers help set up displays, develop and place ads, and conduct special sales promotions (such as two-for-one sales).

2. *Missionary sellers.* Their major responsibility is to increase business from present and potential customers by providing *product information.* Missionary salespeople don't usually take orders. Rather, they persuade customers to buy their firm's products from distributor or wholesale suppliers.

3. *New-business sellers.* Their primary responsibility is to increase business by *obtaining new customers.*

4. *Technical sellers.* Their main responsibility is to increase business by providing *technical information and assistance* to present and potential customers.[8]

Companies using each type of seller are presented in Table 21–1.

These four types of selling jobs are usually found in industrial selling—one business to another. In contrast, retail selling involves selling to consumers for personal use. Retail selling includes door-to-door encyclopedia sales reps, retail store clerks, and life insurance sales reps. For some of these (such as retail clerks), selling may be a minor part of the job. The salesperson may be more of an order taker whose role in selling is passive. Most of our discussion focuses on industrial selling, where personal selling is a major part of the sales rep's job and is a key component of the firm's marketing strategy.

---

[7] Walker et al., "Organizational Determinants," pp. 32–39.

[8] Derek A. Newton, *Sales Force Performance and Turnover* (Cambridge, Mass.: Marketing Science Institute, 1973), p. 5.

Table 21–1: Companies engaged in the four types of selling jobs	Selling job	Company	Customer
	Trade	Kellogg, Procter & Gamble, Kimberly Clark	Supermarkets, convenience store managers
	Missionary	Parke-Davis, Eli Lily, American Hospital Supply	Physicians, pharmacists
	New-Business	Fuller Brush, World Book Encyclopedia	Individual households, consumers
	Technical	3M, Rockwell, International	Manufacturing and retailing executives, public utility executives

Parke-Davis uses missionary sales representatives to promote its products to pharmacists and doctors. This ad illustrates the company's marketing efforts aimed at these target markets.

PARKE-DAVIS

HELPING YOUR PHARMACIST AND YOUR DOCTOR HELP YOUR HEALTH

© 1984 Warner-Lambert Co

3M is a technical seller. This ad highlights the importance of effective listening to customer needs and shows how 3M's technical ability can be used to solve problems for its customers.

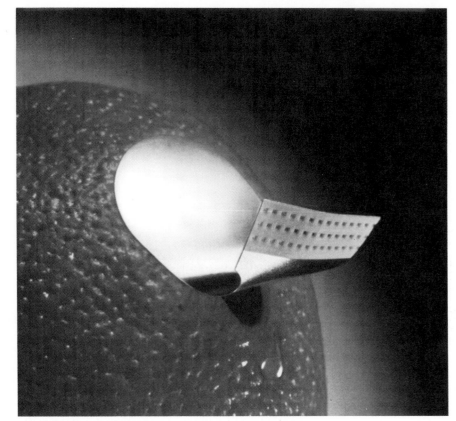

All taste and no tin.

3M invented "Scotchtab" Closure Tape as a convenient opening for canned juices. That was over 20 billion cans ago. Now we've improved on the idea. At the request of a Florida fruit and vegetable-juice packer, we created a tab that even protects the flavors of juices from the thin metal edge exposed when the hole is punched in the top. This helped our customer perfect a new kind of container to better serve its markets.

Listening to people has helped 3M pioneer over 900 products to solve industrial production and maintenance problems. We now make everything from tapes that hold tighter than nuts and bolts to floor coatings tough enough for duty on aircraft carrier flight decks. And it all began by listening.

3M hears you...

For your free 3M Industrial Production Brochure, write: Department 090211/3M, P.O. Box 4039, St. Paul, MN 55104.

Name_____

Address_____

City_____ State_____ Zip_____

Or call toll-free:**1-800-323-1718,** Operator 369. (Illinois residents call 1-800-942-8881.)

H-MS-IPAD-1

Courtesy 3M

THE SELLING PROCESS

Seven steps make up the personal selling process: (1) prospecting, (2) the preapproach, (3) the approach, (4) the presentation, (5) meeting objections, (6) the close, and (7) the follow-up.[9] These steps form a continuous process in which each step should be successfully completed to make a

---

[9] Frederick A. Russell, Frank H. Beach, and Richard H. Buskirk, *Textbook of Salesmanship,* 10th ed. (New York: McGraw-Hill, 1977).

Table 21–2: An overview of the steps and objectives of the personal selling process

	Steps	Objective	Comments
Phase I: Preparation	Prospecting	Locate qualified customers	Techniques used are snowball and referral
	Preapproach	Obtain additional information on prospect to make sales presentation more effective	Sources of information are customers, other sales representatives, newspapers, and personal observations
Phase II: Persuasion	Approach	Gain prospect's attention and make transition to sales presentation	Salesperson introduces self, the company, and the product
	Presentation	Create a desire for the product or service	Salesperson can use a canned or customer-specific presentation; product demonstrations are made; customer is encouraged to use and handle the product
	Meeting objections	Determine customer's true reason for not buying and attempt to remove these reasons	Effective dealing with objections is often considered the heart of the selling process
	The close	Gain a commitment from the prospect	Salesperson "asks for the sale"; some techniques used are the trial close and the assumptive close
Phase III: After-sale service	Follow-up	Resolve any problems that customers has and answer any questions	Effective handling of the follow-up helps to ensure customer satisfaction; it provides an opportunity to make additional sales to the customer, as well

sale. Most important, all selling activities in the steps should reflect the company's overall marketing strategy. In practice the steps overlap, but for discussion purposes we'll consider them individually. Table 21–2 contains an overview of the steps and the objectives in the personal selling process.

Prospecting

The objective of the first step in the selling process is to locate qualified potential customers. *Qualified* means that the prospect has a need or want for the product or service, the money to buy it, and the authority to make a buying decision.

A variety of methods are used to search for prospective customers. One of the more effective is the **snowball technique** (also known as the **endless chain**). With this method, each prospect recommends other prospects to the salesperson. Effectiveness is increased if the sales rep has some type of introduction from the recommender. This variation is called the *referral* method.

Prospects are found in a variety of sources, including newspapers, trade publications, and personal observation. For example, a field sales manager for a waterproofing chemical firm takes walks in residential areas to spot

Advertising and personal selling are often coordinated to enhance a firm's promotional effort. This ad is designed to help the salesperson identify prospects who can be targeted for sales calls.

WE'LL SHOW YOU HOW TO CUT THE COST OF SENDING COMPUTER DATA.

FOR FREE.

Codex, the data communications division of Motorola, introduces a free program for any company, large or small, that has to transmit data from one location to another.

If you have a data communications network now, we'll show you ways to make it more reliable and more cost-effective.

If you're planning a network, we'll show you how to plan for growth to ensure efficiency.

A Codex technical expert will give you all the advice you need to start saving money. You only have to return the coupon or call.

There's no obligation. Except, perhaps, to yourself.

MOTOROLA INC.
Information Systems Group

I'd like the same advice 90 of the Fortune 100 companies depend on.

☐ Have one of your experts contact me right away.

☐ Send your booklet on how to build a data communications network.

Name _____

Title _____

Company _____

Address _____

City _____ State _____ Zip _____

Telephone _____

Mail to: Codex Corporation,
Dept. 707-90, 20 Cabot Blvd., Mansfield, MA 02048.
Or call toll free: **1-800-821-7700** Ext. 890

1487

Courtesy Motorola, Inc.

problems that can be solved by his company's products. He discovered warping window casements in new apartment buildings, and he sold 150,000 linear feet of a stripping material that helped solve this problem.[10]

Company sales records and such promotions as ads with coupons for further information on a product or service also generate prospects. A final technique—often a last resort—is the ***cold canvas approach.*** The cold canvas is least productive, for little is known about the individuals contacted. Companies like Avon and Fuller Brush, which market relatively low-unit-cost products needed in all households, can use cold canvassing best.

The preapproach

The preapproach (1) provides additional information on the prospect, (2) gives insight into the best approach to the prospect, and (3) obtains information to help make the sales reps more effective.[11] This information can be obtained from many sources, including customers, fellow sales reps, newspapers, and observations. Time and effort spent on the preapproach are determined by the importance of the sale. In general, sales reps don't spend enough time on the preapproach. Unfortunately, most are like the life insurance salesman who tried to sell a policy to a man based on the man's affection for his wife and baby. The prospect was "coldly unmoved." The sales rep learned that the prospect lived apart from his wife and was suing for divorce. Their only child had died three years previously.[12]

The approach

The goal of the approach is to gain prospects' attention and interest so they will want to see the presentation. It also serves as a transition into the presentation itself.

Several methods are used to perform this function.[13] Perhaps the most common (but least effective) is the introductory approach: the salesperson first states his/her name and company. The product approach can also be used. This involves engaging in a conversation as the product is simply handed to the prospect. Industrial firms use the consumer-benefit approach, where the product's benefits are stated immediately. Another effective approach uses referral from the prospect's friend. The approach used depends on the information obtained from the preapproach and prospecting steps.

The presentation

The presentation is the core of the selling process and its goal is to obtain a customer by creating a desire for the product or service. Information on the product or service attributes and benefits is communicated

---

[10] *The American Salesman,* February 1962, p. 17.
[11] Russell et al., *Textbook,,* p. 166.
[12] Ibid., p. 168.
[13] Ibid., p. 186–200.

to the prospect. In a good sales presentation the product is shown and its function demonstrated. Whenever feasible, the prospect should participate in such demonstrations. It is essential that the sales rep gain the prospect's confidence and become the influencer in this dyadic relationship. It is then easier to anticipate and overcome objections or attempts by the prospect to sidetrack the presentation.

There is some controversy over which type of sales presentation should be used. In a **canned presentation,** the salesperson depends on company-developed films, flip charts, or memorized messages. A **customer-specific presentation** allows the salesperson flexibility of wording and sequence to describe the product. One study that examined the difference in effectiveness of canned and customer-specific sales presentations found the canned presentations more effective. The canned presentation was more exciting but also more high-pressured. Of the subjects who viewed the canned presentations, 42 percent expressed a definite buying intention. Only 25 percent of those who saw the customer-specific presentation stated a similar intent. Because the research was conducted in a group setting, though, the extent to which the results can be applied to one-on-one situations has been questioned.[14]

A canned sales presentation can be advantageous with new salespeople who are less familiar with the product and the selling process than more experienced staff. It guarantees a comprehensive sales presentation. But the canned presentation lacks spontaneity and flexibility, which does limit its use.

Meeting objections

Objections should be anticipated in the selling process. If no objections are encountered, the prospect is usually not interested. A good sales rep pinpoints the true purpose behind any objections. For example, prospects may object to a product's packaging when it's the price they really don't like. To unearth the true objection, the sales rep must listen carefully and ask probing questions. Arguing with the prospect should be avoided by minimizing objections if possible and—when appropriate—regarding them as requests for more information or clarification.

The close

The closing stage occurs when the purpose of the entire selling process is attained. The goal in closing is to get a commitment from the prospect, preferably in the form of an order. This is the most important step in the selling process and often the most difficult, too, for it is hard to know when the prospect is ready to buy. If closing is attempted too soon or too late, the sale may be lost. The sales rep must be alert to signs from the prospect that she/he is ready. A **trial close** can also be used. A trial close may occur at any time in a sales presentation. The

---

[14] James Reed, "Comments on 'The Underestimated Potential of the Canned Sales Presentation'," *Journal of Marketing* 40 (January 1976), pp. 67–68.

trial close asks the prospect to make a decision on some minor aspect of the purchase or to answer a question that would indicate the prospect's intention to make a purchase: "Do you prefer red or white?" "Are you going to pay cash or do you need financing?"

Many methods are used to close the sale. The two most common are (1) just asking for the order and (2) the assumptive close. The *assumptive close* involves asking for choices on color, size, number, etc., on the assumption that the prospect is going to buy and must make sales-related decisions.

The follow-up

The selling process does not end with taking the order. Salespeople should always follow up to resolve any problems that may have occurred with maintenance, delivery, installation, training, billing, and so on. Servicing the account by resolving these problems and answering questions can reduce customer dissatisfaction or dissonance. The follow-up is an opportune time to suggest accessory equipment and other products. If adequate, the follow-up will ensure customer satisfaction and a repeat sale.

Now let us discuss the management of the sales force. See Figure 21–1 for an overview of the major topics in this process.

MANAGEMENT OF THE SALES FORCE

Sales force objectives

Sales objectives should be coordinated and integrated with the firm's overall marketing strategy. Three purposes of sales objectives are to facilitate the planning of the personal selling program, to provide a focus for sales activities, and to aid in the evaluation of the sales force.

To be effective, sales objectives must meet five criteria. They must be (1) measurable, (2) consistent with each other and the firm's overall

Figure 21–1: An overview of the management of the sales force

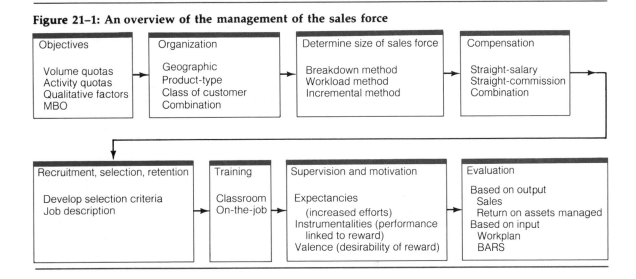

strategy, (3) reasonable, (4) prioritized, and (5) achievable within a specified time period.

Sales force objectives can be stated in a number of ways. Two common methods are volume quotas and activity quotas.[15] **Volume quotas** are measured by dollar sales volume, the number of sales closed, expense-to-sales ratios, and sales of special merchandise. **Activity quotas** are measured by the number of sales calls, the cost per call, and the number of complaints received. Sales performance can also be assessed on *qualitative* factors such as time management, loyalty, honesty, and resourcefulness, but managerial judgment is required to evaluate these objectives. It's important to allow sales reps input into the establishment of sales objectives. Research has found that salespersons who perceive that they have an influence in setting performance and evaluation standards are more satisfied with their jobs and with company policies, supervision, and opportunities for promotion.[16]

One approach to establishing objectives is **management by objectives (MBO).** MBO is a managerial philosophy that involves: the establishment of organizational objectives by top management, the development of sales force objectives by the superior (sales manager) and the subordinate (sales rep) that are consistent with the organizational objectives, and the assessment of the subordinate's performance by both superior and subordinate at a specified date.[17]

Companies that have successfully used MBO for their sales forces include General Electric and Black & Decker. GE used MBO to develop sales volume objectives and plans to achieve them.[18] Black & Decker found that goal priorities established through MBO improved the attitudes and performance of its sales forces.[19]

| **Forms of organizing the sales force** | Sales force activities must be organized for most effective performance. Depending on the firm's goals and strategies, the sales force can be organized using a **geographic, product-type, class of customer,** or **combination** approach. |

Geographic organization. The simplest and most common way to organize the sales force is by geographic territories. In this type of struc-

---

[15] Ben M. Enis, *Personal Selling: Foundations, Process, and Management* (Santa Monica, Calif.: Goodyear Publishing, 1979), p. 250.

[16] Gilbert A. Churchill, Jr., Neil M. Ford, and Orville C. Walker, Jr., "Organizational Climate and Job Satisfaction in the Sales Force," *Journal of Marketing Research* 13 (November 1976), pp. 323–32.

[17] Michael J. Etzel and John M. Ivancevich, "Management by Objectives in Marketing: Philosophy, Process, and Problems," *Journal of Marketing* 38 (October 1974), pp. 47–55.

[18] Robert A. Else, "Selling by Measurable Objectives," *Sales Management,* May 24, 1973, pp. 22–24.

[19] Stephen J. Carroll, Jr. and Henry L. Tosi, Jr., *Management by Objectives* (New York: Macmillan, 1973), p. 41.

ture, each sales rep performs the activities necessary to sell all the products in the firm's line to potential customers in one geographic area. Sales reps from a reasonable number of territories are placed under a territorial executive, typically called a regional, divisional, or district manager. Companies with large sales forces commonly have up to three levels of territorial sales executives. Some form of geographic organization is used by many companies that have grown beyond the small-business stage and sell in broad markets rather than local ones.

The geographic sales organization offers several advantages. It is usually the lowest-cost way to organize a sales force. Because one salesperson covers a specific geographic area, travel time and expenses are minimized. Geographic organization usually promotes better market coverage and better control over salespeople and other operations. Responsibility is more readily placed, and problems are more easily pinpointed. This structure can also adapt more readily to regional needs, habits, and conditions.

The major disadvantage of geographic organization is the loss of benefits from division or specialization of labor. Each salesperson sells the firm's products to all types of customers. He or she must perform all selling functions. Because the structure provides a good deal of individual freedom, sales reps may spend more effort in their best areas or on products and customers they see as most rewarding—whether or not this is consistent with management's policies and objectives.

Product-type organization.   Often the product type is the basis for organizing the sales force. With this structure, salespeople are assigned a product or group of products. For example, IBM has one sales force for computers and a separate one for office equipment.[20]

In the common product-type structure, all salespeople report to the product-line manager. Each division is run as a separate and autonomous unit. The division managers report to a field sales manager, who coordinates selling activities for all product lines.

Perhaps the major advantage of product-type organization is specialization that results from the individual consideration given the products. The sales force becomes familiar with the technical attributes and uses of the product and can then develop more effective ways to sell it. And product-oriented structures offer the advantages of decentralization, as each division controls the selling effort a product receives.

The product-type organization's major drawback is the duplicated effort of several reps calling on customers who use the firm's various products. This duplication is costly in selling and administrative expense and

---

[20] Gilbert A. Churchill, Jr., Neil M. Ford, and Orville C. Walker, Jr., *Sales Force Management: Planning, Implementation, and Control* (Homewood, Ill.: Richard D. Irwin, 1981), p. 94.

in the potential ill will of irritated customers. Product organization thus requires more coordination across the various divisions.

Since the major advantage of a product-type sales structure is specialization, it is best suited for highly technical products that require such expertise. It is also useful when a company offers a large number of products, making it difficult for one person to handle them all. Firms with totally unrelated products use this organization; so do firms whose products require different channels of distribution. A product organization is common in a merger, when the acquired company maintains its own sales force to sell its own product. Green Giant did this when it was acquired by Pillsbury.[21]

Classes of customers. Organizing the sales force by customers is a growing trend. Customers may be classified by sales volume, channels of distribution, or type of industry. In this structure, the sales force sells the full line of products used by their assigned customer group. Ansul Company, which produces fire extinguishers and fire protection equipment, uses this type of organization. It has a separate sales force for end users, governments, and original equipment manufacturers.[22] A customer-specialized organization focuses on the needs of the target market and adapts to those needs.

In firms where a few accounts are critical to the firm's success, a major account management function is common. Its purpose is to make sales and develop long-term relationships with the key accounts.[23] Therefore, special organizational structures handle these accounts.[24] For example, key accounts are often handled by sales executives. A separate key account division can also be created. Some apparel companies have separate divisions that sell private-label clothes to general-merchandise chains such as Sears and Penneys. Other companies assign a separate sales force to the major accounts.

The major advantage of a customer-type organization is the ability to respond more readily to customer needs. Salespeople may then develop new-product ideas or marketing strategies appropriate for the target market. This approach is also more flexible. Each sales force uses the selling approach best suited for their particular customer group. Promotional campaigns are more easily directed at a specific customer group. And management can control selling effort in the various segments simply by specifying the size of each segment's sales force.

---

[21] Ibid., p. 95.

[22] Ibid.

[23] Ibid., p. 98.

[24] Benson P. Shapiro, "Account Management and Sales Organization: New Developments in Practice," in *Sales Management: New Developments from Behavioral and Decision Model Research,* ed. Richard P. Bagozzi (Cambridge, Mass.: Marketing Science Institute, 1979), pp. 265–94.

However, a customer-class organization is subject to the same disadvantage as a product-type structure: efforts are duplicated if territories overlap or if a customer fits into more than one classification. The duplication is costly in executive time and increased overhead expense.

In light of these pros and cons, organization by classes of customers is most beneficial when the target markets have special needs. This is true when a product has several uses or when different selling techniques are needed. IBM, for example, organizes its sales force by type of industry. It has a sales force for the aircraft and missile industry, one for the financial industry, and one for the textile industry.[25] A customer-oriented organization is also advantageous when customers are geographically clustered. IBM's financial sales force sells on Wall Street, its textile force in the South, and its aircraft and missile force in Los Angeles.

Combination organization.   Since different skills are required in different selling activities, the sales force is often organized by selling function. This creates specialization in selling functions. For example, it has been suggested that one sales force specialize in prospecting and developing new customers; another sales force should maintain and service established ones.[26] One functional specialization common in industrial products firms is in developmental specialists.[27] These salespeople help with the development and initial sales of new products.

Organizations such as these may be difficult to maintain, as customers may resent being assigned a different salesperson. And it may be difficult for management to coordinate the functions.

The sales force can be organized on more than one basis. Many firms use a combination of the approaches just discussed; for example, a firm can use a territory–product organization. In any case, the method of organizing the sales force should depend on company objectives.

Sales force size   One of the most productive resources available to a company is its sales force. When the sales force is increased, sales almost always increase. However, the sales force is also one of the firm's most expensive resources; costs can increase significantly when the number of sales reps increases. Thus, for optimal profitability it is important to determine the number of salespeople required. Three methods are widely used to do this: the breakdown, the workload, and the incremental methods.[28]

[25] William J. Stanton and Richard H. Buskirk, *Management of the Sales Force* (Homewood, Ill.: Richard D. Irwin, 1974), pp. 118–19.

[26] George N. Kahn and Abraham Shuchman, "Specialize Your Salesman!" *Harvard Business Review,* January–February 1961, pp. 90–98.

[27] Churchill et al., *Sales Force Management*, p. 97.

[28] The discussion of these methods is based on Churchill et al., *Sales Force Management*, pp. 160–65.

Breakdown method.   The simplest way to determine optimal sales force size is the *breakdown method.* The assumption here is that all salespersons have the potential to produce the same amount of sales in a year. The estimated productivity for one salesperson is divided into the company's total forecasted sales to determine how many sales reps are needed. For example, if a firm forecasted total sales at $10 million and if each salesperson could produce $250,000 in sales, then 40 salespeople would be required.

The major advantage of this method is that it is conceptually simple. But there are some major drawbacks to the breakdown method. For instance, it makes no allowance for turnover. When salespeople quit or are fired, they must be replaced; and the initial productivity of the new reps will be low. Turnover can be included in the formula, but the method then loses some of its simplicity. Another drawback is that it assumes all members of the sales force have equal productivity. It doesn't account for differences in individual abilities or territories.

The most serious shortcoming is that it uses reverse logic. Sales force size is determined by the level of forecasted sales. In reality, sales are a result of marketing effort; sales force size indicates the level of that effort. It is thus more logical to determine sales force size before forecasting sales volume. Another major drawback of the breakdown method is that it considers sales rather than profitability as the desired end result.

Workload method.   The *workload method* is based on an equal workload for all salespeople.[29] To find the number of salespeople needed, management determines the amount of work it takes to cover the target market. It then divides this estimate by the workload the average sales rep can manage. The workload method consists of the following steps:

1. Classify customers and prospects into groups according to the amount of work required to service the group. Classification is usually based on sales volume, but other criteria (such as profitability or customer needs) may be used. For example, firms may classify their accounts in the following manner:

Type	Sales volume	Number of accounts
A	Over $50,000	100
B	$20,000 to $50,000	250
C	Under $20,000	400

[29] Walter J. Talley, Jr., "How to Design Sales Territories," *Journal of Marketing* 25 (January 1961), pp. 7–13.

2. Determine the number of sales calls an account should receive per year and the desired length of these calls. These estimates are obtained through past experience, through experiments varying the length and frequency of the call, or through managerial judgment. The estimates are then multiplied to find the number of contact hours per year necessary for each account type. For example, the firm may have determined the number of contact hours as follows:

					Total contact hours	
Type	Calls per year		Call length (minutes)		minutes	hours
A	25	×	60	=	1,500	= 25
B	15	×	40	=	600	= 10
C	8	×	15	=	120	= 2

3. Calculate the total amount of selling effort required to serve the entire market. The number of accounts in each category is multiplied by the number of contact hours required for each type of account, as follows:

Type	Number of accounts	Contact hours per account	Workload hours
A	120	25	3,000
B	250	10	2,500
C	400	2	800
			6,300

4. Estimate the time available per salesperson. The average hours worked per week is multiplied by the weeks worked per year, taking into account holidays, sickness, and vacation time. For example:

$$40 \text{ hours/week} \times 49 \text{ weeks/year} = 1,960 \text{ hours/year}$$

5. Allocate the time available per salesperson by the functions she or he performs. In our example, this may be done as follows:

Task	Percentage of time	Hours per task
Selling	50	980
Nonselling	30	588
Traveling	20	392
		1,960 hours per year

6. Determine the sales force size by dividing the total workload hours by the selling hours available per salesperson. In this example, seven salespeople would be needed:

$$\frac{6{,}300 \text{ hours}}{980 \text{ hours per salesperson}} = 6.42, \text{ or } 7 \text{ salespeople}$$

The workload method is simple to comprehend. It acknowledges that certain customers require a different level of selling effort. But it still does not consider differences in sales response or profitability of each account. Nor does it allow for differences in the ability of salespeople.

Incremental method. The ***incremental method*** of sales force size determination is based on the principle of diminishing returns. The method recognizes that there will probably be diminishing returns associated with adding more salespeople. For example, while one additional salesperson might add $200,000 to total sales, the addition of two more might add only $350,000.[30]

Semlow found that salespeople in territories with higher sales potential produced more dollar sales than those in smaller sales-potential territories. However, the sales were less than proportionate to the increase in potential sales volume. For example, sales in territories with 1 percent of total national potential were $160,000, where total sales in territories with 5 percent of national potential were $200,000. Thus, only $40,000 of sales per 1 percent of potential were realized in the higher-potential territories versus $160,000 per 1 percent of potential in lower-potential territories. Semlow reached the obvious conclusion that a higher proportion of sales per 1 percent of potential could be realized if territories were made smaller by adding salespeople. The managerial question was to determine the optimum number of salespeople to hire because costs increase as the number of salespeople increases.

The method consists of the following steps:

1. Estimate the sales potential in each territory. Each territory's potential is expressed as a percentage of the total national potential.

2. Determine the dollar sales per 1 percent of territory potential. This figure is derived by dividing the total sales in the territory by the percentage of total potential within the territory and multiplying this value by 1 percent.

3. Estimate the total sales volume for different sizes of the sales force, assuming all territories have equal potential.

---

[30] This discussion of the incremental method is based on the following classic article: Walter J. Semlow, "How Many Salespeople Do You Need?" *Harvard Business Review* 37 (May–June 1959), pp. 126–32; and Churchill et al., *Sales Force Management,* pp. 164–67.

4. Determine the optimal sales force size by converting each total sales volume from step 3 into operating profit on investment. We do this by estimating operating profit before variable selling cost and then deducting variable selling costs of certain sized sales forces. The required investment for each sales volume is then found by estimating the working capital and plant investment required. Operating profit is then expressed as a percentage of required investment. The optimal sales force is determined by the size that produces the highest return on investment.

The incremental method is sound because of the logical idea that salespeople in low-potential territories are expected to achieve more of their potential than those in territories with higher potential. Developing territories with the same potential is also a sound idea. The major drawback to the incremental method is that information necessary to implement it may not be available or may be difficult and costly to obtain.

Sales force compensation

The sales force must be compensated for their efforts, but the development of a suitable compensation plan is difficult. Management's objectives are often not compatible with those of the sales force. Management desires a simple plan that is economical, flexible, includes control of the salesperson's activities, and attracts, retains, and motivates desirable sales reps. The sales force looks for a steady income, reward for superior performance, and a fair compensation plan. Money is not the only reward salespeople desire. They want recognition, opportunity for advancement, and other nonfinancial benefits. These needs must be considered when developing a compensation plan for the sales force. The properly designed plan motivates the sales force to do what management wants, in the manner desired, within a certain time.[31] To do this most effectively, compensation should be linked to the firm's most important sales and marketing objectives.[32]

The level and elements of compensation must be determined when developing a compensation plan. The *level* of compensation should be related to the going market price for the skills and abilities required for the type of selling job that needs to be done. The *elements* of the compensation plan consist of a fixed amount, a variable amount, expense allowances, and fringe benefits. The combination and level of the compensation plan elements depend on the nature of the market and channels of distribution, the nature of the job, the caliber of the people, the company's financial condition, and business conditions in general.[33] Three types of compensation plans are commonly used: straight salary, straight commission, and a combination of the variable and fixed elements.

---

[31] Churchill et al., *Sales Force Management,* pp. 399–401.

[32] Richard C. Smyth and Matthew J. Murphy, *Compensation and Motivating Salespeople* (New York: American Management Association, 1969), pp. 48–49.

[33] Stanton and Buskirk, *Management of the Sales Force.*

Straight salary.   Straight-salary compensation involves a fixed sum of money paid at regular time periods. Payment is determined by the amount of time the salesperson works rather than by specific accomplishments, such as increased sales. Compensation can be given for any expenses incurred.

The major advantage of a straight-salary approach is that management can direct the sales force to perform nonselling tasks. It gives management more control over salespeople's activities. This is particularly desirable when the job requires considerable nonselling activities (such as account servicing) or when sales reps provide a great deal of technical advising. The income security and regularity of a straight salary helps stabilize morale. It may also help develop a more satisfied sales force, which may reduce turnover. And it is easy to understand and administer. The major shortcoming of straight salary is that financial rewards are not based on performance. There is no direct incentive to put forth extra selling effort. Questions arise about salary adjustments for ability and length of service. A heavier burden thus falls upon management to make sure the sales force is properly evaluated, motivated, and rewarded.

The straight-salary approach does not allow the firm to take advantage of changes in the business cycle. During downswings, inflexible selling expenses cut into profits. During upswings, there is no financial incentive to motivate the sales force to take advantage of the increased sales potential. And the lack of a financial incentive makes it difficult to attract achievement-oriented sales people.

The straight-salary compensation plan is best suited to situations where functions other than selling are important and where supervisors are able to motivate the sales force. It is useful when one person's impact on a sale is difficult to measure, as in team selling.[34]

Straight commission.   The straight-commission form of compensation is the direct opposite of straight salary. A straight-commission plan is based entirely on performance. A fixed or sliding rate applied to the sales or profit level produced by a salesperson determines the level of compensation.

In designing a straight-commission plan, three elements must be determined. First, a commission base must be set from which performance is measured and commissions determined. This is usually gross or net sales, profit, or gross margin. Second, a commission rate for each unit of accomplishment must be established. This could be a fixed rate, or it could vary progressively or regressively as sales volume rises. The commission rate can vary by products or customer accounts, with the most profitable sales having a higher commission. Third, a starting point must be set

---

[34] Churchill et al., *Sales Force Management,* p. 406.

These ads indicate the diversity of positions in sales and sales management. The ads announce openings in outdoor advertising, banking, and sporting goods sales.

for the payment of commission. This is usually the first sale or some level of sales thereafter, such as the breakeven point.

The major advantage of a straight commission is that it provides a direct financial incentive. Earnings represent the ability and effort exerted. By using a variable commission rate, management can direct the sales force to focus on certain accounts or products. Selling expense fluctuates with sales volume, so money for sales force compensation is available regardless of the business cycle. Finally, straight commission is easy to compute and administer.

A major disadvantage of this approach is that management has less control over sales force time and effort. It is difficult to induce sales people to perform tasks that do not produce sales (such as servicing an account after a sale). And the sales force may use high-pressure sales tactics that could be detrimental to the company in the long run. Finally, straight commission offers little income security and regularity, which can lower morale when sales volume is down.

To offset this last disadvantage, some firms offer their employees the use of a drawing account. This can be a fixed sum advanced regularly or an account from which a salesperson can make a withdrawal similar to a loan. The money advanced is deducted from the salesperson's earned commissions.

Combination plan.   A combination plan attempts to provide the advantages of a straight salary and a straight commission without their disadvantages. This plan provides a base salary plus commissions, bonuses, or both. It is the most common form of compensation. Currently, 66.3 percent of manufacturing firms use salary-plus-incentive compensation.[35] The proportion of base salary to incentive pay depends on the company's objectives and the nature of the job. If the job requires a lot of nonselling tasks (such as inventory taking or technical advising), a larger base salary is usually needed. On the other hand, if a great deal of selling skill is needed, a larger incentive pay should be given. A rule of thumb is 75 percent base salary and 25 percent incentive.

The base salary provides income stability. It gives management more control to direct the sales force to perform nonselling tasks. The incentive provides direct financial motivation to generate sales. This combination method is appropriate, then, where the sales force's motivation impacts sales volume and where management wants more task control.

A *bonus* is a lump-sum payment awarded at management's discretion for superior performance. It can be offered in addition to or in place of a commission. A bonus is useful when management wants to focus on a particular client or product for a short time. It does not provide as strong an incentive as a commission, though.

Table 21–3 compares the level of payment for straight-salary and salary-plus-incentive compensation for industrial and consumer goods sales. Salary-plus-incentive results in a higher level of payment than a straight salary. And the compensation level increases as a sales rep gains experience. In the table, the compensation level is higher for industrial sales than for consumer goods sales. In addition, incentive payment is a larger percent of compensation for industrial sales.

---

[35] "There Has to Be a Better Way," *Sales and Marketing Management,* November 12, 1979, pp. 41–42.

Table 21–3:
Salespeople's annual
compensation

A. *Consumer goods sales*

Compensation form	Trainee	Sales experience level		Sales management
		Moderate	Senior	
Straight salary	$15,200	$18,100	$28,200	$32,500
Salary plus incentive				
Salary	14,650	19,060	23,820	30,080
Incentive	1,250	4,160	4,560	5,420
Total*	16,250	24,320	30,140	35,420

B. *Industrial goods sales*

Straight salary	$16,650	$24,392	$30,357	$35,825
Salary plus incentive				
Salary	17,375	21,171	25,765	31,687
Incentive	2,825	5,753	7,835	9,120
Total*	20,600	27,771	33,724	41,147

Source: *Sales & Marketing Management Magazine.* Survey of Industrial and Commercial Buying Power. Copyright July 25, 1983.

* The sum of the salary and incentive components will not equal the total compensation because not all respondents provided information on all of the components of compensation.

Administration and management of sales force compensation. As we have said, money is not the only reward desired by salespeople. Other forms of compensation can be just as important. For many salespeople, this means opportunities for promotion and advancement. They also want recognition for their accomplishments. Others desire contact with supervisors and an opportunity to participate in managerial decisions. They seek job enrichment. Salespeople want more responsibility to make their jobs more meaningful. And they seek personal and career development from their jobs. Sales meetings and conventions can enhance the salesperson's knowledge and skills and increase interest in his career. It is essential, then, that management consider nonfinancial rewards when designing and implementing a compensation plan.[36]

In administering the compensation plan, management might consider an ***open-pay policy.*** This means that sales reps are given information on what others in the sales force are paid but without disclosing specific sales person's names. This might be done by publishing the firm's low, overall average, and high merit raises for a year. Research has shown that an open-pay policy can increase salespeople's performance and their satisfaction with pay, promotional policies, and their work.[37] An open-

---

[36] Henry Pruden, William Cunningham, and Wilkie D. English, "Nonfinancial Incentives for Salesmen," *Journal of Marketing* 36 (October 1972), pp. 55–59.

[37] Charles M. Futrell and Omer C. Jenkins, "Pay Secrecy versus Pay Disclosure for Salesmen: A Longitudinal Study," *Journal of Marketing Research* 15 (May 1978), pp. 214–19.

pay policy is one tool management may use to improve job performance and satisfaction.

In administering and managing any compensation plan, it is essential to strike a balance between the needs and objectives of the sales force and those of the company.

Recruitment, selection, and retention

Recruiting is the process of identifying qualified candidates and inducing them to apply for employment. The major tasks involved in recruiting are development of selection criteria, communication with sources of recruits, and selection of recruiting methods.

Selection criteria are based on job qualifications determined from the role of the sales force. The determinants of the sales force are the importance of personal selling within the firm's marketing strategy, the complexity of the selling task, and each salesperson's impact on profits.[38]

Once the sales force is established, a job description can be prepared. A *job description* details the job requirements and lists the products sold, the required selling and nonselling activities, and the salesperson's degree of responsibility and accountability. It identifies the traits and abilities that qualify a prospect for a job.

Managers at various organization levels are responsible for recruiting. In smaller companies, sales executives usually do the recruiting and selecting. Higher-level management may be involved when sales is the training ground for upper-level management. In larger, multilevel sales forces, recruiting is done by district or regional sales managers, often in conjunction with the personnel department.

Job qualifications determine where management looks for recruits. For example, an industrial salesperson may be found among engineering graduates at a university. An experienced person to sell a new product line to a department store may be found through an ad in a trade journal such as *Women's Wear Daily*.[39] Other sources of recruits are general newspaper ads, employment agencies, and current company employees.

Once a pool of qualified applicants has been recruited, the selection process begins. Various selection procedures and tools are used, the most common being personal interviews and application blanks. Physical exams, reference checks, and intelligence, aptitude, and personality tests are used. Firms generally use a combination of these tools plus managerial judgment to evaluate prospective salespersons.

Sales training

One survey found that the average cost to train a sales representative in 1982 was $12,633.[40] To achieve a satisfactory return on this investment,

---

[38] Benson P. Shapiro, *Sales Program Management: Formulation and Implementation* (New York: McGraw-Hill, 1977), p. 450.

[39] Marvin A. Jolson, *Sales Management: A Tactical Approach* (New York: Petrocelli/Charter, 1977), p. 175.

[40] "Average Sales Rep Pay Hits $30,444: Up 12.8 percent over 79," *Marketing News* 15 (February 5, 1982), p. 1.

the sales training program should be tailored to company objectives and marketing strategy.

Sales training involves imparting information, developing skills, and shaping work habits to maximize a salesperson's effectiveness.[41] Its objectives are to increase productivity and improve sales force morale.

Before the actual training begins, the recruit should be made to feel welcome in the firm. The salesperson must respect the company and its products if the training is to be effective. An important function of the training program is to give sales reps extensive knowledge of both. The salespersons should know each product's features, uses, benefits, and limitations. Company history, policies, objectives, operations, and procedures should be understood, as well. Armed with this knowledge, the salesperson is prepared to face customer questions.

Sales training should orient the salesperson to the marketing environment. He or she should become thoroughly familiar with competitors, industry practice, and customer needs.

The skills necessary to the selling process must be developed. This includes learning to prospect, determine customer needs, make a presentation, close a sale, and retain the customer. Sales reps must learn from and build on their own past successes and failures and on those of other salespeople.

Sales training can be formal, off-the-job training (as IBM uses) or informal, on-the-job training. Most companies use a mix of the two. Formal training often uses role-playing and case analysis in which the salesperson is not involved in selling at all. In contrast, on-the-job training involves observing another sales rep perform the job and then performing it under the sales rep's supervision.

The training period can last from a few days to several years, depending on the nature of the products and the position. On-the-job training takes place in the field. The location of formal training varies: regional training centers, manufacturing facilities, corporate headquarters, or home offices can be used.

Sales training is not restricted to new salespersons. Seasoned sales reps are often sent through training as a refresher; to learn about new products, markets, and selling techniques; or to become sales managers.

A properly designed training program can substantially help achieve the organization's objectives. For example, Armour-Dial found that, for well-trained salespeople, the number of calls per day increased 12 percent; new-product retail displays 25 percent; cash sales, 100 percent; display sales, 62 percent; and sales to direct-buying or chain accounts, 25 percent.[42]

---

[41] Jolson, *Sales Management,* p. 198.

[42] "The New Super Salesman: Wired for Success," *Business Week,* January 6, 1973, pp. 45–49.

Sales force supervision and motivation

Sales force supervision is management of the sales force. In the broadest terms, then, sales supervision involves the basic management functions of planning, controlling, directing, and evaluating the sales force to achieve the firm's goals. More narrowly, it is the process where supervisors influence their sales force, just as the sales force influences potential customers.[43]

Sales force supervision can serve several purposes. First, sales managers can provide additional training to help improve and maintain the selling skills of the sales reps. Second, supervision is a way to ensure that company policies are being followed to meet company objectives. Third, sales force supervisors are in a sound position to stimulate the sales force to work better. Fourth, supervisors can give backup and technical assistance when needed. Fifth, they can facilitate communication between the company and the sales force: the sales supervisor is an intermediary who listens to the opinions and problems of the sales force and communicates management's position on various issues and practices. Finally, as a result of these functions, supervisors can have a tremendous impact on sales force morale.

Sales management must determine the appropriate amount of supervision. Oversupervision may be resented by sales reps who select a sales career because of the independence it offers. On the other hand, undersupervision may negatively affect the sales force's morale and performance. Salespeople may feel the firm doesn't care or know what's happening in the field. And any problems a salesperson has may never be resolved unless a supervisor detects or helps correct them.

In most occupations, people prefer less supervision. Research shows that this is not true with industrial salespeople. Industrial sales reps hold a boundary position; that is, they are go-betweens for the firm and its customers. Customer demands often conflict with those of the salesperson's organization, and sales reps are often confronted with challenging new problems. Because of this, industrial salespeople prefer to have relatively close supervision.[44]

Effective sales force supervision can be an important way to motivate the sales force. *Motivation* is defined as the choice to begin a task, to exert effort on a task, and to continue exerting effort on it.[45] For sales reps, motivation is the amount of effort they want to put into a selling-related task.[46]

Motivation can be explained in terms of expectancy theory. This theory proposes that a salesperson's motivation is a function of expectancies,

[43] Jolson, *Sales Management*, p. 244.

[44] Churchill et al., "Organizational Climate," pp. 323–32.

[45] John P. Campbell and Robert C. Pritchard, "Motivation Theory in Industrial and Organizational Psychology," in *Handbook of Industrial Organizational Psychology*, ed. Marvin D. Dunnette (Skokie, Ill.: Rand McNally, 1976), p. 65.

[46] Churchill et al., *Sales Force Management*, p. 379.

instrumentalities, and valences for rewards.[47] ***Expectancies*** are the salesperson's perceptions of how likely exerting effort on a particular task will lead to improved performance in a certain area. For example, a salesperson may perceive that by improving follow-up service after a sale, there is a 50 percent chance the number of customer complaints will decrease.

Instrumentalities are the salesperson's perceptions of how likely improved performance in a certain area will lead to a higher reward. For example, a salesperson may perceive that it is 80 percent likely that a 50 percent increase in sales volume will lead to a promotion.

Valences are the perceptions of how desirable a particular reward is. Different salespeople value and are motivated by different rewards. Valences are a function of the satisfaction with current rewards. For example, a salesperson who makes $40,000 a year may value a $2,000 raise for a 15 percent increase in sales volume less than a salesperson who makes only $16,000 a year and has also increased sales volume 15 percent.

The salesperson's perceptions of these variables—expectancies, instrumentalities, and valences—determine their motivational level. That is, the higher and more accurate the salesperson's perceptions of these variables, the higher the motivation level.

Sales force supervision affects these perceptions and thereby influences motivation. Company policies have a major impact, as well. They determine what rewards are to be given, when, and how often. Therefore, to improve motivation, company policy should set rewards that the sales force desires and give them when performance indicates they are deserved.

Other influences on motivation are job satisfaction, personality, experience, and other personal characteristics. In addition, the products, competition, territory potential, and other environmental variables influence motivation level.

Evaluation of sales force performance

The evaluation of sales force performance is an integral part of the sales management process. The evaluation determines whether the sales force efforts are achieving the company's objectives. It involves comparing the actual results achieved by each salesperson against performance standards. It should result in rewarding those who have attained their objectives and taking measures to correct the problems of those who have not.

Sales force performance evaluation is difficult because factors beyond the sales rep's control affect sales. Sales force evaluation, therefore, is based not only on output (i.e., dollar volume of sales) but also on input (i.e., quality of planning and number of sales calls made).

Objective, quantitative criteria are used to measure performance based

---

[47] This discussion of expectancies, instrumentalities, and valences is based on ibid., pp. 378–82.

on output.[48] One criterion is the salesperson's contribution to company profits. This is the cost plus markup for a product, less all selling expenses. **Return on assets managed (ROAM)** is another measure to evaluate performance. This considers the contribution margin for a certain level of sales along with asset turnover. Consider the following:

$$\text{Return on assets managed} = \frac{\text{Contribution to profit}}{\text{Sales}} \times \frac{\text{Sales}}{\text{Assets employed}}$$

Another evaluation criterion is the sales–cost ratio. This is the ratio of sales expenses to dollar sales volume. Market share can also be used. If other factors that influence market share (pricing, product quality, advertising, competitive environment) are held constant, an increase in share may be attributed to improved sales performance. A final criterion is achievement of company marketing goals, such as sales and profitability objectives.

These output criteria are affected by many factors beyond the salesperson's control, and there is often a time lag between efforts expended and outputs achieved. Therefore, performance measures should also consider the sales reps' *inputs* (efforts expended to meet performance objectives) rather than the actual results achieved. Efforts or desirable behaviors are much more controllable by the salesperson.

One method of assessing performance this way is through the workplan. A **workplan** is a periodic report sales reps submit to their managers about their plans for future activities. It describes the calls the salesperson makes. Evaluation is then based on how well the salesperson has planned his/her activities, how closely the plans have been followed, and how they compare to accomplishments.

BARS (behaviorally anchored rating scales) is another way to evaluate sales force performance. BARS is an evaluation system that focuses on behavior and performance controllable by the individual. It attempts to identify behaviors (inputs) that lead to results (outputs).

A BARS performance measure is constructed in a five-step sequence:[49]

1. *Generate critical incidents.* These are occurrences that are keys to successful performance.[50] They are obtained by asking people familiar with the job to identify successful performance behaviors and to provide examples.

2. *Refine and create dimensions.* The critical incidents are reviewed and refined into 5 to 12 performance dimensions.

---

[48] Henry Porter, "Manage Your Sales Force as a System," *Harvard Business Review,* March–April 1975.

[49] A. Benton Cocanougher and John M. Ivancevich, " 'BARS' Performance Rating for Sales Force Personnel," *Journal of Marketing,* July 1978, pp. 87–95.

[50] John C. Flanagan, "The Critical Incident Technique," *Psychological Bulletin,* August 1954, pp. 327–55.

3. *Retranslate.* A different group of people assign the critical incidents to the performance dimensions. A critical incident is retained if 60 percent of the group assigns it to the same dimension as the first group did.

4. *Weight the incidents.* The second group then rates, on a 7- to 10-point scale, how effectively the behavior in the critical incident reflects performance on the dimension. An incident is retained if it has a low standard deviation on the ratings (which means a high level of agreement among the raters).

5. *Final BARS.* The behaviorally anchored position of each critical incident is determined by its mean rating. The final BARS consist of 5 to 12 performance dimensions anchored by six to eight weighted critical incidents. Figure 21–2 is an example of a BARS scale measuring sales force cooperativeness.

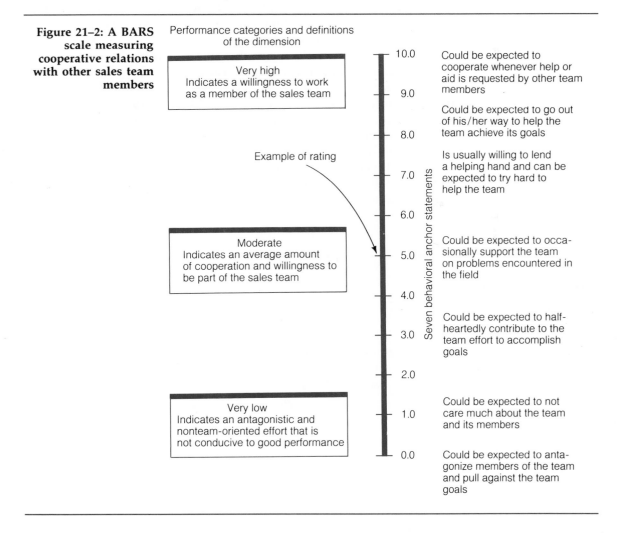

Figure 21–2: A BARS scale measuring cooperative relations with other sales team members

This system has the advantage of involving both sales force and managers. The result is that everyone is aware of the behaviors critical to effective job performance.

Two other types of evaluation systems are often used. One compares actual sales to quotas. The other compares past and present performance.

Table 21–4 shows one way to do both of these. Sales volume produced by each sales rep in a district is compared to sales volume last year and to present sales quotas. The comparisons are simplified through the use of an index.

There are obvious differences in performances and in management expectations. This is reflected in the different sales quotas assigned, which may represent territory potential, experience, competitiveness, etc. The star performer was Thornsen, who not only dramatically increased her sales volume by $600,000 from last year but also far exceeded this year's quota. Martin is responsible for the district not achieving its quota. Martin did not come close to meeting last year's sales volume or this year's quota.

Before any action is taken, a further analysis should be done to determine the causes. This can be done using some of the output criteria suggested earlier. From Table 21–5, it is clear that while Thornsen had the highest dollar sales, she also had the highest expense (expressed as a percentage of sales) and the lowest contribution to profits. Martin's low sales volume may be a result of emphasizing low-margin products and holding down selling costs at the expense of sales. On the other hand, Gillette may be concentrating too heavily on high-margin products. Given this information, management is in a sound position to guide these sales reps and to take corrective action.

Table 21–4:
Performance of sales representatives based on sales volume

Sales representative	Actual sales ($000)	Sales last year ($000)	Sales quota	Performance index* Last year	Quota
Gary Gillette	1,200	1,000	1,200	1.20	1.00
Christopher Martin	500	900	1,100	0.55	0.45
Natalie Thornsen	1,600	1,000	1,200	1.60	1.33
District total	3,300	2,900	3,500	1.14	.94

* Present to past performance is calculated by dividing actual sales by sales last year. For example, Martin:

$$\frac{\$500}{\$900} = 0.55$$

Performance Index for quota performance is calculated by dividing actual sales by quota. For example, Martin:

$$\frac{\$500}{\$1,100} = 0.45$$

Table 21–5: A further analysis of the performance of sales representatives	Sales representative		
	Gillette	**Martin**	**Thornsen**
Sales	100%	100%	100%
— Cost of goods sold	−75	−85	−80
Gross margin	25	15	20
— All other costs	−10	− 5	−12
Contribution to profit	15	10	8
Expense/sales	6	2	10
Market share	16	5	20

TRENDS IN PERSONAL SELLING

Team selling

One trend in personal selling is greater use of **team selling.** Here specialists in production, finance, marketing, and other functions assist the salesperson. Team selling is used with key customers whose large potential purchases require different functional skills to make a purchase decision. In such situations, the purchasing firm also uses a team approach. The buying team consists of people from different functional areas (such as finance and production planning) who are concerned with different aspects of the purchase. It would be extremely difficult for one sales rep to know all these functional areas well enough to answer the buying team's questions. To be most effective, a selling team from functional areas equivalent to the buying team should be organized. Waukesha Motors, which makes combustion engines for construction machinery, petroleum equipment, and marine products, uses team selling for each customer group. Each team consists of a sales rep who knows the industry and a product engineer who knows the product's capabilities. This ensures someone there to install and service an engine once it has been sold.

The major drawback of team selling is its expense. In addition, it is difficult to coordinate the activities of the team members.

Telephone selling

Another trend is the increasing use of telephone selling as either a substitute or a supplement for field selling. In industrial sales, the ratio of outside or field salespeople to inside or telephone salespeople was 3 to 1 in 1973 and 2 to 1 in 1978. And it's expected to be 1 to 2 by the late 1980s.[51] One main reason for this trend is that field selling is more expensive than telephone selling: in 1982 it cost $137.02 to make one industrial sales call,[52] which represents a doubling of costs since 1974.

And telephone selling is usually more efficient than field selling: if a customer isn't available, an inside salesperson can simply phone another

[51] Robert W. Haas, *Industrial Marketing Management* (Boston: Kent Publishing, 1982), p. 246.

[52] Laboratory of Advertising Performance/McGraw-Hill Research as reported in *Business Week,* March 22, 1982, p. 56.

prospect. The telephone can be particularly useful in the prospecting and preapproach stages. Salespeople can contact more potential customers much more quickly and at a lower cost by phone than by personal contact in the field. This saves travel expense and waiting time.

In addition, telephone calls can be efficiently used to make sales, make appointments, deliver news about such things as price deals or product changes, cultivate buyer goodwill, and handle customer problems.[53]

The Bell System has developed a telecommunications system known as **_telemarketing_** to aid sales and service functions. Telemarketing uses an 800 service number or WATS line and an information processing and transfer system that can be tailored to specific elements of the selling process. For example, telemarketing can help qualify prospects, provide product information, handle orders, and provide service. The Chemical Group at B. F. Goodrich uses telemarketing to handle paperwork and allow its reps to concentrate on obtaining new accounts.[54]

Women in personal selling careers

Another trend in selling is the increase of women in sales positions, especially in industrial sales. For 1977, U.S. Department of Labor Statistics indicate that 70.4 percent of the retail sales force were females; only 7.6 percent of the 850,000 industrial (i.e., wholesale and manufacturer) sales reps were females.[55] However, this represented a substantial increase, since women accounted for only 2 percent of industrial sales reps in 1969.[56]

The number of saleswomen in individual companies has significantly increased. Xerox hired over 1,200 people for sales jobs in 1977; 419 (31 percent) were women. And IBM doubled the number of women in their sales force between 1974 and 1978.[57]

Several studies have explored a variety of issues related to women in the sales force. One study surveyed 100 vice presidents of sales in the paper and chemical industries, where male sales reps predominate.[58] These executives felt that women perform very favorably in their personal selling positions. On the issue of making sales, 76 percent felt there was no difference between men and women, and 22 percent felt that men "make more sales" than women. Eight percent felt women had greater absenteeism; 60 percent felt there were no differences between males and females on this dimension. Finally, 26 percent of the responding vice presidents

[53] Charles A. Kirkpatrick and Frederick A. Russ, *Salesmanship,* 6th ed. (Cincinnati: South-Western Publishing, 1976), pp. 442–43.

[54] "The Telemarketing Manual," *Business Week,* March 22, 1982, pp. 55–62.

[55] "Corporate Women," *Business Week,* February 19, 1979, p. 104.

[56] Haas, *Industrial Marketing Management,* p. 245.

[57] "Industrial Sales, like Many Other Fields, Is Opening up to Women," *The Wall Street Journal,* March 28, 1978, pp. 1.

[58] Leslie Kanuk, "Women in Industrial Selling," *Journal of Marketing* 42 (1978), pp. 87–91.

indicated that women had greater turnover than men; 43 percent felt there was no difference.

The vice presidents would recommend industrial sales as a career for female college graduates for the following reasons:

Good opportunity for advancement	49%
Challenging field	37
Good financial rewards	14

Another study compared female and male sales reps from three pharmaceutical companies.[59] To make meaningful comparisons between the men and women, factors such as time on the job, educational level, and age were controlled. There were no differences between males and females on the six job-satisfaction components of pay, supervision, work itself, customers, promotion, and co-workers. Female sales reps were found to have lower role-clarity scores than males. Sales managers should thus try to improve the female roles clarity by improved sales training methods. It is especially important for the women to be able to ask questions freely and openly during training sessions. Experienced sales representatives should be encouraged to provide advice to the women.

Research on personal selling

The trend in research on personal selling is to use a *dyadic approach.*[60] This approach recognizes that personal selling involves a two-way interaction between salesperson and customer. It does not focus on one to the exclusion of the other. Before we discuss the dyadic approach, let's review other research approaches to the personal selling process. This review should help us understand why the dyadic approach developed.

Salesperson behavior and personality. One research approach has attempted to determine what type of sales messages are more effective than others. In one study, six different sales messages were analyzed. The messages differed in the types of information provided: (1) whether the statements on the product were evaluative or nonevaluative; (2) whether the salesperson sought responses from the customer; and (3) whether the salesperson tried to develop a friendly relationship.[61] No significant difference in the effectiveness of these messages was found.

[59] Paul Busch and Ron Bush, "Women Contrasted to Men in the Industrial Sales Force," *Journal of Marketing Research* 15 (August 1978), pp. 438–48.

[60] The discussion of research on personal selling is adapted from Barton Weitz, "Effectiveness in Sales Interactions: A Contingency Approach," *Journal of Marketing* 45 (Winter 1981) pp. 85–103.

[61] Noel Capon, "Persuasive Effects of Sales Messages Developed from Interaction Process Analysis," *Journal of Applied Psychology* 60 (April 1975) pp. 238–44.

Another study found neither a product-oriented message nor a personal-oriented message more effective.[62]

Other studies have attempted to relate personality traits such as forcefulness, achievement orientation, and sociability to sales performance. These studies failed to find a consistent relationship.

Salesperson capability and resources. A second major area of research analyzed the relationship between performance and the salesperson's resources and capabilities. A number of studies examined the relationships between the salesperson's age, education, and intelligence and his/her sales performance. These studies found no consistent relationship between these variables. For example, studies analyzing the relationship between intelligence and sales performance found a positive relationship for stockbrokers, a negative relationship for industrial salespeople, and no relationship for appliance wholesalers.[63]

Other studies explored the relationship between sales performance and specific abilities related to interpersonal persuasion. One study found that effective interpersonal selling is related to the salesperson's ability (1) to accurately perceive the customers' beliefs about the product and (2) to use these perceptions to select an appropriate strategy to influence the customer.[64]

Dyadic studies

The inconclusive results of prior research have led to an interest in the dyadic approach. Dyadic research has explored the effects of the sales rep's expertise and similarities between the customer and the rep. The sales rep's expertise was found to be more important than similarity in influencing the customer.[65] Another study supported the finding that expertise is more important than perceived similarity in eliciting a purchase for technically complex products.[66]

---

[62] John Farley and R. Swinth, "Effects of Choice and Sales Message on Customer–Salesman Interaction," *Journal of Applied Psychology* 51 (April 1967), pp. 107–10.

[63] Edwin E. Ghiselli, "The Validity of Aptitude Tests in Personnel Selection," *Personnel Psychology* 26 (Winter 1973), pp. 461–77; Richard P. Bagozzi, "Sales Force Performance and Satisfaction as a Function of Individual Difference, Interpersonal, and Situational Factors," *Journal of Marketing Research* 15 (November 1978), pp. 517–31; and T. H. Matteiss, Richard M. Durand, Jan R. Muczyk, and Myron Gable, "Personality and the Prediction of Salesmen's Success," in *Contemporary Marketing Thought*, ed. B. Greenberg and D. Bellenger (Chicago: American Marketing Association, 1977), pp. 499–502.

[64] Barton A. Weitz, "The Relationship between Salesperson Performance and Understanding of Customer Decision Making," *Journal of Marketing Research* 15 (November 1978), pp. 501–16.

[65] Paul Busch and David T. Wilson, "An Experimental Analysis of a Salesman's Expert and Referent Bases of Social Power," *Journal of Marketing Research* 13 (February 1976), pp. 3–11.

[66] Arch Woodside and William J. Davenport, "The Effect of Salesman Similarity and Expertise on Consumer Purchasing Behavior," *Journal of Marketing Research* 11 (May 1974), pp. 198–202.

A *contingency approach* to personal selling research is a way to describe the relationship between the salesperson's effectiveness and sales behaviors and a variety of sales rep and customer characteristics.[67] The contingency approach holds considerable promise for improving dyadic personal selling research.

---

[67] Weitz, "Effectiveness in Sales Interactions," p. 89.

SUMMARY

Personal selling can help an organization implement its marketing strategy. However, this role may be difficult for salespeople, who are often caught in the boundary position between conflicting demands of customer and company.

Four types of selling positions can be identified: (1) trade selling, (2) missionary selling, (3) new-business selling, and (4) technical selling. In most selling situations, a seven-step process is followed: (1) prospecting, (2) the preapproach, (3) the approach, (4) the presentation, (5) meeting objections, (6) the close, and (7) the follow-up.

To facilitate the selling process and achieve company goals, objectives are set for the sales force based on volume quotas, activity quotas, or management by objectives (MBO). The sales force is usually organized geographically, by product type, or by class of customer to enable it to perform most effectively. Within this organization, sales force size is generally determined by the breakdown, workload, or incremental method. Straight salary, straight commission or a combination compensation plan is commonly used to reward the sales force for their efforts.

Once qualified candidates have been identified through recruiting, sales training must be given to provide them the knowledge and skills needed to be most effective. Sales force supervision is effective in training as well as in motivating the sales force. Motivation can be determined by using expectancy theory, which includes expectancy, instrumentality, and valence variables. To determine whether the sales force is achieving the company's goals, their performance is evaluated on output criteria (such as sales volume) or on input criteria using a behaviorally anchored rating scale (BARS).

Several trends are evident in the personal selling field: toward more team selling, telephone selling, and more women in personal selling careers. And research on personal selling is emphasizing a dyadic approach, which analyzes significant relationships in the selling process.

KEY CONCEPTS

Boundary position
Trade seller
Missionary seller
New-business seller
Technical seller
Snowball technique
Endless chain

Cold-canvas approach
Canned presentation
Customer-specific presentation
Trial close
Assumptive close
Volume quota
Activity quota

Management by objectives (MBO)
Geographic organization
Product-type organization
Class of customer organization
Combination approach organization
Breakdown method

Workload method	Expectancies	Workplan
Incremental method	Instrumentalities	Team selling
Open-pay policy	Valences	Telemarketing
Job description	Return on assets managed	Dyadic approach
Motivation	(ROAM)	Contingency approach

DISCUSSION QUESTIONS AND EXERCISES

1. In this chapter, Avon and Revlon were contrasted in terms of how much the two companies spend on personal selling. Review the differences in the amounts spent and discuss reasons why these differences exist.

2. Distinguish among and give an example of each of the following: trade sellers, missionary sellers, new-business sellers, technical sellers.

3. The personal selling process is composed of seven stages. Which do you feel is the most important stage? Provide a rationale for your answer.

4. Compare the advantages and disadvantages of the canned and customer-specific sales presentations.

5. List the conditions under which each of the following forms of sales force organization would be used:
    a. Geographic.
    b. Product.
    c. Class of customer.
    d. Combination.

6. Compare and contrast the following three methods of determining sales force size:
    a. Breakdown.
    b. Workload.
    c. Incremental.

7. For which type of selling jobs does straight-commission compensation work the best?

8. What is BARS? What is the rationale for BARS?

9. Which of the trends in personal selling do you regard as most significant? Why?

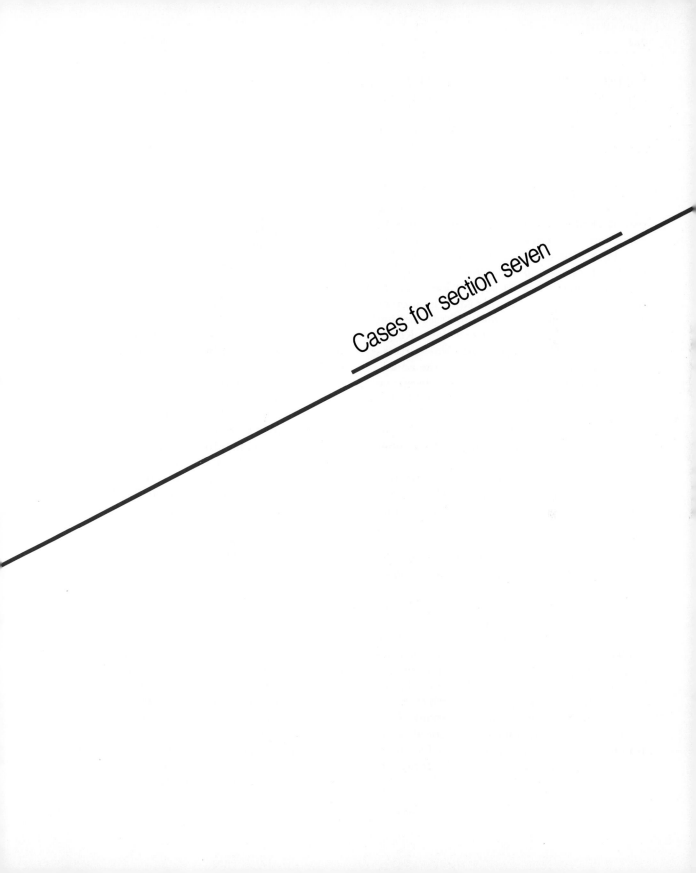

Cases for section seven

Case 13: Burger King, McDonald's, and Wendy's: Advertising in the fast-food industry

In September 1982 Burger King took a big risk: it challenged McDonald's head-on with comparative advertising that named names. In one ad, a little girl says she has "a very big message for grownups" and goes on to explain that McDonald's has 20 percent less meat in their burger than does Burger King. In another ad, a Burger King employee professes feeling sorry for McDonald's because Burger King's hamburger won in a taste test. Not surprisingly, McDonald's filed suit to halt the advertising, claiming that the ads were deceptive because the products were not comparable due to price differences and the taste tests were not well-documented. Under pressure, Burger King withdrew that advertising in November 1982.

Since that time, Burger King has launched a new campaign focusing on the difference between frying (McDonald's) and flame broiling (Burger King). One television advertisement showed a Mr. Rogers (the children's show host) look-alike explaining to the camera the concept of "McFrying," poking fun in an obvious way at McDonald's. This commercial aired only a few days but was removed at the request of the real Mr. Rogers.

McDonald's, the long-time market share leader, has consistently used their advertising to promote their QSC&V motto (quality service, cleanliness, and value). McDonald's responded to Burger King's attack with testimonials from customers talking about food quality, service, and value—all without mentioning the Burger King name. McDonald's, to this date, has refused to play the comparative advertising game.

Kyle T. Craig, executive vice president of Burger King, outlined four criteria that must be met before comparative advertising can be used successfully:

1. Your company should be "tremendously outspent" by the market leader.

2. There should be a clear and meaningful difference that can be exploited.

3. Your company should be large enough to compete credibly with the market leader in the eyes of the consumer.

4. Your company must be willing and able to defend its position in court, if necessary.

A third hamburger chain, Wendy's, used Burger King's ad strategy to "come back with a very strong story in response to the comparative climate Burger King developed, and then take [both McDonald's and Burger King] head on," according to Bruce Ley, Wendy's vice president of national marketing. Ley commented that Burger King's flame broiling versus McDonald's frying was an insignificant rather than meaningful difference. Wendy's ads have focused on the size of the burger and the consumer's preference for a hot and freshly cooked burger, individually dressed. Ley said, "To do this, we used humor to depict the customer as victim at our competitors restaurants." One result: the wildly popular "Where's the beef?" ad campaign featuring octogenarian Clara Peller.

Comparative advertising has paid off for Burger King and Wendy's. Prior to the campaign, studies showed that Burger King had a 7:1 deficiency to McDonald's in top-of-the-mind awareness. That margin has narrowed to 1.5:1. Wendy's is a relatively new chain whose growth has been phenomenal. The first Wendy's opened in 1969. In 1983, Wendy's had 2,678 restaurants, 100,000 employees, and $1.8 billion in sales.

All three chains have made plans for the future: McDonald's licensees voted in 1983 to increase advertising as a percentage of sales.

Burger King's Craig says that "Future comparative ads are going to be based on the positioning—quality food." Wendy's strategy is to broaden their appeal through introduction of new products such as apple dumpling desserts, salad bars, and baked potatoes with toppings. Their new position theme will be "Wendy's has the taste."

References

"Big Mac Ads Hit back at BK." *Advertising Age*, November 1, 1982, p. 1.

"Burger King Beefs up Its Jabs and Jokes." *Business Week*, September 26, 1983, pp. 42–43.

"Burger King's Ads Cook up a Storm." *Business Week*, October 11, 1982, p. 39.

"Comparative Ads Paying off for Burger King." *Marketing News*, p. 18.

"Comparison War Incited Wendy's Ad Campaign." *Marketing News*, p. 19.

"McDonald's 79 Plan: Beat back the Competition." *Advertising Age*, February 19, 1979, p. 1.

Discussion questions

1. What are the four criteria for successful comparative advertising campaigns?

2. Can the market leader benefit from comparative advertising?

3. Both Burger King and Wendy's use humor in their comparison ads. Why do you think they do this?

4. What do you predict the future holds for the three chains in terms of market share?

Case 14:   Avis and Dow Corning: Using telemarketing to improve sales force efficiency and effectiveness

Direct mail and sales calls have historically been the means by which business/industrial marketing is done. Increasingly, however, companies have turned to the telephone to communicate to and persuade the industrial marketing customer. When a systematic approach to the telephone is used, the method is called "telemarketing."

Business Marketing magazine recently teamed with Campaign Communications Institute of America (CCI) to perform the first comprehensive research on the extent of business/industrial marketing by telephone. Their research distinguished between "true telemarketing" and "just making a few calls." True telemarketing is as carefully designed and implemented as advertising, direct mail, or trade show programs, and its practitioners used personnel trained to handle the phone and keep regular call records. By these standards, only 32 percent of the business/industrial firms sampled qualify.

CCI set forth guidelines for a well-designed telemarketing program:

1. Companies should set specific cost and performance objectives and appraise performance against these standards.

2. Structured, pretest scripts should be used.

3. Experienced supervisors should monitor calls on a periodic basis.

The survey found that most business/industrial marketers use the phone to sell or support other selling activities, but that firms who used the above guidelines were most enthusiastic about the medium. Telemarketing offers the interactive benefits of a personal sales call at a much lower cost.

Avis, the car-leasing company, is an example of a firm that has recently started to use telemarketing. Lawrence Mazur, vice president of marketing and sales at Avis, is very enthusiastic about telemarketing. Avis is a true telemarketer in the sense of CCI guidelines. Their first step in outlining a telephone program was to identify its objectives. These were to:

1. Reduce the cost per sale.

2. Provide direction and outside sales call appointments for the fleet sales staff.

3. Provide quality leads for sales force members.

4. Stimulate more contracts and new orders.

5. Obtain an additional lead source.

With these objectives in hand, Avis contacted a telemarketing service company and together they drafted a telephone selling script. The final script was entered on computers to aid the operators who enter prospect data on the CRT terminals. The operators made the calls from a list of companies fitting the target-market criteria used to identify firms who could be leasing 10 to 40 autos, the market Avis can most efficiently serve.

Mazur reports that telemarketing has been very successful for Avis. Since its institution, the average closing time decreased by a month and the sales force had more available selling time. Twenty percent of the calls resulted in appointments with a salesperson. The sales force is now a strong supporter of telemarketing; Mazur says, "They recognize the value of receiving truly qualified leads; it takes the pressure off them and eliminates their confusion about which prospects to call on next."

Mazur reports that Avis will continue with telemarketing, expanding into programs which use direct mail and telemarketing. They expect to use the telephone, also, to further refine their marketing mix and get feedback from customers.

Dow Corning used a similar system to turn routine handling of inquiries into telemarketing. Their objectives were to provide literature quickly to companies requesting it and to identify hot prospects for the sales force. Dow Corning's management is very satisfied with the use of telemarketing for these purposes; the phone is much quicker than mail questionnaires and inside sales people are good at identifying appropriate referrals. An added plus to this program: The inside sales force can actually close many of the sales over the phone. Prior to telemarketing, accounts less than $50,000 were turned away, as the field sales force could not afford to handle them. Now, phone reps service these accounts. Primary results show that each inside sales representative generates $2 million to $3 million in new sales per year, and of course, the cost per sale is much lower than field selling.

References

Maher, Philip. "Dow Corning Blends Inquiry Handling with Telemarketing." *Business Marketing,* October 1983, p. 116.

Mazur, Lawrence D. "How Avis Tries Harder (and Suceeds) with Targeted Telemarketing." *Business Marketing,* October 1983, pp. 114–16.

Roman, Murry, and Bob Donath. "What's Really Happening in Business/Industrial Telemarketing." *Business Marketing,* April 1983, pp. 82–90.

Discussion questions

1. What distinguishes telemarketing from ordinary use of the phone for business purposes?

2. What guidelines did CCI set forth for a well-designed marketing-by-phone program?

3. What were Avis's objectives for their telemarketing program? Were these objectives met?

4. What are the drawbacks to Telemarketing?

5. Compare and contrast Avis and Dow Corning on their use of telemarketing.

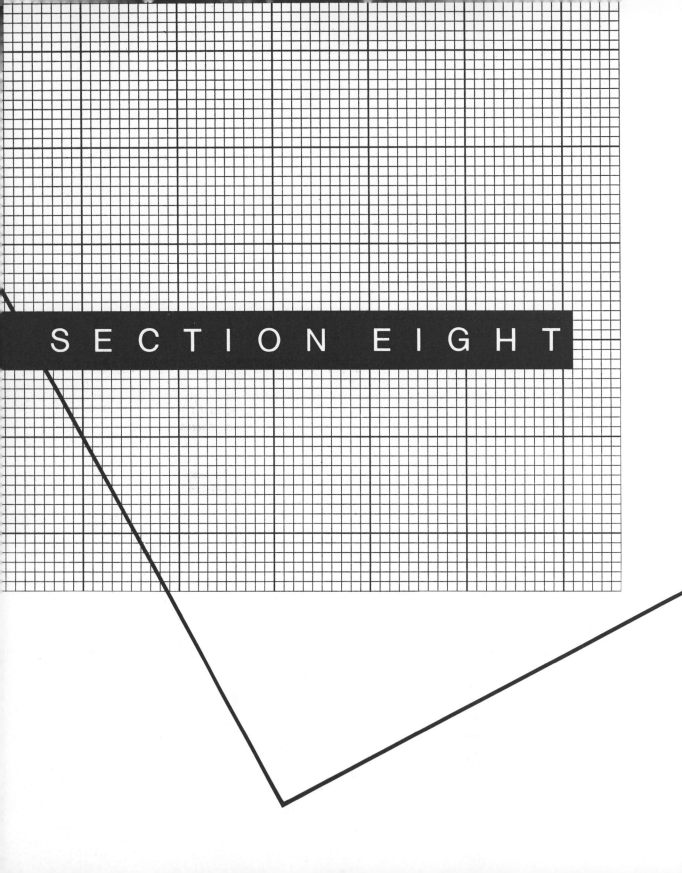

SECTION EIGHT

Evaluation of marketing performance

Marketing plans and strategies are developed with certain objectives in mind. A crucial aspect of marketing management is determining how well these objectives are being met. If objectives are not being met, corrective action must be taken. The control process—the topic of Chapter 22—involves the assessment of marketing performance and the determination of corrective action if performance levels fall short of objectives.

The planning, implementation, and control of marketing strategy require much information on a variety of phenomena from many sources. Chapter 23 examines the informational needs of an organization. Marketing research, as a major source of information, is discussed. The effective management of information through a marketing information system is also considered.

CHAPTER 22

Control of marketing strategy

Nature and definition of control
    Establishment of standards
    Interpretation and evaluation of actual
        performance
    Taking corrective action

Characteristics of effective control systems

Reasons for detailed analysis
    Iceberg principle
    The 80/20 rule

Sales analysis

Variance analysis

Marketing cost analysis
    Unit of analysis
    Sales per unit of analysis
    Full cost versus contribution margin
    Natural versus functional accounts
    Construct unit profit and loss statement

PERT

Budgets

Strategic planning and control
    Profit Impact of Marketing Strategies
        (PIMS)
    Post-action strategic control model
    Contingency planning
    Steering Marketing Control Model
        (STEMCOM)
    The marketing audit

Summary

Key concepts

Discussion questions and exercises

Up to this point, we have concentrated on strategic planning and implementation of the strategic plan. Now, we turn to the managerial task of controlling the plan and implementing the marketing management process. In this chapter, we discuss the nature of control and its components: establishment of standards, interpretation and evaluation, and taking corrective action. Several major methods for analyzing accounting data are presented: sales analysis, variance analysis, and marketing cost analysis. Finally, the marketing audit is presented as a major tool for improving the strategic marketing management process.

NATURE AND DEFINITION OF CONTROL

The control process involves (1) establishment of standards, (2) interpretation and evaluation of information generated by the **feedback** system, and (3) the taking of **corrective action.** Figure 22–1 provides a flowchart illustrating a general model of control of a marketing strategy.

control

> **Control** is that aspect of the managerial process which attempts to ensure that actions and objectives conform to plans.

Establishment of standards

The **standards of performance** flow from the objectives established in the marketing plan. The specific standards depend on the functional area for which they are being established. For example, in the sales management area objectives may be stated in terms of: (1) sales volume as a percentage of sales potential, (2) selling expense as a percentage of sales volume, and (3) the number of customers sold as a percentage of the total number of customers.[1]

For pricing, common objectives may be stated as attempts to: (1) achieve a satisfactory return on investment, (2) maintain market share, and (3) meet a specified profit goal.[2]

Other traditional standards of performance have included gross margin, return on sales, and changes in market share. The main shortcoming of these standards, though, is that they do not take into account the financial resources used by a particular product, customer, sales territory, or market segment. Other, more accurate measures include return on investment, return on equity, and return on assets employed.[3]

---

[1] James F. Engel, Martin T. Warsaw, and Thomas Kinnear, *Promotional Strategy,* 5th ed. (Homewood, Ill.: Richard D. Irwin, 1983), p. 444.

[2] Sand Samiee, "Pricing Objectives of U.S. Manufacturing Firms," in *Proceedings, Southern Marketing Association,* ed. R. S. Franz, R. M. Hopkins, and Al Toma, 1978, pp. 445–47.

[3] Frederick E. Webster, Jr., James A. Largay III, and Clyde P. Stickney, "The Impact of Inflation Accounting on Marketing Decisions," *Journal of Marketing* 44 (Fall 1980), p. 13.

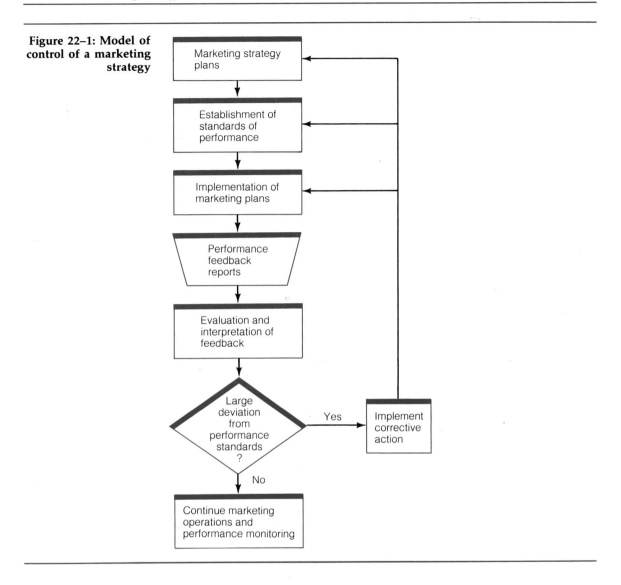

Figure 22–1: Model of control of a marketing strategy

Return on assets has become a more significant measure of marketing performance. Consider the following relationship:

$$\text{Return on assets} = \frac{\text{Operating income}}{\text{Assets}} = \frac{\text{Operating income}}{\text{Sales}} \times \frac{\text{Sales}}{\text{Assets}}$$

The relationship shows that return on assets is determined by profitability or contribution of the sales volume and the turnover rate. Return on assets can be improved by cutting costs while sales remain constant, by reducing the investment in assets, or by increasing sales with the same level of investment.

The performance standards discussed thus far are quantitative. However, some aspects of the marketing manager's job, more subjective and qualitative in nature, include initiative, interpersonal skills, and attitude. The qualitative aspects of the marketing manager's job may contribute most to long-term development of the organization and the individual. Performance standards for these qualitative dimensions should also be established and evaluated.

Development of objectives.   A method for the development of objectives is the ***management by objectives (MBO)*** process. There are three generally accepted steps in the MBO process:

1. Meaningful objectives are established by top management.
2. Superiors and subordinates jointly develop objectives for the subordinates that are consistent with the organizational objectives.
3. Superior and subordinate at some later time assess the subordinate's performance.[4]

Establishing objectives at each level in the organization involves a superior and a subordinate jointly translating the objective that has filtered down from the level above into actions and goals for the subordinate. This is the most important and difficult aspect of the MBO process.

Involving the employee in setting standards improves both performance and job satisfaction. Research has shown that salespeople's perceptions of their influence in setting the standards by which they are supervised and evaluated has the most positive impact on job satisfaction.[5]

Interpretation and evaluation of actual performance

Once performance standards are established, marketing management must develop a system for reporting feedback on actual performance. The feedback must be in a form that is practical and easy to use, and the information must be timely. Managers must have a major input into the design of reports and the overall feedback system. The timeliness of the reports varies significantly. Some reports need to be issued on a daily basis; others are adequate if given monthly or quarterly. In any case, the point is marketing management should receive information often enough to permit corrective action if necessary.

Interpretation and evaluation of feedback is the basis for deciding whether or not to take corrective action. It is, therefore, a key element in the control process.

---

[4] Michael J. Etyd and J. M. Ivancevich, "Management by Objectives in Marketing: Philosophy, Process, and Problems," *Journal of Marketing,* 38 (October 1974), p. 49.

[5] Gilbert A. Churchill, Jr., Neil M. Ford, and Orville C. Walker, Jr., "Organizational Climate and Job Satisfaction in the Sales Force," *Journal of Marketing Research* 13 (November 1976), p. 329.

Taking corrective action
The taking of corrective action links the control process to the planning function. It enables management to accomplish the purpose of control, which is to ensure that planned actions and objectives are being achieved.

Management can make a number of responses to a ***deviation from plan:***

1. Take a corrective action that eliminates the cause for the deviation. An example would be to increase the number of sales representatives in a sales territory to achieve a desired level of dollar sales volume.

2. Adapt to deviations beyond the firm's control and make tactical changes in plans. A common example is reducing price to meet a price cut made by a competitor.

3. Allow both the plan and the condition to continue, but profit by the experience when developing plans and strategy for the next planning period. An example is when a competitor introduces a new product: management may not be able to make any meaningful change in the short run but can only adapt in the longer run.[6]

Before it can take corrective action, management must understand the reason for the deviation, select an approach to solve the problem, and plan to implement it. All this requires that management be an effective decision maker.[7]

CHARACTERISTICS OF EFFECTIVE CONTROL SYSTEMS

In order for a ***marketing control system*** to work effectively, it must (1) utilize current information, (2) use objectives as a standard of comparison to measure performance, (3) point out deviations from the objectives, and (4) report deviations to the individual responsible for the function or activity.[8] Current information must be used, since control is concerned with monitoring and guiding current activities. However, the definition of "current information" may vary. For a purchaser of raw materials subject to frequent price fluctuations, daily information may be required. For others, quarterly or monthly reports may be adequate.

For the control system to be comprehensive, objectives must be developed for all of the organization's units. A unit can vary, depending on the needs of the system but may include departments, products or product lines, sales territories, or customer groups. Thus, if a firm wants to control expenditures for each product, objectives must be established for each product. The goals are necessary in order to evaluate each product's unique

---

[6] David J. Luck and O. C. Ferrell, *Marketing Strategy and Plans* (Englewood Cliffs, N.J.: Prentice-Hall, 1979), pp. 415–16.

[7] Burt K. Scanlan, *Principles of Management and Organizational Behavior* (New York: John Wiley & Sons, 1973), pp. 448–49.

[8] Ibid., p. 449.

contribution. And if the goals are coordinated, the efforts of each product group will be directed toward the overall company objectives.

In *management by exception,* management action is not called for except when a deviation occurs from some objective. This simplifies the manager's work, for the control system itself can point out problems and opportunities as they arise. Management's time can then be spent on the areas requiring the most attention.

Reporting deviations directly to the individual responsible for the operation provides a means for self-evaluation. The deviation could be reported to the individual's superior, but there is less need for supervision when the individual receives feedback directly. The direct feedback fosters an attitude of responsibility; it makes a supervisor's action necessary only when deviations go uncontrolled.

REASONS FOR DETAILED ANALYSIS

Before we present specific methods for interpreting and evaluating accounting data from a marketing management perspective, let's discuss some reasons why this type of analysis is necessary. The *iceberg principle* and the *80/20 rule* are two major reasons why profit and loss statements and total sales figures often require more detailed analysis in order to make them useful to marketing management.

Iceberg principle

Much data and information that marketing managers receive give an impression that may not be consistent with a more detached evaluation of the marketing data. The use of aggregate data like total sales or total costs on an operating statement can be deceiving, for example. Such data do not focus on more specific elements, such as individual products, sales territories, or market segments. Aggregate data allow the marketing manager to focus only on the visible piece of the whole. And visible data may hide certain problems—for small, visible problems are often symptoms of large, unseen ones. Several authors have used the iceberg as an analogy to describe this phenomenon.

Icebergs show only about 10 percent of their mass above the waterline. The submerged and perhaps most dangerous 90 percent remains unseen.

iceberg principle

> The **iceberg principle** applied to business and marketing data means that when we use only aggregate data, we may forget that major difficulties may be submerged.

Detailed data on sales, costs, etc., for each territory, product, or salesperson correspond to the important submerged portion of the iceberg. To rely merely on aggregate data may lead to a misdiagnosis of the true problem. The following example illustrates such a phenomenon:

The annual profit of product X in a company was $800,000, and the annual loss of product Y in the same company was $600,000. Management was pleased with the net profit of $200,000 but was shocked to discover the true status of product Y when accounting by product line was completed.[9]

The iceberg principle is pervasive. The 80/20 rule, or concentration ratio, is one manifestation of this principle.

The 80/20 rule

Often a small percentage of a firm's customers or products provides a relatively large percentage of its sales and profits.

80/20 rule

> The **80/20 rule** states that 80 percent of the sales and/or profit comes from 20 percent of the customers or products.

The 80/20 rule should not be interpreted literally, of course. Its essence is that a small percentage of customers and products yields a large percent of sales. The actual relationship of sales to products may be 65/35, 70/30, or 90/10.

Traditional accounting reports prepared for financial and production analysis often are too general for marketing management. As a result, accounting data are often subjected to more detailed sales and cost analyses so that marketing management can determine the sales and profitability of specific products, sales territories, or customers.

Marketing cost analysis has frequently verified the 80/20 rule. When marketing management identifies the presence of the 80/20 rule in its firm and takes appropriate corrective action, the results are often astounding. For example, one company had 635 (72 percent) unprofitable product items in their product mix of 875 items. The sales staff felt that all items were needed to maintain a complete product mix and to retain customers who bought profitable products. But an experiment in several sales territories resulted in the elimination of 592 of the 635 unprofitable products and a 24 percent increase in net profit.[10]

The control of marketing programs requires feedback to determine their effectiveness and to indicate areas of weakness. There are three major methods of analysis: sales analysis, variance analysis, and marketing cost analysis.

SALES ANALYSIS

Sales analysis is the least expensive and easiest to perform of the three methods.

[9] Patrick Dunne and Harry Wolk, "Marketing Cost Analysis: A Modularized Contribution Approach," *Journal of Marketing* 41 (July 1977), pp. 83–94.

[10] Charles H. Sevin, "Marketing Profits from Financial Analysis," *Financial Executive,* May 1966, p. 26.

sales analysis

> **Sales analysis** is an evaluation on various bases (such as territory, customer class, and product group) to highlight both profitable and problem areas.

Periodic sales analysis gives additional information on trends affecting specific products or market segments. The main uses of sales analysis are: (1) detecting marketing strengths and weaknesses, (2) controlling sales effort and direction, (3) administration of nonmarketing functions such as production, planning, and so on, and (4) overall management with respect to company orientation, expansion, etc.[11]

The sales analysis process simply takes sales figures from company records, divides aggregate sales into the desired units of analysis, and compares the figures. The following example for American Institutional Supply Company illustrates the method.

Table 22–1, a simple sales analysis, shows that each product has exceeded the previous year's sales. In a sales analysis there are no goals against which to compare these results; therefore, management may be satisfied with these figures. Notice, however, that sales are increasing at 20 percent per year for product A, 15 percent per year for product C, and 8 percent per year for product B. This may lead management to analyze product B to determine why it is lagging behind the growth rates of the other products. Management judgment is required in choosing the unit of analysis. In the example, management chose to do the analysis by product. However, an analysis based on market segments, sales territory, chain of distribution, or a number of other bases may have given different results and insights.

The main weaknesses of the sales analysis method are hidden problems, disregard for costs, and lack of goals.

Some problem areas may be undiscovered during the analysis because of underlying conditions. In the American Institutional Supply example, the analysis indicated that product B may be a problem because of its relatively low growth rate. The underlying assumption is that the market for each product has the same potential. But the market may be increasing at a rate of 25 percent per year for product A and only 5 percent per year for product B. Then, to assume that B is lagging behind A would be erroneous. Product B is actually outperforming A in gaining market share. The analysis itself did not indicate that product A (not product B) was a problem area in this case.

A major criticism of sales analysis is that costs are not considered; emphasis is placed on sales without taking into account that higher sales may actually lower profits through increased costs.

---

[11] This list is based on Gilbert A. Churchill, Jr., Neil M. Ford, and Orville C. Walker, Jr., *Sales Force Management* (Homewood, Ill.: Richard D. Irwin, 1981), p. 470.

Table 22–1: Sales analysis by product	Product	1982 actual sales ($ millions)	1983 actual sales ($ millions)	1984 actual sales ($ millions)	Percentage increase per year*
	A	$12.5	$15.0	$18.0	20%
	B	13.1	14.2	15.3	8
	C	12.7	14.6	16.8	15

* The percentage increase per year is calculated as follows: for product A, the percentage increase of 1983 over 1982 sales is determined by

$$\frac{\$(15 - 12.5) \text{ million}}{\$12.5 \text{ million}} = 20 \text{ percent}$$

Similar computations are made for other products and periods.

Sales analysis does not use goals against which actual sales figures can be compared. This is similar to operating without a company objective and leads to inefficient marketing programs and misdirected efforts. Goals help focus marketing efforts and, in addition, help facilitate analysis. In our example, if product A's goal for 1984 was $20 million, it would not have mattered that sales had grown at 20 percent for the previous three years; it would be obvious that A was performing below par.

The next method of analysis uses goals to handle this weakness of sales analysis.

VARIANCE ANALYSIS

This increases the cost of analysis. But in return, variance analysis more effectively addresses the control issue by establishing planned goals against which actual performance can be assessed. Let's continue with the American Institutional Supply Company example.

variance analysis

> **Variance analysis** goes one step beyond sales analysis and *compares* sales figures with *planned* performance. It requires that forecasting and planning be carried out prior to the period of analysis.

Table 22–2 has a variance analysis for American Institutional Supply for 1983. When goals are set for each product, the market growth rates are considered along with many other variables. The variance analysis

Table 22–2: Variance analysis by product	Product	1983 actual sales ($ millions)	1983 planned sales ($ millions)	1983 variance ($ millions)
	A	$15.0	$15.6	$−0.6
	B	14.2	14.1	0.1
	C	14.6	14.6	—0—

Table 22–3: Variance analysis by region, product A	Region	1983 actual sales ($ millions)	1983 planned sales ($ millions)	1983 variance ($ millions)
	I	$ 5.5	$ 5.4	$0.1
	II	5.2	5.2	–0–
	III	4.3	5.0	−0.7
	Totals	15.0	15.6	−0.6

clearly indicates that product A is not achieving its goals. At this point, it is not clear why product A is not meeting expectations, so management may decide to analyze the three regions in which their products are sold (Table 22–3).

The variance analysis by region shows that region III is the major cause of the overall variance. Management should now do more analysis to determine if increased competition, a poor personal selling effort, inaccurate sales forecasting, or some other factor may be causing this failure.

Now let's look at some of the weaknesses of this method. Variance analysis *does* use goals in the analyses. But like sales analysis, it has the weaknesses of hidden problems and disregard for costs.

Problems may still remain hidden in variance analysis, depending on the direction management takes. In our example, once the initial problem area was discovered, management decided to work at product A's sales by region. Management may also analyze by customer groups or any other basis and perhaps uncover other problems.

Both variance and sales analyses ignore costs in the analysis. Even though sales analysis does not take costs into consideration, it is still useful for identifying and solving problems. Our final method of analysis takes into account both sales and costs in an effort to enhance profits.

MARKETING COST ANALYSIS

If a firm's goal is to maximize long-run profits, then costs are an important part of any analysis affecting its decisions.

marketing cost analysis

> **Marketing cost analysis** is a detailed study of a firm's entire distribution cost structure.[12]

Without accurate sales *and* cost analysis, firms can make one of three errors. First, the **marketing budget** may be too large, and diminishing returns may be realized because additional spending does not yield satisfactory additional results. Second, the marketing budget may be too small.

---

[12] William J. Stanton, *Fundamentals of Marketing,* 4th ed. (New York: McGraw-Hill, 1975), p. 659.

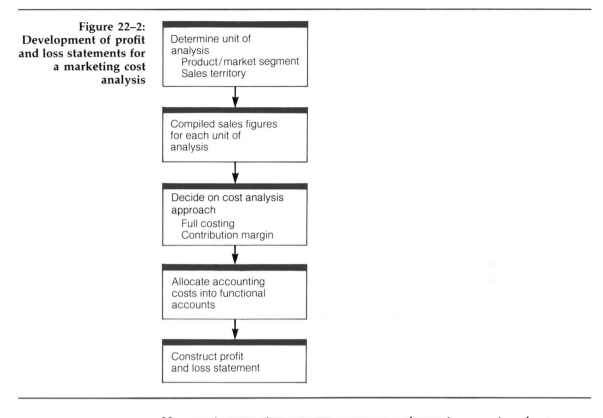

**Figure 22–2:
Development of profit
and loss statements for
a marketing cost
analysis**

Determine unit of
analysis
    Product/market segment
    Sales territory

Compiled sales figures
for each unit of
analysis

Decide on cost analysis
approach
    Full costing
    Contribution margin

Allocate accounting
costs into functional
accounts

Construct profit
and loss statement

Here an increase in costs may generate a larger increase in sales to more than offset the additional costs. Third, the marketing mix may be inefficient. A reallocation of the budget among elements of the marketing mix may be needed. For example, reducing advertising expenditures and lowering prices may be the most cost-effective way to generate sales.[13]

In order to use a marketing cost analysis, management prepares a profit and loss statement for each *unit of analysis.* These units could be product, sales territory, market segment, or other bases. The following are the steps necessary to develop the profit and loss statement (see Figure 22–2 for a flowchart illustration):

1. Determine the unit of analysis.

2. Compile sales figures for each unit of analysis.

3. Decide on using full-cost or contribution margin approach.

4. Allocate accounting costs into functional accounts.

5. Construct unit profit and loss statement.

Let's look at each of these steps in more detail.

---

[13] Adapted from Churchill et al., *Sales Force Management,* pp. 489–90.

Unit of analysis	The basic unit of analysis is determined primarily by the purpose of the analysis. The unit of analysis chosen depends on which unit is of most interest and value to the person to whom the report is directed. For example, if the analysis is to be done for the group product manager, the unit of analysis is likely to be by product; if for the sales manager, by sales territory.
Sales per unit of analysis	The sales for each unit is derived directly from the sales analysis. It is important to match the sales analysis with the cost analysis in terms of unit of analysis and time period.
Full-cost versus contribution margin	A primary purpose of cost analysis is to correctly assign the cost incurred in marketing a product or service. For direct costs, the assignment is simple. ***Direct costs*** are directly associated with the unit of analysis. Thus, advertising costs for one specific product can be directly assigned to that product. The treatment of ***indirect costs*** is more difficult. These are the costs incurred in marketing a product or service which cannot be directly tied to any one product or other unit of analysis. For example, when a company has several product lines, it is difficult to select a basis for assigning the marketing manager's salary among all the products. The problem of assigning indirect costs has given rise to two methods: full costing and contribution margin.

full costing	**Full costing** assigns both direct and indirect costs to the units of analysis.

Supporters of this method argue that all costs incurred in bringing the product to market must be allocated in order to get an accurate picture of how each unit of analysis contributes to the company. There are many methods used in allocating indirect costs; three of the most common are (1) equally among all units, (2) in proportion to the volume of each unit, and (3) prorated on the same proportion as assigned direct costs.

contribution margin	**Contribution margin** assigns only direct costs to the unit of analysis.

Its advocates generally feel that there is no accurate way to assign indirect costs. Since the indirect costs are generally fixed costs, any unit that shows an overall loss may actually be making some contribution toward fixed costs. If the analysis results in the elimination of the unprofitable unit, the burden of those costs is shifted to other products or units.

Table 22–4: Profit and loss statements	**Contribution margin**	**Full cost**
	Sales	Sales
	− Direct costs	− Direct costs
	= Contribution toward indirect costs	− Assigned indirect costs
		= Net profit before taxes

Natural versus functional accounts

Marketing costs must be categorized into useful classifications. Most companies' accounting records only have companywide accounts such as rent, sales salaries, supplies, etc. These are the ***natural accounts.*** For purposes of a marketing cost analysis, marketing managers usually find it necessary to reclassify these expenses according to the marketing functions involved.[14] Thus, if the unit of analysis is the product, the natural account "sales salaries" might be allocated to each product based on the amount of time each sales representative spends on each product. The ***functional account*** here would be "sales salaries per each product." In contrast, if the unit of analysis is sales territories, the natural account "sales salaries" would be allocated according to the sales representatives' salaries within each territory. The functional account would be "sales salaries per territory."

Construct unit profit and loss statement

General formulas for a profit and loss statement using contribution margin and full costing are shown in Table 22–4.

Let's continue with the American Institutional Supply example to show the kinds of additional information that can be obtained through marketing cost analysis.

Step 1.   The unit of analysis is the product because this report is used primarily by marketing management.

Step 2.   Sales for 1982 were:

Product	1982 sales ($ millions)
A	$12.5
B	13.1
C	12.7

Step 3.   In this example, management uses the contribution margin approach.

---

[14] Stanton, *Fundamentals,* p. 660.

Table 22–5: Profit and loss statement for 1985 ($000)

Sales		$38,300
− Directly assigned product costs		25,000
= Gross margin		13,300
− Expenses		
Sales salaries	$1,000	
Advertising	6,000	
Transportation	5,000	
Overhead (other)	1,000	13,000
Net profit before taxes		$ 300

Step 4.   From the company profit and loss statement, we can see that American Institutional Supply made a profit for 1985 of $300,000 before taxes. (See Table 22–5.) In order to complete the analysis, the natural accounts must be reallocated to the functional accounts, in this case by product. (See Table 22–6.) In this example all costs are allocated except for the one cost category, overhead, which is an indirect cost and so is not assigned to the products.

Step 5.   Finally, we can set up the profit and loss statements for each product. (See Table 22–7.) We can see from the individual profit and loss statements that product A is not contributing to indirect costs; it is not even covering costs directly associated with the product. Notice that the *company* profit and loss statement shows a profit of $300,000 with no indication of the problem with product A. This shows the effect of the iceberg principle. The company appears to show a profit, but underneath is an unprofitable product. Product A has higher transportation costs compared to the other products. It may be due to many things, and they may even be necessary— but that is the first place further analysis is indicated.

Clearly, association of costs with sales gives better control for firms using this technique. The next step is to incorporate goals into the market-

Table 22–6: Allocation of natural to functional accounts

	Functional accounts (natural accounts per product, $000)			
Natural accounts	Product A	Product B	Product C	Total
Direct product costs	$8,200	$8,500	$8,300	$25,000
Sales salaries	350	350	300	1,000
Advertising	2,000	2,000	2,000	6,000
Transportation	2,000	1,500	1,500	5,000

Table 22–7: Profit and loss statements by product

Product A		
Sales		$12,500,000
Direct product costs		8,200,000
Gross margin		4,300,000
Expenses (direct)		
Sales salaries	$ 350,000	
Advertising	2,000,000	
Transportation	2,000,000	4,350,000
Contribution to indirect costs		$ (50,000)
Product B		
Sales		$13,100,000
Direct product costs		8,500,000
Gross margin		4,600,000
Expenses (direct)		
Sales salaries	$ 350,000	
Advertising	2,000,000	
Transportation	1,500,000	3,850,000
Contribution to indirect costs		$ 750,000
Product C		
Sales		$12,700,000
Direct product costs		8,300,000
Gross margin		4,400,000
Expenses (direct)		
Sales salaries	$ 300,000	
Advertising	2,000,000	
Transportation	1,500,000	3,800,000
Contribution to indirect costs		$ 600,000
Contribution		
Product A	$ (50,000)	
Product B	750,000	
Product C	600,000	
Less overhead (indirect costs)	(1,000,000)	
Equals net profit before taxes		
(shown on Company P & L statement)	$ 300,000	

ing cost analysis. The method is fairly straightforward but more tedious. The computer has made such analysis much easier to complete and even allows costs to be automatically filed in both natural and functional accounts as they are incurred.

Two other approaches to planning and control deserve mention: PERT and the use of budgets.

PERT

PERT stands for Program Evaluation and Review Technique. PERT provides a framework for coordinating and timing activities to reach stated objectives. The technique uses a flowchart showing activities, intermediate goals, time required for each step, and the interconnecting relations between each. Using PERT, management can realistically compute project completion time, identify critical activities, and determine the effect that delays in each activity will have on the project as a whole.[15] It takes control one step beyond reaching a stated objective to reaching the objective in a timely, coordinated manner.

BUDGETS

Budgets are a projection of income and expenditures over a given time period. *Budgeting* can be thought of as a planning and control function. The budget is the part of the plan that expresses future income and expenditures. From a control perspective, continuous comparisons are made between budget and actual results.

Budgets should be based on the financial resources needed by a department to meet its objectives. Usually, budgets are established by adding a certain percentage to last year's figures. In ***zero-based budgeting,*** management decides what would be needed if the operation were to start from scratch and what would it cost. The idea is to build the budget from the ground up, reflecting the true needs of the operation.[16]

For the marketing function, budgets are based on corporate strategies and objectives. The marketing budget is based on forecasted sales and the costs of obtaining those sales. The marketing budget can be a yardstick against which to measure actual costs of obtaining forecasted sales. Marketing cost analysis (described earlier in this chapter) can use budgeted costs as objectives against which to measure actual costs.

STRATEGIC PLANNING AND CONTROL

Control is an integral part of the strategic marketing management process. Figure 22–3 contains a diagram of the strategic planning model used in this book. It appears that control, as part of the evaluation stage, is the last step in the strategic planning process. However, control may be more correctly designated as one of the first steps in the process because—as a result of control—management may reevaluate the situation analysis and revise objectives.

Another facet of control is that it is a continuous process. Indeed, management may engage in control activities on a daily basis. An example of a product that might require daily control activities is a food product containing raw materials whose prices are very volatile. Oscar Mayer monitors pork and beef prices daily in order to make the best buying decisions.

Control may affect plans on a tactical or on a strategic level. On a tactical level (short term), management might take action by making an adjustment in the original plan. For instance, management may lower the price of the product in response to a price reduction by a major

---

[15] John F. Stolle and Jack C. Page, "Out of Polaris: A Space-Age Technique to Launch New Products," *Sales Management,* July 3, 1964, p. 24.

[16] Paul J. Stonich, "Zero-Base Planning—A Management Tool," *Managerial Planning,* July–August 1976, pp. 1–4.

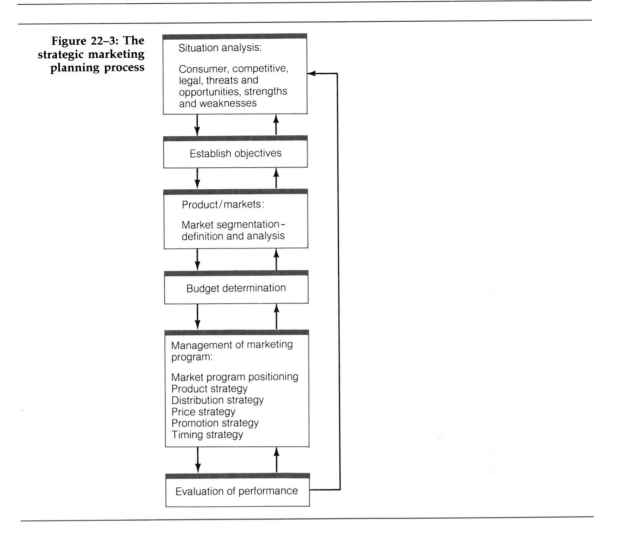

Figure 22–3: The strategic marketing planning process

Situation analysis:

Consumer, competitive, legal, threats and opportunities, strengths and weaknesses

Establish objectives

Product/markets:

Market segmentation – definition and analysis

Budget determination

Management of marketing program:

Market program positioning
Product strategy
Distribution strategy
Price strategy
Promotion strategy
Timing strategy

Evaluation of performance

competitor. On a strategic level (long term), the results of control may be used to maintain or change a strategy after a situation analysis has been performed. If a company failed to accurately assess buyer behavior toward one of its products, the marketing strategy may need to be revised in the next planning cycle to take account of the new information.[17]

Profit Impact of Marketing Strategies (PIMS)

The *PIMS* material has been discussed in Chapter 2. Our purpose here is to look at PIMS as a means of providing useful information for the purpose of strategic control.

PIMS data can provide standards by which marketing performance of an individual company can be judged. Let's consider the relationship

---

[17] Luck and Ferrell, *Marketing Strategy,* pp. 416–17.

Figure 22–4: Relation between return on investment and research and development expenditures

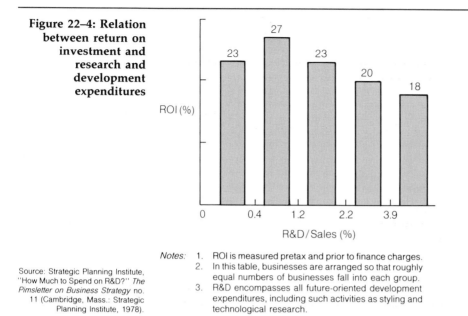

ROI (%)

R&D/Sales (%)

Source: Strategic Planning Institute, "How Much to Spend on R&D?" *The Pimsletter on Business Strategy* no. 11 (Cambridge, Mass.: Strategic Planning Institute, 1978).

Notes:
1. ROI is measured pretax and prior to finance charges.
2. In this table, businesses are arranged so that roughly equal numbers of businesses fall into each group.
3. R&D encompasses all future-oriented development expenditures, including such activities as styling and technological research.

between return on investment (ROI) and R&D expenditures as a percentage of sales. (See Figure 22–4.) If a company was spending over 4 percent of sales on R&D but achieving only an 8 percent ROI, comparison with the PIMS findings would indicate that the company was not performing as well as other firms in a similar situation. Management could then explore reasons for this situation and ways to correct it.[18]

Now let's turn to two specific models that are used for controlling strategic marketing plans: (1) a post-action control model and (2) a steering control model.

Post-action strategic control model

Post-action strategic control models analyze causes of variation between actual and predicted results.[19] This type of model provides planning data for similar projects or future plans. The post-action control model also recognizes that the traditional control techniques have excluded important strategic variables such as market share, size, and growth rate. One author reported that—incredibly—market size is sometimes even omitted from marketing plans![20] A post-action strategic framework has

---

[18] Robert W. Haas, *Industrial Marketing Management* (Boston: Kent Publishing, 1982), p. 365.

[19] This section is based upon James M. Hulbert and Norman E. Toy, "A Strategic Framework for Marketing Control," *Journal of Marketing* 41 (April 1977), pp. 12–20.

[20] F. Beaven Ennis, *Effective Marketing Management* (New York: Association of National Advertisers, 1973), p. 11.

been developed that integrates concepts in marketing strategy and planning with concepts in managerial accounting. This framework comprises two parts. Part one integrates strategic concepts such as market size and market share into a framework for evaluating actual versus planned marketing performance. It thus provides a means of more formally incorporating the marketing plan into the managerial control process.

The second part of the framework incorporates unanticipated events that have occurred during the planning period. It recognizes that a criterion, such as a planned level of sales volume, may no longer be an appropriate basis of comparison to actual or realized sales. The framework recognizes that management usually evaluates performance in terms of what it should have been under the circumstances that actually transpired. It is argued that using this *ex post information* is more sensible than blind adherence to a plan clearly outdated by violation of planning assumptions. Now let's analyze a specific example to learn more about this strategic framework.

Performance versus plan. The first stage in strategic control is to evaluate performance according to standards established in the marketing plan. Table 22–8 contains the operating results for product Alpha. The focus is on analysis of variances in profit contribution. Remember that this variance analysis has limited potential for diagnosing the *causes* of problems; rather, its major benefit lies in the *identification* of areas where problems may exist.

In Table 22–8 we see that product Alpha experienced an unfavorable variance in contribution of $100,000. This variance may be due to differences in (1) actual versus planned total market size, (2) actual versus planned market share penetration, and (3) actual versus planned price and cost per unit. A variance decomposition of these three variables permits us to determine where the variances have occurred.

	Item	Planned	Actual	Variance
Table 22–8: Operating results for product Alpha	Revenues			
	Sales (lbs.)	20,000,000	22,000,000	2,000,000
	Price per lb. ($)	0.50	0.4773	0.0227
	Revenues ($)	10,000,000	10,500,000	500,000
	Total market (lbs.)	40,000,000	50,000,000	10,000,000
	Share of market	50%	44%	(6%)
	Costs			
	Variable cost per lb. ($)	0.30	0.30	—
	Contribution			
	Per lb. ($)	0.20	0.1773	0.0227
	Total ($)	4,000,000	3,900,000	(100,000)

Source: James M. Hulbert and Norman E. Toy, "A Strategic Framework for Marketing Control." *Journal of Marketing* 41 (April 1977), p. 13.

The following symbols are used in the analysis:

S = Share of total market
M = Total market in units
Q = Quantity sold in units
C = Contribution margin per unit
a = Subscript denoting actual values
p = Subscript denoting planned values
v = Subscript denoting variance

In referring to Table 22–8, we see that price/cost variance is given by:

$$(C_a - C_p) \times Q_a = (0.1773 - 0.20) \times 22{,}000{,}000 = -\$500{,}000$$

The volume variance is given by:

$$(Q_a - Q_p) \times C_p = (22{,}000{,}000 - 20{,}000{,}000) \times 0.20 = \$400{,}000$$

The sum of these contribution variances, therefore, yields the overall unfavorable contribution variance of −$100,000 shown in Table 22–8.

The next step is to determine if the volume variance in contribution is due to failure to achieve market share or to underestimating market size. The variance in contribution due to market share is calculated as follows:

$$(S_a - S_p) \times M_a \times C_p = (0.44 - 0.50) \times 50{,}000{,}000 \times 0.2 = -\$600{,}000$$

The variance in contribution due to market size variance is given by:

$$(M_a - M_p) \times S_p \times C_p = (50{,}000{,}000 - 40{,}000{,}000) \times 0.5 \times 0.2$$
$$= \$1{,}000{,}000$$

The sum of the market size and share variances equals an overall favorable volume variance in contribution of $400,000. The variances are summarized in Table 22–9.

Table 22–9: Summary of variances for product Alpha			
Planned profit contribution			$4,000,000
Volume variance			
Share variance	$ (600,000)		
Market-size variance	1,000,000		
	400,000		
Price/cost variance	(500,000)		
Net unfavorable variance		(100,000)	
Actual profit contribution		$3,900,000	

Interpretation. In general, variances can occur because of problems in forecasting or in execution of the marketing plan. Usually, a variance in the total market size is viewed as the responsibility of the market forecasting group. Variances in market share or penetration are more difficult to assign. They may be due to incorrect forecasting or to poor performance itself. The assignment of responsibility is a managerial judgment.

The analysis we reviewed was based on ***ex ante standards,*** which involved a comparison between standards established before the planning period and actual results. The second part of using this framework would involve ***ex post standards.*** Ex post analysis involves revision of planned standards and objectives to take account of unanticipated events and changes. It is argued that such changes should be recognized, not that the plan should be blindly adhered to as established. The ex post analysis is especially important in the strategic planning process for the next period. The unanticipated events in the prior period are considered in the situation analysis. The revised objectives and standards are considered in setting the objectives for the new strategic planning period.

Marketing management may develop contingency plans for unforeseen events during a planning period. Let us briefly discuss the nature and purposes of contingency plans.

Contingency planning

A sound strategic plan should make provision for unforeseen events. ***Contingency planning*** introduces flexibility into the strategic plan. It identifies and plans for alternative future events that may significantly change the assumptions of the original marketing strategy. One way to approach the issue is to identify areas the firm cannot control—interest rates, competitive actions, and consumer buying process. These factors can be analyzed to see how changes in the original assumptions might affect the firm's strategy. Alternative strategies and plans could then be developed.

The 1974 sugar shortage and its effect on the presweetened-cereal market is a good illustration of why contingency planning can be useful. From 1973 to November 1974 sugar prices rose from 9 cents per pound to 58 cents per pound. Presweetened-cereal prices then rose an average of 24 percent. The reaction of the market suggested a relatively high price elasticity for presweetened-cereals, with many consumers shifting their purchases to low-sugar cereals.[21]

Clearly, a contingency plan for changes in prices of raw materials could have helped. Cereal marketers could have made coordinated and controlled changes in marketing efforts.

[21] Scott A. Nelson and Robert W. Shoemaker, "Using a Natural Experiment to Estimate Price Elasticity: The 1974 Sugar Shortage and the Ready-to-Eat Cereal Market," *Journal of Marketing* 47 (Winter 1983), pp. 44–57.

Table 22–10: Mean performance indicators for successful, medium, and unsuccessful indicators in a retail department store	Performance		
Indicator	**Successful**	**Medium**	**Unsuccessful**
Maintained mark-on (%)	41.9	38.8	27.6
Gross margin (%)	47.3	43.7	31.3
Total selling expenses (%)	7.9	9.6	10.9
Total operating expenses (%)	18.9	23.4	28.8
Department margin (%)	28.4	20.2	3.4
Stock turnover	4.2	3.2	2.7
Percent returns (%)	8.7	11.2	13.0
Gross transactions. . . . . (000 units)	70.5	48.2	23.0
Sales per square feet ($)	150.8	97.9	106.1
GMROI (%)	199.4	141.5	77.9
Prior stock (%)	1.5	5.1	8.0
Fashion/Basic . . . . (0, 1 dummy variable)	0.7	0.5	0.3

Source: Subhash Sharma and Dale D. Achabal, "STEMCOM: An Analytical Model for Marketing Control," *Journal of Marketing* 46 (Spring 1982), p. 111.

Steering Marketing Control Model (STEMCOM)

The *Steering Marketing Control Model (STEMCOM)* predicts a final outcome and then monitors progress toward that outcome.[22] The model is open looped, which means that identification of reasons that cause the process to go out of control and the necessary corrective action is external to the model. STEMCOM alerts managers to deviations from some specified level of performance. Management must then determine the cause of the deviation and whether or not corrective action is necessary.

In one application of STEMCOM, management specified the indicators of performance for departments within a retail department store. These 12 indicators, which are commonly furnished by trade associations, are listed in Table 22–10 along with the mean scores for departments that were successful, medium, or unsuccessful in performance. For example, consider stock turnover: for successful departments the rate is 4.2; for medium performance departments the rate is 3.2; and for unsuccessful departments the rate is 2.7.

These indicators were combined into a composite performance index. For successful departments, the composite index ranged from 1 to 2. Management could monitor the performance of a given successful department; and if the performance index dropped below the level of 1, this would signal the need to examine why the deviation occurred and what, if any, corrective action was necessary.

As mentioned earlier, the major objective of STEMCOM is to indicate to management whether actual performance has deviated from target performance. A *control chart* similar to those used in quality control can

---

[22] Subhash Sharma and Dale D. Achabal, "STEMCOM: An Analytical Model for Marketing Control," *Journal of Marketing* 46 (Spring 1982), pp. 104–13.

Figure 22–5: Control chart for STEMCOM, 1976–1979

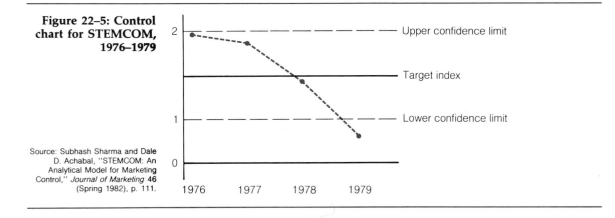

Source: Subhash Sharma and Dale D. Achabal, "STEMCOM: An Analytical Model for Marketing Control," *Journal of Marketing* 46 (Spring 1982), p. 111.

be developed. (See Figure 22–5.) The standard control chart consists of a central line indicating the average or target performance along with both upper and lower control limits. An actual performance index is plotted onto the control chart. If the performance lies within the control limits established, performance is said to be in control. Where the performance index falls outside the control limits, actual performance has then deviated from the target objectives, and management has been alerted that corrective action may be needed. The control chart can also be used to observe trends in the actual performance index. A downward trend would indicate a deterioration in performance over time, and management may decide to take corrective action before performance falls below an acceptable level.

The marketing audit

A marketing audit can be a most useful tool in improving a firm's marketing strategy.

marketing audit

> A **marketing audit** is a systematic, critical, and unbiased review and appraisal of the basic objectives and policies of the marketing function and of the organization, methods, procedures, and personnel used to implement those policies and to achieve those objectives.[23]

There are two basic types of audits: (1) a *functional (or vertical) audit* takes a function within the marketing department such as advertising or sales and makes an in-depth analysis of that area; and (2) a *comprehensive (or horizontal) audit* is necessarily broad and covers all functions within marketing.

[23] Abraham Schuchman, "The Marketing Audit: Its Nature, Purpose, and Problems," *Analyzing and Improving Marketing Performance,* report no. 32 (New York: American Management Association, 1959), p. 13.

Typically, a marketing audit is a blend of both types. First, management desires a broad analysis of the marketing area in order to gain an indication of any problems; then, it may select those areas that seem to require more detailed analysis. The expense of a comprehensive audit often is prohibitive, however.

The individuals who perform the audit can be from within the firm or from the outside. Auditors from within the company may be specialists or executives from an area other than the one being audited. In some smaller firms the manager of the marketing function does a self-audit. The self-audit may be biased and, therefore, less accurate and useful than one done by an outside consultant, though.

The procedure for a marketing audit is a three-step process:

1. Management and the auditor agree on objectives, coverage, depth, data sources, report format, and the time period of the audit.

2. Data are collected. This is the part of the marketing audit which takes most of the auditor's time and effort. Data are limited by the agreement but typically include internal interviews, customer interviews, and secondary sources.

3. The final step is developing the report and presenting it to management.[24]

The marketing audit covers six major areas: *marketing environment, marketing strategy, marketing organization, marketing systems, marketing productivity,* and *marketing functions.* Each of these areas is discussed below and illustrated in Table 22–11.

Marketing environment audit.   This audit covers the firm's customers, competitors, and other factors affecting the firm directly. It includes broader aspects of the environment, such as economic, technological, political, and social factors.

Marketing strategy audit.   The purpose of this audit is to determine if the firm's objectives and strategies are well matched to the environment factors. Often, the firm's objectives and strategies are not clearly stated; then, the auditor must determine the *implied* objectives in order to evaluate them.

Marketing organization audit.   This is an analysis of the marketing organization's ability to carry out the necessary objectives. The audit determines the marketing group's ability to effectively interact with the other areas of the firm, such as research, finance, and purchasing.

---

[24] Much of this section is based on the article by Philip Kotler, William Gregor, and William Rogers, "The Marketing Audit Comes of Age," *Sloan Management Review,* Winter 1977, pp. 25–43.

Table 22–11: Major areas of a marketing audit

The Marketing Environment Audit

I. Macro-Environment

Economic-Demographic
1. What does the company expect in the way of inflation, material shortages, unemployment, and credit availability in the short run, intermediate run, and long run?
2. What effect will forecasted trends in the size, age distribution, and regional distribution of population have on the business?

Technology
1. What major changes are occurring in product technology? In process technology?
2. What are the major generic substitutes that might replace this product?

Political-Legal
1. What laws are being proposed that may affect marketing strategy and tactics?
2. What federal, state, and local agency actions should be watched? What is happening in the areas of pollution control, equal employment opportunity, product safety, advertising, price control, etc., that is relevant to marketing planning?

Social-Cultural
1. What attitudes is the public taking toward business and toward products such as those produced by the company?
2. What changes are occurring in consumer life styles and values that have a bearing on the company's target markets and marketing methods?

II. Task Environment

Markets
1. What is happening to market size, growth, geographical distribution, and profits?
2. What are the major market segments? What are their expected rates of growth? Which are high opportunity and low opportunity segments?

Customers
1. How do current customers and prospects rate the company and its competitors, particularly with respect to reputation, product quality, service, sales force, and price?
2. How do different classes of customers make their buying decisions?
3. What are the evolving needs and satisfactions being sought by the buyers in this market?

Competitors
1. Who are the major competitors? What are the objectives and strategy of each major competitor? What are their strengths and weaknesses? What are the sizes and trends in market shares?
2. What trends can be foreseen in future competition and substitutes for this product?

Distribution and Dealers
1. What are the main trade channels bringing products to customers?

2. What are the efficiency levels and growth potentials of the different trade channels?

Suppliers
1. What is the outlook for the availability of different key resources used in production?
2. What trends are occurring among suppliers in their pattern of selling?

Facilitators
1. What is the outlook for the cost and availability of transportation services?
2. What is the outlook for the cost and availability of warehousing facilities?
3. What is the outlook for the cost and availability of financial resources?
4. How effectively is the advertising agency performing? What trends are occurring in advertising agency services?

Marketing Strategy Audit

Marketing Objectives
1. Are the corporate objectives clearly stated and do they lead logically to the marketing objectives?
2. Are the marketing objectives stated in a clear form to guide marketing planning and subsequent performance measurement?
3. Are the marketing objectives appropriate, given the company's competitive position, resources, and opportunities? Is the appropriate strategic objective to build, hold, harvest, or terminate this business?

Strategy
1. What is the core marketing strategy for achieving the objectives? Is it a sound marketing strategy?
2. Are enough resources (or too much resouces) budgeted to accomplish the marketing objectives?
3. Are the marketing resources allocated optimally to prime market segments, territories, and products of the organization?
4. Are the marketing resources allocated optimally to the major elements of the marketing mix, i.e., product quality, service, sales force, advertising, promotion, and distribution?

Marketing Organization Audit

Formal Structure
1. Is there a high level marketing officer with adequate authority and responsibility over those company activities that affect the customer's satisfaction?
2. Are the marketing responsibilities optimally structured along functional product, end user, and territorial lines?

Functional Efficiency
1. Are there good communication and working relations between marketing and sales?
2. Is the product management system working effectively? Are the product managers able to plan profits or only sales volume?
3. Are there any groups in marketing that need more training, motivation, supervision, or evaluation?

Table 22–11: Major areas of a marketing audit *(concluded)*

Interface Efficiency
1. Are there any problems between marketing and manufacturing that need attention?
2. What about marketing and R&D?
3. What about marketing and financial management?
4. What about marketing and purchasing?

Marketing Systems Audit

Marketing Information System
1. Is the marketing intelligence system producing accurate, sufficient, and timely information about developments in the marketplace?
2. Is marketing research being adequately used by company decision makers?

Marketing Planning System
1. Is the marketing planning system well-conceived and effective?
2. Is sales forecasting and market potential measurement soundly carried out?
3. Are sales quotas set on a proper basis?

Marketing Control System
1. Are the control procedures (monthly, quarterly, etc.) adequate to insure that the annual plan objectives are being achieved?
2. Is provision made to analyze periodically the profitability of different products, markets, territories, and channels of distribution?
3. Is provision made to examine and validate periodically various marketing costs?

New-Product Development System
1. Is the company well-organized to gather, generate, and screen new product ideas?
2. Does the company do adequate concept research and business analysis before investing heavily in a new idea?
3. Does the company carry out adequate product and market testing before launching a new product?

Marketing Productivity Audit

Profitability Analysis
1. What is the profitability of the company's different products, served markets, territories, and channels of distribution?
2. Should the company enter, expand, contract, or withdraw from any business segments and what would be the short- and long-run profit consequences?

Cost-Effectiveness Analysis
1. Do any marketing activities seem to have excessive costs? Are these costs valid? Can cost-reducing steps be taken?

Marketing Function Audits

Products
1. What are the product line objectives? Are these objectives sound? Is the current product line meeting these objectives?
2. Are there particular products that should be phased out?
3. Are there new products that are worth adding?
4. Are any products able to benefit from quality, feature, or style improvements?

Price
1. What are the pricing objectives, policies, strategies, and procedures? To what extent are prices set on sound cost, demand, and competitive criteria?
2. Do the customers see the company's prices as being in line or out of line with the perceived value of its offer?
3. Does the company use price promotions effectively?

Distribution
1. What are the distribution objectives and strategies?
2. Is there adequate market coverage and service?
3. Should the company consider changing its degree of reliance on distributors, sales reps, and direct selling?

Sales Force
1. What are the organization's sales force objectives?
2. Is the sales force large enough to accomplish the company's objectives?
3. Is the sales force organized along the proper principle(s) of specialization (territory, market, product)?
4. Does the sales force show high morale, ability, and effort? Are they sufficiently trained and incentivized?
5. Are the procedures adequate for setting quotas and evaluating performances?
6. How is the company's sales force perceived in relation to competitors' sales forces?

Advertising, Promotion, and Publicity
1. What are the organization's advertising objectives? Are they sound?
2. Is the right amount being spent on advertising? How is the budget determined?
3. Are the ad themes and copy effective? What do customers and the public think about the advertising?
4. Are the advertising media well chosen?
5. Is sales promotion used effectively?
6. Is there a well-conceived publicity program?

Source: Reprinted from "The Marketing Audit Comes of Age," by Philip Kotler, William Gregor, and William Rodgers, in *Sloan Management Review* 18, no. 2, pp. 39–43, by permission of the publisher. Copyright © 1977 by the Sloan Management Review Association.

Marketing systems audit.   This is an analysis of the procedures the firm uses to gather information, plan, and control marketing operations. This refers to actual established methods for routine tasks and whether or not the methods are adequate.

Marketing productivity audit.   This audit analyzes the productivity and profitability of the products, customer groups, or other units of analysis within marketing. Marketing cost analysis (discussed earlier in this chapter) is one method of analyzing the profitability and productivity. Zero-based budgeting is another method.

Marketing function audit.   This is a vertical or in-depth analysis of each of the marketing mix elements: product, price, distribution, sales force, advertising, promotion, and publicity.[25]

In practice, a marketing audit is performed much like audits in other areas of a firm, such as finance or personnel. The marketing audit is often more critical than audits in other areas because of the rapidly changing marketing environment. Economic recessions and recoveries, rapidly climbing advertising costs, consumerism, and the widespread use of computers have contributed to the need for change in marketing. The major U.S. auto manufacturers made a very slow response to the changing needs of consumers with respect to fuel-efficient cars. A marketing audit helps identify the need for such changes in strategy.

Some companies are taking unique approaches to marketing audits. The 3M Company uses an internal auditing group to evaluate marketing plans for products or product lines. The team consists of six executives internal to the firm but external to the marketing group being analyzed. They report the results to the divisional marketing managers; the decision regarding the use of the results resides with that manager. International Telephone & Telegraph Corp. forms teams to evaluate a division of the company. In some cases team members remain in the division as managers after completing the audit in order to implement their recommendations.

The problems with marketing audits concern setting objectives, distortion of data, and implementation of recommendations.

The objectives-setting portion of the audit presupposes that management and the auditors know which areas are going to require in-depth analysis. The only way for an audit to work properly is for the audit itself to be guided by the early results, with frequent communication to management as to the directions the audit is taking. However, because the auditor is often under contract, management sometimes feels the need to control the audit or more precisely outline the details of the audit within the contract. This, of course, limits its flexibility.

The biggest problem does not concern the audit itself but rather the implementation of recommendations derived from it. Organizational

---

[25] Adapted from ibid.

changes are often indicated, and those changes are difficult to accomplish smoothly. Management may accept as true only portions of the audits recommendations and may reject all or part of them. Accepting only part of the recommendations usually weakens their effectiveness.

SUMMARY

Control attempts to ensure that actions and objectives conform to plans. The process includes (1) establishment of standards, (2) interpretation and evaluation of information generated by a feedback system, and (3) taking corrective action.

For a marketing control system to work effectively, it must have current information, use objectives as a standard of comparison to measure performance, point out deviations from the objectives, and report deviations to the individual responsible for the function or activity.

Two analogies point out the need for analysis: the iceberg principle and the 80/20 rule. The iceberg principle implies that without detailed analysis a large percentage of valuable information is not visible, much like an iceberg with 90 percent of its mass submerged. The 80/20 rule states that a small percentage of an organization's customers or products provides a disproportionately large percentage of sales and profits.

Sales analysis is the least expensive and easiest type of analysis to perform. The sales analysis process takes sales figures from company records, divides aggregate sales into desired units of analysis, and then compares the different units of analysis. The main weaknesses of sales analysis are hidden problems, disregard of costs, and lack of goals.

Variance analysis compares sales figures with planned performance. It is more of a control mechanism than sales analysis, for it measures performance related to established goals. Like sales analysis, variance analysis disregards costs of marketing and may not discover hidden problems.

Marketing cost analysis is a detailed study of a firm's entire distribution cost structure. Management input in the marketing cost analysis is required in determining the unit of analysis, choosing full costing or contribution margin, and allocating accounting costs into functional accounts. This approach, when used properly, analyzes both sales and costs and thus places an emphasis on profits instead of sales alone.

Two other approaches that can be useful in control are PERT and budgets. PERT is an activity flowchart that provides a framework for coordination and timing of activities to reach a firm's stated objectives. Budgets express a firm's goals in terms of income and costs for a given time period. Control is obtained by comparing actual results with budgeted figures.

In a marketing management context, control is a continuous process. Control is necessary for current strategies and at the same time provides input into future strategies and objectives. Control may be used on tactical or strategic levels. PIMS data can be used to compare performance with other firms in the industry to indicate areas for improvement.

Post-action strategic control models analyze variations from planned performance and provide a strategic framework. In addition, the post-action model recognizes and compensates for unanticipated events that may occur within the period under control.

Contingency planning attempts to anticipate alternative future strategy. Contingency planning requires identifying factors that are not under control and planning strategies for possible unanticipated variations.

STEMCOM is another method for monitoring performance and alerting management to deviations. STEMCOM uses a composite index of performance and a control chart that establishes upper and lower acceptable performance limits. Over time, the composite index is tracked on the control chart to indicate deviations from targeted objectives.

A marketing audit is very useful in evaluating a firm's current strategies and its ability to reach strategic objectives. A functional audit is an in-depth analysis of one functional area. A comprehensive audit looks at the marketing area as a whole with a broad analysis. Individuals who conduct an audit can be internal or external to the firm. Internal auditors must be unbiased in order for the audit to be accurate and useful. The comprehensive audit typically covers six major areas: environment, strategy, organization, systems, productivity, and functions.

KEY CONCEPTS

Control
Feedback
Corrective action
Standards of performance
Management by objectives (MBO)
Deviation from plans
Marketing control system
Management by exception
Iceberg principle
80/20 rule
Sales analysis
Variance analysis
Marketing cost analysis
Marketing budget

Unit of analysis
Direct cost
Indirect cost
Full costing
Contribution margin
Natural account
Functional account
PERT
Zero-based budgeting
PIMS
Post-action strategic control model
Ex post information
Ex ante standard

Ex post standard
Contingency planning
STEMCOM
Control chart
Marketing audit
Functional (vertical) audit
Comprehensive (horizontal) audit
Marketing environment audit
Marketing strategy audit
Marketing organization audit
Marketing systems audit
Marketing productivity audit
Marketing function audit

DISCUSSION QUESTIONS AND EXERCISES

1. Review the major steps in the control process and relate this process to the strategic planning process as presented in this text.

2. What is the return on assets formula? Discuss the ways in which return on assets can be improved.

3. Compare and contrast the iceberg principle to the 80/20 rule. What is their relationship to the evaluation and control of marketing activities?

4. What is the difference between the contribution margin and full costing? Discuss their implications to strategic marketing management.

5. Compare and contrast a post-action control model with the steering control model.

6. What is a marketing audit? Who should perform it? How often should it be performed?

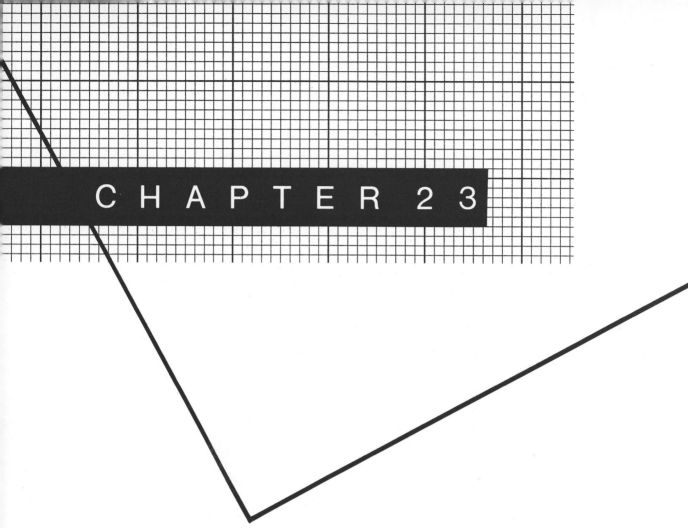

CHAPTER 23

Marketing research and information systems

The marketing information system (MIS)
    The nature of a marketing information
        system
    Components of the MIS
    Design factors in the MIS
    The status of MIS in industry

Summary

Key concepts

Discussion questions and exercises

The role of information in marketing
    management

Sources of marketing information

The nature and scope of marketing research
    The role of marketing research in society

The marketing research process
    Formulate problem
    Propose research design
    Assess value of research
    Implement research
    Interpret findings
    Prepare and present report

It should be quite evident by now that effective marketing management cannot occur in an information vacuum. Knowledge of important events in the environment, marketplace trends, shifts in demand, the real or anticipated impact of marketing variables, and the evaluation of marketing performance are all relevant to marketing decision making. An important component of a company's marketing organization is the set of activities designed to provide informational input to marketing decision making and performance evaluation. This chapter examines the nature and role of marketing information as a critical element in the marketing management process.

THE ROLE OF INFORMATION IN MARKETING MANAGEMENT

One inherent characteristic of marketing management is **uncertainty.** Marketing managers face uncertainty about trends in the environment and in the marketplace. They are uncertain about the ultimate results of marketing decisions. Virtually all aspects of marketing management require an ability to cope with uncertainty.

A manager's ability to cope with uncertainty is most evident when steps are taken to reduce it: when a manager improves his or her knowledge of the environment, the marketplace, the effects of marketing decision variables, or the performance of the marketing program as a whole or some part of it. This knowledge is increased through the acquisition of accurate information. Thus, the essential **role of information** is the reduction of uncertainty that surrounds all aspects of marketing management. (See Figure 23–1.)

Several specific roles of information within the framework of marketing management can be delineated:

1. *Monitoring the environment.* The dynamic nature of the marketing environment and each of its sectors requires that managers continuously monitor the environment and be aware of events that represent potential threats or opportunities. This requires the establishment of a channel of information between the firm and the environment.

2. *Implementation of the marketing concept.* Information is crucial to effectively implement the marketing concept. If companies are to base their marketing offers on the needs and desires of buyers, information about those needs and desires must guide product development, modification, and deletion decisions.

3. *Segmentation.* The formation and analysis of market segments requires information on variables used to form the segments and to develop profiles.

4. *Demand assessment.* Estimates of current and future levels of demand are based on trends and on factors that influence demand. To make these estimates, information on these trends or factors must be obtained.

Figure 23–1: Specific roles of information in marketing management

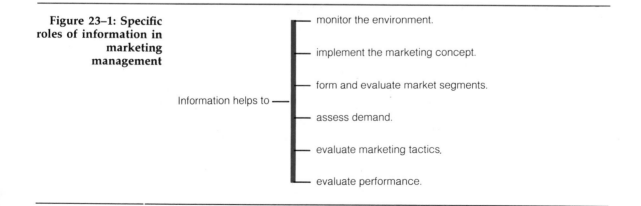

Information helps to —
- monitor the environment.
- implement the marketing concept.
- form and evaluate market segments.
- assess demand.
- evaluate marketing tactics.
- evaluate performance.

5. *Evaluation of marketing decision variables.* The company seeks the optimum level of each marketing decision variable. In setting the levels of variables such as price and promotional efforts, information about the anticipated effects of these variables can be very useful.

6. *Control.* Performance evaluation is a critical stage in strategic planning and control. Information that provides an assessment of performance levels is important to control. And when performance falls below objectives, information about the nature of the problem and likely effects of alternative solutions contributes to the control process.

These are several areas where information plays an important role in marketing management. Its multitude of uses suggest that a broad scope of specific types of information is relevant to marketing. Table 23–1 illus-

---

Table 23–1: Types of information relevant to planning, problem solving, and control

Planning
1. What are the basic trends in the domestic economy? How, specifically, will these affect the market for our products?
2. What changes can we expect in customer purchasing patterns? Will these be based on changes in real income, on changing tastes and values, or on changes in patterns of distribution?
3. What will our needs be over the next three years for sales representatives? branch offices? distribution centers (warehouses)?
4. What new markets are likely to open up? What types of products or services will be needed to serve them? Are there promising markets we are not now serving?

Problem solving
1. Product
   a. Which of several alternative new-product designs is most likely to be successful? What specific features should the final product have?
   b. What action should we take to counter a new-product offering by competitors?
2. Price
   a. How should we price new products? Should we use a penetration (low) price or a skimming (high) price?
   b. What is the shape of our demand curve?
3. Distribution
   a. What types of intermediate deals should be used at the agent, wholesale, or retail levels? How intensive should this coverage be?
   b. How many manufacturing and warehousing facilities should the firm operate? In what locations?
4. Promotion
   a. What should the total promotion budget be? How should it be allocated among products, among geographic areas, and among the various forms of promotion (advertising, personal selling, and so on)?
   b. To what extent should we use such sales stimulants as coupons, premiums, deals, and contests to increase customer traffic in retail stores?

Control
1. What are current sales and market shares for each of our product lines? for each geographic area? for each major customer type?
2. What is our corporate image among present customers? among our potential customers? among our distributors?

Source: Adapted from James H. Myers and Richard R. Mead, *The Management of Marketing Research* (Scranton, Pa.: International Textbook Company, 1969), pp. 27–46.

trates the many types of information that might be important input to planning, problem solving, and control. With such a wide variety of uses and types of information relevant to marketing management, an important organizational task of a firm is to provide the means by which information can be tapped from available sources.

SOURCES OF MARKETING INFORMATION

Figure 23–2 illustrates the various *sources of marketing information* available to a marketing manager. These sources differ in the formality with which they provide information. Marketing research and accounting reports are among the more formal sources of information, for instance. Sources also differ in the scope of information they can provide. Research and development and legal departments are obviously quite narrow in the type of information they provide. Accounting reports provide useful performance evaluation data relating to the efficiency and effectiveness of marketing programs. Intermediaries and marketing intelligence can be sources of information about competitor actions. Marketing research is the source of diverse information. It can provide useful information in virtually every area represented in Table 23–1. For this reason, marketing research is an important support activity in many types of organizations.

Since marketing management is an ongoing task, its need for information is also continuous. Many types of information are useful on a recurring basis; for example, market shares, as performance data, are tracked in recurring fashion. Other information is provided through special, one-time projects. A major consumer-attitude study is an example of such a project.

It should be evident from our discussion that information as input to marketing management is a complex issue:

1.   Several sources of information are available to marketing managers.

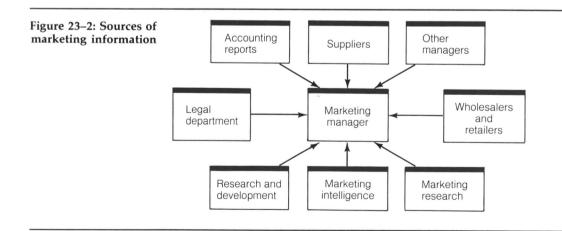

Figure 23–2: Sources of marketing information

2. There are many specific types of information relevant to marketing management.

3. Some of them recur in usefulness, while others are nonrecurring.

With such a complex environment, a major task is to organize the flow, storage, and retrieval of information that supports marketing decision making. This task is accomplished through the use of the marketing information system (MIS). The MIS is a major topic later in this chapter. We'll first examine the special nature of marketing research.

THE NATURE AND SCOPE OF MARKETING RESEARCH

The definition below captures much of the nature and scope of *good* marketing research. *Systematic* emphasizes the need for a well-planned research effort. *Objective* emphasizes that a lack of bias should be present in the research effort. The scope of marketing research includes both the *collection* and *analysis* of information and the *identification* and *solution* of marketing problems. Finally, good marketing research provides *relevant* information. Well-designed research that provides information with little or no relationship to the decision at hand is not good marketing research. Thus, an inherent feature of marketing research is its applied nature. It is problem-oriented.

marketing research

> **Marketing research** is the systematic and objective search for and analysis of information relevant to the identification and solution of marketing problems.

Marketing research requires a good deal of expertise in economic and social science research methods. As you will see in the discussion of the research process, a major research project involves data collection, measurement, sampling, and statistical analysis. Table 23–2 traces the evolution of the nature of marketing research and shows its increasing level of sophistication.

The scope and level of expertise that it takes to effectively conduct marketing research suggests a key decision that a firm must make in this area: should it conduct marketing research through its own internal research department or hire an outside agency to perform the research? The need for marketing research has given rise to **marketing research agencies**—independent firms that specialize in providing marketing research services to client organizations. These firms range in size from one-person consulting shops to major firms, the largest of which is A.C. Nielsen. The larger firms provide a multitude of services, including syndicated research, in which information is collected on a regular basis and sold to interested clients, and customized individual research projects oriented to the specific needs of a single client. The marketing research

	Decade	Technique
Table 23–2: The evolution of marketing research techniques	Prior to 1910	First-hand observation Elementary surveys
	1910–20	Sales analysis Operating-cost analysis
	1920–30	Questionnaire construction Survey technique
	1930–40	Quota sampling Simple correlation analysis Distribution-cost analysis Store auditing techniques
	1940–50	Probability sampling Regression methods Advanced statistical inference Consumer and store panels
	1950–60	Motivation research Operations research Multiple regression and correlation Experimental design Attitude-measuring instruments
	1960–70	Factor analysis and discriminant analysis Mathematical models Bayesian statistical analysis and decision theory Scaling theory Computer data processing and analysis Marketing simulation Information storage and retrieval
	1970–80	Nonmetric multidimensional scaling Econometric models Comprehensive marketing planning models Test-marketing laboratories Multi-attribute attitude models
	1980–	Structural equations Conjoint analysis and trade-off analysis Brain wave analysis Behavior scanning Videotex

Source: Philip Kotler, *Marketing Management: Analysis, Planning, and Control*, 5th ed., © 1984, p. 196. Adapted by permission of Prentice-Hall, Inc., Englewood Cliffs, New Jersey.

industry has grown substantially over the last three decades and represents a major career opportunity for interested students.

Similar growth has characterized the number of internal marketing research departments. The majority of large manufacturers, wholesalers, and retailers maintain formal research departments. Other companies

Table 23–3: The existence of internal marketing research departments	Type of firm	n	Percent with:		
			Formal departments	One-person assignments	No one assigned
	Consumer goods manufacturer	142	83%	14%	3%
	Industrial goods manufacturer	124	69	22	9
	Financial services	105	71	26	3
	Publishers and broadcasters	69	93	7	0
Source: Dik Warren Twedt, *1983 Survey of Marketing Research* (Chicago: American Marketing Association, 1983), p. 11.	Ad agencies	60	85	12	3
	All others	97	65	32	3
	All companies	597	77	20	3

maintain one-person research functions but do formally recognize the need for this activity. See Table 23–3 for a summary of the incidence of internal research departments according to type of organization.

A number of factors go into the decision to do research internally or to hire it done. To do research internally requires trained researchers and the financial resources to maintain them and their activities. Many small firms cannot maintain an ongoing research department; most large firms do. Research agencies maintain this specialized expertise on an ongoing basis, offering many clients a service they could not achieve on their own. Another factor is understanding the problem that the research is to address. Internal personnel are likely to better understand the managerial issues that the research is to support. But this closeness is also more likely to make objectivity more difficult. A research agency is in a better position to ignore the internal politics of a firm and bring objectivity to the research effort. As it turns out, most companies with internal research departments also use research agencies. Table 23–4 summarizes the various types of information that marketing research actually supplies to companies, the extent to which companies obtain each type of information, and the extent to which it is obtained internally or externally.

The role of marketing research in society

While most marketing research is conducted to enhance corporate decision making, it is also playing an increasing role outside corporate boundaries. There are two major nontraditional areas where marketing research is increasingly used. First, the results of marketing research studies are being submitted as evidence in court trials of lawsuits. For example, in a trademark infringement case, a study that shows consumers did (or did not) confuse the two brand names in question might be submitted as evidence. In cases where unfair business practices are charged, market-

Table 23–4: Research activities of companies

	Percent doing	Done by marketing research department	Done by another department	Done by outside firm
Advertising research				
A. Motivation research	47%	30%	2%	15%
B. Copy research	61	30	6	25
C. Media research	68	22	14	32
D. Studies of ad effectiveness	76	42	5	29
E. Studies of competitive advertising	67	36	11	20
Business economics and corporate research				
A. Short-range forecasting (up to one year)	89	51	36	2
B. Long-range forecasting (over one year)	87	49	34	4
C. Studies of business trends	91	68	20	3
D. Pricing studies	83	34	47	2
E. Plant and warehouse location studies	68	29	35	4
F. Acquisition studies	73	33	38	2
G. Export and international studies	49	22	25	2
H. MIS (management information system)	80	25	53	2
I. Operations research	65	14	50	1
J. Internal company employees	76	25	45	6
Corporate responsibility research				
A. Consumers' "right to know" studies	18	7	9	2
B. Ecological impact studies	23	2	17	4
C. Studies of legal constraints on advertising and promotion	46	10	31	5
D. Social values and policies studies	39	19	13	7
Product research				
A. New-product acceptance and potential	76	59	11	6
B. Competitive product studies	87	71	10	6
C. Testing of existing products	80	55	19	6
D. Packaging research: design or physical characteristics	65	44	12	9
Sales and market research				
A. Measurement of market potentials	97	88	4	5
B. Market share analysis	97	85	6	6
C. Determination of market characteristics	97	88	3	6
D. Sales analysis	92	67	23	2
E. Establishment of sales quotas, territories	78	23	54	1
F. Distribution channel studies	71	32	38	1
G. Test markets, store audits	59	43	7	9
H. Consumer panel operations	63	46	2	15
I. Sales compensation studies	60	13	43	4
J. Promotional studies of premiums, coupons, sampling, deals, etc.	58	38	14	6

Source: Dik Warren Twedt, *1983 Survey of Marketing Research* (Chicago: American Marketing Association, 1983), p. 41.

ing research might be used to estimate the damages (e.g., lost revenue) incurred by the plaintiff.[1]

A second area where marketing research is playing a bigger role is in public policymaking. Research can be used in a number of ways in this area. It might be used to determine if consumers have been misled by questionable advertisements.[2] It might be used to examine the effects of a proposed requirement for firms in a particular industry. (For an example, see the antacid warnings study discussed in Chapter 5.) Whatever the application, the role of research in public policy is similar to its role in the corporate world: to enhance the decision-making capabilities of public policymakers.[3]

THE MARKETING RESEARCH PROCESS

In this section we examine the process by which a marketing research investigation occurs. This *marketing research process* occurs in stages, and we will discuss the key issues that enter into each stage. See Figure 23–3 for an overview of the stages in the process.

Formulate problem

Marketing research is problem-driven. It is conducted to provide information to aid in the solution of marketing problems. Therefore, the first step in the research process is to define the *managerial problem* at hand.

The *research problem* is then formulated. The information needed as input to solving the managerial problem is identified.

research problem

> The **research problem** is the specification of variables to be investigated in the research project.

The translation of the managerial problem into a research problem is a crucial step in the research process. A poor translation will yield irrelevant information because the wrong variables were specified. No matter how well the remainder of the process is carried out, the results will be of little or no value.

For an example of the translation of a managerial problem into a research problem, consider a regional printing company in the Midwest

---

[1] For a discussion of the evolution of consumer surveys as evidence in the courts, see Fred W. Morgan, "The Admissibility of Consumer Surveys as Legal Evidence in Courts," *Journal of Marketing,* Fall 1979, pp. 33–40.

[2] For a critical examination of an agency's approach to this issue, see Jacob Jacoby and Constance Small, "The FDA Approach to Defining Misleading Advertising," *Journal of Marketing,* October 1975, pp. 65–73.

[3] For fuller discussions on this role, see William L. Wilkie and David M. Gardner, "The Role of Marketing Research in Public Policy," *Journal of Marketing,* January 1974, pp. 38–47; also see Robert F. Dyer and Terence A. Shimp, "Enhancing the Role of Marketing Research in Public Policy Decision Making," *Journal of Marketing,* January 1977, pp. 63–67.

Figure 23–3: Stages of the research process

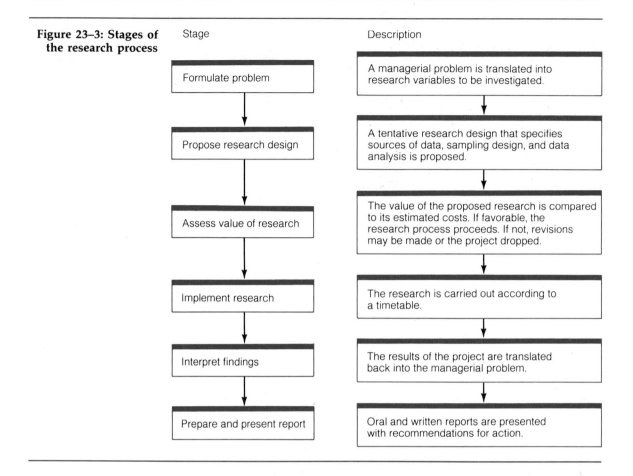

Stage	Description
Formulate problem	A managerial problem is translated into research variables to be investigated.
Propose research design	A tentative research design that specifies sources of data, sampling design, and data analysis is proposed.
Assess value of research	The value of the proposed research is compared to its estimated costs. If favorable, the research process proceeds. If not, revisions may be made or the project dropped.
Implement research	The research is carried out according to a timetable.
Interpret findings	The results of the project are translated back into the managerial problem.
Prepare and present report	Oral and written reports are presented with recommendations for action.

that was contemplating expansion of its services. The major source of the company's business was custom printing jobs for individual firms (company brochures, annual reports). The company had acquired a high-speed printing machine that allowed faster turnaround on major bound reports without a loss of quality or increase in cost over competitors' costs. With this capacity the company could serve more of the printing needs of their existing customers. They were now considering expanding this service to new geographic and organizational markets. However, such expansion would require the purchase of two additional machines. Before making this purchase, the company wanted to assess the feasibility of expansion and the manner in which it should occur. Thus, the managerial problem was whether to expand and, if so, the best manner in which to do it.

Based on this managerial problem, a research problem was formulated. Several key variables were identified:

1. Level of usage of printing of bound reports in selected geographic markets.

2. Level of usage of printing of bound reports by various types of organizations.

3. Importance of speed of service relative to other factors (e.g., price, quality) in the selection of a printing company.

4. Satisfaction with existing suppliers of this printing service on each selection factor.

5. Nature of contractual relationship with present suppliers.

6. Size and nature of buying center.

These general variables were further broken down into more than 200 precise variables that were specified for investigation. Collectively, these variables, when measured and analyzed, would provide an assessment of the receptivity of various market segments to the printing company's service and insights into how to market the service to these segments.

Hypotheses. A key element in the problem formulation of many research investigations is the statement of one or more **hypotheses.**

hypothesis | A **hypothesis** is a conjectural statement of the relationship between two or more variables.[4]

Often a researcher is interested in the relationship between variables—for example, the effect of a price increase on perceptions of product quality. The researcher may, in turn, have an expectation of what this relationship is. The expectation may be based on theory, other findings, or simple intuition. Whatever the basis, the expectation can be in the form of what the research is seeking to confirm or deny. It serves to guide the remainder of the process and allow a test of the hypothesis.

Hypotheses are not always necessary to a research problem, however. If no relationships between variables are of interest or no basis for stating an expected one exists, then a hypothesis will not be developed. In our printing company example, no hypotheses were included in the problem formulation. Hypotheses are more common in theoretically based research or in research that is studying variables that have been the subject of previous studies.

Propose research design | Once the variables to be investigated have been specified (and any hypotheses stated), the next stage is the development of a ***research design.***

---

[4] Fred N. Kerlinger, *Foundations of Behavioral Research,* 2d ed. (New York: Holt, Rinehart & Winston, 1973), p. 18.

research design

> The **research design** is the set of methods and procedures used in collecting and analyzing measures of the variables specified in the research problem.

At this stage, remember, the research procedures for the study are being *planned,* not carried out. A blueprint for the data collection and analysis is being drawn. A framework for the entire research design is established so that the research can be carried out systematically. Given the scope of research design issues, this stage is probably the most extensive in terms of the decisions to be made.

To gain an appreciation for the scope of issues involved in research design plans, we will examine the types and dimensions of research designs. As we do this, keep in mind that the development of a research design is the next crucial step in the research process. Once a relevant research problem has been formulated, a research design must be planned that investigates the problem at hand—and not (inadvertently) something else. Otherwise, the research process breaks down and leads to useless results.

This type of breakdown occurred several years ago in a study conducted by the transit authority of a major midwestern city. The transit authority was interested in determining why passenger usage of the commuter train system had recently declined. The key variables in the research problem were factors leading to the use or nonuse of the train system—that is, attitudes toward *using the train.* In their survey of citizens, the questions measured the value of the train to the community—or attitudes toward the *existence of the system.* This difference is subtle, but it led to an overwhelmingly positive response and no basis at all for determining why people did or did not use the train.

Types of research designs. A common way to classify research designs is by the purpose of the research. (See Table 23–5.) In ***exploratory research designs,*** the emphasis is on the discovery of ideas and insights. Exploratory research is conducted when little is known about the phenomenon being studied. It is conducted to provide a structure to the phenome-

Table 23–5: Research designs classified by purpose

Type of design	Purpose
Exploratory	Discover ideas and insights; provide structure to a phenomenon
Descriptive	Measure levels of variables or associations between variables
Causal	Establish whether a cause–effect relationship exists between variables

non. Such research is usually a prelude to a subsequent study that uses the results of the exploratory study. A currently popular exploratory method is the *focus group.* This method brings a small number (10 to 15) of consumers together in a group setting to discuss their feelings about a product, brand, or some other consumer issue. A moderator initiates a group discussion intended to provide a structure to the issue. The results can suggest hypotheses for further study, questions to ask in a consumer survey, and even tentative consumer reactions to new product concepts.[5]

A *descriptive research design* is more structured. Descriptive designs are concerned with the level of one or more variables or the association between certain variables. A study that establishes profiles of various market segments for a consumer product is one example. Because of their structural nature and interest in association between variables, descriptive studies often contain hypotheses in their problem formulation stage.

The third type of research design is the *causal design.* The purpose of a causal study is to establish the presence or absence of a cause-effect relationship between variables. Causal studies are experiments that allow the isolation of the effect of change in one variable in a change in another variable. Thus, if a company wanted to test the relative effectiveness of a "rational" versus an "emotional" advertising appeal on consumer attitudes, it might use a causal design in which one test group sees a rational ad and a second group sees an emotional ad. Any difference in attitude between the two groups could be attributed to the different appeals.[6]

Dimensions of research design.   The development of a research design involves considerations in three major areas: sources of data, sample design, and data analysis. We will examine the important issues in each of these areas.[7] Figure 23–4 provides an overview of the dimensions of research design.

Sources of data.   Two major sources of marketing research data are *secondary* and *primary data.*

secondary data	**Secondary data** are existing data generated for a problem other than the one at hand.

---

[5] More on the nature of focus groups can be found in James B. Higgenbotham and Keith K. Cox, eds., *Focus Group Interviews: A Reader* (Chicago: American Marketing Association, 1979).

[6] For expanded discussions of the types of designs, see Gilbert A. Churchill, Jr., *Marketing Research: Methodological Foundations,* 3d ed. (Hinsdale, Ill.: Dryden Press, 1983), pp. 59–84.

[7] See the Churchill text for an in-depth discussion of these areas.

**Figure 23–4:
Dimensions of research
design**

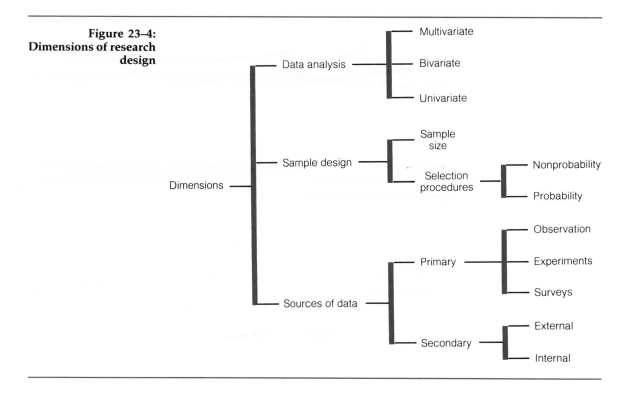

Secondary data can be further distinguished by whether they are generated internally or externally. ***Internal secondary data*** are existing data generated by the firm—for example, accounting reports and reports of previous research projects. Internal secondary data provide valuable performance evaluation information and serve as a foundation for future research efforts. The major advantages of internal secondary data are their accessibility and low costs and the ease with which they can be incorporated into most research projects.

External secondary data are data generated by a source other than the firm. Major types of external secondary data include:

1. ***Published statistics.*** A vast amount of statistical data is published by a variety of public and private sources. The major public source is the federal government and, within it, the Bureau of the Census. Private sources of published statistics include *Sales and Marketing Management's Survey of Buying Power* discussed in Chapter 10. Table 23–6 identifies several public and private sources of statistical data.

2. ***Standardized marketing information services.*** Many research agencies compile data on market trends and consumer behavior and sell the data in standardized form to interested buyers. Key examples of this type of service are summarized in Table 23–7.

Table 23–6: Public and private sources of statistical data	**Public**	**Private**
	Current Population Reports	Almanac of Business and Industrial Financial
	Census of Housing	Ratios
	Census of Retail Trade	Commodity Yearbook
	Census of Service Industries	Consumer Market and Magazine Report
	Census of Wholesale Trade	Editor and Publisher Market Guide
	Census of Manufacturers	Fortune Directory
	Census of Mineral Industries	A Guide to Consumer Markets
	Census of Transportation	Handbook of Basic Economic Statistics
	Census of Agriculture	Million Dollar Directory
	Census of Government	Moody's Manuals
	Business Cycle: Handbook of Indicators	Predicasts
	Survey of Current Business	Sales & Marketing Management Survey of
	County and City Data Book	Buying Power
	Economic Indicators	World Almanac and Book of Facts
	Federal Reserve Bulletin	
	Monthly Labor Review	
	State and Metropolitan Area Data Book	
	Statistical Abstract of the United States	
	Statistics of Income	
	U.S. Industrial Outlook	

3. *Publicly circulated research reports.* This source refers to published reports of research studies conducted on a topic similar to the one at hand. Marketing trade and research journals are typical sources of these reports.

External secondary data are less accessible than internal data and are more costly. But they can be valuable descriptive data for measuring market potential, evaluating a brand's performance, developing sales territories, and profiling market segments. Even in the absence of statistical data, they can provide guidelines for a firm's own research efforts.

Secondary data were a key component of the research for the printing company mentioned earlier. Internal sales records were used to identify the type of businesses that were likely candidates for the specific printing

Table 23–7: Examples of standardized marketing information services	**Dun & Bradstreet "Market Identifiers" (DMI).** DMI is a roster of over 4.3 million establishments that contains descriptive information for each company on the roster. This information includes location, SIC codes, line of business, sales volume, and number of employees. DMI is a useful source for industrial goods manufacturers in planning their marketing operations.
Source: Adapted from Gilbert A. Churchill, Jr., *Marketing Research: Methodological Foundations*, 3d ed. (Hinsdale, Ill.: Dryden Press, 1983), pp. 145–48.	**Nielsen Retail Index.** Every two months, from national samples of 1,600 supermarkets, 750 drugstores, and 150 mass merchandisers, the A. C. Nielsen Company tracks data on individual brands of consumer goods. Information gathered includes inventory change, sales to consumers, price, and the amount of advertising and sales promotion for the brand during the two-month period. This information is broken down by geographic area, store type, and store size. The Nielsen Retail Index is useful to consumer goods manufacturers and wholesalers.

service of concern. External sources were used to pinpoint geographic areas with above-average concentrations of those businesses.

Often, secondary data do not provide sufficient information for the problem being studied or are not in a form appropriate for solving the problem. The researcher must then turn to primary data.

primary data

> **Primary data** are original data tailored specifically to the problem at hand.

There are three major kinds of studies that generate primary data: observational studies, survey research, and experimentation. (See Table 23–8.)

observational studies

> **Observational studies** attempt to study a phenomenon in its natural setting.

Several approaches to observation are available:

1. *Direct observation.* In this approach the researcher observes a phenomenon as it is occurring without interfering with it. An example is found in store location studies where observation of automobile traffic volume and patterns provides information for evaluating the attractiveness of one or more potential sites for a store.

2. *Participation-observation.* In this approach a researcher observes a phenomenon by actually participating in it. In a study of tactics used by retail salespeople, a researcher might pose as a customer in order to observe the behavior of interest.

Table 23–8: Three types of primary research

Type of study	Description	Options	Advantages	Disadvantages
Observation	Study phenomenon in its natural setting	Direct observation Participation-observation Mechanical observation Physical traces	Valid measures	Limited scope of variables
Survey research	Study characteristics of population through questionnaire	Personal interviews Telephone interviews Mail questionnaires Drop-off questionnaires	Wide scope of information can be gathered	Costly Wide scope of expertise needed
Experimentation	Test causal relationship between variables	Field experiments Laboratory experiments	Deep level of inquiry that contributes to understanding	Realism difficult to achieve in lab Control difficult to achieve in field

3. *Mechanical observation.* This approach employs mechanical devices to measure the variables of interest. Instead of directly observing traffic volume on a particular street, a researcher might place a cable across the street to count passing autos.

4. *Physical traces.* In this approach a phenomenon is measured by examining its physical remnants. Liquor preferences in a community where liquor is not sold (but is consumed) could be measured by examining the contents of trash deposited at the city dump.[8]

The major advantage of observational research is that it captures a phenomenon in its natural setting, thereby providing valid measures. Its major drawback is its limited usefulness. Many variables of interest in marketing research—such as consumer beliefs and attitudes—are simply not observable.

The most popular means of generating primary marketing research data is *survey research.*

---

survey research

> **Survey research** attempts to measure a broad array of characteristics of a population of interest by administering a questionnaire to a sample of members of the population.

The major advantage of the survey method is the broad scope of variables that can be studied. Typical categories of variables in a consumer survey include demographic and socioeconomic characteristics, purchase behavior (past, present, and intended), and consumer beliefs and attitudes. It isn't uncommon for a survey questionnaire to measure hundreds of individual variables.

There are two major forms of questionnaire administration: *interviewer-administered* and *self-administered.* Interviewer-administered surveys can occur in one of two ways. In a *personal interview* the interviewer administers the questionnaire to the respondent in a face-to-face situation. This survey approach is the most flexible and offers the greatest quality and scope of respondent data. However, it is also the costliest. The *telephone interview,* in which the interviewer administers the questionnaire over the telephone, is cheaper but much more limited in the scope and quantity of information that can be obtained.

The most common form of self-administered survey is the *mail questionnaire.* Here questionnaires are mailed to a sample; the respondents complete the questionnaire on their own and return the completed questionnaire through the mail. This approach is much cheaper than the others, especially when the population is geographically dispersed. Its major

---

[8] Interesting variations in each of these approaches are provided in Eugene J. Webb, D. T. Campbell, R. D. Schwartz, and L. Sechrest, *Unobtrusive Measures: Nonreactive Research in the Social Sciences* (Chicago: Rand McNally, 1966).

drawbacks are low response rates and incomplete questionnaires. A variation on this approach is the ***drop-off questionnaire,*** in which the form is personally delivered to each sample member and left for the respondent to complete and return (or to be picked up at a later date). The personal delivery is designed to increase the likelihood of response. This approach is an effective alternative to the mail survey when a local population is being studied.

Obviously, a crucial component of the survey method is the questionnaire—the instrument through which the desired information is obtained. Questions cannot be ambiguous, and they must be ordered properly. The physical layout of the questionnaire must be determined. There are many principles of questionnaire construction that should be followed.[9] But questionnaire design is also one place where the creativity of the researcher can play an important role.

More than any other research method, surveys require a wide scope of research skills. As we will see, sampling is important in obtaining a group of respondents representative of the population being studied. The researcher must be knowledgeable about measurement and questionnaire construction issues. The large number of variables being studied requires statistical skills to meaningfully analyze the survey findings.

In our printing company example, the survey method was the major source of data. A mail questionnaire was constructed to obtain the information specified in the problem formulation. It was pretested, revised, and mailed to purchasing agents of sample organizations in the geographic areas of interest. The survey's response rate was 18 percent—about average for institutional samples. Despite the low response, the company was pleased with the type of information obtained because it allowed the company to analyze key market segments of interest.

The final type of primary research is ***experimentation.***

experiment	An **experiment** attempts to isolate and test for the effects of an independent variable on a dependent variable by manipulating the levels of the independent variable, measuring the dependent variable, and controlling the effects of any extraneous variables.

The scope of information being sought in an experiment is much narrower than in the other sources of data. However, the depth of inquiry is potentially much greater. The other sources of data provide exploratory and descriptive information about a phenomenon. An experiment seeks information on cause-effect relationships, thereby contributing to the *understanding* of the phenomenon.

---

[9] For a classic and still meaningful treatment of questionnaire design, see Stanley L. Payne, *The Art of Asking Questions* (Princeton, N.J.: Princeton University Press, 1951). A more current source is Seymour Sudman and Norman M. Bradburn, *Asking Questions: A Practical Guide to Questionnaire Design* (San Francisco: Jossey-Bass Publishers, 1982).

	Type	Description	Advantages	Disadvantages
Table 23–9: Types of field experiments	Field experiment	Occurs in natural setting	Realistic	Lack of control
	Laboratory	Occurs in tightly controlled lab	High level of control	Lack of realism

There are two major types of experiments: field experiments and laboratory experiments. (See Table 23–9.) *Field experiments* test cause-effect relationships in a natural setting. If successfully carried out, a field experiment provides realistic data on what will happen if, for example, a change in a marketing decision variable is implemented. However, field experiments allow little control over the effects of extraneous variables on the dependent variable. *Laboratory experiments* overcome this problem by testing for causation in tightly controlled lab settings. However, they lose the realism of the field, making generalization of laboratory findings to the marketplace tenuous.

The difficulty of field experiments and the lack of realism in lab experiments limited the use of experimentation in marketing research prior to the 1960s. The last three decades have seen a steady growth in its use, however. The major area of application is test marketing of new products and ad campaigns. Other areas of application have included the effects of supermarket shelf-space changes on food sales, the effects of price changes on market share, testing alternative commercials and campaign themes, and advertising copy testing.[10]

Sample design. In many research studies the goal is to draw appropriate conclusions about a population of interest—a segment of buyers, for example. The success of the research design is determined in part by how well the population of interest is represented by the buyers being studied. If they represent a good cross-section of the population, then the conclusions will be valid (assuming other aspects of the research design are sound). If they do not represent the population, then erroneous conclusions are very likely.

One way to ensure representativeness is to take a *census* of the population—collect information from every member of the population. However, cost usually prohibits the census approach. Instead, a *sample* of the population is chosen, and an attempt to collect data from each member of the sample is made.

sample | A **sample** is a subset of the members of a population being studied.

---

[10] Churchill, *Marketing Research,* pp. 105–7.

The representativeness of a sample is determined by the *sample design.*

sample design

> The **sample design** is the set of procedures used to determine the size and composition of a sample.

Two aspects of a sample design determine whether it will yield a sample representative of the population of interest: sample selection procedures and sample size. Sample selection procedures determine the composition of the sample. There are two families of selection procedures: *probability* and *nonprobability sampling* designs.

probability sampling

> In **probability sampling** a sample is chosen such that each member of the population has a known, nonzero probability of being in the sample, and chance mechanisms are used to choose the sample members.

Three types of probability designs exist. (See Table 23–10.) *Random sampling* allows all possible combinations of a given sample size in the population an equal probability of being in the chosen sample. This, in turn, results in an equal probability for each individual in the population of being in the sample. In *stratified sampling,* the population is first broken into mutually exclusive, exhaustive subgroups. Random samples

Table 23–10: Types of sample designs

Types of design	Description	Advantage	Disadvantage
Random	Probability sample that allows each member of population a known, equal chance of inclusion	Easy to select when a list of population is available	May not include sample units from all portions of population May result in high data collection costs
Stratified	Probability sample where population is broken down into subgroups and a sample is taken from each subgroup	Ensures inclusion of sample units from all subgroups	Requires knowledge of value of stratification variable for each population member
Cluster	Probability sample where population is broken down into subgroups (geographic areas) and a sample is taken from only a portion of the subgroups	Lower sample selection and data collection costs	May lose representativeness
Nonprobability	Judgment of researcher determines sample	Easy, inexpensive to select	Cannot generalize results

of a given size are then chosen from each subgroup. This approach ensures the inclusion of population members from each subgroup, making it more accurate than simple random sampling. Stratified samples are very appropriate for market segmentation studies. For example, consider a study conducted by a bank. The bank was interested in customer satisfaction with its services. Since it offered different services to customers based on their account balance, the bank had to make sure that all types of customers were studied. Therefore, it divided its customer base into three strata: customers with high, medium, and low account balances. A stratified sample was taken in which customers were randomly drawn from each stratum.

A *cluster sample* is a probability sample designed to lower the costs of a random sample. In a cluster sample, the population is broken down into subgroups (usually geographic areas) that are each representative of the entire population. The final sample is then drawn from one or more but less than all of the subgroups. In this way the sampling effort focuses on only a portion of the population and cost savings are realized. An example of a cluster sample is provided by a radio station in a study of listenership. The station reached a five-county area, so it broke down the population into counties. Rather than studying listeners in all five counties, the station's researcher randomly chose two of the five counties, and then chose random samples within each of these. The station was able to concentrate its personal interviews in the two counties because all five counties were similar in size and composition. And it spent substantially less on this type of sampling than it would have for a random sample from the five counties together.

nonprobability sampling	**Nonprobability sampling** designs are those that incorporate the judgment of the researcher in selecting sample members.

A common form of nonprobability sample is the *convenience sample,* in which the inclusion of individuals in a sample is based on their ease of access. Nonprobability designs are nonscientific and don't allow generalizations about a population. However, they can be adequate for exploratory studies that identify key issues for further study. For example, a focus group study will employ a nonprobability sample.

The second major aspect of a sample design is the size of a sample. In determining sample size a researcher must balance costs with an adequate number of respondents. Too large a sample will be too costly. Too small a sample will not allow generalization to the population. The major factor dictating the necessary sample size is the heterogeneity of the population being studied: the more heterogeneous the population, the larger the necessary sample. Note that it is not the *size* of the popula-

Table 23–11: Typical sample sizes for different types of studies	Number of subgroups	Individuals or households		Institutions	
		National	Regional or special	National	Regional or special
	None or few	1,000–1,500	200–500	200–500	50–200
Source: Seymour Sudman, *Applied Sampling* (New York: Academic Press, 1976), p. 87.	Average	1,500–2,500	500–1,000	500–1,000	200–500
	Many	2,500+	1,000+	1,000+	500+

tion but its *heterogeneity* that determines appropriate sample size. If everyone in a population is pretty much alike, then it doesn't take a very large sample to find that out. A second factor influencing necessary sample size is the number of subgroups of interest—the larger the number of subgroups, the larger the necessary sample to make sure that each subgroup is adequately represented.

Table 23–11 reflects the influence of population heterogeneity and number of subgroups on typical sample sizes for different types of studies. Regional or local populations, being more homogeneous than national populations, are typically studied with smaller samples, as are organizations versus households or individuals. Within each category, however, as the number of subgroups increases, sample sizes increase.[11]

The sample design of the printing company study employed a stratified sample. Several different types of organizations were of interest. Samples were drawn from each category and combined into a total sample of 3,000 sampling units. While the total sample was fairly large, it resulted from rather small samples (50 to 200) taken from each segment. Variations in sample sizes from each segment were based on the perceived heterogeneity of the segments.

Data analysis. The final major dimension of research design is **data analysis.**

---

data analysis

> **Data analysis** is the set of statistical procedures used to extract meaning from research data and answer the research questions.

The scope of techniques available for data analysis encompasses the entire realm of statistical procedures. The key issue is to select a technique that addresses the research problem and tests any hypotheses that have

---

[11] For an in-depth theoretical treatment of sampling design, see Leslie Kish, *Survey Sampling* (New York: John Wiley & Sons, 1965). For an excellent blend of theory and practice in sampling, see Seymour Sudman, *Applied Sampling* (New York: Academic Press, 1976).

been stated. If the interest is in the behavior of a single variable, some type of *univariate* technique (e.g., computation of a mean) is appropriate. If the interest is in the relationship between two variables, a *bivariate* technique (e.g., simple correlation) would be used. Finally, if the objective is to examine the effects of multiple variables on one or more other variables, *multivariate* analysis (e.g., multiple regression, discriminant analysis) is appropriate.

In our printing company study, the objective was to compare several market segments on a set of buyer behavior variables. Therefore, the major type of analysis was bivariate in the form of cross-tabulation and chi-square analysis. In this way, direct comparisons between segments could be made and key differences and similarities among them identified. Two of these analyses are shown in Table 23–12.

Table 23–12: Examples of data analysis from printing study

a. *Type of organization cross-tabulated with buying center size*

Type of organization	Number of members in buying center		
	One	Two	Three or more
Manufacturer . . .	8%	33%	58%
Association	40	31	29
Hospital	0	0	100
Financial.	25	50	25
Publisher.	38	38	24
Service	31	42	27
Nonprofit.	39	37	24
Industrial service . .	50	33	17
Government. . . .	41	35	24
Other	31	31	38

b. *Type of organization by percent indicating attribute is "very important"*

Type of organization	Attribute				
	Speed	Quality	Price	Meeting deadline	Variety of services
Manufacturer . . .	71%	100%	71%	86%	50%
Association	69	92	74	84	31
Hospital	100	100	100	100	67
Financial.	86	90	57	100	48
Publisher.	56	89	67	78	0
Service	80	85	60	84	22
Nonprofit.	50	75	100	50	25
Industrial service . .	67	100	50	100	100
Government. . . .	56	81	88	94	27
Other	69	87	88	75	44

In Table 23–12a, size of the buying center is cross-tabulated with type of organization. This analysis reveals whether different types of organizations present more formidable marketing tasks based in the number of people involved in the decision. In this case manufacturers and hospitals possess the most complex buying centers.

In Table 23–12b, types of organization are compared according to the percent of respondents indicating "very important" in response to a question on the importance of each of five supplier attributes. The key findings here are the relative lack of importance attached to the ability of suppliers to provide a variety of services and the consistently high importance attached to the quality of services.

Assess value of research

Once a managerial problem has been translated into a research problem and a research design for its investigation has been proposed, an important decision remains—whether or not to conduct the research. The purpose of the value analysis stage is to ascertain whether the problem and research design as presently formulated are worthy of implementation.

The criterion for assessing whether to proceed with the proposed research is fundamental: Will the value of the information provided by the research exceed its cost? With a proposed research design, it's a rather straightforward issue to estimate the dollar costs. The value of information is a more subjective proposition. Three factors should be considered jointly when assessing the **value of information:**[12]

1. *Level of uncertainty.* When uncertainty about the topic of interest is high, the value of information will be high. If, however, much is already known, additional information will be of little value.

2. *Reduction of uncertainty.* For information to be valuable, it must reduce the uncertainty. It must increase knowledge. This point underscores the importance of getting the right information with the proper research design.

3. *Consequences of incorrect decision.* When information will be used to guide a decision in which large absolute or opportunity losses would be associated with a poor decision, it takes on greater value. If an incorrect decision will leave the firm in not much worse shape than a good decision, the information has much less value.[13]

Based on a value analysis, one of three decisions can be made. First, a favorable value-cost assessment might occur and a decision to implement the proposed research made. Second, an unfavorable assessment might occur. The company might then attempt to revise the research design and lower its cost while preserving much of the information. If this were possible, a revised research project would be implemented. Finally, a con-

---

[12] Bertram Schoner and Kenneth Uhl, *Marketing Research: Information Systems and Decision Making,* 2d ed. (New York: John Wiley & Sons, 1975), p. 14.

[13] Bayesian decision theroy is a way to quantify the value of information based on these factors. See Churchill, *Marketing Research,* pp. 30–49, for an exposition.

clusion might be reached that the value-cost relationship was negative without any hope of revising the research to improve the relationship. The firm would then decide not to implement the research.

These three possible decisions are contained within the flow process used by Blue Cross and Blue Shield Association to evaluate research proposals. (See Figure 23–5.) Research proposals go through four levels of review. At each level the project reviewer accepts or rejects the proposal. If rejected, the proposal goes back to the originating department or individual, who has the option of revising or discarding it. Note that research

Figure 23–5: Flow diagram of how Blue Cross and Blue Shield evaluates proposed marketing research

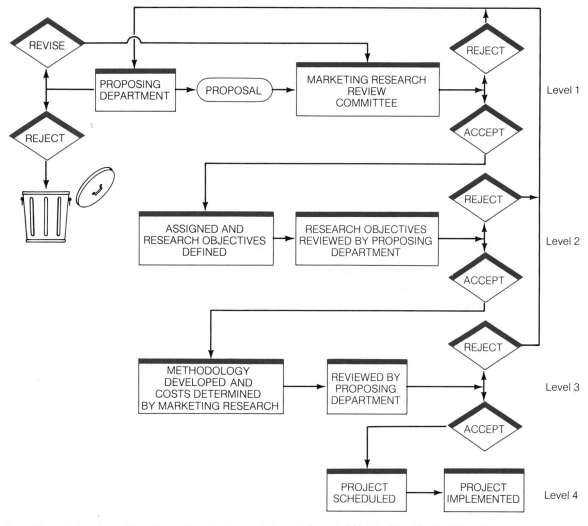

Source: Thomas C. Benedict, Jr., "Flow Diagram Shows How to Evaluate Research Proposals," *Marketing News*, May 14, 1982, p. 11.

objectives are reviewed before methodology and costs are determined. The research design and its costs are then evaluated.

The printing company estimated the cost of their proposed research at approximately $18,000. While not placing a figure on the value, the company concluded that the proposed survey would yield helpful information on market behavior of which they had limited knowledge. The $18,000 research cost was minor compared to the cost the firm would incur if the machines were purchased to serve a market that wasn't there.

Implement research

Once the decision to conduct a proposed research project is made, the next stage is to simply implement the proposed research design. Sample members are selected according to the sample design, and information is collected from them. The data are edited, coded, and analyzed according to the research questions or hypotheses. This stage should be the easiest to complete if the research effort has been planned well and the procedures to follow have been stated clearly and precisely.

A useful first step in the implementation stage is to establish a timeframe for the completion of the project and its component steps. The preferred approach is to estimate the time necessary to complete each stage. The ending date for the final stage is then the completion date for the project. In this way the time needed to complete each stage effectively is more likely to be allocated. However, the time requirements of decision making often necessitate a different approach—where a completion date for decision making is specified first. The timing of each stage is then established by working within the targeted completion date. The details of the timing of the printing company survey are provided in Figure 23–6.

Interpret findings

The completion of data collection and analysis leads to the interpretation stage. The essence of this stage is to link the research findings to the purpose of the research. Recall that a key step early in the research process was the translation of a managerial problem into a research problem. A research design is planned and implemented to investigate the research problem. Now that the design has generated research findings, it is necessary to translate them back into the context of the managerial problem. The researcher must determine the meaning of the findings in terms of the original purpose of the research. It is with this linkage that marketing research provides input to decision making and makes its results actionable. Without it, marketing researchers have lost track of their original purpose.

Our printing company found several interesting results that led them to decide to pursue expansion and purchase the new machines. They identified certain segments who were not aware of the availability of the various printing services offered by the company. Those that were aware perceived costs and speed of service much more negatively than

Figure 23–6: Time frame for completion of printing survey

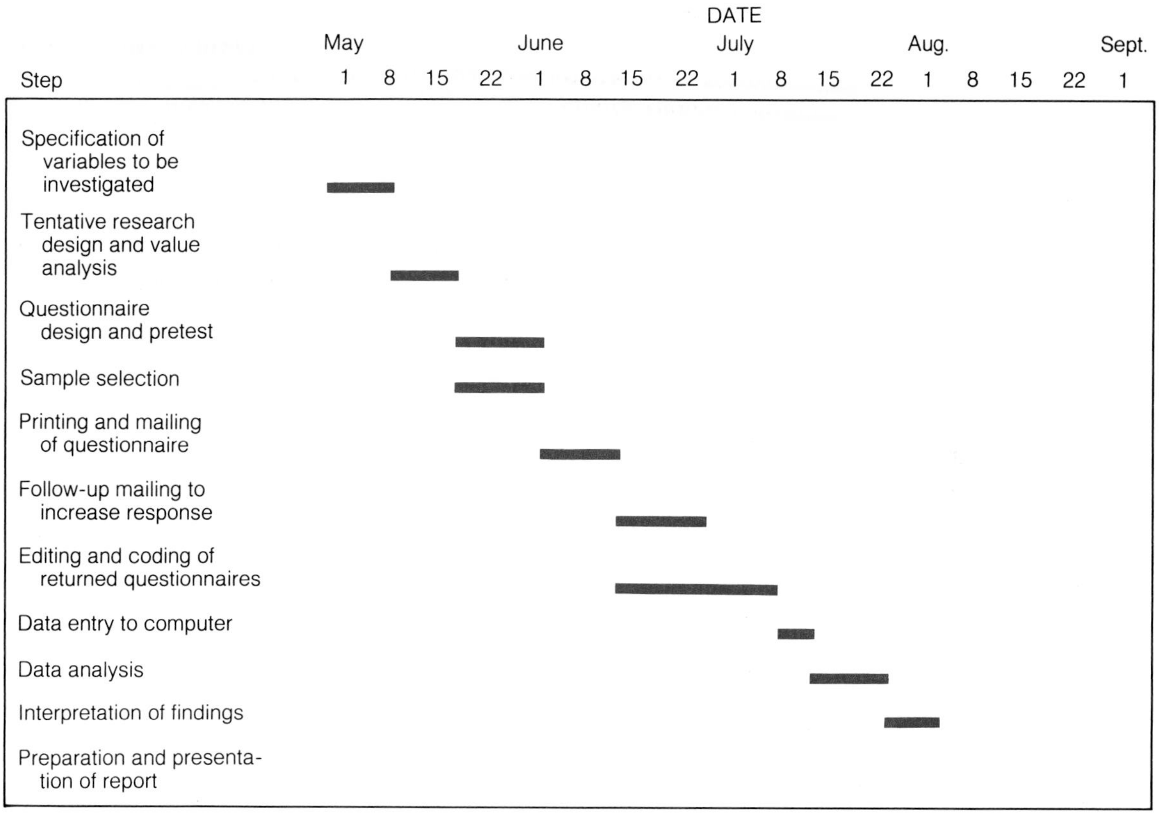

	DATE					
	May	June	July	Aug.	Sept.	

was actually the case. These findings suggested a high level of potential in certain market segments and the nature of the marketing effort appropriate for pursuing it. This effort would involve a program designed to increase awareness through promotional mailings coupled with sales force efforts to change beliefs about the cost and speed of the printing service.

Prepare and present report

The final stage in the research process is to disseminate the research findings and their implications to the appropriate audience. This stage usually entails both an oral and a written audience. The appropriate audience is often a diverse group of individuals—engineers, executives, product managers, other researchers, etc. Some members of the audience are interested only in results. Others are more technically oriented and concerned with the research procedures. Still others just want to know the implications. Sometimes separate reports are generated for each group. Usually, though, a common report to all is the case, and a delicate balance among the diverse interests of the audience must be incorporated into the report. The major criteria in writing a research report are completeness, accuracy, clarity, and conciseness.[14]

This final stage of the research process is critical. For marketing research to perform its support role, research findings and recommendations for action must be effectively communicated to the rest of the organization. Yet, despite the increased capability and versatility of marketing research, its linkage to the remainder of the firm is weak. A study of the performance of marketing research departments cited ineffective communications from research departments to their users as one of the major problems.[15] A more recent study reveals differences between managers and researchers in their perceptions of what makes research useful. Managers see the technical quality of the final report as contributing most to research useful-ness. Researchers see the extent of interaction between managers and researchers and the political acceptability of the research as the most important factors.[16]

A more effective integration of marketing research into the planning and decision-making activities of firms seems to be needed. A first step in this direction would be understanding the role of research within the total marketing information system.

THE MARKETING INFORMATION SYSTEM (MIS)

Earlier in this chapter we emphasized the supportive role of information in marketing decision making. We saw the various types and sources of information available to the marketing manager. We examined market-ing research as an important, versatile source of marketing information. Now it's appropriate to return to a total-information perspective and examine—through the concept of a marketing information system—the management and coordination of marketing information as input to deci-sion making.

MIS

> The **MIS** is structured, interacting complex of persons, machines, and proce-dures designed to generate an orderly flow of information sources for use as input to marketing decision making.[17]

---

[14] William J. Gallagher, *Report Writing for Management* (Reading, Mass.: Addison-Wesley Publishing, 1969).

[15] James R. Krum, "B for Marketing Research Departments," *Journal of Marketing,* Octo-ber 1978, pp. 8–12.

[16] Rohit Deshpande and Gerald Zaltman, "A Comparison of Factors Affecting Researcher and Manager Perceptions of Market Research Use," *Journal of Marketing Research,* February 1984, p. 36.

[17] Adapted from a definition supplied by Richard H. Brien and James E. Stafford, "Market-ing Information Systems: A New Dimension for Marketing Research," *Journal of Marketing* 32 (July 1968), p. 21.

The nature of a marketing information system

This definition implies the importance of a well-planned, coordinated approach to meeting the information needs of an organization. The purpose of the MIS is to bring together relevant information from all sources and make it easily accessible to marketing decision makers. Four major *MIS functions* are performed in the operation of the MIS:

1. *Organize.* With the variety of types and sources of information available to marketing managers, a crucial function of the MIS is to categorize the information as it is collected.

2. *Store.* Not all information is used at the same time or by the same people. Consequently, it is necessary to store the information so it is available to those who need it when they need it.

3. *Analyze.* Some information is not useful until it is analyzed and transformed into a new form. For example, information may enter the system for use in demand assessment. It is not used in its raw form but rather as input to a forecasting model that generates a short-run or long-run forecast of demand.

4. *Transmit.* Raw or transformed information must be transmitted to decision makers in order for it to be used. The MIS must allow for a smooth flow of information to its users on demand.

Components of the MIS

In order to organize, store, analyze, and transmit information, there must be certain key *MIS components:* sources of information, data bank, analytical unit, and display unit. Figure 23–7 shows how these components work together to serve the marketing decision maker.

Sources of information. Figure 23–7 identifies four major sources of information for the MIS. Of these sources, most marketing executives consider *internal accounting* data most important. It is the major source of performance evaluation data. Marketing research, as we have seen, can provide a variety of types of information. *Government affairs* monitors trends in the legal environment. *Marketing intelligence,* as a source of information, is taking on more importance. In fact, a recent study of MIS usage in Fortune 500 companies revealed that more executives identified marketing intelligence as the most important source of information than did marketing research.[18]

marketing intelligence

> **Marketing intelligence** is the day-to-day information concerning pertinent developments in the environment, primarily the competitive sector.[19]

---

[18] Raymond McLeod, Jr. and John Rogers, "Marketing Information Systems: Uses in the Fortune 500," *California Management Review,* Fall 1982, p. 109.

[19] Adapted from Philip Kotler, *Marketing Management: Analysis, Planning, and Control,* 5th ed. (Englewood Cliffs, N.J.: Prentice-Hall, 1984), p. 192.

Figure 23–7: Components of a marketing information system

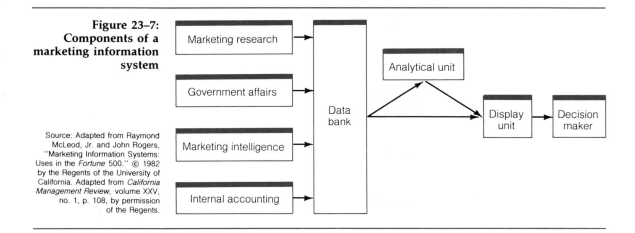

Source: Adapted from Raymond McLeod, Jr. and John Rogers, "Marketing Information Systems: Uses in the *Fortune* 500." © 1982 by the Regents of the University of California. Adapted from *California Management Review*, volume XXV, no. 1, p. 108, by permission of the Regents.

Marketing intelligence is obtained through salesperson call reports, annual reports, suppliers, dealers, trade shows, the press, and a variety of other means.

Internal accounting, marketing research, government affairs, and marketing intelligence generate a vast array of types of information (see Table 23–13) that enter the system.

Data bank.　The data generated by the sources of information enter a *data bank,* which performs the storage and organization functions. A

Table 23–13: Types of information entering the MIS (partial listing)

Internal Accounting	**Marketing research**
Accounts receivable	Invoice data
Accounts payable	Trade association data
Inventory reports	Census data
Cost reports	Audit and panel data
Sales and profitability by	Survey results
Product	Experiments
Product line	Forecasts
Customer class	Market share
Region	**Marketing intelligence**
Salesperson	
Budgets	Salesperson reports
Promotional allowances	Annual reports of
Government affairs	Customers
	Competitors
Lobbyist reports	Suppliers
Pending legislation	Trade journals
Tax law changes	Press clippings
Lawsuits	Competitor decisions
	Trade show data
	Dealer reports

computer enhances the storage and organization functions for internal accounting and marketing research data. However, government affairs and marketing intelligence data do not lend themselves to computer storage. Corporate libraries and file cabinets represent noncomputerized forms of data banks.

Analytical unit. The third key component is the *analytical unit,* which performs the analysis function. The analytical unit contains statistical and mathematical models that transform raw information into statistical summaries, estimates of market response to proposed marketing strategies, forecasts of sales, and other marketing-related analyses.[20]

Display unit. Depending on the needs of the manager, information may be requested directly from the data bank or from the analytical unit after some type of analysis has been formed. Whichever the case, the information is transmitted to the decision maker by the *display unit.* Microcomputer developments now allow quick access to visually displayed information through computer terminals. More and more suppliers of information are making their information available in computer-readable form.

Ideally, a display unit transmits only the information that is requested. Otherwise, the decision maker will be inundated with nonrelevant information. Whirlpool Corporation faced this very problem a few years ago. Its managers received computer printouts daily, weekly, or monthly that dealt with more than 70 areas of analysis. This format so overwhelmed the users that the information had little effect on their decisions. Whirlpool then converted its display unit to video display screens so that information supplied to a particular manager would match his or her specific information needs.[21]

Design factors in the MIS

The development of the MIS so that its components effectively perform its functions requires the consideration of certain design factors. These design factors include:

1. *Information recency.* This refers to the time lapse between the occurrence of an event in the environment and when data describing the event is entered into the MIS. This may range from several weeks in the case of certain market developments to a few hours or minutes in the case of inventory levels.

2. *Information aggregation.* This factor is concerned with the detail level of the information entering the system. For example, sales data may be entered at the individual customer level, sales territory level,

---

[20] For an expanded view of this aspect of the MIS, see David B. Montgomery and Glen L. Urban, "Marketing Decision-Information Systems: An Emerging View," *Journal of Marketing Research* 7 (May 1970), pp. 226–34.

[21] Jack D. Sparks, "Taming the 'Paper Elephant' in Marketing Information Systems," *Journal of Marketing* 40 (July 1976), pp. 83–86.

market segment level, and so on. The level of aggregation may vary with the type of information. Sales data may be entered in very detailed fashion, while census data may be aggregated to the market segment level.

3. ***Analytical sophistication.*** This refers to the level of sophistication built into the analytical unit. At a sample level, we may find analytical capabilities restricted to the aggregation of information or to descriptive statistics. At an advanced level, sophisticated mathematical models that simulate real market conditions may be designed into the system.

4. ***Computer authority.*** The final design factor deals with how much authority is granted to the system in reporting to managers. The lowest level of authority is when the system simply retrieves and displays data. A much higher level of authority exists when the system is designed to provide prognostications of the outcome of planned or contemplated marketing programs.[22]

The levels of these factors vary according to the organization and its management. However, Amstutz specifies four important considerations when designing the MIS:

1. The MIS should be founded on management's conception of the environment.
2. The user must understand the system.
3. The system is based on disaggregated data files.
4. The system is designed to permit expansion and change to higher levels of sophistication.[23]

The general philosophy guiding the design of an MIS should be a user orientation. Too often, MIS designers became enamored with the technical aspects of the MIS and fail to consider user needs in guiding the technical design.

The status of MIS in industry

In the late 1960s the MIS concept received considerable attention as the future structure for dealing with the information explosion. Indeed, several large firms took steps to design and implement the MIS within their operations. Initially, however, the MIS did not realize its promise. This was due in part to the technical requirements that the MIS implies, although it's important to realize that the philosophy of the MIS can still guide the nontechnical management of information. With microcomputers making it easier to meet these technical requirements, the MIS is again emerging as a key consideration in strategic management.[24]

---

[22] Arnold E. Amstutz, "The Marketing Executive and Management Information Systems," in *Science, Technology, and Marketing,* ed. R. M. Haas (Chicago: American Marketing Association, 1966), pp.69–86.

[23] Ibid.

[24] For an account of the nature of the MIS in major corporations, see McLeod and Rogers, "Marketing Information Systems," 1982.

Rather than the emergence of corporatewide information systems, what is happening is the development of information subsystems, each specific to a particular functional area. Information subsystems for finance, production, distribution, marketing, etc., seem to be the primary direction that the development of the information system concept has taken. And marketing, because of its importance and complexity, has shown the greatest interest. The principles of information system design are no less relevant to this type of approach. Even in the absence of formal systems, these principles can guide the coordinated management of information. In fact, as computer technology makes the technical dimension of the MIS concept accessible to more organizations, they become even more relevant and important to understand.

SUMMARY

Uncertainty pervades marketing decision making. Information can help reduce this uncertainty. The activities designed to provide information perform, therefore, an important support role.

There are several sources from which a variety of information is available, including accounting reports, intermediaries, research and development, managers, the sales force, and marketing research. Marketing research is a versatile source of information encompassing internal and external secondary sources. Primary sources of marketing research data include surveys, experiments, and observation. Marketing research occurs through a process that includes the following stages: problem formulation, research design proposal, value analysis, implementation, interpretation of findings, and preparation and presentation of report. Research design is the heart of the research process. Its key dimensions include source of data, sample design, and data analysis.

With the multitude of sources and types of information, it's important to have an orderly flow of information into the firm and to its decision makers. Marketing information systems are designed to provide a coordinated approach to information management. The MIS organizes, stores, analyzes, and transmits information. Components of the MIS include sources of information, data bank, analytical unit, and display unit. These components are designed according to desirable levels of four factors: information recency, information aggregation, analytical sophistication, and computer authority.

KEY CONCEPTS

Uncertainty	Marketing research process	Focus group
Role of information	Managerial problem	Descriptive research design
Sources of marketing information	Research problem	Causal design
Marketing research	Hypothesis	Secondary data
Marketing research agency	Research design	Internal secondary data
	Exploratory research design	External secondary data

Published statistics

Standardized marketing
  information service

Publicly circulated research report

Primary data

Observational studies

Direct observation

Participation-observation

Mechanical observation

Physical traces

Survey research

Interviewer-administered
  survey

Self-administered survey

Personal interviews

Telephone interviews

Mail questionnaire

Drop-off questionnaire

Experimentation

Field experiments

Laboratory experiments

Census

Sample

Sample design

Probability sampling

Random sampling

Stratified sampling

Cluster sample

Nonprobability sampling

Convenience sample

Data analysis

Univariate analysis

Bivariate analysis

Multivariate analysis

Value of information

Marketing information system
  (MIS)

MIS function

MIS components

Internal accounting

Government affairs

Marketing intelligence

Data bank

Analytical unit

Display unit

Information recency

Information aggregation

Analytical sophistication

Computer authority

**DISCUSSION
QUESTIONS AND
EXERCISES**

1. Discuss the general and specific roles of information in marketing strategy planning.

2. Conduct an interview with a marketing executive. Find out the sources and types of information the executive uses in making decisions. Ask him or her to indicate the importance of the various types and sources of information.

3. For each of the following, determine the source of marketing research information you would use. Determine, first, whether you would mainly use primary or secondary data and then, within each category, the specific source you would use.
   a. The radio stations to which customers of an auto service company listen.
   b. The relationship between sales and advertising expenditures.
   c. Consumer beliefs about your brand and your competitors' brands.
   d. Whether consumers notice a predominantly visual or verbal ad the most.
   e. Demographic trends in major market areas.

4. For each of the following survey research projects, discuss the type of sample selection procedure you would use.
   a. A retail department store wants to determine the extent of customers it has in each geographic area of its local market.
   b. An industrial marketer wants to investigate the extent to which Fortune 500 companies use computerized information systems.
   c. A TV station whose signal reaches a three-county area wants to do personal interviews to determine the demographic profile of its viewers.

5. A small retail store owner who can't afford a computer laments that the situation, therefore, precludes designing an MIS for the operation. What is your reaction? Is the MIS beyond the grasp of the store owner? If it is not, design a MIS for such a business.

Cases for section eight

Case 15: Citizens & Southern National Bank: Using MBO to establish a control and evaluation system

C&S was in deep trouble when Bennett Brown took over in February 1978—its 1977 earnings statement showed a $7.8 million loss and its stock had plunged from the 1973 high of $26 to a low of $4 per share. The previous management had operated under a strong autocratic rule which Brown himself described as a "strong, one-man rule."

Brown instituted a classic management by objectives program, described as follows:

> All bank officers participate in setting their own goals—and are held accountable for meeting them. A committee of the bank's top 11 managers meets weekly and distributes the minutes of its meeting throughout the C&S system of 11 banks. There is a quarterly review system in which subordinates are evaluated by the senior managers, who in turn are evaluated by Brown. Brown is reviewed by the executive committee of the board, which measures his progress against his plan.

The impact on C&S has been remarkable. No longer can lower-level managers cover up problems. Decisions are made in a timely manner. Above all, strategy decisions are centralized; no longer can managers set objectives for

their departments that might run counter to the good of the bank.

Managers are given the autonomy to meet the goals set. For example, when Willard Alexander of credit administration was told to cut bad loans as quickly as possible and reduce nonperforming assets by 20 percent annually, he decided to form a 30-member staff that for two years concentrated on pinpointing and eliminating bad loans. The results were that nonperforming assets were slashed by an average of 31 percent over the following three years.

The results of Brown's MBO program have been phenomenal. From its 1977 loss, C&S rebounded to earnings of $37.2 million in 1980. Moreover, the future looks bright—C&S bought four additional banks in 1980 and purchased another 13 in 1983. The best news is that other banks are again viewing C&S as a serious competitor.

Reference

"How One Troubled Bank Turned Itself around." *Business Week,* August 24, 1981, pp. 117–19.

Discussion questions

1. What is management by objectives?

2. MBO worked well for C&S. Could an autocratic program work as well?

3. What is the role of MBO in the evaluation and control process?

4. Can you think of drawbacks to the MBO system? Why doesn't every company use MBO?

Case 16: AMP, Inc.: Effective use of a marketing information system

When AMP, Inc. ran a sales contest in fall 1980, executives of the $1.2 billion manufacturer of electrical connectors found that they could not determine the winner because they did not have the necessary information to do so. Although the Harrisburg, Pennsylvania headquarters regularly received sales reports, it did not have the breakdown by product line needed to find the best salesperson. Indeed, Anthony Zettlemoyer, manager of AMP's statistics and business analysis department, recalled that while many different reports were received, management would seldom have the relevant information at the appropriate time.

Information center at AMP

As a response, AMP established an information center in January 1981, with eight users in three departments. IBM was responsible for promoting the information center concept in 1979. The objective of such centers is to help decisionmakers gather the facts they need and provide the tools for analyzing them quickly.

Most information centers are run as adjuncts to existing data processing departments. However, they operate differently. Instead of funneling all data requests through a team of programmers, information centers allow managers to retrieve and manipulate information on their own. In this way, managers are able to target the information they require and are not overwhelmed with irrelevant data.

The biggest advantage of the information center is its time-saving characteristic. For example, Conway Williams, director of material services for AMP, used to receive a voluminous monthly report listing inventories of each of the company's 170,000 part numbers. So much time was spent plowing through the data that none was left to analyze the problems that arose along the way.

With the information center, however, managers have more time to perform detailed analysis. Williams, for instance, was able to determine how quickly each of AMP's product lines was moving, and how rapid its divisions were in writing off inventory that was not selling. This had not been possible before because AMP found no "easy way to do it with the computer, and it was impossible to do manually."

What next?

By September 1982, AMP's information center serviced 170 users in 26 departments. AMP was able to reorganize its sales records by product line and select its contest winner. Moreover, a restructuring of its inventory was facilitated and domestic sales increased by 25 percent over an 18-month period while shrinking inventories by 2.5 percent. The information center had appeared to significantly improve the quality of management decision making.

Reference

"Helping Decisionmakers Get at Data." *Business Week,* September 13, 1982, pp. 118–23.

Discussion questions

1. What do you think are the requirements for a successful information system? How does an information center like the one used by AMP meet these requirements?

2. It has been said that establishment of an information center must be accompanied by appropriate data organization to facilitate rapid information retrieval. Do you agree? Why? What are the other factors that must be present before the benefits of an information center are realized?

3. The information center concept assumes that managers are able to express their own information needs. Do you see this as a possible impediment to its success in information management and control? Are there any other possible disadvantages in implementing an information center?

4. Aside from inventory control and sales management, what other areas in AMP's operations can be served by an information center? What limits, if any, are there in the information center concept, particularly when applied in a company such as AMP?

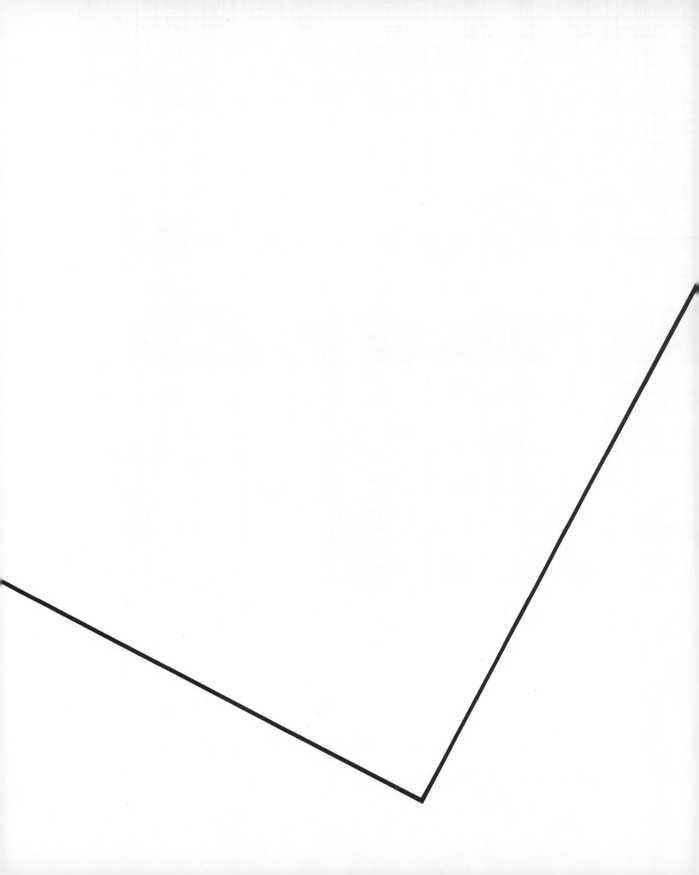

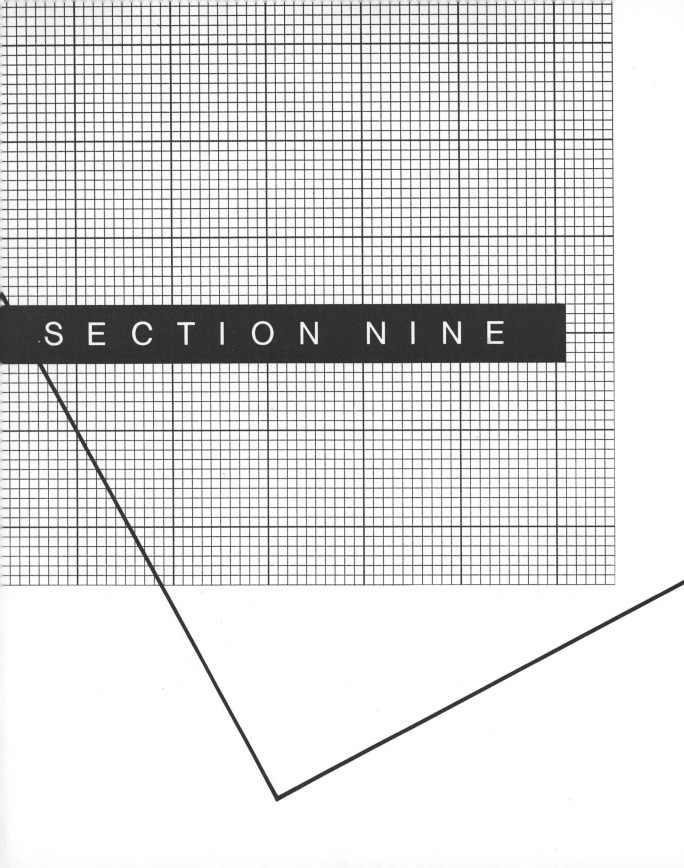

SECTION NINE

Marketing in special fields

Throughout this text we've discussed concepts and examples primarily in the context of product marketing by profit-oriented firms in the U.S. marketplace. We've provided examples outside this context, but we haven't paid separate attention to the special implications of marketing done outside these boundaries. In Section Nine we devote separate attention to important features in three special areas: international marketing, services marketing, and nonprofit marketing.

Many firms view the world as their marketplace. Their marketing efforts cut across multiple countries and multiple cultures. In Chapter 24 we discuss the distinct nature of a multinational marketing effort.

Chapter 25 recognizes two somewhat related special fields of marketing. First, we'll discuss the distinguishing characteristics of services and their implications for strategic marketing. Second, we'll consider the special nature of strategic marketing in nonprofit organizations.

Multinational marketing*

* Surendra Singh's assistance in developing this chapter on multinational marketing is gratefully acknowledged.

Multinational marketing defined

Why firms go beyond domestic markets
    Customers
    Nature of the business
    Lower cost of operating abroad
    Meeting the competition
    Environmental and ecological pressures
    Incentives provided by the host country government
    The stage in the product life cycle (PLC)
    Exchange rate fluctuations

Ways of entering foreign markets
    Exporting
    Licensing
    Joint ventures
    Total ownership

Developing multinational marketing strategies

Multinational environment
    Political environment
    Other forms of political risk
    Legal environment
    Cultural environment
    Economic environment
    Technological environment

Standardized versus nonstandardized marketing plans

Marketing mix variables in multinational setting
    Product considerations
    Pricing considerations
    Promotional considerations
    Distribution considerations

The role of multinational corporations

Summary

Key concepts

Discussion questions and exercises

Today, a growing number of firms in industrialized countries think of the entire world as a marketplace for their products. For such companies, there is no "foreign" or "domestic" market. They think of markets in different countries as simply offering different opportunities and problems, each requiring different strategic and tactical decisions. For example, 60 percent of the total world market for GE-type products is outside the United States; and that market is not only larger than the U.S. market but also growing faster.[1]

This multinationalization of business has increased the complexity of strategic marketing planning and control. Our concerns in this chapter are decisions made in global marketing, reasons to enter such markets, and the changes in strategic marketing necessary to meet global changes.

[1] J. Stanford Smith, *General Electric Investor* (General Electric, Fall 1977), p. 3.

821

MULTINATIONAL MARKETING DEFINED

The terms *international marketing* and *multinational marketing* are often used interchangeably, but there is an important distinction between them.

multinational marketing

> **Multinational marketing** is the process of focusing the resources and objectives of an organization on global market opportunities.[2]

international marketing

> A firm engaged in foreign marketing, but with no direct investment in a foreign country, is involved in **international marketing.**

A company that actually invests in a foreign country is involved in multinational marketing. Thus, a company that exports or imports goods and services is engaged in international marketing but not multinational marketing. The major emphasis in this chapter is on multinational marketing.

Having made this distinction, let's consider the ***multinational corporation (MNC).*** Alas, there is no consensus definition of this term. Some definitions emphasize structural criteria, such as the number of countries a firm operates in or the number of nationalities represented by shareholders. Others define a multinational corporation by the earnings, sales, assets, or employees derived from or committed to foreign operations.[3] Still another way to define MNC is the degree of direct foreign investment made by the firm.

We adopt the definition given by Robock et al.:

multinational corporation

> A **multinational corporation** is a cluster of corporations controlled by one headquarters while operations are spread over many countries. The headquarters invests in the foreign countries in which it operates.

Multinational corporations are largely a product of developed countries. Eight of the 10 largest MNCs are based in the United States. Of a total estimated stock of foreign investment of about $165 billion—most of which is owned by MNCs—the United States owns more than half. Exam-

---

[2] Warren J. Keegan, *Multinational Marketing Management* (Englewood Cliffs, N.J.: Prentice-Hall, 1974).

[3] Stefan H. Robock, Kenneth Simmonds, and Jack Zwick, *International Business and Multinational Enterprises* (Homewood, Ill.: Richard D. Irwin, 1977), p. 7.

ples of U.S.-based MNCs include IBM, ITT, PanAm, American Express, Bank of America, Ford, Mobil Oil, and General Motors.[4]

WHY FIRMS GO BEYOND DOMESTIC MARKETS

Firms market their products beyond domestic markets for several reasons: (1) customers, (2) nature of the business, (3) lower cost of operating abroad, (4) meeting the competition, (5) environmental and ecological pressures, (6) incentives provided by the host governments, (7) stage in the product life cycle, and (8) exchange rate fluctuations. We'll discuss each of these in detail.

Customers

The presence of foreign customers who cannot be served as inexpensively or easily by exports is the most important reason a domestic firm becomes multinational. In large and growing markets, firms may invest in production facilities in foreign markets even if their investment is not immediately profitable. For example, BRY Air Line, an air-conditioning company in Sunbury, Ohio, invested in a joint venture in India: through a local company, it produced dehumidifiers for the rapidly expanding Indian market. But *import licenses* take a long time to make their way through the bureaucracy. Sales were often lost because of the delays. So BRY built a factory in India to serve the Indian market more effectively.[5]

Nature of the business

The very nature of some businesses dictates that they be conducted on a multinational scale. For example, extraction industries (mining and oil drilling) and plantation industries (banana, tea, and coffee) are international in nature. Shell Oil established firms in Indonesia to extract and refine oil that is marketed worldwide. And British tea companies own plantations in India to produce and market tea the world over. United Fruit's banana plantations in Honduras serve the United States' and other countries' fresh-fruit needs.

Lower cost of operating abroad

Often firms go multinational to lower their costs of production and/or marketing. Many developing countries have location economies that provide cheaper raw material, labor, or other inputs of production and marketing. And companies can benefit from such economies simply by being located in countries that have them.

Meeting the competition

Competition is often an important factor when expanding an existing multinational business into other countries. Obviously, more than one firm may attempt to enter the same foreign market. The best way to

---

[4] United Nations Department of Economic and Social Affairs, "Dimensions of Multinational Corporations," in *International Marketing: Managerial Perspectives,* ed. Subhash C. Jain and Lewis R. Tucker, Jr. (Boston: CBI Publishing Company, 1979), p. 38.

[5] *Business Week,* March 1, 1982, p. 36.

prevent a potential competitor from establishing itself in your foreign market is to get there first. A recent example is France's CIT-Alcatel's attempt to capture a major share of India's telecommunications market before British firms could do so. The French company sought a $200 million contract as the first step in a major coup that would give it up to half of India's orders for digital-switching equipment. This market is expected to reach billions of dollars during the 1980s. CIT-Alcatel's success in India would be a shattering blow to the hopes of Britain's System X entrant in the digital-switching race. Four British companies—British Telecom, Standard Telephone and Cables, General Electric, and Plessey—have spent more than $400 million to develop System X. But as of this writing, the British companies have yet to win their first export order. CIT-Alcatel's action angered its international rivals, and the British lobbied hard to prevent the Indians from signing with the French company.[6]

| **Environmental and ecological pressures** | People in *developed countries* usually have high standards of living; they don't want highly polluting manufacturing facilities like steel mills, paper mills, and cement plants in their communities. Government restrictions in these countries have forced such industries into costly environmental cleanups. Many firms in this situation move to *less developed countries,* where government regulations are less restrictive. The governments of many less developed countries welcome these industries because they create jobs and help increase economic prosperity. |

Incentives provided by the host country government

Many countries offer incentives to lure new business from foreign companies. These incentives take a variety of forms including: reduced property costs, import and income tax reductions, protection against competing imports, and unimpeded movement of capital and profit. In some cases, firms may be completely exempt from income taxes.

The stage in the product life cycle (PLC)

Sometimes a firm's degree of multinational involvement is based on the stages its products occupy in the product life cycle (PLC).[7] In the new-product stage of the PLC, the product is developed and manufactured, say, in the United States for export to foreign markets. As you might expect, product development calls for frequent communication among producer, suppliers, and customers—all domestically based. And when the product is new, cost considerations are not so important, since profit margins are high. In the second stage (the mature product stage), however, technology becomes sufficiently routine to be transferred. Other

---

[6] *Business Week,* April 12, 1982, p. 51.

[7] Raymond Vernon, "International Investment and International Trade in the Product Cycle," *Quarterly Journal of Economics,* May 1966, pp. 190–207; also see Igal Ayal, "International Product Life Cycle: A Reassessment and Product Policy Implications," *Journal of Marketing* 45 (Fall 1981), pp. 91–96.

competitors enter the market and threaten the firm's export position. Eventually foreign demand expands so that the firm can justify a production facility abroad—generally in other advanced countries. In the final stage (the standardized product stage), production shifts to low-cost locations in less developed countries. Cost considerations then become the chief determinant of location. The product may, after all, be exported to other markets, including the original home country.

Still, not all companies are guided by the stages of the PLC model. Some firms have a *global perspective* on their markets. They see domestic and foreign markets as part of the same market—and are more likely to plan multinational marketing operations regardless of where their products stand in the life cycle.[8]

Exchange rate fluctuations

Exchange rate fluctuations may force a company to serve a foreign market by direct manufacturing instead of through exports. A classic example of this is Volkswagen's decision to set up a production facility in the United States. Prior to the mid-1970s, VW was successful in penetrating the U.S. market through exports. But from 1970 to 1975 there was an almost 50 percent devaluation in the U.S. dollar in relation to the Deutsche mark. This made the import of Volkswagens into the United States very costly, and VW was thus forced to establish production facilities here. To explain the effect of change in the exchange rate on import prices, let's use the VW example to make some simplistic assumptions.

Let's assume that *prior to 1975,* the exchange rate of one U.S. dollar was four Deutsche marks. The domestic price of a VW (in Germany) was 20,000 DM; hence, the U.S. price = 20,000 DM/4 = $5,000.

Further assume that in 1975 there was a 50 percent *devaluation* of the U.S. dollar in relation to the Deutsche mark (or a 50 percent *revaluation* of the Deutsche mark in relation to the U.S. dollar). Hence, the exchange rate between dollars and DM would be $1 = 2 DM. Assume that the domestic price of a VW (in Germany) was fixed at 20,000 DM. Then the cost of a VW in the United States (at 1975 assumed rate of exchange) = 20,000 DM/2 = $10,000.

Therefore, a 50 percent devaluation of the U.S. dollar in relation to Deustche marks would double the cost of German imports, other things being equal.

WAYS OF ENTERING FOREIGN MARKETS

A company may enter foreign markets in many ways, including exporting, licensing, joint venturing, and creating subsidiaries (total ownership).

---

[8] L. T. Wells, Jr., "Test of a Product Cycle Model of International Trade," *Quarterly Journal of Economics* 83 (February 1969), pp. 152–62.

Exporting   Traditionally, exporting has been the first step in marketing products abroad. It is the least financial commitment to international marketing. There are two principal ways to export: indirectly and directly.[9]

Indirect exporting

indirect exporting

> A firm can **indirectly export** its products by selling to the *local buying office of a foreign department store* or to an *international trading company.*

Trading companies usually prefer to take title to the merchandise. In certain cases, though, trading companies act as a commission agent and provide complete marketing services to the exporting firm.

Another means of indirect exporting is through *export management companies (EMC).* EMCs are independent organizations; they search out and contact customers on behalf of client manufacturers. EMCs provide all necessary marketing services to their clients, similar to those provided by an in-house export department.

The basic problem in using international trading companies and EMCs is that the exporter has little control over such firms. The trading company usually carries competing products; and it may promote competitors' products more than the firm's products in foreign markets.

Direct exporting

direct exporting

> In **direct exporting** the firm's own sales force sells its product in overseas markets.

The technique is useful when customers are easy to locate. Direct sales to foreign markets usually result in more sales—and more control over marketing activities—than indirect selling. The sales force will also gain insights into the needs and wants of foreign consumers, which is useful for both promotional and future product planning. Direct exporting does cost more than indirect exporting, since the firm must perform all marketing functions. The accompanying box shows the top 25 American exporters in 1983.

---

[9] The following sections are adapted from Vern Terpstra, *International Marketing,* 2d ed. (Hinsdale, Ill.: Dryden Press, 1978).

Top 25 American exporters, 1983

Rank (1983)	Company	Products	Exports ($000)	Exports as percent of sales — Percent	Exports as percent of sales — Rank
1	**General Motors** (Detroit)	Motor vehicles and parts, locomotives, diesel engines	6,493,400	8.71	37
2	**Boeing** (Seattle)	Commercial aircraft	4,819,000	43.30	1
3	**Ford Motor** (Dearborn, Mich.)	Motor vehicles and parts	4,732,000	10.64	30
4	**General Electric** (Fairfield, Conn.)	Aircraft engines, generating equipment, locomotives	4,229,000	15.78	17
5	**United Technologies** (Hartford)	Aircraft engines, helicopters, air-conditioning equipment	2,383,411	16.25	16
6	**E. I. du Pont de Nemours** (Wilmington, Del.)	Chemicals, fibers, polymer and petroleum products, coal	2,303,000	6.51	42
7	**International Business Machines** (Armonk, N.Y.)	Information-handling systems, equipment and parts	2,275,000	5.66	44
8	**McDonnell Douglas** (St. Louis)	Aircraft, missiles, space systems	2,104,700	25.95	4
9	**Chrysler** (Highland Park, Mich.)	Motor vehicles and parts	2,078,600	15.70	18
10	**Eastman Kodak** (Rochester, N.Y.)	Photographic equipment and supplies	1,766,000	17.36	13
11	**Caterpillar Tractor** (Peoria, Ill.)	Earthmoving and construction equipment, engines, turbines	1,584,000	29.20	2
12	**Westinghouse Electric** (Pittsburgh)	Generating equipment, defense systems	1,389,223	14.57	20
13	**Hewlett-Packard** (Palo Alto, Calif.)	Computers, electronic equipment	1,105,000	23.46	6
14	**Philip Morris** (New York)	Tobacco products, soft drink ingredients, beer	1,084,000	11.45	28
15	**Signal Companies** (La Jolla, Calif.)	Engines, chemicals, audio-video systems	1,025,000	16.66	15
16	**Exxon** (New York)	Petroleum, chemicals	994,000	1.12	49
17	**Union Carbide** (Danbury, Conn.)	Chemicals, industrial and high-technology products	926,000	10.29	31
18	**General Dynamics** (St. Louis)	Tanks, aircraft, missiles, gun systems	910,900	12.75	27
19	**Archer Daniels Midland** (Decatur, Ill.)	Soybean meal and oil, wheat, flour, corn, corn byproducts	901,000	20.99	8
20	**Monsanto** (St. Louis)	Herbicides, chemicals, polymer products, fibers, silicon	879,000	13.95	23
21	**Weyerhaeuser** (Tacoma, Wash.)	Logs, pulp, paperboard, newsprint, lumber	870,000	17.82	12
22	**Northrop** (Los Angeles)	Aircraft, electronic equipment, related support services	827,700	25.38	5
23	**Dow Chemical** (Midland, Mich.)	Chemicals, plastics, magnesium metal	824,000	7.52	41
24	**Digital Equipment** (Maynard, Mass.)	Computers and related peripheral equipment	816,740	19.12	9
25	**Occidental Petroleum** (Los Angeles)	Agricultural chemical products, coal	803,000	4.20	46

Source: *Fortune*, August 6, 1984, p. 65.

Licensing

Licensing is attractive when a firm does not want to incur heavy capital expenditures on foreign market expansion, where the foreign country is politically unstable, or where the market cannot be adequately served through exports. Companies such as Coca-Cola, Pepsi-Cola, Westinghouse Electric, and Continental Can license their products to foreign firms.

The Coca-Cola Company is a leading user of licensing to foreign firms. Here we see the Coca-Cola trademark translated into a variety of foreign languages.

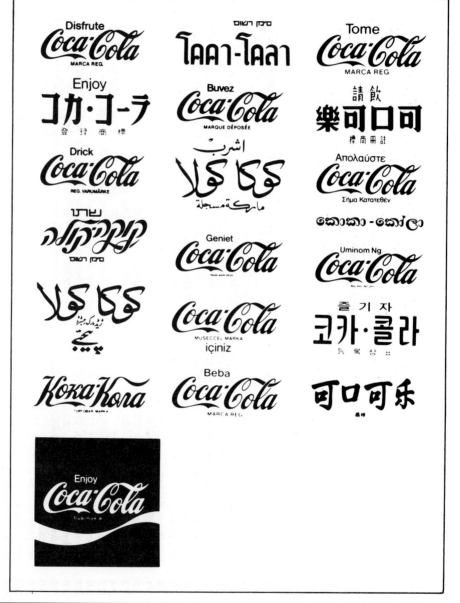

Courtesy The Coca-Cola Company

licensing

> **Licensing** is a contractual agreement. The firm offers the foreign licensees the right to use a manufacturing process, patent, trademark, copyright, or trade secret in exchange for a fee or royalty.

Two serious drawbacks are associated with licensing. A sudden change in the licensing laws of the host country may reduce the control of the licensor over the licensee or may result in substantial financial loss in reduced license fees or royalties on trademarks, etc. And when the licensing period ends, the former licensee may emerge as a formidable competitor because of its access to trade secrets and manufacturing processes.

Joint ventures
joint venture

> A **joint venture** is an agreement between an international firm and a local investor to share the ownership and control of a business.

Joint ventures may take one of several forms.

Contract marketing. Under this plan, a foreign firm permits a local company to manufacture products while retaining the marketing function. Contract marketing is common in the book-publishing business.

Management contracting. In ***management contracting,*** the foreign firm provides consulting services to the host country firm. The manufacturing is done by the local firm. Many hotel chains (such as Hilton) use management contracting.

Joint ownership. In ***joint ownership,*** the foreign company agrees to produce and market its product jointly with the local firm. Usually, the two firms would form a third company. Some examples of joint ventures are those between France's Renault and U.S. American Motors and between Japan's Mitsubishi and U.S. Kentucky Fried Chicken.

There are significant advantages for the international firm engaged in joint venture, including: reduced capital investment, favorable terms from a foreign government, greater control of the producing and marketing of a product, and more accurate feedback on the product's acceptance by the market. But there are major disadvantages, too. The firm must invest more capital and has a greater management involvement than in licensing. And disputes are possible between joint venturing partners due to conflicting interests.

In some situations, joint venturing is the only way to enter a foreign market. Certain governments—especially those in the less developed countries—insist that a foreign firm share ownership with a local company or with the government itself to manufacture or market its products. For example, Brazil requires foreign firms that wish to establish operations in the petrochemical industry to form equal partnerships with local firms.[10] At times, industrialized countries place severe restrictions on joint ventures. For example, Canada has pressured foreign firms to increase Canadian ownership and participation in oil exploration and development in the off-shore Atlantic and Beaufort Sea areas. Canada's energy minister shocked the management of multinationals by asking them to give up 50 percent of the lucrative exploration rights they have accumulated over the last two decades.[11]

Total ownership
total ownership

> In **total ownership,** the company has complete responsibility for producing and marketing the product in foreign countries.

Total ownership has several advantages: direct control of production and marketing, savings in labor and other economies of scale, marketing plans more sensitive to the local needs, and high profit potential.

Total ownership is the riskiest form of business commitment abroad. It is more likely to be subjected to stringent government restrictions, including nationalization. Figure 24–1 arranges the ways of entering foreign markets according to the risk involved.

Figure 24–1: Ways of entering foreign markets arranged according to risk to company doing exporting

Least risk .   .   .   .   Most risk

Exporting   Licensing   Joint   Total
                                       venture   ownership

DEVELOPING MULTINATIONAL MARKETING STRATEGIES

A multinational firm needs a comprehensive strategy to coordinate its marketing operations in different countries. The marketing strategy is based on the degree of involvement in multinational business operations.

There are similarities and differences in all markets, whether domestic or foreign; but the basic concepts, activities, and processes of marketing

---

[10] "Brazil: Local Industry Stops a Big Dow Expansion," *Business Week,* August 25, 1980, p. 46.

[11] "Canada Squeezes More Concessions from Oilmen," *Business Week,* April 12, 1982, p. 51.

Multinational companies must deal with a variety of financial climates. First Interstate Bank helps multinational companies deal with this diversity of financial climates in the Pacific Rim and the Pacific Coast.

Courtesy First Interstate Bancorp

are, with few exceptions, universal.[12] The differences between domestic and foreign marketing occurs because the multinational firm must operate in several countries simultaneously. Figure 24–2 lists factors that differ in domestic and international planning. The beginning point in the development of a global marketing strategy is to analyze the environment of each country in which the multinational corporation markets. Figure 24–3 lists the dimensions that should be considered in this environmental

---

[12] Warren J. Keegan, "A Conceptual Framework for Multinational Marketing," *Columbia Journal of World Business* 8, no. 6 (November–December 1972), pp. 67–76.

Figure 24–2: Domestic versus international planning	Domestic planning	International planning
	Single language and nationality	Multilingual/multinational/multicultural factors
	Relatively homogeneous market	Fragmented and diverse markets
	Data available, usually accurate and easily collected	Data collection a formidable task, requiring significantly higher budgets and personnel allocation
	Political factors relatively unimportant	Political factors frequently vital
	Relative freedom from government interference	Involvement in national economic plans; government influences business decisions
	Individual corporation has little effect on environment	"Gravitational" distortion by large companies
	Chauvinism helps	Chauvinism hinders
	Relatively stable business environment	Multiple environments, many of which are highly unstable (but may be highly profitable)
	Uniform financial climate	Variety of financial climates ranging from over-conservative to wildly inflationary
	Single currency	Currencies differing in stability and real value
	Business "rules of the game" mature and understood	Rules diverse, changeable, and unclear
	Management generally accustomed to sharing responsibilities and using financial controls	Management frequently autonomous and unfamiliar with budgets and controls

Source: William W. Cain, "International Planning: Mission Impossible?" *Columbia Journal of World Business*, July–August, 1970, p. 58.

Figure 24–3: Dimensions of market environment analysis

1. Market characteristics
   a. Size of market, rate of growth
   b. Stage of development
   c. Stage of product life-cycle, saturation levels
   d. Buyer behavior characteristics
   e. Social-cultural factors
   f. Physical environment

2. Marketing institutions
   a. Distribution systems
   b. Communications media
   c. Marketing services (advertising, research, etc.)

3. Industry conditions
   a. Competitive size and practice
   b. Technical development

4. Legal environment (laws, regulations, codes, tariffs, taxes, etc.)

5. Resources
   a. Manpower (availability, skill, potential, cost)
   b. Money (availability, cost)

6. Financial environment (balance of payments, foreign exchange rate, regulations, etc.)

7. Political environment
   a. Current government policies and attitudes
   b. Long-range political environment

Source: Warren J. Keegan, "A Conceptual Framework for Multinational Marketing." *Columbia Journal of World Business* 8, no. 6 (November–December 1972), p. 71.

analysis. This environmental analysis then becomes the first step in the multinational market planning model presented in Figure 24–4.

The model of the multinational market management process starts with environmental analysis. (See Figure 24–4.) Strategic planning begins when this analysis is completed. Key questions for strategic planning include (1) What customers' benefits are provided by our product in the target market? (2) What are our objectives? (3) What is the balance of payment and currency situation in our target markets? Management must organize its resources to achieve its objectives. The organizational structure may be based on customers, products, geographic areas, or some combination of these that best meets the customer's needs. In operational planning, management designs and implements the marketing mix variables to meet the needs of individual countries in which the marketing is done. The final step is control. This involves a comparison of planned versus actual

---

Figure 24–4: The multinational market management process

Key questions for analysis, planning and control of global marketing

Environmental analysis
1. What are the unique characteristics (see Figure 24–3 for characteristics) of each national market? What characteristics does each market have in common with other national markets?
2. Can we cluster national markets for operating and/or planning purposes? What dimensions of markets should we use to cluster markets?

Strategic planning
3. Who should be involved in marketing decisions?
4. What are our major assumptions about target markets? Are they valid?
5. What needs are satisfied by our products in target markets?
6. What customer benefits are provided by our product in target markets?
7. What are the conditions under which our products are used in the target markets?
8. How large is the ability to buy our products in target markets?
9. What are our major strengths and weaknesses relative to existing and potential competition in target markets?
10. Should we extend, adapt, or invent products, prices, advertising, and promotion programs for target markets?
11. What is the balance-of-payments and currency situation in target markets? Will we be able to remit earnings? Is the political climate acceptable?
12. What are our objectives given the alternatives open to us and our assessment of opportunity, risk, and company capability?

Structure
13. How do we structure our organization to optimally achieve our objectives, given our skills and resources? What is the responsibility of each organizational level?

Operational planning
14. Given our objectives, structure, and our assessment of the market environment, how do we implement effective operational marketing plans? What products will we market, at what prices, through what channels, with what communications in which markets and market clusters?

Controlling the marketing program
15. How do we measure and monitor plan performance? What steps should be taken to ensure that marketing objectives are met?

performance of the marketing mix variables. The results of this comparison are fed back into the planning process, and a new planning cycle begins.[13]

MULTINATIONAL ENVIRONMENT

The basic marketing principles apply to all types of markets, domestic or foreign, but the environments in which the firm must operate differ widely. Adoption of the marketing principles in different national environments is thus essential to global marketing strategic planning. Here, we consider some political, legal, cultural, economic, and technological environmental factors.

Political environment

Before entering into major manufacturing or marketing investment in a foreign country, the firm must analyze the political environment of that country. At minimum, the analysis should address the current form of government, the current political party system, the stability and permanence of government policy, and the risks or encouragements to foreign business from political activity.[14]

In many countries, favorable political consideration is given to multinational firms. For example, Singapore and South Korea provide tax incentives and favorable import policies to attract foreign investment. Similarly, during the reign of the Shah multinationals enjoyed favorable treatment in Iran. But when Iranian leadership suddenly changed, several multinationals (especially oil companies) suffered heavy losses. A more recent example of political risk is the change of government in France; when the socialist government took over, about 50 corporations (including multinational firms) were nationalized.

There are four serious *political risks* for a firm with total ownership of a business in a foreign country: confiscation, expropriation, nationalization, and domestication.

Confiscation is an act in which a foreign investment is taken over by a local government without any reimbursement. *Expropriation* occurs when foreign investment is taken over by a local government but some form of reimbursement is made. The firm may not sell the company willingly, and reimbursement may often be less than the full value of the expropriated business. Expropriation and *nationalization* differ in that expropriated businesses are usually handed over to local businesspeople; nationalized businesses are taken over and run by the government. There are numerous examples of these types of risks: Mexico's confiscation of foreign-owned railway systems in 1937 and oil industries in 1938; Guatemala's confiscation of foreign-owned banana plantations in 1953; Cuba's confiscation and nationalization of all industry in 1960; Brazil's

---

[13] Keegan, *Multinational Marketing Management,* pp. 19–21.

[14] Philip R. Cateora and John M. Hess, *International Marketing* (Homewood, Ill.: Richard D. Irwin, 1979), p. 147.

confiscation of U.S.-owned electrical power plants; and Peru's 1969 expropriation of Standard Oil's holdings and the 1973 expropriation and nationalization of the Cerro holdings.[15] Between 1970 and 1974, 34 countries in Latin America, Africa, and Asia expropriated $1.2 billion worth of U.S. overseas investment.[16]

Finally, **domestication** involves a transfer of ownership in part or totally to nationals, forcing foreign firms to place a greater proportion of local managers in higher management levels, granting greater decision-making power to the nationals, increasing the proportion of domestically produced components versus imported components in assembly, and fixing quota(s) for export of the product(s) manufactured locally by a multinational to the world markets.[17]

Malaysia provides a classic example of a government trying to domesticate foreign business. Under its new economic policy, by 1990 30 percent of the corporate sector will be owned by ethnic Malays rather than by foreigners or Malaysian Chinese.[18]

If multinational firms have a choice, they usually prefer domestication to confiscation, expropriation, or nationalization. These latter three capture foreign firms' invested capital, but they drive out managerial know-how, technical expertise, and—often—access to the world market. Domestication, though it results in increased control by nationals, retains all the benefits of the foreign investment.

| **Other forms of political risk** | The following are less severe yet more common types of political risk. |

Exchange controls. When a country's foreign exchange reserves are in short supply, its government may impose *exchange controls* to restrict the movement of foreign currencies out of the country. As Robock and colleagues state:

> With such controls, a nation's currency becomes inconvertible; that is, it is not freely transferable into other currencies. There can be a degree of inconvertibility depending on the nature and extent of the exchange controls. Exchange controls can be limited to import and export transactions or can also cover transfer payments such as profit remittances and capital flows.[19]

The Brazilian cruziero and the Russian ruble are examples of these blocked currencies. Usually, getting profits and investments transferred

---

[15] Ibid., p. 158.

[16] Peter Nehemkis, "Expropriation Has a Silver Lining," *California Management Review,* Fall 1974, p. 15.

[17] Cateora and Hess, *International Marketing,* p. 160.

[18] *Business Week,* March 15, 1982, p. 43.

[19] Robock et al., *International Business,* p. 209.

into the currency of the foreign investor's home country is a severe problem.

Import restrictions. Developing countries may place some restrictions on imports of raw materials, machines, and spare parts. This protects the domestic industries from foreign competition and encourages the foreign industry to purchase locally manufactured products. These ***restrictions*** can be quite harmful if local industries are not developed enough to supply quality raw material. But protectionism is not always bad for foreign investors. For example, Taiwan in April 1982 banned the import of Japanese heavy-duty tractors. Earlier it had prohibited import of Japanese heavy-duty trucks. Both restrictions are aimed at protecting Hua Tung Automotive Corporation, a joint venture company established in 1981—in which General Motors has a 45 percent share![20]

Tax controls. In countries that suffer a chronic shortage of foreign currency, it is common to impose ***tax controls*** by arbitrarily raising corporate taxes. By raising taxes on foreign investment and profits, a significant amount of foreign exchange may be conserved. For example, in the early 1970s Venezuela increased the tax on the profits of all foreign-owned oil companies to 65 percent of net income.[21]

Price controls. During inflationary periods, host governments apply ***price controls*** on products of considerable public interest—drugs, gasoline, and tires. The effect can be disastrous for some firms: sales revenues are limited by price controls, yet costs go up due to inflation.

Labor problems. In countries where organized labor is strong, employees may exert considerable pressure on a multinational firm. Using its influence, organized labor may be able to get legislation passed that would force a multinational to (1) forbid layoffs, (2) share a certain percentage of profits with labor, and (3) provide high-cost fringe benefits.

Ford decided to establish a new plant in Brazil instead of in England, where it already owns plants. The reason is that England had over six times more labor-related stoppages than did existing Brazilian plants.[22]

Legal environment   The legal environment of the host country can impact a foreign firm crucially. A sudden change in regulations can substantially reduce the profits of foreign firms. For example, the harsh treatment of U.S. proprietary drug companies in Canada was a major problem between U.S. trade

---

[20] *Business Week,* April 19, 1982, p. 48.

[21] William H. Cunningham and Isabella C. M. Cunningham, *Marketing: A Managerial Approach* (Cincinnati: South-Western Publishing, 1981), p. 548.

[22] Ibid.

officials and the government of Prime Minister Pierre Trudeau. U.S. drug company executives were angered when profits on some of their most effective products were wiped out by Canadian legislation granting generic manufacturers inexpensive use of international patents. "The law amounts to expropriation of patent rights," complained William M. Robson, president of Smith Kline and French Canada Ltd. Canada is the only industrialized nation in the world doing this. The practice, known as **compulsory licensing,** forces patentholders—nearly always major drug companies—to license their products to Canadian distributors for a 4 percent royalty.[23]

Cultural environment

Foreign markets have a unique character shaped by cultural influences. A marketer dealing with foreign customers must be aware of this. Ignorance of a culture can result in embarrassing personal situations and a substantial financial loss to the firm. Examples abound:

> *In Southeast Asia, Pepsodent toothpaste proved unsuccessful because its ad campaign promised whiter teeth to a culture in which black or yellow teeth are prestige symbols.*[24]

> *In Germany, Maxwell House advertised itself as a great American coffee. But the campaign was a failure—Germans don't have a great deal of respect for American coffee.*[25]

> *Hand gestures are not international in meaning. For example, if you form a circle with thumb and forefinger, most Europeans will know that you mean "it's the best" or "OK." In some Latin American countries, though, the same gesture has a vulgar connotation.*[26]

An intimate knowledge of the language is crucial to understanding a foreign culture. Sometimes, poor knowledge of a customer's language results in "interesting" ads. In Thailand, for instance, a sign advertising a donkey ride for tourists reads, "Would you like to ride on your ass?" A Tokyo hotel sign informed guests, "The flattening of underwear with pressure is the job of the chambermaid—to get it done, turn her on."[27]

These examples underscore the importance of cultural awareness to foreign marketers. Firms can increase cultural awareness by employing foreign personnel in important positions, using foreign researchers, and actively studying cultures.

[23] "A Licensing Law that Hurts U.S. Drugmakers," *Business Week,* March 1, 1982, p. 34.

[24] David Ricks, Marilyn Y. C. Fu, and Jeffery Arpen, *International Business Blunders* (Columbus, Ohio: Grid, 1974), p. 15.

[25] Ibid., p. 16.

[26] S. Watson Funn, "Effects of National Identity on Multinational Promotional Strategy in Europe," *Journal of Marketing* 40 (October 1976), p. 51.

[27] Nino Lo Bello, "Something Funk Would Never Tell Wagnalls," *The Denver Post,* May 1, 1977, p. 45.

Economic environment	Some countries are highly developed and have strong demand for consumer goods and services; others are far less developed and have very little demand for such things. Depending on the stage of the country's economic development, its markets pose qualitatively different kinds of marketing opportunities and problems. (See Table 24–1.)
Technological environment	Many multinational firms try to open manufacturing facilities in technologically less developed countries where labor is relatively cheap. But management must consider the fact that many of these countries have a limited supply of skilled labor. In such cases, cost of training unskilled labor should be considered in planning. Other factors of possible concern are the design of equipment and the conditions in which it operates. For example, U.S. appliances operate on 110 volts of electricity; in Asia and Europe they must operate on 220 volts. And equipment that requires a relatively dry and dust-free atmosphere may not be suited for humid or dusty climates. Such conditions warrant an adaptation of technology to the host country's environment.

Table 24–1: The stages of economic development

Stage	Distinguishing features	Marketing opportunities	Marketing problems
Traditional society	Low productivity; no modern technology; low level of literacy	Market for subsistence goods; basic production goods; raw materials	Limited marketing promotion possible; may not be widespread electricity; few consumers with money for imports
Precondition for take-off	Science beginning to be applied in agriculture and production; public facilities developed	Market for industrial-capital goods (tractors, generators, road-building equipment) and semiprocessed extractive materials	Dealings with foreign governments; training foreign personnel; few consumers can afford luxuries
Take-off	Modernization of existing industry; creation of new industries; rapidly increasing productivity; importance of coal, iron, and railroad industries	Rapidly increasing standard of living; larger markets for consumer goods and complex industrial equipment	Government concern to protect country's industries; higher tariffs and import controls; threats of nationalism; extensive technical assistance required
Drive to maturity	Modern technology in all economic activity; large productivity increases; economy intertwined with other countries; income distributed in more balanced manner	Markets for consumer durables and nondurables; larger market segments; placement of manufacturing facilities into country	Tailoring goods and services to meet market needs
Age of mass consumption	Large proportion of population with high discretionary income and employed in office or skilled factory jobs	Greater markets for consumer durables and nondurables; expansion of manufacturing and sales facilities in country; top quality advertising and marketing research	Tailoring goods and services; competition

Source: Adapted from Walt W. Rostow, The Stages of Economic Growth (London: Cambridge University Press, 1960), pp. 1–11.

STANDARDIZED VERSUS NONSTANDARDIZED MARKETING PLANS

When a firm enters a foreign market, it must decide whether its marketing plans are to be standardized or nonstandardized. A ***standardized plan*** is basically an extension of the home country marketing plan. A ***nonstandardized plan*** involves tailoring the marketing mix variables to the needs of specific host country markets.

The sales potential of a foreign market is an important determinant of standardization. If the sales from the foreign operations will be substantial and permanent, it is wise to adopt a marketing plan sensitive to the needs of the individual foreign markets. But if the foreign markets are not promising in terms of sales volume and permanency, it might be better to use a standardized marketing plan.

Five factors govern the degree of standardization of a marketing plan:[28]

1. *Type of product.* Products such as razor blades, ballpoint pens, automobile tires, and electric irons have universal sales appeal. The marketing plan for such products may thus be more standardized than for such products as cosmetics or clothing.

2. *The homogeneity or heterogeneity of markets.* In homogeneous markets, where customers are relatively similar in income, education, and occupation, the feasibility of using a standardized approach is high.

3. *Media characteristics.* If media characteristics are similar in two cultures, greater standardization of the marketing plan is possible. For example, a firm relying heavily on TV advertising in the United States may not be able to use the same approach in India. Indian television is government controlled and allows only limited advertising. Even then, a very small segment of the Indian population even has TV.

4. *Government restrictions.* In certain countries, government restrictions may influence the degree of standardization. For example, many less developed countries require that a certain percentage of parts used in a manufactured product be made locally. Such a restriction forces a firm to use a production plan sensitive to local market needs.

5. *Availability of marketing services.* Poor availability of marketing research and advertising facilities may also influence a firm's standardization decision. For example, ineffective foreign advertising agencies may force a multinational firm to depend on its home ad agency, thereby increasing the degree of standardization.

A standardized approach has several advantages. Economies-of-scale savings arise because production and promotional overhead is distributed over several markets. Standardization projects a uniform product image in all markets and allows centralized control and reduced expenses in training of foreign personnel. The biggest disadvantage of standardization is that the marketing plan becomes insensitive to the needs of the individual markets.

---

[28] Based in part on Gordon E. Miracle, "International Advertising Principles and Strategies," *Business Topics*, Autumn 1968, pp. 35–36.

A nonstandardized marketing approach treats each market separately. The marketing mix variables change from market to market. This approach is highly sensitive to local market needs. But its biggest disadvantage is increased costs due to the loss of economies of scale in manufacturing and promotion.

Some firms prefer a **mixed approach.** Here, some elements of the marketing mix are standardized across international markets; others remain nonstandardized. This approach attempts to achieve both sensitivity to local market needs and some scale economies resulting from partial standardization.

MARKETING MIX VARIABLES IN MULTINATIONAL SETTING

When a firm follows a standardized approach, elements of its marketing strategy remain relatively invariant from one foreign market to the next. However, as we said before, when a firm uses a nonstandardized approach or a mixed approach, some or all elements of the marketing mix change to a certain degree. In this section, we'll discuss possible alterations of the four Ps: product, pricing, promotion, and placement (distribution).

Product considerations

A firm that decides to sell its product in a foreign market has five product-planning options available.[29]

Option 1. Market the basic product with no modification. This option is viable when consumer needs are the same. This very profitable strategy is practiced by U.S. firms such as Coca-Cola and Pepsi-Cola.

Option 2. Redesign the promotional message while keeping the basic product unaltered. This option is practiced in situations where the same product satisfies (or is perceived as satisfying) a different set of needs. Bicycles are a good example. While bikes are mainly for recreation in the United States, they are the basic means of transportation in many less developed countries. Hence, bicycle promotions in such countries must emphasize transportational values.

Option 3. Adapt the product but keep the same promotional strategy. This is a sound approach where the product's basic appeal remains the same but minor physical changes are needed to adapt it to local needs. For example, an electrical appliance may need its voltage requirement altered from 110 volts and 60 cycles A.C. to 220 volts and 50 cycles D.C. to sell in European and Asian markets. Or a detergent may have to be changed to accommodate the water conditions (hard or soft) of a local market.

---

[29] This section is based on Warren J. Keegan, "Multinational Product Planning: Strategic Alternatives," *Journal of Marketing* 33 (January 1969), pp. 58–62.

This Perugina ad is a good example of designing a promotional message to appeal to the foreign market while maintaining the excellent quality of the product.

This Easter, say something sweet in Italian.

PERUGINA
More great taste from Italy.

Perugina Chocolates, 636 Lexington Avenue at 54th Street, New York, New York 10022 and at other fine stores.
© 1984 Perugina Chocolates and Confections, Inc. Photograph by Phil Marco

Courtesy Perugina Chocolates and Confections, Inc.

Option 4. Use dual adaptation. Here, both product and promotion are changed to meet local market conditions. The clothing industry is a good example of dual adaptation. There are significant differences in clothing from country to country, and the approaches to promoting and advertising clothing must be consistent with the cultural values in each.

Option 5.   Completely redesign a product or create a new one. Product innovation to meet the needs of foreign market consumers is the riskiest option because of the high capital investment, time consumed, and probability of failure.

Pricing considerations

Usually, a standardized pricing policy cannot be followed by a firm unless it operates in a common market such as the **European Economic Community.**

The chief determinants of a pricing policy are the costs of production and distribution, demand for the product, economic condition of the foreign market (such as per capita GNP), exchange rates, tariff and taxes, competition, and government controls.

Canada offers an example of how competition and government controls can influence the pricing policies of multinational firms in a host country. To stimulate price competition among multinationals, Canada permits domestic distributors to import generic duplicates of high-priced drugs in large quantities. Sometimes the drugs are imported from manufacturers in Eastern Europe, where patent enforcement isn't strong. Priced far below proprietary brands, and with similar design and color, the generics can easily capture up to 50 percent of the market.[30]

Another pricing practice used by some firms is called **dumping.** In dumping a product, the manufacturer sells it in the foreign market at a lower price than the prevailing prices in the home country. Sometimes the prices are lower than the cost of production in the home country.[31] However, this price is bounded by the fact that the lower price should always be above variable cost in order to contribute to fixed cost. Japan is often accused of dumping its products in foreign markets to increase its market share. One such case is in the area of computer chips: by dumping, the Japanese have been able to capture about 70 percent of the world market for chips.[32]

Firms engaged in international marketing must decide whether to quote prices in the currency of the home country or of the host country. By quoting home country prices, firms pass the risk of devaluation on to the buyer. But the use of home country prices creates some confusion for the buyers, who must convert the quoted price to local currency units. Some publishing companies use home country pricing, especially on paperback editions of their books.

Promotional considerations

In many cases a firm can use the same theme to promote a product abroad and at home. For example, Avis has successfully used its "We try harder" theme in Europe. Esso's "Tiger in the tank" has been very successful in Germany, Italy, France, and the Netherlands.

---

[30] "Licensing Law," p. 34.

[31] Ibid.

[32] Gene Bylinsky, "Japan's Ominous Chip Victory," *Fortune* December 14, 1981, p. 52.

In many cases, though, a literal translation of the original home advertising theme may not be appropriate (or possible). For example, a national soft drink producer had the company's brand name translated into phonetically correct Chinese characters. They later discovered that the translation's literal meaning was "female horse fattened with wax"—hardly the image the company wanted to portray![33] In many instances, advertising copy must be rewritten or a new campaign must be developed to convey the appropriate image.

When creating an advertising theme, a firm must consider cultural values, labors, and norms prevailing in the target society. Lack of such consideration may prove counterproductive. A manufacturer of canned fish ran an ad repeatedly in the newspapers and magazines of Quebec, showing a woman dressed in shorts and playing golf with her husband. The caption explained that the woman could be on the golf links all day and still prepare a delicious evening dinner by using the advertised product. But the ad contradicted several themes of French-Canadian life. Unfortunately for the advertiser, the wife would not likely be playing golf with her husband, she would not wear shorts, and she would never serve the advertised type of fish as a main course.[34]

Firms must also be careful about labeling and packaging requirements in different countries. In Canada a firm must provide package information in both French and English. Products may be confiscated for failing to provide this information! In France the law is even tougher: "In any offer, presentation, advertisement, written or spoken, instructions for use, specification, or guarantee terms for goods or services, as well as for invoices and receipts, the use of French language is compulsory."[35]

Media considerations are important in deciding how to disseminate information to customers. In many countries a low literacy rate may not permit the use of print advertising at all. The firm may have to opt for broadcast media. Even in broadcast media, choices may be limited. TV advertising may be impractical if few people in the market own TV sets.

Distribution considerations

Firms engaged in international marketing may sell their products either directly or through intermediaries. Usually, a firm might choose direct selling (and hence use its own sales force abroad) for two reasons: to increase sales volume and to increase control over the distribution system.

In some less developed countries a foreign firm may be forced to establish its own distribution network (including warehouse and storage facilities) simply because local facilities aren't available.

Key elements in a firm's distribution decision include availability of

---

[33] Jose de La Torre, "Product Life Cycle Is a Determinant of Global Marketing Strategy," *Atlanta Economic Review,* September–October 1975, p. 13.

[34] Charles Winick, "Anthropology's Contributions to Marketing," *Journal of Marketing,* July 1961, pp. 53–60.

[35] "International Markets," *Business Week,* November 21, 1977, p. 98.

intermediaries, cost of using intermediaries, allocation of distribution functions and the efficiency with which they are performed by the intermediaries, and degree of control executed by manufacturers over the intermediaries.[36]

Sometimes getting access to an established distribution network in a foreign country might even induce a company to enter into a joint venture. For example, Renault, the French automaker, has formed a partnership with American Motors to manufacture cars in the United States. What Renault wants most from this partnership is AMC's dealers.[37]

THE ROLE OF MULTINATIONAL CORPORATIONS

The multinational corporation (MNC) is a vehicle for efficient transfer of world resources (including financial, managerial, marketing and technological expertise) among nations at differing stages of economic development. For example, less developed countries, deficient in capital and technology and with high unemployment, benefit from the MNC's investments. New MNC operations create new jobs and help raise the standard of living in the host country. In return, MNCs obtain low-cost labor and other government-sponsored incentives.

Despite their beneficial role, many multinational corporations have acquired a negative image. They are often perceived as threatening the national sovereignty of the host country, subordinating a nation's economy, and making a nation technologically dependent on MNCs. The list goes on. Such hostility toward MNCs is common in both developed and developing countries.[38]

The part, the negative image is due to MNC's involvement in political events and decision making in host countries. The most publicized cases have been the activities of United Fruit in Central America, ITT in Chile, and the international oil companies in the Middle East. Similarly, Lockheed Corporation's questionable payments to several foreign dignitaries to generate foreign sales is another example of unscrupulous MNC involvement in a foreign country.

Attitudes toward MNCs are mixed. The following excerpt from *The Economist* of London summarizes the love-hate relationship between a MNC and a host government:

The Multinational—A Love-Hate Relationship

It fiddles with its accounts. It avoids or evades its taxes. It rigs its intracompany transfer prices. It is run by foreigners from decision centers thousands of miles away. It imports foreign labor practices. It overpays.

---

[36] Cateora and Hess, *International Marketing,* p. 554.

[37] "American Motors Is about to Blot Itself out to Build New Image around Jeep, Renault," *The Wall Street Journal,* April 16, 1982, p. 23.

[38] S. Prahash Sethi, "Advocacy Advertising and the Multi-national Corporation," *Columbia Journal of World Business,* Fall 1977, pp. 36–37.

Table 24–2: The 10 largest American and non-American multinationals

American multinationals

Rank	Company	Foreign revenue ($ millions)	Total revenue ($ millions)	Foreign as percent of total	Foreign operating profit ($ millions)	Total operating profit ($ millions)	Foreign as percent of total	Foreign assets ($ millions)	Total assets ($ millions)	Foreign as percent of total
1	Exxon	$69,386	$97,173	71.4%	$2,208	$4,343	50.8%	$29,914	$62,289	48.0%
2	Mobil	37,778	60,969	62.0	880	1,380	63.8	18,802	36,439	51.6
3	Texaco	31,118	46,986	66.2	833	1,281	65.0	12,956	27,114	47.8
4	Standard Oil Calif.	16,957	34,362	49.3	404	1,377	29.3	8,861	23,465	37.8
5	Phibro-Salomon	16,600	26,703	62.2	218	337	64.7	4,600	39,669	11.6
6	Ford Motor	16,526	37,067	44.6	460	−658	P/D	14,327	21,956	65.3
7	IBM	15,336	34,364	44.6	1,646	4,409	37.3	14,122	32,541	43.4
8	General Motors.	14,376	60,026	23.9	−107	963	D/P	12,288	41,363	29.7
9	Gulf Oil	11,513	28,427	40.5	300	900	33.3	7,625	20,436	37.3
10	E I du Pont de Nemours	11,057	33,223	33.3	488	1,491	32.7	5,911	24,343	24.3

Non-American multinationals

Rank	Company	Fiscal year-end	Revenue ($ millions)	Net income ($ millions)	Assets ($ millions)	Corporate headquarters	Industry	Employees (000)
1	Royal Dutch/Shell Group	Dec	83,809	$3,489	$69,594	Netherlands/UK	energy	163.0
2	Mitsubishi Corp	Mar	68,721	149	20,355	Tokyo, Japan	wholesaler	15.5
3	Mitsui & Co Ltd	Mar	68,184	5	20,405	Tokyo, Japan	wholesaler	12.3
4	C Itoh & Co Ltd	Mar	55,863	22	15,006	Tokyo, Japan	wholesaler	10.0
5	Marubeni Corp	Mar	52,199	7	15,612	Osaka, Japan	wholesaler	10.4
6	British Petroleum Co Plc	Dec	51,353	1,246	42,403	London, UK	energy	143.4
7	Sumitomo Corp	Mar	48,389	128	10,945	Osaka, Japan	wholesaler	11.0
8	Nissho Iwai Corp	Mar	34,661	16	9,342	Tokyo, Japan	wholesaler	7.8
9	ENI-Ente Nazionale Idrocarburi	Dec	27,525	−1,202	28,810	Rome, Italy	energy	144.0
10	IRI-Istituto Ricostruzione Industriale	Dec	24,833	−1,975	48,558	Rome, Italy	multicompany	525.3

Source: "Spotlight on International Business," *Forbes*, July 4, 1983, pp. 114, 124.

It underpays. It competes unfairly with local firms. It is in cahoots with local firms. It exports jobs from rich countries. It is an instrument of rich countries' imperialism. The technologies it brings to the Third World are old-fashioned. Nobody can control it. It corrects balance of payments. It overturns economic policies. It plays governments off each other to get the biggest investment incentives. Won't it please come and invest? Let it bloody well go home.[39]

Despite these mixed feelings about multinationals, they have grown significantly since World War II. This indicates that benefits offered by multinational firms far outweigh the costs involved to the host and/or home countries. Table 24–2 lists the 10 largest American and 10 largest non-American multinational firms.

---

[39] "Business Brief," *The London Economist,* January 24, 1976, p. 68. Recited from Cateora and Hess, *International Marketing,* p. 43.

SUMMARY

Multinational marketing is the process of focusing the resources and objectives of an organization on global market opportunities. Oftentimes the terms *multinational marketing* and *international marketing* are used interchangeably; but multinational marketing involves a direct investment in a foreign country, while international marketing does not.

A firm expands its product distribution beyond the domestic market for one or more of the following reasons: (1) to gain access to foreign customers, (2) to accommodate the needs of the business, (3) to achieve lower operating costs abroad, (4) to meet a competitive threat, (5) to avoid ecological or environmental pressures, (6) to take advantage of foreign govern-ment incentives, (7) to encourage product growth, or (8) to benefit from exchange-rate fluctuations. Whatever the reason, the firm can enter multinational markets in one of four ways: (1) exporting, (2) licensing, (3) joint venture, and (4) total ownership.

Before a firm can enter foreign distribution, it must evaluate the multinational environment of the country in question. This evaluation analyzes political, legal, cultural, economic, and technological factors. This analysis enables the firm to develop a comprehensive multinational marketing plan. The marketing plan addresses product, pricing, promotional, and placement (distributional) considerations.

KEY CONCEPTS

Multinational marketing

International marketing

Multinational corporation (MNC)

Import licenses

Foreign market

Global perspective

Exchange-rate fluctuations

Devaluation

Revaluation

Exporting

Indirect exporting

International trading company

Export management company (EMC)

Direct exporting

Licensing

Joint venture

Contract marketing

Management contracting   Nationalization   Compulsory licensing
Joint ownership   Domestication   Standardized plan
Total ownership   Exchange controls   Nonstandardized plan
Political risk   Import restrictions   Mixed approach
Confiscation   Tax controls   European Economic Community
Expropriation   Price controls   Dumping

DISCUSSION QUESTIONS AND EXERCISES

1. Review the definition of multinational corporation (MNC) in this chapter. What is the difference between multinational marketing and international marketing?

2. The chapter suggests eight reasons why companies market beyond domestic markets. Consider Caterpillar, McDonald's, and Eli Lilly (drug manufacturer). Which of the eight reasons are most important for each of these companies?

3. List the major methods of entering foreign markets and arrange them in order of risk and payoff to the firm using them.

4. What is political risk and how does it affect multinational marketing activities?

5. Define and illustrate the following:
   a. Confiscation.
   b. Expropriation.
   c. Nationalization.
   d. Domestication.

6. What is the difference between standardized and nonstandardized marketing plans? What are the implications of each for multinational marketing?

7. What product modification might be necessary for IBM when marketing its computers in Europe? Explain.

8. The relationship between a host country and a MNC has been described as a love–hate relationship. Explain.

CHAPTER 25

Marketing of services and
not-for-profit organizations

The concept of exchange and nonprofit
    organizations
Strategic planning in nonprofit
    organizations

Summary

Key concepts

Discussion questions and exercises

Marketing of services
    The nature and importance of services
    Characteristics of services
    Classes of services
    Strategic issues in service marketing
    A comment on the marketing of
        professional services
Marketing in nonprofit organizations
    The nature and scope of nonprofit
        organizations

In this final chapter we turn our attention to two additional special areas of marketing: services and not-for-profit organizations. Marketing examples in each area have appeared in various places throughout the book, but each area is sufficiently different to deserve separate attention. This chapter delineates the important features of services and not-for-profit marketing that set them apart from product-based and profit-oriented marketing.

MARKETING OF SERVICES

The nature and importance of services

Two broad categories of services can be identified: supplemental and central. First, there are services that accompany the purchase of a physical good (such as delivery of furniture purchased at a retail store). In this case, while the service is providing utility, the *good* is the central source of utility the buyer is seeking. The role of the service here is to augment the purchase of the good. Such services are **supplemental services:** their purpose is to enhance the marketing support of the good.

service

> A **service** is an act performed by an individual or organization for the benefit of another individual or organization.

Central services form the second category. As the dominant source of utility, a central service requires a marketing program developed specifically for it. This type of service is the concern of this chapter. Any reference to a "service" from this point on will mean a central service.

central services

> **Central services** represent the dominant and, in some cases, the only source of utility in a purchase.

The specific services available to buyers touch on virtually all aspects of life. The diversity of services available to consumers and industrial buyers is reflected in the examples of service institutions provided in Table 25–1.

The service sector in the U.S. economy (and many other industrialized economies) is large and growing. Several statistics support this fact. First, nearly three fourths of the U.S. nonfarm labor force is employed in the service sector. Second, almost half of every consumer dollar spent goes

Table 25–1: Examples of service institutions

Consumer market		Industrial market
Law firms	Airlines	Market research firms
Hospitals	Hotels–motels	Advertising agencies
Accounting Firms	Travel agencies	Accounting firms
Physicians	Plumbers	Brokers
Barbers and hairdressers	Cable TV and repair	Management consultants
Car washes	Theaters	Engineering firms
Banks and other financial	Funeral homes	Law firms
institutions	Yard and home	Maintenance and cleaning
Auto and appliance repair	maintenance	firms
shops	Real estate brokers	Parts repairs
		Warehouse
		Employment agencies

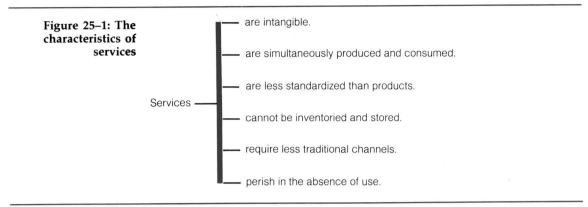

Figure 25–1: The characteristics of services

Services —
- are intangible.
- are simultaneously produced and consumed.
- are less standardized than products.
- cannot be inventoried and stored.
- require less traditional channels.
- perish in the absence of use.

for services.[1] In addition, vast sums of money are spent by businesses and institutions for services like those listed in Table 25–1.

Marketing expertise in the service sector has not kept pace with that in the manufacturing sector, but there is a growing realization that it must improve. In this section we will identify the key characteristics of services and examine them in terms of strategic marketing.

Characteristics of services

The effective implementation of strategic marketing by a service organization requires an understanding of the characteristics of *services* that distinguish them from *products*. Six distinguishing characteristics of services can be identified: intangibility, inseparability of production and consumption, heterogeneity, lack of inventory, distinct channels of distribution, and perishability. (Also see Figure 25–1.)

Intangibility. The central distinguishing feature of services is their *intangibility*—and it is from this that their other unique features emerge.[2]

intangibility

> **Intangibility** refers to the fact that——unlike physical goods—a service cannot be touched, seen, or evaluated prior to its purchase.

The actual purchase and consumption of a service takes little time and is experiential in nature. And the result is not a tangible object that serves as evidence of the exchange process and provides ongoing utility.

[1] Leonard L. Berry, G. Lynn Shostack, Gregory D. Upah, "Preface," in *Emerging Perspectives on Services Marketing,* ed. L. L. Berry et al. (Chicago: American Marketing, Association, 1983), p. 1.

[2] Margaret G. Liechty and Gilbert A. Churchill, Jr., "Conceptual Insights into Consumer Satisfaction with Services," in *1979 Educators' Conference Proceedings*, ed. N. Beckwith et al. (Chicago: American Marketing Association, 1979), p. 510.

Figure 25–2: Types of service production processes

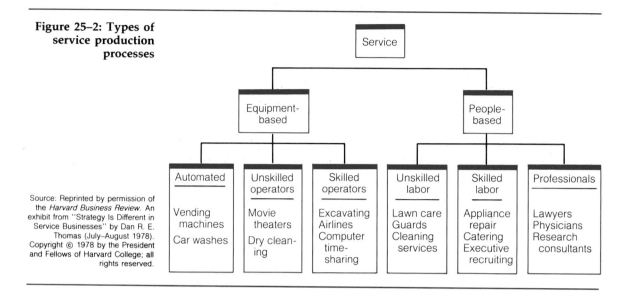

Consider going to a performing arts event, such as a play. You cannot view the play and then decide to go. You may read reviews and consider other indirect sources of information in making the decision to attend, but you cannot directly evaluate the service without purchasing it. Once there, you *experience* the play for a few hours at most. You do not use or apply the play. Finally, upon leaving the theater you do not take the service home with you. Other than a feeling of satisfaction or dissatisfaction and having something to talk about, no further utility is available from the play.

Inseparability of production and consumption

inseparability

> **Inseparability** means that as an act performed for the benefit of the buyer, a service is produced and consumed simultaneously.[3]

This feature often allows the buyer to actually take part in the production process: a buyer can guide the service provider to fit the service more precisely to his or her desires. A haircut is an example. Thus, customized offerings are more often available in the service sector.

The ability to customize services is a function of the manner of production. Services can be distinguished in terms of two general production processes. (See Figure 25–2.)

---

[3] Leonard L. Berry, "Services Marketing Is Different," *Business,* May–June 1980, p. 24.

Such services may be exclusively equipment-based (automated car washes) or involve the use of unskilled operators or skilled operators. In either case some form of equipment represents the major source of the service act.

While equipment may be used in such services, the personal interaction with another individual is the dominant source of the service act.[4] Generally, the more involved a person is with the provision of a service, the greater the opportunity for the buyer to take part in its production and realize a customized offering.

A people-based service that is promoting its nonstandardized nature.

Everybody has legal problems.

Progressive Attorneys at Reasonable Fees

No charge for Consultation — 24 Hour Phone Service
•Criminal Matters • Divorces • Tenant/Landlord
•Immigration Law • Personal Injury
The legislature (usually attorneys) has made the law confusing. The legal profession thus has a duty to provide legal services at reasonable rates.

Scott C. Colky
Hirsch & Colky

Attorneys at Law 372-5300
205 West Randolph, Suite 1150, Chicago, Illinois

Used with permission of Scott C. Colky

---

[4] This distinction is based on that provided in Dan R. E. Thomas, "Strategy Is Different in Service Businesses," *Harvard Business Review,* July–August 1978, pp. 158–65.

Heterogeneity. Services are less standardized than products. Different suppliers vary in the nature and quality of the type of service they provide. We can all think of a favorite hairdresser or barber who does our hair closest to the way we like it. But even the same supplier may differ in the quality of service provided from one occasion to the next. Of course, the opportunity for the buyer to take part in the production of services also contributes to the ***heterogeneity*** of services.

Lack of inventory. Because of their intangible nature, services cannot be inventoried and stored. That is, services are characterized by ***lack of inventory.*** The necessary equipment and labor can be held in readiness to create the service, but they represent the capacity to provide the service, not the service itself.[5] As a result, service organizations must be careful to vary capacity as demand changes. Many tax accountant firms, for example, increase their staffs during the tax season and cut back the rest of the year.

Distinct channels of distribution. Because production and consumption of services occur simultaneously, traditional channels of distribution involving a flow of goods may not exist for services. ***Distinct channels of distribution*** may exist. For people-based services, the channel is usually short and direct. For equipment-based services, unusual forms of distribution can exist. Electronic means of providing a service exist for information-oriented services (e.g., stockbrokers). And banks and other financial institutions are locating customer service outlets in other retail businesses, such as supermarkets and department stores.

Perishability. Many services take on a ***perishable*** nature because of their nonstorage aspect.[6] A service that is available at a particular time but not purchased is lost—but the firm still incurs its costs. Empty seats at a theater or ballpark or on an airplane, missed dental appointments, and empty barber chairs are examples of services that perish in the absence of purchase.

Classes of services

Because services differ considerably from each other, it is useful to distinguish between them and develop a classification scheme. Figure 25–3 presents such a scheme based on two factors: overtness and direct recipient. First, **overtness** refers to how much obvious evidence of the act is present. Second, services are distinguished by who or what is the direct recipient of the act—people or things. These two factors combine to form the four classes of services shown in the figure.

[5] Christopher H. Lovelock, "Why Marketing Management Needs to Be Different for Services," in *Marketing of Services* ed. J. H. Donnelly and William H. George (Chicago: American Marketing Association, 1981), p. 5.

[6] Ibid.

Figure 25–3: Classes of services

	Direct recipient of service act	
	People	**Things**
More overt	Services on people's bodies: Health care Beauty salons Exercise clinics Restaurants Barbershops	Services on physical possessions: Freight service Repair and maintenance Veterinary care Dry cleaning Lawn care
Less overt	Services on people's minds: Education Broadcasting Information services Theaters Museums	Services on intangible assets: Banking Insurance Accounting Legal services

Effect of service act

Source: Adapted from Christopher H. Lovelock, "Classifying Services to Gain Strategic Marketing Insights," *Journal of Marketing,* Summer 1983, p. 12.

A service with overt effects on a physical object.

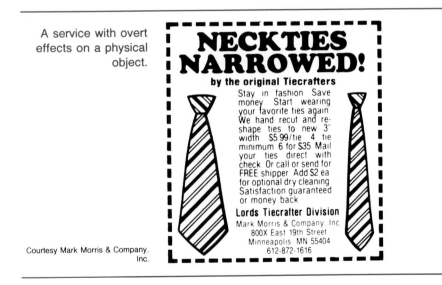

Courtesy Mark Morris & Company, Inc.

Strategic issues in service marketing

Strategic marketing is as relevant to service as it is to products. However, the characteristics of services may call for different considerations when applying the strategic planning process to a service. Figure 25–4 summarizes the key points in the discussion that follows.

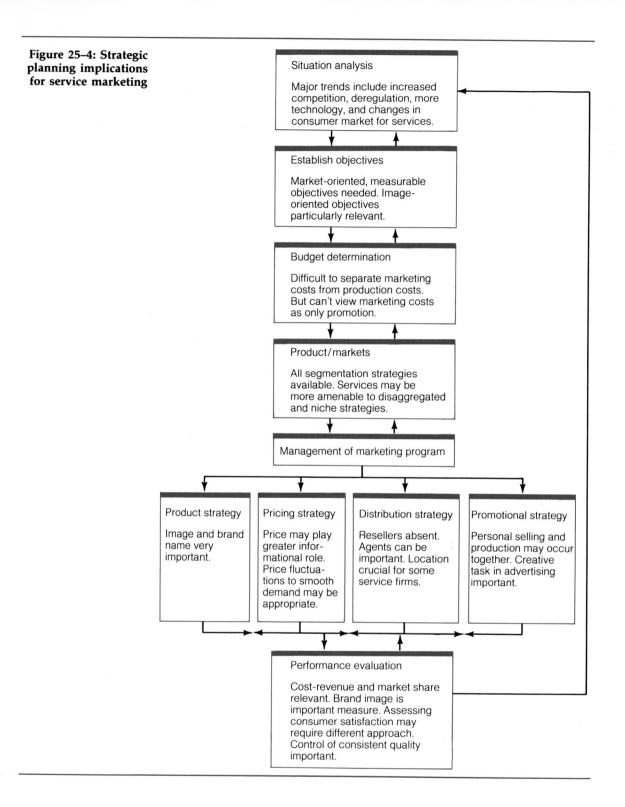

Figure 25–4: Strategic planning implications for service marketing

Situation analysis

Major trends include increased competition, deregulation, more technology, and changes in consumer market for services.

Establish objectives

Market-oriented, measurable objectives needed. Image-oriented objectives particularly relevant.

Budget determination

Difficult to separate marketing costs from production costs. But can't view marketing costs as only promotion.

Product/markets

All segmentation strategies available. Services may be more amenable to disaggregated and niche strategies.

Management of marketing program

Product strategy

Image and brand name very important.

Pricing strategy

Price may play greater informational role. Price fluctuations to smooth demand may be appropriate.

Distribution strategy

Resellers absent. Agents can be important. Location crucial for some service firms.

Promotional strategy

Personal selling and production may occur together. Creative task in advertising important.

Performance evaluation

Cost-revenue and market share relevant. Brand image is important measure. Assessing consumer satisfaction may require different approach. Control of consistent quality important.

Situation analysis.[7] The elements of situation analysis for a service organization are identical to those for a manufacturer of products. The service firm should assess its market, competition, legal environment, and its own strengths and weaknesses much like a product manufacturer would. In fact, it may need to perform situation analysis on a more continuous basis. The service sector and its environment are changing very rapidly. Strategic marketing and a consumer orientation—while they have lagged in the service sector compared to the manufacturing sector—are more important than ever when doing business in the service sector.

The dominant factor calling for strategic marketing in the service sector is its increasingly competitive nature. Performing a situation analysis on the service sector as a whole reveals a variety of factors contributing to the intensified level of competition faced by service firms.

Emerging from the legal environment is the trend toward deregulation. We saw the effects of deregulation on the banking industry in Chapter 3. Other service industries experiencing the effects of deregulation include transportation and telecommunications. Deregulation of airlines, for example, has expanded the number of marketing tools available to an individual firm. A volatile competitive situation has resulted in which pricing policies are more important than ever.

Another rapidly changing area in services is the technological sector of the environment. Innovation is allowing service firms to use sophisticated, customer-oriented machines to provide certain services on a repetitive basis. Examples of such equipment include ticket dispensers, machines that sell travel insurance, self-service gasoline pumps, and automatic bank tellers. This self-service equipment offers productivity savings over the human labor it replaces and a greater consistency over time in the quality of service it provides. However, the firm that implements such equipment may find gaining consumer acceptance difficult.

The interaction of deregulation and technological innovation is contributing to the breakdown of traditional industry and competitive boundaries. Using microwave and satellite transmissions, new telecommunications firms such as MCI are becoming formidable competitors to AT&T in the provision of long-distance telephone services.

Finally, the consumer market for services is changing. Market segments with special service needs (like the elderly) are growing. Consumer attitudes toward service institutions are changing as different service needs and expectations are emerging. Some bankers, for example, believe that the public is becoming less loyal to such well-established service institutions as banks.[8]

---

[7] Material discussed here draws heavily on that presented in Eric Langeard et al., *Services Marketing: New Insights from Consumers and Managers* (Cambridge, Mass.: Marketing Science Institute, 1981), pp. 8–10.

[8] Ibid., p. 10.

These general trends affect some of the more dominant areas in the service sector, and they do point out its dynamic nature. The trends underscore the relative importance of the marketing function within a service organization and the role of situation analysis in planning it.

Establishing objectives. The establishment of the mission and objectives of a service firm should not really be much different than that of a firm marketing products. As in a product firm, service firm objectives should be both *market-oriented* and *measurable*.

Service firms have noticeably lagged behind product firms in bringing a marketing perspective to their missions and objectives. Historically, most service firms have viewed themselves as producers rather than marketers: the emphasis has been on the creation of the service rather than the marketing of it. Many service firms take pride in the quality of their services—the ability to repair a leaky faucet or to conduct good marketing research. But too often they have failed to develop a comprehensive market-oriented way of delivering their service. Of course, there are exceptions. The airline industry includes firms (e.g., Delta) that have been market-oriented.

Given the increasing competition in the service sector, it is becoming even more crucial for service firms to establish market-oriented objectives. In doing so, it is important—though more difficult—for service firms to establish objectives that are *measurable*. Recall that services are not tangible. Thus, while objectives stated in cost-revenue terms are measurable, it is difficult to state other marketing objectives in measurable terms. The intangible nature of services results in objectives stated more in terms of the image that the firm would like to achieve in the marketplace.

An excellent example of the image-oriented nature of service marketing objectives is provided by the hotel industry.[9] Howard Johnson's objective is to upgrade its image from a "roadside rest stop" to that of a "full-service hotel." It is expanding to the luxury segment of the market and intends "to acquire 25 to 30 full-service hotels in choice metropolitan locations in the next five years." Ramada Inn is pursuing a similar objective by opening a luxury line of hotels called Renaissance Hotels. This line will provide a diversified service base aimed at distinct segments of the market: lower-priced Ramada Inns, medium-priced Ramada Hotels, and the luxury-oriented Renaissance Hotels. Other chains (Marriott, Quality Inns) are also pursuing diversification strategies of their own. In any case, the success of these efforts will be measured initially in terms of whether the intended image in each market segment is achieved. Thus, we also see that product/market and market segmentation concepts are just as relevant to service firms as they are to product firms in the development of marketing objectives.

---

[9] *New York Times* Service, "Zeroing In: Hotel Chains Opt for Price Diversification, Market Segmentation," *The Milwaukee Journal,* July 3, 1983, p. 3.

Positioning strategies are appropriate for services. Here a hotel conveys a specific image to business travelers through a word-of-mouth approach.

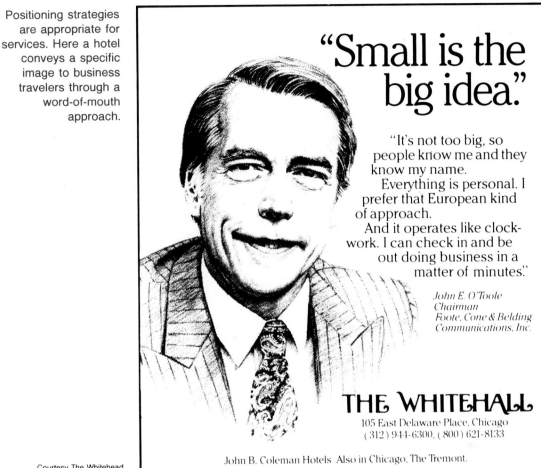

"Small is the big idea."

"It's not too big, so people know me and they know my name.
Everything is personal. I prefer that European kind of approach.
And it operates like clockwork. I can check in and be out doing business in a matter of minutes."

John E. O'Toole
Chairman
Foote, Cone & Belding
Communications, Inc.

THE WHITEHALL
105 East Delaware Place, Chicago
(312) 944-6300, (800) 621-8133

John B. Coleman Hotels Also in Chicago, The Tremont.

Courtesy The Whitehead

Product/markets. All product/market strategies—aggregated, disaggregated, niche—are available to service firms. In fact, the less standardized nature of services makes them more amendable to disaggregated and niche strategies than many products. We saw the use of segmentation in the hotel industry.

Another relatively new service industry recognizing the value of product/market strategies is the express-mail industry. While firms such as Federal Express and the U.S. Postal Service initially pursued this market in aggregated fashion, a more disaggregated strategy is now being used. One firm, Sureway Air Traffic, serves the New York City market with a disaggregated strategy. It targets different types of organizations (law offices, ad agencies) and tailors its courier service to each industry's specific

The financial services industry is one of the most competitive. Companies like E. F. Hutton and Merrill Lynch compete with each other and with other types of financial institutions. Here E. F. Hutton recognizes competition from banks and insurance companies.

ENTER THE WORLD OF WALL ST. WITH A HUTTON ASSET MANAGEMENT PROGRAM.

If you've left a substantial portion of your money resting with a bank or an insurance company, you may be reducing the potential power of your assets.

That is an important reason to consider E.F. Hutton's Asset Management or Asset Reserve Account.

Hutton's two new accounts are, first and foremost, investment vehicles. Their aim is *choice*. A broader choice of investments than any bank or insurance company can bring you.

You can invest in the security of U.S. Government obligations. You can own shares in mutual funds. You can put a portion of your assets into bonds, or stocks, or tax shelters or a score of other opportunities. You can, in short, enter the world of Wall Street.

Just as vital, you can do it without sacrificing flexibility or convenience with a Hutton Asset Management or Asset Reserve Account.

Our Asset Management Account gives you convenient access to your assets through unlimited checkwriting

privileges and the prestigious American Express Gold Card. It provides you with a cogent monthly statement. Cash that accumulates in your account is automatically swept into your choice of three money market funds. And securities held by Hutton in your account are covered by up to $10,000,000 in insurance.

Our Asset Reserve Account has exactly the same features, except for the Gold card.

Finally, there's our secret ingredient: The E.F. Hutton Account Executive. Because, at Hutton, we think you need *ideas* as well as choices. And our ideas are, ultimately, what make people listen.

For a Prospectus and complete information regarding charges and expenses, mail the coupon or call E.F. Hutton.

Read the Prospectus carefully before you invest or send money.

Take me to my broker.

I'd like to read about the details, please send me your free AMA and ARA brochure and a Prospectus.

I have questions, please have an Account Executive get in touch with me.

★ I want action right away, so I'm calling **800-EFH-1212.**

Name

Address

City   State   Zip

Business Phone   Home Phone

E. F. Hutton Account Number

EF Hutton

E. F. Hutton & Company Inc., E.F. Hutton Information Center
P.O. Box 1013 • Des Moines, Iowa 50306
Member SIPC

When E.F. Hutton talks, people listen.

Courtesy E. F. Hutton

needs. For example, for the legal community, services extend to filing documents with government agencies in Washington, D.C.[10]

Budget determination. The budgeting phase of the strategic planning process presents some difficulties for a service firm. The inherent nature

---

[10] Kevin Higgins, "Courier Firm Employs a Brand Approach to Establish a Niche," *Marketing News,* April 27, 1984, pp. 1–13.

of a service makes it difficult to separate marketing-related efforts and attach a cost figure to them. Some of the marketing effort occurs when the service is being produced. The distinct marketing budgets of many service firms consist only of advertising or other promotional expenditures. The fact that other marketing activities may be blurred by their inseparability from production may be one reason for the narrow view of marketing taken by service firms. The realization that marketing efforts are intertwined with production may contribute to more of a broad-based view of marketing management in service firms.

Product strategy.   The counterpart to product strategy in a service organization is the strategy it develops for its service offerings. There are many similarities in the issues faced by both product and service marketers in developing a "product" strategy. We have seen through the hotel and express-mail industries that overall service mixes can be developed with distinct service lines and items based on market segment differences. Members of the financial services industry offer a broad-based mix of services as well. The service mix of one of the most diverse financial services firms, Merrill Lynch, is presented in Figure 25–5.

The important differences between a product strategy and a service strategy are in large part due to the intangibility of services. In some

---

Figure 25–5: The Merrill Lynch network

Merrill Lynch & Co. Inc—The holding company for this worldwide financial services company.

Merrill Lynch, Pierce, Fenner & Smith—As the principal subsidiary, it operates within the realm of securities, investments and financing. Last year, it was divided into two separate groups.

Individual services	**Capital markets**
Sale and purchase of stocks and bonds for individual investors	Investment banking for corporate, institutional and government clients
Cash management account	Trading in government securities
Individual retirement programs	Sale and purchase of commercial paper, certificates of deposit and banker's acceptances
Mutual funds	
Money market funds	Over-the-counter trading
High-yielding certificates	Equipment and real estate financing investments
Tax investment programs	
High-yield annuities	Financing for corporations, financial investors and high net-worth individuals

Merrill Lynch Commodities—Facilitates the trading of precious metal, financial instruments, and energy futures.

Real Estate and Insurance Group—Merrill Lynch provides mortgage-protection life insurance sold to homeowners. Through acquiring a number of real estate firms, Merrill Lynch has become the nation's largest corporate-owned residential real estate firm. The real estate group also handles commercial and industrial brokerage. Its relocation management operation helps to find housing for transferred employees. Its real estate financing arm provides short-term funds at competitive rates.

Source: "The Bull Who Walks by Himself," *Marketing and Media Decisions,* Spring 1982, p. 101.

respects this intangibility makes product strategy development in services more focused. Marketing considerations in the physical nature of a product—color, size, shape, texture—are nonexistent for a service. But this increases the relative importance of other considerations. *Image* becomes a central factor in a service firm's efforts to differentiate itself from competitors. This, in turn, underscores the importance of *brand name* as an element in the service firm's strategy. The customer must be able to link a specific image with a specific brand name if a service firm is to successfully differentiate itself. Merrill Lynch has effectively conveyed a prestige image through mass advertising that characterizes it as "a breed apart" from its competitors.

Pricing strategy. Price may be more important in the overall marketing strategy for a service than for a product. It has been suggested that consumers depend on price information to choose between service competitors to a greater extent than when choosing between *brands* of a product.[11] This is because more nonprice information is available for evaluation of tangible goods. Service marketers should realize this potentially greater informational role of price when developing their marketing strategies.

The discussion in Chapter 18 is as relevant to the pricing of services as it is to the pricing of goods. Cost, competition, and demand are key factors to consider in pricing a service, and each is more important in certain situations. Cost-oriented pricing is prevalent in public utilities, where government regulations constrain pricing practice. The purchase of industrial services is frequently based on competitive bidding. A service marketer whose target market is the quality-conscious buyer may set price according to the price-quality relationship. This relationship may be stronger in the case of services because of the absence of other quality-related cues. Another demand-oriented pricing practice is the peak-load price for electricity service.

Many other pricing practices can be applied to services equally well. Quantity discounts are certainly possible. A season ticket to a concert series usually costs less than the sum of the price for each individual concert. Price penalties are often incurred, as when a monthly bill is paid after a certain date. And prices for services may vary according to when the service is provided: weekend rates for repair services usually exceed weekday rates, for example. Finally, seasonal variations in the demand for some services, coupled with their perishability, may require price fluctuations to smooth out demand.

With the theoretical similarities between the pricing of goods and services, it is interesting to note the terminology that service marketers some-

---

[11] Valerie Zeithaml, "How Consumer Evaluation Processes Differ between Goods and Services," in Donnelly and George, *Marketing of Services,* pp. 186–90.

times use to convey price levels to buyers. The term *price* is often absent. Instead, lawyers, physicians, and consultants charge *fees*. Consumers pay *premiums* for insurance policies. Student pay *tuitions* for education. *Tariffs* are paid for certain transportation services. Public utilities charge *rates*. Their fundamental nature remains one of *price,* however.

Distribution strategy. As noted before, the intangibility and production-consumption inseparability of services result in rather unusual (e.g., electronic) or direct channels of distribution.

Without a physical flow or the need for inventory and storage, resellers do not play a role in the distribution of services. However, in some service industries **agent intermediaries** are a key feature of the distribution system. Travel agencies, insurance agencies, stockbrokers, and entertainment agents (like Ticketron) are intermediaries that enhance the exchange process for producers and buyers. In general, intermediaries in the channel of distribution are feasible for services that do not require direct contact between originator and consumer of the service.[12]

One important consideration in the distribution strategy for many service firms is location. Services that require the consumer to go to the producer must be as accessible as possible. Often, this calls for the establishment of branch offices for consumer service producers (banks, health clinics, hair stylists). Some services are distributed through franchise systems (dance studios, car washes).

Promotional strategy. Service marketing uses many of the same promotional tools as product marketing. The intangibility of services usually eliminates packaging as a form of promotion; but advertising, personal selling, publicity, and sales promotion are all available for developing an overall promotional plan. The use of publicity and sales promotion corresponds quite well with their use in product marketing. Therefore, we'll restrict our discussion to personal selling and advertising services.

Personal selling is inherent in the promotion of services. The inseparability of production and consumption often requires personal, face-to-face contact between buyer and seller. Even when a service is provided through mechanical or electronic means, there is usually an initial personal contact. In general, the degree of personal interaction between a buyer and a seller of a service is proportionally greater than in the case of a product. Furthermore, service personnel frequently perform the dual roles of production and personal selling. The process of providing a service goes a long way in promoting it. As one executive puts it, "In a service business, you're dealing with something that is primarily delivered by

---

[12] James H. Donnelly, Jr., "Marketing Intermediaries in Channels of Distribution for Services," *Journal of Marketing,* January 1976, pp. 55–57.

people—to people. Your people are as much part of your product in the consumer's mind as any other attribute of that service."[13]

Careful training of personnel for the dual role of production and personal selling becomes imperative for the service firm.

The advertising strategy for a service requires the same decisions as a product advertising strategy. Budgeting, media selection, and message content must be determined with specific advertising objectives in mind. The major difference from product-oriented advertising is in the creative area of message content. Services are difficult to show or describe in an advertisement.

Because of the importance of image and brand distinction in a service marketing strategy, service advertisements often attempt to create and convey a distinct corporate image for the firm. Without a tangible product to help convey this image, the creative task is a challenge for a service advertiser. The importance of image and brand differentiation in service advertising is indicated by the five roles assigned to it by an advertising executive for the Young and Rubicam agency: (1) to create the company's world in the mind of the customer, (2) to build the appropriate personality for the company, (3) to identify the company with the customer, (4) to positively influence company personnel in terms of how they deal with customers, and (5) to help open the door for sales representatives.

These roles are most relevant to general services marketed to large groups of consumers. They have been effectively used by Young and Rubicam as creative guidelines in developing campaigns for such clients as Merrill Lynch and Hertz. The Merrill Lynch "a breed apart" campaign indicated the values that Merrill Lynch can bring to a customer in terms of research and financial advice, leading to achievement of financial goals. The Hertz campaign using O.J. Simpson as a spokesperson suggested what Hertz is all about; it promoted the use of the product at airports primarily and the company's expectations that customers would receive efficient, trouble-free service. In both campaigns Young and Rubicam attempted to link an intangible service to a tangible object. For Merrill Lynch it was a bull; for Hertz it was a popular athlete.[14]

Performance evaluation and control.   As with any product firm, a service firm should evaluate its performance by assessing how well its objectives are being met. As noted earlier, it is important that service firms establish measurable, market-oriented objectives to allow effective performance evaluation. Cost-revenue estimates and market share become relevant measures of performance. The intangibility of services suggests

---

[13] Gary Knisely, "Comparing Marketing Management in Package Goods and Service Organizations," in *Services Marketing*, ed. Christopher H. Lovelock (Englewood Cliffs, N.J.: Prentice-Hall, 1984), p. 21.

[14] Sidney H. Firestone, "Why Advertising a Service Is Different," in Berry et al., *Emerging Perspectives*, pp. 86–89.

some other considerations should be weighted more heavily in performance evaluation for a service, though.

First, while brand image is relevant in measuring product performance, it may be especially important in the assessment of a service marketing program. Second, customer satisfaction with a service may be based on a different type of experience than a product offers. One promising approach is to view the consumption of a service as a sequence of actions. For example, in making a deposit at a bank, the following sequence might occur: enter the bank, go to the customers' desk, fill out a deposit slip, endorse the check, wait in line for a teller, complete the transaction, and leave the bank. This sequence may become a set of expectations that the customer has about the service—and significant deviations from it may lead to dissatisfaction.[15] This issue suggests a third consideration in the control process for a service. The intangibility of a service makes it more difficult to offer a consistent level of quality from one purchase situation to the next. Consistent quality should, however, be a prime concern in the control process for a service.

A comment on the marketing of professional services	Professional service organizations (law firms, physicians, dentists, accountants) adopt formal marketing programs. There are a number of reasons, but the dominant one is probably the belief that marketing and advertising are the same and that to advertise would diminish the "professionalism" of the organization.[16] Indeed, until the Supreme Court ruled it illegal, certain professional associations, through codes of ethics (like the American Bar Association's), prohibited advertising by member professionals.

Several comments about the attitude of many professional service organizations toward marketing are in order. First, marketing is much more than advertising. Location, pricing, client interactions, and reputation have been concerns of professional service organizations, and all are related to marketing. Even without advertising, a plan that coordinates other marketing tools would improve operations. Second, there is nothing inherently bad or unprofessional about advertising. Other organizations effectively use it to improve their reputations. Third, competition among professional service organizations is increasing. Health maintenance organizations (HMOs) and legal clinics are new forms of delivery for health and legal services that will increase competition in these areas. Finally, clients of professionals are demanding more information prior to using a particular professional. Professional service organizations should no

---

[15] For the theoretical basis of this argument, see Ruth A. Smith and Michael J. Houston, "Script-Based Evaluations of Satisfaction with Services," in Berry et al., *Emerging Perspectives*, pp. 59–62.

[16] For further discussion, see Philip Kotler and Richard A. Conner, Jr., "Marketing Professional Services," *Journal of Marketing*, January 1977, pp. 71–76.

longer concern themselves with whether or not to practice marketing. Instead, they should accept marketing as a necessary function and determine how it should effectively be implemented within their organizations.

MARKETING IN NONPROFIT ORGANIZATIONS

A logical topic to follow the marketing of services is marketing in **nonprofit organizations.** Most nonprofit organizations offer a service to their markets. Thus, many issues in services marketing apply here also. But there are certain distinctive aspects of nonprofit organizations that affect the role of marketing.

The nature and scope of nonprofit organizations

The essential distinguishing feature of a nonprofit organization is, of course, the absence of a profitability goal. Nonprofit organizations encompass a wide scope of institutions: charitable organizations, the performing arts, museums, the military, hospitals, libraries, universities, churches, credit unions, labor unions, fraternal groups, Girl Scouts, professional societies, and foundations. Some nonprofit institutions are privately owned (private museums, universities, and hospitals). Others are publicly owned and partially supported by taxes (public museums, schools, hospitals, transportation, government agencies). The absence of a profitability goal (i.e., to maximize shareholder wealth) does not alter the importance or relevance of marketing to these organizations.

Other distinguishing features (see Figure 25–6) of nonprofit organizations suggest consequences for the *nature* of their marketing effort:

1. **Multiple publics.** Nonprofit organizations usually have at least two major publics with which they develop a relationship: their clients and their funders. Clients are those to whom resources are allocated; funders are those from whom resources are attracted. Each group calls for a marketing program. In addition, many other publics exist for some organizations. For example, a university's publics include existing, prospective, and former students; parents; faculty; business firms; and government. (Also see Figure 25–7.)

Figure 25–6: Distinguishing features of nonprofit organizations

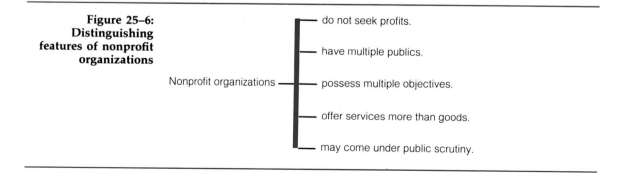

Nonprofit organizations —
- do not seek profits.
- have multiple publics.
- possess multiple objectives.
- offer services more than goods.
- may come under public scrutiny.

Figure 25–7: Multiple publics of a university

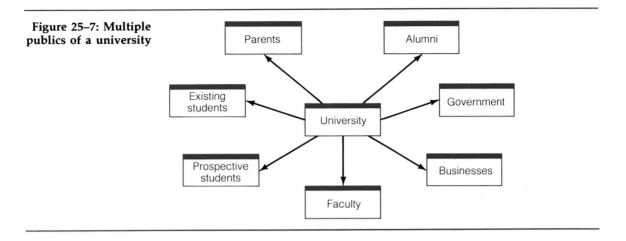

2. *Multiple objectives.* Nonprofit organizations normally possess several important objectives, and distinct strategies for the achievement of each must be implemented. This is true, too, of most business firms; but the multiple objectives are designed to move the firm toward the achievement of a single, central objective—long-run profit maximization.

3. *Service offerings.* Most nonprofit organizations offer services rather than goods. Consequently, many of the points about service marketing are relevant to these organizations.

4. *Public scrutiny.* Many nonprofit organizations are closely scrutinized by the public. This is because they provide public services, are subsidized, and receive tax-exempt status.[17]

We will incorporate the marketing consequence of these characteristics into our discussion of strategic planning for nonprofit organizations.

The concept of exchange and nonprofit organizations

In Chapter 1 we saw the concept of exchange as fundamental to the meaning of marketing. In the traditional commercial context, a buyer and a seller engage in an exchange wherein the buyer gives dollars to the seller, who provides a product or service and its accompanying benefits to the buyer. A classic economic exchange has occurred.

In nonprofit marketing, exchange is also a relevant concept. However, in nonprofit marketing, exchange may occur without the buyer receiving direct benefits from a product or service. For example, consider a charitable organization such as United Way. Local United Way chapters annually engage in a marketing effort directed at one of its key publics—donors from the general public. What is being exchanged when an individual

---

[17] Christopher H. Lovelock and Charles B. Weinberg, "Public and Nonprofit Marketing Comes of Age," in *Review of Marketing 1978*, ed. G. Zaltman and T. V. Bonoma (Chicago: American Marketing Association, 1978), pp. 416–20.

contributes to United Way? United Way (the seller) is receiving dollars to fund and operate its programs to help the needy (the poor, the elderly, the handicapped, etc.). In return, the donor (the buyer) is receiving one or more intangible feelings. First, the individual may feel self-satisfaction from contributing to social welfare. Second, the individual may feel that he or she is hiring United Way to take care of the needy so that the less needy can direct their efforts at other problems and issues of society. The noneconomic nature of exchange in nonprofit organizations is perhaps epitomized by another public of United Way: its unpaid volunteer workers. Here the exchange is time and effort provided by the volunteer in return for self-satisfaction and perhaps even social relationships.

Many types of exchanges are possible with not-for-profit organizations.

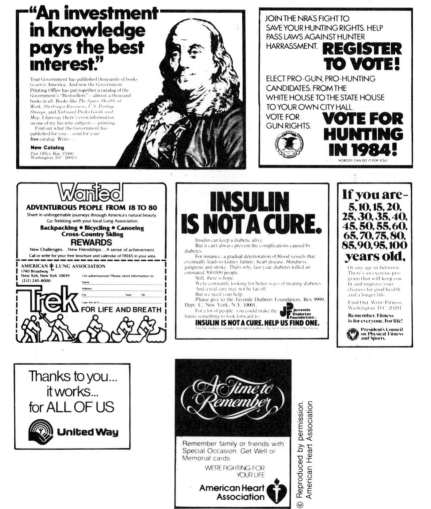

When developing their marketing programs, it is important that non-profit organizations recognize the concept of exchange and the potentially unique meaning it holds for them.[18]

Strategic planning in nonprofit organizations

In this section we examine the strategic planning framework as it applies to nonprofit organizations. Key issues relating to the nature of nonprofit organizations are identified in each phase. Figure 25–8 summarizes our discussion.

Situation analysis. A nonprofit organization should consider the same issues in situation analysis that a profit-oriented firm considers. Two aspects of situation analysis deserve special mention: competition and the organization's strengths and weaknesses.

Understanding the different levels of competition faced by a nonprofit organization is crucial—particularly when examining its funders. Organizations that depend on contributions (charities, universities, medical research foundations) compete at a generic level with each other and with virtually all other potential uses of money. The scope of generic competition for contributions from the *donor market* is thus very wide for a nonprofit organization.

The scope of generic competition for clients also remains wide for some organizations. For example, a performing arts organization faces competition for clients from virtually all forms of leisure-time activities. Product-form and enterprise levels of competition become more salient when considering the *client market:* a touring theater group competes with other forms of entertainment (movies, sporting events, art shows) at the *product-form* level and with other stage productions at the *enterprise* level.

With respect to the organization's strengths and weaknesses, a particularly relevant concern is the organization's attitude toward and practice of marketing. Many nonprofit organizations are composed of individuals with little or no training in business. Consequently, there may be contempt for and unfamiliarity with business techniques, and a formal marketing function will usually be absent. This situation is a major weakness in many nonprofit organizations. Not all though; many hospitals and universities recognize the importance of a formal marketing function.

The nonprofit organization that does recognize the lack of marketing as a weakness should take steps to formally introduce the marketing function. Kotler recommends several strategies for doing so:

1. *Marketing committee.* Establish a **marketing committee** to study the potential nature of the marketing function for the organization.

---

[18] For more on the expanded view of exchange, see Richard P. Bagozzi, "Marketing as Exchange," *Journal of Marketing,* October 1975, pp. 32–39; and Philip Kotler, "A Generic Concept of Marketing," *Journal of Marketing,* April 1972, pp. 46–54.

**Figure 25–8: Strategic
planning implications
for nonprofit
marketing**

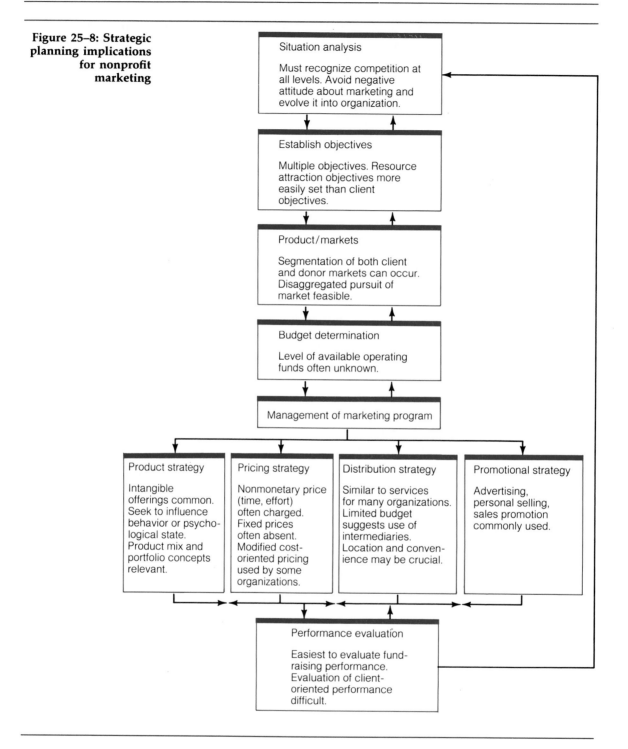

2. *Task forces.* Appoint **task forces** to conduct an institutional audit to assess the image of the organization held by its publics and the relative strength of its various programs.

3. *Marketing specialists/consultants.* Hire ad agencies and research consultants to help identify opportunities, threats, objectives, and strategies.

4. *Marketing director/vice president.* Establish an upper-level management position to guide the marketing function on a continuous basis.[19]

These strategies represent an evolutionary approach to incorporating marketing into the institution. The first three are essentially forms of situation analysis; the fourth is a formal means of recognizing and implementing the marketing function.

Establish objectives. As discussed earlier, an important feature of nonprofit organizations is the need for multiple objectives. This need grows out of the existence of multiple publics. Objectives must be set in the areas of resource attraction and client service. The same criteria relevant to profit-oriented objectives should be applied in setting objectives for nonprofit organizations. Objectives should be prioritized, measurable, consistent, reasonable, and set within a time frame.

For many nonprofit organizations, resource-attraction objectives are more easily set using these criteria than are client-oriented objectives. Consider the case of the American Cancer Society. It is relatively simple for the society to state a measurable, reasonable objective of resource attraction in terms of a dollar amount within a specified time period. It is much more difficult to arrive at objectives that will move it toward the accomplishment of its mission to eradicate cancer. Should the society place priority on finding a cure—or on prevention through the reduction of lifestyles that are related to the incidence of cancer? In either case, how are reasonable objectives determined and stated in measurable terms?

Product/markets. Many nonprofit organizations can segment both donor market and client market and develop marketing strategies for one or more of these segments. On the donor side, the simplest approach would be to form donor and nondonor segments. A distinct strategy to attract new donors could be separate from one aimed at maintaining and enhancing donations from existing donors. Many universities use such an approach in their fund-raising efforts. Universities can further segment their market by type of donor: alumni, business firms, state government,

---

[19] Philip Kotler, "Strategies for Introducing Marketing into Nonprofit Organizations," *Journal of Marketing,* January 1979, pp. 37–44.

Table 25–2: Long Beach, California, performing arts audience segments	Market segment	Type of performance attended	Type of performance not attended
	Classical	Symphony Chamber music Opera Ballet	Experimental theater Rock Comedians
	Country/folk	Country-western Folk/bluegrass Rock	Musicals Plays Symphony
	Theater	Musicals Traditional plays Experimental theater	Rock Chamber music
Source: John R. Nevin and S. Tamer Cavusgil, "Audience Segments for the Performing Arts," in *Marketing of Services*, ed. J. H. Donnelly and William H. George (Chicago: American Marketing Association, 1981), p. 127.	Pop	Jazz Big bands Pop vocalist/group	Gospel
	Recital	Instrumental recitals Solo vocal recitals	Musicals Pop

federal government, and general public. Distinct strategies for each segment can be developed.

On the client side, some performing arts organizations have readily accepted market segmentation as a way to develop their programs. One study segmented the Long Beach, California, market area into five distinct segments based on the types of programs attended and not attended.[20] The five segments are identified and profiled in terms of their attendance behavior in Table 25–2.

Budget determination. One of the greatest difficulties faced by a nonprofit organization is knowing the level of operating funds it will have available. Government-supported groups usually have a reasonable expectation of funds, but this is not the case with organizations dependent on donors. Often they must plan operations with a poor idea of the funding they will have to support these operations. It is not uncommon for the operating budget of a nonprofit organization to be exhausted before the end of the operating period. The adoption of reliable procedures to forecast revenue and expenditures would help alleviate these budgeting problems.

Product strategy. The market offerings of many nonprofit organizations are intangible. As we said before, many offer services, others market ideas (car pooling), information (health groups), and causes (forest fire

---

[20] John R. Nevin and S. Tamer Cavusgil, "Audience Segments for the Performing Arts," in Donnelly and George, *Marketing of Services*, pp. 126–28.

prevention). As with profit-oriented firms, nonprofit organizations try to affect the behavior of their target markets. Usually, they don't aim to affect buying behavior, although the task of some nonprofit organizations is to influence people to *not* purchase a particular product, such as cigarettes or drugs. Rather, they aim for the adoption of a certain type of behavior that will benefit society. They nudge people to stop littering, get medical checkups, and use seat belts, for instance.

In other cases, nonprofit marketing attempts to influence the psychological state of the market. One of the most successful nonprofit marketing efforts in this regard was the "I Love New York" campaign. According to the ad agency responsible for the campaign,

> "I love New York" is a piece of emotion. And it apparently tapped what people actually felt; otherwise, it wouldn't have worked. In fact, a lot of people were very negative about New York, and suddenly somebody was saying, "I love New York."[21]

With total expenditures of $31.7 million from 1977 to 1980, this was an extensive nonprofit marketing effort. Its results were remarkable. Directly attributable to the campaign were the creation of 40,400 new jobs in the New York tourism industry, a 100 percent increase in Broadway ticket sales, a 70 percent increase in statewide resort occupancy, and tax and travel-related revenues to state and local governments of $2.25 billion.[22]

The framework and concepts relevant to product strategy in a commercial firm are also useful to nonprofit organizations. Most nonprofit organizations have multiple products and can think in terms of a *product mix* that has *width, depth,* and *consistency.* For example, see Figure 25–9 for a representation of a zoo's product mix.

Within its total product mix, the nonprofit organization can develop a *product portfolio matrix.* For example, the reader may want to identify departments within his or her university in terms of whether they are stars, problem children, cash cows, or dogs.

The intangibility of many nonprofit offerings makes the application of *packaging* and *branding* similar in principle to that of services marketing.

Pricing strategy. Since, by nature, many nonprofit organizations engage in **nonmonetary exchange,** they find pricing very different. Often, something other than money is being spent by a "buyer"—time, effort, giving up some behavior. When money is involved, the amount is usually determined by the donor. The notion of a fixed price in economic or noneconomic terms is often absent from the pricing strategy of a nonprofit

---

[21] "Luring 'Em with Brass and Class," *Marketing and Media Decisions,* Spring 1982, p. 194.

[22] Ibid., pp. 192–93.

Figure 25–9: Product mix for a zoo

Product lines

Source: Adapted from Philip Kotler, *Marketing for Nonprofit Organizations*, 2d ed., © 1982, p. 290. Adapted by permission of Prentice-Hall, Inc., Englewood Cliffs, New Jersey.

Items

Exhibited animals	Education	Research	Gift shop
5 Lions	10 Classes	2 Basic research projects	Stuffed animals
8 Bears	5 Field trips		Postcards
4 Tigers	50 Public lectures	10 Applied research projects	Glasses
2 Elephants			Posters
1 Gorilla			

organization. Conceptually, the area of pricing is probably the most elusive in nonprofit marketing today.

Of course, some nonprofit organizations use traditional pricing practices based on economic exchanges. Examples include the performing arts, hospitals, and universities. Because of their nonprofit nature, these institutions typically set price on a cost-oriented basis modified by some social objective. For example, tuition paid by an individual student will not cover the entire cost to the school of serving him or her.

Distribution strategy. The intangible offerings of many nonprofit organizations make their distribution situation similar to that of service marketers. No physical flows occur. The need for storage and inventory is absent. However, the channel can still consist of intermediaries. In fact, nonprofit organizations, because of their limited budgets, are often quite dependent on intermediaries in reaching their target markets. Examples include:

1. Use by the American Red Cross of firms, church groups, service clubs, and schools to carry out blood donation drives.

2. Solicitation by the Office of Cancer Communication of the National Cancer Institute of physicians, dentists, and pharmacists to encourage and help their patients and clients quit smoking.

3. Involvement of schools by federal and state agencies to carry out programs related to health education, physical fitness, drug abuse, and the like.[23]

Keep in mind that for some nonprofit organizations physical flows do occur and inventory management is important. Clearly, physical flows

[23] Alan R. Andreasen, "Intermediary Strategies for Nonprofit Organizations," in Donnelly and George, *Marketing of Services*, p. 155.

occur in the U.S. Postal Service's operations. Because of the many products they *buy,* hospitals must manage inventory.

Perhaps the most important factor (other than cost) for a nonprofit organization to consider in formulating a distribution strategy is convenience. The organization should be as accessible as possible to its donor market. The use of payroll deduction and installment payment plans by United Way is an example of a convenience-oriented distribution strategy aimed at donors. The use of mobile blood units by the Red Cross is another example.

Convenience is also important in distributing to the client market. Branch offices make use of the U.S. Postal Service more convenient. Correspondence courses offered by universities make them more accessible to clients.

Promotional strategy.   The one area of marketing strategy that has been readily adopted by nonprofit organizations is promotion. The most relevant forms of promotion include advertising, personal selling, and sales promotion. As with any profit-oriented firm, the managerial task is to effectively integrate the forms of promotion into a mix that enhances the overall marketing strategy.

There is substantial use of advertising by nonprofit organizations directed at both donor markets and client markets. All of the media are available and, for certain public service messages, are free. In most cases, though, the nonprofit advertiser must pay for media time and space. Consequently, media mix and budgeting decisions must be made. The media budget for the "I Love New York" campaign is broken down by media in Table 25–3. Advertising usage by most nonprofit organizations is much less extensive, however. Specific examples of advertising include the national "Smokey the Bear" campaign to prevent forest fires and

Table 25–3: Media mix for New York State tourism campaign— 1981–82	Media	Dollars	Percent of total
	Consumer magazines	$ 313,000	5.2%
	Trade magazines	220,600	3.6
	Network TV	328,200	5.4
	Spot TV	3,360,400	55.6
	Spot radio	303,400	5.0
	Newspapers	461,700	7.6
	Sunday supplements	380,000	6.3
	Foreign magazines	28,500	0.0
Source: Adapted from "Luring 'Em with Brass and Class," *Marketing and Media Decisions*, Spring 1982, p. 194.	Airline co-op	650,000	10.8
	Total	$6,045,800	100%

This billboard appeared near Chicago's O'Hare Airport. It emphasizes the nearness of Drake to Chicago—a major market for potential students.

Courtesy Drake University

direct-mail solicitation of the donor market by universities, churches, and charities. Drake University in Iowa placed a billboard ad near Chicago's O'Hare airport that stated, "Only 65 minutes from O'Hare to Des Moines."

Personal selling is a frequently used form of promotion aimed at the donor market. Many organizations employ door-to-door salespeople to help raise funds. On the client side, universities send recruiters to high schools to promote the generic benefits of higher education as well as the specific advantages of a particular university.

Finally, sales promotion has become a popular tool for nonprofit organizations. Many of them maintain exhibits, donation boxes, and posters at shopping centers, sporting events, and major civic events.

Performance evaluation and control. The problems inherent in setting measurable objectives carry over into performance evaluation. At present, it is easiest to evaluate fund-raising performance and compare it to objectives. On the client side, marketing performance evaluation presents real difficulties for many nonprofit organizations. Many quantitative indices simply do not allow a separation of the effects of the organization. For example, how much of the declining birthrate can be attributed directly to family-planning agencies? In other cases, quantitative indices of performance may not even be available. For example, how do you quantify the quality of life being realized by an institutionalized disabled person?

As the use of marketing in nonprofit organizations matures, perhaps improvements in performance evaluation will also occur. At present, performance evaluation is one of the more challenging tasks that a nonprofit organization faces.

SUMMARY

The service sector is a dynamic, growing part of the economy, but it has yet to develop the marketing sophistication present in the goods sector. The distinct characteristics of services present special challenges to strategic marketing. These characteristics include intangibility, inseparability of production and consumption, heterogeneity, lack of inventory, unique channels of distribution, and perishability. Different types of service can be classified according to the effect of the service act and the direct recipient of the act. The strategic planning process can be applied to the marketing of services. In each stage it is important to recognize the implications of the distinctive nature of services.

Another special area is marketing in nonprofit organizations. Because many nonprofit institutions offer services, issues in the marketing of services are relevant to these organizations. Other distinctive aspects of nonprofit organizations include multiple publics, multiple objectives, public scrutiny, and noneconomic exchange. When applying the strategic planning process in a nonprofit organization, these aspects have important implications in each stage.

KEY CONCEPTS

Service

Supplemental service

Central service

Intangibility

Inseparability of production and
    consumption

Equipment-based service

People-based service

Heterogeneity

Lack of inventory

Distinct channels of distribution

Perishability

Agent intermediaries

Nonprofit organizations

Multiple publics

Multiple objectives

Service offerings

Public scrutiny

Donor market

Client market

Marketing committee

Task force

Nonmonetary exchange

DISCUSSION QUESTIONS AND EXERCISES

1. Discuss the distinguishing characteristics of services. Summarize their implications for the strategic marketing effort of a service company.

2. Look back over the past week and try to identify all the services you bought. Fit each of them into its proper category in Figure 25–2 and then in Figure 25–3.

3. Select a service firm of your choice. Summarize the key trends in the service sector that have affected this firm.

4. Try to obtain an interview with a lawyer, physician, or some other provider of a professional service. Interview this professional about his or her attitudes toward marketing and toward advertising.

5. Identify the various publics of a nonprofit organization of your choice.

6. Try to obtain an interview with the manager of a nonprofit organization. Interview this manager about his or her attitude toward marketing and advertising. Inquire about the steps taken by the organization to incorporate marketing as a function.

7. Describe the nature of any exchange that you have engaged in recently with a nonprofit organization. Describe your level of "consumer satisfaction."

Case 17: Calvin Klein Jeans in Brazil: A case of multinational marketing

With a strong reputation worldwide and falling domestic sales, American manufacturers of designer-label jeans have increasingly turned toward overseas markets. Among their prime targets is Brazil which, with volume sales of 90 million pairs a year, ranks as the second-largest market in the world. Moreover, the Brazilian market is growing 10 percent annually and about 70 percent of its 120 million population is under the age of 30. Indeed, Brazilian consumers appear willing to pay double the U.S. prices for a brand name as an indication of being able to afford a status symbol.

Enter Calvin Klein

Given these market conditions, Calvin Klein launched its line of jeans in late August 1982

879

with a $2 million advertising campaign. Furthermore, Calvin Klein demonstrated its deep commitment to Brazil by entering into its first international licensing agreement outside Japan.

Calvin Klein's decision to employ licensing as the means of entering foreign markets marks a continuing trend by U.S. manufacturers using this method to seek a competitive edge overseas. About $10 billion in retail sales in 1980 were made under licenses, with manufacturers paying around $500 million in royalties, according to the *Licensing Letter,* a trade publication. Calvin Klein's American competitors in Brazil, Gloria Vanderbilt and Jordache, also have licensing agreements with local producers.

Brazilian reaction

Brazilian jeans manufacturers not operating under the license of any of the American companies consider the foreign-inspired product a rip-off. A manager for Alpargatas, Brazil's largest jeans manufacturer, commented that Brazilian consumers will come to realize that they can obtain the same quality and fit in a domestic brand without having to pay a high-price premium for the designer label. Alpargatas markets its jeans for about $10, one-seventh the price of the Calvin Klein brand.

Other local manufacturers have opted to challenge the American products by having their own designer labels such as Don Perignon, Lucky Strike, and Porsche Design. Still others "borrow" high-prestige names like Cartier and Patek Philippe and some even pirate products under foreign names. In fact, prior to introducing its products, Calvin Klein had to buy up more than 1,000 shirts falsely carrying its label to get them out of circulation.

The Brazilian manufacturers are also mimicking U.S. marketing techniques. Just as Calvin Klein increased its U.S. market share by using Brooke Shields in its advertisements,

Staroup, Gloria Vanderbilt's Brazilian licensee, is building its own product image by employing popular film star Sonia Braga in their commercials. Indeed, Staroup has already licensed its trademark to Portuguese and West German manufacturers and is exporting 300,000 pairs annually to other European and South American markets.

Future directions

The designer-jean segment currently represents less than 3 percent of the Brazilian market. However, Calvin Klein is confident of rapid growth by capturing business from other companies that have simply sold their names to local manufacturers. In late 1982, Calvin Klein planned an initial production run of 15,000 pairs of jeans a month to retail at $75 per pair.

References

Rotbart, D. "Licensing Boom Envelopes U.S. Industry as Makers Search for a Competitive Edge." *The Wall Street Journal,* June 1, 1981, p. 29.

"U.S. Jeans Makers Find a Market that Fits." *Business Week,* August 30, 1982, p. 39.

Discussion questions

1. What are the advantages and disadvantages of employing licensing agreements as a method of entry into a foreign market? How do these relate to the Calvin Klein situation in Brazil?

2. Of the remaining methods of foreign market entry discussed in this chapter, which do you consider as viable alternatives for Calvin Klein? Why?

3. From the data presented in the case, what is the size of Calvin Klein's market segment? Its estimated target-market share?

4. Evaluate Calvin Klein's marketing strategy in light of the competitive environment in Brazil. Among its Brazilian competitors, who do you see as providing the most serious challenge to Calvin Klein? Why?

Case 18: Colleges and universities: An increasing use of marketing

Demographic trends have pushed academic institutions into marketing. The influx of students from the baby boom has passed, so there is a smaller pool of potential students. The result is increased competition for students, particularly among the smaller colleges and universities. Marketing strategies can prove helpful for targeting students and refining the college's "marketing mix" to attract them.

Before a school can market itself to potential students, market research should be done. Admissions personnel need to find out what students and their parents know about the institution, its academic reputation, the colleges that compete with it, and the source potential students use to find out about it.

Carleton College of Northfield, Minnesota, was a pioneer in the use of marketing in academic institutions. In the mid-1970s, applications had declined, forcing the acceptance of a greater proportion of applicants. College officials worried that Carleton's reputation as an academically selective school would suffer. Market researchers at Carleton sent out questionnaires to college-bound students. Among the findings: "Prospective students thought the location in southeastern Minnesota was cold and isolated, that Carleton's atmosphere was too cerebral and didn't leave time for socializing, and that the library was too small."

In response, Carleton began to emphasize winter sports in its literature, the fact that Minneapolis–St. Paul was less than an hour away, and that while academic standards are high, there is still plenty of time for recreation and a lot to do. They also photographed the library from a different angle, showing that it was four stories high, not the two it appeared to be from the front.

Research has shown that different classes of students typically value different aspects of an institution and use different sources to make their evaluation. For example, undergraduate students tend to seek information from their peers. Because of this, it is important for a college or university to prevent popular misconceptions. On the other hand, potential graduate students tend to rely more heavily on employers and professors. Both groups use materials requested directly from schools.

Market segmentation strategy was tried at Carleton College in terms of the literature supplied to potential students. Although the brochures sent to each geographic region were the same, the cover letters to students in the East, the West, and locally differed according to the qualities that were valued in a college in each region. As a result, the letter to westerners emphasized outdoor activities and the school's informal atmosphere. Easterners were judged to be more interested in academic prestige, so they received letters emphasizing Carleton's strong academic standing. Minnesotans had indicated that Carleton was too expensive; information supplied locally outlined available financial aid and Carleton's strong national reputation.

References

Bryant, Barbara E. "Universities Conduct Marketing Research to Raise Funds, Recruit Students, Improve Image." *Marketing News,* August 5, 1983, p. 18.

Ingrassia, Lawrence. "College Learns to Use Fine Art of Marketing." *The Wall Street Journal,* February 23, 1981, p. 21.

Discussion questions

1. Why are academic institutions making the move toward marketing?

2. In what way did Carleton College change its marketing mix to reach a target market?

3. Why might there be resistance to marketing techniques in colleges and universities?

4. What other applications can you think of for marketing of nonprofit institutions?

Index of key terms and concepts

A

Absolute income, 134
Accessory equipment, 267
Accordian theory, 525
Account executive, 702
Accounting and control division, 524
Activity quota, 739
Administered vertical marketing system, 488
Adoption process, 445
Advertiser, 702
Advertising, 656
Advertising campaign, 702
Advertising and display allowance, 656
Affective levels, 168
Agent intermediaries, 877
Agents, 38
Aggregated strategy, 313
AIDA, 702
All-you-can-afford approach, 656
Analytical sophistication, 812
Analytical unit, 812
Antitrust, 104
Approaches to message content, 702
A priori segmentation design, 313
Arbitration, 488
Argument, 702
Aspiration groups, 201
Assumptive close, 739
Attitude, 168
Attribute listing, 407
Audience response, 656
Average costs, 580
Average rate of return, 407

B

Bargaining, 488
Base of power, 488
Basing-point pricing, 580
Battle of the brands, 373
Behavior, 168

Behavioral consequences, 313
Belief, 168
Benefit segment, 313
Benefit-structure analysis, 407
Bivariate analysis, 812
Body copy, 702
Boundary position, 739
Brainstorming, 407
Brand, 373, 445
Brand familiarization, 702
Brand image, 168
Brand loyalty, 232
Brand mark, 373
Brand name, 373
Breach of warranty, 445
Breakdown method, 739
Breakeven analysis pricing, 613
Breaking bulk, 525
Brokers, 525
Budgeting, 68
Business analysis, 407
Buy-lease option, 268
Buyers, 38
Buying, 38
Buying allowance, 656
Buying center, 268
Buying center roles, 268
Buying committee, 268
Buying-power index, 343

C

Canned presentation, 739
Capital budgeting, 407
Capital equipment, 267
Cash-and-carry wholesaler, 525
Cash cows, 68
Cash discount, 580
Causal design, 811
Causal techniques, 343
Census, 812
Central service, 877
Central shopping district, 525
Chain discount, 580

Chain-ratio method, 343
Chain store, 525
Channel, 656
Channel of distribution, 488
Channel intermediaries, 104
Channel strategy, 68
Characteristics of marketing functions, 38
Class of customer organization, 739
Classical life-cycle curve, 445
Client market, 877
Cluster sample, 812
Cluster segmentation design, 313
Coefficient of price elasticity of demand, 580
Coercive power, 488
Cognitive dissonance, 232
Cognitive level, 168
Cognitive responses, 232, 656
Cognitive structures, 232
Cold-canvas approach, 739
Combination approach organization, 739
Combination house, 525
Command, 702
Commercialization, 408
Commission houses, 525
Common carrier, 547
Communications-oriented measures of effects, 703
Community shopping center, 525
Comparative advertising, 702
Compatibility, 408
Compensatory decision role, 232
Competitive advertising, 702
Competitive bidding, 613
Competitive intelligence system, 104
Competitive parity approach, 656
Competitive sector, 104
Complementary product, 613
Complementation, 104
Complexity, 408
Component parts and materials, 267

Composite profile, 313
Comprehensive, horizontal, audit, 777
Compulsory licensing, 847
Computer authority, 812
Conative level, 168
Conciliation, 488
Conclusion drawing, 656
Conditions for exchange, 38
Confiscation, 847
Conflict, 488
Conglomerchant, 524
Conjunctive decision model, 232
Consolidated metropolitan statistical area, 134
Conspicuousness of a product, 201
Consumer adoption process, 408
Consumer decision process, 232
Consumer goods, 267, 373
Consumer Goods Pricing Act, 581
Consumer jury, 703
Consumer protection, 104
Consumer rights, 104
Consumer socialization process, 201
Consumerism, 104
Containerization, 547
Contingency approach, 740
Contingency planning, 777
Continuous advertising schedule, 702
Continuous innovation, 401
Contract carrier, 547
Contract marketing, 847
Contractual efficiency, 488
Contractual vertical marketing system, 488
Contribution margin, 777
Control, 777
Control brands, 407
Control chart, 777
Controlled market experiment, 703
Convenience goods, 232, 373
Convenience sample, 812
Convenience store, 524
Conventional marketing channels, 488
Cooperative advertising, 702
Copy, 702
Corporate culture, 104
Corporate vertical marketing system, 488
Corrective action, 777
Corrective-advertising program, 703
Cost per thousand (CPM), 702
Cost trade-off, 547
Counterargument, 656
Criteria for objectives, 68
Critical-path method, 408
Cultural values, 104
Culture, 201
Cumulative quantity discount, 580

Custom product, 445
Customer service, 547
Customer-specific presentation, 739
Cycle-recycle curve, 445

D

Data analysis, 812
Data bank, 812
Decision, 232
Decoding, 232, 656
Decoupling, 547
Delivered pricing, 580
Delphi technique, 343
Demand assessment, 343
Demographics, 104
Department store, 524
Deregulation, 547
Derived demand, 268
Descriptive characteristics, 313
Descriptive research design, 811
Determinant attribute, 168
Devaluation, 846
Deviation, 104
Deviation from plans, 777
Differential advantage, 104
Differentiated product, 445
Diffusion process, 445
Direct cost, 777
Direct exporting, 846
Direct marketing, 524
Direct observation, 812
Discontinuous innovation, 407
Discount store, 524
Discounts, 580
Discretionary income, 134
Disjunctive decision model, 232
Display unit, 812
Disposable income, 134
Distinct channels of distribution, 877
Distributor brands, 373
Dogs, 68
Domain-specific value, 168
Domestication, 847
Donor market, 877
Door-to-door selling, 524
Drop-off questionnaire, 812
Drop shipper, 525
Dual-income households, 134
Dumping, 847
Durable goods, 373
Dyadic approach, 740
Dynamically continuous innovation, 407

E

Econometric models, 343
Economic order quantity (EOQ) model, 547
Economic power, 488
Economic sector, 104

80/20 principle, 445
80/20 rule, 777
Emotional appeal, 656
Emulation, 104
Encoding, 656
Endless chain, 739
Engel's laws, 134
Enterprise competition, 104
Environmental adaptation, 104
Environmental factors, 268
Environmental monitoring, 104
Environmental threat, 104
Equimarginal approach, 656
Equipment-based service, 877
European Economic Community, 847
Evaluative criteria, 168
Evoked set, 232
Ex ante standard, 777
Ex post information, 777
Ex post standard, 777
Exchange controls, 847
Exchange definition of marketing, 38
Exchange rate fluctuation, 846
Exchange relationships, 38
Exclusive-dealing contract, 525
Exclusive distribution, 488
Exclusive territory, 525
Exempt carrier, 547
Expectancies, 740
Expected profit concept, 613
Experience curve, 68
Experience curve pricing, 613
Experimentation, 812
Expert power, 488
Exploratory research, 811
Exponential smoothing, 343
Export management company (EMC), 846
Exporting, 846
Exposure, 656
Express warranty, 445
Expropriation, 847
Extensive problem solving, 232
External search, 232
External secondary data, 811
External support level of environment, 104

F

Facilitating agent, 488
Family brand name strategy, 373
Family decision-making roles, 201
Family life cycle, 313
Fear appeal, 656
Federal Trade Commission Act, 581
Feedback, 656, 777
Field experiments, 812
Financing, 38, 488
Fixed costs, 580
Flighting, 703

Flows in marketing, 38
FOB factory pricing, 580
FOB with freight allowed, 580
Focus group, 811
Foreign market, 846
Form utility, 38
Franchise, 525
Franchising, 488
Free-standing store, 525
Freight absorption pricing, 580
Frequency, 702
Full costing, 777
Full-service advertising agency, 702
Full-service retailer, 524
Fully disaggregated strategy, 313
Functional account, 777
Functional (vertical) audit, 777
Functional organization, 68

G

Gap theory, 38
General behavioral characteristics,
    313
General-line distributor, 525
General-line wholesaler, 525
Generic competition, 104
Generic name, 373
Geographic organization, 739
Geographic pricing, 580
Geographic selectivity, 702
Geographic specialization, 547
Global perspective, 846
Global value, 168
Government affairs, 812
Gross rating points (GRPs), 702
Growth/share matrix, 68

H

Halo effect, 168
Hard-core potential buyer, 407
Headline, 702
Heterogeneity, 877
Heterogeneity between segments, 313
Heterogeneous demands, 38
Heterogeneous supplies, 38
High active strategy, 613
High-involvement process, 232
High passive strategy, 613
Homogeneity within segments, 313
Horizontal agreement, 525
Horizontal cooperative advertising,
    702
Horizontal integration, 488
Horizontal price fixing, 581
Household, 134
Human behavior, 168
Humorous appeal, 656
Hypermarket, 524
Hypothesis, 811

I

Iceberg principle, 777
Identification, 201
Imitation, 702
Implied warranty, 445
Implied warranty of fitness, 445
Implied warranty of merchantability,
    445
Import licenses, 846
Import restrictions, 847
Impressions, 702
Inadvertent cannibalization, 445
Incidental learning, 232
Incremental method, 739
Independent, 525
Indirect exporting, 846
Individual brand name strategy, 373
Individual factors, 268
Industrial distributor, 488, 525
Industrial goods, 267, 373
Industry, 38
Industry attractiveness/business
    strength model, 68
Information, 702
Information aggregation, 812
Information and authority flows, 68
Information receipt, 232
Information recency, 812
Informational message, 702
Informational separation, 38
Informational social influence, 201
Inseparability of production and con-
    sumption, 877
Institutional advertising, 702
Instrumentalities, 740
Intangibility, 877
Intensive distribution, 488
Interbrand competition, 525
Intermediary, 488
Intermediately positioned warehouse,
    547
Intermodal transportation, 547
Internal accounting, 812
Internal search, 232
Internal secondary data, 811
International marketing, 846
International trading company, 846
Interorganizational factors, 268
Interpersonal influence, 268
Interviewer-administered survey, 812
Intrabrand competition, 525
Intraorganizational factors, 268
Intraorganizational level of environ-
    ment, 104
Involvement, 232

J

JND, 168
Job description, 740

Joint ownership, 847
Joint venture, 846
Judgment techniques, 343
Jury of executive opinion method,
    343
Just-in-time (JIT) system, 268

L

Labeling, 373
Laboratory experiments, 812
Laboratory market test, 408
Lack of inventory, 877
Launch, 408
Layout, 702
Leading indicators, 104
Legitimate power, 488
Lexicographic decision rule, 232
Licensing, 846
Lifestyle, 201
Limited problem solving, 232
Limited-service advertising agency,
    702
List price, 580
Loss-leader pricing, 613
Low-active strategy, 613
Low-involvement purchases, 232
Low-passive strategy, 613

M

Macro definition of marketing, 38
Macro level of environment, 104
Macro/micro, 38
Magnuson-Moss Warranty Act of
    1975, 445
Mail-order wholesaler, 525
Mail questionnaire, 812
Make-buy option, 268
Management contracting, 847
Management by exception, 777
Management by objective (MBO),
    739, 777
Managerial problem, 811
Manufacturer brands, 373
Manufacturer-to-consumer sales pro-
    motion, 656
Manufacturer-to-industrial-user
    sales promotion, 656
Manufacturer-to-retailer sales pro-
    motion, 656
Manufacturer-to-wholesaler sales
    promotion, 656
Manufacturers, 38
Manufacturer's agents, 488, 525
Margin, 524
Marginal costs, 580
Market, 38
Market-buildup method, 343
Market-dominated information
    sources, 232
Market forecast, 343

Market heterogeneity, 313
Market organization, 68
Market-positioned warehouse, 547
Market potential, 343
Market program positioning, 68
Market segmentation, 68
Market segmentation process, 313
Market share, 343
Market share approach, 656
Market structure, 580
Market testing, 407
Marketing audit, 777
Marketing budget, 777
Marketing channel, 38
Marketing committee, 877
Marketing concept, 38
Marketing consequences, 313
Marketing control system, 777
Marketing cost analysis, 777
Marketing environment, 38, 104
Marketing environment audit, 777
Marketing flow, 488
Marketing function audit, 777
Marketing functions, 38, 488
Marketing information, 38
Marketing information system (MIS),
    812
Marketing intelligence, 812
Marketing management, 38
Marketing as a matching process, 38
Marketing mix, 38
Marketing organization audit, 777
Marketing productivity audit, 777
Marketing research, 811
Marketing research agency, 811
Marketing research process, 811
Marketing service agencies, 104
Marketing strategy audit, 777
Marketing systems audit, 777
Markup pricing, 613
Material handling, 547
Materials requirement planning, 268
Matrix approach, 68
Mazur plan, 524
Measurability, 313
Mechanical observation, 812
Media, 702
Media-controlled media, 702
Media mix, 702
Media scheduling, 702
Mediation, 488
Membership groups, 201
Merchandising division, 524
Merchant wholesalers, 525
Message acceptance/rejection, 232,
    656
Message content, 656
Message execution, 702
Message format, 656
Message order of presentation, 656

Message sidedness, 656
Message structure, 656
Metropolitan statistical area, 134
Miller-Tydings Act, 581
Minimarket test, 408
MIS components, 812
MIS function, 812
Misrepresentation or fraud, 445
Mission statement, 68
Missionary seller, 739
Mixed approach, 847
Modified rebuy, 268
Monopolistic competition, 580
Monopoly, 580
Motivation, 168, 740
Motivation with psychological ap-
    peals, 702
Moving averages, 343
Multi-attribute attitude model, 168
Multidimensionality of perception,
    168
Multinational corporation (MNC),
    846
Multinational marketing, 846
Multiple channels, 488
Multiple-factor screening methods,
    68
Multiple objectives, 877
Multiple publics, 877
Multiplicity of needs, 168
Multivariate analysis, 811

N

Nationalization, 847
Natural account, 777
Need, 168
Need reduction theory, 168
Negligence theory, 445
Negotiation, 488
Neighborhood shopping center, 525
New business seller, 777
New-product committee, 407
New-product department, 407
New-product manager, 407
New-task buying, 268
Niche strategy, 313
Nine Nations of North America, 313
Noise, 656
Noncompensatory decision rule, 232
Noncumulative quantity discount,
    580
Nondurable goods, 373
Nonmarketer-dominated information
    sources, 232
Nonmonetary exchange, 877
Nonprice competition, 104
Nonprobability sample, 812
Nonprofit organization, 877
Nonstandardized plan, 847
Nonstore retailing, 524

Nonverbal code, 656
Nonverbal elements, 702
Normative marketing, 38
Normative social influence, 201

O

Objective, 68
Objective and task approach, 656
Observability, 408
Observational studies, 812
Odd-numbered pricing, 613
Oligopoly, 580
Open dating, 373
Open-pay policy, 739
Operating supplies, 267
Operations division, 524
Opinion leaders, 201
Order cycle, 547
Orders, 488
Organizational goals and tasks, 268
Organizational service, 268
Organizational structure, 268
Organizational subsystems, 38
Organizational technology, 268
Organized nature of perception, 168
Ownership flow, 488
Ownership separation, 38

P

Packaging, 373
Packaging as promotion, 656
Partially disaggregated strategy, 313
Participation appeal, 656
Participation-observation, 812
Payback period, 407
Payment, 488
Penetration price policy, 580
People-based service, 877
Perceived risk, 168, 636
Perceived-value pricing, 613
Percentage of sales (POS) approach,
    656
Perception, 168
Performance evaluation and control,
    68
Perishability, 877
Personal factors of perception, 168
Personal influence, 201
Personal interviews, 812
Personal selling, 656
Personality, 168
Personality trait, 168
Personality type, 168
Persuasive message, 702
PERT, 777
Physical distribution, 547
Physical possession, 488
Physical traces, 812
Physiological test, 703
PIMS, 777

Pioneer advertising, 702
Place utility, 38
Planned cannibalization, 445
Point-of-purchase (POP) display, 656
Political risk, 847
Portfolio analysis model, 68
Portfolio test, 703
Positive marketing, 38
Positive-normative, 38
Possession utility, 38
Post-action strategic control model, 777
Postdecision, 232
Posttest, 703
Power, 488
Preemptive cannibalization, 445
Present value, 407
PRESS model, 445
Pretest, 703
Price, 580
Price controls, 847
Price discrimination, 581
Price elastic demand, 580
Price elasticity of demand, 580
Price inelastic demand, 580
Price leadership, 613
Price lining, 613
Price-quality relationship, 168, 613
Price strategy, 68
Pricing objectives, 613
Primary data, 812
Primary demand, 104
Primary metropolitan statistical area, 134
Private carrier, 547
Private warehouse, 549
Probability sampling, 812
Problem children, 68
Problem-inventory analysis, 407
Problem recognition, 232
Process versus content of strategy, 68
Producers' cooperative, 525
Product, 373
Product advertising, 702
Product cannibalization, 445
Product class, 445
Product concept, 407
Product defect, 445
Product deletion, 445
Product development, 407
Product form, 445
Product-form competition, 104
Product idea, 407
Product item, 373
Product liability, 445
Product life cycle, 445
Product line, 373
Product management, 68
Product/market, 68

Product mix, 373
Product objectives, 445
Product positioning, 168, 445
Product-positioning map, 445
Product-specific behavioral characteristics, 313
Product-specific value, 168
Product strategy, 68
Product-type organization, 739
Production concept, 38
Production-positioned warehouse, 547
Profit impact of marketing strategy (PIMS), 68
Profit-nonprofit, 38
Proliferation of opportunity, 104
Promotional discount, 580
Promotional flow, 488
Promotional strategy, 68, 656
Psychographics, 201
Public policy sector, 104
Public relations, 656
Public scrutiny, 877
Public warehouse, 547
Publicity, 656
Publicity division, 524
Publicly circulated research report, 812
Published statistics, 812
Pull strategy, 488, 656
Pulsing, 703
Purchasing agent, 268
Pure competition, 580
Push strategy, 488, 656

R

Rack jobbers, 488, 525
Random sampling, 812
Ratchet effect, 134
Rational appeal, 656
Raw materials, 267
Reach, 702
Real income, 134
Recall test, 703
Receiver-controlled media, 702
Reception, 232, 656
Reciprocity, 268
Recognition test, 703
Reference group influence, 201
Reference groups, 201
Referent power, 488
Regional shopping center, 525
Relative advantage, 408
Repeated assertion, 702
Research design, 811
Research problem, 811
Resellers, 267, 488
Resident buyer, 268
Retail buyer, 268

Retail life cycle, 525
Retail-sponsored cooperative, 488
Retailer, 38, 488
Retailer-to-consumer sales promotion, 656
Return on assets managed (ROAM), 740
Return on investment (ROI), 656
Revaluation, 846
Reverse brainstorming, 407
Reverse channel, 547
Risk taking, 38, 488
Robinson-Patman Act, 581
Role, 488
Role of information, 811
Roll-out, 408
Routinized response behavior, 232
Rural population, 134

S

Safety (buffer) stock, 547
Sales agent, 488
Sales analysis, 777
Sales branch, 525
Sales concept, 38
Sales force composite method, 343
Sales forecast, 343
Sales office, 525
Sales-oriented measures of effects, 703
Sales potential, 343
Sales promotion, 656
Sample, 812
Sample design, 812
Saturation, 445
Scrambled merchandising, 525
Screening, 407
Secondary data, 811
Selective demand, 104
Selective distribution, 488
Selective perception, 168
Self-administered survey, 812
Self-image, 168
Selling, 38
Selling agents, 525
Service, 877
Service offering, 877
Shared distribution, 547
Sherman Antitrust Act, 581
Shopping center, 525
Shopping goods, 232, 373
Signature, 702
Situation analysis, 68
Skimming price policy, 580
Smoothing constant, 343
Snowball technique, 739
Social class, 201
Social factors, 168
Socialization process, 201

Sociocultural sector, 104
Socioeconomic characteristics, 104
Sorting, 488
Source, 656
Source credibility, 656
Source derogation, 656
Sources of market information, 811
Spatial separation, 38
Specialization, 38
Specialization agent, 201
Specialty distributor, 525
Specialty goods, 232, 373
Specialty-line wholesaler, 525
Specialty store, 524
Stability, 313
Standard Industrial Classification
    (SIC) system, 313
Standard product, 445
Standard volume, 613
Standardization and grading, 38
Standardized marketing information
    service, 812
Standardized plan, 847
Standards of performance, 777
Starch readership measures, 703
Stars, 68
Statistical demand analysis, 343
Statistical and mathematical model,
    408
STEMCON, 777
Stimulus factors of perception, 168
Stock turnover, 547
Storage, 38
Store atmosphere, 525
Store image, 168, 525
Store location, 525
Straight rebuy, 268
Strategic business unit (SBU), 68
Strategic marketing management, 68
Strategic windows, 68
Strategy, 68
Stratified sampling, 812
Strict liability, 445
Subculture, 104, 201
Subheadline, 702
Substantiality, 313
Substantiation of claims program,
    703

Substitute product, 613
Suburban population, 134
Supermarket, 524
Supplemental service, 877
Support argument, 656
Survey of customer expectations, 343
Survey research, 812
Symbolic association, 702

T

Tactics, 68
Target market, 68
Target-return pricing, 613
Task force, 877
Tax controls, 847
Team selling, 740
Technical seller, 739
Technological forecasting, 104
Technological sector, 104
Telemarketing, 740
Telephone interviews, 812
Time separation, 38
Time-series techniques, 343
Time utility, 38
Timing strategy, 68
Total ownership, 847
Total product concept, 373
Trade advertising, 702
Trade associations, 104
Trade or functional discount, 580
Trade Regulation Rules (TRRs),
    703
Trade seller, 739
Trademark, 373
Transfer pricing, 581
Transportation, 38
Transshipping, 613
Trend fitting, 343
Trial close, 739
Trialability, 408
Truck wholesaler, 525
Turnover, 524
Two-stage usage of decision models,
    232
Two-step flow of communication,
    201
Tying contracts, 525
Type selectivity, 702

U

Unbranded goods, 373
Uncertainty, 811
Uniform delivered pricing, 580
Unit of analysis, 777
Unit pricing, 581
Univariate analysis, 812
Urban population, 134
Used-apple policy, 445
Users, 267
Utility, 38

V

Valence, 740
VALS, 201
Value, 168
Value of information, 812
Value separation, 38
Variable costs, 580
Variance analysis, 777
Variety store, 524
Vending machine, 524
Venture team, 407
Verbal code, 656
Vertical cooperative advertising, 702
Vertical divisions of the market, 525
Vertical marketing systems, 488
Vertical price fixing, 581
Volume quota, 739

W–Z

Want, 168
Warehouse retailing, 524
Wheel of retailing, 525
Wholesaler, 38, 488, 525
Wholesaler-to-organizational user
    sales promotion, 656
Wholesaler-to-retailer sales promo-
    tion, 656
Wholesaler-sponsored voluntary
    group, 488
Wholesalers, 556
Width, depth, consistency of product
    mix, 373
Word-of-mouth communication, 201
Workload method, 739
Workplan, 740
Zero-based budgeting, 777
Zone-delivered pricing, 580

Index of Names

A

Aaker, David A., 87
Abell, Derek F., 42, 51, 54, 55, 60, 590, 591
Abelson, H. I., 640
Abernathy, W., 591
Abrams, Bill, 51, 52, 53
Achabal, Dale D., 770, 771
Achenbaum, Alvin A., 399, 400
Adler, L., 398
Advertising Age, 51
Airline Deregulation Act of 1978, 615–16
Alberto-Culver Co., 179
Alcoa, 560, 603
Alderson, Wroe, 16, 95, 457
Alexander, Ralph S., 459, 513
Allen, Chris T., 132
Allen, J., 398
Allison, N. K., 700
Alpert, M. I., 163, 561, 562
Alter, Jennifer, 402
American Air Lines, 605, 616
American Association of Advertising Agencies, 698
American Can Co., 523
American Cancer Society, 871
American Express, 166
American Institutional Supply Co., 756–57, 762
American Iron and Steel Institute, 75
American Marketing Association, 630
American Motors, 443
Ames, Charles B., 249
AMP, Inc., case study of, 815
Amstutz, Arnold E., 810
Andreasen, Alan R., 874
Anthony, Robert N., 574
Apple Computer Co., 149, 649–50, 653, 655
  case history of, 449
A & P, 46, 498, 604

Arens, William F., 706
Arndt, John, 478
Arpen, Jeffery, 837
ASCIS Tiger Corp., 94
Assad, Henry, 175, 195
Associated Grocers, 476
Association of Home Appliance Manufacturers, 75
Atkin, Charles K., 181, 182
Avis, 476
  case history of, 744–45
Avon Products, 36, 52, 500, 706–7, 713
Axel, H., 128
Ayal, Igal, 824

B

Bagozzi, Richard P., 718, 738, 869
Bailey, Earl L., 320, 332, 341
Bailey, Joseph T., 466
Bannville, G. R., 258
Bar, Robert Drew, 496
Bass, Steven J., 505
Bates, Albert D., 505
Bauer, Raymond, 150, 156
Bausch & Lomb, 681
Bayton, J. A., 147–48
Beach, Frank H., 710
Bearden, William O., 183, 185
Beckwith, N., 666
Beecham, Inc., 55, 160
Beier, Frederick, J., 481
Belch, George E., 647
Bellenger, Danny N., 197
Benedict, Thomas C., Jr., 803
Benner Tire Co., 88
Bennett, Amanda, 564
Bennett, P., 154, 218
Benningson, Lawrence A., and Arnold I., 440
Berman, Barry, 64, 599
Bernhardt, Kenneth, 64
Berry, Leonard L., 851, 852

Best, Roger J., 181
Bettman, J., 162, 204, 226
Biasko, Vincent, 654
Bill Rodgers & Co., 158
Bird, M. M., 263
Birnbaum, Jeffrey H., 53, 504, 512, 558, 576, 605
Black & Decker, 716
Blackwell, Roger D., 156, 209, 231, 307
Blattberg, R., 302
Bloom, Paul N., 604
Bloomingdale's, 190
Blue Cross and Blue Shield, 803
BMW, 6, 7
Bonoma, Thomas V., 237, 252, 254, 867
Boone, L. E., 368
Booz, Allen & Hamilton, 384–85
Borden, Neil, 32
Borden Co., 572
Boston Consulting Group, 57
Bourne, F., 184
Bovee, Courtland L., 706
Bowersox, Donald J., 533, 535, 539
Boyd, Harper, 162, 414
Boyer, Tom, 672
Bozell & Jacobs, 672
Braniff Airways, case study of, 615–16
Brazilian market, 469
Brien, Richard H., 808
Bristol-Meyers, 433–34, 699
Britt, Stewart H., 414
Brogowicz, Andrew A., 531
Bronson, Gail, 52, 706
Brooker, G., 166
Brooks, John, 184
BRY Airline, 823
Bucklin, Louis P., 474
Budget Rent-a-Car, 669
Budweiser, 155, 448
Buell, Victor P., 467

Buesing, L., 302
Burck, Charles G., 8
Bureau of Alcohol, Tobacco, Fire-
    arms, 701
Bureau of the Census, 89, 121, 792
Burger King, case history of, 742
Burley, James R., 523
Burroughs, 55
Busch, Paul, 439, 441, 738
Business Marketing, 744
Business Week, 85, 691
Buskirk, Richard H., 516, 710, 719,
    723
Buss, W. C., 180
Buzzell, Robert B., 62, 378, 413
Bylinsky, Gene, 842
Byrne, Harlan S., 474, 601

C

Cagley, J. W., 368
Cain, William W., 834
Calantone, Roger J., 302
Calder, Bobby J., 152, 175, 434
California Olive Industry, 519
California Retailer Growers and Mer-
    chants Association v. United
    States, 575
Calvert, S., 700
Calvin Klein, case study of, 879–80
Campbell, John H., 528, 543, 545
Carleton College, 881
Carlson, Eugene, 290
Carrefour chain, 366
Carroll, Stephen J., Jr., 716
Carter-Wallace, 464
Cartwright, D., 481
Cash Discount Act, 102
Cassino, Kip D., 334
Cateora, Philip R., 834, 835, 844
Caterpillar Tractor, 36, 244, 245, 472,
    473, 538, 596, 601
  case study of, 549
Cavanaugh, K., 628
Cavinto, Joseph L., 543
Cavusgil, S. Tamer, 872
CF Co., 534
Chesebrough Pond's, Inc., 643
Chevrolet, 609
Child Protection Act, 102
Childers, Terry, 642, 643
Choudbury, Pravat, 700
Christopher, M. G., 529
Chrysler, 215–16, 426, 458
Church, Nancy J., 299
Churchill, Gilbert A., Jr., 155, 264,
    333, 716, 717, 718, 719, 722, 723,
    724, 730, 752, 753, 759, 793, 800,
    802, 851
CIT-Alcatel, 824

Citizens & Southern National Bank,
    case study of, 814
Clarke, Darral G., 341
Claycamp, Henry, 58, 428
Clayton Act, 101, 522–23
Clee, Mona A., 86
Clewett, R. M., 457
Clifford, Donald K., 414, 416
Clyde A. Perkins v. Standard Oil of Cal-
    ifornia, 578
Cocanougher, A. Benton, 732
Cochran, Betty, 378
Cohen, Joel B., 154, 164, 165, 169
Coleman-Rainwater view of social
    class, 187
Coleman, Richard P., 187, 190
Colgate-Palmolive, 606
Colky, Scott C., 853
Computerland, 354
Computers International, Inc., 667
Coney, Kenneth A., 181
Consolidated Metropolitan Statistical
    Area (CMSA), 125–27
Consumer Goods Pricing Act, 577
Consumer Product Safety Act, 102
Consumer Product Safety Commis-
    sion, 372
Consumer Reports, 216, 356, 628
Convair, 609
Convar, John, 522
Cook, Victor, 413, 418
Copeland, Melvin T., 228
Copulsky, William, 609
Cox, R., 462
Cox, William E., Jr., 418
Coyle, J. S., 368
Cravens, David W., 42, 46, 53, 56, 59,
    60, 287, 379, 426, 605, 607, 610
Crawford, Merle, 378
Cross, A. T., 186
Cross, James C., 459, 513
Culley, James D., 529
Cullinet Software, Inc., 638
Cunningham, I. C. M., 182, 188, 512,
    836
Cunningham, M. L., 418, 512
Cunningham, William, 727, 836
Curley, John, 593, 606
Czepiel, J. A., 261

D

Dahl, Robert A., 480
Dalrymple, Douglas J., 341
Darden, Bill R., 588
Davenport, William J., 738
Davidson, J. Hugh, 379
Davidson, William R., 505, 584
Davis, Keith, 482
Day, George S., 58, 87, 427
De la Torre, Jose, 842

Dean, Joel, 418, 567
Deardon, Joel, 574
Del Monte, 199, 371
Delphi technique, 333–34
Delta Air Lines, 74, 616
Deshpande, Rohit, 806
Deutscher, Terry, 507, 508
Dicer, Gary N., 545
Digital Equipment Corp., 74, 427
Dilworth, James B., 249
Direct Marketing Association, 24
Dixon, Jim, 538
Docutel, 55
Dolan, Carrie, 650
Donnelly, James H., Jr., 707, 863, 872
Doody, Alton F., 584
Dornoff, R. J., 258
Dow Chemical, 64, 606
Dow Corning, case study of, 744–45
Doyle, Peter, 428
Drury, Edward A., 337
Duker, Jacob M., 64
Dun & Bradstreet, 793
Duncan, Delbert J., 495, 498, 500, 501,
    502, 507, 510
Dunne, Patrick M., 577, 855
Dunnette, Marvin D., 730
Du Pont, E. I., de Nemours, 68, 560,
    568, 596, 603, 606, 697
Durand, Richard M., 738
Dyer, Robert F., 787

E

Eastman Kodak, 211–13, 303, 366
  case study of, 107–8
Economic Information Services, Inc.,
    323
E. F. Hutton, 860
El-Ansary, Adel I., 30, 454, 457, 462,
    464, 475, 476, 477, 479, 480, 484,
    485, 486, 487, 530, 533, 539
Electronic funds transfer system
    (EFTS), 55
Else, Robert A., 716
Endicott Johnson Corp., 141
Engel, James F., 42, 156, 209, 231, 749
Engel, Peter, 420
Engel's law, 130
Engle, J. F., 679
English, Wilkie D., 727
Enis, Ben M., 428, 598, 716
Ennis, F. Beaven, 766
Equal Credit Opportunity Act, 102
Etgar, Michael, 481
Ethan Allen, Inc., 472
Etyd, Michael J., 752
Etzel, M. J., 183, 185, 716
European Economic Community, 842
Evans, Joel R., 64, 599
Ex-Cello Corp., 330, 332

F

Fair Packaging and Labeling Act, 102, 372–73
Fallon, Walter A., 107–8
Faris, C. W., 266
Farley, John, 738
Farris, Paul, 616
Fauber, Bernard M., 347
Feber, Robert, 399
Federal Communications Agency (FCC), 701
Federal Consumer Product Safety Commission, 102
Federal Express, 605
Federal Food, Drug, and Cosmetics Act, 102
Federal Marketing Order, 519
Federal Meat Inspection Act, 102
Federal Trade Commission (FTC), 87, 100, 101, 102, 139, 575, 699
Federal Trade Commission v. *The Borden Co.*, 578
Feigin, Barbara, 605
Feldman, Laurence P., 443
Ferguson, C. E., 139, 560
Ferrell, O. C., 371, 753, 765
Fetsinger, Leon, 228
Firestone, Sidney H., 864
First Interstate Bancorp, 831
Fishbein, M., 161
Flammable Fabrics Act, 102
Flanagan, John C., 732
Food and Drug Administration, 372
Ford Motor Co., 52, 169–71, 398–99, 434, 445, 456, 567, 609, 773
case study of, 617
Ford, Neil M., 333, 707, 716, 717, 718, 719, 722, 723, 724, 730, 752, 756, 759
Formisano, Roger A., 439, 441
Fortune, 8, 85, 436, 691
Fotomat Corp., 108
Franklin, Ben, 476, 497
Franz, R. S., 750
French, John, 481
French, Warren A., 372
Friedman, Walter F., 538
Fu, Marilyn Y. C., 837
Fuller Brush, 713
Funn, S. Watson, 837
Furse, David H., 303, 304
Futrell, Charles, 378, 727

G

Galbe, Myron, 738
Gallagher, William J., 806
Gardner, David M., 598, 787
Garreau, Joel, 291–92
Geisel, J., 439

General Electric, 53, 56–57, 115–16, 343–44, 449, 489, 632, 671
General Foods, 36, 53, 54, 56, 168, 318, 359, 392
General Mills, 36, 63, 404, 414
General Motors, 27–28, 89, 154, 306–7, 422, 426, 357, 458, 476, 482, 603, 833, 836
case study of, 552–53
Geoffrion, Arthur M., 826
George, William H., 872
Gerber products, 115
Ghiselli, Edwin E., 738
Gilbert, Dennis, 187
Gilbert-Kahl view of social class, 187–88
Gildea, R. L., 628
Gill, Lynn E., 482
Gimbel's, 494
Ginter, Peter M., 530
Gist, Ronald R., 494
Glaskowski, Nicholas A., 531
Gold Circle, 506
Goldberg, Marvin E., 183
Golden, Lawrence, 497
Golden State Foods, 521
Goldstucker, Jack, 400
Goodrich, J. N., 628
Gorman, Elliott S., 332
Gorn, Gerald J., 183
Gould, J. P., 560
Grabner, John R., 529
Granbois, Donald H., 180
Grashof, John F., 531
Gray, R., 216
Greeman v. *Yuba Power Products*, 440
Green, R. T., 180, 182
Green Giant, 627, 718
Gregor, William, 772, 773, 774, 775
Gregory, Russell, 86
Grether, E. T., 462
Greyser, Stephen, 150
GTE, 97
GTE Sylvania case, 523–24
Guenther, Robert, 308
Gultinan, Joseph P., 609

H

Haas, Robert W., 735, 736, 766, 810
Haddock, Rafael, 598
Haley, Russell I., 302
Hall, William K., 56, 57, 60
Hall, William P., 476
Hamelman, Paul W., 437
Hammond, John, 5, 42, 51, 60, 590, 591
Hancock, R. S., 156
Hanes Corp., 371, 391
Hansen, Robert, 507, 508
Harding, Lawrence, 615

Harley-Davidson, 155
Hart, Shaffner & Marx, 360
Hartlye, Robert F., 509
Harvey, Michael G., 433
Hasty, Ronald W., 512
Hauser, John R., 379, 399, 416
Hausir, John, 403
Harvard Business Review, 61–62
Hawkins, Del I., 181, 188, 189
Hayes, Russell I., 399
Henion, Karl E., 86
Hermann, P. W., 218
Herrman, Robert O., 87
Heskett, James L., 521, 531, 543
Hess, John M., 834, 835, 844
Heublein, 83, 479, 605
Hewlett-Packard, 96, 605
Higgins, Kevin, 303, 627, 690, 860
Hill, Richard M., 383, 459, 513
Hills, Gerald E., 46, 287, 379
Hinkle, Joel, 418
Hise, Richard T., 63, 64, 378, 436, 473
Hisrich, Robert D., 378, 380, 381, 383, 388
H. J. Heinz, 302–3, 363, 610–11
Hlavacek, James D., 249, 383
Hoefele, John W., 386
Holiday Inns, Inc., 443–44
Hollander, Stanley C., 495, 498, 500, 501, 502, 504, 507, 510
Home Appliance Manufacturers, Association of, 75
Home Box Office (HBO), 144–45
Honeywell, 55, 543
Hopkins, David S., 378, 382
Hopkins, R. M., 750
Horney, Karen, 164
Horrell, James F., 483
Horton, R. L., 218
Houston, Michael J., 139, 154, 579, 599, 643, 666
Howard, John A., 207–8, 231
Howard Johnson, 476
Hua Tung Automotive Corp., 856
Huber, Joel, 153
Hughes, David G., 399
Hulbert, James M., 439, 766, 767
Human and Environmental Protection Dept., Mead Corp., 89
Hunt, Shelby D., 10, 13, 20–21
Hunt-Wesson Foods, 435, 542
Hurwood, David L., 332

I

Iacocca, Lee, 215–16
IBM (International Business Machines), 36, 47, 74, 95, 96, 143, 149, 208, 238, 296, 430–31, 449, 450, 538, 594, 610, 629, 636, 668, 717, 719, 729, 736

Incollingo v. *Ewing,* 442
Independent Growers Alliance (IGA), 476, 482
Ingrassia, Lawrence, 371
Ingrassia, Paul, 598, 640
Intech System, 300
Interstate Commerce Act, 101
International Harvester, 61, 477
ITT, 844
Iuso, Bill, 395, 404
Ivancevich, John M., 707, 716, 732, 752
Ivie, Robert M., 531

J

Jacoby, Jacob, 598, 787
Jain, Subhash C., 44, 422, 823
J. C. Penney, 190, 482, 499, 510, 602–3
  case study of, 269–70
Jenkins, Omer C., 727
Jewel Food Stores, 367–68
Jobs, Steven, 449
John Deere, 36
Johns Manville, 63
Johnson & Johnson, 64, 84, 120
Johnson, S. C., 103, 211
Johnston, J., 346
Johnston, Wesley J., 237, 252, 254
Jolson, Marvin A., 728, 729, 730
Joseph Schlitz Brewing Co., 155, 470
Joty, O. Maurice, 393

K

Kahl, Joseph A., 187
Kahn, George N., 719
Kaldor, Andrew G., 379
Kanuck, Leslie, 406, 736
Karlins, M., 640
Kassarjian, H., 164, 184
Kastens, Merritt L., 46
Keegan, Warren J., 822, 824, 832, 834, 840
Keith, Robert J., 35
Kellogg, 542
Kelly, Patrick J., 63, 64
Kelman, H. C., 178
Kennecott, 604
Kennedy, John F., 87–88
Kerin, Roger A., 433
Kerlinger, Fred, 789
King, R. L., 264
Kinnear, Thomas C., 42, 679, 750
Kinney Shoe Corp., 496
Kirkpatrick, Charles A., 736
Kirpalani, V. H., 391, 588, 591
Kish, Leslie, 800
Klompmaker, Jay E., 399, 400, 402
Klugman, Ellen, 427

K mart, 190, 362, 607
  case study of, 345–46
Kmoishiroku Co., 108
Knisely, Gary, 864
Kollat, David T., 156
Komatsu, 550–51
Koten, John, 427, 444, 445, 640
Kotler, Phillip, 14, 19, 63–64, 67, 68, 394, 395, 429, 430, 435, 511, 595, 604, 772, 773, 774, 775, 784, 785, 869, 870, 871, 874
Krum, James R., 806

L

La Grace, Raymond, 428
La Lande, Bernard J., 529
Lambert, Douglas M., 486–87
Lambert, Zarrel V., 599
Lamont, L. M., 143
Landro, Laura, 145
Langeard, Eric, 857
Lanham Act of 1946, 360
Lanzillotti, Robert F., 585, 603
Largay, James A., III, 750
Laric, Michael V., 64
Las Vegas Merchant Plumbers Assn., v. *United States,* 575
Lawrence, Paul R., 576
Lazer, William, 85, 422, 529
Lenox, Inc., 53
Leone, Robert P., 697
Lever Brothers, 55, 63, 465, 611
Levi Strauss, 11, 80, 133, 288, 538
Levitt, Theodore, 414–15, 416
Lewis, Edwin H., 467
Lewis, Richard J., 531
Libby, McNeill & Libby, 370
Liechty, Margaret G., 851
Lillian, Gary L., 254
Limited, Inc., 307
Lincoln, D. J., 666
Lisa, 449
Lo Bello, Nino, 837
Lockheed, 237, 845
Locnder, W. B., 218
Lovelock, Christopher H., 854, 855, 864, 867
Luchsinger, L. Louise, 577
Luck, David J., 753, 765
Luick, John F., 630
Lundstrom, William J., 86
Lusch, Robert F., 483
Lutz, R., 162

M

McCammon, Bert C., Jr., 474, 479, 506
McCann, John, 153
McCarthy, Jerome, 517, 531, 577
McConnell, J. Douglas, 598

McDonald's, 44, 175, 476, 521
  case study of, 742–43
McElroy, Neil, 63–64
McGinnis, Michael A., 436
McGraw-Hill, 661
McInnes, William, 15–16
Macintosh, 651
McKinsey and Co., 59
McLeod, Raymond, Jr., 807, 808
MacPherson v. *Buick Motor Co.* case, 440
McTavish, Ronald, 299
Mack, Raymond W., 483
Macy's, 494
Magnuson-Moss Warranty Act, 102, 470
Mahajan, Vijay, 61, 427
Makridakis, Spyros, 328, 336
Malaysia, 835
Maldutis, Julius, 615
Mandell, Maurice, 500
Mark Morris & Co., Inc., 855
Markus, Hazel, 161
Marriott Hotels, 47
Marshall Field's, 494
Maslow, Abraham H., 147
Mason, Joseph B., 483, 494, 502, 504, 511, 579
Mathews, H. L., 190
Matteiss, T. H., 732
Maurice, Charles S., 139
Mayer, Morris L., 483, 494, 502, 504, 511, 579
Mazur, Paul, 495
Mazur plan, 495
Mazze, Edward M., 437
MCI, 329
Mead Corp., 85
Mead, Johnson, 155–56
Mead, Richard R., 781
Meredith, G. E., 401
Merrill Lynch network, 861–62, 864
Mexicana Airlines, 59
Michael, George C., 327, 342
Michaels, Ronald E., 417
Midwest Hospital, case study of, 348–49
Miller Brewing Co., 361, 402
Miller Tydings Act, 577
Miniard, Paul W., 171
Miracle, Gordon E., 839
Mitchell, Arnold, 192–93
Mittelstaedt, R., 666
Mizerski, R. W., 700
Monroe, Kent, 86, 558, 562, 573, 584, 585, 599, 666
Montgomery, David B., 97, 390, 809
Mooney, E., 247
Moore, C., 369
Morgan, Doreen, 497

Morgan, Fred W., 787
Moriarity, Rowland T., 264, 266
Morrison, Donald, 328
Morton Center, 545
Moss-Magnuson Act of 1975, 696
Motor Safety and Cost Savings Authorization, 102
Muczyk, Jan R., 738
Murphy, Matthew J., 723
Murphy, P. E., 293
Murray, H. A., 148
Myers, James H., 388, 445, 781

N

Nabisco Brands, Inc., 25–27, 64, 387
Nader, Ralph, 87
Naisbitt, John, 35, 89, 422
Nash, Henry W., 559
National Advertising Review Board (NARB), 698
National Appliance and Radio TV Dealers Assn., 485
National Association of Broadcasters (NAB), 698
National Association of Manufacturers (NAM), 75
National Cash Register, 237, 250, 431
National Council of Physical Distribution, 528
National Purchase Diary, 398
National Retail Dry Goods Assn., 495
National Traffic & Motor Vehicle Safety Act, 102
Nehemkis, Peter, 835
Nielsen, A. C., 793
Nielsen Retail Index, 793
Neslin, Scott A., 564
Nevin, John R., 872
Newman, Joseph W., 218
Newton, Derek A., 708
Nickels, William G., 578
Niedell, L. A., 368
Nimer, Daniel A., 595, 603
Nishi, Masao, 528, 543, 545
North, B. Q., 99
Nouse, Robert E. M., 378
Novak, Adolph, 511
N. W. Ayer, 402

O

O'Boyle, Thomas F., 604
Office of Consumer Affairs, 87–88
Ogilvy and Mather, 291
Olson, Jerry C., 154, 598
Olsharsky, Richard W., 417
O'Meara, J. T., 392
Osborn, Alex F., 386, 390
Ott, Leland, 605
Outboard Marine Corp., 608

Oxenfeldt, Alfred R., 602
Ozanne, U. B., 264

P

Palda, Kristin S., 339
Palmer, Arnold, 638
Parcels, R., 369
Park, C. W., 226
Parke-Davis, 442, 709
Par Report, 61–62
Patti, Charles H., 654
Patton, Richard B., 610
Paul, Gordon W., 609
Pauly, Helen, 499
Payne, J. W., 226
Payne, Stanley L., 796
Peacock, P., 302
Peller, Clara, 742
Pennebaker, Kenneth J., 54
Perreault, William A., Jr., 517
Perreault, William D., 542
Pessemier, E., 162
Peters, Michael, 378
Peters, Thomas J., 73, 74, 244, 380, 381, 383, 388
Peterson, Esther, 579
Petroleum Marketing Practices Act, 102
Philip Morris, 363
Phillips, Owen R., 139
Pillsbury, 36, 63, 402, 418, 718
Pilot Corp. of America, 173
Playboy, 305–6
Plummer, Joseph T., 192
Poison Prevention Packaging Act, 372
Pokempner, Stanley J., 320, 341
Poli, Rolando, 413, 418
Porter, Henry, 732
Porter, Michael E., 91, 95, 423
Prab Robots, Inc., 377
Pranka, Stephen, 595
Prell, Arthur, 428
Pride, William, 371
Primary Metropolitan Statistical Area (PMSA), 125–27
Prime Time, 119
Printer's Ink, 183, 701
Pritchard, Robert C., 730
Procter & Gamble, 36, 51, 55–56, 63–64, 74, 88, 361, 363, 364, 417, 633, 635
Product Idea Decay Curve, 365
Product Warranty and Uniform Commercial Code, 443
Professional Truckers Buying Service Group, Inc., 241
PPG Industries, 89
Pruder, Henry, 727
Public Health Smoking Act, 102
Puccini, James I., 530

Punj, Girish N., 303, 304
Pure Food and Drug Act, 102
Pyke, D. L., 99

Q–R

Quaker Oats, 65
Qualis, William, 417
Rainwater, Lee P., 187
Ralston Purina, 365, 381, 631–32
Rao, Ashok, 571, 572
Raven, Bertram, 481
Ray, M. L., 162, 640
Reed, James, 714
Reibstien, David J., 610
Reis, Al, 430, 432
Report on Look-Alikes, 62
Republic Airlines, 444
Reve, T., 479, 480
Revlon, 52, 469, 706
Retirement Living, 119
Richardson-Vicks, 84
Ricks, David, 837
Rink, David R., 412, 419, 420
Rippe, Richard, 328
R. J. Reynolds, 298, 427, 469
Robart, Dean, 55
Robertson, Thomas S., 184, 376
Robeson, James F., 529
Robicheaux, Robert A., 559
Robin, Donald P., 559
Robinson-Patman Act, 46, 101, 577–78
Robinson, P. J., 266
Robock, Stefan H., 822, 835
Roedder, Deborah L., 183
Rogers, Everett, 404, 406, 407, 419
Rogers, John, 807, 808
Rogers, William, 772, 773, 774, 775
Rokeach, Milton, 143
Roselius, Ted, 158
Rosen, Dennis L., 180
Rosenberg, Larry J., 500
Rostow, Walt W., 838
Rothe, James T., 433
Rothschild, Michael L., 139, 696
Russ, Frederick A., 542, 736
Russell, Frederick A., 710, 713
Russo, J. Edward, 579

S

Saab, 7, 9, 32
Saab-Scania AB, 7, 8, 9
Sabin, Sharon, 564
Saeed, Samiee, 603, 750
Sales & Marketing Management, 325
Samli, A. C., 666
Sammons, Donna, 632
Scanlon, Sally, 400
Scanlon, Burt K., 753

Schasinger, Charles M., 180, 188, 189, 132
Schellhardt, T. D., 295
Schenley Imports, 177
Scher, Jay, 496
Schewe, Charles D., 391
Schewing, Eberhard S., 381, 382
Schiffman, Leon G., 406, 407, 414
Schonberger, Richard J., 250
Schoner, Bertram, 802
Schuchman, Abraham, 719, 771
Sciglimpaglia, Donald, 86
Scott, J. E., 143
Scott, Nelson A., 769
Sears, Roebuck, 103, 190, 362, 364, 473, 499
Securities and Exchange Commission, 97
Seichow & Righter Co., 641
Sen, S., 302
Sethi, S. Prahash, 844
Sevin, Charles H., 755
Servicemaster, 477
Shapiro, Benson P., 718, 719
Shapiro, Irving, Jr., 455, 456, 461, 476, 512
Shapiro, Stanley, 391, 588, 589
Sharma, Subhash, 770, 771
Shell Oil, 47, 48, 61, 823
Sherif, Muzafer, 484
Sherman Antitrust Act, 101, 522–23, 575, 577
Sheth, Jagdish N., 85, 154, 218, 231
Shimp, Terence A., 787
Shipchandler, Zoher E., 90, 91
Shoemaker, F. Floyd, 404, 406, 407
Shoemaker, Robert W., 564, 769
Shostack, G. Lynn, 851
Simmonds, Kenneth, 822
Simon, Julian L., 675, 678
Simons Market Research Bureau, 690
Singh, Surendra N., 696
Singy, Joseph M., 171
60 Minutes, 119
Slocum, J. W., Jr., 190
Small, Constance, 787
Smallwood, John, 85, 422, 428
Smith, Bruce, 632
Smith-Corona, 212
Smith, Reuben M., 391
Smokey the Bear, 624
Smucker, J. M., 369
Smyth, Richard C., 723
Snyder, Donald, 378
Snyder, Richard C., 483
Social Trends Monitor, 89
Solomon, Michael R., 184
Sonnefeld, Jeffrey, 576
Sony, 47, 92, 420, 610
Sparks, Jack D., 809

Spekman, Robert E., 264
S. S. Kresge, 499
Stafford, James, 598, 806
Standard Industrial Classification (SIC) system, 294–95
Standard Metropolitan Statistical Areas, 125–26, 520
Standard Research Institute (SRI), 192–93
Standard Oil of California, 522
Stanton, Robert, 337
Stanton, W. J., 366, 371, 502, 719, 723, 858, 866
Staples, W. A., 293
Starch readership measures, 696
Starling, Jack M., 530
Steering Marketing Control Systems (STEMCON), 770–71
Stein, Sidney, 269
Steinberg, Bruce, 17
Stern, Louis W., 30, 454, 462, 463, 475, 476, 477, 480, 481, 482, 484, 485, 530, 533, 537, 539
Stewart, D. W., 303, 304
Stickney, Clyde P., 750
Stolle, John F., 764
Stonich, Paul J., 764
Stouffer Foods Corp., 117, 302–3, 420
Strang, Roger A., 630
Strategic Planning Institute, 61–62
Strategy Analysis Report, 62
Strawser, Robert H., 473
Strong, E., 162
Sturdivant, Frederick D., 96
Sudman, Seymour, 800
Sun Belt, 121–22
Sunmaid Raisin Growers Association, 518
Survey of Buying Power, 325–26
Survey of Industrial Purchasing Power, 325
Swan, John E., 412, 419, 420, 598
Swaze, John Cameron, 155
Sweeney, Daniel J., 584
Swinth, R., 738
Sylvania, 97

T

Talarzyk, W. Wayne, 307
Talley, Walter J., 720
Tauber, Edward M., 388, 389, 394, 395, 401, 402, 422
Tennessee Valley Authority (TVA), 607
Teplitz, Charles J., 543
Terpstra, Vern, 826
Texas Instruments, 74, 99, 590
Thomas, Dan R. E., 852–853
Thompson, Donald N., 476, 484
Thompson, G., 378

Thurlow, Michael L., 332
Time, Inc., 424
Toffler, Alvin, 98
Toma, Al, 750
Toman, James, 511
Toni, Henry L., 716
Toy, Norman E., 439, 766, 767
Toyota Industrial Equipment, 544
Tracy, Eleanor Johnson, 498
Trade Regulation Rules (TRRs), 700
Trend Report, 89
Trombetta, W. L., 442, 443
Trout, Jack, 430, 432
TRW, Inc., 99
Tucker, Lewis R., Jr., 823
Twedt, Dik Warren, 785, 786
Tybout, M., 175

U

Udell, Jon G., 559
Uhl, Kenneth, 802
Union Carbide, 63
Union Steel Products, Inc., 17
Uniroyal, 63
   case study of, 271–72
United Air Lines, 669
United Fruit, 884
Upah, Gregory D., 851
Upjohn, 64
Urban, Glen L., 379, 390, 399, 403, 416, 809
U.S. v. American Can Co., et al., 523
U.S. v. Arnold Schwinn & Co., 523
U.S. Department of Agriculture, 624
U.S. Postal Service, 63, 65, 875
U.S. v. Socony-Vacuum Oil Co., 575
U.S. Steel, 604
U.S. v. Utah Pharmaceutical Assn., 575

V

Vaile, R. S., 462
VALS lifestyle framework, 298
VALS typology, 193
Venat, Zal, 512
Venture team, 383–84
Vernon, Raymond, 824
Videojet Systems International, 405
Vinson, D. E., 143
Volancia, Humberto, 197
Volkswagen of America, 432, 825
Von Buytenen, P. M., 529

W

Wackman, Daniel B., 182
Walker, Orville C., 333, 707, 708, 716, 717, 718, 719, 722, 723, 724, 730, 752, 756, 759
Walt Disney Productions, 74
Ward, Scott, 178, 182, 666
Warner-Lambert Co., 700, 709

Warner Publishers Service, 569
Warner & Swasey, 466
Warren, Roland L., 475
Warsaw, Martin T., 750
Warshaw, Martin F., 42, 679
Waterman, Robert H., Jr., 73, 74, 244
Waters, L. L., 545
WATS line, 736
Wayne, Kenneth, 591
Webb, Eugene J., 795
Weber's law, 152
Webster, F. E., Jr., 248, 253, 259, 263, 266, 528, 750
Weigand, Robert E., 466
Weight Watchers, 302–3
Weinberg, Charles B., 97, 867
Weiss, E. B., 362
Weitz, Barton A., 738, 739
Welch, Joe L., 101, 360, 522
Wells, L. T., Jr., 825
Wells, William D., 298
Wendy's, case study of, 742–43
Werner, Ray O., 578
Western Auto, 476

Western Union Corp., 329
Weyerhaeuser, 64
Whalen, Bernie, 7, 32, 33
Wheeler-Lea Amendment of 1938, 699
Wheelwright, Steven C., 328, 336, 341
Whirlpool Corp., 73, 428–29, 809
Whitehall, The, 859
Wholesale House, 515
Wiegner, Kathleen K., 97
Wilkie, E., 162
Wilkie, W. L., 278, 640, 787
Wilkinson, Maurice, 328
Will, R. Ted, 512
Wills, G. S., 529
Wilson, D. L., 738
Wilson, T. L., 442
Wind, J., 253, 259, 266
Wind, Yoram, 58, 61, 254, 259, 266, 310, 395, 396, 427, 428
Winer, Leon, 392
Winick, Charles, 843
Wolk, Harry, 755
Wong, M. Anthony, 254

Woodruff, Robert B., 46, 287, 379
Woods, Lawrence, 372
Woodside A., 154, 218, 738
Woolworth, 497
World Trade Distribution Center, 538
Wotruba, Thomas R., 332
Wozniak, Stephen, 449
Wright, John, 413
Wright, Peter, 646–47

X–Z

Xerox, 53, 366, 367, 449, 736
  case study of, 271–72
Yankelovich, Daniel, 89
Young, Shirley, 605
Yao, M., 368, 369
Young and Rubicam, 864
Zaltman, Gerald, 237, 806, 867
Zajonc, Robert B., 161
Zeithaml, Valerie, 862
Zenith, 27–28, 91
Ziegler, William L., 630
Zimmerman, Donald, 497
Zwick, Jack, 822

Index of Subjects

A

Accordian theory of retail development, 504–5
Account executive, 672
Activities, interests, and opinion (AIO), 191–92
Activity quotas, 716
Actual (marketing) performance, 752–53
Administered vertical marketing system, 475
Adoption process, 418
Advance lifts, 262, 294
Advertisements, types of, 663
Advertiser, 663
Advertising
  agencies, ten largest, 672
  budgets, 671–73
  campaigns, 670–71
  cooperative, 669–70
  copy, 679–82
  definition of, 626
  and display allowance, 631
  expenditures, 662
  layouts, 682–83
  management, 671–72
  measuring effect of, 694–97
  media, 683–91
  message, 673–74, 675–79
  objectives, 673–74
  regulatory environment around, 697–701
  role of, 660–62
  schedules, 692–94
  types of, 663–70
Affective level of beliefs, 160
Age distribution, population, 116–17
Age structure of population, 119
Agent intermediaries, 863
Aggregated strategy, 306, 604–5
AIDA (capture Attention, develop Interest, create Desire, and induce Action) approach, 683

All-you-can-afford approach, 653
Analytical unit, 828
Antitrust laws, 100–103
A priori segmentation design, 309–10
Approaches to message content, 675–76
Assumptive close, 715
Attitudes, 159–65
Attribute listing, 388, 390
Attributes for grocery stores, 508
Audience response, 639–40
Authority flow, 62
Automatic teller machines (ATMs), 54, 55, 81
Automobile industry, 561, 585–86
Average costs, 565–66
Average rate of return, new product, 393

B

Back-alley garages, 518
Banks, 81–83
BARS (behaviorally anchored rating scales), 732–33
Basic transportation modes, 535
Basing-point pricing, 572–73
Behavior, 142, 159–60
Belief, 159
Beliefs, behavior, and attitudes, 647
Believability, 641
Benefit segmentation, 302
Birthrate, declining, 80
Bivariate technique, 801
Black females, 193
Blacks, Hispanics, and whites, demographic traits of, 195
Blind taste tests, 152
Boundaries of the market, 321
Brainstorming, 385–86
Brand(s)
  battle of, 362
  choice and social class, 189

Brand(s)–Cont.
  distribution and manufacture of, 362–63
  extensions in line of, 376
  image, 154–55
  loyalty, 221–24
  mark, 360
  names and generics, 366
  position map, 432
  social status of, 172
Branding, 358–66
Breach of warranty, 440
Breakdown method, 720
Breakeven analysis pricing, 586–89
Breakeven chart, 584
Breakfast cereals, 182
Breaking bulk, 513
Brokers, 517, 520
Budget determination, 473
Budgeting
  as part of management, 51–52
  practices of large advertisers, 654
  for service firm, 860–61
  techniques for decision-making, 391
Budgets, 764
Business travelers, 303
Buyer sophistication, 299–300
Buying allowances, 631
Buying behavior, 236–43, 247
Buying center, 252–55, 271–72, 296
Buying committee, 247
Buying-power-index method, (BPI), 325
Buying stages, 255

C

Campbell soup, 138, 363, 365, 611–12, 627
Canned presentation, 714
Cannibalization, 434–44
Capsule Summaries of the Nine Nations, 518, 627, 631
Car buying, 78

Cash-and-carry wholesalers, 518
Cash discount, 569–70
Cash-flow analysis, 392
Causal design, 791
Causal techniques, 339
Census, 797
Central services, 850
Centralized versus decentralized purchasing, 271–72
Chain discount, 569
Chain-ratio method, 321–22
Chain store, 502
Channel(s)
  agents, 460
  communicative process in, 644
  and conflicts in bargaining, 485–86
  of distribution, 454
  leadership, 482
  management, 479–83, 522
  objectives, 470
  performance evaluation of, 486
  strategy, 53, 467
  system performance, 486–87
Children, 182–83
Cigarette industry, 561
Classes of customers, 718
Classical life-cycle curves, 412
Classification of consumer goods, 228–29
Client market, 869
Close, the, 714
Cluster sample, 799
Cluster segmentation design, 309–10
Coca-Cola, 54, 363, 476, 483, 670, 828
Coefficient of price elasticity of demand, 563–64
Cognitive-affective-conative framework, 161–62
Cognitive dissonance, 228–29
Cognitive level of beliefs, 160
Cognitive responses, 220, 646
Cognitive structure, 213–16
Cold canvas approach, 713
Combination house distributors, 519
Combination plans, 726
Commercialization, 402–3
Commission houses, 517
Commissions, 671
Common carriers, 535
Communication effects, 695–97
Communications-oriented measures of effect, 692
Communications process model, 636
Comparative advertising, 666–67
Compatibility, 404
Compensation of sales force, 723–28
Competition, 90–94
  levels of demand in, 92

Competition–*Cont.*
  and marketing strategy, 45
  nature of, 93–94
  oriented pricing, 501, 592–95
  types of, 91–93
Competitive advantage, 666
Competitive bidding, 594–95
Competitive intelligence system, 96–97
Competitive-parity approach, 652
Complementary products, 608–9
Complementation, 96
Complexity of new product, 404–5
Composite profile of market segment, 305–6
Comprehensive audit, 771–72
Comprehensive product-concept idea, 396
Compulsory licensing, 837
Conative or behavioral level, 160
Concept evaluation procedure, 395
Confiscation and expropriation, 834–35
Conflict within channels, 483–85
Conflict-management strategies, 484–86
Conglomerchant, 500
Conjunctive model, 225
Consumer(s)
  adoption process, 406–7
  attitudes, 161
  basic tasks of, 204–6
  behavior, 138–46, 204, 231
  choice, 206
  and cognitive responsibility, 220
  decision process, 206–7
  decision rules, 222–23
  decisions, 206–10, 221–26
  development of, 209–10
  and external search, 214–16
  goods, 228–30, 355, 724
  goods channel, 457–58
  incidental learning about, 218–19
  information sources, 215–17
  and internal search, 213–14
  involvement of, 209–10
  jury, 695
  market, 114, 295–98, 301–3
  perception, 429
  pretests, 106
  and problem recognition, 210
  rights of, 87
  shopping and specialty goods, 230
  socialization, 178–79
Consumerism, 86–88
Contact efficiency, 454
Containerization, 543
Content of promotional message, 638
Continuous advertising schedule, 693

Contractual vertical marketing system, 475–76
Contribution margin, 760
Control, 750–53
Control brands, 397
Controlled market experiments, 697
Convenience goods, 17, 229, 356–57
Convenience stores, 101, 499
Conventional and vertical marketing systems, 474–79
Cooperative advertising, 669–70
Copy, 679–70
Core values, 74
Corporate culture, 72
Corporate vertical marketing structure, 477
Corrective advertising program, 700
Cost concepts, 565–67
Cost curves, 542
Cost-oriented pricing practices, 584–89
Cost per thousand (CPM), 691
Cost(s)
  average, 565–66
  reductions, 590
  standard, 574
  structure, 565, 587
  trade-offs, 529
  variable, 565
Counterarguing, 220, 646
Creative process, 675
Criteria for effective warnings, 442
Criteria for objectives, 47
Critical-path method (CPM), 403
Cultural values, 85–86
Culture, 194–95
Cumulative quantity discount, 570–71
Curtis-Mathes, 42, 154, 444–45, 472, 607
Custom product, 425
Customer service, 530
Customer-specific presentation, 714
Cycle-recycle curve, 418

D

Data analysis, 800–802
Deal-prone consumers, 301
Decision point, 221
Declining birthrate, 115
Decoding process, 220, 646
Decoupling, 539
Delphi technique, 333–34
Demand, 87
Demand assessment, 299–303, 316–19, 321–27
Demand-oriented pricing, 595–97
Demographics, 84
Department stores, 494–97
Deregulation, 545, 615–16, 857
Derived demand, 244–45

Descriptive research design, 791
Detailed analysis, 754
Determinant attributes, 163
Deutsche marks, 825
Devaluation, 825
Deviation, 95–96, 753
Dichotomies, 10
Differential advantage, 94–95
Differentiated products, 426
Diffusion process, 419
Direct costs, 760
Direct exporting, 826
Direct marketing, 499
Disaggregated strategy, 306–7, 605
Discontinued innovation, 377
Discount stores, 498
Discounts, 568–71
Disjunctive model, 225
Display allowance, 569
Display unit, 809
Disposable/discretionary income, 130
Distribution
    centers, 538
    channels, 457–61, 467
    costs, 530
    exclusive, 472
    international considerations, 843–44
    and service industry, 863
    Shared, 543–44
Distributor(s)
    brands, 362
    combination houses types of, 519
    distinct channels of, 854
    effect, 456
    of multinational corporations, 863
    and nonprofit organizations, 874–75
Domain-specific values, 144–45
Domestication, 835
Donor market, 869
Door-to-door selling, 500
Drop-off questionnaire, 796
Drop shipper, 518
Dual-income household, 85, 132
Dumping, 842
Durable goods, 356, 418
Dyadic approach, 643, 738

E

Econometric models, 340–41
Economic development, 890
Economic order quantity (EOQ), 540–42
Economies of scale, 26
Education, 132–33
Effective control systems, 753–54
Eight male lifestyles, 297–98
80/20 principle, 438, 754–55
Emotional appeal, 640–41

Emulation, 95
Encoding of message, 632
Endless chain, 711
Energy-saving products, 100
Environmental adaptation, 77, 80–82
Environmental monitoring, 79–80
Environmental protection, 530
Equimarginal approach, 651
Equipment-based services, 853
Ethical drugs, 417–18
Evaluation, 55–56, 439
Evaluative criteria, 215
Evolution of marketing techniques, 784
Ex ante standards, 769
Exchange controls, 835
Exchange rate fluctuations, 825
Exchange relationships, 19–20
Exclusive-dealing contracts, 522
Exclusive distribution, 472
Exclusive territories, 523
Exempt carriers, 536
Expectancies, 721
Experience curve pricing, 589
Experience curves, 59
Experiment, 796–97
Exploratory research designs, 790
Exponential smoothing, 335–37
Export management companies, 826
Ex post information, 767–69
Ex post standards, 769
Exposure, 644–45, 686
Express-mail industry, 859–60
External search behavior, 216–17
External secondary data, 792
External support level, 74–75

F

Family brand-name strategy, 363–64
Family decision-making roles, 180
Family influences, 178–79
Family life cycle, 293–94
Fear appeals, 640
Feedback, 648
Field experiments, 794, 797
Fishyback system, 535
Fixed costs, 564
Flighting, 228–29
Flow, 22–23
Flow of communications, 176
FOB (free on board) factory pricing, 571–72
FOB with freight allowed, 572
Focus group, 791
Folding-carton industry, 576
Food consumption, 78–79
Forecasting, 327–41, 342
Foreign customers, 823
Foreign markets, 830
Franchises, 476, 502–3

Freight pricing, 572
Frequency, 687
Full costing, 760
Full-line forcing, 522
Full-service advertising agencies, 671
Full-service retailers, 498
Functional account, 761
Functional organization, 62–63
Functional specialization, 28

G

Gap theory, 15
General-line distributors, 519
General-line wholesalers, 516
Generic products, 148, 188, 366–70
Geographic bases, 289–90
Geographic concentration, 239–40
Geographic distribution, 121, 126
Geographic pricing, 571–74
Geographic selectivity, 688
Global perspective, 143, 825
Governmental regulation, 699–700
Gross rating points (GRP), 687–88
Groups, 183–84
Growth/share matrix, 57–58

H

Halo effect, 153–54
Hard-core potential buyers, 396–97
Headline, 679
Health maintenance organizations (HMOs), 865
Heterogeneity of services, 285–86, 853–54
Heterogeneous supplies and demand, 16
Hierarchy of effects, 674
High active strategy, 607
High price/active strategy, 42
Homogeneity between market segments, 285–86
Horizontal agreement, 523
Horizontal cooperative advertising, 669
Horizontal integration, 479
Horizontal price-fixing, 575–78
Households, 115–16, 129–34
Human behavior, 139–42
Human element, 74
Humorous appeals, 640–41
Husband-wife influence patterns, 180–81
Hypermarkets, 500–501
Hypothesis, 787

I

I Love New York campaign, 873
Iceberg principle, 754–55
Identification, 178–79, 397

Implied warranty of merchantability, 443
Import licenses, 823
Import restrictions, 836
Impressions, 687
Incidental learning, 218–19
Income, 129–30
Incremental method, 722–23
Independent retailers, 501–2
Indirect costs, 760
Indirect exporting, 826
Individual brand-name strategy, 363
Industrial buying, 248–49
Industrial channel of distribution, 549
Industrial distributors, 519
Industrial goods, 240–42, 355, 458–61, 634
Industrial market, 251, 303
Industrial wholesalers, 518–19
Influence of children, 182–83
Information, 780, 782–83
Information flow, 62
Information receipt, 218
Information search, 321
Informational social influence, 172
Innovations, 419
Inseparability, 852
Institutional advertising, 666–68
Intangibility of services, 851
Intensive distribution, 471
Interdependent organizations, 454
Interest rates, 78, 90
Intermediaries, 454–47
Intermediately positioned ware-houses, 536–37
Intermodal transportation, 535
Internal accounting data, 807
Internal marketing research departments, 785
Internal search, 213
Internal secondary data, 792
International marketing, 822
Interorganizational influences, 72, 258–61
Interorganizational relationships and qualitative approach, 486–87
Interorganizational strategy, 485
Intrabrand competition, 524
Inventory, 539
Inventory management, 249, 539, 543
Involvement, 209

J

Japan, 11
Japanese competition, 107
Job description, 728
Joint ventures, 830–32
Judgment techniques, 328
Junk yards, 530

Jury of executive opinion, 328, 332–33
Just-in-time (JIT), 249–50, 552–53
Just noticeable difference (JND), 152–53

L

Labeling, 371–73
Labor problems, 836
Laboratory experiments, 797
Laboratory market test, 423, 424–26
Layout, 682
Leading indicators, 90
Leasing, 251
Legal dimension of management, 522–25
Legal environment, 46, 836–37
Legal sanctions, 11
Lexicographic model, 225
Licensing, 828–29
Life-cycle of products, 428, 505–7, 634
Lifestyle, 190–92, 194–96, 298
Limited-service advertising agencies, 671
Liquid household cleaners, 380
List price, 568
Loss-leader pricing, 598–99
Low active strategy, 607
Low passive strategy, 607

M

Macro level of marketing, 75
Macro versus micro systems, 11, 12, 31
Macroenvironment, 75–79, 81, 83–103
Macromarketing subsystems, 28–29
Magazines, 688
Mail-order wholesalers, 518
Mail questionnaire, 795–96
Major advertisers, 662
Major discount chains, 346
Make or buy option, 250
Management by exception, 757
Management information of competitive strategies (MICS), 97
Management by objectives (MBO), 716, 752, 814
Management of sales force, 715–16
Manufacturer brands, 362
Manufacturer-to-consumer sales promotion, 630
Manufacturer-to-industrial user sales promotion, 630–31
Manufacturer-to-retailer sales promotion, 630
Manufacturer-to-wholesaler public relations, 630
Manufacturers' agents, 517, 519–20

Manufacturing activity, regional shifts in, 239
Margin/turnover classification, 494
Marginal costs, 566–67
Market
    attractiveness, 59–60
    definition of, 28
    environment analysis, dimensions of, 832
    forecast, 317
    heterogeneous, 294–96
    potent, 316
    saturation, 415
Market-buildup method, 322–23
Market segmentation, 51, 54
    approach to, 280
    and consumer market, 288–93
    definition of, 281–82
    implementation of, 286–87
    and industrial market, 296
    key features of, 281
    and K mart, 345–46
    and levels of, for a bank, 283
    in the organizational field, 293
    process, steps in, 309–10
    rationale of, 278–80
    strategies, 306–9, 471
    variables of, 282–86, 287–88, 305–6, 311
Market share, 62, 335–36, 642, 695–96
Market structure, 596–97, 600, 680
Market testing, 398–400
Marketer-dominated information sources, 217
Marketing
    activities, 559
    audit, areas of, 493–97, 771–76
    budget, 758–59
    committee, 869–70
    concept, 34–35
    control systems, 753–54
    cost analysis, 758–63
    definition of, 20–21
    departments, 62–72
    environment, 36, 72, 76–77, 89–97
    flows, 461–66
    functions, 22, 25, 27, 461
    information, 782–83
    institution, 24–25
    management, 31–38, 319–20
    organization, 66
    and its place in society, 15–22
    plans, 839–40
    role of information in, 780–83
    strategies for multinationals, 830–34
    strategy and personal selling, 706–7
    systems, 29–30, 474–79
    uncertainty in management of, 780

Marketing channel(s)
  for consumers, 457–58
  industrial, 458–61
  interorganizational relations
      within, 479–84
  and major flows into, 461–65
  objectives of, 470–74
  performance of, 486–87
  and situation analysis, 467–70
  and strategic decisions, 474–77
  use of intermediaries in, 454–57
Marketing information system (MIS),
      806–11
Marketing mix, 32–33, 840–46
Marketing research, 753, 755–57
  activities, 786
  data analysis of, 800–802
  design, 789–93
  evaluation of, 802–4
  experiments, 796–98
  implementation of, 804–6
  and information services, 793
  and MIS, 806–11
  nature and scope of, 783–85
  process of, 787–89
  role, 785–87
  and sampling, 797–800
  surveys, 795–96
Markup pricing, 584
Matching process, 16
Material flow, 514
Material handling, 543
Materials requirement planning
      (MRP), 249–51
Mathematical models, 400, 402
Matrix approach, 66–67
Measuring advertising effectiveness,
      694–95
Media-controlled message, 691
Media exposure patterns, 295–99
Media mixes, 685, 692, 875
Media scheduling, 692–94
Media selection, 683–85
Media types and estimated revenues,
      684
Median income levels, 132
Megatrends, ten affecting life, 89
Merchant wholesaler, 516
Message acceptance/rejection, 220–
      21, 647
Message elements, 683
Message execution, 679
Message format, 642–45
Message sidedness, 640–42
Metropolitan statistical areas,
      126
Micromarketing issues, 14
Miller Lite Beer, 208–9, 361, 378
  case study of, 448
Minimarket tests, 400

MIS (Marketing Information Sys-
      tem), 806–11
Misrepresentation and fraud, 440–43
Mission and marketing objectives,
      46–47
Mission statement, 47
Missionary sellers, 708
Mixed approach marketing plan, 840
Model of organizational buying, 266
Models of market structure, 562
Monopolistic competition, 561
Monopoly, 368, 559–60
Motivation, 145–46, 730–31
Moving averages, 324–26
Multi-attribute evaluation process,
      222–23
Multi-attribute framework, 161–63
Multidimensional perception, 152–53
Multinational marketing
  corporate role in, 844–46
  and cultural environment, 837
  definition of, 822–23
  and economic environment, 838
  and exports, 826–28
  as joint venture, 829–30
  and legal environment, 836–37
  licensing for, 828–29
  planning for, 839–40
  political environment of, 834–36
  reasons for, 823–25
  strategies for, 830–34
Multiple-factor screening methods,
      59
Multiple marketing channels, 466–67
Multiple nonprofits, 866–67
Multivariate analysis, 801

N

Nationalization, 834
Need-reduction theory of motivation,
      146
Needs, 146–49
Negligence theory of product liabil-
      ity, 440
New product(s)
  average rate of return, 393
  and benefit-structure analysis, 386–
      88
  business analysis of, 391–94
  classification system, 376
  commercial application of, 402–3
  complexity of, 404–5
  and consumer behavior, 404–7
  development, 380–83, 397–402
  evaluation, 393–94
  failures, 378–80
  future of, 378–80
  ideas, 384–91
  import of, 377–78
  and legal aspects of, 439–45

New product(s)–Cont.
  pricing, 567–68
  screening, 390–92
  as sources of revenue, 435
  testing, 394–97, 398–402
  types, 376–77
Niche strategy, 307–9, 425–26, 605
Nine American lifestyles, 193–94
Noise, 648
Noncompensatory procedures, 223–
      25
Noncumulative quantity discount,
      570
Nondurable goods, 356
Nonmarketer-dominated information
      sources, 216
Nonmonetary exchange, 873–74
Nonprice competition, 93–94
Nonprobability sampling, 798–99
Nonprofit organizations, 866–67
  concept of exchange in, 867–69
  performance evaluation of, 876–77
  and pricing, 873
  strategic planning in, 697–703
Nonprofit sector, 13
Nonstandardized marketing plan,
      839–40
Nonstore retailing, 499–501
Nonverbal elements, 642, 680–82
Normative marketing, 11
Normative social influence, 171–72

O

Objective, definition of, 43, 44, 49
Observability of new product, 406
Observational studies, 794–95
Odd-numbered pricing, 599–600
Oligopoly, 561
Open-dating on labels, 371
Open-pay policy, 727
Opinion leaders, 176
Oral warranties, 442
Order cycle, 531
Order processing, quality control for,
      533
Orders filled and inventory, 532
Organizational marketing
  behavior characteristics of, 298–
      300, 303–5
  buyer behavior in, 240–243, 255–62
  and buying center, 252–53
  and buying committee, 247–51
  buying practices of, 245–49
  buying problems of, 262–63
  classification of buying processes
      of, 265–66
  demand characteristics of, 244–45
  and environmental influence, 261–
      62

Organizational marketing–*Cont.*
  interorganizational information about, 259–61
  intraorganizational information about, 258–59
  and problems about buying, 262–63
  purchasing agents for, 251–55
  sources of information about, 263–64
Organizational services, 243
Organizational structure, 46
Organizational subsystem, 7–10
Organizational users, 236
Outdoor advertising, 690
Overtness of services, 854–55
Ownership flow, 462
Ownership of retailing institutions, 501–3

P

Packaging, promotional properties of, 370–71, 627–28
Parity products, 379
Participation appeals, 640
Patent rights, 837
Payback period, 392–93
Penetration price policy, 568
People-based service, 853
Perceived risk, 156–58
Perceived-value pricing, 595–97
Percentage of sales approach (POS), 652
Perception, 150–59
Performance evaluation, 750–53, 864–65
Performance versus planning, 767–68
Performing arts audience, 872
Personal computers, 204–5, 214
Personal factors, 142, 151
Personal influence, 173–76
Personal interview, 795
Personal selling
  and boundary position, 707–8
  classification of jobs in, 708–10
  marketing strategy of, 706–7
  processes in, 710–15
  trends, 626, 706–7, 711, 735–39
Personal values, 142–43
Personality, 163–65
PERT; *see* Program Evaluation and Review Technique
Phantom freight, 573–74
Physical distribution
  and computers, 542
  current issues in, 541–45
  and customer service, 530–31
  inventory aspects of, 539–41
  order cycle of, 531–33

Physical distribution–*Cont.*
  and transportation, 533–36, 536–39, 545–46
Physiological tests, 695
Piggyback combinations, 535
PIMS; *see* Profit impact of marketing strategies
Pioneer advertising, 665–66
Point-of-purchase display, 631
Political environment, 834–36
Pollution-control equipment, 102
Population distribution, 114–16, 119–21, 121–23, 126–28, 129
Portfolio analysis models, 56
Portfolio tests, 695
Positioning, 52
Positive marketing, 10
Positive-normative distinction, 11–13
Possible prices, range of, 567
Post-action strategic control models, 766–67
Posttests, 696–97
Power, 480–81
Present-value method, 393–94
PRESS model rankings of products, 437–39
Pretests, 695–96
Price
  controls, 836
  decisions, 577
  definition of, 594–96
  elasticity of demand, 562–63
  fixing, 575–76
  inelasticity, 563–65
  leadership, 593–94
  lining, 599–600
  positioning, 606–7
  relative, 607–8
  strategy, 53
Pricing
  basic decisions about, 567–75
  basing point of, 572–73
  breakeven analysis for, 586–89
  budget determination of, 605–6
  competition-oriented, 592–93
  and competitive bidding, 593–95
  cost-oriented, 584–89
  costs, 565–67
  definition of, 558
  demand-oriented, 595–97
  discounts, 568–71
  and distribution channel, 609–10
  economic theory of, 559–62
  and elasticity of demand, 562–67
  evaluation of, 611–12
  experience curves of, 589–92
  geographic, 593–94
  leadership, 593–94
  legal aspects of, 575–79
  loss leader, 598–99

Pricing–*Cont.*
  markup, 584
  and multinationals, 842
  of new products, 567–68
  for nonprofit organizations, 873–74
  objectives, 601–3
  odd-numbered, 599
  possible range of, 567
  price lining of, 600–601
  stable, 603
  strategic issues in, 606–9
  strategy for, 604–5, 617, 873–74
  strategy for service organizations, 862–63
  target return of, 584–86
  transfer, 574–78
  uniform delivered, 572
  unit, 578–79
  vertical fixing of, 575–78
Primary data, 794
Priority, 47–49
Private carriers, 536
Private sources of statistical data, 793
Private warehouse, 537
Probability sampling, 798
Problem-inventory analysis, 388–89
Problem recognition, 210–11
Producers' cooperatives, 518
Product
  advertising, 663
  brand position, 430
  brands, 360
  cannibalization, 435–36, 609
  classification, 355–56, 358
  concept, 391
  definition, 354
  deletion, 435–36
  development, 397–98
  idea, 384, 394–401
  item, 358
  liability, 439–40
  life cycle, 412–18, 418–20, 427–29, 635–36, 824–25
  line, 358
  management form of organization of, 63, 717–18
  market, 49, 269, 471
  mix, 358, 494–96, 874
  objective, 422–24
  types of, 354–58, 426
Product portfolio matrix, 873
Product positioning, 155–56, 429–30, 536, 607
Product Review and Evaluation Subsystem (PRESS), 436–38
Product-specific behavior characteristics, 303–4
Product-specific values, 144
Product-type organizations, 717–18

Professional service organizations, 865–66
Profit Impact of Marketing Strategy (PIMS), 61–63, 765–66
Profit and loss statements, 760–63, 811–13
Profit versus nonprofit dichotomy, 14
Profit sector, 12
Profitability advantages of experience, 592
Program Evaluation and Review Technique (PERT), 763–64
Proliferation of opportunity, 95–96
Promotion, 610–11, 626–27
　budget for, 651–55
　channel of, 644–48
　as communications strategy, 622–23, 632–36
　components of, 626–29
　as consideration of multinationals, 842–43
　discounts, 570
　economic view of, 624–25
　goals of, 624–26
　levels of, 624–25
　messages, models for, 636–42
　of multinationals, 842–43
　of nonprofits, 875–76
　and pricing, 610–11
　planning of, 648–51
　and public relations, 628–29
　sales, 639
　of service organizations, 863–64
　source of, 637
　strategies for, 53–54, 463, 490, 622–26, 632–36, 660–64, 671–75, 863–64, 875–76
Prospecting, 711–13
Psychographics, 190
Public policy sector, 100–103
Public relations, 628–29
Public warehouses, 537
Publicity, 628–30
Pull strategy, 463, 465, 634
Pulsing, 694
Purchases and involvement, 209–10
Purchasing agents, 251–52, 271–72
Pure competition, 558, 560
Push strategy, 264, 462, 634

Q–R

Quantitative substantiality test, 522
Quantity discounts, 570
Questionnaires, 795
Rack jobbers, 518
Random sampling, 798
Ratchet effect, 130–33
Rational appeals, 638–39
Reach, 687
Real income, 130

Reasonable consumer, 700
Recall tests, 696
Receiver-controlled media, 691
Reception, 219–20, 645–46
Reciprocity, 251
Recognition tests, 696
Recycling centers, 530
Reference groups and buying, 191–93
Regional discount chains, 346
Regulatory environment, 697–701
Research
　activities, 786
　design, 789–92
　and development, 99, 398
　on personal selling, 737–38
　problem, 787
　process, 788
Reseller, 454
Resident buyers, 247
Responses to information, 220–21
Retail buyer, 246–47
Retailing
　changes confronting, 503–4
　classification of major types of, 494, 523
　conglomerchant, 500
　cooperative, 476
　high- & low-volume, 492
　hypermarkets, 500
　image, 507–9
　institutions, 532
　legal dimensions of, 522–24
　life cycle, 505–7
　management, 553
　nature and scope of, 492–93, 520
　operational methods of, 498–500
　ownership, 501–3
　and prices, 511
　and promotion, 511–12
　service atmosphere of, 509–11
　store sales in, 493, 494–95, 521
Return on assets managed (ROAM), 732
Return on investment (ROI), 61–62, 651–52, 766
Reverse brainstorming, 386
Reverse channel, 530
Right-to-know, consumer's, 100
Risk-reduction methods, 165–66
Routinized response behavior, 208

S

Safety stock, 539–40
Sales
　analysis, 750–51, 755–57
　concept, 34
　effects, 696
　forecast, 317
　oriented measures, 695
　potential, 317–18

Sales–Cont.
　promotion, 629–32
　representatives, performance of, 707–8, 734–35
　and sales management positions, 725
　training, 728–29
　variance analysis, 728–29
Sales force
　compensation of, 723–28
　composite of, 328
　evaluation, 731–35
　management of, 715–16, 730–31
　opinion, 330–31
　organizing of, 716–19
　recruitment and training, 728–30
　size of, 719–28
Sample, 797, 798–800
SBUs, 62–63; see also Strategic business units
Scrambled merchandising, 510
Screening, 390–92
Secondary data, 791–92
Segmentation; see Market segmentation
Selective distribution, 473
Self-image, 165–66, 167
Self-regulation, 697–99
Selling agents, 517
Selling jobs, 708–11
Selling process, 711–15
Semantic differential technique, 156
Separation of producers and consumers, 15–16
Service, 850–52, 854–55
Service firm objectives, 858
Service institutions, 850–58
Service(s)
　budget for, 860
　characteristics of, 852–54
　classes of, 854–55
　marketing of, 850–52, 855–65
　and nonprofits, 866
　pricing of, 862, 873–74
Shared distribution, 543–46
Shopping centers, 501
Shopping goods, 230–31, 356, 357
SIC codes, 322–25, 327, 328
Single-person households, 116
Situation analysis, 44–45, 422, 467–70, 645, 857–58, 870–72
Skimming price policy, 567–68
Smoking, 102
Smoothing constant, 337
Snowball technique, 711
Social class, 185–90
Social factors and behavior, 142
Social influence, 172–75, 176–78, 185–90, 194–98

Social sanctions, 11
Socialization process, 178–79
Sociocultural sector, 83–84, 88–89
Soft drink manufacturers, 121
Source credibility, 637–38
Source derogation, 647
Special-interest magazines, 689
Specialization, 25–26
Specialty distributors, 519
Specialty goods, 230, 356, 357–59
Specialty-line wholesalers, 516
Specialty stores, 496–98
Sporting goods product mix, 497
Stable prices, 603
Standard costs, 612
Standard of living, 6–7
Standard volume, 584
Standardized marketing information
    services, 793
Standardized marketing plan, 839
Standards of performance, 750–52
Statistical data, public and private
    sources of, 793
Statistical demand analysis, 339–40
Statistical models, 400, 402
Stimulus, 151
Stock turnover, 541
Store atmosphere, 510–11
Store image, 507–8
Straight commissions, 724–26
Straight salary, 724
Strategic business units, 56, 58–59
Strategic marketing planning process
    activities of, 319–20
    applied to brands, 363–66, 429
    and channel decisions, 468, 474–79
    and conflicts, 484–86
    control of, 774–79
    applied to distribution, 467–70
    and the environment, 79–83
    and management, 68, 507–9
    models of, 56–62
    and pricing, 601–9
    product decisions about, 420–24
    role of demand, 319–20
    and nonprofits, 869–73
    and specialty markets, 424–27
    product cannibalization and, 433–
        35

Strategic marketing planning process—
    Cont.
    and promotion, 622, 625–26, 632–
        36
    and services, 855–66
Strategies
    and channel decision, 474
    definition of, 474
    and pricing, 606–9
Stratefied sampling, 798
Strict liability, 440
Subculture, 86, 199–200
Substantiation of claims program, 699
Substitute products, 609
Supermarkets, 498–500
Support arguing, 220, 647
Surveys, 328, 795

T

Target(s)
    audience, 673, 688, 734
    consumers, 401–3
    market, 32, 51
    pricing, 584–86
    return on investment, 603
Tax controls, 836
Team selling, 735
Technical sellers, 708
Technological sector, 97–100
Telemarketing, 736, 744–45
Telephone interview, 795
Telephone selling, 735–36
Time series analysis, 334–39
Timing, 54
Total product concept, 354–55
Trade advertising, 667–68
Trade or functional discount, 568
Trade sellers, 708
Trademark, 360
Trading companies, 826
Transfer pricing, 574–78
Transportation, deregulation of, 545
Transportation and distribution, 533–
    36
Transshipping, 616
Trial close, 714
Trialability, 405–6
Truck wholesalers, 518
Tying contracts, 552–53

U

Unbranded goods, 367–77
Uniform commercial code, 443
Uniform delivered pricing, 572
Unit
    of analysis, 759–60
    pricing, 578–79
    profit and loss, 761–72
Univariate technique, 801
Urban-suburban-rural population,
    126–28
Used apple theory, 414
Utility, 17–18, 461

V

Value(s), 143, 145
    cultural, 85–86
    domain-specific, 144
    of information, 802
    and lifestyle, 192–94
    product-specific, 144
Variable costs, 565
Variance analysis, 757–58
Variances for product alpha, 768
Variety stores, 497
Vending machines, 499–500
Verbal codes, 642
Vertical cooperative advertising, 670
Vertical divisions of the market, 523
Vertical price-fixing, 575–78
Volume quotas, 716

W–Z

Warehousing, 500–501, 537–39
Wheel of retailing, 503–4
Wholesaling
    cash and carry, 518
    functions of, 572–76
    legal dimension of, 522–24
    management decision of, 520
    types of, 576–80
Word-of-mouth communications,
    173
Workload method, 720
Workplan, 732
Zip codes, 285, 348–49
Zone-delivered pricing, 572

This book has been set Computer Assisted Photocomp, in 10 and 9 point Palatino, leaded 2 points. Section and chapter numbers are 24 point Helvetica. Section and chapter titles are 20 point Helvetica Light. The size of the type page is 36 by 47 picas.